THE Java™ Developers ALMANAC 1.4

Volume 2

The Java™ Series

Lisa Friendly, Series Editor
Tim Lindholm, Technical Editor
Ken Arnold, Technical Editor of The Jini™ Technology Series
Jim Inscore, Technical Editor of The Java™ Series, Enterprise Edition   **http://www.javaseries.com**

Eric Armstrong, Stephanie Bodoff, Debbie Carson, Maydene Fisher, Dale Green, Kim Haase
The Java™ Web Services Tutorial

Ken Arnold, James Gosling, David Holmes
The Java™ Programming Language, Third Edition

Joshua Bloch
Effective Java™ Programming Language Guide

Mary Campione, Kathy Walrath, Alison Huml
The Java™ Tutorial, Third Edition:
A Short Course on the Basics

Mary Campione, Kathy Walrath, Alison Huml,Tutorial Team
The Java™ Tutorial Continued:
The Rest of the JDK™

Patrick Chan
The Java™ Developers Almanac 1.4, Volume 1

Patrick Chan
The Java™ Developers Almanac 1.4, Volume 2

Patrick Chan, Rosanna Lee
The Java™ Class Libraries, Second Edition, Volume 2:
java.applet, java.awt, java.beans

Patrick Chan, Rosanna Lee, Doug Kramer
The Java™ Class Libraries, Second Edition, Volume 1:
java.io, java.lang, java.math, java.net, java.text, java.util

Patrick Chan, Rosanna Lee, Doug Kramer
The Java˜ Class Libraries, Second Edition, Volume 1:
Supplement for the Java™ 2 Platform,
Standard Edition, v1.2

Kirk Chen, Li Gong
Programming Open Service Gateways with Java™
Embedded Server

Zhiqun Chen
Java Card™ Technology for Smart Cards:
Architecture and Programmer's Guide

Li Gong
Inside Java™ 2 Platform Security:
Architecture, API Design, and Implementation

James Gosling, Bill Joy, Guy Steele, Gilad Bracha
The Java™ Language Specification, Second Edition

Doug Lea
Concurrent Programming in Java™ , Second Edition:
Design Principles and Patterns

Rosanna Lee, Scott Seligman
JNDI API Tutorial and Reference:
Building Directory-Enabled Java™ Applications

Sheng Liang
The Java™ Native Interface:
Programmer's Guide and Specification

Tim Lindholm, Frank Yellin
The Java™ Virtual Machine Specification, Second Edition

Roger Riggs, Antero Taivalsaari, Mark VandenBrink
Programming Wireless Devices with the Java™ 2
Platform, Micro Edition

Henry Sowizral, Kevin Rushforth, Michael Deering
The Java 3D™ API Specification, Second Edition

Sun Microsystems, Inc.
Java™ Look and Feel Design Guidelines: Advanced Topics

Kathy Walrath, Mary Campione
The JFC Swing Tutorial:
A Guide to Constructing GUIs

Seth White, Maydene Fisher, Rick Cattell, Graham Hamilton, Mark Hapner
JDBC™ API Tutorial and Reference, Second Edition:
Universal Data Access for the Java™ 2 Platform

Steve Wilson, Jeff Kesselman
Java™ Platform Performance:
Strategies and Tactics

The Jini™ Technology Series

Eric Freeman, Susanne Hupfer, Ken Arnold
JavaSpaces™ Principles, Patterns, and Practice

Jim Waldo/Jini™ Technology Team
The Jini™ Specifications, Second Edition,
edited by Ken Arnold

The Java™ Series, Enterprise Edition

Stephanie Bodoff, Dale Green, Kim Haase, Eric Jendrock, Monica Pawlan, Beth Stearns
The J2EE™ Tutorial

Rick Cattell, Jim Inscore, Enterprise Partners
J2EE™ Technology in Practice:
Building Business Applications with the Java™ 2 Platform,
Enterprise Edition

Mark Hapner, Rich Burridge, Rahul Sharma, Joseph Fialli, Kim Haase
Java™ Message Service API Tutorial and Reference:
Messaging for the J2EE™ Platform

Inderjeet Singh, Beth Stearns, Mark Johnson, Enterprise Team
Designing Enterprise Applications with the Java™ 2
Platform, Enterprise Edition

Vlada Matena and Beth Stearns
Applying Enterprise JavaBeans™ :
Component-Based Development for the J2EE™ Platform

Bill Shannon, Mark Hapner, Vlada Matena, James Davidson, Eduardo Pelegri-Llopart, Larry Cable, Enterprise Team
Java™ 2 Platform, Enterprise Edition:
Platform and Component Specifications

Rahul Sharma, Beth Stearns, Tony Ng
J2EE™ Connector Architecture and Enterprise Application
Integration

THE Java™ Developers ALMANAC 1.4

Volume 2

Examples and Quick Reference

Patrick Chan

✦Addison-Wesley

Boston • San Francisco • New York • Toronto • Montreal
London • Munich • Paris • Madrid
Capetown • Sydney • Tokyo • Singapore • Mexico City

The publisher offers discounts on this book when ordered in quantity for special sales. For more information, please contact:

U.S. Corporate and Government Sales
(800) 382-3419
corpsales@pearsontechgroup.com

For sales outside of the U.S., please contact:

International Sales
(317) 581-3793
international@pearsontechgroup.com

Visit Addison-Wesley on the Web: www.awprofessional.com

Library of Congress Control Number: 2002102591

ISBN 0-201-76810-0
Text printed on recycled paper
1 2 3 4 5 6 7 8 9 10—CRS—0605040302
First printing, September 2002

To Kevin and Melissa
For the things that really matter.

Contents

Preface

Welcome to the fourth edition of *The Java™ Developers Almanac*.

There was a time when I intimately knew *all* of the Java class libraries. I knew how it all worked and exactly how everything fit together. I knew what subclassed what, what overrode what, and so on (of course, it helped that I was one of the original developers :-). But aside from the occasional inability to remember which argument of `Vector.insertElementAt()` is the index, I rarely had to refer to any reference documentation.

Version 1.1 added 250 classes and my mastery of the Java class libraries was reduced to half. This left me feeling a little disoriented since I no longer knew my way around, and the increased size of the libraries exceeded my ability to recall the details of the signatures.

Since I make my living writing Java code, it was important that I find an efficient way of "navigating" the new libraries. What I wanted was a quick overview of all of the libraries; something that covered every class and briefly showed their relationships; something that would allow me to explore and quickly learn about new packages. This need led to this book.

The Java™ Developers Almanac is like a map of the Java class libraries. It's a compact and portable tool that covers almost all[1] of the libraries, if only from a bird's-eye view. It's great for reminding you of things like method names and parameters. With today's class count at 3000, you're bound to forget a few details now and again. The almanac is great for discovering the relationships between the classes, such as determining all methods that return an image. It's also great for quickly exploring a new package.

While this book is comprehensive, the libraries are so vast that there simply isn't enough room to provide equally comprehensive documentation. So if you're working with a package that is new to you, you'll probably also need a tutorial book such as *The Java Tutorial, Third Edition* (Campione and Walrath, Addison-Wesley, 1998), a detailed reference such as *The Java Class Libraries, Volumes 1 and 2* (Chan, Lee, and Kramer, Addison-Wesley, 1998), and/or the on-line documentation at *http://java.sun.com/docs*.

---

1. Due to size constraints, the `javax.swing.plaf.*` packages are left out of Volume 2.

The book is divided into four parts, briefly described next.

Part 1: Packages

This part covers each package in alphabetical order: a brief description of the package, a description of each class and interface in the package, and a hierarchy diagram showing the relationship between the classes and interfaces in the package. This part is useful when you need an overview of a package or want to see what other related classes are available in a package.

Most packages provide a number of examples demonstrating common usage of classes in the package. The examples are designed to demonstrate a particular task using the smallest amount of code possible. Their main purpose is to show you which classes are involved in the described task and generally how they interact with each other. The code for the examples are available on *http://javaalmanac.com*.

Part 2: Classes

This part contains 500 pages of class tables, one for each class in all the covered packages. Each class table includes a class tree that shows the ancestry of the class and a list of every member in the class. Also included in the member lists are inherited members from superclasses. Thus you have a complete view of all members made available by a class. This part is useful when you're already working with a particular class and want a quick reference to all of the members in the class. New for this edition are example numbers on some of the members. This number refers to an example that demonstrates the use of the member (or a related member).

Part 3: Topics

This part is a set of quick-reference tables on miscellaneous topics. For example, the topic title "Java 1.4" contains a detailed analysis of the API differences between Java 1.3 and Java 1.4.

Part 4: Cross-Reference

This part is a cross-reference of all of the Java classes and interfaces covered in this book. This part is useful when you have questions such as What methods return an `Image` object? or What are all the descendents of `java.io.InputStream`?

Updates

As the title suggests, this book is intended to be updated whenever a new major version of the Java class libraries is released. However, before a new version is published, I will be placing any new material that I manage to write on the *http://javaalmanac.com* website. Since this book is designed for you to use in your everyday programming-related work, I would love to hear how I could improve it for the next version or simply what you thought about it. Although I'm afraid I probably won't be able to reply, I promise to read and consider each suggestion I receive. You can reach me at the following e-mail address:

almanac14@xeo.com

Acknowledgments

First and foremost, I thank Mike Hendrickson, who spent a great deal of time collaborating with me on this project. He helped me hone the ideas in this book and then supported me all of the way. It's been tremendous fun working with him.

Arthur Ogawa (*ogawa@teleport.com*), TeX master extraordinaire, provided me with TeX macros without which this book would have been impossible. Thanks for working with me in the wee hours of the morning trying to get everything just right.

I want to thank Lisa Friendly, the series editor, for all sorts of help getting this book off the ground and for getting me all of the support I needed.

Thanks to Lananh Dang who complained about my java.sql examples and ended up writing the java.sql examples for this edition.

Special thanks to Rosanna, my wife, who helped me with writing examples and many other parts of the book.

Many people gave me feedback or provided some other assistance in the making of this book. Thanks to Jens Alfke, Ken Arnold, Joshua Bloch, Paul Bommarito, David Brownell, Michael Bundschuh, Bartley Calder, Casey Cameron, Norman Chin, Mark Drumm, Robert Field, Janice Heiss, Jeff Jackson, Doug Kramer, Sheng Liang, Tim Lindholm, Hans Muller, John Pampuch, Rob Posadas, Mark Reinhold, Dan Rudman, Georges Saab, Bill Shannon, Ann Sunhachawee, Joanne Stewart-Taylor, Laurence Vanhelsuwe, Bruce Wallace, Kathy Walrath, and Tony Welch.

Finally, I want to thank the wonderful people at Addison-Wesley who made this project a lot of fun: Jacquelyn Doucette, Tracy Russ, and Sarah Weaver.

Patrick Chan
July 2002

Part 1
PACKAGES

This part contains information about each package covered in this book. For each there is a description of the package, a description of each class and interface in that package, and a hierarchy diagram showing the relationships between the classes and interfaces in the packages. The following legend describes each of these pieces.

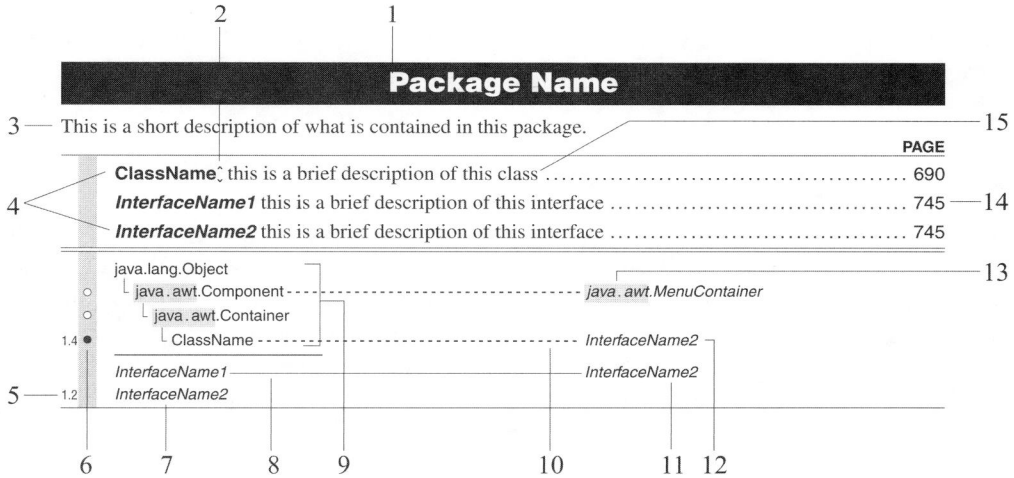

1. The name of the package
2. Has subclass or superclass
   The down-arrow indicator signifies that the class has one or more subclasses. In the case of an interface, it signifies that the interface is extended by one or more interfaces. The up-arrow indicator signifies that the class has a superclass other than `Exception`, `Error`, `Object`, or `RuntimeException`.
3. A brief description of the package
4. A complete list of classes and interfaces (interface names are italicized) in this package
5. The version of Java in which this class or interface was introduced
   You need the specified version of Java or higher in order to use the class. If the field is blank, the class or interface was introduced in Java 1.0. If the field contains a D, the class is deprecated.

6. A symbolic representation of a class's modifier set:
   - ○ An abstract class
   - ● A final class
7. The interfaces in the current package
8. Solid line signifying "extends"
9. The classes in the current package, arranged by inheritance
   A subclass appears below a superclass.
10. Dashed line signifying "implements"
11. Interfaces that are extended by the interfaces on the left
12. Interfaces that are implemented by the classes on the left
13. The shaded background behind a package name indicates that the details of this class is covered in another volume
14. The number of the page on which you will find more information about the class or interface
15. A brief description of a class or interface

Note: The class and interface descriptions were derived from Java Software's online documentation and so some of them may be missing since they have not yet been updated.

Examples

Most packages provide a number of examples demonstrating common usage of classes in the package. The examples are designed to illustrate a particular task using the smallest amount of code possible. Their main purpose is to show you which classes are involved in the described task and generally how they interact with each other. Italicized text in an example indicates the parts that should be replaced if you use it in your program. In some cases, an example may have sufficient detail for you to use directly; in other cases, you may have to look up the involved classes in another reference book for more information.

If the code of an example throws a checked exception, the code is surrounded by a `try`/`catch` statement. However, to reduce space and distraction, the catch clause is left blank. Such catch clauses should always handle the exception in some way and should never be left blank. At the very least, you should include a call to `e.printStackTrace()` to display the exception on the console.

An example is designated a number, for example ε123. You will find these example numbers next to members in the "Classes" part of the book. A member with an example number indicates that the example uses the member.

Finally, the code for the examples are available on *http://javaalmanac.com*. The website provides a search capability for search examples using a class or member name or by a keyword in the description.

Packages

Packages and Examples

3

Examples

javax.swing.table

Packages and Examples

13

Permuted Index of Examples

Packages and Examples

20

Packages and Examples

Packages and Examples

23

Packages and Examples

Packages and Examples

33

Packages and Examples

Packages and Examples

49

Packages and Examples

java.applet

This package contains the classes necessary to create an applet and the classes an applet uses to communicate with its applet context. An applet is an embeddable window with a few additional methods that the applet context uses to initialize, start, and stop the applet. The applet context is an application that is responsible for loading and running applets (e.g., a Web browser or applet development environment).

```
java.lang.Object
 ○   ├ java.awt.Component- - - - - - - - - - - - - - - - - - - - - - - - - - - - - - - - java.awt.MenuContainer, java.awt.image
 │                                                                    .ImageObserver, java.io.Serializable
 │         └ java.awt.Container
 │              └ java.awt.Panel- - - - - - - - - - - - - - - - - - - - - - - - - - - javax.accessibility.Accessible
 │                   └ Applet
1.2 ○   └ javax.accessibility.AccessibleContext
1.3 ○        └ java.awt.Component.AccessibleAWTComponent - - - - - - - - - java.io.Serializable, javax.accessibility
 │                                                                    .AccessibleComponent
1.3              └ java.awt.Container.AccessibleAWTContainer
1.3                   └ java.awt.Panel.AccessibleAWTPanel
1.3                        └ Applet.AccessibleApplet
─────────────────────────────
AppletContext
AppletStub
AudioClip
```

Packages and Examples

ε551. The Quintessential Applet

Every applet must subclass Applet.

```
import java.applet.*;
import java.awt.*;

public class BasicApplet extends Applet {
    // This method is called once by the browser when it starts the applet.
    public void init() {
    }

    // This method is called whenever the page containing this applet is made visible.
    public void start() {
    }

    // This method is called whenever the page containing this applet is not visible.
    public void stop() {
    }

    // This method is called once when the browser destroys this applet.
    public void destroy() {
    }
```

```
        // This method is called whenever this applet needs to repaint itself.
        public void paint(Graphics g) {
        }
    }
```

Here is an example of an HTML file that will cause the browser to load and start the applet:

```
<applet code=BasicApplet width=100 height=100>
</applet>
```

ε552. Getting an Applet Parameter

An applet can be configured through the use of applet *parameters*. For example, the contents for a news ticker applet could be specified through an applet parameter.

Here's how an applet parameter would be specified in an HTML file. The example specifies two applet parameters called *p1* and *p2*:

```
<applet code=AppletClassName width=100 height=100>
    <param name=p1 value="some text">
    <param name=p2 value="some more text">
</applet>
```

Here's how the value of an applet parameter can be retrieved:

```
String parameterName = "p1";
String value = applet.getParameter(parameterName);

parameterName = "p2";
value = applet.getParameter(parameterName);
```

ε553. Making the Browser Visit a URL

```
// See also "ε551. The Quintessential Applet"

try {
    URL url = new URL(getDocumentBase(), "http://hostname.com/page.html");
    applet.getAppletContext().showDocument(url);
} catch (MalformedURLException e) {
}
```

ε554. Showing a Message in the Browser's Status Bar

```
// See also "ε551. The Quintessential Applet"

applet.showStatus("Your Message Here");
```

Sound

ε555. Loading and Playing Audio in an Applet

```
// See also "ε551. The Quintessential Applet"
public void init() {
    // Load audio clip
    AudioClip ac = getAudioClip(getDocumentBase(), "http://hostname.com/audio.au");

    // Play audio clip
    ac.play();
```

Class *Interface* —extends - - -implements   O abstract   ● final   ^—has superclass   ͺ—has subclass   package—see other volume

```
    // Stop playing audio clip
    ac.stop();

    // Play audio clip continuously
    ac.loop();
}
```

ε556. Loading and Playing Audio in an Application

```
try {
    URL url = new URL("http://hostname/audio.au");
    AudioClip ac = Applet.newAudioClip(url);
    ac.play();
} catch (MalformedURLException e) {
}
```

Images

ε557. Loading and Drawing an Image in an Applet

See also "ε551. The Quintessential Applet".

```
Image image;
public void init() {
    // Load image
    image = getImage(getDocumentBase(), "http://hostname/image.gif");
}
public void paint(Graphics g) {
    // Draw image
    g.drawImage(image, 0, 0, this);
}
```

ε558. Animating an Array of Images in an Applet

This is the simplest applet to animate an array of images. In practice, you should use double-buffering (which this example does not use) to eliminate *flickering*.

```
import java.applet.*;
import java.awt.*;

public class AnimApplet extends Applet implements Runnable {
    Image[] images = new Image[2];
    int frame = 0;
    volatile Thread thread;

    public void init() {
        images[0] = getImage(getDocumentBase(), "http://hostname/image0.gif");
        images[1] = getImage(getDocumentBase(), "http://hostname/image1.gif");
    }
    public void start() {
        (thread = new Thread(this)).start();
    }
    public void stop() {
        thread = null;
    }
    public void paint(Graphics g) {
        g.drawImage(images[frame], 0, 0, this);
    }
```

Packages and Examples

```
        public void run() {
            int delay = 1000; // 1 second
            try {
                while (thread == Thread.currentThread()) {
                    frame = (frame+1)%images.length;
                    repaint();
                    Thread.sleep(delay);
                }
            } catch (Exception e) {
            }
        }
    }
```

java.awt

This package is for creating user interfaces and for painting graphics and images. A user interface object such as a button or a scrollbar is called an Abstract Window Toolkit (AWT) component. The AWT package contains classes for various components such as button, scrollbar, and window. Components can be contained in other components called containers. A container can also have a layout manager that controls the visual placement of components in the container. The AWT package contains several layout manager classes.

Class   *Interface*   —extends   - - -implements   ○ abstract   ● final   ^has superclass   ˌhas subclass   package—see other volume

Packages and Examples

Class   *Interface*   —extends   - - -implements   ○ abstract   ● final   ^—has superclass   —has subclass   package—see other volume

```
        java.lang.Object

1.1     ├ AWTEventMulticaster - - - - - - - - - - - - - - - - - - - - - java.awt.event.ActionListener⌣,
                                                                     java.awt.event.AdjustmentListener^,
                                                                     java.awt.event.ComponentListener^,
                                                                     java.awt.event.ContainerListener^,
                                                                     java.awt.event.FocusListener^,
                                                                     java.awt.event.HierarchyBoundsListener^,
                                                                     java.awt.event.HierarchyListener^,
                                                                     java.awt.event.InputMethodListener^,
                                                                     java.awt.event.ItemListener^,
                                                                     java.awt.event.KeyListener^,
                                                                     java.awt.event.MouseListener⌣,
                                                                     java.awt.event.MouseMotionListener⌣,
                                                                     java.awt.event.MouseWheelListener^,
                                                                     java.awt.event.TextListener^,
                                                                     java.awt.event.WindowFocusListener^,
                                                                     java.awt.event.WindowListener^,
                                                                     java.awt.event.WindowStateListener^

1.4     ├ AWTKeyStroke⌣ - - - - - - - - - - - - - - - - - - - - - - java.io.Serializable⌣
1.2 ●   ├ AlphaComposite - - - - - - - - - - - - - - - - - - - - - Composite
1.4     ├ AttributeValue
1.4 ●   │  ├ BufferCapabilities.FlipContents
1.3 ●   │  ├ JobAttributes.DefaultSelectionType
1.3 ●   │  ├ JobAttributes.DestinationType
1.3 ●   │  ├ JobAttributes.DialogType
1.3 ●   │  ├ JobAttributes.MultipleDocumentHandlingType
1.3 ●   │  ├ JobAttributes.SidesType
1.3 ●   │  ├ PageAttributes.ColorType
1.3 ●   │  ├ PageAttributes.MediaType
```

java.lang.Object

1.4 │ ├ AttributeValue
1.3 ● │ │ ├ PageAttributes.OrientationRequestedType
1.3 ● │ │ ├ PageAttributes.OriginType
1.3 ● │ │ └ PageAttributes.PrintQualityType
1.2 │ ├ BasicStroke - *Stroke*
│ ├ BorderLayout - *LayoutManager2^*, *java.io.Serializable*
1.4 │ ├ BufferCapabilities - *java.lang.Cloneable*
│ ├ CardLayout - *LayoutManager2^*, *java.io.Serializable*
│ ├ CheckboxGroup - *java.io.Serializable*
│ ├ Color - *Paint^*, *java.io.Serializable*
1.1 ● │ │ └ SystemColor - *java.io.Serializable*
○ │ ├ Component - *MenuContainer, java.awt.image.ImageObserver,*
│ │ │ *java.io.Serializable*
│ │ ├ Button - *javax.accessibility.Accessible*
│ │ ├ Canvas -
│ │ ├ Checkbox - *ItemSelectable*, *javax.accessibility.Accessible*
│ │ ├ Choice -
│ │ ├ Container
│ │ │ ├ Panel - *javax.accessibility.Accessible*
1.1 │ │ │ ├ ScrollPane -
│ │ │ └ Window -
│ │ │ ├ Dialog
│ │ │ │ └ FileDialog
│ │ │ └ Frame - *MenuContainer*
│ │ ├ Label - *javax.accessibility.Accessible*
│ │ ├ List - *ItemSelectable*, *javax.accessibility.Accessible*
│ │ ├ Scrollbar - *Adjustable, javax.accessibility.Accessible*
│ │ └ TextComponent - *javax.accessibility.Accessible*
│ │ ├ TextArea
│ │ └ TextField
1.3 │ ├ Component.AccessibleAWTComponent - - - - - - - - - - - - - - - - - - *java.awt.event.ComponentListener^*
│ │ .AccessibleAWTComponentHandler
1.3 │ ├ Component.AccessibleAWTComponent - - - - - - - - - - - - - - - - - - *java.awt.event.FocusListener^*
│ │ .AccessibleAWTFocusHandler
1.2 ● │ ├ ComponentOrientation - *java.io.Serializable*
1.3 │ ├ Container.AccessibleAWTContainer - - - - - - - - - - - - - - - - - - *java.awt.event.ContainerListener^*
│ │ .AccessibleContainerHandler
1.1 │ ├ Cursor - *java.io.Serializable*
1.4 ● │ ├ DisplayMode
│ ├ Event -
1.1 │ ├ EventQueue
│ ├ FlowLayout - *LayoutManager*, *java.io.Serializable*
1.4 ○ │ ├ FocusTraversalPolicy
1.4 │ │ └ ContainerOrderFocusTraversalPolicy - - - - - - - - - - - - - - - - *java.io.Serializable*
1.4 │ │ └ DefaultFocusTraversalPolicy
│ ├ Font -
○ │ ├ FontMetrics -
1.2 │ ├ GradientPaint - *Paint^*

Packages and Examples

63

java.lang.Object

○	Graphics	
1.2 ○	└ Graphics2D	
1.2 ○	GraphicsConfigTemplate	*java.io.Serializable*
1.2 ○	GraphicsConfiguration	
1.2 ○	GraphicsDevice	
1.2 ○	GraphicsEnvironment	
	GridBagConstraints	*java.io.Serializable*, *java.lang.Cloneable*
	GridBagLayout	*LayoutManager2^*, *java...o.Serializable*
	GridLayout	*LayoutManager*, *java.io.Serializable*
○	Image	
1.4	ImageCapabilities	*java.lang.Cloneable*
	Insets	*java.io.Serializable*, *java.lang.Cloneable*
1.3 ●	JobAttributes	*java.lang.Cloneable*
1.4 ○	KeyboardFocusManager	*KeyEventDispatcher, KeyEventPostProcessor*
1.4	└ DefaultKeyboardFocusManager	
	MediaTracker	*java.io.Serializable*
○	MenuComponent	
	├ MenuBar	*MenuContainer, javax.accessibility.Accessible*
	└ MenuItem	*javax.accessibility.Accessible*
	├ CheckboxMenuItem	*ItemSelectable*, *javax.accessibility.Accessible*
	└ Menu	*MenuContainer, javax.accessibility.Accessible*
1.1	└ PopupMenu	
1.1	MenuShortcut	*java.io.Serializable*
1.3 ●	PageAttributes	*java.lang.Cloneable*
	Polygon	*Shape, java.io.Serializable*
1.1 ○	PrintJob	
1.2	RenderingHints	*java.lang.Cloneable*, *java.util.Map*
1.2 ○	RenderingHints.Key	
1.3	Robot	
1.4	ScrollPaneAdjustable	*Adjustable, java.io.Serializable*
1.2	TexturePaint	*Paint^*
○	Toolkit	
1.2 ○	java.awt.geom.Dimension2D	*java.lang.Cloneable*
	└ Dimension	*java.io.Serializable*
1.2 ○	java.awt.geom.Point2D	*java.lang.Cloneable*
	└ Point	*java.io.Serializable*
1.2 ○	java.awt.geom.RectangularShape	*Shape, java.lang.Cloneable*
1.2 ○	└ java.awt.geom.Rectangle2D	
	└ Rectangle	*Shape, java.io.Serializable*
1.4 ○	java.awt.image.BufferStrategy	
1.4	├ Component.BltBufferStrategy	
1.4	└ Component.FlipBufferStrategy	
1.2 ○	java.security.Permission	*java.io.Serializable*, *java.security.Guard*
1.2 ○	└ java.security.BasicPermission	*java.io.Serializable*
1.2 ●	└ AWTPermission	

Class   *Interface*   —extends   - - -implements   ○ abstract   ● final   ^—has superclass   ⌄—has subclass   package—see other volume

```
        java.lang.Object                                           - java.io.Serializable
1.1        ┤ java.util.EventObject - - - - - - - - - - - - - - - - - - - - - - - - - - - ┘
1.1  ○      └ AWTEvent
1.2  ○     ┤ javax.accessibility.AccessibleContext
1.3  ○      ┤ Component.AccessibleAWTComponent - - - - - - - - - - - - - - - java.io.Serializable, javax.accessibility
                                                                        .AccessibleComponent
1.3          ┤ Button.AccessibleAWTButton - - - - - - - - - - - - - - - - - - - javax.accessibility.AccessibleAction,
                                                                        javax.accessibility.AccessibleValue
1.3          ┤ Canvas.AccessibleAWTCanvas
1.3          ┤ Checkbox.AccessibleAWTCheckbox - - - - - - - - - - - - - - - - java.awt.event.ItemListener^,
                                                                        javax.accessibility.AccessibleAction,
                                                                        javax.accessibility.AccessibleValue
1.3          ┤ Choice.AccessibleAWTChoice - - - - - - - - - - - - - - - - - - - javax.accessibility.AccessibleAction
1.3          ┤ Container.AccessibleAWTContainer
1.3           ┤ Panel.AccessibleAWTPanel
1.3           ┤ ScrollPane.AccessibleAWTScrollPane
1.3           └ Window.AccessibleAWTWindow
1.3            ┤ Dialog.AccessibleAWTDialog
1.3            └ Frame.AccessibleAWTFrame
1.3          ┤ Label.AccessibleAWTLabel
1.3          ┤ List.AccessibleAWTList - - - - - - - - - - - - - - - - - - - - - - - java.awt.event.ActionListener^,
                                                                        java.awt.event.ItemListener^,
                                                                        javax.accessibility.AccessibleSelection
1.3          ┤ List.AccessibleAWTList.AccessibleAWTListChild - - - - - - - - javax.accessibility.Accessible
1.3          ┤ Scrollbar.AccessibleAWTScrollBar - - - - - - - - - - - - - - - - javax.accessibility.AccessibleValue
1.3          └ TextComponent.AccessibleAWTTextComponent - - - - - - - - java.awt.event.TextListener^,
                                                                        javax.accessibility.AccessibleText
1.3            ┤ TextArea.AccessibleAWTTextArea
1.3            └ TextField.AccessibleAWTTextField
1.3  ○      └ MenuComponent.AccessibleAWTMenuComponent - - - - - - - java.io.Serializable, javax
                                                                        .accessibility.AccessibleComponent,
                                                                        javax.accessibility.AccessibleSelection
1.3          ┤ MenuBar.AccessibleAWTMenuBar
1.3          └ MenuItem.AccessibleAWTMenuItem - - - - - - - - - - - - - - - - javax.accessibility.AccessibleAction,
                                                                        javax.accessibility.AccessibleValue
1.3           ┤ CheckboxMenuItem - - - - - - - - - - - - - - - - - - - - - - -
                .AccessibleAWTCheckboxMenuItem
1.3           └ Menu.AccessibleAWTMenu
1.3            └ PopupMenu.AccessibleAWTPopupMenu
        └ java.lang.Throwable - - - - - - - - - - - - - - - - - - - - - - - - - - - - - java.io.Serializable
          ┤ java.lang.Error
           └ AWTError
          └ java.lang.Exception
            ┤ AWTException
1.3         ┤ FontFormatException
            └ java.lang.RuntimeException
1.1            ┤ java.lang.IllegalStateException
1.1             └ IllegalComponentStateException
1.2            └ java.lang.UnsupportedOperationException
1.4              └ HeadlessException

1.2  ActiveEvent
1.1  Adjustable
```

Frames

ε559. Creating a Frame

A frame is a top-level window with a title bar and buttons for iconizing, maximizing, and closing the frame.
See also "ε733. Creating a JFrame".

```
// Create frame
String title = "Frame Title";
Frame frame = new Frame(title);

// Create a component to add to the frame
Component comp = new TextArea();

// Add the component to the frame; by default, the frame has a border layout
frame.add(comp, BorderLayout.CENTER);

// Show the frame
int width = 300;
int height = 300;
frame.setSize(width, height);
frame.setVisible(true);

// See also "ε560. Setting the Icon for a Frame"
// See also "ε561. Making a Frame Non-Resizable"
```

ε560. Setting the Icon for a Frame

```
// Create frame
String title = "Frame Title";
Frame frame = new Frame(title);

// Set icon
Image icon = Toolkit.getDefaultToolkit().getImage("icon.gif");
frame.setIconImage(icon);
```

ε561. Making a Frame Non-Resizable

By default, a frame can be resized by the user. Use setResizable(false) to freeze a frame's size.

Class   *Interface*   —extends   - - -implements   ○ abstract   ● final   ^—has superclass   ⌐—has subclass   package—see other volume

```
Frame frame = new Frame();
frame.setResizable(false);

// Get the current resizable state
boolean resizable = frame.isResizable();
```

ε562. Removing the Title Bar of a Frame

The title bar and other decorations can be removed from a frame. A frame without decorations looks and behaves like a Window container. However, if the frame never needs the decorations, it is better to use a Window container.

Note: The decorations can only be removed while the frame is not visible.

```
Frame frame = new Frame();
frame.setUndecorated(true);

// Get the current decorated state
boolean undecorated = frame.isUndecorated();
```

ε563. Setting the Bounds for a Maximized Frame

By default, when a frame is maximized, it is resized to cover the entire screen. This example demonstrates how to control the size and location of a frame when it is maximized:

```
// Create frame
Frame frame = new Frame();

// Determine location and size of a maximized frame
int x = 100;
int y = 100;
int width = 300;
int height = 300;
Rectangle bounds = new Rectangle(x, y, width, height);

// Set the maximized bounds
frame.setMaximizedBounds(bounds);
```

ε564. Iconifying and Maximizing a Frame

This example implements methods to iconify, deiconify, minimize, and maximize a frame. In general, you should not make calls such as Frame.setExtendedState(Frame.ICONIFIED) because this would destroy the maximized state of the frame. Instead, the Frame.ICONIFIED state should be combined with the current maximized state of the frame.

```
// This method iconifies a frame; the maximized bits are not affected.
public void iconify(Frame frame) {
    int state = frame.getExtendedState();

    // Set the iconified bit
    state |= Frame.ICONIFIED;

    // Iconify the frame
    frame.setExtendedState(state);
}
// This method deiconifies a frame; the maximized bits are not affected.
public void deiconify(Frame frame) {
    int state = frame.getExtendedState();

    // Clear the iconified bit
    state &= ~Frame.ICONIFIED;
```

```
        // Deiconify the frame
        frame.setExtendedState(state);
    }

    // This method minimizes a frame; the iconified bit is not affected
    public void minimize(Frame frame) {
        int state = frame.getExtendedState();

        // Clear the maximized bits
        state &= ~Frame.MAXIMIZED_BOTH;

        // Maximize the frame
        frame.setExtendedState(state);
    }

    // This method minimizes a frame; the iconified bit is not affected
    public void maximize(Frame frame) {
        int state = frame.getExtendedState();

        // Set the maximized bits
        state |= Frame.MAXIMIZED_BOTH;

        // Maximize the frame
        frame.setExtendedState(state);
    }
```

ε565. Hiding a Frame When Its Close Button Is Clicked

By default, when the close button on a frame is clicked, nothing happens. This example shows how to make the action hide the frame. One reason for hiding rather than disposing a frame would be to reuse the frame later.

```
// Create a frame
Frame frame = new Frame();

// Add a listener for the close event
frame.addWindowListener(new WindowAdapter() {
    public void windowClosing(WindowEvent evt) {
        Frame frame = (Frame)evt.getSource();

        // Hide the frame
        frame.setVisible(false);

        // If the frame is no longer needed, call dispose
        frame.dispose();
    }
});
```

ε566. Exiting an Application When a Frame Is Closed

By default, when the close button on a frame is clicked, nothing happens. This example shows how to exit the application when the frame is closed:

```
// Create a frame
Frame frame = new Frame();

// Add a listener for the close event
frame.addWindowListener(new WindowAdapter() {
    public void windowClosing(WindowEvent evt) {
        // Exit the application
```

```
                    System.exit(0);
            }
    });
```

ε567. Getting All Created Frames in an Application

```
// Retrieve all active frames
Frame[] frames = Frame.getFrames();

for (int i=0; i<frames.length; i++) {
    // Get frame's title
    String title = frames[i].getTitle();

    // Determine if the frame is visible
    boolean isVisible = frames[i].isVisible();
}
```

ε568. Determining When a Frame or Window Is Opened or Closed

```
// Create the frame
Frame frame = new Frame();

// Create a listener for window events
WindowListener listener = new WindowAdapter() {
    // This method is called after a window has been opened
    public void windowOpened(WindowEvent evt) {
        Frame frame = (Frame)evt.getSource();
    }

    // This method is called when the user clicks the close button
    public void windowClosing(WindowEvent evt) {
        Frame frame = (Frame)evt.getSource();

        // By default, nothing happens when the user clicks the close button.
        // To close the frame, see "ε565. Hiding a Frame When Its Close Button Is Clicked"
    }

    // This method is called after a window is closed
    public void windowClosed(WindowEvent evt) {
        Frame frame = (Frame)evt.getSource();
    }
};
// Register the listener with the frame
frame.addWindowListener(listener);
```

ε569. Determining When a Frame or Window Is Iconized or Maximized

```
// Create the frame
Frame frame = new Frame();

// Create a listener
WindowStateListener listener = new WindowAdapter() {
    public void windowStateChanged(WindowEvent evt) {
        int oldState = evt.getOldState();
        int newState = evt.getNewState();

        if ((oldState & Frame.ICONIFIED) == 0
            && (newState & Frame.ICONIFIED) != 0) {
            // Frame was iconized
        } else if ((oldState & Frame.ICONIFIED) != 0
```

```
                && (newState & Frame.ICONIFIED) == 0) {
                // Frame was deiconized
            }

            if ((oldState & Frame.MAXIMIZED_BOTH) == 0
                && (newState & Frame.MAXIMIZED_BOTH) != 0) {
                // Frame was maximized
            } else if ((oldState & Frame.MAXIMIZED_BOTH) != 0
                && (newState & Frame.MAXIMIZED_BOTH) == 0) {
                // Frame was minimized
            }
        }
    };

    // Register the listener with the frame
    frame.addWindowStateListener(listener);
```

Components

ε570. Determining When a Component Has Been Made Visible, Moved, or Resized

A component fires a component event after it is made visible, hidden, moved, or resized.

```
    // Create a listener for component events
    ComponentListener listener = new ComponentAdapter() {
        // This method is called only if the component was hidden and setVisible(true) was called
        public void componentShown(ComponentEvent evt) {
            // Component is now visible
            Component c = (Component)evt.getSource();
        }

        // This method is called only if the component was visible and setVisible(false) was called
        public void componentHidden(ComponentEvent evt) {
            // Component is now hidden
            Component c = (Component)evt.getSource();
        }

        // This method is called after the component's location within its container changes
        public void componentMoved(ComponentEvent evt) {
            Component c = (Component)evt.getSource();

            // Get new location
            Point newLoc = c.getLocation();
        }

        // This method is called after the component's size changes
        public void componentResized(ComponentEvent evt) {
            Component c = (Component)evt.getSource();

            // Get new size
            Dimension newSize = c.getSize();
        }
    };

    // Register the listener with the component
    component.addComponentListener(listener);
```

Class   *Interface*   —extends   - - -implements   ○ abstract   ● final   ⌐—has superclass   ⌐—has subclass   package—see other volume

ε571. Creating a Container

A container holds one or more child components. A container has a layout that determines how the child components are arranged within the container. This example creates a frame with a text area in the center and a row of buttons at the bottom. The buttons are placed in a container.

```java
// Create a container with a flow layout, which arranges its children horizontally
Panel panel = new Panel();

// A container can also be created with a specific layout
panel = new Panel(new FlowLayout(FlowLayout.RIGHT));

// Add several buttons to the container
panel.add(new Button("A"));
panel.add(new Button("B"));
panel.add(new Button("C"));

// Create frame with a text area in the center
Frame frame = new Frame();
Component comp = new TextArea();
frame.add(comp, BorderLayout.CENTER);

// Add the container to the bottom of the frame
frame.add(panel, BorderLayout.SOUTH);

// Show the frame
int width = 300;
int height = 300;
frame.setSize(width, height);
frame.setVisible(true);
```

ε572. Getting the Child Components of a Container

This example retrieves all of a container's children in an array:

```java
// Get children
Component[] components = container.getComponents();

for (int i=0; i<components.length; i++) {
    // Get the component's bounds
    Rectangle bounds = components[i].getBounds();
}
```

This example retrieves all components individually:

```java
// Get number of children
int count = container.getComponentCount();

for (int i=0; i<count; i++) {
    Component c = container.getComponent(i);
}
```

ε573. Determining When a Component Is Added or Removed from a Container

A container fires a container event whenever a component is added or removed.

```java
// Create a listen for container events
ContainerListener listener = new ContainerAdapter() {
    public void componentAdded(ContainerEvent evt) {
        // Get component that was added
```

Packages and Examples

71

```
                Component c = evt.getChild();
        }
        public void componentRemoved(ContainerEvent evt) {
            // Get component that was removed
            Component c = evt.getChild();
        }
    };

    // Register the listener with the container
    container.addContainerListener(listener);
```

Cursors

ε574. Changing the Cursor

A component has a cursor property which controls the shape of the cursor when the cursor is above the component. The component's cursor property can be changed at any time by calling Component.setCursor(). See the Cursor class for available predefined cursor shapes.

```
    // Create a component
    Component comp = new Button("OK");

    // By default, the component's cursor is Cursor.DEFAULT_CURSOR
    Cursor cursor = comp.getCursor();

    // Change the component's cursor to another shape
    comp.setCursor(Cursor.getPredefinedCursor(Cursor.HAND_CURSOR));
```

Drawing

ε575. The Quintessential Drawing Program

To draw on the screen, it is first necessary to subclass a JComponent and override its paint() method. The paint() method is automatically called by the windowing system whenever component's area needs to be repainted.

The paint() method is supplied a *graphics context* which is used to draw shapes and images. The coordinate system of a graphics context is such that the origin is at the northwest corner and x-axis increases toward the right while the y-axis increases toward the bottom.

This example defines a component that draws an oval and installs an instance of this component in a frame. See also "ε586. Drawing Simple Shapes".

```
    import java.awt.*;
    import javax.swing.*;

    public class BasicDraw {
        public static void main(String[] args) {
            new BasicDraw();
        }
        BasicDraw() {
            // Create a frame
            JFrame frame = new JFrame();

            // Add a component with a custom paint method
            frame.getContentPane().add(new MyComponent());
```

```
                    // Display the frame
                    int frameWidth = 300;
                    int frameHeight = 300;
                    frame.setSize(frameWidth, frameHeight);
                    frame.setVisible(true);
            }
            class MyComponent extends JComponent {
                    // This method is called whenever the contents needs to be painted
                    public void paint(Graphics g) {
                            // Retrieve the graphics context; this object is used to paint shapes
                            Graphics2D g2d = (Graphics2D)g;

                            // Draw an oval that fills the window
                            int x = 0;
                            int y = 0;
                            int width = getSize().width-1;
                            int height = getSize().height-1;
                            g2d.drawOval(x, y, width, height);
                    }
            }
    }
```

ε576. Drawing with Alpha

```
    // See "ε575. The Quintessential Drawing Program"
    public void paint(Graphics g) {
            Graphics2D g2d = (Graphics2D)g;

            // Draw background...

            // Set alpha. 0.0f is 100% transparent and 1.0f is 100% opaque.
            float alpha = .3f;
            g2d.setComposite(AlphaComposite.getInstance(AlphaComposite.SRC_OVER, alpha));

            // Draw foreground...
    }
```

ε577. Enabling Antialiasing

```
    // See "ε575. The Quintessential Drawing Program"
    public void paint(Graphics g) {
            // Retrieve the graphics context; this object is used to paint shapes
            Graphics2D g2d = (Graphics2D)g;

            // Determine if antialiasing is enabled
            RenderingHints rhints = g2d.getRenderingHints();
            boolean antialiasOn = rhints.containsValue(RenderingHints.VALUE_ANTIALIAS_ON);

            // Enable antialiasing for shapes
            g2d.setRenderingHint(RenderingHints.KEY_ANTIALIASING,
                                    RenderingHints.VALUE_ANTIALIAS_ON);

            // Disable antialiasing for shapes
            g2d.setRenderingHint(RenderingHints.KEY_ANTIALIASING,
                                    RenderingHints.VALUE_ANTIALIAS_OFF);

            // Draw shapes...; see "ε586. Drawing Simple Shapes"

            // Enable antialiasing for text
            g2d.setRenderingHint(RenderingHints.KEY_TEXT_ANTIALIASING,
```

```
                              RenderingHints.VALUE_TEXT_ANTIALIAS_ON);

      // Draw text...; see "ε591. Drawing Simple Text"

      // Disable antialiasing for text
      g2d.setRenderingHint(RenderingHints.KEY_TEXT_ANTIALIASING,
                              RenderingHints.VALUE_TEXT_ANTIALIAS_OFF);
  }
```

ε578. Setting the Clipping Area with a Shape

This example demonstrates how to set a clipping area using a shape. The example sets an oval for the clipping area and then draws and image. Only those pixels of the image that fall within the oval are displayed.

```
    // See "ε575. The Quintessential Drawing Program"
    public void paint(Graphics g) {
        Graphics2D g2d = (Graphics2D)g;

        // Create an oval shape that's as large as the component
        float fx = 0;
        float fy = 0;
        float fw = getSize().width-1;
        float fh = getSize().height-1;
        Shape shape = new java.awt.geom.Ellipse2D.Float(fx, fy, fw, fh);

        // Set the clipping area
        g2d.setClip(shape);

        // Draw an image
        int x = 0;
        int y = 0;
        g2d.drawImage(image, x, y, this);
    }
```

ε579. Changing the Thickness of the Stroking Pen

dashPhase is the offset to start the dashing pattern.

```
    // See "ε575. The Quintessential Drawing Program"
    public void paint(Graphics g) {
        Graphics2D g2d = (Graphics2D)g;
        float strokeThickness = 5.0f;

        // A solid stroke
        BasicStroke stroke = new BasicStroke(strokeThickness);
        g2d.setStroke(stroke);
        // Draw shapes...; see "ε586. Drawing Simple Shapes"

        // A dashed stroke
        float miterLimit = 10f;
        float[] dashPattern = {10f};
        float dashPhase = 5f;
        stroke = new BasicStroke(strokeThickness, BasicStroke.CAP_BUTT,
            BasicStroke.JOIN_MITER, miterLimit, dashPattern, dashPhase);
        g2d.setStroke(stroke);
        // Draw shapes...; see "ε586. Drawing Simple Shapes"
    }
```

ε580. Stroking or Filling with a Texture

The buffered image used to create the TexturePaint object is scaled down/up to width w and height h. Conceptually, the scaled down/up buffered image is first painted at (x, y) in user space, and then replicated around it.

```
// See "ε575. The Quintessential Drawing Program"
public void paint(Graphics g) {
    Graphics2D g2d = (Graphics2D)g;
    int x = 10;
    int y = 10;
    int width = 50;
    int height = 25;
    TexturePaint texture = new TexturePaint(bufferedImage, new Rectangle(x, y, width, height));
    g2d.setPaint(texture);
    // Draw shapes...; see "ε586. Drawing Simple Shapes"
}
```

ε581. Animating an Array of Images in an Application

This is the simplest application to animate an array of images.

```
import java.awt.*;
import javax.swing.*;

public class AnimApp extends JComponent implements Runnable {
    Image[] images = new Image[2];
    int frame = 0;

    public void paint(Graphics g) {
        Image image = images[frame];
        if (image != null) {
            // Draw the current image
            int x = 0;
            int y = 0;
            g.drawImage(image, x, y, this);
        }
    }

    public void run() {
        // Load the array of images
        images[0] = new ImageIcon("image1.gif").getImage();
        images[1] = new ImageIcon("image2.gif").getImage();

        // Display each image for 1 second
        int delay = 1000; // 1 second

        try {
            while (true) {
                // Move to the next image
                frame = (frame+1)%images.length;

                // Causes the paint() method to be called
                repaint();

                // Wait
                Thread.sleep(delay);
            }
        } catch (Exception e) {
        }
```

```
        }

        public static void main(String[] args) {
            AnimApp app = new AnimApp();

            // Display the animation in a frame
            JFrame frame = new JFrame();
            frame.getContentPane().add(app);
            frame.setSize(300, 300);
            frame.setVisible(true);

            (new Thread(app)).start();
        }
    }
```

Colors

ε582. Drawing with Color

```
public void paint(Graphics g) {
    Graphics2D g2d = (Graphics2D)g;

    // Use a predefined color
    g2d.setColor(Color.red);
    // Draw shapes...; see "ε586. Drawing Simple Shapes"

    // Use a custom color
    int red = 230;
    int green = 45;
    int blue = 67;
    g2d.setColor(new Color(red, green, blue));
    // Draw shapes...; see "ε586. Drawing Simple Shapes"
}
```

ε583. Drawing with a Gradient Color

```
public void paint(Graphics g) {
    Graphics2D g2d = (Graphics2D)g;

    Color startColor = Color.red;
    Color endColor = Color.blue;

    // A non-cyclic gradient
    GradientPaint gradient = new GradientPaint(startX, startY, startColor, endX, endY, endColor);
    g2d.setPaint(gradient);
    // Draw shapes...; see "ε586. Drawing Simple Shapes"

    // A cyclic gradient
    gradient = new GradientPaint(startX, startY, startColor, endX, endY, endColor, true);
    g2d.setPaint(gradient);
    // Draw shapes...; see "ε586. Drawing Simple Shapes"
}
```

ε584. Retrieving a Predefined Color by Name

The Color class contains a number of predefined colors such as red and green. This example demonstrates how to retrieve one of these predefined colors using a string. For example, the predefined color java.awt₂ .Color.red could be retrieved with the string "red".

```java
// Returns a Color based on 'colorName' which must be one of the predefined colors in
// java.awt.Color. Returns null if colorName is not valid.
public Color getColor(String colorName) {
    try {
        // Find the field and value of colorName
        Field field = Class.forName("java.awt.Color").getField(colorName);
        return (Color)field.get(null);
    } catch (Exception e) {
        return null;
    }
}
```

ε585. Converting Between RGB and HSB Colors

This example demonstrates how to convert between a color value in RGB (three integer values in the range 0 to 255 representing red, green, and blue) and HSB (three floating point values in the range 0 to 1.0 representing hue, saturation, and brightness).

```java
// Specify 3 RGB values
int red = 0x33;
int green = 0x66;
int blue = 0x99;

// Convert RGB to HSB
float[] hsb = Color.RGBtoHSB(red, green, blue, null);
float hue = hsb[0]; // .58333
float saturation = hsb[1]; // .66667
float brightness = hsb[2]; // .6

// Convert HSB to RGB value
int rgb = Color.HSBtoRGB(hue, saturation, brightness);
red = (rgb»16)&0xFF;
green = (rgb»8)&0xFF;
blue = rgb&0xFF;
```

Shapes

ε586. Drawing Simple Shapes

There are two ways to draw basic shapes like circles, ovals, lines, arcs, squares, rectangles, rounded rectangles, and polygons. The first is to use specific drawing methods like Graphics.drawOval(). This example uses these methods. The second is to construct a shape and then use Graphics2D.draw() to draw the shape. See the java.awt.geom package for examples that create shapes.

```java
// See "ε575. The Quintessential Drawing Program"
public void paint(Graphics g) {
    Graphics2D g2d = (Graphics2D)g;

    g2d.drawLine(x1, y1, x2, y2);
    g2d.drawOval(x, y, w, h);
    g2d.drawRect(x, y, w, h);
```

```
        // A start angle of 0 represents a 3 o'clock position, 90 represents a 12 o'clock position,
        // and -90 (or 270) represents a 6 o'clock position
        int startAngle = 45;
        int arcAngle = -60;
        g2d.drawArc(x, y, w, h, startAngle, arcAngle);

        g2d.drawRoundRect(x, y, w, h, arcWidth, arcHeight);

        Polygon polygon = new Polygon();
        polygon.addPoint(x, y);
        // Add more points...
        g2d.drawPolygon(polygon);
    }
```

ε587. Filling Basic Shapes

There are two ways to fill basic shapes like lines and rectangles. The first is to use specific drawing methods like Graphics.fillOval(). This example uses these methods. The second is to construct a shape and then use Graphics2D.fill() to fill the shape. See the java.awt.geom package for examples that create shapes.

```
        g2d.fillArc(x, y, w, h, startAngle, arcAngle);
        g2d.fillOval(x, y, w, h);
        g2d.fillRect(x, y, w, h);
        g2d.fillRoundRect(x, y, w, h, arcWidth, arcHeight);

        Polygon polygon = new Polygon();
        polygon.addPoint(x, y);
        // ...continue adding points
        g2d.fillPolygon(polygon);
```

ε588. Creating a Shape from a Stroked Shape

```
        float strokeThickness = 5.0f;
        BasicStroke stroke = new BasicStroke(strokeThickness);
        Shape newShape = stroke.createStrokedShape(shape);
```

ε589. Stroking or Filling a Shape

A stroked shape is an outline of the shape. A filled shape is drawn with filled with a color. See also "ε575. The Quintessential Drawing Program".

```
        public void paint(Graphics g) {
            Graphics2D g2d = (Graphics2D)g;

            // Set pen color for stroked shape
            g2d.setColor(Color.red);

            // Stroke the shape
            g2d.draw(shape);

            // Set fill color for filled shape
            g2d.setColor(Color.blue);

            // Fill the shape
            g2d.fill(shape);
        }
```

Class   *Interface*   —extends   - - -implements   ○ abstract   ● final   ^—has superclass   ⌐—has subclass   package—see other volume

ε590. Drawing a Pie Chart

This example implements a method for drawing a pie chart.

```
// Class to hold a value for a slice
public class PieValue {
    double value;
    Color color;

    public PieValue(double value, Color color) {
        this.value = value;
        this.color = color;
    }
}
// slices is an array of values that represent the size of each slice.
public void drawPie(Graphics2D g, Rectangle area, PieValue[] slices) {
    // Get total value of all slices
    double total = 0.0D;
    for (int i=0; i<slices.length; i++) {
        total += slices[i].value;
    }

    // Draw each pie slice
    double curValue = 0.0D;
    int startAngle = 0;
    for (int i=0; i<slices.length; i++) {
        // Compute the start and stop angles
        startAngle = (int)(curValue * 360 / total);
        int arcAngle = (int)(slices[i].value * 360 / total);

        // Ensure that rounding errors do not leave a gap between the first and last slice
        if (i == slices.length-1) {
            arcAngle = 360 - startAngle;
        }

        // Set the color and draw a filled arc
        g.setColor(slices[i].color);
        g.fillArc(area.x, area.y, area.width, area.height, startAngle, arcAngle);

        curValue += slices[i].value;
    }
}
```

Here's some code that uses the drawPie() method:

```
class MyComponent extends JComponent {
    PieValue[] slices = new PieValue[4];

    MyComponent() {
        slices[0] = new PieValue(25, Color.red);
        slices[1] = new PieValue(33, Color.green);
        slices[2] = new PieValue(20, Color.pink);
        slices[3] = new PieValue(15, Color.blue);
    }

    // This method is called whenever the contents needs to be painted
    public void paint(Graphics g) {
        // Draw the pie
        drawPie((Graphics2D)g, getBounds(), slices);
```

Packages and Examples

```
        }
    }
    // Show the component in a frame
    JFrame frame = new JFrame();
    frame.getContentPane().add(new MyComponent());
    frame.setSize(300, 200);
    frame.setVisible(true);
```

Text

ε591. Drawing Simple Text

See also "ε575. The Quintessential Drawing Program".

```
public void paint(Graphics g) {
    // Set the desired font if different from default font
    String family = "Serif";
    int style = Font.PLAIN;
    int size = 12;
    Font font = new Font(family, style, size);
    g.setFont(font);

    // Draw a string such that its base line is at x, y
    int x = 10;
    int y = 10;
    g.drawString("aString", x, y);


    // Draw a string such that the top-left corner is at x, y
    x = 10;
    y = 30;
    FontMetrics fontMetrics = g.getFontMetrics();
    g.drawString("aString", x, y+fontMetrics.getAscent());
}
```

ε592. Drawing Rotated Text

```
// Draw string rotated clockwise 90 degrees
AffineTransform at = new AffineTransform();
at.setToRotation(Math.PI/2.0);
g2d.setTransform(at);
g2d.drawString("aString", x, y);

// Draw string rotated counter-clockwise 90 degrees
at = new AffineTransform();
at.setToRotation(-Math.PI/2.0);
g2d.setTransform(at);
g2d.drawString("aString", x, y);
```

ε593. Getting the Dimensions of Text

```
// From within the paint() method
public void paint(Graphics g) {
    Graphics2D g2d = (Graphics2D)g;
    Font font = new Font("Serif", Font.PLAIN, 12);
```

Class *Interface* —extends - - -implements ○ abstract ● final ⌐—has superclass ⌐—has subclass package—see other volume

```
        FontMetrics fontMetrics = g2d.getFontMetrics();

        int width = fontMetrics.stringWidth("aString");
        int height = fontMetrics.getHeight();
    }

// From within a component
class MyComponent extends JComponent {
        MyComponent() {
            Font font = new Font("Serif", Font.PLAIN, 12);
            FontMetrics fontMetrics = getFontMetrics(font);

            int width = fontMetrics.stringWidth("aString");
            int height = fontMetrics.getHeight();
        }
    }
```

Images

ε594. Reading an Image or Icon from a File

See also "ε595. Drawing an Image".

```
// This call returns immediately and pixels are loaded in the background
Image image = Toolkit.getDefaultToolkit().getImage("image.gif");
int width = image.getWidth(null);
int height = image.getHeight(null);

if (width >= 0) {
    // The image has been fully loaded
} else {
    // The image has not been fully loaded
}


// This method ensures that all pixels have been loaded before returning
image = new ImageIcon("image.gif").getImage();

// Get the dimensions of the image; these will be non-negative
width = image.getWidth(null);
height = image.getHeight(null);
```

ε595. Drawing an Image

See also "ε575. The Quintessential Drawing Program" and "ε594. Reading an Image or Icon from a File".

```
public void paint(Graphics g) {
    // Draw an Image object
    int x = 0;
    int y = 0;
    g.drawImage(image, x, y, this);

    // Draw an Icon object
    x = 0;
    y = 100;
    icon.paintIcon(this, g, x, y);
}
```

ε596. Scaling, Shearing, Translating, and Rotating a Drawn Image

See also "ε575. The Quintessential Drawing Program" and "ε594. Reading an Image or Icon from a File".

```
public void paint(Graphics g) {
    Graphics2D g2d = (Graphics2D) g;
    AffineTransform tx = new AffineTransform();

    double scalex = .5;
    double scaley = 1;
    tx.scale(scalex, scaley);

    double shiftx = .1;
    double shifty = .3;
    tx.shear(shiftx, shifty);

    double x = 50;
    double y = 50;
    tx.translate(x, y);

    double radians = -Math.PI/4;
    tx.rotate(radians);

    g2d.drawImage(image, tx, this);
}
```

ε597. Creating a Gray Version of an Icon

```
public Icon toGray(Icon icon) {
    if (icon instanceof ImageIcon) {
        Image grayImage = GrayFilter.createDisabledImage(((ImageIcon)icon).getImage());
        return new ImageIcon(grayImage);
    }
    // Cannot convert
    return null;
}
```

The Screen

ε598. Getting the Screen Size

```
// Get the size of the default screen
Dimension dim = Toolkit.getDefaultToolkit().getScreenSize();
```

If more than one screen is available, this example gets the size of each screen:

```
GraphicsEnvironment ge = GraphicsEnvironment.getLocalGraphicsEnvironment();
GraphicsDevice[] gs = ge.getScreenDevices();

// Get size of each screen
for (int i=0; i<gs.length; i++) {
    DisplayMode dm = gs[i].getDisplayMode();
    int screenWidth = dm.getWidth();
    int screenHeight = dm.getHeight();
}
```

Class   *Interface*   —extends   - - -implements   ○ abstract   ● final   ^—has superclass   ⌣—has subclass   package—see other volume

ε599. Centering a Frame, Window, or Dialog on the Screen

```
// Get the size of the screen
Dimension dim = Toolkit.getDefaultToolkit().getScreenSize();

// Determine the new location of the window
int w = window.getSize().width;
int h = window.getSize().height;
int x = (dim.width-w)/2;
int y = (dim.height-h)/2;

// Move the window
window.setLocation(x, y);
```

ε600. Getting the Number of Screens

```
GraphicsEnvironment ge = GraphicsEnvironment.getLocalGraphicsEnvironment();
try {
    GraphicsDevice[] gs = ge.getScreenDevices();

    // Get number of screens
    int numScreens = gs.length;
} catch (HeadlessException e) {
    // Is thrown if there are no screen devices
}
```

ε601. Enabling Full-Screen Mode

In full-screen mode, no window can overlap the full-screen window. Also, when in full-screen mode, the display mode typically can be changed if desired (see "ε605. Setting the Screen Size, Refresh Rate, or Number of Colors").

```
// Determine if full-screen mode is supported directly
GraphicsEnvironment ge = GraphicsEnvironment.getLocalGraphicsEnvironment();
GraphicsDevice gs = ge.getDefaultScreenDevice();
if (gs.isFullScreenSupported()) {
    // Full-screen mode is supported
} else {
    // Full-screen mode will be simulated
}

// Create a button that leaves full-screen mode
Button btn = new Button("OK");
btn.addActionListener(new ActionListener() {
    public void actionPerformed(ActionEvent evt) {
        // Return to normal windowed mode
        GraphicsEnvironment ge = GraphicsEnvironment.getLocalGraphicsEnvironment();
        GraphicsDevice gs = ge.getDefaultScreenDevice();
        gs.setFullScreenWindow(null);
    }
});

// Create a window for full-screen mode; add a button to leave full-screen mode
Frame frame = new Frame(gs.getDefaultConfiguration());
Window win = new Window(frame);
win.add(btn, BorderLayout.CENTER);

try {
    // Enter full-screen mode
    gs.setFullScreenWindow(win);
```

Packages and Examples

```
        win.validate();

        // ...
    } finally {
        // Exit full-screen mode
        gs.setFullScreenWindow(null);
    }
```

ε602. Double-Buffering in Full-Screen Mode

Page-flipping, if supported, is the fastest way to copy a back buffer to the screen. This example demonstrates how to implement double-buffering using page flipping in full-screen mode.

```
    // Determine if page flipping is supported
    GraphicsEnvironment ge = GraphicsEnvironment.getLocalGraphicsEnvironment();
    GraphicsDevice gd = ge.getDefaultScreenDevice();
    GraphicsConfiguration gc = gd.getDefaultConfiguration();
    BufferCapabilities bufCap = gc.getBufferCapabilities();
    boolean page = bufCap.isPageFlipping();

    if (page) {
        // Page flipping is supported
    } else {
        // Page flipping is not supported
    }

    // Create a window for full-screen mode
    Frame frame = new Frame(gd.getDefaultConfiguration());
    Window win = new Window(frame);

    // Configure the window so that a mouse click will exit full-screen mode
    win.addMouseListener(new MouseAdapter() {
        public void mousePressed(MouseEvent evt) {
            // Exit full-screen mode
            GraphicsDevice gd = GraphicsEnvironment.getLocalGraphicsEnvironment()
                .getDefaultScreenDevice();
            gd.setFullScreenWindow(null);
        }
    });

    try {
        // Enter full-screen mode
        gd.setFullScreenWindow(win);
        win.requestFocus();

        // Create the back buffer
        int numBuffers = 2; // Includes front buffer
        win.createBufferStrategy(numBuffers);

        // Determine the state of a back buffer after it has been displayed on the screen.
        // This information is used to optimize performance. For example, if your application
        // needs to initialize a back buffer with a background color, there is
        // no need to do so if the flip contents is BACKGROUND.
        BufferStrategy strategy = win.getBufferStrategy();
        bufCap = strategy.getCapabilities();
        BufferCapabilities.FlipContents flipContents = bufCap.getFlipContents();
        if (flipContents.equals(BufferCapabilities.FlipContents.UNDEFINED)) {
            // The contents is unknown after a flip
```

Class   *Interface*   —extends   - - -implements   ○ abstract   ● final   ^—has superclass   ⌐—has subclass   package—see other volume

```
        } else if (flipContents.equals(BufferCapabilities.FlipContents.BACKGROUND)) {
                // The contents cleared to the component's background color after a flip
        } else if (flipContents.equals(BufferCapabilities.FlipContents.PRIOR)) {
                // The contents is the contents of the front buffer just before the flip
        } else if (flipContents.equals(BufferCapabilities.FlipContents.COPIED)) {
                // The contents is identical to the contents just pushed to the
                // front buffer after a flip
        }

        // Draw loop
        while (true) {
                // Get screen size
                int screenWidth = win.getWidth();
                int screenHeight = win.getHeight();

                // Get graphics context for drawing to the window
                Graphics g = strategy.getDrawGraphics();

                if (!flipContents.equals(BufferCapabilities.FlipContents.BACKGROUND)) {
                        // Clear background
                        g.setColor(Color.white);
                        g.fillRect(0, 0, screenWidth, screenHeight);
                }

                // Draw shapes and images...

                // Done drawing
                g.dispose();

                // Flip the back buffer to the screen
                strategy.show();
        }
} catch (Throwable e) {
        // Process exception...
} finally {
        gd.setFullScreenWindow(null);
}
```

ε603. Getting the Available Screen Sizes, Refresh Rates, and Number of Colors

This example demonstrates how to retrieve all available combinations of screen size, refresh rate, or number of colors for the default screen device. See also "ε605. Setting the Screen Size, Refresh Rate, or Number of Colors".

```
// Determine if the display mode can be changed
GraphicsEnvironment ge = GraphicsEnvironment.getLocalGraphicsEnvironment();
GraphicsDevice gs = ge.getDefaultScreenDevice();

DisplayMode[] dmodes = gs.getDisplayModes();
for (int i=0; i<dmodes.length; i++) {
        int screenWidth = dmodes[i].getWidth();
        int screenHeight = dmodes[i].getHeight();
        int bitDepth = dmodes[i].getBitDepth();
        int refreshRate = dmodes[i].getRefreshRate();
}
```

ε604. Getting the Current Screen Refresh Rate and Number of Colors

This example retrieves the refresh rate (in Hz) and number of supported colors for all screens.

```
GraphicsEnvironment ge = GraphicsEnvironment.getLocalGraphicsEnvironment();
GraphicsDevice[] gs = ge.getScreenDevices();

for (int i=0; i<gs.length; i++) {
    DisplayMode dm = gs[i].getDisplayMode();

    // Get refresh rate in Hz
    int refreshRate = dm.getRefreshRate();
    if (refreshRate == DisplayMode.REFRESH_RATE_UNKNOWN) {
        // Unknown rate
    }

    // Get number of colors
    int bitDepth = dm.getBitDepth();
    if (bitDepth == DisplayMode.BIT_DEPTH_MULTI) {
        // Multiple bit depths are supported in this display mode
    } else {
        int numColors = (int)Math.pow(2, bitDepth);
    }
}
```

ε605. Setting the Screen Size, Refresh Rate, or Number of Colors

Typically, the properties of the screen can only be changed while in full-screen mode (see "ε601. Enabling Full-Screen Mode". See also "ε603. Getting the Available Screen Sizes, Refresh Rates, and Number of Colors".

```
// Determine if the display mode can be changed
GraphicsEnvironment ge = GraphicsEnvironment.getLocalGraphicsEnvironment();
GraphicsDevice gs = ge.getDefaultScreenDevice();

// Determine if the display mode can be changed
boolean canChg = gs.isDisplayChangeSupported();
if (canChg) {
    // Change the screen size and number of colors
    DisplayMode displayMode = gs.getDisplayMode();
    int screenWidth = 640;
    int screenHeight = 480;
    int bitDepth = 8;
    displayMode = new DisplayMode(
        screenWidth, screenHeight, bitDepth, displayMode.getRefreshRate());
    try {
        gs.setDisplayMode(displayMode);
    } catch (Throwable e) {
        // Desired display mode is not supported; leave full-screen mode
        gs.setFullScreenWindow(null);
    }
} else if (gs.getFullScreenWindow() != null) {
    // Try enabling full-screen mode;
    // see "ε601. Enabling Full-Screen Mode"
} else {
    // Display mode cannot be changed
}
```

Class   *Interface*   —extends   - - -implements   ○ abstract   ● final   ˆ—has superclass   ˎ—has subclass   package—see other volume

Focus

ε606. Determining Which Component or Window Has the Focus

```
// null is returned if none of the components in this application has the focus
Component compFocusOwner =
    KeyboardFocusManager.getCurrentKeyboardFocusManager().getFocusOwner();
```

```
// null is returned if none of the windows in this application has the focus
Window windowFocusOwner =
    KeyboardFocusManager.getCurrentKeyboardFocusManager().getFocusedWindow();
```

```
// Use this method to determine whether a particular component has the focus
boolean b = component.isFocusOwner();
```

ε607. Preventing a Component from Gaining the Focus

When setFocusable() is called, the user will not be able to give the component the focus (by clicking on it or through focus traversal), nor be able to acquire the focus.

```
component.setFocusable(false);
```

ε608. Preventing a Window from Gaining the Focus

If Window.setFocusableWindowState(false) is called on a window, neither the window nor any of its children components can gain the focus. However, components like buttons can still invoke actions.

On some platforms, if the non-focusable window is the only window visible in the application, the non-focusable window will gain the focus. However, none of the children components will gain the focus.

```
frame.setFocusableWindowState(false);
```

ε609. Listening to All Focus Changes Between Components in an Application

To listen to focus change events between components, install a listener with the keyboard focus manager. If you need the ability to veto (reject) a focus change, install a vetoable listener with the keyboard focus manager.

```
KeyboardFocusManager.getCurrentKeyboardFocusManager()
    .addPropertyChangeListener(new FocusChangeListener());
KeyboardFocusManager.getCurrentKeyboardFocusManager()
    .addVetoableChangeListener(new FocusVetoableChangeListener());

class FocusChangeListener implements PropertyChangeListener {
    public void propertyChange(PropertyChangeEvent evt) {
        Component oldComp = (Component)evt.getOldValue();
        Component newComp = (Component)evt.getNewValue();

        if ("focusOwner".equals(evt.getPropertyName())) {
            if (oldComp == null) {
                // the newComp component gained the focus
            } else {
                // the oldComp component lost the focus
            }
        } else if ("focusedWindow".equals(evt.getPropertyName())) {
            if (oldComp == null) {
                // the newComp window gained the focus
            } else {
                // the oldComp window lost the focus
            }
```

```
                }
            }
        }
        class FocusVetoableChangeListener implements VetoableChangeListener {
            public void vetoableChange(PropertyChangeEvent evt) throws PropertyVetoException {
                Component oldComp = (Component)evt.getOldValue();
                Component newComp = (Component)evt.getNewValue();

                if ("focusOwner".equals(evt.getPropertyName())) {
                    if (oldComp == null) {
                        // the newComp component will gain the focus
                    } else {
                        // the oldComp component will lose the focus
                    }
                } else if ("focusedWindow".equals(evt.getPropertyName())) {
                    if (oldComp == null) {
                        // the newComp window will gain the focus
                    } else {
                        // the oldComp window will lose the focus
                    }
                }

                boolean vetoFocusChange = false;
                if (vetoFocusChange) {
                    throw new PropertyVetoException("message", evt);
                }
            }
        }
```

ε610. Setting Focus Traversal Keys in a Component

When the focus is on a component, any focus traversal keys set for that component override the default focus traversal keys. For an example of how to change the focus traversal keys for the entire application, see "ε611. Setting Focus Traversal Keys for the Entire Application".

```
// Change the forward focus traversal keys for a component
Set set = new HashSet(component.getFocusTraversalKeys(
    KeyboardFocusManager.FORWARD_TRAVERSAL_KEYS));
set.clear(); // Call clear() if you want to eliminate the current key set
set.add(KeyStroke.getKeyStroke("F2"));
component.setFocusTraversalKeys(KeyboardFocusManager.FORWARD_TRAVERSAL_KEYS, set);
```

ε611. Setting Focus Traversal Keys for the Entire Application

This example changes the focus traversal keys for the entire application. For an example of how to change the focus traversal keys for a particular component, see "ε610. Setting Focus Traversal Keys in a Component".

```
// Change the forward focus traversal keys for the application
Set set = new HashSet(
    KeyboardFocusManager.getCurrentKeyboardFocusManager().getDefaultFocusTraversalKeys(
        KeyboardFocusManager.FORWARD_TRAVERSAL_KEYS));
set.clear(); // Call clear() if you want to eliminate the current key set
set.add(KeyStroke.getKeyStroke("F2"));
KeyboardFocusManager.getCurrentKeyboardFocusManager().setDefaultFocusTraversalKeys(
    KeyboardFocusManager.FORWARD_TRAVERSAL_KEYS, set);

// Change the backward focus traversal keys for the application
```

```
set = new HashSet(
    KeyboardFocusManager.getCurrentKeyboardFocusManager().getDefaultFocusTraversalKeys(
        KeyboardFocusManager.BACKWARD_TRAVERSAL_KEYS));
set.clear(); // Call clear() if you want to eliminate the current key set
set.add(KeyStroke.getKeyStroke("F3"));
KeyboardFocusManager.getCurrentKeyboardFocusManager().setDefaultFocusTraversalKeys(
    KeyboardFocusManager.BACKWARD_TRAVERSAL_KEYS, set);

// Remove all forward and backward focus traversal keys for the application
set.clear();
KeyboardFocusManager.getCurrentKeyboardFocusManager().setDefaultFocusTraversalKeys(
    KeyboardFocusManager.FORWARD_TRAVERSAL_KEYS, set);
KeyboardFocusManager.getCurrentKeyboardFocusManager().setDefaultFocusTraversalKeys(
    KeyboardFocusManager.BACKWARD_TRAVERSAL_KEYS, set);
```

ε612. Moving the Focus to the Next or Previous Focusable Component

The methods to move the focus to the next or to the previous focusable component are Component$_2$ .transferFocus() and Component.transferFocusBackward().

This example modifies a component so that pressing the space bar or pressing F2 moves the focus to the next focusable component. Pressing shift space or shift F2 moves the focus to the previous focusable component.

```
// Bind space and shift space
component.getInputMap(JComponent.WHEN_FOCUSED).put(
    KeyStroke.getKeyStroke("SPACE"), nextFocusAction.getValue(Action.NAME));
component.getInputMap(JComponent.WHEN_FOCUSED).put(
    KeyStroke.getKeyStroke("shift SPACE"), prevFocusAction.getValue(Action.NAME));

// This key binding is required for text components. It hides the
// default typed space key binding in a text component. If you don't
// hide this key binding, typing the space key will insert a space into
// the text component (as well as move the focus).
// See "ε1003. Overriding a Few Default Typed Key Bindings in a JTextComponent" for more details.
component.getInputMap(JComponent.WHEN_FOCUSED).put(
    KeyStroke.getKeyStroke(new Character(' '), 0), "unbound");

// Bind F2 and shift F2
component.getInputMap(JComponent.WHEN_FOCUSED).put(
    KeyStroke.getKeyStroke("F2"), nextFocusAction.getValue(Action.NAME));
component.getInputMap(JComponent.WHEN_FOCUSED).put(
    KeyStroke.getKeyStroke("shift F2"), prevFocusAction.getValue(Action.NAME));

// Add actions
component.getActionMap().put(nextFocusAction.getValue(Action.NAME), nextFocusAction);
component.getActionMap().put(prevFocusAction.getValue(Action.NAME), prevFocusAction);

// The actions
public Action nextFocusAction = new AbstractAction("Move Focus Forwards") {
    public void actionPerformed(ActionEvent evt) {
        ((Component)evt.getSource()).transferFocus();
    }
};
public Action prevFocusAction = new AbstractAction("Move Focus Backwards") {
    public void actionPerformed(ActionEvent evt) {
        ((Component)evt.getSource()).transferFocusBackward();
    }
};
```

Packages and Examples

ε613. Modifying the Focus Traversal Order

```
JFrame frame = new JFrame();
JButton component1 = new JButton("1");
JButton component2 = new JButton("2");
JButton component3 = new JButton("3");

// By default, the focus traversal order is the same as the insertion order
frame.getContentPane().setLayout(new FlowLayout());
frame.getContentPane().add(component1);
frame.getContentPane().add(component2);
frame.getContentPane().add(component3);

// Change the order from 1,2,3 to 1,3,2
component1.setNextFocusableComponent(component3);
component3.setNextFocusableComponent(component2);
component2.setNextFocusableComponent(component1);

// Restore the order to 1,2,3
component1.setNextFocusableComponent(null);
component2.setNextFocusableComponent(null);
component3.setNextFocusableComponent(null);
```

ε614. Setting the Initial Focused Component in a Window

There is no straightforward way to set the initial focused component in a window. The typical method is to add a window listener to listen for the window opened event and then make the desired component request the focus.

```
// Create frame and three buttons
JFrame frame = new JFrame();
JButton component1 = new JButton("1");
JButton component2 = new JButton("2");
JButton component3 = new JButton("3");

// Set component with initial focus; must be done before the frame is made visible
InitialFocusSetter.setInitialFocus(frame, component2);

class InitialFocusSetter {
    public static void setInitialFocus(Window w, Component c) {
        w.addWindowListener(new FocusSetter(c));
    }

    public static class FocusSetter extends WindowAdapter {
        Component initComp;
        FocusSetter(Component c) {
            initComp = c;
        }
        public void windowOpened(WindowEvent e) {
            initComp.requestFocus();

            // Since this listener is no longer needed, remove it
            e.getWindow().removeWindowListener(this);
        }
    }
}
```

Class   *Interface*   —extends   - - -implements   ○ abstract   ● final   ^—has superclass   ⌄—has subclass   package—see other volume

ε615. Finding the Next Focusable Component

```
public Component findNextFocus() {
    // Find focus owner
    Component c = KeyboardFocusManager.getCurrentKeyboardFocusManager().getFocusOwner();
    Container root = c == null ? null : c.getFocusCycleRootAncestor();

    if (root != null) {
        FocusTraversalPolicy policy = root.getFocusTraversalPolicy();
        Component nextFocus = policy.getComponentAfter(root, c);
        if (nextFocus == null) {
            nextFocus = policy.getDefaultComponent(root);
        }
        return nextFocus;
    }
    return null;
}
public Component findPrevFocus() {
    // Find focus owner
    Component c = KeyboardFocusManager.getCurrentKeyboardFocusManager().getFocusOwner();
    Container root = c == null ? null : c.getFocusCycleRootAncestor();

    if (root != null) {
        FocusTraversalPolicy policy = root.getFocusTraversalPolicy();
        Component prevFocus = policy.getComponentBefore(root, c);
        if (prevFocus == null) {
            prevFocus = policy.getDefaultComponent(root);
        }
        return prevFocus;
    }
    return null;
}
```

ε616. Determining If a Focus Lost Is Temporary or Permanent

A temporary focus-lost event occurs if the focus moves to another window. It's temporary because the component will gain the focus when its window becomes active again.

A permanent focus-lost event occurs if the focus moves to another component in the same window.

An example where this distinction might come in handy is in text field validation; a text field might not validate its contents in the case of a temporary loss of focus.

```
component.addFocusListener(new MyFocusListener());

public class MyFocusListener extends FocusAdapter {
    public void focusGained(FocusEvent evt) {
        // The component gained the focus.
    }
    public void focusLost(FocusEvent evt) {
        // The component lost the focus.
        boolean isTemporary = evt.isTemporary();
    }
}
```

ε617. Determining the Opposite Component of a Focus Event

The opposite component is the other component affected in a focus event. Specifically, in a focus-lost event, the opposite component is the one gaining the focus. In a focus-gain event, the opposite component is the one losing the focus.

Sometimes the opposite component is null, which indicates that the component is in some other application.

```
component.addFocusListener(new MyFocusListener());

public class MyFocusListener extends FocusAdapter {
    public void focusGained(FocusEvent evt) {
        // The component that lost the focus
        Component c = evt.getOppositeComponent();
    }

    public void focusLost(FocusEvent evt) {
        // The component that gained the focus
        Component c = evt.getOppositeComponent();
    }
}
```

ε618. Validating a JTextField When Permanently Losing the Focus

This example demonstrates a text field that validates its contents when it receives a permanent focus-lost event. If the contents are invalid, it displays a modal dialog with an error message and regains the focus.

```
JTextField component = new JTextField(10);
component.addFocusListener(new MyFocusListener());

public class MyFocusListener extends FocusAdapter {
    boolean showingDialog = false;

    public void focusGained(FocusEvent evt) {
        final JTextComponent c = (JTextComponent)evt.getSource();
        String s = c.getText();

        // Position the caret at the 1st non-digit character
        for (int i=0; i<s.length(); i++) {
            // Ensure validity
            if (!Character.isDigit(s.charAt(i))) {
                c.setSelectionStart(i);
                c.setSelectionEnd(i);
                break;
            }
        }
    }
    public void focusLost(FocusEvent evt) {
        final JTextComponent c = (JTextComponent)evt.getSource();
        String s = c.getText();

        if (evt.isTemporary()) {
            return;
        }
        for (int i=0; i<s.length(); i++) {
            // Ensure validity
            if (!Character.isDigit(s.charAt(i))) {
                // Find top-level window
                Component par = c;
```

```
        while (par.getParent() != null) {
            par = par.getParent();
        }
        final Frame frame = (Frame)par;

        // Create and display an error message
        JOptionPane optionPane = new JOptionPane("The value must only contain digits",
            JOptionPane.ERROR_MESSAGE, JOptionPane.DEFAULT_OPTION);
        optionPane.createDialog(frame, null).show();

        // Regain the focus
        c.requestFocus();
        break;
      }
    }
  }
}
```

ε619. Removing the Focus from the Application

```
KeyboardFocusManager.getCurrentKeyboardFocusManager().clearGlobalFocusOwner();
```

ε620. Activating a Keystroke When Any Component in the Window Has Focus

Normally, a keystroke registered to a component is activated when the component has the focus. This type of activation condition is called WHEN_FOCUSED. It is possible to specify that a keystroke be activated if any component (including itself) in the window has the focus. This type of keystroke activation condition is called WHEN_IN_FOCUSED_WINDOW.

Keyboard accelerators use this type of keystroke activation condition. For example, in many applications, regardless of which component has the focus, typing F1 in an active window causes a help window to appear.

There are three types of activation conditions available: WHEN_FOCUSED, WHEN_ANCESTOR_OF_ _FOCUSED_COMPONENT, and WHEN_IN_FOCUSED_WINDOW. When a key is typed, the focused component is checked for a registered keystroke to handle the typed key. If found, the action bound to the keystroke is invoked. If not found, the set of WHEN_ANCESTOR_OF_FOCUSED_COMPONENT keystrokes is searched for a handler of the typed key. WHEN_ANCESTOR_OF_FOCUSED_COMPONENT is described in "ε621. Activating a Keystroke When Any Child Component Has Focus". If none are found still, the set of WHEN_IN_FOCUSED_WINDOW keystrokes is searched for a handler of the typed key.

In non-WHEN_FOCUSED activated keystrokes, the source of the resulting action event is the component to which the keystroke is registered, not the focused component.

```
    // To create an action, see "ε855. Creating an Action"

    // Register keystroke
component.getInputMap(JComponent.WHEN_IN_FOCUSED_WINDOW).put(
    KeyStroke.getKeyStroke("F2"), action.getValue(Action.NAME));

    // Register action
component.getActionMap().put(action.getValue(Action.NAME), action);
```

ε621. Activating a Keystroke When Any Child Component Has Focus

Normally, a keystroke registered on a component is activated when the component has the focus. This type of activation condition is called WHEN_FOCUSED. It is possible to specify that a keystroke be activated if it or any child or descendant component has the focus. This type of keystroke activation condition is called WHEN_ANCESTOR_OF_FOCUSED_COMPONENT.

Packages and Examples

An example where this type of keystroke activation condition is useful is in the case of a scrollpane that handles scrolling navigation keystrokes even when the child component has the focus.

There are three types of activation conditions available: WHEN_FOCUSED, WHEN_ANCESTOR_OF‚ _FOCUSED_COMPONENT, and WHEN_IN_FOCUSED_WINDOW. See "ε620. Activating a Keystroke When Any Component in the Window Has Focus" for more details about these activation conditions.

```
// To create an action, see "ε855. Creating an Action"

// Register keystroke
component.getInputMap(JComponent.WHEN_ANCESTOR_OF_FOCUSED_COMPONENT).put(
    KeyStroke.getKeyStroke("F2"), action.getValue(Action.NAME));

// Register action
component.getActionMap().put(action.getValue(Action.NAME), action);
```

GridBagLayout

ε622. Creating a GridBagLayout

A gridbag layout is the most sophisticated layout manager in Java's UI toolkit. This example demonstrates how to create and set a gridbag layout and how to set gridbag constraints on components added to the layout. See other examples for code that demonstrates the usage of available gridbag constraints.

```
JFrame frame = new JFrame();
Container container = frame.getContentPane();

// Create the layout
GridBagLayout gbl = new GridBagLayout();

// Set layout on container
container.setLayout(gbl);

// Place a component at cell location (1,1)
GridBagConstraints gbc = new GridBagConstraints();
gbc.gridx = 1;
gbc.gridy = 1;
// Add other gridbag constraints here

// Associate the gridbag constraints with the component
gbl.setConstraints(component, gbc);

// Add the component to the container
container.add(component);

// Show the frame
frame.pack();
frame.setVisible(true);
```

ε623. Setting the Location of a Component in a GridBagLayout

A gridbag layout arranges components in a two-dimensional grid of *cells*. The northwest-most cell has position (0,0). The cell to the right or east has position (1,0); the cell to the bottom or south has position (0,1).

The size of the grid grows dynamically. For example, if you place a component at position (2,1) in a new empty gridbag layout, the layout will automatically have a size of 3 cells across by 2 cells down.

Class   *Interface*   —extends   - - -implements   ○ abstract   ● final   ˆ—has superclass   ˌ—has subclass   package—see other volume

See "ε622. Creating a GridBagLayout" for an example on how to use a gridbag layout with gridbag constraints.

```
GridBagConstraints gbc = new GridBagConstraints();

// Place a component at (1,1)
gbc.gridx = 1;
gbc.gridy = 1;
gbl.setConstraints(component1, gbc);
container.add(component1);
// The layout now has 4 cells

// Place a component at (0,0)
gbc.gridx = 0;
gbc.gridy = 0;
gbl.setConstraints(component2, gbc);
container.add(component2);
```

ε624. Getting the Number of Rows and Columns of Cells in a GridBagLayout

The number of rows and columns in a GridBagLayout automatically grows as needed when components are added. The current number of rows and columns can be determined by calling getLayoutDimensions(). However, it won't return the correct values until the components have been laid out at least once before the call to getLayoutDimensions(). Unless you can be sure the components have been laid out at least once, you should explicitly call layoutContainer() to force a layout of the components.

```
GridBagLayout gbl = new GridBagLayout();
container.setLayout(gbl);

// Add components to container and gbl

// Force the layout of components before calling getLayoutDimensions()
gbl.layoutContainer(container);

// Get the dimensions
int[][] dim = gbl.getLayoutDimensions();
int cols = dim[0].length;
int rows = dim[1].length;
```

ε625. Making a GridBagLayout Fill the Container

By default, a gridbag layout arranges its components in the smallest area that satisfies the preferred sizes of the components. If the container is larger than this area, the cluster of components is centered within the container. This example demonstrates how to spread the excess space among all the cells in the gridbag layout.

It is possible to control exactly how much excess space is distributed among the gridbag layout cells. See "ε626. Setting the Stretchyness of Rows and Columns in a GridBagLayout Using Layout Weights" for more details.

```
GridBagLayout gbl = new GridBagLayout();
container.setLayout(gbl);

// Add components to container and gbl

// Force the layout of components before calling getLayoutWeights()
// otherwise the result of getLayoutWeights() is not valid
gbl.layoutContainer(container);

// Set weights of all columns and rows to 1
double[][] weights = gbl.getLayoutWeights();
```

```
for (int i=0; i<2; i++) {
    for (int j=0; j<weights[i].length; j++) {
        weights[i][j] = 1;
    }
}
gbl.columnWeights = weights[0];
gbl.rowWeights = weights[1];
```

ε626. Setting the Stretchyness of Rows and Columns in a GridBagLayout Using Layout Weights

Column and row stretchyness is controlled by the *weight* of specific columns and rows. A column with zero weight does not stretch; it is given just enough space to accommodate the component with the widest preferred width in that column; this also applies to a row with zero weight.

When a single column has a non-zero weight, it is given all the excess horizontal space; it is the only column that stretches. In this case, the value of the weight doesn't matter

When more than one column has a non-zero weight, the excess space is distributed among the non-zero weight columns using the weight values. In particular, if the excess space is P pixels, and the column weights for column^i is weight^i, then column^i gets exactly (weight^i * P) / (sum-of-all-column-weights). For example, if column 1 has weight 1 and column 2 has weight 2 and the excess space is 90 pixels, column 1 will get 30 extra pixels and column 2 will get 60 extra pixels. Rows with a non-zero *weight* behave in similar fashion.

There are two ways to set the weight of a column or row. The first is to set the weights using the GridBagLayout object. The second way is to assign weights to components. The weight of a column is determined by the maximum of all the weights of all components in that column including the assigned weight of the column in the GridBagLayout object. So, if the maximum weight of all the components in the column is 2 and the weight for that column in the GridBagLayout object is 3, the column weight is 3. The weight of a row is determined in similar fashion.

Typically, weights are set using either method, not both. In particular, if only one row or column needs to be stretchy, it is usually more convenient to assign a non-zero weight to the stretchy component. Then the right thing happens. Whereas, if two or more columns or rows are stretchy and the weights are not the same, it is sometimes more convenient to set the weights in the GridBadLayout object.

This example demonstrates how to assign weights in the GridBagLayout object. See "ε627. Setting the Stretchyness of Columns and Rows in a GridBagLayout Using Component Weights" for an example of how to set weights on a component.

See "ε622. Creating a GridBagLayout" for an example on how to use a gridbag layout with gridbag constraints.

```
GridBagLayout gbl = new GridBagLayout();

// We assume that the grid has 2 rows and 3 columns.
// The 1st column and row do not stretch.
// The 2nd column gets 1/3 of the excess horizontal space.
// The 3rd column gets 2/3 of the excess horizontal space.
// The 2nd row gets all of the excess vertical space.
gbl.columnWeights = new double[]{0.0f, 1.0f, 2.0f};
gbl.rowWeights = new double[]{0.0f, 1.0f};
```

Class   *Interface*   —extends   - - -implements   ○ abstract   ● final   ^—has superclass   ⌄—has subclass   package—see other volume

ε627. Setting the Stretchyness of Columns and Rows in a GridBagLayout Using Component Weights

See "ε626. Setting the Stretchyness of Rows and Columns in a GridBagLayout Using Layout Weights" for an explanation of stretchyness and weights. This example demonstrates how to set the weight of a row or column by assigning the weight on a component.

See "ε622. Creating a GridBagLayout" for an example on how to use a gridbag layout with gridbag constraints.

```
GridBagLayout gbl = new GridBagLayout();
container.setLayout(gbl);

// Place a component at (0,1) with a column weight 1 and
// a row weight of 2
GridBagConstraints gbc = new GridBagConstraints();
gbc.gridx = 0;
gbc.gridy = 1;
gbc.weightx = 1;
gbc.weighty = 2;
gbl.setConstraints(component, gbc);
container.add(component);
```

ε628. Setting the Stretchyness of a Component Within the Cell of a GridBagLayout Using Fill

By default, when the cell is larger than the preferred size of a component, the component is centered within the cell. You can stretch a component horizontally or vertically, or in both directions within the cell by setting its fill constraint.

See "ε622. Creating a GridBagLayout" for an example on how to use a gridbag layout with gridbag constraints.

```
GridBagLayout gbl = new GridBagLayout();
container.setLayout(gbl);

GridBagConstraints gbc = new GridBagConstraints();

// Make the component on stretchable
gbc.fill = GridBagConstraints.NONE;

// Make the component only stretch horizontally
gbc.fill = GridBagConstraints.HORIZONTAL;

// Make the component only stretch vertically
gbc.fill = GridBagConstraints.VERTICAL;

// Make the component stretch in both directions
gbc.fill = GridBagConstraints.BOTH;

gbl.setConstraints(component, gbc);
container.add(component);
```

ε629. Setting the Location of a Component Within the Cell of a GridBagLayout Using Anchors

By default, when the cell is larger than the preferred size of a component, the component is centered within the cell. You can specify other relative positions using the anchor constraint. For example, specifying an anchor of NORTH causes the component to be horizontally centered with the top edge of the component aligned with the top edge of the cell. Specifying an anchor of NORTHEAST causes the northeast corner of the component to coincide with the northeast corner of the cell.

See "ε622. Creating a GridBagLayout" for an example on how to use a gridbag layout with gridbag constraints.

```
GridBagConstraints gbc = new GridBagConstraints();

// These are the nine possible anchor values
gbc.anchor = GridBagConstraints.CENTER;
gbc.anchor = GridBagConstraints.NORTH;
gbc.anchor = GridBagConstraints.NORTHEAST;
gbc.anchor = GridBagConstraints.EAST;
gbc.anchor = GridBagConstraints.SOUTHEAST;
gbc.anchor = GridBagConstraints.SOUTH;
gbc.anchor = GridBagConstraints.SOUTHWEST;
gbc.anchor = GridBagConstraints.WEST;
gbc.anchor = GridBagConstraints.NORTHWEST;
```

ε630. Setting the Space around a Component Within the Cell of the GridBagLayout Using Insets

With insets, you can add space around a component. The cell dimensions expand to accommodate this extra space.

See "ε622. Creating a GridBagLayout" for an example on how to use a gridbag layout with gridbag constraints.

```
GridBagConstraints gbc = new GridBagConstraints();

int top = 2;
int left = 2;
int bottom = 2;
int right = 2;
gbc.insets = new Insets(top, left, bottom, right);
```

ε631. Adjusting the Size of a Component in a GridBadLayout Using Internal Padding

With internal padding, you can increase or decrease the minimum size of a component. For example, if the minimum width of a component is 10 and ipadx is 2, the minimum width of the component within the gridbag layout becomes 14.

See "ε622. Creating a GridBagLayout" for an example on how to use a gridbag layout with gridbag constraints.

```
GridBagConstraints gbc = new GridBagConstraints();

gbc.ipadx = 2;
gbc.ipady = 4;
```

ε632. Setting a Row or Column of a GridBadLayout to a Particular Size

By default, the width of a column in a gridbag layout is set to the widest component in the component. This example demonstrates how to increase the width of the column to a particular size. The same applies to rows of a gridbag layout.

See "ε622. Creating a GridBagLayout" for an example on how to use a gridbag layout.

Class   *Interface*   —extends   - - -implements   ○ abstract   ● final   ^—has superclass   ‿—has subclass   package—see other volume

```
// Sets the minimum width for column c to be w pixels wide
public void setColumnMinWidth(GridBagLayout gbl, int c, int w) {
    int[] ws = gbl.columnWidths;
    if (ws == null) {
        ws = new int[c+1];
    } else if (ws.length < c+1) {
        ws = new int[c+1];
        System.arraycopy(gbl.columnWidths, 0, ws, 0, gbl.columnWidths.length);
    }
    ws[c] = w;
    gbl.columnWidths = ws;
}

// Sets the minimum height for row r to be h pixels high
public void setRowMinHeight(GridBagLayout gbl, int r, int h) {
    int[] hs = gbl.rowHeights;
    if (hs == null) {
        hs = new int[r+1];
    } else if (hs.length < r+1) {
        hs = new int[r+1];
        System.arraycopy(gbl.rowHeights, 0, hs, 0, gbl.rowHeights.length);
    }
    hs[r] = h;
    gbl.rowHeights = hs;
}
```

ε633. Setting Gap Sizes in a GridBadLayout

Unlike most of the other layout managers, the gridbag layout manager does not have a property for controlling the size of the gaps between cells. You could implement gaps using insets (see "ε630. Setting the Space around a Component Within the Cell of the GridBagLayout Using Insets". However, this method is tedious and any change in the layout requires major changes with the insets.

The next best method is to create a blank column or row explicitly for the desired gaps.

```
// Assume components have been added in cells
// (0,0), (0,2), (2,0), (2,2)
```

```
// Create a 10 pixel gap between columns 0 and 2
setColumnMinWidth(gbl, 1, 10);
```

```
// Create a 10 pixel gap between rows 0 and 2
setRowMinHeight(gbl, 1, 10);
```

```
// setColumnMinWidth() and setRowMinHeight() are defined in
// "ε632. Setting a Row or Column of a GridBadLayout to a Particular Size"
```

Simulating Events

ε634. Moving the Cursor on the Screen

```
try {
    // These coordinates are screen coordinates
    int xCoord = 500;
    int yCoord = 500;

    // Move the cursor
    Robot robot = new Robot();
```

```
        robot.mouseMove(xCoord, yCoord);
    } catch (AWTException e) {
    }
```

ε635. Simulating Mouse and Key Presses

This feature is useful for tools that test windowing applications.

```
    try {
        Robot robot = new Robot();

        // Simulate a mouse click
        robot.mousePress(InputEvent.BUTTON1_MASK);
        robot.mouseRelease(InputEvent.BUTTON1_MASK);

        // Simulate a key press
        robot.keyPress(KeyEvent.VK_A);
        robot.keyRelease(KeyEvent.VK_A);
    } catch (AWTException e) {
    }
```

Events

ε636. Listening to All Key Events Before Delivery to Focused Component

Registering a key event dispatcher with the keyboard focus manager allows you to see all key events before they are sent to the focused component. It is possible to modify the event or even prevent the event from being delivered.

```
    KeyboardFocusManager.getCurrentKeyboardFocusManager().addKeyEventDispatcher(
        new KeyEventDispatcher() {
            public boolean dispatchKeyEvent(KeyEvent e) {
                // This example converts all typed keys to upper case
                if (e.getID() == KeyEvent.KEY_TYPED) {
                    e.setKeyChar(Character.toUpperCase(e.getKeyChar()));
                }

                // If the key should not be dispatched to the
                // focused component, set discardEvent to true
                boolean discardEvent = false;
                return discardEvent;
            }
        });
```

java.awt.color

This package contains classes for color spaces. It contains an implementation of a color space based on the International Color Consortium (ICC) Profile Format Specification, Version 3.4, August 15, 1997. It also contains color profiles based on the ICC Profile Format Specification.

Class   *Interface*   —extends   - - -implements   ○ abstract   ● final   ˆ—has superclass   ˏ—has subclass   package—see other volume

```
       java.lang.Object
1.2 ○   ├ ColorSpace ----------------------------------------- java.io.Serializable ˇ
1.2     │  └ ICC_ColorSpace
1.2     ├ ICC_Profile ------------------------------------┐
1.2     │  ├ ICC_ProfileGray                              ┊
1.2     │  └ ICC_ProfileRGB                               ┊
        └ java.lang.Throwable -----------------------------┘
           └ java.lang.Exception
              └ java.lang.RuntimeException
1.2              ├ CMMException
1.2              └ ProfileDataException
```

java.awt.datatransfer

This package contains interfaces and classes for transferring data between and within applications. It defines the notion of a clipboard, which is an object that temporarily holds data as it is being transferred between or within an application. It is typically used in copy and paste operations. Although it is possible to create a clipboard to use within an applications, most applications will use the system clipboard.

Packages and Examples

	java . lang.Object	
1.1	├ Clipboard	
1.1	├ DataFlavor -	*java . io.Externalizable˘, java . lang.Cloneable˘*
1.1	├ StringSelection -	*ClipboardOwner, Transferable*
1.2 ●	├ SystemFlavorMap -	*FlavorMap˘, FlavorTable^*
	└ java . lang.Throwable -	*java . io.Serializable˘*
	└ java . lang.Exception	
1.3	├ MimeTypeParseException	
1.1	└ UnsupportedFlavorException	
1.1	*ClipboardOwner*	
1.2	*FlavorMap˘*	
1.4	*FlavorTable* ——————————————————————————	*FlavorMap*
1.1	*Transferable*	

ε637. Getting and Setting Text on the System Clipboard

This examples defines methods for getting and setting text on the system clipboard.

```
// If a string is on the system clipboard, this method returns it;
// otherwise it returns null.
public static String getClipboard() {
    Transferable t = Toolkit.getDefaultToolkit().getSystemClipboard().getContents(null);

    try {
        if (t != null && t.isDataFlavorSupported(DataFlavor.stringFlavor)) {
            String text = (String)t.getTransferData(DataFlavor.stringFlavor);
            return text;
        }
    } catch (UnsupportedFlavorException e) {
    } catch (IOException e) {
    }
    return null;
}

// This method writes a string to the system clipboard.
// otherwise it returns null.
public static void setClipboard(String str) {
    StringSelection ss = new StringSelection(str);
    Toolkit.getDefaultToolkit().getSystemClipboard().setContents(ss, null);
}
```

ε638. Getting and Setting an Image on the System Clipboard

```
// If an image is on the system clipboard, this method returns it;
// otherwise it returns null.
public static Image getClipboard() {
    Transferable t = Toolkit.getDefaultToolkit().getSystemClipboard().getContents(null);

    try {
        if (t != null && t.isDataFlavorSupported(DataFlavor.imageFlavor)) {
            Image text = (Image)t.getTransferData(DataFlavor.imageFlavor);
            return text;
        }
```

Class   *Interface*   ——extends   - - -implements   ○ abstract   ● final   ^—has superclass ˘—has subclass package—see other volume

```
            } catch (UnsupportedFlavorException e) {
            } catch (IOException e) {
            }
            return null;
    }
```

Setting an image on the system clipboard requires a custom Transferable object to hold the image while on the clipboard.

```
    // This method writes a image to the system clipboard.
    // otherwise it returns null.
    public static void setClipboard(Image image) {
        ImageSelection imgSel = new ImageSelection(image);
        Toolkit.getDefaultToolkit().getSystemClipboard().setContents(imgSel, null);
    }

    // This class is used to hold an image while on the clipboard.
    public static class ImageSelection implements Transferable {
        private Image image;

        public ImageSelection(Image image) {
            this.image = image;
        }

        // Returns supported flavors
        public DataFlavor[] getTransferDataFlavors() {
            return new DataFlavor[]{DataFlavor.imageFlavor};
        }

        // Returns true if flavor is supported
        public boolean isDataFlavorSupported(DataFlavor flavor) {
            return DataFlavor.imageFlavor.equals(flavor);
        }

        // Returns image
        public Object getTransferData(DataFlavor flavor) throws UnsupportedFlavorException, IOException {
            if (!DataFlavor.imageFlavor.equals(flavor)) {
                throw new UnsupportedFlavorException(flavor);
            }
            return image;
        }
    }
}
```

ε639. Determining When an Item Is No Longer on the System Clipboard

When an item is set on the system clipboard, it is possible to be notified when that item is no longer on the clipboard. This is done by including a *clipboard owner* object when setting the item.

```
    // This class serves as the clipboard owner.
    class MyClipboardOwner implements ClipboardOwner {
        // This method is called when this object is no longer
        // the owner of the item on the system clipboard.
        public void lostOwnership(Clipboard clipboard, Transferable contents) {
            // To retrieve the contents, see
            // "ε637. Getting and Setting Text on the System Clipboard"
        }
    }
```

Here's some code that uses the clipboard owner:

Packages and Examples

```
// Create a clipboard owner
ClipboardOwner owner = new MyClipboardOwner();
```

```
// Set a string on the system clipboard and include the owner object
StringSelection ss = new StringSelection("A String");
Toolkit.getDefaultToolkit().getSystemClipboard().setContents(ss, owner);
```

java.awt.dnd

This package contains interfaces and classes for supporting drag-and-drop operations. It defines classes for the drag-source and the drop-target, as well as events for transferring the data being dragged, and giving visual feedback to the user performing the operation.

Class   *Interface*   —extends   - - -implements   ○ abstract   ● final   ^—has superclass   ⌄—has subclass   package—see other volume

```
        java.lang.Object
1.2 ●    ├ DnDConstants
1.2 ○    ├ DragGestureRecognizer ----------------------------- java.io.Serializable⌐
1.2 ○    │  └ MouseDragGestureRecognizer ------------------- java.awt.event.MouseListenerˆ,
                                                              java.awt.event.MouseMotionListenerˆ
1.2      ├ DragSource-------------------------------------- java.io.Serializable⌐
1.4 ○    ├ DragSourceAdapter ------------------------------ DragSourceListenerˆ, DragSourceMotionListenerˆ
1.2      ├ DragSourceContext ------------------------------ DragSourceListenerˆ,
                                                              DragSourceMotionListenerˆ,
                                                              java.io.Serializable⌐
1.2      ├ DropTarget ------------------------------------- DropTargetListenerˆ, java.io.Serializable⌐
1.2      ├ DropTarget.DropTargetAutoScroller -------------- java.awt.event.ActionListenerˆ
1.4 ○    ├ DropTargetAdapter ------------------------------ DropTargetListenerˆ
1.2      ├ DropTargetContext ------------------------------ java.io.Serializable⌐
1.2      ├ DropTargetContext.TransferableProxy ------------ java.awt.datatransfer.Transferable
1.1      ├ java.util.EventObject -------------------------- java.io.Serializable⌐
1.2      │   ├ DragGestureEvent
1.2      │   ├ DragSourceEvent
1.2      │   │  ├ DragSourceDragEvent
1.2      │   │  └ DragSourceDropEvent
1.2      │   └ DropTargetEvent
1.2      │      ├ DropTargetDragEvent
1.2      │      └ DropTargetDropEvent
1.2      └ java.lang.Throwable ---------------------------
              └ java.lang.Exception
                  └ java.lang.RuntimeException
1.1                   └ java.lang.IllegalStateException
1.2                       └ InvalidDnDOperationException

1.2     Autoscroll
1.2     DragGestureListener ──────────────────────────── java.util.EventListener
1.2     DragSourceListener ───────────────────────────
1.4     DragSourceMotionListener ─────────────────────
1.2     DropTargetListener ───────────────────────────
```

ε640. Making a Component Draggable

This example demonstrates the code needed to make a component draggable. The object being transferred in this example is a string.

```java
public class DraggableComponent extends JComponent
        implements DragGestureListener, DragSourceListener {
    DragSource dragSource;

    public DraggableComponent() {
        dragSource = new DragSource();
        dragSource.createDefaultDragGestureRecognizer(
            this, DnDConstants.ACTION_COPY_OR_MOVE, this);
    }
    public void dragGestureRecognized(DragGestureEvent evt) {
        Transferable t = new StringSelection("aString");
```

```
                dragSource.startDrag (evt, DragSource.DefaultCopyDrop, t, this);
            }
            public void dragEnter(DragSourceDragEvent evt) {
                // Called when the user is dragging this drag source and enters
                // the drop target.
            }
            public void dragOver(DragSourceDragEvent evt) {
                // Called when the user is dragging this drag source and moves
                // over the drop target.
            }
            public void dragExit(DragSourceEvent evt) {
                // Called when the user is dragging this drag source and leaves
                // the drop target.
            }
            public void dropActionChanged(DragSourceDragEvent evt) {
                // Called when the user changes the drag action between copy or move.
            }
            public void dragDropEnd(DragSourceDropEvent evt) {
                // Called when the user finishes or cancels the drag operation.
            }
        }
```

ε641. Making a Component a Drop Target

```
        public class DropTargetComponent extends JComponent implements DropTargetListener {
            public DropTargetComponent() {
                new DropTarget(this, this);
            }
            public void dragEnter(DropTargetDragEvent evt) {
                // Called when the user is dragging and enters this drop target.
            }
            public void dragOver(DropTargetDragEvent evt) {
                // Called when the user is dragging and moves over this drop target.
            }
            public void dragExit(DropTargetEvent evt) {
                // Called when the user is dragging and leaves this drop target.
            }
            public void dropActionChanged(DropTargetDragEvent evt) {
                // Called when the user changes the drag action between copy or move.
            }
            public void drop(DropTargetDropEvent evt) {
                // Called when the user finishes or cancels the drag operation.
            }
        }
```

ε642. Handling a Drop Event

The drop target in this example only accepts dropped String objects. A drop target must implement DropTargetListener and supply an implementation for drop().

```
        public void drop(DropTargetDropEvent evt) {
            try {
                Transferable t = evt.getTransferable();

                if (t.isDataFlavorSupported(DataFlavor.stringFlavor)) {
```

```
                evt.acceptDrop(DnDConstants.ACTION_COPY_OR_MOVE);
                String s = (String)t.getTransferData(DataFlavor.stringFlavor);
                evt.getDropTargetContext().dropComplete(true);
                process(s);
            } else {
                evt.rejectDrop();
            }
        } catch (IOException e) {
            evt.rejectDrop();
        } catch (UnsupportedFlavorException e) {
            evt.rejectDrop();
        }
    }
}
```

java.awt.event

This package contains interfaces and classes for dealing with different types of events fired by AWT components. See the java.awt.AWTEvent class for details on the AWT event model. Events are fired by event sources. An event listener registers with an event source to receive notifications about the events of a particular type. This package defines events and event listeners, as well as event listener adapters, which are convenience classes to make easier the process of writing event listeners.

Packages and Examples

107

	java.lang.Object	
1.1 ○	├ ComponentAdapter ----------------------------------	*ComponentListener*^
1.1 ○	├ ContainerAdapter -----------------------------------	*ContainerListener*^
1.1 ○	├ FocusAdapter ---------------------------------------	*FocusListener*^
1.3 ○	├ HierarchyBoundsAdapter -----------------------------	*HierarchyBoundsListener*^
1.1 ○	├ KeyAdapter ---	*KeyListener*^
1.1 ○	├ MouseAdapter ---------------------------------------	*MouseListener*
1.1 ○	├ MouseMotionAdapter ---------------------------------	*MouseMotionListener*
1.1 ○	├ WindowAdapter --------------------------------------	*WindowFocusListener*^, *WindowListener*^, *WindowStateListener*^
1.4 ○	├ java.util.EventListenerProxy -----------------------	*java.util.EventListener*
1.4	└ AWTEventListenerProxy -----------------------------	*AWTEventListener*^
1.1	└ java.util.EventObject -----------------------------	*java.io.Serializable*
1.1 ○	└ java.awt.AWTEvent	
1.1	├ ActionEvent	
1.1	├ AdjustmentEvent	
1.1	├ ComponentEvent	
1.1	├ ContainerEvent	
1.1	├ FocusEvent	
1.1 ○	├ InputEvent	
1.1	├ KeyEvent	
1.1	└ MouseEvent	
1.4	└ MouseWheelEvent	
1.1	├ PaintEvent	

Class   *Interface*   —extends   - - -implements   ○ abstract   ● final   ^—has superclass   —has subclass   package—see other volume

```
       java.lang.Object
1.1      └ java.util.EventObject - - - - - - - - - - - - - - - - - - - - - - - - - - - - - - java.io.Serializable
1.1  ○       └ java.awt.AWTEvent
1.1             ├ ComponentEvent
1.1             │   └ WindowEvent
1.3             ├ HierarchyEvent
1.2             ├ InputMethodEvent
1.2             ├ InvocationEvent - - - - - - - - - - - - - - - - - - - - - - - - - - - java.awt.ActiveEvent
1.1             ├ ItemEvent
1.1             └ TextEvent

1.2      AWTEventListener ──────────────────────────────── java.util.EventListener
1.1      ActionListener
1.1      AdjustmentListener
1.1      ComponentListener
1.1      ContainerListener
1.1      FocusListener
1.3      HierarchyBoundsListener
1.3      HierarchyListener
1.2      InputMethodListener
1.1      ItemListener
1.1      KeyListener
1.1      MouseListener
1.1      MouseMotionListener
1.4      MouseWheelListener
1.1      TextListener
1.4      WindowFocusListener
1.1      WindowListener
1.4      WindowStateListener
```

ε643. Handling Events with an Anonymous Class

If an event handler is specific to a component (that is, not shared by other components), there is no need to declare a class to handle the event. The event handler can be implemented using an anonymous inner class. This example demonstrates an anonymous inner class to handle key events for a component.

```
component.addKeyListener(new KeyAdapter() {
    public void keyPressed(KeyEvent evt) {
    }
});
```

ε644. Handling Action Events

Action events are fired by subclasses of AbstractButton and includes buttons, checkboxes, and menus.

```
AbstractButton button = new JButton("OK");
button.addActionListener(new MyActionListener());

public class MyActionListener implements ActionListener {
    public void actionPerformed(ActionEvent evt) {
        // Determine which abstract button fired the event.
        AbstractButton button = (AbstractButton)evt.getSource();
    }
}
```

Packages and Examples

109

ε645. Handling Key Presses

You can get the key that was pressed either as a key character (which is a Unicode character) or as a key code (a special value representing a particular key on the keyboard).

```java
component.addKeyListener(new MyKeyListener());

public class MyKeyListener extends KeyAdapter {
    public void keyPressed(KeyEvent evt) {
        // Check for key characters.
        if (evt.getKeyChar() == 'a') {
            process(evt.getKeyChar());
        }

        // Check for key codes.
        if (evt.getKeyCode() == KeyEvent.VK_HOME) {
            process(evt.getKeyCode());
        }
    }
}
```

ε646. Handling Mouse Clicks

```java
component.addMouseListener(new MyMouseListener());

public class MyMouseListener extends MouseAdapter {
    public void mouseClicked(MouseEvent evt) {
        if ((evt.getModifiers() & InputEvent.BUTTON1_MASK) != 0) {
            processLeft(evt.getPoint());
        }
        if ((evt.getModifiers() & InputEvent.BUTTON2_MASK) != 0) {
            processMiddle(evt.getPoint());
        }
        if ((evt.getModifiers() & InputEvent.BUTTON3_MASK) != 0) {
            processRight(evt.getPoint());
        }
    }
}
```

ε647. Handling Mouse Motion

```java
component.addMouseMotionListener(new MyMouseMotionListener());

public class MyMouseMotionListener extends MouseMotionAdapter {
    public void mouseMoved(MouseEvent evt) {
        // Process current position of cursor while all mouse buttons are up.
        process(evt.getPoint());
    }
    public void mouseDragged(MouseEvent evt) {
        // Process current position of cursor while mouse button is pressed.
        process(evt.getPoint());
    }
}
```

Class   *Interface*   —extends   - - -implements   O abstract   ● final   ^—has superclass   ‿—has subclass   package—see other volume

ε648. Detecting Double and Triple Clicks

```
component.addMouseListener(new MyMouseListener());

public class MyMouseListener extends MouseAdapter {
    public void mouseClicked(MouseEvent evt) {
        if (evt.getClickCount() == 3) {
            // triple-click
        } else if (evt.getClickCount() == 2) {
            // double-click
        }
    }
}
```

ε649. Handling Focus Changes

```
component.addFocusListener(new MyFocusListener());

public class MyFocusListener extends FocusAdapter {
    public void focusGained(FocusEvent evt) {
        // The component gained the focus
    }
    public void focusLost(FocusEvent evt) {
        // The component lost the focus
    }
}
```

ε650. Firing Item Events

An object wishing to fire item events must implement ItemSelectable. This example shows typical code that an object must implement to fire item events. When an item event is to be fired, fireItemEvent() should be called.

```
public class MyComponent implements ItemSelectable {
    protected EventListenerList listenerList = new EventListenerList();

    public Object[] getSelectedObjects() {
        return selectedObjects;
    }

    public void addItemListener(ItemListener l) {
        listenerList.add(ItemListener.class, l);
    }

    public void removeItemListener(ItemListener l) {
        listenerList.remove(ItemListener.class, l);
    }

    // If the item is selected, sel should be true.
    void fireItemEvent(Object item, boolean sel) {
        ItemEvent evt = new ItemEvent(this, ItemEvent.ITEM_STATE_CHANGED,
            item, sel ? ItemEvent.SELECTED : ItemEvent.DESELECTED);

        // Get list of listeners
        Object[] listeners = listenerList.getListenerList();

        // Send event to all listeners
        for (int i=0; i<listeners.length-2; i+=2) {
            if (listeners[i] == ItemListener.class) {
                ((ItemListener)listeners[i+1]).itemStateChanged(evt);
            }
```

Packages and Examples

111

```
            }
        }
    }
```

java.awt.font

This package contains classes and interfaces relating to fonts. It contains support for representing Type 1, Type 1 Multiple Master fonts, OpenType fonts, and TrueType fonts.

```
          java.lang.Object
1.2         ├ FontRenderContext
1.2 ●       ├ GlyphJustificationInfo
1.2 ●       ├ GlyphMetrics
1.2 ○       ├ GlyphVector - - - - - - - - - - - - - - - - - - - - - - - - - - - - - - - - - - - java.lang.Cloneable
1.2 ○       ├ GraphicAttribute
1.2 ●          ├ ImageGraphicAttribute
1.2 ●          └ ShapeGraphicAttribute
1.2 ●       ├ LineBreakMeasurer
```

Class   *Interface*   —extends   - - -implements   ○ abstract   ● final   ^—has superclass   ⌄—has subclass   package—see other volume

java . lang.Object

1.2 ○	⊢ LineMetrics	
1.4 ●	⊢ NumericShaper -	*java . io.Serializable*
1.2 ●	⊢ TextHitInfo	
1.2 ●	⊢ TextLayout -	*java . lang.Cloneable*
1.2	⊢ TextLayout.CaretPolicy	
1.3 ●	⊢ TextMeasurer -	
1.2 ●	⊢ TransformAttribute -	*java . io.Serializable*
1.2	⌊ java . text.AttributedCharacterIterator.Attribute - - - - - - - - - - - -	
1.2 ●	⌊ TextAttribute	
1.2	*MultipleMaster*	
1.2	*OpenType*	

ε651. Listing All Available Font Families

A font family refers to a set of font faces with a related typographic design. For example, the font faces in the family *Lucida Sans Typewriter* might be *Lucida Sans Typewriter Bold*, and *Lucida Sans Typewriter Regular*. This example lists all available font family names.

Note: J2SE 1.4 only supports True Type fonts.

```
// Get all font family names
GraphicsEnvironment ge = GraphicsEnvironment.getLocalGraphicsEnvironment();
String fontNames[] = ge.getAvailableFontFamilyNames();

// Iterate the font family names
for (int i=0; i<fontNames.length; i++) {
}
// Aria
// Comic Sans MS
// Verdana
// ...
```

ε652. Getting the Font Faces for a Font Family

To create a Font object to draw text, it is necessary to specify the font face name. This example demonstrates how to retrieve all the font face names from a font family name. Unfortunately, the method is somewhat inefficient since it involves creating one-point size Font objects for every available font in the system. The example caches all the information by creating a hash table that maps a font family name to an array of font face names.

See also "ε651. Listing All Available Font Families". Note: J2SE 1.4 only support True Type fonts.

```
Map fontFaceNames = new HashMap();

// Get all available font faces names
GraphicsEnvironment ge = GraphicsEnvironment.getLocalGraphicsEnvironment();
Font[] fonts = ge.getAllFonts();

// Process each font
for (int i=0; i<fonts.length; i++) {
    // Get font's family and face
    String familyName = fonts[i].getFamily();
    String faceName = fonts[i].getName();

    // Add font to table
    java.util.List list = (java.util.List)fontFaceNames.get(familyName);
```

```
            if (list == null) {
                list = new ArrayList();
                fontFaceNames.put(familyName, list);

            }
            list.add(faceName);
        }

        // Replace the face name lists with string arrays,
        // which are more compact and convenient to use
        for (Iterator it=fontFaceNames.keySet().iterator(); it.hasNext(); ) {
            String familyName = (String)it.next();
            java.util.List list = (java.util.List)fontFaceNames.get(familyName);
            fontFaceNames.put(familyName, list.toArray(new String[list.size()]));
        }


        // Use the table
        String[] faces = (String[])fontFaceNames.get("Verdana");
```

ε653. Drawing a Paragraph of Text

In order to change the font of the text, you need to supply an attributed string to the LineBreakMeasurer. See "ε655. Drawing Text with Mixed Styles" for an example.

```
        public void drawParagraph(Graphics2D g, String paragraph, float width) {
            LineBreakMeasurer linebreaker = new LineBreakMeasurer(
                new AttributedString(paragraph).getIterator(), g.getFontRenderContext());

            float y = 0.0f;
            while (linebreaker.getPosition() < paragraph.length()) {
                TextLayout tl = linebreaker.nextLayout(width);

                y += tl.getAscent();
                tl.draw(g, 0, y);
                y += tl.getDescent() + tl.getLeading();
            }
        }
```

ε654. Getting the Shape from the Outline of Text

```
        Shape getTextShape(Graphics2D g2d, String str, Font font) {
            FontRenderContext frc = g2d.getFontRenderContext();
            TextLayout tl = new TextLayout(str, font, frc);
            return tl.getOutline(null);
        }
```

ε655. Drawing Text with Mixed Styles

This example applies a new font and background color to a part of the text. You can apply styles to as many parts of the text as you need. See TextAttributes for available styles.

```
        // Apply styles to text
        AttributedString astr = new AttributedString("aString");
        astr.addAttribute(TextAttribute.FONT, font, start, end);
        astr.addAttribute(TextAttribute.BACKGROUND, color, start, end);

        // Draw mixed-style text
```

TextLayout tl = new TextLayout(astr.getIterator(), *g2d*.getFontRenderContext());
tl.draw(*g2d*, *x*, *y*);

java.awt.geom

This package contains classes for creating and representing various shapes such as points, lines, arcs, curves, ellipses, and rectangles. Also included are transformation classes used to transform shapes and drawing coordinates (see java.awt.Graphics2D).

Packages and Examples

115

```
        java.lang.Object
1.2       ├ AffineTransform -------------------------------- java.io.Serializable, java.lang.Cloneable
1.2       ├ Area----------------------------------------- java.awt.Shape, java.lang.Cloneable
1.2 ○     ├ CubicCurve2D--------------------------------┐
1.2       │   ├ CubicCurve2D.Double                      │
1.2       │   └ CubicCurve2D.Float                       │
1.2 ○     ├ Dimension2D --------------------------------- java.lang.Cloneable
1.2       ├ FlatteningPathIterator ----------------------- PathIterator
1.2 ●     ├ GeneralPath --------------------------------┐ java.awt.Shape, java.lang.Cloneable
1.2 ○     ├ Line2D -------------------------------------┘
1.2       │   ├ Line2D.Double
1.2       │   └ Line2D.Float
1.2 ○     ├ Point2D ------------------------------------- java.lang.Cloneable
1.2       │   ├ Point2D.Double
1.2       │   └ Point2D.Float
1.2 ○     ├ QuadCurve2D---------------------------------- java.awt.Shape, java.lang.Cloneable
1.2       │   ├ QuadCurve2D.Double                       │
1.2       │   └ QuadCurve2D.Float                        │
1.2 ○     ├ RectangularShape ---------------------------┘
1.2 ○     │   ├ Arc2D
1.2       │   │   ├ Arc2D.Double
1.2       │   │   └ Arc2D.Float
1.2 ○     │   ├ Ellipse2D
1.2       │   │   ├ Ellipse2D.Double
1.2       │   │   └ Ellipse2D.Float
1.2 ○     │   ├ Rectangle2D
1.2       │   │   ├ Rectangle2D.Double
1.2       │   │   └ Rectangle2D.Float
1.2 ○     │   └ RoundRectangle2D
1.2       │       ├ RoundRectangle2D.Double
1.2       │       └ RoundRectangle2D.Float
          └ java.lang.Throwable -------------------------- java.io.Serializable
              └ java.lang.Exception
                  ├ NoninvertibleTransformException
                  ├ java.lang.RuntimeException
1.2                   └ IllegalPathStateException

1.2     PathIterator
```

ε656. Creating Basic Shapes

```
Shape line = new Line2D.Float(x1, y1, x2, y2);
Shape arc = new Arc2D.Float(x, y, w, h, start, extent, type);
```

Class *Interface* —extends - - -implements ○ abstract ● final ˆ—has superclass ⌣—has subclass package—see other volume

```
Shape oval = new Ellipse2D.Float(x, y, w, h);
Shape rectangle = new Rectangle2D.Float(x, y, w, h);
Shape roundRectangle = new RoundRectangle2D.Float(x, y, w, h, arcWidth, arcHeight);
```

ε657. Creating a Shape Using Lines and Curves

```
GeneralPath shape = new GeneralPath();
shape.moveTo(x, y);
shape.lineTo(x, y);
shape.quadTo(controlPointX, controlPointY, x, y);
shape.curveTo(controlPointX1, controlPointY1, controlPointX2, controlPointY2, x, y);
shape.closePath();
```

ε658. Combining Shapes

```
Area shape = new Area(shape1);
shape.add(new Area(shape2));
shape.subtract(new Area(shape3));
shape.intersect(new Area(shape4));
shape.exclusiveOr(new Area(shape5));
```

ε659. Scaling, Shearing, Translating, and Rotating a Shape

```
AffineTransform tx = new AffineTransform();
tx.scale(scalex, scaley);
tx.shear(shiftx, shifty);
tx.translate(x, y);
tx.rotate(radians);
Shape newShape = tx.createTransformedShape(shape);
```

java.awt.im

This package contains classes and interfaces for the input method framework. This framework enables users to enter thousands of different characters using keyboards with far fewer keys. Characters (in many Asian languages such as Japanese and Chinese) are entered using a sequence of several key strokes to text-editing components.

```
java.lang.Object
1.2      ├ InputContext
1.2      ├ InputMethodHighlight
1.2      └ java.lang.Character.Subset
1.2 ●         └ InputSubset

1.2   InputMethodRequests
```

java.awt.im.spi

This package provides interfaces that enable the development of input methods that can be used with any Java runtime environment. Input methods are software components that let the user enter text in ways other than simple typing on a keyboard. They are commonly used to enter Japanese, Chinese, or Korean - languages using thousands of different characters - on keyboards with far fewer keys. However, this package also allows the development of input methods for other languages and the use of entirely different input mechanisms, such as handwriting recognition.

java.awt.image

This package contains classes for creating and modifying images. Images are processed using a streaming framework that involves an image producer, optional image filters, and an image consumer. This framework makes it possible to progressively render an image while it is being fetched and generated. Moreover, the framework allows an application to discard the storage used by an image and to regenerate it at any time. This package provides a number of image producers, consumers, and filters that you can configure for your image processing needs.

Class   *Interface*   —extends   - - -implements   ○ abstract   ● final   ˆ—has superclass   ˎ—has subclass   package—see other volume

Packages and Examples

	java.lang.Object	
1.2	├ AffineTransformOp - *BufferedImageOp, RasterOp*	
1.2	├ BandCombineOp - *RasterOp*	
1.4 ○	├ BufferStrategy	
1.2	├ ColorConvertOp - *BufferedImageOp, RasterOp*	
○	├ ColorModel - *java.awt.Transparency*	
1.2	│ ├ ComponentColorModel	
	│ ├ IndexColorModel	
1.2 ○	│ └ PackedColorModel	
	│ └ DirectColorModel	
1.2	├ ConvolveOp - *BufferedImageOp, RasterOp*	
1.2 ○	├ DataBuffer	
1.2 ●	│ ├ DataBufferByte	
1.4 ●	│ ├ DataBufferDouble	
1.4 ●	│ ├ DataBufferFloat	
1.2 ●	│ ├ DataBufferInt	
1.2 ●	│ ├ DataBufferShort	
1.2 ●	│ └ DataBufferUShort	
	├ FilteredImageSource - *ImageProducer*	
	├ ImageFilter - *ImageConsumer, java.lang.Cloneable*	
1.2	│ ├ BufferedImageFilter - *java.lang.Cloneable*	
	│ ├ CropImageFilter	
○	│ ├ RGBImageFilter	
1.1	│ └ ReplicateScaleFilter	
1.1	│ └ AreaAveragingScaleFilter	
1.2	├ Kernel -	
1.2	├ LookupOp - *BufferedImageOp, RasterOp*	
1.2 ○	├ LookupTable	
1.2	│ ├ ByteLookupTable	
1.2	│ └ ShortLookupTable	

Class   *Interface*   —extends   - - -implements   ○ abstract   ● final   ^has superclass   ‿has subclass   package—see other volume

```
        java.lang.Object
        ├ MemoryImageSource ----------------------------- ImageProducer
        ├ PixelGrabber ---------------------------------- ImageConsumer
1.2     ├ Raster
1.2     │ └ WritableRaster
1.2     ├ RescaleOp ------------------------------------- BufferedImageOp, RasterOp
1.2 ○   ├ SampleModel
1.2     │ ├ ComponentSampleModel
1.2 ●   │ │ ├ BandedSampleModel
1.2     │ │ └ PixelInterleavedSampleModel
1.2     │ ├ MultiPixelPackedSampleModel
1.2     │ └ SinglePixelPackedSampleModel
    ○   ├ java.awt.Image
1.2     │ ├ BufferedImage ------------------------------- WritableRenderedImage^
1.4 ○   │ └ VolatileImage
        └ java.lang.Throwable --------------------------- java.io.Serializable
          └ java.lang.Exception
            └ java.lang.RuntimeException
1.2           ├ ImagingOpException
1.2           └ RasterFormatException

1.2     BufferedImageOp
        ImageConsumer
        ImageObserver
        ImageProducer
1.2     RasterOp
1.2     RenderedImage
1.2     TileObserver
1.2     WritableRenderedImage —————————————————————————— RenderedImage
```

Images

ε660. Creating an Image from an Array of Color-Indexed Pixel Values

This example demonstrates how to convert a byte array of pixel values that are indices to a color table into an Image. In particular, the example generates the Mandelbrot set in a byte buffer and uses the MemoryImageSource image producer to create an image from the pixel data in the byte buffer. A 16-color index color model is used to represent the pixel colors.

```
import java.awt.*;
import java.awt.event.*;
import java.awt.geom.*;
import java.awt.image.*;

// Instantiate this class and then use the draw() method to draw the
// generated on the graphics context.
public class Mandelbrot {
    // Holds the generated image
    Image image;

    // 16-color model
    ColorModel colorModel = generateColorModel();
```

Packages and Examples

```java
public Mandelbrot(int width, int height) {
    // Initialize with default location
    this(width, height, new Rectangle2D.Float(-2.0f, -1.2f, 3.2f, 2.4f));
}

public Mandelbrot(int width, int height, Rectangle2D.Float loc) {
    image = Toolkit.getDefaultToolkit().createImage(
        new MemoryImageSource(width, height,
        colorModel, generatePixels(width, height, loc), 0, width));
}

public void draw(Graphics g, int x, int y) {
    g.drawImage(image, x, y, null);
}

private byte[] generatePixels(int w, int h, Rectangle2D.Float loc) {
    float xmin = loc.x;
    float ymin = loc.y;
    float xmax = loc.x+loc.width;
    float ymax = loc.y+loc.height;

    byte[] pixels = new byte[w * h];
    int plx = 0;
    float[] p = new float[w];
    float q = ymin;
    float dp = (xmax-xmin)/w;
    float dq = (ymax-ymin)/h;

    p[0] = xmin;
    for (int i=1; i<w; i++) {
        p[i] = p[i-1] + dp;
    }

    for (int r=0; r<h; r++) {
        for (int c=0; c<w; c++) {
            int color = 1;
            float x = 0.0f;
            float y = 0.0f;
            float xsqr = 0.0f;
            float ysqr = 0.0f;
            do {
                xsqr = x*x;
                ysqr = y*y;
                y = 2*x*y + q;
                x = xsqr - ysqr + p[c];
                color++;
            } while (color < 512 && xsqr + ysqr < 4);
            pixels[plx++] = (byte)(color % 16);
        }
        q += dq;
    }
    return pixels;
}

private static ColorModel generateColorModel() {
    // Generate 16-color model
    byte[] r = new byte[16];
```

```
            byte[] g = new byte[16];
            byte[] b = new byte[16];

            r[0] = 0; g[0] = 0; b[0] = 0;
            r[1] = 0; g[1] = 0; b[1] = (byte)192;
            r[2] = 0; g[2] = 0; b[2] = (byte)255;
            r[3] = 0; g[3] = (byte)192; b[3] = 0;
            r[4] = 0; g[4] = (byte)255; b[4] = 0;
            r[5] = 0; g[5] = (byte)192; b[5] = (byte)192;
            r[6] = 0; g[6] = (byte)255; b[6] = (byte)255;
            r[7] = (byte)192; g[7] = 0; b[7] = 0;
            r[8] = (byte)255; g[8] = 0; b[8] = 0;
            r[9] = (byte)192; g[9] = 0; b[9] = (byte)192;
            r[10] = (byte)255; g[10] = 0; b[10] = (byte)255;
            r[11] = (byte)192; g[11] = (byte)192; b[11] = 0;
            r[12] = (byte)255; g[12] = (byte)255; b[12] = 0;
            r[13] = (byte)80; g[13] = (byte)80; b[13] = (byte)80;
            r[14] = (byte)192; g[14] = (byte)192; b[14] = (byte)192;
            r[15] = (byte)255; g[15] = (byte)255; b[15] = (byte)255;

            return new IndexColorModel(4, 16, r, g, b);
        }
    }
```

Here's some code that uses the Mandelbrot class:

```
    class RunMandelbrot {
        static public void main(String[] args) {
            new RunMandelbrot();
        }
        RunMandelbrot() {
            Frame frame = new Frame("Mandelbrot Set");
            frame.add(new MyCanvas());
            frame.setSize(300, 200);
            frame.setVisible(true);
        }

        class MyCanvas extends Canvas {
            Mandelbrot mandelbrot;

            MyCanvas() {
                // Add a listener for resize events
                addComponentListener(new ComponentAdapter() {
                    // This method is called when the component's size changes
                    public void componentResized(ComponentEvent evt) {
                        Component c = (Component)evt.getSource();

                        // Get new size
                        Dimension newSize = c.getSize();

                        // Regenerate the image
                        mandelbrot = new Mandelbrot(newSize.width, newSize.height);
                        c.repaint();
                    }
                });
            }
            public void paint(Graphics g) {
                if (mandelbrot != null) {
```

```
                    mandelbrot.draw(g, 0, 0);
                }
            }
        }
    }
```

ε661. Determining If an Image Has Transparent Pixels

```
// This method returns true if the specified image has transparent pixels
public static boolean hasAlpha(Image image) {
    // If buffered image, the color model is readily available
    if (image instanceof BufferedImage) {
        BufferedImage bimage = (BufferedImage)image;
        return bimage.getColorModel().hasAlpha();
    }

    // Use a pixel grabber to retrieve the image's color model;
    // grabbing a single pixel is usually sufficient
    PixelGrabber pg = new PixelGrabber(image, 0, 0, 1, 1, false);
    try {
        pg.grabPixels();
    } catch (InterruptedException e) {
    }

    // Get the image's color model
    ColorModel cm = pg.getColorModel();
    return cm.hasAlpha();
}
```

ε662. Getting the Color Model of an Image

```
// This method returns the color model of an image
public static ColorModel getColorModel(Image image) {
    // If buffered image, the color model is readily available
    if (image instanceof BufferedImage) {
        BufferedImage bimage = (BufferedImage)image;
        return bimage.getColorModel();
    }

    // Use a pixel grabber to retrieve the image's color model;
    // grabbing a single pixel is usually sufficient
    PixelGrabber pg = new PixelGrabber(image, 0, 0, 1, 1, false);
    try {
        pg.grabPixels();
    } catch (InterruptedException e) {
    }
    ColorModel cm = pg.getColorModel();
    return cm;
}
```

ε663. Getting the Transparent Pixel and Number of Colors Used in a GIF Image

A IndexColorModel is used to represent the color table of a GIF image.

```
// Get GIF image
Image image = new ImageIcon("image.gif").getImage();
```

```
// Get the color model; this method is implemented in
// "ε662. Getting the Color Model of an Image"
IndexColorModel colorModel = (IndexColorModel)getColorModel(image);

// Get transparent pixel
int trans = colorModel.getTransparentPixel();
if (trans == -1) {
    // There is no transparent pixel
}

// Get the number of colors
int numColors = colorModel.getMapSize();
```

ε664. Getting a Sub-Image of an Image

```
// From an Image
image = createImage(new FilteredImageSource(image.getSource(), new CropImageFilter(x, y, w, h)));

// From a BufferedImage
bufferedImage = bufferedImage.getSubimage(x, y, w, h);
```

ε665. Filtering the RGB Values in an Image

This example demonstrates how to create a filter that can modify any of the RGB pixel values in an image.

```
// This filter removes all but the red values in an image
class GetRedFilter extends RGBImageFilter {
    public GetRedFilter() {
        // When this is set to true, the filter will work with images
        // whose pixels are indices into a color table (IndexColorModel).
        // In such a case, the color values in the color table are filtered.
        canFilterIndexColorModel = true;
    }
    // This method is called for every pixel in the image
    public int filterRGB(int x, int y, int rgb) {
        if (x == -1) {
            // The pixel value is from the image's color table rather than the image itself
        }
        // Return only the red component
        return rgb & 0xffff0000;
    }
}
```

Here's some code that uses the filter:

```
// Get image
Image image = new ImageIcon("image.gif").getImage();

// Create the filter
ImageFilter filter = new GetRedFilter();
FilteredImageSource filteredSrc = new FilteredImageSource(image.getSource(), filter);

// Create the filtered image
image = Toolkit.getDefaultToolkit().createImage(filteredSrc);
```

Buffered Images

ε666. Creating a Buffered Image

A buffered image is a type of image whose pixels can be modified. For example, you can draw on a buffered image and then draw the resulting buffered image on the screen or save it to a file. A buffered image supports many formats for storing pixels. Although a buffered image of any format can be drawn on the screen, it is best to choose a format that is the most compatible with the screen to allow efficient drawing. This example demonstrates several ways of creating a buffered image.

If the buffered image will not be drawn, it can simply be constructed with a specific format; TYPE_INT_RGB and TYPE_INT_ARGB are typically used. See BufferedImage for a list of available formats.

See also "ε667. Creating a Buffered Image from an Image".

```
int width = 100;
int height = 100;

// Create buffered image that does not support transparency
BufferedImage bimage = new BufferedImage(width, height, BufferedImage.TYPE_INT_RGB);

// Create a buffered image that supports transparency
bimage = new BufferedImage(width, height, BufferedImage.TYPE_INT_ARGB);
```

These examples create buffered images that are compatible with the screen:

```
GraphicsEnvironment ge = GraphicsEnvironment.getLocalGraphicsEnvironment();
GraphicsDevice gs = ge.getDefaultScreenDevice();
GraphicsConfiguration gc = gs.getDefaultConfiguration();

// Create an image that does not support transparency
bimage = gc.createCompatibleImage(width, height, Transparency.OPAQUE);

// Create an image that supports transparent pixels
bimage = gc.createCompatibleImage(width, height, Transparency.BITMASK);

// Create an image that supports arbitrary levels of transparency
bimage = gc.createCompatibleImage(width, height, Transparency.TRANSLUCENT);
```

A screen compatible buffered image can also be created from a graphics context:

```
public void paint(Graphics g) {
    Graphics2D g2d = (Graphics2D)g;
    int width = 100;
    int height = 100;

    // Create an image that does not support transparency
    BufferedImage bimage = g2d.getDeviceConfiguration().createCompatibleImage(
        width, height, Transparency.OPAQUE);

    // Create an image that supports transparent pixels
    bimage = g2d.getDeviceConfiguration().createCompatibleImage(
        width, height, Transparency.BITMASK);

    // Create an image that supports arbitrary levels of transparency
    bimage = g2d.getDeviceConfiguration().createCompatibleImage(
        width, height, Transparency.TRANSLUCENT);
}
```

Class   *Interface*   —extends   - - -implements   O abstract   ● final   ˆ—has superclass   ˌ—has subclass   package—see other volume

One last way of creating a buffered image is using Component.createImage(). This method can be used only if the component is visible on the screen. Also, this method returns buffered images that do not support transparent pixels.

```
BufferedImage bimage = (BufferedImage)component.createImage(width, height);
if (bimage == null) {
    // The component is not visible on the screen
}
```

ε667. Creating a Buffered Image from an Image

An Image object cannot be converted to a BufferedImage object. The closest equivalent is to create a buffered image and then draw the image on the buffered image. This example defines a method that does this.

```
// This method returns a buffered image with the contents of an image
public static BufferedImage toBufferedImage(Image image) {
    if (image instanceof BufferedImage) {
        return (BufferedImage)image;
    }

    // This code ensures that all the pixels in the image are loaded
    image = new ImageIcon(image).getImage();

    // Determine if the image has transparent pixels; for this method's
    // implementation, see "ε661. Determining If an Image Has Transparent Pixels"
    boolean hasAlpha = hasAlpha(image);

    // Create a buffered image with a format that's compatible with the screen
    BufferedImage bimage = null;
    GraphicsEnvironment ge = GraphicsEnvironment.getLocalGraphicsEnvironment();
    try {
        // Determine the type of transparency of the new buffered image
        int transparency = Transparency.OPAQUE;
        if (hasAlpha) {
            transparency = Transparency.BITMASK;
        }

        // Create the buffered image
        GraphicsDevice gs = ge.getDefaultScreenDevice();
        GraphicsConfiguration gc = gs.getDefaultConfiguration();
        bimage = gc.createCompatibleImage(
            image.getWidth(null), image.getHeight(null), transparency);
    } catch (HeadlessException e) {
        // The system does not have a screen
    }

    if (bimage == null) {
        // Create a buffered image using the default color model
        int type = BufferedImage.TYPE_INT_RGB;
        if (hasAlpha) {
            type = BufferedImage.TYPE_INT_ARGB;
        }
        bimage = new BufferedImage(image.getWidth(null), image.getHeight(null), type);
    }

    // Copy image to buffered image
    Graphics g = bimage.createGraphics();

    // Paint the image onto the buffered image
    g.drawImage(image, 0, 0, null);
```

```
            g.dispose();
            return bimage;
        }
```

ε668. Creating a Buffered Image from an Array of Color-Indexed Pixel Values

This example demonstrates how to convert a byte array of pixel values that are indices to a color table into a BufferedImage. In particular, the example generates the Mandelbrot set in a byte buffer and combines this data with a SampleModel, ColorModel, and Raster into a BufferedImage. A 16-color index color model is used to represent the pixel colors.

```java
import java.awt.*;
import java.awt.event.*;
import java.awt.geom.*;
import java.awt.image.*;

// Instantiate this class and then use the draw() method to draw the
// generated on the graphics context.
public class Mandelbrot2 {
    // Holds the generated image
    Image image;

    // 16-color model; this method is defined in
    // "ε660. Creating an Image from an Array of Color-Indexed Pixel Values"
    ColorModel colorModel = generateColorModel();

    public Mandelbrot2(int width, int height) {
        // Initialize with default location
        this(width, height, new Rectangle2D.Float(-2.0f, -1.2f, 3.2f, 2.4f));
    }

    public Mandelbrot2(int width, int height, Rectangle2D.Float loc) {
        // Generate the pixel data; this method is defined in
        // "ε660. Creating an Image from an Array of Color-Indexed Pixel Values"
        byte[] pixels = generatePixels(width, height, loc);

        // Create a data buffer using the byte buffer of pixel data.
        // The pixel data is not copied; the data buffer uses the byte buffer array.
        DataBuffer dbuf = new DataBufferByte(pixels, width*height, 0);

        // The number of banks should be 1
        int numBanks = dbuf.getNumBanks(); // 1

        // Prepare a sample model that specifies a storage 4-bits of
        // pixel datavd in an 8-bit data element
        int bitMasks[] = new int[]{(byte)0xf};
        SampleModel sampleModel = new SinglePixelPackedSampleModel(
            DataBuffer.TYPE_BYTE, width, height, bitMasks);

        // Create a raster using the sample model and data buffer
        WritableRaster raster = Raster.createWritableRaster(sampleModel, dbuf, null);

        // Combine the color model and raster into a buffered image
        image = new BufferedImage(colorModel, raster, false, null);//new java.util.Hashtable());
    }

    public void draw(Graphics g, int x, int y) {
        g.drawImage(image, x, y, null);
```

```
            }
        }
```

Here's some code that uses the Mandelbrot2 class:

```
class RunMandelbrot2 {
    static public void main(String[] args) {
        new RunMandelbrot2();
    }
    RunMandelbrot2() {
        Frame frame = new Frame("Mandelbrot2 Set");
        frame.add(new MyCanvas());
        frame.setSize(300, 200) ;
        frame.setVisible(true);
    }

    class MyCanvas extends Canvas {
        Mandelbrot2 mandelbrot;

        MyCanvas() {
            // Add a listener for resize events
            addComponentListener(new ComponentAdapter() {
                // This method is called when the component's size changes
                public void componentResized(ComponentEvent evt) {
                    Component c = (Component)evt.getSource();

                    // Get new size
                    Dimension newSize = c.getSize();

                    // Regenerate the image
                    mandelbrot = new Mandelbrot2(newSize.width, newSize.height);
                    c.repaint();
                }
            });
        }
        public void paint(Graphics g) {
            if (mandelbrot != null) {
                mandelbrot.draw(g, 0, 0);
            }
        }
    }
}
```

ε669. Drawing on a Buffered Image

To draw on a buffered image, create a graphics context on the buffered image.

```
// Create a graphics context on the buffered image
Graphics2D g2d = bimage.createGraphics();

// Draw on the image
g2d.setColor(Color.red);
g2d.fill(new Ellipse2D.Float(0, 0, 200, 100));
g2d.dispose();
```

If the buffered image supports transparency, (see "ε661. Determining If an Image Has Transparent Pixels"), pixels can be made transparent:

Packages and Examples

```
g2d = bimage.createGraphics();

// Make all filled pixels transparent
Color transparent = new Color(0, 0, 0, 0);
g2d.setColor(transparent);
g2d.setComposite(AlphaComposite.Src);
g2d.fill(new Rectangle2D.Float(20, 20, 100, 20));
g2d.dispose();
```

ε670. Converting a Buffered Image to an Image

```
// This method returns an Image object from a buffered image
public static Image toImage(BufferedImage bufferedImage) {
    return Toolkit.getDefaultToolkit().createImage(bufferedImage.getSource());
}
```

ε671. Getting and Setting Pixels in a Buffered Image

```
// Get a pixel
int rgb = bufferedImage.getRGB(x, y);

// Get all the pixels
int w = bufferedImage.getWidth(null);
int h = bufferedImage.getHeight(null);
int[] rgbs = new int[w*h];
bufferedImage.getRGB(0, 0, w, h, rgbs, 0, w);

// Set a pixel
rgb = 0xFF00FF00; // green
bufferedImage.setRGB(x, y, rgb);
```

ε672. Scaling, Shearing, Translating, and Rotating a Buffered Image

```
AffineTransform tx = new AffineTransform();
tx.scale(scalex, scaley);
tx.shear(shiftx, shifty);
tx.translate(x, y);
tx.rotate(radians, bufferedImage.getWidth()/2, bufferedImage.getHeight()/2);

AffineTransformOp op = new AffineTransformOp(tx, AffineTransformOp.TYPE_BILINEAR);
bufferedImage = op.filter(bufferedImage, null);
```

Volatile Images

ε673. Getting Amount of Free Accelerated Image Memory

Images in accelerated memory are much faster to draw on the screen. However, accelerated memory is typically limited and it is usually necessary for an application to manage the images residing in this space. This example demonstrates how to determine the amount free accelerated available.

Note: There appears to be a problem with GraphicsDevice.getAvailableAcceleratedMemory() on some systems. The method returns 0 even if accelerated image memory is available. A workaround is to create a temporary volatile image on the graphics device before calling the method. Once the volatile image is created, the method appears to return the correct value on all subsequent calls.

See also "ε601. Enabling Full-Screen Mode" and "ε674. Creating and Drawing an Accelerated Image".

Class *Interface* —extends - - -implements ○ abstract ● final ^—has superclass ⌐—has subclass package—see other volume

```
GraphicsEnvironment ge = GraphicsEnvironment.getLocalGraphicsEnvironment();
try {
    GraphicsDevice[] gs = ge.getScreenDevices();

    // Get current amount of available memory in bytes for each screen
    for (int i=0; i<gs.length; i++) {
        // Workaround; see description
        VolatileImage im = gs[i].getDefaultConfiguration().createCompatibleVolatileImage(1, 1);

        // Retrieve available free accelerated image memory
        int bytes = gs[i].getAvailableAcceleratedMemory();
        if (bytes < 0) {
            // Amount of memory is unlimited
        }

        // Release the temporary volatile image
        im.flush();
    }
} catch (HeadlessException e) {
    // Is thrown if there are no screen devices
}
```

ε674. Creating and Drawing an Accelerated Image

Images in accelerated memory are much faster to draw on the screen. This example demonstrates how to take an image and make an accelerated copy of it and then use it to draw on the screen.

The problem with images in accelerated memory is that they can disappear at any time. The system is free to free accelerated memory at any time. Such images are called volatile images. To deal with this issue, it is necessary to check whether a volatile image is still valid immediately after drawing it. If it is no longer valid, it is then necessary to reconstruct the image and then attempt to draw with it again.

This example implements a convenient method for drawing volatile images. It automatically handles the task of reconstructing the volatile image when necessary.

```
// This method draws a volatile image and returns it or possibly a
// newly created volatile image object. Subsequent calls to this method
// should always use the returned volatile image.
// If the contents of the image is lost, it is recreated using orig.
// img may be null, in which case a new volatile image is created.
public VolatileImage drawVolatileImage(Graphics2D g, VolatileImage img,
                                       int x, int y, Image orig) {
    final int MAX_TRIES = 100;
    for (int i=0; i<MAX_TRIES; i++) {
        if (img != null) {
            // Draw the volatile image
            g.drawImage(img, x, y, null);

            // Check if it is still valid
            if (!img.contentsLost()) {
                return img;
            }
        } else {
            // Create the volatile image
            img = g.getDeviceConfiguration().createCompatibleVolatileImage(
                orig.getWidth(null), orig.getHeight(null));
        }

        // Determine how to fix the volatile image
```

```
                    switch (img.validate(g.getDeviceConfiguration())) {
                    case VolatileImage.IMAGE_OK:
                        // This should not happen
                        break;
                    case VolatileImage.IMAGE_INCOMPATIBLE:
                        // Create a new volatile image object;
                        // this could happen if the component was moved to another device
                        img.flush();
                        img = g.getDeviceConfiguration().createCompatibleVolatileImage(
                            orig.getWidth(null), orig.getHeight(null));
                    case VolatileImage.IMAGE_RESTORED:
                        // Copy the original image to accelerated image memory
                        Graphics2D gc = (Graphics2D)img.createGraphics();
                        gc.drawImage(orig, 0, 0, null);
                        gc.dispose();
                        break;
                    }
                }

                // The image failed to be drawn after MAX_TRIES;
                // draw with the non-accelerated image
                g.drawImage(orig, x, y, null);
                return img;
            }
```

Here's a component that uses the method:

```
        // Declare a component that draws a volatile image
        class MyComponent extends Canvas {
            VolatileImage volImage;
            Image origImage = null;

            MyComponent() {
                // Get image to move into accelerated image memory
                origImage = new ImageIcon("image.gif").getImage();
            }
            public void paint(Graphics g) {
                // Draw accelerated image
                int x = 0;
                int y = 0;
                volImage = drawVolatileImage((Graphics2D)g, volImage, x, y, origImage);
            }
        }
```

Effects

ε675. Flipping a Buffered Image

```
        // To create a buffered image, see "ε666. Creating a Buffered Image"

        // Flip the image vertically
        AffineTransform tx = AffineTransform.getScaleInstance(1, -1);
        tx.translate(0, -image.getHeight(null));
        AffineTransformOp op = new AffineTransformOp(tx, AffineTransformOp.TYPE_NEAREST_NEIGHBOR);
```

```
bufferedImage = op.filter(bufferedImage, null);

// Flip the image horizontally
tx = AffineTransform.getScaleInstance(-1, 1);
tx.translate(-image.getWidth(null), 0);
op = new AffineTransformOp(tx, AffineTransformOp.TYPE_NEAREST_NEIGHBOR);
bufferedImage = op.filter(bufferedImage, null);

// Flip the image vertically and horizontally;
// equivalent to rotating the image 180 degrees
tx = AffineTransform.getScaleInstance(-1, -1);
tx.translate(-image.getWidth(null), -image.getHeight(null));
op = new AffineTransformOp(tx, AffineTransformOp.TYPE_NEAREST_NEIGHBOR);
bufferedImage = op.filter(bufferedImage, null);
```

ε676. Converting a Colored Buffered Image to Gray

```
ColorSpace cs = ColorSpace.getInstance(ColorSpace.CS_GRAY);
ColorConvertOp op = new ColorConvertOp(cs, null);
bufferedImage = op.filter(bufferedImage, null);
```

ε677. Blurring a Buffered Image

This example demonstrates a 3x3 kernel that blurs an image.

```
Kernel kernel = new Kernel(3, 3,
    new float[] {
        1f/9f, 1f/9f, 1f/9f,
        1f/9f, 1f/9f, 1f/9f,
        1f/9f, 1f/9f, 1f/9f});
BufferedImageOp op = new ConvolveOp(kernel);
bufferedImage = op.filter(bufferedImage, null);
```

ε678. Sharpening a Buffered Image

This example demonstrates a 3x3 kernel that sharpens an image.

```
Kernel kernel = new Kernel(3, 3,
    new float[] {
        -1, -1, -1,
        -1, 9, -1,
        -1, -1, -1});
BufferedImageOp op = new ConvolveOp(kernel);
bufferedImage = op.filter(bufferedImage, null);
```

ε679. Embossing a Buffered Image

This example demonstrates a 3x3 kernel that embosses an image.

```
Kernel kernel = new Kernel(3, 3,
    new float[] {
        -2, 0, 0,
        0, 1, 0,
        0, 0, 2});
BufferedImageOp op = new ConvolveOp(kernel);
bufferedImage = op.filter(bufferedImage, null);
```

Packages and Examples

ε680. Brightening or Darkening an RGB Buffered Image

This example demonstrates how to brighten or darken an RGB buffered image by scaling the red, green, and blue values in the image.

```
// To create a buffered image, see "ε666. Creating a Buffered Image"

// Brighten the image by 30%
float scaleFactor = 1.3f;
RescaleOp op = new RescaleOp(scaleFactor, 0, null);
bufferedImage = op.filter(bufferedImage, null);

// Darken the image by 10%
scaleFactor = .9f;
op = new RescaleOp(scaleFactor, 0, null);
bufferedImage = op.filter(bufferedImage, null);
```

If the image is not an RGB image, the following code converts a non-RGB image to an RGB buffered image:

```
// Get non-RGB image
Image image = new ImageIcon("image.gif").getImage();

// Create an RGB buffered image
BufferedImage bimage = new BufferedImage(image.getWidth(null), image.getHeight(null), BufferedIm-
age.TYPE_INT_RGB);

// Copy non-RGB image to the RGB buffered image
Graphics2D g = bimage.createGraphics();
g.drawImage(image, 0, 0, null);
g.dispose();
```

java.awt.image.renderable

This package contains classes and interfaces for producing rendering-independent images.

Class *Interface* —extends - - -implements ○ abstract ● final ^—has superclass ‿—has subclass package—see other volume

```
    java.lang.Object
1.2    ├ ParameterBlock - - - - - - - - - - - - - - - - - - - - - - - - - - - - - - - - - java.io.Serializable◦, java.lang.Cloneable◦
1.2    ├ RenderContext - - - - - - - - - - - - - - - - - - - - - - - - - - - - - - - - - java.lang.Cloneable◦
1.2    ├ RenderableImageOp - - - - - - - - - - - - - - - - - - - - - - - - - - - - - - RenderableImage
1.2    └ RenderableImageProducer - - - - - - - - - - - - - - - - - - - - - - - - - java.awt.image.ImageProducer,
                                                                    java.lang.Runnable
```

```
1.2    ContextualRenderedImageFactory ─────────────── RenderedImageFactory
1.2    RenderableImage
1.2    RenderedImageFactory◦
```

java.awt.peer

This package is for interfacing with the underlying window system. It is for accessing the platform-specific facilities in order to build AWT toolkits. It is only used by AWT toolkit developers.

```
    ButtonPeer ─────────────────────────┐ ComponentPeer
    CanvasPeer ─────────────────────────┤
    CheckboxMenuItemPeer ───────────────────── MenuItemPeer^
```

Packages and Examples

	CheckboxPeer ————————————————	*ComponentPeer*
	ChoicePeer	
	ComponentPeer ˬ	
	ContainerPeer ˬ	
	DialogPeer ˬ ————————————————	*WindowPeer* ˆ
	FileDialogPeer ————————————————	*DialogPeer* ˆ
1.1	*FontPeer*	
	FramePeer ————————————————	*WindowPeer* ˆ
	LabelPeer ————————————————	*ComponentPeer*
1.1	*LightweightPeer*	
	ListPeer	
	MenuBarPeer ————————————————	*MenuComponentPeer*
	MenuComponentPeer ˬ	
	MenuItemPeer ˬ	
	MenuPeer ˬ ————————————————	*MenuItemPeer* ˆ
	PanelPeer ————————————————	*ContainerPeer* ˆ
1.1	*PopupMenuPeer* ————————————————	*MenuPeer* ˆ
1.3	*RobotPeer*	
1.1	*ScrollPanePeer* ————————————————	*ContainerPeer* ˆ
	ScrollbarPeer ————————————————	*ComponentPeer*
	TextAreaPeer ————————————————	*TextComponentPeer* ˆ
	TextComponentPeer ˬ ————————————————	*ComponentPeer*
	TextFieldPeer ————————————————	*TextComponentPeer* ˆ
	WindowPeer ˬ ————————————————	*ContainerPeer* ˆ

java.awt.print

This package contains classes and interfaces for printing AWT components. It defines the notion of a book, which consists of a list of pages to be printed. Each page is described using its page format and a printable object.

java . lang . Object

1.2	├ Book - *Pageable*
1.2	├ PageFormat - ┐ *java . lang . Cloneable* ˬ
1.2	├ Paper - ┘
1.2 ○	├ PrinterJob

```
java.lang.Object
  └ java.lang.Throwable - - - - - - - - - - - - - - - - - - - - - - - - - - - - - - - java.io.Serializable
        └ java.lang.Exception
1.2          └ PrinterException
1.2             ├ PrinterAbortException
1.2             └ PrinterIOException

1.2   Pageable
1.2   Printable
1.2   PrinterGraphics
```

ε681. The Quintessential Printing Program

Note that (0, 0) of the Graphics object is at the top-left of the actual page, outside the printable area. In this example, the Graphics object is translated so that (0, 0) becomes the top-left corner of the printable area.

```java
import java.awt.*;
import java.awt.print.*;

public class BasicPrint extends JComponent implements Printable {
    public int print(Graphics g, PageFormat pf, int pageIndex) {
        if (pageIndex > 0) {
            return Printable.NO_SUCH_PAGE;
        }
        Graphics2D g2d = (Graphics2D)g;
        g2d.translate(pf.getImageableX(), pf.getImageableY());
        drawGraphics(g2d, pf);
        return Printable.PAGE_EXISTS;
    }

    public static void main(String[] args) {
        PrinterJob pjob = PrinterJob.getPrinterJob();
        PageFormat pf = pjob.defaultPage();
        pjob.setPrintable(new BasicPrint(), pf);
        try {
            pjob.print();
        } catch (PrinterException e) {
        }
    }
}
```

ε682. Getting the Dimensions of a Printed Page

Note that (0, 0) of the Graphics object is at the top-left of the actual page, which is outside the printable area.

```java
public int print(Graphics g, PageFormat pf, int pageIndex) {
    // The area of the printable area.
    double ix = pf.getImageableX();
    double iy = pf.getImageableY();
    double iw = pf.getImageableWidth();
    double ih = pf.getImageableHeight();

    // The area of the actual page.
    double x = 0;
    double y = 0;
    double w = pf.getWidth();
    double h = pf.getHeight();
```

Packages and Examples

```
        return Printable.NO_SUCH_PAGE;
    }
```

ε683. Setting the Orientation of a Printed Page

```
PrinterJob pjob = PrinterJob.getPrinterJob();
PageFormat pf = pjob.defaultPage();

if (portrait) {
    pf.setOrientation(PageFormat.PORTRAIT);
} else {
    pf.setOrientation(PageFormat.LANDSCAPE);
}

pjob.setPrintable(printable, pf);
try {
    pjob.print();
} catch (PrinterException e) {
}
```

ε684. Printing Pages with Different Formats

A Book object is used when printing pages with different page formats. This example prints the first page in landscape and five more pages in portrait.

```
public class PrintBook {
    public static void main(String[] args) {
        PrinterJob pjob = PrinterJob.getPrinterJob();
        Book book = new Book();

        // First part.
        PageFormat landscape = pjob.defaultPage();
        landscape.setOrientation(PageFormat.LANDSCAPE);
        book.append(new Printable1(), landscape);

        // Second part.
        PageFormat portrait = pjob.defaultPage();
        portrait.setOrientation(PageFormat.PORTRAIT);
        book.append(new Printable2(), portrait, 5);

        pjob.setPageable(book);
        try {
            pjob.print();
        } catch (PrinterException e) {
        }
    }
    static class Printable1 implements Printable {
        public int print(Graphics g, PageFormat pf, int pageIndex) {
            drawGraphics(g, pf);
            return Printable.PAGE_EXISTS;
        }
    }
    static class Printable2 implements Printable {
        public int print(Graphics g, PageFormat pf, int pageIndex) {
            drawGraphics(g, pf);
            return Printable.PAGE_EXISTS;
        }
    }
```

Class *Interface* —extends - - -implements ○ abstract ● final ˆ—has superclass ˌ—has subclass package—see other volume

```
        }
    }
```

ε685. Displaying the Page Format Dialog

The page format dialog allows the user to change the default page format values such as the orientation and paper size.

```
PrinterJob pjob = PrinterJob.getPrinterJob();

// Get and change default page format settings if necessary.
PageFormat pf = pjob.defaultPage();
pf.setOrientation(PageFormat.LANDSCAPE);

// Show page format dialog with page format settings.
pf = pjob.pageDialog(pf);
```

ε686. Displaying the Print Dialog

The print dialog allows the user to change the default printer settings such as the default printer, number of copies, range of pages, etc.

```
PrinterJob pjob = PrinterJob.getPrinterJob();
PageFormat pf = pjob.defaultPage();
pjob.setPrintable(new PrintableClass(), pf);
try {
    if (pjob.printDialog()) {
        pjob.print();
    }
} catch (PrinterException e) {
}
```

javax.accessibility

This package provides support for building AWT and Swing user interfaces for use by people with and without physical disabilities. It provides an interface between UI objects and screen access products (such as screen readers and Braille terminals).

Packages and Examples

```
        java.lang.Object
1.2 O   ├ AccessibleBundle
1.3     │   ├ AccessibleRelation
1.2     │   ├ AccessibleRole
1.2     │   └ AccessibleState
1.2 O   ├ AccessibleContext⌄
1.2 O   ├ AccessibleHyperlink⌄ - - - - - - - - - - - - - - - - - - - - - - - - - - - - - - - AccessibleAction
1.3     ├ AccessibleRelationSet
1.2     ├ AccessibleStateSet
1.1 O   └ java.util.ResourceBundle
1.1 O       └ java.util.ListResourceBundle
D               └ AccessibleResourceBundle
        ─────────────────────────────
1.2     Accessible
1.2     AccessibleAction
1.2     AccessibleComponent⌄
1.4     AccessibleEditableText ───────────────────── AccessibleText
1.4     AccessibleExtendedComponent ─────────────── AccessibleComponent
1.4     AccessibleExtendedTable ───────────────── AccessibleTable
1.2     AccessibleHypertext ──────────────────── AccessibleText
1.3     AccessibleIcon
1.4     AccessibleKeyBinding
1.2     AccessibleSelection
1.3     AccessibleTable⌄
1.3     AccessibleTableModelChange
```

Class   *Interface*   ──extends   - - -implements   O abstract   ● final   ^—has superclass   ⌄—has subclass   package—see other volume

ε687. The Quintessential Accessible Object

You should try to subclass from JComponent or one of its descendants since that will automatically make your object accessible. If that is not possible, your object should implement Accessible.

```
import javax.accessibility.*;

public class BasicAccessible implements Accessible {
    public AccessibleContext getAccessibleContext() {
        return new AccessibleContext() {
            // Implement all the abstract methods in this abstract class.
        };
    }
}
```

ε688. Setting an Accessible Name for an Image Button

You should also set the accessible name for components that only show an image. The tool tip text, if set, serves as the accessible name for a component. However, if the tool tip text is being used for something else, set the component's accessible name.

```
JButton button = new JButton(new ImageIcon("image.gif"));
button.setToolTipText("Button Name");

// If tool tip is being used for something else, set the accessible name.
button.getAccessibleContext().setAccessibleName("Button Name");
```

ε689. Setting a Description for Image Icons

Image icons can be inserted in a variety of places such as in a text or tree component. You should set a description for image icons to help blind users.

```
ImageIcon icon = new ImageIcon("image.gif");
icon.setDescription("Description of Image");
```

ε690. Setting a Mnemonic for Buttons

```
JButton button = new JButton("Button");
button.setMnemonic('B');
JCheckBox checkBox = new JCheckBox("CheckBox");
checkBox.setMnemonic('C');
```

ε691. Setting a Mnemonic for a Menu

At least one menu in a menu bar should have a mnemonic. This makes all the menus and menu items accessible.

```
JMenu menu = new JMenu("Menu");
menu.setMnemonic('M');
```

ε692. Associating a Label with a Component

When a label is associated with a component, you should call setLabelFor() to make the association explicit and then set a mnemonic on the label. The associated component will get the focus when the mnemonic is activated.

Packages and Examples

```
JLabel label = new JLabel("Name:");
label.setDisplayedMnemonic('N');
label.setLabelFor(component);
```

ε693. Setting a Keyboard Accelerator for a Menu Item

At least one menu in a menu bar should have a mnemonic. This makes all the menus and menu items accessible.

```
JMenuItem item = new JMenuItem("Item");
item.setAccelerator(KeyStroke.getKeyStroke(KeyEvent.VK_I, KeyEvent.SHIFT_MASK));
```

javax.imageio

This package contains classes and interfaces for reading and writing images.

```
      java.lang.Object
1.4     ├ IIOImage
1.4 ○   ├ IIOParam
1.4        ├ ImageReadParam
1.4        └ ImageWriteParam
1.4 ●   ├ ImageIO
1.4 ○   ├ ImageReader
1.4     ├ ImageTypeSpecifier
1.4 ○   ├ ImageWriter - - - - - - - - - - - - - - - - - - - - - - - - - - - - - ImageTranscoder
        └ java.lang.Throwable - - - - - - - - - - - - - - - - - - - - - - - - - java.io.Serializable
           └ java.lang.Exception
              └ java.io.IOException
1.4              └ IIOException
      ─────────────────────────────
1.4  IIOParamController
1.4  ImageTranscoder
```

Class *Interface* —extends - - -implements ○ abstract ● final ˆ—has superclass ˎ—has subclass package—see other volume

ε694. Reading an Image from a File, InputStream, or URL

This example demonstrates how to use the javax.imageio package to read an image from a file, input stream, or URL. The example also demonstrates how to display the image on the screen.

GIF, PNG, and JPEG formats are supported by the javax.imageio package by default.

This example works only in J2SE 1.4. For a method that works since J2SE 1.3, see "ε594. Reading an Image or Icon from a File".

```
Image image = null;
try {
    // Read from a file
    File file = new File("image.gif");
    image = ImageIO.read(file);

    // Read from an input stream
    InputStream is = new BufferedInputStream(
        new FileInputStream("image.gif"));
    image = ImageIO.read(is);

    // Read from a URL
    URL url = new URL("http://hostname.com/image.gif");
    image = ImageIO.read(url);
} catch (IOException e) {
}

// Use a label to display the image
JFrame frame = new JFrame();
JLabel label = new JLabel(new ImageIcon(image));
frame.getContentPane().add(label, BorderLayout.CENTER);
frame.pack();
frame.setVisible(true);
```

ε695. Saving a Generated Graphic to a PNG or JPEG File

This example demonstrates how to create a generated image and save it as a PNG or JPEG file.

```
// Create an image to save
RenderedImage rendImage = myCreateImage();

// Write generated image to a file
try {
    // Save as PNG
    File file = new File("newimage.png");
    ImageIO.write(rendImage, "png", file);

    // Save as JPEG
    file = new File("newimage.jpg");
    ImageIO.write(rendImage, "jpg", file);
} catch (IOException e) {
}
// Returns a generated image.
public RenderedImage myCreateImage() {
    int width = 100;
    int height = 100;

    // Create a buffered image in which to draw
    BufferedImage bufferedImage = new BufferedImage(width, height, BufferedImage.TYPE_INT_RGB);

    // Create a graphics contents on the buffered image
```

Packages and Examples

```
Graphics2D g2d = bufferedImage.createGraphics();

// Draw graphics
g2d.setColor(Color.white);
g2d.fillRect(0, 0, width, height);
g2d.setColor(Color.black);
g2d.fillOval(0, 0, width, height);

// Graphics context no longer needed so dispose it
g2d.dispose();

return bufferedImage;
}
```

ε696. Listing the Image Formats That Can Be Read and Written

By default, the javax.imageio package can read GIF, PNG, and JPEG images and can write PNG and JPEG images. The complete list of available readable and writeable formats can be retrieved by calling ImageIO₂ .getReaderFormatNames() and ImageIO.getWriterFormatNames().

Note: These methods may return the format name in both lowercase and uppercase. This example implements a unique() method that removes duplicates, regardless of case.

```
// Get list of unique supported read formats
String[] formatNames = ImageIO.getReaderFormatNames();
formatNames = unique(formatNames);
// e.g. png jpeg gif jpg

// Get list of unique supported write formats
formatNames = ImageIO.getWriterFormatNames();
formatNames = unique(formatNames);
// e.g. png jpeg jpg

// Get list of unique MIME types that can be read
formatNames = ImageIO.getReaderMIMETypes();
formatNames = unique(formatNames);
// e.g image/jpeg image/png image/x-png image/gif

// Get list of unique MIME types that can be written
formatNames = ImageIO.getWriterMIMETypes();
formatNames = unique(formatNames);
// e.g. image/jpeg image/png image/x-png

// Converts all strings in 'strings' to lowercase
// and returns an array containing the unique values.
// All returned values are lowercase.
public static String[] unique(String[] strings) {
    Set set = new HashSet();
    for (int i=0; i<strings.length; i++) {
        String name = strings[i].toLowerCase();
        set.add(name);
    }
    return (String[])set.toArray(new String[0]);
}
```

Class   *Interface*   —extends   - - -implements   ○ abstract   ● final   ˉ—has superclass   ˍ—has subclass   package—see other volume

*ε*697. Determining If an Image Format Can Be Read or Written

By default, the javax.imageio package can read GIF, PNG, and JPEG images and can write PNG and JPEG images. This example demonstrates how to determine if a particular image format can be either read or written using the javax.imageio package.

```
boolean b;

// Check availability using a format name
b = canReadFormat("foo"); // false
b = canReadFormat("gif"); // true
b = canReadFormat("giF"); // true
b = canWriteFormat("foo"); // false
b = canWriteFormat("gif"); // false
b = canWriteFormat("PNG"); // true
b = canWriteFormat("jPeG"); // true

// Get extension from a File object
File f = new File("image.jpg");
String s = f.getName().substring(f.getName().lastIndexOf('.')+1);

// Check availability using a filename extension
b = canReadExtension(s);
b = canWriteExtension(s);

// Check availability using a MIME type
b = canReadMimeType("image/jpg"); // false
b = canReadMimeType("image/jpeg"); // true
b = canWriteMimeType("image/gif"); // false
b = canWriteMimeType("image/jPeg"); // true

// Returns true if the specified format name can be read
public static boolean canReadFormat(String formatName) {
    Iterator iter = ImageIO.getImageReadersByFormatName(formatName);
    return iter.hasNext();
}

// Returns true if the specified format name can be written
public static boolean canWriteFormat(String formatName) {
    Iterator iter = ImageIO.getImageWritersByFormatName(formatName);
    return iter.hasNext();
}

// Returns true if the specified file extension can be read
public static boolean canReadExtension(String fileExt) {
    Iterator iter = ImageIO.getImageReadersBySuffix(fileExt);
    return iter.hasNext();
}

// Returns true if the specified file extension can be written
public static boolean canWriteExtension(String fileExt) {
    Iterator iter = ImageIO.getImageWritersBySuffix(fileExt);
    return iter.hasNext();
}

// Returns true if the specified mime type can be read
public static boolean canReadMimeType(String mimeType) {
    Iterator iter = ImageIO.getImageReadersByMIMEType(mimeType);
    return iter.hasNext();
}
```

Packages and Examples

```
    // Returns true if the specified mime type can be written
    public static boolean canWriteMimeType(String mimeType) {
        Iterator iter = ImageIO.getImageWritersByMIMEType(mimeType);
        return iter.hasNext();
    }
```

ε698. Determining the Format of an Image in a File

The javax.imageio package can determine the type of image in a file or input stream.

```
    try {
        // Get image format in a file
        File file = new File("image.gif");
        String formatName = getFormatName(file);
        // e.g. gif

        // Get image format from an input stream
        InputStream is = new FileInputStream(file);
        formatName = getFormatName(is);
        is.close();
    } catch (IOException e) {
    }

    // Returns the format of the image in the file 'f'.
    // Returns null if the format is not known.
    public static String getFormatInFile(File f) {
        return getFormatName(f);
    }

    // Returns the format of the image in the input stream 'is'.
    // Returns null if the format is not known.
    public static String getFormatFromStream(InputStream is) {
        return getFormatName(is);
    }

    // Returns the format name of the image in the object 'o'.
    // 'o' can be either a File or InputStream object.
    // Returns null if the format is not known.
    private static String getFormatName(Object o) {
        try {
            // Create an image input stream on the image
            ImageInputStream iis = ImageIO.createImageInputStream(o);

            // Find all image readers that recognize the image format
            Iterator iter = ImageIO.getImageReaders(iis);
            if (!iter.hasNext()) {
                // No readers found
                return null;
            }

            // Use the first reader
            ImageReader reader = (ImageReader)iter.next();

            // Close stream
            iis.close();

            // Return the format name
            return reader.getFormatName();
```

Class   *Interface*   —extends   - - -implements   ○ abstract   ● final   ^—has superclass   ‿—has subclass   package—see other volume

```
        } catch (IOException e) {
        }
        // The image could not be read
        return null;
    }
```

*ε*699. Compressing a JPEG File

This example implements a method for writing a JPEG file with a specific compression quality. In J2SE 1.4, the compression capability is not functioning properly. This example demonstrates a workaround.

```
    // Reads the jpeg image in infile, compresses the image,
    // and writes it back out to outfile.
    // compressionQuality ranges between 0 and 1,
    // 0-lowest, 1-highest.
    public void compressJpegFile(File infile, File outfile, float compressionQuality) {
        try {
            // Retrieve jpg image to be compressed
            RenderedImage rendImage = ImageIO.read(infile);

            // Find a jpeg writer
            ImageWriter writer = null;
            Iterator iter = ImageIO.getImageWritersByFormatName("jpg");
            if (iter.hasNext()) {
                writer = (ImageWriter)iter.next();
            }

            // Prepare output file
            ImageOutputStream ios = ImageIO.createImageOutputStream(outfile);
            writer.setOutput(ios);

            // Set the compression quality
            ImageWriteParam iwparam = new MyImageWriteParam();
            iwparam.setCompressionMode(ImageWriteParam.MODE_EXPLICIT) ;
            iwparam.setCompressionQuality(compressionQuality);

            // Write the image
            writer.write(null, new IIOImage(rendImage, null, null), iwparam);

            // Cleanup
            ios.flush();
            writer.dispose();
            ios.close();
        } catch (IOException e) {
        }
    }

    // This class overrides the setCompressionQuality() method to workaround
    // a problem in compressing JPEG images using the javax.imageio package.
    public class MyImageWriteParam extends JPEGImageWriteParam {
        public MyImageWriteParam() {
            super(Locale.getDefault());
        }

        // This method accepts quality levels between 0 (lowest) and 1 (highest) and simply converts
        // it to a range between 0 and 256; this is not a correct conversion algorithm.
        // However, a proper alternative is a lot more complicated.
        // This should do until the bug is fixed.
        public void setCompressionQuality(float quality) {
```

Packages and Examples

147

```
                    if (quality < 0.0F || quality > 1.0F) {
                        throw new IllegalArgumentException("Quality out-of-bounds!");
                    }
                    this.compressionQuality = 256 - (quality * 256);
                }
            }
```

javax.imageio.event

This package contains listener interfaces for receiving event notification during the reading and writing of images.

1.4	*IIOReadProgressListener* ————————————— *java . util.EventListener*
1.4	*IIOReadUpdateListener* ————————
1.4	*IIOReadWarningListener* ————————
1.4	*IIOWriteProgressListener* ————————
1.4	*IIOWriteWarningListener* ————————

javax.imageio.metadata

This package contains classes and interfaces for reading and writing metadata associated with images.

	java . lang.Object
1.4 ○	IIOMetadata
1.4 ○	IIOMetadataFormatImpl - *IIOMetadataFormat*
1.4	IIOMetadataNode - *org . w3c . dom . Element* ^, *org . w3c . dom . NodeList*

Class   *Interface*   ——extends   - - -implements   ○ abstract   ● final   ^—has superclass   ⌐—has subclass   package—see other volume

javax.imageio.plugins.jpeg

This package contains classes used by the JPEG plug-in for reading and writing of JPEG formatted images.

javax.imageio.spi

This package contains the classes and interfaces which must be implemented by plug-in modules for the javax.imageio packages.

Packages and Examples

java.lang.Object

1.4 ○   ├ IIOServiceProvider - *RegisterableService*
1.4 ○   │   ├ ImageInputStreamSpi
1.4 ○   │   ├ ImageOutputStreamSpi
1.4 ○   │   ├ ImageReaderWriterSpi
1.4 ○   │   │   ├ ImageReaderSpi
1.4 ○   │   │   └ ImageWriterSpi
1.4 ○   │   └ ImageTranscoderSpi
1.4   └ ServiceRegistry
1.4 ●   └ IIORegistry

1.4   *RegisterableService*
1.4   *ServiceRegistry.Filter*

javax.imageio.stream

This package contains classes and interfaces for reading and writing images to and from IO streams and files.

PAGE

java.lang.Object

1.4   ├ IIOByteBuffer
1.4 ○   └ ImageInputStreamImpl - *ImageInputStream*˘
1.4   ├ FileCacheImageInputStream
1.4   ├ FileImageInputStream
1.4 ○   ├ ImageOutputStreamImpl - *ImageOutputStream*^
1.4   │   ├ FileCacheImageOutputStream
1.4   │   ├ FileImageOutputStream

Class   *Interface*   —extends   - - -implements   ○ abstract   ● final   ^—has superclass   ˘—has subclass   package—see other volume

```
       java . lang.Object
1.4 ○    └ ImageInputStreamImpl - - - - - - - - - - - - - - - - - - - - - - - - - - - - - - - - - ImageInputStream˄
1.4 ○      ├ ImageOutputStreamImpl - - - - - - - - - - - - - - - - - - - - - - - - - - - ImageOutputStream˄
1.4          └ MemoryCacheImageOutputStream
1.4        └ MemoryCacheImageInputStream
```

1.4	*ImageInputStream*˅ ───────────────────────────	*java . io.DataInput*
1.4	*ImageOutputStream* ─────────────────────────	*ImageInputStream*˄, *java . io.DataOutput*

javax.print

This package contains the main classes and interfaces for printing.

	java.lang.Object
1.4	┬ DocFlavor - *java.io.Serializable,, java.lang.Cloneable,*
1.4	├ DocFlavor.BYTE_ARRAY
1.4	├ DocFlavor.CHAR_ARRAY
1.4	├ DocFlavor.INPUT_STREAM
1.4	├ DocFlavor.READER
1.4	├ DocFlavor.SERVICE_FORMATTED
1.4	├ DocFlavor.STRING
1.4	└ DocFlavor.URL
1.4 ○	├ PrintServiceLookup
1.4	├ ServiceUI
1.4 ○	├ ServiceUIFactory
1.4 ●	├ SimpleDoc - *Doc*
1.4 ○	├ StreamPrintService - *PrintService,*
1.4 ○	├ StreamPrintServiceFactory
	└ java.lang.Throwable - *java.io.Serializable,*
	└ java.lang.Exception
1.4	└ PrintException
1.4	*AttributeException*
1.4	*CancelablePrintJob* ──────────────────────────── *DocPrintJob*
1.4	*Doc*
1.4	*DocPrintJob,*
1.4	*FlavorException*
1.4	*MultiDoc*
1.4	*MultiDocPrintJob* ────────────────────────────
1.4	*MultiDocPrintService* ─────────────────────────── *PrintService*
1.4	*PrintService,*
1.4	*URIException*

ε700. The Quintessential Printing Program Using a Printing Service

This example demonstrates a program that prints an image on the default print service.

Since DocPrintJob.print() is not guaranteed to be synchronous, it is necessary to watch for a print job completion event before closing the input stream.

```
import java.io.*;
import javax.print.*;
import javax.print.attribute.*;
import javax.print.attribute.standard.*;
import javax.print.event.*;

public class BasicPrint {
    public static void main(String[] args) {
        try {
            // Open the image file
```

```
        InputStream is = new BufferedInputStream(
            new FileInputStream("filename.gif"));

        // Find the default service
        DocFlavor flavor = DocFlavor.INPUT_STREAM.GIF;
        PrintService service = PrintServiceLookup.lookupDefaultPrintService();

        // Create the print job
        DocPrintJob job = service.createPrintJob();
        Doc doc = new SimpleDoc(is, flavor, null);

        // Monitor print job events; for the implementation of PrintJobWatcher,
        // see "ε702. Determining When a Print Job Has Finished"
        PrintJobWatcher pjDone = new PrintJobWatcher(job);

        // Print it
        job.print(doc, null);

        // Wait for the print job to be done
        pjDone.waitForDone();

        // It is now safe to close the input stream
        is.close();
      } catch (PrintException e) {
      } catch (IOException e) {
      }
    }
  }
```

ε701. The Quintessential Printing Program Using a Streaming Printing Service

A streaming print service is used to convert print data from one format to another. Unlike a print service that prints to a printer, a streaming print service writes to an output stream. This example demonstrates a program that prints an image to a postscript-generating streaming print service.

```
import java.io.*;
import javax.print.*;

public class BasicStream {
    public static void main(String[] args) {
        try {
            // Open the image file
            InputStream is = new BufferedInputStream(
                new FileInputStream("filename.gif"));

            // Prepare the output file to receive the postscript
            OutputStream fos = new BufferedOutputStream(
                new FileOutputStream("filename.ps"));

            // Find a factory that can do the conversion
            DocFlavor flavor = DocFlavor.INPUT_STREAM.GIF;
            StreamPrintServiceFactory[] factories =
                StreamPrintServiceFactory.lookupStreamPrintServiceFactories(
                    flavor,
                    DocFlavor.BYTE_ARRAY.POSTSCRIPT.getMimeType());

            if (factories.length > 0) {
                StreamPrintService service = factories[0].getPrintService(fos);

                // Create the print job
                DocPrintJob job = service.createPrintJob();
```

```
                        Doc doc = new SimpleDoc(is, flavor, null);

                        // Monitor print job events; for the implementation of PrintJobWatcher,
                        // see "ε702. Determining When a Print Job Has Finished"
                        PrintJobWatcher pjDone = new PrintJobWatcher(job);

                        // Print it
                        job.print(doc, null);

                        // Wait for the print job to be done
                        pjDone.waitForDone();
                        // It is now safe to close the streams
                    }
                    is.close();
                    fos.close();
                } catch (PrintException e) {
                } catch (IOException e) {
                }
            }
        }
```

ε702. Determining When a Print Job Has Finished

Since DocPrintJob.print() is not guaranteed to be synchronous, it is necessary to watch for a print job completion event before closing the input stream. This example implements a convenient class that you can use while waiting for a print job to finish.

```
    try {
        // Open the image file
        InputStream is = new BufferedInputStream(
            new FileInputStream("filename.gif"));
        // Create the print job
        DocPrintJob job = service.createPrintJob();
        Doc doc = new SimpleDoc(is, flavor, null);

        // Monitor print job events
        PrintJobWatcher pjDone = new PrintJobWatcher(job);

        // Print it
        job.print(doc, null);

        // Wait for the print job to be done
        pjDone.waitForDone();

        // It is now safe to close the input stream
        is.close();
    } catch (PrintException e) {
    } catch (IOException e) {
    }

    class PrintJobWatcher {
        // true iff it is safe to close the print job's input stream
        boolean done = false;

        PrintJobWatcher(DocPrintJob job) {
            // Add a listener to the print job
            job.addPrintJobListener(new PrintJobAdapter() {
                public void printJobCanceled(PrintJobEvent pje) {
```

```
                    allDone();
                }
                public void printJobCompleted(PrintJobEvent pje) {
                    allDone();
                }
                public void printJobFailed(PrintJobEvent pje) {
                    allDone();
                }
                public void printJobNoMoreEvents(PrintJobEvent pje) {
                    allDone();
                }
                void allDone() {
                    synchronized (PrintJobWatcher.this) {
                        done = true;
                        PrintJobWatcher.this.notify();
                    }
                }
            });
        }
        public synchronized void waitForDone() {
            try {
                while (!done) {
                    wait();
                }
            } catch (InterruptedException e) {
            }
        }
    }
}
```

*ε*703. Discovering Available Print Services

```
// Look up all services
PrintService[] services = PrintServiceLookup.lookupPrintServices(null, null);

// Look up the default print service
PrintService service = PrintServiceLookup.lookupDefaultPrintService();

// Find all services that can support a particular
// input format; in this case, a GIF
services = PrintServiceLookup.lookupPrintServices(
    DocFlavor.INPUT_STREAM.GIF, null);

// Find a particular service by name;
// in this case "HP LaserJet 6MP PS"
AttributeSet aset = new HashAttributeSet();
aset.add(new PrinterName("HP LaserJet 6MP PS", null));
services = PrintServiceLookup.lookupPrintServices(null, aset);

// Find all services that support a set of print job capabilities;
// in this case, color
aset = new HashAttributeSet();
aset.add(ColorSupported.SUPPORTED);
services = PrintServiceLookup.lookupPrintServices(null, aset);
```

*ε*704. Discovering Available Streaming Print Services

```
// Look up all streaming factories
StreamPrintServiceFactory[] factories
```

```
        = StreamPrintServiceFactory.lookupStreamPrintServiceFactories(null, null);

    // Find all streaming factories that support particular input formats;
    // in this case, GIF and postscript
    factories = StreamPrintServiceFactory.lookupStreamPrintServiceFactories(
        DocFlavor.INPUT_STREAM.GIF,
        DocFlavor.BYTE_ARRAY.POSTSCRIPT.getMimeType());

    // Use a factory to create a print service.
    // An output stream is required to create a print service.
    OutputStream fos = new BufferedOutputStream(
        new FileOutputStream("outfile.ps"));
    StreamPrintService service = factories[0].getPrintService(fos);
```

ε705. Cancelling a Print Job

Not all print jobs can be cancelled. A print job can be cancelled if the PrintJob object implements CancelablePrintJob.

This example shows a cancel button if the print job can be cancelled.

```
    try {
        // Create the print job
        final DocPrintJob job = service.createPrintJob();
        Doc doc = new SimpleDoc(is, flavor, null);

        // Monitor print job events.
        // See "ε702. Determining When a Print Job Has Finished"
        // for the implementation of PrintJobWatcher.
        PrintJobWatcher pjDone = new PrintJobWatcher(job);

        // Sample code to display a cancel button
        JFrame frame = new JFrame();
        if (job instanceof CancelablePrintJob) {
            JButton btn = new JButton("Cancel Print Job");
            btn.addActionListener(new ActionListener() {
                public void actionPerformed(ActionEvent evt) {
                    CancelablePrintJob cancelJob = (CancelablePrintJob)job;
                    try {
                        cancelJob.cancel();
                    } catch (PrintException e) {
                        // Possible reason is job was already finished
                    }
                }
            });

            frame.getContentPane().add(btn, BorderLayout.CENTER);
            frame.pack();
            frame.setVisible(true);
        }

        // Print it
        job.print(doc, null);

        // Wait for the print job to be done
        pjDone.waitForDone();

        // Remove frame
        frame.setVisible(false);
```

Class   *Interface*   —extends   - - -implements   ○ abstract   ● final   ^—has superclass   ‿—has subclass   package—see other volume

```
        // It is now safe to close the input stream
        is.close();
    } catch (PrintException e) {
        if (e.getCause() instanceof java.awt.print.PrinterAbortException) {
            // Print job was cancelled
        }
    }
}
```

javax.print.attribute

This package contains classes and interfaces that describe the types of printing attributes and how they can be collected into attribute sets.

Packages and Examples

```
       java.lang.Object
1.4 ●    ├ AttributeSetUtilities
1.4 ○    ├ DateTimeSyntax - - - - - - - - - - - - - - - - - - - - - - - - - - - - - : java.io.Serializable, java.lang.Cloneable
1.4 ○    ├ EnumSyntax - - - - - - - - - - - - - - - - - - - - - - - - - - - - - - :
1.4      ├ HashAttributeSet - - - - - - - - - - - - - - - - - - - - - - - AttributeSet, java.io.Serializable
1.4      │  ├ HashDocAttributeSet - - - - - - - - - - - - - - - - - - - DocAttributeSet^, java.io.Serializable
1.4      │  ├ HashPrintJobAttributeSet - - - - - - - - - - - - - - - - PrintJobAttributeSet^, java.io.Serializable
1.4      │  ├ HashPrintRequestAttributeSet - - - - - - - - - - - - - PrintRequestAttributeSet^, java.io.Serializable
1.4      │  └ HashPrintServiceAttributeSet - - - - - - - - - - - - - PrintServiceAttributeSet^, java.io.Serializable
1.4 ○    ├ IntegerSyntax - - - - - - - - - - - - - - - - - - - - - - - - - - : java.io.Serializable, java.lang.Cloneable
1.4 ○    ├ ResolutionSyntax - - - - - - - - - - - - - - - - - - - - - - - :
1.4 ○    ├ SetOfIntegerSyntax - - - - - - - - - - - - - - - - - - - - - - :
1.4 ○    ├ Size2DSyntax - - - - - - - - - - - - - - - - - - - - - - - - - :
1.4 ○    ├ TextSyntax - - - - - - - - - - - - - - - - - - - - - - - - - - :
1.4 ○    ├ URISyntax - - - - - - - - - - - - - - - - - - - - - - - - - - - :
         ├ java.lang.Throwable - - - - - - - - - - - - - - - - - - - - - - java.io.Serializable
         │  └ java.lang.Exception
         │     └ java.lang.RuntimeException
1.4      │        └ UnmodifiableSetException

1.4    Attribute ————————————————————————— java.io.Serializable
1.4    AttributeSet
1.4    DocAttribute ——————————————————————— Attribute^
1.4    DocAttributeSet ————————————————————— AttributeSet
1.4    PrintJobAttribute —————————————————————— Attribute^
1.4    PrintJobAttributeSet ————————————————————— AttributeSet
1.4    PrintRequestAttribute ———————————————————— Attribute^
1.4    PrintRequestAttributeSet ——————————————————— AttributeSet
1.4    PrintServiceAttribute ————————————————————— Attribute^
1.4    PrintServiceAttributeSet ——————————————————— AttributeSet
1.4    SupportedValuesAttribute —————————————————— Attribute^
```

*ε*706. Determining the Capabilities of a Print Service

The capabilities of a print service are called print service *attributes*. Examples of print service attributes include: color-supported, printer-name, and queued-job-count. This example demonstrates how to retrieve the current attributes of a print service. To monitor changes to these attributes, see "*ε*713. Listening for Print Service Status Changes".

Class   *Interface*   —extends   - - -implements   ○ abstract   ● final   ^—has superclass   ⌙—has subclass   package—see other volume

```
Attribute[] attrs = service.getAttributes().toArray();
for (int j=0; j<attrs.length; j++) {
    String attrName = attrs[j].getName();

    // Retrieve the string version of the attribute value
    String attrValue = attrs[j].toString();

    process(service, attrName, attrValue);
}
```

ε707. Determining Print Job Capabilities Supported by a Print Service

The capabilities of a print job are called print job *attributes*. Examples of print job attributes include–Copies, OrientationRequested, and Destination. This example demonstrates how to retrieve the supported print job attributes of a print service.

```
// Get all print job attributes of a print service
Class[] cats = service.getSupportedAttributeCategories();
for (int j=0; j<cats.length; j++) {
    Attribute attr = (Attribute)service.getDefaultAttributeValue(cats[j]);

    if (attr != null) {
        // Get attribute name and values
        String attrName = attr.getName();
        String attrValue = attr.toString();

        Object o = service.getSupportedAttributeValues(attr.getCategory(), null, null);
        if (o.getClass().isArray()) {
            for (int k=0; k<Array.getLength(o); k++) {
                Object o2 = Array.get(o, k);
            }
        }
    }
}
```

ε708. Getting the Default Value of a Print Job Capability

The capabilities of a print job are called print job *attributes*. Examples of print job attributes include: Copies, OrientationRequested, and Destination. This example demonstrates how to retrieve the default value of a particular attribute.

```
Attribute attr = (Attribute)service.getDefaultAttributeValue(Destination.class);

// attr == null if the attribute is not supported
if (attr != null) {
    String attrName = attr.getName();
    // Get string representation of default value
    String attrValue = attr.toString();
    process(service, attrName, attrValue);
}
```

ε709. Getting the Possible Values for a Print Job Capability

The capabilities of a print job are called print job *attributes*. Examples of print job attributes include: Copies, OrientationRequested, and Destination. This example demonstrates how to retrieve the possible values of a print job attribute.

PrintService.getSupportedAttributeValues() is the method to use. This method returns 3 possible types of objects: 1) an instance of the attribute which indicates arbitrary values (e.g., Destination); 2) an array of instances of the attribute that indicates a set of specific values (e.g., OrientationRequested); and 3) an instance of something other than the attribute type that indicates that the values are limited to a particular range of values (the documentation is not clear about this particular return value).

```
Class category = OrientationRequested.class;
Object o = service.getSupportedAttributeValues(category, null, null);
if (o == null) {
    // Attribute is not supported
} else if (o.getClass() == category) {
    // Attribute value is arbitrary; the actual value in o is irrelevant
} else if (o.getClass().isArray()) {
    // Attribute values are a set of values
    for (int i=0; i<Array.getLength(o); i++) {
        Object v = Array.get(o, i);
        // v is one of the possible values
    }
} else {
    // Attribute value is limited to a range of values represented by o
}
```

javax.print.attribute.standard

This package contains classes for specific printing attributes.

Class   *Interface*   —extends   - - -implements   ○ abstract   ● final   ˆ—has superclass   ‿—has subclass   package—see other volume

Packages and Examples

Class *Interface* —extends - - -implements ○ abstract ● final ^—has superclass ⌐—has subclass package—see other volume

	java . lang . Object	
1.4 ●	├ MediaPrintableArea -	*javax.print.attribute.DocAttribute*ˆ, *javax.print.attribute.PrintJobAttribute*ˆ, *javax.print.attribute.PrintRequestAttribute*ˆ
1.4 ●	├ MediaSize.Engineering	
1.4 ●	├ MediaSize.ISO	
1.4 ●	├ MediaSize.JIS	
1.4 ●	├ MediaSize.NA	
1.4 ●	├ MediaSize.Other	
1.2 ○	├ java . util . AbstractCollection -	*java . util . Collection*˅
1.2 ○	│ └ java . util . AbstractSet -	*java . util . Set*˚
1.2	│ └ java . util . HashSet -	*java . io . Serializable*˅, *java . lang . Cloneable*˅, *java . util . Set*˚
1.4 ●	│ └ JobStateReasons -	*javax.print.attribute.PrintJobAttribute*ˆ
1.2 ○	├ java . util . AbstractMap -	*java . util . Map*˅
1.2	│ └ java . util . HashMap -	*java . io . Serializable*˅, *java . lang . Cloneable*˅, *java . util . Map*˅
1.4 ●	│ └ PrinterStateReasons -	*javax.print.attribute.PrintServiceAttribute*ˆ
1.4 ○	├ javax.print.attribute.DateTimeSyntax - - - - - - - - - - - - - - - - -	*java . io . Serializable*˅, *java . lang . Cloneable*˅
1.4 ●	│ ├ DateTimeAtCompleted -	*javax.print.attribute.PrintJobAttribute*ˆ
1.4 ●	│ ├ DateTimeAtCreation -	
1.4 ●	│ ├ DateTimeAtProcessing -	
1.4 ●	│ └ JobHoldUntil -	*javax.print.attribute.PrintJobAttribute*ˆ, *javax.print.attribute.PrintRequestAttribute*ˆ
1.4 ○	├ javax.print.attribute.EnumSyntax -	*java . io . Serializable*˅, *java . lang . Cloneable*˅
1.4 ●	│ ├ Chromaticity -	*javax.print.attribute.DocAttribute*ˆ, *javax.print.attribute.PrintJobAttribute*ˆ, *javax.print.attribute.PrintRequestAttribute*ˆ
1.4 ●	│ ├ ColorSupported -	*javax.print.attribute.PrintServiceAttribute*ˆ
1.4	│ ├ Compression -	*javax.print.attribute.DocAttribute*ˆ
1.4 ●	│ ├ Fidelity -	*javax.print.attribute.PrintJobAttribute*ˆ, *javax.print.attribute.PrintRequestAttribute*ˆ
1.4	│ ├ Finishings -	*javax.print.attribute.DocAttribute*ˆ, *javax.print.attribute.PrintJobAttribute*ˆ, *javax.print.attribute.PrintRequestAttribute*ˆ
1.4	│ ├ JobSheets -	*javax.print.attribute.PrintJobAttribute*ˆ, *javax.print.attribute.PrintRequestAttribute*ˆ
1.4	│ ├ JobState -	*javax.print.attribute.PrintJobAttribute*ˆ
1.4	│ ├ JobStateReason -	*javax.print.attribute.Attribute*˚
1.4 ○	│ ├ Media -	*javax.print.attribute.DocAttribute*ˆ, *javax.print.attribute.PrintJobAttribute*ˆ, *javax.print.attribute.PrintRequestAttribute*ˆ
1.4	│ │ ├ MediaName -	*javax.print.attribute.Attribute*˚
1.4	│ │ ├ MediaSizeName	
1.4	│ │ └ MediaTray -	
1.4	│ ├ MultipleDocumentHandling -	*javax.print.attribute.PrintJobAttribute*ˆ, *javax.print.attribute.PrintRequestAttribute*ˆ

Packages and Examples

		java.lang.Object	
1.4 ○		javax.print.attribute.EnumSyntax -	*java.io.Serializable*, *java.lang.Cloneable*
1.4 ●		OrientationRequested -	*javax.print.attribute.DocAttribute^,* *javax.print.attribute.PrintJobAttribute^,* *javax.print.attribute.PrintRequestAttribute^*
1.4		PDLOverrideSupported -	*javax.print.attribute.PrintServiceAttribute^*
1.4 ●		PresentationDirection -	*javax.print.attribute.PrintJobAttribute^,* *javax.print.attribute.PrintRequestAttribute^*
1.4		PrintQuality -	*javax.print.attribute.DocAttribute^,* *javax.print.attribute.PrintJobAttribute^,* *javax.print.attribute.PrintRequestAttribute^*
1.4 ●		PrinterIsAcceptingJobs -	*javax.print.attribute.PrintServiceAttribute^*
1.4 ●		PrinterState -	
1.4		PrinterStateReason -	*javax.print.attribute.Attribute*
1.4		ReferenceUriSchemesSupported -	
1.4 ●		Severity -	
1.4 ●		SheetCollate -	*javax.print.attribute.DocAttribute^,* *javax.print.attribute.PrintJobAttribute^,* *javax.print.attribute.PrintRequestAttribute^*
1.4 ●		Sides -	
1.4 ○		javax.print.attribute.IntegerSyntax -	*java.io.Serializable*, *java.lang.Cloneable*
1.4 ●		Copies -	*javax.print.attribute.PrintJobAttribute^,* *javax.print.attribute.PrintRequestAttribute^*
1.4 ●		JobImpressions -	
1.4 ●		JobImpressionsCompleted -	*javax.print.attribute.PrintJobAttribute^*
1.4 ●		JobKOctets -	*javax.print.attribute.PrintJobAttribute^,* *javax.print.attribute.PrintRequestAttribute^*
1.4 ●		JobKOctetsProcessed -	*javax.print.attribute.PrintJobAttribute^*
1.4		JobMediaSheets -	*javax.print.attribute.PrintJobAttribute^,* *javax.print.attribute.PrintRequestAttribute^*
1.4 ●		JobMediaSheetsCompleted -	*javax.print.attribute.PrintJobAttribute^*
1.4 ●		JobPriority -	*javax.print.attribute.PrintJobAttribute^,* *javax.print.attribute.PrintRequestAttribute^*
1.4 ●		JobPrioritySupported -	*javax.print.attribute.SupportedValuesAttribute^*
1.4 ●		NumberOfDocuments -	*javax.print.attribute.PrintJobAttribute^*
1.4 ●		NumberOfInterveningJobs -	
1.4 ●		NumberUp -	*javax.print.attribute.DocAttribute^,* *javax.print.attribute.PrintJobAttribute^,* *javax.print.attribute.PrintRequestAttribute^*
1.4 ●		PagesPerMinute -	*javax.print.attribute.PrintServiceAttribute^*
1.4 ●		PagesPerMinuteColor -	
1.4 ●		QueuedJobCount -	
1.4 ○		javax.print.attribute.ResolutionSyntax - - - - - - - - - - - - - - - - -	*java.io.Serializable*, *java.lang.Cloneable*
1.4 ●		PrinterResolution -	*javax.print.attribute.DocAttribute^,* *javax.print.attribute.PrintJobAttribute^,* *javax.print.attribute.PrintRequestAttribute^*
1.4 ○		javax.print.attribute.SetOfIntegerSyntax - - - - - - - - - - - - - - - -	*java.io.Serializable*, *java.lang.Cloneable*
1.4 ●		CopiesSupported -	*javax.print.attribute.SupportedValuesAttribute^*
1.4 ●		JobImpressionsSupported -	
1.4 ●		JobKOctetsSupported -	
1.4 ●		JobMediaSheetsSupported -	
1.4 ●		NumberUpSupported -	

```
        java.lang.Object
1.4 ○    ├ javax.print.attribute.SetOfIntegerSyntax ------------------ java.io.Serializable↓, java.lang.Cloneable↓
1.4 ●    │  └ PageRanges ------------------------------------- javax.print.attribute.DocAttribute^,
         │                                                          javax.print.attribute.PrintJobAttribute^,
         │                                                          javax.print.attribute.PrintRequestAttribute^
1.4 ○    ├ javax.print.attribute.Size2DSyntax --------------------- java.io.Serializable↓, java.lang.Cloneable↓
1.4      │  └ MediaSize ------------------------------------- javax.print.attribute.Attribute↑
1.4 ○    ├ javax.print.attribute.TextSyntax ----------------------- java.io.Serializable↓, java.lang.Cloneable↓
1.4 ●    │  ├ DocumentName ----------------------------------- javax.print.attribute.DocAttribute^
1.4 ●    │  ├ JobMessageFromOperator ---------------------------- javax.print.attribute.PrintJobAttribute^
1.4 ●    │  ├ JobName --------------------------------------- javax.print.attribute.PrintJobAttribute^,
         │                                                          javax.print.attribute.PrintRequestAttribute^
1.4 ●    │  ├ JobOriginatingUserName --------------------------┬-- javax.print.attribute.PrintJobAttribute^
1.4 ●    │  ├ OutputDeviceAssigned ----------------------------┤
1.4 ●    │  ├ PrinterInfo -----------------------------------┬-- javax.print.attribute.PrintServiceAttribute^
1.4 ●    │  ├ PrinterLocation --------------------------------┤
1.4 ●    │  ├ PrinterMakeAndModel ------------------------------┤
1.4 ●    │  ├ PrinterMessageFromOperator ------------------------┤
1.4 ●    │  ├ PrinterName ----------------------------------┘
1.4 ●    │  └ RequestingUserName ------------------------------- javax.print.attribute.PrintRequestAttribute^
1.4 ○    └ javax.print.attribute.URISyntax ----------------------- java.io.Serializable↓, java.lang.Cloneable↓
1.4 ●       ├ Destination ---------------------------------- javax.print.attribute.PrintJobAttribute^,
            │                                                       javax.print.attribute.PrintRequestAttribute^
1.4 ●       ├ PrinterMoreInfo -------------------------------┬-- javax.print.attribute.PrintServiceAttribute^
1.4 ●       ├ PrinterMoreInfoManufacturer ----------------------┤
1.4 ●       └ PrinterURI ------------------------------------┘
```

*ε*710. Setting the Orientation of a Print Job – Portrait or Landscape

Print job attributes are delivered to the print service via the print request attribute set supplied to DocPrintJob₂ .print(). See "*ε*700. The Quintessential Printing Program Using a Printing Service" to see how to set up a print job.

```
try {
    // Set up the attribute set
    PrintRequestAttributeSet aset = new HashPrintRequestAttributeSet();
    if (portrait) {
        aset.add(OrientationRequested.PORTRAIT);
    } else {
        aset.add(OrientationRequested.LANDSCAPE);
    }
    // Print it
    job.print(doc, aset);
} catch (PrintException e) {
}
```

*ε*711. Setting the Number of Copies of a Print Job

Print job attributes are delivered to the print service via the print request attribute set supplied to DocPrintJob₂ .print(). See "*ε*700. The Quintessential Printing Program Using a Printing Service" to see how to set up a print job.

```
try {
    // Set up the attribute set
```

```
            PrintRequestAttributeSet aset = new HashPrintRequestAttributeSet();
            aset.add(new Copies(2));

            // Print it
            job.print(doc, aset);
        } catch (PrintException e) {
        }
```

ε712. Printing to a File

There are two ways to print to a file. One way is to use a streaming print service (see "ε701. The Quintessential Printing Program Using a Streaming Printing Service") that writes to an output stream that you supply. The other is to request that the print service write directly into a specified file.

This example demonstrates the latter, by using a Destination print job attribute to specify the destination filename. The example prints to a file called e:\temp\out.ps.

Print job attributes are delivered to the print service via the print request attribute set supplied to DocPrintJob$_2$ .print(). See "ε700. The Quintessential Printing Program Using a Printing Service" to see how to set up a print job.

```
        try {
            // Set up destination attribute
            PrintRequestAttributeSet aset = new HashPrintRequestAttributeSet();
            aset.add(new Destination(new java.net.URI("file:e:/temp/out.ps")));

            // Print it
            job.print(doc, aset);
        } catch (PrintException e) {
        } catch (java.net.URISyntaxException e) {
        }
```

javax.print.event

This package contains event classes and listener interfaces for supporting event notifications related to printing.

```
        java.lang.Object
1.4 ○    ├ PrintJobAdapter - - - - - - - - - - - - - - - - - - - - - - - - - - - - - - - - PrintJobListener
```

Class   *Interface*   —extends   - - -implements   ○ abstract   ● final   ^—has superclass   ̲—has subclass   package—see other volume

```
      java.lang.Object
1.1     └ java.util.EventObject - - - - - - - - - - - - - - - - - - - - - - - - - - - - - - java.io.Serializable
1.4         └ PrintEvent
1.4             ├ PrintJobAttributeEvent
1.4             ├ PrintJobEvent
1.4             └ PrintServiceAttributeEvent

1.4     PrintJobAttributeListener
1.4     PrintJobListener
1.4     PrintServiceAttributeListener
```

ε713. Listening for Print Service Status Changes

Examples of print service status include PrinterIsAcceptingJobs (indicates if a print service will accept new print jobs) and QueuedJobCount (the number of print jobs to be processed by the print service). Use a PrintServiceAttributeListener to get status changes on a print server. This example adds a listener to all print services.

To obtain detailed status changes for a print job, see "ε714. Listening for Print Job Status Changes".

```java
// Add a listener to all print services
PrintService[] services = PrintServiceLookup.lookupPrintServices(null, null);
for (int i=0; i<services.length; i++) {
    services[i].addPrintServiceAttributeListener(new MyPrintServiceAttributeListener());
}

class MyPrintServiceAttributeListener implements PrintServiceAttributeListener {
    public void attributeUpdate(PrintServiceAttributeEvent psae) {
        // Some event occurred with a print service
        PrintService service = psae.getPrintService();

        Attribute[] attrs = psae.getAttributes().toArray();
        for (int i=0; i<attrs.length; i++) {
            String attrName = attrs[i].getName();

            // New value
            String attrValue = attrs[i].toString();
            process(service, attrName, attrValue);
        }
    }
}
```

ε714. Listening for Print Job Status Changes

In order to get status on a print job, a print job listener must be added to the print job before it is submitted to the print service.

These status changes are common to all print jobs. A print service may support other types of print job status changes and these are delivered through a print job attribute listener rather than a print job listener; see "ε715. Listening for Print Job Attribute Changes".

```java
// Create the print job
DocPrintJob job = service.createPrintJob();
job.addPrintJobListener(new MyPrintJobListener());

class MyPrintJobListener implements PrintJobListener {
    public void printDataTransferCompleted(PrintJobEvent pje) {
        // The print data has been transferred to the print service
    }
```

```
        public void printJobCanceled(PrintJobEvent pje) {
            // The print job was cancelled
        }

        public void printJobCompleted(PrintJobEvent pje) {
            // The print job was completed
        }

        public void printJobFailed(PrintJobEvent pje) {
            // The print job has failed
        }

        public void printJobNoMoreEvents(PrintJobEvent pje) {
            // No more events will be delivered from this
            // print service for this print job.
            // This event is fired in cases where the print service
            // is not able to determine when the job completes.
        }

        public void printJobRequiresAttention(PrintJobEvent pje) {
            // The print service requires some attention to repair
            // some problem. E.g. running out of paper would
            // cause this event to be fired.
        }
    }
```

ε715. Listening for Print Job Attribute Changes

Status changes that are common to all print jobs are delivered through a print job listener; see "ε714. Listening for Print Job Status Changes".

However, if a print service supports a status that is not supported by the print job listener (e.g., JobMediaSheetsCompleted), it delivers status changes through a print job attribute listener.

```
    // Create the print job
    DocPrintJob job = service.createPrintJob();
    PrintJobAttributeSet set = new HashPrintJobAttributeSet(job.getAttributes());
    set.add(new JobMediaSheetsCompleted(0));
    job.addPrintJobAttributeListener(new MyPrintJobAttributeListener(), set);

    class MyPrintJobAttributeListener implements PrintJobAttributeListener {
        public void attributeUpdate(PrintJobAttributeEvent pjae) {
            // Get the set of attributes that have changed
            Attribute[] attrs = pjae.getAttributes().toArray();

            for (int i=0; i<attrs.length; i++) {
                String attrName = attrs[i].getName();
                String attrValue = attrs[i].toString();
                process(pjae, attrName, attrValue);
            }
        }
    }
```

Class   *Interface*   —extends   - - -implements   ○ abstract   ● final   ⌐—has superclass   ⌐—has subclass   package—see other volume

javax.sound.midi

This package provides interfaces and classes for I/O, sequencing, and synthesis of MIDI (Musical Instrument Digital Interface) data.

java . lang.Object

1.3 ├ MidiDevice.Info

	java . lang.Object
1.3	– MidiEvent
1.3	– MidiFileFormat
1.3 ○	– MidiMessage - *java . lang.Cloneable*
1.3	– MetaMessage
1.3	– ShortMessage
1.3	└ SysexMessage
1.3	– MidiSystem
1.3	– Patch
1.3	– Sequence
1.3	– Sequencer.SyncMode
1.3 ○	– SoundbankResource
1.3 ○	└ Instrument
1.3	– Track
1.3	– VoiceStatus
	└ java . lang.Throwable - *java . io.Serializable*
	└ java . lang.Exception
1.3	– InvalidMidiDataException
1.3	└ MidiUnavailableException

1.3	*ControllerEventListener* —————————————— *java . util.EventListener*
1.3	*MetaEventListener* ———————
1.3	*MidiChannel*
1.3	*MidiDevice*
1.3	*Receiver*
1.3	*Sequencer* ——————————————— *MidiDevice*
1.3	*Soundbank*
1.3	*Synthesizer* ———————————
1.3	*Transmitter*

Playing

*ε*716. Loading and Playing Midi Audio

Supported audio file formats: mid. See also "*ε*717. Playing Streaming Midi Audio".

```
try {
    // From file
    Sequence sequence = MidiSystem.getSequence(new File("midifile"));

    // From URL
    sequence = MidiSystem.getSequence(new URL("http://hostname/midifile"));

    // Create a sequencer for the sequence
    Sequencer sequencer = MidiSystem.getSequencer();
    sequencer.open();
    sequencer.setSequence(sequence);

    // Start playing
    sequencer.start();
} catch (MalformedURLException e) {
} catch (IOException e) {
```

Class *Interface* —extends - - -implements ○ abstract ● final ˆ—has superclass ⌐—has subclass package—see other volume

```
        } catch (MidiUnavailableException e) {
        } catch (InvalidMidiDataException e) {
        }
```

ε717. Playing Streaming Midi Audio

Supported audio file formats: mid, rmf

```
        try {
            Sequencer sequencer = MidiSystem.getSequencer();
            sequencer.open();

            // From file
            InputStream is = new BufferedInputStream(
                new FileInputStream(new File("midifile")));

            // From URL
            is = new BufferedInputStream(
                new URL("http://hostname/rmffile").openStream());

            sequencer.setSequence(is);

            // Start playing
            sequencer.start();
        } catch (MalformedURLException e) {
        } catch (IOException e) {
        } catch (MidiUnavailableException e) {
        } catch (InvalidMidiDataException e) {
        }
```

Properties

ε718. Determining the File Format of a Midi Audio File

```
        try {
            // From file
            MidiFileFormat fformat = MidiSystem.getMidiFileFormat(new File("midifile"));

            // From URL
            fformat = MidiSystem.getMidiFileFormat(new URL("http://hostname/midifile"));

            // Get file format
            switch (fformat.getType()) {
            case 0:
                // mid
                break;
            case 1:
                // rmf
                break;
            }
        } catch (MalformedURLException e) {
        } catch (IOException e) {
        } catch (InvalidMidiDataException e) {
            // File format is not supported.
        }
```

ε719. Determining the Duration of a Midi Audio File

To create a Sequencer object, see "ε716. Loading and Playing Midi Audio".

// To create a Sequencer object, see "ε716. Loading and Playing Midi Audio"

double durationInSecs = *sequencer*.getMicrosecondLength() / 1000000.0;

ε720. Determining the Position of a Midi Sequencer

// To create a Sequencer object, see "ε716. Loading and Playing Midi Audio"

double seconds = *sequencer*.getMicrosecondPosition() / 1000000.0;

ε721. Setting the Volume of Playing Midi Audio

// To create a Sequencer object, see "ε716. Loading and Playing Midi Audio"

```
if (sequencer instanceof Synthesizer) {
    Synthesizer synthesizer = (Synthesizer)sequencer;
    MidiChannel[] channels = synthesizer.getChannels();

    // gain is a value between 0 and 1 (loudest)
    double gain = 0.9D;
    for (int i=0; i<channels.length; i++) {
        channels[i].controlChange(7, (int)(gain * 127.0));
    }
}
```

Events

ε722. Determining When a Midi Audio Player Has Finished Playing

A sequencer fires a meta message event when a midi file has finished playing.

// To create a Sequencer object, see "ε716. Loading and Playing Midi Audio"

```
// Add a listener for meta message events
sequencer.addMetaEventListener(
    new MetaEventListener() {
        public void meta(MetaMessage event) {
            if (event.getType() == 47) {
                // Sequencer is done playing
            }
        }
    });
```

javax.sound.midi.spi

This package supplies interfaces for service providers to implement when offering new MIDI devices, MIDI file readers and writers, or sound bank readers.

Class   *Interface*   —extends   - - -implements   ○ abstract   ● final   ^—has superclass   _—has subclass   package—see other volume

```
       java.lang.Object
1.3 ○    ├ MidiDeviceProvider
1.3 ○    ├ MidiFileReader
1.3 ○    ├ MidiFileWriter
1.3 ○    └ SoundbankReader
```

javax.sound.sampled

This package provides interfaces and classes for capture, processing, and playback of sampled audio data.

PAGE

Packages and Examples

java . lang.Object

1.3   ├ AudioFileFormat

1.3   ├ AudioFileFormat.Type

1.3   ├ AudioFormat

1.3   ├ AudioFormat.Encoding

1.3   ├ AudioSystem

1.3 ○   ├ Control

1.3 ○   ├ BooleanControl

1.3 ○   ├ CompoundControl

1.3 ○   ├ EnumControl

1.3 ○   └ FloatControl

1.3   ├ Control.Type

1.3   ├ BooleanControl.Type

1.3   ├ CompoundControl.Type

1.3   ├ EnumControl.Type

1.3   └ FloatControl.Type

1.3   ├ Line.Info

1.3   ├ DataLine.Info

1.3   └ Port.Info

1.3   ├ LineEvent.Type

1.3   ├ Mixer.Info

1.3   ├ ReverbType

○   ├ java . io.InputStream

1.3   └ AudioInputStream

1.2 ○   ├ java . security.Permission - *java . io.Serializable* , *java . security.Guard*

1.2 ○   ├ java . security.BasicPermission - *java . io.Serializable*

1.3   └ AudioPermission

1.1   ├ java . util.EventObject -

1.3   └ LineEvent

     └ java . lang.Throwable -

       └ java . lang.Exception

1.3   ├ LineUnavailableException

1.3   └ UnsupportedAudioFileException

1.3   *Clip* ——————————————————————— *DataLine*ˆ

1.3   *DataLine* , ——————————————————————— *Line*

1.3   *Line* ,

Class   *Interface*   —extends   - - -implements   ○ abstract   ● final   ˆ—has superclass   ,—has subclass   package—see other volume

1.3	LineListener ————————————————————————————————	java . util.EventListener
1.3	Mixer ——————————————————————————————— Line	
1.3	Port ————————————————————————	
1.3	SourceDataLine ———————————————————————— DataLineˆ	
1.3	TargetDataLine ————————————————————————	

ε723. Loading and Playing Sampled Audio

Supported audio file formats: aif, au, and wav. See also "ε724. Playing Streaming Sampled Audio".

```
try {
    // From file
    AudioInputStream stream = AudioSystem.getAudioInputStream(new File("audiofile"));

    // From URL
    stream = AudioSystem.getAudioInputStream(new URL("http://hostname/audiofile"));

    // At present, ALAW and ULAW encodings must be converted
    // to PCM_SIGNED before it can be played
    AudioFormat format = stream.getFormat();
    if (format.getEncoding() != AudioFormat.Encoding.PCM_SIGNED) {
        format = new AudioFormat(
                AudioFormat.Encoding.PCM_SIGNED,
                format.getSampleRate(),
                format.getSampleSizeInBits()*2,
                format.getChannels(),
                format.getFrameSize()*2,
                format.getFrameRate(),
                true); // big endian
        stream = AudioSystem.getAudioInputStream(format, stream);
    }

    // Create the clip
    DataLine.Info info = new DataLine.Info(
        Clip.class, stream.getFormat(), ((int)stream.getFrameLength()*format.getFrameSize()));
    Clip clip = (Clip) AudioSystem.getLine(info);

    // This method does not return until the audio file is completely loaded
    clip.open(stream);

    // Start playing
    clip.start();
} catch (MalformedURLException e) {
} catch (IOException e) {
} catch (LineUnavailableException e) {
} catch (UnsupportedAudioFileException e) {
}
```

ε724. Playing Streaming Sampled Audio

```
try {
    // From file
    AudioInputStream stream = AudioSystem.getAudioInputStream(new File("audiofile"));

    // From URL
    stream = AudioSystem.getAudioInputStream(new URL("http://hostname/audiofile"));
```

Packages and Examples

```
        // At present, ALAW and ULAW encodings must be converted
        // to PCM_SIGNED before it can be played
        AudioFormat format = stream.getFormat();
        if (format.getEncoding() != AudioFormat.Encoding.PCM_SIGNED) {
            format = new AudioFormat(
                    AudioFormat.Encoding.PCM_SIGNED,
                    format.getSampleRate(),
                    format.getSampleSizeInBits()*2,
                    format.getChannels(),
                    format.getFrameSize()*2,
                    format.getFrameRate(),
                    true); // big endian
            stream = AudioSystem.getAudioInputStream(format, stream);
        }

        // Create line
        SourceDataLine.Info info = new DataLine.Info(
            SourceDataLine.class, stream.getFormat(),
            ((int)stream.getFrameLength()*format.getFrameSize())));
        SourceDataLine line = (SourceDataLine) AudioSystem.getLine(info);
        line.open(stream.getFormat());
        line.start();

        // Continuously read and play chunks of audio
        int numRead = 0;
        byte[] buf = new byte[line.getBufferSize()];
        while ((numRead = stream.read(buf, 0, buf.length)) >= 0) {
            int offset = 0;
            while (offset < numRead) {
                offset += line.write(buf, offset, numRead-offset);
            }
        }
        line.drain();
        line.stop();
    } catch (MalformedURLException e) {
    } catch (IOException e) {
    } catch (LineUnavailableException e) {
    } catch (UnsupportedAudioFileException e) {
    }
```

ε725. Continuously Playing a Sampled Audio File

Only DataLine objects that are of type Clip can be repeated. To create a clip, see "ε723. Loading and Playing Sampled Audio".

```
    // Play once
    clip.start();

    // Play and loop forever
    clip.loop(Clip.LOOP_CONTINUOUSLY);

    // Play and repeat for a certain number of times
    int numberOfPlays = 3;
    clip.loop(numberOfPlays-1);
```

Class   *Interface*   —extends   - - -implements   ○ abstract   ● final   ^—has superclass   .—has subclass   package—see other volume

Properties

ε726. Determining the File Format of a Sampled Audio File

```
try {
    // From file
    AudioFileFormat fformat = AudioSystem.getAudioFileFormat(new File("audiofile"));

    // From URL
    fformat = AudioSystem.getAudioFileFormat(new URL("http://hostname/audiofile"));

    if (fformat.getType() == AudioFileFormat.Type.AIFC) {
    } else if (fformat.getType() == AudioFileFormat.Type.AIFF) {
    } else if (fformat.getType() == AudioFileFormat.Type.AU) {
    } else if (fformat.getType() == AudioFileFormat.Type.WAVE) {
    }
} catch (MalformedURLException e) {
} catch (IOException e) {
} catch (UnsupportedAudioFileException e) {
    // File format is not supported.
}
```

ε727. Determining the Encoding of a Sampled Audio File

```
try {
    // From file
    AudioInputStream stream = AudioSystem.getAudioInputStream(new File("audiofile"));

    // From URL
    stream = AudioSystem.getAudioInputStream(new URL("http://hostname/audiofile"));

    AudioFormat format = stream.getFormat();
    if (format.getEncoding() == AudioFormat.Encoding.ULAW) {
    } else if (format.getEncoding() == AudioFormat.Encoding.ULAW) {
    }
} catch (MalformedURLException e) {
} catch (IOException e) {
} catch (UnsupportedAudioFileException e) {
    // Audio format is not supported.
}
```

ε728. Determining the Duration of a Sampled Audio File

```
// To create a Clip object, see "ε723. Loading and Playing Sampled Audio"

double durationInSecs = clip.getBufferSize() /
    (clip.getFormat().getFrameSize() * clip.getFormat().getFrameRate());
```

ε729. Determining the Position of a Sampled Audio Player

```
// To create a Clip object, see "ε723. Loading and Playing Sampled Audio"

double timeInSeconds = clip.getMicrosecondPosition()/1000000.0d;
```

ε730. Setting the Volume of a Sampled Audio Player

```
// To create a Clip object, see "ε723. Loading and Playing Sampled Audio"

// Set Volume
FloatControl gainControl = (FloatControl)clip.getControl(FloatControl.Type.MASTER_GAIN);
```

Packages and Examples

177

```
double gain = .5D; // number between 0 and 1 (loudest)
float dB = (float)(Math.log(gain)/Math.log(10.0)*20.0);
gainControl.setValue(dB);

// Mute On
BooleanControl muteControl = (BooleanControl)clip.getControl(BooleanControl.Type.MUTE);
muteControl.setValue(true);

// Mute Off
muteControl.setValue(false);
```

Events

ε731. Determining When a Sampled Audio Player Has Finished Playing

An audio clip fires a line event when the audio sample has finished playing. If the audio clip is played in a loop (see "ε725. Continuously Playing a Sampled Audio File"), the event is fired only after the loop is finished.

```
// To create a Clip object, see "ε723. Loading and Playing Sampled Audio"

// Add a listener for line events
clip.addLineListener(new LineListener() {
    public void update(LineEvent evt) {
        if (evt.getType() == LineEvent.Type.STOP) {
        }
    }
});
```

javax.sound.sampled.spi

This package supplies abstract classes for service providers to subclass when offering new audio devices, sound file readers and writers, or audio format converters.

		PAGE
1.3 ○	**AudioFileReader** is a provider for audio file reading services	413
1.3 ○	**AudioFileWriter** is a provider for audio file writing services	414
1.3 ○	**FormatConversionProvider** provides format conversion services from one or more input formats to one or more output formats	531
1.3 ○	**MixerProvider** is a provider or factory for a particular mixer type	695

```
java.lang.Object
```
1.3 ○	├ AudioFileReader
1.3 ○	├ AudioFileWriter
1.3 ○	├ FormatConversionProvider
1.3 ○	└ MixerProvider

javax.swing

This package extends the java.awt package by adding interfaces and classes for creating completely portable graphical user interfaces written entirely in Java (without any window-system-specific code). User interfaces

Class   *Interface*   —extends   - - -implements   ○ abstract   ● final   ^—has superclass   ⌐—has subclass   package—see other volume

built using this and related packages have a "pluggable" look and feel that can be changed dynamically by the user and/or application.

Packages and Examples

Class   *Interface*   —extends   - - -implements   ○ abstract   ● final   ^-has superclass   ˎ-has subclass   package—see other volume

Class   *Interface*   —extends   - - -implements   ○ abstract   ● final   ˆ—has superclass   ˛—has subclass   package—see other volume

Packages and Examples

Class   *Interface*   —extends   - - -implements   ○ abstract   ● final   ^—has superclass   ˛—has subclass   package—see other volume

java . lang.Object

1.2 O ├─ AbstractAction - *Action^, java.io.Serializable,*
                                                                              java . lang.Cloneable

1.2   ├─ AbstractButton.ButtonChangeListener - - - - - - - - - - - - - - - - - - *java . io.Serializable, javax.swing.event*
                                                                              *.ChangeListener^*

1.3 O ├─ AbstractCellEditor - *CellEditor, java . io.Serializable*

1.2   │ └─ DefaultCellEditor - *javax.swing.table.TableCellEditor^,*
                                                                              *javax.swing.tree.TreeCellEditor^*

1.2 O ├─ AbstractListModel - *ListModel, java . io.Serializable*

1.2   │ ├─ DefaultComboBoxModel - *MutableComboBoxModel^, java . io.Serializable*

1.2   │ └─ DefaultListModel

1.4 O ├─ AbstractSpinnerModel - *SpinnerModel*

1.4   │ ├─ SpinnerDateModel - *java . io.Serializable*

1.4   │ ├─ SpinnerListModel -

1.4   │ └─ SpinnerNumberModel -

1.3   ├─ ActionMap -

1.2   ├─ BorderFactory

1.2   ├─ BoxLayout - *java.awt.LayoutManager2^, java . io.Serializable*

1.2   ├─ ButtonGroup - *java . io.Serializable*

1.2   ├─ DefaultBoundedRangeModel - *BoundedRangeModel, java . io.Serializable*

1.2   ├─ DefaultButtonModel - *ButtonModel^, java . io.Serializable*

1.2   │ └─ JToggleButton.ToggleButtonModel

1.2   ├─ DefaultCellEditor.EditorDelegate - - - - - - - - - - - - - - - - - - - *java.awt.event.ActionListener^,*
                                                                              java.awt.event.ItemListener^,
                                                                              java . io.Serializable

1.2   ├─ DefaultDesktopManager - *DesktopManager, java . io.Serializable*

1.2   ├─ DefaultListSelectionModel - *ListSelectionModel, java . io.Serializable,*
                                                                              java . lang.Cloneable

1.2   ├─ DefaultSingleSelectionModel - *SingleSelectionModel, java . io.Serializable*

1.2   ├─ ImageIcon - *Icon, java . io.Serializable,*
                                                                              javax.accessibility.Accessible

1.3   ├─ InputMap - *java . io.Serializable*

1.3   │ └─ ComponentInputMap

1.3 O ├─ InputVerifier

1.2   ├─ JComponent.AccessibleJComponent - - - - - - - - - - - - - - - - - *java.awt.event.ContainerListener^*
          .AccessibleContainerHandler

1.3   ├─ JComponent.AccessibleJComponent.AccessibleFocusHandler - *java.awt.event.FocusListener^*

1.4 O ├─ JFormattedTextField.AbstractFormatter - - - - - - - - - - - - - - - *java . io.Serializable*

```
            java . lang. Object
1.4 ○       ├ JFormattedTextField.AbstractFormatterFactory ⌄
1.2         ├ JRootPane.RootLayout - - - - - - - - - - - - - - - - - - - - - - - - - - - - java.awt.LayoutManager2^, java . io.Serializable ⌄
1.2         ├ JTabbedPane.ModelListener - - - - - - - - - - - - - - - - - - - - - - - - java . io. Serializable ⌄, javax.swing.event⟩
                                                                                         .ChangeListener^
1.3         ├ JTable.AccessibleJTable.AccessibleJTableModelChange - - - - - - javax.accessibility.AccessibleTableModelChange
1.2         ├ JTree.TreeModelHandler - - - - - - - - - - - - - - - - - - - - - - - - - - - javax.swing.event. TreeModelListener^
1.2         ├ JTree.TreeSelectionRedirector - - - - - - - - - - - - - - - - - - - - - - java . io. Serializable ⌄, javax.swing.event⟩
                                                                                         .TreeSelectionListener^
1.2 ○       ├ LookAndFeel ⌄
1.2         ├ MenuSelectionManager
1.2         ├ OverlayLayout - - - - - - - - - - - - - - - - - - - - - - - - - - - - - - - - - java.awt.LayoutManager2^, java . io.Serializable ⌄
1.4         ├ Popup
1.4         ├ PopupFactory
1.2         ├ ProgressMonitor
1.2         ├ RepaintManager
1.2         ├ ScrollPaneLayout - - - - - - - - - - - - - - - - - - - - - - - - - - - - - - ScrollPaneConstants, java.awt.LayoutManager ⌄,
                                                                                         java . io. Serializable ⌄
1.2         │  └ ScrollPaneLayout.UIResource - - - - - - - - - - - - - - - - - - - - - javax.swing.plaf.UIResource
1.2         ├ SizeRequirements - - - - - - - - - - - - - - - - - - - - - - - - - - - - - - java . io. Serializable ⌄
1.3         ├ SizeSequence
1.4 ○       ├ Spring
1.4         ├ SpringLayout - - - - - - - - - - - - - - - - - - - - - - - - - - - - - - - - - java.awt.LayoutManager2^
1.4         ├ SpringLayout.Constraints
1.2         ├ SwingUtilities - - - - - - - - - - - - - - - - - - - - - - - - - - - - - - - - SwingConstants
1.2         ├ Timer - - - - - - - - - - - - - - - - - - - - - - - - - - - - - - - - - - - - - - java . io. Serializable ⌄
1.2         ├ ToolTipManager.insideTimerAction - - - - - - - - - - - - - - - - - - - - java.awt.event.ActionListener^
1.2         ├ ToolTipManager.outsideTimerAction - - - - - - - - - - - - - - - - - ⌐
1.2         ├ ToolTipManager.stillInsideTimerAction - - - - - - - - - - - - - - - - ┘
1.4         ├ TransferHandler - - - - - - - - - - - - - - - - - - - - - - - - - - - - - - - java . io. Serializable ⌄
1.3         ├ UIDefaults.LazyInputMap - - - - - - - - - - - - - - - - - - - - - - - - - - UIDefaults.LazyValue
1.3         ├ UIDefaults.ProxyLazyValue - - - - - - - - - - - - - - - - - - - - - - - ┘
1.2         ├ UIManager - - - - - - - - - - - - - - - - - - - - - - - - - - - - - - - - - - java . io. Serializable ⌄
1.2         ├ UIManager.LookAndFeelInfo
1.2         ├ ViewportLayout - - - - - - - - - - - - - - - - - - - - - - - - - - - - - - - - java.awt.LayoutManager ⌄, java . io. Serializable ⌄
1.4         ├ java.awt.AWTKeyStroke - - - - - - - - - - - - - - - - - - - - - - - - - - java . io. Serializable ⌄
1.2         │  └ KeyStroke
    ○       ├ java.awt.Component - - - - - - - - - - - - - - - - - - - - - - - - - - - - java.awt.MenuContainer, java.awt.image⟩
                                                                                         .ImageObserver, java . io. Serializable ⌄
               └ java.awt.Container
1.2              ├ CellRendererPane - - - - - - - - - - - - - - - - - - - - - - - - - - javax.accessibility.Accessible
1.2 ○            ├ JComponent - - - - - - - - - - - - - - - - - - - - - - - - - - - - - - java . io. Serializable ⌄
1.2 ○               ├ AbstractButton - - - - - - - - - - - - - - - - - - - - - - - - - - SwingConstants, java.awt.ItemSelectable ⌄
1.2                    ├ JButton ⌄ - - - - - - - - - - - - - - - - - - - - - - - - - - - - javax.accessibility.Accessible
1.2                    ├ JMenuItem - - - - - - - - - - - - - - - - - - - - - - - - - - - MenuElement, javax.accessibility.Accessible
1.2                       ├ JCheckBoxMenuItem - - - - - - - - - - - - - - - - - - - SwingConstants, javax.accessibility.Accessible
1.2                       ├ JMenu - - - - - - - - - - - - - - - - - - - - - - - - - - - - MenuElement, javax.accessibility.Accessible
1.2                       └ JRadioButtonMenuItem - - - - - - - - - - - - - - - - - javax.accessibility.Accessible
```

Class   *Interface*   —extends   - - -implements   ○ abstract   ● final   ^—has superclass   ⌄—has subclass   package—see other volume

```
        java . lang.Object
  O      ├ java.awt.Component - - - - - - - - - - - - - - - - - - - - - - - - - - -   java.awt.MenuContainer, java.awt.image
                                                                                      .ImageObserver, java . io.Serializable
         └ java.awt.Container
1.2 O        ├ JComponent - - - - - - - - - - - - - - - - - - - - - - - - - - - - -   java . io.Serializable
1.2 O           ├ AbstractButton - - - - - - - - - - - - - - - - - - - - - - - - - - - - -   SwingConstants, java.awt.ItemSelectable
                                                                                      javax.accessibility.Accessible
1.2               └ JToggleButton - - - - - - - - - - - - - - - - - - - - - -
1.2                  ├ JCheckBox - - - - - - - - - - - - - - - - - - - - - -
1.2                  └ JRadioButton - - - - - - - - - - - - - - - - - - - -
1.2            ├ Box - - - - - - - - - - - - - - - - - - - - - - - - - - - - - -
1.2            ├ Box.Filler - - - - - - - - - - - - - - - - - - - - - - - - - -
1.2            ├ JColorChooser - - - - - - - - - - - - - - - - - - - - - - - -
1.2            ├ JComboBox - - - - - - - - - - - - - - - - - - - - - - - - -   java.awt.ItemSelectable , java.awt.event
                                                                                      .ActionListener , javax.accessibility.Accessible,
                                                                                      javax.swing.event.ListDataListener^
1.2            ├ JFileChooser - - - - - - - - - - - - - - - - - - - - - - - - -   javax.accessibility.Accessible
1.2            ├ JInternalFrame - - - - - - - - - - - - - - - - - - - - - - - -   RootPaneContainer, WindowConstants,
                                                                                      javax.accessibility.Accessible
1.2            ├ JInternalFrame.JDesktopIcon - - - - - - - - - - - - - - -   javax.accessibility.Accessible
1.2            ├ JLabel - - - - - - - - - - - - - - - - - - - - - - - - - - - - -   SwingConstants, javax.accessibility.Accessible
1.2               └ DefaultListCellRenderer - - - - - - - - - - - - - - - -   ListCellRenderer, java . io.Serializable
1.2                  └ DefaultListCellRenderer.UIResource - - - - - - - - -   javax.swing.plaf.UIResource
1.2            ├ JLayeredPane - - - - - - - - - - - - - - - - - - - - - - - - -   javax.accessibility.Accessible
1.2               └ JDesktopPane - - - - - - - - - - - - - - - - - - - - - - -
1.2            ├ JList - - - - - - - - - - - - - - - - - - - - - - - - - - - - - -   Scrollable, javax.accessibility.Accessible
1.2            ├ JMenuBar - - - - - - - - - - - - - - - - - - - - - - - - - - - -   MenuElement, javax.accessibility.Accessible
1.2            ├ JOptionPane - - - - - - - - - - - - - - - - - - - - - - - - - -   javax.accessibility.Accessible
1.2            ├ JPanel - - - - - - - - - - - - - - - - - - - - - - - - - - - - -
1.4               └ JSpinner.DefaultEditor - - - - - - - - - - - - - - - - - - - -   java.awt.LayoutManager ,
                                                                                      java . beans.PropertyChangeListener^,
                                                                                      javax.swing.event.ChangeListener^
1.4                  ├ JSpinner.DateEditor
1.4                  ├ JSpinner.ListEditor
1.4                  └ JSpinner.NumberEditor
1.2            ├ JPopupMenu - - - - - - - - - - - - - - - - - - - - - - - - - -   MenuElement, javax.accessibility.Accessible
1.2            ├ JProgressBar - - - - - - - - - - - - - - - - - - - - - - - - -   SwingConstants, javax.accessibility.Accessible
1.2            ├ JRootPane - - - - - - - - - - - - - - - - - - - - - - - - - - -   javax.accessibility.Accessible
1.2            ├ JScrollBar - - - - - - - - - - - - - - - - - - - - - - - - - - -   java.awt.Adjustable, javax.accessibility.Accessible
1.2               └ JScrollPane.ScrollBar - - - - - - - - - - - - - - - - - - -   javax.swing.plaf.UIResource
1.2            ├ JScrollPane - - - - - - - - - - - - - - - - - - - - - - - - - -   ScrollPaneConstants, javax.accessibility
                                                                                      .Accessible
1.2            ├ JSeparator - - - - - - - - - - - - - - - - - - - - - - - - - - -   SwingConstants, javax.accessibility.Accessible
1.2               ├ JPopupMenu.Separator
1.2               └ JToolBar.Separator
1.2            ├ JSlider - - - - - - - - - - - - - - - - - - - - - - - - - - - - - -
1.4            ├ JSpinner
1.2            ├ JSplitPane - - - - - - - - - - - - - - - - - - - - - - - - - - -   javax.accessibility.Accessible
1.2            ├ JTabbedPane - - - - - - - - - - - - - - - - - - - - - - - - -   SwingConstants, java . io.Serializable ,
                                                                                      javax.accessibility.Accessible
```

```
            java.lang.Object
      ○     ├ java.awt.Component- - - - - - - - - - - - - - - - - - - - - - - - - - - - - - - java.awt.MenuContainer, java.awt.image
                                                                              .ImageObserver, java.io.Serializable
            │    └ java.awt.Container
 1.2  ○     │         ├ JComponent- - - - - - - - - - - - - - - - - - - - - - - - - - - - - - java.io.Serializable
 1.2        │         │    ├ JTable- - - - - - - - - - - - - - - - - - - - - - - - - - - - - - Scrollable, javax.accessibility.Accessible,
                                                                              javax.swing.event.CellEditorListener^,
                                                                              javax.swing.event.ListSelectionListener^,
                                                                              javax.swing.event.TableColumnModelListener^,
                                                                              javax.swing.event.TableModelListener^
 1.2        │         │    ├ JToolBar- - - - - - - - - - - - - - - - - - - - - - - - - - - - - SwingConstants, javax.accessibility.Accessible
 1.2        │         │    ├ JToolTip- - - - - - - - - - - - - - - - - - - - - - - - - - - - - javax.accessibility.Accessible
 1.2        │         │    ├ JTree- - - - - - - - - - - - - - - - - - - - - - - - - - - - - - - Scrollable, javax.accessibility.Accessible
 1.2        │         │    ├ JViewport- - - - - - - - - - - - - - - - - - - - - - - - - - - - - javax.accessibility.Accessible
 1.2  ○     │         │    └ javax.swing.text.JTextComponent- - - - - - - - - - - - - - - - - Scrollable, javax.accessibility.Accessible
 1.2        │         │         ├ JEditorPane
 1.2        │         │         │    └ JTextPane
 1.2        │         │         ├ JTextArea
 1.2        │         │         └ JTextField- - - - - - - - - - - - - - - - - - - - - - - - - SwingConstants
 1.4        │         │              ├ JFormattedTextField
 1.2        │         │              └ JPasswordField
            │         ├ java.awt.Panel- - - - - - - - - - - - - - - - - - - - - - - - - - - - javax.accessibility.Accessible
            │         │    └ java.applet.Applet
 1.2        │         │         └ JApplet- - - - - - - - - - - - - - - - - - - - - - - - - - - RootPaneContainer, javax.accessibility.Accessible
            │         └ java.awt.Window- - - - - - - - - - - - - - - - - - - - - - - - - - - javax.accessibility.Accessible
 1.2        │              ├ JWindow- - - - - - - - - - - - - - - - - - - - - - - - - - - - - RootPaneContainer, javax.accessibility.Accessible
            │              ├ java.awt.Dialog
 1.2        │              │    └ JDialog- - - - - - - - - - - - - - - - - - - - - - - - - - - RootPaneContainer, WindowConstants,
                                                                              javax.accessibility.Accessible
            │              └ java.awt.Frame- - - - - - - - - - - - - - - - - - - - - - - - - java.awt.MenuContainer
 1.2        │                   └ JFrame- - - - - - - - - - - - - - - - - - - - - - - - - - - RootPaneContainer, WindowConstants,
                                                                              javax.accessibility.Accessible
 1.4  ○     ├ java.awt.FocusTraversalPolicy
 1.4  ○     │ └ InternalFrameFocusTraversalPolicy
 1.4        │    └ SortingFocusTraversalPolicy
 1.4        │         └ LayoutFocusTraversalPolicy- - - - - - - - - - - - - - - - - - - - - java.io.Serializable
      ○     ├ java.awt.Graphics
 1.2        │ └ DebugGraphics
 1.4  ○     ├ java.awt.KeyboardFocusManager- - - - - - - - - - - - - - - - - - - - - - - - java.awt.KeyEventDispatcher,
                                                                              java.awt.KeyEventPostProcessor
 1.4        │ └ java.awt.DefaultKeyboardFocusManager
 1.2  ○     │    └ FocusManager
 1.2        │         └ DefaultFocusManager
 1.1  ○     ├ java.awt.event.ComponentAdapter- - - - - - - - - - - - - - - - - - - - - - - java.awt.event.ComponentListener^
 1.2        │ └ JViewport.ViewListener- - - - - - - - - - - - - - - - - - - - - - - - - - - java.io.Serializable
 1.1  ○     ├ java.awt.event.MouseAdapter- - - - - - - - - - - - - - - - - - - - - - - - - java.awt.event.MouseListener^
 1.2        │ └ ToolTipManager- - - - - - - - - - - - - - - - - - - - - - - - - - - - - - - java.awt.event.MouseMotionListener^
 1.1  ○     ├ java.awt.event.WindowAdapter- - - - - - - - - - - - - - - - - - - - - - - - - java.awt.event.WindowFocusListener^,
                                                                              java.awt.event.WindowListener^,
                                                                              java.awt.event.WindowStateListener^
 1.2        └ JMenu.WinListener- - - - - - - - - - - - - - - - - - - - - - - - - - - - - - - java.io.Serializable
```

Class   *Interface*   —extends   - - -implements   ○ abstract   ● final   ^—has superclass   ⌣—has subclass   package—see other volume

```
        java.lang.Object
           ├ java.awt.image.ImageFilter ---------------------------- java.awt.image.ImageConsumer,
           │                                                          java.lang.Cloneable,
     ○     │   └ java.awt.image.RGBImageFilter
    1.2    │        └ GrayFilter
     ○     ├ java.io.InputStream
           │   └ java.io.FilterInputStream
    1.2    │        └ ProgressMonitorInputStream
     ○     ├ java.util.Dictionary
           │   ├ java.util.Hashtable ------------------------------- java.io.Serializable, java.lang.Cloneable,
           │   │                                                     java.util.Map,
    1.2    │   └ UIDefaults
    1.2 ○  ├ javax.accessibility.AccessibleContext
    1.3    │   ├ ImageIcon.AccessibleImageIcon --------------------- java.io.Serializable, javax.accessibility
           │   │                                                     .AccessibleIcon
    1.2    │   ├ JList.AccessibleJList.AccessibleJListChild -------┐ javax.accessibility.Accessible,
           │   │                                                   ┊ javax.accessibility.AccessibleComponent,
    1.2    │   ├ JTable.AccessibleJTable.AccessibleJTableCell -----┘
    1.2    │   ├ JTree.AccessibleJTree.AccessibleJTreeNode ---------- javax.accessibility.Accessible,
           │   │                                                      javax.accessibility.AccessibleAction,
           │   │                                                      javax.accessibility.AccessibleComponent,
           │   │                                                      javax.accessibility.AccessibleSelection
    1.3 ○  │   └ java.awt.Component.AccessibleAWTComponent --------- java.io.Serializable, javax.accessibility
           │                                                         .AccessibleComponent,
    1.2    │       ├ Box.Filler.AccessibleBoxFiller
    1.3    │       └ java.awt.Container.AccessibleAWTContainer
    1.2    │           ├ Box.AccessibleBox
    1.2    │           ├ CellRendererPane.AccessibleCellRendererPane
    1.2 ○  │           ├ JComponent.AccessibleJComponent ------------- javax.accessibility
           │           │                                               .AccessibleExtendedComponent^
    1.2 ○  │           │   ├ AbstractButton.AccessibleAbstractButton -------- javax.accessibility.AccessibleAction, javax
           │           │   │                                                  .accessibility.AccessibleExtendedComponent^,
           │           │   │                                                  javax.accessibility.AccessibleText,
           │           │   │                                                  javax.accessibility.AccessibleValue
    1.2    │           │   │   ├ JButton.AccessibleJButton
    1.2    │           │   │   ├ JMenuItem.AccessibleJMenuItem ------------ javax.swing.event.ChangeListener^
    1.2    │           │   │   │   ├ JCheckBoxMenuItem
           │           │   │   │   │    .AccessibleJCheckBoxMenuItem
    1.2    │           │   │   │   ├ JMenu.AccessibleJMenu ---------------- javax.accessibility.AccessibleSelection
    1.2    │           │   │   │   └ JRadioButtonMenuItem
           │           │   │   │        .AccessibleJRadioButtonMenuItem
    1.2    │           │   │   └ JToggleButton.AccessibleJToggleButton -------- java.awt.event.ItemListener^
    1.2    │           │   │       ├ JCheckBox.AccessibleJCheckBox
    1.2    │           │   │       └ JRadioButton.AccessibleJRadioButton
    1.2    │           │   ├ JColorChooser.AccessibleJColorChooser
    1.2    │           │   ├ JComboBox.AccessibleJComboBox ----------- javax.accessibility.AccessibleAction,
           │           │   │                                           javax.accessibility.AccessibleSelection
    1.2    │           │   ├ JDesktopPane.AccessibleJDesktopPane
    1.2    │           │   ├ JFileChooser.AccessibleJFileChooser
    1.2    │           │   ├ JInternalFrame.AccessibleJInternalFrame -------┐ javax.accessibility.AccessibleValue
    1.2    │           │   ├ JInternalFrame.JDesktopIcon -----------------┘
           │           │   │    .AccessibleJDesktopIcon
```

java . lang.Object

1.2 ○	├ javax.accessibility.AccessibleContext
1.3 ○	└ java.awt.Component.AccessibleAWTComponent - - - - - - - - - *java . io.Serializable*⌄, *javax.accessibility*⌐
	.AccessibleComponent⌄
1.3	└ java.awt.Container.AccessibleAWTContainer
1.2 ○	├ JComponent.AccessibleJComponent - - - - - - - - - - - - - *javax.accessibility*⌐
	.AccessibleExtendedComponent^
1.2	├ JLabel.AccessibleJLabel - - - - - - - - - - - - - - - - - - - *javax.accessibility*⌐
	.AccessibleExtendedComponent^,
	javax.accessibility.AccessibleText⌄
1.2	├ JLayeredPane.AccessibleJLayeredPane
1.2	├ JList.AccessibleJList - *java . beans.PropertyChangeListener*^,
	javax.accessibility.AccessibleSelection,
	javax.swing.event.ListDataListener^,
	javax.swing.event.ListSelectionListener^
1.2	├ JMenuBar.AccessibleJMenuBar - - - - - - - - - - - - - - - *javax.accessibility.AccessibleSelection*
1.2	├ JOptionPane.AccessibleJOptionPane
1.2	├ JPanel.AccessibleJPanel
1.2	├ JPopupMenu.AccessibleJPopupMenu
1.2	├ JProgressBar.AccessibleJProgressBar - - - - - - - - - ┐ *javax.accessibility.AccessibleValue*
1.2	├ JRootPane.AccessibleJRootPane ┊
1.2	├ JScrollBar.AccessibleJScrollBar - - - - - - - - - - - - - ┘
1.2	├ JScrollPane.AccessibleJScrollPane - - - - - - - - - - - - *javax.swing.event.ChangeListener*^
1.2	├ JSeparator.AccessibleJSeparator
1.2	├ JSlider.AccessibleJSlider - - - - - - - - - - - - - - - - - - ┐ *javax.accessibility.AccessibleValue*
1.2	├ JSplitPane.AccessibleJSplitPane - - - - - - - - - - - - - ┘
1.2	├ JTabbedPane.AccessibleJTabbedPane - - - - - - - - - - *javax.accessibility.AccessibleSelection*,
	javax.swing.event.ChangeListener^
1.2	├ JTable.AccessibleJTable - - - - - - - - - - - - - - - - - - - *java . beans.PropertyChangeListener*^,
	javax.accessibility.AccessibleExtendedTable^,
	javax.accessibility.AccessibleSelection,
	javax.swing.event.CellEditorListener^,
	javax.swing.event.ListSelectionListener^,
	javax.swing.event.TableColumnModelListener^,
	javax.swing.event.TableModelListener^
1.2	├ JToolBar.AccessibleJToolBar
1.2	├ JToolTip.AccessibleJToolTip
1.2	├ JTree.AccessibleJTree - *javax.accessibility.AccessibleSelection*,
	javax.swing.event.TreeExpansionListener^,
	javax.swing.event.TreeModelListener^,
	javax.swing.event.TreeSelectionListener^
1.2	├ JViewport.AccessibleJViewport
1.2	└ javax.swing.text.JTextComponent⌐ - - - - - - - - - - - - - *javax.accessibility.AccessibleAction*,
	.AccessibleJTextComponent	*javax.accessibility.AccessibleEditableText*^,
	javax.accessibility.AccessibleText⌄,
	javax.swing.event.CaretListener^,
	javax.swing.event.DocumentListener^
1.2	├ JEditorPane.AccessibleJEditorPane
1.2	├ JEditorPane.AccessibleJEditorPaneHTML
1.2	└ JEditorPane⌐ - *javax.accessibility.AccessibleHypertext*^
	.JEditorPaneAccessibleHypertextSupport
1.2	├ JTextArea.AccessibleJTextArea
1.2	└ JTextField.AccessibleJTextField
1.2	└ JPasswordField.AccessibleJPasswordField

Class *Interface* —extends - - -implements ○ abstract ● final ^—has superclass ⌄—has subclass package—see other volume

```
              java . lang.Object
1.2  ○       ├ javax.accessibility.AccessibleContext
1.3  ○       │  └ java.awt.Component.AccessibleAWTComponent - - - - - - - - -  *java . io.Serializable* , *javax.accessibility* ₂
             │                                                                    *.AccessibleComponent* ˌ
1.3          │     └ java.awt.Container.AccessibleAWTContainer
1.3          │        ├ java.awt.Panel.AccessibleAWTPanel
1.3          │        │  └ java.applet.Applet.AccessibleApplet
1.2          │        │     └ JApplet.AccessibleJApplet
1.3          │        └ java.awt.Window.AccessibleAWTWindow
1.2          │           ├ JWindow.AccessibleJWindow
1.3          │           ├ java.awt.Dialog.AccessibleAWTDialog
1.2          │           │  └ JDialog.AccessibleJDialog
1.3          │           ├ java.awt.Frame.AccessibleAWTFrame
1.2          │              └ JFrame.AccessibleJFrame
1.2  ○       ├ javax.accessibility.AccessibleHyperlink - - - - - - - - - - - - - - - - - -  *javax.accessibility.AccessibleAction*
1.2          │  └ JEditorPane.JEditorPaneAccessibleHypertextSupport ₂
             │     .HTMLLink
1.2          ├ javax.swing.tree.DefaultMutableTreeNode - - - - - - - - - - - - - - - - -  *java . io.Serializable* ˌ , *java . lang.Cloneable* ˌ ,
             │                                                                    *javax.swing.tree.MutableTreeNode* ˆ
1.2          │  └ JTree.DynamicUtilTreeNode
1.2          ├ javax.swing.tree.DefaultTreeSelectionModel - - - - - - - - - - - - - - -  *java . io.Serializable* ˌ , *java . lang.Cloneable* ˌ ,
             │                                                                    *javax.swing.tree.TreeSelectionModel*
1.2          │  └ JTree.EmptySelectionModel
1.2          └ java . lang.Throwable - - - - - - - - - - - - - - - - - - - - - - - - - - - -  *java . io.Serializable* ˌ
1.2             └ java . lang.Exception
1.2                └ UnsupportedLookAndFeelException
```

```
1.2    *Action* ─────────────────────────────────────────  *java.awt.event.ActionListener* ˆ
1.2    *BoundedRangeModel*
1.2    *ButtonModel* ────────────────────────────────────  *java.awt.ItemSelectable*
1.2    *CellEditor* ˌ
1.2    *ComboBoxEditor*
1.2    *ComboBoxModel* ˌ ──────────────────────────────  *ListModel*
1.2    *DesktopManager*
1.2    *Icon*
1.2    *JComboBox.KeySelectionManager*
1.2    *ListCellRenderer*
1.2    *ListModel* ˌ
1.2    *ListSelectionModel*
1.2    *MenuElement*
1.2    *MutableComboBoxModel* ──────────────────────────  *ComboBoxModel* ˆ
1.2    *Renderer*
1.2    *RootPaneContainer*
1.2    *ScrollPaneConstants*
1.2    *Scrollable*
1.2    *SingleSelectionModel*
1.4    *SpinnerModel*
1.2    *SwingConstants*
1.2    *UIDefaults.ActiveValue*
1.2    *UIDefaults.LazyValue*
1.2    *WindowConstants*
```

ε732. The Quintessential Swing User Interface

This example creates and shows a frame with a button. To enable the button to respond to button clicks, see "ε743. Creating a JButton Component".

```java
import java.awt.*;
import javax.swing.*;

public class BasicUI {
    public static void main(String[] args) {
        JButton button = new JButton("Label");
        JFrame frame = new JFrame();

        // Add button to the frame
        frame.getContentPane().add(button, BorderLayout.CENTER);

        // Set initial size
        int frameWidth = 300;
        int frameHeight = 300;
        frame.setSize(frameWidth, frameHeight);

        // Show the frame
        frame.setVisible(true);
    }
}
```

JFrame, JWindow, JDialog

ε733. Creating a JFrame

A frame is a component container that displays its contents in a top-level window with a title bar and buttons to resize, iconify, maximize, and close the frame.

Unlike most Swing containers, adding a component to a frame is not done with the JFrame.add() method. This is because the frame holds several panes and it is necessary to specify a particular pane to which to add the component. The pane that holds child components is called the content pane. This example adds a text area to the content pane of a frame.

See also "ε559. Creating a Frame".

```java
// Create the frame
String title = "Frame Title";
JFrame frame = new JFrame(title);

// Create a component to add to the frame
JComponent comp = new JTextArea();

// Add the component to the frame's content pane;
// by default, the content pane has a border layout
frame.getContentPane().add(comp, BorderLayout.CENTER);

// Show the frame
int width = 300;
int height = 300;
frame.setSize(width, height);
frame.setVisible(true);
```

Class   *Interface*   —extends   - - -implements   ○ abstract   ● final   ˆ—has superclass   ˍ—has subclass   package—see other volume

ε734. Exiting an Application When a JFrame Is Closed

By default, when the close button on a frame is clicked, the frame hides itself. This example shows how to exit the application when the frame is closed:

```
// Create a frame
JFrame frame = new JFrame();

// Get default close operation
int op = frame.getDefaultCloseOperation(); // HIDE_ON_CLOSE

// Set to exit on close
frame.setDefaultCloseOperation(JFrame.EXIT_ON_CLOSE);
```

ε735. Disabling the Close Button on a JFrame

By default, when the close button on a frame is clicked, the frame hides itself. This example shows how to disable the close button:

```
// Create a frame
JFrame frame = new JFrame();

// Get default close operation
int op = frame.getDefaultCloseOperation(); // HIDE_ON_CLOSE

// Set to ignore the button
frame.setDefaultCloseOperation(JFrame.DO_NOTHING_ON_CLOSE);
```

ε736. Creating a Borderless Window

```
JWindow window = new JWindow();

// Add component to the window
window.getContentPane().add(component, BorderLayout.CENTER);

// Set initial size
window.setSize(300, 300);

// Show the window
window.setVisible(true);
```

ε737. Showing a Dialog Box

```
// Modal dialog with OK button
String message = "Line1\nLine2";
JOptionPane.showMessageDialog(frame, message);

// Modal dialog with yes/no button
int answer = JOptionPane.showConfirmDialog(frame, message);
if (answer == JOptionPane.YES_OPTION) {
    // User clicked YES.
} else if (answer == JOptionPane.NO_OPTION) {
    // User clicked NO.
}

// Modal dialog with OK/cancel and a text field
String text = JOptionPane.showInputDialog(frame, message);
if (text == null) {
    // User clicked cancel
}
```

Packages and Examples

ε738. Getting the JFrame of a Component

In order to find the frame that contains a component, it is necessary to walk up the component's parents until the frame is encountered. SwingUtilities.getRoot() is a convenience method that finds the frame.

This example implements an action that finds and hides the frame of the component that triggered the action. See also "ε743. Creating a JButton Component".

```
// Create an action
Action action = new AbstractAction("Action Label") {
        // This method is called when the action is triggered
        public void actionPerformed(ActionEvent evt) {
            Component c = (Component)evt.getSource();

            // Get the frame
            Component frame = SwingUtilities.getRoot(c);

            // Hide the frame
            frame.setVisible(false);
        }
};
```

JLabel

ε739. Creating a JLabel Component

```
// The text is left-justified and vertically centered
JLabel label = new JLabel("Text Label");

// The text is horizontally and vertically centered
label = new JLabel("Text Label", JLabel.CENTER);

// The text is right-justified and vertically centered
label = new JLabel("Text Label", JLabel.RIGHT);

// The text is left-justified and top-aligned
label = new JLabel("Text Label", JLabel.LEFT);
label.setVerticalAlignment(JLabel.TOP);

// The text is right-justified and top-aligned
label = new JLabel("Text Label", JLabel.RIGHT);
label.setVerticalAlignment(JLabel.TOP);

// The text is left-justified and bottom-aligned
label = new JLabel("Text Label", JLabel.LEFT);
label.setVerticalAlignment(JLabel.BOTTOM);

// The text is right-justified and bottom-aligned
label = new JLabel("Text Label", JLabel.RIGHT);
label.setVerticalAlignment(JLabel.BOTTOM);
```

ε740. Adding an Icon to a JLabel Component

This example creates a JLabel component with an icon.

```
// Fetch icon
Icon icon = new ImageIcon("icon.gif");

// Create a label with text and an icon; the icon appears to the left of the text
JLabel label = new JLabel("Text Label", icon, JLabel.CENTER);
```

Class   *Interface*   —extends   - - -implements   ○ abstract   ● final   ˆ—has superclass   �‿—has subclass   package—see other volume

// Create a label with only an icon
label = new JLabel(icon);

This example adds or replaces the icon in an existing JLabel component:

// Add an icon to an existing label
label.setIcon(icon);

The methods to control the position of the icon and text within a JLabel component are identical to those of a JButton. See also "ε747. Moving the Icon in a JButton Component", "ε748. Moving the Label/Icon Pair in a JButton Component", "ε749. Setting the Gap Size Between the Label and Icon in a JButton Component", and "ε750. Adding a Disabled Icon to a JButton Component".

ε741. Setting the Focus of a JTextField Component Using a JLabel Component

This example associates a label with a text field using setLabelFor(). A mnemonic is set on the label. When the mnemonic keystroke is pressed, the text field will gain the focus.

In the following example, when ALT-L is pressed, the text field gains the focus.

```
// Create text field
JTextField textfield = new JTextField(25);

// Create label and associate with text field
JLabel label = new JLabel("Text Label");
label.setDisplayedMnemonic(KeyEvent.VK_L);
label.setLabelFor(textfield);
```

ε742. Adding Drag-and-Drop Support to a JLabel Component

This example demonstrates how to modify a label component so that its text can be dragged and dropped to another component.

```
// Create a label
JLabel label = new JLabel("Label Text");

// Specify that the label's text property be transferable; the value of
// this property will be used in any drag-and-drop involving this label
final String propertyName = "text";
label.setTransferHandler(new TransferHandler(propertyName));

// Listen for mouse clicks
label.addMouseListener(new MouseAdapter() {
    public void mousePressed(MouseEvent evt) {
        JComponent comp = (JComponent)evt.getSource();
        TransferHandler th = comp.getTransferHandler();

        // Start the drag operation
        th.exportAsDrag(comp, evt, TransferHandler.COPY);
    }
});
```

JButton

ε743. Creating a JButton Component

Although it is possible to create a button with just a label, it is highly recommended to use an action to create a button. The action can then be shared by other components such as a toolbar.

```
// Create an action
Action action = new AbstractAction("Button Label") {
    // This method is called when the button is pressed
    public void actionPerformed(ActionEvent evt) {
        // Perform action...
    }
};

// Create the button
JButton button = new JButton(action);
```

ε744. Changing the Label of a JButton Component

See also "ε745. Creating a Multiline Label for a JButton Component".

```
// To create a button, see "ε743. Creating a JButton Component"
// Change the label
button.setText("New Label");
```

```
// Remove the label; this is useful for a button with only an icon
button.setText(null);
```

ε745. Creating a Multiline Label for a JButton Component

A button label can show simple HTML tags when surrounded by the tags <HTML> and </HTML>. This example shows how to create multiple lines by using the <BR> tag. See the javax.swing.text.html.HTML class documentation for a list of supported tags.

```
String label = "<html>"+"This is a"+"<br>"+"swing button"+"</html>";
```

```
// Create an action with the label
Action action = new AbstractAction(label) {
    // This method is called when the button is pressed
    public void actionPerformed(ActionEvent evt) {
        // Perform action
    }
};

// Create the button
JButton button = new JButton(action);
```

By default, the lines are left justified. This label text will center the lines:

```
button.setText("<html><center>"+"This is a"+"<br>"+"swing button"+"</center></html>");
```

This label text italicizes the second line:

```
button.setText("<html>"+"This is a"+"<br><i>"+"swing button"+"</i></html>");
```

ε746. Adding an Icon to a JButton Component

If the action used to create the button contains an icon, the button will be created using that icon. The icon will appear to the left of the text; to change the icon's position, see "ε747. Moving the Icon in a JButton Component".

```
// Retrieve the icon
Icon icon = new ImageIcon("icon.gif");
```

```
// Create an action with an icon
Action action = new AbstractAction("Button Label", icon) {
```

Class *Interface* —extends - - -implements ○ abstract ● final ^—has superclass ⌐—has subclass package—see other volume

```
        // This method is called when the button is pressed
        public void actionPerformed(ActionEvent evt) {
            // Perform action
        }
    };
    // Create the button; the icon will appear to the left of the label
    JButton button = new JButton(action);
```

If the action does not have an icon or a different icon must be used, add or change the icon using setIcon():

```
    // Add or change the icon; it will appear to the left of the text
    button.setIcon(icon);

    // Set to null to remove icon
    button.setIcon(null);
```

ε747. Moving the Icon in a JButton Component

There are two methods for controlling the position of the text relative to the icon—setVerticalTextPosition() and setHorizontalTextPosition(). There are three settings for each axis, which allows for a total of nine positions.

To control the gap between the text and icon, see "ε749. Setting the Gap Size Between the Label and Icon in a JButton Component".

Note: Not all placements are possible. For example, it is not possible to place the text above the icon with their left edges aligned. The nine possible placements are demonstrated below.

```
    // To create a button with an icon, see "ε746. Adding an Icon to a JButton Component"

    // Place text over center of icon; they both occupy the same space
    button.setVerticalTextPosition(SwingConstants.CENTER);
    button.setHorizontalTextPosition(SwingConstants.CENTER);

    // Place text above icon
    button.setVerticalTextPosition(SwingConstants.TOP);
    button.setHorizontalTextPosition(SwingConstants.CENTER);

    // Place text below icon
    button.setVerticalTextPosition(SwingConstants.BOTTOM);
    button.setHorizontalTextPosition(SwingConstants.CENTER);

    // Place text to the left of icon, vertically centered
    button.setVerticalTextPosition(SwingConstants.CENTER);
    button.setHorizontalTextPosition(SwingConstants.LEFT);

    // Place text to the left of icon and align their tops
    button.setVerticalTextPosition(SwingConstants.TOP);
    button.setHorizontalTextPosition(SwingConstants.LEFT);

    // Place text to the left of icon and align their bottoms
    button.setVerticalTextPosition(SwingConstants.BOTTOM);
    button.setHorizontalTextPosition(SwingConstants.LEFT);

    // Place text to the right of icon, vertically centered
    button.setVerticalTextPosition(SwingConstants.CENTER);
    button.setHorizontalTextPosition(SwingConstants.RIGHT);

    // Place text to the right of icon and align their tops
    button.setVerticalTextPosition(SwingConstants.TOP);
    button.setHorizontalTextPosition(SwingConstants.RIGHT);
```

```
// Place text to the right of icon and align their bottoms
button.setVerticalTextPosition(SwingConstants.BOTTOM);
button.setHorizontalTextPosition(SwingConstants.RIGHT);
```

ε748. Moving the Label/Icon Pair in a JButton Component

When the size of the button component is larger than its contents, the label and icon are always kept together. In fact, the gap size (see "ε749. Setting the Gap Size Between the Label and Icon in a JButton Component") determines the fixed distance between them. Using two alignment methods, you can place the label/icon pair in one of nine possible locations.

```
// To create a button with an icon, see "ε746. Adding an Icon to a JButton Component"

// Place the contents in the nw corner
button.setVerticalAlignment(SwingConstants.TOP);
button.setHorizontalAlignment(SwingConstants.LEFT);

// Place the contents centered at the top
button.setVerticalAlignment(SwingConstants.TOP);
button.setHorizontalAlignment(SwingConstants.CENTER);

// Place the contents in the ne corner
button.setVerticalAlignment(SwingConstants.BOTTOM);
button.setHorizontalAlignment(SwingConstants.RIGHT);

// Place the contents in the sw corner
button.setVerticalAlignment(SwingConstants.BOTTOM);
button.setHorizontalAlignment(SwingConstants.LEFT);

// Place the contents centered at the bottom
button.setVerticalAlignment(SwingConstants.BOTTOM);
button.setHorizontalAlignment(SwingConstants.CENTER);

// Place the contents in the se corner
button.setVerticalAlignment(SwingConstants.BOTTOM);
button.setHorizontalAlignment(SwingConstants.RIGHT);

// Place the contents vertically centered on the left
button.setVerticalAlignment(SwingConstants.CENTER);
button.setHorizontalAlignment(SwingConstants.LEFT);

// Place the contents directly in the center
button.setVerticalAlignment(SwingConstants.CENTER);
button.setHorizontalAlignment(SwingConstants.CENTER);

// Place the contents vertically centered on the right
button.setVerticalAlignment(SwingConstants.CENTER);
button.setHorizontalAlignment(SwingConstants.RIGHT);
```

ε749. Setting the Gap Size Between the Label and Icon in a JButton Component

```
// To create a button with an icon, see "ε743. Creating a JButton Component"

// Get gap size; default is 4
int gapSize = button.getIconTextGap();

// Set gap size
button.setIconTextGap(8);
```

Class *Interface* —extends - - -implements   ○ abstract   ● final   ^—has superclass   ⌣—has subclass   package—see other volume

ε750. Adding a Disabled Icon to a JButton Component

By default, when a button is disabled, it automatically generates a grayed-out version of the installed icon. However, it is possible to set a specific icon to use when the button is disabled.

```
// To create a button with an icon, see "ε746. Adding an Icon to a JButton Component"

// Icon will appear gray
button.setEnabled(false);

// Set a disabled version of icon
Icon disabledIcon = new ImageIcon("dicon.gif");
button.setDisabledIcon(disabledIcon);

// To remove the disabled version of the icon, set to null
button.setDisabledIcon(null);

// If original icon is set as the disabled icon, disabling
// the button will have no effect on the icon
button.setDisabledIcon(icon);
```

ε751. Adding a Rollover and Pressed Icon to a JButton Component

The rollover icon is displayed when the cursor is moved over the button. If no rollover icon is set, the default icon is displayed when the cursor is moved over the button.

The pressed icon is displayed when the button is armed (i.e., the mouse button is down while the cursor is on the button). If no pressed icon is set, the default icon is displayed when the button is armed.

The rollover and pressed icons are never displayed if the button is disabled.

```
// To create a button with an icon, see "ε746. Adding an Icon to a JButton Component"

// Add rollover icon
Icon rolloverIcon = new ImageIcon("ricon.gif");
button.setRolloverIcon(rolloverIcon);

// Add pressed icon
Icon pressedIcon = new ImageIcon("picon.gif");
button.setPressedIcon(pressedIcon);

// To remove rollover icon, set to null
button.setRolloverIcon(null);

// To remove pressed icon, set to null
button.setPressedIcon(null);
```

JCheckBox

ε752. Creating a JCheckbox Component

By default, the state of the checkbox is off; to change the state, see "ε753. Getting and Setting the State of a JCheckbox Component". Also by default, the checkbox is left-justified and vertically centered. The methods to control the text alignment are identical to those of a JButton; see "ε748. Moving the Label/Icon Pair in a JButton Component".

```
// Create an action
Action action = new AbstractAction("CheckBox Label") {
    // This method is called when the button is pressed
    public void actionPerformed(ActionEvent evt) {
        // Perform action
```

Packages and Examples

199

```
            JCheckBox cb = (JCheckBox)evt.getSource();

            // Determine status
            boolean isSel = cb.isSelected();
            if (isSel) {
                // The checkbox is now selected
            } else {
                // The checkbox is now deselected
            }
        }
    };
    // Create the checkbox
    JCheckBox checkBox = new JCheckBox(action);
```

ε753. Getting and Setting the State of a JCheckbox Component

// To create a checkbox, see "ε752. Creating a JCheckbox Component"

// Get the current state of the checkbox
boolean b = *checkbox*.isSelected();

// Set the state of the checkbox to off
checkbox.setSelected(false);

// Set the state of the checkbox to on
checkbox.setSelected(true);

ε754. Adding an Icon to the Label of a JCheckBox Component

Unlike a button, setIcon() does not add an icon to the text label. Rather, in a checkbox, the method is used to customize the icons used to depict its state. However, by using the HTML capabilities in a label, it is possible to add an icon to the label without affecting the state-depicting icons. This example demonstrates the technique.

```
// Define an HTML fragment with an icon on the left and text on the right.
// The elements are embedded in a 3-column table.
String label = "<html><table cellpadding=0><tr><td><img src=file:"
    // The location of the icon
    + icon.gif"
    + "/></td><td width="

    // The gap, in pixels, between icon and text
    + 3
    + "><td>"

    // Retrieve the current label text
    + checkbox.getText()
    + "</td></tr></table></html>";
// Add the icon
checkbox.setText(label);
```

ε755. Customizing the Icons in a JCheckBox Component

The icons used to depict the selected state of a checkbox component can be customized. The simplest customization requires two icons, one to depict the selected state and one to depict the unselected state.

```
// Set the unselected state icon
Icon unsellcon = new ImageIcon("nosel-icon.gif");
checkbox.setIcon(unsellcon);
```

```
// Set the selected state icon
Icon sellcon = new ImageIcon("sel-icon.gif");
checkbox.setSelectedIcon(sellcon);
```

If the checkbox is disabled, grayed out icons are automatically generated for the customized icons. Here's how to customize these disabled icons:

```
// Set the unselected state icon
Icon unselDisIcon = new ImageIcon("nosel-dis-icon.gif");
checkbox.setDisabledIcon(unselDisIcon);
```

```
// Set the selected state icon
Icon selDisIcon = new ImageIcon("sel-dis-icon.gif");
checkbox.setDisabledSelectedIcon(selDisIcon);
```

By default, when the user clicks on a checkbox, the pressed icon (if set) is displayed. Here's how to set it:

```
Icon pressedIcon = new ImageIcon("pres-icon.gif");
checkbox.setPressedIcon(pressedIcon);
```

Finally, it is possible to display an icon when the cursor is moved over the checkbox. This is called the rollover icon.

```
Icon rollIcon = new ImageIcon("roll-icon.gif");
checkbox.setRolloverIcon(rollIcon);
```

JComboBox

ε756. Creating a JComboBox Component

```
// Create a read-only combobox
String[] items = {"item1", "item2"};
JComboBox readOnlyCB = new JComboBox(items);
```

By default, a combobox only allows the user to select from a predefined list of values. The combobox can be made editable which not only allows the user to select from the predefined list but also to type in any string.

```
// Create an editable combobox
items = new String[]{"item1", "item2"};
JComboBox editableCB = new JComboBox(items);
editableCB.setEditable(true);
```

ε757. Getting and Setting the Selected Item in a JComboBox Component

```
// Create a read-only combobox
String[] items = {"item1", "item2"};
JComboBox cb = new JComboBox(items);
```

```
// Get current value
Object obj = cb.getSelectedItem(); // item1
```

```
// Set a new value
cb.setSelectedItem("item2");
obj = cb.getSelectedItem(); // item2
```

Packages and Examples

```
// If the new value is not in the list of valid items, the call is ignored
cb.setSelectedItem("item3");
obj = cb.getSelectedItem(); // item2

// However, if the combobox is editable, the new value can be any value
cb.setEditable(true);
cb.setSelectedItem("item3");
obj = cb.getSelectedItem(); // item3
```

ε758. Getting the Items in a JComboBox Component

```
// Create a read-only combobox
String[] items = {"item1", "item2", "item3"};
JComboBox cb = new JComboBox(items);

// Get number of items
int num = cb.getItemCount();

// Get items
for (int i=0; i<num; i++) {
    Object item = cb.getItemAt(i);
}
// [item1, item2, item3]
```

ε759. Adding and Removing an Item in a JComboBox Component

There is no method for replacing an item. To replace an item, first remove the item and then insert the new one.

```
// Create a read-only combobox; the combobox is read-only
// in that it does not allow the user to type in a new item.
// The combobox still allows programmatic changes to its items.
String[] items = {"item1", "item2"};
JComboBox cb = new JComboBox(items);

// Add an item to the start of the list
cb.insertItemAt("item0", 0);

// Add an item after the first item
cb.insertItemAt("item0.5", 1);

// Add an item to the end of the list
cb.addItem("item3");

// Remove first item
cb.removeItemAt(0);

// Remove the last item
cb.removeItemAt(cb.getItemCount()-1);

// Remove all items
cb.removeAllItems();
```

ε760. Selecting an Item in a JComboBox Component with Multiple Keystrokes

By default, when the user types a keystroke in a read-only combobox and an item in the combobox starts with the typed keystroke, the combobox will select that item. This behavior is not ideal if there are multiple items that start with the same letter.

Class *Interface* —extends - - -implements ○ abstract ● final ^—has superclass ⌐—has subclass package—see other volume

This example demonstrates how to customize a combobox so that it will select an item based on multiple keystrokes. More specifically, if a keystroke is typed within 300 milliseconds of the previous keystroke, the new keystroke is appended to the previous keystroke, and the combobox will select an item that starts with both keystrokes.

```
// Create a read-only combobox
String[] items = {"Ant", "Ape", "Bat", "Boa", "Cat", "Cow"};
JComboBox cb = new JComboBox(items);

// Install the custom key selection manager
cb.setKeySelectionManager(new MyKeySelectionManager());

// This key selection manager will handle selections based on multiple keys.
class MyKeySelectionManager implements JComboBox.KeySelectionManager {
    long lastKeyTime = 0;
    String pattern = "";
    public int selectionForKey(char aKey, ComboBoxModel model) {
        // Find index of selected item
        int sellx = 01;
        Object sel = model.getSelectedItem();
        if (sel != null) {
            for (int i=0; i<model.getSize(); i++) {
                if (sel.equals(model.getElementAt(i))) {
                    sellx = i;
                    break;
                }
            }
        }

        // Get the current time
        long curTime = System.currentTimeMillis();

        // If last key was typed less than 300 ms ago, append to current pattern
        if (curTime - lastKeyTime < 300) {
            pattern += ("" + aKey).toLowerCase();
        } else {
            pattern = ("" + aKey).toLowerCase();
        }

        // Save current time
        lastKeyTime = curTime;

        // Search forward from current selection
        for (int i=sellx+1; i<model.getSize(); i++) {
            String s = model.getElementAt(i).toString().toLowerCase();
            if (s.startsWith(pattern)) {
                return i;
            }
        }

        // Search from top to current selection
        for (int i=0; i<sellx ; i++) {
            if (model.getElementAt(i) != null) {
                String s = model.getElementAt(i).toString().toLowerCase();
                if (s.startsWith(pattern)) {
                    return i;
                }
            }
        }
```

```
                }
                return -1;
            }
        }
```

ε761. Determining If the Menu of a JComboBox Component Is Visible

```
// Create a read-only combobox
String[] items = {"item1", "item2"};
JComboBox cb = new JComboBox(items);

// Determine if the menu is visible
boolean isVisible = cb.isPopupVisible();
```

ε762. Displaying the Menu in a JComboBox Component Using a Keystroke

By default, typing a key in a read-only combobox selects an item that starts with the typed key. This example demonstrates how to display the drop-down menu when a key is typed.

```
// Create a read-only combobox
String[] items = {"Ant", "Ape", "Bat", "Boa", "Cat", "Cow"};
JComboBox cb = new JComboBox(items);

// Create and register the key listener
cb.addKeyListener(new MyKeyListener());

// This key listener displays the menu when a key is pressed.
// To display the menu only if the pressed key matches or does not match an item,
// see "ε763. Displaying the Menu in a JComboBox Component Using a Keystroke If the Selected Item Is
// Not Unique".
class MyKeyListener extends KeyAdapter {
    public void keyPressed(KeyEvent evt) {
        JComboBox cb = (JComboBox)evt.getSource();

        // Get pressed character
        char ch = evt.getKeyChar();

        // If not a printable character, return
        if (ch != KeyEvent.CHAR_UNDEFINED) {
            cb.showPopup();
        }
    }
}
```

ε763. Displaying the Menu in a JComboBox Component Using a Keystroke If the Selected Item Is Not Unique

This example registers a key listener in a read-only combobox that displays the menu if the newly selected item is not unique.

```
// Create a read-only combobox
String[] items = {"Ant", "Ape", "Bat", "Boa", "Cat"};
JComboBox cb = new JComboBox(items);

// Create and register the key listener
cb.addKeyListener(new MyKeyListener());

// This key listener displays the menu only if the pressed key
// does not select a new item or if the selected item is not unique.
```

Class   *Interface*   —extends   - - -implements   ○ abstract   ● final   ^—has superclass   ⌐—has subclass   package—see other volume

```
class MyKeyListener extends KeyAdapter {
    public void keyPressed(KeyEvent evt) {
        JComboBox cb = (JComboBox)evt.getSource();

        // At this point, the selection in the combobox has already been
        // changed; get the index of the new selection
        int curIx = cb.getSelectedIndex();

        // Get pressed character
        char ch = evt.getKeyChar();

        // Get installed key selection manager
        JComboBox.KeySelectionManager ksm = cb.getKeySelectionManager();
        if (ksm != null) {
            // Determine if another item has the same prefix
            int ix = ksm.selectionForKey(ch, cb.getModel());
            boolean noMatch = ix < 0;
            boolean uniqueItem = ix == curIx;

            // Display menu if no matching items or the if the selection is not unique
            if (noMatch || !uniqueItem) {
                cb.showPopup();
            }
        }
    }
}
```

ε764. Setting the Number of Visible Items in the Menu of a JComboBox Component

By default, the menu of a combobox only shows eight items. If there are more items in the menu, a scrollbar is automatically created. To change the default of eight, use JComboBox.setMaximumRowCount().

```
// Create a read-only combobox with lots of items
String[] items = new String[50];
for (int i=0; i<items.length; i++) {
    items[i] = "" + Math.random();
}
JComboBox cb = new JComboBox(items);

// Retrieve the current max visible rows
int maxVisibleRows = cb.getMaximumRowCount();

// Change the current max visible rows
maxVisibleRows = 20;
cb.setMaximumRowCount(maxVisibleRows);
```

ε765. Listening for Changes to the Selected Item in a JComboBox Component

Item events are generated whenever the selected item changes. These events are generated even while the user is moving through items in the displayed popup menu. If the combobox is editable, this event does not indicate whether the new item is taken from the predefined list or not. If this information is necessary, see "ε766. Listening for Action Events from a JComboBox Component".

```
// Create an editable combobox
String[] items = {"item1", "item2"};
JComboBox cb = new JComboBox(items);
cb.setEditable(true);

// Create and register listener
MyItemListener actionListener = new MyItemListener();
```

```
cb.addItemListener(actionListener);

class MyItemListener implements ItemListener {
    // This method is called only if a new item has been selected.
    public void itemStateChanged(ItemEvent evt) {
        JComboBox cb = (JComboBox)evt.getSource();

        // Get the affected item
        Object item = evt.getItem();

        if (evt.getStateChange() == ItemEvent.SELECTED) {
            // Item was just selected
        } else if (evt.getStateChange() == ItemEvent.DESELECTED) {
            // Item is no longer selected
        }
    }
}
```

ε766. Listening for Action Events from a JComboBox Component

Action events are generated whenever the selected item changes. These events are generated even while the user is moving through items in the displayed popup menu. Unlike item events (see "ε765. Listening for Changes to the Selected Item in a JComboBox Component"), action events are generated even if the new item is the same as the old item.

```
// Create component
String[] items = {"item1", "item2"};
JComboBox cb = new JComboBox(items);
cb.setEditable(true);

// Create and register listener
MyActionListener actionListener = new MyActionListener();
cb.addActionListener(actionListener);

class MyActionListener implements ActionListener {
    // Retain the previously selected item in order to determine whether
    // the new item is the same
    Object oldItem;

    // This method is called whenever the user or program changes the selected item.
    // Note: The new item may be the same as the previous item.
    public void actionPerformed(ActionEvent evt) {
        JComboBox cb = (JComboBox)evt.getSource();

        // Get the new item
        Object newItem = cb.getSelectedItem();

        // Determine if different from previously selected item
        boolean same = newItem.equals(oldItem);
        oldItem = newItem;

        if ("comboBoxEdited".equals(evt.getActionCommand())) {
            // User has typed in a string; only possible with an editable combobox
        } else if ("comboBoxChanged".equals(evt.getActionCommand())) {
            // User has selected an item; it may be the same item
        }
    }
}
```

Class   *Interface*   —extends   - - -implements   ○ abstract   ● final   ^—has superclass   ‿—has subclass   package—see other volume

ε767. Determining When the Menu of a JComboBox Component Is Displayed

```
// Create component
String[] items = {"item1", "item2"};
JComboBox cb = new JComboBox(items);
cb.setEditable(true);

// Create and register listener
MyPopupMenuListener actionListener = new MyPopupMenuListener();
cb.addPopupMenuListener(actionListener);

class MyPopupMenuListener implements PopupMenuListener {
    // This method is called just before the menu becomes visible
    public void popupMenuWillBecomeVisible(PopupMenuEvent evt) {
        JComboBox cb = (JComboBox)evt.getSource();
    }

    // This method is called just before the menu becomes hidden
    public void popupMenuWillBecomeInvisible(PopupMenuEvent evt) {
        JComboBox cb = (JComboBox)evt.getSource();
    }

    // This method is called when menu is hidden because the user cancelled it
    public void popupMenuCanceled(PopupMenuEvent evt) {
        JComboBox cb = (JComboBox)evt.getSource();
    }
}
```

JRadioButton

ε768. Creating a JRadioButton Component

```
// Create an action for each radio button
Action action1 = new AbstractAction("RadioButton Label1") {
    // This method is called whenever the radio button is pressed,
    // even if it is already selected; this method is not called
    // if the radio button was selected programmatically
    public void actionPerformed(ActionEvent evt) {
        // Perform action
    }
};
Action action2 = new AbstractAction("RadioButton Label2") {
    // See above
    public void actionPerformed(ActionEvent evt) {
        // Perform action
    }
};

// Create the radio buttons using the actions
JRadioButton b1 = new JRadioButton(action1);
JRadioButton b2 = new JRadioButton(action2);

// Associate the two buttons with a button group
ButtonGroup group = new ButtonGroup();
group.add(b1);
group.add(b2);
```

```
// Neither radio button is selected; to select a radio button,
// see "ε769. Selecting a JRadioButton Component in a Button Group"
```

ε769. Selecting a JRadioButton Component in a Button Group

```
// To create a radio button and button group,
// see "ε768. Creating a JRadioButton Component"

// Select the radio button; the currently selected radio button is deselected.
// This operation does not cause any action events to be fired.
ButtonModel model = radioButton.getModel();
group.setSelected(model, true);
```

ε770. Determining the Selected JRadioButton in a Button Group

When you ask a button group for the currently selected radio button, it returns the selected radio button's model (rather than the selected radio button itself). Fortunately, the button group maintains the list of buttons and so you can iterate over this list looking for one with the same model.

```
// This method returns the selected radio button in a button group
public static JRadioButton getSelection(ButtonGroup group) {
    for (Enumeration e=group.getElements(); e.hasMoreElements(); ) {
        JRadioButton b = (JRadioButton)e.nextElement();
        if (b.getModel() == group.getSelection()) {
            return b;
        }
    }
    return null;
}
```

ε771. Determining If a JRadioButton Component Is Selected

```
// This method returns true if btn is selected; false otherwise
public static boolean isSelected(JRadioButton btn) {
    DefaultButtonModel model = (DefaultButtonModel)btn.getModel();
    return model.getGroup().isSelected(model);
}
```

ε772. Adding an Icon to the Label of a JRadioButton Component

Unlike a JButton, setIcon() does not add an icon to the text label. Rather, in a radio button, the method is used to customize the icons used to depict its state. However, by using the HTML capabilities in a label, it is possible to add an icon to the label without affecting the state-depicting icons. This technique is identical to the one used for checkboxes. For more information, see "ε754. Adding an Icon to the Label of a JCheckBox Component".

ε773. Customizing the Icons in a JRadioButton Component

The icons used to depict the selected state of a radio button can be customized. The customization of radio button icons is identical to the customization of checkboxes. For more information, see "ε755. Customizing the Icons in a JCheckBox Component".

JList

ε774. Creating a JList Component

By default, a list allows more than one item to be selected. Also, the selected items need not be contiguous. To change this default, see "ε781. Setting the Selection Mode of a JList Component".

A list selection event is fired when the set of selected items is changed (see "ε784. Listening for Changes to the Selection in a JList Component").

```
// Create a list with some items
String[] items = {"A", "B", "C", "D"};
JList list = new JList(items);
```

The items can be arbitrary objects. The toString() method of the objects is displayed in the list component.

```
// Create a list with two items - "123" and "Sun May 19 21:15:38 PDT 2002"
Object[] items2 = {new Integer(123), new java.util.Date()};
list = new JList(items2);
```

By default, a list does not automatically display a scrollbar when there are more items than can be displayed. The list must be wrapped in a scroll pane:

```
JScrollPane scrollingList = new JScrollPane(list);
```

ε775. Setting the Dimensions of an Item in a JList Component

By default, the width of the list is determined by the longest item and the height is determined by the number of visible lines multiplied by the tallest item. This example demonstrates how to override these values.

```
// Create a list
String[] items = {"A", "B", "C", "D"};
JList list = new JList(items);

// Set the item width
int cellWidth = 200;
list.setFixedCellWidth(cellWidth);

// Set the item height
int cellHeight = 18;
list.setFixedCellHeight(cellHeight);
```

It is also possible to set the item dimensions using a sample value:

```
String protoCellValue = "My Sample Item Value";
list.setPrototypeCellValue(protoCellValue);
```

ε776. Setting a Tool Tip for an Item in a JList Component

```
// Create a list, overriding the getToolTipText() method
String[] items = {"A", "B", "C", "D"};
JList list = new JList(items) {
    // This method is called as the cursor moves within the list.
    public String getToolTipText(MouseEvent evt) {
        // Get item index
        int index = locationToIndex(evt.getPoint());

        // Get item
        Object item = getModel().getElementAt(index);

        // Return the tool tip text
        return "tool tip for "+item;
```

Packages and Examples

209

```
        }
    };
```

ε777. Getting the Items in a JList Component

```
// Create a list
String[] items = {"A", "B", "C", "D"};
JList list = new JList(items);

// Get number of items in the list
int size = list.getModel().getSize(); // 4

// Get all item objects
for (int i=0; i<size; i++) {
    Object item = list.getModel().getElementAt(i);
}
```

These methods are used to find an item:

```
// The prefix is case-insensitive
String prefix = "b";

// Search forward, starting from index 0, looking for an item that starts with "b"
int start = 0;
javax.swing.text.Position.Bias direction = javax.swing.text.Position.Bias.Forward;
int itemIx = list.getNextMatch(prefix, start, direction);

// Search backward, starting from the last item, looking for an item that starts with "b"
start = list.getModel().getSize()-1;
direction = javax.swing.text.Position.Bias.Backward;
itemIx = list.getNextMatch(prefix, start, direction);
```

These methods can be used to find the range of visible items:

```
// Get number of visible items
int visibleSize = list.getVisibleRowCount();

// Get index of first visible item
itemIx = list.getFirstVisibleIndex();
if (itemIx < 0) {
    // List is either not visible or there are no items
}

// Get index of last visible item
itemIx = list.getLastVisibleIndex();
if (itemIx < 0) {
    // List is either not visible or there are no items
}
```

ε778. Adding and Removing an Item in a JList Component

The default model for a list does not allow the addition and removal of items. The list must be created with a DefaultListModel.

```
// Create a list that allows adds and removes
DefaultListModel model = new DefaultListModel();
JList list = new JList(model);

// Initialize the list with items
String[] items = {"A", "B", "C", "D"};
```

```
    for (int i=0; i<items.length; i++) {
        model.add(i, items[i]);
    }

    // Append an item
    int pos = list.getModel().getSize();
    model.add(pos, "E");

    // Insert an item at the beginning
    pos = 0;
    model.add(pos, "a");
```

This method replaces an item:

```
    // Replace the 2nd item
    pos = 1;
    model.set(pos, "b");
```

These methods are used to remove items:

```
    // Remove the first item
    pos = 0;
    model.remove(pos);

    // Remove the last item
    pos = model.getSize()-1;
    if (pos >= 0) {
        model.remove(pos);
    }

    // Remove all items
    model.clear();
```

ε779. Getting the Selected Items in a JList Component

The following methods return the indices of the selected items:

```
    // To create a list, see "ε774. Creating a JList Component"

    // Get the index of all the selected items
    int[] selectedIx = list.getSelectedIndices();

    // Get all the selected items using the indices
    for (int i=0; i<selectedIx.length; i++) {
        Object sel = list.getModel().getElementAt(selectedIx[i]);
    }

    // Get the index of the first selected item
    int firstSelIx = list.getSelectedIndex();

    // Get the index of the last selected item
    int lastSelIx = list.getMaxSelectionIndex();

    // Determine if the third item is selected
    int index = 2;
    boolean isSel = list.isSelectedIndex(index);

    // Determine if there are any selected items
    boolean anySelected = !list.isSelectionEmpty();
```

The following methods return the selected item objects:

```
// Get the first selected item
Object firstSel = list.getSelectedValue();

// Get all selected items without using indices
Object[] selected = list.getSelectedValues();
```

ε780. Setting the Selected Items in a JList Component

List selection events are fired when the following methods are used to change the set of selected items (see "ε774. Creating a JList Component").

```
// Create a list and get the model
String[] items = {"A", "B", "C", "D"};
JList list = new JList(items);

// Select the second item
int start = 1;
int end = 1;
list.setSelectionInterval(start, end); // B

// Select the first 3 items
start = 0;
end = 2;
list.setSelectionInterval(start, end); // A, B, C

// Select all the items
start = 0;
end = list.getModel().getSize()-1;
if (end >= 0) {
    list.setSelectionInterval(start, end); // A, B, C, D
}

// Clear all selections
list.clearSelection();

// Select the first item
start = 0;
end = 0;
list.setSelectionInterval(start, end); // A

// Add another selection - the third item
start = 2;
end = 2;
list.addSelectionInterval(start, end); // A, C

// Deselect the first item
start = 0;
end = 0;
list.removeSelectionInterval(start, end); // C

// Select a single item
boolean scrollIntoView = true;
list.setSelectedValue("B", scrollIntoView); // B
```

ε781. Setting the Selection Mode of a JList Component

```
// The default mode is MULTIPLE_INTERVAL_SELECTION
String[] items = {"A", "B", "C", "D"};
JList list = new JList(items);
```

```
// Get the current selection model mode
int mode = list.getSelectionMode(); // MULTIPLE_INTERVAL_SELECTION

// Only one item can be selected
list.setSelectionMode(DefaultListSelectionModel.SINGLE_SELECTION);

// The selected items must be in a contiguous range
list.setSelectionMode(DefaultListSelectionModel.SINGLE_INTERVAL_SELECTION);

// Multiple ranges of selected items are allowed
list.setSelectionMode(DefaultListSelectionModel.MULTIPLE_INTERVAL_SELECTION);
```

ε782. Arranging Items in a JList Component

By default, the items in a list are arranged vertically, in a single column, as in:

```
item1
item2
...
```

It is possible to arrange the items left-to-right and top-to-bottom, as in:

```
item1 item2
item3 item4
item5 ...
```

This example creates and configures a list that displays its items left-to-right and top-to-bottom. Note that the number of columns can change as the width of the list changes.

```
// Create a scrollable list
String[] items = {"A", "B", "C", "D"};
JList list = new JList(items);
JScrollPane scrollingList = new JScrollPane(list);

// The default layout orientation is JList.VERTICAL
int orient = list.getLayoutOrientation();

// Change the layout orientation to left-to-right, top-to-bottom
list.setLayoutOrientation(JList.HORIZONTAL_WRAP);
```

The items can also be arranged top-to-bottom and left-to-right, as in:

```
item1 item4
item2 item5
item3 ...
```

This example changes the layout orientation so that its items are displayed top-to-bottom and left-to-right.

```
// Change orientation to top-to-bottom, left-to-right layout
list.setLayoutOrientation(JList.VERTICAL_WRAP);
```

With some look and feels, a list is set to display a fixed number of rows. In order to make the number of visible rows dependent on the height of the list, the visibleRowCount property must be set to 0:

```
// Make the number of rows dynamic
list.setVisibleRowCount(0);
```

ε783. Detecting Double and Triple Clicks on an Item in a JList Component

```
// Create a list
String[] items = {"A", "B", "C", "D"};
JList list = new JList(items);
```

```
// Add a listener for mouse clicks
list.addMouseListener(new MouseAdapter() {
    public void mouseClicked(MouseEvent evt) {
        JList list = (JList)evt.getSource();
        if (evt.getClickCount() == 2) { // Double-click
            // Get item index
            int index = list.locationToIndex(evt.getPoint());
        } else if (evt.getClickCount() == 3) { // Triple-click
            // Get item index
            int index = list.locationToIndex(evt.getPoint());

            // Note that this list will receive a double-click event before this triple-click event
        }
    }
});
```

ε784. Listening for Changes to the Selection in a JList Component

When the set of selected items is changed, either by the user or programmatically, a list selection event is fired.

```
// Create a list
String[] items = {"A", "B", "C", "D"};
JList list = new JList(items);

// Register a selection listener
list.addListSelectionListener(new MyListSelectionListener());

class MyListSelectionListener implements ListSelectionListener {
    // This method is called each time the user changes the set of selected items
    public void valueChanged(ListSelectionEvent evt) {
        // When the user release the mouse button and completes the selection,
        // getValueIsAdjusting() becomes false
        if (!evt.getValueIsAdjusting()) {
            JList list = (JList)evt.getSource();

            // Get all selected items
            Object[] selected = list.getSelectedValues();

            // Iterate all selected items
            for (int i=0; i<selected.length; i++) {
                Object sel = selected[i];
            }
        }
    }
}
```

ε785. Listening for Changes to the Items in a JList Component

When the set of items in a list component is changed, a list data event is fired.

```
// Create a list that allows adds and removes;
// see "ε778. Adding and Removing an Item in a JList Component"

// Register a list data listener
DefaultListModel model = (DefaultListModel)list.getModel();
model.addListDataListener(new MyListDataListener());

class MyListDataListener implements ListDataListener {
```

```
    // This method is called when new items have been added to the list
    public void intervalAdded(ListDataEvent evt) {
        DefaultListModel model = (DefaultListModel)evt.getSource();

        // Get range of new items
        int start = evt.getIndex0();
        int end = evt.getIndex1();
        int count = end-start+1;

        // Get new items
        for (int i=start; i<=end; i++) {
            Object item = model.getElementAt(i);
        }
    }
    // This method is called when items have been removed from the list
    public void intervalRemoved(ListDataEvent evt) {
        // Get range of removed items
        int start = evt.getIndex0();
        int end = evt.getIndex1();
        int count = end-start+1;

        // The removed items are not available
    }


    // This method is called when items in the list are replaced
    public void contentsChanged(ListDataEvent evt) {
        DefaultListModel model = (DefaultListModel)evt.getSource();

        // Get range of changed items
        int start = evt.getIndex0();
        int end = evt.getIndex1();
        int count = end-start+1;

        // Get changed items
        for (int i=start; i<=end; i++) {
            Object item = model.getElementAt(i);
        }
    }
}
```

JSpinner

ε786. Creating a JSpinner Component

This example demonstrates how to build three kinds of spinners. A number spinner:

```
// Create a number spinner
JSpinner spinner = new JSpinner();

// Set its value
spinner.setValue(new Integer(100));
```

A list spinner:

```
// Create a list spinner
SpinnerListModel listModel = new SpinnerListModel(
    new String[]{"red", "green", "blue"});
spinner = new JSpinner(listModel);
```

```
// Set its value
spinner.setValue("blue");
```

A date spinner:

```
// Create a date spinner
SpinnerDateModel dateModel = new SpinnerDateModel();
spinner = new JSpinner(dateModel);

// Set its value to jan 1 2000
Calendar calendar = new GregorianCalendar(2000, Calendar.JANUARY, 1);
spinner.setValue(calendar.getTime());
```

ε787. Creating an Hour JSpinner Component

```
// Create a calendar object and initialize to a particular hour if desired
Calendar calendar = new GregorianCalendar();
calendar.set(Calendar.HOUR_OF_DAY, 13); // 1pm

// Create a date spinner that controls the hours
SpinnerDateModel dateModel = new SpinnerDateModel(
        calendar.getTime(), null, null, Calendar.HOUR_OF_DAY);
JSpinner spinner = new JSpinner(dateModel);

// Get the date formatter
JFormattedTextField tf =
        ((JSpinner.DefaultEditor)spinner.getEditor()).getTextField();
DefaultFormatterFactory factory =
        (DefaultFormatterFactory)tf.getFormatterFactory();
DateFormatter formatter = (DateFormatter)factory.getDefaultFormatter();

// Change the date format to only show the hours
formatter.setFormat(new SimpleDateFormat("hh:00 a"));

// Or use 24 hour mode
formatter.setFormat(new SimpleDateFormat("HH:00 a"));
```

ε788. Disabling Keyboard Editing in a JSpinner Component

```
// Create a nummber spinner
JSpinner spinner = new JSpinner();

// Disable keyboard edits in the spinner
JFormattedTextField tf =
        ((JSpinner.DefaultEditor)spinner.getEditor()).getTextField();
tf.setEditable(false);

// The previous call sets the background to a disabled
// color (usually gray). To change this disabled color,
// reset the background color.
tf.setBackground(Color.white);

// The value of the spinner can still be programmatically changed
spinner.setValue(new Integer(100));
```

ε789. Limiting the Values in a Number JSpinner Component

```
// Create a number spinner that only handles values in the range [0,100]
int min = 0;
int max = 100;
```

```
int step = 5;
int initValue = 50;
SpinnerModel model = new SpinnerNumberModel(initValue, min, max, step);
JSpinner spinner = new JSpinner(model);
```

ε790. Setting the Margin Space on a JSpinner Component

```
// Create a number spinner
JSpinner spinner = new JSpinner();

// Get the text field
JFormattedTextField tf =
    ((JSpinner.DefaultEditor)spinner.getEditor()).getTextField();

// Set the margin (add two spaces to the left and right side of the value)
int top = 0;
int left = 2;
int bottom = 0;
int right = 2;
Insets insets = new Insets(top, left, bottom, right);
tf.setMargin(insets);
```

ε791. Customizing the Editor in a JSpinner Component

This example replaces the default editor (a JFormattedTextField) in a spinner component with a custom editor. The custom editor is simply a panel that displays a color. The name of the color to display is stored in a SpinnerListModel.

```
// Create a color spinner
ColorSpinner spinner = new ColorSpinner(
    new String[]{"red", "green", "blue"});

// Change the selected color
spinner.setValue("blue");

public class ColorSpinner extends JSpinner {
    public ColorSpinner(String[] colorNames) {
        super();
        setModel(new SpinnerListModel(colorNames));
        setEditor(new Editor(this));
    }

    public class Editor extends JPanel implements ChangeListener {
        int preferredWidth = 30;
        int preferredHeight = 16;

        Editor(JSpinner spinner) {
            // Add the listener
            spinner.addChangeListener(this);

            // Set the preferred size
            setPreferredSize(new Dimension(preferredWidth, preferredHeight));

            // Display the current color
            setColor((String)spinner.getValue());
        }

        // Handles changes to the value stored in the model
        public void stateChanged(ChangeEvent evt) {
            JSpinner spinner = (JSpinner)evt.getSource();
```

217

```
            // Get the new value
            String value = (String)spinner.getValue();

            // Update the displayed color
            setColor(value);
        }

        // Updates the displayed color to 'colorName' which must be one
        // of the predefined colors in java.awt.Color.
        public void setColor(String colorName) {
            try {
                // Find the field and value of colorName
                Field field = Class.forName("java.awt.Color").getField(colorName);
                Color color = (Color)field.get(null);

                // Display the color
                setBackground(color);
            } catch (Exception e) {
            }
        }
    }
}
```

ε792. Creating a SpinnerListModel That Loops Through Its Values

By default, if the user is browsing the values in a SpinnerListModel, the iteration stops when either end is reached. This example demonstrates a subclass that allows the user to continuously loop through the values.

```
SpinnerCircularListModel listModel = new SpinnerCircularListModel(
    new String[]{"red", "green", "blue"});
JSpinner spinner = new JSpinner(listModel);

public class SpinnerCircularListModel extends SpinnerListModel {
    public SpinnerCircularListModel(Object[] items) {
        super(items);
    }

    // Returns the next value. If the current value is at the end
    // of the list, returns the first value.
    // There must be at least one item in the list.
    public Object getNextValue() {
        java.util.List list = getList();
        int index = list.indexOf(getValue());

        index = (index >= list.size()-1) ? 0 : index+1;
        return list.get(index);
    }

    // Returns the previous value. If the current value is at the
    // start of the list, returns the last value.
    // There must be at least one item in the list.
    public Object getPreviousValue() {
        java.util.List list = getList();
        int index = list.indexOf(getValue());

        index = (index <= 0) ? list.size()-1 : index-1;
        return list.get(index);
    }
}
```

ε793. Listening for Changes to the Value in a JSpinner Component

```
// Create a nummber spinner
JSpinner spinner = new JSpinner();

// Add the listener
spinner.addChangeListener(new SpinnerListener());

// Changing the value programmatically also fires an event
spinner.setValue(new Integer(100));

public class SpinnerListener implements ChangeListener {
    public void stateChanged(ChangeEvent evt) {
        JSpinner spinner = (JSpinner)evt.getSource();

        // Get the new value
        Object value = spinner.getValue();
    }
}
```

JSlider

ε794. Creating a JSlider Component

```
// Create a horizontal slider with min=0, max=100, value=50
JSlider slider = new JSlider();

// Create a horizontal slider with custom min and max; value is set to the middle
int minimum = -255;
int maximum = 256;
slider = new JSlider(minimum, maximum);

// Create a horizontal slider with custom min, max, and value
int initValue = 0;
slider = new JSlider(minimum, maximum, initValue);

// Create a vertical slider with min=0, max=100, value=50
slider = new JSlider(JSlider.VERTICAL);

// Create a vertical slider with custom min, max, and value
slider = new JSlider(JSlider.VERTICAL, minimum, maximum, initValue);
```

In addition to allowing the user to drag the slider, some look and feels allow the user *page* the slider by a fixed amount. This amount is called the extent.

```
// Set an extent
int extent = 10;
slider.setExtent(extent);
```

For most look and feels, the slider appears as a knob on a track. In this case, it is possible to hide the track:

```
slider.setPaintTrack(false);
```

ε795. Getting and Setting the Values of a JSlider Component

```
// To create a slider, see "ε794. Creating a JSlider Component"

// Get the current value
int value = slider.getValue();

// Get the minimum value
int min = slider.getMinimum();
```

```
// Get the maximum value
int max = slider.getMaximum();

// Get the extent
int extent = slider.getExtent();
// Change the minimum value
int newMin = 0;
slider.setMinimum(newMin);

// Change the maximum value
int newMax = 256;
slider.setMaximum(newMax);

// Set the value; the new value will be forced into the bar's range
int newValue = 33;
slider.setValue(newValue);

// Set the extent
int newExtent = 10;
slider.setExtent(newExtent);
```

It is also possible to set all the values at once by using the model:

```
slider.getModel().setRangeProperties(newValue, newExtent, newMin, newMax, false);
```

ε796. Setting the Orientation of a JSlider Component

Besides being either horizontal or vertical, a slider can also be inverted. An inverted horizontal slider moves from right-to-left. An inverted vertical slider moves from top-to-bottom.

```
// Create a horizontal slider that moves left-to-right
JSlider slider = new JSlider();

// Make the horizontal slider move right-to-left
slider.setInverted(true);

// Make it vertical and move bottom-to-top
slider.setOrientation(JSlider.VERTICAL);
slider.setInverted(false);

// Make it vertical and move top-to-bottom
slider.setOrientation(JSlider.VERTICAL);
slider.setInverted(true);
```

ε797. Showing Tick Marks on a JSlider Component

The slider supports two levels of tick marks, major and minor. Typically, the minor tick-mark spacing is smaller than the major tick-mark spacing. Also, the minor tick-mark spacing is a multiple of the major tick-mark spacing. However, the slider does not enforce any of these constraints.

```
// Create a horizontal slider that moves left-to-right
JSlider slider = new JSlider();
// Determine if currently showing ticks
boolean b = slider.getPaintTicks(); // false

// Show tick marks
slider.setPaintTicks(true);

// Set major tick marks every 25 units
int tickSpacing = 25;
```

```
slider.setMajorTickSpacing(tickSpacing);

// Set minor tick marks every 5 units
tickSpacing = 5;
slider.setMinorTickSpacing(tickSpacing);
```

ε798. Showing Tick-Mark Labels on a JSlider Component

This example demonstrates how to display labels (numerical values) at the major ticks (see "ε797. Showing Tick Marks on a JSlider Component").

```
// Create a horizontal slider that moves left-to-right
JSlider slider = new JSlider();

// Set major tick marks every 25 units
int tickSpacing = 25;
slider.setMajorTickSpacing(tickSpacing);

// Determine if currently painting labels
boolean b = slider.getPaintLabels(); // false

// Paint labels at the major ticks - 0, 25, 50, 75, and 100
slider.setPaintLabels(true);
```

The slider allows you to use an arbitrary label at any particular major tick mark. This example configures a slider that shows an icon at the minimum and maximum positions. The component is only used to render the label and so it can be used at more than one position. Unfortunately, it also means that if the component is interactive (e.g., a button), it will not respond to mouse and keyboard gestures.

```
// Retrieve current table
java.util.Dictionary table = slider.getLabelTable();

// Create icon
ImageIcon icon = new ImageIcon("icon.gif");
JLabel label = new JLabel(icon);

// Set at desired positions
table.put(new Integer(slider.getMinimum()), label);
table.put(new Integer(slider.getMaximum()), label);

// Force the slider to use the new labels
slider.setLabelTable(table);
```

ε799. Constraining JSlider Component Values to Tick Marks

By default, the slider can take on any value from the minimum to the maximum. It is possible to configure the slider to allow only values at tick marks (see "ε797. Showing Tick Marks on a JSlider Component"). This is done by calling JSlider.setSnapToTicks(true).

The slider's minimum and minor tick-mark spacing determines what values are possible. For example, if the minimum is 3 and the minor tick-mark spacing is 10, only the values, 3, 13, 23, and so forth, are allowed. If a minor tick-mark spacing has not been set, the major tick-mark spacing is used. If neither a minor nor a major tick mark spacing has been set, a tick-mark spacing of 1 is assumed.

Calling setSnapToTicks() also has the effect of causing the slider's knob to snap to the closest tick mark whenever it is dragged or programmatically moved to a spot between tick marks.

```
// Create a horizontal slider that moves left-to-right
JSlider slider = new JSlider();
// Set major tick marks every 25 units
int tickSpacing = 25;
```

Packages and Examples

```
    slider.setMajorTickSpacing(tickSpacing);

    // Set minor tick marks every 5 units
    tickSpacing = 5;
    slider.setMinorTickSpacing(tickSpacing);

    // Show tick marks
    slider.setPaintTicks(true);

    // Determine if currently snapping to tick marks
    boolean b = slider.getSnapToTicks(); // false

    // Snap to tick marks
    slider.setSnapToTicks(true);

    // Set to a spot between tick marks; the value moves to closest tick mark
    slider.setValue(27);
    int value = slider.getValue(); // 25
```

ε800. Listening for Value Changes in a JSlider Component

```
    // Create horizontal slider
    JSlider slider = new JSlider();

    // Register a change listener
    slider.addChangeListener(new ChangeListener() {
        // This method is called whenever the slider's value is changed
        public void stateChanged(ChangeEvent evt) {
            JSlider slider = (JSlider)evt.getSource();

            if (!slider.getValueIsAdjusting()) {
                // Get new value
                int value = slider.getValue();
            }
        }
    });
```

JProgressBar

ε801. Creating a JProgressBar Component

A progress bar is used to visually indicate how much a task has been progressed. A progress bar can be oriented horizontally (left-to-right) or vertically (bottom-to-top). By default, the orientation is horizontal.

See also "ε806. Creating a Progress Monitor Dialog".

```
    // Create a horizontal progress bar
    int minimum = 0;
    int maximum = 100;
    JProgressBar progress = new JProgressBar(minimum, maximum);

    // Create a vertical progress bar
    minimum = 0;
    maximum = 100;
    progress = new JProgressBar(JProgressBar.VERTICAL, minimum, maximum);
```

ε802. Creating a JProgressBar Component with an Unknown Maximum

A progress bar with an unknown maximum typically displays an animation until the task is complete.

Class   *Interface*   —extends   - - -implements   ○ abstract   ● final   ^—has superclass   ⌐—has subclass   package—see other volume

Note: The percentage display should not be enabled when the maximum is not known ("ε804. Displaying the Percentage Done on a JProgressBar Component").

```
// Create a horizontal progress bar
int min = 0;
int max = 100;
JProgressBar progress = new JProgressBar(min, max);

// Play animation
progress.setIndeterminate(true);
```

When information on the task's progress is available, the progress bar can be made determinate:

```
int value = 33;
progress.setValue(value);
progress.setIndeterminate(false);
```

ε803. Getting and Setting the Values of a JProgressBar Component

```
// To create a progress bar, see "ε801. Creating a JProgressBar Component"

// Get the current value
int value = progress.getValue();

// Get the minimum value
int min = progress.getMinimum();

// Get the maximum value
int max = progress.getMaximum();


// Change the minimum value
int newMin = 0;
progress.setMinimum(newMin);

// Change the maximum value
int newMax = 256;
progress.setMaximum(newMax);

// Set the value; the new value will be forced into the bar's range
int newValue = 33;
progress.setValue(newValue);
```

It is also possible to set all the values at once by using the model:

```
progress.getModel().setRangeProperties(newValue, 0, newMin, newMax, false);
```

ε804. Displaying the Percentage Done on a JProgressBar Component

The progress bar offers the ability to display the actual value of the bar as a percentage. This example demonstrates how to enable this display.

Note: The percentage display should not be enabled when the maximum is not known ("ε802. Creating a JProgressBar Component with an Unknown Maximum").

```
// Create a horizontal progress bar
int minimum = 0;
int maximum = 100;
JProgressBar progress = new JProgressBar(minimum, maximum);

// Overlay a string showing the percentage done
progress.setStringPainted(true);
```

ε805. Listening for Value Changes in a JProgressBar Component

Whenever the value of a progress bar is changed, a change event is fired. In fact, the event is also fired when the minimum or maximum values are changed. However, the event does not specify which values were changed.

```
// Create a horizontal progress bar
int minimum = 0;
int maximum = 100;
JProgressBar progress = new JProgressBar(minimum, maximum);

progress.addChangeListener(new ChangeListener() {
    // This method is called when the value, minimum, or maximum is changed.
    public void stateChanged(ChangeEvent evt) {
        JProgressBar comp = (JProgressBar)evt.getSource();

        // The old value is not available

        // Get new values
        int value = comp.getValue();
        int min = comp.getMinimum();
        int max = comp.getMaximum();
    }
});
```

Progress Monitor

ε806. Creating a Progress Monitor Dialog

A common feature of a user interface is to show a progress dialog that visually displays the progress of a long-running task. The dialog automatically disappears when the task is done. The ProgressMonitor class is a convenient dialog that implements a progress dialog.

The progress monitor contains a message which describes the long-running task. The message does not change for the duration of the task. The progress monitor also allows for a *note* which is a description of the current subtask. For example, if the task is copying a set of files, the note could be the name of the current file being copied.

Note: A progress monitor should not be reused. The properties that control when the dialog should appear are set when the monitor is constructed and cannot be reset.

See also "ε801. Creating a JProgressBar Component".

```
// This message describes the task that is running
String message = "Description of Task";

// This string describes a subtask; set to null if not needed
String note = "subtask";

// Set the title of the dialog if desired
String title = "Task Title";
UIManager.put("ProgressMonitor.progressText", title);

// Create a progress monitor dialog.
// The dialog will use the supplied component's frame as the parent.
int min = 0;
int max = 100;
ProgressMonitor pm = new ProgressMonitor(component, message, note, min, max);
```

Class   *Interface*   —extends   - - -implements   ○ abstract   ● final   ^—has superclass   ⌐—has subclass   package—see other volume

As the task progresses, check to see if the task has been cancelled and if not, call setProgress() and supply its current state.

```
// Check if the dialog has been cancelled
boolean cancelled = pm.isCanceled();

if (cancelled) {
    // Stop task
} else {
    // Set new state
    pm.setProgress(newValue);

    // Change the note if desired
    pm.setNote("New Note");
}
```

ε807. Setting the Popup Delay of a Progress Monitor Dialog

By default, the progress monitor delays for a short period before it is displayed. There are two properties that control when the dialog is displayed—millisToPopup and millisToDecideToPopup. The progress monitor computes a time-to-completion based on the how fast the value changes. The dialog will not appear as long as the predicted time-to-completion is less than millisToPopup. millisToDecideToPopup determines a minimum time, since the progress monitor was created, before the dialog can appear.

In summary, the dialog is shown only if it has been millisToDecideToPopup milliseconds after the progress monitor was created *and* the predicted time-to-completion is greater than millisToPopup.

```
// Get delay based on time-to-completion
int millisToPopup = pm.getMillisToPopup(); // 2000

// Get minimum delay
int millisToDecideToPopup = pm.getMillisToDecideToPopup(); // 500

// To make progress monitor popup immediately, set both to 0
pm.setMillisToPopup(0);
pm.setMillisToDecideToPopup(0);
```

Packages and Examples

Menus

ε808. Creating a JMenuBar, JMenu, and JMenuItem Component

When the user selects a menu item, it fires an action event.

```
// Create the menu bar
JMenuBar menuBar = new JMenuBar();

// Create a menu
JMenu menu = new JMenu("Menu Label");
menuBar.add(menu);

// Create a menu item
JMenuItem item = new JMenuItem("Item Label");
item.addActionListener(actionListener);
menu.add(item);

// Install the menu bar in the frame
frame.setJMenuBar(menuBar);
```

ε809. Separating Menu Items in a Menu

A separator typically appears as a horizontal line. It is used to group related sets of menu items in a menu.

```
// Create a menu
JMenu menu = new JMenu("Menu Label");

// Add a menu item
JMenuItem item1 = new JMenuItem("Item Label");
menu.add(item1);

// Add separator
menu.add(new JSeparator());

// Add another menu item
JMenuItem item2 = new JMenuItem("Item Label");
menu.add(item2);
```

ε810. Creating a Popup Menu

```
final JPopupMenu menu = new JPopupMenu();

// Create and add a menu item
JMenuItem item = new JMenuItem("Item Label");
item.addActionListener(actionListener);
menu.add(item);

// Set the component to show the popup menu
component.addMouseListener(new MouseAdapter() {
    public void mousePressed(MouseEvent evt) {
        if (evt.isPopupTrigger()) {
            menu.show(evt.getComponent(), evt.getX(), evt.getY());
        }
    }
    public void mouseReleased(MouseEvent evt) {
        if (evt.isPopupTrigger()) {
            menu.show(evt.getComponent(), evt.getX(), evt.getY());
        }
    }
});
```

ε811. Creating a Popup Menu with Nested Menus

See "ε810. Creating a Popup Menu" for an example on how to display a popup menu.

```
final JPopupMenu popupMenu = new JPopupMenu();

// Create a submenu with items
JMenu submenu = new JMenu("SubMenu1");
submenu.add(action1);
submenu.add(action2);

// Add submenu to popup menu
popupMenu.add(submenu);
```

ε812. Forcing a Popup Menu to Be a Heavyweight Component

By default, Swing popup menus used by JMenu and JPopupMenu are lightweight. If heavyweight components are used in the same frame, the popup menus may appear behind the heavyweight components.

This example demonstrates how to force a JPopupMenu to use heavyweight components:

Class   *Interface*   —extends   - - -implements   O abstract   ● final   ^—has superclass   ⌐—has subclass   package—see other volume

```
JPopupMenu popupMenu = new JPopupMenu();

// Retrieve current setting
boolean lwPopup = popupMenu.isLightWeightPopupEnabled(); // true

// Force the popup menu to use heavyweight components
popupMenu.setLightWeightPopupEnabled(false);
// To use the popup menu, see "ε810. Creating a Popup Menu"
```

This example demonstrates how to force the popup menu of a JMenu to be heavyweight:

```
// Create a menu with a menu item
JMenu menu = new JMenu("Menu Label");
menu.add(new JMenuItem("Item Label"));

// Retrieve current setting
lwPopup = menu.getPopupMenu().isLightWeightPopupEnabled(); // true

// Force the menu's popup menu to be heavyweight
menu.getPopupMenu().setLightWeightPopupEnabled(false);
// To use the menu, see "ε808. Creating a JMenuBar, JMenu, and JMenuItem Component"
```

This example configures all popup menus to be heavyweight:

```
// Retrieve current setting
lwPopup = JPopupMenu.getDefaultLightWeightPopupEnabled(); // true

// Globally use heavyweight components for all popup menus
JPopupMenu.setDefaultLightWeightPopupEnabled(false);
```

ε813. Getting the Currently Selected Menu or Menu Item

The currently selected menu or menu item in a JMenu or JPopupMenu is tracked by MenuSelectionManager and can be retrieved by calling MenuSelectionManager.getSelectedPath(). This method returns an array of MenuElement objects, representing all the menu objects that are part of the selected menu or menu item. For example, when a menu is opened in a menu bar, the sequence of elements in the path is: JMenuBar, JMenu, and JPopupMenu. If a menu item in the open menu is then selected, there will be fourth element, a JMenuItem.

The menu path also includes nested menus. For example, if the currently selected menu item is part of a nested menu in a menu bar, the sequence of elements is: JMenuBar, JMenu, JPopupMenu, JMenu, JPopupMenu, and JMenuItem. Note that a JMenu is always followed by a JPopupMenu.

If a menu item in a popup menu is selected, the sequence of menu objects is simply JPopupMenu and JMenuItem. If the menu item is part of a nest menu, the sequence is, JPopupMenu, JMenu, JPopupMenu, and JMenuItem.

```
// Get the selected menu path
MenuElement[] path = MenuSelectionManager.defaultManager().getSelectedPath();

if (path.length == 0) {
    // No menus are opened or menu items selected
}

// Retrieve the labels of all the menu elements in the path
for (int i=0; i<path.length; i++) {
    Component c = path[i].getComponent();

    if (c instanceof JMenuItem) {
        JMenuItem mi = (JMenuItem)c;
        String label = mi.getText();
```

```
          // Note: JMenu is a subclass of JMenuItem; also JMenuBar does not have a label
     }
}
```

ε814. Creating a Menu Item That Listens for Changes to Its Selection Status

A menu item can receive notification of selection changes by overriding its menuSelectionChanged() method.
See also "ε808. Creating a JMenuBar, JMenu, and JMenuItem Component".

```
JMenuItem item = new JMenuItem("Label") {
     // This method is called whenever the selection status of
     // this menu item is changed
     public void menuSelectionChanged(boolean isSelected) {
          // Always forward the event
          super.menuSelectionChanged(isSelected);

          if (isSelected) {
               // The menu item is selected
          } else {
               // The menu item is no longer selected
          }
     }
};
```

ε815. Listening for Changes to the Currently Selected Menu or Menu Item

The currently selected menu or menu item in a JMenu or JPopupMenu is tracked by MenuSelectionManager.
To receive notification of changes to the currently selected menu or menu item, a change listener must be
registered with the MenuSelectionManager.

```
// Create a change listener and register with the menu selection manager
MenuSelectionManager.defaultManager().addChangeListener(
     new ChangeListener() {
          public void stateChanged(ChangeEvent evt) {
               // Get the selected menu or menu item
               MenuSelectionManager msm = (MenuSelectionManager)evt.getSource();
               MenuElement[] path = msm.getSelectedPath();
               // To interpret path, see
               // "ε813. Getting the Currently Selected Menu or Menu Item"

               if (path.length == 0) {
                    // All menus are hidden
               }
          }
     }
);
```

JToolBar

ε816. Creating a JToolbar Container

A toolbar can be either horizontal or vertical. When the orientation is horizontal, the objects in the toolbar
are displayed left-to-right. When the orientation is vertical, the objects in the toolbar are displayed top-
to-bottom. This orientation is automatically changed when the toolbar is moved to the top or side of a
container.

Class   *Interface*   —extends   - - -implements   ○ abstract   ● final   ^—has superclass   ⌐—has subclass   package—see other volume

```
// Create a horizontal toolbar
JToolBar toolbar = new JToolBar();

// Create a vertical toolbar
toolbar = new JToolBar(null, JToolBar.VERTICAL);

// Get current orientation
int orient = toolbar.getOrientation();
```

The following code adds various buttons to the toolbar:

```
// Get icon
ImageIcon icon = new ImageIcon("icon.gif");

// Create an action with an icon
Action action = new AbstractAction("Button Label", icon) {
    // This method is called when the button is pressed
    public void actionPerformed(ActionEvent evt) {
        // Perform action
    }
};


// Add a button to the toolbar; remove the label and margin before adding
JButton c1 = new JButton(action);
c1.setText(null);
c1.setMargin(new Insets(0, 0, 0, 0));
toolbar.add(c1);


// Add a toggle button; remove the label and margin before adding
JToggleButton c2 = new JToggleButton(action);
c2.setText(null);
c2.setMargin(new Insets(0, 0, 0, 0));
toolbar.add(c2);


// Add a combobox
JComboBox c3 = new JComboBox(new String[]{"A", "B", "C"});
c3.setPrototypeDisplayValue("XXXXXXXX"); // Set a desired width
c3.setMaximumSize(c3.getMinimumSize());
toolbar.add(c3);
// See also "ε765. Listening for Changes to the Selected Item in a JComboBox Component"
```

If the toolbar is to be floatable (see "ε818. Preventing a JToolbar Container from Floating"), it must be added to a container with a BorderLayout.

```
// Add the toolbar to a frame
JFrame frame = new JFrame();
frame.getContentPane().add(toolbar, BorderLayout.NORTH);
frame.pack();
frame.setVisible(true);
```

ε817. Determining When a Floatable JToolBar Container Changes Orientation

When the orientation of a toolbar is changed, either by the user or programmatically, the toolbar fires a property change event.

```
// Create a floatable horizontal toolbar
JToolBar toolbar = new JToolBar();
```

```
// Register for orientation property change events
toolbar.addPropertyChangeListener(new java.beans.PropertyChangeListener() {
    // This method is called whenever the orientation of the toolbar is changed
    public void propertyChange(java.beans.PropertyChangeEvent evt) {
        String propName = evt.getPropertyName();
        if ("orientation".equals(propName)) {
            // Get the old orientation
            Integer oldValue = (Integer)evt.getOldValue();

            // Get the new orientation
            Integer newValue = (Integer)evt.getNewValue();

            if (newValue.intValue() == JToolBar.HORIZONTAL) {
                // toolbar now has horizontal orientation
            } else {
                // toolbar now has vertical orientation
            }
        }
    }
});
```

ε818. Preventing a JToolbar Container from Floating

By default, a toolbar can *float*, that is, it can be dragged to a different edge in its container or it can be moved into a top-level window.

```
// Create a horizontal toolbar
JToolBar toolbar = new JToolBar();

// Get current floatability
boolean b = toolbar.isFloatable();

// Disable floatability
toolbar.setFloatable(false);
```

ε819. Highlighting Buttons in a JToolbar Container While Under the Cursor

By default, a button in a toolbar does not change its appearance when the cursor is over the button. However, if the toolbar is in *rollover* mode, the buttons will highlight while under a cursor.

```
// Create a horizontal toolbar
JToolBar toolbar = new JToolBar();

// Get current rollover mode
boolean b = toolbar.isRollover();

// Enable rollover mode
toolbar.setRollover(true);
```

JScrollPane

ε820. Creating a JScrollPane Container

The Swing components do not typically have scroll bars. In order to automatically display scroll bars, you need to wrap the component in a scroll pane.

```
// Create a scrollable text area
JTextArea textArea = new JTextArea();
```

Class   *Interface*   —extends   - - -implements   O abstract   ● final   ⌐—has superclass   ⌐—has subclass   package—see other volume

```
JScrollPane scrollableTextArea = new JScrollPane(textArea);

// Create a scrollable list
JList list = new JList();
JScrollPane scrollableList = new JScrollPane(list);
```

ε821. Setting the Scrollbar Policy of a JScrollPane Container

A scroll bar in a scroll pane can be set to appear only as needed, always appear, or never appear. By default, both the vertical and horizontal scrollbars in a scroll pane appear only when needed.

```
// Create a scrollable text area
JTextArea textArea = new JTextArea();
JScrollPane pane = new JScrollPane(textArea);

// Get the default scrollbar policy
int hpolicy = pane.getHorizontalScrollBarPolicy();
// JScrollPane.HORIZONTAL_SCROLLBAR_AS_NEEDED;

int vpolicy = pane.getVerticalScrollBarPolicy();
// JScrollPane.VERTICAL_SCROLLBAR_AS_NEEDED;


// Make the scrollbars always appear
pane.setHorizontalScrollBarPolicy(JScrollPane.HORIZONTAL_SCROLLBAR_ALWAYS);
pane.setVerticalScrollBarPolicy(JScrollPane.VERTICAL_SCROLLBAR_ALWAYS);

// Make the scrollbars never appear
pane.setHorizontalScrollBarPolicy(JScrollPane.HORIZONTAL_SCROLLBAR_NEVER);
pane.setVerticalScrollBarPolicy(JScrollPane.VERTICAL_SCROLLBAR_NEVER);
```

ε822. Listening for Scrollbar Value Changes in a JScrollPane Container

A scrollbar in a scroll pane fires adjustment events whenever its value changes.

```
// Create a scrollable text area
JTextArea textArea = new JTextArea();
JScrollPane pane = new JScrollPane(textArea);

// Listen for value changes in the scroll pane's scrollbars
AdjustmentListener listener = new MyAdjustmentListener();
pane.getHorizontalScrollBar().addAdjustmentListener(listener);
pane.getVerticalScrollBar().addAdjustmentListener(listener);

class MyAdjustmentListener implements AdjustmentListener {
    // This method is called whenever the value of a scrollbar is changed,
    // either by the user or programmatically.
    public void adjustmentValueChanged(AdjustmentEvent evt) {
        Adjustable source = evt.getAdjustable();

        // getValueIsAdjusting() returns true if the user is currently
        // dragging the scrollbar's knob and has not picked a final value
        if (evt.getValueIsAdjusting()) {
            // The user is dragging the knob
            return;
        }

        // Determine which scrollbar fired the event
        int orient = source.getOrientation();
        if (orient == Adjustable.HORIZONTAL) {
            // Event from horizontal scrollbar
```

```
            } else {
                // Event from vertical scrollbar
            }

            // Determine the type of event
            int type = evt.getAdjustmentType();
            switch (type) {
            case AdjustmentEvent.UNIT_INCREMENT:
                // Scrollbar was increased by one unit
                break;
            case AdjustmentEvent.UNIT_DECREMENT:
                // Scrollbar was decreased by one unit
                break;
            case AdjustmentEvent.BLOCK_INCREMENT:
                // Scrollbar was increased by one block
                break;
            case AdjustmentEvent.BLOCK_DECREMENT:
                // Scrollbar was decreased by one block
                break;
            case AdjustmentEvent.TRACK:
                // The knob on the scrollbar was dragged
                break;
            }

            // Get current value
            int value = evt.getValue();
        }
    }
```

JSplitPane

ε823. Creating a JSplitPane Container

A split pane divides its space between two components. The split pane contains a divider that allows the user to control the amount of space distributed to each component.

```
// Create a left-right split pane
JSplitPane hpane = new JSplitPane(JSplitPane.HORIZONTAL_SPLIT, leftComponent, rightComponent);

// Create a top-bottom split pane
JSplitPane vpane = new JSplitPane(JSplitPane.VERTICAL_SPLIT, topComponent, bottomComponent);
```

By default, when the divider is dragged, a shadow is displayed to indicate where the divider would be when the mouse is released. It is possible for the split pane to continuously move the divider and resize its child components while the user is dragging the divider.

```
boolean b = vpane.isContinuousLayout(); // false by default

// Set the split pane to continuously resize the child components
// which the divider is dragged
vpane.setContinuousLayout(true);
```

The split pane supports a *one-touch-expandable* capability that allows the user to conveniently move the divider to either end with a single click. This capability is enabled by setting the following property:

Class *Interface* —extends - - -implements ○ abstract ● final ˆ—has superclass ˌ—has subclass package—see other volume

b = vpane.isOneTouchExpandable(); // false by default

vpane.setOneTouchExpandable(true);

ε824. Getting the Setting the Children in a JSplitPane Container

```
// Create a left-right split pane
JSplitPane hpane = new JSplitPane(JSplitPane.HORIZONTAL_SPLIT, leftComponent, rightComponent);

// Create a top-bottom split pane
JSplitPane vpane = new JSplitPane(JSplitPane.VERTICAL_SPLIT, topComponent, bottomComponent);


// Get the children from the horizontal split pane
leftComponent = hpane.getLeftComponent();
rightComponent = hpane.getRightComponent();

// Get the children from the vertical split pane
topComponent = vpane.getTopComponent();
bottomComponent = vpane.getBottomComponent();

// Replace the children in the horizontal split pane
hpane.setLeftComponent(comp1);
hpane.setRightComponent(comp2);

// Replace the children in the vertical split pane
vpane.setTopComponent(comp3);
vpane.setBottomComponent(comp4);
```

ε825. Distributing Space When a JSplitPane Container Is Resized

The *weight* of a split pane controls the behavior of the divider when the split pane is resized. If the weight is 0, all extra space is given to the right or bottom component. If the weight is 1, all extra space is given to the left or top component. A weight of .3 specifies that the left or top component gets one-third of the extra space. The weight also determines how the children lose space when the size of the split pane is reduced. For example, a weight of 0 means that the left or top component does not lose any space.

The weight also controls the starting location of the divider. For example, if the weight is .5, the divider is placed in the center.

```
// Create a left-right split pane
JSplitPane pane = new JSplitPane(JSplitPane.HORIZONTAL_SPLIT, leftComponent, rightComponent);

// Get current weight
double weight = pane.getResizeWeight(); // 0.0 by default

// Keep the size of the right component constant
weight = 1D;
pane.setResizeWeight(weight);

// Split the space evenly
weight = .5D;
pane.setResizeWeight(weight);
```

ε826. Getting and Setting the Divider Location in a JSplitPane Container

The location of a divider is measured in pixels from either the left edge (in the case of a horizontal split pane) or the top edge (in the case of a vertical split pane).

There are two ways to set the location of the divider. The first is to specify an absolute location based on the distance in pixels from the left or top edge. The second is to specify a proportional location based on

Packages and Examples

the distance from the left or top edge. For example, a proportional location of 0 sets the divider at the left or top edge. A proportional location of 1 sets the divider at the right or bottom edge. A proportional location of .5 sets the divider at the center.

```
// Create a left-right split pane
JSplitPane pane = new JSplitPane(JSplitPane.HORIZONTAL_SPLIT, leftComponent, rightComponent);

// Get current location; result is number of pixels from the left edge
int loc = pane.getDividerLocation();

// Set a new location using an absolution location; center the divider
loc = (int)((pane.getBounds().getWidth()-pane.getDividerSize())/2);
pane.setDividerLocation(loc);

double propLoc = .5D;
// Set a proportional location
pane.setDividerLocation(propLoc);
```

ε827. Setting the Size of the Divider in a JSplitPane Container

A divider can be no less than one pixel in size.

```
// Create a left-right split pane
JSplitPane pane = new JSplitPane(JSplitPane.HORIZONTAL_SPLIT, leftComponent, rightComponent);

// Get current size; it is look and feel dependent
int size = pane.getDividerSize();

// Set a new size
size = 1;
pane.setDividerSize(size);
```

JTabbedPane

ε828. Creating a JTabbedPane Container

A tabbed pane is a container that displays only one child component at a time. Typically, the children are themselves containers of other components. Each child is associated with a visible *tab* on the tabbed pane. The user can choose a child to display by selecting the tab associated with that child.

```
// Create a child container which is to be associated with a tab
JPanel panel = new JPanel();
// Add components to the panel...

// Specify on which edge the tabs should appear
int location = JTabbedPane.TOP; // or BOTTOM, LEFT, RIGHT

// Create the tabbed pane
JTabbedPane pane = new JTabbedPane();

// Add a tab
String label = "Tab Label";
pane.addTab(label, panel);
```

ε829. Getting and Setting the Selected Tab in a JTabbedPane Container

```
// To create a tabbed pane, see "ε828. Creating a JTabbedPane Container"

// Get the index of the currently selected tab
```

Class   *Interface*   —extends   - - -implements   ○ abstract   ● final   ^—has superclass   ˸—has subclass   package—see other volume

```
int selIndex = pane.getSelectedIndex();

// Select the last tab
selIndex = pane.getTabCount()-1;
pane.setSelectedIndex(selIndex);
```

ε830. Adding a Tab to a JTabbedPane Container

This example demonstrates various ways to add a tab to a tabbed pane.

```
// Create a tabbed pane
JTabbedPane pane = new JTabbedPane();
```

```
// Add a tab with a label taken from the name of the component
component1.setName("Tab Label");
pane.add(component1);
```

```
// Add a tab with a label at the end of all tabs
String label = "Tab Label";
pane.addTab(label, component2);
```

```
// Add a tab with a label and icon at the end of all tabs
Icon icon = new ImageIcon("icon.gif");
pane.addTab(label, icon, component3);
```

```
// Add a tab with a label, icon, and tool tip at the end of all tabs
String tooltip = "Tool Tip Text";
pane.addTab(label, icon, component4, tooltip);
```

```
// Insert a tab after the first tab
int index = 1;
pane.insertTab(label, icon, component5, tooltip, index);
```

ε831. Removing a Tab in a JTabbedPane Container

```
// To create a tabbed pane, see "ε828. Creating a JTabbedPane Container"
```

```
// Remove the last tab
pane.remove(pane.getTabCount()-1);
```

```
// Remove the tab with the specified child component
pane.remove(component);
```

```
// Remove all the tabs
pane.removeAll();
```

ε832. Moving a Tab in a JTabbedPane Container

To move a tab, it must first be removed and then reinserted into the tabbed pane as a new tab. Unfortunately, since there is no object that represents a tab, it is necessary to record all of the tab's properties before moving it and to restore them after the new tab has been created.

This example moves the last tab to the first position:

```
// To create a tabbed pane, see "ε828. Creating a JTabbedPane Container"
```

```
int src = pane.getTabCount()-1;
int dst = 0;
```

```
// Get all the properties
Component comp = pane.getComponentAt(src);
String label = pane.getTitleAt(src);
Icon icon = pane.getIconAt(src);
```

```
Icon iconDis = pane.getDisabledIconAt(src);
String tooltip = pane.getToolTipTextAt(src);
boolean enabled = pane.isEnabledAt(src);
int keycode = pane.getMnemonicAt(src);
int mnemonicLoc = pane.getDisplayedMnemonicIndexAt(src);
Color fg = pane.getForegroundAt(src);
Color bg = pane.getBackgroundAt(src);

// Remove the tab
pane.remove(src);

// Add a new tab
pane.insertTab(label, icon, comp, tooltip, dst);

// Restore all properties
pane.setDisabledIconAt(dst, iconDis);
pane.setEnabledAt(dst, enabled);
pane.setMnemonicAt(dst, keycode);
pane.setDisplayedMnemonicIndexAt(dst, mnemonicLoc);
pane.setForegroundAt(dst, fg);
pane.setBackgroundAt(dst, bg);
```

ε833. Getting the Tabs in a JTabbedPane Container

This example retrieves all the tabs in a tabbed pane:

```
// To create a tabbed pane, see "ε828. Creating a JTabbedPane Container"

// Get number of tabs
int count = pane.getTabCount();

// Get the properties of each tab
for (int i=0; i<count; i++) {
    // Get label
    String label = pane.getTitleAt(i);

    // Get icon
    Icon icon = pane.getIconAt(i);

    // Get tool tip
    String tooltip = pane.getToolTipTextAt(i);

    // Is enabled?
    boolean enabled = pane.isEnabledAt(i);

    // Get mnemonic
    int keycode = pane.getMnemonicAt(i);

    // Get component associated with tab
    Component comp = pane.getComponentAt(i);
}
```

Most of the methods that allow the properties of a tab to be changed require the index of the tab. The index of a tab can change as tabs are added, removed, or moved. Here are three ways to retrieve the index of a tab when needed.

```
// Get the index of the first tab that matches a label
String label = "Tab Label";
int index = pane.indexOfTab(label);
```

Class   *Interface*   —extends   - - -implements   ○ abstract   ● final   ˆ—has superclass   ˍ—has subclass   package—see other volume

```
// Get the index of the first tab that matches an icon; the supplied
// icon must be the same instance that was used to create the tab
index = pane.indexOfTab(icon);
```

```
// Get the index of the tab by matching the child component; the supplied
// component must be the same instance that was used to create the tab
index = pane.indexOfComponent(component);
```

```
if (index < 0) {
    // The tab could not be found
}
```

ε834. Setting the Location of the Tabs in a JTabbedPane Container

The tabs of a tabbed pane can be placed on one of the four edges of its container. By default, when a tabbed pane is created, the tabs are placed on top.

```
// Create a tabbed pane with the tabs on top
JTabbedPane pane = new JTabbedPane();
```

```
// Get current location
int loc = pane.getTabPlacement(); // TOP
```

```
// Create a tabbed pane with tabs at a particular location
int location = JTabbedPane.LEFT; // or TOP, BOTTOM, RIGHT
pane = new JTabbedPane(location);
```

```
// Change the tab location
pane.setTabPlacement(JTabbedPane.BOTTOM);
```

ε835. Enabling and Disabling a Tab in a JTabbedPane Container

By default, all new tabs are enabled, which means the user can select them. A tab can be disabled to prevent the user from selecting it.

```
// Create a tabbed pane
JTabbedPane pane = new JTabbedPane();
```

```
// Add a tab
pane.addTab("Tab Label", component);
```

```
// Get index of the new tab
int index = pane.getTabCount()-1;
```

```
// Determine whether the tab is enabled
boolean enabled = pane.isEnabledAt(index);
```

```
// Disable the tab
pane.setEnabledAt(index, false);
```

ε836. Setting the Tool Tip for a Tab in a JTabbedPane Container

There are two ways to set a tool tip on a tab. The first is to specify it when the tab is created; the second way is to set it using JTabbedPane.setToolTipTextAt().

```
// Create a tabbed pane
JTabbedPane pane = new JTabbedPane();
```

```
// Add a tab with a tool tip
String label = "Tab Label";
String tooltip = "Tool Tip Text";
pane.addTab(label, null, component, tooltip);
```

```
// Get index of new tab
int index = pane.getTabCount()-1;

// Get current tool tip
tooltip = pane.getToolTipTextAt(index);

// Change tool tip
tooltip = "New Tool Tip Text";
pane.setToolTipTextAt(index, tooltip);
```

ε837. Setting the Color of a Tab in a JTabbedPane Container

```
// Create a tabbed pane
JTabbedPane pane = new JTabbedPane();

// Set the text color for all tabs
pane.setForeground(Color.YELLOW);

// Set the background color for all tabs
pane.setBackground(Color.MAGENTA);

// Add a tab
String label = "Tab Label";
pane.addTab(label, component);

// Get index of the new tab
int index = pane.getTabCount()-1;

// Set text color for the new tab
pane.setForegroundAt(index, Color.ORANGE);

// Set background color for the new tab
pane.setBackgroundAt(index, Color.GREEN);
```

ε838. Enabling the Selection of a Tab in a JTabbedPane Container Using a Keystroke

Setting a mnemonic on a tab allows the tab to be selected with a keystroke. For example, if the mnemonic for a tab were the key L, then typing ALT-L (on Windows) would select the tab.

```
// Create a tabbed pane
JTabbedPane pane = new JTabbedPane();

// Add a tab
pane.addTab("Tab Label", component);

// Get index of the new tab
int index = pane.getTabCount()-1;

// Set the mnemonic; on some look and feels, the L in the label will be underlined
int keycode = KeyEvent.VK_L;
pane.setMnemonicAt(index, keycode);
```

ε839. Enable Scrolling Tabs in a JTabbedPane Container

By default, all the tabs in a tabbed pane are displayed. When the tabs are wider than the width of the tabbed pane, they are displayed in rows. If space is an issue, it is possible to configure the tabs to appear in a single row along with a scroller that allows the tabs to be scrolled into view.

```
// Create a tabbed pane
JTabbedPane pane = new JTabbedPane();

// Add some tabs...; see "ε830. Adding a Tab to a JTabbedPane Container"
```

Class   *Interface*   —extends   - - -implements   ○ abstract   ● final   ^—has superclass   ˌ—has subclass   package—see other volume

```
// Get the number of rows of tabs
int rows = pane.getTabRunCount();
```

```
// Get the current layout policy
int policy = pane.getTabLayoutPolicy(); // WRAP_TAB_LAYOUT
```

```
// Configure the tabs to scroll
pane.setTabLayoutPolicy(JTabbedPane.SCROLL_TAB_LAYOUT);
```

ε840. Determining When the Selected Tab Changes in a JTabbedPane Container

A tabbed pane fires a change event whenever the selected tab is changed either by the user or programmatically.

```
// Create the tabbed pane
JTabbedPane pane = new JTabbedPane();
```

```
// Add tabs...; see "ε830. Adding a Tab to a JTabbedPane Container"
```

```
// Register a change listener
pane.addChangeListener(new ChangeListener() {
    // This method is called whenever the selected tab changes
    public void stateChanged(ChangeEvent evt) {
        JTabbedPane pane = (JTabbedPane)evt.getSource();

        // Get current tab
        int sel = pane.getSelectedIndex();
    }
});
```

JDesktop and JInternalFrame

ε841. Creating a JDesktopPane Container

A desktop is a container that can only hold internal frames (JInternalFrame objects). This example creates a desktop with an internal frame.

```
// Create an internal frame
boolean resizable = true;
boolean closeable = true;
boolean maximizable = true;
boolean iconifiable = true;
String title = "Frame Title";
JInternalFrame iframe = new JInternalFrame(title, resizable, closeable, maximizable, iconifiable);
```

```
// Set an initial size
int width = 200;
int height = 50;
iframe.setSize(width, height);
```

```
// By default, internal frames are not visible; make it visible
iframe.setVisible(true);
```

```
// Add components to internal frame...
iframe.getContentPane().add(new JTextArea());
```

```
// Add internal frame to desktop
JDesktopPane desktop = new JDesktopPane();
desktop.add(iframe);
```

```
// Display the desktop in a top-level frame
```

Packages and Examples

239

```
JFrame frame = new JFrame();
frame.getContentPane().add(desktop, BorderLayout.CENTER);
frame.setSize(300, 300);
frame.setVisible(true);
```

ε842. Getting All Frames in a JDesktopPane Container

```
// To create a desktop, see "ε841. Creating a JDesktopPane Container"

// Retrieve all internal frames
JInternalFrame[] frames = desktop.getAllFrames();

for (int i=0; i<frames.length; i++) {
    // Get internal frame's title
    String title = frames[i].getTitle();

    // Determine if the internal frame is visible
    boolean isVisible = frames[i].isVisible();

    // Get other properties
    boolean isCloseable = frames[i].isClosable();
    boolean isResizeable = frames[i].isResizable();
    boolean isIconifiable = frames[i].isIconifiable();
    boolean isIcon = frames[i].isIcon();
    boolean isMaximizable = frames[i].isMaximizable();
    boolean isSelected = frames[i].isSelected();
}
```

Tool Tips

ε843. Setting a Tool Tip

If a JComponent such as a JButton is created using an action, the component will be created with the tool tip text in the action (see "ε855. Creating an Action").

However, if the action does not have any tool tip text or if it must be changed, use JComponent.setToolTipText() is used.

```
JComponent button = new JButton("Label");

// Set tool tip text
button.setToolTipText("tool tip text");
```

ε844. Setting the Location of a Tool Tip

By default, when a tool tip of a component appears, its northwest corner appears at the same x-coordinate as the cursor and 20 pixels lower than the y-coordinate of the cursor. To change this default location for a component, the getToolTipLocation() method of the component must be overridden.

```
// Set the location of the tool tip such that its nw corner
// coincides with the nw corner of the button
JButton button = new JButton("My Button") {
    public Point getToolTipLocation(MouseEvent event) {
        return new Point(0, 0);
    }
};

// Set the location of the tool tip such that its nw corner
```

```
// coincides with the bottom center of the button
button = new JButton("My Button") {
    public Point getToolTipLocation(MouseEvent event) {
        return new Point(getWidth()/2, getHeight());
    }
};
// Use the default tool tip location
button = new JButton("My Button") {
    public Point getToolTipLocation(MouseEvent event) {
        return null;
    }
};
// Set the tool tip text
button.setToolTipText("aString");
```

ε845. Enabling and Disabling Tool Tips

By default, tool tips are enabled for the entire application. So if a component has a tool tip text, it will be displayed. To enable or disable tool tips for the entire application, ToolTipManager.setEnabled() is used.

Note: Enabling or disabling the tool tip for a particular component can be done only by adding or removing the tool tip text on the component.

```
// Enable tool tips for the entire application
ToolTipManager.sharedInstance().setEnabled(true);

// Disable tool tips for the entire application
ToolTipManager.sharedInstance().setEnabled(false);
```

ε846. Making Tool Tips Appear Immediately

By default, when the cursor enters a component, there is a 750-millisecond delay before the tool tip is displayed. This example demonstrates how to show the tool tip immediately.

```
// Get current delay
int initialDelay = ToolTipManager.sharedInstance().getInitialDelay();

// Show tool tips immediately
ToolTipManager.sharedInstance().setInitialDelay(0);

// Show tool tips after a second
initialDelay = 1000;
ToolTipManager.sharedInstance().setInitialDelay(initialDelay);
```

ε847. Making Tool Tips Remain Visible

By default, a tool tip stays visible for 4 seconds. This example demonstrates how to keep the tool tip showing as long as the cursor is in the component.

```
// Get current delay
int dismissDelay = ToolTipManager.sharedInstance().getDismissDelay();

// Keep the tool tip showing
dismissDelay = Integer.MAX_VALUE;
ToolTipManager.sharedInstance().setDismissDelay(dismissDelay);
```

ε848. Showing Multiple Lines in a Tool Tip

A tool tip can show simple HTML tags when surrounded by the tags <HTML> and </HTML>. This example shows how to create multiple lines by using the <BR> tag. See the javax.swing.text.html.HTML class documentation for a list of supported tags.

```
// Show two lines in the tool tip
component.setToolTipText("<html>"+"This is a"+"<br>"+"tool tip"+"</html>");
```

```
// By default, the lines are left justified. Center the lines.
component.setToolTipText("<html><center>"+"This is a"+"<br>"+"tool tip"+"</center></html>");
```

```
// Italicize the second line
component.setToolTipText("<html>"+"This is a"+"<br><i>"+"tool tip"+"</i></html>");
```

ε849. Showing an Image in a Tool Tip

A tool tip can show simple HTML tags when surrounded by the tags <HTML> and </HTML). This example shows how to include an image in a tool tip by using the <IMG> tag. See the javax.swing.text.html.HTML class documentation for a list of other supported tags.

```
String imageName = "file:image.jpg";
component.setToolTipText("<html>Here is an image <img src="+imageName+"></html>");
```

Layout

ε850. Laying Out Components in a Row or Column

A horizontal box container arranges the components left-to-right in their preferred sizes. The row of components are vertically centered.

```
// Create horizontal box container
Box box = new Box(BoxLayout.X_AXIS);
```

```
// Here is a another way to create a horizontal box container
box = Box.createHorizontalBox();
```

```
// Add components
box.add(component1);
box.add(component2);
```

A vertical box container arranges the components top-to-bottom aligned in their preferred sizes. The column of components are left-aligned.

```
// Create vertical box container
box = new Box(BoxLayout.Y_AXIS);
```

```
// Here is a another way to create a vertical box container
box = Box.createVerticalBox();
```

```
// Add components
box.add(component1);
box.add(component2);
```

ε851. Separating Components in a Row or Column

```
Box box = new Box(BoxLayout.X_AXIS);
```

```
// Glue spreads the components as far apart as possible.
```

```
box.add(component1);
box.add(Box.createGlue());
box.add(component2);

// Strut spreads the components apart by a fixed distance.
int width = 10;
box.add(Box.createHorizontalStrut(width));
box.add(component3);
```

ε852. Laying Out Components in a Flow (Left-to-Right, Top-to-Bottom)

```
int align = FlowLayout.CENTER; // or LEFT, RIGHT
JPanel panel = new JPanel(new FlowLayout(align));
panel.add(component1);
panel.add(component2);
```

ε853. Laying Out Components in a Grid

When components are added to the container, they fill the grid left-to-right, top-to-bottom.

```
int rows = 2;
int cols = 2;
JPanel panel = new JPanel(new GridLayout(rows, cols));
panel.add(component1);
panel.add(component2);
```

ε854. Laying Out Components Using Absolute Coordinates

```
JPanel panel = new JPanel(null);
component.setBounds(x, y, w, h);
panel.add(component);
```

Actions

ε855. Creating an Action

An action is used by a Swing component to invoke a method. To create an action, the actionPerformed() method must be overridden. The action is then attached to a component such as a button or bound to a keystroke in a text component. When the button is activated or the keystroke is pressed, the action's actionPerformed() method is called. Actions can be attached to more than one component or keystroke.

Actions can also contain other optional information, such as a label, icon, or tool tip text. When the action is attached to a component, the component may use this information if present. For example, if the action has a label and icon, a button created using that action will use that label and icon.

This example defines an action and creates a button using the action.

```
// Create an action object
public Action action = new AbstractAction("Action Name") {
    // This is an instance initializer; it is executed just after the
    // constructor of the superclass is invoked
    {
        // The following values are completely optional

        // Set tool tip text
        putValue(Action.SHORT_DESCRIPTION, "Tool Tip Text");

        // This text is not directly used by any Swing component;
        // however, this text could be used in a help system
```

```
                putValue(Action.LONG_DESCRIPTION, "Context-Sensitive Help Text");

            // Set an icon
            Icon icon = new ImageIcon("icon.gif");
            putValue(Action.SMALL_ICON, icon);

            // Set a mnemonic character. In most look and feels, this causes the
            // specified character to be underlined This indicates that if the component
            // using this action has the focus and In some look and feels, this causes
            // the specified character in the label to be underlined and
            putValue(Action.MNEMONIC_KEY, new Integer(java.awt.event.KeyEvent.VK_A));

            // Set an accelerator key; this value is used by menu items
            putValue(Action.ACCELERATOR_KEY, KeyStroke.getKeyStroke("control F2"));
        }

        // This method is called when the action is invoked
        public void actionPerformed(ActionEvent evt) {
            // Perform action
        }
    };
```

Create a button using the action object:

```
    JButton button = new JButton(action);
```

ε856. Listing the Actions in a Component

This example demonstrates how to list all the actions in a component.

```
    ActionMap map = component.getActionMap();

    // List actions in the component
    list(map, map.keys());

    // List actions in the component and in all parent action maps
    list(map, map.allKeys());

    public static void list(ActionMap map, Object[] actionKeys) {
        if (actionKeys == null) {
            return;
        }
        for (int i=0; i<actionKeys.length; i++) {
            // Get the action bound to this action key
            while (map.get(actionKeys[i]) == null) {
                map = map.getParent();
            }
            Action action = (Action)map.get(actionKeys[i]);
        }
    }
```

A text component not only has an action map with actions, it also has keymaps with actions. Moreover, every keymap has a default action to handle any typed character key events not handled by any input map or keymap. The following code retrieves actions from these objects:

```
    // List the actions in the keymaps
    if (component instanceof JTextComponent) {
        JTextComponent textComp = (JTextComponent)component;
        Keymap keymap = textComp.getKeymap();
```

Class *Interface* —extends - - -implements ○ abstract ● final ⌐—has superclass ˪—has subclass package—see other volume

```
    while (keymap != null) {
        // Get actions in the keymap
        Action[] actions = keymap.getBoundActions();
        for (int i=0; i<actions.length; i++) {
            Action action = actions[i];
        }

        // Get the default action in the keymap
        Action defaultAction = keymap.getDefaultAction();
        keymap = keymap.getResolveParent();
    }
}
```

ε857. Enabling an Action

Actions can be bound to many different kinds of components. When an action is enabled or disabled, components that are bound to that action may automatically alter its display to match the enabled state of the action.

This example creates three components: a button, a text component, and a menu item—all bound to the same action. When the action is disabled, the button and menu item will appear disabled and the text component will not be able to invoke the action.

```
    JFrame frame = new JFrame();

    // Button
    JButton button = new JButton(action);

    // Text Component
    JTextField textfield = new JTextField();
    textfield.getInputMap(JComponent.WHEN_FOCUSED).put(
        KeyStroke.getKeyStroke("F2"), action.getValue(Action.NAME));
    textfield.getActionMap().put(action.getValue(Action.NAME), action);

    // Menu Item
    JMenuBar menuBar = new JMenuBar();
    JMenu menu = new JMenu("Menu Label");
    menu.add(new JMenuItem(action));
    menuBar.add(menu);
    frame.setJMenuBar(menuBar);

    // The action
    public Action action = new AbstractAction("Action Name") {
        public void actionPerformed(ActionEvent evt) {
            // Perform action
        }
    };
```

Keystrokes and Input Maps

ε858. Creating a KeyStroke and Binding It to an Action

This example creates a number of keystrokes and adds them to the input map of a component. When a keystroke is added to an input map, an action name must be supplied. This action is invoked when the keystroke is pressed while the component has the focus.

```
    // Create some keystrokes and bind them all to the same action
    component.getInputMap().put(KeyStroke.getKeyStroke("F2"), "actionName");
```

Packages and Examples

```
component.getInputMap().put(KeyStroke.getKeyStroke("control A"), "actionName");
component.getInputMap().put(KeyStroke.getKeyStroke("shift F2"), "actionName");
component.getInputMap().put(KeyStroke.getKeyStroke('/'), "actionName");
component.getInputMap().put(KeyStroke.getKeyStroke("button3 F"), "actionName");
component.getInputMap().put(KeyStroke.getKeyStroke("typed x"), "actionName");
component.getInputMap().put(KeyStroke.getKeyStroke("released DELETE"), "actionName");
component.getInputMap().put(KeyStroke.getKeyStroke("shift UP"), "actionName");

// Add the action to the component
component.getActionMap().put("actionName",
    new AbstractAction("actionName") {
        public void actionPerformed(ActionEvent evt) {
            process(evt);
        }
    }
);
```

ε859. Converting a KeyStroke to a String

The KeyStroke.toString() method does not return a string that can be parsed by KeyStroke.getKeyStroke(). The method keyStroke2String() in this example returns a string that is parseable by KeyStroke.getKeyStroke().

However, there is one keystroke that cannot be represented as a string that can be parsed back to a keystroke––a typed space character. In order to bind an action to a typed space character, KeyStroke.getKeyStroke(new Character(' '), 0) needs to be called.

```
public static String keyStroke2String(KeyStroke key) {
    StringBuffer s = new StringBuffer(50);
    int m = key.getModifiers();

    if ((m & (InputEvent.SHIFT_DOWN_MASK|InputEvent.SHIFT_MASK)) != 0) {
        s.append("shift ");
    }
    if ((m & (InputEvent.CTRL_DOWN_MASK|InputEvent.CTRL_MASK)) != 0) {
        s.append("ctrl ");
    }
    if ((m & (InputEvent.META_DOWN_MASK|InputEvent.META_MASK)) != 0) {
        s.append("meta ");
    }
    if ((m & (InputEvent.ALT_DOWN_MASK|InputEvent.ALT_MASK)) != 0) {
        s.append("alt ");
    }
    if ((m & (InputEvent.BUTTON1_DOWN_MASK|InputEvent.BUTTON1_MASK)) != 0) {
        s.append("button1 ");
    }
    if ((m & (InputEvent.BUTTON2_DOWN_MASK|InputEvent.BUTTON2_MASK)) != 0) {
        s.append("button2 ");
    }
    if ((m & (InputEvent.BUTTON3_DOWN_MASK|InputEvent.BUTTON3_MASK)) != 0) {
        s.append("button3 ");
    }

    switch (key.getKeyEventType()) {
    case KeyEvent.KEY_TYPED:
        s.append("typed ");
        s.append(key.getKeyChar() + " ");
```

```
            break;
        case KeyEvent.KEY_PRESSED:
            s.append("pressed ");
            s.append(getKeyText(key.getKeyCode()) + " ");
            break;
        case KeyEvent.KEY_RELEASED:
            s.append("released ");
            s.append(getKeyText(key.getKeyCode()) + " ");
            break;
        default:
            s.append("unknown-event-type ");
            break;
        }

        return s.toString();
    }

    public static String getKeyText(int keyCode) {
        if (keyCode >= KeyEvent.VK_0 && keyCode <= KeyEvent.VK_9 ||
            keyCode >= KeyEvent.VK_A && keyCode <= KeyEvent.VK_Z) {
            return String.valueOf((char)keyCode);
        }

        switch(keyCode) {
        case KeyEvent.VK_COMMA: return "COMMA";
        case KeyEvent.VK_PERIOD: return "PERIOD";
        case KeyEvent.VK_SLASH: return "SLASH";
        case KeyEvent.VK_SEMICOLON: return "SEMICOLON";
        case KeyEvent.VK_EQUALS: return "EQUALS";
        case KeyEvent.VK_OPEN_BRACKET: return "OPEN_BRACKET";
        case KeyEvent.VK_BACK_SLASH: return "BACK_SLASH";
        case KeyEvent.VK_CLOSE_BRACKET: return "CLOSE_BRACKET";

        case KeyEvent.VK_ENTER: return "ENTER";
        case KeyEvent.VK_BACK_SPACE: return "BACK_SPACE";
        case KeyEvent.VK_TAB: return "TAB";
        case KeyEvent.VK_CANCEL: return "CANCEL";
        case KeyEvent.VK_CLEAR: return "CLEAR";
        case KeyEvent.VK_SHIFT: return "SHIFT";
        case KeyEvent.VK_CONTROL: return "CONTROL";
        case KeyEvent.VK_ALT: return "ALT";
        case KeyEvent.VK_PAUSE: return "PAUSE";
        case KeyEvent.VK_CAPS_LOCK: return "CAPS_LOCK";
        case KeyEvent.VK_ESCAPE: return "ESCAPE";
        case KeyEvent.VK_SPACE: return "SPACE";
        case KeyEvent.VK_PAGE_UP: return "PAGE_UP";
        case KeyEvent.VK_PAGE_DOWN: return "PAGE_DOWN";
        case KeyEvent.VK_END: return "END";
        case KeyEvent.VK_HOME: return "HOME";
        case KeyEvent.VK_LEFT: return "LEFT";
        case KeyEvent.VK_UP: return "UP";
        case KeyEvent.VK_RIGHT: return "RIGHT";
        case KeyEvent.VK_DOWN: return "DOWN";

        // numpad numeric keys handled below
        case KeyEvent.VK_MULTIPLY: return "MULTIPLY";
        case KeyEvent.VK_ADD: return "ADD";
```

Packages and Examples

```
                case KeyEvent.VK_SEPARATOR: return "SEPARATOR";
                case KeyEvent.VK_SUBTRACT: return "SUBTRACT";
                case KeyEvent.VK_DECIMAL: return "DECIMAL";
                case KeyEvent.VK_DIVIDE: return "DIVIDE";
                case KeyEvent.VK_DELETE: return "DELETE";
                case KeyEvent.VK_NUM_LOCK: return "NUM_LOCK";
                case KeyEvent.VK_SCROLL_LOCK: return "SCROLL_LOCK";

                case KeyEvent.VK_F1: return "F1";
                case KeyEvent.VK_F2: return "F2";
                case KeyEvent.VK_F3: return "F3";
                case KeyEvent.VK_F4: return "F4";
                case KeyEvent.VK_F5: return "F5";
                case KeyEvent.VK_F6: return "F6";
                case KeyEvent.VK_F7: return "F7";
                case KeyEvent.VK_F8: return "F8";
                case KeyEvent.VK_F9: return "F9";
                case KeyEvent.VK_F10: return "F10";
                case KeyEvent.VK_F11: return "F11";
                case KeyEvent.VK_F12: return "F12";
                case KeyEvent.VK_F13: return "F13";
                case KeyEvent.VK_F14: return "F14";
                case KeyEvent.VK_F15: return "F15";
                case KeyEvent.VK_F16: return "F16";
                case KeyEvent.VK_F17: return "F17";
                case KeyEvent.VK_F18: return "F18";
                case KeyEvent.VK_F19: return "F19";
                case KeyEvent.VK_F20: return "F20";
                case KeyEvent.VK_F21: return "F21";
                case KeyEvent.VK_F22: return "F22";
                case KeyEvent.VK_F23: return "F23";
                case KeyEvent.VK_F24: return "F24";

                case KeyEvent.VK_PRINTSCREEN: return "PRINTSCREEN";
                case KeyEvent.VK_INSERT: return "INSERT";
                case KeyEvent.VK_HELP: return "HELP";
                case KeyEvent.VK_META: return "META";
                case KeyEvent.VK_BACK_QUOTE: return "BACK_QUOTE";
                case KeyEvent.VK_QUOTE: return "QUOTE";

                case KeyEvent.VK_KP_UP: return "KP_UP";
                case KeyEvent.VK_KP_DOWN: return "KP_DOWN";
                case KeyEvent.VK_KP_LEFT: return "KP_LEFT";
                case KeyEvent.VK_KP_RIGHT: return "KP_RIGHT";

                case KeyEvent.VK_DEAD_GRAVE: return "DEAD_GRAVE";
                case KeyEvent.VK_DEAD_ACUTE: return "DEAD_ACUTE";
                case KeyEvent.VK_DEAD_CIRCUMFLEX: return "DEAD_CIRCUMFLEX";
                case KeyEvent.VK_DEAD_TILDE: return "DEAD_TILDE";
                case KeyEvent.VK_DEAD_MACRON: return "DEAD_MACRON";
                case KeyEvent.VK_DEAD_BREVE: return "DEAD_BREVE";
                case KeyEvent.VK_DEAD_ABOVEDOT: return "DEAD_ABOVEDOT";
                case KeyEvent.VK_DEAD_DIAERESIS: return "DEAD_DIAERESIS";
                case KeyEvent.VK_DEAD_ABOVERING: return "DEAD_ABOVERING";
                case KeyEvent.VK_DEAD_DOUBLEACUTE: return "DEAD_DOUBLEACUTE";
```

```
case KeyEvent.VK_DEAD_CARON: return "DEAD_CARON";
case KeyEvent.VK_DEAD_CEDILLA: return "DEAD_CEDILLA";
case KeyEvent.VK_DEAD_OGONEK: return "DEAD_OGONEK";
case KeyEvent.VK_DEAD_IOTA: return "DEAD_IOTA";
case KeyEvent.VK_DEAD_VOICED_SOUND: return "DEAD_VOICED_SOUND";
case KeyEvent.VK_DEAD_SEMIVOICED_SOUND: return "DEAD_SEMIVOICED_SOUND";

case KeyEvent.VK_AMPERSAND: return "AMPERSAND";
case KeyEvent.VK_ASTERISK: return "ASTERISK";
case KeyEvent.VK_QUOTEDBL: return "QUOTEDBL";
case KeyEvent.VK_LESS: return "LESS";
case KeyEvent.VK_GREATER: return "GREATER";
case KeyEvent.VK_BRACELEFT: return "BRACELEFT";
case KeyEvent.VK_BRACERIGHT: return "BRACERIGHT";
case KeyEvent.VK_AT: return "AT";
case KeyEvent.VK_COLON: return "COLON";
case KeyEvent.VK_CIRCUMFLEX: return "CIRCUMFLEX";
case KeyEvent.VK_DOLLAR: return "DOLLAR";
case KeyEvent.VK_EURO_SIGN: return "EURO_SIGN";
case KeyEvent.VK_EXCLAMATION_MARK: return "EXCLAMATION_MARK";
case KeyEvent.VK_INVERTED_EXCLAMATION_MARK:
        return "INVERTED_EXCLAMATION_MARK";
case KeyEvent.VK_LEFT_PARENTHESIS: return "LEFT_PARENTHESIS";
case KeyEvent.VK_NUMBER_SIGN: return "NUMBER_SIGN";
case KeyEvent.VK_MINUS: return "MINUS";
case KeyEvent.VK_PLUS: return "PLUS";
case KeyEvent.VK_RIGHT_PARENTHESIS: return "RIGHT_PARENTHESIS";
case KeyEvent.VK_UNDERSCORE: return "UNDERSCORE";

case KeyEvent.VK_FINAL: return "FINAL";
case KeyEvent.VK_CONVERT: return "CONVERT";
case KeyEvent.VK_NONCONVERT: return "NONCONVERT";
case KeyEvent.VK_ACCEPT: return "ACCEPT";
case KeyEvent.VK_MODECHANGE: return "MODECHANGE";
case KeyEvent.VK_KANA: return "KANA";
case KeyEvent.VK_KANJI: return "KANJI";
case KeyEvent.VK_ALPHANUMERIC: return "ALPHANUMERIC";
case KeyEvent.VK_KATAKANA: return "KATAKANA";
case KeyEvent.VK_HIRAGANA: return "HIRAGANA";
case KeyEvent.VK_FULL_WIDTH: return "FULL_WIDTH";
case KeyEvent.VK_HALF_WIDTH: return "HALF_WIDTH";
case KeyEvent.VK_ROMAN_CHARACTERS: return "ROMAN_CHARACTERS";
case KeyEvent.VK_ALL_CANDIDATES: return "ALL_CANDIDATES";
case KeyEvent.VK_PREVIOUS_CANDIDATE: return "PREVIOUS_CANDIDATE";
case KeyEvent.VK_CODE_INPUT: return "CODE_INPUT";
case KeyEvent.VK_JAPANESE_KATAKANA: return "JAPANESE_KATAKANA";
case KeyEvent.VK_JAPANESE_HIRAGANA: return "JAPANESE_HIRAGANA";
case KeyEvent.VK_JAPANESE_ROMAN: return "JAPANESE_ROMAN";
case KeyEvent.VK_KANA_LOCK: return "KANA_LOCK";
case KeyEvent.VK_INPUT_METHOD_ON_OFF: return "INPUT_METHOD_ON_OFF";

case KeyEvent.VK_AGAIN: return "AGAIN";
case KeyEvent.VK_UNDO: return "UNDO";
case KeyEvent.VK_COPY: return "COPY";
case KeyEvent.VK_PASTE: return "PASTE";
case KeyEvent.VK_CUT: return "CUT";
```

Packages and Examples

```
        case KeyEvent.VK_FIND: return "FIND";
        case KeyEvent.VK_PROPS: return "PROPS";
        case KeyEvent.VK_STOP: return "STOP";

        case KeyEvent.VK_COMPOSE: return "COMPOSE";
        case KeyEvent.VK_ALT_GRAPH: return "ALT_GRAPH";
    }
    if (keyCode >= KeyEvent.VK_NUMPAD0 && keyCode <= KeyEvent.VK_NUMPAD9) {
        char c = (char)(keyCode - KeyEvent.VK_NUMPAD0 + '0');
        return "NUMPAD"+c;
    }
    return "unknown(0x" + Integer.toString(keyCode, 16) + ")";
}
```

ε860. Listing the Key Bindings in a Component

This example demonstrates how to list all the key bindings in a component. Text components have an additional set of key bindings called a keymap. See "ε1005. Listing the Key Bindings in a JTextComponent Keymap" for an example on how to list those key bindings.

```
// List keystrokes in the WHEN_FOCUSED input map of the component
InputMap map = component.getInputMap(JComponent.WHEN_FOCUSED);
list(map, map.keys());
// List keystrokes in the component and in all parent input maps
list(map, map.allKeys());

// List keystrokes in the WHEN_ANCESTOR_OF_FOCUSED_COMPONENT input map of the component
map = component.getInputMap(JComponent.WHEN_ANCESTOR_OF_FOCUSED_COMPONENT);
list(map, map.keys());
// List keystrokes in all related input maps
list(map, map.allKeys());

// List keystrokes in the WHEN_IN_FOCUSED_WINDOW input map of the component
map = component.getInputMap(JComponent.WHEN_IN_FOCUSED_WINDOW);
list(map, map.keys());
// List keystrokes in all related input maps
list(map, map.allKeys());

public static void list(InputMap map, KeyStroke[] keys) {
    if (keys == null) {
        return;
    }
    for (int i=0; i<keys.length; i++) {
        // This method is defined in "ε859. Converting a KeyStroke to a String"
        String keystrokeStr = keyStroke2String(keys[i]);

        // Get the action name bound to this keystroke
        while (map.get(keys[i]) == null) {
            map = map.getParent();
        }
        if (map.get(keys[i]) instanceof String) {
            String actionName = (String)map.get(keys[i]);
        } else {
            Action action = (Action)map.get(keys[i]);
        }
```

Class *Interface* —extends - - -implements ○ abstract ● final ˆ—has superclass ˌ—has subclass package—see other volume

```
        }
    }
```

ε861. Sharing an InputMap or an ActionMap Between Two Components

By sharing an InputMap or ActionMap, any change to the shared InputMap or ActionMap will affect all components sharing the InputMap or ActionMap.

WHEN_FOCUSED and WHEN_ANCESTOR_OF_FOCUSED_COMPONENT types of InputMaps can be shared. WHEN_IN_FOCUSED_WINDOW InputMaps cannot be shared.

```
// Get an InputMap from the desired type of component and initialize it
InputMap im = new JTextArea().getInputMap(JComponent.WHEN_FOCUSED);
im.put(KeyStroke.getKeyStroke("F2"), "actionName");

// Get an ActionMap from the desired type of component and initialize it
ActionMap am = new JTextArea().getActionMap();
am.put("actionName",
    new AbstractAction("actionName") {
        public void actionPerformed(ActionEvent evt) {
            process((JTextComponent)evt.getSource());
        }
    }
);

// Use the shared InputMap and ActionMap
component1.setInputMap(JComponent.WHEN_FOCUSED, im);
component2.setInputMap(JComponent.WHEN_FOCUSED, im);

component1.setActionMap(am);
component2.setActionMap(am);

// Now, any change to the shared InputMap or ActionMap will affect both component1 and component2
im.put(KeyStroke.getKeyStroke("F3"), "actionName2");
am.put("actionName2",
    new AbstractAction("actionName2") {
        public void actionPerformed(ActionEvent evt) {
            process((JTextComponent)evt.getSource());
        }
    }
);
```

ε862. Finding a Key Binding in a Component

This example searches all of a component's inputmaps and keymaps (if the component is a text component) for a particular keystroke.

```
FindResult r = find(KeyStroke.getKeyStroke("ctrl pressed C"), component);
r = find(KeyStroke.getKeyStroke("ctrl released C"), component);
r = find(KeyStroke.getKeyStroke("C"), component);
r = find(KeyStroke.getKeyStroke("typed C"), component);
r = find(KeyStroke.getKeyStroke(new Character('\u0002'), 0), component);

// The results of a find are returned in a FindResult object
static class FindResult {
    // Non-null if the keystroke is in an inputmap
    InputMap inputMap;

    // Non-null if the keystroke is in an keymap or default action
    Keymap keymap;
```

Packages and Examples

251

```
                    // Non-null if the keystroke is in a default action
                    // The keymap field holds the keymap containing the default action
                    Action defaultAction;

                    // If true, the keystroke is in the component's inputMap or keymap
                    // and not in one of the inputMap's or keymap's parent.
                    boolean isLocal;

                    public String toString() {
                        StringBuffer b = new StringBuffer();

                        b.append("inputmap="+inputMap+",keymap="+keymap
                                +",defaultAction="+defaultAction+",isLocal="+isLocal);
                        return b.toString();
                    }
                }
                // Returns null if not found
                public static FindResult find(KeyStroke k, JComponent c) {
                    FindResult result;

                    result = find(k, c.getInputMap(JComponent.WHEN_FOCUSED));
                    if (result != null) {
                        return result;
                    }
                    result = find(k, c.getInputMap(JComponent.WHEN_ANCESTOR_OF_FOCUSED_COMPONENT));
                    if (result != null) {
                        return result;
                    }
                    result = find(k, c.getInputMap(JComponent.WHEN_IN_FOCUSED_WINDOW));
                    if (result != null) {
                        return result;
                    }


                    // Check keymaps
                    if (c instanceof JTextComponent) {
                        JTextComponent tc = (JTextComponent)c;
                        result = new FindResult();

                        // Check local keymap
                        Keymap kmap = tc.getKeymap();
                        if (kmap.isLocallyDefined(k)) {
                            result.keymap = kmap;
                            result.isLocal = true;
                            return result;
                        }

                        // Check parent keymaps
                        kmap = kmap.getResolveParent();
                        while (kmap != null) {
                            if (kmap.isLocallyDefined(k)) {
                                result.keymap = kmap;
                                return result;
                            }
                            kmap = kmap.getResolveParent();
                        }
```

```
                    // Look for default action
                    if (k.getKeyEventType() == KeyEvent.KEY_TYPED) {
                        // Check local keymap
                        kmap = tc.getKeymap();
                        if (kmap.getDefaultAction() != null) {
                            result.keymap = kmap;
                            result.defaultAction = kmap.getDefaultAction();
                            result.isLocal = true;
                            return result;
                        }

                        // Check parent keymaps
                        kmap = kmap.getResolveParent();
                        while (kmap != null) {
                            if (kmap.getDefaultAction() != null) {
                                result.keymap = kmap;
                                result.defaultAction = kmap.getDefaultAction();
                                return result;
                            }
                            kmap = kmap.getResolveParent();
                        }
                    }
                }
            }
        return null;
    }

    public static FindResult find(KeyStroke k, InputMap map) {
        // Check local inputmap
        KeyStroke[] keys = map.keys();
        for (int i=0; keys != null && i<keys.length; i++) {
            if (k.equals(keys[i])) {
                FindResult result = new FindResult();
                result.inputMap = map;
                result.isLocal = true;
                return result;
            }
        }

        // Check parent inputmap
        map = map.getParent();
        while (map != null) {
            keys = map.keys();
            for (int i=0; keys != null && i<keys.length; i++) {
                if (k.equals(keys[i])) {
                    FindResult result = new FindResult();
                    result.inputMap = map;
                    return result;
                }
            }
            map = map.getParent();
        }
        return null;
    }
```

ε863. Adding an InputMap to a Component

```
InputMap inputMap = new InputMap();

// Add a KeyStroke
inputMap.put(KeyStroke.getKeyStroke("F2"), "actionName");

inputMap.setParent(component.getInputMap(JComponent.WHEN_FOCUSED));
component.setInputMap(JComponent.WHEN_FOCUSED, inputMap);
```

The Screen

ε864. Capturing a Screen Shot

See also "ε670. Converting a Buffered Image to an Image".

```
try {
    Robot robot = new Robot();

    // Capture a particular area on the screen
    int x = 100;
    int y = 100;
    int width = 200;
    int height = 200;
    Rectangle area = new Rectangle(x, y, width, height);
    BufferedImage bufferedImage = robot.createScreenCapture(area);

    // Capture the whole screen
    area = new Rectangle(Toolkit.getDefaultToolkit().getScreenSize());
    bufferedImage = robot.createScreenCapture(area);
} catch (AWTException e) {
}
```

ε865. Converting Between Component and Screen Coordinates

This example demonstrates how to convert a coordinate within a component to a coordinate on the screen and visa versa.

```
// Convert a coordinate relative to a component's bounds to screen coordinates
Point pt = new Point(component.getLocation());
SwingUtilities.convertPointToScreen(pt, component);

// Convert a coordinate on a screen to a coordinate relative to a component's bounds
SwingUtilities.convertPointFromScreen(pt, component);
```

Look and Feel

ε866. Determining the Available Look and Feels

```
UIManager.LookAndFeelInfo[] info = UIManager.getInstalledLookAndFeels();
for (int i=0; i<info.length; i++) {
    // Get the name of the look and feel that is suitable for display to the user
    String humanReadableName = info[i].getName();

    String className = info[i].getClassName();
    // The className is used with UIManager.setLookAndFeel()
```

Class *Interface* —extends - - -implements   O abstract   ● final   ˆ—has superclass   ˌ—has subclass   package—see other volume

```
    // See "ε867. Getting and Setting a Look and Feel"
}
```

ε867. Getting and Setting a Look and Feel

To change the look and feel, you need to know the class name of the new look and feel. This example installs the Windows look and feel. See also "ε866. Determining the Available Look and Feels".

```
// Get the currently installed look and feel
LookAndFeel lf = UIManager.getLookAndFeel();

// Install a different look and feel; specifically, the Windows look and feel
try {
    UIManager.setLookAndFeel("com.sun.java.swing.plaf.windows.WindowsLookAndFeel");
} catch (InstantiationException e) {
} catch (ClassNotFoundException e) {
} catch (UnsupportedLookAndFeelException e) {
} catch (IllegalAccessException e) {
}
```

ε868. Getting and Setting a Native Look and Feel

By default, Swing uses a cross-platform look and feel called *Metal*. In most cases, it is more desirable to use a look and feel that is closer to the platform on which the application is being run. This example demonstrates how to retrieve and install the look and feel that most closely resembles the current platform.

```
// Get the native look and feel class name
String nativeLF = UIManager.getSystemLookAndFeelClassName();

// Install the look and feel
try {
    UIManager.setLookAndFeel(nativeLF);
} catch (InstantiationException e) {
} catch (ClassNotFoundException e) {
} catch (UnsupportedLookAndFeelException e) {
} catch (IllegalAccessException e) {
}
```

It is also possible to retrieve the cross-platform look and feel:

```
String javaLF = UIManager.getCrossPlatformLookAndFeelClassName();
```

ε869. Setting the Default Look and Feel Using a System Property or Property File

By default, Swing uses a cross-platform look and feel called *Metal*. This default can be changed with a system property on the command line, an entry in a properties file, or programmatically (see "ε867. Getting and Setting a Look and Feel").

The following example demonstrates how to set the look and feel using a system property on the command line:

```
> java -Dswing.defaultlaf=com.sun.java.swing.plaf.windows.WindowsLookAndFeel MyApp
```

Alternatively, the default look and feel can be set in a properties file called 'swing.properties' located in the '<JAVAHOME>/lib' directory. The name of the property is swing.defaultlaf.

```
# Specify the default look and feel
swing.defaultlaf=com.sun.java.swing.plaf.windows.WindowsLookAndFeel
```

Packages and Examples

UI Default Values

ε870. Getting the Default Values for a Look and Feel

This example demonstrates how to retrieve all the default values for the current look and feel.

```
// Get the currently installed look and feel
UIDefaults uidefs = UIManager.getLookAndFeelDefaults();

// Retrieve the keys. Can't use an iterator since the map
// may be modified during the iteration. So retrieve all at once.
String[] keys = (String[])uidefs.keySet().toArray(new String[0]);

for (int i=0; i<keys.length; i++) {
    Object v = uidefs.get(keys[i]);

    if (v instanceof Integer) {
        int intVal = uidefs.getInt(keys[i]);
    } else if (v instanceof Boolean) {
        boolean boolVal = uidefs.getBoolean(keys[i]);
    } else if (v instanceof String) {
        String strVal = uidefs.getString(keys[i]);
    } else if (v instanceof Dimension) {
        Dimension dimVal = uidefs.getDimension(keys[i]);
    } else if (v instanceof Insets) {
        Insets insetsVal = uidefs.getInsets(keys[i]);
    } else if (v instanceof Color) {
        Color colorVal = uidefs.getColor(keys[i]);
    } else if (v instanceof Font) {
        Font fontVal = uidefs.getFont(keys[i]);
    } else if (v instanceof Border) {
        Border borderVal = uidefs.getBorder(keys[i]);
    } else if (v instanceof Icon) {
        Icon iconVal = uidefs.getIcon(keys[i]);
    } else if (v instanceof javax.swing.text.JTextComponent.KeyBinding[]) {
        javax.swing.text.JTextComponent.KeyBinding[] keyBindsVal =
            (javax.swing.text.JTextComponent.KeyBinding[])uidefs.get(keys[i]);
    } else if (v instanceof InputMap) {
        InputMap imapVal = (InputMap)uidefs.get(keys[i]);
    } else {
        // Unknown type
    }
}
```

ε871. Setting a UI Default Value That Is Created When Fetched

When a UI default value is fairly large and may never be used, the value should be *lazily* created. This means that the value should be created only when the value is fetched. The UIDefaults table allows for such values.

For values that are created every time they are fetched, see "ε872. Setting a UI Default Value That Is Created at Every Fetch".

This example declares a lazy value (a JPanel) that is created only when fetched.

```
// Create a lazy value
Object lazyValue = new UIDefaults.LazyValue() {
```

Class   *Interface*   —extends   - - -implements   ○ abstract   ● final   ˆ—has superclass   ‿—has subclass   package—see other volume

```
    // This method is called once, when the value is fetched.
    // If this method can be called no more than once, it must be synchronized.
    public Object createValue(UIDefaults table) {
        // The returned value will be permanently stored in the UI default table
        return new JPanel();
    }
};

// Add the lazy value to the UI defaults table
UIManager.put("key", lazyValue);

// Fetch the value; this causes the value to be created
Object value = UIManager.get("key");
```

ε872. Setting a UI Default Value That Is Created at Every Fetch

The UIDefaults table supports values that are created every time they are fetched. Such values are called *active* values.

For values that are created only once, see "ε871. Setting a UI Default Value That Is Created When Fetched".

This example declares an active value (a Date) that is created every time it is fetched.

```
// Create an active value
Object activeValue = new UIDefaults.ActiveValue() {
    // This method is called every time the value is fetched.
    // If this method can be called no more than once, it must be synchronized.
    public Object createValue(UIDefaults table) {
        return new Date();
    }
};

// Add the active value to the UI defaults table
UIManager.put("key", activeValue);

// Fetch the value twice; this causes the value to be created twice
Date d1 = (Date)UIManager.get("key");
Date d2 = (Date)UIManager.get("key");
boolean b = d1.equals(d2); // false
```

---

javax.swing.border

This package contains classes and interfaces for drawing specialized borders around a Swing component. You can subclass these classes to create customized borders for your components instead of using the default borders provided by the look-and-feel being used. If you want to create one of the default borders that Swing provides, used java.swing.BorderFactory.

Packages and Examples

```
java.lang.Object
 └ AbstractBorder - - - - - - - - - - - - - - - - - - - - - - - - - - - - - - - - - Border, java.io.Serializable
     ├ BevelBorder
     │  └ SoftBevelBorder
     ├ CompoundBorder
     ├ EmptyBorder - - - - - - - - - - - - - - - - - - - - - - - - - - - - - - - - java.io.Serializable
     │  └ MatteBorder
     ├ EtchedBorder
     ├ LineBorder
     └ TitledBorder

 Border
```

ε873. Creating and Setting a Border

There are several types of borders available, each represented by its own class. A border can be created using the class' constructor or using a border factory. The border factory is the typical method for creating a border since it creates the border using values that are compatible with the current look and feel. However, if custom values are required, the border should be created using a constructor.

This example creates one of each of the available borders. See also "ε874. Adding a Title to a Border".

```
// Create a border
EmptyBorder emptyBorder = (EmptyBorder)BorderFactory.createEmptyBorder();

LineBorder lineBorder = (LineBorder)BorderFactory.createLineBorder(Color.black);

EtchedBorder etchedBorder = (EtchedBorder)BorderFactory.createEtchedBorder();

BevelBorder raisedBevelBorder = (BevelBorder)BorderFactory.createRaisedBevelBorder();

BevelBorder loweredBevelBorder = (BevelBorder)BorderFactory.createLoweredBevelBorder();

ImageIcon icon = new ImageIcon("image.gif");
MatteBorder matteBorder = (MatteBorder)BorderFactory.createMatteBorder(-1, -1, -1, -1, icon);


// Set the border
component.setBorder(emptyBorder);
```

ε874. Adding a Title to a Border

```
// Use default border
TitledBorder titledBorder = BorderFactory.createTitledBorder("Title");

// Create the title around existing border
titledBorder = BorderFactory.createTitledBorder(border, "Title");

// Also available: DEFAULT_JUSTIFICATION, LEFT, RIGHT
titledBorder.setTitleJustification(TitledBorder.CENTER);
```

Class   *Interface*   —extends   - - -implements   ○ abstract   ● final   ^—has superclass   ˅—has subclass   package —see other volume

```
// Also available: DEFAULT_POSITION, ABOVE_TOP, TOP,
// ABOVE_BOTTOM, BOTTOM, BELOW_BOTTOM
titledBorder.setTitlePosition(TitledBorder.BELOW_TOP);

component.setBorder(titledBorder);
```

ε875. Creating a Compound Border

```
// border1 is around border2
Border newBorder = BorderFactory.createCompoundBorder(border1, border2);
component.setBorder(newBorder);
```

javax.swing.colorchooser

This package contains classes and interfaces used by the JColorChooser component.

```
     java.lang.Object
1.2    ├ ColorChooserComponentFactory
1.2    ├ DefaultColorSelectionModel - - - - - - - - - - - - - - - - - - - - - ColorSelectionModel, java.io.Serializable
   ○   └ java.awt.Component - - - - - - - - - - - - - - - - - - - - - java.awt.MenuContainer, java.awt.image
                                                                         .ImageObserver, java.io.Serializable
         └ java.awt.Container
1.2 ○       └ javax.swing.JComponent - - - - - - - - - - - - - - - - - - java.io.Serializable
1.2            └ javax.swing.JPanel - - - - - - - - - - - - - - - - - - - javax.accessibility.Accessible
1.2 ○             └ AbstractColorChooserPanel

1.2    ColorSelectionModel
```

ε876. Creating a JColorChooser Dialog

The following example creates a temporary color chooser dialog and shows it:

```
Color initialColor = Color.red;

// Show the dialog; this method does not return until the dialog is closed
Color newColor = JColorChooser.showDialog(frame, "Dialog Title", initialColor);
```

Here is a more elaborate example that defines an action that creates and shows a color chooser dialog. This action can be used in components such as a button or a menu item.

```
// This action creates and shows a modeless color chooser dialog.
public class ShowColorChooserAction extends AbstractAction {
    JColorChooser chooser;
    JDialog dialog;

    ShowColorChooserAction(JFrame frame, JColorChooser chooser) {
        super("Color Chooser...");
        this.chooser = chooser;
```

Packages and Examples

```
            // Choose whether dialog is modal or modeless
            boolean modal = false;

            // Create the dialog that contains the chooser
            dialog = JColorChooser.createDialog(frame, "Dialog Title", modal,
                chooser, null, null);
        }
        public void actionPerformed(ActionEvent evt) {
            // Show dialog
            dialog.setVisible(true);

            // Disable the action; to enable the action when the dialog is closed, see
            // "ε884. Listening for OK and Cancel Events in a JColorChooser Dialog"
            setEnabled(false);
        }
    };
```

Here's some code that demonstrates the use of the action:

```
    JFrame frame = new JFrame();

    // Create a color chooser dialog
    Color initialColor = Color.white;
    JColorChooser chooser = new JColorChooser(initialColor);

    // Create a button using the action
    JButton button = new JButton(new ShowColorChooserAction(frame, chooser));
```

ε877. Getting and Setting the Selected Color in a JColorChooser Dialog

Normally, the color is retrieved from a color chooser dialog when the dialog is closed. See "ε884. Listening for OK and Cancel Events in a JColorChooser Dialog" for an example of how to determine when the dialog is closed.

```
    // Create the chooser
    JColorChooser chooser = new JColorChooser();

    // Set the selected color
    chooser.setColor(Color.red);

    // Create and show dialog.
    // See "ε876. Creating a JColorChooser Dialog".

    // Get current selected color
    Color color = chooser.getColor();
```

Preview Panel

ε878. Customizing the Preview Panel of a JColorChooser Dialog

The preview panel shows the selected color in a particular context. The default preview panel colors some text with the selected color.

It may be desirable to change the preview panel to a more relevant setting. For example, if the color chooser is used to color an image, a miniature version of the image can be shown in the preview panel.

```
    JColorChooser chooser = new JColorChooser();
    chooser.setPreviewPanel(new MyPreviewPanel(chooser));
```

Class   *Interface*   —extends   - - -implements   O abstract   ● final   ^—has superclass   ‿—has subclass   package—see other volume

```
// This preview panel simply displays the currently selected color.
public class MyPreviewPanel extends JComponent {
    // The currently selected color
    Color curColor;

    public MyPreviewPanel(JColorChooser chooser) {
        // Initialize the currently selected color
        curColor = chooser.getColor();

        // Add listener on model to detect changes to selected color
        ColorSelectionModel model = chooser.getSelectionModel();
        model.addChangeListener(new ChangeListener() {
            public void stateChanged(ChangeEvent evt) {
                ColorSelectionModel model = (ColorSelectionModel)evt.getSource();

                // Get the new color value
                curColor = model.getSelectedColor();
            }
        }) ;
        // Set a preferred size
        setPreferredSize(new Dimension(50, 50));
    }
    // Paint current color
    public void paint(Graphics g) {
        g.setColor(curColor);
        g.fillRect(0, 0, getWidth()-1, getHeight()-1);
    }
}
```

ε879. Removing the Preview Panel from a JColorChooser Dialog

The preview panel can be removed by setting a do-nothing component.

```
JColorChooser chooser = new JColorChooser();
chooser.setPreviewPanel(new JPanel());

// This preview panel simply displays the currently selected color.
public class MyPreviewPanel extends JComponent {
    // The currently selected color
    Color curColor;

    public MyPreviewPanel(JColorChooser chooser) {
        // Initialize the currently selected color
        curColor = chooser.getColor();

        // Add listener on model to detect changes to selected color
        ColorSelectionModel model = chooser.getSelectionModel();
        model.addChangeListener(new ChangeListener() {
            public void stateChanged(ChangeEvent evt) {
                ColorSelectionModel model = (ColorSelectionModel)evt.getSource();

                // Get the new color value
                curColor = model.getSelectedColor();
            }
        }) ;
        // Set a preferred size
        setPreferredSize(new Dimension(50, 50));
    }
```

Packages and Examples

261

```
            // Paint current color
            public void paint(Graphics g) {
                g.setColor(curColor);
                g.fillRect(0, 0, getWidth()-1, getHeight()-1);
            }
        }
```

Color Chooser Panel

ε880. Retrieving the Color Chooser Panels in a JColorChooser Dialog

There are three chooser panels in the default JColorChooser dialog. Although each is implemented by a class in the javax.swing.colorchooser package, these classes are not public. This example demonstrates how to identify these panels by class name.

```
JColorChooser chooser = new JColorChooser();

// Retrieve the swatch chooser
findPanel(chooser, "javax.swing.colorchooser.DefaultSwatchChooserPanel");

// Retrieve the HSB chooser
findPanel(chooser, "javax.swing.colorchooser.DefaultHSBChooserPanel");

// Retrieve the RGB chooser
findPanel(chooser, "javax.swing.colorchooser.DefaultRGBChooserPanel");

// Returns the panel instance with the specified name.
// Returns null if not found.
public AbstractColorChooserPanel findPanel(JColorChooser chooser, String name) {
    AbstractColorChooserPanel[] panels = chooser.getChooserPanels();

    for (int i=0; i<panels.length; i++) {
        String clsName = panels[i].getClass().getName();

        if (clsName.equals(name)) {
            return panels[i];
        }
    }
    return null;
}
```

ε881. Removing a Color Chooser Panel from a JColorChooser Dialog

Removing chooser panels is simply a matter of removeChooserPanel(). The issue is to identify the panels that are to be kept. There are three chooser panels in the default JColorChooser dialog. Although each is implemented by a class in the javax.swing.colorchooser package, these classes are not public. This example demonstrates how to identify these panels by class name.

```
JColorChooser chooser = new JColorChooser();

// Retrieve the current set of panels
AbstractColorChooserPanel[] oldPanels = chooser.getChooserPanels();

// Remove panels
for (int i=0; i<oldPanels.length; i++) {
    String clsName = oldPanels[i].getClass().getName();
    if (clsName.equals("javax.swing.colorchooser.DefaultSwatchChooserPanel")) {
        // Remove swatch chooser if desired
```

```
                chooser.removeChooserPanel(oldPanels[i]);
        } else if (clsName.equals("javax.swing.colorchooser.DefaultRGBChooserPanel")) {
                // Remove rgb chooser if desired
                chooser.removeChooserPanel(oldPanels[i]);
        } else if (clsName.equals("javax.swing.colorchooser.DefaultHSBChooserPanel")) {
                // Remove hsb chooser if desired
                chooser.removeChooserPanel(oldPanels[i]);
        }
    }

    // This preview pane simply displays the currently selected color.
    public class MyPreviewPane extends JComponent {
        // The currently selected color
        Color curColor;

        public MyPreviewPane(JColorChooser chooser) {
            // Initialize the currently selected color
            curColor = chooser.getColor();

            // Add listener on model to detect changes to selected color
            ColorSelectionModel model = chooser.getSelectionModel();
            model.addChangeListener(new ChangeListener() {
                public void stateChanged(ChangeEvent evt) {
                    ColorSelectionModel model = (ColorSelectionModel)evt.getSource();

                    // Get the new color value
                    curColor = model.getSelectedColor();
                }
            }) ;
            // Set a preferred size
            setPreferredSize(new Dimension(50, 50));
        }
        // Paint current color
        public void paint(Graphics g) {
            g.setColor(curColor);
            g.fillRect(0, 0, getWidth()-1, getHeight()-1);
        }
    }
}
```

ε882. Setting the Order of the Color Chooser Panel Tabs in a JColorChooser Dialog

The default order of chooser panels is: swatch chooser, HSB chooser, and RGB chooser. This example demonstrates how to change the ordering.

```
JColorChooser chooser = new JColorChooser();

// Retrieve the number of panels
int numPanels = chooser.getChooserPanels().length;

// Create an array with the desired order of panels
// findPanel() is defined in
// "ε880. Retrieving the Color Chooser Panels in a JColorChooser Dialog".
AbstractColorChooserPanel[] newPanels = new AbstractColorChooserPanel[numPanels];
newPanels[0] = findPanel(chooser, "javax.swing.colorchooser.DefaultHSBChooserPanel");
newPanels[1] = findPanel(chooser, "javax.swing.colorchooser.DefaultRGBChooserPanel");
newPanels[2] = findPanel(chooser, "javax.swing.colorchooser.DefaultSwatchChooserPanel");
```

Packages and Examples

263

```
                // Set the new order of panels
                chooser.setChooserPanels(newPanels);
```

ε883. Adding a Custom Color Chooser Panel to a JColorChooser Dialog

This example creates a color chooser panel with three colored buttons. Clicking on a button changes the selected color to the color of the button.

```
        JColorChooser chooser = new JColorChooser();
        chooser.addChooserPanel(new MyChooserPanel());

        public class MyChooserPanel extends AbstractColorChooserPanel {
            // These are the methods that must be implemented
            // in order to create a color chooser panel.

            // This is called once to initialize the panel.
            public void buildChooser() {
                setLayout(new GridLayout(0, 3));
                makeAddButton("Red", Color.red);
                makeAddButton("Green", Color.green);
                makeAddButton("Blue", Color.blue);
            }

            // This method is called whenever the user chooses this panel.
            // This method should retrieve the currently selected color.
            public void updateChooser() {
            }

            // This method is called to retrieve the label used
            // in the tab that selects this panel.
            public String getDisplayName() {
                return "MyChooserPanel";
            }

            // This method is currently not used.
            public Icon getSmallDisplayIcon() {
                return null;
            }

            // This method is currently not used.
            public Icon getLargeDisplayIcon() {
                return null;
            }

            // These are helper methods specifically for this example

            // Creates a color button and adds it to this panel.
            private void makeAddButton(String name, Color color) {
                JButton button = new JButton(name);
                button.setBackground(color);
                button.setAction(setColorAction);
                add(button);
            }

            // This action takes the background color of the button
            // and uses it to set the selected color.
            Action setColorAction = new AbstractAction() {
                public void actionPerformed(ActionEvent evt) {
                    JButton button = (JButton)evt.getSource();
```

```
                getColorSelectionModel().setSelectedColor(button.getBackground());
        }
    };

}
```

Events

ε884. Listening for OK and Cancel Events in a JColorChooser Dialog

This example defines an action that creates and shows a color chooser dialog.

```
// Create the chooser
final JColorChooser chooser = new JColorChooser();

// Define listener for ok events
ActionListener okListener = new ActionListener() {
    // Called when user clicks ok
    public void actionPerformed(ActionEvent evt) {
        // Note: The source is an internal button in the dialog
        // and should not be used

        // Get selected color
        Color newColor = chooser.getColor();
    }
};
// Define listener for cancel events
ActionListener cancelListener = new ActionListener() {
    // Called when user clicks cancel
    public void actionPerformed(ActionEvent evt) {
        // Note: The source is an internal button in the dialog
        // and should not be used

        // Note: The original color is not restored.
        // getColor() returns the latest selected color.
        Color newColor = chooser.getColor();
    }
};
// Choose whether dialog is modal or modeless
boolean modal = false;

// Create the dialog that contains the chooser
dialog = JColorChooser.createDialog(null, "Dialog Title", modal,
        chooser, okListener, cancelListener);

// Add listener for clicks to the close-window icon
dialog.addWindowListener(new WindowAdapter() {
    // Called when user clicks the close-window icon.
    // This type of event is usually treated like a cancel.
    public void windowClosing(WindowEvent evt) {
        // Note: The original color is not restored.
        // getColor() returns the latest selected color.
        Color newColor = chooser.getColor();
    }
});
```

Packages and Examples

265

ε885. Listening for Changes to the Selected Color in a JColorChooser Dialog

```
JColorChooser chooser = new JColorChooser();
ColorSelectionModel model = chooser.getSelectionModel();

// Add listener on model to detect changes to selected color
model.addChangeListener(new ChangeListener() {
    public void stateChanged(ChangeEvent evt) {
        ColorSelectionModel model = (ColorSelectionModel)evt.getSource();

        // Get the new color value
        Color newColor = model.getSelectedColor();
    }
});
```

javax.swing.event

This package contains event classes and corresponding event listener interfaces for events fired by Swing components.

Class *Interface* —extends - - -implements ○ abstract ● final ^—has superclass ⌄—has subclass package—see other volume

java.lang.Object

1.2 ● ├ DocumentEvent.EventType

1.2 ├ EventListenerList - *java.io.Serializable*

1.2 ● ├ HyperlinkEvent.EventType

1.2 ○ ├ InternalFrameAdapter - *InternalFrameListener*^

1.2 ○ ├ MouseInputAdapter - *MouseInputListener*^

1.1 ├ java.beans.PropertyChangeSupport - - - - - - - - - - - - - - - - -┐ *java.io.Serializable*

1.2 ● └ SwingPropertyChangeSupport   ┊

1.1 └ java.util.EventObject -┘

1.2 ○ ├ CaretEvent

1.2 ├ ChangeEvent

1.2 ├ HyperlinkEvent

1.2 ├ ListDataEvent

1.2 ├ ListSelectionEvent

Packages and Examples

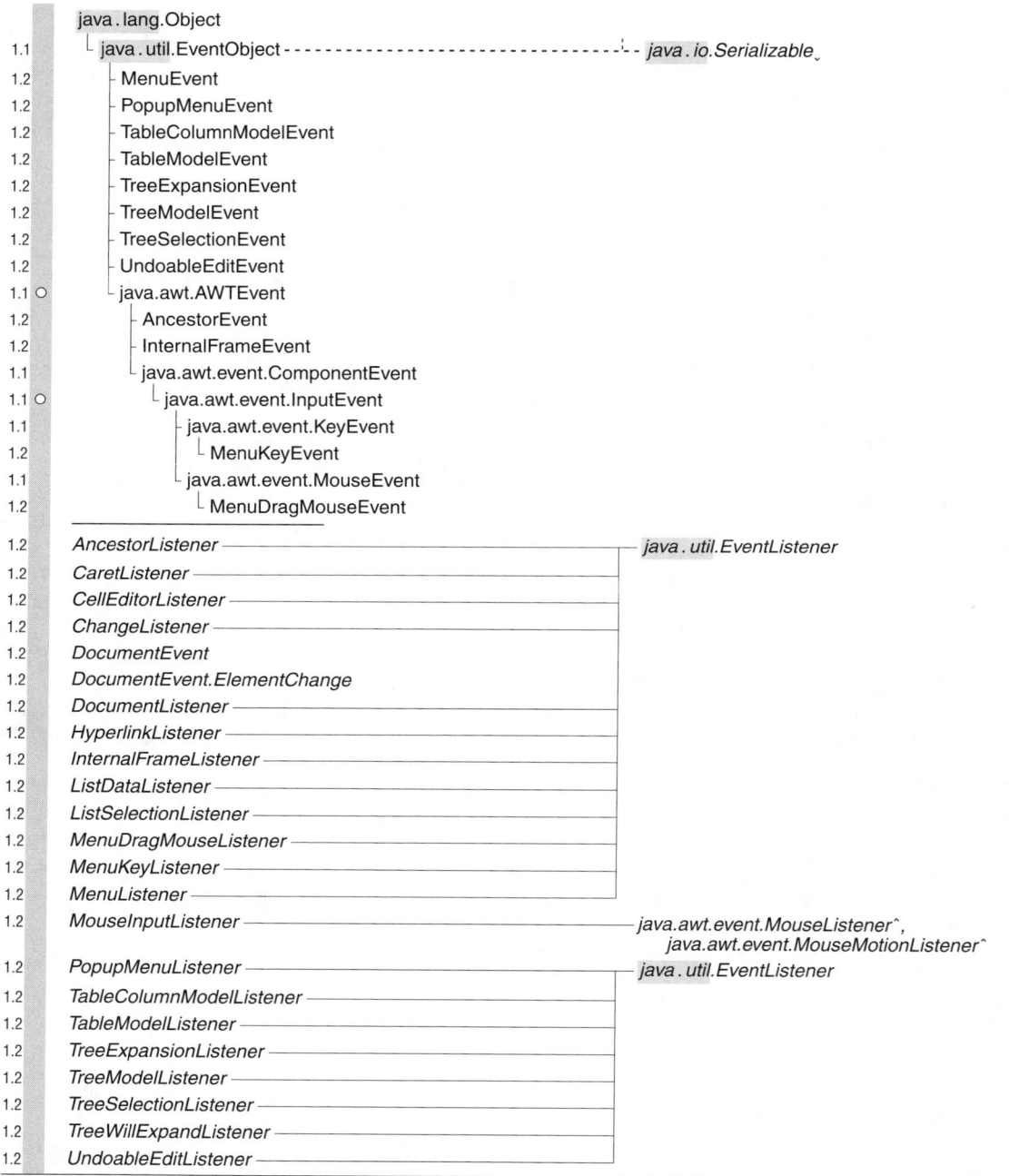

java.lang.Object
1.1 └ java.util.EventObject -'- - java.io.Serializable ⌄
1.2   ├ MenuEvent
1.2   ├ PopupMenuEvent
1.2   ├ TableColumnModelEvent
1.2   ├ TableModelEvent
1.2   ├ TreeExpansionEvent
1.2   ├ TreeModelEvent
1.2   ├ TreeSelectionEvent
1.2   ├ UndoableEditEvent
1.1 ○   └ java.awt.AWTEvent
1.2   ├ AncestorEvent
1.2   ├ InternalFrameEvent
1.1   └ java.awt.event.ComponentEvent
1.1 ○   └ java.awt.event.InputEvent
1.1   ├ java.awt.event.KeyEvent
1.2   │   └ MenuKeyEvent
1.1   └ java.awt.event.MouseEvent
1.2   └ MenuDragMouseEvent

1.2 AncestorListener —————————————————————————————— java.util.EventListener
1.2 CaretListener ——————————————————————————————
1.2 CellEditorListener —————————————————————————————
1.2 ChangeListener —————————————————————————————
1.2 DocumentEvent —————————————————————————————
1.2 DocumentEvent.ElementChange ———————————————————
1.2 DocumentListener —————————————————————————————
1.2 HyperlinkListener —————————————————————————————
1.2 InternalFrameListener ————————————————————————————
1.2 ListDataListener ——————————————————————————————
1.2 ListSelectionListener —————————————————————————————
1.2 MenuDragMouseListener ————————————————————————
1.2 MenuKeyListener —————————————————————————————
1.2 MenuListener ——————————————————————————————
1.2 MouseInputListener ———————————————————————————— java.awt.event.MouseListenerˆ,
                                                                                    java.awt.event.MouseMotionListenerˆ
1.2 PopupMenuListener ———————————————————————————— java.util.EventListener
1.2 TableColumnModelListener ——————————————————————
1.2 TableModelListener ————————————————————————————
1.2 TreeExpansionListener ———————————————————————————
1.2 TreeModelListener —————————————————————————————
1.2 TreeSelectionListener —————————————————————————————
1.2 TreeWillExpandListener ————————————————————————————
1.2 UndoableEditListener ——————————————————————————

ε886. Listening for Hyperlink Events from a JEditorPane Component

Hyperlink events are fired by a JEditorPane when the user clicks on a hyperlink.

```
try {
    String url = "http://java.sun.com";
```

Class   *Interface*   —extends   - - -implements   ○ abstract   ● final   ˆ—has superclass   ⌄—has subclass   package—see other volume

```
        JEditorPane editorPane = new JEditorPane(url);
        editorPane.setEditable(false);
        editorPane.addHyperlinkListener(new MyHyperlinkListener());
    } catch (IOException e) {
    }

    class MyHyperlinkListener implements HyperlinkListener {
        public void hyperlinkUpdate(HyperlinkEvent evt) {
            if (evt.getEventType() == HyperlinkEvent.EventType.ACTIVATED) {
                JEditorPane pane = (JEditorPane)evt.getSource();
                try {
                    // Show the new page in the editor pane.
                    pane.setPage(evt.getURL());
                } catch (IOException e) {
                }
            }
        }
    }
```

javax.swing.filechooser

This package contains classes and interfaces used by the JFileChooser component.

```
            java.lang.Object
1.2 O        ├ FileFilter
1.2 O        ├ FileSystemView
1.2 O        └ FileView
```

ε887. Creating a JFileChooser Dialog

The following example creates a file chooser and displays it as first an open-file dialog and then as a save-file dialog:

```
String filename = File.separator+"tmp";
JFileChooser fc = new JFileChooser(new File(filename));

// Show open dialog; this method does not return until the dialog is closed
fc.showOpenDialog(frame);
File selFile = fc.getSelectedFile();

// Show save dialog; this method does not return until the dialog is closed
fc.showSaveDialog(frame);
selFile = fc.getSelectedFile();
```

Here is a more elaborate example that creates two buttons that create and show file chooser dialogs.

```
// This action creates and shows a modal open-file dialog.
public class OpenFileAction extends AbstractAction {
    JFrame frame;
    JFileChooser chooser;

    OpenFileAction(JFrame frame, JFileChooser chooser) {
```

```
                super("Open...");
                this.chooser = chooser;
                this.frame = frame;
            }

            public void actionPerformed(ActionEvent evt) {
                // Show dialog; this method does not return until dialog is closed
                chooser.showOpenDialog(frame);

                // Get the selected file
                File file = chooser.getSelectedFile();
            }
        };

        // This action creates and shows a modal save-file dialog.
        public class SaveFileAction extends AbstractAction {
            JFileChooser chooser;
            JFrame frame;

            SaveFileAction(JFrame frame, JFileChooser chooser) {
                super("Save As...");
                this.chooser = chooser;
                this.frame = frame;
            }

            public void actionPerformed(ActionEvent evt) {
                // Show dialog; this method does not return until dialog is closed
                chooser.showSaveDialog(frame);

                // Get the selected file
                File file = chooser.getSelectedFile();
            }
        };
```

Here's some code that demonstrates the use of the actions:

```
        JFrame frame = new JFrame();

        // Create a file chooser
        String filename = File.separator+"tmp";
        JFileChooser fc = new JFileChooser(new File(filename));

        // Create the actions
        Action openAction = new OpenFileAction(frame, fc);
        Action saveAction = new SaveFileAction(frame, fc);

        // Create buttons for the actions
        JButton openButton = new JButton(openAction);
        JButton saveButton = new JButton(saveAction);

        // Add the buttons to the frame and show the frame
        frame.getContentPane().add(openButton, BorderLayout.NORTH);
        frame.getContentPane().add(saveButton, BorderLayout.SOUTH);
        frame.pack();
        frame.setVisible(true);
```

ε888. Displaying Only Directories in a File Chooser Dialog

```
        JFileChooser fileChooser = new JFileChooser(file);
        fileChooser.setFileSelectionMode(JFileChooser.DIRECTORIES_ONLY);
```

Class   *Interface*   —extends   - - -implements   ○ abstract   ● final   ^—has superclass   ˌ—has subclass   package—see other volume

ε889. Adding a Filter to a File Chooser Dialog

This example add a filter for .java files to the file chooser.

```
JFileChooser fileChooser = new JFileChooser(new File(filename));
fileChooser.addChoosableFileFilter(new MyFilter());

// Open file dialog.
fileChooser.showOpenDialog(frame);
openFile(fileChooser.getSelectedFile());

class MyFilter extends javax.swing.filechooser.FileFilter {
    public boolean accept(File file) {
        String filename = file.getName();
        return filename.endsWith(".java");
    }
    public String getDescription() {
        return "*.java";
    }
}
```

ε890. Determining If the Approve or Cancel Button Was Clicked in a JFileChooser Dialog

```
JFileChooser chooser = new JFileChooser();

// Show the dialog; wait until dialog is closed
int result = chooser.showOpenDialog(frame);

// Determine which button was clicked to close the dialog
switch (result) {
case JFileChooser.APPROVE_OPTION:
    // Approve (Open or Save) was clicked
    break;
case JFileChooser.CANCEL_OPTION:
    // Cancel or the close-dialog icon was clicked
    break;
case JFileChooser.ERROR_OPTION:
    // The selection process did not complete successfully
    break;
}
```

ε891. Getting and Setting the Current Directory of a JFileChooser Dialog

```
JFileChooser chooser = new JFileChooser();

try {
    // Create a File object containing the canonical path of the
    // desired directory
    File f = new File(new File(".").getCanonicalPath());

    // Set the current directory
    chooser.setCurrentDirectory(f);
} catch (IOException e) {
}

// The following method call sets the current directory to the home directory
chooser.setCurrentDirectory(null);

// Show the dialog; wait until dialog is closed
chooser.showOpenDialog(frame);
```

Packages and Examples

271

```
// Get the current directory
File curDir = chooser.getCurrentDirectory();
```

ε892. Getting and Setting the Selected File of a JFileChooser Dialog

When setting the selected file, the file chooser dialog automatically sets the current directory.

```
JFileChooser chooser = new JFileChooser();

// Set the current directory to the application's current directory
try {
    // Create a File object containing the canonical path of the
    // desired file
    File f = new File(new File("filename.txt").getCanonicalPath());

    // Set the selected file
    chooser.setSelectedFile(f);
} catch (IOException e) {
}

// Show the dialog; wait until dialog is closed
chooser.showOpenDialog(frame);

// Get the currently selected file
File curFile = chooser.getSelectedFile();
```

ε893. Getting the File-Type Name of a File

Files and directories have a type, usually based on their extension. This example retrieves the name of the file type. Examples of file-type names include *Java Source* and *Shortcut*. This name is displayed with the filename in a file chooser dialog.

```
JFileChooser chooser = new JFileChooser();

// Create a File instance of the file
File file = new File("filename.txt");

// Get the file type name
String fileTypeName = chooser.getTypeDescription(file);
// Text Document
```

ε894. Copying the Filename Path from a JFileChooser Dialog to the Clipboard

Typing control-c in a file chooser dialog copies the names of the selected files to the clipboard. If there is only a single selected file, the absolute path of the file is copied to the clipboard. Here is an example:

```
C:\Documents and Settings\Administrator\Start Menu\Programs\Internet Explorer.lnk
```

If there are multiple selected files, the absolute paths of the selected files are wrapped in HTML code and copied to the clipboard. Here is an example of the HTML code:

```
<html><ol>
<li>C:\Documents and Settings\Administrator\Start Menu\Programs\Internet Explorer.lnk
<li>C:\Documents and Settings\Administrator\Start Menu\Programs\MSN Messenger Service.lnk
<li>C:\Documents and Settings\Administrator\Start Menu\Programs\Outlook Express.lnk
<li>C:\Documents and Settings\Administrator\Start Menu\Programs\Windows Media Player.lnk
</ol></html>
```

Selections

ε895. Enabling Multiple Selections in a JFileChooser Dialog

```
JFileChooser chooser = new JFileChooser();

// Enable multiple selections
chooser.setMultiSelectionEnabled(true);

// Show the dialog; wait until dialog is closed
chooser.showOpenDialog(frame);

// Retrieve the selected files. This method returns empty
// if multiple-selection mode is not enabled.
File[] files = chooser.getSelectedFiles();
```

Hidden Files

ε896. Showing Hidden Files in a JFileChooser Dialog

By default, hidden files are not shown in a file chooser dialog.

```
JFileChooser chooser = new JFileChooser();

// By default, hidingEnabled is true
boolean hidingEnabled = chooser.isFileHidingEnabled();

// Display hidden files
chooser.setFileHidingEnabled(false);

// Show the dialog; wait until dialog is closed
chooser.showOpenDialog(frame);
```

ε897. Determining If a File Is Hidden

```
JFileChooser chooser = new JFileChooser();

// Create a File instance of the file
File file = new File("c:\\Program Files");
// (this file is not hidden)

file = new File("c:\\IO.SYS");
// (this file is hidden)

// Check if file is hidden
boolean isHidden = chooser.getFileSystemView().isHiddenFile(file);
```

Layout

ε898. Changing the Text of the Approve Button in a JFileChooser Dialog

The *approve* button is clicked by the user to indicate that the file has been selected. The default label for the approve button is either Open or Save, depending on the dialog type. This label can be changed.

```
JFileChooser chooser = new JFileChooser();

// Set the text
chooser.setApproveButtonText("New Approve Text");

// Set the mnemonic
chooser.setApproveButtonMnemonic('a');
```

Packages and Examples

```
// Set the tool tip
chooser.setApproveButtonToolTipText("New Approve Tool Tip");

// Show the dialog; wait until dialog is closed
chooser.showOpenDialog(frame);
```

ε899. Setting an Accessory Component in a JFileChooser Dialog

The *accessory* is an optional component that can be added to a file chooser dialog to show a preview image of the selected file. By default, a file chooser dialog does not have an accessory installed. This example demonstrates how to install an accessory component.

```
JFileChooser chooser = new JFileChooser();

// Create and set the accessory
chooser.setAccessory(new MyAccessory(chooser));

// Show the dialog; wait until dialog is closed
chooser.showOpenDialog(frame);

public class MyAccessory extends JComponent implements PropertyChangeListener {
    public MyAccessory(JFileChooser chooser) {
        // Listen for changes to the selected file
        chooser.addPropertyChangeListener(this);

        // Set a preferred size
        setPreferredSize(new Dimension(50, 50));
    }

    // This listener listens for changes to the selected file
    public void propertyChange(PropertyChangeEvent evt) {
        if (JFileChooser.SELECTED_FILE_CHANGED_PROPERTY.equals(
                evt.getPropertyName())) {
            JFileChooser chooser = (JFileChooser)evt.getSource();

            // Get the new selected file
            File newFile = (File)evt.getNewValue();

            // Prepare the preview data based on the new selected file

            // Repaint this component
            repaint();
        }
    }
    public void paint(Graphics g) {
        // Paint a preview of the selected file
    }
}
```

ε900. Displaying the Current Directory in the Title of a JFileChooser Dialog

This example displays the complete path of the current directory in the title whenever the current directory changes.

```
final JFileChooser chooser = new JFileChooser();

// Initialize title with current directory
File curDir = chooser.getCurrentDirectory();
chooser.setDialogTitle(""+curDir.getAbsolutePath());
```

Class   *Interface*   —extends   - - -implements   ○ abstract   ● final   ^—has superclass   ⌐—has subclass   package—see other volume

```
// Add listener on chooser to detect changes to current directory
chooser.addPropertyChangeListener(new PropertyChangeListener() {
    public void propertyChange(PropertyChangeEvent evt) {
        if (JFileChooser.DIRECTORY_CHANGED_PROPERTY.equals(evt.getPropertyName())) {
            File curDir = chooser.getCurrentDirectory();

            chooser.setDialogTitle(""+curDir.getAbsolutePath());
        }
    }
}) ;
```

Icons

ε901. Getting the File-Type Icon of a File

The icon displayed next to directories and filenames in a file chooser dialog can be retrieved and used in other applications.

```
JFileChooser chooser = new JFileChooser();

// Create a File instance of the file
File file = new File("filename.txt");

// Get the icon
Icon icon = chooser.getIcon(file);

// Some sample code to display the icon in a window
JLabel label = new JLabel(""+file);
label.setIcon(icon);
JFrame frame = new JFrame();
frame.getContentPane().add(label, BorderLayout.CENTER);
frame.pack();
frame.setVisible(true);
```

ε902. Getting the Large File-Type Icon of a File

This example uses an unsupported class—sun.awt.shell.ShellFolder—and therefore will not work in all virtual machines.

```
// Create a File instance of the file
File file = new File("filename.txt");

try {
    sun.awt.shell.ShellFolder sf = sun.awt.shell.ShellFolder.getShellFolder(file);

    // Get large icon
    Icon icon = new ImageIcon(sf.getIcon(true), sf.getFolderType());
} catch (FileNotFoundException e) {
}
```

Events

ε903. Listening for Changes to the Selected File in a JFileChooser Dialog

A property change event is fired whenever the selected file is changed. However, the selected file can be null if the selected item does not match the selection mode of the chooser. For example, if the selection mode is JFileChooser.FILES_ONLY and a directory is selected, the fired event will have a new value of null.

Packages and Examples

Note: SELECTED_FILE_CHANGED_PROPERTY events are fired only if a single item is selected. In particular, if multiple items are selected while multiple-selection mode is enabled, this event is not fired. But if a single item is selected while in multiple-selection mode, this event is fired.

When in multiple-selection mode, SELECTED_FILES_CHANGED_PROPERTY events are always fired regardless of whether a single or multiple files have been selected.

```
JFileChooser chooser = new JFileChooser();

// Add listener on chooser to detect changes to selected file
chooser.addPropertyChangeListener(new PropertyChangeListener() {
    public void propertyChange(PropertyChangeEvent evt) {
        if (JFileChooser.SELECTED_FILE_CHANGED_PROPERTY
                .equals(evt.getPropertyName())) {
            JFileChooser chooser = (JFileChooser)evt.getSource();
            File oldFile = (File)evt.getOldValue();
            File newFile = (File)evt.getNewValue();

            // The selected file should always be the same as newFile
            File curFile = chooser.getSelectedFile();
        } else if (JFileChooser.SELECTED_FILES_CHANGED_PROPERTY.equals(
                evt.getPropertyName())) {
            JFileChooser chooser = (JFileChooser)evt.getSource();
            File[] oldFiles = (File[])evt.getOldValue();
            File[] newFiles = (File[])evt.getNewValue();

            // Get list of selected files
            // The selected files should always be the same as newFiles
            File[] files = chooser.getSelectedFiles();
        }
    }
}) ;
```

ε904. Listening for Changes to the Current Directory in a JFileChooser Dialog

```
final JFileChooser chooser = new JFileChooser();

// Add listener on chooser to detect changes to current directory
chooser.addPropertyChangeListener(new PropertyChangeListener() {
    public void propertyChange(PropertyChangeEvent evt) {
        if (JFileChooser.DIRECTORY_CHANGED_PROPERTY.equals(evt.getPropertyName())) {
            JFileChooser chooser = (JFileChooser)evt.getSource();
            File oldDir = (File)evt.getOldValue();
            File newDir = (File)evt.getNewValue();

            // The current directory should always be the same as newDir
            File curDir = chooser.getCurrentDirectory();
        }
    }
}) ;
```

ε905. Listening for Approve and Cancel Events in a JFileChooser Dialog

When the user clicks on the approve button (Open or Save) or the Cancel button, an action event is fired.

Unfortunately, if the user clicks on the close-dialog icon in the title bar, an event is not fired. In order to listen for this event, it is necessary to add a window event listener to the dialog. This means that JFileChooser₂

.showDialog() cannot be used because it creates the dialog internally. The workaround is to override the createDialog() method to make it public and then call it to create the dialog.

With this deficiency, we recommend that you simply wait until showDialog() returns and then use its return value. See "ε890. Determining If the Approve or Cancel Button Was Clicked in a JFileChooser Dialog" for more information.

```
// Create customized chooser
MyFileChooser chooser = new MyFileChooser();

// Set dialog type if not OPEN_DIALOG
chooser.setDialogType(JFileChooser.SAVE_DIALOG);

// Create dialog containing the chooser
final JDialog dialog = chooser.createDialog(frame);

// Add listener for approve and cancel events
chooser.addActionListener(new AbstractAction() {
    public void actionPerformed(ActionEvent evt) {
        JFileChooser chooser = (JFileChooser)evt.getSource();
        if (JFileChooser.APPROVE_SELECTION.equals(evt.getActionCommand())) {
            // Open or Save was clicked

            // Hide dialog
            dialog.setVisible(false);
        } else if (JFileChooser.CANCEL_SELECTION.equals(evt.getActionCommand())) {
            // Cancel was clicked

            // Hide dialog
            dialog.setVisible(false);
        }
    }
});

// Add listener for window closing events
dialog.addWindowListener(new WindowAdapter() {
    public void windowClosing(WindowEvent e) {
        // Close-dialog icon was clicked

        // Hide dialog
        dialog.setVisible(false);
    }
});

// Show the dialog; wait until dialog is closed
dialog.show();

// This version of JFileChooser simply makes createDialog a public method.
public class MyFileChooser extends JFileChooser {
    public JDialog createDialog(Component parent) throws HeadlessException {
        return super.createDialog(parent);
    }
}
```

javax.swing.plaf

This package contains one interface and many abstract classes that Swing uses to provide its pluggable look-and-feel capabilities. Its classes are subclassed and implemented by look-and-feel UIs like Basic and

Metal. This package is used only by look-and-feel developers who cannot create a new look-and-feel by subclassing existing look-and-feel components.

Class *Interface* —extends - - -implements O abstract ● final ^ has superclass — has subclass package—see other volume

java.lang.Object	

1.2 ├ BorderUIResource - *UIResource, java.io.Serializable,*
                                                                                  javax.swing.border.Border

1.2 ○ ├ ComponentUI
1.2 ○ │ ├ ButtonUI
1.2 ○ │ │ └ MenuItemUI
1.2 ○ │ ├ ColorChooserUI
1.2 ○ │ ├ ComboBoxUI
1.2 ○ │ ├ DesktopIconUI
1.2 ○ │ ├ DesktopPaneUI
1.2 ○ │ ├ FileChooserUI
1.2 ○ │ ├ InternalFrameUI
1.2 ○ │ ├ LabelUI
1.2 ○ │ ├ ListUI
1.2 ○ │ ├ MenuBarUI
1.2 ○ │ ├ OptionPaneUI
1.2 ○ │ ├ PanelUI
1.2 ○ │ ├ PopupMenuUI
1.2 ○ │ ├ ProgressBarUI
1.3 ○ │ ├ RootPaneUI
1.2 ○ │ ├ ScrollBarUI
1.2 ○ │ ├ ScrollPaneUI
1.2 ○ │ ├ SeparatorUI
1.2 ○ │ ├ SliderUI
1.4 ○ │ ├ SpinnerUI
1.2 ○ │ ├ SplitPaneUI
1.2 ○ │ ├ TabbedPaneUI
1.2 ○ │ ├ TableHeaderUI
1.2 ○ │ ├ TableUI
1.2 ○ │ ├ TextUI
1.2 ○ │ ├ ToolBarUI
1.2 ○ │ ├ ToolTipUI
1.2 ○ │ ├ TreeUI
1.2 ○ │ └ ViewportUI
1.2 ├ IconUIResource - *UIResource, java.io.Serializable,*
                                                                     javax.swing.Icon
├ java.awt.Color - *java.awt.Paint, java.io.Serializable*
1.2 │ └ ColorUIResource - *UIResource*
├ java.awt.Font - *java.io.Serializable*
1.2 │ └ FontUIResource - *UIResource*

Packages and Examples

```
        java.lang.Object
          ├ java.awt.Insets -------------------------------------- java.io.Serializable, java.lang.Cloneable
1.2       │    └ InsetsUIResource ------------------------------- UIResource
1.2  ○    ├ java.awt.geom.Dimension2D --------------------------- java.lang.Cloneable
          │    └ java.awt.Dimension -------------------------------- java.io.Serializable
1.2       │        └ DimensionUIResource ---------------------- UIResource
1.3       ├ javax.swing.ActionMap------------------------------- java.io.Serializable
1.3       │    └ ActionMapUIResource -------------------------- UIResource
1.3       ├ javax.swing.InputMap-------------------------------- java.io.Serializable
1.3       ├ InputMapUIResource ---------------------------------- UIResource
1.3       └ javax.swing.ComponentInputMap
1.3            └ ComponentInputMapUIResource -----------------
1.2  ○    └ javax.swing.border.AbstractBorder -------------------- java.io.Serializable, javax.swing.border.Border
1.2       ├ javax.swing.border.BevelBorder
1.2       │    └ BorderUIResource.BevelBorderUIResource ----------- UIResource
1.2       ├ javax.swing.border.CompoundBorder
1.2       │    └ BorderUIResource.CompoundBorderUIResource -----
1.2       ├ javax.swing.border.EmptyBorder --------------------- java.io.Serializable
1.2       ├ BorderUIResource.EmptyBorderUIResource ----------- UIResource
1.2       │ javax.swing.border.MatteBorder
1.2       │    └ BorderUIResource.MatteBorderUIResource -------
1.2       ├ javax.swing.border.EtchedBorder
1.2       │    └ BorderUIResource.EtchedBorderUIResource --------
1.2       ├ javax.swing.border.LineBorder
1.2       │    └ BorderUIResource.LineBorderUIResource -----------
1.2       └ javax.swing.border.TitledBorder
1.2            └ BorderUIResource.TitledBorderUIResource ---------

1.2    UIResource
```

javax.swing.table

This package contains classes and interfaces for dealing with javax.swing.JTable. You use these classes and interfaces if you want control over how tables are constructed, updated, and rendered, as well as how data associated with the tables are viewed and managed.

Class *Interface* —extends - - -implements ○ abstract ● final ˆ—has superclass ˌ—has subclass package—see other volume

```
java.lang.Object
1.2 O  ├ AbstractTableModel - - - - - - - - - - - - - - - - - - - - - - - - - - - - - - TableModel, java.io.Serializable
1.2    │  └ DefaultTableModel - - - - - - - - - - - - - - - - - - - - - - - - - - - - - - java.io.Serializable
1.2    ├ DefaultTableColumnModel - - - - - - - - - - - - - - - - - - - - - - - - - - - TableColumnModel, java.beans
                                                                    .PropertyChangeListener^,
                                                                    java.io.Serializable, javax.swing.event
                                                                    .ListSelectionListener^
1.2    ├ TableColumn - - - - - - - - - - - - - - - - - - - - - - - - - - - - - - - - - java.io.Serializable
   O   ├ java.awt.Component - - - - - - - - - - - - - - - - - - - - - - - - - - - - - java.awt.MenuContainer, java.awt.image
                                                                    .ImageObserver, java.io.Serializable
       │  └ java.awt.Container
1.2 O  │     └ javax.swing.JComponent - - - - - - - - - - - - - - - - - - - - - - - - java.io.Serializable
1.2    │        ├ JTableHeader - - - - - - - - - - - - - - - - - - - - - - - - - - - - javax.accessibility.Accessible,
                                                                    javax.swing.event.TableColumnModelListener^
1.2    │        └ javax.swing.JLabel - - - - - - - - - - - - - - - - - - - - - - - - - javax.accessibility.Accessible,
                                                                    javax.swing.SwingConstants
1.2    │           └ DefaultTableCellRenderer - - - - - - - - - - - - - - - - - - - TableCellRenderer, java.io.Serializable
1.2    │              └ DefaultTableCellRenderer.UIResource - - - - - - - - - javax.swing.plaf.UIResource
1.2 O  └ javax.accessibility.AccessibleContext
1.2       ├ JTableHeader.AccessibleJTableHeader - - - - - - - - - - - - - - - - javax.accessibility.Accessible,
             .AccessibleJTableHeaderEntry                                       javax.accessibility.AccessibleComponent
1.3 O     └ java.awt.Component.AccessibleAWTComponent - - - - - - - - - - java.io.Serializable, javax.accessibility
                                                                    .AccessibleComponent
1.3          └ java.awt.Container.AccessibleAWTContainer
1.2 O           └ javax.swing.JComponent.AccessibleJComponent - - - - - javax.accessibility
                                                                    .AccessibleExtendedComponent^
1.2                └ JTableHeader.AccessibleJTableHeader

1.2  TableCellEditor ─────────────────────────────── javax.swing.CellEditor
1.2  TableCellRenderer
1.2  TableColumnModel
1.2  TableModel
```

Packages and Examples

ε906. Creating a JTable Component

The following creates a table that uses an efficient underlying storage implementation. Although cell values can be changed, rows and columns cannot be added or deleted.

```
// Create with initial data
Object[][] cellData = {
    {"row1-col1", "row1-col2"},
    {"row2-col1", "row2-col2"}};
String[] columnNames = {"col1", "col2"};
```

```
JTable table = new JTable(cellData, columnNames);
```

The following creates tables that allow rows and columns to be added or deleted:

```
// Create a table with empty cells
int rows = 10;
int cols = 5;
table = new JTable(rows, cols);

// Create a table with initial data
Vector rowData = new Vector();
for (int i=0; i<cellData.length; i++) {
    Vector colData = new Vector(Arrays.asList(cellData[i]));
    rowData.add(colData);
}
Vector columnNamesV = new Vector(Arrays.asList(columnNames));

table = new JTable(rowData, columnNamesV);
```

Rows

ε907. Getting the Number of Rows and Columns in a JTable Component

```
int rows = table.getRowCount();
int cols = table.getColumnCount();
```

ε908. Appending a Row to a JTable Component

To add a row of data to a JTable component, you need to add it to its table model. A simple implementation of a table model that supports appending row data is DefaultTableModel. By default, a table uses a DefaultTableModel.

```
DefaultTableModel model = new DefaultTableModel();
JTable table = new JTable(model);

// Create a couple of columns
model.addColumn("Col1");
model.addColumn("Col2");

// Append a row
model.addRow(new Object[]{"v1", "v2"});
// there are now 2 rows with 2 columns

// Append a row with fewer values than columns.
// The left-most fields in the new row are populated
// with the supplied values (left-to-right) and fields
// without values are set to null.
model.addRow(new Object[]{"v1"});
// there are now 3 rows with 2 columns

// Append a row with more values than columns.
// The extra values are ignored.
model.addRow(new Object[]{"v1", "v2", "v3"});
// there are now 4 rows with 2 columns
```

ε909. Inserting a Row in a JTable Component

To insert a row of data to a JTable component, you need to insert it to its table model. A simple implementation of a table model that supports the insertion of row data is DefaultTableModel.

When inserting a row using DefaultTableModel.insertRow(), the position of the new row must be specified. Positions are locations between rows. For example, if there are 2 rows in a table, there are 3 possible positions—0, 1,and 2. Inserting a row at position 0 makes the new row the first row. Inserting a row at position 2 makes the new row the last row.

When inserting a row with fewer values than columns, the left-most fields in the new row are populated with the supplied values (left-to-right) and the fields without values are set to null. When inserting a row with more values than columns, the extra values are ignored.

```
DefaultTableModel model = new DefaultTableModel();
JTable table = new JTable(model);

// Create a couple of columns
model.addColumn("Col1");
model.addColumn("Col2");

// Create the first row
model.insertRow(0, new Object[]{"r1"});

// Insert a row so that it becomes the first row
model.insertRow(0, new Object[]{"r2"});

// Insert a row at position p
int p = 2;
model.insertRow(p, new Object[]{"r3"});

// Insert a row before the second row
int r = 1;
model.insertRow(r, new Object[]{"r4"});
// the new row is now the second row

// Insert a row after the second row
r = 1;
model.insertRow(r+1, new Object[]{"r5"});
// the new row is now the third row

// Append a row
model.insertRow(model.getRowCount(), new Object[]{"r5"});
```

ε910. Removing a Row from a JTable Component

To remove a row of data from a JTable component, you need to remove it from its table model. A simple implementation of a table model that supports the removal of row data is DefaultTableModel.

When removing a row using DefaultTableModel.removeRow(), the index of the row must be specified. Row indices start from 0. For example, if there are 2 rows in a table, the index of the first row is 0 and the index of the second row is 1. Removing a row at index 0 removes the first row.

```
DefaultTableModel model = new DefaultTableModel();
JTable table = new JTable(model);

// Create some data
model.addColumn("Col1");
model.addRow(new Object[]{"r1"});
model.addRow(new Object[]{"r2"});
model.addRow(new Object[]{"r3"});
```

```
// Remove the first row
model.removeRow(0);
```

```
// Remove the last row
model.removeRow(model.getRowCount()-1);
```

ε911. Moving a Row in a JTable Component

To move a row of data to a JTable component, you need to move it in its table model. A simple implementation of a table model that supports the moving of row data is DefaultTableModel.

When moving one or more rows using DefaultTableModel.moveRow(), the set of the rows to be moved and the destination position must be specified. The contiguous set of rows to be moved is specified with the index of the starting row and the index of the end row. Row indices start from 0. For example, if there are 2 rows in a table, the index of the first row is 0 and the index of the second row is 1.

The destination is also a position. Positions are locations between rows. For example, if there are 2 rows in a table, there are 3 possible positions—0, 1,and 2. The important thing to remember about the destination position is that it specifies the position in the row data *after* the rows to be moved are taken out of the row data. For example, if you want to move the first row to the end of the table, the destination position is not getRowCount(), it is getRowCount()-1. Similarly, if you want to move the first 2 lines to the end of the table, the destination position is getRowCount()-2.

The way in which the parameters are interpreted is somewhat awkward. The more conventional method is to either make the end index exclusive (like String.substring()) or replace end with a length. Also, it is easier to specify the destination as it exists before the operation, and not have to pretend that the rows to be moved are taken out. A version of moveRow() with more conventional parameter interpretation is provided in betterMoveRow().

```
DefaultTableModel model = new DefaultTableModel();
JTable table = new JTable(model);

// Create some data
model.addColumn("Col1");
model.addRow(new Object[]{"r1"});
model.addRow(new Object[]{"r2"});
model.addRow(new Object[]{"r3"});

// Move the first row to the end of the table
model.moveRow(0, 0, model.getRowCount()-1);
betterMoveRow(model, 0, 1, model.getRowCount());

// Move the last row to the beginning of the table
model.moveRow(model.getRowCount()-1, model.getRowCount()-1, 0);
betterMoveRow(model, model.getRowCount()-1, model.getRowCount(), 0);

// Move the first two rows to the end of the table
model.moveRow(0, 1, model.getRowCount()-2);
betterMoveRow(model, 0, 2, model.getRowCount());

// Move the last two rows to the start of the table
model.moveRow(model.getRowCount()-2, model.getRowCount()-1, 0);
betterMoveRow(model, model.getRowCount()-2, model.getRowCount(), 0);

// A better version of moveRow().
// Moves all rows contained between the positions start and end
// to the position specified by dest.
public static void betterMoveRow(DefaultTableModel model, int start, int end, int dest) {
```

Class   *Interface*   —extends   - - -implements   ○ abstract   ● final   ^—has superclass   ⌄—has subclass   package—see other volume

```
        int count = end - start;
        if (count <= 0) {
            return;
        }
        if (dest > start) {
            dest = Math.max(start, dest-count);
        }
        end–;
        model.moveRow(start, end, dest);
    }
```

ε912. Copying a Row or Column in a JTable Component

This example demonstrates how to copy a column or row of data in a DefaultTableModel.

```
DefaultTableModel model = new DefaultTableModel();
JTable table = new JTable(model);

// Create some data

// Get all the table data
Vector data = model.getDataVector();

// Copy the second row
Vector row = (Vector)data.elementAt(1);
row = (Vector)row.clone();

// Overwrite the first row with the copy
Vector firstRow = (Vector)data.elementAt(0);
for (int i=0; i<row.size(); i++) {
    firstRow.set(i, row.get(i));
}

// Append the copy to the end of the table.
// Note that a copy is NOT made of 'row'.
model.addRow(row);


// Copy the first column
int mColIndex = 0;
java.util.List colData = new ArrayList(table.getRowCount());
for (int i=0; i<table.getRowCount(); i++) {
    row = (Vector)data.elementAt(i);
    colData.add(row.get(mColIndex));
}
// Copy it to the second column
for (int i=0; i<colData.size(); i++) {
    row = (Vector)data.elementAt(i);
    row.set(1, colData.get(i));
}
// Append a new column with copied data
model.addColumn("Col3", colData.toArray());
```

ε913. Setting the Height of a Row in a JTable Component

The height of a row in a JTable component is based on an assigned value rather than on the preferred height of the renderers used in that row. You can either set a default height for all rows or set the heights for individual rows.

This example demonstrates a few routines that can be used to adjust the height of rows in applications where the row heights can vary.

```
int rows = 10;
int cols = 5;
JTable table = new JTable(rows, cols);

// Set the 1st row to 60 pixels high
table.setRowHeight(0, 60);

// Set the height of all rows to 32 pixels high,
// regardless if any heights were assigned to particular rows
table.setRowHeight(32);
// the height of the 1st row is set to 32 pixels high

// Returns the preferred height of a row.
// The result is equal to the tallest cell in the row.
public int getPreferredRowHeight(JTable table, int rowIndex, int margin) {
    // Get the current default height for all rows
    int height = table.getRowHeight();

    // Determine highest cell in the row
    for (int c=0; c<table.getColumnCount(); c++) {
        TableCellRenderer renderer = table.getCellRenderer(rowIndex, c);
        Component comp = table.prepareRenderer(renderer, rowIndex, c);
        int h = comp.getPreferredSize().height + 2*margin;
        height = Math.max(height, h);
    }
    return height;
}

// The height of each row is set to the preferred height of the
// tallest cell in that row.
public void packRows(JTable table, int margin) {
    packRows(table, 0, table.getRowCount(), margin);
}

// For each row >= start and < end, the height of a
// row is set to the preferred height of the tallest cell
// in that row.
public void packRows(JTable table, int start, int end, int margin) {
    for (int r=0; r<table.getRowCount(); r++) {
        // Get the preferred height
        int h = getPreferredRowHeight(table, r, margin);

        // Now set the row height using the preferred height
        if (table.getRowHeight(r) != h) {
            table.setRowHeight(r, h);
        }
    }
}
```

ε914. Shading Rows and Columns in a JTable Component

The simplest way of shading alternate rows or columns in a JTable component is to override the prepareRenderer() method. The table calls this method for every cell, just prior to displaying it. The override should call the

---

Class   *Interface*   —extends   - - -implements   ○ abstract   ● final   ˆ—has superclass   ˌ—has subclass   package—see other volume

superclass and retrieve the prepared component. It can then modify the background and foreground colors to achieve any desired pattern of shaded rows and columns.

```
// This table shades every other row yellow
JTable table = new JTable() {
    public Component prepareRenderer(TableCellRenderer renderer,
                                     int rowIndex, int vColIndex) {
        Component c = super.prepareRenderer(renderer, rowIndex, vColIndex);
        if (rowIndex % 2 == 0 && !isCellSelected(rowIndex, vColIndex)) {
            c.setBackground(Color.yellow);
        } else {
            // If not shaded, match the table's background
            c.setBackground(getBackground());
        }
        return c;
    }
};
// This table shades every other column yellow
table = new JTable() {
    public Component prepareRenderer(TableCellRenderer renderer,
                                     int rowIndex, int vColIndex) {
        Component c = super.prepareRenderer(renderer, rowIndex, vColIndex);
        if (vColIndex % 2 == 0 && !isCellSelected(rowIndex, vColIndex)) {
            c.setBackground(Color.yellow);
        } else {
            // If not shaded, match the table's background
            c.setBackground(getBackground());
        }
        return c;
    }
};
```

Columns

ε915. Converting a Column Index Between the View and Model in a JTable Component

A column in a JTable component has two types of indices, a visible index and a model index. The visible index of a column is its visible location on the screen. The model index of a column is its permanent position in a TableModel, which contains the actual data. This example demonstrates how to convert a column index between the two forms.

```
// Converts a visible column index to a column index in the model.
// Returns -1 if the index does not exist.
public int toModel(JTable table, int vColIndex) {
    if (vColIndex >= table.getColumnCount()) {
        return -1;
    }
    return table.getColumnModel().getColumn(vColIndex).getModelIndex();
}

// Converts a column index in the model to a visible column index.
// Returns -1 if the index does not exist.
public int toView(JTable table, int mColIndex) {
    for (int c=0; c<table.getColumnCount(); c++) {
        TableColumn col = table.getColumnModel().getColumn(c);
```

```
              if (col.getModelIndex() == mColIndex) {
                  return c;
              }
          }
          return -1;
      }
```

ε916. Enumerating the Columns in a JTable Component

Column information such as the name of a column and the cell renderer are kept in ρ TableColumn object. The values in a column are not kept in a TableColumn object; they are kept in a TableModel object. There is one TableColumn object for each visible column. All the TableColumn objects in a JTable are maintained by a single TableColumnModel object kept by the JTable component.

This example demonstrates how to enumerate TableColumn objects in both model order (order of creation) and view order (modifiable by the user).

Note: The number of columns in a TableModel can be greater than the number of TableColumns. The reason is that if you remove a column from a JTable (or TableColumnModel), you are only removing the visual representation of the column; the column of data still exists in the TableModel.

```
// Returns the visible columns in the order that they appear in the model
public TableColumn[] getColumnsInModel(JTable table) {
    java.util.List result = new ArrayList();
    Enumeration enum = table.getColumnModel().getColumns();
    for (; enum.hasMoreElements(); ) {
        result.add((TableColumn)enum.nextElement());
    }

    // Sort the columns based on the model index
    Collections.sort(result, new Comparator() {
        public int compare(Object a, Object b) {
            TableColumn c1 = (TableColumn)a;
            TableColumn c2 = (TableColumn)b;
            if (c1.getModelIndex() < c2.getModelIndex()) {
                return -1;
            } else if (c1.getModelIndex() == c2.getModelIndex()) {
                return 0;
            } else {
                return 1;
            }
        }
    });
    return (TableColumn[])result.toArray(new TableColumn[result.size()]);
}

// Returns the columns in the order that they appear in the view
public TableColumn[] getColumnsInView(JTable table) {
    TableColumn[] result = new TableColumn[table.getColumnCount()];

    // Use an enumeration
    Enumeration enum = table.getColumnModel().getColumns();
    for (int i=0; enum.hasMoreElements(); i++) {
        result[i] = (TableColumn)enum.nextElement();
    }

    // Use a for loop
```

```
        for (int c=0; c<table.getColumnCount(); c++) {
            result[c] = table.getColumnModel().getColumn(c);
        }
        return result;
    }

    // Returns the TableColumn associated with the specified column
    // index in the model
    public TableColumn findTableColumn(JTable table, int columnModelIndex) {
        Enumeration enum = table.getColumnModel().getColumns();
        for (; enum.hasMoreElements(); ) {
            TableColumn col = (TableColumn)enum.nextElement();
            if (col.getModelIndex() == columnModelIndex) {
                return col;
            }
        }
        return null;
    }
```

ε917. Setting the Width of a Column in a JTable Component

By default, the column widths of all columns are equal. In order for column width adjustments to be made, autoResizeMode must be disabled.

```
int rows = 3;
int cols = 3;
JTable table = new JTable(rows, cols);

// Disable auto resizing
table.setAutoResizeMode(JTable.AUTO_RESIZE_OFF);

// Set the first visible column to 100 pixels wide
int vColIndex = 0;
TableColumn col = table.getColumnModel().getColumn(vColIndex);
int width = 100;
col.setPreferredWidth(width);
```

ε918. Setting the Column Resize Mode of a JTable Component

Resizing the width of a column can affect the widths of the other columns in the table. There are several resizing modes available. The default is AUTO_RESIZE_SUBSEQUENT_COLUMNS.

```
// Disable auto resizing
table.setAutoResizeMode(JTable.AUTO_RESIZE_OFF);

// When the width of a column is changed,
// the width of the right-most column is changed
// so that the width of the entire table does not change
table.setAutoResizeMode(JTable.AUTO_RESIZE_LAST_COLUMN);

// When the width of a column is changed,
// all columns to the right are resized so that the width
// of the entire table does not change
table.setAutoResizeMode(JTable.AUTO_RESIZE_SUBSEQUENT_COLUMNS);

// When the width of a column is changed,
// only the columns to the left and right of the
// margin change
table.setAutoResizeMode(JTable.AUTO_RESIZE_NEXT_COLUMN);
```

Packages and Examples

```
// When the width of a column is changed,
// the widths of all columns are changed
// so that the width of the entire table does not change
table.setAutoResizeMode(JTable.AUTO_RESIZE_ALL_COLUMNS);
```

ε919. Locking the Width of a Column in a JTable Component

This example demonstrates how to set the width of a column and prevent it from being resized by the user.

```
int rows = 3;
int cols = 3;
JTable table = new JTable(rows, cols);

// Add data here

// Lock the second column of the table to be 100 pixels wide
int vColIndex = 1;
int width = 100;
TableColumn col = table.getColumnModel().getColumn(vColIndex);
col.setMinWidth(width);
col.setMaxWidth(width);
col.setPreferredWidth(width);
```

ε920. Appending a Column to a JTable Component

To add a column to a JTable component, the component must use a table model that supports this operation. A simple implementation of such a table model is DefaultTableModel.

The simplest way to add a column to a JTable component using a DefaultTableModel table model is to call DefaultTableModel.addColumn(). You need only supply the name and data for the new column and a new visible column will appear in the table. However, this method of column creation is not suitable after existing columns have undergone customizations or after the user has made adjustments to the existing columns. All customizations and adjustments are lost after the new column is added. For example, if you've installed a special renderer on one of the columns or if the user has moved a column, all these changes will be lost when the new column is added. In fact, if you remove a column (but did not remove the column data), the column will reappear after the new column is added.

This example provides a routine that will add a column without affecting the state of the existing columns. In order for the routine to work, the autoCreateColumnsFromModel property must be set to false. This property causes the table component to rebuild all the columns when a column is added to the table model. When set to false, the table component will no longer add a visible column when a column is added to the table model. This step must now be done explicitly.

```
DefaultTableModel model = new DefaultTableModel();
JTable table = new JTable(model);

// Add a column using the simple method
model.addColumn("Col1");

// Add a column with values.
// The list of values are appended to the end of the
// existing rows. However, if there are more column values
// than there are rows, new rows with null values are
// created to accommodate the extra column values.
model.addColumn("Col2", new Object[]{"v2"});
// there is now 1 row with 2 columns
```

```
// Disable autoCreateColumnsFromModel
table.setAutoCreateColumnsFromModel(false);

// Add a column without affecting existing columns
betterAddColumn(table, "Col3", new Object[]{"v3"});

// This method adds a new column to table without reconstructing
// all the other columns.
public void betterAddColumn(JTable table, Object headerLabel,
                            Object[] values) {
    DefaultTableModel model = (DefaultTableModel)table.getModel();
    TableColumn col = new TableColumn(model.getColumnCount());

    // Ensure that auto-create is off
    if (table.getAutoCreateColumnsFromModel()) {
        throw new IllegalStateException();
    }
    col.setHeaderValue(headerLabel);
    table.addColumn(col);
    model.addColumn(headerLabel.toString(), values);
}
```

ε921. Inserting a Column in a JTable Component

There is no insertColumn method like DefaultTableModel.insertRow() for inserting rows. In order to insert a column at a particular position, you must append the column using DefaultTable.addColumn() and then move the new column into the desired position.

See "ε920. Appending a Column to a JTable Component" and "ε923. Moving a Column in a JTable Component" for more information.

```
int rows = 10;
int cols = 5;
JTable table = new JTable(rows, cols);

// Disable autoCreateColumnsFromModel
table.setAutoCreateColumnsFromModel(false);

// Add data

// Insert a new column at position 2 (becomes 3rd column)
insertColumn(table, "New Column", null, 2);

// Insert a new column at the end
insertColumn(table, "New Column", null, table.getColumnCount());

// Creates a new column at position vColIndex
public void insertColumn(JTable table, Object headerLabel,
                         Object[] values, int vColIndex) {
    // This method is defined in
    // "ε920. Appending a Column to a JTable Component"
    betterAddColumn(table, headerLabel, values);

    table.moveColumn(table.getColumnCount()-1, vColIndex);
}
```

ε922. Removing a Column from a JTable Component

To remove a column to a JTable component, the component must use a table model that supports this operation. A simple implementation of such a table model is DefaultTableModel.

DefaultTableModel.removeColumn() removes the visible column, but leaves the column data in the table model. This example provides a routine that removes both the visible column and the column data.

```
DefaultTableModel model = new MyDefaultTableModel();
JTable table = new JTable(model);
table.setModel(model);

// Create 3 columns
model.addColumn("Col1");
model.addColumn("Col2");
model.addColumn("Col3");
model.addRow(new Object[]{"v1"});

// Remove the first visible column without removing the underlying data
table.removeColumn(table.getColumnModel().getColumn(0));

// Disable autoCreateColumnsFromModel to prevent
// the reappearance of columns that have been removed but
// whose data is still in the table model
table.setAutoCreateColumnsFromModel(false);

// Remove the first visible column and its data
removeColumnAndData(table, 0);

// Remove the last visible column and its data
removeColumnAndData(table, table.getColumnCount()-1);

// Removes the specified column from the table and the associated
// call data from the table model.
public void removeColumnAndData(JTable table, int vColIndex) {
    MyDefaultTableModel model = (MyDefaultTableModel)table.getModel();
    TableColumn col = table.getColumnModel().getColumn(vColIndex);
    int columnModelIndex = col.getModelIndex();
    Vector data = model.getDataVector();
    Vector colIds = model.getColumnIdentifiers();

    // Remove the column from the table
    table.removeColumn(col);

    // Remove the column header from the table model
    colIds.removeElementAt(columnModelIndex);

    // Remove the column data
    for (int r=0; r<data.size(); r++) {
        Vector row = (Vector)data.get(r);
        row.removeElementAt(columnModelIndex);
    }
    model.setDataVector(data, colIds);

    // Correct the model indices in the TableColumn objects
    // by decrementing those indices that follow the deleted column
    Enumeration enum = table.getColumnModel().getColumns();
    for (; enum.hasMoreElements(); ) {
        TableColumn c = (TableColumn)enum.nextElement();
        if (c.getModelIndex() >= columnModelIndex) {
            c.setModelIndex(c.getModelIndex()-1);
        }
    }
    model.fireTableStructureChanged();
```

Class   *Interface*   —extends   - - -implements   O abstract   ● final   ^—has superclass   ⌐—has subclass   package—see other volume

```
    }
    // This subclass adds a method to retrieve the columnIdentifiers
    // which is needed to implement the removal of
    // column data from the table model
    class MyDefaultTableModel extends DefaultTableModel {
        public Vector getColumnIdentifiers() {
            return columnIdentifiers;
        }
    }
}
```

ε923. Moving a Column in a JTable Component

Moving a column requires the index of the column to be moved and a position specified. The index of a column is 0-based; the first column has index 0. Positions are locations between columns. For example, if there are 2 columns in a table, there are 3 possible position—0, 1,and 2. Moving a column to position 0 makes the column the first column. Moving a column to position 2 makes the column the last column.

```
int rows = 10;
int cols = 5;
JTable table = new JTable(rows, cols);

// Move the last visible column so it becomes the first visible column
int vSrcColIndex = table.getColumnCount()-1;
int vDstColIndex = 0;
table.moveColumn(vSrcColIndex, vDstColIndex);
```

ε924. Allowing the User to Move a Column in a JTable Component

By default, a table allows the user to reorder its columns. This example demonstrates how to disable this feature.

```
int rows = 3;
int cols = 3;
JTable table = new JTable(rows, cols);

table.getTableHeader().setReorderingAllowed(false);

// Programmatically moving a column is still possible
table.moveColumn(table.getColumnCount()-1, 0);
// the last column is moved to the first position
```

ε925. Allowing the User to Resize a Column in a JTable Component

By default, a table allows the user to size its columns. This example demonstrates how to disable this feature.

```
int rows = 3;
int cols = 3;
JTable table = new JTable(rows, cols);

table.getTableHeader().setResizingAllowed(false);
```

Cells

ε926. Getting and Setting a Cell Value in a JTable Component

```
// Retrieve the value in the visible cell (1,2)
int rowIndex = 1;
int vColIndex = 2;
```

```
Object o = table.getValueAt(rowIndex, vColIndex);

// Retrieve the value in cell (1,2) from the model
rowIndex = 1;
int mColIndex = 2;
o = table.getModel().getValueAt(rowIndex, mColIndex);

// Change a cell in the 2nd visible column
rowIndex = 2;
vColIndex = 1;
table.setValueAt("New Value", rowIndex, vColIndex);

// Change a cell in the 3rd column in the model
rowIndex = 3;
mColIndex = 2;
table.getModel().setValueAt("New Value", rowIndex, mColIndex);
```

ε927. Using Built-In Cell Renderers and Editors in a JTable Component

There are built-in cell renderers and editors available for seven types: Boolean, Date, Double, Float, Icon, Number, and Object. By default every column uses the Object cell renderer and editor, regardless of the column data type. There are two typical ways to force a column to use a particular cell renderer and editor.

The first way is to have the table model's getColumnClass() method return the Class object for the column data type. Typically, this method is overridden to return the Class object of the first cell in that column. The Class object is then used to fetch the appropriate cell renderer and editor.

The second way is to find the TableColumn associated with the column data in the table model and explicitly set a cell renderer and editor. This method must be used if two columns have different cell renderers yet their data type is the same.

```
DefaultTableModel model = new DefaultTableModel() {
    // This method returns the Class object of the first
    // cell in specified column in the table model.
    // Unless this method is overridden, all values are
    // assumed to be the type Object.
    public Class getColumnClass(int columnIndex) {
        Object o = getValueAt(0, columnIndex);
        if (o == null) {
            return Object.class;
        } else {
            return o.getClass();
        }
    }
};
JTable table = new JTable(model);

// Add a column for each of the available renderers
model.addColumn("Boolean", new Object[]{Boolean.TRUE});
model.addColumn("Date", new Object[]{new Date()});
model.addColumn("Double", new Object[]{new Double(Math.PI)});
model.addColumn("Float", new Object[]{new Float(1.2)});
model.addColumn("Icon", new Object[]{new ImageIcon("icon.gif")});
model.addColumn("Number", new Object[]{new Integer(1)});
model.addColumn("Object", new Object[]{"object"});

// Explicitly set the Boolean cell renderer and editor on the
```

```
// TableColumn showing the first column in the table model
int mColIndex = 0;
findTableColumn(table, mColIndex).setCellRenderer(table.getDefaultRenderer(Boolean.class));
findTableColumn(table, mColIndex).setCellEditor(table.getDefaultEditor(Boolean.class));

// Returns the TableColumn associated with the specified column
// index in the model
public TableColumn findTableColumn(JTable table, int columnModelIndex) {
    Enumeration enum = table.getColumnModel().getColumns();
    for (; enum.hasMoreElements(); ) {
        TableColumn col = (TableColumn)enum.nextElement();
        if (col.getModelIndex() == columnModelIndex) {
            return col;
        }
    }
    return null;
}
```

ε928. Creating a Custom Cell Renderer in a JTable Component

A table cell renderer needs to implement a single method, TableCellRenderer.getTableCellRendererComponent() that returns a component. For performance reasons, the renderer should not create a new component each time getTableCellRendererComponent() is called. Rather, it should return the same component (or one from a set) every time. Typically, the renderer can either hold onto a component instance and return that component or it can be a subclass of a component and return itself.

The job of getTableCellRendererComponent() is to configure the component based on the coordinates and value in the cell. The table then uses the configured component and paints it on the screen. After painting it, the table no longer needs the component.

```
JTable table = new JTable();
// Add data...

// Install the custom renderer on the first visible column
int vColIndex = 0;
TableColumn col = table.getColumnModel().getColumn(vColIndex);
col.setCellRenderer(new MyTableCellRenderer());

// This renderer extends a component. It is used each time a
// cell must be displayed.
public class MyTableCellRenderer extends JLabel implements TableCellRenderer {
    // This method is called each time a cell in a column
    // using this renderer needs to be rendered.
    public Component getTableCellRendererComponent(JTable table, Object value,
            boolean isSelected, boolean hasFocus, int rowIndex, int vColIndex) {
        // 'value' is value contained in the cell located at
        // (rowIndex, vColIndex)

        if (isSelected) {
            // cell (and perhaps other cells) are selected
        }

        if (hasFocus) {
            // this cell is the anchor and the table has the focus
        }

        // Configure the component with the specified value
        setText(value.toString());
```

```
                    // Set tool tip if desired
                    setToolTipText((String)value);

                    // Since the renderer is a component, return itself
                    return this;
                }

                // The following methods override the defaults for performance reasons
                public void validate() {}
                public void revalidate() {}
                protected void firePropertyChange(String propertyName, Object oldValue, Object newValue) {}
                public void firePropertyChange(String propertyName, boolean oldValue, boolean newValue) {}
            }
```

ε929. Creating a Class-Based Custom Cell Renderer in a JTable Component

See "ε928. Creating a Custom Cell Renderer in a JTable Component" for information on how to implement a custom table cell renderer.

There are two ways to associate a custom table cell renderer with a column. The first is to explicitly assign the renderer to the column; the example cited above demonstrates this method. The second is to associate the renderer with a type; this example demonstrates this method. The example installs a renderer for values of the type Color.

```
DefaultTableModel model = new DefaultTableModel() {
    // This method returns the Class object of the first
    // cell in specified column in the table model.
    // Unless this method is overridden, all values are
    // assumed to be the type Object.
    public Class getColumnClass(int mColIndex) {
        int rowIndex = 0;
        Object o = getValueAt(rowIndex, mColIndex);
        if (o == null) {
            return Object.class;
        } else {
            return o.getClass();
        }
    }
};
JTable table = new JTable(model);

// Add data
model.addColumn("Col1", new Object[]{Color.red});
model.addRow(new Object[]{Color.green});
model.addRow(new Object[]{Color.blue});

table.setDefaultRenderer(Color.class, new ColorTableCellRenderer());

public class ColorTableCellRenderer extends JComponent implements TableCellRenderer {
    // The current color to display
    Color curColor;

    public Component getTableCellRendererComponent(JTable table, Object value,
            boolean isSelected, boolean hasFocus, int rowIndex, int vColIndex) {
        // Set the color to paint
        if (curColor instanceof Color) {
            curColor = (Color)value;
```

```
        } else {
            // If color unknown, use table's background
            curColor = table.getBackground();
        }
        return this;
    }
    // Paint current color
    public void paint(Graphics g) {
        g.setColor(curColor);
        g.fillRect(0, 0, getWidth()-1, getHeight()-1);
    }
}
```

ε930. Copying Cell Values to the Clipboard from a JTable Component

Given the cell values in the example code below, typing control-c in a table component while all cells have been selected causes the following text to be copied to the clipboard. In particular, the cell values are formatted as an HTML table.

Note: Control-c only works if the selected cells do not contain a null value.

```
<html>
<table>
<tr>
<th id=0>A
<th id=1>B
<th id=2>C
<tr id=0>
<td>A1
<td>B1
<td>C1
<tr id=1>
<td>A2
<td>B2
<td>C2
<tr id=2>
<td>A3
<td>B3
<td>C3
</table>
</html>
```

Here is the example code with initial cell values.

```
JTable table = new JTable();

// Add data
DefaultTableModel model = (DefaultTableModel)table.getModel();
model.addColumn("A");
model.addColumn("B");
model.addColumn("C");
model.addRow(new Object[]{"A1", "B1", "C1"});
model.addRow(new Object[]{"A2", "B2", "C2"});
model.addRow(new Object[]{"A3", "B3", "C3"});
```

Column Heads

ε931. Showing the Table Header in a Non-Scrollable JTable Component

By default, if you don't place a table component in a scroll pane, the table header is not shown. You need to explicitly display it.

```
int rows = 10;
int cols = 5;
JTable table = new JTable(rows, cols);
JTableHeader header = table.getTableHeader();

container.setLayout(new BorderLayout());

// Add header in NORTH slot
container.add(header, BorderLayout.NORTH);

// Add table itself to CENTER slot
container.add(table, BorderLayout.CENTER);
```

ε932. Changing the Name of a Column in a JTable Component

```
DefaultTableModel model = new DefaultTableModel();
JTable table = new JTable(model);

// Create 2 columns
model.addColumn("Col1");
model.addColumn("Col2");

// Change name of first visible column
int vColIndex = 0;
table.getColumnModel().getColumn(vColIndex).setHeaderValue("New Name");

// Force the header to resize and repaint itself
table.getTableHeader().resizeAndRepaint();
```

ε933. Displaying an Icon in a Column Head of a JTable Component

Although the default renderer for a table header is a JLabel, the default renderer will only display text. This example demonstrates how to install a custom renderer that can display text as well as icons.

```
DefaultTableModel model = new DefaultTableModel();
JTable table = new JTable(model);

// Create 2 columns
model.addColumn("Col1");
model.addColumn("Col2");
// the header value for this column will be overwritten
// with a TextandIcon object

// Set the icon renderer on the second column
table.getTableHeader().getColumnModel()
    .getColumn(1).setHeaderRenderer(iconHeaderRenderer);

// Set the text and icon values on the second column for the icon render
table.getColumnModel().getColumn(1).setHeaderValue(
    new TextAndIcon("Col2", new ImageIcon("icon.gif")));

// This class is used to hold the text and icon values
// used by the renderer that renders both text and icons
```

```
class TextAndIcon {
    TextAndIcon(String text, Icon icon) {
        this.text = text;
        this.icon = icon;
    }
    String text;
    Icon icon;
}

// This customized renderer can render objects of the type TextandIcon
TableCellRenderer iconHeaderRenderer = new DefaultTableCellRenderer() {
    public Component getTableCellRendererComponent(JTable table, Object value,
            boolean isSelected, boolean hasFocus, int row, int column) {
        // Inherit the colors and font from the header component
        if (table != null) {
            JTableHeader header = table.getTableHeader();
            if (header != null) {
                setForeground(header.getForeground());
                setBackground(header.getBackground());
                setFont(header.getFont());
            }
        }

        if (value instanceof TextAndIcon) {
            setIcon(((TextAndIcon)value).icon);
            setText(((TextAndIcon)value).text);
        } else {
            setText((value == null) ? "" : value.toString());
            setIcon(null);
        }
        setBorder(UIManager.getBorder("TableHeader.cellBorder"));
        setHorizontalAlignment(JLabel.CENTER);
        return this;
    }
};
```

ε934. Implementing Variable-Height Column Headers in a JTable Component

The default table header renderer for a table is assumed to render all column heads with the same preferred height. If you install a default header renderer that breaks this assumption, your column heads may not be rendered correctly. In particular, the height of the entire header is made just high enough to satisfy the first column head. If the preferred height of any other column head is higher, that column will not be given enough area to display its contents properly.

Here is how the height of the header is determined. Check the first visible column for an installed header renderer. If one exists, it is used to compute a height. Otherwise, the default header renderer is used to compute a height. Now check every other column for a header renderer and if one exists, use it to compute a height. The final height is the maximum of all computed heights.

Therefore, if a column other than the first lacks a header renderer and produces a taller height with the default header renderer, it will never be computed and so won't be given the correct height. The solution to this problem is to assign a header renderer to the column to ensure that a height is computed for that column, even if the renderer is identical to the default header renderer.

This example implements a header renderer that can display either text or an icon, depending on what is set in the column header value. Since the height of a column head with an icon depends on the height of the icon, this icon renderer is set on all columns with icons.

```
DefaultTableModel model = new DefaultTableModel();
JTable table = new JTable(model);

// Create 2 columns
model.addColumn("Col1");
model.addColumn("Icon Here");
// the header value for this column will be overwritten
// with an Icon object. There is no point supplying the
// Icon object in the addColumn() call because it will be
// converted to a string.

// Now set the second column with an Icon as the column header value
int vColIndex = 1;
table.getColumnModel().getColumn(vColIndex).setHeaderValue(
    new ImageIcon("image.gif"));

// Finally, set the icon header renderer on the second column
table.getColumnModel().getColumn(vColIndex)
    .setHeaderRenderer(iconHeaderRenderer);

// Use this renderer for table headers that contain icons
TableCellRenderer iconHeaderRenderer = new DefaultTableCellRenderer() {
    public Component getTableCellRendererComponent(JTable table, Object value,
            boolean isSelected, boolean hasFocus, int row, int column) {
        // Inherit the colors and font from the header component
        if (table != null) {
            JTableHeader header = table.getTableHeader();
            if (header != null) {
                setForeground(header.getForeground());
                setBackground(header.getBackground());
                setFont(header.getFont());
            }
        }

        if (value instanceof Icon) {
            // Value is an Icon
            setIcon((Icon)value);
            setText("");
        } else {
            // Value is text
            setText((value == null) ? "" : value.toString());
            setIcon(null);
        }
        setBorder(UIManager.getBorder("TableHeader.cellBorder"));
        setHorizontalAlignment(JLabel.CENTER);
        return this;
    }
};
```

Class   *Interface*   —extends   - - -implements   ○ abstract   ● final   ^—has superclass   ⌐—has subclass   package—see other volume

ε935. Removing the Column Headers from a Scrollable in a JTable Component

```
JTable table = new JTable();

// Remove the column headers
table.setTableHeader(null);
```

ε936. Creating a Custom Column Header Renderer in a JTable Component

The default column header renderer simply display a single line of text. If you need to display something other than this, you will need to build and install your own column header renderer. This example defines a generic renderer and installs it on a column.

See "ε928. Creating a Custom Cell Renderer in a JTable Component" for more information about renderers.

```
JTable table = new JTable();
// Add data...

// Install the custom header renderer on the first visible column
int vColIndex = 0;
TableColumn col = table.getColumnModel().getColumn(vColIndex);
col.setHeaderRenderer(new MyTableHeaderRenderer());


public class MyTableHeaderRenderer extends JLabel implements TableCellRenderer {
    // This method is called each time a column header
    // using this renderer needs to be rendered.
    public Component getTableCellRendererComponent(JTable table, Object value,
            boolean isSelected, boolean hasFocus, int rowIndex, int vColIndex) {
        // 'value' is column header value of column 'vColIndex'
        // rowIndex is always -1
        // isSelected is always false
        // hasFocus is always false

        // Configure the component with the specified value
        setText(value.toString());

        // Set tool tip if desired
        setToolTipText((String)value);

        // Since the renderer is a component, return itself
        return this;
    }

    // The following methods override the defaults for performance reasons
    public void validate() {}
    public void revalidate() {}
    protected void firePropertyChange(String propertyName, Object oldValue, Object newValue) {}
    public void firePropertyChange(String propertyName, boolean oldValue, boolean newValue) {}
}
```

Tool Tips

ε937. Setting Column Header Tool Tips in a JTable Components

To display a tool tip for a column header, install a mouse motion listener on the header component and change its tool tip based on which column header is under the cursor.

```
int rows = 10;
int cols = 5;
```

```
JTable table = new JTable(rows, cols);
JTableHeader header = table.getTableHeader();

ColumnHeaderToolTips tips = new ColumnHeaderToolTips();

// Assign a tooltip for each of the columns
for (int c=0; c<table.getColumnCount(); c++) {
    TableColumn col = table.getColumnModel().getColumn(c);
    tips.setToolTip(col, "Col "+c);
}
header.addMouseMotionListener(tips);

public class ColumnHeaderToolTips extends MouseMotionAdapter {
    // Current column whose tooltip is being displayed.
    // This variable is used to minimize the calls to setToolTipText().
    TableColumn curCol;

    // Maps TableColumn objects to tooltips
    Map tips = new HashMap();

    // If tooltip is null, removes any tooltip text.
    public void setToolTip(TableColumn col, String tooltip) {
        if (tooltip == null) {
            tips.remove(col);
        } else {
            tips.put(col, tooltip);
        }
    }

    public void mouseMoved(MouseEvent evt) {
        TableColumn col = null;
        JTableHeader header = (JTableHeader)evt.getSource();
        JTable table = header.getTable();
        TableColumnModel colModel = table.getColumnModel();
        int vColIndex = colModel.getColumnIndexAtX(evt.getX());

        // Return if not clicked on any column header
        if (vColIndex >= 0) {
            col = colModel.getColumn(vColIndex);
        }

        if (col != curCol) {
            header.setToolTipText((String)tips.get(col));
            curCol = col;
        }
    }
}
```

ε938. Setting Tool Tips on Cells in a JTable Component

Unfortunately, there is no setToolTipText() method for cells in a JTable component. For a cell to show a tool tip, the renderer for that cell must set the tool tip text on the returned component. See "ε928. Creating a Custom Cell Renderer in a JTable Component" for an example of a renderer that sets a tool tip.

If you cannot modify the renderer, you can override the table's prepareRenderer() method and explicitly set the tool tip on the returned component.

```
// This table displays a tool tip text based on the string
// representation of the cell value
```

```
JTable table = new JTable() {
    public Component prepareRenderer(TableCellRenderer renderer,
                                     int rowIndex, int vColIndex) {
        Component c = super.prepareRenderer(renderer, rowIndex, vColIndex);
        if (c instanceof JComponent) {
            JComponent jc = (JComponent)c;
            jc.setToolTipText((String)getValueAt(rowIndex, vColIndex));
        }
        return c;
    }
};
```

Selection

ε939. Enabling Row, Column, or Cell Selections in a JTable Component

With row selections enabled, clicking on any cell selects the entire row containing that cell. This also applies to columns. With cell selections enabled, rectangular blocks of cells can be selected.

```
JTable table = new JTable();

// Enable row selection (default)
table.setColumnSelectionAllowed(false);
table.setRowSelectionAllowed(true);

// Enable column selection
table.setColumnSelectionAllowed(true);
table.setRowSelectionAllowed(false);

// Enable cell selection
table.setColumnSelectionAllowed(true);
table.setRowSelectionAllowed(true);
```

ε940. Enabling Single or Multiple Selections in a JTable Component

By default, a table component allows multiple selections. To control the selection behavior, see "ε939. Enabling Row, Column, or Cell Selections in a JTable Component".

```
JTable table = new JTable();

// Get default selection mode
int selMode = table.getSelectionModel().getSelectionMode();
// MULTIPLE_INTERVAL_SELECTION

// Allow only single a selection
table.setSelectionMode(ListSelectionModel.SINGLE_SELECTION);

// Allow selection to span one contiguous set of rows,
// visible columns, or block of cells
table.setSelectionMode(ListSelectionModel.SINGLE_INTERVAL_SELECTION);

// Allow multiple selections of rows, visible columns, or cell blocks (default)
table.setSelectionMode(ListSelectionModel.MULTIPLE_INTERVAL_SELECTION);
```

ε941. Programmatically Making Selections in a JTable Component

To select columns, setColumnSelectionInterval(), addColumnSelectionInterval(), and removeColumnSelectionInterval() are available. However, these only work if columnSelectionAllowed is true and rowSelectionAllowed is false. This also applies to rows.

To select individual cells or blocks of cells, use changeSelection(). However, both columnSelectionAllowed and rowSelectionAllowed must be false.

These selection methods observe the setting of the selection mode. For example, if the selection mode is SINGLE_SELECTION, only a single row, column, or cell can be made. See "ε940. Enabling Single or Multiple Selections in a JTable Component" for more information on selection modes.

```
int rows = 10;
int cols = 5;
JTable table = new JTable(rows, cols);

// Use this mode to demonstrate the following examples
table.setSelectionMode(ListSelectionModel.MULTIPLE_INTERVAL_SELECTION);

// The following column selection methods work only if these
// properties are set this way
table.setColumnSelectionAllowed(true);
table.setRowSelectionAllowed(false);

// Select a column - column 0
table.setColumnSelectionInterval(0, 0);

// Select an additional range of columns - columns 1 to 2
table.addColumnSelectionInterval(1, 2);

// Deselect a range of columns - columns 0 to 1
table.removeColumnSelectionInterval(0, 1);


// The following row selection methods work only if these
// properties are set this way
table.setColumnSelectionAllowed(false);
table.setRowSelectionAllowed(true);

// Select a row - row 0
table.setRowSelectionInterval(0, 0);

// Select an additional range of rows - rows 1 to 2
table.addRowSelectionInterval(1, 2);

// Deselect a range of rows - rows 0 to 1
table.removeRowSelectionInterval(0, 1);


// The following cell selection methods work only if these
// properties are set this way
table.setColumnSelectionAllowed(true);
table.setRowSelectionAllowed(true);

// Select a cell: cell (2,1)
int row = 2;
int col = 1;
boolean toggle = false;
boolean extend = false;
table.changeSelection(row, col, toggle, extend);

// Extend the selection to include all cells between (2,1) to (5,3)
row = 5;
col = 3;
toggle = false;
```

```
extend = true;
table.changeSelection(row, col, toggle, extend);

// Deselect a cell: cell (3,2)
// All cells in the row and column containing (3,2) are deselected.
row = 3;
col = 2;
toggle = true;
extend = false;
table.changeSelection(row, col, toggle, extend);

// This method actually toggles the selection state so that
// if it were called again, it exactly reverses the first call.
// Select cell (3,2) as well as the other cells that
// were deselected in the first call.
toggle = true;
extend = false;
table.changeSelection(row, col, toggle, extend);

// Select all cells
table.selectAll();

// Deselect all cells
table.clearSelection();
```

ε942. Getting the Selected Cells in a JTable Component

The method for determining the selected cells depends on whether column, row, or cell selection is enabled.

```
JTable table = new JTable();

if (table.getColumnSelectionAllowed()
        && !table.getRowSelectionAllowed()) {
    // Column selection is enabled
    // Get the indices of the selected columns
    int[] vColIndices = table.getSelectedColumns();
} else if (!table.getColumnSelectionAllowed()
        && table.getRowSelectionAllowed()) {
    // Row selection is enabled
    // Get the indices of the selected rows
    int[] rowIndices = table.getSelectedRows();
} else if (table.getCellSelectionEnabled()) {
    // Individual cell selection is enabled

    // In SINGLE_SELECTION mode, the selected cell can be retrieved using
    table.setSelectionMode(ListSelectionModel.SINGLE_SELECTION);
    int rowIndex = table.getSelectedRow();
    int colIndex = table.getSelectedColumn();

    // In the other modes, the set of selected cells can be retrieved using
    table.setSelectionMode(ListSelectionModel.SINGLE_INTERVAL_SELECTION);
    table.setSelectionMode(ListSelectionModel.MULTIPLE_INTERVAL_SELECTION);

    // Get the min and max ranges of selected cells
    int rowIndexStart = table.getSelectedRow();
    int rowIndexEnd = table.getSelectionModel().getMaxSelectionIndex();
    int colIndexStart = table.getSelectedColumn();
    int colIndexEnd = table.getColumnModel().getSelectionModel()
        .getMaxSelectionIndex();
```

```
            // Check each cell in the range
            for (int r=rowIndexStart; r<=rowIndexEnd; r++) {
                for (int c=colIndexStart; c<=colIndexEnd; c++) {
                    if (table.isCellSelected(r, c)) {
                        // cell is selected
                    }
                }
            }
        }
```

ε943. Disabling Selections in a JTable Component

The only way to completely prevent a selection in a JTable component is to prevent it from getting the focus using setFocusable(false). However, if you still need keystrokes to work in the component, this method is not an option.

The next closest way to disable selections is to call setCellSelectionEnabled(false). After this call, isCellSelected() correctly returns false for every cell. However, getSelectedRows() and getSelectedColumns() do not return empty arrays as expected. Instead, the anchor cell ("ε944. Getting the Anchor Cell in a JTable Component") will be considered selected. Therefore, if you are using these methods, make sure you ignore the results if getCellSelectionEnabled() returns false.

```
        int rows = 10;
        int cols = 5;
        JTable table = new JTable(rows, cols);

        // Do this only if there's no need for the component to have the focus
        table.setFocusable(false);

        // Partially disables selections (see description above)
        table.setCellSelectionEnabled(false);
```

ε944. Getting the Anchor Cell in a JTable Component

The anchor cell in a table component is the cell that received the most recent mouse click. In some applications, the content of the anchor cell is automatically displayed in another larger and more convenient editing text area.

```
        public void getAnchorCell(JTable table) {
            int rowIndex = table.getSelectionModel().getAnchorSelectionIndex();
            int vColIndex = table.getColumnModel().getSelectionModel()
                .getAnchorSelectionIndex();
        }
```

Scrolling

ε945. Creating a Scrollable JTable Component

```
        // Create a table with 10 rows and 5 columns
        JTable table = new JTable(10, 5);

        // Make the table vertically scrollable
        JScrollPane scrollPane = new JScrollPane(table);
```

By default, a table is created with auto resize enabled. This means that if the user changes the width of the table, the columns automatically expand or shrink so that all the columns are entirely visible. In this mode, there is no need for a horizontal scrollbar. In order to get horizontal scrolling, auto resize must be disabled.

```
// Disable auto resizing to make the table horizontal scrollable
table.setAutoResizeMode(JTable.AUTO_RESIZE_OFF);
```

ε946. Determining If a Cell Is Visible in a JTable Component

```
// Check if the cell (1,2) is completely visible
int rowIndex = 1;
int vColIndex = 2;
isCellVisible(table, rowIndex, vColIndex);

// Assumes table is contained in a JScrollPane. Returns true iff the
// cell (rowIndex, vColIndex) is completely visible within the viewport.
public boolean isCellVisible(JTable table, int rowIndex, int vColIndex) {
    if (!(table.getParent() instanceof JViewport)) {
        return false;
    }
    JViewport viewport = (JViewport)table.getParent();

    // This rectangle is relative to the table where the
    // northwest corner of cell (0,0) is always (0,0)
    Rectangle rect = table.getCellRect(rowIndex, vColIndex, true);

    // The location of the viewport relative to the table
    Point pt = viewport.getViewPosition();

    // Translate the cell location so that it is relative
    // to the view, assuming the northwest corner of the
    // view is (0,0)
    rect.setLocation(rect.x-pt.x, rect.y-pt.y);

    // Check if view completely contains cell
    return new Rectangle(viewport.getExtentSize()).contains(rect);
}
```

ε947. Making a Cell Visible in a JTable Component

```
// Ensure that the cell (1,2) is visible
int rowIndex = 1;
int vColIndex = 2;
scrollToVisible(table, rowIndex, vColIndex);

// Assumes table is contained in a JScrollPane. Scrolls the
// cell (rowIndex, vColIndex) so that it is visible within the viewport.
public void scrollToVisible(JTable table, int rowIndex, int vColIndex) {
    if (!(table.getParent() instanceof JViewport)) {
        return;
    }
    JViewport viewport = (JViewport)table.getParent();

    // This rectangle is relative to the table where the
    // northwest corner of cell (0,0) is always (0,0).
    Rectangle rect = table.getCellRect(rowIndex, vColIndex, true);

    // The location of the viewport relative to the table
    Point pt = viewport.getViewPosition();

    // Translate the cell location so that it is relative
```

Packages and Examples

307

```
        // to the view, assuming the northwest corner of the
        // view is (0,0)
        rect.setLocation(rect.x-pt.x, rect.y-pt.y);

        // Scroll the area into view
        viewport.scrollRectToVisible(rect);
```

ε948. Scrolling a Cell to the Center of a JTable Component

This example demonstrates how to scroll the view so that a specified cell appears in the center of the view.

```
    // Make the cell (1,2) is appear in the center of the view
    int rowIndex = 1;
    int vColIndex = 2;
    scrollToCenter(table, rowIndex, vColIndex);

    // Assumes table is contained in a JScrollPane. Scrolls the
    // cell (rowIndex, vColIndex) so that it is visible at the center of viewport.
    public void scrollToCenter(JTable table, int rowIndex, int vColIndex) {
        if (!(table.getParent() instanceof JViewport)) {
            return;
        }
        JViewport viewport = (JViewport)table.getParent();

        // This rectangle is relative to the table where the
        // northwest corner of cell (0,0) is always (0,0).
        Rectangle rect = table.getCellRect(rowIndex, vColIndex, true);

        // The location of the view relative to the table
        Rectangle viewRect = viewport.getViewRect();

        // Translate the cell location so that it is relative
        // to the view, assuming the northwest corner of the
        // view is (0,0).
        rect.setLocation(rect.x-viewRect.x, rect.y-viewRect.y);

        // Calculate location of rect if it were at the center of view
        int centerX = (viewRect.width-rect.width)/2;
        int centerY = (viewRect.height-rect.height)/2;

        // Fake the location of the cell so that scrollRectToVisible
        // will move the cell to the center
        if (rect.x < centerX) {
            centerX = -centerX;
        }
        if (rect.y < centerY) {
            centerY = -centerY;
        }
        rect.translate(centerX, centerY);

        // Scroll the area into view.
        viewport.scrollRectToVisible(rect);
    }
```

Layout

ε949. Packing a JTable Component

This example demonstrates how to adjust the preferred size of a JTable to be just large enough to accommodate the preferred size of all cells.

```
int rows = 10;
int cols = 5;
JTable table = new JTable(rows, cols) {
        // Override this method so that it returns the preferred
        // size of the JTable instead of the default fixed size
        public Dimension getPreferredScrollableViewportSize() {
            return getPreferredSize();
        }
};

// Allow columns to be resized
table.setAutoResizeMode(JTable.AUTO_RESIZE_OFF);

// Add data...

// These packing methods are defined in "ε950. Packing a Column of a JTable Component"
// and "ε913. Setting the Height of a Row in a JTable Component"
packColumns(table, 2);
packRows(table, 0);
```

ε950. Packing a Column of a JTable Component

This example demonstrates how to adjust the width of a column to be just wide enough to show all of the column header and the widest cell in the column.

```
int rows = 3;
int cols = 3;
JTable table = new JTable(rows, cols);

// Disable auto resizing
table.setAutoResizeMode(JTable.AUTO_RESIZE_OFF);

// Add data here

// Pack the second column of the table
int vColIndex = 1;
int margin = 2;
packColumn(table, vColIndex, margin);
public void packColumns(JTable table, int margin) {
    for (int c=0; c<table.getColumnCount(); c++) {
        packColumn(table, c, 2);
    }
}

// Sets the preferred width of the visible column specified by vColIndex. The column
// will be just wide enough to show the column head and the widest cell in the column.
// margin pixels are added to the left and right
// (resulting in an additional width of 2*margin pixels).
public void packColumn(JTable table, int vColIndex, int margin) {
    TableModel model = table.getModel();
    DefaultTableColumnModel colModel = (DefaultTableColumnModel)table.getColumnModel();
    TableColumn col = colModel.getColumn(vColIndex);
    int width = 0;
```

```
    // Get width of column header
    TableCellRenderer renderer = col.getHeaderRenderer();
    if (renderer == null) {
        renderer = table.getTableHeader().getDefaultRenderer();
    }
    Component comp = renderer.getTableCellRendererComponent(
        table, col.getHeaderValue(), false, false, 0, 0);
    width = comp.getPreferredSize().width;

    // Get maximum width of column data
    for (int r=0; r<table.getRowCount(); r++) {
        renderer = table.getCellRenderer(r, vColIndex);
        comp = renderer.getTableCellRendererComponent(
            table, table.getValueAt(r, vColIndex), false, false, r, vColIndex);
        width = Math.max(width, comp.getPreferredSize().width);
    }

    // Add margin
    width += 2*margin;

    // Set the width
    col.setPreferredWidth(width);
}
```

ε951. Setting Grid Line Properties in a JTable Component

```
JTable table = new JTable();

// Add data here

// Show both horizontal and vertical grid lines (the default)
table.setShowGrid(true);

// Don't show any grid lines
table.setShowGrid(false);

// Show only vertical grid lines
table.setShowGrid(false);
table.setShowVerticalLines(true);

// Show only horizontal grid lines
table.setShowGrid(false);
table.setShowHorizontalLines(true);

// Set the grid color
table.setGridColor(Color.red);
```

ε952. Setting the Gap Size Between Cells in a JTable Component

The horizontal space (column margin) and vertical space (row margin) between cells can be customized. If you increase the column margin, the cell widths automatically increase by the same amount. However, if you increase the row margin, the cell heights do not automatically increase. In order to increase the cell heights, you need to call setRowHeight() explicitly.

```
JTable table = new JTable();

// Add data here
// Get defaults
Dimension d = table.getIntercellSpacing();
```

Class   *Interface*   —extends   - - -implements   ○ abstract   ● final   ^—has superclass   ‿—has subclass   package—see other volume

```
// d.width == 1, d.height == 1
```

```
// Add 5 spaces to the left and right sides of a cell.
// Add 2 spaces to the top and bottom sides of a cell.
int gapWidth = 10;
int gapHeight = 4;
table.setIntercellSpacing(new Dimension(gapWidth, gapHeight));
```

```
// Increase the row height
table.setRowHeight(table.getRowHeight()+gapHeight);
```

Editing

ε953. Creating a Custom Table Cell Editor in a JTable Component

A table cell editor needs to implement the TableCellEditor interface. This interface supports listeners. The listener code is conveniently provided by the class AbstractCellEditor so that most table cell editors extend from this class.

Like a renderer (see "ε928. Creating a Custom Cell Renderer in a JTable Component"), an editor returns a component used to edit the value in the cell. For performance reasons, the editor should not create a new component each time getTableCellEditorComponent() is called. Rather, it should return the same component (or one from a set) every time.

The job of getTableCellEditorComponent() is to configure the component based on the coordinates and value in the cell. The table then uses the configured component and paints it on the screen. After painting it, the table no longer needs the component.

```
JTable table = new JTable();

// Add some data...

// Install the custom editor on the first column
int vColIndex = 0;
TableColumn col = table.getColumnModel().getColumn(vColIndex);
col.setCellEditor(new MyTableCellEditor());

public class MyTableCellEditor extends AbstractCellEditor implements TableCellEditor {
    // This is the component that will handle the editing of the cell value
    JComponent component = new JTextField();

    // This method is called when a cell value is edited by the user.
    public Component getTableCellEditorComponent(JTable table, Object value,
            boolean isSelected, int rowIndex, int vColIndex) {
        // 'value' is value contained in the cell located at (rowIndex, vColIndex)

        if (isSelected) {
            // cell (and perhaps other cells) are selected
        }

        // Configure the component with the specified value
        ((JTextField)component).setText((String)value);

        // Return the configured component
        return component;
    }

    // This method is called when editing is completed.
    // It must return the new value to be stored in the cell.
    public Object getCellEditorValue() {
```

```
                    return ((JTextField)component).getText();
            }
    }
```

*ε*954. Preventing Invalid Values in a Cell in a JTable Component

This example demonstrates how to modify a custom table cell editor to prevent invalid values from being saved. See "*ε*953. Creating a Custom Table Cell Editor in a JTable Component" for more information about table cell editors.

```
public class MyTableCellEditor extends AbstractCellEditor implements TableCellEditor {
    // See "ε953. Creating a Custom Table Cell Editor in a JTable Component"
    // for other methods that need to be implemented.

    // This method is called just before the cell value
    // is saved. If the value is not valid, false should be returned.
    public boolean stopCellEditing() {
        String s = (String)getCellEditorValue();

        if (!isValid(s)) {
            // Should display an error message at this point
            return false;
        }
        return super.stopCellEditing();
    }
}
```

*ε*955. Setting the Activation Click Count for a Table Cell Editor in a JTable Component

By default, a table cell editor is activated with a double-click. The activation behavior is controlled by the renderer, not by a table property. To change this, override the isCellEditable() method of the editor. See "*ε*953. Creating a Custom Table Cell Editor in a JTable Component" for more information about table cell editors.

```
public class MyTableCellEditor extends AbstractCellEditor implements TableCellEditor {
    // See "ε953. Creating a Custom Table Cell Editor in a JTable Component"
    // for other methods that need to be implemented.
    public boolean isCellEditable(EventObject evt) {
        if (evt instanceof MouseEvent) {
            int clickCount;

            // For single-click activation
            clickCount = 1;

            // For double-click activation
            clickCount = 2;

            // For triple-click activation
            clickCount = 3;

            return ((MouseEvent)evt).getClickCount() >= clickCount;
        }
        return true;
    }
}
```

ε956. Programmatically Starting and Stopping Cell Editing in a JTable Component

Normally, the table component automatically starts and stops the editing of table cells based on user input. However, when building table commands, it may be necessary to programmatically enable and disable editing of cells. The following code demonstrates how to set a cell in edit mode:

```
// Create table
int rows = 10;
int cols = 5;
JTable table = new JTable(rows, cols);

// Enable the ability to select a single cell
table.setColumnSelectionAllowed(true);
table.setRowSelectionAllowed(true);

// Set the cell on the 2nd row, 4th column in edit mode
int row = 1;
int col = 3;
boolean success = table.editCellAt(row, col);
if (success) {
    // Select cell
    boolean toggle = false;
    boolean extend = false;
    table.changeSelection(row, col, toggle, extend);
} else {
    // Cell could not be edited
}
```

The following code saves the current value in the cell being edited and stops the editing process:

```
if (table.getCellEditor() != null) {
    table.getCellEditor().stopCellEditing();
}
```

The following code discards any changes made by the user and stops the editing process:

```
if (table.getCellEditor() != null) {
    table.getCellEditor().cancelCellEditing();
}
```

ε957. Creating a Text Field That Mirrors the Value in the Anchor Cell in a JTable Component

In some spreadsheet applications, the value of the current cell (anchor) is mirrored in a separate and conveniently larger text field. Any changes to the current cell are immediately reflected in the text field and vice versa. This example demonstrates how to set up a mirror text field for the anchor cell in a table component.

In order to detect changes to the anchor cell, a selection-changed listener and a cell-value-changed listener must be added to the table.

See "ε944. Getting the Anchor Cell in a JTable Component" for more information about the anchor cell.

```
JTable table = new JTable();

// Add data

// Create text field and add action
JTextField textField = new JTextField();
textField.setAction(new UpdateAnchorAction(table));
```

```
// Add selection listener to table
SelectionListener listener = new SelectionListener(table, textField);
table.getSelectionModel().addListSelectionListener(listener);
table.getColumnModel().getSelectionModel()
    .addListSelectionListener(listener);

// Add value changed listener to table
table.getModel().addTableModelListener(new MyTableModelListener(table, textField));

// Create a frame and add both components to the frame
JFrame frame = new JFrame();
frame.getContentPane().add(new JScrollPane(table), BorderLayout.CENTER);
frame.getContentPane().add(textField, BorderLayout.NORTH);
frame.pack();
frame.setVisible(true);

public class SelectionListener implements ListSelectionListener {
    JTable table;
    JTextField textField;

    // It is necessary to keep the table since it is not possible
    // to determine the table from the event's source
    SelectionListener(JTable table, JTextField textField) {
        this.table = table;
        this.textField = textField;
    }

    // Update the text field whenever the anchor cell changes
    public void valueChanged(ListSelectionEvent e) {
        int rowIndex = table.getSelectionModel().getAnchorSelectionIndex();
        int vColIndex = table.getColumnModel().getSelectionModel()
            .getAnchorSelectionIndex();

        // Get the value and set the text field
        textField.setText((String)table.getValueAt(rowIndex, vColIndex));
    }
}

public class MyTableModelListener implements TableModelListener {
    JTable table;
    JTextField textField;

    // It is necessary to keep the table since it is not possible
    // to determine the table from the event's source
    MyTableModelListener(JTable table, JTextField textField) {
        this.table = table;
        this.textField = textField;
    }

    // Update the text field whenever the value in the anchor cell changes
    public void tableChanged(TableModelEvent e) {
        // Get anchor cell location
        int rAnchor = table.getSelectionModel().getAnchorSelectionIndex();
        int vcAnchor = table.getColumnModel().getSelectionModel()
            .getAnchorSelectionIndex();

        // This method is defined in
        // "ε915. Converting a Column Index Between the View and Model in a JTable Component"
```

```
            int mcAnchor = toModel(table, vcAnchor);

            // Get affected rows and columns
            int firstRow = e.getFirstRow();
            int lastRow = e.getLastRow();
            int mColIndex = e.getColumn();

            if (firstRow != TableModelEvent.HEADER_ROW
                    && rAnchor >= firstRow
                    && rAnchor <= lastRow
                    && (mColIndex == TableModelEvent.ALL_COLUMNS
                        || mColIndex == mcAnchor)) {
                // Set the text field with the new value
                textField.setText((String)table.getValueAt(rAnchor, vcAnchor));
            }
        }
    }
}

public class UpdateAnchorAction extends AbstractAction {
    JTable table;
    UpdateAnchorAction(JTable table) {
        super("Set Anchor");
        this.table = table;
    }

    // Update the value in the anchor cell whenever the text field changes
    public void actionPerformed(ActionEvent evt) {
        JTextField textField = (JTextField)evt.getSource();

        // Get anchor cell location
        int rAnchor = table.getSelectionModel().getAnchorSelectionIndex();
        int vcAnchor = table.getColumnModel().getSelectionModel()
            .getAnchorSelectionIndex();

        table.setValueAt(textField.getText(), rAnchor, vcAnchor);
    }
}
```

ε958. Disabling User Edits in a JTable Component

User editing can be disabled in two places. By disabling edits in the model, no table component using that model will allow editing by the user. By disabling edits in the table component, only that component disallows edits; other table components using the same model will allow editing.

Disabling edits requires subclassing either the JTable or TableModel class.

Note: Although user editing is disabled, programmatically changing values in the model is still possible.

```
// Create a JTable that disallow edits
JTable table1 = new JTable() {
    public boolean isCellEditable(int rowIndex, int vColIndex) {
        return false;
    }
};

// Create a JTable based on the same model as table1 but allows edits
JTable table2 = new JTable(table1.getModel());

// Create a model that disallows edits; JTable's using this model will not allow edits
TableModel model = new DefaultTableModel() {
    public boolean isCellEditable(int rowIndex, int mColIndex) {
```

315

```
                    return false;
            }
    };
```

ε959. Using a JComboBox in a Cell in a JTable Component

If the possible values allowed in a column must be one from a small fixed set of values, a combobox might be appropriate as the cell editor for that column. By using a combobox, it is impossible for the user to input an invalid value.

```
JTable table = new JTable();
DefaultTableModel model = (DefaultTableModel)table.getModel();

// Add some columns
model.addColumn("A", new Object[]{"item1"});
model.addColumn("B", new Object[]{"item2"});

// These are the combobox values
String[] values = new String[]{"item1", "item2", "item3"};

// Set the combobox editor on the 1st visible column
int vColIndex = 0;
TableColumn col = table.getColumnModel().getColumn(vColIndex);
col.setCellEditor(new MyComboBoxEditor(values));

// If the cell should appear like a combobox in its
// non-editing state, also set the combobox renderer
col.setCellRenderer(new MyComboBoxRenderer(values));

public class MyComboBoxRenderer extends JComboBox implements TableCellRenderer {
    public MyComboBoxRenderer(String[] items) {
        super(items);
    }

    public Component getTableCellRendererComponent(JTable table, Object value,
            boolean isSelected, boolean hasFocus, int row, int column) {
        if (isSelected) {
            setForeground(table.getSelectionForeground());
            super.setBackground(table.getSelectionBackground());
        } else {
            setForeground(table.getForeground());
            setBackground(table.getBackground());
        }

        // Select the current value
        setSelectedItem(value);
        return this;
    }
}

public class MyComboBoxEditor extends DefaultCellEditor {
    public MyComboBoxEditor(String[] items) {
        super(new JComboBox(items));
    }
}
```

ε960. Using a List JSpinner as a Cell Editor in a JTable Component

If the possible values allowed in a column must be from a small fixed set of values, a spinner might be appropriate as the cell editor for that column. By using a list spinner, it is impossible for the user to input an invalid value.

```
JTable table = new JTable();
DefaultTableModel model = (DefaultTableModel)table.getModel();

// Add some columns
model.addColumn("A", new Object[]{"item1"});
model.addColumn("B", new Object[]{"item2"});

// These are the spinner values
String[] values = new String[]{"item1", "item2", "item3"};

// Set the spinner editor on the 1st visible column
int vColIndex = 0;
TableColumn col = table.getColumnModel().getColumn(vColIndex);
col.setCellEditor(new SpinnerEditor(values));

// If you want to make the cell appear like a spinner in its
// non-editing state, also set the spinner renderer
col.setCellRenderer(new SpinnerRenderer(values));

public class SpinnerEditor extends AbstractCellEditor
        implements TableCellEditor {
    final JSpinner spinner = new JSpinner();

    // Initializes the spinner.
    public SpinnerEditor(String[] items) {
        spinner.setModel(new SpinnerListModel(java.util.Arrays.asList(items)));
    }

    // Prepares the spinner component and returns it.
    public Component getTableCellEditorComponent(JTable table, Object value,
            boolean isSelected, int row, int column) {
        spinner.setValue(value);
        return spinner;
    }

    // Enables the editor only for double-clicks.
    public boolean isCellEditable(EventObject evt) {
        if (evt instanceof MouseEvent) {
            return ((MouseEvent)evt).getClickCount() >= 2;
        }
        return true;
    }

    // Returns the spinners current value.
    public Object getCellEditorValue() {
        return spinner.getValue();
    }
}
```

Packages and Examples

317

Sorting

ε961. Sorting the Rows in a JTable Component Based on a Column

This example implements a method that sorts all the rows in a DefaultTableModel based on the values of the column.

```
DefaultTableModel model = new DefaultTableModel();
JTable table = new JTable(model);

// Add data here...

// Disable autoCreateColumnsFromModel otherwise all the column customizations
// and adjustments will be lost when the model data is sorted
table.setAutoCreateColumnsFromModel(false);

// Sort all the rows in descending order based on the
// values in the second column of the model
sortAllRowsBy(model, 1, false);

// Regardless of sort order (ascending or descending), null values always appear last.
// colIndex specifies a column in model.
public void sortAllRowsBy(DefaultTableModel model, int colIndex, boolean ascending) {
    Vector data = model.getDataVector();
    Collections.sort(data, new ColumnSorter(colIndex, ascending));
    model.fireTableStructureChanged();
}

// This comparator is used to sort vectors of data
public class ColumnSorter implements Comparator {
    int colIndex;
    boolean ascending;
    ColumnSorter(int colIndex, boolean ascending) {
        this.colIndex = colIndex;
        this.ascending = ascending;
    }
    public int compare(Object a, Object b) {
        Vector v1 = (Vector)a;
        Vector v2 = (Vector)b;
        Object o1 = v1.get(colIndex);
        Object o2 = v2.get(colIndex);

        // Treat empty strains like nulls
        if (o1 instanceof String && ((String)o1).length() == 0) {
            o1 = null;
        }
        if (o2 instanceof String && ((String)o2).length() == 0) {
            o2 = null;
        }

        // Sort nulls so they appear last, regardless
        // of sort order
        if (o1 == null && o2 == null) {
            return 0;
        } else if (o1 == null) {
            return 1;
        } else if (o2 == null) {
```

```
                return -1;
        } else if (o1 instanceof Comparable) {
            if (ascending) {
                return ((Comparable)o1).compareTo(o2);
            } else {
                return ((Comparable)o2).compareTo(o1);
            }
        } else {
            if (ascending) {
                return o1.toString().compareTo(o2.toString());
            } else {
                return o2.toString().compareTo(o1.toString());
            }
        }
    }
}
```

ε962. Sorting a Column in a JTable Component

This example implements a method that sorts the data of a particular column of a DefaultTableModel.

```
DefaultTableModel model = new DefaultTableModel();
JTable table = new JTable(model);

// Add data here...

// Disable autoCreateColumnsFromModel otherwise all the column customizations
// and adjustments will be lost when the model data is sorted
table.setAutoCreateColumnsFromModel(false);

// Sort the values in the second column of the model
// in descending order
int mColIndex = 1;
boolean ascending = false;
sortColumn(model, mColIndex, ascending);

// Regardless of sort order (ascending or descending), null values always appear last.
// colIndex specifies a column in model.
public void sortColumn(DefaultTableModel model, int colIndex, boolean ascending) {
    Vector data = model.getDataVector();
    Object[] colData = new Object[model.getRowCount()];

    // Copy the column data in an array
    for (int i=0; i<colData.length; i++) {
        colData[i] = ((Vector)data.get(i)).get(colIndex);
    }

    // Sort the array of column data
    Arrays.sort(colData, new ColumnSorter(ascending));

    // Copy the sorted values back into the table model
    for (int i=0; i<colData.length; i++) {
        ((Vector)data.get(i)).set(colIndex, colData[i]);
    }
    model.fireTableStructureChanged();
}
public class ColumnSorter implements Comparator {
    boolean ascending;
    ColumnSorter(boolean ascending) {
```

319

```
            this.ascending = ascending;
        }
        public int compare(Object a, Object b) {
            // Treat empty strains like nulls
            if (a instanceof String && ((String)a).length() == 0) {
                a = null;
            }
            if (b instanceof String && ((String)b).length() == 0) {
                b = null;
            }

            // Sort nulls so they appear last, regardless
            // of sort order
            if (a == null && b == null) {
                return 0;
            } else if (a == null) {
                return 1;
            } else if (b == null) {
                return -1;
            } else if (a instanceof Comparable) {
                if (ascending) {
                    return ((Comparable)a).compareTo(b);
                } else {
                    return ((Comparable)b).compareTo(a);
                }
            } else {
                if (ascending) {
                    return a.toString().compareTo(b.toString());
                } else {
                    return b.toString().compareTo(a.toString());
                }
            }
        }
    }
}
```

Table Model

ε963. Sharing a Table Model Between JTable Components

When you share a table model between two table components, any changes made to values in the model will appear in both table components. However, any changes to the visible columns in one table component will not affect the columns in the other table component.

```
DefaultTableModel model = new DefaultTableModel();
JTable table1 = new JTable(model);
JTable table2 = new JTable(model);

// Add data here

// Place the two tables in a split pane
JSplitPane splitPane = new JSplitPane(JSplitPane.HORIZONTAL_SPLIT);
splitPane.add(new JScrollPane(table1));
splitPane.add(new JScrollPane(table2));

// Remove the first visible column from table1;
```

Class   *Interface*   —extends   - - -implements   ○ abstract   ● final   ˆ—has superclass   ˏ—has subclass   package—see other volume

```
// the column will not be removed from table2
table1.getColumnModel().removeColumn(table1.getColumnModel().getColumn(0));
```

ε964. Listening for Selection Events in a JTable Component

To listen for selection changes, you need to add a listener to both the JTable's table model and to the table column model.

A selection change event has a first and last property that specifies the range of affected rows (or columns). For example, if the 5th row is selected and the user selects the 7th row, the first property is 4 and the last is property 6. There is not enough information in the event to determine exactly which cells have changed. See "ε942. Getting the Selected Cells in a JTable Component" for an example of how to determine the selected cells.

Changing the selection programmatically (see "ε941. Programmatically Making Selections in a JTable Component") causes selection change events to be fired.

```
SelectionListener listener = new SelectionListener(table);
table.getSelectionModel().addListSelectionListener(listener);
table.getColumnModel().getSelectionModel()
    .addListSelectionListener(listener);

public class SelectionListener implements ListSelectionListener {
    JTable table;

    // It is necessary to keep the table since it is not possible
    // to determine the table from the event's source
    SelectionListener(JTable table) {
        this.table = table;
    }
    public void valueChanged(ListSelectionEvent e) {
        // If cell selection is enabled, both row and column change events are fired
        if (e.getSource() == table.getSelectionModel()
            && table.getRowSelectionAllowed()) {
            // Column selection changed
            int first = e.getFirstIndex();
            int last = e.getLastIndex();
        } else if (e.getSource() == table.getColumnModel().getSelectionModel()
            && table.getColumnSelectionAllowed() ){
            // Row selection changed
            int first = e.getFirstIndex();
            int last = e.getLastIndex();
        }

        if (e.getValueIsAdjusting()) {
            // The mouse button has not yet been released
        }
    }
}
```

ε965. Listening for Changes to the Rows and Columns of a JTable Component

This example demonstrates how to detect row and columns being added, deleted, or changed in a table component. To listen for these events, a listener must be added to the JTable's table model.

Note: When a column is added, the type of the event is UPDATE.

```
table.getModel().addTableModelListener(new MyTableModelListener(table));

public class MyTableModelListener implements TableModelListener {
    JTable table;

    // It is necessary to keep the table since it is not possible
    // to determine the table from the event's source
    MyTableModelListener(JTable table) {
        this.table = table;
    }

    public void tableChanged(TableModelEvent e) {
        int firstRow = e.getFirstRow();
        int lastRow = e.getLastRow();
        int mColIndex = e.getColumn();

        switch (e.getType()) {
        case TableModelEvent.INSERT:
            // The inserted rows are in the range [firstRow, lastRow]
            for (int r=firstRow; r<=lastRow; r++) {
                // Row r was inserted
            }
            break;
        case TableModelEvent.UPDATE:
            if (firstRow == TableModelEvent.HEADER_ROW) {
                if (mColIndex == TableModelEvent.ALL_COLUMNS) {
                    // A column was added
                } else {
                    // Column mColIndex in header changed
                }
            } else {
                // The rows in the range [firstRow, lastRow] changed
                for (int r=firstRow; r<=lastRow; r++) {
                    // Row r was changed

                    if (mColIndex == TableModelEvent.ALL_COLUMNS) {
                        // All columns in the range of rows have changed
                    } else {
                        // Column mColIndex changed
                    }
                }
            }
            break;
        case TableModelEvent.DELETE:
            // The rows in the range [firstRow, lastRow] changed
            for (int r=firstRow; r<=lastRow; r++) {
                // Row r was deleted
            }
            break;
        }
    }
}
```

ε966. Listening for Column-Related Changes in a JTable Component

Events are fired whenever a column is added, removed, resized, or moved.

```
table.getColumnModel().addColumnModelListener(
    new MyTableColumnModelListener(table));

public class MyTableColumnModelListener implements TableColumnModelListener {
    JTable table;

    // It is necessary to keep the table since it is not possible
    // to determine the table from the event's source
    public MyTableColumnModelListener(JTable table) {
        this.table = table;
    }
    public void columnAdded(TableColumnModelEvent e) {
        int fromIndex = e.getFromIndex();
        int toIndex = e.getToIndex();
        // fromIndex and toIndex identify the range of added columns
    }
    public void columnRemoved(TableColumnModelEvent e) {
        int fromIndex = e.getFromIndex();
        int toIndex = e.getToIndex();
        // fromIndex and toIndex identify the range of removed columns
    }
    public void columnMoved(TableColumnModelEvent e) {
        int fromIndex = e.getFromIndex();
        int toIndex = e.getToIndex();
        // fromIndex and toIndex identify the range of columns being moved.
        // In the case of a user dragging a column, this event is fired as
        // the column is being dragged to its new position. Also, if the
        // column displaces another during dragging, the fromIndex and
        // toIndex show its new position; this new position is only
        // temporary until the user stops dragging the column.
    }
    public void columnMarginChanged(ChangeEvent e) {
        // The width of some column has changed.
        // The event does not identify which column.
    }
    public void columnSelectionChanged(ListSelectionEvent e) {
        // See "ε964. Listening for Selection Events in a JTable Component"
    }
}
```

ε967. Listening for Clicks on a Column Header in a JTable Component

```
int rows = 10;
int cols = 5;
JTable table = new JTable(rows, cols);
JTableHeader header = table.getTableHeader();

header.addMouseListener(new ColumnHeaderListener());

public class ColumnHeaderListener extends MouseAdapter {
    public void mouseClicked(MouseEvent evt) {
        JTable table = ((JTableHeader)evt.getSource()).getTable();
```

```
                TableColumnModel colModel = table.getColumnModel();

                // The index of the column whose header was clicked
                int vColIndex = colModel.getColumnIndexAtX(evt.getX());
                int mColIndex = table.convertColumnIndexToModel(vColIndex);

                // Return if not clicked on any column header
                if (vColIndex == -1) {
                    return;
                }

                // Determine if mouse was clicked between column heads
                Rectangle headerRect = table.getTableHeader().getHeaderRect(vColIndex);
                if (vColIndex == 0) {
                    headerRect.width -= 3; // Hard-coded constant
                } else {
                    headerRect.grow(-3, 0); // Hard-coded constant
                }
                if (!headerRect.contains(evt.getX(), evt.getY())) {
                    // Mouse was clicked between column heads
                    // vColIndex is the column head closest to the click

                    // vLeftColIndex is the column head to the left of the click
                    int vLeftColIndex = vColIndex;
                    if (evt.getX() < headerRect.x) {
                        vLeftColIndex--;
                    }
                }
            }
        }
    }
```

---

javax.swing.text

This package contains classes and interfaces that deal with editable and noneditable text components. Examples of text components are text fields and text areas, of which password fields and document editors are special instantiations. Features that are supported by this package include selection/highlighting, editing, style, and key mapping.

Class   *Interface*   —extends   - - -implements   ○ abstract   ● final   ^—has superclass   ˏ—has subclass   package—see other volume

Packages and Examples

Class   *Interface*   —extends   - - -implements   ○ abstract   ● final   ^-has superclass   ⌄-has subclass   package—see other volume

java.lang.Object

1.2 ○ ├ AbstractDocument ------------------------------------- *Document*, *java.io.Serializable*
1.2   │ ├ DefaultStyledDocument ----------------------------- *StyledDocumentˆ*
1.2   │ └ PlainDocument
1.2 ○ ├ AbstractDocument.AbstractElement --------------------- *Element, MutableAttributeSetˆ, java.io.Serializable, javax.swing.tree.TreeNode*
1.2   │ ├ AbstractDocument.BranchElement
1.2   │ │ └ DefaultStyledDocument.SectionElement
1.2   │ └ AbstractDocument.LeafElement
1.2 ○ ├ AbstractWriter
1.3   ├ AsyncBoxView.ChildLocator
1.3   ├ AsyncBoxView.ChildState ---------------------------- *java.lang.Runnable*
1.2   ├ DefaultStyledDocument.ElementBuffer ---------------- *java.io.Serializable*
1.2   ├ DefaultStyledDocument.ElementSpec
1.4   ├ DocumentFilter
1.4 ○ ├ DocumentFilter.FilterBypass
1.2 ○ ├ EditorKit -- *java.io.Serializable, java.lang.Cloneable*
1.2   │ └ DefaultEditorKit
1.2   │   └ StyledEditorKit
1.2   ├ ElementIterator ------------------------------------ *java.lang.Cloneable*
1.3   ├ FlowView.FlowStrategy
1.2   ├ GapVector -- *java.io.Serializable*
1.2   │ └ GapContent --------------------------------------- *AbstractDocument.Content, java.io.Serializable*
1.3 ○ ├ GlyphView.GlyphPainter
1.2   ├ JTextComponent.KeyBinding
1.2 ○ ├ LayeredHighlighter --------------------------------- *Highlighter*
1.2   │ └ DefaultHighlighter
1.2 ○ ├ LayeredHighlighter.LayerPainter -------------------- *Highlighter.HighlightPainter*
1.2   │ └ DefaultHighlighter.DefaultHighlightPainter
1.3   ├ LayoutQueue
1.4   ├ NavigationFilter
1.4 ○ ├ NavigationFilter.FilterBypass
1.2 ● ├ Position.Bias
1.2   ├ Segment -- *java.lang.Cloneable, java.text.CharacterIteratorˆ*
1.2   ├ SimpleAttributeSet --------------------------------- *MutableAttributeSetˆ, java.io.Serializable, java.lang.Cloneable*
1.2 ● ├ StringContent -------------------------------------- *AbstractDocument.Content, java.io.Serializable*

Class   *Interface*   —extends   - - -implements   ○ abstract   ● final   ˆ—has superclass   —has subclass   package—see other volume

```
           java.lang.Object
1.2          ┬ StyleConstants
1.2          │   ┬ StyleConstants.CharacterConstants ------------------ AttributeSet.CharacterAttribute
1.2          │   ┬ StyleConstants.ColorConstants ----------------------- AttributeSet.CharacterAttribute,
                                                                          AttributeSet.ColorAttribute
1.2          │   ┬ StyleConstants.FontConstants ----------------------- AttributeSet.CharacterAttribute,
                                                                          AttributeSet.FontAttribute
1.2          │   └ StyleConstants.ParagraphConstants ----------------- AttributeSet.ParagraphAttribute
1.2          ┬ StyleContext ------------------------------------------- AbstractDocument.AttributeContext,
                                                                          java.io.Serializable
1.2          ┬ StyleContext.NamedStyle ----------------------------- Style^, java.io.Serializable
1.2          ┬ StyleContext.SmallAttributeSet ----------------------- AttributeSet
1.2          ┬ TabSet ------------------------------------------------ java.io.Serializable
1.2          ┬ TabStop ------------------------------------------------
1.2          ┬ Utilities
1.2    ○     ┬ View -------------------------------------------------- javax.swing.SwingConstants
1.3          │   ┬ AsyncBoxView
1.2          │   ┬ ComponentView
1.2    ○     │   ┬ CompositeView
1.2          │   │   └ BoxView
1.3    ○     │   │       ┬ FlowView
1.2          │   │       │   └ ParagraphView --------------------------- TabExpander
1.2    ○     │   │       ┬ TableView
D            │   │       ┬ TableView.TableCell
1.2          │   │       ┬ TableView.TableRow
1.2          │   │       ┬ WrappedPlainView -------------------------- TabExpander
1.3          │   │       └ ZoneView
1.3          │   ┬ GlyphView ------------------------------------------- TableView, java.lang.Cloneable
1.2          │   │   └ LabelView ----------------------------------------- TableView
1.2          │   ┬ IconView
1.2          │   └ PlainView -------------------------------------------- TabExpander
1.2          │       └ FieldView
1.2          │           └ PasswordView
       ○     ┬ java.awt.Component ------------------------------------- java.awt.MenuContainer, java.awt.image
                                                                          .ImageObserver, java.io.Serializable
             │   └ java.awt.Container
1.2    ○     │       └ javax.swing.JComponent ------------------------- java.io.Serializable
1.2    ○     │           └ JTextComponent --------------------------- javax.accessibility.Accessible,
                                                                          javax.swing.Scrollable
1.2    ○     ┬ java.awt.geom.RectangularShape ---------------------- java.awt.Shape, java.lang.Cloneable
1.2    ○     └ java.awt.geom.Rectangle2D
             │   └ java.awt.Rectangle ------------------------------- java.awt.Shape, java.io.Serializable
1.2          │       └ DefaultCaret ----------------------------------- Caret, java.awt.event.FocusListener^,
                                                                          java.awt.event.MouseListener^,
                                                                          java.awt.event.MouseMotionListener^
```

Packages and Examples

329

```
        java.lang.Object
1.2 ○    ├ javax.accessibility.AccessibleContext
1.3 ○    │  └ java.awt.Component.AccessibleAWTComponent --------- java.io.Serializable ⌄, javax.accessibility ⌃
        │                                                              .AccessibleComponent ⌄
1.3     │     └ java.awt.Container.AccessibleAWTContainer
1.2 ○    │        └ javax.swing.JComponent.AccessibleJComponent ----- javax.accessibility ⌃
        │                                                              .AccessibleExtendedComponent ^
1.2     │           └ JTextComponent.AccessibleJTextComponent ⌄ ----- javax.accessibility.AccessibleAction,
        │                                                              javax.accessibility.AccessibleEditableText ^,
        │                                                              javax.accessibility.AccessibleText ⌄,
        │                                                              javax.swing.event.CaretListener ^,
        │                                                              javax.swing.event.DocumentListener ^
1.2 ○    ├ javax.swing.AbstractAction ---------------------------- java.io.Serializable ⌄, java.lang.Cloneable ⌄,
        │                                                              javax.swing.Action ^
1.2 ○    │  └ TextAction
1.2     │     ├ DefaultEditorKit.BeepAction
1.2     │     ├ DefaultEditorKit.CopyAction
1.2     │     ├ DefaultEditorKit.CutAction
1.2     │     ├ DefaultEditorKit.DefaultKeyTypedAction
1.2     │     ├ DefaultEditorKit.InsertBreakAction
1.2     │     ├ DefaultEditorKit.InsertContentAction
1.2     │     ├ DefaultEditorKit.InsertTabAction
1.2     │     ├ DefaultEditorKit.PasteAction
1.2 ○    │     └ StyledEditorKit.StyledTextAction
1.2     │        ├ StyledEditorKit.AlignmentAction
1.2     │        ├ StyledEditorKit.BoldAction
1.2     │        ├ StyledEditorKit.FontFamilyAction
1.2     │        ├ StyledEditorKit.FontSizeAction
1.2     │        ├ StyledEditorKit.ForegroundAction
1.2     │        ├ StyledEditorKit.ItalicAction
1.2     │        └ StyledEditorKit.UnderlineAction
1.4 ○    ├ javax.swing.JFormattedTextField.AbstractFormatter --------- java.io.Serializable ⌄
1.4     │  └ DefaultFormatter -------------------------------------- java.io.Serializable ⌄, java.lang.Cloneable ⌄
1.4     │     ├ InternationalFormatter
1.4     │     │  ├ DateFormatter
1.4     │     │  └ NumberFormatter
1.4     │     └ MaskFormatter
1.4 ○    ├ javax.swing.JFormattedTextField.AbstractFormatterFactory
1.4     │  └ DefaultFormatterFactory ------------------------------ java.io.Serializable ⌄
1.2 ○    ├ javax.swing.plaf.ComponentUI
1.2 ○    │  └ javax.swing.plaf.TextUI
1.2 ○    │     └ javax.swing.plaf.basic.BasicTextUI ----------------- ViewFactory
D   ○    │        └ DefaultTextUI
1.2     ├ javax.swing.undo.AbstractUndoableEdit ------------------- java.io.Serializable ⌄, javax.swing.undo ⌃
        │                                                              .UndoableEdit
1.2     │  ├ AbstractDocument.ElementEdit ---------------------- javax.swing.event.DocumentEvent.ElementChange
1.2     │  ├ DefaultStyledDocument.AttributeUndoableEdit
1.2     │  └ javax.swing.undo.CompoundEdit
1.2     │     └ AbstractDocument.DefaultDocumentEvent ------------ javax.swing.event.DocumentEvent
```

Class   *Interface*   —extends   - - -implements   ○ abstract   ● final   ^—has superclass   ⌄—has subclass   package—see other volume

```
java.lang.Object
  └ java.lang.Throwable ------------------------------ java.io.Serializable
      └ java.lang.Exception
1.2        ├ BadLocationException
1.2        └ java.io.IOException
1.2              └ ChangedCharSetException
```

1.2	*AbstractDocument.AttributeContext*
1.2	*AbstractDocument.Content*
1.2	*AttributeSet*
1.2	*AttributeSet.CharacterAttribute*
1.2	*AttributeSet.ColorAttribute*
1.2	*AttributeSet.FontAttribute*
1.2	*AttributeSet.ParagraphAttribute*
1.2	*Caret*
1.2	*Document*
1.2	*Element*
1.2	*Highlighter*
1.2	*Highlighter.Highlight*
1.2	*Highlighter.HighlightPainter*
1.2	*Keymap*
1.2	*MutableAttributeSet* ———————————————— *AttributeSet*
1.2	*Position*
1.2	*Style* ————————————————————— *MutableAttributeSet*
1.2	*StyledDocument* ————————————————— *Document*
1.2	*TabExpander*
1.2	*TabableView*
1.2	*ViewFactory*

JTextComponent

ε968. Retrieving Text from a JTextComponent

This example works for all types of text components.

```
// Create the text component
JTextComponent tc = new JTextArea("Initial Text");

// Get length
int docLength = tc.getDocument().getLength();

// Get all text
String text = tc.getText();

try {
    // Get the first 3 characters
    int offset = 0;
    int len = 3;
    text = tc.getText(offset, len);

    // Get the last 3 characters
    offset = docLength-3;
    len = 3;
    text = tc.getText(offset, len);
```

```
    } catch (BadLocationException e) {
    }
```

ε969. Retrieving All the Text from a JTextComponent Efficiently

The text contained in a text component is not always stored contiguously. Therefore, retrieving text using getText() may cause a new String object to be created and the text copied to the new string. If you do not need the text in one contiguous chunk, the most efficient way to retrieve the text is in pieces called segments. This example retrieves the entire contents of a text component in segments.

```
    // Create the text component
    JTextComponent textComp = new JTextPane();
    Document doc = textComp.getDocument();

    // Create a segment to hold the characters in the document
    Segment segment = new Segment();
    int pos = 0;
    segment.setPartialReturn(true);

    try {
        // Retrieve all segments
        while (pos < doc.getLength()) {
            // Ask for the remainder of the document text
            doc.getText(pos, doc.getLength()-pos, segment);

            // You can access the contents directly from the array in the segment.
            // Never modify the contents of the array
            for (int i=0; i<segment.count; i++) {
                int positionInDoc = pos+i;
                char charAtPos = segment.array[i+segment.offset];
            }

            // Or use the segment as a character iterator
            int i=0;
            for(char c=segment.first(); c != CharacterIterator.DONE; c=segment.next(), i++) {
                int positionInDoc = pos+i;
                char charAtPos = c;
            }

            // Increment pos by the actual number of characters retrieved
            pos += segment.count;
        }
    } catch (BadLocationException e) {
    }
```

ε970. Modifying Text in a JTextComponent

```
    // Create the text component
    JTextComponent textComp = new JTextField("Initial Text");
    Document doc = textComp.getDocument();

    try {
        // Insert some text at the beginning
        int pos = 0;
        doc.insertString(pos, "some text", null);

        // Insert some text after the 5th character
        pos = 5;
```

```
        doc.insertString(pos, "some text", null);

        // Append some text
        doc.insertString(doc.getLength(), "some text", null);

        // Delete the first 5 characters
        pos = 0;
        int len = 5;
        doc.remove(pos, len);

        // Replace the first 3 characters with some text
        pos = 0;
        len = 3;
        doc.remove(pos, len);
        doc.insertString(pos, "new text", null);
    } catch (BadLocationException e) {
    }
```

ε971. Asynchronously Reading the Contents of a Visible JTextComponent

When a text component is visible on the screen, you cannot simply call getText() on the document model to retrieve the text. The reason is that the user may be modifying the text at the same time. There are two ways to safely access the contents of the text component. One is by using SwingUtilities.invokeLater() and the other is by using Document.render(). This example demonstrates the latter.

```
// Create and display the component
JTextComponent textComp = new JTextArea();
Document doc = textComp.getDocument();

JFrame frame = new JFrame();
frame.getContentPane().add(textComp, BorderLayout.CENTER);
frame.pack();
frame.setVisible(true);

// Read the contents
try {
    process(read(doc));
} catch (InterruptedException e) {
} catch (Exception e) {
}

// This method returns the contents of a Document using a renderer.
public static String read(Document doc) throws InterruptedException, Exception {
    Renderer r = new Renderer(doc);
    doc.render(r);

    synchronized (r) {
        while (!r.done) {
            r.wait();
            if (r.err != null) {
                throw new Exception(r.err);
            }
        }
    }
    return r.result;
}

static class Renderer implements Runnable {
    Document doc;
    String result;
```

```
            Throwable err;
            boolean done;

            Renderer(Document doc) {
                this.doc = doc;
            }
            public synchronized void run() {
                try {
                    result = doc.getText(0, doc.getLength());
                } catch (Throwable e) {
                    err = e;
                    e.printStackTrace();
                }
                done = true;
                // When done, notify the creator of this object
                notify();
            }
        }
```

ε972. Finding Word Boundaries in a JTextComponent

This example demonstrates an action that selects the word adjacent to the caret. If the caret is adjacent to two words, the word following the caret is selected. The implementation uses BreakIterator.getWordInstance() to find word boundaries.

```
    public TextAction selectWordAction = new TextAction("Select Word") {
        public void actionPerformed(ActionEvent evt) {
            JTextComponent c = getTextComponent(evt);
            if (c == null) {
                return;
            }
            int pos = c.getCaretPosition();

            try {
                // Find start of word from caret
                int start = Utilities.getWordStart(c, pos);

                // Check if start precedes whitespace
                if (start < c.getDocument().getLength()
                    && Character.isWhitespace(c.getDocument().getText(start, 1).charAt(0))) {
                    // Check if caret is at end of word
                    if (pos > 0
                        && !Character.isWhitespace(c.getDocument().getText(pos-1, 1).charAt(0))) {
                        // Start searching before the caret
                        start = Utilities.getWordStart(c, pos-1);
                    } else {
                        // Caret is not adjacent to a word
                        start = -1;
                    }
                }
                if (start != -1) {
                    // A non-whitespace character follows start.
                    // Find end of word from start.
                    int end = Utilities.getWordEnd(c, start);

                    // Set selection
```

```
                    c.setSelectionStart(start);
                    c.setSelectionEnd(end);
                }
            } catch (BadLocationException e) {
            }
        }
    };

    public TextAction selectNextWordAction = new TextAction("Select Next Word") {
        public void actionPerformed(ActionEvent evt) {
            JTextComponent c = getTextComponent(evt);
            if (c == null) {
                return;
            }
            int pos = c.getSelectionStart();
            int len = c.getDocument().getLength();

            try {
                // Find start of next word from selection.
                // getNextWord() throws BadLocationException if no word follows pos.
                int start = Utilities.getNextWord(c, pos);

                // Find end of word from start
                int end = Utilities.getWordEnd(c, start);

                // Set selection
                c.setSelectionStart(start);
                c.setSelectionEnd(end);
            } catch (BadLocationException e) {
            }
        }
    };

    public TextAction selectPrevWordAction = new TextAction("Select Previous Word") {
        public void actionPerformed(ActionEvent evt) {
            JTextComponent c = getTextComponent(evt);
            if (c == null) {
                return;
            }
            int pos = c.getSelectionStart();
            int len = c.getDocument().getLength();

            try {
                // Find start of previous word from selection.
                // getPreviousWord() throws BadLocationException if no word precedes pos.
                int start = Utilities.getPreviousWord(c, pos);

                // Find end of word from start
                int end = Utilities.getWordEnd(c, start);

                // Set selection
                c.setSelectionStart(start);
                c.setSelectionEnd(end);
            } catch (BadLocationException e) {
            }
        }
    };
```

Packages and Examples

335

ε973. Retrieving the Visible Lines in a JTextComponent

There are *hard* and *soft* line breaks when viewing the contents of a text component. Hard line breaks are caused by a newline character in the contents. Soft line breaks are a result of word wrapping by the text component. Word wrapping occurs strictly on the display; it does not change the contents (i.e., newlines are not inserted into the contents).

This example demonstrates how to retrieve the contents with soft line breaks. The retrieval does not modify the contents; it returns the contents with additional newlines for soft line breaks.

Note: getWrappedLines() can be used directly if called within an event thread. To call it on a visible text component outside an event thread, use the Document.render() method to safely retrieve the text. See "ε971. Asynchronously Reading the Contents of a Visible JTextComponent" for an example.

```java
// Returns null if comp does not have a size
public static String getWrappedText(JTextComponent c) {
    int len = c.getDocument().getLength();
    int offset = 0;

    // Increase 10% for extra newlines
    StringBuffer buf = new StringBuffer((int)(len*1.10));

    try {
        while (offset < len) {
            int end = Utilities.getRowEnd(c, offset);
            if (end < 0) {
                break;
            }

            // Include the last character on the line
            end = Math.min(end+1, len);

            String s = c.getDocument().getText(offset, end-offset);
            buf.append(s);

            // Add a newline if s does not have one
            if (!s.endsWith("\n")) {
                buf.append('\n');
            }
            offset = end;
        }
    } catch (BadLocationException e) {
    }
    return buf.toString();
}
```

ε974. Using a Position in a JTextComponent

A position marks a location between two characters in a JTextComponent. The position attempts to remain between the same two characters despite edits to the JTextComponent. For example, if the position is at location 10 and the first character is deleted, the new location of the position becomes 9.

When text is inserted at the position, a position's bias determines whether it remains in the same location or is moved to the end of the new text. By default, createPosition() returns a position with a right bias, which means inserting text at the position causes it to move to the end of the inserted text. There is no way to change the bias at present.

```
JTextComponent textComp = new JTextArea();
Document doc = textComp.getDocument();

Position p = null;
try {
    // Create a right-bias Position object
    int location = 3;
    p = doc.createPosition(location);
} catch (BadLocationException e) {
}

// Retrieve the current location of the Position object
int location = p.getOffset();
```

ε975. Limiting the Capacity of a JTextComponent

Prior to J2SE 1.4, limiting the capacity of a text component involved overriding the insertString() method of the component's model. Here's an example:

```
JTextComponent textComp = new JTextField();
textComp.setDocument(new FixedSizePlainDocument(10));

class FixedSizePlainDocument extends PlainDocument {
    int maxSize;

    public FixedSizePlainDocument(int limit) {
        maxSize = limit;
    }

    public void insertString(int offs, String str, AttributeSet a) throws BadLocationException {
        if ((getLength() + str.length()) <= maxSize) {
            super.insertString(offs, str, a);
        } else {
            throw new BadLocationException("Insertion exceeds max size of document", offs);
        }
    }
}
```

J2SE 1.4 allows the ability to filter all editing operations on a text component. Here's an example that uses the new filtering capability to limit the capacity of the text component:

```
JTextComponent textComponent = new JTextField();
AbstractDocument doc = (AbstractDocument)textComponent.getDocument();
doc.setDocumentFilter(new FixedSizeFilter(10));

class FixedSizeFilter extends DocumentFilter {
    int maxSize;

    // limit is the maximum number of characters allowed.
    public FixedSizeFilter(int limit) {
        maxSize = limit;
    }

    // This method is called when characters are inserted into the document
    public void insertString(DocumentFilter.FilterBypass fb, int offset, String str,
            AttributeSet attr) throws BadLocationException {
        replace(fb, offset, 0, str, attr);
    }

    // This method is called when characters in the document are replace with other characters
    public void replace(DocumentFilter.FilterBypass fb, int offset, int length,
```

Packages and Examples

337

```
                  String str, AttributeSet attrs) throws BadLocationException {
              int newLength = fb.getDocument().getLength()-length+str.length();
              if (newLength <= maxSize) {
                  fb.replace(offset, length, str, attrs);
              } else {
                  throw new BadLocationException("New characters exceeds max size of document", offset);
              }
          }
      }
```

ε976. Enabling Text-Dragging on a JTextComponent

With text-dragging enabled, the user can select some text and drag the selected text to another part of the text component (or to another text component). During dragging, the text component's caret follows the cursor (but caret events are not fired). When the user releases the mouse, the selected text is deleted and inserted into the location of the caret. If the control key is pressed at the time the mouse button is released, the selected text is instead copied to the new location.

```
JTextComponent textComp = new JTextArea();
textComp.setDragEnabled(true);
```

ε977. Sharing a Document Between JTextComponents

When you share a document between two text components, any edits made in one text component will show up in the other.

```
JTextComponent textComp1 = new JTextArea();
JTextComponent textComp2 = new JTextArea();

textComp2.setDocument(textComp1.getDocument());
```

ε978. Enumerating All the Views in a JTextComponent

```
// Create a text component
JTextComponent textComp = new JTextPane();

// Get the root view
View v = textComp.getUI().getRootView(textComp);

// Walk the view hierarchy
walkView(v, 0);
// Recursively walks a view hierarchy
public void walkView(View view, int level) {
    // Process view...

    // Get number of children views
    int n = view.getViewCount();

    // Visit the children of this view
    for (int i=0; i<n; i++) {
        walkView(view.getView(i), level+1);
    }
}
```

JTextField

ε979. Creating a JTextField Component

When the user hits RETURN, the text field fires an action event.

```
// Create a text field with some initial text
JTextField textfield = new JTextField("Initial Text");

// Create a text field with some initial text and a default number of columns.
// The number of columns controls the preferred width of the component;
// each column is rougly the size of an M in the current font.
int cols = 30;
textfield = new JTextField("Initial Text", cols);

// Listen for action events, which are fired when the user hits RETURN
textfield.addActionListener(new MyActionListener());

class MyActionListener implements ActionListener {
    public void actionPerformed(ActionEvent evt) {
        JTextField textfield = (JTextField)evt.getSource();
        process(textfield.getText());
    }
}
```

ε980. Creating a Password JTextField Component

When the user hits RETURN, the text field fires an action event.

```
JPasswordField textfield = new JPasswordField("Initial Text");
textfield.setEchoChar('#');
textfield.addActionListener(actionListener);
```

ε981. Aligning the Text in a JTextField Component

```
// Create a text field with some initial text
JTextField textfield = new JTextField("Initial Text");

// Left-justify the text
textfield.setHorizontalAlignment(JTextField.LEFT);

// Center the text
textfield.setHorizontalAlignment(JTextField.CENTER);

// Right-justify the text
textfield.setHorizontalAlignment(JTextField.RIGHT);
```

JTextArea

ε982. Creating a JTextArea Component

```
// Create a text area with some initial text
JTextArea textarea = new JTextArea("Initial Text");

// Create a text area with some initial text and a default number of rows and columns.
// This number of rows and columns controls the preferred width and height of the component;
// each row and column is rougly the size of an M in the current font.
int rows = 20;
int cols = 30;
textarea = new JTextArea("Initial Text", rows, cols);
```

Packages and Examples

ε983. Modifying Text in a JTextArea Component

The text in a text area can be modified using the method described in "ε970. Modifying Text in a JTextComponent". However, the text area supports a similar set of convenience editing methods that are demonstrated in this example.

```
// Create the text area
JTextArea ta = new JTextArea("Initial Text");

// Insert some text at the beginning
int pos = 0;
ta.insert("some text", pos);

// Insert some text after the 5th character
pos = 5;
ta.insert("some text", pos);

// Append some text
ta.append("some text");

// Replace the first 3 characters with some text
int start = 0;
int end = 3;
ta.replaceRange("new text", start, end);

// Delete the first 5 characters
start = 0;
end = 5;
ta.replaceRange(null, start, end);
```

ε984. Enumerating the Lines in a JTextArea Component

The contents of a text component are stored in a Document object that, in turn, breaks the content into a hierarchy of Element objects. In the case of a text area, each line of text (a contiguous span of characters terminated by a single newline) is stored in a content element. For example, if the last line of the contents is terminated by a newline and there are 100 new lines, there will be 100 content elements. All content elements are stored under a single paragraph element.

This example demonstrates how to retrieve the paragraph element and enumerate all children content elements.

See also "ε973. Retrieving the Visible Lines in a JTextComponent".

```
// Create a text area
JTextArea textArea = new JTextArea("word1 word2\nword3\nword4");

// Get paragraph element
Element paragraph = textArea.getDocument().getDefaultRootElement();

// Get number of content elements
int contentCount = paragraph.getElementCount();

// Get index ranges for each content element.
// Each content element represents one line.
// Each line includes the terminating newline.
for (int i=0; i<contentCount; i++) {
    Element e = paragraph.getElement(i);
    int rangeStart = e.getStartOffset();
    int rangeEnd = e.getEndOffset();
    try {
```

```
            String line = textArea.getText(rangeStart, rangeEnd-rangeStart);
        } catch (BadLocationException ex) {
        }
    }
}
```

Here is another way to enumerate the content elements with a ElementIterator:

```
// Get the text area's document
Document doc = textArea.getDocument();

// Create an iterator using the root element
ElementIterator it = new ElementIterator(doc.getDefaultRootElement());

// Iterate all content elements (which are leaves)
Element e;
while ((e=it.next()) != null) {
    if (e.isLeaf()) {
        int rangeStart = e.getStartOffset();
        int rangeEnd = e.getEndOffset();
        try {
            String line = textArea.getText(rangeStart, rangeEnd-rangeStart);
        } catch (BadLocationException ex) {
        }
    }
}
```

ε985. Setting the Tab Size of a JTextArea Component

When a tab character (\t) is inserted into a text area, it is represented by a space that is wide enough to reach the next tab stop. The space expands or contracts, if the text preceding it is modified. A tab space cannot be zero-width or wider than a tab stop.

By default, each tab stop is the same width and appears at regular intervals. The tab stop width is controlled by the \metatab size. The tab size specifies a number of characters. The tab width is this value multiplied by the maximal character width in the current font. For example, if the widest character in the current font is 20 pixels and the tab size is 8, the tab width is 160 pixels; tab stops will appear every 160 pixels in the text area.

All tab stops in a JTextArea are left-aligned. For other types of tab stops, a JTextPane must be used; see "ε993. Customizing Tab Stops in a JTextPane Component".

```
// Create a text area
JTextArea textarea = new JTextArea();

// Get the default tab size
int tabSize = textarea.getTabSize(); // 8

// Change the tab size
tabSize = 4;
textarea.setTabSize(tabSize);

Font font = textarea.getFont();
```

ε986. Moving the Focus with the TAB Key in a JTextArea Component

By default, typing TAB in a JTextArea inserts a TAB character. This example demonstrates how to modify the behavior so that typing TAB moves the focus to the next focusable component.

Rather than try to find the inputmap or keymap with the TAB binding and remove it, it is better to add an overriding key binding that will move the focus. The reason is that the location of the default TAB binding might change in some future version.

```
JTextArea component = new JTextArea();

// Add actions
component.getActionMap().put(nextFocusAction.getValue(Action.NAME), nextFocusAction);
component.getActionMap().put(prevFocusAction.getValue(Action.NAME), prevFocusAction);

// The actions
public Action nextFocusAction = new AbstractAction("Move Focus Forwards") {
    public void actionPerformed(ActionEvent evt) {
        ((Component)evt.getSource()).transferFocus();
    }
};
public Action prevFocusAction = new AbstractAction("Move Focus Backwards") {
    public void actionPerformed(ActionEvent evt) {
        ((Component)evt.getSource()).transferFocusBackward();
    }
};
```

ε987. Enabling Word-Wrapping and Line-Wrapping in a JTextArea Component

With line-wrapping, breaks are allowed to occur in the middle of words. With word-wrapping, breaks are only allowed between words.

```
JTextArea c = new JTextArea();

// Enable line-wrapping
c.setLineWrap(true);
c.setWrapStyleWord(false);

// Enable word-wrapping
c.setLineWrap(true);
c.setWrapStyleWord(true);
```

ε988. Implementing a Console Window with a JTextArea Component

This example creates a console window using a JTextArea which shows all output printed to System.out and System.err. System.out and System.err are replaced with piped io streams. Two reader threads are created that retrieve the output from these piped io streams and append it to the JTextArea component.

```
import java.awt.*;
import java.awt.event.*;
import java.io.*;
import javax.swing.*;
import javax.swing.event.*;
import javax.swing.text.*;

public class Console extends JFrame {
    PipedInputStream piOut;
    PipedInputStream piErr;
    PipedOutputStream poOut;
    PipedOutputStream poErr;
    JTextArea textArea = new JTextArea();

    public Console() throws IOException {
```

Class   *Interface*   —extends   - - -implements   ○ abstract   ● final   ˆ—has superclass   ˏ—has subclass   `package`—see other volume

```
        // Set up System.out
        piOut = new PipedInputStream();
        poOut = new PipedOutputStream(piOut);
        System.setOut(new PrintStream(poOut, true));

        // Set up System.err
        piErr = new PipedInputStream();
        poErr = new PipedOutputStream(piErr);
        System.setErr(new PrintStream(poErr, true));

        // Add a scrolling text area
        textArea.setEditable(false);
        textArea.setRows(20);
        textArea.setColumns(50);
        getContentPane().add(new JScrollPane(textArea), BorderLayout.CENTER);
        pack();
        setVisible(true);

        // Create reader threads
        new ReaderThread(piOut).start();
        new ReaderThread(piErr).start();
    }

    class ReaderThread extends Thread {
        PipedInputStream pi;

        ReaderThread(PipedInputStream pi) {
            this.pi = pi;
        }

        public void run() {
            final byte[] buf = new byte[1024];
            try {
                while (true) {
                    final int len = pi.read(buf);
                    if (len == -1) {
                        break;
                    }
                    SwingUtilities.invokeLater(new Runnable() {
                        public void run() {
                            textArea.append(new String(buf, 0, len));

                            // Make sure the last line is always visible
                            textArea.setCaretPosition(textArea.getDocument().getLength());

                            // Keep the text area down to a certain character size
                            int idealSize = 1000;
                            int maxExcess = 500;
                            int excess = textArea.getDocument().getLength() - idealSize;
                            if (excess >= maxExcess) {
                                textArea.replaceRange("", 0, excess);
                            }
                        }
                    });
                }
            } catch (IOException e) {
            }
        }
```

```
        }
    }
```

The console window is created using

```
try {
    new Console();
} catch (IOException e) {
}
```

JTextPane

ε989. Inserting Styled Text in a JTextPane Component

See the StyleConstants class for more attributes.

```
try {
    // Get the text pane's document
    JTextPane textPane = new JTextPane();
    StyledDocument doc = (StyledDocument)textPane.getDocument();

    // Create a style object and then set the style attributes
    Style style = doc.addStyle("StyleName", null);

    // Italic
    StyleConstants.setItalic(style, true);

    // Bold
    StyleConstants.setBold(style, true);

    // Font family
    StyleConstants.setFontFamily(style, "SansSerif");

    // Font size
    StyleConstants.setFontSize(style, 30);

    // Background color
    StyleConstants.setBackground(style, Color.blue);

    // Foreground color
    StyleConstants.setForeground(style, Color.white);

    // Append to document
    doc.insertString(doc.getLength(), "Some Text", style);
} catch (BadLocationException e) {
}
```

ε990. Enumerating the Paragraphs of a JTextPane Component

The contents of a text component are stored in a Document object that in turn, breaks the content into a hierarchy of Element objects. In the case of a text pane, the content elements contain *runs* of characters. A run of characters is a contiguous span of characters with the same attributes. Adjacent runs of characters will have different sets of attributes. If the attributes of one run is modified so that it becomes identical to an adjacent run, both runs will be combined into a single run.

Adjacent runs that make up a line of text (a contiguous span of characters terminated by a single newline) are stored under one paragraph element. In other words, a paragraph element will have at most one run (the last run) with a single newline (only the very last line of the contents may lack a newline). Note that the adjacency rule does not apply to runs in different paragraph elements.

Finally, all paragraph elements in a text pane are stored under a single section element.

See also "ε973. Retrieving the Visible Lines in a JTextComponent".

```java
// Create a text pane
JTextPane textPane = new JTextPane();

// Get section element
Element section = textPane.getDocument().getDefaultRootElement();

// Get number of paragraphs.
// In a text pane, a span of characters terminated by single
// newline is typically called a paragraph.
int paraCount = section.getElementCount();

// Get index ranges for each paragraph
for (int i=0; i<paraCount; i++) {
    Element e = section.getElement(i);
    int rangeStart = e.getStartOffset();
    int rangeEnd = e.getEndOffset();
    try {
        String para = textPane.getText(rangeStart, rangeEnd-rangeStart);
    } catch (BadLocationException ex) {
    }
}
```

ε991. Inserting an Image into a JTextPane Component

```java
try {
    // Get the text pane's document
    JTextPane textPane = new JTextPane();
    StyledDocument doc = (StyledDocument)textPane.getDocument();

    // The image must first be wrapped in a style
    Style style = doc.addStyle("StyleName", null);
    StyleConstants.setIcon(style, new ImageIcon("imagefile"));

    // Insert the image at the end of the text
    doc.insertString(doc.getLength(), "ignored text", style);
} catch (BadLocationException e) {
}
```

ε992. Inserting a Component into a JTextPane Component

This example inserts a button into a text pane.

```java
try {
    // Get the text pane's document
    JTextPane textPane = new JTextPane();
    StyledDocument doc = (StyledDocument)textPane.getDocument();

    // The component must first be wrapped in a style
    Style style = doc.addStyle("StyleName", null);
    StyleConstants.setComponent(style, new JButton("OK"));

    // Insert the component at the end of the text
    doc.insertString(doc.getLength(), "ignored text", style);
} catch (BadLocationException e) {
}
```

Packages and Examples

345

ε993. Customizing Tab Stops in a JTextPane Component

This example demonstrates the four types of tabs that can be used in a JTextPane. In a left-aligned tab, characters appear after the tab. In a right-aligned tab, characters appear in front of the tab. In a center-aligned tab, characters appear centered around the tab. In a decimal-aligned tab, the decimal point is anchored at the tab.

```
// Create a text pane
JTextPane textPane = new JTextPane();

// Create one of each type of tab stop
java.util.List list = new ArrayList();

// Create a left-aligned tab stop at 100 pixels from the left margin
float pos = 100;
int align = TabStop.ALIGN_LEFT;
int leader = TabStop.LEAD_NONE;
TabStop tstop = new TabStop(pos, align, leader);
list.add(tstop);

// Create a right-aligned tab stop at 200 pixels from the left margin
pos = 200;
align = TabStop.ALIGN_RIGHT;
leader = TabStop.LEAD_NONE;
tstop = new TabStop(pos, align, leader);
list.add(tstop);

// Create a center-aligned tab stop at 300 pixels from the left margin
pos = 300;
align = TabStop.ALIGN_CENTER;
leader = TabStop.LEAD_NONE;
tstop = new TabStop(pos, align, leader);
list.add(tstop);

// Create a decimal-aligned tab stop at 400 pixels from the left margin
pos = 400;
align = TabStop.ALIGN_DECIMAL;
leader = TabStop.LEAD_NONE;
tstop = new TabStop(pos, align, leader);
list.add(tstop);

// Create a tab set from the tab stops
TabStop[] tstops = (TabStop[])list.toArray(new TabStop[0]);
TabSet tabs = new TabSet(tstops);

// Add the tab set to the logical style;
// the logical style is inherited by all paragraphs
Style style = textPane.getLogicalStyle();
StyleConstants.setTabSet(style, tabs);
textPane.setLogicalStyle(style);
```

JEditorPane

ε994. Displaying Simple HTML Files

```
try {
    String url = "http://java.sun.com";
```

```
        JEditorPane editorPane = new JEditorPane(url);
        editorPane.setEditable(false);

        JFrame frame = new JFrame();
        frame.getContentPane().add(editorPane, BorderLayout.CENTER);
        frame.setSize(width, height);
        frame.setVisible(true);
    } catch (IOException e) {
    }
```

JFormattedTextField

ε995. Creating a Text Field to Display and Edit a Number

This example uses a JFormattedTextField to allow the display and editing of a number. By default, when the component loses the focus and the modified value is a valid date, the modified value is saved. Otherwise, if the modified value is not a valid date, the modified value is discarded and the old value is displayed.

```
// Support an integer number; if a decimal point is typed,
// the decimal point and all following characters are discarded
JFormattedTextField tft1 = new JFormattedTextField(NumberFormat.getIntegerInstance());
tft1.setValue(new Integer(123));

// Retrieve the value from the text field
Integer intValue = (Integer)tft1.getValue();


// Support a decimal number with one digit following the decimal point;
// if more digits after the decimal point is typed, the value is rounded to one decimal place
JFormattedTextField tft2 = new JFormattedTextField(new DecimalFormat("#.0"));
tft2.setValue(new Float(123.4F));

// Retrieve the value from the text field
Float floatValue = (Float)tft2.getValue();
```

By default, if the type of the value is not one of Byte, Short, Integer, Long , Float, or Double, the object is automatically converted to a Double after it has been edited. To prevent this, a custom formatter must be used. This example demonstrates this by using a BigDecimal object.

```
// Support a decimal number with arbitrary number of decimal digits.
// Actually, this isn't technically possible using DecimalFormat;
// the best that we can do is to specify lots of #'s
JFormattedTextField tft3 = new JFormattedTextField(new BigDecimal("123.4567"));
DefaultFormatter fmt = new NumberFormatter(new DecimalFormat("#.0##############"));
fmt.setValueClass(tft3.getValue().getClass());
DefaultFormatterFactory fmtFactory = new DefaultFormatterFactory(fmt, fmt, fmt);
tft3.setFormatterFactory(fmtFactory);

// Retrieve the value from the text field
BigDecimal bigValue = (BigDecimal)tft3.getValue();
```

ε996. Creating a Text Field to Display and Edit a Date

This example uses a JFormattedTextField to allow the display and editing of a date. By default, when the component loses the focus and the modified value is a valid date, the modified value is saved. Otherwise, if the modified value is not a valid date, the modified value is discarded and the old value is displayed.

```
// Support a date in the MEDIUM format in the current locale;
// see "ε322. Formatting and Parsing a Date Using Default Formats".
// For Locale.ENGLISH, the format would be Feb 8, 2002.
JFormattedTextField tft1 = new JFormattedTextField(new Date());

// Support a date in the SHORT format using the current locale.
// For Locale.ENGLISH, the format would be 2/8/02.
JFormattedTextField tft2 = new JFormattedTextField(DateFormat.getDateInstance(DateFormat.SHORT));
tft2.setValue(new Date());

// Support a date with the custom format: 2002-8-2
JFormattedTextField tft3 = new JFormattedTextField(new SimpleDateFormat("yyyy-M-d"));
tft3.setValue(new Date());
// See also "ε320. Formatting a Date Using a Custom Format"

// Retrieve the date from the text field
Date date = (Date)tft3.getValue();
```

The following example demonstrates how to dynamically change the format:

```
// Change the format to: 2/8/2002
DateFormatter fmt = (DateFormatter)tft3.getFormatter();
fmt.setFormat(new SimpleDateFormat("d/M/yyyy"));

// Reformat the display
tft3.setValue(tft3.getValue());
```

ε997. Creating a Text Field to Display and Edit a Phone Number

This example uses a JFormattedTextField to allow the display and editing of certain fixed-string patterns. By default, when the component loses the focus and the modified value is valid, the modified value is saved. Otherwise, if the modified value is not valid, the modified value is discarded and the old value is displayed.

The pattern is specified using one of the following characters: # represents a decimal digit, H represents a hex digit, U represents an uppercase letter, L represents a lowercase letter, A represents a number or letter, ? represents a letter in any case, and * represents any character. Any other character in the pattern represents itself. If it is necessary to use one of the special characters, it can be escaped by preceding it with a quote (').

```
MaskFormatter fmt = null;

// A phone number
try {
    fmt = new MaskFormatter("###-###-####");
} catch (java.text.ParseException e) {
}
JFormattedTextField tft1 = new JFormattedTextField(fmt);


// A social security number
try {
    fmt = new MaskFormatter("###-##-####");
} catch (java.text.ParseException e) {
}
JFormattedTextField tft2 = new JFormattedTextField(fmt);
```

The spot where a character or digit is expected is called a placeholder. By default, a placeholder is represented with a space character. The space is automatically replaced as the user fills in the field. This example demonstrates how to use an asterisk as the placeholder character.

```
// A social security number
fmt.setPlaceholderCharacter('*');
JFormattedTextField tft3 = new JFormattedTextField(fmt);
```

Caret and Selection

ε998. Moving the Caret of a JTextComponent

```
JTextComponent c = new JTextArea();

// Get position of the caret
c.getCaretPosition();

// Get the character following the caret
if (c.getCaretPosition() < c.getDocument().getLength()) {
    try {
        char ch = c.getText(c.getCaretPosition(), 1).charAt(0);
    } catch (BadLocationException e) {
    }
}

// Move the caret
int newPosition = 0;
c.moveCaretPosition(newPosition);

// Set the caret color
c.setCaretColor(Color.red);
```

ε999. Setting the Blink Rate of a JTextComponent's Caret

The blink rate is specified in milliseconds. In particular, the blink rate causes the caret to appear for T milliseconds and disappear for T milliseconds.

```
JTextComponent c = new JTextArea();

// Set rate to blink once a second
c.getCaret().setBlinkRate(1000);

// Set the caret to stop blinking
c.getCaret().setBlinkRate(0);
```

ε1000. Using the Selection of a JTextComponent

```
JTextComponent c = new JTextArea();

// Get text inside selection
c.getSelectedText();

// Replace selected text
c.replaceSelection("replacement text");

// Set the start of the selection; ignored if new start is < end
c.setSelectionStart(10);

// Set the end of the selection; ignored if new end is > start
c.setSelectionEnd(20);

// Better way to set the selection
```

Packages and Examples

349

```
c.select(10, 20);

// Set the color of text inside the selection
c.setSelectedTextColor(Color.red);

// Set the color behind the selected text
c.setSelectionColor(Color.green);
```

Actions and Key Bindings

ε1001. Overriding the Default Action of a JTextComponent

The default action in a text component keymap receives all typed characters that are not handled in any inputmap or keymap. This example demonstrates how to wrap the default action of a text component with a custom default action.

```
JTextArea component = new JTextArea();
Action defAction = findDefaultAction(component);

// Install the overriding default action
component.getKeymap().setDefaultAction(new MyDefaultAction(defAction));

public class MyDefaultAction extends AbstractAction {
    Action defAction;
    public MyDefaultAction(Action a) {
        super("My Default Action");
        defAction = a;
    }
    public void actionPerformed(ActionEvent e) {
        // Perform customizations here
        // This example upper cases all typed characters
        if (e.getActionCommand() != null) {
            String command = e.getActionCommand();
            if (command != null) {
                command = command.toUpperCase();
            }
            e = new ActionEvent(e.getSource(), e.getID(), command, e.getModifiers());
        }

        // Now call the installed default action
        if (defAction != null) {
            defAction.actionPerformed(e);
        }
    }
}

public Action findDefaultAction(JTextComponent c) {
    // Look for default action
    // Check local keymap
    Keymap kmap = c.getKeymap();
    if (kmap.getDefaultAction() != null) {
        return kmap.getDefaultAction();
    }

    // Check parent keymaps
    kmap = kmap.getResolveParent();
```

Class   *Interface*   —extends   - - -implements   ○ abstract   ● final   ^—has superclass   ⌐—has subclass   package—see other volume

```
        while (kmap != null) {
            if (kmap.getDefaultAction() != null) {
                return kmap.getDefaultAction();
            }
            kmap = kmap.getResolveParent();
        }
        return null;
    }
```

ε1002. Creating a Custom Editing Command for a JTextComponent

This example demonstrates how to implement an editing command. There are two steps when creating a custom command. The first is to create an action object that executes the desired functionality and then installs the action object in the component. The second is to bind a keystroke to the action object using an inputmap.

Text component actions should extend from TextAction. TextAction has a convenience method for finding the appropriate text component on which to operate.

This example implements a *Lowercase* command that converts characters to lowercase. If the selection is empty, the command converts the character following the caret and then moves the caret forward one space. If the selection is not empty, the command converts the characters in the selection.

```
JTextArea comp = new JTextArea();

// Bind F2 to the lowercase action
String actionName = "Lowercase";
comp.getInputMap().put(KeyStroke.getKeyStroke("F2"), actionName);

// Install the action
comp.getActionMap().put(actionName,
    new TextAction(actionName) {
        public void actionPerformed(ActionEvent evt) {
            lowercaseSelection(getTextComponent(evt));
        }
    }
);
public static void lowercaseSelection(JTextComponent comp) {
    if (comp.getSelectionStart() == comp.getSelectionEnd()) {
        // There is no selection, only a caret
        if (comp.getCaretPosition() < comp.getDocument().getLength()) {
            // The caret must be at least one position left of the end
            try {
                int pos = comp.getCaretPosition();
                Document doc = comp.getDocument();
                String str = doc.getText(pos, 1).toLowerCase();

                doc.remove(pos, 1);
                doc.insertString(pos, str, null);
                comp.moveCaretPosition(pos+1);
            } catch (BadLocationException e) {
            }
        }
    } else {
        // There is a selection
        int s = comp.getSelectionStart();
        int e = comp.getSelectionEnd();
```

```
                comp.replaceSelection(comp.getSelectedText().toLowerCase());
                comp.select(s, e);
            }
        }
```

ε1003. Overriding a Few Default Typed Key Bindings in a JTextComponent

Hitting a key on the keyboard can fire one of three types of key events: KeyEvent.PRESSED, KeyEvent.TYPED, or KeyEvent.RELEASED. Briefly, hitting a key will first fire a PRESSED key event for the key and then, if the key represents an ASCII character (e.g., 'a' or 'control-f'), a TYPED key event containing the character is fired as well. When the key is released, the RELEASED key event is fired.

Rather than have an action and key bindings for every ASCII character, a text component uses a single default action installed in its keymap. When an ASCII character is typed and no key binding exists in any inputmap or keymap for that character, the default action is invoked (which inserts the character into the text component).

Therefore, to override the behavior of a typed character in a text component, you bind a TYPED keystroke to the new action in the text component's inputmap.

There are two ways to override the default key bindings in a JTextComponent. This example demonstrates a technique for overriding a few characters. See "ε1004. Overriding Many Default Typed Key Bindings in a JTextComponent" for a technique suitable for overriding many characters.

```
    JTextField component = new JTextField(10);

    // Override a, A, 9, -, $
    component.getInputMap(JComponent.WHEN_FOCUSED).put(
        KeyStroke.getKeyStroke("typed a"), "actionName");
    component.getInputMap(JComponent.WHEN_FOCUSED).put(
        KeyStroke.getKeyStroke("typed A"), "actionName");
    component.getInputMap(JComponent.WHEN_FOCUSED).put(
        KeyStroke.getKeyStroke("typed 9"), "actionName");
    component.getInputMap(JComponent.WHEN_FOCUSED).put(
        KeyStroke.getKeyStroke("typed -"), "actionName");
    component.getInputMap(JComponent.WHEN_FOCUSED).put(
        KeyStroke.getKeyStroke("typed $"), "actionName");

    // Overriding space must be done this way
    component.getInputMap(JComponent.WHEN_FOCUSED).put(
        KeyStroke.getKeyStroke(new Character(' '), 0), "actionName");

    // Disable a character so that no action is invoked.
    // The action name "none" is conventionally used to mean no action.
    component.getInputMap(JComponent.WHEN_FOCUSED).put(
        KeyStroke.getKeyStroke("typed X"), "none");

    // If you want to bind a keystroke to shift-space (which generates
    // a space character), you need to use a pressed-type keystroke.
    component.getInputMap(JComponent.WHEN_FOCUSED).put(
        KeyStroke.getKeyStroke("shift pressed SPACE"), "actionName");

    // However, the above is not sufficient. Although it binds the action to shift-space,
    // it does not mask the generated space character. So, not only will the action
    // be invoked, a space character will be inserted into the text component.
    // You need to disable the typed space character.
    // This will prevent the space from being inserted when shift-space is pressed.
```

```
component.getInputMap(JComponent.WHEN_FOCUSED).put(
    KeyStroke.getKeyStroke(new Character(' '), 0), "none");

// But if you still want a non-modified spaced key to insert
// a space, you need to add a pressed-type keystroke for space.
component.getInputMap(JComponent.WHEN_FOCUSED).put(
    KeyStroke.getKeyStroke("pressed SPACE"), insertSpaceAction.getValue(Action.NAME));

// Add action
component.getActionMap().put(insertSpaceAction.getValue(Action.NAME), insertSpaceAction);

public Action insertSpaceAction = new AbstractAction("Insert Space") {
    public void actionPerformed(ActionEvent evt) {
        JTextComponent c = (JTextComponent)evt.getSource();

        try {
            c.getDocument().insertString(c.getCaretPosition(), " ", null);
        } catch (BadLocationException e) {
        }
    }
};
```

ε1004. Overriding Many Default Typed Key Bindings in a JTextComponent

See "ε1003. Overriding a Few Default Typed Key Bindings in a JTextComponent" for information about default typed key bindings in a text component.

There are two ways to override the default key bindings in a text component. This example demonstrates a technique when many characters need to be overridden. This example converts all lowercase characters to uppercase. See "ε1004. Overriding Many Default Typed Key Bindings in a JTextComponent" for a technique suitable for overriding a few characters.

```
JTextField component = new JTextField();
component.addKeyListener(new MyKeyListener());

public class MyKeyListener extends KeyAdapter {
    public void keyTyped(KeyEvent evt) {
        JTextComponent c = (JTextComponent)evt.getSource();
        char ch = evt.getKeyChar();

        if (Character.isLowerCase(ch)) {
            try {
                c.getDocument().insertString(
                    c.getCaretPosition(), ""+Character.toUpperCase(ch), null);
                evt.consume();
            } catch (BadLocationException e) {
            }
        }
    }
}
```

ε1005. Listing the Key Bindings in a JTextComponent Keymap

A text component has an additional list of key bindings that is searched after its inputmaps. This additional list is called a *keymap*. The inputmap mechanism is newer but keymaps were left in place for backwards compatibility.

```
JTextArea component = new JTextArea();
Keymap map = component.getKeymap();
```

```
while (map != null) {
    KeyStroke[] keys = map.getBoundKeyStrokes();

    for (int i=0; i<keys.length; i++) {
        // This method is defined in "ε859. Converting a KeyStroke to a String"
        String keystrokeStr = keyStroke2String(keys[i]);
        // Get the action name bound to this keystroke
        Action action = (Action)map.getAction(keys[i]);
    }

    // The default action is invoked if a character is typed
    // and no key binding exists in the component's InputMap or Keymap.
    Action defAction = map.getDefaultAction();

    // Process all parent keymaps as well
    map = map.getResolveParent();
}
```

Styles

ε1006. Highlighting Words in a JTextComponent

This example demonstrates how to highlight a range of characters in a text component using highlights. The example uses a text component's highlighter to create and manage the highlights. Since one of the highlights in the highlighter is the selection, we must be careful when removing highlights not to remove the selection.

The way in which we identify our highlights is to create the highlight using a private painter. So when removing highlights from the highlighter, we remove only the ones whose painter is an instance of the private painter.

If many different highlight styles are required, it is necessary to use styles with a JTextPane. See "ε1007. Setting the Font and Color of Text in a JTextPane Using Styles" for more details.

```
JTextArea textComp = new JTextArea();

// Highlight the occurrences of the word "public"
highlight(textComp, "public");

// Creates highlights around all occurrences of pattern in textComp
public void highlight(JTextComponent textComp, String pattern) {
    // First remove all old highlights
    removeHighlights(textComp);

    try {
        Highlighter hilite = textComp.getHighlighter();
        Document doc = textComp.getDocument();
        String text = doc.getText(0, doc.getLength());
        int pos = 0;

        // Search for pattern
        while ((pos = text.indexOf(pattern, pos)) >= 0) {
            // Create highlighter using private painter and apply around pattern
            hilite.addHighlight(pos, pos+pattern.length(), myHighlightPainter);
            pos += pattern.length();
        }
    } catch (BadLocationException e) {
```

```
        }
    }
    // Removes only our private highlights
    public void removeHighlights(JTextComponent textComp) {
        Highlighter hilite = textComp.getHighlighter();
        Highlighter.Highlight[] hilites = hilite.getHighlights();

        for (int i=0; i<hilites.length; i++) {
            if (hilites[i].getPainter() instanceof MyHighlightPainter) {
                hilite.removeHighlight(hilites[i]);
            }
        }
    }
}
    // An instance of the private subclass of the default highlight painter
    Highlighter.HighlightPainter myHighlightPainter = new MyHighlightPainter(Color.red);

    // A private subclass of the default highlight painter
    class MyHighlightPainter extends DefaultHighlighter.DefaultHighlightPainter {
        public MyHighlightPainter(Color color) {
            super(color);
        }
    }
}
```

ε1007. Setting the Font and Color of Text in a JTextPane Using Styles

A style is a set of text attributes, such as font size and color. A style can be applied any number of times to the contents of a text pane. When a style is applied to a word in the text pane, the style is not associated with the word. Rather, the contents of the style, namely the attributes, are associated with the word. This means that if the style is changed, the set of attributes associated with the word does not change.

Styles can be stored in a text pane so that they can be retrieved, modified, and applied later. It is not necessary for a style to be stored with a text pane in order to use the style on the text pane.

This example demonstrates the creation and application of styles in the contents of a JTextPane. See StyleConstants for a complete set of available attributes.

```
JTextPane textPane = new JTextPane();
StyledDocument doc = textPane.getStyledDocument();

// Makes text red
Style style = textPane.addStyle("Red", null);
StyleConstants.setForeground(style, Color.red);

// Inherits from "Red"; makes text red and underlined
style = textPane.addStyle("Red Underline", style);
StyleConstants.setUnderline(style, true);

// Makes text 24pts
style = textPane.addStyle("24pts", null);
StyleConstants.setFontSize(style, 24);

// Makes text 12pts
style = textPane.addStyle("12pts", null);
StyleConstants.setFontSize(style, 12);

// Makes text italicized
style = textPane.addStyle("Italic", null);
StyleConstants.setItalic(style, true);
```

```
// A style can have multiple attributes; this one makes text bold and italic
style = textPane.addStyle("Bold Italic", null);
StyleConstants.setBold(style, true);
StyleConstants.setItalic(style, true);

// Set text in the range [5, 7) red
doc.setCharacterAttributes(5, 2, textPane.getStyle("Red"), true);

// Italicize the entire paragraph containing the position 12
doc.setParagraphAttributes(12, 1, textPane.getStyle("Italic"), true);
```

ε1008. Sharing Styles Between JTextPanes

Styles are stored in a style context. By default, text panes do not share style contexts, so any styles created for a text pane are available only in that text pane. This example creates two text panes that share a style context. Any new styles created in one text pane are available in the other. This also applies to changes in a shared style.

```
JTextPane c1 = new JTextPane();
JTextPane c2 = new JTextPane();

// Create new styled documents with the same style context
StyleContext styleContext = new StyleContext();
c1.setDocument(new DefaultStyledDocument(styleContext));
c2.setDocument(new DefaultStyledDocument(styleContext));

// Create a new style with one text pane
Style style = c1.addStyle("style name", null);
StyleConstants.setForeground(style, Color.red);

// Modify an existing style using the other text pane
style = c2.getStyle("style name");
StyleConstants.setBold(style, true);
```

ε1009. Listing the Styles Associated with a JTextPane

This example lists the styles that have been associated with a text pane.

```
DefaultStyledDocument doc = (DefaultStyledDocument)textPane.getDocument();
Enumeration enum = doc.getStyleNames();
while (enum.hasMoreElements()) {
    String styleName = (String)enum.nextElement();

    // Get style object
    Style style = doc.getStyle(styleName);
}
```

ε1010. Listing the Attributes in a Style

The way to retrieve the attributes in a style is to enumerate all the attribute names in the style and then use the specific attribute name to retrieve its value. The attribute name can be either a string or an object of type StyleConstants.

```
// To retrieve a style from a text pane, see
// "ε1009. Listing the Styles Associated with a JTextPane"

// Get number of attributes
int count = style.getAttributeCount();

// Get enumeration of attribute names; an attribute name can be
```

```
// either a string or a StyleConstants object
Enumeration enum = style.getAttributeNames();
while (enum.hasMoreElements()) {
    Object o = enum.nextElement();
    if (o instanceof String) {
        String attrName = (String)o;
        Object attrValue = style.getAttribute(attrName);
    } else if (o == StyleConstants.NameAttribute) {
        // Retrieve the style's name
        String styleName = (String)style.getAttribute(o);
    } else if (o == StyleConstants.ResolveAttribute) {
        // Retrieve the style's parent
        Style parent = (Style)style.getAttribute(o);
    } else {
        // Retrieve the style constant name and value
        String attrName = o.toString();
        Object attrValue = style.getAttribute(o);
    }
}
```

ε1011. Using a Popup to Apply Styles to a JTextPane

This example implements a text pane that allows the user to display a popup of available styles. If the user
selects a style in the popup, the characters in the selection are formatted with the attributes in the style.

```
JTextPane textPane = new JTextPane();

// Makes text red
Style style = textPane.addStyle("Red", null);
StyleConstants.setForeground(style, Color.red);

// Inherits from "Red"; makes text red and underlined
style = textPane.addStyle("Red Underline", style);
StyleConstants.setUnderline(style, true);

// Makes text 24pts
style = textPane.addStyle("24pts", null);
StyleConstants.setFontSize(style, 24);

// Makes text 12pts
style = textPane.addStyle("12pts", null);
StyleConstants.setFontSize(style, 12);

// Makes text italicized
style = textPane.addStyle("Italics", null);
StyleConstants.setItalic(style, true);

// Makes text bold
style = textPane.addStyle("Bold", null);
StyleConstants.setBold(style, true);

JTextPane c = textPane;
// Construct a sorted list of style names
DefaultStyledDocument doc = (DefaultStyledDocument)textPane.getDocument();
java.util.List l = new ArrayList();
Enumeration enum = doc.getStyleNames();
while (enum.hasMoreElements()) {
    l.add(enum.nextElement());
}
```

```
        Collections.sort(l);

        // First sub menu applies character attributes
        final JPopupMenu menu = new JPopupMenu();
        JMenu submenu = new JMenu("Character");
        for (int i=0; i<l.size(); i++) {
            submenu.add(new JMenuItem(new DoStyleAction((String)l.get(i), CHARACTER)));
        }
        menu.add(submenu);

        // Second sub menu applies paragraph attributes
        submenu = new JMenu("Paragraph");
        for (int i=0; i<l.size(); i++) {
            submenu.add(new JMenuItem(new DoStyleAction((String)l.get(i), PARAGRAPH)));
        }
        menu.add(submenu);

        // Third submenu applies logical attributes
        submenu = new JMenu("Logical");
        for (int i=0; i<l.size(); i++) {
            submenu.add(new JMenuItem(new DoStyleAction((String)l.get(i), LOGICAL)));
        }
        menu.add(submenu);

        // Add a listener to display pop-up
        textPane.addMouseListener(new MouseAdapter() {
            public void mousePressed(MouseEvent evt) {
                if (evt.isPopupTrigger()) {
                    menu.show(evt.getComponent(), evt.getX(), evt.getY());
                }
            }
            public void mouseReleased(MouseEvent evt) {
                if (evt.isPopupTrigger()) {
                    menu.show(evt.getComponent(), evt.getX(), evt.getY());
                }
            }
        });

    static final int CHARACTER = 1;
    static final int PARAGRAPH = 2;
    static final int LOGICAL = 3;

    // Assumes the style name is the same as the action name.
    // The type specifies how the style should be applied.
    // The style is applied to the text within the selection.
    public static class DoStyleAction extends StyledEditorKit.StyledTextAction {
        int type;
        public DoStyleAction(String styleName, int type) {
            super(styleName);
            this.type = type;
        }
        public void actionPerformed(ActionEvent e) {
            JTextPane c = (JTextPane)getEditor(e);
            if (c != null) {
                String styleName = e.getActionCommand();
                StyledDocument doc = (StyledDocument)c.getDocument();
```

```
                    switch (type) {
                    case CHARACTER:
                        c.setCharacterAttributes(doc.getStyle(styleName), true);
                        break;
                    case PARAGRAPH:
                        c.setParagraphAttributes(doc.getStyle(styleName), true);
                        break;
                    case LOGICAL:
                        c.setLogicalStyle(doc.getStyle(styleName));
                        break;
                    }
                }
            }
        }
```

ε1012. Retaining the Logical Style When Setting a New Paragraph Style

Logical styles are a collection of attributes that apply after the attributes of the paragraph style are applied. A common misconception of logical and paragraph styles is that they are independent. That is, setting a new logical style does not affect the current paragraph style and vice versa.

However, a logical style is nothing more than the parent of a paragraph style. If you replace the paragraph style, the logical style is replaced or removed as well. If you set a new logical style, the current parent of the current paragraph style (if any), is replaced with the new logical style.

In order to retain the logical style when setting a new paragraph style in non-replace mode, it is necessary to get the current logical style and restore it after setting the new paragraph style.

```
JTextPane textPane = new JTextPane();

// Set logical style
Style style = textPane.addStyle(null, null);
StyleConstants.setForeground(style, Color.red);
textPane.setLogicalStyle(style);
// paragraph is now red

// Set paragraph style; removes logical style
style = textPane.addStyle(null, null);
StyleConstants.setUnderline(style, true);
textPane.setParagraphAttributes(style, true);
// paragraph is now underlined, not red

// Set logical style; replaces paragraph style's parent
style = textPane.addStyle(null, null);
StyleConstants.setForeground(style, Color.red);
textPane.setLogicalStyle(style);
// paragraph is now red and underlined

// Get logical style and restore it after new paragraph style
Style logicalStyle = textPane.getLogicalStyle();
style = textPane.addStyle(null, null);
StyleConstants.setBold(style, true);
textPane.setParagraphAttributes(style, true);
textPane.setLogicalStyle(logicalStyle);
// paragraph is now red and bold
```

ε1013. Automatically Updating Styled Text When a Style Is Updated

When a style is applied to text in a text pane, the text is set with the attributes of the style. If the style is changed, the set of attributes associated with the range of text does not change.

This example demonstrates how to have styled text automatically updated when the style object used to style the text is changed. When a named style is applied to text, the name of the style is included in the set of attributes that are associated with the text. Hence, it is possible to find all the places where a named style has been applied in a text pane. The reapplyStyle() method takes a style object and searches the text pane for all uses of the style (by name) and reapplies it.

In order to detect changes to a style, a change listener is added to it. Whenever the style is changed, the style's change listener will call reapplyStyle() to update the text pane.

```
final JTextPane textPane = new JTextPane();
ChangeListener changeListener = new ChangeListener() {
    public void stateChanged(ChangeEvent e) {
        reapplyStyles(textPane, (Style)e.getSource());
    }
};

// Make paragraph red
Style style = textPane.addStyle("Highlight", null);
style.addChangeListener(changeListener);
StyleConstants.setForeground(style, Color.red);
textPane.setParagraphAttributes(style, true);
// paragraph appears red

style = textPane.getStyle("Highlight");
StyleConstants.setUnderline(style, true);
// paragraph becomes red and underlined

// This method traverses every paragraph and content element
// and reapplies any style that matches the specified style
public static void reapplyStyles(JTextPane c, Style style) {
    // Get section element
    Element sectionElem = c.getDocument().getDefaultRootElement();

    // Get number of paragraphs.
    int paraCount = sectionElem.getElementCount();

    for (int i=0; i<paraCount; i++) {
        Element paraElem = sectionElem.getElement(i);
        AttributeSet attr = paraElem.getAttributes();

        // Get the name of the style applied to this paragraph element; may be null
        String sn = (String)attr.getAttribute(StyleConstants.NameAttribute);

        // Check if style name match
        if (style.getName().equals(sn)) {
            // Reapply the paragraph style
            int rangeStart = paraElem.getStartOffset();
            int rangeEnd = paraElem.getEndOffset();
            c.getStyledDocument().setParagraphAttributes(
                rangeStart, rangeEnd-rangeStart, style, true);
        }

        // Enumerate the content elements
        for (int j=0; j<paraElem.getElementCount(); j++) {
```

```
Element contentElem = paraElem.getElement(j);
attr = contentElem.getAttributes();

// Get the name of the style applied to this content element; may be null
sn = (String)attr.getAttribute(StyleConstants.NameAttribute);

// Check if style name match
if (style.getName().equals(sn)) {
    // Reapply the content style
    int rangeStart = contentElem.getStartOffset();
    int rangeEnd = contentElem.getEndOffset();
    c.getStyledDocument().setCharacterAttributes(
        rangeStart, rangeEnd-rangeStart, style, true);
    }
}
}
}
```

*ε*1014. Determining If a Style Attribute Applies to a Character or the Paragraph

All style attributes as defined in StyleConstants are either character- or paragraph-based attributes. See also "*ε*1010. Listing the Attributes in a Style".

```
boolean b;

// Check if character-based attribute
b = StyleConstants.Italic instanceof AttributeSet.CharacterAttribute; // true
b = StyleConstants.LineSpacing instanceof AttributeSet.CharacterAttribute; // false

// Check if paragraph-based attribute
b = StyleConstants.LineSpacing instanceof AttributeSet.ParagraphAttribute; // true
b = StyleConstants.Italic instanceof AttributeSet.ParagraphAttribute; // false
```

It is also possible to determine if the attribute is a color or a font-related attribute.

```
// Check if color-based attribute
b = StyleConstants.Foreground instanceof AttributeSet.ColorAttribute; // true
b = StyleConstants.Italic instanceof AttributeSet.ColorAttribute; // false

// Check if font-based attribute
b = StyleConstants.Italic instanceof AttributeSet.FontAttribute; // true
b = StyleConstants.Foreground instanceof AttributeSet.FontAttribute; // false
```

Packages and Examples

Events

*ε*1015. Listening for Caret Movement Events in a JTextComponent

A caret event is fired whenever the caret is moved, either by the user or by setCaretPosition(). Caret events are not fired while the mouse is being dragged. When calling setCaretPosition(), a caret event is fired only if the new position is different from the old position.

```
JTextComponent textComp = new JTextArea();
textComp.addCaretListener(new CaretListener() {
    public void caretUpdate(CaretEvent e) {
        // dot is the caret position
        int dot = e.getDot();

        // mark is the non-caret end of the selection
        int mark = e.getMark();
```

```
    }
});
```

ε1016. Listening for Editing Changes in a JTextComponent

A DocumentEvent is fired each time characters are inserted or removed from a text component. The event is also fired if the set of attributes in the text component is changed.

```java
JTextComponent textcomp = new JTextPane();
textcomp.setText("Initial Text");
textcomp.getDocument().addDocumentListener(new DocumentListener() {
    // This method is called after an insert into the document
    public void insertUpdate(DocumentEvent evt) {
        // Get index of newly inserted characters
        int off = evt.getOffset();

        // Get length of new inserted characters
        int len = evt.getLength();

        try {
            // Get inserted string
            String str = evt.getDocument().getText(off, len);
        } catch (BadLocationException e) {
        }
    }

    // This method is called after a removal from the document
    public void removeUpdate(DocumentEvent evt) {
        // Get starting index of removed characters
        int off = evt.getOffset();

        // Get length of removed characters
        int len = evt.getLength();

        // The removed characters are not available
    }

    // This method is called after one or more attributes have changed.
    // This method is not called when characters are inserted with attributes.
    public void changedUpdate(DocumentEvent evt) {
        // Get starting index of characters whose attributes have changed
        int off = evt.getOffset();

        // Get length of characters whose attributes have changed
        int len = evt.getLength();
    }
});
```

javax.swing.text.html

This package contains the class (HTMLEditorKit) and supporting classes for creating HTML text editors.

Class   *Interface*   —extends   - - -implements   O abstract   ● final   ˆ—has superclass   ‿—has subclass   package—see other volume

Packages and Examples

```
java.lang.Object
1.2       ├ CSS------------------------------------------ java.io.Serializable
1.2 ●     ├ CSS.Attribute
1.2       ├ HTML
1.2 ●     ├ HTML.Attribute
1.2       ├ HTML.Tag
1.2       │  └ HTML.UnknownTag---------------------------
1.2       ├ HTMLDocument.HTMLReader.TagAction
1.2       │  ├ HTMLDocument.HTMLReader.BlockAction
1.2       │  │  ├ HTMLDocument.HTMLReader.ParagraphAction
1.2       │  │  └ HTMLDocument.HTMLReader.PreAction
1.2       │  ├ HTMLDocument.HTMLReader.CharacterAction
1.2       │  ├ HTMLDocument.HTMLReader.HiddenAction
1.2       │  ├ HTMLDocument.HTMLReader.IsindexAction
1.2       │  ├ HTMLDocument.HTMLReader.SpecialAction
1.2       │     └ HTMLDocument.HTMLReader.FormAction
1.2 ○     ├ HTMLDocument.Iterator
1.2       ├ HTMLEditorKit.HTMLFactory-------------------- javax.swing.text.ViewFactory
1.2 ○     ├ HTMLEditorKit.Parser
1.2       ├ HTMLEditorKit.ParserCallback
1.2       │  └ HTMLDocument.HTMLReader
1.2       ├ Option
1.2       ├ StyleSheet.BoxPainter----------------------- java.io.Serializable
1.2       ├ StyleSheet.ListPainter----------------------
1.1 ○     ├ java.awt.event.MouseAdapter----------------- java.awt.event.MouseListener^
1.2       │  ├ FormView.MouseEventListener
1.2       │  └ HTMLEditorKit.LinkController------------- java.awt.event.MouseMotionListener^,
          │                                              java.io.Serializable
1.1       ├ java.util.EventObject----------------------- java.io.Serializable
1.2       │  └ javax.swing.event.HyperlinkEvent
1.2       │     └ HTMLFrameHyperlinkEvent
1.2 ○     ├ javax.swing.AbstractAction------------------ java.io.Serializable, java.lang.Cloneable,
          │                                              javax.swing.Action^
1.2 ○     │  └ javax.swing.text.TextAction
1.2 ○     │     └ javax.swing.text.StyledEditorKit.StyledTextAction
1.2 ○     │        └ HTMLEditorKit.HTMLTextAction
1.2       │           └ HTMLEditorKit.InsertHTMLTextAction
```

Class   *Interface*   —extends   - - -implements   ○ abstract   ● final   ^—has superclass   ⌣—has subclass   package—see other volume

```
          java . lang.Object
1.2  ○    ├ javax.swing.text.AbstractDocument- - - - - - - - - - - - - - - - - - - - java . io.Serializable ˬ, javax.swing.text.Document ˬ
1.2       │ └ javax.swing.text.DefaultStyledDocument- - - - - - - - - - - - - - - javax.swing.text.StyledDocument^
1.2       │   └ HTMLDocument
1.2  ○    ├ javax.swing.text.AbstractDocument.AbstractElement - - - - - - - - java . io.Serializable ˬ, javax.swing.text.Element,
                                                                              javax.swing.text.MutableAttributeSet ͨ,
                                                                              javax.swing.tree.TreeNode ˬ
1.2       │ ├ javax.swing.text.AbstractDocument.BranchElement
1.2       │ │ └ HTMLDocument.BlockElement
1.2       │ └ javax.swing.text.AbstractDocument.LeafElement
1.2       │   └ HTMLDocument.RunElement
1.2  ○    ├ javax.swing.text.AbstractWriter
1.2       │ ├ HTMLWriter
1.2       │ └ MinimalHTMLWriter
1.2  ○    ├ javax.swing.text.EditorKit- - - - - - - - - - - - - - - - - - - - - - - - - - java . io.Serializable ˬ, java . lang.Cloneable ˬ
1.2       │ └ javax.swing.text.DefaultEditorKit
1.2       │   └ javax.swing.text.StyledEditorKit
1.2       │     └ HTMLEditorKit - - - - - - - - - - - - - - - - - - - - - - - - - - - javax.accessibility.Accessible
1.2       ├ javax.swing.text.StyleContext - - - - - - - - - - - - - - - - - - - - - java . io.Serializable ˬ, javax.swing.text ₂
                                                                              .AbstractDocument.AttributeContext
1.2       │ └ StyleSheet
1.2  ○    └ javax.swing.text.View - - - - - - - - - - - - - - - - - - - - - - - - - - - javax.swing.SwingConstants
1.4         ├ ImageView
1.2         ├ javax.swing.text.ComponentView
1.2         │ ├ FormView - - - - - - - - - - - - - - - - - - - - - - - - - - - - - - - - java.awt.event.ActionListener ͨ
1.2         │ └ ObjectView
1.2  ○      ├ javax.swing.text.CompositeView
1.2         │ └ javax.swing.text.BoxView
1.2         │   ├ BlockView
1.2         │   │ └ ListView
1.3  ○      │   └ javax.swing.text.FlowView
1.2         │     └ javax.swing.text.ParagraphView - - - - - - - - - - - - - - - - javax.swing.text.TabExpander
1.2         │       └ ParagraphView
1.3         └ javax.swing.text.GlyphView - - - - - - - - - - - - - - - - - - - - - - java . lang.Cloneable ˬ, javax.swing.text ₂
                                                                              .TabableView
1.2           └ javax.swing.text.LabelView - - - - - - - - - - - - - - - - - - - - - javax.swing.text.TabableView
1.2             └ InlineView
```

ε1017. Getting the Links in an HTML Document

```
// This method takes a URI which can be either a filename (e.g. file://c:/dir/file.html)
// or a URL (e.g. http://host.com/page.html) and returns all HREF links in the document.
public static String[] getLinks(String uriStr) {
    List result = new ArrayList();

    try {
        // Create a reader on the HTML content
        URL url = new URI(uriStr).toURL();
        URLConnection conn = url.openConnection();
        Reader rd = new InputStreamReader(conn.getInputStream());

        // Parse the HTML
        EditorKit kit = new HTMLEditorKit();
        HTMLDocument doc = (HTMLDocument)kit.createDefaultDocument();
```

```
            kit.read(rd, doc, 0);

            // Find all the A elements in the HTML document
            HTMLDocument.Iterator it = doc.getIterator(HTML.Tag.A);
            while (it.isValid()) {
                SimpleAttributeSet s = (SimpleAttributeSet)it.getAttributes();

                String link = (String)s.getAttribute(HTML.Attribute.HREF);
                if (link != null) {
                    // Add the link to the result list
                    result.add(link);
                }
                it.next();
            }
        } catch (MalformedURLException e) {
        } catch (URISyntaxException e) {
        } catch (BadLocationException e) {
        } catch (IOException e) {
        }

        // Return all found links
        return (String[])result.toArray(new String[result.size()]);
    }
```

ε1018. Getting the Text in an HTML Document

```
    // This method takes a URI which can be either a filename (e.g. file://c:/dir/file.html)
    // or a URL (e.g. http://host.com/page.html) and returns all text in the document.
    public static String getText(String uriStr) {
        final StringBuffer buf = new StringBuffer(1000);

        try {
            // Create an HTML document that appends all text to buf
            HTMLDocument doc = new HTMLDocument() {
                public HTMLEditorKit.ParserCallback getReader(int pos) {
                    return new HTMLEditorKit.ParserCallback() {
                        // This method is whenever text is encountered in the HTML file
                        public void handleText(char[] data, int pos) {
                            buf.append(data);
                            buf.append('\n');
                        }
                    };
                }
            };

            // Create a reader on the HTML content
            URL url = new URI(uriStr).toURL();
            URLConnection conn = url.openConnection();
            Reader rd = new InputStreamReader(conn.getInputStream());

            // Parse the HTML
            EditorKit kit = new HTMLEditorKit();
            kit.read(rd, doc, 0);
        } catch (MalformedURLException e) {
        } catch (URISyntaxException e) {
        } catch (BadLocationException e) {
        } catch (IOException e) {
```

```
    }
    // Return the text
    return buf.toString();
}
```

javax.swing.text.html.parser

This package contains a default HTML parser and supporting classes for writing an HTML parser.

```
        java.lang.Object
1.2 ●     ├ AttributeList - - - - - - - - - - - - - - - - - - - - - - - - - - - - - - - - - - - DTDConstants, java.io.Serializable ˏ
1.2 ●     ├ ContentModel - - - - - - - - - - - - - - - - - - - - - - - - - - - - - - - - - - - - java.io.Serializable ˏ
1.2       ├ DTD - - - - - - - - - - - - - - - - - - - - - - - - - - - - - - - - - - - - - - - - - DTDConstants
1.2 ●     ├ Element - - - - - - - - - - - - - - - - - - - - - - - - - - - - - - - - - - - - - - - DTDConstants, java.io.Serializable ˏ
1.2 ●     ├ Entity - - - - - - - - - - - - - - - - - - - - - - - - - - - - - - - - - - - - -ˏ- - DTDConstants
1.2       ├ Parser - - - - - - - - - - - - - - - - - - - - - - - - - - - - - - - - - - - - -¦
1.2       │  └ DocumentParser
1.2       ├ TagElement
1.2 ○     └ javax.swing.text.html.HTMLEditorKit.Parser
1.2          └ ParserDelegator - - - - - - - - - - - - - - - - - - - - - - - - - - - - - - - java.io.Serializable ˏ

1.2       DTDConstants
```

javax.swing.text.rtf

This package contains a class (RTFEditorKit) for creating Rich-Text-Format text editors.

```
        java.lang.Object
1.2 ○     └ javax.swing.text.EditorKit - - - - - - - - - - - - - - - - - - - - - - - - - - - - - java.io.Serializable ˏ, java.lang.Cloneable ˏ
1.2          └ javax.swing.text.DefaultEditorKit
1.2             └ javax.swing.text.StyledEditorKit
1.2                └ RTFEditorKit
```

Packages and Examples

367

```
java.lang.Object
1.2 O   ├ AbstractLayoutCache - - - - - - - - - - - - - - - - - - - - - - - - - - RowMapper
1.2     │  ├ FixedHeightLayoutCache
1.2     │  └ VariableHeightLayoutCache
1.2 O   ├ AbstractLayoutCache.NodeDimensions
1.2     ├ DefaultMutableTreeNode - - - - - - - - - - - - - - - - - - - - - - - MutableTreeNode^, java.io.Serializable,
                                                                                java.lang.Cloneable
1.2     ├ DefaultTreeCellEditor - - - - - - - - - - - - - - - - - - - - - - - - TreeCellEditor^, java.awt.event.ActionListener^,
                                                                                javax.swing.event.TreeSelectionListener^
1.2     ├ DefaultTreeModel - - - - - - - - - - - - - - - - - - - - - - - - - - TreeModel, java.io.Serializable
1.2     ├ DefaultTreeSelectionModel - - - - - - - - - - - - - - - - - - - - - TreeSelectionModel, java.io.Serializable,
                                                                                java.lang.Cloneable
1.2     ├ TreePath - - - - - - - - - - - - - - - - - - - - - - - - - - - - - - java.io.Serializable
    O   ├ java.awt.Component - - - - - - - - - - - - - - - - - - - - - - - - - java.awt.MenuContainer, java.awt.image
                                                                                .ImageObserver, java.io.Serializable
            └ java.awt.Container
1.2            ├ DefaultTreeCellEditor.EditorContainer
```

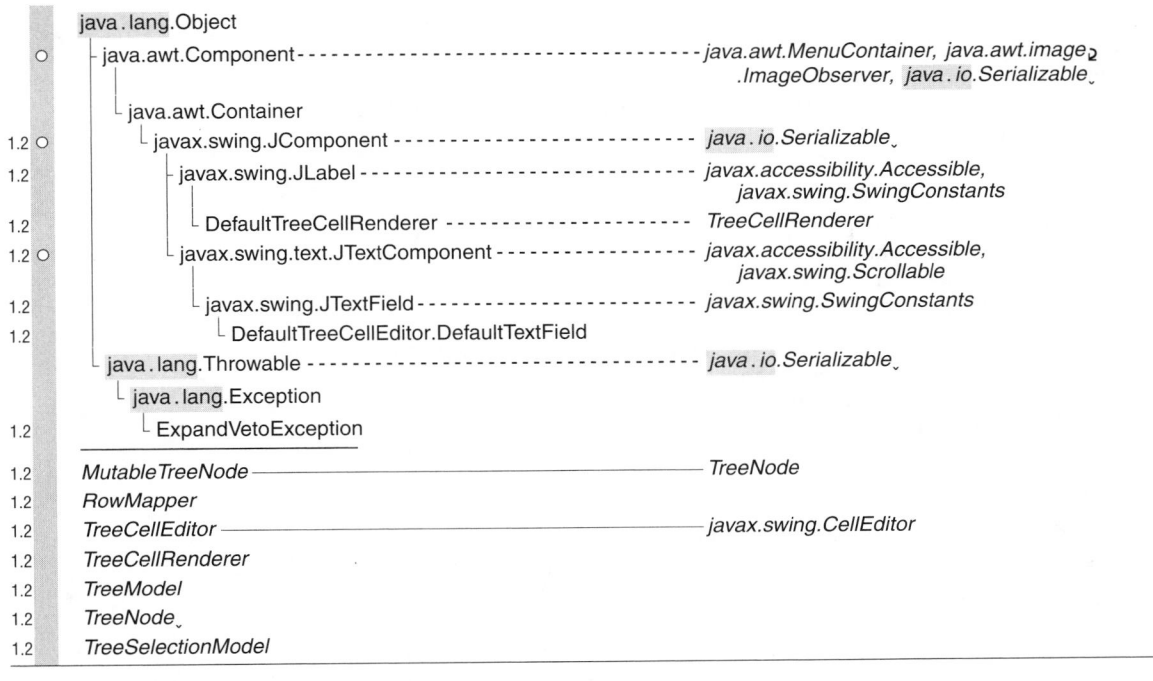

ε1019. Creating a JTree Component

This example creates a tree component with a root node and a child of the root node. You build the tree hierarchy by adding nodes to nodes.

```
DefaultMutableTreeNode root = new DefaultMutableTreeNode("Root Label");
root.add(new DefaultMutableTreeNode("Node Label"));

JTree tree = new JTree(root);
```

ε1020. Changing and Removing the Default Icons in a JTree Component

There are three icons used by the default tree component. The open icon is used to display an open internal node that can contain children. The closed icon is used to display a closed internal node that can contain children. The leaf icon is used for nodes that cannot contain children.

These icons can be changed individually. However, it is more typical that if one needs to be changed, all three are changed together. The reason is that each look and feel installs its own set of icons, often with differing dimensions. If you change only one of the three icons, the new icon may visibly match one look and feel but it will not match the others.

There are two ways to change the icons. The first is to override the UI defaults. With this method, all new tree components will have the new icons. The second method is to update the renderer for a particular tree component. This method only affects that tree component and no other.

When overriding the icons, you should set the row height. See "ε1031. Setting the Row Height of a JTree Component" for more information.

```
// Retrieve the three icons
Icon leafIcon = new ImageIcon("leaf.gif");
Icon openIcon = new ImageIcon("open.gif");
Icon closedIcon = new ImageIcon("closed.gif");
```

369

```
// Create tree
JTree tree = new JTree();

// Update only one tree instance
DefaultTreeCellRenderer renderer = (DefaultTreeCellRenderer)tree.getCellRenderer();
renderer.setLeafIcon(leafIcon);
renderer.setClosedIcon(closedIcon);
renderer.setOpenIcon(openIcon);

// Remove the icons
renderer.setLeafIcon(null);
renderer.setClosedIcon(null);
renderer.setOpenIcon(null);

// Change defaults so that all new tree components will have new icons
UIManager.put("Tree.leafIcon", leafIcon);
UIManager.put("Tree.openIcon", openIcon);
UIManager.put("Tree.closedIcon", closedIcon);

// Create tree with new icons
tree = new JTree();

// Update row height based on new icons;
// see "ε1031. Setting the Row Height of a JTree Component"
```

Selections

ε1021. Getting the Selected Nodes in a JTree Component

```
// Create tree
JTree tree = new JTree();

// Get paths of all selected nodes
TreePath[] paths = tree.getSelectionPaths();
```

ε1022. Enabling and Disabling Multiple Selections in a JTree Component

```
// Create tree
JTree tree = new JTree();

// Allow only a single node to be selected (default)
tree.getSelectionModel().setSelectionMode(
    TreeSelectionModel.SINGLE_TREE_SELECTION);

// Allow selection to span one vertical contiguous set of visible nodes
tree.getSelectionModel().setSelectionMode(
    TreeSelectionModel.CONTIGUOUS_TREE_SELECTION);

// Allow multiple selections of visible nodes
tree.getSelectionModel().setSelectionMode(
    TreeSelectionModel.DISCONTIGUOUS_TREE_SELECTION);
```

Class   *Interface*   —extends   - - -implements   ○ abstract   ● final   ˆ—has superclass   ⌐—has subclass   package—see other volume

Nodes

ε1023. Visiting All the Nodes in a JTree Component

```java
// Create tree
JTree tree = new JTree();

// Add the nodes...

// Visit all nodes
visitAllNodes(tree);

// Visit only expanded nodes
visitAllExpandedNodes(tree);

// Traverse all nodes in tree
public void visitAllNodes(JTree tree) {
    TreeNode root = (TreeNode)tree.getModel().getRoot();
    visitAllNodes(root);
}
public void visitAllNodes(TreeNode node) {
    // node is visited exactly once
    process(node);

    if (node.getChildCount() >= 0) {
        for (Enumeration e=node.children(); e.hasMoreElements(); ) {
            TreeNode n = (TreeNode)e.nextElement();
            visitAllNodes(n);
        }
    }
}

// Traverse all expanded nodes in tree
public void visitAllExpandedNodes(JTree tree) {
    TreeNode root = (TreeNode)tree.getModel().getRoot();
    visitAllExpandedNodes(tree, new TreePath(root));
}
public void visitAllExpandedNodes(JTree tree, TreePath parent) {
    // Return if node is not expanded
    if (!tree.isVisible(parent)) {
        return;
    }

    // node is visible and is visited exactly once
    TreeNode node = (TreeNode)parent.getLastPathComponent();
    process(node);

    // Visit all children
    if (node.getChildCount() >= 0) {
        for (Enumeration e=node.children(); e.hasMoreElements(); ) {
            TreeNode n = (TreeNode)e.nextElement();
            TreePath path = parent.pathByAddingChild(n);
            visitAllExpandedNodes(tree, path);
        }
    }
}
```

ε1024. Finding a Node in a JTree Component

```
// Create tree
JTree tree = new JTree();

// Search forward from first visible row looking for any visible node
// whose name starts with prefix.
int startRow = 0;
String prefix = "b";
TreePath path = tree.getNextMatch(prefix, startRow, Position.Bias.Forward);

// Search backward from last visible row looking for any visible node
// whose name starts with prefix.
startRow = tree.getRowCount()-1;
prefix = "b";
path = tree.getNextMatch(prefix, startRow, Position.Bias.Backward);

// Find the path (regardless of visibility) that matches the
// specified sequence of names
path = findByName(tree, new String[]{"JTree", "food", "bananas"});

// Finds the path in tree as specified by the node array. The node array is a sequence
// of nodes where nodes[0] is the root and nodes[i] is a child of nodes[i-1].
// Comparison is done using Object.equals(). Returns null if not found.
public TreePath find(JTree tree, Object[] nodes) {
    TreeNode root = (TreeNode)tree.getModel().getRoot();
    return find2(tree, new TreePath(root), nodes, 0, false);
}

// Finds the path in tree as specified by the array of names. The names array is a
// sequence of names where names[0] is the root and names[i] is a child of names[i-1].
// Comparison is done using String.equals(). Returns null if not found.
public TreePath findByName(JTree tree, String[] names) {
    TreeNode root = (TreeNode)tree.getModel().getRoot();
    return find2(tree, new TreePath(root), names, 0, true);
}
private TreePath find2(JTree tree, TreePath parent, Object[] nodes, int depth, boolean byName) {
    TreeNode node = (TreeNode)parent.getLastPathComponent();
    Object o = node;

    // If by name, convert node to a string
    if (byName) {
        o = o.toString();
    }

    // If equal, go down the branch
    if (o.equals(nodes[depth])) {
        // If at end, return match
        if (depth == nodes.length-1) {
            return parent;
        }

        // Traverse children
        if (node.getChildCount() >= 0) {
            for (Enumeration e=node.children(); e.hasMoreElements(); ) {
                TreeNode n = (TreeNode)e.nextElement();
                TreePath path = parent.pathByAddingChild(n);
                TreePath result = find2(tree, path, nodes, depth+1, byName);
```

```
                    // Found a match
                    if (result != null) {
                        return result;
                    }
                }
            }
        }
        // No match at this branch
        return null;
    }
```

ε1025. Adding a Node to a JTree Component

```
// Create tree
JTree tree = new JTree();
DefaultTreeModel model = (DefaultTreeModel)tree.getModel();

// Find node to which new node is to be added
int startRow = 0;
String prefix = "J";
TreePath path = tree.getNextMatch(prefix, startRow, Position.Bias.Forward);
MutableTreeNode node = (MutableTreeNode)path.getLastPathComponent();

// Create new node
MutableTreeNode newNode = new DefaultMutableTreeNode("green");

// Insert new node as last child of node
model.insertNodeInto(newNode, node, node.getChildCount());
```

ε1026. Removing a Node to a JTree Component

```
// Create tree
JTree tree = new JTree();
DefaultTreeModel model = (DefaultTreeModel)tree.getModel();

// Find node to remove
int startRow = 0;
String prefix = "b";
TreePath path = tree.getNextMatch(prefix, startRow, Position.Bias.Forward);
MutableTreeNode node = (MutableTreeNode)path.getLastPathComponent();

// Remove node; if node has descendants, all descendants are removed as well
model.removeNodeFromParent(node);

// The root cannot be removed with removeNodeFromParent();
// use the following to remove the root
model.setRoot(null);
```

ε1027. Converting a Node in a JTree Component to a TreePath

```
// Returns a TreePath containing the specified node.
public TreePath getPath(TreeNode node) {
    List list = new ArrayList();

    // Add all nodes to list
    while (node != null) {
        list.add(node);
        node = node.getParent();
    }
```

```
        Collections.reverse(list);

        // Convert array of nodes to TreePath
        return new TreePath(list.toArray());
    }
```

ε1028. Converting All Nodes in a JTree Component to a TreePath Array

```
    // If expanded, return only paths of nodes that are expanded.
    public TreePath[] getPaths(JTree tree, boolean expanded) {
        TreeNode root = (TreeNode)tree.getModel().getRoot();

        // Create array to hold the treepaths
        List list = new ArrayList();

        // Traverse tree from root adding treepaths for all nodes to list
        getPaths(tree, new TreePath(root), expanded, list);

        // Convert list to array
        return (TreePath[])list.toArray(new TreePath[list.size()]);
    }
    public void getPaths(JTree tree, TreePath parent, boolean expanded, List list) {
        // Return if node is not expanded
        if (expanded && !tree.isVisible(parent)) {
            return;
        }

        // Add node to list
        list.add(parent);

        // Create paths for all children
        TreeNode node = (TreeNode)parent.getLastPathComponent();
        if (node.getChildCount() >= 0) {
            for (Enumeration e=node.children(); e.hasMoreElements(); ) {
                TreeNode n = (TreeNode)e.nextElement();
                TreePath path = parent.pathByAddingChild(n);
                getPaths(tree, path, expanded, list);
            }
        }
    }
```

Node Expansion

ε1029. Expanding or Collapsing All Nodes in a JTree Component

```
    // If expand is true, expands all nodes in the tree.
    // Otherwise, collapses all nodes in the tree.
    public void expandAll(JTree tree, boolean expand) {
        TreeNode root = (TreeNode)tree.getModel().getRoot();

        // Traverse tree from root
        expandAll(tree, new TreePath(root), expand);
    }
    private void expandAll(JTree tree, TreePath parent, boolean expand) {
        // Traverse children
        TreeNode node = (TreeNode)parent.getLastPathComponent();
        if (node.getChildCount() >= 0) {
```

Class   *Interface*   —extends   - - -implements   O abstract   ● final   ^—has superclass   ﹎—has subclass   package—see other volume

```
    for (Enumeration e=node.children(); e.hasMoreElements(); ) {
        TreeNode n = (TreeNode)e.nextElement();
        TreePath path = parent.pathByAddingChild(n);
        expandAll(tree, path, expand);
    }
}

// Expansion or collapse must be done bottom-up
if (expand) {
    tree.expandPath(parent);
} else {
    tree.collapsePath(parent);
}
}
```

ε1030. Preventing the Expansion or Collapse of a Node in a JTree Component

There are two ways to prevent the expansion or collapse of a node. The first way is to listen to expansion events and veto those events that expand or collapse particular nodes. This method allows any listener to prevent expansion of collapse of a node (see "ε1032. Listening for Expansion and Collapse Events in a JTree Component").

The second way is to override JTree.setExpandedState(). This method is suitable if the tree wants to impose particular expansion or collapse rules. This method is demonstrated in this example.

```
JTree tree = new JTree() {
    protected void setExpandedState(TreePath path, boolean state) {
        // Ignore all collapse requests; collapse events will not be fired
        if (state) {
            super.setExpandedState(path, state);
        }
    }
};
```

Layout

ε1031. Setting the Row Height of a JTree Component

The tree component's row height property controls the height of every displayed node. If the row height is greater than 0, all rows will be given the specified height. However, if the rows can be of differing heights, it is necessary to set the row height to 0. With a 0 row height, all heights of all rows are computed individually.

```
// Create tree
JTree tree = new JTree();

// All rows will be given 15 pixels of height
tree.setRowHeight(15);

// Have the row height for each row computed individually
tree.setRowHeight(0);

// If the row height is 0 and the height of a row has dynamically changed, it is necessary
// to flush the internal cache of row heights. The following calls flush the internal cache.
if (tree.getRowHeight() <= 0) {
    // Temporary change to non-zero height
    tree.setRowHeight(1);
}
tree.setRowHeight(0);
```

Events

ε1032. Listening for Expansion and Collapse Events in a JTree Component

The tree component allows you to get events before and after a node has been expanded or collapsed. The events that are fired before a node is expanded or collapsed can be vetoed, thereby preventing the operation.

```
// Create tree
JTree tree = new JTree();

// Add pre-expansion event listener
tree.addTreeWillExpandListener(new MyTreeWillExpandListener());

// Add post-expansion event listener
tree.addTreeExpansionListener(new MyTreeExpansionListener());

// Pre-expansion/collapse event listener
public class MyTreeWillExpandListener implements TreeWillExpandListener {
    public void treeWillExpand(TreeExpansionEvent evt) throws ExpandVetoException {
        JTree tree = (JTree)evt.getSource();

        // Get the path that will be expanded
        TreePath path = evt.getPath();

        // Cancel the operation if desired
        boolean veto = false;
        if (veto) {
            throw new ExpandVetoException(evt);
        }
    }
    public void treeWillCollapse(TreeExpansionEvent evt) throws ExpandVetoException {
        JTree tree = (JTree)evt.getSource();

        // Get the path that will be collapsed
        TreePath path = evt.getPath();

        // Cancel the operation if desired
        boolean veto = false;
        if (veto) {
            throw new ExpandVetoException(evt);
        }
    }
}

// Post-expansion/collapse event listener
public class MyTreeExpansionListener implements TreeExpansionListener {
    public void treeExpanded(TreeExpansionEvent evt) {
        JTree tree = (JTree)evt.getSource();

        // Get the path that was expanded
        TreePath path = evt.getPath();
    }
    public void treeCollapsed(TreeExpansionEvent evt) {
        JTree tree = (JTree)evt.getSource();

        // Get the path that was collapsed
        TreePath path = evt.getPath();
```

Class   *Interface*   —extends   - - -implements   ○ abstract   ● final   ˆ—has superclass   �‿—has subclass   package—see other volume

```
        }
    }
```

ε1033. Listening for Selection Events in a JTree Component

This example adds a listener for selection events to a tree component.

```
tree.addTreeSelectionListener(new TreeSelectionListener() {
    public void valueChanged(TreeSelectionEvent evt) {
        // Get all nodes whose selection status has changed
        TreePath[] paths = evt.getPaths();

        // Iterate through all affected nodes
        for (int i=0; i<paths.length; i++) {
            if (evt.isAddedPath(i)) {
                // This node has been selected
            } else {
                // This node has been deselected
            }
        }
    }
});
```

This package provides support for undo/redo capabilities in an application such as a text editor. It is for developers that provide undo/redo capabilities in their application.

```
     java.lang.Object
1.2    ├ AbstractUndoableEdit ----------------------------- UndoableEdit, java.io.Serializable
1.2    │  ├ CompoundEdit
1.2    │  │  └ UndoManager --------------------------------- javax.swing.event.UndoableEditListener
1.2    │  └ StateEdit
1.2    ├ UndoableEditSupport
```

```
      java.lang.Object
        └ java.lang.Throwable - - - - - - - - - - - - - - - - - - - - - - - - - - - - - - - java.io.Serializable
            └ java.lang.Exception
                └ java.lang.RuntimeException
1.2                 ├ CannotRedoException
1.2                 └ CannotUndoException

1.2   StateEditable
1.2   UndoableEdit
```

ε1034. Adding Undo and Redo to a Text Component

```java
JTextComponent textcomp = new JTextArea();
final UndoManager undo = new UndoManager();
Document doc = textcomp.getDocument();

// Listen for undo and redo events
doc.addUndoableEditListener(new UndoableEditListener() {
    public void undoableEditHappened(UndoableEditEvent evt) {
        undo.addEdit(evt.getEdit());
    }
});

// Create an undo action and add it to the text component
textcomp.getActionMap().put("Undo",
    new AbstractAction("Undo") {
        public void actionPerformed(ActionEvent evt) {
            try {
                if (undo.canUndo()) {
                    undo.undo();
                }
            } catch (CannotUndoException e) {
            }
        }
    });

// Bind the undo action to ctl-Z
textcomp.getInputMap().put(KeyStroke.getKeyStroke("control Z"), "Undo");

// Create a redo action and add it to the text component
textcomp.getActionMap().put("Redo",
    new AbstractAction("Redo") {
        public void actionPerformed(ActionEvent evt) {
            try {
                if (undo.canRedo()) {
                    undo.redo();
                }
            } catch (CannotRedoException e) {
            }
        }
    });

// Bind the redo action to ctl-Y
textcomp.getInputMap().put(KeyStroke.getKeyStroke("control Y"), "Redo");
```

Class   *Interface*   —extends   - - -implements   ○ abstract   ● final   ^—has superclass   ⌐—has subclass   package—see other volume

Part 2
CLASSES

This part contains information about each class in every package. For easy lookup, the classes are arranged alphabetically by class name without regard to package. The following legend describes the layout of the class information.

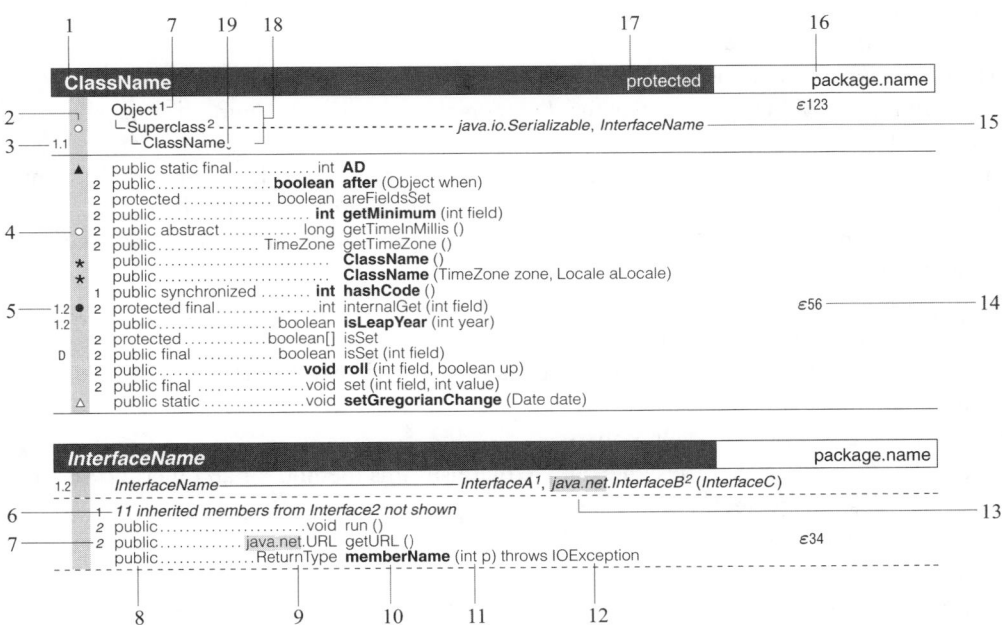

1. The class or interface name (interface names are italicized)
2. A symbolic representation of a class's modifier set:

   ○   An abstract class

   ●   A final class
3. The version of Java in which this class or interface was introduced

   You need the specified version of Java or higher in order to use the class. If the field is blank, the class or interface was introduced in Java 1.0.
4. A symbolic representation of a member's modifier set, which is used to quickly locate members by their modifiers:

○　An abstract member

●　A final member

△　A static member

▲　A static final member

*　A constructor

5. The version of Java in which this member was introduced

   You need the specified version of Java or higher in order to use the member. If the field is blank, the version is the same as that of the current class or interface. If the field contains a D, the member has been deprecated.

6. The number and source of inherited members that are not shown in the member list

7. The tree-reference

   The number in this field corresponds to one of the classes or interfaces in the class tree. If this member has been inherited, the tree-reference refers to the class from which the member was inherited. If this member is an override, the tree-reference refers to the class that contains the overridden member. If this is a declared method and the method is required because of an interface, the tree-reference shows which interface.

8. The list of modifiers of a member

9. The return type of a member

   A return type in bold type signifies that the member overrides a member from a superclass.

10. The member name

    A member name in bold type signifies that the member has been declared in the current class or interface. A non-bold member name signifies that the member was inherited from a superclass. Inherited members from `java.lang.Object` and `java.lang.Throwable` are not shown (in order to save space).

11. The list of parameters of a member

12. The declared exceptions of a member

13. The shaded background behind a package name indicates that the details of this class is covered in another volume

14. A list of one or more example numbers

    The example number identifies an example that uses this method, or an inherited version of it. The examples are located in the "Packages" part of this book.

15. A list of interfaces implemented by a class

16. Package name

    The name of the package that contains this class or interface

17. Class modifiers

    Currently, only the modifier "protected" can appear in this space.

18. The class tree

    If the current entity is a class, the class tree shows the superclasses of the current class. Also shown are the interfaces that each class implements, if any. If the current entity is an interface, the class tree shows all of the interfaces from which the current interface extends, if any.

    A solid line means "extends" and a dotted line means "implements."

19. Has subclass

    When on a class, the indicator signifies that the class has one or more subclasses. When on an interface, the indicator signifies that the interface is extended by one or more interfaces.

Note: For types appearing in a method's or constructor's signature, unless the type is from the same package or from the `java.lang` package, it is qualified with its package name.

Legend

A legend appears on all left-hand pages to remind you of the meanings of the symbols. Here are the symbols shown in the legend:

Class	Class names are not italicized
Interface	Interface names are italicized
○	An abstract member or class
●	A final member
△	A static member
▲	A static final member
*	A constructor
----	Implements
—	Extends
x x	Inherited
x x	Declared
x x	Overridden
ε N	A list of examples that use this class or member
ˇ	Has one or more subclasses

The x x's represent the pattern of light and bold type for the return type and member name. Spelled out, this pattern is:

return type	member name	Inherited
return type	**member name**	Declared
return type	**member name**	Overridden

Classes Not Shown

To save space, all classes in the `javax.swing.plaf.*` packages are not included. All subclasses of `javax.accessibility.AccessibleContext` are not included as well.

AbstractAction

AbstractAction				javax.swing

Object [1]
1.2 ○ └AbstractAction ----------------------- Action [2] (java.awt.event.ActionListener [3] (java.util.EventListener)),
Cloneable, java.io.Serializable

	2	8 inherited members from Action not shown	
✱		public.........................	**AbstractAction** ()	ε883,905
✱		public.........................	**AbstractAction** (String name)	ε738,743,745,752,768
✱		public.........................	**AbstractAction** (String name, *Icon* icon)	ε746,816
○	3	public abstract ....void	actionPerformed (java.awt.event.ActionEvent e)	ε855,738,743,745,746
	2	public synchronized ....void	**addPropertyChangeListener** (*java.beans.PropertyChangeListener* listener)	
		protected...................... .... java.swing.event.Swing- PropertyChangeSupport	**changeSupport**	
	1	protected..............**Object**	**clone** () throws CloneNotSupportedException	
		protected .... boolean	**enabled**	
		protected ....void	**firePropertyChange** (String propertyName, Object oldValue, Object newValue)	
1.3		public............... Object[]	**getKeys** ()	
1.4		public synchronized .... java.beans.- PropertyChangeListener[]	**getPropertyChangeListeners** ()	
	2	public................. Object	**getValue** (String key)	ε857,960,986,1003,612
	2	public................ boolean	**isEnabled** ()	
	2	public......................void	**putValue** (String key, Object newValue)	
	2	public synchronized ....void	**removePropertyChangeListener** (*java.beans.PropertyChangeListener* listener)	
	2	public......................void	**setEnabled** (boolean newValue)	

AbstractBorder				javax.swing.border

Object ε873
1.2 ○ └AbstractBorder ----------------------- *Border* [1], java.io.Serializable

✱		public.........................	**AbstractBorder** ()
	1	public...........java.awt.Insets	**getBorderInsets** (java.awt.Component c)
		public...........java.awt.Insets	**getBorderInsets** (java.awt.Component c, java.awt.Insets insets)
		public...... java.awt.Rectangle	**getInteriorRectangle** (java.awt.Component c, int x, int y, int width, int height)
△		public static .... java.awt.Rectangle	**getInteriorRectangle** (java.awt.Component c, *Border* b, int x, int y, int width, int height)
	1	public................. boolean	**isBorderOpaque** ()
	1	public......................void	**paintBorder** (java.awt.Component c, java.awt.Graphics g, int x, int y, int width, int height)

AbstractButton				javax.swing

Object ε45
○ └java.awt.Component [1] ------------------- *java.awt.image.ImageObserver* [4], *java.awt.MenuContainer*,
java.io.Serializable
 └java.awt.Container [2]
1.2 ○ └JComponent [3]
1.2 ○   └AbstractButton ------------------- *java.awt.ItemSelectable* [5], *SwingConstants* [6]

	1	*142 inherited members from java.awt.Component not shown*	
	2	*51 inherited members from java.awt.Container not shown*	
	3	*143 inherited members from JComponent not shown*	
	6	*19 inherited members from SwingConstants not shown*	
	4	*8 inherited members from java.awt.image.ImageObserver not shown*	
✱		public.........................	**AbstractButton** ()	
		protected .... java. .awt.event.ActionListener	**actionListener**	
		public......................void	**addActionListener** (java.awt.event.ActionListener l)	ε644
		public......................void	**addChangeListener** (javax.swing.event.ChangeListener l)	
	5	public......................void	**addItemListener** (java.awt.event.ItemListener l)	ε650,765
▲		public static final ....String	**BORDER_PAINTED_CHANGED_PROPERTY** = "borderPainted"	
		protected transient...... javax. .swing.event.ChangeEvent	**changeEvent**	

Class *Interface* —extends - - -implements ○ abstract ● final △ static ▲ static final ✱ constructor x x—inherited x **x**—declared **x x**—overridden
ε*n*—examples of usage —has subclass package—see other volume

	protected . . . . *javax.swing*	**changeListener**		
	.event.ChangeListener			
	protected . . . . .int	**checkHorizontalKey** (int key, String exception)		
	protected . . . . .int	**checkVerticalKey** (int key, String exception)		
1.3	protected . . . . .void	**configurePropertiesFromAction** (*Action* a)		
▲	public static final . . . . String	**CONTENT_AREA_FILLED_CHANGED_PROPERTY** = "contentAreaFilled"		
	protected . . . . *java*	**createActionListener** ()		
	.awt.event.ActionListener			
1.3	protected . . . . *java.beans*	**createActionPropertyChangeListener** (*Action* a)		
	.PropertyChangeListener			
	protected . . . . *javax.swing*	**createChangeListener** ()		
	.event.ChangeListener			
	protected	**createItemListener** ()		
	. . java.awt.event.ItemListener			
▲	public static final . . . . String	**DISABLED_ICON_CHANGED_PROPERTY** = "disabledIcon"		
▲	public static final . . . . String	**DISABLED_SELECTED_ICON_CHANGED_PROPERTY** = "disabledSelectedIcon"		
	public .void	**doClick** ()		
	public .void	**doClick** (int pressTime)		
	protected . . . . .void	**fireActionPerformed** (java.awt.event.ActionEvent event)		
	protected . . . . .void	**fireItemStateChanged** (java.awt.event.ItemEvent event)		
	protected . . . . .void	**fireStateChanged** ()		
▲	public static final . . . . String	**FOCUS_PAINTED_CHANGED_PROPERTY** = "focusPainted"		
1.3	public . . . . *Action*	**getAction** ()		
	public . . . . .String	**getActionCommand** ()		
1.4	public . . . . *java*	**getActionListeners** ()		
	.awt.event.ActionListener[]			
1.4	public . . . . *javax.swing*	**getChangeListeners** ()		
	.event.ChangeListener[]			
	public . . . . *Icon*	**getDisabledIcon** ()		
	public . . . . *Icon*	**getDisabledSelectedIcon** ()		
1.4	public . . . . .int	**getDisplayedMnemonicIndex** ()		
	public . . . . .int	**getHorizontalAlignment** ()		
	public . . . . .int	**getHorizontalTextPosition** ()		
	public . . . . *Icon*	**getIcon** ()		
1.4	public . . . . .int	**getIconTextGap** ()		ε749
1.4	public	**getItemListeners** ()		
	java.awt.event.ItemListener[]			
D	public . . . . .String	**getLabel** ()		
	public . . . . java.awt.Insets	**getMargin** ()		
	public . . . . .int	**getMnemonic** ()		
	public . . . . *ButtonModel*	**getModel** ()		ε769,770,771
1.4	public .long	**getMultiClickThreshhold** ()		
	public . . . . *Icon*	**getPressedIcon** ()		
	public . . . . *Icon*	**getRolloverIcon** ()		
	public . . . . *Icon*	**getRolloverSelectedIcon** ()		
	public . . . . *Icon*	**getSelectedIcon** ()		
5	public . . . . Object[]	**getSelectedObjects** ()		ε650
	public . . . . .String	**getText** ()		ε754,813
	public	**getUI** ()		
	. . . . javax.swing.plaf.ButtonUI			
	public . . . . .int	**getVerticalAlignment** ()		
	public . . . . .int	**getVerticalTextPosition** ()		
▲	public static final . . . . String	**HORIZONTAL_ALIGNMENT_CHANGED_PROPERTY** = "horizontalAlignment"		
▲	public static final . . . . String	**HORIZONTAL_TEXT_POSITION_CHANGED_PROPERTY** = "horizontalTextPosition"		
▲	public static final . . . . String	**ICON_CHANGED_PROPERTY** = "icon"		
1	public . . . .**boolean**	**imageUpdate** (java.awt.Image img, int infoflags, int x, int y, int w, int h)		
	protected . . . . .void	**init** (String text, *Icon* icon)		
	public . . . . boolean	**isBorderPainted** ()		
	public . . . . boolean	**isContentAreaFilled** ()		
	public . . . . boolean	**isFocusPainted** ()		
	public . . . . boolean	**isRolloverEnabled** ()		
	public . . . . boolean	**isSelected** ()		ε752,753
	protected	**itemListener**		
	. . java.awt.event.ItemListener			
▲	public static final . . . . String	**MARGIN_CHANGED_PROPERTY** = "margin"		
▲	public static final . . . . String	**MNEMONIC_CHANGED_PROPERTY** = "mnemonic"		
▲	protected . . . . *ButtonModel*	**model**		
▲	public static final . . . . String	**MODEL_CHANGED_PROPERTY** = "model"		
3	protected . . . . **void**	**paintBorder** (java.awt.Graphics g)		
3	protected . . . . **String**	**paramString** ()		
▲	public static final . . . . String	**PRESSED_ICON_CHANGED_PROPERTY** = "pressedIcon"		
	public .void	**removeActionListener** (*java.awt.event.ActionListener* l)		

AbstractButton

	public	void	**removeChangeListener** (*javax.swing.event.ChangeListener* l)	
5	public	void	**removeItemListener** (*java.awt.event.ItemListener* l)	ε650
▲	public static final	String	**ROLLOVER_ENABLED_CHANGED_PROPERTY** = "rolloverEnabled"	
▲	public static final	String	**ROLLOVER_ICON_CHANGED_PROPERTY** = "rolloverIcon"	
▲	public static final	String	**ROLLOVER_SELECTED_ICON_CHANGED_PROPERTY** = "rolloverSelectedIcon"	
▲	public static final	String	**SELECTED_ICON_CHANGED_PROPERTY** = "selectedIcon"	
1.3	public	void	**setAction** (*Action* a)	ε883
	public	void	**setActionCommand** (String actionCommand)	
	public	void	**setBorderPainted** (boolean b)	
	public	void	**setContentAreaFilled** (boolean b)	
	public	void	**setDisabledIcon** (*Icon* disabledIcon)	ε750,755
	public	void	**setDisabledSelectedIcon** (*Icon* disabledSelectedIcon)	ε755
1.4	public	void	**setDisplayedMnemonicIndex** (int index) throws IllegalArgumentException	
3	public	**void**	**setEnabled** (boolean b)	ε750
	public	void	**setFocusPainted** (boolean b)	
	public	void	**setHorizontalAlignment** (int alignment)	ε748
	public	void	**setHorizontalTextPosition** (int textPosition)	ε747
	public	void	**setIcon** (*Icon* defaultIcon)	ε746,755
1.4	public	void	**setIconTextGap** (int iconTextGap)	ε749
D	public	void	**setLabel** (String label)	
	public	void	**setMargin** (java.awt.Insets m)	ε816
	public	void	**setMnemonic** (char mnemonic)	ε690,691
	public	void	**setMnemonic** (int mnemonic)	
	public	void	**setModel** (*ButtonModel* newModel)	
1.4	public	void	**setMultiClickThreshhold** (long threshhold)	
	public	void	**setPressedIcon** (*Icon* pressedIcon)	ε751,755
	public	void	**setRolloverEnabled** (boolean b)	
	public	void	**setRolloverIcon** (*Icon* rolloverIcon)	ε751,755
	public	void	**setRolloverSelectedIcon** (*Icon* rolloverSelectedIcon)	
	public	void	**setSelected** (boolean b)	ε753
	public	void	**setSelectedIcon** (*Icon* selectedIcon)	ε755
	public	void	**setText** (String text)	ε744,745,754,816
	public	void	**setUI** (javax.swing.plaf.ButtonUI ui)	
	public	void	**setVerticalAlignment** (int alignment)	ε748
	public	void	**setVerticalTextPosition** (int textPosition)	ε747
▲	public static final	String	**TEXT_CHANGED_PROPERTY** = "text"	
3	public	**void**	**updateUI** ()	
▲	public static final	String	**VERTICAL_ALIGNMENT_CHANGED_PROPERTY** = "verticalAlignment"	
▲	public static final	String	**VERTICAL_TEXT_POSITION_CHANGED_PROPERTY** = "verticalTextPosition"	

AbstractButton.ButtonChangeListener protected javax.swing

Object
  └AbstractButton.ButtonChangeListener ------ *javax.swing.event.ChangeListener* [1] (*java.util.EventListener*), *java.io.Serializable*

1.2

1	public	void	**stateChanged** (javax.swing.event.ChangeEvent e)	ε791,793,800,805,815

AbstractCellEditor javax.swing

Object ε959
1.3 ○ └AbstractCellEditor ------------------- *CellEditor* [1], *java.io.Serializable*

*	public		**AbstractCellEditor** ()	
1	public	void	**addCellEditorListener** (*javax.swing.event.CellEditorListener* l)	
1	public	void	**cancelCellEditing** ()	ε956
	protected transient	javax. swing.event.ChangeEvent	**changeEvent**	
	protected	void	**fireEditingCanceled** ()	
	protected	void	**fireEditingStopped** ()	
1.4	public	javax.swing. event.CellEditorListener[]	**getCellEditorListeners** ()	
○ 1	public abstract	Object	getCellEditorValue ()	ε953,954,960
1	public	boolean	**isCellEditable** (java.util.EventObject e)	ε955,960
	protected	javax.swing. event.EventListenerList	**listenerList**	
1	public	void	**removeCellEditorListener** (*javax.swing.event.CellEditorListener* l)	
1	public	boolean	**shouldSelectCell** (java.util.EventObject anEvent)	

Class *Interface* —extends - - -implements ○ abstract ● final △ static ▲ static final ✳ constructor x x—inherited x **x**—declared **x x**—overridden
εn—examples of usage ‿—has subclass package—see other volume

1	public.................. boolean	**stopCellEditing** ()		ε954,956

AbstractColorChooserPanel

javax.swing.colorchooser

ε882

```
Object
○   └─java.awt.Component 1 - - - - - - - - - - - - - - - - - - - java.awt.image.ImageObserver 5, java.awt.MenuContainer,
                                                                   java.io.Serializable
        └─java.awt.Container 2
1.2 ○       └─javax.swing.JComponent 3
1.2           └─javax.swing.JPanel 4 - - - - - - - - - - - - - - - javax.accessibility.Accessible
1.2 ○             └─AbstractColorChooserPanel
```

	1	*143 inherited members from java.awt.Component not shown*		
	2	*51 inherited members from java.awt.Container not shown*		
	3	*142 inherited members from javax.swing.JComponent not shown*		
	5	*8 inherited members from java.awt.image.ImageObserver not shown*		
✳		public........................	**AbstractColorChooserPanel** ()	
○		protected abstract ....void	**buildChooser** ()	ε883
	4	public......javax.accessibility ⊋ .AccessibleContext	getAccessibleContext ()	
		protected ....java.awt.Color	**getColorFromModel** ()	
		public.... *ColorSelectionModel*	**getColorSelectionModel** ()	
1.4		public.........................int	**getDisplayedMnemonicIndex** ()	
○		public abstract ....String	**getDisplayName** ()	ε883
○		public abstract ....*javax.swing.Icon*	**getLargeDisplayIcon** ()	ε883
1.4		public.........................int	**getMnemonic** ()	
○		public abstract ....*javax.swing.Icon*	**getSmallDisplayIcon** ()	ε883
1.4	4	public javax.swing.plaf.PanelUI	getUI ()	
	4	public......................String	getUIClassID ()	
		public........................void	**installChooserPanel** (javax.swing.JColorChooser enclosingChooser)	
	3	public........................ **void**	**paint** (java.awt.Graphics g)	
	4	protected ....String	paramString ()	
1.4	4	public........................void	setUI (javax.swing.plaf.PanelUI ui)	
		public........................void	**uninstallChooserPanel** (javax.swing.JColorChooser enclosingChooser)	
○		public abstract ....void	**updateChooser** ()	ε883
	4	public........................void	updateUI ()	

AbstractDocument

javax.swing.text

```
Object
1.2 ○   └─AbstractDocument - - - - - - - - - - - - - - - - - - - Document 1, java.io.Serializable
```

✳		protected	**AbstractDocument** (*AbstractDocument.Content* data)	
✳		protected	**AbstractDocument** (*AbstractDocument.Content* data, *AbstractDocument.AttributeContext* context)	
	1	public......................void	**addDocumentListener** (*javax.swing.event.DocumentListener* listener) ε1016	
	1	public......................void	**addUndoableEditListener** (*javax.swing.event.UndoableEditListener* listener) ε1034	
▲		protected static final .....String	**BAD_LOCATION**	
▲		public static final ....String	**BidiElementName** = "bidi level"	
▲		public static final ....String	**ContentElementName** = "content"	
		protected .... *Element*	**createBranchElement** (*Element* parent, *AttributeSet* a)	
		protected .... *Element*	**createLeafElement** (*Element* parent, *AttributeSet* a, int p0, int p1)	
	1	public synchronized ...*Position*	**createPosition** (int offs) throws BadLocationException ε974	
		public........................void	**dump** (java.io.PrintStream out)	
▲		public static final ....String	**ElementNameAttribute** = "$ename"	
		protected ....void	**fireChangedUpdate** (*javax.swing.event.DocumentEvent* e)	
		protected ....void	**fireInsertUpdate** (*javax.swing.event.DocumentEvent* e)	
		protected ....void	**fireRemoveUpdate** (*javax.swing.event.DocumentEvent* e)	
		protected ....void	**fireUndoableEditUpdate** (javax.swing.event.UndoableEditEvent e)	
		public...........................int	**getAsynchronousLoadPriority** ()	
●		protected final................. .... *AbstractDocument* ⊋ .AttributeContext	**getAttributeContext** ()	
		public............... *Element*	**getBidiRootElement** ()	
●		protected final................. .. *AbstractDocument.Content*	**getContent** ()	

AbstractDocument

●		protected final synchronized .. .. Thread	**getCurrentWriter** ()	
○ 1		public abstract .... *Element*	**getDefaultRootElement** ()	ε984,990,1013
1.4		public.......... DocumentFilter	**getDocumentFilter** ()	
1.4		public.............. *javax.swing₂ .event.DocumentListener[]*	**getDocumentListeners** ()	
		public....... java.util.Dictionary	**getDocumentProperties** ()	
● 1		public final ....*Position*	**getEndPosition** ()	
1		public.......................int	**getLength** ()	ε968,969,970,971,972
1.3		public . *java.util.EventListener[]*	**getListeners** (Class listenerType)	
○		public abstract .... *Element*	**getParagraphElement** (int pos)	
● 1		public final .... Object	**getProperty** (Object key)	
1		public.................*Element[]*	**getRootElements** ()	
● 1		public final ....*Position*	**getStartPosition** ()	
1		public.....................String	**getText** (int offset, int length) throws BadLocationException	ε971,972,973,1002,1006
1		public.....................void	**getText** (int offset, int length, Segment txt) throws BadLocationException	ε969
1.4		public...... *javax.swing.event₂ .UndoableEditListener[]*	**getUndoableEditListeners** ()	
1		public.....................void	**insertString** (int offs, String str, *AttributeSet* a) throws BadLocationException	ε975,970,989,991,992
		protected ....void	**insertUpdate** (AbstractDocument.DefaultDocumentEvent chng, *AttributeSet* attr)	
		protected .... javax.swing₂ .event.EventListenerList	**listenerList**	
▲		public static final .... String	**ParagraphElementName** = "paragraph"	
		protected ....void	**postRemoveUpdate** (AbstractDocument.DefaultDocumentEvent chng)	
● 1		public final ....void	**putProperty** (Object key, Object value)	
●		public final synchronized ..void	**readLock** ()	
●		public final synchronized ..void	**readUnlock** ()	
1		public.....................void	**remove** (int offs, int len) throws BadLocationException	ε970,1002
1		public.....................void	**removeDocumentListener** (*javax.swing.event.DocumentListener* listener)	
1		public.....................void	**removeUndoableEditListener** (*javax.swing.event.UndoableEditListener* listener)	
		protected ....void	**removeUpdate** (AbstractDocument.DefaultDocumentEvent chng)	
1		public.....................void	**render** (*Runnable* r)	ε971
1.4		public.....................void	**replace** (int offset, int length, String text, *AttributeSet* attrs) throws BadLocationException	
▲		public static final .... String	**SectionElementName** = "section"	
		public.....................void	**setAsynchronousLoadPriority** (int p)	
1.4		public.....................void	**setDocumentFilter** (DocumentFilter filter)	ε975
		public.....................void	**setDocumentProperties** (java.util.Dictionary x)	
▲ 1		public static final .... String	StreamDescriptionProperty = "stream"	
▲ 1		public static final .... String	TitleProperty = "title"	
●		protected final synchronized .. ..void	**writeLock** ()	
●		protected final synchronized .. ..void	**writeUnlock** ()	

AbstractDocument.AbstractElement | javax.swing.text

Object [1]
1.2 ○ └AbstractDocument.AbstractElement‚ - - - - - - - - *Element* [2], *MutableAttributeSet* [3] (*AttributeSet* [4]),
java.io.Serializable‚, *javax.swing.tree.TreeNode*‚ [5]

∗		public.........................	**AbstractDocument.AbstractElement** (*Element* parent, *AttributeSet* a)	
3		public.......................void	**addAttribute** (Object name, Object value)	
3		public.......................void	**addAttributes** (*AttributeSet* attr)	
○ 5		public abstract .... *java.util.Enumeration*	**children** ()	ε1023,1024,1028,1029
4		public................. boolean	**containsAttribute** (Object name, Object value)	
4		public................. boolean	**containsAttributes** (*AttributeSet* attrs)	
4		public............. *AttributeSet*	**copyAttributes** ()	
		public.......................void	**dump** (java.io.PrintStream psOut, int indentAmount)	
1		protected .... **void**	**finalize** () throws Throwable	
○ 5		public abstract .... boolean	**getAllowsChildren** ()	
4		public................... Object	**getAttribute** (Object attrName)	ε1010,1013,1017
4		public.......................int	**getAttributeCount** ()	ε1010
4		public.... *java.util.Enumeration*	**getAttributeNames** ()	ε1010
2		public............. *AttributeSet*	**getAttributes** ()	ε1013

Class   *Interface*   —extends   - - -implements   ○ abstract   ● final   △ static   ▲ static final   ∗ constructor   x x—inherited   x **x**—declared   **x x**—overridden
ε*n*—examples of usage   ‚—has subclass   package—see other volume

	5	public........................	**getChildAt** (int childIndex)	
		...javax.swing.tree.TreeNode		
	5	public........................int	**getChildCount** ()	ε1023,1024,1025,1028,1029
	2	public..............*Document*	**getDocument** ()	
○	2	public abstract.........*Element*	**getElement** (int index)	ε984,990,1013
○	2	public abstract..............int	**getElementCount** ()	ε984,990,1013
○	2	public abstract..............int	**getElementIndex** (int offset)	
○	2	public abstract..............int	**getEndOffset** ()	ε984,990,1013
	5	public........................int	**getIndex** (*javax.swing.tree.TreeNode* node)	
	2	public......................String	**getName** ()	
	5	public........................	**getParent** ()	ε1027
		...javax.swing.tree.TreeNode		
	2	public................*Element*	**getParentElement** ()	
	4	public.............*AttributeSet*	**getResolveParent** ()	
○	2	public abstract..............int	**getStartOffset** ()	ε984,990,1013
	4	public................boolean	**isDefined** (Object attrName)	
	4	public................boolean	**isEqual** (*AttributeSet* attr)	
○	2	public abstract........boolean	**isLeaf** ()	ε984
▲	4	public static final........Object	NameAttribute	
	3	public......................void	**removeAttribute** (Object name)	
	3	public......................void	**removeAttributes** (*java.util.Enumeration* names)	
	3	public......................void	**removeAttributes** (*AttributeSet* attrs)	
▲	4	public static final........Object	ResolveAttribute	
	3	public......................void	**setResolveParent** (*AttributeSet* parent)	

AbstractDocument.AttributeContext   javax.swing.text

1.2   *AbstractDocument.AttributeContext*

public.............*AttributeSet*	**addAttribute** (*AttributeSet* old, Object name, Object value)
public.............*AttributeSet*	**addAttributes** (*AttributeSet* old, *AttributeSet* attr)
public.............*AttributeSet*	**getEmptySet** ()
public......................void	**reclaim** (*AttributeSet* a)
public.............*AttributeSet*	**removeAttribute** (*AttributeSet* old, Object name)
public.............*AttributeSet*	**removeAttributes** (*AttributeSet* old, *java.util.Enumeration* names)
public.............*AttributeSet*	**removeAttributes** (*AttributeSet* old, *AttributeSet* attrs)

AbstractDocument.BranchElement   javax.swing.text

Object[1]
1.2 ○ └AbstractDocument.AbstractElement[2] - - - - - - *Element, MutableAttributeSet*⌐ (*AttributeSet*[3]), *java.io.Serializable*⌐,
                                javax.swing.tree.TreeNode⌐
1.2   └AbstractDocument.BranchElement⌐

	2	public......................void	addAttribute (Object name, Object value)	
	2	public......................void	addAttributes (*AttributeSet* attr)	
*		public........................	**AbstractDocument.BranchElement** (*Element* parent, *AttributeSet* a)	ε1023,1024,1028,1029
	2	public.. *java.util.Enumeration*	**children** ()	
	2	public................boolean	containsAttribute (Object name, Object value)	
	2	public................boolean	containsAttributes (*AttributeSet* attrs)	
	2	public.............*AttributeSet*	copyAttributes ()	
	2	public......................void	dump (java.io.PrintStream psOut, int indentAmount)	
	2	protected ....void	finalize () throws Throwable	
	2	public................**boolean**	**getAllowsChildren** ()	
	2	public....................Object	getAttribute (Object attrName)	ε1010,1013,1017
	2	public........................int	getAttributeCount ()	ε1010
	2	public.... *java.util.Enumeration*	getAttributeNames ()	ε1010
	2	public.............*AttributeSet*	getAttributes ()	ε1013
	2	public........................	getChildAt (int childIndex)	
		...javax.swing.tree.TreeNode		
	2	public........................int	getChildCount ()	ε1023,1024,1025,1028,1029
	2	public..............*Document*	getDocument ()	
	2	public................***Element***	**getElement** (int index)	ε984,990,1013
	2	public...................**int**	**getElementCount** ()	ε984,990,1013
	2	public...................**int**	**getElementIndex** (int offset)	
	2	public...................**int**	**getEndOffset** ()	ε984,990,1013
	2	public........................int	getIndex (*javax.swing.tree.TreeNode* node)	
	2	public................**String**	**getName** ()	
	2	public........................	getParent ()	ε1027
		...javax.swing.tree.TreeNode		
	2	public................*Element*	getParentElement ()	
	2	public.............*AttributeSet*	getResolveParent ()	

AbstractDocument.BranchElement

2	public	**int**	**getStartOffset** ()		ε984,990,1013
2	public	boolean	isDefined (Object attrName)		
2	public	boolean	isEqual (*AttributeSet* attr)		
2	public	**boolean**	**isLeaf** ()		ε984
▲ 3	public static final	Object	NameAttribute		
	public	*Element*	**positionToElement** (int pos)		
2	public	void	removeAttribute (Object name)		
2	public	void	removeAttributes (*java.util.Enumeration* names)		
2	public	void	removeAttributes (*AttributeSet* attrs)		
	public	void	**replace** (int offset, int length, *Element[]* elems)		
▲ 3	public static final	Object	ResolveAttribute		
2	public	void	setResolveParent (*AttributeSet* parent)		
1	public	**String**	**toString** ()		

AbstractDocument.Content   javax.swing.text

1.2   *AbstractDocument.Content*

public	*Position*	**createPosition** (int offset) throws BadLocationException
public	void	**getChars** (int where, int len, Segment txt) throws BadLocationException
public	String	**getString** (int where, int len) throws BadLocationException
public	*javax₂ .swing.undo.UndoableEdit*	**insertString** (int where, String str) throws BadLocationException
public	int	**length** ()
public	*javax₂ .swing.undo.UndoableEdit*	**remove** (int where, int nitems) throws BadLocationException

AbstractDocument.DefaultDocumentEvent   javax.swing.text

```
       Object
1.2    └javax.swing.undo.AbstractUndoableEdit 1 - - - - javax.swing.undo.UndoableEdit, java.io.Serializable
1.2      └javax.swing.undo.CompoundEdit 2
1.2        └AbstractDocument₂ - - - - - - - - - - - - - - - javax.swing.event.DocumentEvent 3
                .DefaultDocumentEvent
```

2	public	**boolean**	**addEdit** (*javax.swing.undo.UndoableEdit* anEdit)		ε1034
2	public	boolean	canRedo ()		ε1034
2	public	boolean	canUndo ()		ε1034
✳	public		**AbstractDocument.DefaultDocumentEvent** (int offs, int len, javax.swing.event.DocumentEvent.EventType type)		
2	public	void	die ()		
2	protected	java.util.Vector	edits		
2	public	void	end ()		
3	public	*javax.swing₂ .event.DocumentEvent₂ .ElementChange*	**getChange** (*Element* elem)		
3	public	Document	**getDocument** ()		ε1016
3	public	int	**getLength** ()		ε1016
3	public	int	**getOffset** ()		ε1016
2	public	**String**	**getPresentationName** ()		
2	public	**String**	**getRedoPresentationName** ()		
3	public	*javax.swing.event₂ .DocumentEvent.EventType*	**getType** ()		
2	public	**String**	**getUndoPresentationName** ()		
2	public	boolean	isInProgress ()		
2	public	**boolean**	**isSignificant** ()		
2	protected	*javax₂ .swing.undo.UndoableEdit*	lastEdit ()		
2	public	**void**	**redo** () throws javax.swing.undo.CannotRedoException		ε1034
▲ 1	protected static final	String	RedoName		
1	public	boolean	replaceEdit (*javax.swing.undo.UndoableEdit* anEdit)		
2	public	**String**	**toString** ()		
2	public	**void**	**undo** () throws javax.swing.undo.CannotUndoException		ε1034
▲ 1	protected static final	String	UndoName		

Class   *Interface*   —extends   - - -implements   ○ abstract   ● final   △ static   ▲ static final   ✳ constructor   x x—inherited   x **x**—declared   **x x**—overridden
ε*n*—examples of usage   ⌐—has subclass   package—see other volume

		AbstractDocument.ElementEdit		javax.swing.text

Object
1.2 └─javax.swing.undo.AbstractUndoableEdit [1] ---- *javax.swing.undo.UndoableEdit*, *java.io.Serializable*
1.2   └─AbstractDocument.ElementEdit --------- *javax.swing.event.DocumentEvent.ElementChange* [2]

1	public	boolean	addEdit (*javax.swing.undo.UndoableEdit* anEdit)	ε1034
1	public	boolean	canRedo ()	ε1034
1	public	boolean	canUndo ()	ε1034
1	public	void	die ()	
*	public		**AbstractDocument.ElementEdit** (*Element* e, int index, *Element[]* removed, *Element[]* added)	
2	public	*Element[]*	**getChildrenAdded** ()	
2	public	*Element[]*	**getChildrenRemoved** ()	
2	public	*Element*	**getElement** ()	
2	public	int	**getIndex** ()	
1	public	String	getPresentationName ()	
1	public	String	getRedoPresentationName ()	
1	public	String	getUndoPresentationName ()	
1	public	boolean	isSignificant ()	
1	public	**void**	**redo** () throws javax.swing.undo.CannotRedoException	ε1034
▲ 1	protected static final	String	RedoName	
1	public	boolean	replaceEdit (*javax.swing.undo.UndoableEdit* anEdit)	
1	public	String	toString ()	
1	public	**void**	**undo** () throws javax.swing.undo.CannotUndoException	ε1034
▲ 1	protected static final	String	UndoName	

	AbstractDocument.LeafElement			javax.swing.text

Object [1]
1.2 ○ └─AbstractDocument.AbstractElement [2] ------ *Element*, *MutableAttributeSet* (*AttributeSet* [3]), *java.io.Serializable*, *javax.swing.tree.TreeNode*
1.2   └─AbstractDocument.LeafElement

2	public	void	addAttribute (Object name, Object value)	
2	public	void	addAttributes (*AttributeSet* attr)	
2	public	**java.util.Enumeration**	**children** ()	ε1023,1024,1028,1029
2	public	boolean	containsAttribute (Object name, Object value)	
2	public	boolean	containsAttributes (*AttributeSet* attrs)	
2	public	*AttributeSet*	copyAttributes ()	
2	public	void	dump (java.io.PrintStream psOut, int indentAmount)	
2	protected	void	finalize () throws Throwable	
2	public	**boolean**	**getAllowsChildren** ()	
2	public	Object	getAttribute (Object attrName)	ε1010,1013,1017
2	public	int	getAttributeCount ()	ε1010
2	public	*java.util.Enumeration*	getAttributeNames ()	ε1010
2	public	*AttributeSet*	getAttributes ()	ε1013
2	public	*...javax.swing.tree.TreeNode*	getChildAt (int childIndex)	
2	public	int	getChildCount ()	ε1023,1024,1025,1028,1029
2	public	*Document*	getDocument ()	
2	public	**Element**	**getElement** (int index)	ε984,990,1013
2	public	**int**	**getElementCount** ()	ε984,990,1013
2	public	**int**	**getElementIndex** (int pos)	
2	public	**int**	**getEndOffset** ()	ε984,990,1013
2	public	int	getIndex (*javax.swing.tree.TreeNode* node)	
2	public	**String**	**getName** ()	ε1027
2	public	*...javax.swing.tree.TreeNode*	getParent ()	
2	public	*Element*	getParentElement ()	
2	public	*AttributeSet*	getResolveParent ()	
2	public	**int**	**getStartOffset** ()	ε984,990,1013
2	public	boolean	isDefined (Object attrName)	
2	public	boolean	isEqual (*AttributeSet* attr)	ε984
2	public	**boolean**	**isLeaf** ()	
*	public		**AbstractDocument.LeafElement** (*Element* parent, *AttributeSet* a, int offs0, int offs1)	
▲ 3	public static final	Object	NameAttribute	
2	public	void	removeAttribute (Object name)	
2	public	void	removeAttributes (*java.util.Enumeration* names)	
2	public	void	removeAttributes (*AttributeSet* attrs)	
▲ 3	public static final	Object	ResolveAttribute	
2	public	void	setResolveParent (*AttributeSet* parent)	

AbstractDocument.LeafElement

	1	public	**String toString** ()

AbstractLayoutCache

Object
1.2 ○ └AbstractLayoutCache ------------------ *RowMapper* [1]

*	public...........................	**AbstractLayoutCache** ()
○	public abstract .... java.awt.Rectangle	**getBounds** (TreePath path, java.awt.Rectangle placeIn)
○	public abstract .... boolean	**getExpandedState** (TreePath path)
	public................ *TreeModel*	**getModel** ()
	public.. AbstractLayoutCache ₂ .NodeDimensions	**getNodeDimensions** ()
	protected .. java.awt.Rectangle	**getNodeDimensions** (Object value, int row, int depth, boolean expanded, java.awt.Rectangle placeIn)
○	public abstract ....TreePath	**getPathClosestTo** (int x, int y)
○	public abstract ....TreePath	**getPathForRow** (int row)
	public................int	**getPreferredHeight** ()
	public................int	**getPreferredWidth** (java.awt.Rectangle bounds)
○	public abstract ....int	**getRowCount** ()
○	public abstract ....int	**getRowForPath** (TreePath path)
	public...............int	**getRowHeight** ()
1	public....................int[]	**getRowsForPaths** (TreePath[] paths)
	public..... *TreeSelectionModel*	**getSelectionModel** ()
○	public abstract ....int	**getVisibleChildCount** (TreePath path)
○	public abstract .... *java.util.Enumeration*	**getVisiblePathsFrom** (TreePath path)
○	public abstract ....void	**invalidatePathBounds** (TreePath path)
○	public abstract ....void	**invalidateSizes** ()
○	public abstract .... boolean	**isExpanded** (TreePath path)
	protected .... boolean	**isFixedRowHeight** ()
	public................. boolean	**isRootVisible** ()
	protected...................... ....AbstractLayoutCache ₂ .NodeDimensions	**nodeDimensions**
	protected .... boolean	**rootVisible**
	protected ....int	**rowHeight**
○	public abstract ....void	**setExpandedState** (TreePath path, boolean isExpanded)
	public.................void	**setModel** (*TreeModel* newModel)
	public.................void	**setNodeDimensions** (AbstractLayoutCache.NodeDimensions nd)
	public.................void	**setRootVisible** (boolean rootVisible)
	public.................void	**setRowHeight** (int rowHeight)
	public.................void	**setSelectionModel** (*TreeSelectionModel* newLSM)
	protected .... *TreeModel*	**treeModel**
○	public abstract ....void	**treeNodesChanged** (javax.swing.event.TreeModelEvent e)
○	public abstract ....void	**treeNodesInserted** (javax.swing.event.TreeModelEvent e)
○	public abstract ....void	**treeNodesRemoved** (javax.swing.event.TreeModelEvent e)
	protected . *TreeSelectionModel*	**treeSelectionModel**
○	public abstract ....void	**treeStructureChanged** (javax.swing.event.TreeModelEvent e)

AbstractLayoutCache.NodeDimensions

Object
1.2 ○ └AbstractLayoutCache.NodeDimensions

○	public abstract .... java.awt.Rectangle	**getNodeDimensions** (Object value, int row, int depth, boolean expanded, java.awt.Rectangle bounds)
*	public...........................	**AbstractLayoutCache.NodeDimensions** ()

AbstractListModel

Object
1.2 ○ └AbstractListModel ----------------- *ListModel* [1], *java.io.Serializable*

*	public...........................	**AbstractListModel** ()	
1	public......................void	**addListDataListener** (*javax.swing.event.ListDataListener* l)	ε785

Class *Interface* —extends - - -implements ○ abstract ● final △ static ▲ static final ✳ constructor x x—inherited x **x**—declared x **x**—overridden
ε*n*—examples of usage ͺ—has subclass package—see other volume

		protected .... void	**fireContentsChanged** (Object source, int index0, int index1)	
		protected .... void	**fireIntervalAdded** (Object source, int index0, int index1)	
		protected .... void	**fireIntervalRemoved** (Object source, int index0, int index1)	
○	1	public abstract .... Object	getElementAt (int index)	ε760,776,777,779,785
1.4		public .... *javax.swing*ᗒ	**getListDataListeners** ()	
		.event.ListDataListener[]		
1.3		public. *java.util.EventListener[]*	**getListeners** (Class listenerType)	
○	1	public abstract .... int	getSize ()	ε760,777,778,780
		protected .... javax.swingᗒ	**listenerList**	
		.event.EventListenerList		
	1	public .... void	**removeListDataListener** (*javax.swing.event.ListDataListener* l)	

Object
1.4 ○ └ AbstractSpinnerModel ᵥ - - - - - - - - - - - - - - - - - - *SpinnerModel* ¹

*		public	**AbstractSpinnerModel** ()	
	1	public .... void	**addChangeListener** (*javax.swing.event.ChangeListener* l)	
		protected .... void	**fireStateChanged** ()	
		public .... *javax.swing*ᗒ	**getChangeListeners** ()	
		.event.ChangeListener[]		
		public. *java.util.EventListener[]*	**getListeners** (Class listenerType)	
○	1	public abstract .... Object	getNextValue ()	ε792
○	1	public abstract .... Object	getPreviousValue ()	ε792
○	1	public abstract .... Object	getValue ()	
		protected .... javax.swingᗒ	**listenerList**	
		.event.EventListenerList		
	1	public .... void	**removeChangeListener** (*javax.swing.event.ChangeListener* l)	
○	1	public abstract .... void	setValue (Object value)	

Object
1.2 ○ └ AbstractTableModel ᵥ - - - - - - - - - - - - - - - - - - - *TableModel* ¹, *java.io.Serializable* ᵥ

*		public	**AbstractTableModel** ()	
	1	public .... void	**addTableModelListener** (*javax.swing.event.TableModelListener* l)	ε957,965
		public .... int	**findColumn** (String columnName)	
		public .... void	**fireTableCellUpdated** (int row, int column)	
		public .... void	**fireTableChanged** (javax.swing.event.TableModelEvent e)	
		public .... void	**fireTableDataChanged** ()	
		public .... void	**fireTableRowsDeleted** (int firstRow, int lastRow)	
		public .... void	**fireTableRowsInserted** (int firstRow, int lastRow)	
		public .... void	**fireTableRowsUpdated** (int firstRow, int lastRow)	
		public .... void	**fireTableStructureChanged** ()	ε961,962
	1	public .... Class	**getColumnClass** (int columnIndex)	ε927,929
○	1	public abstract .... int	getColumnCount ()	ε920,921
	1	public .... String	**getColumnName** (int column)	
1.3		public. *java.util.EventListener[]*	**getListeners** (Class listenerType)	
○	1	public abstract .... int	getRowCount ()	ε911,909,910,962
1.4		public .... *javax.swing*ᗒ	**getTableModelListeners** ()	
		.event.TableModelListener[]		
○	1	public abstract .... Object	getValueAt (int rowIndex, int columnIndex)	ε926
	1	public .... boolean	**isCellEditable** (int rowIndex, int columnIndex)	ε958
		protected .... javax.swingᗒ	**listenerList**	
		.event.EventListenerList		
	1	public .... void	**removeTableModelListener** (*javax.swing.event.TableModelListener* l)	
	1	public .... void	**setValueAt** (Object aValue, int rowIndex, int columnIndex)	ε926

Object ¹
1.2 └ AbstractUndoableEdit ᵥ - - - - - - - - - - - - - - - - - - *UndoableEdit* ², *java.io.Serializable* ᵥ

*		public	**AbstractUndoableEdit** ()	
	2	public .... boolean	**addEdit** (*UndoableEdit* anEdit)	ε1034
	2	public .... boolean	**canRedo** ()	ε1034
	2	public .... boolean	**canUndo** ()	ε1034

AbstractUndoableEdit

2	public	void	**die** ()	
2	public	String	**getPresentationName** ()	
2	public	String	**getRedoPresentationName** ()	
2	public	String	**getUndoPresentationName** ()	
2	public	boolean	**isSignificant** ()	
2	public	void	**redo** () throws CannotRedoException	ε1034
▲	protected static final	String	**RedoName**	
2	public	boolean	**replaceEdit** (*UndoableEdit* anEdit)	
1	public	**String**	**toString** ()	
2	public	void	**undo** () throws CannotUndoException	ε1034
▲	protected static final	String	**UndoName**	

AbstractWriter
javax.swing.text

Object
└AbstractWriter⌄
1.2 ○

✳	protected		**AbstractWriter** (java.io.Writer w, *Document* doc)
✳	protected		**AbstractWriter** (java.io.Writer w, *Element* root)
✳	protected		**AbstractWriter** (java.io.Writer w, *Element* root, int pos, int len)
✳	protected		**AbstractWriter** (java.io.Writer w, *Document* doc, int pos, int len)
	protected	void	**decrIndent** ()
1.3	protected	boolean	**getCanWrapLines** ()
1.3	protected	int	**getCurrentLineLength** ()
	protected	*Document*	**getDocument** ()
	protected	ElementIterator	**getElementIterator** ()
1.3	public	int	**getEndOffset** ()
1.3	protected	int	**getIndentLevel** ()
1.3	protected	int	**getIndentSpace** ()
1.3	protected	int	**getLineLength** ()
1.3	public	String	**getLineSeparator** ()
1.3	public	int	**getStartOffset** ()
	protected	String	**getText** (*Element* elem) throws BadLocationException
1.3	protected	java.io.Writer	**getWriter** ()
	protected	void	**incrIndent** ()
	protected	void	**indent** () throws java.io.IOException
	protected	boolean	**inRange** (*Element* next)
1.3	protected	boolean	**isLineEmpty** ()
▲	protected static final	char	**NEWLINE**
1.3	protected	void	**output** (char[] content, int start, int length) throws java.io.IOException
1.3	protected	void	**setCanWrapLines** (boolean newValue)
1.3	protected	void	**setCurrentLineLength** (int length)
	protected	void	**setIndentSpace** (int space)
	protected	void	**setLineLength** (int l)
1.3	public	void	**setLineSeparator** (String value)
	protected	void	**text** (*Element* elem) throws BadLocationException, java.io.IOException
○	protected abstract	void	**write** () throws java.io.IOException, BadLocationException
	protected	void	**write** (char ch) throws java.io.IOException
	protected	void	**write** (String content) throws java.io.IOException
1.3	protected	void	**write** (char[] chars, int startIndex, int length) throws java.io.IOException
	protected	void	**writeAttributes** (*AttributeSet* attr) throws java.io.IOException
1.3	protected	void	**writeLineSeparator** () throws java.io.IOException

---

Accessible
javax.accessibility

Accessible
1.2

public	AccessibleContext	**getAccessibleContext** ()	ε687

AccessibleAction
javax.accessibility

AccessibleAction
1.2

public	boolean	**doAccessibleAction** (int i)	
public	int	**getAccessibleActionCount** ()	
public	String	**getAccessibleActionDescription** (int i)	

Class *Interface* —extends - - -implements ○ abstract ● final △ static ▲ static final ✳ constructor x x—inherited x **x**—declared **x x**—overridden
ε*n*—examples of usage ⌄—has subclass package—see other volume

AccessibleBundle | javax.accessibility

Object [1]
1.2 ○ └─AccessibleBundle␣

```
 *      public.......................... AccessibleBundle ()
        protected ................String key
        public.....................String toDisplayString ()
        public.....................String toDisplayString (java.util.Locale locale)
        protected ................String toDisplayString (String resourceBundleName, java.util.Locale locale)
     1  public................... String toString ()
```

AccessibleComponent | javax.accessibility

1.2   *AccessibleComponent*␣

```
        public......................void addFocusListener (java.awt.event.FocusListener l)
        public.................. boolean contains (java.awt.Point p)
        public.............. Accessible getAccessibleAt (java.awt.Point p)
        public..........java.awt.Color getBackground ()
        public...... java.awt.Rectangle getBounds ()
        public...... java.awt.Cursor getCursor ()
        public............java.awt.Font getFont ()
        public.... java.awt.FontMetrics getFontMetrics (java.awt.Font f)
        public..........java.awt.Color getForeground ()
        public..........java.awt.Point getLocation ()
        public..........java.awt.Point getLocationOnScreen ()
        public......java.awt.Dimension getSize ()
        public................. boolean isEnabled ()
        public................. boolean isFocusTraversable ()
        public................. boolean isShowing ()
        public................. boolean isVisible ()
        public......................void removeFocusListener (java.awt.event.FocusListener l)
        public......................void requestFocus ()
        public......................void setBackground (java.awt.Color c)
        public......................void setBounds (java.awt.Rectangle r)
        public......................void setCursor (java.awt.Cursor cursor)
        public......................void setEnabled (boolean b)
        public......................void setFont (java.awt.Font f)
        public......................void setForeground (java.awt.Color c)
        public......................void setLocation (java.awt.Point p)
        public......................void setSize (java.awt.Dimension d)
        public......................void setVisible (boolean b)
```

AccessibleContext | javax.accessibility

Object
1.2 ○ └─AccessibleContext␣

```
1.3 ▲   public static final ........String ACCESSIBLE_ACTION_PROPERTY = "accessibleActionProperty"
    ▲   public static final ........String ACCESSIBLE_ACTIVE_DESCENDANT_PROPERTY
                                           = "AccessibleActiveDescendant"
    ▲   public static final ........String ACCESSIBLE_CARET_PROPERTY = "AccessibleCaret"
    ▲   public static final ........String ACCESSIBLE_CHILD_PROPERTY = "AccessibleChild"
    ▲   public static final ........String ACCESSIBLE_DESCRIPTION_PROPERTY = "AccessibleDescription"
1.4 ▲   public static final ........String ACCESSIBLE_HYPERTEXT_OFFSET = "AccessibleHypertextOffset"
    ▲   public static final ........String ACCESSIBLE_NAME_PROPERTY = "AccessibleName"
    ▲   public static final ........String ACCESSIBLE_SELECTION_PROPERTY = "AccessibleSelection"
    ▲   public static final ........String ACCESSIBLE_STATE_PROPERTY = "AccessibleState"
    ▲   public static final ........String ACCESSIBLE_TABLE_CAPTION_CHANGED = "accessibleTableCaptionChanged"
1.3 ▲   public static final ........String ACCESSIBLE_TABLE_COLUMN_DESCRIPTION_CHANGED
                                           = "accessibleTableColumnDescriptionChanged"
1.3 ▲   public static final ........String ACCESSIBLE_TABLE_COLUMN_HEADER_CHANGED
                                           = "accessibleTableColumnHeaderChanged"
1.3 ▲   public static final ........String ACCESSIBLE_TABLE_MODEL_CHANGED = "accessibleTableModelChanged"
1.3 ▲   public static final ........String ACCESSIBLE_TABLE_ROW_DESCRIPTION_CHANGED
                                           = "accessibleTableRowDescriptionChanged"
1.3 ▲   public static final ........String ACCESSIBLE_TABLE_ROW_HEADER_CHANGED
                                           = "accessibleTableRowHeaderChanged"
1.3 ▲   public static final ........String ACCESSIBLE_TABLE_SUMMARY_CHANGED =
                                           "accessibleTableSummaryChanged"
    ▲   public static final ........String ACCESSIBLE_TEXT_PROPERTY = "AccessibleText"
```

A

Classes

AccessibleContext

▲	public static final	String	**ACCESSIBLE_VALUE_PROPERTY**	= "AccessibleValue"
▲	public static final	String	**ACCESSIBLE_VISIBLE_DATA_PROPERTY**	= "AccessibleVisibleData"
✳	public		**AccessibleContext** ()	ε687
	protected	String	**accessibleDescription**	
	protected	String	**accessibleName**	
	protected	Accessible	**accessibleParent**	
	public	void	**addPropertyChangeListener** (*java.beans.PropertyChangeListener* listener)	
	public	void	**firePropertyChange** (String propertyName, Object oldValue, Object newValue)	
	public	AccessibleAction	**getAccessibleAction** ()	
○	public abstract	Accessible	**getAccessibleChild** (int i)	
○	public abstract	int	**getAccessibleChildrenCount** ()	
	public	AccessibleComponent	**getAccessibleComponent** ()	
	public	String	**getAccessibleDescription** ()	
1.4	public	AccessibleEditableText	**getAccessibleEditableText** ()	
1.3	public	AccessibleIcon[]	**getAccessibleIcon** ()	
○	public abstract	int	**getAccessibleIndexInParent** ()	
	public	String	**getAccessibleName** ()	
	public	Accessible	**getAccessibleParent** ()	
1.3	public	AccessibleRelationSet	**getAccessibleRelationSet** ()	
○	public abstract	AccessibleRole	**getAccessibleRole** ()	
	public	AccessibleSelection	**getAccessibleSelection** ()	
○	public abstract	AccessibleStateSet	**getAccessibleStateSet** ()	
1.3	public	AccessibleTable	**getAccessibleTable** ()	
	public	AccessibleText	**getAccessibleText** ()	
	public	AccessibleValue	**getAccessibleValue** ()	
	public abstract	java.util.Locale	**getLocale** () throws java.awt.IllegalComponentStateException	
	public	void	**removePropertyChangeListener** (*java.beans.PropertyChangeListener* listener)	
	public	void	**setAccessibleDescription** (String s)	
	public	void	**setAccessibleName** (String s)	ε688
	public	void	**setAccessibleParent** (*Accessible* a)	

AccessibleEditableText   javax.accessibility

1.4   *AccessibleEditableText*────────── *AccessibleText* ₌ [1]

▲	[1]	public static final	int	CHARACTER = 1
		public	void	**cut** (int startIndex, int endIndex)
		public	void	**delete** (int startIndex, int endIndex)
	[1]	public	String	getAfterIndex (int part, int index)
	[1]	public	String	getAtIndex (int part, int index)
	[1]	public	String	getBeforeIndex (int part, int index)
	[1]	public	int	getCaretPosition ()
	[1]	public	*javax.swing.text.AttributeSet*	getCharacterAttribute (int i)
	[1]	public	java.awt.Rectangle	getCharacterBounds (int i)
	[1]	public	int	getCharCount ()
	[1]	public	int	getIndexAtPoint (java.awt.Point p)
	[1]	public	String	getSelectedText ()
	[1]	public	int	getSelectionEnd ()
	[1]	public	int	getSelectionStart ()
		public	String	**getTextRange** (int startIndex, int endIndex)
		public	void	**insertTextAtIndex** (int index, String s)
		public	void	**paste** (int startIndex)
		public	void	**replaceText** (int startIndex, int endIndex, String s)
		public	void	**selectText** (int startIndex, int endIndex)
▲	[1]	public static final	int	SENTENCE = 3
		public	void	**setAttributes** (int startIndex, int endIndex, *javax.swing.text.AttributeSet* as)
		public	void	**setTextContents** (String s)
▲	[1]	public static final	int	WORD = 2

AccessibleExtendedComponent   javax.accessibility

1.4   *AccessibleExtendedComponent*────────── *AccessibleComponent* ₌ [1]

	[1]	*27 inherited members from AccessibleComponent not shown*	
	public	AccessibleKeyBinding	**getAccessibleKeyBinding** ()
	public	String	**getTitledBorderText** ()
	public	String	**getToolTipText** ()

Class   *Interface*   —extends   - - -implements   ○ abstract   ● final   △ static   ▲ static final   ✳ constructor   x x—inherited   x **x**—declared   **x x**—overridden
ε*n*—examples of usage   ‿—has subclass   package—see other volume

A

		AccessibleExtendedTable	javax.accessibility

1.4   *AccessibleExtendedTable*——————————————— *AccessibleTable* [1]

1	public	*Accessible*	getAccessibleAt (int r, int c)
1	public	*Accessible*	getAccessibleCaption ()
	public	int	**getAccessibleColumn** (int index)
1	public	int	getAccessibleColumnCount ()
1	public	*Accessible*	getAccessibleColumnDescription (int c)
1	public	int	getAccessibleColumnExtentAt (int r, int c)
1	public	*AccessibleTable*	getAccessibleColumnHeader ()
	public	int	**getAccessibleIndex** (int r, int c)
	public	int	**getAccessibleRow** (int index)
1	public	int	getAccessibleRowCount ()
1	public	*Accessible*	getAccessibleRowDescription (int r)
1	public	int	getAccessibleRowExtentAt (int r, int c)
1	public	*AccessibleTable*	getAccessibleRowHeader ()
1	public	*Accessible*	getAccessibleSummary ()
1	public	int[]	getSelectedAccessibleColumns ()
1	public	int[]	getSelectedAccessibleRows ()
1	public	boolean	isAccessibleColumnSelected (int c)
1	public	boolean	isAccessibleRowSelected (int r)
1	public	boolean	isAccessibleSelected (int r, int c)
1	public	void	setAccessibleCaption (*Accessible* a)
1	public	void	setAccessibleColumnDescription (int c, *Accessible* a)
1	public	void	setAccessibleColumnHeader (*AccessibleTable* table)
1	public	void	setAccessibleRowDescription (int r, *Accessible* a)
1	public	void	setAccessibleRowHeader (*AccessibleTable* table)
1	public	void	setAccessibleSummary (*Accessible* a)

AccessibleHyperlink	javax.accessibility

Object
1.2 ○   └AccessibleHyperlink - - - - - - - - - - - - - - - - - - - *AccessibleAction* [1]

＊	public		**AccessibleHyperlink** ()
○ *1*	public abstract	boolean	**doAccessibleAction** (int i)
○	public abstract	Object	**getAccessibleActionAnchor** (int i)
○ *1*	public abstract	int	**getAccessibleActionCount** ()
○ *1*	public abstract	String	**getAccessibleActionDescription** (int i)
○	public abstract	Object	**getAccessibleActionObject** (int i)
○	public abstract	int	**getEndIndex** ()
○	public abstract	int	**getStartIndex** ()
○	public abstract	boolean	**isValid** ()

AccessibleHypertext	javax.accessibility

1.2   *AccessibleHypertext*——————————————— *AccessibleText* [1]

▲ *1*	public static final	int	CHARACTER = 1
1	public	String	getAfterIndex (int part, int index)
1	public	String	getAtIndex (int part, int index)
1	public	String	getBeforeIndex (int part, int index)
1	public	int	getCaretPosition ()
1	public		getCharacterAttribute (int i)
	. *javax.swing.text.AttributeSet*		
1	public	java.awt.Rectangle	getCharacterBounds (int i)
1	public	int	getCharCount ()
1	public	int	getIndexAtPoint (java.awt.Point p)
	public	AccessibleHyperlink	**getLink** (int linkIndex)
	public	int	**getLinkCount** ()
	public	int	**getLinkIndex** (int charIndex)
1	public	String	getSelectedText ()
1	public	int	getSelectionEnd ()
1	public	int	getSelectionStart ()
▲ *1*	public static final	int	SENTENCE = 3
▲ *1*	public static final	int	WORD = 2

Classes

AccessibleIcon

		javax.accessibility

1.3   *AccessibleIcon*

public	String	**getAccessibleIconDescription** ()
public	int	**getAccessibleIconHeight** ()
public	int	**getAccessibleIconWidth** ()
public	void	**setAccessibleIconDescription** (String description)

AccessibleKeyBinding

	javax.accessibility

1.4   *AccessibleKeyBinding*

public	Object	**getAccessibleKeyBinding** (int i)
public	int	**getAccessibleKeyBindingCount** ()

AccessibleRelation

	javax.accessibility

Object
1.2 ○   └AccessibleBundle [1]
1.3   └AccessibleRelation

✳	public		**AccessibleRelation** (String key)
✳	public		**AccessibleRelation** (String key, Object target)
✳	public		**AccessibleRelation** (String key, Object[] target)
▲	public static final	String	**CONTROLLED_BY** = "controlledBy"
▲	public static final	String	**CONTROLLED_BY_PROPERTY** = "controlledByProperty"
▲	public static final	String	**CONTROLLER_FOR** = "controllerFor"
▲	public static final	String	**CONTROLLER_FOR_PROPERTY** = "controllerForProperty"
	public	String	**getKey** ()
	public	Object[]	**getTarget** ()
1	protected	String	key
▲	public static final	String	**LABEL_FOR** = "labelFor"
▲	public static final	String	**LABEL_FOR_PROPERTY** = "labelForProperty"
▲	public static final	String	**LABELED_BY** = "labeledBy"
▲	public static final	String	**LABELED_BY_PROPERTY** = "labeledByProperty"
▲	public static final	String	**MEMBER_OF** = "memberOf"
▲	public static final	String	**MEMBER_OF_PROPERTY** = "memberOfProperty"
	public	void	**setTarget** (Object target)
	public	void	**setTarget** (Object[] target)
1	public	String	toDisplayString ()
1	public	String	toDisplayString (java.util.Locale locale)
1	protected	String	toDisplayString (String resourceBundleName, java.util.Locale locale)
1	public	String	toString ()

AccessibleRelationSet

	javax.accessibility

Object [1]
1.3   └AccessibleRelationSet

✳	public		**AccessibleRelationSet** ()
✳	public		**AccessibleRelationSet** (AccessibleRelation[] relations)
	public	boolean	**add** (AccessibleRelation relation)
	public	void	**addAll** (AccessibleRelation[] relations)
	public	void	**clear** ()
	public	boolean	**contains** (String key)
	public	AccessibleRelation	**get** (String key)
	protected	java.util.Vector	**relations**
	public	boolean	**remove** (AccessibleRelation relation)
	public	int	**size** ()
	public	AccessibleRelation[]	**toArray** ()
1	public	**String**	**toString** ()

Class   *Interface*   —extends   - - -implements   ○ abstract   ● final   △ static   ▲ static final   ✳ constructor   x x—inherited   x **x**—declared   **x x**—overridden
εn—examples of usage   ⌐—has subclass   package—see other volume

396

			AccessibleResourceBundle	javax.accessibility

```
          Object
1.1  O    └ java.util.ResourceBundle 1
1.1  O      └ java.util.ListResourceBundle 2
D             └ AccessibleResourceBundle
```

D	✳		public.........................	**AccessibleResourceBundle** ()
D	▲	1	public static final..............	getBundle (String baseName)
			.... java.util.ResourceBundle	
D	▲	1	public static final..............	getBundle (String baseName, java.util.Locale locale)
			.... java.util.ResourceBundle	
D	△	1	public static	getBundle (String baseName, java.util.Locale locale, ClassLoader loader)
			.... java.util.ResourceBundle	
D		2	public............... **Object[][]**	**getContents** ()
D		2	public.... *java.util.Enumeration*	getKeys ()
D		1	public......... java.util.Locale	getLocale ()
D	●	1	public final ....Object	getObject (String key)
D	●	1	public final ....String	getString (String key)
D	●	1	public final ....String[]	getStringArray (String key)
D	●	2	public final ....Object	handleGetObject (String key)
D		1	protected	parent
			.... java.util.ResourceBundle	
D		1	protected ....void	setParent (java.util.ResourceBundle parent)

			AccessibleRole	javax.accessibility

```
          Object
1.2  O    └ AccessibleBundle 1
1.2         └ AccessibleRole
```

	✳		protected	**AccessibleRole** (String key)
	▲		public static final .... AccessibleRole	**ALERT**
	▲		public static final .... AccessibleRole	**AWT_COMPONENT**
1.3	▲		public static final .... AccessibleRole	**CANVAS**
	▲		public static final .... AccessibleRole	**CHECK_BOX**
	▲		public static final .... AccessibleRole	**COLOR_CHOOSER**
	▲		public static final .... AccessibleRole	**COLUMN_HEADER**
	▲		public static final .... AccessibleRole	**COMBO_BOX**
1.4	▲		public static final .... AccessibleRole	**DATE_EDITOR**
	▲		public static final .... AccessibleRole	**DESKTOP_ICON**
	▲		public static final .... AccessibleRole	**DESKTOP_PANE**
	▲		public static final .... AccessibleRole	**DIALOG**
	▲		public static final .... AccessibleRole	**DIRECTORY_PANE**
	▲		public static final .... AccessibleRole	**FILE_CHOOSER**
	▲		public static final .... AccessibleRole	**FILLER**
1.4	▲		public static final .... AccessibleRole	**FONT_CHOOSER**
	▲		public static final .... AccessibleRole	**FRAME**
	▲		public static final .... AccessibleRole	**GLASS_PANE**
1.4	▲		public static final .... AccessibleRole	**GROUP_BOX**
1.4	▲		public static final .... AccessibleRole	**HYPERLINK**
1.3	▲		public static final .... AccessibleRole	**ICON**
	▲		public static final .... AccessibleRole	**INTERNAL_FRAME**
		1	protected .... String	key
	▲		public static final .... AccessibleRole	**LABEL**
	▲		public static final .... AccessibleRole	**LAYERED_PANE**
	▲		public static final .... AccessibleRole	**LIST**
1.3	▲		public static final .... AccessibleRole	**LIST_ITEM**
	▲		public static final .... AccessibleRole	**MENU**
	▲		public static final .... AccessibleRole	**MENU_BAR**
	▲		public static final .... AccessibleRole	**MENU_ITEM**
	▲		public static final .... AccessibleRole	**OPTION_PANE**
	▲		public static final .... AccessibleRole	**PAGE_TAB**
	▲		public static final .... AccessibleRole	**PAGE_TAB_LIST**
	▲		public static final .... AccessibleRole	**PANEL**
	▲		public static final .... AccessibleRole	**PASSWORD_TEXT**
	▲		public static final .... AccessibleRole	**POPUP_MENU**
	▲		public static final .... AccessibleRole	**PROGRESS_BAR**
	▲		public static final .... AccessibleRole	**PUSH_BUTTON**
	▲		public static final .... AccessibleRole	**RADIO_BUTTON**
	▲		public static final .... AccessibleRole	**ROOT_PANE**
	▲		public static final .... AccessibleRole	**ROW_HEADER**

AccessibleRole

▲		public static final	AccessibleRole	**SCROLL_BAR**
▲		public static final	AccessibleRole	**SCROLL_PANE**
▲		public static final	AccessibleRole	**SEPARATOR**
▲		public static final	AccessibleRole	**SLIDER**
1.4 ▲		public static final	AccessibleRole	**SPIN_BOX**
▲		public static final	AccessibleRole	**SPLIT_PANE**
1.4 ▲		public static final	AccessibleRole	**STATUS_BAR**
▲		public static final	AccessibleRole	**SWING_COMPONENT**
▲		public static final	AccessibleRole	**TABLE**
▲		public static final	AccessibleRole	**TEXT**
	1	public	String	toDisplayString ()
	1	public	String	toDisplayString (java.util.Locale locale)
	1	protected	String	toDisplayString (String resourceBundleName, java.util.Locale locale)
▲		public static final	AccessibleRole	**TOGGLE_BUTTON**
▲		public static final	AccessibleRole	**TOOL_BAR**
▲		public static final	AccessibleRole	**TOOL_TIP**
	1	public	String	toString ()
▲		public static final	AccessibleRole	**TREE**
▲		public static final	AccessibleRole	**UNKNOWN**
▲		public static final	AccessibleRole	**VIEWPORT**
▲		public static final	AccessibleRole	**WINDOW**

AccessibleSelection   javax.accessibility

1.2		*AccessibleSelection*		
		public .... void	**addAccessibleSelection** (int i)
		public .... void	**clearAccessibleSelection** ()
		public .... *Accessible*	**getAccessibleSelection** (int i)
		public .... int	**getAccessibleSelectionCount** ()
		public .... boolean	**isAccessibleChildSelected** (int i)
		public .... void	**removeAccessibleSelection** (int i)
		public .... void	**selectAllAccessibleSelection** ()

AccessibleState   javax.accessibility

Object
1.2 ○ └AccessibleBundle [1]
1.2   └AccessibleState

✳		protected		**AccessibleState** (String key)
▲		public static final	AccessibleState	**ACTIVE**
▲		public static final	AccessibleState	**ARMED**
▲		public static final	AccessibleState	**BUSY**
▲		public static final	AccessibleState	**CHECKED**
▲		public static final	AccessibleState	**COLLAPSED**
▲		public static final	AccessibleState	**EDITABLE**
▲		public static final	AccessibleState	**ENABLED**
▲		public static final	AccessibleState	**EXPANDABLE**
▲		public static final	AccessibleState	**EXPANDED**
▲		public static final	AccessibleState	**FOCUSABLE**
▲		public static final	AccessibleState	**FOCUSED**
▲		public static final	AccessibleState	**HORIZONTAL**
▲		public static final	AccessibleState	**ICONIFIED**
	1	protected	String	key
▲		public static final	AccessibleState	**MODAL**
▲		public static final	AccessibleState	**MULTI_LINE**
▲		public static final	AccessibleState	**MULTISELECTABLE**
▲		public static final	AccessibleState	**OPAQUE**
▲		public static final	AccessibleState	**PRESSED**
▲		public static final	AccessibleState	**RESIZABLE**
▲		public static final	AccessibleState	**SELECTABLE**
▲		public static final	AccessibleState	**SELECTED**
▲		public static final	AccessibleState	**SHOWING**
▲		public static final	AccessibleState	**SINGLE_LINE**
	1	public	String	toDisplayString ()
	1	public	String	toDisplayString (java.util.Locale locale)

Class   *Interface*   —extends   - - -implements   ○ abstract   ● final   △ static   ▲ static final   ✳ constructor   x x—inherited   x **x**—declared   **x x**—overridden
ε*n*—examples of usage   ⌐—has subclass   package—see other volume

1	protected	.... String	toDisplayString (String resourceBundleName, java.util.Locale locale)
1	public	.... String	toString ()
▲	public static final	.... AccessibleState	**TRANSIENT**
▲	public static final	.... AccessibleState	**VERTICAL**
▲	public static final	.... AccessibleState	**VISIBLE**

AccessibleStateSet			javax.accessibility

1.2

```
Object 1
 └ AccessibleStateSet
```

✳	public	....	**AccessibleStateSet** ()
✳	public	....	**AccessibleStateSet** (AccessibleState[] states)
	public	.... boolean	**add** (AccessibleState state)
	public	.... void	**addAll** (AccessibleState[] states)
	public	.... void	**clear** ()
	public	.... boolean	**contains** (AccessibleState state)
	public	.... boolean	**remove** (AccessibleState state)
	protected	.... java.util.Vector	**states**
	public	.... AccessibleState[]	**toArray** ()
1	public	.... String	**toString** ()

AccessibleTable			javax.accessibility

1.3 *AccessibleTable*

public	.... *Accessible*	**getAccessibleAt** (int r, int c)
public	.... *Accessible*	**getAccessibleCaption** ()
public	.... int	**getAccessibleColumnCount** ()
public	.... *Accessible*	**getAccessibleColumnDescription** (int c)
public	.... int	**getAccessibleColumnExtentAt** (int r, int c)
public	.... *AccessibleTable*	**getAccessibleColumnHeader** ()
public	.... int	**getAccessibleRowCount** ()
public	.... *Accessible*	**getAccessibleRowDescription** (int r)
public	.... int	**getAccessibleRowExtentAt** (int r, int c)
public	.... *AccessibleTable*	**getAccessibleRowHeader** ()
public	.... *Accessible*	**getAccessibleSummary** ()
public	.... int[]	**getSelectedAccessibleColumns** ()
public	.... int[]	**getSelectedAccessibleRows** ()
public	.... boolean	**isAccessibleColumnSelected** (int c)
public	.... boolean	**isAccessibleRowSelected** (int r)
public	.... boolean	**isAccessibleSelected** (int r, int c)
public	.... void	**setAccessibleCaption** (*Accessible* a)
public	.... void	**setAccessibleColumnDescription** (int c, *Accessible* a)
public	.... void	**setAccessibleColumnHeader** (*AccessibleTable* table)
public	.... void	**setAccessibleRowDescription** (int r, *Accessible* a)
public	.... void	**setAccessibleRowHeader** (*AccessibleTable* table)
public	.... void	**setAccessibleSummary** (*Accessible* a)

AccessibleTableModelChange			javax.accessibility

1.3 *AccessibleTableModelChange*

▲	public static final	.... int	**DELETE** = -1
	public	.... int	**getFirstColumn** ()
	public	.... int	**getFirstRow** ()
	public	.... int	**getLastColumn** ()
	public	.... int	**getLastRow** ()
	public	.... int	**getType** ()
▲	public static final	.... int	**INSERT** = 1
▲	public static final	.... int	**UPDATE** = 0

AccessibleText			javax.accessibility

1.2 *AccessibleText*

▲	public static final	.... int	**CHARACTER** = 1
	public	.... String	**getAfterIndex** (int part, int index)
	public	.... String	**getAtIndex** (int part, int index)
	public	.... String	**getBeforeIndex** (int part, int index)

AccessibleText

public	int	**getCaretPosition** ()
public		**getCharacterAttribute** (int i)
. javax.swing.text.AttributeSet		
public	java.awt.Rectangle	**getCharacterBounds** (int i)
public	int	**getCharCount** ()
public	int	**getIndexAtPoint** (java.awt.Point p)
public	String	**getSelectedText** ()
public	int	**getSelectionEnd** ()
public	int	**getSelectionStart** ()
▲ public static final	int	**SENTENCE** = 3
▲ public static final	int	**WORD** = 2

AccessibleValue

javax.accessibility

1.2 *AccessibleValue*

public	Number	**getCurrentAccessibleValue** ()
public	Number	**getMaximumAccessibleValue** ()
public	Number	**getMinimumAccessibleValue** ()
public	boolean	**setCurrentAccessibleValue** (Number n)

Action

javax.swing

1.2 *Action* ────────────────── *java.awt.event.ActionListener* [1]   ε738,743,745,746,752
(*java.util.EventListener*)

1.3 ▲	public static final	String	**ACCELERATOR_KEY** = "AcceleratorKey"	ε855
1.3 ▲	public static final	String	**ACTION_COMMAND_KEY** = "ActionCommandKey"	
1	public	void	actionPerformed (java.awt.event.ActionEvent e)	ε1001,855,644,738,743
	public	void	**addPropertyChangeListener** (*java.beans.PropertyChangeListener* listener)	
▲	public static final	String	**DEFAULT** = "Default"	
	public	Object	**getValue** (String key)	ε857,960,986,1003,612
	public	boolean	**isEnabled** ()	
▲	public static final	String	**LONG_DESCRIPTION** = "LongDescription"	ε855
1.3 ▲	public static final	String	**MNEMONIC_KEY** = "MnemonicKey"	ε855
▲	public static final	String	**NAME** = "Name"	ε857,986,1003,612,620
	public	void	**putValue** (String key, Object value)	
	public	void	**removePropertyChangeListener** (*java.beans.PropertyChangeListener* listener)	
	public	void	**setEnabled** (boolean b)	
▲	public static final	String	**SHORT_DESCRIPTION** = "ShortDescription"	ε855
▲	public static final	String	**SMALL_ICON** = "SmallIcon"	ε855

ActionEvent

java.awt.event

Object   ε601,705,743,745,746
1.1 └ java.util.EventObject [1] - - - - - - - - - - - - - - - - - - - *java.io.Serializable*
1.1 ○ └ java.awt.AWTEvent [2]
1.1 └ ActionEvent

	2	*26 inherited members from java.awt.AWTEvent not shown*		
▲		public static final	int	**ACTION_FIRST** = 1001	
▲		public static final	int	**ACTION_LAST** = 1001	
▲		public static final	int	**ACTION_PERFORMED** = 1001	
✳		public		**ActionEvent** (Object source, int id, String command)	
✳		public		**ActionEvent** (Object source, int id, String command, int modifiers)	ε1001
1.4 ✳		public		**ActionEvent** (Object source, int id, String command, long when, int modifiers)	
▲		public static final	int	**ALT_MASK** = 8	
▲		public static final	int	**CTRL_MASK** = 2	
		public	String	**getActionCommand** ()	ε766,905,1001,1011
	2	public	int	getID ()	ε1001,636
		public	int	**getModifiers** ()	ε1001
	1	public	Object	getSource ()	ε644,612,738,752,766
1.4		public	long	**getWhen** ()	
▲		public static final	int	**META_MASK** = 4	
	2	public	String	**paramString** ()	
▲		public static final	int	**SHIFT_MASK** = 1	
	1	protected transient	Object	source	

Class   *Interface*   —extends   - - -implements   ○ abstract   ● final   △ static   ▲ static final   ✳ constructor   x x—inherited   x **x**—declared   **x x**—overridden
ε*n*—examples of usage   ↳—has subclass   package—see other volume

ActionListener
java.awt.event

1.1	*ActionListener* ──────────────────── *java.util.EventListener*		ε738,743,745,746,752
	public.....................void **actionPerformed** (ActionEvent e)		ε644,601,705,766,884

ActionMap
javax.swing

Object
└ActionMap ------------------------- *java.io.Serializable*

1.3			
*	public.......................... **ActionMap** ()		
	public.................. Object[] **allKeys** ()		ε856
	public.....................void **clear** ()		
	public.................. *Action* **get** (Object key)		ε856
	public.............. ActionMap **getParent** ()		ε856
	public.................. Object[] **keys** ()		ε856
	public.....................void **put** (Object key, *Action* action)		ε857,858,861,863,937
	public.....................void **remove** (Object key)		
	public.....................void **setParent** (ActionMap map)		
	public........................int **size** ()		

ActionMapUIResource
javax.swing.plaf

Object
└javax.swing.ActionMap [1] ----------------- *java.io.Serializable*
    └ActionMapUIResource ----------------- *UIResource*

1.3			
1.3			
*	public.......................... **ActionMapUIResource** ()		
1	public.................. Object[] allKeys ()		ε856
1	public.....................void clear ()		
1	public.......*javax.swing.Action* get (Object key)		ε856
1	public..javax.swing.ActionMap getParent ()		ε856
1	public.................. Object[] keys ()		ε856
1	public.....................void put (Object key, *javax.swing.Action* action)		ε857,858,861,863,937
1	public.....................void remove (Object key)		
1	public.....................void setParent (javax.swing.ActionMap map)		
1	public........................int size ()		

ActiveEvent
java.awt

1.2	*ActiveEvent*		
	public.....................void **dispatch** ()		

Adjustable
java.awt

1.1	*Adjustable*		
	public.....................void **addAdjustmentListener** (*java.awt.event.AdjustmentListener* l)	ε822
	public........................int **getBlockIncrement** ()		
	public........................int **getMaximum** ()		
	public........................int **getMinimum** ()		
	public........................int **getOrientation** ()		ε822
	public........................int **getUnitIncrement** ()		
	public........................int **getValue** ()		
	public........................int **getVisibleAmount** ()		
▲	public static final ....int **HORIZONTAL** = 0		ε822
1.4 ▲	public static final ....int **NO_ORIENTATION** = 2		
	public.....................void **removeAdjustmentListener** (*java.awt.event.AdjustmentListener* l)	
	public.....................void **setBlockIncrement** (int b)		
	public.....................void **setMaximum** (int max)		
	public.....................void **setMinimum** (int min)		
	public.....................void **setUnitIncrement** (int u)		
	public.....................void **setValue** (int v)		
	public.....................void **setVisibleAmount** (int v)		
▲	public static final ....int **VERTICAL** = 1		

A

Classes

AdjustmentEvent

		AdjustmentEvent		java.awt.event

Object   ε640,641,643,649,566

- 1.1 └ java.util.EventObject[1] - *java.io.Serializable*
- 1.1 ○ └ java.awt.AWTEvent[2]
- 1.1 └ AdjustmentEvent

2 *27 inherited members from java.awt.AWTEvent not shown*

▲	public static final	int	**ADJUSTMENT_FIRST** = 601	
▲	public static final	int	**ADJUSTMENT_LAST** = 601	
▲	public static final	int	**ADJUSTMENT_VALUE_CHANGED** = 601	
∗	public		**AdjustmentEvent** (*java.awt.Adjustable* source, int id, int type, int value)	
1.4 ∗	public		**AdjustmentEvent** (*java.awt.Adjustable* source, int id, int type, int value, boolean isAdjusting)	
▲	public static final	int	**BLOCK_DECREMENT** = 3	ε822
▲	public static final	int	**BLOCK_INCREMENT** = 4	ε822
	public	*java.awt.Adjustable*	**getAdjustable** ()	ε822
	public	int	**getAdjustmentType** ()	ε822
1	public	Object	getSource ()	ε644,886,565,568,570
	public	int	**getValue** ()	ε822
1.4	public	boolean	**getValueIsAdjusting** ()	ε822
2	public	String	**paramString** ()	
1	protected transient	Object	source	
▲	public static final	int	**TRACK** = 5	ε822
▲	public static final	int	**UNIT_DECREMENT** = 2	ε822
▲	public static final	int	**UNIT_INCREMENT** = 1	ε822

		AdjustmentListener		java.awt.event

- 1.1 *AdjustmentListener* ——————————————— *java.util.EventListener*   ε738,743,745,746,752

	public	void	**adjustmentValueChanged** (AdjustmentEvent e)	ε822

		AffineTransform		java.awt.geom

Object[1]

- 1.2 └ AffineTransform - *Cloneable*, *java.io.Serializable*

∗	public		**AffineTransform** ()	ε659,592,596,672
∗	public		**AffineTransform** (double[] flatmatrix)	
∗	public		**AffineTransform** (float[] flatmatrix)	
∗	public		**AffineTransform** (AffineTransform Tx)	
∗	public		**AffineTransform** (double m00, double m10, double m01, double m11, double m02, double m12)	
∗	public		**AffineTransform** (float m00, float m10, float m01, float m11, float m02, float m12)	
1	public	Object	**clone** ()	
	public	void	**concatenate** (AffineTransform Tx)	
	public	AffineTransform	**createInverse** () throws NoninvertibleTransformException	
	public	*java.awt.Shape*	**createTransformedShape** (*java.awt.Shape* pSrc)	ε659
	public	Point2D	**deltaTransform** (Point2D ptSrc, Point2D ptDst)	
	public	void	**deltaTransform** (double[] srcPts, int srcOff, double[] dstPts, int dstOff, int numPts)	
1	public	boolean	**equals** (Object obj)	
	public	double	**getDeterminant** ()	
	public	void	**getMatrix** (double[] flatmatrix)	
△	public static	AffineTransform	**getRotateInstance** (double theta)	
△	public static	AffineTransform	**getRotateInstance** (double theta, double x, double y)	
△	public static	AffineTransform	**getScaleInstance** (double sx, double sy)	ε675
	public	double	**getScaleX** ()	
	public	double	**getScaleY** ()	
△	public static	AffineTransform	**getShearInstance** (double shx, double shy)	
	public	double	**getShearX** ()	
	public	double	**getShearY** ()	
△	public static	AffineTransform	**getTranslateInstance** (double tx, double ty)	
	public	double	**getTranslateX** ()	
	public	double	**getTranslateY** ()	
	public	int	**getType** ()	
1	public	int	**hashCode** ()	
	public	Point2D	**inverseTransform** (Point2D ptSrc, Point2D ptDst) throws NoninvertibleTransformException	

Class   *Interface*   —extends - - -implements ○ abstract ● final △ static ▲ static final ∗ constructor x x—inherited x **x**—declared **x x**—overridden
εn—examples of usage ⌐—has subclass package—see other volume

public	void	**inverseTransform** (double[] srcPts, int srcOff, double[] dstPts, int dstOff, int numPts) throws NoninvertibleTransformException	
public	boolean	**isIdentity** ()	
public	void	**preConcatenate** (AffineTransform Tx)	
public	void	**rotate** (double theta)	ε659,596
public	void	**rotate** (double theta, double x, double y)	ε672
public	void	**scale** (double sx, double sy)	ε659,596,672
public	void	**setToIdentity** ()	
public	void	**setToRotation** (double theta)	ε592
public	void	**setToRotation** (double theta, double x, double y)	
public	void	**setToScale** (double sx, double sy)	
public	void	**setToShear** (double shx, double shy)	
public	void	**setToTranslation** (double tx, double ty)	
public	void	**setTransform** (AffineTransform Tx)	
public	void	**setTransform** (double m00, double m10, double m01, double m11, double m02, double m12)	
public	void	**shear** (double shx, double shy)	ε659,596,672
1 public	String	**toString** ()	
public	Point2D	**transform** (Point2D ptSrc, Point2D ptDst)	
public	void	**transform** (double[] srcPts, int srcOff, float[] dstPts, int dstOff, int numPts)	
public	void	**transform** (double[] srcPts, int srcOff, double[] dstPts, int dstOff, int numPts)	
public	void	**transform** (float[] srcPts, int srcOff, double[] dstPts, int dstOff, int numPts)	
public	void	**transform** (float[] srcPts, int srcOff, float[] dstPts, int dstOff, int numPts)	
public	void	**transform** (Point2D[] ptSrc, int srcOff, Point2D[] ptDst, int dstOff, int numPts)	
public	void	**translate** (double tx, double ty)	ε659,596,672,675
▲ public static final	int	**TYPE_FLIP** = 64	
▲ public static final	int	**TYPE_GENERAL_ROTATION** = 16	
▲ public static final	int	**TYPE_GENERAL_SCALE** = 4	
▲ public static final	int	**TYPE_GENERAL_TRANSFORM** = 32	
▲ public static final	int	**TYPE_IDENTITY** = 0	
▲ public static final	int	**TYPE_MASK_ROTATION** = 24	
▲ public static final	int	**TYPE_MASK_SCALE** = 6	
▲ public static final	int	**TYPE_QUADRANT_ROTATION** = 8	
▲ public static final	int	**TYPE_TRANSLATION** = 1	
▲ public static final	int	**TYPE_UNIFORM_SCALE** = 2	

AffineTransformOp   java.awt.image

Object
  └AffineTransformOp - - - - - - - - - - - - - - - - - - - *BufferedImageOp* [1], *RasterOp* [2]
1.2

* public		**AffineTransformOp** (java.awt.geom.AffineTransform xform, java.awt.RenderingHints hints)	
* public		**AffineTransformOp** (java.awt.geom.AffineTransform xform, int interpolationType)	ε672,675
1 public	BufferedImage	**createCompatibleDestImage** (BufferedImage src, ColorModel destCM)	
2 public	WritableRaster	**createCompatibleDestRaster** (Raster src)	
● 1 public final	BufferedImage	**filter** (BufferedImage src, BufferedImage dst)	ε672,675,676,677,678
● 2 public final	WritableRaster	**filter** (Raster src, WritableRaster dst)	
● 1 public final . java.awt.geom.Rectangle2D		**getBounds2D** (BufferedImage src)	
● 2 public final . java.awt.geom.Rectangle2D		**getBounds2D** (Raster src)	
● public final	int	**getInterpolationType** ()	
● 1 public final java.awt.geom.Point2D		**getPoint2D** (java.awt.geom.Point2D srcPt, java.awt.geom.Point2D dstPt)	
● 1 public final ..... java.awt.RenderingHints		**getRenderingHints** ()	
● public final .... java.awt.geom.AffineTransform		**getTransform** ()	
▲ public static final	int	**TYPE_BILINEAR** = 2	ε672
▲ public static final	int	**TYPE_NEAREST_NEIGHBOR** = 1	ε675

AlphaComposite   java.awt

Object [1]
  └AlphaComposite - *Composite* [2]
1.2 ●

▲ public static final .... AlphaComposite		**Clear**
▲ public static final	int	**CLEAR** = 1

AlphaComposite

	2	public . . . . *CompositeContext*	**createContext** (java.awt.image.ColorModel srcColorModel, java.awt.image.ColorModel dstColorModel, RenderingHints hints)
1.4 ▲		public static final . . . . AlphaComposite	**Dst**
1.4 ▲		public static final . . . . int	**DST** = 9
1.4 ▲		public static final . . . . int	**DST_ATOP** = 11
▲		public static final . . . . int	**DST_IN** = 6
▲		public static final . . . . int	**DST_OUT** = 8
▲		public static final . . . . int	**DST_OVER** = 4
1.4 ▲		public static final . . . . AlphaComposite	**DstAtop**
▲		public static final . . . . AlphaComposite	**DstIn**
▲		public static final . . . . AlphaComposite	**DstOut**
▲		public static final . . . . AlphaComposite	**DstOver**
	1	public . . . . **boolean**	**equals** (Object obj)
		public . . . . float	**getAlpha** ()
△		public static . . AlphaComposite	**getInstance** (int rule)
△		public static . . AlphaComposite	**getInstance** (int rule, float alpha) ε576
		public . . . . int	**getRule** ()
	1	public . . . . **int**	**hashCode** ()
▲		public static final	**Src** ε669
▲		public static final . . . . AlphaComposite	**SRC** = 2
1.4 ▲		public static final . . . . int	**SRC_ATOP** = 10
▲		public static final . . . . int	**SRC_IN** = 5
▲		public static final . . . . int	**SRC_OUT** = 7
▲		public static final . . . . int	**SRC_OVER** = 3 ε576
1.4 ▲		public static final . . . . AlphaComposite	**SrcAtop**
▲		public static final . . . . AlphaComposite	**SrcIn**
▲		public static final . . . . AlphaComposite	**SrcOut**
▲		public static final . . . . AlphaComposite	**SrcOver**
1.4 ▲		public static final . . . . AlphaComposite	**Xor**
1.4 ▲		public static final . . . . int	**XOR** = 12

AncestorEvent
javax.swing.event

ε640,641,643,649,566

```
      Object
1.1   └ java.util.EventObject¹ - - - - - - - - - - - - - - - - - - - java.io.Serializable
1.1 ○   └java.awt.AWTEvent²
1.2       └AncestorEvent
```

	2	*28 inherited members from java.awt.AWTEvent not shown*	
▲		public static final . . . . int	**ANCESTOR_ADDED** = 1
▲		public static final . . . . int	**ANCESTOR_MOVED** = 3
▲		public static final . . . . int	**ANCESTOR_REMOVED** = 2
✳		public	**AncestorEvent** (javax.swing.JComponent source, int id, java.awt.Container ancestor, java.awt.Container ancestorParent)
		public . . . . java.awt.Container	**getAncestor** ()
		public . . . . java.awt.Container	**getAncestorParent** ()
		public . . . . javax.swing.JComponent	**getComponent** ()
	1	public . . . . Object	getSource () ε644,886,565,568,570
	1	protected transient . . . . . . Object	source

AncestorListener
javax.swing.event

1.2		*AncestorListener*———————————*java.util.EventListener* ε738,743,745,746,752	
		public . . . . void	**ancestorAdded** (AncestorEvent event)
		public . . . . void	**ancestorMoved** (AncestorEvent event)

Class *Interface* —extends - - -implements ○ abstract ● final △ static ▲ static final ✳ constructor x x—inherited x **x**—declared **x x**—overridden
ε*n*—examples of usage ↳—has subclass package—see other volume

public . . . . void **ancestorRemoved** (AncestorEvent event)

Applet
java.applet

Object
  └java.awt.Component[1] - - - - - - - - - - - - - - - - - - - *java.awt.image.ImageObserver* [4], *java.awt.MenuContainer*,
                                                       java.io.Serializable
    └java.awt.Container[2]
      └java.awt.Panel[3] - - - - - - - - - - - - - - - - - - - *javax.accessibility.Accessible*
       └Applet

	1	*173 inherited members from java.awt.Component not shown*		
	2	*65 inherited members from java.awt.Container not shown*		
	4	*8 inherited members from java.awt.image.ImageObserver not shown*		
	3	public . . . . void	addNotify ()	
*		public	**Applet** () throws java.awt.HeadlessException	
		public . . . . void	**destroy** ()	ε551
1.3	3	public . . . . **javax.accessibility**₂ **.AccessibleContext**	**getAccessibleContext** ()	
		public . . . . *AppletContext*	**getAppletContext** ()	
		public . . . . String	**getAppletInfo** ()	
		public . . . . *AudioClip*	**getAudioClip** (java.net.URL url)	
		public . . . . *AudioClip*	**getAudioClip** (java.net.URL url, String name)	
		public . . . . java.net.URL	**getCodeBase** ()	
		public . . . . java.net.URL	**getDocumentBase** ()	
		public . . . . java.awt.Image	**getImage** (java.net.URL url)	
		public . . . . java.awt.Image	**getImage** (java.net.URL url, String name)	
1.1	1	public . . . . **java.util.Locale**	**getLocale** ()	
		public . . . . String	**getParameter** (String name)	ε552
		public . . . . String[][]	**getParameterInfo** ()	
		public . . . . void	**init** ()	ε551,555,557,558
		public . . . . boolean	**isActive** ()	
1.2 ▲		public static final . . . . *AudioClip*	**newAudioClip** (java.net.URL url)	ε556
	2	public . . . . void	paint (java.awt.Graphics g)	ε551,557,558,575,878
		public . . . . void	**play** (java.net.URL url)	
		public . . . . void	**play** (java.net.URL url, String name)	
	1	public . . . . **void**	**resize** (java.awt.Dimension d)	
	1	public . . . . **void**	**resize** (int width, int height)	
●		public final . . . . **void**	**setStub** (*AppletStub* stub)	
		public . . . . void	**showStatus** (String msg)	ε554
		public . . . . void	**start** ()	ε551,558
		public . . . . void	**stop** ()	ε551,558

AppletContext
java.applet

AppletContext

	public . . . . Applet	**getApplet** (String name)	
	public . . . . *java.util.Enumeration*	**getApplets** ()	
	public . . . . *AudioClip*	**getAudioClip** (java.net.URL url)	
	public . . . . java.awt.Image	**getImage** (java.net.URL url)	
1.4	public . . . . . . java.io.InputStream	**getStream** (String key)	
1.4	public . . . . *java.util.Iterator*	**getStreamKeys** ()	
1.4	public . . . . void	**setStream** (String key, java.io.InputStream stream) throws java.io.IOException	
	public . . . . void	**showDocument** (java.net.URL url)	ε553
	public . . . . void	**showDocument** (java.net.URL url, String target)	
	public . . . . void	**showStatus** (String status)	

AppletStub
java.applet

AppletStub

public . . . . void	**appletResize** (int width, int height)
public . . . . *AppletContext*	**getAppletContext** ()
public . . . . java.net.URL	**getCodeBase** ()
public . . . . java.net.URL	**getDocumentBase** ()
public . . . . String	**getParameter** (String name)
public . . . . boolean	**isActive** ()

Arc2D

				java.awt.geom

```
Arc2D                                                                              java.awt.geom
```

Object   ε572
1.2 ○ └─RectangularShape[1] ------------------- *java.awt.Shape*[2], *Cloneable*
1.2 ○   └─Arc2D

✱		protected	**Arc2D** (int type)	
▲		public static final ....int	**CHORD** = 1	
	1	public.................... Object	clone ()	
	1	public.................. boolean	contains (Point2D p)	
	1	public................. **boolean**	**contains** (Rectangle2D r)	
	2	public................. boolean	**contains** (double x, double y)	
	2	public................. boolean	**contains** (double x, double y, double w, double h)	
		public................. boolean	**containsAngle** (double angle)	
○		public abstract ....double	**getAngleExtent** ()	
○		public abstract ....double	**getAngleStart** ()	
		public....................int	**getArcType** ()	
	1	public...... java.awt.Rectangle	getBounds ()	
	2	public............. Rectangle2D	**getBounds2D** ()	
	1	public.................double	getCenterX ()	
	1	public.................double	getCenterY ()	
		public...................Point2D	**getEndPoint** ()	
	1	public............. Rectangle2D	getFrame ()	
○	1	public abstract ....double	getHeight ()	
	1	public.................double	getMaxX ()	
	1	public.................double	getMaxY ()	
	1	public.................double	getMinX ()	
	1	public.................double	getMinY ()	
	2	public............. *PathIterator*	**getPathIterator** (AffineTransform at)	
	1	public............. *PathIterator*	getPathIterator (AffineTransform at, double flatness)	
		public...................Point2D	**getStartPoint** ()	
○	1	public abstract ....double	getWidth ()	ε826
○	1	public abstract ....double	getX ()	
○	1	public abstract ....double	getY ()	
	1	public................. boolean	intersects (Rectangle2D r)	
	2	public................. boolean	**intersects** (double x, double y, double w, double h)	
○	1	public abstract .... boolean	isEmpty ()	
○		protected abstract Rectangle2D	**makeBounds** (double x, double y, double w, double h)	
▲		public static final ....int	**OPEN** = 0	
▲		public static final ....int	**PIE** = 2	
○		public abstract ....void	**setAngleExtent** (double angExt)	
		public....................void	**setAngles** (Point2D p1, Point2D p2)	
		public....................void	**setAngles** (double x1, double y1, double x2, double y2)	
○		public abstract ....void	**setAngleStart** (double angSt)	
		public....................void	**setAngleStart** (Point2D p)	
		public....................void	**setArc** (Arc2D a)	
		public....................void	**setArc** (Rectangle2D rect, double angSt, double angExt, int closure)	
		public....................void	**setArc** (Point2D loc, Dimension2D size, double angSt, double angExt, int closure)	
○		public abstract ....void	**setArc** (double x, double y, double w, double h, double angSt, double angExt, int closure)	
		public....................void	**setArcByCenter** (double x, double y, double radius, double angSt, double angExt, int closure)	
		public....................void	**setArcByTangent** (Point2D p1, Point2D p2, Point2D p3, double radius)	
		public....................void	**setArcType** (int type)	
	1	public....................void	setFrame (Rectangle2D r)	
	1	public....................void	setFrame (Point2D loc, Dimension2D size)	
	1	public.................... **void setFrame**	(double x, double y, double w, double h)	
	1	public....................void	setFrameFromCenter (Point2D center, Point2D corner)	
	1	public....................void	setFrameFromCenter (double centerX, double centerY, double cornerX, double cornerY)	
	1	public....................void	setFrameFromDiagonal (Point2D p1, Point2D p2)	
	1	public....................void	setFrameFromDiagonal (double x1, double y1, double x2, double y2)	

Class *Interface* —extends - - -implements ○ abstract ● final △ static ▲ static final ✱ constructor x x—inherited x **x**—declared **x x**—overridden
εn—examples of usage —has subclass package—see other volume

Arc2D.Double				java.awt.geom

ε572

```
      Object
1.2 ○  └RectangularShape 1 - - - - - - - - - - - - - - - - - - - java.awt.Shape, Cloneable
1.2 ○     └Arc2D 2
1.2         └Arc2D.Double
```

▲	2	public static final .... int	CHORD = 1
	1	public .... Object	clone ()
	1	public .... boolean	contains (Point2D p)
	1	public .... boolean	contains (Rectangle2D r)
	2	public .... boolean	contains (double x, double y)
	2	public .... boolean	contains (double x, double y, double w, double h)
	2	public .... boolean	containsAngle (double angle)
*		public	**Arc2D.Double** ()
*		public	**Arc2D.Double** (int type)
*		public	**Arc2D.Double** (Rectangle2D ellipseBounds, double start, double extent, int type)
*		public	**Arc2D.Double** (double x, double y, double w, double h, double start, double extent, int type)
		public .... double	**extent**
	2	public .... **double**	**getAngleExtent** ()
	2	public .... **double**	**getAngleStart** ()
	2	public .... int	getArcType ()
	1	public ...... java.awt.Rectangle	getBounds ()
	2	public Rectangle2D	getBounds2D ()
	1	public .... double	getCenterX ()
	1	public .... double	getCenterY ()
	2	public Point2D	getEndPoint ()
	1	public Rectangle2D	getFrame ()
	1	public .... **double**	**getHeight** ()
	1	public .... double	getMaxX ()
	1	public .... double	getMaxY ()
	1	public .... double	getMinX ()
	1	public .... double	getMinY ()
	2	public .... PathIterator	getPathIterator (AffineTransform at)
	1	public .... PathIterator	getPathIterator (AffineTransform at, double flatness)
	2	public Point2D	getStartPoint ()
	1	public .... **double**	**getWidth** ()
	1	public .... **double**	**getX** ()
	1	public .... **double**	**getY** ()
		public .... double	**height**
	1	public .... boolean	intersects (Rectangle2D r)
	2	public .... boolean	intersects (double x, double y, double w, double h)
	1	public .... **boolean**	**isEmpty** ()
	2	protected **Rectangle2D**	**makeBounds** (double x, double y, double w, double h)
▲	2	public static final .... int	OPEN = 0
▲	2	public static final .... int	PIE = 2
	2	public .... **void**	**setAngleExtent** (double angExt)
	2	public .... void	setAngles (Point2D p1, Point2D p2)
	2	public .... void	setAngles (double x1, double y1, double x2, double y2)
	2	public .... **void**	**setAngleStart** (double angSt)
	2	public .... void	setAngleStart (Point2D p)
	2	public .... void	setArc (Arc2D a)
	2	public .... void	setArc (Rectangle2D rect, double angSt, double angExt, int closure)
	2	public .... void	setArc (Point2D loc, Dimension2D size, double angSt, double angExt, int closure)
	2	public .... **void**	**setArc** (double x, double y, double w, double h, double angSt, double angExt, int closure)
	2	public .... void	setArcByCenter (double x, double y, double radius, double angSt, double angExt, int closure)
	2	public .... void	setArcByTangent (Point2D p1, Point2D p2, Point2D p3, double radius)
	2	public .... void	setArcType (int type)
	1	public .... void	setFrame (Rectangle2D r)
	1	public .... void	setFrame (Point2D loc, Dimension2D size)
	2	public .... void	setFrame (double x, double y, double w, double h)
	1	public .... void	setFrameFromCenter (Point2D center, Point2D corner)
	1	public .... void	setFrameFromCenter (double centerX, double centerY, double cornerX, double cornerY)
	1	public .... void	setFrameFromDiagonal (Point2D p1, Point2D p2)
	1	public .... void	setFrameFromDiagonal (double x1, double y1, double x2, double y2)
		public .... double	**start**
		public .... double	**width**
		public .... double	**x**
		public .... double	**y**

ε826

A

Classes

Arc2D.Float

```
Object                                                            ε572
  └ RectangularShape¹ - - - - - - - - - - - - - - - - - - - java.awt.Shape, Cloneable
      └ Arc2D²
          └ Arc2D.Float
```

▲	2	public static final ....int	CHORD = 1
	1	public.....................Object	clone ()
	1	public...................... boolean	contains (Point2D p)
	2	public................. boolean	contains (Rectangle2D r)
	2	public................. boolean	contains (double x, double y)
	2	public................. boolean	contains (double x, double y, double w, double h)
	2	public................. boolean	containsAngle (double angle)
		public.......................float	**extent**
*		public.......................	**Arc2D.Float** ()
*		public.......................	**Arc2D.Float** (int type)
*		public.......................	**Arc2D.Float** (Rectangle2D ellipseBounds, float start, float extent, int type)
*		public.......................	**Arc2D.Float** (float x, float y, float w, float h, float start, float extent, int type)
			ε656
	2	public................. **double**	**getAngleExtent** ()
	2	public................. **double**	**getAngleStart** ()
	2	public.......................int	getArcType ()
	1	public...... java.awt.Rectangle	getBounds ()
	2	public.............Rectangle2D	getBounds2D ()
	1	public...................double	getCenterX ()
	1	public...................double	getCenterY ()
	2	public...................Point2D	getEndPoint ()
	1	public.............Rectangle2D	getFrame ()
		public................. **double**	**getHeight** ()
	1	public...................double	getMaxX ()
	1	public...................double	getMaxY ()
	1	public...................double	getMinX ()
	1	public...................double	getMinY ()
	2	public....... *PathIterator*	getPathIterator (AffineTransform at)
	1	public............. *PathIterator*	getPathIterator (AffineTransform at, double flatness)
	2	public...................Point2D	getStartPoint ()
	1	public................. **double**	**getWidth** ()	ε826
	1	public................. **double**	**getX** ()
	1	public................. **double**	**getY** ()
		public.......................float	**height**
	1	public................. boolean	intersects (Rectangle2D r)
	2	public................. boolean	intersects (double x, double y, double w, double h)
	1	public................. **boolean**	**isEmpty** ()
	2	protected........ **Rectangle2D**	**makeBounds** (double x, double y, double w, double h)
▲	2	public static final ....int	OPEN = 0
▲	2	public static final ....int	PIE = 2
	2	public................. **void**	**setAngleExtent** (double angExt)
	2	public...................void	setAngles (Point2D p1, Point2D p2)
	2	public...................void	setAngles (double x1, double y1, double x2, double y2)
	2	public................. **void**	**setAngleStart** (double angSt)
	2	public...................void	setAngleStart (Point2D p)
	2	public...................void	setArc (Arc2D a)
	2	public...................void	setArc (Rectangle2D rect, double angSt, double angExt, int closure)
	2	public...................void	setArc (Point2D loc, Dimension2D size, double angSt, double angExt, int closure)
	2	public................. **void**	**setArc** (double x, double y, double w, double h, double angSt, double angExt, int closure)
	2	public...................void	setArcByCenter (double x, double y, double radius, double angSt, double angExt, int closure)
	2	public...................void	setArcByTangent (Point2D p1, Point2D p2, Point2D p3, double radius)
	2	public...................void	setArcType (int type)
	1	public...................void	setFrame (Rectangle2D r)
	1	public...................void	setFrame (Point2D loc, Dimension2D size)
	2	public...................void	setFrame (double x, double y, double w, double h)
	1	public...................void	setFrameFromCenter (Point2D center, Point2D corner)
	1	public...................void	setFrameFromCenter (double centerX, double centerY, double cornerX, double cornerY)
	1	public...................void	setFrameFromDiagonal (Point2D p1, Point2D p2)
	1	public...................void	setFrameFromDiagonal (double x1, double y1, double x2, double y2)
		public.......................float	**start**

Class *Interface* —extends - - -implements ○ abstract ● final △ static ▲ static final ✳ constructor x x—inherited x **x**—declared **x x**—overridden
ε*n*—examples of usage ⌄—has subclass package—see other volume

public	float	**width**	
public	float	**x**	
public	float	**y**	

Area

java.awt.geom

Object[1]
1.2 └ Area `- - - - - - - - - - - - - - - - - - - - - - - - - - -` *java.awt.Shape*[2], *Cloneable*

	public	void	**add** (Area rhs)	ε658
✳	public		**Area** ()	
✳	public		**Area** (*java.awt.Shape* s)	ε658
1	public	**Object**	**clone** ()	
2	public	boolean	**contains** (Point2D p)	
2	public	boolean	**contains** (Rectangle2D p)	
2	public	boolean	**contains** (double x, double y)	
2	public	boolean	**contains** (double x, double y, double w, double h)	
	public	Area	**createTransformedArea** (AffineTransform t)	
	public	boolean	**equals** (Area other)	
	public	void	**exclusiveOr** (Area rhs)	ε658
2	public	java.awt.Rectangle	**getBounds** ()	
2	public	Rectangle2D	**getBounds2D** ()	
2	public	*PathIterator*	**getPathIterator** (AffineTransform at)	
2	public	*PathIterator*	**getPathIterator** (AffineTransform at, double flatness)	
	public	void	**intersect** (Area rhs)	ε658
2	public	boolean	**intersects** (Rectangle2D p)	
2	public	boolean	**intersects** (double x, double y, double w, double h)	
	public	boolean	**isEmpty** ()	
	public	boolean	**isPolygonal** ()	
	public	boolean	**isRectangular** ()	
	public	boolean	**isSingular** ()	
	public	void	**reset** ()	
	public	void	**subtract** (Area rhs)	ε658
	public	void	**transform** (AffineTransform t)	

AreaAveragingScaleFilter

java.awt.image

ε665

Object
└ ImageFilter[1] `- - - - - - - - - - - - - - - - - - - - - - - - -` *ImageConsumer*[3], *Cloneable*
1.1 └ ReplicateScaleFilter[2]
1.1   └ AreaAveragingScaleFilter

3	*9 inherited members from ImageConsumer not shown*		
✳	public		**AreaAveragingScaleFilter** (int width, int height)
1	public	Object	clone ()
1	protected	*ImageConsumer*	consumer
2	protected	int	destHeight
2	protected	int	destWidth
1	public	ImageFilter	getFilterInstance (*ImageConsumer* ic)
1	public	void	imageComplete (int status)
2	protected	Object	outpixbuf
1	public	void	resendTopDownLeftRight (*ImageProducer* ip)
1	public	void	setColorModel (ColorModel model)
2	public	void	setDimensions (int w, int h)
1	public	**void**	**setHints** (int hints)
2	public	**void**	**setPixels** (int x, int y, int w, int h, ColorModel model, int[] pixels, int off, int scansize)
2	public	**void**	**setPixels** (int x, int y, int w, int h, ColorModel model, byte[] pixels, int off, int scansize)
2	public	void	setProperties (java.util.Hashtable props)
2	protected	int[]	srccols
2	protected	int	srcHeight
2	protected	int[]	srcrows
2	protected	int	srcWidth

AsyncBoxView

javax.swing.text

Object
1.2 ○ └ View[1] `- - - - - - - - - - - - - - - - - - - - - - - - -` *javax.swing.SwingConstants*[2]
1.3   └ AsyncBoxView

AsyncBoxView

	1		*36 inherited members from View not shown*	
	2		*19 inherited members from javax.swing.SwingConstants not shown*	
	*	public...........................	**AsyncBoxView** (*Element* elem, int axis)	
		protected.......................	**createChildState** (View v)	
		....AsyncBoxView.ChildState		
		protected..................void	**flushRequirementChanges** ()	
		public......................float	**getBottomInset** ()	
	1	public.........***java.awt.Shape***	**getChildAllocation** (int index, *java.awt.Shape* a)	
		protected.......................	**getChildState** (int index)	
		....AsyncBoxView.ChildState		
1.4		protected.............. boolean	**getEstimatedMajorSpan** ()	
1.4		protected................float	**getInsetSpan** (int axis)	
		protected........ LayoutQueue	**getLayoutQueue** ()	
		public.....................float	**getLeftInset** ()	
		public.......................int	**getMajorAxis** ()	
	1	public.................... **float**	**getMaximumSpan** (int axis)	
	1	public.................... **float**	**getMinimumSpan** (int axis)	
		public.......................int	**getMinorAxis** ()	
	1	public...................... **int**	**getNextVisualPositionFrom** (int pos, Position.Bias b, *java.awt.Shape* a,	
			int direction, Position.Bias[] biasRet) throws BadLocationException	
	1	public.................... **float**	**getPreferredSpan** (int axis)	
		public.....................float	**getRightInset** ()	
		public.....................float	**getTopInset** ()	
	1	public.................... **View**	**getView** (int n)	*ε978*
	1	public...................... **int**	**getViewCount** ()	*ε978*
	1	public...................... **int**	**getViewIndex** (int pos, Position.Bias b)	
		protected synchronized .....int	**getViewIndexAtPosition** (int pos, Position.Bias b)	
		protected..................void	**loadChildren** (*ViewFactory* f)	
		protected.......................	**locator**	
		. AsyncBoxView.ChildLocator		
		protected synchronized ...void	**majorRequirementChange** (AsyncBoxView.ChildState cs, float delta)	
		protected synchronized ...void	**minorRequirementChange** (AsyncBoxView.ChildState cs)	
	1	public.........***java.awt.Shape***	**modelToView** (int pos, *java.awt.Shape* a, Position.Bias b)	
			throws BadLocationException	
	1	public.................... **void**	**paint** (java.awt.Graphics g, *java.awt.Shape* alloc)	
	1	public synchronized ...... **void**	**preferenceChanged** (View child, boolean width, boolean height)	
	1	public.................... **void**	**replace** (int offset, int length, View[] views)	
		public.....................void	**setBottomInset** (float i)	
1.4		protected..................void	**setEstimatedMajorSpan** (boolean isEstimated)	
		public.....................void	**setLeftInset** (float i)	
	1	public.................... **void**	**setParent** (View parent)	
		public.....................void	**setRightInset** (float i)	
	1	public.................... **void**	**setSize** (float width, float height)	
		public.....................void	**setTopInset** (float i)	
	1	protected................. **void**	**updateLayout** (*javax.swing.event.DocumentEvent.ElementChange* ec,	
			javax.swing.event.DocumentEvent e, *java.awt.Shape* a)	
	1	public...................... **int**	**viewToModel** (float x, float y, *java.awt.Shape* a, Position.Bias[] biasReturn)	

AsyncBoxView.ChildLocator | javax.swing.text

		Object	
1.3		└AsyncBoxView.ChildLocator	
		protected.. java.awt.Rectangle	**childAlloc**
		public synchronized ....void	**childChanged** (AsyncBoxView.ChildState cs)
	*	public...........................	**AsyncBoxView.ChildLocator** ()
		protected...... *java.awt.Shape*	**getChildAllocation** (int index)
		public synchronized	**getChildAllocation** (int index, *java.awt.Shape* a)
		.... *java.awt.Shape*	
		public.......................int	**getViewIndexAtPoint** (float x, float y, *java.awt.Shape* a)
		protected..................int	**getViewIndexAtVisualOffset** (float targetOffset)
		protected.. java.awt.Rectangle	**lastAlloc**
		protected.......................	**lastValidOffset**
		....AsyncBoxView.ChildState	
		public synchronized ....void	**paintChildren** (java.awt.Graphics g)
		protected..................void	**setAllocation** (*java.awt.Shape* a)

AsyncBoxView.ChildState | javax.swing.text

```
        Object
1.3     └─AsyncBoxView.ChildState --------------- Runnable 1
```

*	public	....	**AsyncBoxView.ChildState** (View v)
	public	.... View	**getChildView** ()
	public	.... float	**getMajorOffset** ()
	public	.... float	**getMajorSpan** ()
	public	.... float	**getMinorOffset** ()
	public	.... float	**getMinorSpan** ()
	public	.... boolean	**isLayoutValid** ()
	public	.... void	**preferenceChanged** (boolean width, boolean height)
1	public	.... void	**run** ()
	public	.... void	**setMajorOffset** (float offs)

---

*Attribute*② | javax.print.attribute

```
1.4     Attribute ──────────────────── java.io.Serializable
```

public	.... Class	**getCategory** ()	ε707
public	.... String	**getName** ()	ε706,707,708

AttributeException | javax.print

```
1.4     AttributeException
```

public	.... Class[]	**getUnsupportedAttributes** ()
public	.... javax	**getUnsupportedValues** ()
.print.attribute.Attribute[]		

AttributeList① | javax.swing.text.html.parser

```
        Object 1
1.2 ●   └─AttributeList ------------------------- DTDConstants 2, java.io.Serializable
```

	2	*35 inherited members from DTDConstants not shown*		
*		public	....	**AttributeList** (String name)
*		public	....	**AttributeList** (String name, int type, int modifier, String value, java.util.Vector values, AttributeList next)
		public	.... int	**getModifier** ()
		public	.... String	**getName** ()
		public	.... AttributeList	**getNext** ()
		public	.... int	**getType** ()
		public	.... String	**getValue** ()
		public	.... java.util.Enumeration	**getValues** ()
		public	.... int	**modifier**
		public	.... String	**name**
△		public static	.... int	**name2type** (String nm)
		public	.... AttributeList	**next**
	1	public	.... String	**toString** ()
		public	.... int	**type**
△		public static	.... String	**type2name** (int tp)
		public	.... String	**value**
		public	.... java.util.Vector	**values**

AttributeSet ① | javax.print.attribute

```
1.4     AttributeSet
```

public	.... boolean	**add** (*Attribute* attribute)	ε703
public	.... boolean	**addAll** (*AttributeSet* attributes)	
public	.... void	**clear** ()	
public	.... boolean	**containsKey** (Class category)	
public	.... boolean	**containsValue** (*Attribute* attribute)	
public	.... boolean	**equals** (Object object)	
public	.... *Attribute*	**get** (Class category)	
public	.... int	**hashCode** ()	
public	.... boolean	**isEmpty** ()	
public	.... boolean	**remove** (Class category)	

Classes

AttributeSet ❶

```
public................. boolean  remove (Attribute attribute)
public.......................int  size ()
public............... Attribute[]  toArray ()                                    ε706
```

AttributeSet ❷   javax.swing.text

1.2 *AttributeSet*   ε975

```
public................. boolean  containsAttribute (Object name, Object value)
public................. boolean  containsAttributes (AttributeSet attributes)
public.............. AttributeSet  copyAttributes ()
public..................Object  getAttribute (Object key)                        ε1013
public.......................int  getAttributeCount ()                           ε1010
public.... java.util.Enumeration  getAttributeNames ()                          ε1010
public.............. AttributeSet  getResolveParent ()
public................. boolean  isDefined (Object attrName)
public................. boolean  isEqual (AttributeSet attr)
▲  public static final........Object  NameAttribute
▲  public static final........Object  ResolveAttribute
```

AttributeSet.CharacterAttribute   javax.swing.text

1.2 *AttributeSet.CharacterAttribute*   ε1014

AttributeSet.ColorAttribute   javax.swing.text

1.2 *AttributeSet.ColorAttribute*   ε1014

AttributeSet.FontAttribute   javax.swing.text

1.2 *AttributeSet.FontAttribute*   ε1014

AttributeSet.ParagraphAttribute   javax.swing.text

1.2 *AttributeSet.ParagraphAttribute*   ε1014

AttributeSetUtilities   javax.print.attribute

```
      Object
1.4 ●  └AttributeSetUtilities
```

```
△  public static ....... AttributeSet  synchronizedView (AttributeSet attributeSet)
△  public static ... DocAttributeSet  synchronizedView (DocAttributeSet attributeSet)
△  public static ....................  synchronizedView (PrintJobAttributeSet attributeSet)
         .......... PrintJobAttributeSet
△  public static ....................  synchronizedView (PrintRequestAttributeSet attributeSet)
      ..... PrintRequestAttributeSet
△  public static ....................  synchronizedView (PrintServiceAttributeSet attributeSet)
      ...... PrintServiceAttributeSet
△  public static ....... AttributeSet  unmodifiableView (AttributeSet attributeSet)
△  public static ... DocAttributeSet  unmodifiableView (DocAttributeSet attributeSet)
△  public static ....................  unmodifiableView (PrintJobAttributeSet attributeSet)
         .......... PrintJobAttributeSet
△  public static ....................  unmodifiableView (PrintRequestAttributeSet attributeSet)
      ..... PrintRequestAttributeSet
△  public static ....................  unmodifiableView (PrintServiceAttributeSet attributeSet)
      ...... PrintServiceAttributeSet
△  public static ............. Class  verifyAttributeCategory (Object object, Class interfaceName)
△  public static ........... Attribute  verifyAttributeValue (Object object, Class interfaceName)
△  public static ...............void  verifyCategoryForValue (Class category, Attribute attribute)
```

Class   *Interface*   —extends   - - -implements   ○ abstract   ● final   △ static   ▲ static final   ✳ constructor   x x—inherited   x **x**—declared   **x x**—overridden
ε*n*—examples of usage   ‿—has subclass   package—see other volume

AttributeValue

java.awt

```
        Object¹
1.4     └AttributeValue
```

∗	protected		**AttributeValue** (int, String[])
1	public	**int**	**hashCode** ()
1	public	**String**	**toString** ()

AudioClip

java.applet

```
        AudioClip
```

public . . . . void	**loop** ()	ε555
public . . . . void	**play** ()	ε555,556
public . . . . void	**stop** ()	ε555

AudioFileFormat

javax.sound.sampled

```
        Object¹
1.3     └AudioFileFormat
```

∗	public		**AudioFileFormat** (AudioFileFormat.Type type, AudioFormat format, int frameLength)
∗	protected		**AudioFileFormat** (AudioFileFormat.Type type, int byteLength, AudioFormat format, int frameLength)
	public . . . . int	**getByteLength** ()	
	public . . . . AudioFormat	**getFormat** ()	
	public . . . . int	**getFrameLength** ()	
	public . . . AudioFileFormat.Type	**getType** ()	ε726
1	public . . . . **String**	**toString** ()	

AudioFileFormat.Type

javax.sound.sampled

```
        Object¹
1.3     └AudioFileFormat.Type
```

▲	public static final . . . . AudioFileFormat.Type	**AIFC**	ε726
▲	public static final . . . . AudioFileFormat.Type	**AIFF**	ε726
▲	public static final . . . . AudioFileFormat.Type	**AU**	ε726
● 1	public final . . . . **boolean**	**equals** (Object obj)	
	public . . . . String	**getExtension** ()	
● 1	public final . . . . **int**	**hashCode** ()	
▲	public static final . . . . AudioFileFormat.Type	**SND**	
● 1	public final . . . . **String**	**toString** ()	
∗	protected	**AudioFileFormat.Type** (String name, String extension)	
▲	public static final . . . . AudioFileFormat.Type	**WAVE**	ε726

AudioFileReader

javax.sound.sampled.spi

```
        Object
1.3 ○   └AudioFileReader
```

∗	public	**AudioFileReader** ()
○	public abstract . . . javax.sound ͻ .sampled.AudioFileFormat	**getAudioFileFormat** (java.io.File file) throws javax.sound.sampled ͻ .UnsupportedAudioFileException, java.io.IOException
○	public abstract . . . javax.sound ͻ .sampled.AudioFileFormat	**getAudioFileFormat** (java.io.InputStream stream) throws javax.sound.sampled.UnsupportedAudioFileException, java.io.IOException
○	public abstract . . . javax.sound ͻ .sampled.AudioFileFormat	**getAudioFileFormat** (java.net.URL url) throws javax.sound.sampled ͻ .UnsupportedAudioFileException, java.io.IOException
○	public abstract . . . javax.sound ͻ .sampled.AudioInputStream	**getAudioInputStream** (java.io.File file) throws javax.sound.sampled ͻ .UnsupportedAudioFileException, java.io.IOException
○	public abstract . . . javax.sound ͻ .sampled.AudioInputStream	**getAudioInputStream** (java.io.InputStream stream) throws javax.sound.sampled.UnsupportedAudioFileException, java.io.IOException

AudioFileReader

○	public abstract . . . javax.sound₂	**getAudioInputStream** (java.net.URL url) throws javax.sound.sampled₂
	.sampled.AudioInputStream	.UnsupportedAudioFileException, java.io.IOException

AudioFileWriter
javax.sound.sampled.spi

Object
1.3 ○ └AudioFileWriter

✳	public.	**AudioFileWriter** ()
○	public abstract	**getAudioFileTypes** ()
	. . . . javax.sound.sampled₂	
	.AudioFileFormat.Type[]	
○	public abstract	**getAudioFileTypes** (javax.sound.sampled.AudioInputStream stream)
	. . . . javax.sound.sampled₂	
	.AudioFileFormat.Type[]	
	public. . . . . boolean	**isFileTypeSupported** (javax.sound.sampled.AudioFileFormat.Type fileType)
	public. . . . . boolean	**isFileTypeSupported** (javax.sound.sampled.AudioFileFormat.Type fileType,
		javax.sound.sampled.AudioInputStream stream)
○	public abstract . . . . int	**write** (javax.sound.sampled.AudioInputStream stream,
		javax.sound.sampled.AudioFileFormat.Type fileType, java.io.OutputStream out)
		throws java.io.IOException
○	public abstract . . . . int	**write** (javax.sound.sampled.AudioInputStream stream, javax.sound.sampled₂
		.AudioFileFormat.Type fileType, java.io.File out) throws java.io.IOException

AudioFormat
javax.sound.sampled

Object[1]
1.3 └AudioFormat

✳	public.	**AudioFormat** (float sampleRate, int sampleSizeInBits, int channels, boolean signed,
		boolean bigEndian)
✳	public.	**AudioFormat** (AudioFormat.Encoding encoding, float sampleRate,
		int sampleSizeInBits, int channels, int frameSize, float frameRate,
		boolean bigEndian) ε723,724
	protected . . . . boolean	**bigEndian**
	protected . . . . .int	**channels**
	protected	**encoding**
	. . . . . . .AudioFormat.Encoding	
	protected . . . . .float	**frameRate**
	protected . . . . .int	**frameSize**
	public. .int	**getChannels** () ε723,724
	public. . AudioFormat.Encoding	**getEncoding** () ε723,724,727
	public. . . . . .float	**getFrameRate** () ε723,724,728
	public. .int	**getFrameSize** () ε723,724,728
	public. . . . . .float	**getSampleRate** () ε723,724
	public. .int	**getSampleSizeInBits** () ε723,724
	public. . . . . boolean	**isBigEndian** ()
	public. . . . . boolean	**matches** (AudioFormat format)
	protected . . . . .float	**sampleRate**
	protected . . . . .int	**sampleSizeInBits**
1	public. . . . . **String**	**toString** ()

AudioFormat.Encoding
javax.sound.sampled

Object[1]
1.3 └AudioFormat.Encoding

▲	public static final	**ALAW**
	. . . . . . .AudioFormat.Encoding	
✳	protected	**AudioFormat.Encoding** (String name)
● 1	public final . . . . **boolean**	**equals** (Object obj)
● 1	public final . . . . **int**	**hashCode** ()
▲	public static final	**PCM_SIGNED** ε723,724
	. . . . . . .AudioFormat.Encoding	
▲	public static final	**PCM_UNSIGNED**
	. . . . . . .AudioFormat.Encoding	
● 1	public final . . . . **String**	**toString** ()

Class *Interface* —extends - - -implements ○ abstract ● final △ static ▲ static final ✳ constructor ⨯ ⨯—inherited ⨯ **x**—declared **x x**—overridden
ε*n*—examples of usage ₂—has subclass package—see other volume

▲	public static final	**ULAW**	ε727
	. . . . AudioFormat.Encoding		

AudioInputStream   javax.sound.sampled

Object
○ └ java.io.InputStream[1]
1.3   └ AudioInputStream

*	public	**AudioInputStream** (*TargetDataLine* line)	
*	public	**AudioInputStream** (java.io.InputStream stream, AudioFormat format, long length)	
1	public . . . . int	**available** () throws java.io.IOException	
1	public . . . . **void**	**close** () throws java.io.IOException	
	protected . . . . AudioFormat	**format**	
	protected . . . . long	**frameLength**	
	protected . . . . long	**framePos**	
	protected . . . . int	**frameSize**	
	public . . . . AudioFormat	**getFormat** ()	ε723,724,727,728
	public . . . . long	**getFrameLength** ()	ε723,724
1	public . . . . **void**	**mark** (int readlimit)	
1	public . . . . **boolean**	**markSupported** ()	
1	public . . . . int	**read** () throws java.io.IOException	
1	public . . . . int	**read** (byte[] b) throws java.io.IOException	
1	public . . . . int	**read** (byte[] b, int off, int len) throws java.io.IOException	ε724
1	public . . . . **void**	**reset** () throws java.io.IOException	
1	public . . . . **long**	**skip** (long n) throws java.io.IOException	

AudioPermission   javax.sound.sampled

Object
1.2 ○ └ java.security.Permission[1] - - - - - - - - - - - - - - - - *java.security.Guard*, *java.io.Serializable*
1.2 ○   └ java.security.BasicPermission[2]
1.3   └ AudioPermission

*	public	**AudioPermission** (String name)	
*	public	**AudioPermission** (String name, String actions)	
1	public . . . . void	checkGuard (Object object) throws SecurityException	
2	public . . . . boolean	equals (Object obj)	
2	public . . . . String	getActions ()	
● 1	public final . . . . String	getName ()	
2	public . . . . int	hashCode ()	
2	public . . . . boolean	implies (java.security.Permission p)	
2	public . . . . java.security.	newPermissionCollection ()	
	.PermissionCollection		
1	public . . . . String	toString ()	

AudioSystem   javax.sound.sampled

Object
1.3 └ AudioSystem

△	public static . . AudioFileFormat	**getAudioFileFormat** (java.io.File file) throws UnsupportedAudioFileException, java.io.IOException	ε726
△	public static . . AudioFileFormat	**getAudioFileFormat** (java.io.InputStream stream) throws UnsupportedAudioFileException, java.io.IOException	
△	public static . . AudioFileFormat	**getAudioFileFormat** (java.net.URL url) throws UnsupportedAudioFileException, java.io.IOException	ε726
△	public static . . . . AudioFileFormat.Type[]	**getAudioFileTypes** ()	
△	public static . . . . AudioFileFormat.Type[]	**getAudioFileTypes** (AudioInputStream stream)	
△	public static AudioInputStream	**getAudioInputStream** (java.io.File file) throws UnsupportedAudioFileException, java.io.IOException	ε723,724,727
△	public static AudioInputStream	**getAudioInputStream** (java.io.InputStream stream) throws UnsupportedAudioFileException, java.io.IOException	
△	public static AudioInputStream	**getAudioInputStream** (java.net.URL url) throws UnsupportedAudioFileException, java.io.IOException	ε723,724,727
△	public static AudioInputStream	**getAudioInputStream** (AudioFormat targetFormat, AudioInputStream sourceStream)	ε723,724

AudioSystem

△	public static	AudioInputStream	**getAudioInputStream** (AudioFormat.Encoding targetEncoding, AudioInputStream sourceStream)
△	public static	...............*Line*	**getLine** (Line.Info info) throws LineUnavailableException ε723,724
△	public static	...........*Mixer*	**getMixer** (Mixer.Info info)
△	public static	........Mixer.Info[]	**getMixerInfo** ()
△	public static	........Line.Info[]	**getSourceLineInfo** (Line.Info info)
△	public static	.... AudioFormat.Encoding[]	**getTargetEncodings** (AudioFormat sourceFormat)
△	public static	.... AudioFormat.Encoding[]	**getTargetEncodings** (AudioFormat.Encoding sourceEncoding)
△	public static	.... AudioFormat[]	**getTargetFormats** (AudioFormat.Encoding targetEncoding, AudioFormat sourceFormat)
△	public static	.... Line.Info[]	**getTargetLineInfo** (Line.Info info)
△	public static	..........boolean	**isConversionSupported** (AudioFormat targetFormat, AudioFormat sourceFormat)
△	public static	..........boolean	**isConversionSupported** (AudioFormat.Encoding targetEncoding, AudioFormat sourceFormat)
△	public static	..........boolean	**isFileTypeSupported** (AudioFileFormat.Type fileType)
△	public static	..........boolean	**isFileTypeSupported** (AudioFileFormat.Type fileType, AudioInputStream stream)
△	public static	..........boolean	**isLineSupported** (Line.Info info)
▲	public static final	...........int	**NOT_SPECIFIED** = -1
△	public static	.................int	**write** (AudioInputStream stream, AudioFileFormat.Type fileType, java.io.File out) throws java.io.IOException
△	public static	.................int	**write** (AudioInputStream stream, AudioFileFormat.Type fileType, java.io.OutputStream out) throws java.io.IOException

---

Autoscroll   java.awt.dnd

1.2   *Autoscroll*

public	.......................void	**autoscroll** (java.awt.Point cursorLocn)
public	...........java.awt.Insets	**getAutoscrollInsets** ()

AWTError   java.awt

Object
└Throwable - *java.io.Serializable*
  └Error
    └AWTError

✳	public..........................**AWTError** (String msg)	

AWTEvent   java.awt

Object   ε640,641,643,649,566
1.1 └java.util.EventObject[1] - - - - - - - - - - - - - - - - - - - *java.io.Serializable*
1.1 ○   └AWTEvent

▲	public static final	.........long	**ACTION_EVENT_MASK** = 128
▲	public static final	.........long	**ADJUSTMENT_EVENT_MASK** = 256
✳	public	..........................long	**AWTEvent** (Event event)
✳	public	..........................long	**AWTEvent** (Object source, int id)
▲	public static final	.........long	**COMPONENT_EVENT_MASK** = 1
	protected	...................void	**consume** () ε1004
	protected	.............boolean	**consumed**
▲	public static final	.........long	**CONTAINER_EVENT_MASK** = 2
▲	public static final	.........long	**FOCUS_EVENT_MASK** = 4
	public	..........................int	**getID** () ε636,1001
1	public	..........................Object	getSource () ε644,886,565,568,570
1.3 ▲	public static final	.........long	**HIERARCHY_BOUNDS_EVENT_MASK** = 65536
1.3 ▲	public static final	.........long	**HIERARCHY_EVENT_MASK** = 32768
	protected	...................int	**id**
1.2 ▲	public static final	.........long	**INPUT_METHOD_EVENT_MASK** = 2048
1.3 ▲	public static final	.........long	**INVOCATION_EVENT_MASK** = 16384
	protected	.............boolean	**isConsumed** ()
▲	public static final	.........long	**ITEM_EVENT_MASK** = 512
▲	public static final	.........long	**KEY_EVENT_MASK** = 8
▲	public static final	.........long	**MOUSE_EVENT_MASK** = 16
▲	public static final	.........long	**MOUSE_MOTION_EVENT_MASK** = 32

Class   *Interface*   —extends   - - -implements   ○ abstract   ● final   △ static   ▲ static final   ✳ constructor   x x—inherited   x **x**—declared   **x x**—overridden
ε*n*—examples of usage   ˌ—has subclass   package—see other volume

1.4 ▲	public static final .... long	**MOUSE_WHEEL_EVENT_MASK** = 131072
1.3 ▲	public static final .... long	**PAINT_EVENT_MASK** = 8192
	public....................String	**paramString** ()
▲	public static final ....int	**RESERVED_ID_MAX** = 1999
1.4	public......................void	**setSource** (Object newSource)
1	protected transient......Object	source
▲	public static final .... long	**TEXT_EVENT_MASK** = 1024
1	public.................. **String**	**toString** ()
▲	public static final .... long	**WINDOW_EVENT_MASK** = 64
1.4 ▲	public static final .... long	**WINDOW_FOCUS_EVENT_MASK** = 524288
1.4 ▲	public static final .... long	**WINDOW_STATE_EVENT_MASK** = 262144

AWTEventListener java.awt.event

1.2	*AWTEventListener*————————————————— *java.util.EventListener* ⌄	ε738,743,745,746,752

public........................void **eventDispatched** (java.awt.AWTEvent event)

AWTEventListenerProxy java.awt.event

Object
1.4 ○ └ *java.util.EventListenerProxy* [1] - - - - - - - - - - - - - *java.util.EventListener* ⌄
1.4   └ AWTEventListenerProxy - - - - - - - - - - - - - - - *AWTEventListener* [2] (*java.util.EventListener*)

*	public...........................	**AWTEventListenerProxy** (long eventMask, *AWTEventListener* listener)
2	public........................void	**eventDispatched** (java.awt.AWTEvent evt)
	public...................... long	**getEventMask** ()
1	public... *java.util.EventListener*	getListener ()

AWTEventMulticaster java.awt

Object
1.1 └ AWTEventMulticaster - - - - - - - - - - - - - - - - - - - *java.awt.event.ComponentListener* [1] (*java.util.EventListener*),
                                                     java.awt.event.ContainerListener [2] (*java.util.EventListener*),
                                                     java.awt.event.FocusListener [3] (*java.util.EventListener*),
                                                     java.awt.event.KeyListener [4] (*java.util.EventListener*),
                                                     java.awt.event.MouseListener ⌄ [5] (*java.util.EventListener*),
                                                     java.awt.event.MouseMotionListener ⌄ [6] (*java.util.EventListener*),
                                                     java.awt.event.WindowListener [7] (*java.util.EventListener*),
                                                     java.awt.event.WindowFocusListener [8] (*java.util.EventListener*),
                                                    java.awt.event.WindowStateListener [9] (*java.util.EventListener*),
                                                    java.awt.event.ActionListener ⌄ [10] (*java.util.EventListener*),
                                                    java.awt.event.ItemListener [11] (*java.util.EventListener*),
                                                    java.awt.event.AdjustmentListener [12] (*java.util.EventListener*),
                                                    java.awt.event.TextListener [13] (*java.util.EventListener*), java⌇
                                                   .awt.event.InputMethodListener [14] (*java.util.EventListener*), java⌇
                                                   .awt.event.HierarchyListener [15] (*java.util.EventListener*), java⌇
                                                   .awt.event.HierarchyBoundsListener [16] (*java.util.EventListener*),
                                                   java.awt.event.MouseWheelListener [17] (*java.util.EventListener*)

●	protected final.................. *java.util.EventListener*	**a**	
10	public......................void	**actionPerformed** (java.awt.event.ActionEvent e)	ε855,644,738,743,745
△	public static .... *java⌇.awt.event.ActionListener*	**add** (*java.awt.event.ActionListener* a, *java.awt.event.ActionListener* b)	
△	public static ....*java.awt⌇.event.AdjustmentListener*	**add** (*java.awt.event.AdjustmentListener* a, *java.awt.event.AdjustmentListener* b)	
△	public static ....*java.awt⌇.event.ComponentListener*	**add** (*java.awt.event.ComponentListener* a, *java.awt.event.ComponentListener* b)	
△	public static ....*java.awt⌇.event.ContainerListener*	**add** (*java.awt.event.ContainerListener* a, *java.awt.event.ContainerListener* b)	
△	public static .... *java.awt.event.FocusListener*	**add** (*java.awt.event.FocusListener* a, *java.awt.event.FocusListener* b)	
1.3 △	public static ... *java.awt.event⌇.HierarchyBoundsListener*	**add** (*java.awt.event.HierarchyBoundsListener* a, *java.awt.event⌇.HierarchyBoundsListener* b)	
1.3 △	public static ....*java.awt⌇.event.HierarchyListener*	**add** (*java.awt.event.HierarchyListener* a, *java.awt.event.HierarchyListener* b)	

AWTEventMulticaster

1.2	△		public static .... java.awt. *.event.InputMethodListener*	**add** (*java.awt.event.InputMethodListener* a, *java.awt.event.InputMethodListener* b)
	△		public static .... *java.awt.event.ItemListener*	**add** (*java.awt.event.ItemListener* a, *java.awt.event.ItemListener* b)
	△		public static ....*java.awt.event.KeyListener*	**add** (*java.awt.event.KeyListener* a, *java.awt.event.KeyListener* b)
	△		public static .... *java. .awt.event.MouseListener*	**add** (*java.awt.event.MouseListener* a, *java.awt.event.MouseListener* b)
	△		public static .... *java.awt. .event.MouseMotionListener*	**add** (*java.awt.event.MouseMotionListener* a, *java.awt.event.MouseMotionListener* b)
1.4	△		public static .... *java.awt. .event.MouseWheelListener*	**add** (*java.awt.event.MouseWheelListener* a, *java.awt.event.MouseWheelListener* b)
	△		public static .... *java.awt.event.TextListener*	**add** (*java.awt.event.TextListener* a, *java.awt.event.TextListener* b)
1.4	△		public static .... *java.awt .event.WindowFocusListener*	**add** (*java.awt.event.WindowFocusListener* a, *java.awt.event.WindowFocusListener* b)
	△		public static .... *java. .awt.event.WindowListener*	**add** (*java.awt.event.WindowListener* a, *java.awt.event.WindowListener* b)
1.4	△		public static .... *java.awt .event.WindowStateListener*	**add** (*java.awt.event.WindowStateListener* a, *java.awt.event.WindowStateListener* b)
	△		protected static .... *java.util.EventListener*	**addInternal** (*java.util.EventListener* a, *java.util.EventListener* b)
		12	public...................void	**adjustmentValueChanged** (java.awt.event.AdjustmentEvent e) ε822
1.3		16	public...................void	**ancestorMoved** (java.awt.event.HierarchyEvent e)
1.3		16	public...................void	**ancestorResized** (java.awt.event.HierarchyEvent e)
	*		protected	**AWTEventMulticaster** (*java.util.EventListener* a, *java.util.EventListener* b)
	●		protected final................... .... *java.util.EventListener*	**b**
1.2		14	public...................void	**caretPositionChanged** (java.awt.event.InputMethodEvent e)
		2	public...................void	**componentAdded** (java.awt.event.ContainerEvent e) ε573
		1	public...................void	**componentHidden** (java.awt.event.ComponentEvent e) ε570
		1	public...................void	**componentMoved** (java.awt.event.ComponentEvent e) ε570
		2	public...................void	**componentRemoved** (java.awt.event.ContainerEvent e) ε573
		1	public...................void	**componentResized** (java.awt.event.ComponentEvent e) ε570
		1	public...................void	**componentShown** (java.awt.event.ComponentEvent e) ε570
		3	public...................void	**focusGained** (java.awt.event.FocusEvent e) ε649,616,617,618
		3	public...................void	**focusLost** (java.awt.event.FocusEvent e) ε649,616,617,618
1.4	△		public static .... *java.util.EventListener[]*	**getListeners** (*java.util.EventListener* l, Class listenerType)
1.3		15	public...................void	**hierarchyChanged** (java.awt.event.HierarchyEvent e)
1.2		14	public...................void	**inputMethodTextChanged** (java.awt.event.InputMethodEvent e)
		11	public...................void	**itemStateChanged** (java.awt.event.ItemEvent e) ε650,765
		4	public...................void	**keyPressed** (java.awt.event.KeyEvent e) ε643,645,762,763
		4	public...................void	**keyReleased** (java.awt.event.KeyEvent e)
		4	public...................void	**keyTyped** (java.awt.event.KeyEvent e) ε1004
		5	public...................void	**mouseClicked** (java.awt.event.MouseEvent e) ε646,648,783,967
		6	public...................void	**mouseDragged** (java.awt.event.MouseEvent e) ε647
		5	public...................void	**mouseEntered** (java.awt.event.MouseEvent e)
		5	public...................void	**mouseExited** (java.awt.event.MouseEvent e)
		6	public...................void	**mouseMoved** (java.awt.event.MouseEvent e) ε647,937
		5	public...................void	**mousePressed** (java.awt.event.MouseEvent e) ε602,742,810,1011
		5	public...................void	**mouseReleased** (java.awt.event.MouseEvent e) ε810,1011
1.4		17	public...................void	**mouseWheelMoved** (java.awt.event.MouseWheelEvent e)
			protected...................... .... *java.util.EventListener*	**remove** (*java.util.EventListener* oldl)
	△		public static .... *java. .awt.event.ActionListener*	**remove** (*java.awt.event.ActionListener* l, *java.awt.event.ActionListener* oldl)
	△		public static .... *java.awt .event.AdjustmentListener*	**remove** (*java.awt.event.AdjustmentListener* l, *java.awt.event.AdjustmentListener* oldl)
	△		public static .... *java.awt .event.ComponentListener*	**remove** (*java.awt.event.ComponentListener* l, *java.awt.event.ComponentListener* oldl)
	△		public static .... *java.awt .event.ContainerListener*	**remove** (*java.awt.event.ContainerListener* l, *java.awt.event.ContainerListener* oldl)
	△		public static .... *java.awt.event.FocusListener*	**remove** (*java.awt.event.FocusListener* l, *java.awt.event.FocusListener* oldl)
1.3	△		public static ... *java.awt.event .HierarchyBoundsListener*	**remove** (*java.awt.event.HierarchyBoundsListener* l, *java.awt.event.HierarchyBoundsListener* oldl)
1.3	△		public static .... *java.awt .event.HierarchyListener*	**remove** (*java.awt.event.HierarchyListener* l, *java.awt.event.HierarchyListener* oldl)

Class   *Interface*   —extends   - - -implements   ○ abstract   ● final   △ static   ▲ static final   ✱ constructor   x x—inherited   x **x**—declared   **x x**—overridden
ε*n*—examples of usage   ⌐—has subclass   package—see other volume

1.2	△	public static .... java.awt₂ .event.InputMethodListener	**remove** (java.awt.event.InputMethodListener l, java.awt.event.InputMethodListener oldl)		
	△	public static .... java.awt.event.ItemListener	**remove** (java.awt.event.ItemListener l, java.awt.event.ItemListener oldl)		
	△	public static .... java.awt.event.KeyListener	**remove** (java.awt.event.KeyListener l, java.awt.event.KeyListener oldl)		
	△	public static .... java₂ .awt.event.MouseListener	**remove** (java.awt.event.MouseListener l, java.awt.event.MouseListener oldl)		
	△	public static .... java.awt₂ .event.MouseMotionListener	**remove** (java.awt.event.MouseMotionListener l, java.awt.event₂ .MouseMotionListener oldl)		
1.4	△	public static .... java.awt₂ .event.MouseWheelListener	**remove** (java.awt.event.MouseWheelListener l, java.awt.event.MouseWheelListener oldl)		
	△	public static .... java.awt.event.TextListener	**remove** (java.awt.event.TextListener l, java.awt.event.TextListener oldl)		
1.4	△	public static .... java.awt₂ .event.WindowFocusListener	**remove** (java.awt.event.WindowFocusListener l, java.awt.event₂ .WindowFocusListener oldl)		
	△	public static .... java₂ .awt.event.WindowListener	**remove** (java.awt.event.WindowListener l, java.awt.event.WindowListener oldl)		
1.4	△	public static .... java.awt₂ .event.WindowStateListener	**remove** (java.awt.event.WindowStateListener l, java.awt.event.WindowStateListener oldl)		
	△	protected static .... java.util.EventListener	**removeInternal** (java.util.EventListener l, java.util.EventListener oldl)		
	△	protected static ....void	**save** (java.io.ObjectOutputStream s, String k, java.util.EventListener l) throws java.io.IOException		
		protected ....void	**saveInternal** (java.io.ObjectOutputStream s, String k) throws java.io.IOException		
	13	public ....void	**textValueChanged** (java.awt.event.TextEvent e)		
	7	public ....void	**windowActivated** (java.awt.event.WindowEvent e)		
	7	public ....void	**windowClosed** (java.awt.event.WindowEvent e)	ε568	
	7	public ....void	**windowClosing** (java.awt.event.WindowEvent e)	ε565,566,568,884,905	
	7	public ....void	**windowDeactivated** (java.awt.event.WindowEvent e)		
	7	public ....void	**windowDeiconified** (java.awt.event.WindowEvent e)		
1.4	8	public ....void	**windowGainedFocus** (java.awt.event.WindowEvent e)		
	7	public ....void	**windowIconified** (java.awt.event.WindowEvent e)		
1.4	8	public ....void	**windowLostFocus** (java.awt.event.WindowEvent e)		
	7	public ....void	**windowOpened** (java.awt.event.WindowEvent e)	ε568	
1.4	9	public ....void	**windowStateChanged** (java.awt.event.WindowEvent e)	ε569	

AWTException		java.awt
		ε634,635,864

```
Object
└Throwable ------------------------- java.io.Serializable
  └Exception
    └AWTException
```

✳	public...........................	**AWTException** (String msg)	

AWTKeyStroke		java.awt
	Object¹	ε860
1.4	└AWTKeyStroke ------------------------- java.io.Serializable	

✳		protected	**AWTKeyStroke** ()	
✳		protected	**AWTKeyStroke** (char keyChar, int keyCode, int modifiers, boolean onKeyRelease)	
●	1	public final ....boolean	**equals** (Object anObject)	ε862
△		public static .... AWTKeyStroke	**getAWTKeyStroke** (char keyChar)	
△		public static .... AWTKeyStroke	**getAWTKeyStroke** (String s)	
△		public static .... AWTKeyStroke	**getAWTKeyStroke** (int keyCode, int modifiers)	
△		public static .... AWTKeyStroke	**getAWTKeyStroke** (Character keyChar, int modifiers)	
△		public static .... AWTKeyStroke	**getAWTKeyStroke** (int keyCode, int modifiers, boolean onKeyRelease)	
△		public static .... AWTKeyStroke	**getAWTKeyStrokeForEvent** (java.awt.event.KeyEvent anEvent)	
●		public final .... char	**getKeyChar** ()	ε859
●		public final ....int	**getKeyCode** ()	ε859
●		public final ....int	**getKeyEventType** ()	ε859,862
●		public final ....int	**getModifiers** ()	ε859
	1	public........................ int	**hashCode** ()	
●		public final .... boolean	**isOnKeyRelease** ()	
		protected .... Object	**readResolve** () throws java.io.ObjectStreamException	
△		protected static ....void	**registerSubclass** (Class subclass)	
	1	public.................. String	**toString** ()	

AWTPermission

		AWTPermission	java.awt

```
           Object
1.2 ○      └java.security.Permission 1 ----------------- java.security.Guard, java.io.Serializable ⌟
1.2 ○        └java.security.BasicPermission 2
1.2 ●          └AWTPermission
```

✳	public.........................		**AWTPermission** (String name)
✳	public.........................		**AWTPermission** (String name, String actions)
1	public.....................void		checkGuard (Object object) throws SecurityException
2	public.................. boolean		equals (Object obj)
2	public......................String		getActions ()
● 1	public final ....String		getName ()
2	public.........................int		hashCode ()
2	public.................. boolean		implies (java.security.Permission p)
2	public............. java.security ⌟ .PermissionCollection		newPermissionCollection ()
1	public....................String		toString ()

		BadLocationException	javax.swing.text

ε968,969,970,972,973

```
           Object
           └Throwable 1 --------------------------- java.io.Serializable ⌟
             └Exception
1.2            └BadLocationException
```

✳	public.........................		**BadLocationException** (String s, int offs)	ε975
	public.........................int		**offsetRequested** ()	
1	public.....................void		printStackTrace ()	ε971

		BandCombineOp	java.awt.image

```
           Object
1.2        └BandCombineOp ---------------------- RasterOp 1
```

✳	public.........................		**BandCombineOp** (float[][] matrix, java.awt.RenderingHints hints)
1	public........... WritableRaster		**createCompatibleDestRaster** (Raster src)
1	public........... WritableRaster		**filter** (Raster src, WritableRaster dst)
● 1	public final java.awt.geom.Rectangle2D		**getBounds2D** (Raster src)
●	public final .... float[][]		**getMatrix** ()
● 1	public final java.awt.geom.Point2D		**getPoint2D** (java.awt.geom.Point2D srcPt, java.awt.geom.Point2D dstPt)
● 1	public final .... java.awt.RenderingHints		**getRenderingHints** ()

		BandedSampleModel	java.awt.image

ε668

```
           Object
1.2 ○      └SampleModel 1
1.2          └ComponentSampleModel 2
1.2 ●          └BandedSampleModel
```

✳	public.........................		**BandedSampleModel** (int dataType, int w, int h, int numBands)
✳	public.........................		**BandedSampleModel** (int dataType, int w, int h, int scanlineStride, int[] bankIndices, int[] bandOffsets)
2	protected .... int[]		bandOffsets
2	protected .... int[]		bankIndices
2	public........... **SampleModel**		**createCompatibleSampleModel** (int w, int h)
2	public.............. **DataBuffer**		**createDataBuffer** ()
2	public........... **SampleModel**		**createSubsetSampleModel** (int[] bands)
1	protected ....int		dataType
2	public.................. boolean		equals (Object o)
● 2	public final .... int[]		getBandOffsets ()
● 2	public final .... int[]		getBankIndices ()
2	public.................. **Object**		**getDataElements** (int x, int y, Object obj, DataBuffer data)
1	public.................. Object		getDataElements (int x, int y, int w, int h, Object obj, DataBuffer data)

Class *Interface* —extends - - -implements ○ abstract ● final △ static ▲ static final ✳ constructor x x—inherited x **x**—declared **x x**—overridden
ε*n*—examples of usage ⌟—has subclass package—see other volume

●	1	public final .... int	getDataType ()
●	1	public final .... int	getHeight ()
●	1	public final .... int	getNumBands ()
●	2	public final .... int	getNumDataElements ()
	2	public....................... int	getOffset (int x, int y)
	2	public....................... int	getOffset (int x, int y, int b)
	2	public....................... **int[] getPixel** (int x, int y, int[] iArray, DataBuffer data)
	1	public....................... float[] getPixel (int x, int y, float[] fArray, DataBuffer data)
	1	public.................... double[] getPixel (int x, int y, double[] dArray, DataBuffer data)
	2	public....................... **int[] getPixels** (int x, int y, int w, int h, int[] iArray, DataBuffer data)
	1	public....................... float[] getPixels (int x, int y, int w, int h, float[] fArray, DataBuffer data)
	1	public.................... double[] getPixels (int x, int y, int w, int h, double[] dArray, DataBuffer data)
●	2	public final .... int	getPixelStride ()
	2	public....................... **int getSample** (int x, int y, int b, DataBuffer data)
	2	public.................... **double getSampleDouble** (int x, int y, int b, DataBuffer data)
	2	public....................... **float getSampleFloat** (int x, int y, int b, DataBuffer data)
	2	public....................... **int[] getSamples** (int x, int y, int w, int h, int b, int[] iArray, DataBuffer data)
	1	public....................... float[] getSamples (int x, int y, int w, int h, int b, float[] fArray, DataBuffer data)
	1	public.................... double[] getSamples (int x, int y, int w, int h, int b, double[] dArray, DataBuffer data)
●	2	public final .... int[]	getSampleSize ()
●	2	public final .... int	getSampleSize (int band)
●	2	public final .... int	getScanlineStride ()
	1	public....................... int	getTransferType ()
●	1	public final .... int	getWidth ()
	2	public....................... **int hashCode** ()
	1	protected .... int	height
	2	protected .... int	numBands
	2	protected .... int	numBanks
	2	protected .... int	pixelStride
	2	protected .... int	scanlineStride
	2	public....................... **void setDataElements** (int x, int y, Object obj, DataBuffer data)
	1	public....................... void setDataElements (int x, int y, int w, int h, Object obj, DataBuffer data)
	2	public....................... **void setPixel** (int x, int y, int[] iArray, DataBuffer data)
	1	public....................... void setPixel (int x, int y, float[] fArray, DataBuffer data)
	1	public....................... void setPixel (int x, int y, double[] dArray, DataBuffer data)
	2	public....................... **void setPixels** (int x, int y, int w, int h, int[] iArray, DataBuffer data)
	1	public....................... void setPixels (int x, int y, int w, int h, float[] fArray, DataBuffer data)
	1	public....................... void setPixels (int x, int y, int w, int h, double[] dArray, DataBuffer data)
	2	public....................... **void setSample** (int x, int y, int b, double s, DataBuffer data)
	2	public....................... **void setSample** (int x, int y, int b, int s, DataBuffer data)
	2	public....................... **void setSample** (int x, int y, int b, float s, DataBuffer data)
	2	public....................... **void setSamples** (int x, int y, int w, int h, int b, int[] iArray, DataBuffer data)
	1	public....................... void setSamples (int x, int y, int w, int h, int b, float[] fArray, DataBuffer data)
	1	public....................... void setSamples (int x, int y, int w, int h, int b, double[] dArray, DataBuffer data)
	1	protected .... int	width

BasicStroke

Object[1]
1.2 └BasicStroke - Stroke[2]

*		public...........................	**BasicStroke** ()	
*		public...........................	**BasicStroke** (float width)	ε579,588
*		public...........................	**BasicStroke** (float width, int cap, int join)	
*		public...........................	**BasicStroke** (float width, int cap, int join, float miterlimit)	
*		public...........................	**BasicStroke** (float width, int cap, int join, float miterlimit, float[] dash, float dash_phase)	ε579
				ε579
▲		public static final .... int	**CAP_BUTT** = 0	
▲		public static final .... int	**CAP_ROUND** = 1	
▲		public static final .... int	**CAP_SQUARE** = 2	
	2	public.................... Shape	**createStrokedShape** (Shape s)	ε588
	1	public.................... **boolean equals** (Object obj)	
		public.................... float[]	**getDashArray** ()	
		public.................... float	**getDashPhase** ()	
		public.................... int	**getEndCap** ()	
		public.................... int	**getLineJoin** ()	
		public.................... float	**getLineWidth** ()	
		public.................... float	**getMiterLimit** ()	
	1	public.................... **int hashCode** ()	
▲		public static final .... int	**JOIN_BEVEL** = 2	
▲		public static final .... int	**JOIN_MITER** = 0	ε579
▲		public static final .... int	**JOIN_ROUND** = 1	

BevelBorder

BevelBorder

javax.swing.border

```
        Object
1.2 ○   └AbstractBorder 1 --------------------- Border, java.io.Serializable.
1.2          └BevelBorder .
```

ε873

✱	public		**BevelBorder** (int bevelType)
✱	public		**BevelBorder** (int bevelType, java.awt.Color highlight, java.awt.Color shadow)
✱	public		**BevelBorder** (int bevelType, java.awt.Color highlightOuterColor, java.awt.Color highlightInnerColor, java.awt.Color shadowOuterColor, java.awt.Color shadowInnerColor)
	protected	int	**bevelType**
	public	int	**getBevelType** ()
1	public	**java.awt.Insets**	**getBorderInsets** (java.awt.Component c)
1	public	**java.awt.Insets**	**getBorderInsets** (java.awt.Component c, java.awt.Insets insets)
1.3	public	java.awt.Color	**getHighlightInnerColor** ()
	public	java.awt.Color	**getHighlightInnerColor** (java.awt.Component c)
1.3	public	java.awt.Color	**getHighlightOuterColor** ()
	public	java.awt.Color	**getHighlightOuterColor** (java.awt.Component c)
1	public	java.awt.Rectangle	getInteriorRectangle (java.awt.Component c, int x, int y, int width, int height)
△ 1	public static	java.awt.Rectangle	getInteriorRectangle (java.awt.Component c, Border b, int x, int y, int width, int height)
1.3	public	java.awt.Color	**getShadowInnerColor** ()
	public	java.awt.Color	**getShadowInnerColor** (java.awt.Component c)
1.3	public	java.awt.Color	**getShadowOuterColor** ()
	public	java.awt.Color	**getShadowOuterColor** (java.awt.Component c)
	protected	java.awt.Color	**highlightInner**
	protected	java.awt.Color	**highlightOuter**
1	public	boolean	**isBorderOpaque** ()
▲	public static final	int	**LOWERED** = 1
1	public	void	**paintBorder** (java.awt.Component c, java.awt.Graphics g, int x, int y, int width, int height)
	protected	void	**paintLoweredBevel** (java.awt.Component c, java.awt.Graphics g, int x, int y, int width, int height)
	protected	void	**paintRaisedBevel** (java.awt.Component c, java.awt.Graphics g, int x, int y, int width, int height)
▲	public static final	int	**RAISED** = 0
	protected	java.awt.Color	**shadowInner**
	protected	java.awt.Color	**shadowOuter**

BlockView

javax.swing.text.html

```
        Object
1.2 ○   └javax.swing.text.View 1 ----------------- javax.swing.SwingConstants 4
1.2 ○       └javax.swing.text.CompositeView 2
1.2            └javax.swing.text.BoxView 3
1.2                 └BlockView .
```

	1	*31 inherited members from javax.swing.text.View not shown*	
	2	*17 inherited members from javax.swing.text.CompositeView not shown*	
	3	*26 inherited members from javax.swing.text.BoxView not shown*	
	4	*19 inherited members from javax.swing.SwingConstants not shown*	
✱	public		**BlockView** (*javax.swing.text.Element* elem, int axis)
3	protected	javax₂ .swing.SizeRequirements	**calculateMajorAxisRequirements** (int axis, javax.swing.SizeRequirements r)
3	protected	javax₂ .swing.SizeRequirements	**calculateMinorAxisRequirements** (int axis, javax.swing.SizeRequirements r)
1	public	void	**changedUpdate** (*javax.swing.event.DocumentEvent* changes, *java.awt.Shape* a, *javax.swing.text.ViewFactory* f)
3	public	float	**getAlignment** (int axis)
1	public	javax₂ .swing.text.AttributeSet	**getAttributes** ()
3	public	float	**getMaximumSpan** (int axis)
3	public	float	**getMinimumSpan** (int axis)
3	public	float	**getPreferredSpan** (int axis)
3	public	int	**getResizeWeight** (int axis)
	protected	StyleSheet	**getStyleSheet** ()
3	protected	void	**layoutMinorAxis** (int targetSpan, int axis, int[] offsets, int[] spans)
3	public	void	**paint** (java.awt.Graphics g, *java.awt.Shape* allocation)

Class   *Interface*   —extends   - - -implements   ○ abstract   ● final   △ static   ▲ static final   ✱ constructor   x x—inherited   x **x**—declared   **x x**—overridden
ε*n*—examples of usage   .—has subclass   package—see other volume

2	public	**void**	**setParent** (javax.swing.text.View parent)		
	protected	void	**setPropertiesFromAttributes** ()		

Book

java.awt.print

Object
1.2 └Book - *Pageable* [1]

	public	void	**append** (*Printable* painter, PageFormat page)	ε684
	public	void	**append** (*Printable* painter, PageFormat page, int numPages)	ε684
*	public		**Book** ()	ε684
1	public	int	**getNumberOfPages** ()	
1	public	PageFormat	**getPageFormat** (int pageIndex) throws IndexOutOfBoundsException	
1	public	*Printable*	**getPrintable** (int pageIndex) throws IndexOutOfBoundsException	
	public	void	**setPage** (int pageIndex, *Printable* painter, PageFormat page)	
			throws IndexOutOfBoundsException	
▲ 1	public static final	int	UNKNOWN_NUMBER_OF_PAGES = -1	

BooleanControl

javax.sound.sampled

Object
1.3 ○ └Control [1]
1.3 ○   └BooleanControl

*	protected		**BooleanControl** (BooleanControl.Type type, boolean initialValue)	
*	protected		**BooleanControl** (BooleanControl.Type type, boolean initialValue,	
			String trueStateLabel, String falseStateLabel)	
	public	String	**getStateLabel** (boolean state)	
1	public	Control.Type	getType ()	
	public	boolean	**getValue** ()	
	public	void	**setValue** (boolean value)	ε730
1	public	**String**	**toString** ()	

BooleanControl.Type

javax.sound.sampled

Object
1.3 └Control.Type [1]
1.3   └BooleanControl.Type

▲	public static final		**APPLY_REVERB**	
		BooleanControl.Type		
● 1	public final	boolean	equals (Object obj)	
● 1	public final	int	hashCode ()	
▲	public static final		**MUTE**	ε730
		BooleanControl.Type		
● 1	public final	String	toString ()	
*	protected		**BooleanControl.Type** (String name)	

Border

javax.swing.border
ε875,870

1.2 *Border*

	public	java.awt.Insets	**getBorderInsets** (java.awt.Component c)
	public	boolean	**isBorderOpaque** ()
	public	void	**paintBorder** (java.awt.Component c, java.awt.Graphics g, int x, int y, int width,
			int height)

BorderFactory

javax.swing

Object
1.2 └BorderFactory

△	public static		**createBevelBorder** (int type)
	... javax.swing.border.Border		
△	public static		**createBevelBorder** (int type, java.awt.Color highlight, java.awt.Color shadow)
	... javax.swing.border.Border		
△	public static		**createBevelBorder** (int type, java.awt.Color highlightOuter, java.awt.Color
	... javax.swing.border.Border		highlightInner, java.awt.Color shadowOuter, java.awt.Color shadowInner)

Classes
B

BorderFactory

△	public static ...... javax.swing ⊃.border.CompoundBorder	**createCompoundBorder** ()	
△	public static ...... javax.swing ⊃.border.CompoundBorder	**createCompoundBorder** (*javax.swing.border.Border* outsideBorder, *javax.swing.border.Border* insideBorder)	ε875
△	public static ... *javax.swing.border.Border*	**createEmptyBorder** ()	ε873
△	public static ... *javax.swing.border.Border*	**createEmptyBorder** (int top, int left, int bottom, int right)	
△	public static ... *javax.swing.border.Border*	**createEtchedBorder** ()	ε873
1.3 △	public static ... *javax.swing.border.Border*	**createEtchedBorder** (int type)	
△	public static ... *javax.swing.border.Border*	**createEtchedBorder** (java.awt.Color highlight, java.awt.Color shadow)	
1.3 △	public static ... *javax.swing.border.Border*	**createEtchedBorder** (int type, java.awt.Color highlight, java.awt.Color shadow)	
△	public static ... *javax.swing.border.Border*	**createLineBorder** (java.awt.Color color)	ε873
△	public static ... *javax.swing.border.Border*	**createLineBorder** (java.awt.Color color, int thickness)	
△	public static ... *javax.swing.border.Border*	**createLoweredBevelBorder** ()	ε873
△	public static .... javax ⊃.swing.border.MatteBorder	**createMatteBorder** (int top, int left, int bottom, int right, java.awt.Color color)	
△	public static .... javax ⊃.swing.border.MatteBorder	**createMatteBorder** (int top, int left, int bottom, int right, *Icon* tileIcon)	ε873
△	public static ... *javax.swing.border.Border*	**createRaisedBevelBorder** ()	ε873
△	public static .... javax ⊃.swing.border.TitledBorder	**createTitledBorder** (String title)	ε874
△	public static .... javax ⊃.swing.border.TitledBorder	**createTitledBorder** (*javax.swing.border.Border* border)	
△	public static .... javax ⊃.swing.border.TitledBorder	**createTitledBorder** (*javax.swing.border.Border* border, String title)	ε874
△	public static .... javax ⊃.swing.border.TitledBorder	**createTitledBorder** (*javax.swing.border.Border* border, String title, int titleJustification, int titlePosition)	
△	public static .... javax ⊃.swing.border.TitledBorder	**createTitledBorder** (*javax.swing.border.Border* border, String title, int titleJustification, int titlePosition, java.awt.Font titleFont)	
△	public static .... javax ⊃.swing.border.TitledBorder	**createTitledBorder** (*javax.swing.border.Border* border, String title, int titleJustification, int titlePosition, java.awt.Font titleFont, java.awt.Color titleColor)	

BorderLayout

java.awt

Object [1]
└ BorderLayout - *LayoutManager2* [2] (*LayoutManager* [3]), *java.io.Serializable* ⌄

1.1	2	public.....................void	**addLayoutComponent** (Component comp, Object constraints)	
D	3	public.....................void	**addLayoutComponent** (String name, Component comp)	
1.2 ▲		public static final........String	**AFTER_LAST_LINE** = "Last"	
1.2 ▲		public static final........String	**AFTER_LINE_ENDS** = "After"	
1.2 ▲		public static final........String	**BEFORE_FIRST_LINE** = "First"	
1.2 ▲		public static final........String	**BEFORE_LINE_BEGINS** = "Before"	
✳		public...........................	**BorderLayout** ()	ε931
✳		public...........................	**BorderLayout** (int hgap, int vgap)	
1.1 ▲		public static final........String	**CENTER** = "Center"	ε559,571,601,694,705
1.1 ▲		public static final........String	**EAST** = "East"	
1.1		public........................int	**getHgap** ()	
1.1	2	public......................float	**getLayoutAlignmentX** (Container parent)	
1.1	2	public......................float	**getLayoutAlignmentY** (Container parent)	
1.1		public........................int	**getVgap** ()	
1.1	2	public.....................void	**invalidateLayout** (Container target)	
	3	public.....................void	**layoutContainer** (Container target)	ε624,625
1.4 ▲		public static final........String	**LINE_END** = "After"	
1.4 ▲		public static final........String	**LINE_START** = "Before"	
1.1	2	public...............Dimension	**maximumLayoutSize** (Container target)	
	3	public...............Dimension	**minimumLayoutSize** (Container target)	
1.1 ▲		public static final........String	**NORTH** = "North"	ε816,887,931,957
1.4 ▲		public static final........String	**PAGE_END** = "Last"	
1.4 ▲		public static final........String	**PAGE_START** = "First"	

Class   *Interface*   —extends   - - -implements   ○ abstract   ● final   △ static   ▲ static final   ✳ constructor   x x—inherited   x **x**—declared   **x x**—overridden
ε*n*—examples of usage   ⌄—has subclass   package—see other volume

	3	public..............Dimension	**preferredLayoutSize** (Container target)	
	3	public.....................void	**removeLayoutComponent** (Component comp)	
1.1		public.......................void	**setHgap** (int hgap)	
1.1		public.......................void	**setVgap** (int vgap)	
1.1 ▲		public static final.........String	**SOUTH** = "South"	ε571,887
	1	public...............**String**	**toString** ()	
1.1 ▲		public static final.........String	**WEST** = "West"	

BorderUIResource · javax.swing.plaf

Object
1.2 └BorderUIResource -------------------- *javax.swing.border.Border* [1], *UIResource*, java.io.Serializable

*	public..........................	**BorderUIResource** (*javax.swing.border.Border* delegate)	
△	public static	**getBlackLineBorderUIResource** ()	
	... *javax.swing.border.Border*		
	1	public...........java.awt.Insets	**getBorderInsets** (java.awt.Component c)
△	public static	**getEtchedBorderUIResource** ()	
	... *javax.swing.border.Border*		
△	public static	**getLoweredBevelBorderUIResource** ()	
	... *javax.swing.border.Border*		
△	public static	**getRaisedBevelBorderUIResource** ()	
	... *javax.swing.border.Border*		
	1	public................ boolean	**isBorderOpaque** ()
	1	public.......................void	**paintBorder** (java.awt.Component c, java.awt.Graphics g, int x, int y, int width, int height)

BorderUIResource.BevelBorderUIResource · javax.swing.plaf

ε873

Object
1.2 ○ └javax.swing.border.AbstractBorder [1] ------- *javax.swing.border.Border*, java.io.Serializable
1.2 └javax.swing.border.BevelBorder [2]
1.2 └BorderUIResource [2] ------------------- *UIResource*
.BevelBorderUIResource

*		public..........................	**BorderUIResource.BevelBorderUIResource** (int bevelType)
*		public..........................	**BorderUIResource.BevelBorderUIResource** (int bevelType, java.awt.Color highlight, java.awt.Color shadow)
*		public..........................	**BorderUIResource.BevelBorderUIResource** (int bevelType, java.awt.Color highlightOuter, java.awt.Color highlightInner, java.awt.Color shadowOuter, java.awt.Color shadowInner)
	2	protected ....int	bevelType
	2	public..........................int	getBevelType ()
	2	public..........java.awt.Insets	getBorderInsets (java.awt.Component c)
	2	public..........java.awt.Insets	getBorderInsets (java.awt.Component c, java.awt.Insets insets)
1.3	2	public............java.awt.Color	getHighlightInnerColor ()
	2	public............java.awt.Color	getHighlightInnerColor (java.awt.Component c)
1.3	2	public............java.awt.Color	getHighlightOuterColor ()
	2	public............java.awt.Color	getHighlightOuterColor (java.awt.Component c)
	1	public...... java.awt.Rectangle	getInteriorRectangle (java.awt.Component c, int x, int y, int width, int height)
△ 1		public static	getInteriorRectangle (java.awt.Component c, *javax.swing.border.Border* b, int x,
		.... java.awt.Rectangle	int y, int width, int height)
1.3	2	public............java.awt.Color	getShadowInnerColor ()
	2	public............java.awt.Color	getShadowInnerColor (java.awt.Component c)
1.3	2	public............java.awt.Color	getShadowOuterColor ()
	2	public............java.awt.Color	getShadowOuterColor (java.awt.Component c)
	2	protected ....java.awt.Color	highlightInner
	2	protected ....java.awt.Color	highlightOuter
	2	public.................. boolean	isBorderOpaque ()
▲ 2		public static final ....int	LOWERED = 1
	2	public.......................void	paintBorder (java.awt.Component c, java.awt.Graphics g, int x, int y, int width, int height)
	2	protected ....void	paintLoweredBevel (java.awt.Component c, java.awt.Graphics g, int x, int y, int width, int height)
	2	protected ....void	paintRaisedBevel (java.awt.Component c, java.awt.Graphics g, int x, int y, int width, int height)
▲ 2		public static final ....int	RAISED = 0
	2	protected ....java.awt.Color	shadowInner
	2	protected ....java.awt.Color	shadowOuter

BorderUIResource.CompoundBorderUIResource

javax.swing.plaf

```
Object
1.2 ○ └javax.swing.border.AbstractBorder¹ ------- javax.swing.border.Border, java.io.Serializable↵
1.2      └javax.swing.border.CompoundBorder²
1.2          └BorderUIResource↵ ----------------- UIResource
                .CompoundBorderUIResource
```

✱	public..........................	**BorderUIResource.CompoundBorderUIResource** (*javax.swing.border.Border* outsideBorder, *javax.swing.border.Border* insideBorder)
2	public..........java.awt.Insets	getBorderInsets (java.awt.Component c)
2	public..........java.awt.Insets	getBorderInsets (java.awt.Component c, java.awt.Insets insets)
2	public.......................... *... javax.swing.border.Border*	getInsideBorder ()
1	public...... java.awt.Rectangle	getInteriorRectangle (java.awt.Component c, int x, int y, int width, int height)
△ 1	public static ....java.awt.Rectangle	getInteriorRectangle (java.awt.Component c, *javax.swing.border.Border* b, int x, int y, int width, int height)
2	public.......................... *... javax.swing.border.Border*	getOutsideBorder ()
2	protected..................... *... javax.swing.border.Border*	insideBorder
2	public.................. boolean	isBorderOpaque ()
2	protected..................... *... javax.swing.border.Border*	outsideBorder
2	public......................void	paintBorder (java.awt.Component c, java.awt.Graphics g, int x, int y, int width, int height)

BorderUIResource.EmptyBorderUIResource

javax.swing.plaf

```
Object
1.2 ○ └javax.swing.border.AbstractBorder¹ ------- javax.swing.border.Border, java.io.Serializable↵
1.2      └javax.swing.border.EmptyBorder²
1.2          └BorderUIResource↵ ----------------- UIResource
                .EmptyBorderUIResource
```

2	protected ....int	bottom
✱	public..........................	**BorderUIResource.EmptyBorderUIResource** (java.awt.Insets insets)
✱	public..........................	**BorderUIResource.EmptyBorderUIResource** (int top, int left, int bottom, int right)
1.3 2	public..........java.awt.Insets	getBorderInsets ()
2	public..........java.awt.Insets	getBorderInsets (java.awt.Component c)
2	public..........java.awt.Insets	getBorderInsets (java.awt.Component c, java.awt.Insets insets)
1	public...... java.awt.Rectangle	getInteriorRectangle (java.awt.Component c, int x, int y, int width, int height)
△ 1	public static ....java.awt.Rectangle	getInteriorRectangle (java.awt.Component c, *javax.swing.border.Border* b, int x, int y, int width, int height)
2	public.................. boolean	isBorderOpaque ()
2	protected ....int	left
2	public......................void	paintBorder (java.awt.Component c, java.awt.Graphics g, int x, int y, int width, int height)
2	protected ....int	right
2	protected ....int	top

BorderUIResource.EtchedBorderUIResource

javax.swing.plaf

```
Object
1.2 ○ └javax.swing.border.AbstractBorder¹ ------- javax.swing.border.Border, java.io.Serializable↵
1.2      └javax.swing.border.EtchedBorder²
1.2          └BorderUIResource↵ ----------------- UIResource
                .EtchedBorderUIResource
```

✱	public..........................	**BorderUIResource.EtchedBorderUIResource** ()
✱	public..........................	**BorderUIResource.EtchedBorderUIResource** (int etchType)
✱	public..........................	**BorderUIResource.EtchedBorderUIResource** (java.awt.Color highlight, java.awt.Color shadow)
✱	public..........................	**BorderUIResource.EtchedBorderUIResource** (int etchType, java.awt.Color highlight, java.awt.Color shadow)
2	protected ....int	etchType
2	public..........java.awt.Insets	getBorderInsets (java.awt.Component c)

Class *Interface* —extends - - -implements ○ abstract ● final △ static ▲ static final ✱ constructor x x—inherited x **x**—declared **x x**—overridden
ε*n*—examples of usage ↵—has subclass package—see other volume

	2	public	java.awt.Insets	getBorderInsets (java.awt.Component c, java.awt.Insets insets)
	2	public	int	getEtchType ()
1.3	2	public	java.awt.Color	getHighlightColor ()
	2	public	java.awt.Color	getHighlightColor (java.awt.Component c)
	1	public	java.awt.Rectangle	getInteriorRectangle (java.awt.Component c, int x, int y, int width, int height)
△	1	public static		getInteriorRectangle (java.awt.Component c, *javax.swing.border.Border* b, int x,
			java.awt.Rectangle	int y, int width, int height)
1.3	2	public	java.awt.Color	getShadowColor ()
	2	public	java.awt.Color	getShadowColor (java.awt.Component c)
	2	protected	java.awt.Color	highlight
	2	public	boolean	isBorderOpaque ()
▲	2	public static final	int	LOWERED = 1
	2	public	void	paintBorder (java.awt.Component c, java.awt.Graphics g, int x, int y, int width,
				int height)
▲	2	public static final	int	RAISED = 0
	2	protected	java.awt.Color	shadow

BorderUIResource.LineBorderUIResource javax.swing.plaf

ε873

Object
  1.2 ○ └ javax.swing.border.AbstractBorder [1] - - - - - - - *javax.swing.border.Border*, java.io.Serializable
  1.2   └ javax.swing.border.LineBorder [2]
  1.2   └ BorderUIResource - - - - - - - - - - - - - - *UIResource*
            .LineBorderUIResource

△	2	public static		createBlackLineBorder ()
			javax.swing.border.Border	
△	2	public static		createGrayLineBorder ()
			javax.swing.border.Border	
	2	public	java.awt.Insets	getBorderInsets (java.awt.Component c)
	2	public	java.awt.Insets	getBorderInsets (java.awt.Component c, java.awt.Insets insets)
	1	public	java.awt.Rectangle	getInteriorRectangle (java.awt.Component c, int x, int y, int width, int height)
△	1	public static		getInteriorRectangle (java.awt.Component c, *javax.swing.border.Border* b, int x,
			java.awt.Rectangle	int y, int width, int height)
	2	public	java.awt.Color	getLineColor ()
1.3	2	public	boolean	getRoundedCorners ()
	2	public	int	getThickness ()
	2	public	boolean	isBorderOpaque ()
*		public		**BorderUIResource.LineBorderUIResource** (java.awt.Color color)
*		public		**BorderUIResource.LineBorderUIResource** (java.awt.Color color, int thickness)
	2	protected	java.awt.Color	lineColor
	2	public	void	paintBorder (java.awt.Component c, java.awt.Graphics g, int x, int y, int width,
				int height)
	2	protected	boolean	roundedCorners
	2	protected	int	thickness

BorderUIResource.MatteBorderUIResource javax.swing.plaf

ε873

Object
  1.2 ○ └ javax.swing.border.AbstractBorder [1] - - - - - - - *javax.swing.border.Border*, java.io.Serializable
  1.2   └ javax.swing.border.EmptyBorder [2]
  1.2   └ javax.swing.border.MatteBorder [3]
  1.2   └ BorderUIResource - - - - - - - - - - - - - - *UIResource*
                .MatteBorderUIResource

	2	protected	int	bottom
	3	protected	java.awt.Color	color
1.3	3	public	java.awt.Insets	getBorderInsets ()
	3	public	java.awt.Insets	getBorderInsets (java.awt.Component c)
	3	public	java.awt.Insets	getBorderInsets (java.awt.Component c, java.awt.Insets insets)
	1	public	java.awt.Rectangle	getInteriorRectangle (java.awt.Component c, int x, int y, int width, int height)
△	1	public static		getInteriorRectangle (java.awt.Component c, *javax.swing.border.Border* b, int x,
			java.awt.Rectangle	int y, int width, int height)
1.3	3	public	java.awt.Color	getMatteColor ()
1.3	3	public	*javax.swing.Icon*	getTileIcon ()
	3	public	boolean	isBorderOpaque ()
	2	protected	int	left
*		public		**BorderUIResource.MatteBorderUIResource** (*javax.swing.Icon* tileIcon)
*		public		**BorderUIResource.MatteBorderUIResource** (int top, int left, int bottom, int right,
				javax.swing.Icon tileIcon)

BorderUIResource.MatteBorderUIResource

✳	public		**BorderUIResource.MatteBorderUIResource** (int top, int left, int bottom, int right, java.awt.Color color)
3	public	void	paintBorder (java.awt.Component c, java.awt.Graphics g, int x, int y, int width, int height)
2	protected	int	right
3	protected	*javax.swing.Icon*	tileIcon
2	protected	int	top

BorderUIResource.TitledBorderUIResource

```
        Object                                                                    ε873
1.2 ○   └─javax.swing.border.AbstractBorder¹ - - - - - - - - javax.swing.border.Border, java.io.Serializable
1.2         └─javax.swing.border.TitledBorder²
1.2             └─BorderUIResource⊃ - - - - - - - - - - - - - - - - - UIResource
                  .TitledBorderUIResource
```

2		*40 inherited members from javax.swing.border.TitledBorder not shown*	
1	public	java.awt.Rectangle	getInteriorRectangle (java.awt.Component c, int x, int y, int width, int height)
△ 1	public static	java.awt.Rectangle	getInteriorRectangle (java.awt.Component c, *javax.swing.border.Border* b, int x, int y, int width, int height)
✳	public		**BorderUIResource.TitledBorderUIResource** (String title)
✳	public		**BorderUIResource.TitledBorderUIResource** (*javax.swing.border.Border* border)
✳	public		**BorderUIResource.TitledBorderUIResource** (*javax.swing.border.Border* border, String title)
✳	public		**BorderUIResource.TitledBorderUIResource** (*javax.swing.border.Border* border, String title, int titleJustification, int titlePosition)
✳	public		**BorderUIResource.TitledBorderUIResource** (*javax.swing.border.Border* border, String title, int titleJustification, int titlePosition, java.awt.Font titleFont)
✳	public		**BorderUIResource.TitledBorderUIResource** (*javax.swing.border.Border* border, String title, int titleJustification, int titlePosition, java.awt.Font titleFont, java.awt.Color titleColor)

BoundedRangeModel

```
1.2     BoundedRangeModel
```

	public	void	**addChangeListener** (*javax.swing.event.ChangeListener* x)
	public	int	**getExtent** ()
	public	int	**getMaximum** ()
	public	int	**getMinimum** ()
	public	int	**getValue** ()
	public	boolean	**getValueIsAdjusting** ()
	public	void	**removeChangeListener** (*javax.swing.event.ChangeListener* x)
	public	void	**setExtent** (int newExtent)
	public	void	**setMaximum** (int newMaximum)
	public	void	**setMinimum** (int newMinimum)
	public	void	**setRangeProperties** (int value, int extent, int min, int max, boolean adjusting)
			ε795,803
	public	void	**setValue** (int newValue)
	public	void	**setValueIsAdjusting** (boolean b)

Box

```
        Object
○       └─java.awt.Component¹ - - - - - - - - - - - - - - - - - - java.awt.image.ImageObserver⁴, java.awt.MenuContainer,
                                                                  java.io.Serializable
            └─java.awt.Container²
1.2 ○           └─JComponent³
1.2                 └─Box - - - - - - - - - - - - - - - - - - - - - - - javax.accessibility.Accessible
```

1		*143 inherited members from java.awt.Component not shown*	
2		*49 inherited members from java.awt.Container not shown*	
3		*145 inherited members from JComponent not shown*	
4		*8 inherited members from java.awt.image.ImageObserver not shown*	
3	protected	javax.accessibility⊃ .AccessibleContext	accessibleContext
2	public	java.awt.Component	add (java.awt.Component comp)
			ε850,851,571,575,581

Class *Interface* —extends - - -implements ○ abstract ● final △ static ▲ static final ✳ constructor x x—inherited x **x**—declared **x x**—overridden
ε*n*—examples of usage ⌐—has subclass package—see other volume

✱	public........................	**Box** (int axis)		ε850,851
△	public static	**createGlue** ()		ε851
	.... java.awt.Component			
△	public static .... Box	**createHorizontalBox** ()		ε850
△	public static	**createHorizontalGlue** ()		
	.... java.awt.Component			
△	public static	**createHorizontalStrut** (int width)		ε851
	.... java.awt.Component			
△	public static	**createRigidArea** (java.awt.Dimension d)		
	.... java.awt.Component			
△	public static .... Box	**createVerticalBox** ()		ε850
△	public static	**createVerticalGlue** ()		
	.... java.awt.Component			
△	public static	**createVerticalStrut** (int height)		
	.... java.awt.Component			
3	public.... **javax.accessibility₂**	**getAccessibleContext** ()		
	.AccessibleContext			
2	public.................... **void**	**setLayout** (*java.awt.LayoutManager* l)		ε613,622,624,625,627

Box.Filler   javax.swing

Object
└─java.awt.Component[1] - - - - - - - - - - - - - - - - - - - *java.awt.image.ImageObserver* [4], *java.awt.MenuContainer*,
○   *java.io.Serializable*

    └─java.awt.Container[2]
1.2 ○   └─JComponent[3]
1.2   └─Box.Filler - *javax.accessibility.Accessible*

1	*143 inherited members from java.awt.Component not shown*		
2	*51 inherited members from java.awt.Container not shown*		
3	*142 inherited members from JComponent not shown*		
4	*8 inherited members from java.awt.image.ImageObserver not shown*		
3	protected **javax.accessibility₂**	**accessibleContext**	
	.AccessibleContext		
	public........................void	**changeShape** (java.awt.Dimension min, java.awt.Dimension pref,	
		java.awt.Dimension max)	
✱	public........................	**Box.Filler** (java.awt.Dimension min, java.awt.Dimension pref,	
		java.awt.Dimension max)	
3	public.... **javax.accessibility₂**	**getAccessibleContext** ()	
	.AccessibleContext		
3	public.... **java.awt.Dimension**	**getMaximumSize** ()	
3	public.... **java.awt.Dimension**	**getMinimumSize** ()	
3	public.... **java.awt.Dimension**	**getPreferredSize** ()	

BoxLayout   javax.swing

Object
1.2 └─BoxLayout - *java.awt.LayoutManager2* [1] (*java.awt.LayoutManager* [2]),
                                                                        java.io.Serializable

	1	public........................void	**addLayoutComponent** (java.awt.Component comp, Object constraints)	
	2	public........................void	**addLayoutComponent** (String name, java.awt.Component comp)	
✱		public........................	**BoxLayout** (java.awt.Container target, int axis)	
	1	public synchronized ....float	**getLayoutAlignmentX** (java.awt.Container target)	
	1	public synchronized ....float	**getLayoutAlignmentY** (java.awt.Container target)	
	1	public synchronized ....void	**invalidateLayout** (java.awt.Container target)	
	2	public........................void	**layoutContainer** (java.awt.Container target)	ε624,625
1.4 ▲		public static final...........int	**LINE_AXIS** = 2	
	1	public...... java.awt.Dimension	**maximumLayoutSize** (java.awt.Container target)	
	2	public...... java.awt.Dimension	**minimumLayoutSize** (java.awt.Container target)	
1.4 ▲		public static final...........int	**PAGE_AXIS** = 3	
	2	public...... java.awt.Dimension	**preferredLayoutSize** (java.awt.Container target)	
	2	public........................void	**removeLayoutComponent** (java.awt.Component comp)	
▲		public static final...........int	**X_AXIS** = 0	ε850,851
▲		public static final...........int	**Y_AXIS** = 1	ε850

BoxView

	BoxView		javax.swing.text

```
        Object
1.2 ○   └View 1 - - - - - - - - - - - - - - - - - - - - - - - - - - - - - - javax.swing.SwingConstants 3
1.2 ○     └CompositeView 2
1.2         └BoxView⌄
```

	1	*33 inherited members from View not shown*	
	2	*18 inherited members from CompositeView not shown*	
	3	*19 inherited members from javax.swing.SwingConstants not shown*	
		protected . . . . void	**baselineLayout** (int targetSpan, int axis, int[] offsets, int[] spans)
		protected . . . . javax₂ .swing.SizeRequirements	**baselineRequirements** (int axis, javax.swing.SizeRequirements r)
*		public	**BoxView** (*Element* elem, int axis)
		protected . . . . javax₂ .swing.SizeRequirements	**calculateMajorAxisRequirements** (int axis, javax.swing.SizeRequirements r)
		protected . . . . javax₂ .swing.SizeRequirements	**calculateMinorAxisRequirements** (int axis, javax.swing.SizeRequirements r)
	2	protected . . . . **void**	**childAllocation** (int index, java.awt.Rectangle alloc)
	2	protected . . . . **boolean**	**flipEastAndWestAtEnds** (int position, Position.Bias bias)
1.3	1	protected . . . . **void**	**forwardUpdate** (*javax.swing.event.DocumentEvent.ElementChange* ec, *javax.swing.event.DocumentEvent* e, *java.awt.Shape* a, *ViewFactory* f)
	1	public . . . . **float**	**getAlignment** (int axis)
1.3		public . . . . int	**getAxis** ()
	2	public . . . . ***java.awt.Shape***	**getChildAllocation** (int index, *java.awt.Shape* a)
		public . . . . int	**getHeight** ()
	1	public . . . . **float**	**getMaximumSpan** (int axis)
	1	public . . . . **float**	**getMinimumSpan** (int axis)
		protected . . . . int	**getOffset** (int axis, int childIndex)
	1	public . . . . **float**	**getPreferredSpan** (int axis)
	1	public . . . . **int**	**getResizeWeight** (int axis)
		protected . . . . int	**getSpan** (int axis, int childIndex)
	2	protected . . . . **View**	**getViewAtPoint** (int x, int y, java.awt.Rectangle alloc)
		public . . . . int	**getWidth** ()
	2	protected . . . . **boolean**	**isAfter** (int x, int y, java.awt.Rectangle innerAlloc)
		protected . . . . boolean	**isAllocationValid** ()
	2	protected . . . . **boolean**	**isBefore** (int x, int y, java.awt.Rectangle innerAlloc)
1.4		protected . . . . boolean	**isLayoutValid** (int axis)
		protected . . . . void	**layout** (int width, int height)
1.3		public . . . . void	**layoutChanged** (int axis)
		protected . . . . void	**layoutMajorAxis** (int targetSpan, int axis, int[] offsets, int[] spans)
		protected . . . . void	**layoutMinorAxis** (int targetSpan, int axis, int[] offsets, int[] spans)
	2	public . . . . ***java.awt.Shape***	**modelToView** (int pos, *java.awt.Shape* a, Position.Bias b) throws BadLocationException
	1	public . . . . **void**	**paint** (java.awt.Graphics g, *java.awt.Shape* allocation)
		protected . . . . void	**paintChild** (java.awt.Graphics g, java.awt.Rectangle alloc, int index)
	1	public . . . . **void**	**preferenceChanged** (View child, boolean width, boolean height)
	2	public . . . . **void**	**replace** (int index, int length, View[] elems)
1.3		public . . . . void	**setAxis** (int axis)
	1	public . . . . **void**	**setSize** (float width, float height)
	2	public . . . . **int**	**viewToModel** (float x, float y, *java.awt.Shape* a, Position.Bias[] bias)

	BufferCapabilities		java.awt

```
        Object 1
1.4     └BufferCapabilities - - - - - - - - - - - - - - - - - - - - - Cloneable⌄
```

*		public	**BufferCapabilities** (ImageCapabilities frontCaps, ImageCapabilities backCaps, BufferCapabilities.FlipContents flipContents)	
	1	public . . . . **Object**	**clone** ()	
		public . . . . ImageCapabilities	**getBackBufferCapabilities** ()	
		public . . . . . . BufferCapabilities₂ .FlipContents	**getFlipContents** ()	ε602
		public . . . . ImageCapabilities	**getFrontBufferCapabilities** ()	
		public . . . . boolean	**isFullScreenRequired** ()	
		public . . . . boolean	**isMultiBufferAvailable** ()	
		public . . . . boolean	**isPageFlipping** ()	ε602

Class   *Interface*   —extends   - - -implements   ○ abstract   ● final   △ static   ▲ static final   ✱ constructor   x x—inherited   x **x**—declared   **x x**—overridden
ε*n*—examples of usage   ⌄—has subclass   package—see other volume

430

	BufferCapabilities.FlipContents			java.awt

```
        Object
1.4     └AttributeValue 1
1.4 ●     └BufferCapabilities.FlipContents
```

▲		public static final . . BufferCapabilities.FlipContents	**BACKGROUND**	ε602
▲		public static final . . BufferCapabilities.FlipContents	**COPIED**	ε602
	1	public . . . . int	hashCode ()	
▲		public static final . . BufferCapabilities.FlipContents	**PRIOR**	ε602
	1	public . . . . String	toString ()	
▲		public static final . . BufferCapabilities.FlipContents	**UNDEFINED**	ε602

	BufferedImage			java.awt.image
				ε864,560,581,597,638

```
        Object 1
  ○     └java.awt.Image 2
1.2       └BufferedImage ----------------------- WritableRenderedImage 3 (RenderedImage 4)
```

3	public . . . . void	**addTileObserver** (*TileObserver* to)	
*	public	**BufferedImage** (int width, int height, int imageType)	ε666,667,680,695
*	public	**BufferedImage** (int width, int height, int imageType, IndexColorModel cm)	
*	public	**BufferedImage** (ColorModel cm, WritableRaster raster,	
		boolean isRasterPremultiplied, java.util.Hashtable properties)	ε668
	public . . . . void	**coerceData** (boolean isAlphaPremultiplied)	
4	public . . . . WritableRaster	**copyData** (WritableRaster outRaster)	
	public java.awt.Graphics2D	**createGraphics** ()	ε667,669,680,695
2	public . . . . **void**	**flush** ()	ε673,674
	public . . . . WritableRaster	**getAlphaRaster** ()	
4	public . . . . ColorModel	**getColorModel** ()	ε661,662
4	public . . . . Raster	**getData** ()	
4	public . . . . Raster	**getData** (java.awt.Rectangle rect)	
2	public . . . . **java.awt.Graphics**	**getGraphics** ()	
4	public . . . . int	**getHeight** ()	ε672
2	public . . . . **int**	**getHeight** (*ImageObserver* observer)	ε671,594,667,674,675
4	public . . . . int	**getMinTileX** ()	
4	public . . . . int	**getMinTileY** ()	
4	public . . . . int	**getMinX** ()	
4	public . . . . int	**getMinY** ()	
4	public . . . . int	**getNumXTiles** ()	
4	public . . . . int	**getNumYTiles** ()	
4	public . . . . Object	**getProperty** (String name)	
2	public . . . . **Object**	**getProperty** (String name, *ImageObserver* observer)	
4	public . . . . String[]	**getPropertyNames** ()	
	public . . . . WritableRaster	**getRaster** ()	
	public . . . . int	**getRGB** (int x, int y)	ε671
	public . . . . int[]	**getRGB** (int startX, int startY, int w, int h, int[] rgbArray, int offset, int scansize)	
			ε671
4	public . . . . SampleModel	**getSampleModel** ()	
2	public . . . . java.awt.Image	getScaledInstance (int width, int height, int hints)	ε670,664,665
2	public . . . . **ImageProducer**	**getSource** ()	
4	public . . . . java.util.Vector	**getSources** ()	
	public . . . . BufferedImage	**getSubimage** (int x, int y, int w, int h)	ε664
4	public . . . . Raster	**getTile** (int tileX, int tileY)	
4	public . . . . int	**getTileGridXOffset** ()	
4	public . . . . int	**getTileGridYOffset** ()	
4	public . . . . int	**getTileHeight** ()	
4	public . . . . int	**getTileWidth** ()	
	public . . . . int	**getType** ()	
4	public . . . . int	**getWidth** ()	ε672
2	public . . . . **int**	**getWidth** (*ImageObserver* observer)	ε671,594,667,674,675
3	public . . . . WritableRaster	**getWritableTile** (int tileX, int tileY)	
3	public . . . . java.awt.Point[]	**getWritableTileIndices** ()	
3	public . . . . boolean	**hasTileWriters** ()	
	public . . . . boolean	**isAlphaPremultiplied** ()	
3	public . . . . boolean	**isTileWritable** (int tileX, int tileY)	
3	public . . . . void	**releaseWritableTile** (int tileX, int tileY)	
3	public . . . . void	**removeTileObserver** (*TileObserver* to)	
▲ 2	public static final . . . . int	SCALE_AREA_AVERAGING = 16	
▲ 2	public static final . . . . int	SCALE_DEFAULT = 1	
▲ 2	public static final . . . . int	SCALE_FAST = 2	
▲ 2	public static final . . . . int	SCALE_REPLICATE = 8	

BufferedImage

```
▲  2  public static final............int  SCALE_SMOOTH  = 4
   3  public.......................void  setData (Raster r)
      public synchronized .......void  setRGB (int x, int y, int rgb)                                    ε671
      public.......................void  setRGB (int startX, int startY, int w, int h, int[] rgbArray, int offset, int scansize)
   1  public....................  String  toString ()
▲     public static final............int  TYPE_3BYTE_BGR = 5
▲     public static final............int  TYPE_4BYTE_ABGR = 6
▲     public static final............int  TYPE_4BYTE_ABGR_PRE = 7
▲     public static final............int  TYPE_BYTE_BINARY = 12
▲     public static final............int  TYPE_BYTE_GRAY = 10
▲     public static final............int  TYPE_BYTE_INDEXED = 13
▲     public static final............int  TYPE_CUSTOM = 0
▲     public static final............int  TYPE_INT_ARGB = 2                                              ε666,667
▲     public static final............int  TYPE_INT_ARGB_PRE = 3
▲     public static final............int  TYPE_INT_BGR = 4
▲     public static final............int  TYPE_INT_RGB = 1                                              ε666,667,680,695
▲     public static final............int  TYPE_USHORT_555_RGB = 9
▲     public static final............int  TYPE_USHORT_565_RGB = 8
▲     public static final............int  TYPE_USHORT_GRAY = 11
▲  2  public static final........Object  UndefinedProperty
```

BufferedImageFilter   java.awt.image

```
      Object                                                                                            ε665
      └ImageFilter 1 - - - - - - - - - - - - - - - - - - - - - - - - ImageConsumer 2, Cloneable
1.2      └BufferedImageFilter
```

```
   2  9 inherited members from ImageConsumer not shown
*     public.......................  BufferedImageFilter (BufferedImageOp op)
   1  public.....................Object  clone ()
   1  protected .....ImageConsumer  consumer
      public.......BufferedImageOp  getBufferedImageOp ()
   1  public..............ImageFilter  getFilterInstance (ImageConsumer ic)
   1  public.....................  void  imageComplete (int status)
   1  public.......................void  resendTopDownLeftRight (ImageProducer ip)
   1  public.....................  void  setColorModel (ColorModel model)
   1  public.....................  void  setDimensions (int width, int height)
   1  public.......................void  setHints (int hints)
   1  public.....................  void  setPixels (int x, int y, int w, int h, ColorModel model, int[] pixels, int off, int scansize)
   1  public.....................  void  setPixels (int x, int y, int w, int h, ColorModel model, byte[] pixels, int off, int scansize)
   1  public.......................void  setProperties (java.util.Hashtable props)
```

BufferedImageOp   java.awt.image

```
1.2    BufferedImageOp
```

```
      public...........BufferedImage  createCompatibleDestImage (BufferedImage src, ColorModel destCM)
      public...........BufferedImage  filter (BufferedImage src, BufferedImage dest)                    ε677,678,679
      public...........              getBounds2D (BufferedImage src)
      . java.awt.geom.Rectangle2D
      public..java.awt.geom.Point2D  getPoint2D (java.awt.geom.Point2D srcPt, java.awt.geom.Point2D dstPt)
      public java.awt.RenderingHints  getRenderingHints ()
```

BufferStrategy   java.awt.image

```
      Object
1.4 ○  └BufferStrategy
```

```
*     public.......................  BufferStrategy ()
○     public abstract ........boolean  contentsLost ()
○     public abstract ........boolean  contentsRestored ()
○     public abstract ...............  getCapabilities ()                                               ε602
      ...java.awt.BufferCapabilities
○     public abstract ...............  getDrawGraphics ()                                               ε602
      ............java.awt.Graphics
○     public abstract ............void  show ()                                                         ε602
```

Class *Interface* —extends - - -implements ○ abstract ● final △ static ▲ static final * constructor x x—inherited x **x**—declared **x x**—overridden
ε*n*—examples of usage ╷—has subclass package—see other volume

Button

```
        Object
    ○   └Component 1 ------------------------- java.awt.image.ImageObserver 2, MenuContainer,
                                                java.io.Serializable
              └Button ---------------------------- javax.accessibility.Accessible
```

	1	206 inherited members from Component not shown		
	2	8 inherited members from java.awt.image.ImageObserver not shown		
1.1		public synchronized .... void	**addActionListener** (java.awt.event.ActionListener l)	ε601
	1	public..................... **void**	**addNotify** ()	
*		public..........................	**Button** () throws HeadlessException	
*		public..........................	**Button** (String label) throws HeadlessException	ε571,574,601
1.3	1	public.... **javax.accessibility₂ .AccessibleContext**	**getAccessibleContext** ()	
1.1		public....................String	**getActionCommand** ()	
1.4		public synchronized ..... java₂ .awt.event.ActionListener[]	**getActionListeners** ()	
		public....................String	**getLabel** ()	
1.3	1	public..........................	**getListeners** (Class listenerType)	
		.... **java.util.EventListener[]**		
	1	protected .... **String**	**paramString** ()	
1.1	1	protected ....void	**processActionEvent** (java.awt.event.ActionEvent e)	
1.1	1	protected .... **void**	**processEvent** (AWTEvent e)	
1.1		public synchronized .... void	**removeActionListener** (java.awt.event.ActionListener l)	
1.1		public....................void	**setActionCommand** (String command)	
		public....................void	**setLabel** (String label)	

ButtonGroup

```
        Object
    1.2 └ButtonGroup ------------------------ java.io.Serializable
```

	public....................void	**add** (AbstractButton b)	ε768
*	public..........................	**ButtonGroup** ()	ε768
	protected .... java.util.Vector	**buttons**	
1.3	public....................int	**getButtonCount** ()	
	public.... java.util.Enumeration	**getElements** ()	ε770
	public............ ButtonModel	**getSelection** ()	ε770
	public............... boolean	**isSelected** (ButtonModel m)	ε771
	public....................void	**remove** (AbstractButton b)	
	public....................void	**setSelected** (ButtonModel m, boolean b)	ε769

ButtonModel

1.2	*ButtonModel*————————————————java.awt.ItemSelectable 1		ε769
	public....................void	**addActionListener** (java.awt.event.ActionListener l)	
	public....................void	**addChangeListener** (javax.swing.event.ChangeListener l)	
1	public....................void	**addItemListener** (java.awt.event.ItemListener l)	ε650,765
	public....................String	**getActionCommand** ()	
	public.......................int	**getMnemonic** ()	
1	public.................. Object[]	getSelectedObjects ()	ε650
	public.............. boolean	**isArmed** ()	
	public.............. boolean	**isEnabled** ()	
	public.............. boolean	**isPressed** ()	
	public.............. boolean	**isRollover** ()	
	public.............. boolean	**isSelected** ()	
	public....................void	**removeActionListener** (java.awt.event.ActionListener l)	
	public....................void	**removeChangeListener** (javax.swing.event.ChangeListener l)	
1	public....................void	**removeItemListener** (java.awt.event.ItemListener l)	ε650
	public....................void	**setActionCommand** (String s)	
	public....................void	**setArmed** (boolean b)	
	public....................void	**setEnabled** (boolean b)	
	public....................void	**setGroup** (ButtonGroup group)	
	public....................void	**setMnemonic** (int key)	
	public....................void	**setPressed** (boolean b)	
	public....................void	**setRollover** (boolean b)	
	public....................void	**setSelected** (boolean b)	

ButtonPeer

	java.awt.peer

ButtonPeer————————————————————*ComponentPeer* [1]

---
1 *42 inherited members from ComponentPeer not shown*
public.....................void **setLabel** (String label)

ButtonUI

	javax.swing.plaf

Object
1.2 ○ └ComponentUI [1]
1.2 ○   └ButtonUI

---
1 *11 inherited members from ComponentUI not shown*
✳ public........................... **ButtonUI** ()

ByteLookupTable

	java.awt.image

Object
1.2 ○ └LookupTable [1]
1.2   └ByteLookupTable

✳ public........................... **ByteLookupTable** (int offset, byte[][] data)
✳ public........................... **ByteLookupTable** (int offset, byte[] data)
1 public.........................int getNumComponents ()
1 public.........................int getOffset ()
● public final .... byte[][] **getTable** ()
  public....................byte[] **lookupPixel** (byte[] src, byte[] dst)
1 public.........................**int[]** **lookupPixel** (int[] src, int[] dst)

CancelablePrintJob

	javax.print

1.4 *CancelablePrintJob*————————————————*DocPrintJob* [1]

---
1 public.........................void addPrintJobAttributeListener (*javax.print.event.PrintJobAttributeListener* listener,
    javax.print.attribute.PrintJobAttributeSet attributes) ε715
1 public.........................void addPrintJobListener (*javax.print.event.PrintJobListener* listener) ε714
  public.........................void **cancel** () throws PrintException ε705
1 public.....*javax.print.attribute* getAttributes () ε715
    .PrintJobAttributeSet
1 public..............*PrintService* getPrintService ()
1 public.........................void print (*Doc* doc, *javax.print.attribute.PrintRequestAttributeSet* attributes)
    throws PrintException ε700,702,710,711,712
1 public.........................void removePrintJobAttributeListener (*javax.print.event.PrintJobAttributeListener* listener)
1 public.........................void removePrintJobListener (*javax.print.event.PrintJobListener* listener)

CannotRedoException

	javax.swing.undo

Object   ε1034
└Throwable - *java.io.Serializable*
  └Exception
    └RuntimeException
1.2   └CannotRedoException

✳ public........................... **CannotRedoException** ()

CannotUndoException

	javax.swing.undo

Object   ε1034
└Throwable - *java.io.Serializable*
  └Exception
    └RuntimeException
1.2   └CannotUndoException

✳ public........................... **CannotUndoException** ()

Class *Interface* —extends - - -implements ○ abstract ● final △ static ▲ static final ✳ constructor x x—inherited x **x**—declared **x x**—overridden
εn—examples of usage ˌ—has subclass package—see other volume

	Canvas		java.awt

```
        Object
   o    └─Component 1 ------------------------- java.awt.image.ImageObserver 2, MenuContainer,
                                                    java.io.Serializable
              └─Canvas -------------------------- javax.accessibility.Accessible
```

	1	*207 inherited members from Component not shown*		
	2	*8 inherited members from java.awt.image.ImageObserver not shown*		
	1	public..................... **void**	**addNotify** ()	
✱		public.........................	**Canvas** ()	
1.2 ✱		public.........................	**Canvas** (GraphicsConfiguration config)	
1.4		public.....................void	**createBufferStrategy** (int numBuffers)	
1.4		public.....................void	**createBufferStrategy** (int numBuffers, BufferCapabilities caps)	
			throws AWTException	
1.3	1	public.... **javax.accessibility ⊃**	**getAccessibleContext** ()	
		.AccessibleContext		
1.4		public..................java ⊃	**getBufferStrategy** ()	
		.awt.image.BufferStrategy		
	1	public..................... **void**	**paint** (Graphics g)	ε674
	1	public..................... **void**	**update** (Graphics g)	

	CanvasPeer		java.awt.peer

```
        CanvasPeer————————————ComponentPeer 1
```

1	*42 inherited members from ComponentPeer not shown*

	CardLayout		java.awt

```
        Object 1
        └─CardLayout ------------------------- LayoutManager2 2 (LayoutManager 3), java.io.Serializable
```

1.1	2	public.....................void	**addLayoutComponent** (Component comp, Object constraints)	
D	3	public.....................void	**addLayoutComponent** (String name, Component comp)	
✱		public.........................	**CardLayout** ()	
✱		public.........................	**CardLayout** (int hgap, int vgap)	
		public.....................void	**first** (Container parent)	
1.1		public......................int	**getHgap** ()	
1.1	2	public.....................float	**getLayoutAlignmentX** (Container parent)	
1.1	2	public.....................float	**getLayoutAlignmentY** (Container parent)	
1.1		public......................int	**getVgap** ()	
1.1	2	public.....................void	**invalidateLayout** (Container target)	
		public.....................void	**last** (Container parent)	
	3	public.....................void	**layoutContainer** (Container parent)	ε624,625
1.1	2	public.................Dimension	**maximumLayoutSize** (Container target)	
	3	public.................Dimension	**minimumLayoutSize** (Container parent)	
		public.....................void	**next** (Container parent)	
	3	public.................Dimension	**preferredLayoutSize** (Container parent)	
		public.....................void	**previous** (Container parent)	
	3	public.....................void	**removeLayoutComponent** (Component comp)	
1.1		public.....................void	**setHgap** (int hgap)	
1.1		public.....................void	**setVgap** (int vgap)	
		public.....................void	**show** (Container parent, String name)	
	1	public............. **String**	**toString** ()	

	Caret		javax.swing.text

1.2	*Caret*	

public.....................void	**addChangeListener** (*javax.swing.event.ChangeListener* l)
public.....................void	**deinstall** (JTextComponent c)
public......................int	**getBlinkRate** ()
public......................int	**getDot** ()
public............java.awt.Point	**getMagicCaretPosition** ()
public......................int	**getMark** ()
public.....................void	**install** (JTextComponent c)
public...................boolean	**isSelectionVisible** ()
public...................boolean	**isVisible** ()
public.....................void	**moveDot** (int dot)
public.....................void	**paint** (java.awt.Graphics g)

public.......................void	**removeChangeListener** (*javax.swing.event.ChangeListener* l)	
public.......................void	**setBlinkRate** (int rate)	ε999
public.......................void	**setDot** (int dot)	
public.......................void	**setMagicCaretPosition** (java.awt.Point p)	
public.......................void	**setSelectionVisible** (boolean v)	
public.......................void	**setVisible** (boolean v)	

CaretEvent   javax.swing.event

Object	ε640,641,643,649,566
1.1 └ java.util.EventObject[1] - - - - - - - - - - - - - - - - - - - *java.io.Serializable*	
1.2 ○ └ CaretEvent	

✳	public........................	**CaretEvent** (Object source)	
○	public abstract...............int	**getDot** ()	ε1015
○	public abstract...............int	**getMark** ()	ε1015
1	public....................Object	getSource ()	ε644,886,565,568,570
1	protected transient......Object	source	
1	public....................String	toString ()	

CaretListener   javax.swing.event

1.2	*CaretListener*————————————*java.util.EventListener*	ε738,743,745,746,752

public........................void	**caretUpdate** (CaretEvent e)	ε1015

CellEditor   javax.swing

1.2	*CellEditor*

public........................void	**addCellEditorListener** (*javax.swing.event.CellEditorListener* l)	
public........................void	**cancelCellEditing** ()	ε956
public........................Object	**getCellEditorValue** ()	ε953,954,960
public........................boolean	**isCellEditable** (java.util.EventObject anEvent)	ε955,960
public........................void	**removeCellEditorListener** (*javax.swing.event.CellEditorListener* l)	
public........................boolean	**shouldSelectCell** (java.util.EventObject anEvent)	
public........................boolean	**stopCellEditing** ()	ε954,956

CellEditorListener   javax.swing.event

1.2	*CellEditorListener*————————————*java.util.EventListener*	ε738,743,745,746,752

public........................void	**editingCanceled** (ChangeEvent e)	
public........................void	**editingStopped** (ChangeEvent e)	

CellRendererPane   javax.swing

Object	ε606,618,733,953,988
○ └ java.awt.Component[1] - - - - - - - - - - - - - - - - - - - *java.awt.image.ImageObserver* [3], *java.awt.MenuContainer*,	
java.io.Serializable	
└ java.awt.Container[2]	
1.2 └ CellRendererPane - - - - - - - - - - - - - - - - - - - *javax.accessibility.Accessible*	

1	*176 inherited members from java.awt.Component not shown*		
2	*63 inherited members from java.awt.Container not shown*		
3	*8 inherited members from java.awt.image.ImageObserver not shown*		
	protected .. javax.accessibility	**accessibleContext**	
	.AccessibleContext		
✳ 2	protected .... **void**	**addImpl** (java.awt.Component x, Object constraints, int index)	
	public........................	**CellRendererPane** ()	
1	public.... **javax.accessibility**	getAccessibleContext ()	
	.AccessibleContext		
2	public........................ **void**	invalidate ()	
2	public........................ **void**	**paint** (java.awt.Graphics g)	ε575,551,557,558,878
	public........................void	**paintComponent** (java.awt.Graphics g, java.awt.Component c,	
		java.awt.Container p, java.awt.Rectangle r)	

---

public	void	**paintComponent** (java.awt.Graphics g, java.awt.Component c, java.awt.Container p, int x, int y, int w, int h)
public	void	**paintComponent** (java.awt.Graphics g, java.awt.Component c, java.awt.Container p, int x, int y, int w, int h, boolean shouldValidate)
2 public	**void**	**update** (java.awt.Graphics g)

ChangedCharSetException · javax.swing.text

```
Object
└Throwable ------------------------- java.io.Serializable
   └Exception
      └ java.io.IOException
         └ChangedCharSetException
```
1.2

* public		**ChangedCharSetException** (String charSetSpec, boolean charSetKey)
public	String	**getCharSetSpec** ()
public	boolean	**keyEqualsCharSet** ()

ChangeEvent · javax.swing.event

ε966,640,641,643,649

```
Object
1.1 └ java.util.EventObject 1 ------------------- java.io.Serializable
1.2    └ChangeEvent
```

*	public		**ChangeEvent** (Object source)
1	public	Object	getSource ()	ε791,793,800,805,815
1	protected transient	Object	source
1	public	String	toString ()

ChangeListener · javax.swing.event

ε738,743,745,746,752

1.2 *ChangeListener* ——————————— *java.util.EventListener*

public	void	**stateChanged** (ChangeEvent e)	ε791,793,800,805,815

Checkbox · java.awt

```
Object
○ └Component 1 ------------------------- java.awt.image.ImageObserver 2, MenuContainer,
                                         java.io.Serializable
     └Checkbox ----------------------- ItemSelectable 3, javax.accessibility.Accessible
```

	1	206 inherited members from Component not shown		
	2	8 inherited members from java.awt.image.ImageObserver not shown		
1.1	3	public synchronized ...... void	**addItemListener** (java.awt.event.ItemListener l)	ε650,765
	1	public .... **void**	**addNotify** ()	
*		public	**Checkbox** () throws HeadlessException	
*		public	**Checkbox** (String label) throws HeadlessException	
1.1 *		public	**Checkbox** (String label, boolean state) throws HeadlessException	
1.1 *		public	**Checkbox** (String label, boolean state, CheckboxGroup group) throws HeadlessException	
*		public	**Checkbox** (String label, CheckboxGroup group, boolean state) throws HeadlessException	
1.3	1	public .... **javax.accessibility .AccessibleContext**	**getAccessibleContext** ()	
		public .... CheckboxGroup	**getCheckboxGroup** ()	
1.4		public synchronized .... *java.awt.event.ItemListener[]*	**getItemListeners** ()	
		public .... String	**getLabel** ()	
1.3	1	public .... *.... java.util.EventListener[]*	**getListeners** (Class listenerType)	
1.1	3	public .... Object[]	**getSelectedObjects** ()	ε650
		public .... boolean	**getState** ()	
	1	protected .... **String**	**paramString** ()	
1.1	1	protected .... **void**	**processEvent** (AWTEvent e)	
1.1		protected .... void	**processItemEvent** (java.awt.event.ItemEvent e)	
1.1	3	public synchronized ......void	**removeItemListener** (java.awt.event.ItemListener l)	ε650
		public ....void	**setCheckboxGroup** (CheckboxGroup g)	
		public ....void	**setLabel** (String label)	

Checkbox

	public	void	**setState** (boolean state)

CheckboxGroup · java.awt

Object[1]
└CheckboxGroup - *java.io.Serializable*

	*	public		**CheckboxGroup** ()	
D		public	Checkbox	**getCurrent** ()	
1.1		public	Checkbox	**getSelectedCheckbox** ()	
D		public synchronized	void	**setCurrent** (Checkbox box)	
1.1		public	void	**setSelectedCheckbox** (Checkbox box)	
	1	public	**String**	**toString** ()	

CheckboxMenuItem · java.awt

Object
○ └MenuComponent[1] - *java.io.Serializable*
  └MenuItem[2] - *javax.accessibility.Accessible*
    └CheckboxMenuItem - - - - - - - - - - - - - - - - - *ItemSelectable*[3]

1.1	2	public synchronized	void	addActionListener (*java.awt.event.ActionListener* l)	
1.1	3	public synchronized	void	**addItemListener** (*java.awt.event.ItemListener* l)	ε650,765
	2	public	**void**	**addNotify** ()	
1.1	*	public		**CheckboxMenuItem** () throws HeadlessException	
	*	public		**CheckboxMenuItem** (String label) throws HeadlessException	
1.1	*	public		**CheckboxMenuItem** (String label, boolean state) throws HeadlessException	
1.1	2	public	void	deleteShortcut ()	
1.1	● 2	protected final	void	disableEvents (long eventsToDisable)	
1.1	● 1	public final	void	dispatchEvent (AWTEvent e)	
1.1	● 2	protected final	void	enableEvents (long eventsToEnable)	
1.3	2	public.... **javax.accessibility .AccessibleContext**		getAccessibleContext ()	
1.1	2	public	String	getActionCommand ()	
1.4	2	public synchronized	*java .awt.event.ActionListener[]*	getActionListeners ()	
	1	public	Font	getFont ()	
1.4		public synchronized	*java.awt.event.ItemListener[]*	**getItemListeners** ()	
	2	public	String	getLabel ()	
1.3	2	public	.... *java.util.EventListener[]*	**getListeners** (Class listenerType)	
1.1	1	public	String	getName ()	
	1	public	*MenuContainer*	getParent ()	
1.1	3	public synchronized	Object[]	**getSelectedObjects** ()	ε650
1.1	2	public	MenuShortcut	getShortcut ()	
		public	boolean	**getState** ()	
1.2	● 1	protected final	Object	getTreeLock ()	
	2	public	boolean	isEnabled ()	
	2	public	**String**	**paramString** ()	
1.1	2	protected	void	processActionEvent (java.awt.event.ActionEvent e)	
1.1	2	protected	**void**	**processEvent** (AWTEvent e)	
1.1		protected	void	**processItemEvent** (java.awt.event.ItemEvent e)	
1.1	2	public synchronized	void	removeActionListener (*java.awt.event.ActionListener* l)	
1.1	3	public synchronized	void	**removeItemListener** (*java.awt.event.ItemListener* l)	ε650
	1	public	void	removeNotify ()	
1.1	2	public	void	setActionCommand (String command)	
1.1	2	public synchronized	void	setEnabled (boolean b)	
	1	public	void	setFont (Font f)	
	2	public synchronized	void	setLabel (String label)	
1.1	1	public	void	setName (String name)	
1.1	2	public	void	setShortcut (MenuShortcut s)	
		public synchronized	void	**setState** (boolean b)	
	1	public	String	toString ()	

Class · *Interface* · —extends · - - -implements · ○ abstract · ● final · △ static · ▲ static final · * constructor · x x—inherited · x **x**—declared · **x x**—overridden
ε*n*—examples of usage · —has subclass · package—see other volume

CheckboxMenuItemPeer | java.awt.peer

CheckboxMenuItemPeer ———————————— *MenuItemPeer* ⌐[1] *(MenuComponentPeer* [2]*)*

- -

> 1 *4 inherited members from MenuItemPeer not shown*
> 2 *1 inherited members from MenuComponentPeer not shown*
>   public.......................void **setState** (boolean t)

- -

C

CheckboxPeer | java.awt.peer

CheckboxPeer ———————————————— *ComponentPeer* ⌐[1]

- -

> 1 *42 inherited members from ComponentPeer not shown*
>   public.......................void **setCheckboxGroup** (java.awt.CheckboxGroup g)
>   public.......................void **setLabel** (String label)
>   public.......................void **setState** (boolean state)

- -

Choice | java.awt

Object
  ○ └─Component[1] - *java.awt.image.ImageObserver* [2], *MenuContainer*,
                                        java.io.Serializable⌐
             └─Choice - *ItemSelectable* ⌐[3], *javax.accessibility.Accessible*

	1	*206 inherited members from Component not shown*		
	2	*8 inherited members from java.awt.image.ImageObserver not shown*		
1.1		public.......................void **add** (String item)		
		public.......................void **addItem** (String item)		
1.1	3	public synchronized ....void **addItemListener** (java.awt.event.ItemListener l)		ε650,765
	1	public....................... **void addNotify** ()		
*		public......................... **Choice** () throws HeadlessException		
D		public.......................int **countItems** ()		
1.3	1	public.... **javax.accessibility₂** **getAccessibleContext** ()		
		.AccessibleContext		
		public.......................String **getItem** (int index)		
1.1		public.......................int **getItemCount** ()		
1.4		public synchronized .... **getItemListeners** ()		
		java.awt.event.ItemListener[]		
1.3	1	public......................... **getListeners** (Class listenerType)		
		.... *java.util.EventListener[]*		
		public.......................int **getSelectedIndex** ()		
		public synchronized .....String **getSelectedItem** ()		
1.1	3	public synchronized .. Object[] **getSelectedObjects** ()		ε650
1.1		public.......................void **insert** (String item, int index)		
	1	protected................ **String paramString** ()		
1.1	1	protected................. **void processEvent** (AWTEvent e)		
1.1		protected...................void **processItemEvent** (java.awt.event.ItemEvent e)		
1.1		public.......................void **remove** (int position)		
1.1		public.......................void **remove** (String item)		
1.1		public.......................void **removeAll** ()		
1.1	3	public synchronized ....void **removeItemListener** (java.awt.event.ItemListener l)		ε650
		public synchronized ......void **select** (int pos)		
		public synchronized ....void **select** (String str)		

Classes

ChoicePeer | java.awt.peer

ChoicePeer ———————————————— *ComponentPeer* ⌐[1]

- -

> 1 *42 inherited members from ComponentPeer not shown*
> | 1.1 | public.......................void **add** (String item, int index) |
> | | public.......................void **addItem** (String item, int index) |
> | 1.1 | public.......................void **remove** (int index) |
> | 1.3 | public.......................void **removeAll** () |
> | | public.......................void **select** (int index) |

- -

Chromaticity

Chromaticity			javax.print.attribute.standard

Object
1.4 ○ └─*javax.print.attribute.EnumSyntax*[1] - - - - - - - - - *java.io.Serializable*⌄, *Cloneable*⌄
1.4 ●   └─Chromaticity - *javax.print.attribute.DocAttribute* (*javax.print.attribute.Attribute*[2]
                                                     (*java.io.Serializable*)), *javax.print.attribute.PrintRequestAttribute*
                                                     (*javax.print.attribute.Attribute*[2] (*java.io.Serializable*)),
                                                     javax.print.attribute.PrintJobAttribute
                                                     (*javax.print.attribute.Attribute*[2] (*java.io.Serializable*))

✻		protected	**Chromaticity** (int value)	
	1	public . . . . Object	clone ()	
▲		public static final . Chromaticity	**COLOR**	
●	2	public final . . . . Class	**getCategory** ()	ε707
	1	protected . . . . **javax.print**₂	**getEnumValueTable** ()	
		.attribute.EnumSyntax[]		
●	2	public final . . . . String	**getName** ()	ε706,707,708
	1	protected . . . . int	getOffset ()	
	1	protected . . . . **String[]**	**getStringTable** ()	
	1	public . . . . int	getValue ()	
	1	public . . . . int	hashCode ()	
▲		public static final . Chromaticity	**MONOCHROME**	
	1	protected . . . . Object	readResolve () throws java.io.ObjectStreamException	
	1	public . . . . String	toString ()	

Clip			javax.sound.sampled

1.3   *Clip* ─────────────── *DataLine*⌄[1] (*Line*[2])

	2	public . . . . void	addLineListener (*LineListener* listener)	ε731
	1	public . . . . int	available ()	
	2	public . . . . void	close ()	
	1	public . . . . void	drain ()	ε724
	1	public . . . . void	flush ()	
	1	public . . . . int	getBufferSize ()	ε724,728
	2	public . . . . Control	getControl (Control.Type control)	ε730
	2	public . . . . Control[]	getControls ()	
	1	public . . . . AudioFormat	getFormat ()	ε728
		public . . . . int	**getFrameLength** ()	
	1	public . . . . int	getFramePosition ()	
	1	public . . . . float	getLevel ()	
	2	public . . . . Line.Info	getLineInfo ()	
		public . . . . long	**getMicrosecondLength** ()	
	1	public . . . . long	getMicrosecondPosition ()	ε729
	1	public . . . . boolean	isActive ()	
	2	public . . . . boolean	isControlSupported (Control.Type control)	
	2	public . . . . boolean	isOpen ()	
	1	public . . . . boolean	isRunning ()	
		public . . . . void	**loop** (int count)	ε725
▲		public static final . . . . int	**LOOP_CONTINUOUSLY** = -1	ε725
	2	public . . . . void	open () throws LineUnavailableException	
		public . . . . void	**open** (AudioInputStream stream) throws LineUnavailableException,	
			java.io.IOException	ε723
		public . . . . void	**open** (AudioFormat format, byte[] data, int offset, int bufferSize)	
			throws LineUnavailableException	
	2	public . . . . void	removeLineListener (*LineListener* listener)	
		public . . . . void	**setFramePosition** (int frames)	
		public . . . . void	**setLoopPoints** (int start, int end)	
		public . . . . void	**setMicrosecondPosition** (long microseconds)	
	1	public . . . . void	start ()	ε723,725,724
	1	public . . . . void	stop ()	ε724

Clipboard			java.awt.datatransfer

Object
1.1   └─Clipboard

Class   *Interface*   —extends   - - -implements   ○ abstract   ● final   △ static   ▲ static final   ✻ constructor   x x—inherited   x **x**—declared   **x x**—overridden
ε*n*—examples of usage   ⌄—has subclass   package—see other volume

*	public	**Clipboard** (String name)	
	protected . . . . *Transferable*	**contents**	
	public synchronized	**getContents** (Object requestor)	ε637,638
	. . . . *Transferable*		
	public . . . . String	**getName** ()	
	protected . . . . . *ClipboardOwner*	**owner**	
	public synchronized . . . . void	**setContents** (*Transferable* contents, *ClipboardOwner* owner)	ε637,638,639

C

ClipboardOwner		java.awt.datatransfer
1.1	*ClipboardOwner*	
	public . . . . void **lostOwnership** (Clipboard clipboard, *Transferable* contents)	ε639

CMMException	java.awt.color

```
Object
└Throwable ------------------------- java.io.Serializable
  └Exception
    └RuntimeException
      └CMMException
```

1.2		
*	public	**CMMException** (String s)

Color	java.awt

```
Object 1                                                    ε584,791,832,870,878
└Color ------------------------------- Paint 2 (Transparency 3), java.io.Serializable
```

1.2	▲	3	public static final . . . . int	BITMASK = 2	ε666,667
1.4	▲		public static final . . . . Color	**BLACK** = new Color(0, 0, 0)	
	▲		public static final . . . . Color	**black** = new Color(0, 0, 0)	ε695,873
	▲		public static final . . . . Color	**blue** = new Color(0, 0, 255)	ε583,589,590,883,929
1.4	▲		public static final . . . . Color	**BLUE** = new Color(0, 0, 255)	
			public . . . . Color	**brighter** ()	
	*		public	**Color** (int rgb)	
1.2	*		public	**Color** (int rgba, boolean hasalpha)	
	*		public	**Color** (float r, float g, float b)	
	*		public	**Color** (int r, int g, int b)	ε582
1.2	*		public	**Color** (java.awt.color.ColorSpace cspace, float[] components, float alpha)	
1.2	*		public	**Color** (float r, float g, float b, float a)	
1.2	*		public	**Color** (int r, int g, int b, int a)	ε669
1.2		2	public synchronized	**createContext** (java.awt.image.ColorModel cm, Rectangle r, java.awt.geom
			. . . . *PaintContext*	.Rectangle2D r2d, java.awt.geom.AffineTransform xform, RenderingHints hints)
	▲		public static final . . . . Color	**cyan** = new Color(0, 255, 255)	
1.4	▲		public static final . . . . Color	**CYAN** = new Color(0, 255, 255)	
1.4	▲		public static final . . . . Color	**DARK_GRAY** = new Color(64, 64, 64)	
			public . . . . Color	**darker** ()	
	▲		public static final . . . . Color	**darkGray** = new Color(64, 64, 64)	
1.1	△		public static . . . . Color	**decode** (String nm) throws NumberFormatException	
		1	public . . . . **boolean**	**equals** (Object obj)	
1.2			public . . . . int	**getAlpha** ()	
			public . . . . int	**getBlue** ()	
	△		public static . . . . Color	**getColor** (String nm)	
	△		public static . . . . Color	**getColor** (String nm, Color v)	
	△		public static . . . . Color	**getColor** (String nm, int v)	
1.2			public . . . . float[]	**getColorComponents** (float[] compArray)	
1.2			public . . . . float[]	**getColorComponents** (java.awt.color.ColorSpace cspace, float[] compArray)	
1.2			public	**getColorSpace** ()	
			. . . java.awt.color.ColorSpace		
1.2			public . . . . float[]	**getComponents** (float[] compArray)	
1.2			public . . . . float[]	**getComponents** (java.awt.color.ColorSpace cspace, float[] compArray)	
			public . . . . int	**getGreen** ()	
	△		public static . . . . Color	**getHSBColor** (float h, float s, float b)	
			public . . . . int	**getRed** ()	
			public . . . . int	**getRGB** ()	
1.2			public . . . . float[]	**getRGBColorComponents** (float[] compArray)	
1.2			public . . . . float[]	**getRGBComponents** (float[] compArray)	
1.2		3	public . . . . int	**getTransparency** ()	
	▲		public static final . . . . Color	**gray** = new Color(128, 128, 128)	
1.4	▲		public static final . . . . Color	**GRAY** = new Color(128, 128, 128)	

Classes

Color

▲	public static final	Color	**green** = new Color(0, 255, 0)		ε590,883,929,1000
1.4 ▲	public static final	Color	**GREEN** = new Color(0, 255, 0)		ε837
1	public	**int**	**hashCode** ()		
△	public static	int	**HSBtoRGB** (float hue, float saturation, float brightness)		ε585
1.4 ▲	public static final	Color	**LIGHT_GRAY** = new Color(192, 192, 192)		
▲	public static final	Color	**lightGray** = new Color(192, 192, 192)		
▲	public static final	Color	**magenta** = new Color(255, 0, 255)		
1.4 ▲	public static final	Color	**MAGENTA** = new Color(255, 0, 255)		ε837
1.2 ▲ 3	public static final	int	OPAQUE = 1		ε666,667
▲	public static final	Color	**orange** = new Color(255, 200, 0)		
1.4 ▲	public static final	Color	**ORANGE** = new Color(255, 200, 0)		ε837
▲	public static final	Color	**pink** = new Color(255, 175, 175)		ε590
1.4 ▲	public static final	Color	**PINK** = new Color(255, 175, 175)		
▲	public static final	Color	**red** = new Color(255, 0, 0)		ε582,583,585,589,590
1.4 ▲	public static final	Color	**RED** = new Color(255, 0, 0)		
△	public static	float[]	**RGBtoHSB** (int r, int g, int b, float[] hsbvals)		ε585
1	public	**String**	**toString** ()		
1.2 ▲ 3	public static final	int	TRANSLUCENT = 3		ε666
1.4 ▲	public static final	Color	**WHITE** = new Color(255, 255, 255)		
▲	public static final	Color	**white** = new Color(255, 255, 255)		ε602,695,788,876,989
▲	public static final	Color	**yellow** = new Color(255, 255, 0)		ε914
1.4 ▲	public static final	Color	**YELLOW** = new Color(255, 255, 0)		ε837

ColorChooserComponentFactory javax.swing.colorchooser

Object
1.2 └ColorChooserComponentFactory

△	public static	Abstract-ColorChooserPanel[]	**getDefaultChooserPanels** ()
△	public static	javax.swing.JComponent	**getPreviewPanel** ()

ColorChooserUI javax.swing.plaf

Object
1.2 ○ └ComponentUI [1]
1.2 ○   └ColorChooserUI

1 *11 inherited members from ComponentUI not shown*
∗ public   **ColorChooserUI** ()

ColorConvertOp java.awt.image

Object
1.2 └ColorConvertOp - *BufferedImageOp [1], RasterOp [2]*

∗	public		**ColorConvertOp** (java.awt.RenderingHints hints)	
∗	public		**ColorConvertOp** (java.awt.color.ColorSpace cspace, java.awt.RenderingHints hints)	ε676
∗	public		**ColorConvertOp** (java.awt.color.ICC_Profile[] profiles, java.awt.RenderingHints hints)	
∗	public		**ColorConvertOp** (java.awt.color.ColorSpace srcCspace, java.awt.color.ColorSpace dstCspace, java.awt.RenderingHints hints)	
1	public	BufferedImage	**createCompatibleDestImage** (BufferedImage src, ColorModel destCM)	
2	public	WritableRaster	**createCompatibleDestRaster** (Raster src)	
● 1	public final	BufferedImage	**filter** (BufferedImage src, BufferedImage dest)	ε676,672,675,677,678
● 2	public final	WritableRaster	**filter** (Raster src, WritableRaster dest)	
● 1	public final	java.awt.geom.Rectangle2D	**getBounds2D** (BufferedImage src)	
● 2	public final	java.awt.geom.Rectangle2D	**getBounds2D** (Raster src)	
●	public final	java.awt.color.ICC_Profile[]	**getICC_Profiles** ()	
● 1	public final	java.awt.geom.Point2D	**getPoint2D** (java.awt.geom.Point2D srcPt, java.awt.geom.Point2D dstPt)	

Class   *Interface*   —extends   - - -implements   ○ abstract   ● final   △ static   ▲ static final   ∗ constructor   x x—inherited   x **x**—declared   **x x**—overridden
ε*n*—examples of usage   ⌄—has subclass   package—see other volume

●	*1*	public final . . . . **getRenderingHints** ()	
		. . . . . java.awt.RenderingHints	

ColorModel — java.awt.image `C`

		Object[1]		ε660,662,668
○		└ ColorModel - *java.awt.Transparency* [2]	

1.2	▲	*2*	public static final . . . . int	BITMASK = 2	ε666,667
1.2			public . . . . ColorModel	**coerceData** (WritableRaster raster, boolean isAlphaPremultiplied)	
	＊		public	**ColorModel** (int bits)	
1.2	＊		protected	**ColorModel** (int pixel_bits, int[] bits, java.awt.color.ColorSpace cspace, boolean hasAlpha, boolean isAlphaPremultiplied, int transparency, int transferType)	
1.2			public . . . . SampleModel	**createCompatibleSampleModel** (int w, int h)	
1.2			public . . . . WritableRaster	**createCompatibleWritableRaster** (int w, int h)	
		1	public . . . . **boolean**	**equals** (Object obj)	
		1	public . . . . **void**	**finalize** ()	
	○		public abstract . . . . int	**getAlpha** (int pixel)	
1.2			public . . . . int	**getAlpha** (Object inData)	
1.2			public . . . . WritableRaster	**getAlphaRaster** (WritableRaster raster)	
	○		public abstract . . . . int	**getBlue** (int pixel)	
1.2			public . . . . int	**getBlue** (Object inData)	
1.2	●		public final	**getColorSpace** ()	
			. . . java.awt.color.ColorSpace		
1.2			public . . . . int[]	**getComponents** (int pixel, int[] components, int offset)	
1.2			public . . . . int[]	**getComponents** (Object pixel, int[] components, int offset)	
1.2			public . . . . int[]	**getComponentSize** ()	
1.2			public . . . . int	**getComponentSize** (int componentIdx)	
1.4			public . . . . int	**getDataElement** (float[] normComponents, int normOffset)	
1.2			public . . . . int	**getDataElement** (int[] components, int offset)	
1.2			public . . . . Object	**getDataElements** (int rgb, Object pixel)	
1.4			public . . . . Object	**getDataElements** (float[] normComponents, int normOffset, Object obj)	
1.2			public . . . . Object	**getDataElements** (int[] components, int offset, Object obj)	
	○		public abstract . . . . int	**getGreen** (int pixel)	
1.2			public . . . . int	**getGreen** (Object inData)	
1.4			public . . . . float[]	**getNormalizedComponents** (Object pixel, float[] normComponents, int normOffset)	
1.2			public . . . . float[]	**getNormalizedComponents** (int[] components, int offset, float[] normComponents, int normOffset)	
1.2			public . . . . int	**getNumColorComponents** ()	
1.2			public . . . . int	**getNumComponents** ()	
			public . . . . int	**getPixelSize** ()	
	○		public abstract . . . . int	**getRed** (int pixel)	
1.2			public . . . . int	**getRed** (Object inData)	
			public . . . . int	**getRGB** (int pixel)	
1.2			public . . . . int	**getRGB** (Object inData)	
	△		public static . . . . ColorModel	**getRGBdefault** ()	
1.3	●		public final . . . . int	**getTransferType** ()	
1.2		*2*	public . . . . int	**getTransparency** ()	
1.2			public . . . . int[]	**getUnnormalizedComponents** (float[] normComponents, int normOffset, int[] components, int offset)	
1.2	●		public final . . . . boolean	**hasAlpha** ()	ε661
		1	public . . . . **int**	**hashCode** ()	
1.2	●		public final . . . . boolean	**isAlphaPremultiplied** ()	
1.2			public . . . . boolean	**isCompatibleRaster** (Raster raster)	
1.2			public . . . . boolean	**isCompatibleSampleModel** (SampleModel sm)	
1.2	▲	*2*	public static final . . . . int	OPAQUE = 1	ε666,667
			protected . . . . int	**pixel_bits**	
		1	public . . . . **String**	**toString** ()	
1.2			protected . . . . int	**transferType**	
1.2	▲	*2*	public static final . . . . int	TRANSLUCENT = 3	ε666

ColorSelectionModel — javax.swing.colorchooser

1.2		*ColorSelectionModel*	

	public . . . . void	**addChangeListener** (*javax.swing.event.ChangeListener* listener)	
			ε878,879,881,885
	public . . . . java.awt.Color	**getSelectedColor** ()	ε878,879,881,885
	public . . . . void	**removeChangeListener** (*javax.swing.event.ChangeListener* listener)	
	public . . . . void	**setSelectedColor** (java.awt.Color color)	ε883

ColorSpace

Object
1.2 ○ └ColorSpace, - *java.io.Serializable*,

✳	protected		**ColorSpace** (int type, int numcomponents)	
▲	public static final	int	**CS_CIEXYZ** = 1001	
▲	public static final	int	**CS_GRAY** = 1003	ε676
▲	public static final	int	**CS_LINEAR_RGB** = 1004	
▲	public static final	int	**CS_PYCC** = 1002	
▲	public static final	int	**CS_sRGB** = 1000	
○	public abstract	float[]	**fromCIEXYZ** (float[] colorvalue)	
○	public abstract	float[]	**fromRGB** (float[] rgbvalue)	
△	public static	ColorSpace	**getInstance** (int colorspace)	ε676
1.4	public	float	**getMaxValue** (int component)	
1.4	public	float	**getMinValue** (int component)	
	public	String	**getName** (int idx)	
	public	int	**getNumComponents** ()	
	public	int	**getType** ()	
	public	boolean	**isCS_sRGB** ()	
○	public abstract	float[]	**toCIEXYZ** (float[] colorvalue)	
○	public abstract	float[]	**toRGB** (float[] colorvalue)	
▲	public static final	int	**TYPE_2CLR** = 12	
▲	public static final	int	**TYPE_3CLR** = 13	
▲	public static final	int	**TYPE_4CLR** = 14	
▲	public static final	int	**TYPE_5CLR** = 15	
▲	public static final	int	**TYPE_6CLR** = 16	
▲	public static final	int	**TYPE_7CLR** = 17	
▲	public static final	int	**TYPE_8CLR** = 18	
▲	public static final	int	**TYPE_9CLR** = 19	
▲	public static final	int	**TYPE_ACLR** = 20	
▲	public static final	int	**TYPE_BCLR** = 21	
▲	public static final	int	**TYPE_CCLR** = 22	
▲	public static final	int	**TYPE_CMY** = 11	
▲	public static final	int	**TYPE_CMYK** = 9	
▲	public static final	int	**TYPE_DCLR** = 23	
▲	public static final	int	**TYPE_ECLR** = 24	
▲	public static final	int	**TYPE_FCLR** = 25	
▲	public static final	int	**TYPE_GRAY** = 6	
▲	public static final	int	**TYPE_HLS** = 8	
▲	public static final	int	**TYPE_HSV** = 7	
▲	public static final	int	**TYPE_Lab** = 1	
▲	public static final	int	**TYPE_Luv** = 2	
▲	public static final	int	**TYPE_RGB** = 5	
▲	public static final	int	**TYPE_XYZ** = 0	
▲	public static final	int	**TYPE_YCbCr** = 3	
▲	public static final	int	**TYPE_Yxy** = 4	

Object
1.4 ○ └javax.print.attribute.EnumSyntax[1] - - - - - - - - - *java.io.Serializable*,, *Cloneable*,
1.4 ●   └ColorSupported - *javax.print.attribute.PrintServiceAttribute*
                                  (*javax.print.attribute.Attribute*[2] (*java.io.Serializable*))

	1	public	Object	clone ()	
✳		protected		**ColorSupported** (int value)	
●	2	public final	Class	**getCategory** ()	ε707
	1	protected	**javax.print**₂**.attribute.EnumSyntax[]**	**getEnumValueTable** ()	
●	2	public final	String	**getName** ()	ε706,707,708
	1	protected	int	getOffset ()	
	1	protected	**String[]**	**getStringTable** ()	
	1	public	int	getValue ()	
	1	public	int	hashCode ()	
▲		public static final		**NOT_SUPPORTED**	
			ColorSupported		
	1	protected	Object	readResolve () throws java.io.ObjectStreamException	
▲		public static final		**SUPPORTED**	ε703
			ColorSupported		

Class   *Interface* —extends - - -implements ○ abstract ● final △ static ▲ static final ✳ constructor x x—inherited x **x**—declared **x x**—overridden
ε*n*—examples of usage ,—has subclass package—see other volume

1	public . . . . String	toString ()

ColorUIResource   javax.swing.plaf

Object
└java.awt.Color[1] - *java.awt.Paint (java.awt.Transparency [2]), java.io.Serializable*
1.2 └ColorUIResource - *UIResource*

ε584,791,832,870,878

	1	*52 inherited members from java.awt.Color not shown*		
▲	2	public static final . . . . int	BITMASK = 2	ε666,667
*		public	**ColorUIResource** (int rgb)	
*		public	**ColorUIResource** (java.awt.Color c)	
*		public	**ColorUIResource** (float r, float g, float b)	
*		public	**ColorUIResource** (int r, int g, int b)	
▲	2	public static final . . . . int	OPAQUE = 1	ε666,667
▲	2	public static final . . . . int	TRANSLUCENT = 3	ε666

ComboBoxEditor   javax.swing

1.2   *ComboBoxEditor*

public . . . . void	**addActionListener** (*java.awt.event.ActionListener* l)
public . . . . java.awt.Component	**getEditorComponent** ()
public . . . . Object	**getItem** ()
public . . . . void	**removeActionListener** (*java.awt.event.ActionListener* l)
public . . . . void	**selectAll** ()
public . . . . void	**setItem** (Object anObject)

ComboBoxModel   javax.swing

1.2   *ComboBoxModel* ────────────────── *ListModel* [1]

1	public . . . . void	addListDataListener (*javax.swing.event.ListDataListener* l)	ε785
1	public . . . . Object	getElementAt (int index)	ε760,776,777,779,785
	public . . . . Object	**getSelectedItem** ()	ε760
1	public . . . . int	getSize ()	ε760,777,778,780
1	public . . . . void	removeListDataListener (*javax.swing.event.ListDataListener* l)	
	public . . . . void	**setSelectedItem** (Object anItem)	

ComboBoxUI   javax.swing.plaf

Object
1.2 ○ └ComponentUI [1]
1.2 ○ └ComboBoxUI

	1	*11 inherited members from ComponentUI not shown*	
*		public	**ComboBoxUI** ()
○		public abstract . . . . boolean	**isFocusTraversable** (javax.swing.JComboBox c)
○		public abstract . . . . boolean	**isPopupVisible** (javax.swing.JComboBox c)
○		public abstract . . . . void	**setPopupVisible** (javax.swing.JComboBox c, boolean v)

Component   java.awt

Object [1]
○ └Component - *java.awt.image.ImageObserver [2], MenuContainer [3],*
                                                                          java.io.Serializable

ε559,571,573,606,609

	2	*8 inherited members from java.awt.image.ImageObserver not shown*		
D		public . . . . boolean	**action** (Event evt, Object what)	
1.1		public synchronized . . . . void	**add** (PopupMenu popup)	
1.1		public synchronized . . . . void	**addComponentListener** (*java.awt.event.ComponentListener* l)	ε570
1.1		public synchronized . . . . void	**addFocusListener** (*java.awt.event.FocusListener* l)	
1.3		public . . . . void	**addHierarchyBoundsListener** (*java.awt.event.HierarchyBoundsListener* l)	
1.3		public . . . . void	**addHierarchyListener** (*java.awt.event.HierarchyListener* l)	
1.2		public synchronized . . . . void	**addInputMethodListener** (*java.awt.event.InputMethodListener* l)	
1.1		public synchronized . . . . void	**addKeyListener** (*java.awt.event.KeyListener* l)	
1.1		public synchronized . . . . void	**addMouseListener** (*java.awt.event.MouseListener* l)	
1.1		public synchronized . . . . void	**addMouseMotionListener** (*java.awt.event.MouseMotionListener* l)	
1.4		public synchronized . . . . void	**addMouseWheelListener** (*java.awt.event.MouseWheelListener* l)	

C

Classes

445

Component

Ver		Modifiers / Return	Member
		public .... void	**addNotify** ()
1.2		public synchronized .... void	**addPropertyChangeListener** (*java.beans.PropertyChangeListener* listener)
1.2		public synchronized .... void	**addPropertyChangeListener** (String propertyName, *java.beans.PropertyChangeListener* listener)
1.4		public .... void	**applyComponentOrientation** (ComponentOrientation orientation)
1.4		public .... boolean	**areFocusTraversalKeysSet** (int id)
1.1	▲	public static final .... float	**BOTTOM_ALIGNMENT** = 1.0
D		public .... Rectangle	**bounds** ()
1.1	▲	public static final .... float	**CENTER_ALIGNMENT** = 0.5
		public .... int	**checkImage** (Image image, *java.awt.image.ImageObserver* observer)
		public .... int	**checkImage** (Image image, int width, int height, *java.awt.image.ImageObserver* observer)
1.2		protected .... AWTEvent	**coalesceEvents** (AWTEvent existingEvent, AWTEvent newEvent)
1.1	*	protected	**Component** ()
1.1		public .... boolean	**contains** (Point p)
1.1		public .... boolean	**contains** (int x, int y)
		public .... Image	**createImage** (*java.awt.image.ImageProducer* producer)
		public .... Image	**createImage** (int width, int height) ε666
1.4		public .... java. awt.image.VolatileImage	**createVolatileImage** (int width, int height)
1.4		public .... java. awt.image.VolatileImage	**createVolatileImage** (int width, int height, ImageCapabilities caps) throws AWTException
D		public .... void	**deliverEvent** (Event e)
D		public .... void	**disable** ()
1.1	●	protected final .... void	**disableEvents** (long eventsToDisable)
1.1	●	public final .... void	**dispatchEvent** (AWTEvent e)
1.1		public .... void	**doLayout** ()
D		public .... void	**enable** ()
D		public .... void	**enable** (boolean b)
1.1	●	protected final .... void	**enableEvents** (long eventsToEnable)
1.2		public .... void	**enableInputMethods** (boolean enable)
1.2		protected .... void	**firePropertyChange** (String propertyName, Object oldValue, Object newValue)
1.4		protected .... void	**firePropertyChange** (String propertyName, int oldValue, int newValue)
1.4		protected .... void	**firePropertyChange** (String propertyName, boolean oldValue, boolean newValue)
1.3		public .... javax.accessibility. AccessibleContext	**getAccessibleContext** ()
1.1		public .... float	**getAlignmentX** ()
1.1		public .... float	**getAlignmentY** ()
		public .... Color	**getBackground** ()
1.1		public .... Rectangle	**getBounds** () ε572
1.2		public .... Rectangle	**getBounds** (Rectangle rv)
		public .... java.awt.image.ColorModel	**getColorModel** ()
1.1		public .... Component	**getComponentAt** (Point p)
1.1		public .... Component	**getComponentAt** (int x, int y)
1.4		public synchronized . *java.awt. event.ComponentListener[]*	**getComponentListeners** ()
1.2		public .. ComponentOrientation	**getComponentOrientation** ()
1.1		public .... Cursor	**getCursor** () ε574
1.2		public synchronized .... java.awt.dnd.DropTarget	**getDropTarget** ()
1.4		public .... Container	**getFocusCycleRootAncestor** () ε615
1.4		public synchronized ..... *java. awt.event.FocusListener[]*	**getFocusListeners** ()
1.4		public .... *java.util.Set*	**getFocusTraversalKeys** (int id)
1.4		public .... boolean	**getFocusTraversalKeysEnabled** ()
3		public .... Font	**getFont** ()
		public .... FontMetrics	**getFontMetrics** (Font font)
		public .... Color	**getForeground** ()
		public .... Graphics	**getGraphics** ()
1.3		public .. GraphicsConfiguration	**getGraphicsConfiguration** ()
1.2		public .... int	**getHeight** ()
1.4		public synchronized .... *java.awt.event.- HierarchyBoundsListener[]*	**getHierarchyBoundsListeners** ()
1.4		public synchronized . *java.awt. event.HierarchyListener[]*	**getHierarchyListeners** ()
1.4		public .... boolean	**getIgnoreRepaint** ()
1.2		public .... java.awt.im.InputContext	**getInputContext** ()

Class *Interface* —extends - - -implements   ○ abstract   ● final   △ static   ▲ static final   * constructor   x x—inherited   x **x**—declared   **x x**—overridden
ε*n*—examples of usage   ⌐—has subclass   package—see other volume

Since	Modifiers / Return	Member	Ref
1.4	public synchronized . java.awt.event.InputMethodListener[]	**getInputMethodListeners** ()	
1.2	public java.awt.im.InputMethodRequests	**getInputMethodRequests** ()	
1.4	public synchronized . java.awt.event.KeyListener[]	**getKeyListeners** ()	
1.3	public . java.util.EventListener[]	**getListeners** (Class listenerType)	
1.1	public java.util.Locale	**getLocale** ()	
1.1	public Point	**getLocation** ()	ε570
1.2	public Point	**getLocation** (Point rv)	
1.1	public Point	**getLocationOnScreen** ()	
1.1	public Dimension	**getMaximumSize** ()	
1.1	public Dimension	**getMinimumSize** ()	
1.4	public synchronized java.awt.event.MouseListener[]	**getMouseListeners** ()	
1.4	public synchronized java.awt.event.MouseMotionListener[]	**getMouseMotionListeners** ()	
1.4	public synchronized java.awt.event.MouseWheelListener[]	**getMouseWheelListeners** ()	
1.1	public String	**getName** ()	
	public Container	**getParent** ()	ε618
D	public java.awt.peer.ComponentPeer	**getPeer** ()	
1.1	public Dimension	**getPreferredSize** ()	ε913,950
1.4	public synchronized java.beans.-PropertyChangeListener[]	**getPropertyChangeListeners** ()	
1.4	public synchronized java.beans.-PropertyChangeListener[]	**getPropertyChangeListeners** (String propertyName)	
1.1	public Dimension	**getSize** ()	ε570
1.2	public Dimension	**getSize** (Dimension rv)	
	public Toolkit	**getToolkit** ()	
1.1 ●	public final Object	**getTreeLock** ()	
1.2	public int	**getWidth** ()	
1.2	public int	**getX** ()	
1.2	public int	**getY** ()	
D	public boolean	**gotFocus** (Event evt, Object what)	
D	public boolean	**handleEvent** (Event evt)	
1.2	public boolean	**hasFocus** ()	
D	public void	**hide** ()	
2	public boolean	**imageUpdate** (Image img, int infoflags, int x, int y, int w, int h)	
D	public boolean	**inside** (int x, int y)	
	public void	**invalidate** ()	
1.4	public boolean	**isBackgroundSet** ()	
1.4	public boolean	**isCursorSet** ()	
1.2	public boolean	**isDisplayable** ()	
1.2	public boolean	**isDoubleBuffered** ()	
	public boolean	**isEnabled** ()	
1.4	public boolean	**isFocusable** ()	
1.4	public boolean	**isFocusCycleRoot** (Container container)	
1.4	public boolean	**isFocusOwner** ()	
D	public boolean	**isFocusTraversable** ()	
1.4	public boolean	**isFontSet** ()	
1.4	public boolean	**isForegroundSet** ()	
1.2	public boolean	**isLightweight** ()	
1.2	public boolean	**isOpaque** ()	
	public boolean	**isShowing** ()	
	public boolean	**isValid** ()	
	public boolean	**isVisible** ()	
D	public boolean	**keyDown** (Event evt, int key)	
D	public boolean	**keyUp** (Event evt, int key)	
D	public void	**layout** ()	
1.1 ▲	public static final float	**LEFT_ALIGNMENT** = 0.0	
	public void	**list** ()	
	public void	**list** (java.io.PrintStream out)	
1.1	public void	**list** (java.io.PrintWriter out)	
	public void	**list** (java.io.PrintStream out, int indent)	
1.1	public void	**list** (java.io.PrintWriter out, int indent)	
D	public Component	**locate** (int x, int y)	
D	public Point	**location** ()	

Component

D		public .... boolean	**lostFocus** (Event evt, Object what)
D		public .... Dimension	**minimumSize** ()
D		public .... boolean	**mouseDown** (Event evt, int x, int y)
D		public .... boolean	**mouseDrag** (Event evt, int x, int y)
D		public .... boolean	**mouseEnter** (Event evt, int x, int y)
D		public .... boolean	**mouseExit** (Event evt, int x, int y)
D		public .... boolean	**mouseMove** (Event evt, int x, int y)
D		public .... boolean	**mouseUp** (Event evt, int x, int y)
D		public .... void	**move** (int x, int y)
D		public .... void	**nextFocus** ()
		public .... void	**paint** (Graphics g)
		public .... void	**paintAll** (Graphics g)
		protected .... String	**paramString** ()
D	3	public .... boolean	**postEvent** (Event e)
D		public .... Dimension	**preferredSize** ()
		public .... boolean	**prepareImage** (Image image, *java.awt.image.ImageObserver* observer)
		public .... boolean	**prepareImage** (Image image, int width, int height, *java.awt.image.ImageObserver* observer)
		public .... void	**print** (Graphics g)
		public .... void	**printAll** (Graphics g)
1.1		protected .... void	**processComponentEvent** (java.awt.event.ComponentEvent e)
1.1		protected .... void	**processEvent** (AWTEvent e)
1.1		protected .... void	**processFocusEvent** (java.awt.event.FocusEvent e)
1.3		protected .... void	**processHierarchyBoundsEvent** (java.awt.event.HierarchyEvent e)
1.3		protected .... void	**processHierarchyEvent** (java.awt.event.HierarchyEvent e)
1.2		protected .... void	**processInputMethodEvent** (java.awt.event.InputMethodEvent e)
1.1		protected .... void	**processKeyEvent** (java.awt.event.KeyEvent e)
1.1		protected .... void	**processMouseEvent** (java.awt.event.MouseEvent e)
1.1		protected .... void	**processMouseMotionEvent** (java.awt.event.MouseEvent e)
1.4		protected .... void	**processMouseWheelEvent** (java.awt.event.MouseWheelEvent e)
1.1	3	public synchronized .... void	**remove** (MenuComponent popup)
1.1		public synchronized .... void	**removeComponentListener** (*java.awt.event.ComponentListener* l)
1.1		public synchronized .... void	**removeFocusListener** (*java.awt.event.FocusListener* l)
1.3		public .... void	**removeHierarchyBoundsListener** (*java.awt.event.HierarchyBoundsListener* l)
1.3		public .... void	**removeHierarchyListener** (*java.awt.event.HierarchyListener* l)
1.2		public synchronized .... void	**removeInputMethodListener** (*java.awt.event.InputMethodListener* l)
1.1		public synchronized .... void	**removeKeyListener** (*java.awt.event.KeyListener* l)
1.1		public synchronized .... void	**removeMouseListener** (*java.awt.event.MouseListener* l)
1.1		public synchronized .... void	**removeMouseMotionListener** (*java.awt.event.MouseMotionListener* l)
1.4		public synchronized .... void	**removeMouseWheelListener** (*java.awt.event.MouseWheelListener* l)
		public .... void	**removeNotify** ()
1.2		public synchronized .... void	**removePropertyChangeListener** (*java.beans.PropertyChangeListener* listener)
1.2		public synchronized .... void	**removePropertyChangeListener** (String propertyName, *java.beans.PropertyChangeListener* listener)
		public .... void	**repaint** ()
		public .... void	**repaint** (long tm)
		public .... void	**repaint** (int x, int y, int width, int height)
		public .... void	**repaint** (long tm, int x, int y, int width, int height)
		public .... void	**requestFocus** ()
1.4		protected .... boolean	**requestFocus** (boolean temporary)
1.4		public .... boolean	**requestFocusInWindow** ()
1.4		protected .... boolean	**requestFocusInWindow** (boolean temporary)
D		public .... void	**reshape** (int x, int y, int width, int height)
D		public .... void	**resize** (Dimension d)
D		public .... void	**resize** (int width, int height)
1.1 ▲		public static final ...... float	**RIGHT_ALIGNMENT** = 1.0
		public .... void	**setBackground** (Color c)
1.1		public .... void	**setBounds** (Rectangle r)
1.1		public .... void	**setBounds** (int x, int y, int width, int height)
1.2		public .... void	**setComponentOrientation** (ComponentOrientation o)
1.1		public .... void	**setCursor** (Cursor cursor)
1.2		public synchronized .... void	**setDropTarget** (java.awt.dnd.DropTarget dt)
1.1		public .... void	**setEnabled** (boolean b)
1.4		public .... void	**setFocusable** (boolean focusable)
1.4		public .... void	**setFocusTraversalKeys** (int id, *java.util.Set* keystrokes)
1.4		public .... void	**setFocusTraversalKeysEnabled** (boolean focusTraversalKeysEnabled)
		public .... void	**setFont** (Font f)
		public .... void	**setForeground** (Color c)
1.4		public .... void	**setIgnoreRepaint** (boolean ignoreRepaint)
1.1		public .... void	**setLocale** (java.util.Locale l)
1.1		public .... void	**setLocation** (Point p)

ε914 (setBackground)
ε574 (setCursor)

1.1	public ....void	**setLocation** (int x, int y)	
1.1	public ....void	**setName** (String name)	ε830
1.1	public ....void	**setSize** (Dimension d)	
1.1	public ....void	**setSize** (int width, int height)	
1.1	public ....void	**setVisible** (boolean b)	ε738
D	public ....void	**show** ()	
D	public ....void	**show** (boolean b)	
D	public ....Dimension	**size** ()	
1.1 ▲	public static final ....float	**TOP_ALIGNMENT** = 0.0	
1	public ....String	**toString** ()	
1.1	public ....void	**transferFocus** ()	ε612,986
1.4	public ....void	**transferFocusBackward** ()	ε612,986
1.4	public ....void	**transferFocusUpCycle** ()	
	public ....void	**update** (Graphics g)	
	public ....void	**validate** ()	

Component.AccessibleAWTComponent.AccessibleAWTComponentHandler protect | java.awt

Object
1.3 └─Component.AccessibleAWTComponent ₂ - - - - *java.awt.event.ComponentListener* [1] (*java.util.EventListener*)
.AccessibleAWTComponentHandler

*	protected	**Component.AccessibleAWTComponent.AccessibleAWTComponentHandler** ()	
1	public ....void	**componentHidden** (java.awt.event.ComponentEvent e)	ε570
1	public ....void	**componentMoved** (java.awt.event.ComponentEvent e)	ε570
1	public ....void	**componentResized** (java.awt.event.ComponentEvent e)	ε570
1	public ....void	**componentShown** (java.awt.event.ComponentEvent e)	ε570

Component.AccessibleAWTComponent.AccessibleAWTFocusHandler | protected | java.awt

Object
1.3 └─Component.AccessibleAWTComponent ₂ - - - - *java.awt.event.FocusListener* [1] (*java.util.EventListener*)
.AccessibleAWTFocusHandler

*	protected	**Component.AccessibleAWTComponent.AccessibleAWTFocusHandler** ()	
1	public ....void	**focusGained** (java.awt.event.FocusEvent event)	ε649,616,617,618
1	public ....void	**focusLost** (java.awt.event.FocusEvent event)	ε649,616,617,618

Component.BltBufferStrategy | protected | java.awt

Object
1.4 ○ └─java.awt.image.BufferStrategy [1]
1.4 └─Component.BltBufferStrategy

	protected .... java ₂ .awt.image.VolatileImage[]	**backBuffers**	
*	protected	**Component.BltBufferStrategy** (int numBuffers, BufferCapabilities caps)	
	protected ....BufferCapabilities	**caps**	
1	public ....**boolean**	**contentsLost** ()	
1	public ....**boolean**	**contentsRestored** ()	
	protected ....void	**createBackBuffers** (int numBuffers)	
1	public ......**BufferCapabilities**	**getCapabilities** ()	ε602
1	public ....**Graphics**	**getDrawGraphics** ()	ε602
	protected ....int	**height**	
	protected ....void	**revalidate** ()	
1	public .... **void**	**show** ()	ε602
	protected .... boolean	**validatedContents**	
	protected ....int	**width**	

Component.FlipBufferStrategy | protected | java.awt

Object
1.4 ○ └─java.awt.image.BufferStrategy [1]
1.4 └─Component.FlipBufferStrategy

	protected ....BufferCapabilities	**caps**	
1	public ....**boolean**	**contentsLost** ()	
1	public ....**boolean**	**contentsRestored** ()	
	protected ....void	**createBuffers** (int numBuffers, BufferCapabilities caps) throws AWTException	

Component.FlipBufferStrategy

	protected . . . . void	**destroyBuffers** ()	
	protected . . . . Image	**drawBuffer**	
	protected . . . . java.	**drawVBuffer**	
	.awt.image.VolatileImage		
	protected . . . . void	**flip** (BufferCapabilities.FlipContents flipAction)	
*	protected	**Component.FlipBufferStrategy** (int numBuffers, BufferCapabilities caps) throws AWTException	
	protected . . . . Image	**getBackBuffer** ()	
1	public . . . . . . **BufferCapabilities**	**getCapabilities** ()	ε602
1	public . . . . **Graphics**	**getDrawGraphics** ()	ε602
	protected . . . . int	**numBuffers**	
	protected . . . . void	**revalidate** ()	
1	public . . . . **void**	**show** ()	ε602
	protected . . . . boolean	**validatedContents**	

ComponentAdapter   java.awt.event

Object
1.1 ○ └─ComponentAdapter ─ ─ ─ ─ ─ ─ ─ ─ ─ ─ ─ ─ ─ ─ ─ ─ ─ ─ *ComponentListener* [1] (*java.util.EventListener*)

*	public	**ComponentAdapter** ()	ε570
1	public . . . . void	**componentHidden** (ComponentEvent e)	ε570
1	public . . . . void	**componentMoved** (ComponentEvent e)	ε570
1	public . . . . void	**componentResized** (ComponentEvent e)	ε570
1	public . . . . void	**componentShown** (ComponentEvent e)	ε570

ComponentColorModel   java.awt.image

Object   ε660,662,668
○ └─ColorModel [1] ─ *java.awt.Transparency* [2]
1.2   └─ComponentColorModel

▲	2	public static final . . . . int	BITMASK = 2	ε666,667
	1	public . . . . **ColorModel**	**coerceData** (WritableRaster raster, boolean isAlphaPremultiplied)	
1.4	*	public	**ComponentColorModel** (java.awt.color.ColorSpace colorSpace, boolean hasAlpha, boolean isAlphaPremultiplied, int transparency, int transferType)	
	*	public	**ComponentColorModel** (java.awt.color.ColorSpace colorSpace, int[] bits, boolean hasAlpha, boolean isAlphaPremultiplied, int transparency, int transferType)	
	1	public . . . . **SampleModel**	**createCompatibleSampleModel** (int w, int h)	
	1	public . . . . **WritableRaster**	**createCompatibleWritableRaster** (int w, int h)	
	1	public . . . . **boolean**	**equals** (Object obj)	
	1	public . . . . void	finalize ()	
	1	public . . . . **int**	**getAlpha** (int pixel)	
	1	public . . . . **int**	**getAlpha** (Object inData)	
	1	public . . . . **WritableRaster**	**getAlphaRaster** (WritableRaster raster)	
	1	public . . . . **int**	**getBlue** (int pixel)	
	1	public . . . . **int**	**getBlue** (Object inData)	
●	1	public final	getColorSpace ()	
		. . . java.awt.color.ColorSpace		
	1	public . . . . **int[]**	**getComponents** (int pixel, int[] components, int offset)	
	1	public . . . . **int[]**	**getComponents** (Object pixel, int[] components, int offset)	
	1	public . . . . int[]	getComponentSize ()	
	1	public . . . . int	getComponentSize (int componentIdx)	
1.4	1	public . . . . **int**	**getDataElement** (float[] normComponents, int normOffset)	
	1	public . . . . **int**	**getDataElement** (int[] components, int offset)	
	1	public . . . . **Object**	**getDataElements** (int rgb, Object pixel)	
1.4	1	public . . . . **Object**	**getDataElements** (float[] normComponents, int normOffset, Object obj)	
	1	public . . . . **Object**	**getDataElements** (int[] components, int offset, Object obj)	
	1	public . . . . **int**	**getGreen** (int pixel)	
	1	public . . . . **int**	**getGreen** (Object inData)	
1.4	1	public . . . . **float[]**	**getNormalizedComponents** (Object pixel, float[] normComponents, int normOffset)	
	1	public . . . . **float[]**	**getNormalizedComponents** (int[] components, int offset, float[] normComponents, int normOffset)	
	1	public . . . . int	getNumColorComponents ()	
	1	public . . . . int	getNumComponents ()	
	1	public . . . . int	getPixelSize ()	
	1	public . . . . **int**	**getRed** (int pixel)	
	1	public . . . . **int**	**getRed** (Object inData)	

Class   *Interface*   —extends   - - -implements   ○ abstract   ● final   △ static   ▲ static final   ✳ constructor   x x—inherited   x **x**—declared   **x x**—overridden
ε*n*—examples of usage   ‿—has subclass   package—see other volume

450

	1	public........................	**int**	**getRGB** (int pixel)	
	1	public........................	**int**	**getRGB** (Object inData)	
△	1	public static .... ColorModel		getRGBdefault ()	
1.3 ●	1	public final ....int		getTransferType ()	
	1	public........................int		getTransparency ()	
	1	public.......................	**int[]**	**getUnnormalizedComponents** (float[] normComponents, int normOffset, int[] components, int offset)	
●	1	public final .... boolean		hasAlpha ()	ε661
	1	public........................int		hashCode ()	
●	1	public final .... boolean		isAlphaPremultiplied ()	
	1	public.................	**boolean**	**isCompatibleRaster** (Raster raster)	
	1	public.................	**boolean**	**isCompatibleSampleModel** (SampleModel sm)	
▲	2	public static final ....int		OPAQUE = 1	ε666,667
	1	protected.....................int		pixel_bits	
	1	public....................String		toString ()	
	1	protected.....................int		transferType	
▲	2	public static final ....int		TRANSLUCENT = 3	ε666

ComponentEvent
java.awt.event

	Object	ε640,641,643,649,566
1.1	└ java.util.EventObject [1] - - - - - - - - - - - - - - - - - - - *java.io.Serializable*	
1.1 ○	└ java.awt.AWTEvent [2]	
1.1	└ ComponentEvent	

	2	*27 inherited members from java.awt.AWTEvent not shown*		
▲		public static final ....int	**COMPONENT_FIRST** = 100	
▲		public static final ....int	**COMPONENT_HIDDEN** = 103	
▲		public static final ....int	**COMPONENT_LAST** = 103	
▲		public static final ....int	**COMPONENT_MOVED** = 100	
▲		public static final ....int	**COMPONENT_RESIZED** = 101	
▲		public static final ....int	**COMPONENT_SHOWN** = 102	
✳		public........................	**ComponentEvent** (java.awt.Component source, int id)	
		public.... java.awt.Component	**getComponent** ()	ε810,813,1011
	1	public....................Object	getSource ()	ε570,644,886,565,568
	2	public.................	**String paramString** ()	
	1	protected transient......Object	source	

ComponentInputMap
javax.swing

	Object	ε870
1.3	└ InputMap [1] - *java.io.Serializable*	
1.3	└ ComponentInputMap	

	1	public............. KeyStroke[]	allKeys ()	ε860
	1	public....................	**void clear** ()	
✳		public........................	**ComponentInputMap** (JComponent component)	
	1	public....................Object	get (KeyStroke keyStroke)	ε860
		public............. JComponent	**getComponent** ()	
	1	public.............InputMap	getParent ()	ε860,862
	1	public............. KeyStroke[]	keys ()	ε860,862
	1	public.................	**void put** (KeyStroke keyStroke, Object actionMapKey)	ε857,858,861,863,937
	1	public.................	**void remove** (KeyStroke key)	
	1	public.................	**void setParent** (InputMap map)	ε863
	1	public........................int	size ()	

ComponentInputMapUIResource
javax.swing.plaf

	Object	ε870
1.3	└ javax.swing.InputMap [1] - - - - - - - - - - - - - - - - - - - *java.io.Serializable*	
1.3	└ javax.swing.ComponentInputMap [2]	
1.3	└ ComponentInputMapUIResource - - - - - - - *UIResource*	

	1	public. javax.swing.KeyStroke[]	allKeys ()	ε860
	2	public........................void	clear ()	
✳		public........................	**ComponentInputMapUIResource** (javax.swing.JComponent component)	
	1	public....................Object	get (javax.swing.KeyStroke keyStroke)	ε860
	2	public........................	getComponent ()	
		.... javax.swing.JComponent		
	1	public... javax.swing.InputMap	getParent ()	ε860,862

C

Classes

ComponentInputMapUIResource

1	public . javax.swing.KeyStroke[]		keys ()	ε860,862
2	public......................void		put (javax.swing.KeyStroke keyStroke, Object actionMapKey)	ε857,858,861,863,937
2	public......................void		remove (javax.swing.KeyStroke key)	
2	public......................void		setParent (javax.swing.InputMap map)	ε863
1	public........................int		size ()	

ComponentListener — java.awt.event

1.1	*ComponentListener* ———————————— *java.util.EventListener*	ε570,738,743,745,746

public....................void	**componentHidden** (ComponentEvent e)	ε570
public....................void	**componentMoved** (ComponentEvent e)	ε570
public....................void	**componentResized** (ComponentEvent e)	ε570
public....................void	**componentShown** (ComponentEvent e)	ε570

ComponentOrientation — java.awt

Object
└─ComponentOrientation - - - - - - - - - - - - - - - - - *java.io.Serializable*

1.2 ●

△	public static .... ComponentOrientation	**getOrientation** (java.util.Locale locale)
D △	public static .... ComponentOrientation	**getOrientation** (java.util.ResourceBundle bdl)
	public................. boolean	**isHorizontal** ()
	public................. boolean	**isLeftToRight** ()
▲	public static final .... ComponentOrientation	**LEFT_TO_RIGHT**
▲	public static final .... ComponentOrientation	**RIGHT_TO_LEFT**
▲	public static final .... ComponentOrientation	**UNKNOWN**

ComponentPeer — java.awt.peer

ComponentPeer

1.4	public................. boolean	**canDetermineObscurity** ()
	public........................int	**checkImage** (java.awt.Image img, int w, int h, *java.awt.image.ImageObserver* o)
1.3	public.......................void	**coalescePaintEvent** (java.awt.event.PaintEvent e)
1.4	public.......................void	**createBuffers** (int numBuffers, java.awt.BufferCapabilities caps) throws java.awt.AWTException
	public......... java.awt.Image	**createImage** (*java.awt.image.ImageProducer* producer)
	public......... java.awt.Image	**createImage** (int width, int height)
1.4	public....................... java .awt.image.VolatileImage	**createVolatileImage** (int width, int height)
1.4	public.......................void	**destroyBuffers** ()
	public.......................void	**disable** ()
	public.......................void	**dispose** ()
	public.......................void	**enable** ()
1.4	public.......................void	**flip** (java.awt.BufferCapabilities.FlipContents flipAction)
1.4	public......... java.awt.Image	**getBackBuffer** ()
	public.......... java.awt.image.ColorModel	**getColorModel** ()
	public.... java.awt.FontMetrics	**getFontMetrics** (java.awt.Font font)
	public....... java.awt.Graphics	**getGraphics** ()
1.3	public....................... java .awt.GraphicsConfiguration	**getGraphicsConfiguration** ()
1.1	public.............java.awt.Point	**getLocationOnScreen** ()
1.1	public......java.awt.Dimension	**getMinimumSize** ()
1.1	public......java.awt.Dimension	**getPreferredSize** ()
	public...........java.awt.Toolkit	**getToolkit** ()
1.1	public.......................void	**handleEvent** (java.awt.AWTEvent e)
1.4	public................. boolean	**handlesWheelScrolling** ()
	public.......................void	**hide** ()
1.4	public................. boolean	**isFocusable** ()
1.4	public................. boolean	**isObscured** ()
	public......java.awt.Dimension	**minimumSize** ()

Class   *Interface*   —extends   - - -implements   ○ abstract   ● final   △ static   ▲ static final   ✳ constructor   x x—inherited   x **x**—declared   **x x**—overridden
ε*n*—examples of usage   ⌐—has subclass   package—see other volume

	public	void	**paint** (java.awt.Graphics g)
	public	java.awt.Dimension	**preferredSize** ()
	public	boolean	**prepareImage** (java.awt.Image img, int w, int h, *java.awt.image.ImageObserver* o)
	public	void	**print** (java.awt.Graphics g)
	public	void	**repaint** (long tm, int x, int y, int width, int height)
1.4	public	boolean	**requestFocus** (java.awt.Component lightweightChild, boolean temporary, boolean focusedWindowChangeAllowed, long time)
	public	void	**reshape** (int x, int y, int width, int height)
	public	void	**setBackground** (java.awt.Color c)
1.1	public	void	**setBounds** (int x, int y, int width, int height)
1.1	public	void	**setEnabled** (boolean b)
	public	void	**setFont** (java.awt.Font f)
	public	void	**setForeground** (java.awt.Color c)
1.1	public	void	**setVisible** (boolean b)
	public	void	**show** ()
1.4	public	void	**updateCursorImmediately** ()

ComponentSampleModel

Object [1]
1.2 O └SampleModel [2]
1.2   └ComponentSampleModel

	protected	int[]	**bandOffsets**
	protected	int[]	**bankIndices**
*	public		**ComponentSampleModel** (int dataType, int w, int h, int pixelStride, int scanlineStride, int[] bandOffsets)
*	public		**ComponentSampleModel** (int dataType, int w, int h, int pixelStride, int scanlineStride, int[] bankIndices, int[] bandOffsets)
2	public	**SampleModel**	**createCompatibleSampleModel** (int w, int h)
2	public	**DataBuffer**	**createDataBuffer** ()
2	public	**SampleModel**	**createSubsetSampleModel** (int[] bands)
2	protected	int	dataType
1	public	**boolean**	**equals** (Object o)
●	public final	int[]	**getBandOffsets** ()
●	public final	int[]	**getBankIndices** ()
2	public	**Object**	**getDataElements** (int x, int y, Object obj, DataBuffer data)
2	public	Object	getDataElements (int x, int y, int w, int h, Object obj, DataBuffer data)
● 2	public final	int	**getDataType** ()
● 2	public final	int	getHeight ()
● 2	public final	int	getNumBands ()
● 2	public final	**int**	**getNumDataElements** ()
	public	int	**getOffset** (int x, int y)
	public	int	**getOffset** (int x, int y, int b)
2	public	**int[]**	**getPixel** (int x, int y, int[] iArray, DataBuffer data)
2	public	float[]	getPixel (int x, int y, float[] fArray, DataBuffer data)
2	public	double[]	getPixel (int x, int y, double[] dArray, DataBuffer data)
2	public	**int[]**	**getPixels** (int x, int y, int w, int h, int[] iArray, DataBuffer data)
2	public	float[]	getPixels (int x, int y, int w, int h, float[] fArray, DataBuffer data)
2	public	double[]	getPixels (int x, int y, int w, int h, double[] dArray, DataBuffer data)
●	public final	int	**getPixelStride** ()
2	public	**int**	**getSample** (int x, int y, int b, DataBuffer data)
2	public	**double**	**getSampleDouble** (int x, int y, int b, DataBuffer data)
2	public	**float**	**getSampleFloat** (int x, int y, int b, DataBuffer data)
2	public	**int[]**	**getSamples** (int x, int y, int w, int h, int b, int[] iArray, DataBuffer data)
2	public	float[]	getSamples (int x, int y, int w, int h, int b, float[] fArray, DataBuffer data)
2	public	double[]	getSamples (int x, int y, int w, int h, int b, double[] dArray, DataBuffer data)
● 2	public final	**int[]**	**getSampleSize** ()
● 2	public final	**int**	**getSampleSize** (int band)
●	public final	int	**getScanlineStride** ()
2	public	int	getTransferType ()
● 2	public final	int	getWidth ()
1	public	**int**	**hashCode** ()
2	protected	int	height
2	protected	**int**	**numBands**
	protected	int	**numBanks**
	protected	int	**pixelStride**
	protected	int	**scanlineStride**
2	public	**void**	**setDataElements** (int x, int y, Object obj, DataBuffer data)
2	public	void	setDataElements (int x, int y, int w, int h, Object obj, DataBuffer data)
2	public	**void**	**setPixel** (int x, int y, int[] iArray, DataBuffer data)
2	public	void	setPixel (int x, int y, float[] fArray, DataBuffer data)
2	public	void	setPixel (int x, int y, double[] dArray, DataBuffer data)

ComponentSampleModel

2	public	**void**	**setPixels** (int x, int y, int w, int h, int[] iArray, DataBuffer data)
2	public	void	setPixels (int x, int y, int w, int h, float[] fArray, DataBuffer data)
2	public	void	setPixels (int x, int y, int w, int h, double[] dArray, DataBuffer data)
2	public	**void**	**setSample** (int x, int y, int b, double s, DataBuffer data)
2	public	**void**	**setSample** (int x, int y, int b, float s, DataBuffer data)
2	public	**void**	**setSample** (int x, int y, int b, int s, DataBuffer data)
2	public	**void**	**setSamples** (int x, int y, int w, int h, int b, int[] iArray, DataBuffer data)
2	public	void	setSamples (int x, int y, int w, int h, int b, float[] fArray, DataBuffer data)
2	public	void	setSamples (int x, int y, int w, int h, int b, double[] dArray, DataBuffer data)
2	protected	int	width

ComponentUI — javax.swing.plaf

```
Object
 └ComponentUI
```
1.2 ○

✳	public		**ComponentUI** ()
	public	boolean	**contains** (javax.swing.JComponent c, int x, int y)
△	public static	ComponentUI	**createUI** (javax.swing.JComponent c)
	public	javax.accessibility.Accessible	**getAccessibleChild** (javax.swing.JComponent c, int i)
	public	int	**getAccessibleChildrenCount** (javax.swing.JComponent c)
	public	java.awt.Dimension	**getMaximumSize** (javax.swing.JComponent c)
	public	java.awt.Dimension	**getMinimumSize** (javax.swing.JComponent c)
	public	java.awt.Dimension	**getPreferredSize** (javax.swing.JComponent c)
	public	void	**installUI** (javax.swing.JComponent c)
	public	void	**paint** (java.awt.Graphics g, javax.swing.JComponent c)
	public	void	**uninstallUI** (javax.swing.JComponent c)
	public	void	**update** (java.awt.Graphics g, javax.swing.JComponent c)

ComponentView — javax.swing.text

```
Object
 └View 1 - - - - - - - - - - - - - - - - - - - - - - - - - - - javax.swing.SwingConstants 2
    └ComponentView
```
1.2 ○
1.2

1	*44 inherited members from View not shown*		
2	*19 inherited members from javax.swing.SwingConstants not shown*		
✳	public		**ComponentView** (*Element* elem)
	protected	java.awt.Component	**createComponent** ()
1	public	**float**	**getAlignment** (int axis)
●	public final	java.awt.Component	**getComponent** ()
1	public	**float**	**getMaximumSpan** (int axis)
1	public	**float**	**getMinimumSpan** (int axis)
1	public	**float**	**getPreferredSpan** (int axis)
1	public	***java.awt.Shape***	**modelToView** (int pos, *java.awt.Shape* a, Position.Bias b) throws BadLocationException
1	public	**void**	**paint** (java.awt.Graphics g, *java.awt.Shape* a)
1	public	**void**	**setParent** (View p)
1	public	**int**	**viewToModel** (float x, float y, *java.awt.Shape* a, Position.Bias[] bias)

Composite — java.awt

Composite
1.2

	public	*CompositeContext*	**createContext** (java.awt.image.ColorModel srcColorModel, java.awt.image.ColorModel dstColorModel, RenderingHints hints)

CompositeContext — java.awt

CompositeContext
1.2

	public	void	**compose** (java.awt.image.Raster src, java.awt.image.Raster dstIn, java.awt.image.WritableRaster dstOut)
	public	void	**dispose** ()

Class   *Interface*   —extends   - - -implements   ○ abstract   ● final   △ static   ▲ static final   ✳ constructor   x x—inherited   x **x**—declared   **x x**—overridden
ε*n*—examples of usage   ⌄—has subclass   package—see other volume

CompositeView

```
        Object
1.2 ○   └View 1 ---------------------------- javax.swing.SwingConstants 2
1.2 ○      └CompositeView ↲
```

	1	*42 inherited members from View not shown*	
	2	*19 inherited members from javax.swing.SwingConstants not shown*	
○		protected abstract ....void	**childAllocation** (int index, java.awt.Rectangle a)
*		public........................	**CompositeView** (*Element* elem)
		protected.............. boolean	**flipEastAndWestAtEnds** (int position, Position.Bias bias)
		protected ....short	**getBottomInset** ()
	1	public......... ***java.awt.Shape***	**getChildAllocation** (int index, *java.awt.Shape* a)
		protected .. java.awt.Rectangle	**getInsideAllocation** (*java.awt.Shape* a)
		protected ....short	**getLeftInset** ()
		protected ....int	**getNextEastWestVisualPositionFrom** (int pos, Position.Bias b, *java.awt.Shape* a, int direction, Position.Bias[] biasRet) throws BadLocationException
		protected ....int	**getNextNorthSouthVisualPositionFrom** (int pos, Position.Bias b, *java.awt.Shape* a, int direction, Position.Bias[] biasRet) throws BadLocationException
	1	public..................... **int**	**getNextVisualPositionFrom** (int pos, Position.Bias b, *java.awt.Shape* a, int direction, Position.Bias[] biasRet) throws BadLocationException
		protected ....short	**getRightInset** ()
		protected ....short	**getTopInset** ()
	1	public..................... **View**	**getView** (int n) ε978
○		protected abstract .... View	**getViewAtPoint** (int x, int y, java.awt.Rectangle alloc)
		protected .... View	**getViewAtPosition** (int pos, java.awt.Rectangle a)
	1	public..................... **int**	**getViewCount** () ε978
1.3	1	public..................... **int**	**getViewIndex** (int pos, Position.Bias b)
		protected ....int	**getViewIndexAtPosition** (int pos)
○		protected abstract .... boolean	**isAfter** (int x, int y, java.awt.Rectangle alloc)
○		protected abstract .... boolean	**isBefore** (int x, int y, java.awt.Rectangle alloc)
		protected ....void	**loadChildren** (*ViewFactory* f)
	1	public......... ***java.awt.Shape***	**modelToView** (int pos, *java.awt.Shape* a, Position.Bias b) throws BadLocationException
	1	public......... ***java.awt.Shape***	**modelToView** (int p0, Position.Bias b0, int p1, Position.Bias b1, *java.awt.Shape* a) throws BadLocationException
	1	public..................... **void**	**replace** (int offset, int length, View[] views)
		protected ....void	**setInsets** (short top, short left, short bottom, short right)
		protected ....void	**setParagraphInsets** (*AttributeSet* attr)
	1	public..................... **void**	**setParent** (View parent)
	1	public..................... **int**	**viewToModel** (float x, float y, *java.awt.Shape* a, Position.Bias[] bias)

CompoundBorder

ε873

```
        Object
1.2 ○   └AbstractBorder 1 --------------------- Border, java.io.Serializable ↲
1.2        └CompoundBorder ↲
```

*		public........................	**CompoundBorder** ()
*		public........................	**CompoundBorder** (*Border* outsideBorder, *Border* insideBorder)
	1	public......... **java.awt.Insets**	**getBorderInsets** (java.awt.Component c)
	1	public......... **java.awt.Insets**	**getBorderInsets** (java.awt.Component c, java.awt.Insets insets)
		public.................. *Border*	**getInsideBorder** ()
	1	public...... java.awt.Rectangle	getInteriorRectangle (java.awt.Component c, int x, int y, int width, int height)
△	1	public static .... java.awt.Rectangle	getInteriorRectangle (java.awt.Component c, *Border* b, int x, int y, int width, int height)
		public.................. *Border*	**getOutsideBorder** ()
		protected .... *Border*	**insideBorder**
	1	public.................. **boolean**	**isBorderOpaque** ()
		protected .... *Border*	**outsideBorder**
	1	public..................... **void**	**paintBorder** (java.awt.Component c, java.awt.Graphics g, int x, int y, int width, int height)

CompoundControl

```
        Object
1.3 ○   └Control 1
1.3 ○      └CompoundControl
```

*		protected	**CompoundControl** (CompoundControl.Type type, Control[] memberControls)
		public.................Control[]	**getMemberControls** ()

CompoundControl

1	public	Control.Type	getType ()
1	public	**String**	**toString** ()

CompoundControl.Type

Object
1.3 └Control.Type [1]
1.3   └CompoundControl.Type

●	1	public final	boolean	equals (Object obj)
●	1	public final	int	hashCode ()
●	1	public final	String	toString ()
✳		protected		**CompoundControl.Type** (String name)

CompoundEdit

Object
1.2 └AbstractUndoableEdit [1] - - - - - - - - - - - - - - - - - - *UndoableEdit*, *java.io.Serializable*⌄
1.2   └CompoundEdit⌄

	1	public	**boolean**	**addEdit** (*UndoableEdit* anEdit)	ε1034
	1	public	**boolean**	**canRedo** ()	ε1034
	1	public	**boolean**	**canUndo** ()	ε1034
✳		public		**CompoundEdit** ()	
	1	public	**void**	**die** ()	
		protected	java.util.Vector	**edits**	
		public	void	**end** ()	
	1	public	**String**	**getPresentationName** ()	
	1	public	**String**	**getRedoPresentationName** ()	
	1	public	**String**	**getUndoPresentationName** ()	
		public	boolean	**isInProgress** ()	
	1	public	**boolean**	**isSignificant** ()	
		protected	*UndoableEdit*	**lastEdit** ()	
	1	public	**void**	**redo** () throws CannotRedoException	ε1034
▲	1	protected static final	String	RedoName	
	1	public	boolean	replaceEdit (*UndoableEdit* anEdit)	
	1	public	**String**	**toString** ()	
	1	public	**void**	**undo** () throws CannotUndoException	ε1034
▲	1	protected static final	String	UndoName	

Compression

javax.print.attribute.standard

Object
1.4 ○ └javax.print.attribute.EnumSyntax [1] - - - - - - - - - *java.io.Serializable*⌄, *Cloneable*⌄
1.4   └Compression - *javax.print.attribute.DocAttribute* (*javax.print.attribute.Attribute* [2]
                       (*java.io.Serializable*))

	1	public	Object	clone ()	
▲		public static final	.Compression	**COMPRESS**	
✳		protected		**Compression** (int value)	
▲		public static final	.Compression	**DEFLATE**	
●	2	public final	Class	**getCategory** ()	ε707
	1	protected	**javax.print** [2] **.attribute.EnumSyntax[]**	**getEnumValueTable** ()	
●	2	public final	String	**getName** ()	ε706,707,708
	1	protected	int	**getOffset** ()	
	1	protected	**String[]**	**getStringTable** ()	
	1	public	int	getValue ()	
▲		public static final	.Compression	**GZIP**	
	1	public	int	hashCode ()	
▲		public static final	.Compression	**NONE**	
	1	protected	Object	readResolve () throws java.io.ObjectStreamException	
	1	public	String	toString ()	

Class *Interface* —extends - - -implements ○ abstract ● final △ static ▲ static final ✳ constructor x x—inherited x **x**—declared **x x**—overridden
ε*n*—examples of usage ⌄—has subclass package—see other volume

		Container	java.awt

ε606,618,733,953,988

```
Object
 └─Component¹ ------------------------ java.awt.image.ImageObserver², MenuContainer,
                                       java.io.Serializable
    └─Container
```

C

1 177 inherited members from Component not shown
2 8 inherited members from java.awt.image.ImageObserver not shown

Ver	1	Modifiers / Return	Member	ε refs
		public Component	**add** (Component comp)	ε575,581,590,610,611
1.1		public void	**add** (Component comp, Object constraints)	ε733,694,705,732,778
		public Component	**add** (Component comp, int index)	
		public Component	**add** (String name, Component comp)	
1.1		public void	**add** (Component comp, Object constraints, int index)	
1.1		public synchronized void	**addContainerListener** (java.awt.event.ContainerListener l)	ε573
1.1		protected void	**addImpl** (Component comp, Object constraints, int index)	
	1	public void	**addNotify** ()	
1.2	1	public void	**addPropertyChangeListener** (java.beans.PropertyChangeListener listener)	
1.2	1	public void	**addPropertyChangeListener** (String propertyName, java.beans.PropertyChangeListener listener)	
1.4	1	public void	**applyComponentOrientation** (ComponentOrientation o)	
1.4	1	public boolean	**areFocusTraversalKeysSet** (int id)	
1.1 *		public	**Container** ()	
D		public int	**countComponents** ()	
D	1	public void	**deliverEvent** (Event e)	
1.1	1	public void	**doLayout** ()	
1.2		public Component	**findComponentAt** (Point p)	
1.2		public Component	**findComponentAt** (int x, int y)	
1.1	1	public float	**getAlignmentX** ()	
1.1	1	public float	**getAlignmentY** ()	
		public Component	**getComponent** (int n)	ε572
1.1	1	public Component	**getComponentAt** (Point p)	
1.1	1	public Component	**getComponentAt** (int x, int y)	
1.1		public int	**getComponentCount** ()	ε572
		public Component[]	**getComponents** ()	ε572
1.4		public synchronized java.awt.event.ContainerListener[]	**getContainerListeners** ()	
1.4	1	public java.util.Set	**getFocusTraversalKeys** (int id)	ε610
1.4		public FocusTraversalPolicy	**getFocusTraversalPolicy** ()	ε615
1.1		public Insets	**getInsets** ()	
		public LayoutManager	**getLayout** ()	
1.3	1	public java.util.EventListener[]	**getListeners** (Class listenerType)	
1.1	1	public Dimension	**getMaximumSize** ()	
1.1	1	public Dimension	**getMinimumSize** ()	
1.1	1	public Dimension	**getPreferredSize** ()	
D		public Insets	**insets** ()	
	1	public void	**invalidate** ()	
1.1		public boolean	**isAncestorOf** (Component c)	
1.4		public boolean	**isFocusCycleRoot** ()	
1.4	1	public boolean	**isFocusCycleRoot** (Container container)	
1.4		public boolean	**isFocusTraversalPolicySet** ()	
D	1	public void	**layout** ()	
	1	public void	**list** (java.io.PrintStream out, int indent)	
1.1	1	public void	**list** (java.io.PrintWriter out, int indent)	
D	1	public Component	**locate** (int x, int y)	
D	1	public Dimension	**minimumSize** ()	
	1	public void	**paint** (Graphics g)	ε575,551,557,558,878
		public void	**paintComponents** (Graphics g)	
	1	protected String	**paramString** ()	
D	1	public Dimension	**preferredSize** ()	
	1	public void	**print** (Graphics g)	
		public void	**printComponents** (Graphics g)	
1.1		protected void	**processContainerEvent** (java.awt.event.ContainerEvent e)	
1.1	1	protected void	**processEvent** (AWTEvent e)	
1.1		public void	**remove** (int index)	ε831,832
		public void	**remove** (Component comp)	ε831
		public void	**removeAll** ()	ε831
1.1		public synchronized void	**removeContainerListener** (java.awt.event.ContainerListener l)	
	1	public void	**removeNotify** ()	
1.4		public void	**setFocusCycleRoot** (boolean focusCycleRoot)	
1.4	1	public void	**setFocusTraversalKeys** (int id, java.util.Set keystrokes)	ε610
1.4		public void	**setFocusTraversalPolicy** (FocusTraversalPolicy policy)	

Classes

Container

	1	public.....................**void setFont** (Font f)		
		public.....................void **setLayout** (*LayoutManager* mgr)		ε613,622,624,625,627
1.4	1	public.....................**void transferFocusBackward** ()		
1.4		public.....................void **transferFocusDownCycle** ()		
	1	public.....................**void update** (Graphics g)		
	1	public.....................**void validate** ()		ε601,674,928,936
1.1		protected.....................void **validateTree** ()		

Container.AccessibleAWTContainer.AccessibleContainerHandler protecte java.awt

Object
1.3 └─Container.AccessibleAWTContainer ₂ - - - - - - - *java.awt.event.ContainerListener* [1] (*java.util.EventListener*)
　　　.AccessibleContainerHandler

*	protected.....................**Container.AccessibleAWTContainer.AccessibleContainerHandler** ()		
	1	public.....................void **componentAdded** (java.awt.event.ContainerEvent e)	ε573
	1	public.....................void **componentRemoved** (java.awt.event.ContainerEvent e)	ε573

ContainerAdapter java.awt.event

Object
1.1 ○ └─ContainerAdapter - - - - - - - - - - - - - - - - - - - *ContainerListener* [1] (*java.util.EventListener*)

	1	public.....................void **componentAdded** (ContainerEvent e)	ε573
	1	public.....................void **componentRemoved** (ContainerEvent e)	ε573
*		public.....................**ContainerAdapter** ()	ε573

ContainerEvent java.awt.event

Object　　　　　　　　　　　　　　　　　　　　　　　　　　　　　ε640,641,643,649,566
1.1 └─ java.util.EventObject [1] - - - - - - - - - - - - - - - - - *java.io.Serializable* ⌄
1.1 ○　└─java.awt.AWTEvent [2]
1.1　　　└─ComponentEvent [3]
1.1　　　　　└─ContainerEvent

	2	*27 inherited members from java.awt.AWTEvent not shown*	
▲		public static final.............int **COMPONENT_ADDED** = 300	
▲	3	public static final.............int COMPONENT_FIRST = 100	
▲	3	public static final.............int COMPONENT_HIDDEN = 103	
▲	3	public static final.............int COMPONENT_LAST = 103	
▲	3	public static final.............int COMPONENT_MOVED = 100	
▲		public static final.............int **COMPONENT_REMOVED** = 301	
▲	3	public static final.............int COMPONENT_RESIZED = 101	
▲	3	public static final.............int COMPONENT_SHOWN = 102	
▲		public static final.............int **CONTAINER_FIRST** = 300	
▲		public static final.............int **CONTAINER_LAST** = 301	
*		public.....................**ContainerEvent** (java.awt.Component source, int id, java.awt.Component child)	
		public.... java.awt.Component **getChild** ()	ε573
	3	public.... java.awt.Component getComponent ()	ε810,813,1011
		public.......java.awt.Container **getContainer** ()	
	1	public.....................Object getSource ()	ε644,886,565,568,570
	3	public.....................**String paramString** ()	
	1	protected transient......Object source	

ContainerListener java.awt.event

1.1 *ContainerListener*──────────────────── *java.util.EventListener* ⌄　　ε573,738,743,745,746

	public.....................void **componentAdded** (ContainerEvent e)	ε573
	public.....................void **componentRemoved** (ContainerEvent e)	ε573

Class　*Interface*　—extends　- - -implements　○ abstract　● final　△ static　▲ static final　✴ constructor　x x—inherited　x **x**—declared　**x x**—overridden
εn—examples of usage　⌄—has subclass　package—see other volume

ContainerOrderFocusTraversalPolicy　　　　　　java.awt

```
        Object
1.4 O   └FocusTraversalPolicy 1
1.4         └ContainerOrderFocusTraversalPolicy ----- java.io.Serializable
```

	protected .... boolean	**accept** (Component aComponent)	
*	public..........................	**ContainerOrderFocusTraversalPolicy** ()	
1	public............ **Component**	**getComponentAfter** (Container focusCycleRoot, Component aComponent)	ε615
1	public............ **Component**	**getComponentBefore** (Container focusCycleRoot, Component aComponent)	ε615
1	public............ **Component**	**getDefaultComponent** (Container focusCycleRoot)	ε615
1	public............ **Component**	**getFirstComponent** (Container focusCycleRoot)	
	public............. boolean	**getImplicitDownCycleTraversal** ()	
1	public............. Component	getInitialComponent (Window window)	
1	public............ **Component**	**getLastComponent** (Container focusCycleRoot)	
	public......................void	**setImplicitDownCycleTraversal** (boolean implicitDownCycleTraversal)	

ContainerPeer　　　　　　java.awt.peer

```
        ContainerPeer ─────────────── ComponentPeer 1
    1  42 inherited members from ComponentPeer not shown
```

1.4	public.....................void	**beginLayout** ()
1.1	public.....................void	**beginValidate** ()
1.4	public.....................void	**endLayout** ()
1.1	public.....................void	**endValidate** ()
1.1	public.......... java.awt.Insets	**getInsets** ()
	public.......... java.awt.Insets	**insets** ()
1.4	public........... boolean	**isPaintPending** ()

ContentModel　　　　　　javax.swing.text.html.parser

```
        Object 1
1.2 ●   └ContentModel ----------------------- java.io.Serializable
```

	public...................Object	**content**
*	public........................	**ContentModel** ()
*	public........................	**ContentModel** (Element content)
*	public........................	**ContentModel** (int type, ContentModel content)
*	public........................	**ContentModel** (int type, Object content, ContentModel next)
	public................ boolean	**empty** ()
	public................ Element	**first** ()
	public................ boolean	**first** (Object token)
	public.....................void	**getElements** (java.util.Vector elemVec)
	public.........ContentModel	**next**
1	public................... **String**	**toString** ()
	public........................int	**type**

ContextualRenderedImageFactory　　　　　　java.awt.image.renderable

```
1.2     ContextualRenderedImageFactory────── RenderedImageFactory 1
```

1	public................. java.awt.ᵒ image.RenderedImage	create (ParameterBlock paramBlock, java.awt.RenderingHints hints)
	public................. java.awt.ᵒ image.RenderedImage	**create** (RenderContext renderContext, ParameterBlock paramBlock)
	public................. . java.awt.geom.Rectangle2D	**getBounds2D** (ParameterBlock paramBlock)
	public...................Object	**getProperty** (ParameterBlock paramBlock, String name)
	public................. String[]	**getPropertyNames** ()
	public................ boolean	**isDynamic** ()
	public..........RenderContext	**mapRenderContext** (int i, RenderContext renderContext, ParameterBlock paramBlock, *RenderableImage* image)

Control❷

			javax.sound.sampled

Object[1]
1.3 ○ └Control⌄

*	protected	**Control** (Control.Type type)
	public .... Control.Type	**getType** ()
1	public .... **String**	**toString** ()

Control.Type

			javax.sound.sampled

Object[1]
1.3 └Control.Type⌄

●	1	public final .... **boolean**	**equals** (Object obj)
●	1	public final .... **int**	**hashCode** ()
●	1	public final .... **String**	**toString** ()
*		protected	**Control.Type** (String name)

ControllerEventListener

			javax.sound.midi

1.3 *ControllerEventListener*————————————*java.util.EventListener*⌄   ε738,743,745,746,752

	public .... void	**controlChange** (ShortMessage event)

ConvolveOp

			java.awt.image

Object
1.2 └ConvolveOp - *BufferedImageOp*[1], *RasterOp*[2]

*		public	**ConvolveOp** (Kernel kernel)	ε677,678,679
*		public	**ConvolveOp** (Kernel kernel, int edgeCondition, java.awt.RenderingHints hints)	
	1	public .... BufferedImage	**createCompatibleDestImage** (BufferedImage src, ColorModel destCM)	
	2	public .... WritableRaster	**createCompatibleDestRaster** (Raster src)	
▲		public static final .... int	**EDGE_NO_OP** = 1	
▲		public static final .... int	**EDGE_ZERO_FILL** = 0	
●	1	public final ..... BufferedImage	**filter** (BufferedImage src, BufferedImage dst)	ε672,675,676,677,678
●	2	public final ..... WritableRaster	**filter** (Raster src, WritableRaster dst)	
●	1	public final	**getBounds2D** (BufferedImage src)	
		. java.awt.geom.Rectangle2D		
●	2	public final	**getBounds2D** (Raster src)	
		. java.awt.geom.Rectangle2D		
		public .... int	**getEdgeCondition** ()	
●		public final .... Kernel	**getKernel** ()	
●	1	public final	**getPoint2D** (java.awt.geom.Point2D srcPt, java.awt.geom.Point2D dstPt)	
		.... java.awt.geom.Point2D		
●	1	public final	**getRenderingHints** ()	
		..... java.awt.RenderingHints		

Copies

			javax.print.attribute.standard

Object
1.4 ○ └javax.print.attribute.IntegerSyntax[1] - - - - - - - - *java.io.Serializable*⌄, *Cloneable*⌄
1.4 ● └Copies - *javax.print.attribute.PrintRequestAttribute*
　　　　　　　　　　　　　　　　　　　　　　　　(*javax.print.attribute.Attribute*[2] (*java.io.Serializable*)),
　　　　　　　　　　　　　　　　　　　　　　　　javax.print.attribute.PrintJobAttribute
　　　　　　　　　　　　　　　　　　　　　　　　(*javax.print.attribute.Attribute*[2] (*java.io.Serializable*))

*		public	**Copies** (int value)	ε711
	1	public .... **boolean**	**equals** (Object object)	
●	2	public final .... Class	**getCategory** ()	ε707
●	2	public final .... String	**getName** ()	ε706,707,708
	1	public .... int	getValue ()	
	1	public .... int	hashCode ()	
	1	public .... String	toString ()	

Class　*Interface*　—extends　- - -implements　○ abstract　● final　△ static　▲ static final　✻ constructor　× x—inherited　× **x**—declared　**x x**—overridden
ε*n*—examples of usage　⌄—has subclass　package—see other volume

CopiesSupported

javax.print.attribute.standard

```
        Object
1.4 ○   └─javax.print.attribute.SetOfIntegerSyntax¹ - - - - java.io.Serializable⌄, Cloneable⌄
1.4 ●       └─CopiesSupported - - - - - - - - - - - - - - - - - - - - javax.print.attribute.SupportedValuesAttribute
                                    (javax.print.attribute.Attribute² (java.io.Serializable))
```

	1	public.................	boolean	contains (int x)	
	1	public.................	boolean	contains (javax.print.attribute.IntegerSyntax attribute)	
*		public........................		**CopiesSupported** (int member)	
*		public........................		**CopiesSupported** (int lowerBound, int upperBound)	
	1	public.................	**boolean**	**equals** (Object object)	
●	2	public final	Class	**getCategory** ()	ε707
	1	public.................	int[][]	getMembers ()	
●	2	public final	String	**getName** ()	ε706,707,708
	1	public........................	int	hashCode ()	
	1	public........................	int	next (int x)	
	1	public.................	String	toString ()	

CropImageFilter

java.awt.image
ε665

```
        Object
        └─ImageFilter¹ - - - - - - - - - - - - - - - - - - - - - - - - ImageConsumer², Cloneable⌄
            └─CropImageFilter
```

	2	9 inherited members from ImageConsumer not shown			
	1	public....................	Object	clone ()	
	1	protected	ImageConsumer	consumer	
*		public........................		**CropImageFilter** (int x, int y, int w, int h)	ε664
	1	public.................	ImageFilter	getFilterInstance (ImageConsumer ic)	
	1	public........................	void	imageComplete (int status)	
	1	public........................	void	resendTopDownLeftRight (ImageProducer ip)	
	1	public........................	void	setColorModel (ColorModel model)	
	1	public........................	**void**	**setDimensions** (int w, int h)	
	1	public........................	void	setHints (int hints)	
	1	public........................	**void**	**setPixels** (int x, int y, int w, int h, ColorModel model, byte[] pixels, int off, int scansize)	
	1	public........................	**void**	**setPixels** (int x, int y, int w, int h, ColorModel model, int[] pixels, int off, int scansize)	
	1	public........................	**void**	**setProperties** (java.util.Hashtable props)	

CSS

javax.swing.text.html

```
        Object
1.2     └─CSS - - - - - - - - - - - - - - - - - - - - - - - - - - - - - - java.io.Serializable⌄
```

*	public........................		**CSS** ()	
△	public static	CSS.Attribute[]	**getAllAttributeKeys** ()	
▲	public static final	CSS.Attribute	**getAttribute** (String name)	

CSS.Attribute

javax.swing.text.html

```
        Object¹
1.2 ●   └─CSS.Attribute
```

▲	public static final	CSS.Attribute	**BACKGROUND**
▲	public static final	CSS.Attribute	**BACKGROUND_ATTACHMENT**
▲	public static final	CSS.Attribute	**BACKGROUND_COLOR**
▲	public static final	CSS.Attribute	**BACKGROUND_IMAGE**
▲	public static final	CSS.Attribute	**BACKGROUND_POSITION**
▲	public static final	CSS.Attribute	**BACKGROUND_REPEAT**
▲	public static final	CSS.Attribute	**BORDER**
▲	public static final	CSS.Attribute	**BORDER_BOTTOM**
▲	public static final	CSS.Attribute	**BORDER_BOTTOM_WIDTH**
▲	public static final	CSS.Attribute	**BORDER_COLOR**
▲	public static final	CSS.Attribute	**BORDER_LEFT**
▲	public static final	CSS.Attribute	**BORDER_LEFT_WIDTH**
▲	public static final	CSS.Attribute	**BORDER_RIGHT**
▲	public static final	CSS.Attribute	**BORDER_RIGHT_WIDTH**
▲	public static final	CSS.Attribute	**BORDER_STYLE**
▲	public static final	CSS.Attribute	**BORDER_TOP**
▲	public static final	CSS.Attribute	**BORDER_TOP_WIDTH**

C

Classes

CSS.Attribute

▲		public static final	CSS.Attribute	**BORDER_WIDTH**
▲		public static final	CSS.Attribute	**CLEAR**
▲		public static final	CSS.Attribute	**COLOR**
▲		public static final	CSS.Attribute	**DISPLAY**
▲		public static final	CSS.Attribute	**FLOAT**
▲		public static final	CSS.Attribute	**FONT**
▲		public static final	CSS.Attribute	**FONT_FAMILY**
▲		public static final	CSS.Attribute	**FONT_SIZE**
▲		public static final	CSS.Attribute	**FONT_STYLE**
▲		public static final	CSS.Attribute	**FONT_VARIANT**
▲		public static final	CSS.Attribute	**FONT_WEIGHT**
		public	String	**getDefaultValue** ()
▲		public static final	CSS.Attribute	**HEIGHT**
		public	boolean	**isInherited** ()
▲		public static final	CSS.Attribute	**LETTER_SPACING**
▲		public static final	CSS.Attribute	**LINE_HEIGHT**
▲		public static final	CSS.Attribute	**LIST_STYLE**
▲		public static final	CSS.Attribute	**LIST_STYLE_IMAGE**
▲		public static final	CSS.Attribute	**LIST_STYLE_POSITION**
▲		public static final	CSS.Attribute	**LIST_STYLE_TYPE**
▲		public static final	CSS.Attribute	**MARGIN**
▲		public static final	CSS.Attribute	**MARGIN_BOTTOM**
▲		public static final	CSS.Attribute	**MARGIN_LEFT**
▲		public static final	CSS.Attribute	**MARGIN_RIGHT**
▲		public static final	CSS.Attribute	**MARGIN_TOP**
▲		public static final	CSS.Attribute	**PADDING**
▲		public static final	CSS.Attribute	**PADDING_BOTTOM**
▲		public static final	CSS.Attribute	**PADDING_LEFT**
▲		public static final	CSS.Attribute	**PADDING_RIGHT**
▲		public static final	CSS.Attribute	**PADDING_TOP**
▲		public static final	CSS.Attribute	**TEXT_ALIGN**
▲		public static final	CSS.Attribute	**TEXT_DECORATION**
▲		public static final	CSS.Attribute	**TEXT_INDENT**
▲		public static final	CSS.Attribute	**TEXT_TRANSFORM**
	1	public	String	**toString** ()
▲		public static final	CSS.Attribute	**VERTICAL_ALIGN**
▲		public static final	CSS.Attribute	**WHITE_SPACE**
▲		public static final	CSS.Attribute	**WIDTH**
▲		public static final	CSS.Attribute	**WORD_SPACING**

CubicCurve2D java.awt.geom

Object[1]
1.2 ○ └CubicCurve2D - *java.awt.Shape*[2], *Cloneable*

	1	public	**Object**	**clone** ()
	2	public	boolean	**contains** (Point2D p)
	2	public	boolean	**contains** (Rectangle2D r)
	2	public	boolean	**contains** (double x, double y)
	2	public	boolean	**contains** (double x, double y, double w, double h)
*		protected		**CubicCurve2D** ()
	2	public	java.awt.Rectangle	**getBounds** ()
○	2	public abstract	Rectangle2D	getBounds2D ()
○		public abstract	Point2D	**getCtrlP1** ()
○		public abstract	Point2D	**getCtrlP2** ()
○		public abstract	double	**getCtrlX1** ()
○		public abstract	double	**getCtrlX2** ()
○		public abstract	double	**getCtrlY1** ()
○		public abstract	double	**getCtrlY2** ()
		public	double	**getFlatness** ()
△		public static	double	**getFlatness** (double[] coords, int offset)
△		public static	double	**getFlatness** (double x1, double y1, double ctrlx1, double ctrly1, double ctrlx2, double ctrly2, double x2, double y2)
		public	double	**getFlatnessSq** ()
△		public static	double	**getFlatnessSq** (double[] coords, int offset)
△		public static	double	**getFlatnessSq** (double x1, double y1, double ctrlx1, double ctrly1, double ctrlx2, double ctrly2, double x2, double y2)
○		public abstract	Point2D	**getP1** ()
○		public abstract	Point2D	**getP2** ()
	2	public	*PathIterator*	**getPathIterator** (AffineTransform at)

Class *Interface* —extends - - -implements ○ abstract ● final △ static ▲ static final ✳ constructor x x—inherited x **x**—declared **x x**—overridden
εn—examples of usage ˽—has subclass package—see other volume

2	public..............	*PathIterator*	**getPathIterator** (AffineTransform at, double flatness)
○	public abstract.........	double	**getX1** ()
○	public abstract.........	double	**getX2** ()
○	public abstract.........	double	**getY1** ()
○	public abstract.........	double	**getY2** ()
2	public.................	boolean	**intersects** (Rectangle2D r)
2	public.................	boolean	**intersects** (double x, double y, double w, double h)
	public......................	void	**setCurve** (CubicCurve2D c)
	public......................	void	**setCurve** (double[] coords, int offset)
	public......................	void	**setCurve** (Point2D[] pts, int offset)
	public......................	void	**setCurve** (Point2D p1, Point2D cp1, Point2D cp2, Point2D p2)
○	public abstract.............	void	**setCurve** (double x1, double y1, double ctrlx1, double ctrly1, double ctrlx2, double ctrly2, double x2, double y2)
△	public static	int	**solveCubic** (double[] eqn)
1.3 △	public static	int	**solveCubic** (double[] eqn, double[] res)
	public......................	void	**subdivide** (CubicCurve2D left, CubicCurve2D right)
△	public static	void	**subdivide** (CubicCurve2D src, CubicCurve2D left, CubicCurve2D right)
△	public static	void	**subdivide** (double[] src, int srcoff, double[] left, int leftoff, double[] right, int rightoff)

CubicCurve2D.Double   java.awt.geom

Object
1.2 ○	└CubicCurve2D [1] - *java.awt.Shape* [2], *Cloneable*
1.2	└CubicCurve2D.Double

1	*25 inherited members from CubicCurve2D not shown*		
	public..................	double	**ctrlx1**
	public..................	double	**ctrlx2**
	public..................	double	**ctrly1**
	public..................	double	**ctrly2**
✳	public........................		**CubicCurve2D.Double** ()
✳	public........................		**CubicCurve2D.Double** (double x1, double y1, double ctrlx1, double ctrly1, double ctrlx2, double ctrly2, double x2, double y2)
2	public.............	Rectangle2D	**getBounds2D** ()
1	public.................	**Point2D**	**getCtrlP1** ()
1	public.................	**Point2D**	**getCtrlP2** ()
1	public.................	**double**	**getCtrlX1** ()
1	public.................	**double**	**getCtrlX2** ()
1	public.................	**double**	**getCtrlY1** ()
1	public.................	**double**	**getCtrlY2** ()
1	public.................	**Point2D**	**getP1** ()
1	public.................	**Point2D**	**getP2** ()
1	public.................	**double**	**getX1** ()
1	public.................	**double**	**getX2** ()
1	public.................	**double**	**getY1** ()
1	public.................	**double**	**getY2** ()
1	public.................	**void**	**setCurve** (double x1, double y1, double ctrlx1, double ctrly1, double ctrlx2, double ctrly2, double x2, double y2)
	public..................	double	**x1**
	public..................	double	**x2**
	public..................	double	**y1**
	public..................	double	**y2**

CubicCurve2D.Float   java.awt.geom

Object
1.2 ○	└CubicCurve2D [1] - *java.awt.Shape* [2], *Cloneable*
1.2	└CubicCurve2D.Float

1	*25 inherited members from CubicCurve2D not shown*		
	public......................	float	**ctrlx1**
	public......................	float	**ctrlx2**
	public......................	float	**ctrly1**
	public......................	float	**ctrly2**
✳	public........................		**CubicCurve2D.Float** ()
✳	public........................		**CubicCurve2D.Float** (float x1, float y1, float ctrlx1, float ctrly1, float ctrlx2, float ctrly2, float x2, float y2)
2	public.............	Rectangle2D	**getBounds2D** ()
1	public.................	**Point2D**	**getCtrlP1** ()
1	public.................	**Point2D**	**getCtrlP2** ()
1	public.................	**double**	**getCtrlX1** ()
1	public.................	**double**	**getCtrlX2** ()

CubicCurve2D.Float

1	public	**double**	**getCtrlY1** ()	
1	public	**double**	**getCtrlY2** ()	
1	public	**Point2D**	**getP1** ()	
1	public	**Point2D**	**getP2** ()	
1	public	**double**	**getX1** ()	
1	public	**double**	**getX2** ()	
1	public	**double**	**getY1** ()	
1	public	**double**	**getY2** ()	
1	public	**void**	**setCurve** (double x1, double y1, double ctrlx1, double ctrly1, double ctrlx2, double ctrly2, double x2, double y2)	
	public	void	**setCurve** (float x1, float y1, float ctrlx1, float ctrly1, float ctrlx2, float ctrly2, float x2, float y2)	
	public	float	**x1**	
	public	float	**x2**	
	public	float	**y1**	
	public	float	**y2**	

Cursor   java.awt

Object[1]
1.1 └Cursor - *java.io.Serializable*

▲	public static final	int	**CROSSHAIR_CURSOR** = 1	
✳	public		**Cursor** (int type)	
1.2 ✳	protected		**Cursor** (String name)	
1.2 ▲	public static final	int	**CUSTOM_CURSOR** = -1	
▲	public static final	int	**DEFAULT_CURSOR** = 0	
▲	public static final	int	**E_RESIZE_CURSOR** = 11	
1	protected	**void**	**finalize** () throws Throwable	
△	public static	Cursor	**getDefaultCursor** ()	
1.2	public	String	**getName** ()	
△	public static	Cursor	**getPredefinedCursor** (int type)	ε574
1.2 △	public static	Cursor	**getSystemCustomCursor** (String name) throws AWTException, HeadlessException	
	public	int	**getType** ()	
▲	public static final	int	**HAND_CURSOR** = 12	ε574
▲	public static final	int	**MOVE_CURSOR** = 13	
▲	public static final	int	**N_RESIZE_CURSOR** = 8	
1.2	protected	String	**name**	
▲	public static final	int	**NE_RESIZE_CURSOR** = 7	
▲	public static final	int	**NW_RESIZE_CURSOR** = 6	
△	protected static	Cursor[]	**predefined**	
▲	public static final	int	**S_RESIZE_CURSOR** = 9	
▲	public static final	int	**SE_RESIZE_CURSOR** = 5	
▲	public static final	int	**SW_RESIZE_CURSOR** = 4	
▲	public static final	int	**TEXT_CURSOR** = 2	
1	public	**String**	**toString** ()	
▲	public static final	int	**W_RESIZE_CURSOR** = 10	
▲	public static final	int	**WAIT_CURSOR** = 3	

DataBuffer   java.awt.image

Object
1.2 ○ └DataBuffer

	protected	int	**banks**	
✳	protected		**DataBuffer** (int dataType, int size)	
✳	protected		**DataBuffer** (int dataType, int size, int numBanks)	
✳	protected		**DataBuffer** (int dataType, int size, int numBanks, int[] offsets)	
✳	protected		**DataBuffer** (int dataType, int size, int numBanks, int offset)	
	protected	int	**dataType**	
	public	int	**getDataType** ()	
△	public static	int	**getDataTypeSize** (int type)	
	public	int	**getElem** (int i)	
○	public abstract	int	**getElem** (int bank, int i)	
	public	double	**getElemDouble** (int i)	
	public	double	**getElemDouble** (int bank, int i)	
	public	float	**getElemFloat** (int i)	
	public	float	**getElemFloat** (int bank, int i)	
	public	int	**getNumBanks** ()	ε668

Class *Interface* —extends - - -implements ○ abstract ● final △ static ▲ static final ✳ constructor x x—inherited x **x**—declared **x x**—overridden
ε*n*—examples of usage ‿—has subclass package—see other volume

```
   public........................int  getOffset ()
   public.....................int[]  getOffsets ()
   public........................int  getSize ()
   protected ....................int  offset
   protected ..................int[]  offsets
   public.......................void  setElem (int i, int val)
○  public abstract ............void  setElem (int bank, int i, int val)
   public.......................void  setElemDouble (int i, double val)
   public.......................void  setElemDouble (int bank, int i, double val)
   public.......................void  setElemFloat (int i, float val)
   public.......................void  setElemFloat (int bank, int i, float val)
   protected ....................int  size
▲  public static final .........int  TYPE_BYTE  = 0                              ε668
▲  public static final .........int  TYPE_DOUBLE  = 5
▲  public static final .........int  TYPE_FLOAT  = 4
▲  public static final .........int  TYPE_INT  = 3
▲  public static final .........int  TYPE_SHORT  = 2
▲  public static final .........int  TYPE_UNDEFINED  = 32
▲  public static final .........int  TYPE_USHORT  = 1
```

DataBufferByte   java.awt.image

```
       Object
1.2 ○  └DataBuffer 1
1.2 ●    └DataBufferByte

    1  26 inherited members from DataBuffer not shown
 ∗     public........................  DataBufferByte (int size)
 ∗     public........................  DataBufferByte (byte[] dataArray, int size)
 ∗     public........................  DataBufferByte (byte[][] dataArray, int size)
 ∗     public........................  DataBufferByte (int size, int numBanks)
 ∗     public........................  DataBufferByte (byte[] dataArray, int size, int offset)    ε668
 ∗     public........................  DataBufferByte (byte[][] dataArray, int size, int[] offsets)
       public................byte[][]  getBankData ()
       public..................byte[]  getData ()
       public..................byte[]  getData (int bank)
    1  public.....................int  getElem (int i)
    1  public.....................int  getElem (int bank, int i)
    1  public....................void  setElem (int i, int val)
    1  public....................void  setElem (int bank, int i, int val)
```

DataBufferDouble   java.awt.image

```
       Object
1.2 ○  └DataBuffer 1
1.4 ●    └DataBufferDouble

    1  protected ....................int  banks
 ∗     public...........................  DataBufferDouble (int size)
 ∗     public...........................  DataBufferDouble (double[] dataArray, int size)
 ∗     public...........................  DataBufferDouble (double[][] dataArray, int size)
 ∗     public...........................  DataBufferDouble (int size, int numBanks)
 ∗     public...........................  DataBufferDouble (double[] dataArray, int size, int offset)
 ∗     public...........................  DataBufferDouble (double[][] dataArray, int size, int[] offsets)
    1  protected ....................int  dataType
       public.................double[][]  getBankData ()
       public...................double[]  getData ()
       public...................double[]  getData (int bank)
    1  public.....................int  getDataType ()
  △ 1  public static .............int  getDataTypeSize (int type)
    1  public.....................int  getElem (int i)
    1  public.....................int  getElem (int bank, int i)
    1  public..................double  getElemDouble (int i)
    1  public..................double  getElemDouble (int bank, int i)
    1  public...................float  getElemFloat (int i)
    1  public...................float  getElemFloat (int bank, int i)
    1  public.....................int  getNumBanks ()                          ε668
    1  public.....................int  getOffset ()
    1  public...................int[]  getOffsets ()
    1  public.....................int  getSize ()
    1  protected ..................int  offset
    1  protected ................int[]  offsets
```

DataBufferDouble

	1	public.....................	**void setElem** (int i, int val)	
	1	public.....................	**void setElem** (int bank, int i, int val)	
	1	public.....................	**void setElemDouble** (int i, double val)	
	1	public.....................	**void setElemDouble** (int bank, int i, double val)	
	1	public.....................	**void setElemFloat** (int i, float val)	
	1	public.....................	**void setElemFloat** (int bank, int i, float val)	
	1	protected	int size	
▲	1	public static final	int TYPE_BYTE = 0	ε668
▲	1	public static final	int TYPE_DOUBLE = 5	
▲	1	public static final	int TYPE_FLOAT = 4	
▲	1	public static final	int TYPE_INT = 3	
▲	1	public static final	int TYPE_SHORT = 2	
▲	1	public static final	int TYPE_UNDEFINED = 32	
▲	1	public static final	int TYPE_USHORT = 1	

DataBufferFloat   java.awt.image

```
        Object
1.2 ○   └DataBuffer 1
1.4 ●     └DataBufferFloat
```

	1	protected	int banks	
✳		public.........................	**DataBufferFloat** (int size)	
✳		public.........................	**DataBufferFloat** (float[] dataArray, int size)	
✳		public.........................	**DataBufferFloat** (float[][] dataArray, int size)	
✳		public.........................	**DataBufferFloat** (int size, int numBanks)	
✳		public.........................	**DataBufferFloat** (float[] dataArray, int size, int offset)	
✳		public.........................	**DataBufferFloat** (float[][] dataArray, int size, int[] offsets)	
	1	protected	int dataType	
		public................. float[][]	**getBankData** ()	
		public................... float[]	**getData** ()	
		public................... float[]	**getData** (int bank)	
	1	public.....................	int getDataType ()	
△	1	public static	int getDataTypeSize (int type)	
	1	public................. **int getElem** (int i)		
	1	public................. **int getElem** (int bank, int i)		
	1	public........... **double getElemDouble** (int i)		
	1	public........... **double getElemDouble** (int bank, int i)		
	1	public............. **float getElemFloat** (int i)		
	1	public............. **float getElemFloat** (int bank, int i)		
	1	public.....................	int getNumBanks ()	ε668
	1	public.....................	int getOffset ()	
	1	public................... int[]	getOffsets ()	
	1	public.....................	int getSize ()	
	1	protected	int offset	
	1	protected	int[] offsets	
	1	public.....................	**void setElem** (int i, int val)	
	1	public.....................	**void setElem** (int bank, int i, int val)	
	1	public.....................	**void setElemDouble** (int i, double val)	
	1	public.....................	**void setElemDouble** (int bank, int i, double val)	
	1	public.....................	**void setElemFloat** (int i, float val)	
	1	public.....................	**void setElemFloat** (int bank, int i, float val)	
	1	protected	int size	
▲	1	public static final	int TYPE_BYTE = 0	ε668
▲	1	public static final	int TYPE_DOUBLE = 5	
▲	1	public static final	int TYPE_FLOAT = 4	
▲	1	public static final	int TYPE_INT = 3	
▲	1	public static final	int TYPE_SHORT = 2	
▲	1	public static final	int TYPE_UNDEFINED = 32	
▲	1	public static final	int TYPE_USHORT = 1	

DataBufferInt   java.awt.image

```
        Object
1.2 ○   └DataBuffer 1
1.2 ●     └DataBufferInt
```

	1	*26 inherited members from DataBuffer not shown*	
✳		public........................	**DataBufferInt** (int size)

Class *Interface* —extends - - -implements ○ abstract ● final △ static ▲ static final ✳ constructor x x—inherited x **x**—declared **x x**—overridden
ε*n*—examples of usage ˻—has subclass package—see other volume

*	public.........................	**DataBufferInt** (int size, int numBanks)	
*	public.........................	**DataBufferInt** (int[] dataArray, int size)	
*	public.........................	**DataBufferInt** (int[][] dataArray, int size)	
*	public.........................	**DataBufferInt** (int[] dataArray, int size, int offset)	
*	public.........................	**DataBufferInt** (int[][] dataArray, int size, int[] offsets)	
	public................... int[][]	**getBankData** ()	
	public..................... int[]	**getData** ()	
	public..................... int[]	**getData** (int bank)	
1	public...................... **int**	**getElem** (int i)	
1	public...................... **int**	**getElem** (int bank, int i)	
1	public.................... **void**	**setElem** (int i, int val)	
1	public.................... **void**	**setElem** (int bank, int i, int val)	

DataBufferShort   java.awt.image

Object
1.2 ○ └DataBuffer¹
1.2 ●   └DataBufferShort

1	*26 inherited members from DataBuffer not shown*		
*	public.........................	**DataBufferShort** (int size)	
*	public.........................	**DataBufferShort** (int size, int numBanks)	
*	public.........................	**DataBufferShort** (short[] dataArray, int size)	
*	public.........................	**DataBufferShort** (short[][] dataArray, int size)	
*	public.........................	**DataBufferShort** (short[] dataArray, int size, int offset)	
*	public.........................	**DataBufferShort** (short[][] dataArray, int size, int[] offsets)	
	public............... short[][]	**getBankData** ()	
	public................. short[]	**getData** ()	
	public................. short[]	**getData** (int bank)	
1	public...................... **int**	**getElem** (int i)	
1	public...................... **int**	**getElem** (int bank, int i)	
1	public.................... **void**	**setElem** (int i, int val)	
1	public.................... **void**	**setElem** (int bank, int i, int val)	

DataBufferUShort   java.awt.image

Object
1.2 ○ └DataBuffer¹
1.2 ●   └DataBufferUShort

1	*26 inherited members from DataBuffer not shown*		
*	public.........................	**DataBufferUShort** (int size)	
*	public.........................	**DataBufferUShort** (int size, int numBanks)	
*	public.........................	**DataBufferUShort** (short[] dataArray, int size)	
*	public.........................	**DataBufferUShort** (short[][] dataArray, int size)	
*	public.........................	**DataBufferUShort** (short[] dataArray, int size, int offset)	
*	public.........................	**DataBufferUShort** (short[][] dataArray, int size, int[] offsets)	
	public............... short[][]	**getBankData** ()	
	public................. short[]	**getData** ()	
	public................. short[]	**getData** (int bank)	
1	public...................... **int**	**getElem** (int i)	
1	public...................... **int**	**getElem** (int bank, int i)	
1	public.................... **void**	**setElem** (int i, int val)	
1	public.................... **void**	**setElem** (int bank, int i, int val)	

DataFlavor   java.awt.datatransfer

Object¹
1.1 └DataFlavor ------------------------- *java.io.Externalizable*²ˇ (*java.io.Serializable*), *Cloneable*ˇ

1	public................**Object clone** () throws CloneNotSupportedException		
1.2 *	public.........................	**DataFlavor** ()	
1.2 *	public.........................	**DataFlavor** (String mimeType) throws ClassNotFoundException	
*	public.........................	**DataFlavor** (Class representationClass, String humanPresentableName)	
*	public.........................	**DataFlavor** (String mimeType, String humanPresentableName)	
1.2 *	public.........................	**DataFlavor** (String mimeType, String humanPresentableName, ClassLoader classLoader) throws ClassNotFoundException	
	public................. boolean	**equals** (DataFlavor that)	ε638
1	public................**boolean equals** (Object o)		
D	public................. boolean	**equals** (String s)	

D

Classes

467

DataFlavor

1.3 ●	public final	Class	**getDefaultRepresentationClass** ()	
1.3 ●	public final	String	**getDefaultRepresentationClassAsString** ()	
	public	String	**getHumanPresentableName** ()	
	public	String	**getMimeType** ()	
1.2	public	String	**getParameter** (String paramName)	
1.2	public	String	**getPrimaryType** ()	
1.3	public	java.io.Reader	**getReaderForText** (*Transferable* transferable) throws UnsupportedFlavorException, java.io.IOException	
	public	Class	**getRepresentationClass** ()	
1.2	public	String	**getSubType** ()	
1.3 ▲	public static final	DataFlavor	**getTextPlainUnicodeFlavor** ()	
	1 public	int	**hashCode** ()	
1.4	public static final	DataFlavor	**imageFlavor**	ε638
1.2	public	boolean	**isFlavorJavaFileListType** ()	
1.2	public	boolean	**isFlavorRemoteObjectType** ()	
1.2	public	boolean	**isFlavorSerializedObjectType** ()	
1.4	public	boolean	**isFlavorTextType** ()	
●	public final	boolean	**isMimeTypeEqual** (DataFlavor dataFlavor)	
	public	boolean	**isMimeTypeEqual** (String mimeType)	
1.2	public	boolean	**isMimeTypeSerializedObject** ()	
1.4	public	boolean	**isRepresentationClassByteBuffer** ()	
1.4	public	boolean	**isRepresentationClassCharBuffer** ()	
1.2	public	boolean	**isRepresentationClassInputStream** ()	
1.4	public	boolean	**isRepresentationClassReader** ()	
1.2	public	boolean	**isRepresentationClassRemote** ()	
1.2	public	boolean	**isRepresentationClassSerializable** ()	
1.2 ▲	public static final	DataFlavor	**javaFileListFlavor**	
1.2 ▲	public static final	String	**javaJVMLocalObjectMimeType** = "application/x-java-jvm-local-objectref"	
1.2 ▲	public static final	String	**javaRemoteObjectMimeType** = "application/x-java-remote-object"	
1.2 ▲	public static final	String	**javaSerializedObjectMimeType** = "application/x-java-serialized-object"	
1.3	public	boolean	**match** (DataFlavor that)	
D	protected	String	**normalizeMimeType** (String mimeType)	
D	protected	String	**normalizeMimeTypeParameter** (String parameterName, String parameterValue)	
D ▲	public static final	DataFlavor	**plainTextFlavor**	
1.2	2 public synchronized	void	**readExternal** (*java.io.ObjectInput* is) throws java.io.IOException, ClassNotFoundException	
1.3 ▲	public static final	DataFlavor	**selectBestTextFlavor** (DataFlavor[] availableFlavors)	
	public	void	**setHumanPresentableName** (String humanPresentableName)	
▲	public static final	DataFlavor	**stringFlavor**	ε637,642
	1 public	**String**	**toString** ()	
1.2 ▲	protected static final	Class	**tryToLoadClass** (String className, ClassLoader fallback) throws ClassNotFoundException	
1.2	2 public synchronized	void	**writeExternal** (*java.io.ObjectOutput* os) throws java.io.IOException	

DataLine	javax.sound.sampled

1.3 *DataLine* ──────────────── *Line* [1]

	1 public	void	addLineListener (*LineListener* listener)	ε731
	public	int	**available** ()	
	1 public	void	close ()	
	public	void	**drain** ()	ε724
	public	void	**flush** ()	
	public	int	**getBufferSize** ()	ε728
	1 public	Control	getControl (Control.Type control)	ε730
	1 public	Control[]	getControls ()	
	public	AudioFormat	**getFormat** ()	ε728
	public	int	**getFramePosition** ()	
	public	float	**getLevel** ()	
	1 public	Line.Info	getLineInfo ()	
	public	long	**getMicrosecondPosition** ()	ε729
	public	boolean	**isActive** ()	
	1 public	boolean	isControlSupported (Control.Type control)	
	1 public	boolean	isOpen ()	
	public	boolean	**isRunning** ()	
	1 public	void	open () throws LineUnavailableException	
	1 public	void	removeLineListener (*LineListener* listener)	
	public	void	**start** ()	ε723,724,725
	public	void	**stop** ()	ε724

Class *Interface* —extends - - -implements ○ abstract ● final △ static ▲ static final ✳ constructor x x—inherited x **x**—declared **x x**—overridden
ε*n*—examples of usage ⌄—has subclass package—see other volume

DataLine.Info   javax.sound.sampled

```
        Object
1.3     └Line.Info 1
1.3        └DataLine.Info
```

	public	AudioFormat[]	**getFormats** ()	
1	public	Class	getLineClass ()	
	public	int	**getMaxBufferSize** ()	
	public	int	**getMinBufferSize** ()	
*	public		**DataLine.Info** (Class lineClass, AudioFormat format)	
*	public		**DataLine.Info** (Class lineClass, AudioFormat format, int bufferSize)	ε723,724
*	public		**DataLine.Info** (Class lineClass, AudioFormat[] formats, int minBufferSize, int maxBufferSize)	
	public	boolean	**isFormatSupported** (AudioFormat format)	
1	public	**boolean**	**matches** (Line.Info info)	
1	public	**String**	**toString** ()	

DateFormatter   javax.swing.text

```
        Object
1.4 ○   └javax.swing.JFormattedTextField 2 ---------- java.io.Serializable ┘
           .AbstractFormatter 1
1.4        └DefaultFormatter 2 ------------------- Cloneable ┘
1.4           └InternationalFormatter 3
1.4              └DateFormatter
```

3	public	Object	clone () throws CloneNotSupportedException	
*	public		**DateFormatter** ()	
*	public		**DateFormatter** (java.text.DateFormat format)	
3	protected .	javax.swing.Action[]	getActions ()	
2	public	boolean	getAllowsInvalid ()	
2	public	boolean	getCommitsOnValidEdit ()	
2	protected	DocumentFilter	getDocumentFilter ()	
3	public	java.text.Format.Field[]	getFields (int offset)	
3	public	java.text.Format	getFormat ()	
1	protected	javax 2 .swing.JFormattedTextField	getFormattedTextField ()	
3	public	Comparable	getMaximum ()	
3	public	Comparable	getMinimum ()	
2	protected	NavigationFilter	getNavigationFilter ()	
2	public	boolean	getOverwriteMode ()	
2	public	Class	getValueClass ()	
3	public	void	install (javax.swing.JFormattedTextField ftf)	
1	protected	void	invalidEdit ()	
2	public	void	setAllowsInvalid (boolean allowsInvalid)	
2	public	void	setCommitsOnValidEdit (boolean commit)	
1	protected	void	setEditValid (boolean valid)	
	public	void	**setFormat** (java.text.DateFormat format)	ε996,787
3	public	void	setFormat (java.text.Format format)	
3	public	void	setMaximum (Comparable max)	
3	public	void	setMinimum (Comparable minimum)	
2	public	void	setOverwriteMode (boolean overwriteMode)	
2	public	void	setValueClass (Class valueClass)	ε995
3	public	Object	stringToValue (String text) throws java.text.ParseException	
1	public	void	uninstall ()	
3	public	String	valueToString (Object value) throws java.text.ParseException	

DateTimeAtCompleted   javax.print.attribute.standard

```
        Object
1.4 ○   └javax.print.attribute.DateTimeSyntax 1 ------- java.io.Serializable ┘, Cloneable ┘
1.4 ●      └DateTimeAtCompleted ----------------- javax.print.attribute.PrintJobAttribute (javax.print.attribute.Attribute 2
                                                        (java.io.Serializable))
```

*	public		**DateTimeAtCompleted** (java.util.Date dateTime)	
1	public	**boolean**	**equals** (Object object)	
● 2	public final	Class	**getCategory** ()	ε707
● 2	public final	String	**getName** ()	ε706,707,708

DateTimeAtCompleted

```
  1  public............java.util.Date  getValue ()
  1  public........................int  hashCode ()
  1  public...................String  toString ()
```

DateTimeAtCreation   javax.print.attribute.standard

Object
1.4 O └─*java.io.Serializable*., *Cloneable*. ─ ─ ─ ─ ─ ─ *java.io.Serializable*., *Cloneable*.
1.4 ● └─DateTimeAtCreation ─ ─ ─ ─ ─ ─ ─ ─ ─ ─ ─ *javax.print.attribute.PrintJobAttribute (javax.print.attribute.Attribute* [2]
                                                         (*java.io.Serializable*))

```
  *  public........................  DateTimeAtCreation (java.util.Date dateTime)
  1  public................boolean  equals (Object object)
● 2  public final ..............Class  getCategory ()                              ε707
● 2  public final .............String  getName ()                                  ε706,707,708
  1  public............java.util.Date  getValue ()
  1  public........................int  hashCode ()
  1  public...................String  toString ()
```

DateTimeAtProcessing   javax.print.attribute.standard

Object
1.4 O └─javax.print.attribute.DateTimeSyntax [1] ─ ─ ─ ─ *java.io.Serializable*., *Cloneable*.
1.4 ● └─DateTimeAtProcessing ─ ─ ─ ─ ─ ─ ─ ─ ─ ─ ─ *javax.print.attribute.PrintJobAttribute (javax.print.attribute.Attribute* [2]
                                                         (*java.io.Serializable*))

```
  *  public........................  DateTimeAtProcessing (java.util.Date dateTime)
  1  public................boolean  equals (Object object)
● 2  public final ..............Class  getCategory ()                              ε707
● 2  public final .............String  getName ()                                  ε706,707,708
  1  public............java.util.Date  getValue ()
  1  public........................int  hashCode ()
  1  public...................String  toString ()
```

DateTimeSyntax   javax.print.attribute

Object [1]
1.4 O └─DateTimeSyntax. ─ ─ ─ ─ ─ ─ ─ ─ ─ ─ ─ ─ ─ *java.io.Serializable*., *Cloneable*.

```
  *  protected .....................  DateTimeSyntax (java.util.Date value)
  1  public................boolean  equals (Object object)
     public............java.util.Date  getValue ()
  1  public................. int  hashCode ()
  1  public................. String  toString ()
```

DebugGraphics   javax.swing

Object   ε575,576,577,578,579
  O └─java.awt.Graphics [1]
1.2 └─DebugGraphics

```
  ▲  public static final ............int  BUFFERED_OPTION  = 4
  1  public....................  void  clearRect (int x, int y, int width, int height)
  1  public....................  void  clipRect (int x, int y, int width, int height)
  1  public....................  void  copyArea (int x, int y, int width, int height, int destX, int destY)
  1  public......  java.awt.Graphics  create ()
  1  public......  java.awt.Graphics  create (int x, int y, int width, int height)
  *  public........................  DebugGraphics ()
  *  public........................  DebugGraphics (java.awt.Graphics graphics)
  *  public........................  DebugGraphics (java.awt.Graphics graphics, JComponent component)
  1  public....................  void  dispose ()                                 ε602,667,669,674,680
  1  public....................  void  draw3DRect (int x, int y, int width, int height, boolean raised)
  1  public....................  void  drawArc (int x, int y, int width, int height, int startAngle, int arcAngle)
                                                                                   ε586
  1  public....................  void  drawBytes (byte[] data, int offset, int length, int x, int y)
  1  public....................  void  drawChars (char[] data, int offset, int length, int x, int y)
```

1	public	**boolean**	**drawImage** (java.awt.Image img, int x, int y, *java.awt.image.ImageObserver* observer)	*ε*578,581,595,660,667
1	public	**boolean**	**drawImage** (java.awt.Image img, int x, int y, java.awt.Color bgcolor, *java.awt.image.ImageObserver* observer)	
1	public	**boolean**	**drawImage** (java.awt.Image img, int x, int y, int width, int height, *java.awt.image.ImageObserver* observer)	
1	public	**boolean**	**drawImage** (java.awt.Image img, int x, int y, int width, int height, java.awt.Color bgcolor, *java.awt.image.ImageObserver* observer)	
1	public	**boolean**	**drawImage** (java.awt.Image img, int dx1, int dy1, int dx2, int dy2, int sx1, int sy1, int sx2, int sy2, *java.awt.image.ImageObserver* observer)	
1	public	**boolean**	**drawImage** (java.awt.Image img, int dx1, int dy1, int dx2, int dy2, int sx1, int sy1, int sx2, int sy2, java.awt.Color bgcolor, *java.awt.image.ImageObserver* observer)	
1	public	**void**	**drawLine** (int x1, int y1, int x2, int y2)	*ε*586
1	public	**void**	**drawOval** (int x, int y, int width, int height)	*ε*586,575
1	public	void	drawPolygon (java.awt.Polygon p)	*ε*586
1	public	**void**	**drawPolygon** (int[] xPoints, int[] yPoints, int nPoints)	
1	public	**void**	**drawPolyline** (int[] xPoints, int[] yPoints, int nPoints)	
1	public	**void**	**drawRect** (int x, int y, int width, int height)	*ε*586
1	public	**void**	**drawRoundRect** (int x, int y, int width, int height, int arcWidth, int arcHeight)	*ε*586
1	public	**void**	**drawString** (String aString, int x, int y)	*ε*591
1	public	**void**	**drawString** (*java.text.AttributedCharacterIterator* iterator, int x, int y)	
1	public	**void**	**fill3DRect** (int x, int y, int width, int height, boolean raised)	
1	public	**void**	**fillArc** (int x, int y, int width, int height, int startAngle, int arcAngle)	*ε*587,590
1	public	**void**	**fillOval** (int x, int y, int width, int height)	*ε*587,695
1	public	void	fillPolygon (java.awt.Polygon p)	*ε*587
1	public	**void**	**fillPolygon** (int[] xPoints, int[] yPoints, int nPoints)	
1	public	**void**	**fillRect** (int x, int y, int width, int height)	*ε*587,602,695,878,879
1	public	**void**	**fillRoundRect** (int x, int y, int width, int height, int arcWidth, int arcHeight)	*ε*587
1	public	void	finalize ()	
▲	public static final	int	**FLASH_OPTION** = 2	
△	public static	java.awt.Color	**flashColor** ()	
△	public static	int	**flashCount** ()	
△	public static	int	**flashTime** ()	
1	public	***java.awt.Shape***	**getClip** ()	
1	public	**java.awt.Rectangle**	**getClipBounds** ()	
1	public	java.awt.Rectangle	getClipBounds (java.awt.Rectangle r)	
1	public	**java.awt.Color**	**getColor** ()	
	public	int	**getDebugOptions** ()	
1	public	**java.awt.Font**	**getFont** ()	
1	public	**java.awt.FontMetrics**	**getFontMetrics** ()	*ε*591,593
1	public	**java.awt.FontMetrics**	**getFontMetrics** (java.awt.Font f)	
1	public	boolean	hitClip (int x, int y, int width, int height)	
	public	boolean	isDrawingBuffer ()	
▲	public static final	int	**LOG_OPTION** = 1	
△	public static		**logStream** ()	
		java.io.PrintStream		
▲	public static final	int	**NONE_OPTION** = -1	
1	public	**void**	**setClip** (*java.awt.Shape* clip)	*ε*578
1	public	**void**	**setClip** (int x, int y, int width, int height)	
1	public	**void**	**setColor** (java.awt.Color aColor)	*ε*582,589,590,602,669
	public	void	**setDebugOptions** (int options)	
△	public static	void	**setFlashColor** (java.awt.Color flashColor)	
△	public static	void	**setFlashCount** (int flashCount)	
△	public static	void	**setFlashTime** (int flashTime)	
1	public	**void**	**setFont** (java.awt.Font aFont)	*ε*591
△	public static	void	**setLogStream** (java.io.PrintStream stream)	
1	public	**void**	**setPaintMode** ()	
1	public	**void**	**setXORMode** (java.awt.Color aColor)	
1	public	String	toString ()	
1	public	**void**	**translate** (int x, int y)	

D

Classes

DefaultBoundedRangeModel			javax.swing

Object[1]
1.2 └DefaultBoundedRangeModel - - - - - - - - - - - - - *BoundedRangeModel*[2], *java.io.Serializable*

2	public	void	**addChangeListener** (*javax.swing.event.ChangeListener* l)
	protected transient	javax[2] .swing.event.ChangeEvent	**changeEvent**
*	public		**DefaultBoundedRangeModel** ()

DefaultBoundedRangeModel

✳		public		**DefaultBoundedRangeModel** (int value, int extent, int min, int max)
		protected	void	**fireStateChanged** ()
1.4		public	*javax.swing₂* *.event.ChangeListener[]*	**getChangeListeners** ()
	2	public	int	**getExtent** ()
1.3		public	*java.util.EventListener[]*	**getListeners** (Class listenerType)
	2	public	int	**getMaximum** ()
	2	public	int	**getMinimum** ()
	2	public	int	**getValue** ()
	2	public	boolean	**getValueIsAdjusting** ()
		protected	*javax.swing₂* *.event.EventListenerList*	**listenerList**
	2	public	void	**removeChangeListener** (*javax.swing.event.ChangeListener* l)
	2	public	void	**setExtent** (int n)
	2	public	void	**setMaximum** (int n)
	2	public	void	**setMinimum** (int n)
	2	public	void	**setRangeProperties** (int newValue, int newExtent, int newMin, int newMax, boolean adjusting) ε795,803
	2	public	void	**setValue** (int n)
	2	public	void	**setValueIsAdjusting** (boolean b)
	1	public	String	**toString** ()

DefaultButtonModel   javax.swing

Object
└ DefaultButtonModel `- - - - - - - - - - - - - - - - - - -` *ButtonModel [1]* (*java.awt.ItemSelectable [2]*), *java.io.Serializable*   (1.2)

		protected	String	**actionCommand**
	1	public	void	**addActionListener** (*java.awt.event.ActionListener* l)
	1	public	void	**addChangeListener** (*javax.swing.event.ChangeListener* l)
	1	public	void	**addItemListener** (*java.awt.event.ItemListener* l) ε650,765
▲		public static final	int	**ARMED** = 1
		protected transient	*javax₂* *.swing.event.ChangeEvent*	**changeEvent**
✳		public		**DefaultButtonModel** ()
▲		public static final	int	**ENABLED** = 8
		protected	void	**fireActionPerformed** (java.awt.event.ActionEvent e)
		protected	void	**fireItemStateChanged** (java.awt.event.ItemEvent e)
		protected	void	**fireStateChanged** ()
	1	public	String	**getActionCommand** ()
1.4		public	*java₂* *.awt.event.ActionListener[]*	**getActionListeners** ()
1.4		public	*javax.swing₂* *.event.ChangeListener[]*	**getChangeListeners** ()
1.3		public	ButtonGroup	**getGroup** () ε771
1.4		public	*java.awt.event.ItemListener[]*	**getItemListeners** ()
1.3		public	*java.util.EventListener[]*	**getListeners** (Class listenerType)
	1	public	int	**getMnemonic** ()
	2	public	Object[]	**getSelectedObjects** () ε650
		protected	ButtonGroup	**group**
	1	public	boolean	**isArmed** ()
	1	public	boolean	**isEnabled** ()
	1	public	boolean	**isPressed** ()
	1	public	boolean	**isRollover** ()
	1	public	boolean	**isSelected** ()
		protected	*javax.swing₂* *.event.EventListenerList*	**listenerList**
		protected	int	**mnemonic**
▲		public static final	int	**PRESSED** = 4
	1	public	void	**removeActionListener** (*java.awt.event.ActionListener* l)
	1	public	void	**removeChangeListener** (*javax.swing.event.ChangeListener* l)
	1	public	void	**removeItemListener** (*java.awt.event.ItemListener* l) ε650
▲		public static final	int	**ROLLOVER** = 16
▲		public static final	int	**SELECTED** = 2
	1	public	void	**setActionCommand** (String actionCommand)
	1	public	void	**setArmed** (boolean b)
	1	public	void	**setEnabled** (boolean b)
	1	public	void	**setGroup** (ButtonGroup group)

Class   *Interface*   —extends   - - -implements   ○ abstract   ● final   △ static   ▲ static final   ✳ constructor   x x—inherited   x **x**—declared   **x x**—overridden
ε*n*—examples of usage   ˷—has subclass   package—see other volume

472

1	public	void	**setMnemonic** (int key)
1	public	void	**setPressed** (boolean b)
1	public	void	**setRollover** (boolean b)
1	public	void	**setSelected** (boolean b)
	protected	int	**stateMask**

DefaultCaret — javax.swing.text · D

ε572

```
Object
1.2 ○  └─java.awt.geom.RectangularShape 1 --------- java.awt.Shape, Cloneable
1.2 ○     └─java.awt.geom.Rectangle2D 2
             └─java.awt.Rectangle 3 --------------- java.io.Serializable
1.2             └─DefaultCaret --------------------- Caret 4, java.awt.event.FocusListener 5 ( java.util.EventListener),
                                                      java.awt.event.MouseListener 6 ( java.util.EventListener),
                                                      java.awt.event.MouseMotionListener 7 ( java.util.EventListener)
```

	3	*39 inherited members from java.awt.Rectangle not shown*		
	2	public	void	add (java.awt.geom.Point2D pt)
	2	public	void	add (java.awt.geom.Rectangle2D r)
	2	public	void	add (double newx, double newy)
	4	public	void	**addChangeListener** (*javax.swing.event.ChangeListener* l)
		protected	void	**adjustVisibility** (java.awt.Rectangle nloc)
		protected transient	javax.swing.event.ChangeEvent	**changeEvent**
	1	public	Object	clone ()
	1	public	boolean	contains (java.awt.geom.Point2D p)
	1	public	boolean	contains (java.awt.geom.Rectangle2D r)
	2	public	boolean	contains (double x, double y)
	2	public	boolean	contains (double x, double y, double w, double h)
		protected synchronized	void	**damage** (java.awt.Rectangle r)
*		public		**DefaultCaret** ()
	4	public	void	**deinstall** (JTextComponent c)
	3	public	**boolean**	**equals** (Object obj)
		protected	void	**fireStateChanged** ()
	5	public	void	**focusGained** (java.awt.event.FocusEvent e) — ε649,616,617,618
	5	public	void	**focusLost** (java.awt.event.FocusEvent e) — ε649,616,617,618
	4	public	int	**getBlinkRate** ()
	1	public	double	getCenterX ()
	1	public	double	getCenterY ()
1.4		public	javax.swing.event.ChangeListener[]	**getChangeListeners** ()
●		protected final	JTextComponent	**getComponent** ()
	4	public	int	**getDot** ()
	1	public	java.awt.geom.Rectangle2D	getFrame ()
1.3		public	*java.util.EventListener[]*	**getListeners** (Class listenerType)
	4	public	java.awt.Point	**getMagicCaretPosition** ()
	4	public	int	**getMark** ()
	1	public	double	getMaxX ()
	1	public	double	getMaxY ()
	1	public	double	getMinX ()
	1	public	double	getMinY ()
	2	public	...java.awt.geom.PathIterator	getPathIterator (java.awt.geom.AffineTransform at)
	2	public	...java.awt.geom.PathIterator	getPathIterator (java.awt.geom.AffineTransform at, double flatness)
		protected	..Highlighter.HighlightPainter	**getSelectionPainter** ()
	2	public	int	hashCode ()
	4	public	void	**install** (JTextComponent c)
△	2	public static	void	intersect (java.awt.geom.Rectangle2D src1, java.awt.geom.Rectangle2D src2, java.awt.geom.Rectangle2D dest)
	1	public	boolean	intersects (java.awt.geom.Rectangle2D r)
	2	public	boolean	intersects (double x, double y, double w, double h)
	2	public	boolean	intersectsLine (java.awt.geom.Line2D l)
	2	public	boolean	intersectsLine (double x1, double y1, double x2, double y2)
	4	public	boolean	**isSelectionVisible** ()
	4	public	boolean	**isVisible** ()
		protected	javax.swing.event.EventListenerList	**listenerList**
	6	public	void	**mouseClicked** (java.awt.event.MouseEvent e) — ε646,648,783,967

DefaultCaret

7	public	void	**mouseDragged** (java.awt.event.MouseEvent e)	ε647
6	public	void	**mouseEntered** (java.awt.event.MouseEvent e)	
6	public	void	**mouseExited** (java.awt.event.MouseEvent e)	
7	public	void	**mouseMoved** (java.awt.event.MouseEvent e)	ε647,937
6	public	void	**mousePressed** (java.awt.event.MouseEvent e)	ε602,742,810,1011
6	public	void	**mouseReleased** (java.awt.event.MouseEvent e)	ε810,1011
	protected	void	**moveCaret** (java.awt.event.MouseEvent e)	
4	public	void	**moveDot** (int dot)	
▲ 2	public static final	int	OUT_BOTTOM = 8	
▲ 2	public static final	int	OUT_LEFT = 1	
▲ 2	public static final	int	OUT_RIGHT = 4	
▲ 2	public static final	int	OUT_TOP = 2	
2	public	int	outcode (java.awt.geom.Point2D p)	
4	public	void	**paint** (java.awt.Graphics g)	
	protected	void	**positionCaret** (java.awt.event.MouseEvent e)	
4	public	void	**removeChangeListener** (*javax.swing.event.ChangeListener* l)	
●	protected final synchronized	void	**repaint** ()	
4	public	void	**setBlinkRate** (int rate)	ε999
4	public	void	**setDot** (int dot)	
1	public	void	setFrame (java.awt.geom.Rectangle2D r)	
1	public	void	setFrame (java.awt.geom.Point2D loc, java.awt.geom.Dimension2D size)	
2	public	void	setFrame (double x, double y, double w, double h)	
1	public	void	setFrameFromCenter (java.awt.geom.Point2D center, java.awt.geom.Point2D corner)	
1	public	void	setFrameFromCenter (double centerX, double centerY, double cornerX, double cornerY)	
1	public	void	setFrameFromDiagonal (java.awt.geom.Point2D p1, java.awt.geom.Point2D p2)	
1	public	void	setFrameFromDiagonal (double x1, double y1, double x2, double y2)	
4	public	void	**setMagicCaretPosition** (java.awt.Point p)	
2	public	void	setRect (java.awt.geom.Rectangle2D r)	
4	public	void	**setSelectionVisible** (boolean vis)	
4	public	void	**setVisible** (boolean e)	
3	public	**String**	**toString** ()	
△ 2	public static	void	union (java.awt.geom.Rectangle2D src1, java.awt.geom.Rectangle2D src2, java.awt.geom.Rectangle2D dest)	

DefaultCellEditor

javax.swing

```
Object                                                                    ε959
1.3 ○  └AbstractCellEditor 1 --------------------- CellEditor ⌄2, java.io.Serializable⌄
1.2        └DefaultCellEditor -------------------- javax.swing.table.TableCellEditor 3 (CellEditor 2),
                                                   javax.swing.tree.TreeCellEditor 4 (CellEditor 2)
```

	1	public	void	addCellEditorListener (*javax.swing.event.CellEditorListener* l)	
	1	public	**void**	**cancelCellEditing** ()	ε956
1.3	1	protected transient	javax⌄.swing.event.ChangeEvent	changeEvent	
		protected	int	**clickCountToStart**	
	✳	public		**DefaultCellEditor** (JCheckBox checkBox)	
	✳	public		**DefaultCellEditor** (JComboBox comboBox)	
	✳	public		**DefaultCellEditor** (JTextField textField)	
		protected	DefaultCellEditor⌄.EditorDelegate	**delegate**	
		protected	JComponent	**editorComponent**	
1.3	1	protected	void	fireEditingCanceled ()	
1.3	1	protected	void	fireEditingStopped ()	
1.4	1	public	*javax.swing⌄.event.CellEditorListener[]*	getCellEditorListeners ()	
	2	public	Object	**getCellEditorValue** ()	ε953,954,960
		public	int	**getClickCountToStart** ()	
		public	java.awt.Component	**getComponent** ()	
	3	public	java.awt.Component	**getTableCellEditorComponent** (JTable table, Object value, boolean isSelected, int row, int column)	ε953,960
	4	public	java.awt.Component	**getTreeCellEditorComponent** (JTree tree, Object value, boolean isSelected, boolean expanded, boolean leaf, int row)	
	1	public	**boolean**	**isCellEditable** (java.util.EventObject anEvent)	ε955,960
1.3	1	protected	javax.swing⌄.event.EventListenerList	listenerList	

Class *Interface* —extends - - -implements ○ abstract ● final △ static ▲ static final ✳ constructor x x—inherited x **x**—declared **x x**—overridden
ε*n*—examples of usage ⌄—has subclass package—see other volume

1	public	.... void	removeCellEditorListener (*javax.swing.event.CellEditorListener* l)	
	public	.... void	**setClickCountToStart** (int count)	
1	public	.... **boolean**	**shouldSelectCell** (java.util.EventObject anEvent)	
1	public	.... **boolean**	**stopCellEditing** ()	ε954,956

DefaultCellEditor.EditorDelegate protected javax.swing

Object

1.2 └─DefaultCellEditor.EditorDelegate - - - - - - - - - - *java.awt.event.ActionListener* ˌ[1] (*java.util.EventListener*),
java.awt.event.ItemListener [2] (*java.util.EventListener*),
java.io.Serializable ˌ

	1	public	.... void	**actionPerformed** (java.awt.event.ActionEvent e)	ε855,644,738,743,745
		public	.... void	**cancelCellEditing** ()	
*		protected	....	**DefaultCellEditor.EditorDelegate** ()	
		public	.... Object	**getCellEditorValue** ()	ε960
		public	.... boolean	**isCellEditable** (java.util.EventObject anEvent)	
	2	public	.... void	**itemStateChanged** (java.awt.event.ItemEvent e)	ε650,765
		public	.... void	**setValue** (Object value)	ε960
1.3		public	.... boolean	**shouldSelectCell** (java.util.EventObject anEvent)	
		public	.... boolean	**startCellEditing** (java.util.EventObject anEvent)	
		public	.... boolean	**stopCellEditing** ()	
		protected	.... Object	**value**	

DefaultColorSelectionModel javax.swing.colorchooser

Object

1.2 └─DefaultColorSelectionModel - - - - - - - - - - - - - - *ColorSelectionModel* [1], *java.io.Serializable* ˌ

	1	public	.... void	**addChangeListener** (*javax.swing.event.ChangeListener* l)	ε878,879,881,885
		protected transient	...... javax.ˌ swing.event.ChangeEvent	**changeEvent**	
*		public	....	**DefaultColorSelectionModel** ()	
*		public	....	**DefaultColorSelectionModel** (java.awt.Color color)	
		protected	.... void	**fireStateChanged** ()	
1.4		public	.... javax.swingˌ .event.ChangeListener[]	**getChangeListeners** ()	
	1	public	.... java.awt.Color	**getSelectedColor** ()	ε878,879,881,885
		protected	.... javax.swingˌ .event.EventListenerList	**listenerList**	
	1	public	.... void	**removeChangeListener** (*javax.swing.event.ChangeListener* l)	
	1	public	.... void	**setSelectedColor** (java.awt.Color color)	ε883

DefaultComboBoxModel javax.swing

Object

1.2 ○ └─AbstractListModel [1] - *ListModel* ˌ[2], *java.io.Serializable* ˌ

1.2 └─DefaultComboBoxModel - - - - - - - - - - - - - - - *MutableComboBoxModel* [3] (*ComboBoxModel* [4] (*ListModel* [2]))

	3	public	.... void	**addElement** (Object anObject)	
	1	public	.... void	addListDataListener (*javax.swing.event.ListDataListener* l)	ε785
*		public	....	**DefaultComboBoxModel** ()	
*		public	....	**DefaultComboBoxModel** (Object[] items)	
*		public	....	**DefaultComboBoxModel** (java.util.Vector v)	
	1	protected	.... void	fireContentsChanged (Object source, int index0, int index1)	
	1	protected	.... void	fireIntervalAdded (Object source, int index0, int index1)	
	1	protected	.... void	fireIntervalRemoved (Object source, int index0, int index1)	
	2	public	.... Object	**getElementAt** (int index)	ε760,776,777,779,785
		public	.... int	**getIndexOf** (Object anObject)	
1.4	1	public	.... javax.swingˌ .event.ListDataListener[]	getListDataListeners ()	
1.3	1	public	... *java.util.EventListener*[]	getListeners (Class listenerType)	ε760
	4	public	.... Object	**getSelectedItem** ()	ε760,777,778,780
	2	public	.... int	**getSize** ()	
	3	public	.... void	**insertElementAt** (Object anObject, int index)	
	1	protected	.... javax.swingˌ .event.EventListenerList	listenerList	
		public	.... void	**removeAllElements** ()	
	3	public	.... void	**removeElement** (Object anObject)	
	3	public	.... void	**removeElementAt** (int index)	

DefaultComboBoxModel

1 public	void	removeListDataListener (*javax.swing.event.ListDataListener* l)
4 public	void	**setSelectedItem** (Object anObject)

DefaultDesktopManager   javax.swing

Object
  └─DefaultDesktopManager ----------------- *DesktopManager* [1], *java.io.Serializable*

D   1.2

1	public	void	**activateFrame** (JInternalFrame f)
1	public	void	**beginDraggingFrame** (JComponent f)
1	public	void	**beginResizingFrame** (JComponent f, int direction)
1	public	void	**closeFrame** (JInternalFrame f)
1	public	void	**deactivateFrame** (JInternalFrame f)
✱	public		**DefaultDesktopManager** ()
1	public	void	**deiconifyFrame** (JInternalFrame f)
1	public	void	**dragFrame** (JComponent f, int newX, int newY)
1	public	void	**endDraggingFrame** (JComponent f)
1	public	void	**endResizingFrame** (JComponent f)
	protected	java.awt.Rectangle	**getBoundsForIconOf** (JInternalFrame f)
	protected	java.awt.Rectangle	**getPreviousBounds** (JInternalFrame f)
1	public	void	**iconifyFrame** (JInternalFrame f)
1	public	void	**maximizeFrame** (JInternalFrame f)
1	public	void	**minimizeFrame** (JInternalFrame f)
1	public	void	**openFrame** (JInternalFrame f)
	protected	void	**removeIconFor** (JInternalFrame f)
1	public	void	**resizeFrame** (JComponent f, int newX, int newY, int newWidth, int newHeight)
1	public	void	**setBoundsForFrame** (JComponent f, int newX, int newY, int newWidth, int newHeight)
	protected	void	**setPreviousBounds** (JInternalFrame f, java.awt.Rectangle r)
	protected	void	**setWasIcon** (JInternalFrame f, Boolean value)
	protected	boolean	**wasIcon** (JInternalFrame f)

DefaultEditorKit   javax.swing.text

Object
1.2 ○ └─EditorKit [1] ---------------------------- *Cloneable*, *java.io.Serializable*
1.2   └─DefaultEditorKit

▲	public static final	String	**backwardAction** = "caret-backward"
▲	public static final	String	**beepAction** = "beep"
▲	public static final	String	**beginAction** = "caret-begin"
▲	public static final	String	**beginLineAction** = "caret-begin-line"
▲	public static final	String	**beginParagraphAction** = "caret-begin-paragraph"
▲	public static final	String	**beginWordAction** = "caret-begin-word"
1	public	Object	clone ()
▲	public static final	String	**copyAction** = "copy-to-clipboard"
1	public	*Caret*	**createCaret** ()
1	public	*Document*	**createDefaultDocument** () ε1017
▲	public static final	String	**cutAction** = "cut-to-clipboard"
✱	public		**DefaultEditorKit** ()
▲	public static final	String	**defaultKeyTypedAction** = "default-typed"
1	public	void	deinstall (javax.swing.JEditorPane c)
▲	public static final	String	**deleteNextCharAction** = "delete-next"
▲	public static final	String	**deletePrevCharAction** = "delete-previous"
▲	public static final	String	**downAction** = "caret-down"
▲	public static final	String	**endAction** = "caret-end"
▲	public static final	String	**endLineAction** = "caret-end-line"
▲	public static final	String	**EndOfLineStringProperty** = "__EndOfLine__"
▲	public static final	String	**endParagraphAction** = "caret-end-paragraph"
▲	public static final	String	**endWordAction** = "caret-end-word"
▲	public static final	String	**forwardAction** = "caret-forward"
1	public	*javax.swing.Action[]*	**getActions** ()
1	public	String	**getContentType** ()
1	public	*ViewFactory*	**getViewFactory** ()
▲	public static final	String	**insertBreakAction** = "insert-break"
▲	public static final	String	**insertContentAction** = "insert-content"
▲	public static final	String	**insertTabAction** = "insert-tab"
1	public	void	install (javax.swing.JEditorPane c)
▲	public static final	String	**nextWordAction** = "caret-next-word"

Class *Interface* —extends - - -implements ○ abstract ● final △ static ▲ static final ✱ constructor x x—inherited x **x**—declared **x x**—overridden
ε*n*—examples of usage —has subclass package—see other volume

▲	public static final	........String	**pageDownAction**	= "page-down"
▲	public static final	........String	**pageUpAction**	= "page-up"
▲	public static final	........String	**pasteAction**	= "paste-from-clipboard"
▲	public static final	........String	**previousWordAction**	= "caret-previous-word"

| 1 | public | .... | **void** **read** (java.io.InputStream in, *Document* doc, int pos) |
| | | | throws java.io.IOException, BadLocationException |

| 1 | public | .... | **void** **read** (java.io.Reader in, *Document* doc, int pos) throws java.io.IOException, BadLocationException | ε1017,1018 |

D

▲	public static final	........String	**readOnlyAction**	= "set-read-only"
▲	public static final	........String	**selectAllAction**	= "select-all"
▲	public static final	........String	**selectionBackwardAction**	= "selection-backward"
▲	public static final	........String	**selectionBeginAction**	= "selection-begin"
▲	public static final	........String	**selectionBeginLineAction**	= "selection-begin-line"
▲	public static final	........String	**selectionBeginParagraphAction**	= "selection-begin-paragraph"
▲	public static final	........String	**selectionBeginWordAction**	= "selection-begin-word"
▲	public static final	........String	**selectionDownAction**	= "selection-down"
▲	public static final	........String	**selectionEndAction**	= "selection-end"
▲	public static final	........String	**selectionEndLineAction**	= "selection-end-line"
▲	public static final	........String	**selectionEndParagraphAction**	= "selection-end-paragraph"
▲	public static final	........String	**selectionEndWordAction**	= "selection-end-word"
▲	public static final	........String	**selectionForwardAction**	= "selection-forward"
▲	public static final	........String	**selectionNextWordAction**	= "selection-next-word"
▲	public static final	........String	**selectionPreviousWordAction**	= "selection-previous-word"
▲	public static final	........String	**selectionUpAction**	= "selection-up"
▲	public static final	........String	**selectLineAction**	= "select-line"
▲	public static final	........String	**selectParagraphAction**	= "select-paragraph"
▲	public static final	........String	**selectWordAction**	= "select-word"
▲	public static final	........String	**upAction**	= "caret-up"
▲	public static final	........String	**writableAction**	= "set-writable"

| 1 | public | .... | **void** **write** (java.io.OutputStream out, *Document* doc, int pos, int len) |
| | | | throws java.io.IOException, BadLocationException |

| 1 | public | .... | **void** **write** (java.io.Writer out, *Document* doc, int pos, int len) |
| | | | throws java.io.IOException, BadLocationException |

DefaultEditorKit.BeepAction   javax.swing.text

Object
1.2 ○ └javax.swing.AbstractAction[1] - - - - - - - - - - - - - - *javax.swing.Action*[3] (*java.awt.event.ActionListener*[4]
                                                (*java.util.EventListener*)), *Cloneable*, *java.io.Serializable*.

1.2 ○   └TextAction[2]
1.2   └DefaultEditorKit.BeepAction

1	*12 inherited members from javax.swing.AbstractAction not shown*
2	*3 inherited members from TextAction not shown*
3	*8 inherited members from javax.swing.Action not shown*
4	public.....................void **actionPerformed** (java.awt.event.ActionEvent e)	ε855,644,738,743,745
✳	public......................... **DefaultEditorKit.BeepAction** ()

Classes

DefaultEditorKit.CopyAction   javax.swing.text

Object
1.2 ○ └javax.swing.AbstractAction[1] - - - - - - - - - - - - - - *javax.swing.Action*[3] (*java.awt.event.ActionListener*[4]
                                                (*java.util.EventListener*)), *Cloneable*, *java.io.Serializable*.

1.2 ○   └TextAction[2]
1.2   └DefaultEditorKit.CopyAction

1	*12 inherited members from javax.swing.AbstractAction not shown*
2	*3 inherited members from TextAction not shown*
3	*8 inherited members from javax.swing.Action not shown*
4	public.....................void **actionPerformed** (java.awt.event.ActionEvent e)	ε855,644,738,743,745
✳	public......................... **DefaultEditorKit.CopyAction** ()

DefaultEditorKit.CutAction	javax.swing.text

```
      Object
1.2 ○  └javax.swing.AbstractAction¹ - - - - - - - - - - - - - - javax.swing.Action³ (java.awt.event.ActionListener⁴
                                                         (java.util.EventListener)), Cloneable., java.io.Serializable.
1.2 ○      └TextAction²
1.2          └DefaultEditorKit.CutAction
```

```
     1  12 inherited members from javax.swing.AbstractAction not shown
     2  3 inherited members from TextAction not shown
     3  8 inherited members from javax.swing.Action not shown
     4  public......................void actionPerformed (java.awt.event.ActionEvent e)          ε855,644,738,743,745
  *     public......................... DefaultEditorKit.CutAction ()
```

DefaultEditorKit.DefaultKeyTypedAction	javax.swing.text

```
      Object
1.2 ○  └javax.swing.AbstractAction¹ - - - - - - - - - - - - - - javax.swing.Action³ (java.awt.event.ActionListener⁴
                                                         (java.util.EventListener)), Cloneable., java.io.Serializable.
1.2 ○      └TextAction²
1.2          └DefaultEditorKit.DefaultKeyTypedAction
```

```
     1  12 inherited members from javax.swing.AbstractAction not shown
     2  3 inherited members from TextAction not shown
     3  8 inherited members from javax.swing.Action not shown
     4  public......................void actionPerformed (java.awt.event.ActionEvent e)          ε855,644,738,743,745
  *     public......................... DefaultEditorKit.DefaultKeyTypedAction ()
```

DefaultEditorKit.InsertBreakAction	javax.swing.text

```
      Object
1.2 ○  └javax.swing.AbstractAction¹ - - - - - - - - - - - - - - javax.swing.Action³ (java.awt.event.ActionListener⁴
                                                         (java.util.EventListener)), Cloneable., java.io.Serializable.
1.2 ○      └TextAction²
1.2          └DefaultEditorKit.InsertBreakAction
```

```
     1  12 inherited members from javax.swing.AbstractAction not shown
     2  3 inherited members from TextAction not shown
     3  8 inherited members from javax.swing.Action not shown
     4  public......................void actionPerformed (java.awt.event.ActionEvent e)          ε855,644,738,743,745
  *     public......................... DefaultEditorKit.InsertBreakAction ()
```

DefaultEditorKit.InsertContentAction	javax.swing.text

```
      Object
1.2 ○  └javax.swing.AbstractAction¹ - - - - - - - - - - - - - - javax.swing.Action³ (java.awt.event.ActionListener⁴
                                                         (java.util.EventListener)), Cloneable., java.io.Serializable.
1.2 ○      └TextAction²
1.2          └DefaultEditorKit.InsertContentAction
```

```
     1  12 inherited members from javax.swing.AbstractAction not shown
     2  3 inherited members from TextAction not shown
     3  8 inherited members from javax.swing.Action not shown
     4  public......................void actionPerformed (java.awt.event.ActionEvent e)          ε855,644,738,743,745
  *     public......................... DefaultEditorKit.InsertContentAction ()
```

DefaultEditorKit.InsertTabAction	javax.swing.text

```
      Object
1.2 ○  └javax.swing.AbstractAction¹ - - - - - - - - - - - - - - javax.swing.Action³ (java.awt.event.ActionListener⁴
                                                         (java.util.EventListener)), Cloneable., java.io.Serializable.
1.2 ○      └TextAction²
1.2          └DefaultEditorKit.InsertTabAction
```

Class *Interface* —extends - - -implements ○ abstract ● final △ static ▲ static final * constructor x x—inherited x **x**—declared **x x**—overridden
εn—examples of usage .—has subclass package—see other volume

478

1	*12 inherited members from javax.swing.AbstractAction not shown*		
2	*3 inherited members from TextAction not shown*		
3	*8 inherited members from javax.swing.Action not shown*		
4	public.....................void **actionPerformed** (java.awt.event.ActionEvent e)		ε855,644,738,743,745
*	public.......................... **DefaultEditorKit.InsertTabAction** ()		

DefaultEditorKit.PasteAction   javax.swing.text   D

Object
1.2 O └─javax.swing.AbstractAction[1] - - - - - - - - - - - - - *javax.swing.Action*[3] (*java.awt.event.ActionListener*[4]
                                                (*java.util.EventListener*)), *Cloneable*, *java.io.Serializable*
1.2 O   └─TextAction[2]
1.2   └─DefaultEditorKit.PasteAction

1	*12 inherited members from javax.swing.AbstractAction not shown*		
2	*3 inherited members from TextAction not shown*		
3	*8 inherited members from javax.swing.Action not shown*		
4	public.....................void **actionPerformed** (java.awt.event.ActionEvent e)		ε855,644,738,743,745
*	public.......................... **DefaultEditorKit.PasteAction** ()		

DefaultFocusManager   javax.swing

Object
1.4 O └─java.awt.KeyboardFocusManager[1] - - - - - - - - - *java.awt.KeyEventDispatcher*, *java.awt.KeyEventPostProcessor*
1.4   └─java.awt.DefaultKeyboardFocusManager[2]
1.2 O   └─FocusManager[3]
1.2   └─DefaultFocusManager

	1	*51 inherited members from java.awt.KeyboardFocusManager not shown*		
		public................. boolean **compareTabOrder** (java.awt.Component a, java.awt.Component b)		
	*	public.......................... **DefaultFocusManager** ()		
1.4	2	protected synchronized ...void dequeueKeyEvents (long after, java.awt.Component untilFocused)		
1.4	2	protected synchronized ...void discardKeyEvents (java.awt.Component comp)		
1.4	2	public................. boolean dispatchEvent (java.awt.AWTEvent e)		
1.4	2	public................. boolean dispatchKeyEvent (java.awt.event.KeyEvent e)		ε636
1.4	2	public.......................void downFocusCycle (java.awt.Container aContainer)		
1.4	2	protected synchronized ...void enqueueKeyEvents (long after, java.awt.Component untilFocused)		
▲	3	public static final ....String FOCUS_MANAGER_CLASS_PROPERTY = "FocusManagerClassName"		
1.4	2	public.......................void focusNextComponent (java.awt.Component aComponent)		
1.4	2	public.......................void focusPreviousComponent (java.awt.Component aComponent)		
		public.... java.awt.Component **getComponentAfter** (java.awt.Container aContainer, java.awt.Component aComponent)		
		public.... java.awt.Component **getComponentBefore** (java.awt.Container aContainer, java.awt.Component aComponent)		
△	3	public static ....FocusManager getCurrentManager ()		
		public.... java.awt.Component **getFirstComponent** (java.awt.Container aContainer)		
		public.... java.awt.Component **getLastComponent** (java.awt.Container aContainer)		
1.4	2	public................. boolean postProcessKeyEvent (java.awt.event.KeyEvent e)		
1.4	2	public.......................void processKeyEvent (java.awt.Component focusedComponent, java.awt.event.KeyEvent e)		
△	3	public static ....void setCurrentManager (FocusManager aFocusManager) throws SecurityException		
1.4	2	public.......................void upFocusCycle (java.awt.Component aComponent)		

DefaultFocusTraversalPolicy   java.awt

Object
1.4 O └─FocusTraversalPolicy[1]
1.4   └─ContainerOrderFocusTraversalPolicy[2] - - - - - *java.io.Serializable*
1.4   └─DefaultFocusTraversalPolicy

2	protected .... **boolean accept** (Component aComponent)		
*	public.......................... **DefaultFocusTraversalPolicy** ()		
2	public............. Component getComponentAfter (Container focusCycleRoot, Component aComponent)		
			ε615
2	public............. Component getComponentBefore (Container focusCycleRoot, Component aComponent)		
			ε615
2	public............. Component getDefaultComponent (Container focusCycleRoot)		ε615
2	public............. Component getFirstComponent (Container focusCycleRoot)		
2	public................. boolean getImplicitDownCycleTraversal ()		

DefaultFocusTraversalPolicy

1 public.............. Component getInitialComponent (Window window)
2 public.............. Component getLastComponent (Container focusCycleRoot)
2 public........................void setImplicitDownCycleTraversal (boolean implicitDownCycleTraversal)

DefaultFormatter — javax.swing.text

D

Object
1.4 ○ └javax.swing.JFormattedTextField - - - - - - - - - - *java.io.Serializable*
.AbstractFormatter [1]
1.4 └DefaultFormatter - *Cloneable*

1 public.................... **Object** **clone** () throws CloneNotSupportedException
* public............................ **DefaultFormatter** ()
1 protected . *javax.swing.Action[]* getActions ()
public.................. boolean **getAllowsInvalid** ()
public.................. boolean **getCommitsOnValidEdit** ()
1 protected ..... **DocumentFilter** **getDocumentFilter** ()
1 protected .... javax.swing.JFormattedTextField getFormattedTextField ()
1 protected .....**NavigationFilter** **getNavigationFilter** ()
public.................. boolean **getOverwriteMode** ()
public..................... Class **getValueClass** ()
1 public...................... **void** **install** (javax.swing.JFormattedTextField ftf)
1 protected ....void invalidEdit ()
public.......................void **setAllowsInvalid** (boolean allowsInvalid)
public.......................void **setCommitsOnValidEdit** (boolean commit)
1 protected ....void setEditValid (boolean valid)
public.......................void **setOverwriteMode** (boolean overwriteMode)
public.......................void **setValueClass** (Class valueClass) ε995
1 public.................... **Object** **stringToValue** (String string) throws java.text.ParseException
1 public.......................void uninstall ()
1 public.................... **String** **valueToString** (Object value) throws java.text.ParseException

DefaultFormatterFactory — javax.swing.text

Object
1.4 ○ └javax.swing.JFormattedTextField
.AbstractFormatterFactory [1]
1.4 └DefaultFormatterFactory - - - - - - - - - - - - - - - - *java.io.Serializable*

* public........................... **DefaultFormatterFactory** ()
* public........................... **DefaultFormatterFactory** (javax.swing.JFormattedTextField.AbstractFormatter defaultFormat)
* public........................... **DefaultFormatterFactory** (javax.swing.JFormattedTextField.AbstractFormatter defaultFormat, javax.swing.JFormattedTextField.AbstractFormatter displayFormat)
* public........................... **DefaultFormatterFactory** (javax.swing.JFormattedTextField.AbstractFormatter defaultFormat, javax.swing.JFormattedTextField.AbstractFormatter displayFormat, javax.swing.JFormattedTextField.AbstractFormatter editFormat) ε995
* public........................... **DefaultFormatterFactory** (javax.swing.JFormattedTextField.AbstractFormatter defaultFormat, javax.swing.JFormattedTextField.AbstractFormatter displayFormat, javax.swing.JFormattedTextField.AbstractFormatter editFormat, javax.swing.JFormattedTextField.AbstractFormatter nullFormat)
public.................... javax.swing.JFormattedTextField.AbstractFormatter **getDefaultFormatter** () ε787
public.................... javax.swing.JFormattedTextField.AbstractFormatter **getDisplayFormatter** ()
public.................... javax.swing.JFormattedTextField.AbstractFormatter **getEditFormatter** ()
1 public............ **javax.swing.JFormattedTextField.AbstractFormatter** **getFormatter** (javax.swing.JFormattedTextField source)

Class *Interface* —extends - - -implements ○ abstract ● final △ static ▲ static final ✻ constructor x x—inherited x **x**—declared **x x**—overridden
εn—examples of usage ˯—has subclass package—see other volume

```
     public ..................... javax ⊋  getNullFormatter ()
         .swing.JFormattedTextField ⊋
             .AbstractFormatter
     public ....................... void  setDefaultFormatter (javax.swing.JFormattedTextField.AbstractFormatter atf)
     public ....................... void  setDisplayFormatter (javax.swing.JFormattedTextField.AbstractFormatter atf)
     public ....................... void  setEditFormatter (javax.swing.JFormattedTextField.AbstractFormatter atf)
     public ....................... void  setNullFormatter (javax.swing.JFormattedTextField.AbstractFormatter atf)
```

D

DefaultHighlighter — javax.swing.text

```
         Object
1.2 ○    └LayeredHighlighter 1 - - - - - - - - - - - - - - - - - - - Highlighter 2
1.2          └DefaultHighlighter
```

```
     2   public ................... Object  addHighlight (int p0, int p1, Highlighter.HighlightPainter p)        ε1006
                                              throws BadLocationException
     2   public ....................... void  changeHighlight (Object tag, int p0, int p1) throws BadLocationException
  *      public ...........................      DefaultHighlighter ()
  ▲      public static final ..............      DefaultPainter
             ......... LayeredHighlighter ⊋
                 .LayerPainter
     2   public ................... void  deinstall (JTextComponent c)
         public ................. boolean  getDrawsLayeredHighlights ()
     2   public ... Highlighter.Highlight[]  getHighlights ()                                                   ε1006
     2   public ................... void  install (JTextComponent c)
     2   public ................... void  paint (java.awt.Graphics g)
     1   public ................... void  paintLayeredHighlights (java.awt.Graphics g, int p0, int p1,
                                              java.awt.Shape viewBounds, JTextComponent editor, View view)
     2   public ....................... void  removeAllHighlights ()
     2   public ....................... void  removeHighlight (Object tag)                                       ε1006
         public ....................... void  setDrawsLayeredHighlights (boolean newValue)
```

DefaultHighlighter.DefaultHighlightPainter — javax.swing.text

ε1006

```
         Object
1.2 ○    └LayeredHighlighter.LayerPainter 1 - - - - - - - - - - Highlighter.HighlightPainter 2
1.2          └DefaultHighlighter.DefaultHighlightPainter
```

```
  *      public ...........................      DefaultHighlighter.DefaultHighlightPainter (java.awt.Color c)
         public ......... java.awt.Color  getColor ()
     2   public ....................... void  paint (java.awt.Graphics g, int offs0, int offs1, java.awt.Shape bounds,
                                              JTextComponent c)
     1   public ......... java.awt.Shape  paintLayer (java.awt.Graphics g, int offs0, int offs1, java.awt.Shape bounds,
                                              JTextComponent c, View view)
```

DefaultKeyboardFocusManager — java.awt

Classes

```
         Object
1.4 ○    └KeyboardFocusManager 1 - - - - - - - - - - - - - - - KeyEventDispatcher, KeyEventPostProcessor
1.4          └DefaultKeyboardFocusManager
```

```
     1   51 inherited members from KeyboardFocusManager not shown
  *      public ...........................      DefaultKeyboardFocusManager ()
     1   protected synchronized .. void  dequeueKeyEvents (long after, Component untilFocused)
     1   protected synchronized .. void  discardKeyEvents (Component comp)
     1   public ................. boolean  dispatchEvent (AWTEvent e)
     1   public ................. boolean  dispatchKeyEvent (java.awt.event.KeyEvent e)                          ε636
     1   public ................... void  downFocusCycle (Container aContainer)
     1   protected synchronized .. void  enqueueKeyEvents (long after, Component untilFocused)
     1   public ................... void  focusNextComponent (Component aComponent)
     1   public ................... void  focusPreviousComponent (Component aComponent)
     1   public ................. boolean  postProcessKeyEvent (java.awt.event.KeyEvent e)
     1   public ................... void  processKeyEvent (Component focusedComponent, java.awt.event.KeyEvent e)
     1   public ................... void  upFocusCycle (Component aComponent)
```

DefaultListCellRenderer

DefaultListCellRenderer	javax.swing

```
Object
○  └java.awt.Component¹ ------------------- java.awt.image.ImageObserver ⁵, java.awt.MenuContainer,
                                                    java.io.Serializable.
        └java.awt.Container²
1.2 ○      └JComponent³
1.2         └JLabel⁴ ----------------------- SwingConstants ⁶, javax.accessibility.Accessible
1.2            └DefaultListCellRenderer. --------- ListCellRenderer ⁷
```

1	*142 inherited members from java.awt.Component not shown*	
2	*50 inherited members from java.awt.Container not shown*	
3	*131 inherited members from JComponent not shown*	
4	*33 inherited members from JLabel not shown*	
6	*19 inherited members from SwingConstants not shown*	
5	*8 inherited members from java.awt.image.ImageObserver not shown*	
*	public.........................	**DefaultListCellRenderer** ()
3	public..................... **void**	**firePropertyChange** (String propertyName, float oldValue, float newValue)
3	public..................... **void**	**firePropertyChange** (String propertyName, short oldValue, short newValue)
3	public..................... **void**	**firePropertyChange** (String propertyName, boolean oldValue, boolean newValue)
3	public..................... **void**	**firePropertyChange** (String propertyName, char oldValue, char newValue)
3	protected .... **void**	**firePropertyChange** (String propertyName, Object oldValue, Object newValue)
3	public..................... **void**	**firePropertyChange** (String propertyName, long oldValue, long newValue)
3	public..................... **void**	**firePropertyChange** (String propertyName, byte oldValue, byte newValue)
3	public..................... **void**	**firePropertyChange** (String propertyName, double oldValue, double newValue)
3	public..................... **void**	**firePropertyChange** (String propertyName, int oldValue, int newValue)
7	public.... java.awt.Component	**getListCellRendererComponent** (JList list, Object value, int index, boolean isSelected, boolean cellHasFocus)
△	protected static	**noFocusBorder** *... javax.swing.border.Border*
3	public..................... **void**	**repaint** (java.awt.Rectangle r)
3	public..................... **void**	**repaint** (long tm, int x, int y, int width, int height)
3	public..................... **void**	**revalidate** ()
2	public..................... **void**	**validate** ()

ε601,674,928,936

DefaultListCellRenderer.UIResource	javax.swing

```
Object
○  └java.awt.Component¹ ------------------- java.awt.image.ImageObserver ⁶, java.awt.MenuContainer,
                                                    java.io.Serializable.
        └java.awt.Container²
1.2 ○      └JComponent³
1.2         └JLabel⁴ ----------------------- SwingConstants ⁷, javax.accessibility.Accessible
1.2            └DefaultListCellRenderer⁵ --------- ListCellRenderer
1.2               └DefaultListCellRenderer₂ ------- javax.swing.plaf.UIResource
                     .UIResource
```

1	*142 inherited members from java.awt.Component not shown*	
2	*50 inherited members from java.awt.Container not shown*	
3	*131 inherited members from JComponent not shown*	
4	*33 inherited members from JLabel not shown*	
7	*19 inherited members from SwingConstants not shown*	
6	*8 inherited members from java.awt.image.ImageObserver not shown*	
5	public.....................void	firePropertyChange (String propertyName, short oldValue, short newValue)
5	public.....................void	firePropertyChange (String propertyName, long oldValue, long newValue)
5	protected ....void	firePropertyChange (String propertyName, Object oldValue, Object newValue)
5	public.....................void	firePropertyChange (String propertyName, int oldValue, int newValue)
5	public.....................void	firePropertyChange (String propertyName, float oldValue, float newValue)
5	public.....................void	firePropertyChange (String propertyName, double oldValue, double newValue)
5	public.....................void	firePropertyChange (String propertyName, char oldValue, char newValue)
5	public.....................void	firePropertyChange (String propertyName, byte oldValue, byte newValue)
5	public.....................void	firePropertyChange (String propertyName, boolean oldValue, boolean newValue)
5	public.... java.awt.Component	getListCellRendererComponent (JList list, Object value, int index, boolean isSelected, boolean cellHasFocus)
△ 5	protected static	noFocusBorder *... javax.swing.border.Border*
5	public.....................void	repaint (java.awt.Rectangle r)
5	public.....................void	repaint (long tm, int x, int y, int width, int height)

Class *Interface* —extends - - -implements ○ abstract ● final △ static ▲ static final ✳ constructor x x—inherited x **x**—declared **x x**—overridden
εn—examples of usage .—has subclass package—see other volume

482

5	public.....................void	revalidate ()		
*	public.....................	**DefaultListCellRenderer.UIResource** ()		
5	public.....................void	validate ()		ε601,674,928,936

DefaultListModel   javax.swing

Object [1]
1.2 ○ └ AbstractListModel [2] - *ListModel* ⌐ [3], *java.io.Serializable* ⌐
1.2   └ DefaultListModel

	public.....................void	**add** (int index, Object element)	ε778
	public.....................void	**addElement** (Object obj)	
2	public.....................void	addListDataListener (*javax.swing.event.ListDataListener* l)	ε785
	public.......................int	**capacity** ()	
	public.....................void	**clear** ()	ε778
	public............... boolean	**contains** (Object elem)	
	public.....................void	**copyInto** (Object[] anArray)	
*	public.....................	**DefaultListModel** ()	ε778
	public..................Object	**elementAt** (int index)	
	public.... *java.util.Enumeration*	**elements** ()	
	public.....................void	**ensureCapacity** (int minCapacity)	
2	protected.................void	fireContentsChanged (Object source, int index0, int index1)	
2	protected.................void	fireIntervalAdded (Object source, int index0, int index1)	
2	protected.................void	fireIntervalRemoved (Object source, int index0, int index1)	
	public..................Object	**firstElement** ()	
	public..................Object	**get** (int index)	
3	public..................Object	**getElementAt** (int index)	ε785,760,776,777,779
1.4 2	public............. *javax.swing* ⌐	getListDataListeners ()	
	.event.ListDataListener[]		
1.3 2	public. *java.util.EventListener[]*	getListeners (Class listenerType)	ε778,760,777,780
3	public.......................int	**getSize** ()	
	public.......................int	**indexOf** (Object elem)	
	public.......................int	**indexOf** (Object elem, int index)	
	public.....................void	**insertElementAt** (Object obj, int index)	
	public............... boolean	**isEmpty** ()	
	public..................Object	**lastElement** ()	
	public.......................int	**lastIndexOf** (Object elem)	
	public.......................int	**lastIndexOf** (Object elem, int index)	
2	protected......... *javax.swing* ⌐	listenerList	
	.event.EventListenerList		
	public..................Object	**remove** (int index)	ε778
	public.....................void	**removeAllElements** ()	
	public............... boolean	**removeElement** (Object obj)	
	public.....................void	**removeElementAt** (int index)	
2	public.....................void	removeListDataListener (*javax.swing.event.ListDataListener* l)	
	public.....................void	**removeRange** (int fromIndex, int toIndex)	
	public..................Object	**set** (int index, Object element)	ε778
	public.....................void	**setElementAt** (Object obj, int index)	
	public.....................void	**setSize** (int newSize)	
	public.......................int	**size** ()	
	public..................Object[]	**toArray** ()	
1	public................**String**	**toString** ()	
	public.....................void	**trimToSize** ()	

DefaultListSelectionModel   javax.swing

Object [1]
1.2 └ DefaultListSelectionModel - - - - - - - - - - - - - - - *ListSelectionModel* [2], *Cloneable* ⌐, *java.io.Serializable* ⌐

2	public.....................void	**addListSelectionListener** (*javax.swing.event.ListSelectionListener* l)	
			ε957,964
2	public.....................void	**addSelectionInterval** (int index0, int index1)	
2	public.....................void	**clearSelection** ()	
1	public..................**Object**	**clone** () throws CloneNotSupportedException	
*	public.....................	**DefaultListSelectionModel** ()	
	protected.................void	**fireValueChanged** (boolean isAdjusting)	
	protected.................void	**fireValueChanged** (int firstIndex, int lastIndex)	
	protected.................void	**fireValueChanged** (int firstIndex, int lastIndex, boolean isAdjusting)	
2	public.......................int	**getAnchorSelectionIndex** ()	ε944,957
2	public.......................int	**getLeadSelectionIndex** ()	
1.3	public. *java.util.EventListener[]*	**getListeners** (Class listenerType)	

D

Classes

DefaultListSelectionModel

1.4	public	*javax.swing* *.event.ListSelectionListener[]*	**getListSelectionListeners** ()	
2	public	int	**getMaxSelectionIndex** ()	ε942
2	public	int	**getMinSelectionIndex** ()	
2	public	int	**getSelectionMode** ()	ε940
2	public	boolean	**getValueIsAdjusting** ()	
2	public	void	**insertIndexInterval** (int index, int length, boolean before)	
	public	boolean	**isLeadAnchorNotificationEnabled** ()	
2	public	boolean	**isSelectedIndex** (int index)	
2	public	boolean	**isSelectionEmpty** ()	
	protected	boolean	**leadAnchorNotificationEnabled**	
	protected	*javax.swing* *.event.EventListenerList*	**listenerList**	
▲ 2	public static final	int	MULTIPLE_INTERVAL_SELECTION = 2	ε781,940,941,942
2	public	void	**removeIndexInterval** (int index0, int index1)	
2	public	void	**removeListSelectionListener** (*javax.swing.event.ListSelectionListener* l)	
2	public	void	**removeSelectionInterval** (int index0, int index1)	
2	public	void	**setAnchorSelectionIndex** (int anchorIndex)	
	public	void	**setLeadAnchorNotificationEnabled** (boolean flag)	
2	public	void	**setLeadSelectionIndex** (int leadIndex)	
2	public	void	**setSelectionInterval** (int index0, int index1)	
2	public	void	**setSelectionMode** (int selectionMode)	
2	public	void	**setValueIsAdjusting** (boolean isAdjusting)	
▲ 2	public static final	int	SINGLE_INTERVAL_SELECTION = 1	ε781,940,942
▲ 2	public static final	int	SINGLE_SELECTION = 0	ε781,940,942
1	public	String	**toString** ()	

DefaultMutableTreeNode
javax.swing.tree

Object[1]
1.2 └─DefaultMutableTreeNode — - - - - - - - - - - - - - - - - *Cloneable*, *MutableTreeNode*[2] (*TreeNode*[3]), *java.io.Serializable*

	public	void	**add** (*MutableTreeNode* newChild)	ε1019
	protected	boolean	**allowsChildren**	
	public	*java.util.Enumeration*	**breadthFirstEnumeration** ()	
3	public	*java.util.Enumeration*	**children** ()	ε1023,1024,1028,1029
	protected	java.util.Vector	**children**	
1	public	**Object**	**clone** ()	
*	public		**DefaultMutableTreeNode** ()	
*	public		**DefaultMutableTreeNode** (Object userObject)	ε1019,1025
*	public		**DefaultMutableTreeNode** (Object userObject, boolean allowsChildren)	
	public	*java.util.Enumeration*	**depthFirstEnumeration** ()	
▲	public static final	*java.util.Enumeration*	**EMPTY_ENUMERATION**	
3	public	boolean	**getAllowsChildren** ()	
	public	*TreeNode*	**getChildAfter** (*TreeNode* aChild)	
3	public	*TreeNode*	**getChildAt** (int index)	
	public	*TreeNode*	**getChildBefore** (*TreeNode* aChild)	
3	public	int	**getChildCount** ()	ε1023,1024,1025,1028,1029
	public	int	**getDepth** ()	
	public	*TreeNode*	**getFirstChild** ()	
	public	DefaultMutableTreeNode	**getFirstLeaf** ()	
3	public	int	**getIndex** (*TreeNode* aChild)	
	public	*TreeNode*	**getLastChild** ()	
	public	DefaultMutableTreeNode	**getLastLeaf** ()	
	public	int	**getLeafCount** ()	
	public	int	**getLevel** ()	
	public	DefaultMutableTreeNode	**getNextLeaf** ()	
	public	DefaultMutableTreeNode	**getNextNode** ()	
	public	DefaultMutableTreeNode	**getNextSibling** ()	
3	public	*TreeNode*	**getParent** ()	ε1027
	public	*TreeNode[]*	**getPath** ()	
	protected	*TreeNode[]*	**getPathToRoot** (*TreeNode* aNode, int depth)	

Class   *Interface*   —extends   - - -implements   ○ abstract   ● final   △ static   ▲ static final   ✳ constructor   x x—inherited   x **x**—declared   **x x**—overridden
ε*n*—examples of usage   ⌐—has subclass   package—see other volume

public		**getPreviousLeaf** ()
.....*DefaultMutableTreeNode*		
public		**getPreviousNode** ()
.....*DefaultMutableTreeNode*		
public		**getPreviousSibling** ()
.....*DefaultMutableTreeNode*		
public	*TreeNode*	**getRoot** ()
public	*TreeNode*	**getSharedAncestor** (DefaultMutableTreeNode aNode)
public	int	**getSiblingCount** ()
public	Object	**getUserObject** ()
public	Object[]	**getUserObjectPath** ()
2 public	void	**insert** (*MutableTreeNode* newChild, int childIndex)
3 public	boolean	**isLeaf** ()
public	boolean	**isNodeAncestor** (*TreeNode* anotherNode)
public	boolean	**isNodeChild** (*TreeNode* aNode)
public	boolean	**isNodeDescendant** (DefaultMutableTreeNode anotherNode)
public	boolean	**isNodeRelated** (DefaultMutableTreeNode aNode)
public	boolean	**isNodeSibling** (*TreeNode* anotherNode)
public	boolean	**isRoot** ()
protected	*MutableTreeNode*	**parent**
public	*java.util.Enumeration*	**pathFromAncestorEnumeration** (*TreeNode* ancestor)
public	*java.util.Enumeration*	**postorderEnumeration** ()
public	*java.util.Enumeration*	**preorderEnumeration** ()
2 public	void	**remove** (int childIndex)
2 public	void	**remove** (*MutableTreeNode* aChild)
public	void	**removeAllChildren** ()
2 public	void	**removeFromParent** ()
public	void	**setAllowsChildren** (boolean allows)
2 public	void	**setParent** (*MutableTreeNode* newParent)
2 public	void	**setUserObject** (Object userObject)
1 public	**String**	**toString** ()
protected transient	Object	**userObject**

DefaultSingleSelectionModel

Object
1.2 └─DefaultSingleSelectionModel ------------- *SingleSelectionModel* [1], *java.io.Serializable*

1 public	void	**addChangeListener** (*javax.swing.event.ChangeListener* l)
protected transient	javax	**changeEvent**
.swing.event.ChangeEvent		
1 public	void	**clearSelection** ()
* public		**DefaultSingleSelectionModel** ()
protected	void	**fireStateChanged** ()
1.4 public	*javax.swing*	**getChangeListeners** ()
.event.ChangeListener[]		
1.3 public	*java.util.EventListener[]*	**getListeners** (Class listenerType)
1 public	int	**getSelectedIndex** ()
1 public	boolean	**isSelected** ()
protected	javax.swing	**listenerList**
.event.EventListenerList		
1 public	void	**removeChangeListener** (*javax.swing.event.ChangeListener* l)
1 public	void	**setSelectedIndex** (int index)

DefaultStyledDocument

Object
1.2 ○ └─AbstractDocument[1] -------------------- *Document* [2], *java.io.Serializable*
1.2   └─DefaultStyledDocument ---------------- *StyledDocument* [3] (*Document* [2])

1	*47 inherited members from AbstractDocument not shown*	
1 public	void	**addDocumentListener** (*javax.swing.event.DocumentListener* listener)
		ε1016
3 public	*Style*	**addStyle** (String nm, *Style* parent)
protected		**buffer**
.....DefaultStyledDocument		ε989,991,992
.ElementBuffer		
▲ public static final	int	**BUFFER_SIZE_DEFAULT** = 4096
protected	void	**create** (DefaultStyledDocument.ElementSpec[] data)
protected . AbstractDocument		**createDefaultRoot** ()
.AbstractElement		

DefaultStyledDocument

*		public	....	**DefaultStyledDocument** ()	
*		public	....	**DefaultStyledDocument** (StyleContext styles)	ε1008
*		public	....	**DefaultStyledDocument** (*AbstractDocument.Content* c, StyleContext styles)	
	3	public	............java.awt.Color	**getBackground** (*AttributeSet* attr)	
	3	public	..................*Element*	**getCharacterElement** (int pos)	
	1	public	..................***Element***	**getDefaultRootElement** ()	ε984,990,1013
	3	public	............java.awt.Font	**getFont** (*AttributeSet* attr)	
	3	public	............java.awt.Color	**getForeground** (*AttributeSet* attr)	
	3	public	....................*Style*	**getLogicalStyle** (int p)	
	1	public	..................***Element***	**getParagraphElement** (int pos)	
	3	public	....................*Style*	**getStyle** (String nm)	ε1009,1007,1008,1011,1013
		public	..*java.util.Enumeration*	**getStyleNames** ()	ε1009,1011
		protected	...................void	**insert** (int offset, DefaultStyledDocument.ElementSpec[] data)	
				throws BadLocationException	
	1	protected	...............**void**	**insertUpdate** (AbstractDocument.DefaultDocumentEvent chng, *AttributeSet* attr)	
	1	public	...............**void**	**removeDocumentListener** (*javax.swing.event.DocumentListener* listener)	
	3	public	...................void	**removeStyle** (String nm)	
	1	protected	...............**void**	**removeUpdate** (AbstractDocument.DefaultDocumentEvent chng)	
	3	public	...................void	**setCharacterAttributes** (int offset, int length, *AttributeSet* s, boolean replace)	
					ε1007,1013
	3	public	...................void	**setLogicalStyle** (int pos, *Style* s)	
	3	public	...................void	**setParagraphAttributes** (int offset, int length, *AttributeSet* s, boolean replace)	
					ε1007,1013
▲	2	public static final	.........String	StreamDescriptionProperty = "stream"	
		protected	...................void	**styleChanged** (*Style* style)	
▲	2	public static final	.........String	TitleProperty = "title"	

DefaultStyledDocument.AttributeUndoableEdit

javax.swing.text

Object
1.2 └javax.swing.undo.AbstractUndoableEdit [1] - - - - *javax.swing.undo.UndoableEdit*, *java.io.Serializable*╷
1.2 └DefaultStyledDocument╻
.AttributeUndoableEdit

	1	public	.... boolean	addEdit (*javax.swing.undo.UndoableEdit* anEdit)	ε1034
*		public	....	**DefaultStyledDocument.AttributeUndoableEdit** (*Element* element,	
				AttributeSet newAttributes, boolean isReplacing)	
	1	public	.... boolean	canRedo ()	ε1034
	1	public	.... boolean	canUndo ()	ε1034
		protected	.... *AttributeSet*	**copy**	
	1	public	.......................void	die ()	
		protected	.... *Element*	**element**	
	1	public	.... String	getPresentationName ()	
	1	public	.... String	getRedoPresentationName ()	
	1	public	.... String	getUndoPresentationName ()	
		protected	.... boolean	**isReplacing**	
	1	public	.... boolean	isSignificant ()	
		protected	.... *AttributeSet*	**newAttributes**	
	1	public	.... **void**	redo () throws javax.swing.undo.CannotRedoException	ε1034
▲	1	protected static final	.....String	RedoName	
	1	public	.... boolean	replaceEdit (*javax.swing.undo.UndoableEdit* anEdit)	
	1	public	.... String	toString ()	
	1	public	.... **void**	undo () throws javax.swing.undo.CannotUndoException	ε1034
▲	1	protected static final	.....String	UndoName	

DefaultStyledDocument.ElementBuffer

javax.swing.text

Object
1.2 └DefaultStyledDocument.ElementBuffer - - - - - - *java.io.Serializable*╷

	public	.......................void	**change** (int offset, int length, AbstractDocument.DefaultDocumentEvent de)	
	protected	...................void	**changeUpdate** ()	
	public	..................*Element*	**clone** (*Element* parent, *Element* clonee)	
*	public	....	**DefaultStyledDocument.ElementBuffer** (*Element* root)	
	public	..................*Element*	**getRootElement** ()	
	public	.......................void	**insert** (int offset, int length, DefaultStyledDocument.ElementSpec[] data,	
			AbstractDocument.DefaultDocumentEvent de)	
	protected	...................void	**insertUpdate** (DefaultStyledDocument.ElementSpec[] data)	

Class *Interface* —extends - - -implements ○ abstract ● final △ static ▲ static final ＊ constructor x x—inherited x **x**—declared x **x**—overridden
εn—examples of usage ╷—has subclass package—see other volume

public	void	**remove** (int offset, int length, AbstractDocument.DefaultDocumentEvent de)
protected	void	**removeUpdate** ()

DefaultStyledDocument.ElementSpec

Object [1]
1.2 └DefaultStyledDocument.ElementSpec

D

▲	public static final	short	**ContentType**
＊	public		**DefaultStyledDocument.ElementSpec** (*AttributeSet* a, short type)
＊	public		**DefaultStyledDocument.ElementSpec** (*AttributeSet* a, short type, int len)
＊	public		**DefaultStyledDocument.ElementSpec** (*AttributeSet* a, short type, char[] txt,
			int offs, int len)
▲	public static final	short	**EndTagType**
	public	char[]	**getArray** ()
	public	*AttributeSet*	**getAttributes** ()
	public	short	**getDirection** ()
	public	int	**getLength** ()
	public	int	**getOffset** ()
	public	short	**getType** ()
▲	public static final	short	**JoinFractureDirection**
▲	public static final	short	**JoinNextDirection**
▲	public static final	short	**JoinPreviousDirection**
▲	public static final	short	**OriginateDirection**
	public	void	**setDirection** (short direction)
	public	void	**setType** (short type)
▲	public static final	short	**StartTagType**
1	public	String	**toString** ()

DefaultStyledDocument.SectionElement

protected

Object
1.2 ○ └AbstractDocument.AbstractElement [1] ------ *Element*, *MutableAttributeSet* ⌐ (*AttributeSet* [3]), *java.io.Serializable* ⌐,
           javax.swing.tree.TreeNode ⌐

1.2   └AbstractDocument.BranchElement [2]
1.2   └DefaultStyledDocument.SectionElement

1	public	void	addAttribute (Object name, Object value)	
1	public	void	addAttributes (*AttributeSet* attr)	
2	public	*java.util.Enumeration*	children ()	ε1023,1024,1028,1029
1	public	boolean	containsAttribute (Object name, Object value)	
1	public	boolean	containsAttributes (*AttributeSet* attrs)	
1	public	*AttributeSet*	copyAttributes ()	
1	public	void	dump (java.io.PrintStream psOut, int indentAmount)	
1	protected	void	finalize () throws Throwable	
2	public	boolean	getAllowsChildren ()	
1	public	Object	getAttribute (Object attrName)	ε1010,1013,1017
1	public	int	getAttributeCount ()	ε1010
1	public	*java.util.Enumeration*	getAttributeNames ()	ε1010
1	public	*AttributeSet*	getAttributes ()	ε1013
1	public	*javax.swing.tree.TreeNode*	getChildAt (int childIndex)	
1	public	int	getChildCount ()	ε1023,1024,1025,1028,1029
1	public	Document	getDocument ()	
2	public	Element	getElement (int index)	ε984,990,1013
2	public	int	getElementCount ()	ε984,990,1013
2	public	int	getElementIndex (int offset)	
2	public	int	getEndOffset ()	ε984,990,1013
1	public	int	getIndex (*javax.swing.tree.TreeNode* node)	
2	public	String	**getName** ()	
1	public	*javax.swing.tree.TreeNode*	getParent ()	ε1027
1	public	Element	getParentElement ()	
1	public	*AttributeSet*	getResolveParent ()	
2	public	int	getStartOffset ()	ε984,990,1013
1	public	boolean	isDefined (Object attrName)	
1	public	boolean	isEqual (*AttributeSet* attr)	
2	public	boolean	isLeaf ()	ε984
▲ 3	public static final	Object	NameAttribute	
2	public	Element	positionToElement (int pos)	
1	public	void	removeAttribute (Object name)	

Classes

DefaultStyledDocument.SectionElement

	1	public	void	removeAttributes (*java.util.Enumeration* names)
	1	public	void	removeAttributes (*AttributeSet* attrs)
	2	public	void	replace (int offset, int length, *Element[]* elems)
▲	3	public static final	Object	ResolveAttribute
✳		public		**DefaultStyledDocument.SectionElement** ()
	1	public	void	setResolveParent (*AttributeSet* parent)
	2	public	String	toString ()

D

DefaultTableCellRenderer   javax.swing.table

Object
└ java.awt.Component[1] - - - - - - - - - - - - - - - - - - *java.awt.image.ImageObserver* [5], *java.awt.MenuContainer*,
　　　　　　　　　　　　　　　　　　　　　　　　　java.io.Serializable
　　└ java.awt.Container[2]
1.2 ○　　　└ javax.swing.JComponent[3]
1.2　　　　　└ javax.swing.JLabel[4] - - - - - - - - - - - - - - - *javax.swing.SwingConstants* [6], *javax.accessibility.Accessible*
1.2　　　　　　└ DefaultTableCellRenderer - - - - - - - - *TableCellRenderer* [7]

	1	*142 inherited members from java.awt.Component not shown*		
	2	*50 inherited members from java.awt.Container not shown*		
	3	*135 inherited members from javax.swing.JComponent not shown*		
	4	*32 inherited members from javax.swing.JLabel not shown*		
	6	*19 inherited members from javax.swing.SwingConstants not shown*		
	5	*8 inherited members from java.awt.image.ImageObserver not shown*		
✳		public		**DefaultTableCellRenderer** ()　　　　　　ε933,934
	3	protected	**void**	**firePropertyChange** (String propertyName, Object oldValue, Object newValue)
	3	public	**void**	**firePropertyChange** (String propertyName, boolean oldValue, boolean newValue)
	7	public	java.awt.Component	**getTableCellRendererComponent** (javax.swing.JTable table, Object value, boolean isSelected, boolean hasFocus, int row, int column)　ε933,934,928,929,936
	3	public	**boolean**	**isOpaque** ()
△		protected static		**noFocusBorder**
		... javax.swing.border.Border		
	3	public	**void**	**repaint** (java.awt.Rectangle r)
	3	public	**void**	**repaint** (long tm, int x, int y, int width, int height)
	3	public	**void**	**revalidate** ()
	3	public	**void**	**setBackground** (java.awt.Color c)
	3	public	**void**	**setForeground** (java.awt.Color c)
		protected	void	**setValue** (Object value)
	4	public	**void**	**updateUI** ()
	2	public	**void**	**validate** ()　　　　　　　　　　ε601,674,928,936

DefaultTableCellRenderer.UIResource   javax.swing.table

Object
└ java.awt.Component[1] - - - - - - - - - - - - - - - - - - *java.awt.image.ImageObserver* [6], *java.awt.MenuContainer*,
　　　　　　　　　　　　　　　　　　　　　　　　　java.io.Serializable
　　└ java.awt.Container[2]
1.2 ○　　　└ javax.swing.JComponent[3]
1.2　　　　　└ javax.swing.JLabel[4] - - - - - - - - - - - - - - - *javax.swing.SwingConstants* [7], *javax.accessibility.Accessible*
1.2　　　　　　└ DefaultTableCellRenderer[5] - - - - - - - - *TableCellRenderer*
1.2　　　　　　　└ DefaultTableCellRenderer - - - - - - *javax.swing.plaf.UIResource*
　　　　　　　　　　.UIResource

	1	*142 inherited members from java.awt.Component not shown*		
	2	*50 inherited members from java.awt.Container not shown*		
	3	*135 inherited members from javax.swing.JComponent not shown*		
	4	*32 inherited members from javax.swing.JLabel not shown*		
	7	*19 inherited members from javax.swing.SwingConstants not shown*		
	6	*8 inherited members from java.awt.image.ImageObserver not shown*		
	5	protected	void	firePropertyChange (String propertyName, Object oldValue, Object newValue)
	5	public	void	firePropertyChange (String propertyName, boolean oldValue, boolean newValue)
	5	public	java.awt.Component	getTableCellRendererComponent (javax.swing.JTable table, Object value, boolean isSelected, boolean hasFocus, int row, int column)　ε928,929,933,934,936
	5	public	boolean	isOpaque ()
△	5	protected static		noFocusBorder
		... javax.swing.border.Border		
	5	public	void	repaint (java.awt.Rectangle r)

5	public	void	repaint (long tm, int x, int y, int width, int height)
5	public	void	revalidate ()
5	public	void	setBackground (java.awt.Color c)
5	public	void	setForeground (java.awt.Color c)
5	protected	void	setValue (Object value)
*	public		**DefaultTableCellRenderer.UIResource** ()
5	public	void	updateUI ()
5	public	void	validate () ε601,674,928,936

D

DefaultTableColumnModel   javax.swing.table

Object
1.2 └DefaultTableColumnModel - - - - - - - - - - - - - - - *TableColumnModel* [1], *java.beans.PropertyChangeListener* [2] (*java .util.EventListener*), *javax.swing.event.ListSelectionListener* [3] (*java.util.EventListener*), *java.io.Serializable*

1	public	void	**addColumn** (TableColumn aColumn)
1	public	void	**addColumnModelListener** (*javax.swing.event.TableColumnModelListener* x)
			ε966
	protected transient	javax. swing.event.ChangeEvent	**changeEvent**
	protected	int	**columnMargin**
	protected	boolean	**columnSelectionAllowed**
	protected	*javax. swing.ListSelectionModel*	**createSelectionModel** ()
*	public		**DefaultTableColumnModel** ()
	protected	void	**fireColumnAdded** (javax.swing.event.TableColumnModelEvent e)
	protected	void	**fireColumnMarginChanged** ()
	protected	void	**fireColumnMoved** (javax.swing.event.TableColumnModelEvent e)
	protected	void	**fireColumnRemoved** (javax.swing.event.TableColumnModelEvent e)
	protected	void	**fireColumnSelectionChanged** (javax.swing.event.ListSelectionEvent e)
1	public	TableColumn	**getColumn** (int columnIndex) ε950,915,916,917,919
1	public	int	**getColumnCount** ()
1	public	int	**getColumnIndex** (Object identifier)
1	public	int	**getColumnIndexAtX** (int x) ε937,967
1	public	int	**getColumnMargin** ()
1.4	public	*javax.swing.event.- TableColumnModelListener[]*	**getColumnModelListeners** ()
1	public	*java.util.Enumeration*	**getColumns** () ε916,922,927
1	public	boolean	**getColumnSelectionAllowed** ()
1.3	public	*java.util.EventListener[]*	**getListeners** (Class listenerType)
1	public	int	**getSelectedColumnCount** ()
1	public	int[]	**getSelectedColumns** ()
1	public	*javax. swing.ListSelectionModel*	**getSelectionModel** () ε942,944,957,964
1	public	int	**getTotalColumnWidth** ()
	protected	*javax.swing. event.EventListenerList*	**listenerList**
1	public	void	**moveColumn** (int columnIndex, int newIndex)
2	public	void	**propertyChange** (java.beans.PropertyChangeEvent evt)
	protected	void	**recalcWidthCache** ()
1	public	void	**removeColumn** (TableColumn column) ε963
1	public	void	**removeColumnModelListener** (*javax.swing.event.TableColumnModelListener* x)
	protected	*javax. swing.ListSelectionModel*	**selectionModel**
1	public	void	**setColumnMargin** (int newMargin)
1	public	void	**setColumnSelectionAllowed** (boolean flag)
1	public	void	**setSelectionModel** (*javax.swing.ListSelectionModel* newModel)
	protected	java.util.Vector	**tableColumns**
	protected	int	**totalColumnWidth**
3	public	void	**valueChanged** (javax.swing.event.ListSelectionEvent e) ε784,957,964

DefaultTableModel   javax.swing.table

Object
1.2 ○ └AbstractTableModel [1] - - - - - - - - - - - - - - - - - - - *TableModel* [2], *java.io.Serializable*
1.2   └DefaultTableModel

	public	void	**addColumn** (Object columnName) ε920,908,909,910,911
	public	void	**addColumn** (Object columnName, Object[] columnData) ε920,912,927,929,959
	public	void	**addColumn** (Object columnName, java.util.Vector columnData)

Classes

DefaultTableModel

	public	void	**addRow** (Object[] rowData)	ε908,910,911,912,922
	public	void	**addRow** (java.util.Vector rowData)	ε912
1	public	void	addTableModelListener (*javax.swing.event.TableModelListener* l)	
				ε957,965
	protected	java.util.Vector	**columnIdentifiers**	
△	protected static	java.util.Vector	**convertToVector** (Object[] anArray)	
△	protected static	java.util.Vector	**convertToVector** (Object[][] anArray)	
	protected	java.util.Vector	**dataVector**	
✳	public		**DefaultTableModel** ()	ε908,909,910,911,912
✳	public		**DefaultTableModel** (int rowCount, int columnCount)	
✳	public		**DefaultTableModel** (Object[] columnNames, int rowCount)	
✳	public		**DefaultTableModel** (Object[][] data, Object[] columnNames)	
✳	public		**DefaultTableModel** (java.util.Vector data, java.util.Vector columnNames)	
✳	public		**DefaultTableModel** (java.util.Vector columnNames, int rowCount)	
1	public	int	findColumn (String columnName)	
1	public	void	fireTableCellUpdated (int row, int column)	
1	public	void	fireTableChanged (javax.swing.event.TableModelEvent e)	
1	public	void	fireTableDataChanged ()	
1	public	void	fireTableRowsDeleted (int firstRow, int lastRow)	
1	public	void	fireTableRowsInserted (int firstRow, int lastRow)	
1	public	void	fireTableRowsUpdated (int firstRow, int lastRow)	
1	public	void	fireTableStructureChanged ()	ε961,962
1	public	Class	getColumnClass (int columnIndex)	ε927,929
2	public	int	**getColumnCount** ()	ε920,921
1	public	String	**getColumnName** (int column)	
	public	java.util.Vector	**getDataVector** ()	ε912,961,962
1.3 1	public	*java.util.EventListener[]*	getListeners (Class listenerType)	
2	public	int	**getRowCount** ()	ε911,909,910,962
1.4 1	public	*javax.swing.event.TableModelListener[]*	getTableModelListeners ()	
2	public	Object	**getValueAt** (int row, int column)	ε926
	public	void	**insertRow** (int row, Object[] rowData)	ε909
	public	void	**insertRow** (int row, java.util.Vector rowData)	
1	public	boolean	**isCellEditable** (int row, int column)	ε958
1	protected	javax.swing.event.EventListenerList	listenerList	
	public	void	**moveRow** (int start, int end, int to)	ε911
	public	void	**newDataAvailable** (javax.swing.event.TableModelEvent event)	
	public	void	**newRowsAdded** (javax.swing.event.TableModelEvent e)	
	public	void	**removeRow** (int row)	ε910
1	public	void	removeTableModelListener (*javax.swing.event.TableModelListener* l)	
	public	void	**rowsRemoved** (javax.swing.event.TableModelEvent event)	
1.3	public	void	**setColumnCount** (int columnCount)	
	public	void	**setColumnIdentifiers** (Object[] newIdentifiers)	
	public	void	**setColumnIdentifiers** (java.util.Vector columnIdentifiers)	
	public	void	**setDataVector** (Object[][] dataVector, Object[] columnIdentifiers)	
	public	void	**setDataVector** (java.util.Vector dataVector, java.util.Vector columnIdentifiers)	
	public	void	**setNumRows** (int rowCount)	
1.3	public	void	**setRowCount** (int rowCount)	
1	public	void	**setValueAt** (Object aValue, int row, int column)	ε926

DefaultTextUI

javax.swing.text

```
      Object
1.2 ○  └─javax.swing.plaf.ComponentUI 1
1.2 ○     └─javax.swing.plaf.TextUI
1.2 ○        └─javax.swing.plaf.basic.BasicTextUI 2 - - - - - ViewFactory
D   ○           └─DefaultTextUI
```

1	*4 inherited members from javax.swing.plaf.ComponentUI not shown*		
2	*37 inherited members from javax.swing.plaf.basic.BasicTextUI not shown*		
D ✳	public	**DefaultTextUI** ()	

Class *Interface* —extends - - -implements ○ abstract ● final △ static ▲ static final ✳ constructor × x—inherited × **x**—declared **x x**—overridden
ε*n*—examples of usage ‿—has subclass package—see other volume

490

DefaultTreeCellEditor				javax.swing.tree

Object
1.2 └ DefaultTreeCellEditor - *java.awt.event.ActionListener* [1] (*java.util.EventListener*),
  TreeCellEditor [2] (*javax.swing.CellEditor* [3]), *javax.swing.event* [2]
  .TreeSelectionListener [4] (*java.util.EventListener*)

1	public......................void	**actionPerformed** (java.awt.event.ActionEvent e)	ε855,644,738,743,745
3	public......................void	**addCellEditorListener** (*javax.swing.event.CellEditorListener* l)	
	protected........java.awt.Color	**borderSelectionColor**	
3	public......................void	**cancelCellEditing** ()	ε956
	protected.............. boolean	**canEdit**	
	protected.............. boolean	**canEditImmediately** (java.util.EventObject event)	
	protected...java.awt.Container	**createContainer** ()	
	protected........ *TreeCellEditor*	**createTreeCellEditor** ()	
*	public..........................	**DefaultTreeCellEditor** (javax.swing.JTree tree, DefaultTreeCellRenderer renderer)	
*	public..........................	**DefaultTreeCellEditor** (javax.swing.JTree tree, DefaultTreeCellRenderer renderer, *TreeCellEditor* editor)	
	protected..................void	**determineOffset** (javax.swing.JTree tree, Object value, boolean isSelected, boolean expanded, boolean leaf, int row)	
	protected transient............ .... java.awt.Component	**editingComponent**	
	protected...java.awt.Container	**editingContainer**	
	protected transient............ ....*javax.swing.Icon*	**editingIcon**	
	protected........java.awt.Font	**font**	
	public............java.awt.Color	**getBorderSelectionColor** ()	
1.4	public............ *javax.swing* [2] *.event.CellEditorListener[]*	**getCellEditorListeners** ()	
3	public...................Object	**getCellEditorValue** ()	ε953,954,960
	public............java.awt.Font	**getFont** ()	
2	public.... java.awt.Component	**getTreeCellEditorComponent** (javax.swing.JTree tree, Object value, boolean isSelected, boolean expanded, boolean leaf, int row)	
	protected.............. boolean	**inHitRegion** (int x, int y)	
3	public.................. boolean	**isCellEditable** (java.util.EventObject event)	ε955,960
	protected transient....TreePath	**lastPath**	
	protected transient...........int	**lastRow**	
	protected transient...........int	**offset**	
	protected..................void	**prepareForEditing** ()	
	protected........ *TreeCellEditor*	**realEditor**	
3	public......................void	**removeCellEditorListener** (*javax.swing.event.CellEditorListener* l)	
	protected...................... ..... DefaultTreeCellRenderer	**renderer**	
	public......................void	**setBorderSelectionColor** (java.awt.Color newColor)	
	public......................void	**setFont** (java.awt.Font font)	
	protected..................void	**setTree** (javax.swing.JTree newTree)	
3	public.................. boolean	**shouldSelectCell** (java.util.EventObject event)	
	protected.............. boolean	**shouldStartEditingTimer** (java.util.EventObject event)	
	protected..................void	**startEditingTimer** ()	
3	public.................. boolean	**stopCellEditing** ()	ε954,956
	protected transient............ .... javax.swing.Timer	**timer**	
	protected transient............ ....javax.swing.JTree	**tree**	
4	public......................void	**valueChanged** (javax.swing.event.TreeSelectionEvent e)	ε1033

DefaultTreeCellEditor.DefaultTextField			javax.swing.tree

Object   ε861
○ └ java.awt.Component [1] - *java.awt.image.ImageObserver* [6], *java.awt.MenuContainer*,
  java.io.Serializable

  └ java.awt.Container [2]
1.2 ○   └ javax.swing.JComponent [3]
1.2 ○   └ javax.swing.text.JTextComponent [4] - - - - *javax.swing.Scrollable, javax.accessibility.Accessible*
1.2   └ javax.swing.JTextField [5] - - - - - - - - - - - *javax.swing.SwingConstants* [7]
1.2   └ DefaultTreeCellEditor [2]
            .DefaultTextField

1 *138 inherited members from java.awt.Component not shown*
2 *51 inherited members from java.awt.Container not shown*
3 *135 inherited members from javax.swing.JComponent not shown*

DefaultTreeCellEditor.DefaultTextField

4		*70 inherited members from javax.swing.text.JTextComponent not shown*	
5		*28 inherited members from javax.swing.JTextField not shown*	
7		*19 inherited members from javax.swing.SwingConstants not shown*	
6		*8 inherited members from java.awt.image.ImageObserver not shown*	

protected .... **border**
... *javax.swing.border.Border*

✴ public .... **DefaultTreeCellEditor.DefaultTextField** (*javax.swing.border.Border* border)

3 public .... **getBorder** ()
. ***javax.swing.border.Border***

1 public .... **java.awt.Font** **getFont** ()

5 public .... **java.awt.Dimension** **getPreferredSize** ()

3 public .... **void** **setBorder** (*javax.swing.border.Border* border)

DefaultTreeCellEditor.EditorContainer · javax.swing.tree

Object
○ └java.awt.Component [1] - - - - - - - - - - - - - - - - - - *java.awt.image.ImageObserver* [3], *java.awt.MenuContainer*,
java.io.Serializable
└java.awt.Container [2]
1.2 └DefaultTreeCellEditor.EditorContainer

ε606,618,733,953,988

1		*177 inherited members from java.awt.Component not shown*	
2		*64 inherited members from java.awt.Container not shown*	
3		*8 inherited members from java.awt.image.ImageObserver not shown*	

2 public .... **void** **doLayout** ()

✴ public .... **DefaultTreeCellEditor.EditorContainer** ()

public .... void **EditorContainer** ()

2 public .... **java.awt.Dimension** **getPreferredSize** ()

2 public .... **void** **paint** (java.awt.Graphics g)

ε575,551,557,558,878

DefaultTreeCellRenderer · javax.swing.tree

Object
○ └java.awt.Component [1] - - - - - - - - - - - - - - - - - - *java.awt.image.ImageObserver* [5], *java.awt.MenuContainer*,
java.io.Serializable
└java.awt.Container [2]
1.2 ○ └javax.swing.JComponent [3]
1.2 └javax.swing.JLabel [4] - - - - - - - - - - - - - - *javax.swing.SwingConstants* [6], *javax.accessibility.Accessible*
1.2 └DefaultTreeCellRenderer - - - - - - - - - *TreeCellRenderer* [7]

1		*141 inherited members from java.awt.Component not shown*	
2		*50 inherited members from java.awt.Container not shown*	
3		*127 inherited members from javax.swing.JComponent not shown*	
4		*33 inherited members from javax.swing.JLabel not shown*	
6		*19 inherited members from javax.swing.SwingConstants not shown*	
5		*8 inherited members from java.awt.image.ImageObserver not shown*	

protected ....java.awt.Color **backgroundNonSelectionColor**

protected ....java.awt.Color **backgroundSelectionColor**

protected ....java.awt.Color **borderSelectionColor**

protected transient .... **closedIcon**
.... *javax.swing.Icon*

✴ public .... **DefaultTreeCellRenderer** ()

3 public .... **void** **firePropertyChange** (String propertyName, char oldValue, char newValue)

3 public .... **void** **firePropertyChange** (String propertyName, double oldValue, double newValue)

3 public .... **void** **firePropertyChange** (String propertyName, long oldValue, long newValue)

3 public .... **void** **firePropertyChange** (String propertyName, byte oldValue, byte newValue)

3 protected .... **void** **firePropertyChange** (String propertyName, Object oldValue, Object newValue)

3 public .... **void** **firePropertyChange** (String propertyName, int oldValue, int newValue)

3 public .... **void** **firePropertyChange** (String propertyName, float oldValue, float newValue)

3 public .... **void** **firePropertyChange** (String propertyName, short oldValue, short newValue)

3 public .... **void** **firePropertyChange** (String propertyName, boolean oldValue, boolean newValue)

public ....java.awt.Color **getBackgroundNonSelectionColor** ()

public ....java.awt.Color **getBackgroundSelectionColor** ()

public ....java.awt.Color **getBorderSelectionColor** ()

public ....*javax.swing.Icon* **getClosedIcon** ()

public ....*javax.swing.Icon* **getDefaultClosedIcon** ()

public ....*javax.swing.Icon* **getDefaultLeafIcon** ()

public ....*javax.swing.Icon* **getDefaultOpenIcon** ()

Class   *Interface*   —extends   - - -implements   ○ abstract   ● final   △ static   ▲ static final   ✴ constructor   x x—inherited   x **x**—declared   **x x**—overridden
εn—examples of usage   ⌄—has subclass   package—see other volume

492

	1	public............**java.awt.Font**	**getFont** ()	
		public.........*javax.swing.Icon*	**getLeafIcon** ()	
		public.........*javax.swing.Icon*	**getOpenIcon** ()	
	3	public.... **java.awt.Dimension**	**getPreferredSize** ()	
		public............java.awt.Color	**getTextNonSelectionColor** ()	
		public............java.awt.Color	**getTextSelectionColor** ()	
	7	public.... java.awt.Component	**getTreeCellRendererComponent** (javax.swing.JTree tree, Object value,	
			boolean sel, boolean expanded, boolean leaf, int row, boolean hasFocus)	
1.3		protected.............. boolean	**hasFocus**	
		protected transient.............	**leafIcon**	
		............*javax.swing.Icon*		
		protected transient.............	**openIcon**	
		............*javax.swing.Icon*		
	3	public.................... **void**	**paint** (java.awt.Graphics g)	
	3	public.................... **void**	**repaint** (java.awt.Rectangle r)	
	3	public.................... **void**	**repaint** (long tm, int x, int y, int width, int height)	
	3	public.................... **void**	**revalidate** ()	
		protected.............. boolean	**selected**	
	3	public.................... **void**	**setBackground** (java.awt.Color color)	
		public....................void	**setBackgroundNonSelectionColor** (java.awt.Color newColor)	
		public....................void	**setBackgroundSelectionColor** (java.awt.Color newColor)	
		public....................void	**setBorderSelectionColor** (java.awt.Color newColor)	
		public....................void	**setClosedIcon** (*javax.swing.Icon* newIcon)	ε1020
	3	public.................... **void**	**setFont** (java.awt.Font font)	
		public....................void	**setLeafIcon** (*javax.swing.Icon* newIcon)	ε1020
		public....................void	**setOpenIcon** (*javax.swing.Icon* newIcon)	ε1020
		public....................void	**setTextNonSelectionColor** (java.awt.Color newColor)	
		public....................void	**setTextSelectionColor** (java.awt.Color newColor)	
		protected.......java.awt.Color	**textNonSelectionColor**	
		protected.......java.awt.Color	**textSelectionColor**	
	2	public.................... **void**	**validate** ()	ε601,674,928,936

DefaultTreeModel				javax.swing.tree

		Object		
1.2		└ DefaultTreeModel - *java.io.Serializable* ⌐, TreeModel [1]		
	1	public....................void	**addTreeModelListener** (*javax.swing.event.TreeModelListener* l)	
		protected.............. boolean	**asksAllowsChildren**	
		public................. boolean	**asksAllowsChildren** ()	
*		public...........................	**DefaultTreeModel** (*TreeNode* root)	
*		public...........................	**DefaultTreeModel** (*TreeNode* root, boolean asksAllowsChildren)	
		protected....................void	**fireTreeNodesChanged** (Object source, Object[] path, int[] childIndices,	
			Object[] children)	
		protected....................void	**fireTreeNodesInserted** (Object source, Object[] path, int[] childIndices,	
			Object[] children)	
		protected....................void	**fireTreeNodesRemoved** (Object source, Object[] path, int[] childIndices,	
			Object[] children)	
		protected....................void	**fireTreeStructureChanged** (Object source, Object[] path, int[] childIndices,	
			Object[] children)	
	1	public....................Object	**getChild** (Object parent, int index)	
	1	public........................int	**getChildCount** (Object parent)	
	1	public........................int	**getIndexOfChild** (Object parent, Object child)	
1.3		public. *java.util.EventListener[]*	**getListeners** (Class listenerType)	
		public.............. *TreeNode[]*	**getPathToRoot** (*TreeNode* aNode)	
		protected.......... *TreeNode[]*	**getPathToRoot** (*TreeNode* aNode, int depth)	
	1	public....................Object	**getRoot** ()	ε1023,1024,1028,1029
1.4		public.............*javax.swing* ⌐	**getTreeModelListeners** ()	
		.*event.TreeModelListener[]*		
		public....................void	**insertNodeInto** (*MutableTreeNode* newChild, *MutableTreeNode* parent, int index)	
				ε1025
	1	public............. boolean	**isLeaf** (Object node)	
		protected......... javax.swing ⌐	**listenerList**	
		.event.EventListenerList		
		public....................void	**nodeChanged** (*TreeNode* node)	
		public....................void	**nodesChanged** (*TreeNode* node, int[] childIndices)	
		public....................void	**nodeStructureChanged** (*TreeNode* node)	
		public....................void	**nodesWereInserted** (*TreeNode* node, int[] childIndices)	
		public....................void	**nodesWereRemoved** (*TreeNode* node, int[] childIndices,	
			Object[] removedChildren)	
		public....................void	**reload** ()	
		public....................void	**reload** (*TreeNode* node)	

DefaultTreeModel

	public	void	**removeNodeFromParent** (*MutableTreeNode* node)	ε1026
1	public	void	**removeTreeModelListener** (*javax.swing.event.TreeModelListener* l)	
	protected	*TreeNode*	**root**	
	public	void	**setAsksAllowsChildren** (boolean newValue)	
	public	void	**setRoot** (*TreeNode* root)	ε1026
1	public	void	**valueForPathChanged** (TreePath path, Object newValue)	

DefaultTreeSelectionModel				javax.swing.tree

Object [1]
1.2　└DefaultTreeSelectionModel - - - - - - - - - - - - - - *Cloneable*, *java.io.Serializable*, *TreeSelectionModel* [2]

2	public synchronized	void	**addPropertyChangeListener** (*java.beans.PropertyChangeListener* listener)	
2	public	void	**addSelectionPath** (TreePath path)	
2	public	void	**addSelectionPaths** (TreePath[] paths)	
2	public	void	**addTreeSelectionListener** (*javax.swing.event.TreeSelectionListener* x)	
	protected	boolean	**arePathsContiguous** (TreePath[] paths)	
	protected	boolean	**canPathsBeAdded** (TreePath[] paths)	
	protected	boolean	**canPathsBeRemoved** (TreePath[] paths)	
	protected .... javax.swing.event.Swing-PropertyChangeSupport		**changeSupport**	
2	public	void	**clearSelection** ()	
1	public	**Object**	**clone** () throws CloneNotSupportedException	
▲ 2	public static final	int	CONTIGUOUS_TREE_SELECTION = 2	ε1022
✱	public		**DefaultTreeSelectionModel** ()	
▲ 2	public static final	int	DISCONTIGUOUS_TREE_SELECTION = 4	ε1022
	protected	void	**fireValueChanged** (javax.swing.event.TreeSelectionEvent e)	
2	public	TreePath	**getLeadSelectionPath** ()	
2	public	int	**getLeadSelectionRow** ()	
1.3	public. *java.util.EventListener[]*		**getListeners** (Class listenerType)	
2	public	int	**getMaxSelectionRow** ()	
2	public	int	**getMinSelectionRow** ()	
1.4	public. *java.beans.-PropertyChangeListener[]*		**getPropertyChangeListeners** ()	
2	public	*RowMapper*	**getRowMapper** ()	
2	public	int	**getSelectionCount** ()	
2	public	int	**getSelectionMode** ()	
2	public	TreePath	**getSelectionPath** ()	
2	public	TreePath[]	**getSelectionPaths** ()	
2	public	int[]	**getSelectionRows** ()	
1.4	public. *javax.swing.event.TreeSelectionListener[]*		**getTreeSelectionListeners** ()	
	protected	void	**insureRowContinuity** ()	
	protected	void	**insureUniqueness** ()	
2	public	boolean	**isPathSelected** (TreePath path)	
2	public	boolean	**isRowSelected** (int row)	
2	public	boolean	**isSelectionEmpty** ()	
	protected	int	**leadIndex**	
	protected	TreePath	**leadPath**	
	protected	int	**leadRow**	
	protected. *javax.swing.event.EventListenerList*		**listenerList**	
	protected. javax.swing.-DefaultListSelectionModel		**listSelectionModel**	
	protected	void	**notifyPathChange** (java.util.Vector changedPaths, TreePath oldLeadSelection)	
2	public synchronized	void	**removePropertyChangeListener** (*java.beans.PropertyChangeListener* listener)	
2	public	void	**removeSelectionPath** (TreePath path)	
2	public	void	**removeSelectionPaths** (TreePath[] paths)	
2	public	void	**removeTreeSelectionListener** (*javax.swing.event.TreeSelectionListener* x)	
2	public	void	**resetRowSelection** ()	
	protected transient	*RowMapper*	**rowMapper**	
	protected	TreePath[]	**selection**	
▲	public static final	String	**SELECTION_MODE_PROPERTY** = "selectionMode"	
	protected	int	**selectionMode**	
2	public	void	**setRowMapper** (*RowMapper* newMapper)	
2	public	void	**setSelectionMode** (int mode)	ε1022
2	public	void	**setSelectionPath** (TreePath path)	

Class　*Interface*　—extends　- - -implements　○ abstract　● final　△ static　▲ static final　✱ constructor　x x—inherited　x **x**—declared　**x x**—overridden
ε*n*—examples of usage　.—has subclass　package—see other volume

```
    2  public ..................... void  setSelectionPaths (TreePath[] pPaths)
▲   2  public static final ............. int  SINGLE_TREE_SELECTION = 1                            ε1022
    1  public ................... String  toString ()
       protected ................. void  updateLeadIndex ()
```

DesktopIconUI

```
        Object
1.2 ○   └ComponentUI 1
1.2 ○      └DesktopIconUI ,
```

```
     1  11 inherited members from ComponentUI not shown
 ✳   public ........................  DesktopIconUI ()
```

DesktopManager

```
1.2     DesktopManager
```

```
        public ..................... void  activateFrame (JInternalFrame f)
        public ..................... void  beginDraggingFrame (JComponent f)
        public ..................... void  beginResizingFrame (JComponent f, int direction)
        public ..................... void  closeFrame (JInternalFrame f)
        public ..................... void  deactivateFrame (JInternalFrame f)
        public ..................... void  deiconifyFrame (JInternalFrame f)
        public ..................... void  dragFrame (JComponent f, int newX, int newY)
        public ..................... void  endDraggingFrame (JComponent f)
        public ..................... void  endResizingFrame (JComponent f)
        public ..................... void  iconifyFrame (JInternalFrame f)
        public ..................... void  maximizeFrame (JInternalFrame f)
        public ..................... void  minimizeFrame (JInternalFrame f)
        public ..................... void  openFrame (JInternalFrame f)
        public ..................... void  resizeFrame (JComponent f, int newX, int newY, int newWidth, int newHeight)
        public ..................... void  setBoundsForFrame (JComponent f, int newX, int newY, int newWidth,
                                           int newHeight)
```

DesktopPaneUI

```
        Object
1.2 ○   └ComponentUI 1
1.2 ○      └DesktopPaneUI ,
```

```
     1  11 inherited members from ComponentUI not shown
 ✳   public ........................  DesktopPaneUI ()
```

Destination

```
        Object
1.4 ○   └javax.print.attribute.URISyntax 1 ----------- java.io.Serializable ,, Cloneable ,
1.4 ●      └Destination - - - - - - - - - - - - - - - - - - - - - - - - - javax.print.attribute.PrintJobAttribute (javax.print.attribute.Attribute 2
                                                         (java.io.Serializable)), javax.print.attribute.PrintRequestAttribute
                                                         (javax.print.attribute.Attribute 2 (java.io.Serializable))
```

```
 ✳   public ........................      Destination (java.net.URI uri)                            ε712
     1  public ................. boolean  equals (Object object)
 ●   2  public final .............. Class  getCategory ()                                            ε707
 ●   2  public final ............. String  getName ()                                                ε706,707,708
     1  public ........... java.net.URI  getURI ()
     1  public ..................... int  hashCode ()
     1  public ................. String  toString ()
```

495

Dialog

Dialog   java.awt

```
        Object                                                              ε606,618,733,953,988
   ○    └Component¹ - - - - - - - - - - - - - - - - - - - - - - - - - java.awt.image.ImageObserver⁴, MenuContainer,
                                                                    java.io.Serializable
          └Container²
            └Window³ - - - - - - - - - - - - - - - - - - - - - - - javax.accessibility.Accessible
              └Dialog
```

	1	*166 inherited members from Component not shown*	
	2	*58 inherited members from Container not shown*	
	3	*47 inherited members from Window not shown*	
	4	*8 inherited members from java.awt.image.ImageObserver not shown*	
	3	public . . . . **void addNotify** ()	
1.2 ✳		public . . . . **Dialog** (Dialog owner)	
1.1 ✳		public . . . . **Dialog** (Frame owner)	
1.2 ✳		public . . . . **Dialog** (Dialog owner, String title)	
✳		public . . . . **Dialog** (Frame owner, boolean modal)	
1.1 ✳		public . . . . **Dialog** (Frame owner, String title)	
1.2 ✳		public . . . . **Dialog** (Dialog owner, String title, boolean modal)	
✳		public . . . . **Dialog** (Frame owner, String title, boolean modal)	
1.4 ✳		public . . . . **Dialog** (Dialog owner, String title, boolean modal, GraphicsConfiguration gc)	
1.4 ✳		public . . . . **Dialog** (Frame owner, String title, boolean modal, GraphicsConfiguration gc)	
	3	public . . . . **void dispose** () ε565	
1.3	3	public . . . . **javax.accessibility .AccessibleContext getAccessibleContext** ()	
		public . . . . String **getTitle** ()	
	3	public . . . . **void hide** ()	
		public . . . . boolean **isModal** ()	
		public . . . . boolean **isResizable** ()	
1.4		public . . . . boolean **isUndecorated** ()	
	2	protected . . . . **String paramString** ()	
1.1		public . . . . void **setModal** (boolean b)	
		public . . . . void **setResizable** (boolean resizable)	
		public . . . . void **setTitle** (String title)	
1.4		public . . . . void **setUndecorated** (boolean undecorated)	
	3	public . . . . **void show** () ε905,618	

DialogPeer   java.awt.peer

```
    DialogPeer ──────────────── WindowPeer¹ (ContainerPeer² (ComponentPeer³))
```

	3	*42 inherited members from ComponentPeer not shown*
	2	*7 inherited members from ContainerPeer not shown*
	1	*2 inherited members from WindowPeer not shown*
		public . . . . void **setResizable** (boolean resizeable)
		public . . . . void **setTitle** (String title)

Dimension   java.awt

```
        Object¹                                                              ε570,598,870,949
1.2 ○   └java.awt.geom.Dimension2D² - - - - - - - - - - - - Cloneable
          └Dimension - - - - - - - - - - - - - - - - - - - - - - - java.io.Serializable
```

	2	public . . . . Object clone ()	
✳		public . . . . **Dimension** ()	
✳		public . . . . **Dimension** (Dimension d)	
✳		public . . . . **Dimension** (int width, int height)	ε791,878,879,881,899
	1	public . . . . **boolean equals** (Object obj)	
1.2	2	public . . . . **double getHeight** ()	
1.1		public . . . . Dimension **getSize** ()	
1.2	2	public . . . . **double getWidth** ()	
	1	public . . . . **int hashCode** ()	
		public . . . . int **height**	ε575,578,599,913
1.1		public . . . . void **setSize** (Dimension d)	
1.2	2	public . . . . void setSize (java.awt.geom.Dimension2D d)	
1.2	2	public . . . . **void setSize** (double width, double height)	
1.1		public . . . . void **setSize** (int width, int height)	

Class   *Interface*   —extends   - - -implements   ○ abstract   ● final   △ static   ▲ static final   ✳ constructor   x x—inherited   x **x**—declared   **x x**—overridden
ε*n*—examples of usage   —has subclass   package—see other volume

1	public..................	**String**	**toString** ()	
	public.......................int		**width**	ε575,578,599,950

Dimension2D

Object[1]
ε570,598,870,949

1.2 ○ └Dimension2D ------------------------ *Cloneable*

1	public.................. **Object**	**clone** ()	
*	protected......................	**Dimension2D** ()	
○	public abstract..........double	**getHeight** ()	
○	public abstract..........double	**getWidth** ()	
	public......................void	**setSize** (Dimension2D d)	
○	public abstract.............void	**setSize** (double width, double height)	

DimensionUIResource

Object
ε570,598,870,949

1.2 ○ └java.awt.geom.Dimension2D[1] ------------ *Cloneable*

  └java.awt.Dimension[2] ------------------ *java.io.Serializable*

1.2   └DimensionUIResource -------------- *UIResource*

1	public....................Object	clone ()		
*	public......................	**DimensionUIResource** (int width, int height)		
2	public..................boolean	equals (Object obj)		
2	public..................double	getHeight ()		
2	public......java.awt.Dimension	getSize ()		
2	public..................double	getWidth ()		
2	public......................int	hashCode ()		
2	public......................int	height		ε575,578,599,913
2	public......................void	setSize (java.awt.Dimension d)		
1	public......................void	setSize (java.awt.geom.Dimension2D d)		
2	public......................void	setSize (double width, double height)		
2	public......................void	setSize (int width, int height)		
2	public....................String	toString ()		ε575,578,599,950
2	public......................int	width		

DirectColorModel

Object
ε660,662,668

○ └ColorModel[1] -------------------------- *java.awt.Transparency* [3]

1.2 ○ └PackedColorModel[2]

  └DirectColorModel

1.2	▲	3	public static final.............int	BITMASK = 2	ε666,667
1.2	●	1	public final ....**ColorModel**	**coerceData** (WritableRaster raster, boolean isAlphaPremultiplied)	
1.2	●	2	public............SampleModel	createCompatibleSampleModel (int w, int h)	
1.2	●	1	public final ....**WritableRaster**	**createCompatibleWritableRaster** (int w, int h)	
	*		public.........................	**DirectColorModel** (int bits, int rmask, int gmask, int bmask)	
	*		public.........................	**DirectColorModel** (int bits, int rmask, int gmask, int bmask, int amask)	
1.2	*		public.........................	**DirectColorModel** (java.awt.color.ColorSpace space, int bits, int rmask, int gmask, int amask, int bmask, int amask, boolean isAlphaPremultiplied, int transferType)	
		2	public.................. boolean	equals (Object obj)	
		1	public......................void	finalize ()	
	●	1	public final ....**int**	**getAlpha** (int pixel)	
1.2		1	public......................int	**getAlpha** (Object inData)	
	●		public final ....int	**getAlphaMask** ()	
1.2		2	public.......... WritableRaster	getAlphaRaster (WritableRaster raster)	
	●	1	public final ....**int**	**getBlue** (int pixel)	
1.2		1	public......................int	**getBlue** (Object inData)	
	●		public final ....int	**getBlueMask** ()	
1.2	●	1	public final .... java.awt.color.ColorSpace	getColorSpace ()	
1.2	●	1	public final ....**int[]**	**getComponents** (int pixel, int[] components, int offset)	
1.2	●	1	public final ....**int[]**	**getComponents** (Object pixel, int[] components, int offset)	
1.2		1	public......................int[]	getComponentSize ()	
1.2		1	public......................int	getComponentSize (int componentIdx)	
1.4		1	public......................int	getDataElement (float[] normComponents, int normOffset)	
1.2		1	public.................. **int**	**getDataElement** (int[] components, int offset)	
1.2		1	public....................**Object**	**getDataElements** (int rgb, Object pixel)	

497

DirectColorModel

1.4		1	public	Object	getDataElements (float[] normComponents, int normOffset, Object obj)
1.2		1	public	**Object**	**getDataElements** (int[] components, int offset, Object obj)
	●	1	public final	**int**	**getGreen** (int pixel)
1.2		1	public	**int**	**getGreen** (Object inData)
	●		public final	int	**getGreenMask** ()
1.2	●	2	public final	int	getMask (int index)
1.2	●	2	public final	int[]	getMasks ()
1.4		1	public	float[]	getNormalizedComponents (Object pixel, float[] normComponents, int normOffset)
1.2		1	public	float[]	getNormalizedComponents (int[] components, int offset, float[] normComponents, int normOffset)
1.2		1	public	int	getNumColorComponents ()
1.2		1	public	int	getNumComponents ()
		1	public	int	getPixelSize ()
	●	1	public final	**int**	**getRed** (int pixel)
1.2		1	public	**int**	**getRed** (Object inData)
	●		public final	int	**getRedMask** ()
	●	1	public final	**int**	**getRGB** (int pixel)
1.2		1	public	**int**	**getRGB** (Object inData)
	△	1	public static	ColorModel	getRGBdefault ()
1.3	●	1	public final	int	getTransferType ()
1.2		1	public	int	getTransparency ()
1.2		1	public	int[]	getUnnormalizedComponents (float[] normComponents, int normOffset, int[] components, int offset)
1.2	●	1	public final	boolean	hasAlpha ()	ε661
		1	public	int	hashCode ()
1.2	●	1	public final	boolean	isAlphaPremultiplied ()
1.2		1	public	**boolean**	**isCompatibleRaster** (Raster raster)
1.2		2	public	boolean	isCompatibleSampleModel (SampleModel sm)
1.2	▲	3	public static final	int	OPAQUE = 1	ε666,667
		1	protected	int	pixel_bits
		1	public	**String**	**toString** ()
1.2		1	protected	int	transferType
1.2	▲	3	public static final	int	TRANSLUCENT = 3	ε666

DisplayMode   java.awt

Object[1]
└ DisplayMode   (1.4 ●)

	▲		public static final	int	**BIT_DEPTH_MULTI** = -1	ε604
	✳		public		**DisplayMode** (int width, int height, int bitDepth, int refreshRate)	ε605
			public	boolean	**equals** (DisplayMode dm)
			public	int	**getBitDepth** ()	ε603,604
			public	int	**getHeight** ()	ε598,603
			public	int	**getRefreshRate** ()	ε603,604,605
			public	int	**getWidth** ()	ε598,603
		1	public	**int**	**hashCode** ()
	▲		public static final	int	**REFRESH_RATE_UNKNOWN** = 0	ε604

DnDConstants   java.awt.dnd

Object
└ DnDConstants   (1.2 ●)

	▲		public static final	int	**ACTION_COPY** = 1
	▲		public static final	int	**ACTION_COPY_OR_MOVE** = 3	ε640,642
	▲		public static final	int	**ACTION_LINK** = 1073741824
	▲		public static final	int	**ACTION_MOVE** = 2
	▲		public static final	int	**ACTION_NONE** = 0
	▲		public static final	int	**ACTION_REFERENCE** = 1073741824

Doc   javax.print

Doc   (1.4)   ε700,701,702,705

		public	*javax.print₂*	**getAttributes** ()
			.attribute.DocAttributeSet	
		public	DocFlavor	**getDocFlavor** ()

Class   *Interface*   —extends   - - -implements   ○ abstract   ● final   △ static   ▲ static final   ✳ constructor   x x—inherited   x **x**—declared   **x x**—overridden
εn—examples of usage   ⌄—has subclass   package—see other volume

```
public . . . . . . . . . . . . . . . . . . Object getPrintData () throws java.io.IOException
public . . . . . . . . . . . java.io.Reader getReaderForText () throws java.io.IOException
public . . . . . . java.io.InputStream getStreamForBytes () throws java.io.IOException
```

DocAttribute   javax.print.attribute

1.4	*DocAttribute* ———————————— *Attribute* ,[1] (*java.io.Serializable*)	
1	public . . . . Class getCategory ()	ε707
1	public . . . . String getName ()	ε706,707,708

DocAttributeSet   javax.print.attribute

1.4	*DocAttributeSet* ———————————— *AttributeSet* ,[1]	
1	public . . . . boolean **add** (*Attribute* attribute)	ε710,711,712,703,715
1	public . . . . boolean **addAll** (*AttributeSet* attributes)	
1	public . . . . void clear ()	
1	public . . . . boolean containsKey (Class category)	
1	public . . . . boolean containsValue (*Attribute* attribute)	
1	public . . . . boolean equals (Object object)	
1	public . . . . *Attribute* get (Class category)	
1	public . . . . int hashCode ()	
1	public . . . . boolean isEmpty ()	
1	public . . . . boolean remove (Class category)	
1	public . . . . boolean remove (*Attribute* attribute)	
1	public . . . . int size ()	
1	public . . . . *Attribute[]* toArray ()	ε706

DocFlavor   javax.print

```
         Object[1]
1.4      └ DocFlavor ------------------------- java.io.Serializable , Cloneable
```

*	public . . . . **DocFlavor** (String mimeType, String className)	
1	public . . . . **boolean equals** (Object obj)	
	public . . . . String **getMediaSubtype** ()	
	public . . . . String **getMediaType** ()	
	public . . . . String **getMimeType** ()	ε701,704
	public . . . . String **getParameter** (String paramName)	
	public . . . . String **getRepresentationClassName** ()	
1	public . . . . **int hashCode** ()	
▲	public static final . . . . String **hostEncoding** = "Cp1252"	
1	public . . . . **String toString** ()	

DocFlavor.BYTE_ARRAY   javax.print

```
         Object
1.4      └ DocFlavor[1] ------------------------- java.io.Serializable , Cloneable
1.4        └ DocFlavor.BYTE_ARRAY
```

▲	public static final . . . . DocFlavor.BYTE_ARRAY **AUTOSENSE**	
*	public . . . . **DocFlavor.BYTE_ARRAY** (String mimeType)	
1	public . . . . boolean equals (Object obj)	
1	public . . . . String getMediaSubtype ()	
1	public . . . . String getMediaType ()	
1	public . . . . String getMimeType ()	ε701,704
1	public . . . . String getParameter (String paramName)	
1	public . . . . String getRepresentationClassName ()	
▲	public static final . . . . DocFlavor.BYTE_ARRAY **GIF**	
1	public . . . . int hashCode ()	
▲ 1	public static final . . . . String hostEncoding = "Cp1252"	
▲	public static final . . . . DocFlavor.BYTE_ARRAY **JPEG**	
▲	public static final . . . . DocFlavor.BYTE_ARRAY **PCL**	
▲	public static final . . . . DocFlavor.BYTE_ARRAY **PDF**	
▲	public static final . . . . DocFlavor.BYTE_ARRAY **PNG**	
▲	public static final . . . . DocFlavor.BYTE_ARRAY **POSTSCRIPT**	
▲	public static final . . . . DocFlavor.BYTE_ARRAY **TEXT_HTML_HOST**	
▲	public static final . . . . DocFlavor.BYTE_ARRAY **TEXT_HTML_US_ASCII**	
▲	public static final . . . . DocFlavor.BYTE_ARRAY **TEXT_HTML_UTF_16**	
▲	public static final . . . . DocFlavor.BYTE_ARRAY **TEXT_HTML_UTF_16BE**	

D

Classes

DocFlavor.BYTE_ARRAY

▲	public static final .... DocFlavor.BYTE_ARRAY	**TEXT_HTML_UTF_16LE**
▲	public static final .... DocFlavor.BYTE_ARRAY	**TEXT_HTML_UTF_8**
▲	public static final .... DocFlavor.BYTE_ARRAY	**TEXT_PLAIN_HOST**
▲	public static final .... DocFlavor.BYTE_ARRAY	**TEXT_PLAIN_US_ASCII**
▲	public static final .... DocFlavor.BYTE_ARRAY	**TEXT_PLAIN_UTF_16**
▲	public static final .... DocFlavor.BYTE_ARRAY	**TEXT_PLAIN_UTF_16BE**
▲	public static final .... DocFlavor.BYTE_ARRAY	**TEXT_PLAIN_UTF_16LE**
▲	public static final .... DocFlavor.BYTE_ARRAY	**TEXT_PLAIN_UTF_8**
1	public .... String	toString ()

DocFlavor.CHAR_ARRAY   javax.print

Object
1.4 └DocFlavor[1] - *java.io.Serializable*˅, *Cloneable*˅
1.4   └DocFlavor.CHAR_ARRAY

*	public	**DocFlavor.CHAR_ARRAY** (String mimeType)
1	public .... boolean	equals (Object obj)
1	public .... String	getMediaSubtype ()
1	public .... String	getMediaType ()
1	public .... String	getMimeType ()
1	public .... String	getParameter (String paramName)
1	public .... String	getRepresentationClassName ()
1	public .... int	hashCode ()
▲ 1	public static final .... String	hostEncoding = "Cp1252"
▲	public static final	**TEXT_HTML**
	.... DocFlavor.CHAR_ARRAY	
▲	public static final	**TEXT_PLAIN**
	.... DocFlavor.CHAR_ARRAY	
1	public .... String	toString ()

ε701,704

DocFlavor.INPUT_STREAM   javax.print

Object
1.4 └DocFlavor[1] - *java.io.Serializable*˅, *Cloneable*˅
1.4   └DocFlavor.INPUT_STREAM

▲	public static final ...... DocFlavor.INPUT_STREAM	**AUTOSENSE**
1	public .... boolean	equals (Object obj)
1	public .... String	getMediaSubtype ()
1	public .... String	getMediaType ()
1	public .... String	getMimeType ()
1	public .... String	getParameter (String paramName)
1	public .... String	getRepresentationClassName ()
▲	public static final ...... DocFlavor.INPUT_STREAM	**GIF**
1	public .... int	hashCode ()
▲ 1	public static final .... String	hostEncoding = "Cp1252"
*	public	**DocFlavor.INPUT_STREAM** (String mimeType)
▲	public static final ...... DocFlavor.INPUT_STREAM	**JPEG**
▲	public static final ...... DocFlavor.INPUT_STREAM	**PCL**
▲	public static final ...... DocFlavor.INPUT_STREAM	**PDF**
▲	public static final ...... DocFlavor.INPUT_STREAM	**PNG**
▲	public static final ...... DocFlavor.INPUT_STREAM	**POSTSCRIPT**
▲	public static final ...... DocFlavor.INPUT_STREAM	**TEXT_HTML_HOST**
▲	public static final ...... DocFlavor.INPUT_STREAM	**TEXT_HTML_US_ASCII**
▲	public static final ...... DocFlavor.INPUT_STREAM	**TEXT_HTML_UTF_16**
▲	public static final ...... DocFlavor.INPUT_STREAM	**TEXT_HTML_UTF_16BE**
▲	public static final ...... DocFlavor.INPUT_STREAM	**TEXT_HTML_UTF_16LE**
▲	public static final ...... DocFlavor.INPUT_STREAM	**TEXT_HTML_UTF_8**
▲	public static final ...... DocFlavor.INPUT_STREAM	**TEXT_PLAIN_HOST**
▲	public static final ...... DocFlavor.INPUT_STREAM	**TEXT_PLAIN_US_ASCII**
▲	public static final ...... DocFlavor.INPUT_STREAM	**TEXT_PLAIN_UTF_16**
▲	public static final ...... DocFlavor.INPUT_STREAM	**TEXT_PLAIN_UTF_16BE**
▲	public static final ...... DocFlavor.INPUT_STREAM	**TEXT_PLAIN_UTF_16LE**
▲	public static final ...... DocFlavor.INPUT_STREAM	**TEXT_PLAIN_UTF_8**
1	public .... String	toString ()

ε701,704

GIF ε700,701,703,704

Class   *Interface*   —extends   - - -implements   ○ abstract   ● final   △ static   ▲ static final   ✴ constructor   x x—inherited   x **x**—declared   **x x**—overridden
εn—examples of usage   ˅—has subclass   package—see other volume

DocFlavor.READER — javax.print

```
      Object
1.4   └DocFlavor¹ --------------------------- java.io.Serializable, Cloneable
1.4     └DocFlavor.READER
```

```
  1 public................. boolean equals (Object obj)
  1 public.................... String getMediaSubtype ()
  1 public.................... String getMediaType ()
  1 public.................... String getMimeType ()                          ε701,704
  1 public.................... String getParameter (String paramName)
  1 public.................... String getRepresentationClassName ()
  1 public....................... int hashCode ()
▲ 1 public static final......... String hostEncoding = "Cp1252"
*   public..........................  DocFlavor.READER (String mimeType)
▲   public static final..............  TEXT_HTML
        .......... DocFlavor.READER
▲   public static final..............  TEXT_PLAIN
        .......... DocFlavor.READER
  1 public.................... String toString ()
```

DocFlavor.SERVICE_FORMATTED — javax.print

```
      Object
1.4   └DocFlavor¹ --------------------------- java.io.Serializable, Cloneable
1.4     └DocFlavor.SERVICE_FORMATTED
```

```
  1 public................. boolean equals (Object obj)
  1 public.................... String getMediaSubtype ()
  1 public.................... String getMediaType ()
  1 public.................... String getMimeType ()                          ε701,704
  1 public.................... String getParameter (String paramName)
  1 public.................... String getRepresentationClassName ()
  1 public....................... int hashCode ()
▲ 1 public static final......... String hostEncoding = "Cp1252"
▲   public static final...DocFlavor PAGEABLE
           .SERVICE_FORMATTED
▲   public static final...DocFlavor PRINTABLE
           .SERVICE_FORMATTED
▲   public static final...DocFlavor RENDERABLE_IMAGE
           .SERVICE_FORMATTED
*   public..........................  DocFlavor.SERVICE_FORMATTED (String className)
  1 public.................... String toString ()
```

DocFlavor.STRING — javax.print

```
      Object
1.4   └DocFlavor¹ --------------------------- java.io.Serializable, Cloneable
1.4     └DocFlavor.STRING
```

```
  1 public................. boolean equals (Object obj)
  1 public.................... String getMediaSubtype ()
  1 public.................... String getMediaType ()
  1 public.................... String getMimeType ()                          ε701,704
  1 public.................... String getParameter (String paramName)
  1 public.................... String getRepresentationClassName ()
  1 public....................... int hashCode ()
▲ 1 public static final......... String hostEncoding = "Cp1252"
*   public..........................  DocFlavor.STRING (String mimeType)
▲   public static final..............  TEXT_HTML
        ........... DocFlavor.STRING
▲   public static final..............  TEXT_PLAIN
        ........... DocFlavor.STRING
  1 public.................... String toString ()
```

DocFlavor.URL   javax.print

Object
1.4 └─DocFlavor [1] - *java.io.Serializable* ., *Cloneable* .
1.4   └─DocFlavor.URL

▲		public static final ....DocFlavor.URL	**AUTOSENSE**	
	1	public.................................... boolean	equals (Object obj)	
	1	public..String	getMediaSubtype ()	
	1	public..String	getMediaType ()	
	1	public..String	getMimeType ()	ε701,704
	1	public..String	getParameter (String paramName)	
	1	public..String	getRepresentationClassName ()	
▲		public static final ....DocFlavor.URL	**GIF**	
	1	public..int	hashCode ()	
▲	1	public static final ....String	hostEncoding = "Cp1252"	
▲		public static final ....DocFlavor.URL	**JPEG**	
▲		public static final ....DocFlavor.URL	**PCL**	
▲		public static final ....DocFlavor.URL	**PDF**	
▲		public static final ....DocFlavor.URL	**PNG**	
▲		public static final ....DocFlavor.URL	**POSTSCRIPT**	
▲		public static final ....DocFlavor.URL	**TEXT_HTML_HOST**	
▲		public static final ....DocFlavor.URL	**TEXT_HTML_US_ASCII**	
▲		public static final ....DocFlavor.URL	**TEXT_HTML_UTF_16**	
▲		public static final ....DocFlavor.URL	**TEXT_HTML_UTF_16BE**	
▲		public static final ....DocFlavor.URL	**TEXT_HTML_UTF_16LE**	
▲		public static final ....DocFlavor.URL	**TEXT_HTML_UTF_8**	
▲		public static final ....DocFlavor.URL	**TEXT_PLAIN_HOST**	
▲		public static final ....DocFlavor.URL	**TEXT_PLAIN_US_ASCII**	
▲		public static final ....DocFlavor.URL	**TEXT_PLAIN_UTF_16**	
▲		public static final ....DocFlavor.URL	**TEXT_PLAIN_UTF_16BE**	
▲		public static final ....DocFlavor.URL	**TEXT_PLAIN_UTF_16LE**	
▲		public static final ....DocFlavor.URL	**TEXT_PLAIN_UTF_8**	
	1	public...String	toString ()	
✳		public...	**DocFlavor.URL** (String mimeType)	

DocPrintJob   javax.print

1.4 *DocPrintJob* .

public......................void **addPrintJobAttributeListener** (*javax.print.event.PrintJobAttributeListener* listener,
  javax.print.attribute.PrintJobAttributeSet attributes) ε715
public......................void **addPrintJobListener** (*javax.print.event.PrintJobListener* listener)
                                                                         ε714
public.....*javax.print.attribute* . **getAttributes** () ε715
        .PrintJobAttributeSet
public..............*PrintService* **getPrintService** ()
public......................void **print** (*Doc* doc, *javax.print.attribute.PrintRequestAttributeSet* attributes)
          throws PrintException ε700,702,710,711,712
public......................void **removePrintJobAttributeListener** (*javax.print.event.PrintJobAttributeListener*
          listener)
public......................void **removePrintJobListener** (*javax.print.event.PrintJobListener* listener)

Document ❶   javax.swing.text

1.2 *Document* .

public......................void **addDocumentListener** (*javax.swing.event.DocumentListener* listener)
                                                                         ε1016
public......................void **addUndoableEditListener** (*javax.swing.event.UndoableEditListener* listener)
                                                                         ε1034
public..................*Position* **createPosition** (int offs) throws BadLocationException ε974
public.................*Element* **getDefaultRootElement** () ε984,990,1013
public..................*Position* **getEndPosition** ()
public...........................int **getLength** () ε968,969,970,971,972
public..................Object **getProperty** (Object key)
public.................*Element[]* **getRootElements** ()
public..................*Position* **getStartPosition** ()
public.........................String **getText** (int offset, int length) throws BadLocationException ε971,972,973,1002,1006

Class *Interface* —extends - - -implements ○ abstract ● final △ static ▲ static final ✳ constructor x x—inherited x **x**—declared **x x**—overridden
εn—examples of usage   .—has subclass   package—see other volume

public	void	**getText** (int offset, int length, Segment txt) throws BadLocationException	
			ε969
public	void	**insertString** (int offset, String str, *AttributeSet* a) throws BadLocationException	
			ε970,1002,1003,1004
public	void	**putProperty** (Object key, Object value)	
public	void	**remove** (int offs, int len) throws BadLocationException	ε970,1002
public	void	**removeDocumentListener** (*javax.swing.event.DocumentListener* listener)	
public	void	**removeUndoableEditListener** (*javax.swing.event.UndoableEditListener* listener)	
public	void	**render** (*Runnable* r)	ε971
▲ public static final	String	**StreamDescriptionProperty** = "stream"	
▲ public static final	String	**TitleProperty** = "title"	

D

DocumentEvent
javax.swing.event

1.2   *DocumentEvent*

public	*DocumentEvent₂ .ElementChange*	**getChange** (*javax.swing.text.Element* elem)	
public	*.. javax.swing.text.Document*	**getDocument** ()	ε1016
public	int	**getLength** ()	ε1016
public	int	**getOffset** ()	ε1016
public	*.. DocumentEvent.EventType*	**getType** ()	

DocumentEvent.ElementChange
javax.swing.event

1.2   *DocumentEvent.ElementChange*

public	*... javax.swing.text.Element[]*	**getChildrenAdded** ()
public	*... javax.swing.text.Element[]*	**getChildrenRemoved** ()
public	*..... javax.swing.text.Element*	**getElement** ()
public	int	**getIndex** ()

DocumentEvent.EventType
javax.swing.event

Object[1]
1.2 ●   └ DocumentEvent.EventType

▲ public static final		**CHANGE**	
	.. DocumentEvent.EventType		
▲ public static final		**INSERT**	
	.. DocumentEvent.EventType		
▲ public static final		**REMOVE**	
	.. DocumentEvent.EventType		
1 public	String	**toString** ()	

DocumentFilter
javax.swing.text

Object
1.4   └ DocumentFilter

* public		**DocumentFilter** ()	
public	void	**insertString** (DocumentFilter.FilterBypass fb, int offset, String string,	
		AttributeSet attr) throws BadLocationException	ε975
public	void	**remove** (DocumentFilter.FilterBypass fb, int offset, int length)	
		throws BadLocationException	
public	void	**replace** (DocumentFilter.FilterBypass fb, int offset, int length, String text,	
		AttributeSet attrs) throws BadLocationException	ε975

DocumentFilter.FilterBypass
javax.swing.text

Object
1.4 ○   └ DocumentFilter.FilterBypass

Classes

DocumentFilter.FilterBypass

✳	public..........................		**DocumentFilter.FilterBypass** ()	
○	public abstract......	Document	**getDocument** ()	ε975
○	public abstract............void		**insertString** (int offset, String string, *AttributeSet* attr) throws BadLocationException	
○	public abstract............void		**remove** (int offset, int length) throws BadLocationException	
○	public abstract............void		**replace** (int offset, int length, String string, *AttributeSet* attrs)	
			throws BadLocationException	ε975

D

DocumentListener — javax.swing.event

1.2	*DocumentListener* ———————————— *java.util.EventListener*	ε738,743,745,746,752
	public......................void **changedUpdate** (*DocumentEvent* e)	ε1016
	public......................void **insertUpdate** (*DocumentEvent* e)	ε1016
	public......................void **removeUpdate** (*DocumentEvent* e)	ε1016

DocumentName — javax.print.attribute.standard

Object
1.4 ○	└javax.print.attribute.TextSyntax [1] - - - - - - - - - - *java.io.Serializable*, *Cloneable*
1.4 ●	└DocumentName - - - - - - - - - - - - - - - - *javax.print.attribute.DocAttribute* (*javax.print.attribute.Attribute* [2] (*java.io.Serializable*))

✳	public..........................		**DocumentName** (String documentName, java.util.Locale locale)	
	1	public..................**boolean**	**equals** (Object object)	
●	2	public final ....Class	**getCategory** ()	ε707
	1	public.......... java.util.Locale	getLocale ()	
●	2	public final ....String	**getName** ()	ε706,707,708
	1	public....................String	getValue ()	
	1	public.......................int	hashCode ()	
	1	public....................String	toString ()	

DocumentParser — javax.swing.text.html.parser

Object
1.2	└Parser [1] - *DTDConstants* [2]
1.2	└DocumentParser

	2	*35 inherited members from DTDConstants not shown*	
✳		public..........................	**DocumentParser** (DTD dtd)
	1	protected .... DTD	dtd
	1	protected ....void	endTag (boolean omitted)
	1	protected ....void	error (String err)
	1	protected ....void	error (String err, String arg1)
	1	protected ....void	error (String err, String arg1, String arg2)
	1	protected ....void	error (String err, String arg1, String arg2, String arg3)
	1	protected ....void	flushAttributes ()
	1	protected .... javax.swing, .text.SimpleAttributeSet	getAttributes ()
	1	protected ....int	getCurrentLine ()
	1	protected ....int	getCurrentPos ()
	1	protected .... **void**	**handleComment** (char[] text)
	1	protected .... **void**	**handleEmptyTag** (TagElement tag) throws javax.swing.text, .ChangedCharSetException
	1	protected .... **void**	**handleEndTag** (TagElement tag)
	1	protected ....void	handleEOFInComment ()
	1	protected .... **void**	**handleError** (int ln, String errorMsg)
	1	protected .... **void**	**handleStartTag** (TagElement tag)
	1	protected .... **void**	**handleText** (char[] data)
	1	protected ....void	handleTitle (char[] text)
	1	protected .... TagElement	makeTag (Element elem)
	1	protected .... TagElement	makeTag (Element elem, boolean fictional)
	1	protected ....void	markFirstTime (Element elem)
	1	public synchronized ......void	parse (java.io.Reader in) throws java.io.IOException
		public.......................void	**parse** (java.io.Reader in, javax.swing.text.html.HTMLEditorKit.ParserCallback callback, boolean ignoreCharSet) throws java.io.IOException
	1	public....................String	parseDTDMarkup () throws java.io.IOException
	1	protected .... boolean	parseMarkupDeclarations (StringBuffer strBuff) throws java.io.IOException

---

Class *Interface* —extends - - -implements ○ abstract ● final △ static ▲ static final ✳ constructor x x—inherited x **x**—declared **x x**—overridden
ε*n*—examples of usage ‿—has subclass package—see other volume

1	protected ....void	startTag (TagElement tag) throws javax.swing.text.ChangedCharSetException
1	protected ....boolean	strict

DragGestureEvent
java.awt.dnd

Object ε640,641,643,649,566
1.1 └ java.util.EventObject [1] ------------------- *java.io.Serializable*
1.2 └ DragGestureEvent

*	public...........................	**DragGestureEvent** (DragGestureRecognizer dgr, int act, java.awt.Point ori, *java.util.*List evs)
	public.... java.awt.Component	**getComponent** ()
	public.............................int	**getDragAction** ()
	public...........java.awt.Point	**getDragOrigin** ()
	public.............DragSource	**getDragSource** ()
1	public..................Object	getSource () ε644,886,565,568,570
	public DragGestureRecognizer	**getSourceAsDragGestureRecognizer** ()
	public...........................	**getTriggerEvent** ()
	....java.awt.event.InputEvent	
	public........... *java.util.Iterator*	**iterator** ()
1	protected transient......Object	source
1.4	public.....................void	**startDrag** (java.awt.Cursor dragCursor, *java.awt.datatransfer.Transferable* transferable) throws InvalidDnDOperationException
	public.....................void	**startDrag** (java.awt.Cursor dragCursor, *java.awt.datatransfer.Transferable* transferable, *DragSourceListener* dsl) throws InvalidDnDOperationException
	public.....................void	**startDrag** (java.awt.Cursor dragCursor, java.awt.Image dragImage, java.awt.Point imageOffset, *java.awt.datatransfer.Transferable* transferable, *DragSourceListener* dsl) throws InvalidDnDOperationException
	public.................Object[]	**toArray** ()
	public.................Object[]	**toArray** (Object[] array)
1	public....................String	toString ()

DragGestureListener
java.awt.dnd

1.2 *DragGestureListener* ──────────────── *java.util.EventListener* ε738,743,745,746,752

public.....................void **dragGestureRecognized** (DragGestureEvent dge) ε640

DragGestureRecognizer
java.awt.dnd

Object
1.2 ○ └ DragGestureRecognizer ---------------- *java.io.Serializable*

	public synchronized ....void	**addDragGestureListener** (*DragGestureListener* dgl) throws java.util.TooManyListenersException
	protected synchronized ...void	**appendEvent** (java.awt.event.InputEvent awtie)
	protected java.awt.Component	**component**
	protected transient.............	**dragGestureListener**
	.... *DragGestureListener*	
*	protected......................	**DragGestureRecognizer** (DragSource ds)
*	protected......................	**DragGestureRecognizer** (DragSource ds, java.awt.Component c)
*	protected......................	**DragGestureRecognizer** (DragSource ds, java.awt.Component c, int sa)
*	protected......................	**DragGestureRecognizer** (DragSource ds, java.awt.Component c, int sa, *DragGestureListener* dgl)
	protected..........DragSource	**dragSource**
	protected....java.util.ArrayList	**events**
	protected synchronized ...void	**fireDragGestureRecognized** (int dragAction, java.awt.Point p)
	public synchronized	**getComponent** ()
	.... java.awt.Component	
	public..............DragSource	**getDragSource** ()
	public synchronized ....int	**getSourceActions** ()
	public...........................	**getTriggerEvent** ()
	....java.awt.event.InputEvent	
○	protected abstract ....void	**registerListeners** ()
	public synchronized ....void	**removeDragGestureListener** (*DragGestureListener* dgl)
	public.....................void	**resetRecognizer** ()
	public synchronized ....void	**setComponent** (java.awt.Component c)
	public synchronized ....void	**setSourceActions** (int actions)
	protected....................int	**sourceActions**
○	protected abstract ....void	**unregisterListeners** ()

DragSource

		java.awt.dnd

Object
1.2 └─DragSource - *java.io.Serializable*

1.4	public......................void	**addDragSourceListener** (*DragSourceListener* dsl)	
1.4	public......................void	**addDragSourceMotionListener** (*DragSourceMotionListener* dsml)	
	public DragGestureRecognizer	**createDefaultDragGestureRecognizer** (java.awt.Component c, int actions, *DragGestureListener* dgl)	ε640
	public DragGestureRecognizer	**createDragGestureRecognizer** (Class recognizerAbstractClass, java.awt.Component c, int actions, *DragGestureListener* dgl)	
	protected . DragSourceContext	**createDragSourceContext** (java.awt.dnd.peer.DragSourceContextPeer dscp, DragGestureEvent dgl, java.awt.Cursor dragCursor, java.awt.Image dragImage, java.awt.Point imageOffset, *java.awt.datatransfer.Transferable* t, *DragSourceListener* dsl)	
▲	public static final.............. ....java.awt.Cursor	**DefaultCopyDrop**	ε640
▲	public static final.............. ....java.awt.Cursor	**DefaultCopyNoDrop**	
▲	public static final.............. ....java.awt.Cursor	**DefaultLinkDrop**	
▲	public static final.............. ....java.awt.Cursor	**DefaultLinkNoDrop**	
▲	public static final.............. ....java.awt.Cursor	**DefaultMoveDrop**	
▲	public static final.............. ....java.awt.Cursor	**DefaultMoveNoDrop**	
＊	public..............	**DragSource** () throws java.awt.HeadlessException	ε640
△	public static .... DragSource	**getDefaultDragSource** ()	
1.4	public... *DragSourceListener[]*	**getDragSourceListeners** ()	
1.4	public.................... . *DragSourceMotionListener[]*	**getDragSourceMotionListeners** ()	
	public.................*java.awt*₂ .*datatransfer.FlavorMap*	**getFlavorMap** ()	
1.4	public. *java.util.EventListener[]*	**getListeners** (Class listenerType)	
△	public static .... boolean	**isDragImageSupported** ()	
1.4	public......................void	**removeDragSourceListener** (*DragSourceListener* dsl)	
1.4	public......................void	**removeDragSourceMotionListener** (*DragSourceMotionListener* dsml)	
	public......................void	**startDrag** (DragGestureEvent trigger, java.awt.Cursor dragCursor, *java.awt.datatransfer.Transferable* transferable, *DragSourceListener* dsl) throws InvalidDnDOperationException	ε640
	public......................void	**startDrag** (DragGestureEvent trigger, java.awt.Cursor dragCursor, *java.awt.datatransfer.Transferable* transferable, *DragSourceListener* dsl, *java*₂ .*awt.datatransfer.FlavorMap* flavorMap) throws InvalidDnDOperationException	
	public......................void	**startDrag** (DragGestureEvent trigger, java.awt.Cursor dragCursor, java.awt.Image dragImage, java.awt.Point dragOffset, *java.awt.datatransfer.Transferable* transferable, *DragSourceListener* dsl) throws InvalidDnDOperationException	
	public......................void	**startDrag** (DragGestureEvent trigger, java.awt.Cursor dragCursor, java.awt.Image dragImage, java.awt.Point imageOffset, *java.awt.datatransfer.Transferable* transferable, *DragSourceListener* dsl, *java.awt.datatransfer.FlavorMap* flavorMap) throws InvalidDnDOperationException	

---

		java.awt.dnd

Object
1.4 ○ └─DragSourceAdapter - *DragSourceListener* [1] (*java.util.EventListener*), *DragSourceMotionListener* [2] (*java.util.EventListener*)

1	public......................void	**dragDropEnd** (DragSourceDropEvent dsde)	ε640
1	public......................void	**dragEnter** (DragSourceDragEvent dsde)	ε640
1	public......................void	**dragExit** (DragSourceEvent dse)	ε640
2	public......................void	**dragMouseMoved** (DragSourceDragEvent dsde)	
1	public......................void	**dragOver** (DragSourceDragEvent dsde)	ε640
＊	public..............	**DragSourceAdapter** ()	
1	public......................void	**dropActionChanged** (DragSourceDragEvent dsde)	ε640

Class *Interface* —extends - - -implements ○ abstract ● final △ static ▲ static final ＊ constructor x x—inherited x **x**—declared **x x**—overridden
ε*n*—examples of usage ⌐has subclass package—see other volume

DragSourceContext		java.awt.dnd

Object
1.2 └DragSourceContext - *DragSourceListener* [1] (*java.util.EventListener*),
DragSourceMotionListener [2] (*java.util.EventListener*),
java.io.Serializable

D

	public synchronized ....void	**addDragSourceListener** (*DragSourceListener* dsl)	
		throws java.util.TooManyListenersException	
▲	protected static final ....int	**CHANGED**	
▲	protected static final ....int	**DEFAULT**	
1	public.......................void	**dragDropEnd** (DragSourceDropEvent dsde)	ε640
1	public.......................void	**dragEnter** (DragSourceDragEvent dsde)	ε640
1	public.......................void	**dragExit** (DragSourceEvent dse)	ε640
1.4 2	public.......................void	**dragMouseMoved** (DragSourceDragEvent dsde)	
1	public.......................void	**dragOver** (DragSourceDragEvent dsde)	ε640
*	public........................	**DragSourceContext** (java.awt.dnd.peer.DragSourceContextPeer dscp,	
		DragGestureEvent trigger, java.awt.Cursor dragCursor,	
		java.awt.Image dragImage, java.awt.Point offset,	
		java.awt.datatransfer.Transferable t, *DragSourceListener* dsl)	
1	public.......................void	**dropActionChanged** (DragSourceDragEvent dsde)	ε640
▲	protected static final ....int	**ENTER**	
	public.... java.awt.Component	**getComponent** ()	
	public.......... java.awt.Cursor	**getCursor** ()	
	public.............. DragSource	**getDragSource** ()	
	public........................int	**getSourceActions** ()	
	public.................*java.awt*	**getTransferable** ()	
	.datatransfer.Transferable		
	public........DragGestureEvent	**getTrigger** ()	
▲	protected static final ....int	**OVER**	
	public synchronized ....void	**removeDragSourceListener** (*DragSourceListener* dsl)	
	public synchronized ....void	**setCursor** (java.awt.Cursor c)	
	public.......................void	**transferablesFlavorsChanged** ()	
	protected synchronized ...void	**updateCurrentCursor** (int dropOp, int targetAct, int status)	

DragSourceDragEvent		java.awt.dnd
		ε640,641,643,649,566

Object
1.1 └ java.util.EventObject [1] - - - - - - - - - - - - - - - - - - - *java.io.Serializable*
1.2 └DragSourceEvent [2]
1.2 └DragSourceDragEvent

*	public........................	**DragSourceDragEvent** (DragSourceContext dsc, int dropAction, int actions,	
		int modifiers)	
1.4 *	public........................	**DragSourceDragEvent** (DragSourceContext dsc, int dropAction, int actions,	
		int modifiers, int x, int y)	
2	public..... DragSourceContext	getDragSourceContext ()	
	public........................int	**getDropAction** ()	
	public........................int	**getGestureModifiers** ()	
1.4	public........................int	**getGestureModifiersEx** ()	
1.4 2	public.............java.awt.Point	getLocation ()	
1	public.................Object	getSource ()	ε644,886,565,568,570
	public........................int	**getTargetActions** ()	
	public........................int	**getUserAction** ()	
1.4 2	public........................int	getX ()	
1.4 2	public........................int	getY ()	
1	protected transient......Object	source	
1	public....................String	toString ()	

Classes

DragSourceDropEvent		java.awt.dnd
		ε640,641,643,649,566

Object
1.1 └ java.util.EventObject [1] - - - - - - - - - - - - - - - - - - - *java.io.Serializable*
1.2 └DragSourceEvent [2]
1.2 └DragSourceDropEvent

*	public........................	**DragSourceDropEvent** (DragSourceContext dsc)
*	public........................	**DragSourceDropEvent** (DragSourceContext dsc, int action, boolean success)
1.4 *	public........................	**DragSourceDropEvent** (DragSourceContext dsc, int action, boolean success,
		int x, int y)

DragSourceDropEvent

	2	public..... DragSourceContext	**getDragSourceContext** ()		
		public.........................int	**getDropAction** ()		
		public......................... boolean	**getDropSuccess** ()		
1.4	2	public............ java.awt.Point	getLocation ()		
	1	public.....................Object	getSource ()		ε644,886,565,568,570
1.4	2	public.........................int	getX ()		
1.4	2	public.........................int	getY ()		
	1	protected transient...... Object	source		
	1	public.....................String	toString ()		

DragSourceEvent   java.awt.dnd

Object   ε640,641,643,649,566

1.1 └ java.util.EventObject [1] - - - - - - - - - - - - - - - - - - *java.io.Serializable*
1.2   └ DragSourceEvent

*	public...........................	**DragSourceEvent** (DragSourceContext dsc)		
1.4 *	public...........................	**DragSourceEvent** (DragSourceContext dsc, int x, int y)		
	public..... DragSourceContext	**getDragSourceContext** ()		
1.4	public............ java.awt.Point	**getLocation** ()		
1	public.....................Object	getSource ()		ε644,886,565,568,570
1.4	public.........................int	**getX** ()		
1.4	public.........................int	**getY** ()		
1	protected transient...... Object	source		
1	public.....................String	toString ()		

DragSourceListener   java.awt.dnd

1.2 *DragSourceListener*————————————*java.util.EventListener*   ε738,743,745,746,752

public.......................void	**dragDropEnd** (DragSourceDropEvent dsde)	ε640	
public.......................void	**dragEnter** (DragSourceDragEvent dsde)	ε640	
public.......................void	**dragExit** (DragSourceEvent dse)	ε640	
public.......................void	**dragOver** (DragSourceDragEvent dsde)	ε640	
public.......................void	**dropActionChanged** (DragSourceDragEvent dsde)	ε640	

DragSourceMotionListener   java.awt.dnd

1.4 *DragSourceMotionListener*————————*java.util.EventListener*   ε738,743,745,746,752

public.......................void	**dragMouseMoved** (DragSourceDragEvent dsde)

DropTarget   java.awt.dnd

Object
1.2 └ DropTarget - *DropTargetListener* [1] (*java.util.EventListener*), *java.io.Serializable*

	public synchronized ....void	**addDropTargetListener** (*DropTargetListener* dtl) throws	
		java.util.TooManyListenersException	
	public.......................void	**addNotify** (*java.awt.peer.ComponentPeer* peer)	
	protected ....void	**clearAutoscroll** ()	
	protected ....DropTarget	**createDropTargetAutoScroller** (java.awt.Component c, java.awt.Point p)	
	.DropTargetAutoScroller		
	protected .. DropTargetContext	**createDropTargetContext** ()	
1	public synchronized ......void	**dragEnter** (DropTargetDragEvent dtde)	ε641
1	public synchronized ......void	**dragExit** (DropTargetEvent dte)	ε641
1	public synchronized ......void	**dragOver** (DropTargetDragEvent dtde)	ε641
1	public synchronized ......void	**drop** (DropTargetDropEvent dtde)	ε642,641
1	public synchronized ......void	**dropActionChanged** (DropTargetDragEvent dtde)	ε641
*	public...........................	**DropTarget** () throws java.awt.HeadlessException	
*	public...........................	**DropTarget** (java.awt.Component c, *DropTargetListener* dtl)	
		throws java.awt.HeadlessException	ε641
*	public...........................	**DropTarget** (java.awt.Component c, int ops, *DropTargetListener* dtl)	
		throws java.awt.HeadlessException	
*	public...........................	**DropTarget** (java.awt.Component c, int ops, *DropTargetListener* dtl, boolean act)	
		throws java.awt.HeadlessException	

Class   *Interface*   —extends   - - -implements   ○ abstract   ● final   △ static   ▲ static final   ✳ constructor   x x—inherited   x **x**—declared   **x x**—overridden
εn—examples of usage   —has subclass   package—see other volume

*	public.........................	**DropTarget** (java.awt.Component c, int ops, *DropTargetListener* dtl, boolean act, *java.awt.datatransfer.FlavorMap* fm) throws java.awt.HeadlessException
	public synchronized .... java.awt.Component	**getComponent** ()
	public........................int	**getDefaultActions** ()
	public...... DropTargetContext	**getDropTargetContext** ()
	public...............*java.awt* .datatransfer.FlavorMap	**getFlavorMap** ()
	protected ....void	**initializeAutoscrolling** (java.awt.Point p)
	public .... boolean	**isActive** ()
	public synchronized ......void	**removeDropTargetListener** (*DropTargetListener* dtl)
	public.......................void	**removeNotify** (*java.awt.peer.ComponentPeer* peer)
	public synchronized ......void	**setActive** (boolean isActive)
	public synchronized ......void	**setComponent** (java.awt.Component c)
	public.......................void	**setDefaultActions** (int ops)
	public.......................void	**setFlavorMap** (*java.awt.datatransfer.FlavorMap* fm)
	protected ....void	**updateAutoscroll** (java.awt.Point dragCursorLocn)

DropTarget.DropTargetAutoScroller	protected	java.awt.dnd

1.2   Object
      └DropTarget.DropTargetAutoScroller - - - - - - - - *java.awt.event.ActionListener* ↙[1] (*java.util.EventListener*)

1	public synchronized ....void	**actionPerformed** (java.awt.event.ActionEvent e)	ε855,644,738,743,745
*	protected......................	**DropTarget.DropTargetAutoScroller** (java.awt.Component c, java.awt.Point p)	
	protected..................void	**stop** ()	
	protected synchronized ...void	**updateLocation** (java.awt.Point newLocn)	

DropTargetAdapter		java.awt.dnd

1.4 ○   Object
      └DropTargetAdapter - *DropTargetListener* [1] (*java.util.EventListener*)

1	public.......................void	**dragEnter** (DropTargetDragEvent dtde)	ε641
1	public.......................void	**dragExit** (DropTargetEvent dte)	ε641
1	public.......................void	**dragOver** (DropTargetDragEvent dtde)	ε641
○ 1	public abstract ....void	drop (DropTargetDropEvent dtde)	ε642,641
1	public.......................void	**dropActionChanged** (DropTargetDragEvent dtde)	ε641
*	public..........................	**DropTargetAdapter** ()	

DropTargetContext		java.awt.dnd

1.2   Object
      └DropTargetContext - *java.io.Serializable*

	protected ....void	**acceptDrag** (int dragOperation)
	protected ....void	**acceptDrop** (int dropOperation)
	public.......................void	**addNotify** (java.awt.dnd.peer.DropTargetContextPeer dtcp)
	protected ....*java.awt* .datatransfer.*Transferable*	**createTransferableProxy** (*java.awt.datatransfer.Transferable* t, boolean local)
	public.......................void	**dropComplete** (boolean success) throws InvalidDnDOperationException ε642
	public.... java.awt.Component	**getComponent** ()
	protected ....*java.awt* .datatransfer.DataFlavor[]	**getCurrentDataFlavors** ()
	protected ....*java.util.List*	**getCurrentDataFlavorsAsList** ()
	public...............DropTarget	**getDropTarget** ()
	protected ....int	**getTargetActions** ()
	protected ....*java.awt* .datatransfer.*Transferable*	**getTransferable** () throws InvalidDnDOperationException
	protected .... boolean	**isDataFlavorSupported** (java.awt.datatransfer.DataFlavor df)
	protected ....void	**rejectDrag** ()
	protected ....void	**rejectDrop** ()
	public.......................void	**removeNotify** ()
	protected ....void	**setTargetActions** (int actions)

DropTargetContext.TransferableProxy	protected	java.awt.dnd

Object
1.2 └─DropTargetContext.TransferableProxy - - - - - - - *java.awt.datatransfer.Transferable* [1]

1	public.................Object	**getTransferData** (java.awt.datatransfer.DataFlavor df) throws java.awt.datatransfer $_\supset$ .UnsupportedFlavorException, java.io.IOException	*ε*637,638,642
1	public.............java.awt $_\supset$ .datatransfer.DataFlavor[]	**getTransferDataFlavors** ()	*ε*638
1	public................boolean	**isDataFlavorSupported** (java.awt.datatransfer.DataFlavor flavor)	*ε*637,638,642
	protected.............boolean	**isLocal**	
	protected.............java.awt $_\supset$ .datatransfer.Transferable	**transferable**	

DropTargetDragEvent		java.awt.dnd

Object *ε*641,640,643,649,566
1.1 └─ java.util.EventObject [1] - - - - - - - - - - - - - - - - - *java.io.Serializable* ↲
1.2   └─DropTargetEvent [2]
1.2   └─DropTargetDragEvent

	public........................void	**acceptDrag** (int dragOperation)	
2	protected .. DropTargetContext	context	
*	public..........................	**DropTargetDragEvent** (DropTargetContext dtc, java.awt.Point cursorLocn, int dropAction, int srcActions)	
	public.................java.awt $_\supset$ .datatransfer.DataFlavor[]	**getCurrentDataFlavors** ()	
	public............. *java.util.List*	**getCurrentDataFlavorsAsList** ()	
	public........................int	**getDropAction** ()	
2	public...... DropTargetContext	getDropTargetContext ()	*ε*642
	public...........java.awt.Point	**getLocation** ()	
1	public................Object	getSource ()	*ε*644,886,565,568,570
	public........................int	**getSourceActions** ()	
	public................boolean	**isDataFlavorSupported** (java.awt.datatransfer.DataFlavor df)	*ε*642
	public........................void	**rejectDrag** ()	
1	protected transient......Object	source	
1	public.................String	toString ()	

DropTargetDropEvent		java.awt.dnd

Object *ε*641,640,643,649,566
1.1 └─ java.util.EventObject [1] - - - - - - - - - - - - - - - - - *java.io.Serializable* ↲
1.2   └─DropTargetEvent [2]
1.2   └─DropTargetDropEvent

	public........................void	**acceptDrop** (int dropAction)	*ε*642
2	protected .. DropTargetContext	context	
	public........................void	**dropComplete** (boolean success)	
*	public..........................	**DropTargetDropEvent** (DropTargetContext dtc, java.awt.Point cursorLocn, int dropAction, int srcActions)	
*	public..........................	**DropTargetDropEvent** (DropTargetContext dtc, java.awt.Point cursorLocn, int dropAction, int srcActions, boolean isLocal)	
	public.................java.awt $_\supset$ .datatransfer.DataFlavor[]	**getCurrentDataFlavors** ()	
	public............. *java.util.List*	**getCurrentDataFlavorsAsList** ()	
	public........................int	**getDropAction** ()	
2	public...... DropTargetContext	getDropTargetContext ()	*ε*642
	public...........java.awt.Point	**getLocation** ()	
1	public................Object	getSource ()	*ε*644,886,565,568,570
	public........................int	**getSourceActions** ()	
	public.................java.awt $_\supset$ .datatransfer.Transferable	**getTransferable** ()	*ε*642
	public................boolean	**isDataFlavorSupported** (java.awt.datatransfer.DataFlavor df)	
	public................boolean	**isLocalTransfer** ()	
	public........................void	**rejectDrop** ()	*ε*642
1	protected transient......Object	source	

Class *Interface* —extends - - -implements ○ abstract ● final △ static ▲ static final ✳ constructor x x—inherited x **x**—declared **x x**—overridden
εn—examples of usage ↲—has subclass package—see other volume

D

1	public..................... String	toString ()	

DropTargetEvent

ε641,640,643,649,566

```
      Object
1.1   └ java.util.EventObject¹ - - - - - - - - - - - - - - - - - - java.io.Serializable
1.2     └ DropTargetEvent
```

	protected .. DropTargetContext	**context**	
*	public................................	**DropTargetEvent** (DropTargetContext dtc)	
	public...... DropTargetContext	**getDropTargetContext** ()	ε642
1	public.................... Object	getSource ()	ε644,886,565,568,570
1	protected transient...... Object	source	
1	public.................... String	toString ()	

DropTargetListener

ε738,743,745,746,752

```
1.2   DropTargetListener ———————————— java.util.EventListener
```

	public..........................void	**dragEnter** (DropTargetDragEvent dtde)	ε641
	public..........................void	**dragExit** (DropTargetEvent dte)	ε641
	public..........................void	**dragOver** (DropTargetDragEvent dtde)	ε641
	public..........................void	**drop** (DropTargetDropEvent dtde)	ε642,641
	public..........................void	**dropActionChanged** (DropTargetDragEvent dtde)	ε641

DTD

```
      Object¹
1.2   └ DTD - - - - - - - - - - - - - - - - - - - - - - - - - - - DTDConstants²
```

2	*35 inherited members from DTDConstants not shown*		
●	public final .... Element	**applet**	
●	public final .... Element	**base**	
●	public final .... Element	**body**	
	protected .... AttributeList	**defAttributeList** (String name, int type, int modifier, String value, String values, AttributeList atts)	
	protected ....ContentModel	**defContentModel** (int type, Object obj, ContentModel next)	
	protected .... Element	**defElement** (String name, int type, boolean omitStart, boolean omitEnd, ContentModel content, String[] exclusions, String[] inclusions, AttributeList atts)	
	protected .... Entity	**defEntity** (String name, int type, String str)	
	public...................... Entity	**defEntity** (String name, int type, int ch)	
	public.......................void	**defineAttributes** (String name, AttributeList atts)	
	public.................. Element	**defineElement** (String name, int type, boolean omitStart, boolean omitEnd, ContentModel content, java.util.BitSet exclusions, java.util.BitSet inclusions, AttributeList atts)	
	public...................... Entity	**defineEntity** (String name, int type, char[] data)	
*	protected.........................	**DTD** (String name)	
	public....... java.util.Hashtable	**elementHash**	
	public........... java.util.Vector	**elements**	
	public....... java.util.Hashtable	**entityHash**	
△	public static ....int	**FILE_VERSION**	
△	public static .... DTD	**getDTD** (String name) throws java.io.IOException	
	public................. Element	**getElement** (int index)	
	public................. Element	**getElement** (String name)	
	public.................. Entity	**getEntity** (int ch)	
	public.................. Entity	**getEntity** (String name)	
	public.................... String	**getName** ()	
●	public final .... Element	**head**	
●	public final .... Element	**html**	
●	public final .... Element	**isindex**	
●	public final .... Element	**meta**	
	public...................... String	**name**	
●	public final .... Element	**p**	
●	public final .... Element	**param**	
●	public final .... Element	**pcdata**	
△	public static ....void	**putDTDHash** (String name, DTD dtd)	
	public.......................void	**read** (java.io.DataInputStream in) throws java.io.IOException	
●	public final .... Element	**title**	
1	public.................... **String**	**toString** ()	

DTDConstants

		javax.swing.text.html.parser

1.2 *DTDConstants*

▲	public static final . . . . int	**ANY** = 19
▲	public static final . . . . int	**CDATA** = 1
▲	public static final . . . . int	**CONREF** = 4
▲	public static final . . . . int	**CURRENT** = 3
▲	public static final . . . . int	**DEFAULT** = 131072
▲	public static final . . . . int	**EMPTY** = 17
▲	public static final . . . . int	**ENDTAG** = 14
▲	public static final . . . . int	**ENTITIES** = 3
▲	public static final . . . . int	**ENTITY** = 2
▲	public static final . . . . int	**FIXED** = 1
▲	public static final . . . . int	**GENERAL** = 65536
▲	public static final . . . . int	**ID** = 4
▲	public static final . . . . int	**IDREF** = 5
▲	public static final . . . . int	**IDREFS** = 6
▲	public static final . . . . int	**IMPLIED** = 5
▲	public static final . . . . int	**MD** = 16
▲	public static final . . . . int	**MODEL** = 18
▲	public static final . . . . int	**MS** = 15
▲	public static final . . . . int	**NAME** = 7
▲	public static final . . . . int	**NAMES** = 8
▲	public static final . . . . int	**NMTOKEN** = 9
▲	public static final . . . . int	**NMTOKENS** = 10
▲	public static final . . . . int	**NOTATION** = 11
▲	public static final . . . . int	**NUMBER** = 12
▲	public static final . . . . int	**NUMBERS** = 13
▲	public static final . . . . int	**NUTOKEN** = 14
▲	public static final . . . . int	**NUTOKENS** = 15
▲	public static final . . . . int	**PARAMETER** = 262144
▲	public static final . . . . int	**PI** = 12
▲	public static final . . . . int	**PUBLIC** = 10
▲	public static final . . . . int	**RCDATA** = 16
▲	public static final . . . . int	**REQUIRED** = 2
▲	public static final . . . . int	**SDATA** = 11
▲	public static final . . . . int	**STARTTAG** = 13
▲	public static final . . . . int	**SYSTEM** = 17

EditorKit

		javax.swing.text

Object [1]

1.2 ○ └EditorKit ----------------------------- *Cloneable* ˸, *java.io.Serializable* ˸

	1	public . . . . **Object clone** ()	
○		public abstract . . . . *Caret* **createCaret** ()	
○		public abstract . . . . . . *Document* **createDefaultDocument** ()	ε1017
		public . . . . void **deinstall** (javax.swing.JEditorPane c)	
∗		public . . . . **EditorKit** ()	
○		public abstract . . . . **getActions** ()	
		. . . . *javax.swing.Action[]*	
○		public abstract . . . . String **getContentType** ()	
○		public abstract . . . . *ViewFactory* **getViewFactory** ()	
		public . . . . void **install** (javax.swing.JEditorPane c)	
○		public abstract . . . . void **read** (java.io.InputStream in, *Document* doc, int pos)	
		throws java.io.IOException, BadLocationException	
○		public abstract . . . . void **read** (java.io.Reader in, *Document* doc, int pos) throws java.io.IOException,	
		BadLocationException	ε1017,1018
○		public abstract . . . . void **write** (java.io.OutputStream out, *Document* doc, int pos, int len)	
		throws java.io.IOException, BadLocationException	
○		public abstract . . . . void **write** (java.io.Writer out, *Document* doc, int pos, int len)	
		throws java.io.IOException, BadLocationException	

Class   *Interface*   —extends   - - -implements   ○ abstract   ● final   △ static   ▲ static final   ∗ constructor   x x—inherited   x **x**—declared   **x x**—overridden
ε*n*—examples of usage   ˸—has subclass   package—see other volume

		Element ❶	javax.swing.text

1.2   *Element*

```
public............... AttributeSet getAttributes ()                           ε1013
public................. Document getDocument ()
public................... Element getElement (int index)                      ε984,990,1013
public....................... int getElementCount ()                          ε984,990,1013
public....................... int getElementIndex (int offset)
public....................... int getEndOffset ()                             ε984,990,1013
public.................... String getName ()
public................... Element getParentElement ()
public....................... int getStartOffset ()                           ε984,990,1013
public................... boolean isLeaf ()                                   ε984
```

Element ❷		javax.swing.text.html.parser

Object[1]
1.2 ●   └Element - *DTDConstants*[2], *java.io.Serializable*⌄

```
   2   35 inherited members from DTDConstants not shown
       public............... AttributeList atts
       public............... ContentModel content
       public.................... Object data
       public......... java.util.BitSet exclusions
       public............... AttributeList getAttribute (String name)
       public............... AttributeList getAttributeByValue (String name)
       public............... AttributeList getAttributes ()
       public............... ContentModel getContent ()
       public....................... int getIndex ()
       public.................... String getName ()
       public....................... int getType ()
       public......... java.util.BitSet inclusions
       public....................... int index
       public................... boolean isEmpty ()
       public.................... String name
   △   public static ................. int name2type (String nm)
       public................... boolean oEnd
       public................... boolean omitEnd ()
       public................... boolean omitStart ()
       public................... boolean oStart
   1   public.................... String toString ()
       public....................... int type
```

ElementIterator		javax.swing.text

Object[1]
1.2   └ElementIterator - *Cloneable*⌄

```
   1   public synchronized ....Object clone ()
       public................... Element current ()
       public....................... int depth ()
   *   public....................... ElementIterator (Document document)
   *   public....................... ElementIterator (Element root)          ε984
       public................... Element first ()
       public................... Element next ()                             ε984
       public................... Element previous ()
```

Ellipse2D		java.awt.geom

                                                                          ε572

Object
1.2 ○   └RectangularShape[1] - - - - - - - - - - - - - - - - - - - *java.awt.Shape*[2], *Cloneable*⌄
1.2 ○   └Ellipse2D⌄

```
   1   25 inherited members from RectangularShape not shown
   2   public................... boolean contains (double x, double y)
   2   public................... boolean contains (double x, double y, double w, double h)
   *   protected ....................... Ellipse2D ()
 ○ 2   public abstract ...Rectangle2D getBounds2D ()
   2   public............... PathIterator getPathIterator (AffineTransform at)
   2   public................... boolean intersects (double x, double y, double w, double h)
```

		Ellipse2D.Double	java.awt.geom
		Object	ε572
1.2 ○		└RectangularShape[1] - *java.awt.Shape*[3], *Cloneable* ⌄	
1.2 ○		└Ellipse2D[2]	
1.2		└Ellipse2D.Double	

1	public.................Object	clone ()	
1	public.................boolean	contains (Point2D p)	
1	public.................boolean	contains (Rectangle2D r)	
2	public.................boolean	contains (double x, double y)	
2	public.................boolean	contains (double x, double y, double w, double h)	
✳	public............................	**Ellipse2D.Double** ()	
✳	public............................	**Ellipse2D.Double** (double x, double y, double w, double h)	
1	public......java.awt.Rectangle	getBounds ()	
3	public.............Rectangle2D	**getBounds2D** ()	
1	public.................double	getCenterX ()	
1	public.................double	getCenterY ()	
1	public.............Rectangle2D	getFrame ()	
1	public.............**double getHeight** ()		
1	public.................double	getMaxX ()	
1	public.................double	getMaxY ()	
1	public.................double	getMinX ()	
1	public.................double	getMinY ()	
2	public..............*PathIterator*	getPathIterator (AffineTransform at)	
1	public..............*PathIterator*	getPathIterator (AffineTransform at, double flatness)	
1	public.............**double getWidth** ()		ε826
1	public.............**double getX** ()		
1	public.............**double getY** ()		
	public.................double	**height**	
1	public.................boolean	intersects (Rectangle2D r)	
2	public.................boolean	intersects (double x, double y, double w, double h)	
1	public.............**boolean isEmpty** ()		
1	public.................void	setFrame (Rectangle2D r)	
1	public.................void	setFrame (Point2D loc, Dimension2D size)	
1	public.............**void setFrame** (double x, double y, double w, double h)		
1	public.................void	setFrameFromCenter (Point2D center, Point2D corner)	
1	public.................void	setFrameFromCenter (double centerX, double centerY, double cornerX, double cornerY)	
1	public.................void	setFrameFromDiagonal (Point2D p1, Point2D p2)	
1	public.................void	setFrameFromDiagonal (double x1, double y1, double x2, double y2)	
	public.................double	**width**	
	public.................double	**x**	
	public.................double	**y**	

		Ellipse2D.Float	java.awt.geom
		Object	ε572
1.2 ○		└RectangularShape[1] - *java.awt.Shape*[3], *Cloneable* ⌄	
1.2 ○		└Ellipse2D[2]	
1.2		└Ellipse2D.Float	

1	public.................Object	clone ()	
1	public.................boolean	contains (Point2D p)	
1	public.................boolean	contains (Rectangle2D r)	
2	public.................boolean	contains (double x, double y)	
2	public.................boolean	contains (double x, double y, double w, double h)	
✳	public............................	**Ellipse2D.Float** ()	
✳	public............................	**Ellipse2D.Float** (float x, float y, float w, float h)	ε656,578,669
1	public......java.awt.Rectangle	getBounds ()	
3	public.............Rectangle2D	**getBounds2D** ()	
1	public.................double	getCenterX ()	
1	public.................double	getCenterY ()	
1	public.............Rectangle2D	getFrame ()	
1	public.............**double getHeight** ()		
1	public.................double	getMaxX ()	
1	public.................double	getMaxY ()	
1	public.................double	getMinX ()	
1	public.................double	getMinY ()	

Class *Interface* —extends - - -implements ○ abstract ● final △ static ▲ static final ✳ constructor x x—inherited x **x**—declared **x x**—overridden
ε*n*—examples of usage ⌄—has subclass package—see other volume

2	public............	*PathIterator*	getPathIterator (AffineTransform at)
1	public............	*PathIterator*	getPathIterator (AffineTransform at, double flatness)
1	public...............	**double**	**getWidth** ()
1	public...............	**double**	**getX** ()
1	public...............	**double**	**getY** ()
	public...............	float	**height**
1	public...............	boolean	intersects (Rectangle2D r)
2	public...............	boolean	intersects (double x, double y, double w, double h)
1	public...............	**boolean**	**isEmpty** ()
1	public...............	void	setFrame (Rectangle2D r)
1	public...............	void	setFrame (Point2D loc, Dimension2D size)
1	public...............	**void**	**setFrame** (double x, double y, double w, double h)
	public...............	void	**setFrame** (float x, float y, float w, float h)
1	public...............	void	setFrameFromCenter (Point2D center, Point2D corner)
1	public...............	void	setFrameFromCenter (double centerX, double centerY, double cornerX, double cornerY)
1	public...............	void	setFrameFromDiagonal (Point2D p1, Point2D p2)
1	public...............	void	setFrameFromDiagonal (double x1, double y1, double x2, double y2)
	public...............	float	**width**
	public...............	float	**x**
	public...............	float	**y**

ε826

E

EmptyBorder
javax.swing.border

ε873

Object
 └AbstractBorder[1] ----------------------- *Border*, *java.io.Serializable*
  └EmptyBorder

	protected...............	int	**bottom**
*	public...............		**EmptyBorder** (java.awt.Insets borderInsets)
*	public...............		**EmptyBorder** (int top, int left, int bottom, int right)
1.3	public..........	java.awt.Insets	**getBorderInsets** ()
1	public..........	**java.awt.Insets**	**getBorderInsets** (java.awt.Component c)
1	public..........	**java.awt.Insets**	**getBorderInsets** (java.awt.Component c, java.awt.Insets insets)
1	public......	java.awt.Rectangle	getInteriorRectangle (java.awt.Component c, int x, int y, int width, int height)
△ 1	public static	java.awt.Rectangle	getInteriorRectangle (java.awt.Component c, *Border* b, int x, int y, int width, int height)
1	public...............	**boolean**	**isBorderOpaque** ()
	protected...............	int	**left**
1	public...............	**void**	**paintBorder** (java.awt.Component c, java.awt.Graphics g, int x, int y, int width, int height)
	protected...............	int	**right**
	protected...............	int	**top**

Entity ➊
javax.swing.text.html.parser

Object
 └Entity -------------------------------- *DTDConstants*[1]

1.2 ●

1	*35 inherited members from DTDConstants not shown*		
	public...............	char[]	**data**
*	public...............		**Entity** (String name, int type, char[] data)
	public...............	char[]	**getData** ()
	public...............	String	**getName** ()
	public...............	String	**getString** ()
	public...............	int	**getType** ()
	public...............	boolean	**isGeneral** ()
	public...............	boolean	**isParameter** ()
	public...............	String	**name**
△	public static...............	int	**name2type** (String nm)
	public...............	int	**type**

EnumControl
javax.sound.sampled

Object
 └Control[1]
  └EnumControl

1.3 ○
1.3 ○

*	protected...............		**EnumControl** (EnumControl.Type type, Object[] values, Object value)
1	public............	Control.Type	**getType** ()

EnumControl

	public	Object	**getValue** ()
	public	Object[]	**getValues** ()
	public	void	**setValue** (Object value)
1	public	**String**	**toString** ()

EnumControl.Type

Object
1.3 └ Control.Type [1]
1.3   └ EnumControl.Type

●	1	public final	boolean	equals (Object obj)
●	1	public final	int	hashCode ()
▲		public static final		**REVERB**
			EnumControl.Type	
●	1	public final	String	toString ()
✳		protected		**EnumControl.Type** (String name)

EnumSyntax

Object [1]
1.4 ○ └ EnumSyntax - *java.io.Serializable*, *Cloneable*

✳	1	public	**Object**	**clone** ()
		protected		**EnumSyntax** (int value)
		protected	EnumSyntax[]	**getEnumValueTable** ()
		protected	int	**getOffset** ()
		protected	String[]	**getStringTable** ()
		public	int	**getValue** ()
	1	public	**int**	**hashCode** ()
		protected	Object	**readResolve** () throws java.io.ObjectStreamException
	1	public	**String**	**toString** ()

EtchedBorder

Object   ε873
1.2 ○ └ AbstractBorder [1] - *Border*, *java.io.Serializable*
1.2   └ EtchedBorder

✳		public		**EtchedBorder** ()
✳		public		**EtchedBorder** (int etchType)
✳		public		**EtchedBorder** (java.awt.Color highlight, java.awt.Color shadow)
✳		public		**EtchedBorder** (int etchType, java.awt.Color highlight, java.awt.Color shadow)
		protected	int	**etchType**
	1	public	**java.awt.Insets**	**getBorderInsets** (java.awt.Component c)
	1	public	**java.awt.Insets**	**getBorderInsets** (java.awt.Component c, java.awt.Insets insets)
		public	int	**getEtchType** ()
1.3		public	java.awt.Color	**getHighlightColor** ()
		public	java.awt.Color	**getHighlightColor** (java.awt.Component c)
	1	public	java.awt.Rectangle	getInteriorRectangle (java.awt.Component c, int x, int y, int width, int height)
△	1	public static		getInteriorRectangle (java.awt.Component c, *Border* b, int x, int y, int width, int height)
			java.awt.Rectangle	
1.3		public	java.awt.Color	**getShadowColor** ()
		public	java.awt.Color	**getShadowColor** (java.awt.Component c)
		protected	java.awt.Color	**highlight**
	1	public	**boolean**	**isBorderOpaque** ()
▲		public static final	int	**LOWERED** = 1
	1	public	**void**	**paintBorder** (java.awt.Component c, java.awt.Graphics g, int x, int y, int width, int height)
▲		public static final	int	**RAISED** = 0
		protected	java.awt.Color	**shadow**

Class   *Interface*   —extends   - - -implements   ○ abstract   ● final   △ static   ▲ static final   ✳ constructor   x x—inherited   x **x**—declared   **x x**—overridden
ε*n*—examples of usage   —has subclass   package—see other volume

```
         Object¹
         └─Event - - - - - - - - - - - - - - - - - - - - - - - - - - - - - - - - - java.io.Serializable
```

▲	public static final	int	**ACTION_EVENT** = 1001
▲	public static final	int	**ALT_MASK** = 8
	public	Object	**arg**
1.1 ▲	public static final	int	**BACK_SPACE** = 8
1.1 ▲	public static final	int	**CAPS_LOCK** = 1022
	public	int	**clickCount**
	public	boolean	**controlDown** ()
▲	public static final	int	**CTRL_MASK** = 2
1.1 ▲	public static final	int	**DELETE** = 127
▲	public static final	int	**DOWN** = 1005
▲	public static final	int	**END** = 1001
1.1 ▲	public static final	int	**ENTER** = 10
1.1 ▲	public static final	int	**ESCAPE** = 27
*	public		**Event** (Object target, int id, Object arg)
* *	public		**Event** (Object target, long when, int id, int x, int y, int key, int modifiers)
* *	public		**Event** (Object target, long when, int id, int x, int y, int key, int modifiers, Object arg)
	public	Event	**evt**
▲	public static final	int	**F1** = 1008
▲	public static final	int	**F10** = 1017
▲	public static final	int	**F11** = 1018
▲	public static final	int	**F12** = 1019
▲	public static final	int	**F2** = 1009
▲	public static final	int	**F3** = 1010
▲	public static final	int	**F4** = 1011
▲	public static final	int	**F5** = 1012
▲	public static final	int	**F6** = 1013
▲	public static final	int	**F7** = 1014
▲	public static final	int	**F8** = 1015
▲	public static final	int	**F9** = 1016
▲	public static final	int	**GOT_FOCUS** = 1004
▲	public static final	int	**HOME** = 1000
	public	int	**id**
1.1 ▲	public static final	int	**INSERT** = 1025
	public	int	**key**
▲	public static final	int	**KEY_ACTION** = 403
▲	public static final	int	**KEY_ACTION_RELEASE** = 404
▲	public static final	int	**KEY_PRESS** = 401
▲	public static final	int	**KEY_RELEASE** = 402
▲	public static final	int	**LEFT** = 1006
▲	public static final	int	**LIST_DESELECT** = 702
▲	public static final	int	**LIST_SELECT** = 701
▲	public static final	int	**LOAD_FILE** = 1002
▲	public static final	int	**LOST_FOCUS** = 1005
▲	public static final	int	**META_MASK** = 4
	public	boolean	**metaDown** ()
	public	int	**modifiers**
▲	public static final	int	**MOUSE_DOWN** = 501
▲	public static final	int	**MOUSE_DRAG** = 506
▲	public static final	int	**MOUSE_ENTER** = 504
▲	public static final	int	**MOUSE_EXIT** = 505
▲	public static final	int	**MOUSE_MOVE** = 503
▲	public static final	int	**MOUSE_UP** = 502
1.1 ▲	public static final	int	**NUM_LOCK** = 1023
	protected	String	**paramString** ()
1.1 ▲	public static final	int	**PAUSE** = 1024
▲	public static final	int	**PGDN** = 1003
▲	public static final	int	**PGUP** = 1002
1.1 ▲	public static final	int	**PRINT_SCREEN** = 1020
▲	public static final	int	**RIGHT** = 1007
▲	public static final	int	**SAVE_FILE** = 1003
▲	public static final	int	**SCROLL_ABSOLUTE** = 605
1.1 ▲	public static final	int	**SCROLL_BEGIN** = 606
1.1 ▲	public static final	int	**SCROLL_END** = 607
▲	public static final	int	**SCROLL_LINE_DOWN** = 602
▲	public static final	int	**SCROLL_LINE_UP** = 601
1.1 ▲	public static final	int	**SCROLL_LOCK** = 1021
▲	public static final	int	**SCROLL_PAGE_DOWN** = 604
▲	public static final	int	**SCROLL_PAGE_UP** = 603
▲	public static final	int	**SHIFT_MASK** = 1

E

Classes

Event

	public .... boolean	**shiftDown** ()
1.1 ▲	public static final .... int	**TAB** = 9
	public .... Object	**target**
1	public .... **String**	**toString** ()
	public .... void	**translate** (int x, int y)
▲	public static final .... int	**UP** = 1004
	public .... long	**when**
▲	public static final .... int	**WINDOW_DEICONIFY** = 204
▲	public static final .... int	**WINDOW_DESTROY** = 201
▲	public static final .... int	**WINDOW_EXPOSE** = 202
▲	public static final .... int	**WINDOW_ICONIFY** = 203
▲	public static final .... int	**WINDOW_MOVED** = 205
	public .... int	**x**
	public .... int	**y**

EventListenerList · javax.swing.event

Object [1]
 └EventListenerList - *java.io.Serializable*
1.2

✳	public synchronized .... void	**add** (Class t, *java.util.EventListener* l)	ε333,650
	public	**EventListenerList** ()	ε333,650
	public .... int	**getListenerCount** ()	
	public .... int	**getListenerCount** (Class t)	
	public .... Object[]	**getListenerList** ()	ε333,650
1.3	public . *java.util.EventListener[]*	**getListeners** (Class t)	
	protected transient.... Object[]	**listenerList**	
	public synchronized .... void	**remove** (Class t, *java.util.EventListener* l)	ε333,650
1	public .... **String**	**toString** ()	

EventQueue · java.awt

Object
 └EventQueue
1.1

1.2	protected .... void	**dispatchEvent** (AWTEvent event)
✳	public	**EventQueue** ()
1.4 △	public static .... AWTEvent	**getCurrentEvent** ()
1.4 △	public static .... long	**getMostRecentEventTime** ()
	public .... AWTEvent	**getNextEvent** () throws InterruptedException
1.2 △	public static .... void	**invokeAndWait** (*Runnable* runnable) throws InterruptedException, *java.lang.reflect.InvocationTargetException*
1.2 △	public static .... void	**invokeLater** (*Runnable* runnable)
1.2 △	public static .... boolean	**isDispatchThread** ()
	public synchronized AWTEvent	**peekEvent** ()
	public synchronized AWTEvent	**peekEvent** (int id)
1.2	protected .... void	**pop** () throws *java.util.EmptyStackException*
	public .... void	**postEvent** (AWTEvent theEvent)
1.2	public synchronized .... void	**push** (EventQueue newEventQueue)

ExpandVetoException · javax.swing.tree

Object
 └Throwable - *java.io.Serializable*
  └Exception
   └ExpandVetoException
1.2

	protected .... javax.swing .event.TreeExpansionEvent	**event**
✳	public	**ExpandVetoException** (javax.swing.event.TreeExpansionEvent event)
		ε1032
✳	public	**ExpandVetoException** (javax.swing.event.TreeExpansionEvent event, String message)

Class *Interface* —extends - - -implements ○ abstract ● final △ static ▲ static final ✳ constructor x x—inherited x **x**—declared **x x**—overridden
ε*n*—examples of usage ˻—has subclass package —see other volume

Fidelity | javax.print.attribute.standard

```
        Object
1.4 ○   └─javax.print.attribute.EnumSyntax 1 - - - - - - - - -  java.io.Serializable , Cloneable
1.4 ●       └─Fidelity - - - - - - - - - - - - - - - - - - - - - -  javax.print.attribute.PrintJobAttribute (javax.print.attribute.Attribute 2
                                                                    (java.io.Serializable)), javax.print.attribute.PrintRequestAttribute
                                                                    (javax.print.attribute.Attribute 2 (java.io.Serializable))
```

	1	public	Object	clone ()	
*		protected		**Fidelity** (int value)	
▲		public static final	Fidelity	**FIDELITY_FALSE**	
▲		public static final	Fidelity	**FIDELITY_TRUE**	
●	2	public final	Class	**getCategory** ()	ε707
	1	protected	**javax.print** 2 **.attribute.EnumSyntax[]**	**getEnumValueTable** ()	
●	2	public final	String	**getName** ()	ε706,707,708
	1	protected	int	getOffset ()	
	1	protected	**String[]**	**getStringTable** ()	
	1	public	int	getValue ()	
	1	public	int	hashCode ()	
	1	protected	Object	readResolve () throws java.io.ObjectStreamException	
	1	public	String	toString ()	

FieldView | javax.swing.text

```
        Object
1.2 ○   └─View 1 - - - - - - - - - - - - - - - - - - - - - - - - - - -  javax.swing.SwingConstants 3
1.2       └─PlainView 2 - - - - - - - - - - - - - - - - - - - - - -  TabExpander
1.2           └─FieldView
```

	1	*43 inherited members from View not shown*		
	3	*19 inherited members from javax.swing.SwingConstants not shown*		
		protected	java.awt.Shape	**adjustAllocation** (java.awt.Shape a)
	2	public	void	changedUpdate (javax.swing.event.DocumentEvent changes, java.awt.Shape a, ViewFactory f)
1.4	2	protected	void	damageLineRange (int line0, int line1, java.awt.Shape a, java.awt.Component host)
	2	protected	void	drawLine (int lineIndex, java.awt.Graphics g, int x, int y)
	2	protected	int	drawSelectedText (java.awt.Graphics g, int x, int y, int p0, int p1) throws BadLocationException
	2	protected	int	drawUnselectedText (java.awt.Graphics g, int x, int y, int p0, int p1) throws BadLocationException
*		public		**FieldView** (*Element* elem)
		protected	java.awt.FontMetrics	**getFontMetrics** ()
●	2	protected final	Segment	getLineBuffer ()
	2	public	**float**	**getPreferredSpan** (int axis)
	1	public	**int**	**getResizeWeight** (int axis)
	2	protected	int	getTabSize ()
	2	public	**void**	**insertUpdate** (javax.swing.event.DocumentEvent changes, java.awt.Shape a, ViewFactory f)
1.4	2	protected	java.awt.Rectangle	lineToRect (java.awt.Shape a, int line)
	2	protected	java.awt.FontMetrics	metrics
	2	public	**java.awt.Shape**	**modelToView** (int pos, java.awt.Shape a, Position.Bias b) throws BadLocationException
	2	public	float	nextTabStop (float x, int tabOffset)
	2	public	**void**	**paint** (java.awt.Graphics g, java.awt.Shape a)
	2	public	**void**	**removeUpdate** (javax.swing.event.DocumentEvent changes, java.awt.Shape a, ViewFactory f)
	2	public	void	setSize (float width, float height)
1.4	2	protected	void	updateDamage (javax.swing.event.DocumentEvent changes, java.awt.Shape a, ViewFactory f)
1.4	2	protected	void	updateMetrics ()
	2	public	**int**	**viewToModel** (float fx, float fy, java.awt.Shape a, Position.Bias[] bias)

FileCacheImageInputStream | javax.imageio.stream

```
        Object
1.4 ○   └─ImageInputStreamImpl 1 - - - - - - - - - - - - - - -  ImageInputStream  (java.io.DataInput)
1.4       └─FileCacheImageInputStream
```

FileCacheImageInputStream

F

FileCacheImageOutputStream
javax.imageio.stream

Object
1.4 O └ImageInputStreamImpl[1] - - - - - - - - - - - - - - - - *ImageInputStream* (*java.io.DataInput*)
1.4 O   └ImageOutputStreamImpl[2] - - - - - - - - - - - - - *ImageOutputStream* (*ImageInputStream* (*java.io.DataInput*), *java.io.DataOutput*)
1.4   └FileCacheImageOutputStream

FileChooserUI
javax.swing.plaf

Object
1.2 O └ComponentUI[1]
1.2 O   └FileChooserUI

Class *Interface* —extends - - -implements ○ abstract ● final △ static ▲ static final * constructor x x—inherited **x x**—declared **x x**—overridden
ε*n*—examples of usage ‿—has subclass package—see other volume

o	public abstract . . . . String	**getDialogTitle** (javax.swing.JFileChooser fc)
o	public abstract . . . . javax₂	**getFileView** (javax.swing.JFileChooser fc)
	.swing.filechooser.FileView	
o	public abstract . . . . void	**rescanCurrentDirectory** (javax.swing.JFileChooser fc)

FileDialog | java.awt

ε606,618,733,953,988

Object
└Component[1] - *java.awt.image.ImageObserver* [5], *MenuContainer*,
                                             java.io.Serializable
  └Container[2]
    └Window[3] - *javax.accessibility.Accessible*
      └Dialog[4]
        └FileDialog

	1	*166 inherited members from Component not shown*		
	2	*58 inherited members from Container not shown*		
	3	*47 inherited members from Window not shown*		
	5	*8 inherited members from java.awt.image.ImageObserver not shown*		
	4	public . . . . **void**	**addNotify** ()	
	4	public . . . . void	dispose ()	ε565
1.1 ✻		public	**FileDialog** (Frame parent)	
✻		public	**FileDialog** (Frame parent, String title)	
✻		public	**FileDialog** (Frame parent, String title, int mode)	
1.3	4	public . . . . . . javax.accessibility₂	getAccessibleContext ()	
		.AccessibleContext		
		public . . . . String	**getDirectory** ()	
		public . . . . String	**getFile** ()	
		public . . . *java.io.FilenameFilter*	**getFilenameFilter** ()	
		public . . . . int	**getMode** ()	
	4	public . . . . String	getTitle ()	
	4	public . . . . void	hide ()	
	4	public . . . . boolean	isModal ()	
	4	public . . . . boolean	isResizable ()	
1.4	4	public . . . . boolean	isUndecorated ()	
▲		public static final . . . . int	**LOAD** = 0	
	4	protected . . . . **String**	**paramString** ()	
▲		public static final . . . . int	**SAVE** = 1	
		public . . . . void	**setDirectory** (String dir)	
		public . . . . void	**setFile** (String file)	
		public synchronized . . . . void	**setFilenameFilter** (*java.io.FilenameFilter* filter)	
1.1	4	public . . . . void	setModal (boolean b)	
1.1	4	public . . . . void	**setMode** (int mode)	
	4	public . . . . void	setResizable (boolean resizable)	
	4	public . . . . void	setTitle (String title)	
1.4	4	public . . . . void	setUndecorated (boolean undecorated)	
	4	public . . . . void	show ()	ε905,618

FileDialogPeer | java.awt.peer

FileDialogPeer ——————————————— *DialogPeer* [1] (*WindowPeer* [2] (*ContainerPeer* [3] (*ComponentPeer* [4])))

4	*42 inherited members from ComponentPeer not shown*	
1	*2 inherited members from DialogPeer not shown*	
3	*7 inherited members from ContainerPeer not shown*	
2	*2 inherited members from WindowPeer not shown*	
	public . . . . void	**setDirectory** (String dir)
	public . . . . void	**setFile** (String file)
	public . . . . void	**setFilenameFilter** (*java.io.FilenameFilter* filter)

FileFilter❷ | javax.swing.filechooser

Object
1.2 └FileFilter

o	public abstract . . . . boolean	**accept** (java.io.File f)	ε889
✻	public	**FileFilter** ()	
o	public abstract . . . . String	**getDescription** ()	ε889

FileImageInputStream

			javax.imageio.stream

Object
1.4 ○ └ImageInputStreamImpl [1] - - - - - - - - - - - - - - - - - - *ImageInputStream* (*java.io.DataInput*)
1.4   └FileImageInputStream

---

[1] *46 inherited members from ImageInputStreamImpl not shown*
[1] public..................... **void close** () throws java.io.IOException   ε698,699
*   public.......................... **FileImageInputStream** (java.io.File f) throws java.io.FileNotFoundException,
                                       java.io.IOException
*   public.......................... **FileImageInputStream** (java.io.RandomAccessFile raf)
[1] public.................... **long length** ()
[1] public.................... **int read** () throws java.io.IOException
[1] public.................... **int read** (byte[] b, int off, int len) throws java.io.IOException
[1] public.................... **void seek** (long pos) throws java.io.IOException

---

FileImageOutputStream

			javax.imageio.stream

Object
1.4 ○ └ImageInputStreamImpl [1] - - - - - - - - - - - - - - - - - - *ImageInputStream* (*java.io.DataInput*)
1.4 ○   └ImageOutputStreamImpl [2] - - - - - - - - - - - - - - *ImageOutputStream* (*ImageInputStream* (*java.io.DataInput*),
                                                  java.io.DataOutput)
1.4   └FileImageOutputStream

---

[1] *46 inherited members from ImageInputStreamImpl not shown*
[1] public..................... **void close** () throws java.io.IOException   ε698,699
*   public.......................... **FileImageOutputStream** (java.io.File f) throws java.io.FileNotFoundException,
                                       java.io.IOException
*   public.......................... **FileImageOutputStream** (java.io.RandomAccessFile raf)
● [2] protected final................void flushBits () throws java.io.IOException
[1] public.................... **long length** ()
[1] public.................... **int read** () throws java.io.IOException
[1] public.................... **int read** (byte[] b, int off, int len) throws java.io.IOException
[1] public.................... **void seek** (long pos) throws java.io.IOException
[2] public....................void write (byte[] b) throws java.io.IOException
[2] public.................... **void write** (int b) throws java.io.IOException
[2] public.................... **void write** (byte[] b, int off, int len) throws java.io.IOException
[2] public....................void writeBit (int bit) throws java.io.IOException
[2] public....................void writeBits (long bits, int numBits) throws java.io.IOException
[2] public....................void writeBoolean (boolean v) throws java.io.IOException
[2] public....................void writeByte (int v) throws java.io.IOException
[2] public....................void writeBytes (String s) throws java.io.IOException
[2] public....................void writeChar (int v) throws java.io.IOException
[2] public....................void writeChars (String s) throws java.io.IOException
[2] public....................void writeChars (char[] c, int off, int len) throws java.io.IOException
[2] public....................void writeDouble (double v) throws java.io.IOException
[2] public....................void writeDoubles (double[] d, int off, int len) throws java.io.IOException
[2] public....................void writeFloat (float v) throws java.io.IOException
[2] public....................void writeFloats (float[] f, int off, int len) throws java.io.IOException
[2] public....................void writeInt (int v) throws java.io.IOException
[2] public....................void writeInts (int[] i, int off, int len) throws java.io.IOException
[2] public....................void writeLong (long v) throws java.io.IOException
[2] public....................void writeLongs (long[] l, int off, int len) throws java.io.IOException
[2] public....................void writeShort (int v) throws java.io.IOException
[2] public....................void writeShorts (short[] s, int off, int len) throws java.io.IOException
[2] public....................void writeUTF (String s) throws java.io.IOException

---

FileSystemView

			javax.swing.filechooser

Object
1.2 ○ └FileSystemView

---

   public............... java.io.File **createFileObject** (String path)
   public............... java.io.File **createFileObject** (java.io.File dir, String filename)
1.4 protected .... java.io.File **createFileSystemRoot** (java.io.File f)
○   public abstract ..... java.io.File **createNewFolder** (java.io.File containingDir) throws java.io.IOException

---

Class   *Interface*   —extends   - - -implements   ○ abstract   ● final   △ static   ▲ static final   * constructor   x x—inherited   x **x**—declared   **x x**—overridden
ε*n*—examples of usage   ‿—has subclass   package—see other volume

✱	public		**FileSystemView** ()	
1.4	public	java.io.File	**getChild** (java.io.File parent, String fileName)	
1.4	public	java.io.File	**getDefaultDirectory** ()	
	public	java.io.File[]	**getFiles** (java.io.File dir, boolean useFileHiding)	
△	public static ...	FileSystemView	**getFileSystemView** ()	
	public	java.io.File	**getHomeDirectory** ()	
	public	java.io.File	**getParentDirectory** (java.io.File dir)	
	public	java.io.File[]	**getRoots** ()	
1.4	public	String	**getSystemDisplayName** (java.io.File f)	
1.4	public	*javax.swing.Icon*	**getSystemIcon** (java.io.File f)	
1.4	public	String	**getSystemTypeDescription** (java.io.File f)	
1.4	public	boolean	**isComputerNode** (java.io.File dir)	
1.4	public	boolean	**isDrive** (java.io.File dir)	
1.4	public	boolean	**isFileSystem** (java.io.File f)	
1.4	public	boolean	**isFileSystemRoot** (java.io.File dir)	
1.4	public	boolean	**isFloppyDrive** (java.io.File dir)	
	public	boolean	**isHiddenFile** (java.io.File f)	ε897
1.4	public	boolean	**isParent** (java.io.File folder, java.io.File file)	
	public	boolean	**isRoot** (java.io.File f)	
1.4	public	Boolean	**isTraversable** (java.io.File f)	

F

FileView

javax.swing.filechooser

	Object
1.2 ○	└ FileView␣

✱	public		**FileView** ()
	public	String	**getDescription** (java.io.File f)
	public	*javax.swing.Icon*	**getIcon** (java.io.File f)
	public	String	**getName** (java.io.File f)
	public	String	**getTypeDescription** (java.io.File f)
	public	Boolean	**isTraversable** (java.io.File f)

FilteredImageSource

java.awt.image

	Object
	└ FilteredImageSource - - - - - - - - - - - - - - - - - - - *ImageProducer* [1]

	[1]	public synchronized .... void	**addConsumer** (*ImageConsumer* ic)	
✱		public	**FilteredImageSource** (*ImageProducer* orig, ImageFilter imgf)	ε664,665
	[1]	public synchronized .. boolean	**isConsumer** (*ImageConsumer* ic)	
	[1]	public synchronized .... void	**removeConsumer** (*ImageConsumer* ic)	
	[1]	public .... void	**requestTopDownLeftRightResend** (*ImageConsumer* ic)	
	[1]	public .... void	**startProduction** (*ImageConsumer* ic)	

Finishings

javax.print.attribute.standard

	Object
1.4 ○	└ javax.print.attribute.EnumSyntax[1] - - - - - - - - - *java.io.Serializable*␣, *Cloneable*␣
1.4	└ Finishings - *javax.print.attribute.DocAttribute* (*javax.print.attribute.Attribute* [2]
	(*java.io.Serializable*)), *javax.print.attribute.PrintRequestAttribute*
	(*javax.print.attribute.Attribute* [2] (*java.io.Serializable*)),
	javax.print.attribute.PrintJobAttribute
	(*javax.print.attribute.Attribute* [2] (*java.io.Serializable*))

▲		public static final .... Finishings	**BIND**	
	[1]	public .... Object	clone ()	
▲		public static final .... Finishings	**COVER**	
▲		public static final .... Finishings	**EDGE_STITCH**	
▲		public static final .... Finishings	**EDGE_STITCH_BOTTOM**	
▲		public static final .... Finishings	**EDGE_STITCH_LEFT**	
▲		public static final .... Finishings	**EDGE_STITCH_RIGHT**	
▲		public static final .... Finishings	**EDGE_STITCH_TOP**	
✱		protected	**Finishings** (int value)	
●	[2]	public final .... Class	**getCategory** ()	ε707
	[1]	protected .... **javax.print** [2] **.attribute.EnumSyntax[]**	**getEnumValueTable** ()	
●	[2]	public final .... String	**getName** ()	ε706,707,708
	[1]	protected .... **int**	**getOffset** ()	

Classes

Finishings

1	protected	String[]	**getStringTable** ()
1	public	int	getValue ()
1	public	int	hashCode ()
▲	public static final	Finishings	**NONE**
1	protected	Object	readResolve () throws java.io.ObjectStreamException
▲	public static final	Finishings	**SADDLE_STITCH**
▲	public static final	Finishings	**STAPLE**
▲	public static final	Finishings	**STAPLE_BOTTOM_LEFT**
▲	public static final	Finishings	**STAPLE_BOTTOM_RIGHT**
▲	public static final	Finishings	**STAPLE_DUAL_BOTTOM**
▲	public static final	Finishings	**STAPLE_DUAL_LEFT**
▲	public static final	Finishings	**STAPLE_DUAL_RIGHT**
▲	public static final	Finishings	**STAPLE_DUAL_TOP**
▲	public static final	Finishings	**STAPLE_TOP_LEFT**
▲	public static final	Finishings	**STAPLE_TOP_RIGHT**
1	public	String	toString ()

FixedHeightLayoutCache javax.swing.tree

```
      Object
1.2 ○  └AbstractLayoutCache 1 ------------------ RowMapper
1.2       └FixedHeightLayoutCache
```

✳	public		**FixedHeightLayoutCache** ()
1	public	java.awt.Rectangle	**getBounds** (TreePath path, java.awt.Rectangle placeIn)
1	public	boolean	**getExpandedState** (TreePath path)
1	public	TreeModel	getModel ()
1	public	AbstractLayoutCache₂.NodeDimensions	getNodeDimensions ()
1	protected	java.awt.Rectangle	getNodeDimensions (Object value, int row, int depth, boolean expanded, java.awt.Rectangle placeIn)
1	public	TreePath	**getPathClosestTo** (int x, int y)
1	public	TreePath	**getPathForRow** (int row)
1	public	int	getPreferredHeight ()
1	public	int	getPreferredWidth (java.awt.Rectangle bounds)
1	public	int	**getRowCount** ()
1	public	int	**getRowForPath** (TreePath path)
1	public	int	getRowHeight ()
1	public	int[]	getRowsForPaths (TreePath[] paths)
1	public	TreeSelectionModel	getSelectionModel ()
1	public	int	**getVisibleChildCount** (TreePath path)
1	public	java.util.Enumeration	**getVisiblePathsFrom** (TreePath path)
1	public	void	**invalidatePathBounds** (TreePath path)
1	public	void	**invalidateSizes** ()
1	public	boolean	**isExpanded** (TreePath path)
1	protected	boolean	isFixedRowHeight ()
1	public	boolean	isRootVisible ()
1	protected	AbstractLayoutCache₂.NodeDimensions	nodeDimensions
1	protected	boolean	rootVisible
1	protected	int	rowHeight
1	public	void	**setExpandedState** (TreePath path, boolean isExpanded)
1	public	void	**setModel** (TreeModel newModel)
1	public	void	setNodeDimensions (AbstractLayoutCache.NodeDimensions nd)
1	public	void	**setRootVisible** (boolean rootVisible)
1	public	void	**setRowHeight** (int rowHeight)
1	public	void	setSelectionModel (TreeSelectionModel newLSM)
1	protected	TreeModel	treeModel
1	public	void	**treeNodesChanged** (javax.swing.event.TreeModelEvent e)
1	public	void	**treeNodesInserted** (javax.swing.event.TreeModelEvent e)
1	public	void	**treeNodesRemoved** (javax.swing.event.TreeModelEvent e)
1	protected	TreeSelectionModel	treeSelectionModel
1	public	void	**treeStructureChanged** (javax.swing.event.TreeModelEvent e)

Class *Interface* —extends - - -implements ○ abstract ● final △ static ▲ static final ✳ constructor x x—inherited x **x**—declared **x x**—overridden
εn—examples of usage ⌄—has subclass package—see other volume

FlatteningPathIterator | java.awt.geom

```
        Object
1.2     └─FlatteningPathIterator - - - - - - - - - - - - - - - - - - - - PathIterator 1
```

1	*7 inherited members from PathIterator not shown*		
1	public.........................int	**currentSegment** (double[] coords)
1	public.........................int	**currentSegment** (float[] coords)
*	public..........................	**FlatteningPathIterator** (*PathIterator* src, double flatness)
*	public..........................	**FlatteningPathIterator** (*PathIterator* src, double flatness, int limit)
	public.................double	**getFlatness** ()
	public.........................int	**getRecursionLimit** ()
1	public.........................int	**getWindingRule** ()
1	public.................boolean	**isDone** ()
1	public.....................void	**next** ()

FlavorException | javax.print

```
1.4     FlavorException
```
```
        public.............. DocFlavor[] getUnsupportedFlavors ()
```

FlavorMap | java.awt.datatransfer

```
1.2     FlavorMap
```
```
        public............. java.util.Map getFlavorsForNatives (String[] natives)
        public............. java.util.Map getNativesForFlavors (DataFlavor[] flavors)
```

FlavorTable | java.awt.datatransfer

```
1.4     FlavorTable───────────────────FlavorMap 1
```
```
        public............. java.util.List getFlavorsForNative (String nat)
      1 public............. java.util.Map getFlavorsForNatives (String[] natives)
        public............. java.util.List getNativesForFlavor (DataFlavor flav)
      1 public............. java.util.Map getNativesForFlavors (DataFlavor[] flavors)
```

FloatControl | javax.sound.sampled

```
        Object
1.3 ○   └─Control 1
1.3 ○     └─FloatControl
```

*	protected	**FloatControl** (FloatControl.Type type, float minimum, float maximum, float precision, int updatePeriod, float initialValue, String units)
*	protected	**FloatControl** (FloatControl.Type type, float minimum, float maximum, float precision, int updatePeriod, float initialValue, String units, String minLabel, String midLabel, String maxLabel)
	public.....................float	**getMaximum** ()
	public...................String	**getMaxLabel** ()
	public...................String	**getMidLabel** ()
	public.....................float	**getMinimum** ()
	public...................String	**getMinLabel** ()
	public.....................float	**getPrecision** ()
1	public............. Control.Type	getType ()
	public...................String	**getUnits** ()
	public.........................int	**getUpdatePeriod** ()
	public.....................float	**getValue** ()
	public.....................void	**setValue** (float newValue) ε730
	public.....................void	**shift** (float from, float to, int microseconds)
1	public................... **String**	**toString** ()

FloatControl.Type | javax.sound.sampled

```
        Object
1.3     └─Control.Type 1
1.3       └─FloatControl.Type
```

FloatControl.Type

▲		public static final	FloatControl.Type	**AUX_RETURN**
▲		public static final	FloatControl.Type	**AUX_SEND**
▲		public static final	FloatControl.Type	**BALANCE**
●	1	public final	boolean	equals (Object obj)
●	1	public final	int	hashCode ()
▲		public static final	FloatControl.Type	**MASTER_GAIN**
▲		public static final	FloatControl.Type	**PAN**
▲		public static final	FloatControl.Type	**REVERB_RETURN**
▲		public static final	FloatControl.Type	**REVERB_SEND**
▲		public static final	FloatControl.Type	**SAMPLE_RATE**
●	1	public final	String	toString ()
✳		protected		**FloatControl.Type** (String name)
▲		public static final	FloatControl.Type	**VOLUME**

ε730 (against MASTER_GAIN row)

F

FlowLayout   java.awt

Object[1]
└FlowLayout - *LayoutManager*[2], *java.io.Serializable*

	2	public	void	**addLayoutComponent** (String name, Component comp)	
▲		public static final	int	**CENTER** = 1	ε852
✳		public		**FlowLayout** ()	ε613
✳		public		**FlowLayout** (int align)	ε571,852
✳		public		**FlowLayout** (int align, int hgap, int vgap)	
1.1		public	int	**getAlignment** ()	
1.1		public	int	**getHgap** ()	
1.1		public	int	**getVgap** ()	
1.2 ▲	2	public	void	**layoutContainer** (Container target)	ε624,625
1.2 ▲		public static final	int	**LEADING** = 3	
▲		public static final	int	**LEFT** = 0	
	2	public	Dimension	**minimumLayoutSize** (Container target)	
	2	public	Dimension	**preferredLayoutSize** (Container target)	
	2	public	void	**removeLayoutComponent** (Component comp)	
▲		public static final	int	**RIGHT** = 2	ε571
1.1		public	void	**setAlignment** (int align)	
1.1		public	void	**setHgap** (int hgap)	
1.1		public	void	**setVgap** (int vgap)	
	1	public	**String**	**toString** ()	
1.2 ▲		public static final	int	**TRAILING** = 4	

FlowView   javax.swing.text

Object
1.2 ○ └View[1] - *javax.swing.SwingConstants*[4]
1.2 ○   └CompositeView[2]
1.2   └BoxView[3]
1.3 ○   └FlowView

	1			*30 inherited members from View not shown*
	2			*16 inherited members from CompositeView not shown*
	3			*33 inherited members from BoxView not shown*
	4			*19 inherited members from javax.swing.SwingConstants not shown*
	3	protected	**javax** **.swing.SizeRequirements**	**calculateMinorAxisRequirements** (int axis, javax.swing.SizeRequirements r)
	1	public	**void**	**changedUpdate** (*javax.swing.event.DocumentEvent* changes, *java.awt.Shape* a, *ViewFactory* f)
○		protected abstract	View	**createRow** ()
✳		public		**FlowView** (*Element* elem, int axis)
		public	int	**getFlowAxis** ()
		public	int	**getFlowSpan** (int index)
		public	int	**getFlowStart** (int index)
	2	protected	**int**	**getViewIndexAtPosition** (int pos)
	1	public	**void**	**insertUpdate** (*javax.swing.event.DocumentEvent* changes, *java.awt.Shape* a, *ViewFactory* f)
	3	protected	**void**	**layout** (int width, int height)
		protected	View	**layoutPool**
		protected	int	**layoutSpan**
	2	protected	**void**	**loadChildren** (*ViewFactory* f)

Class *Interface* —extends - - -implements ○ abstract ● final △ static ▲ static final ✳ constructor x x—inherited x **x**—declared **x x**—overridden
εn—examples of usage ⌡—has subclass package—see other volume

526

1	public	**void removeUpdate** (*javax.swing.event.DocumentEvent* changes, *java.awt.Shape* a, *ViewFactory* f)	
	protected	**strategy**	
	.... FlowView.FlowStrategy		

FlowView.FlowStrategy
javax.swing.text

Object
1.3 └ FlowView.FlowStrategy

	protected	void **adjustRow** (FlowView fv, int rowIndex, int desiredSpan, int x)	
	public	void **changedUpdate** (FlowView fv, *javax.swing.event.DocumentEvent* e, *java.awt.Rectangle* alloc)	
	protected	View **createView** (FlowView fv, int startOffset, int spanLeft, int rowIndex)	
*	public	**FlowView.FlowStrategy** ()	
	protected	View **getLogicalView** (FlowView fv)	
	public	void **insertUpdate** (FlowView fv, *javax.swing.event.DocumentEvent* e, *java.awt.Rectangle* alloc)	
	public	void **layout** (FlowView fv)	
	protected	int **layoutRow** (FlowView fv, int rowIndex, int pos)	
	public	void **removeUpdate** (FlowView fv, *javax.swing.event.DocumentEvent* e, *java.awt.Rectangle* alloc)	

FocusAdapter
java.awt.event

Object
1.1 O └ FocusAdapter ------------------------- *FocusListener* [1] (*java.util.EventListener*)

*	public	**FocusAdapter** ()	
1	public	void **focusGained** (FocusEvent e)	ε649,616,617,618
1	public	void **focusLost** (FocusEvent e)	ε649,616,617,618

FocusEvent
java.awt.event
ε649,640,641,643,566

Object
1.1 └ java.util.EventObject [1] ------------------- *java.io.Serializable*
1.1 O └ java.awt.AWTEvent [2]
1.1 └ ComponentEvent [3]
1.1 └ FocusEvent

2	*27 inherited members from java.awt.AWTEvent not shown*		
▲ 3	public static final	int COMPONENT_FIRST = 100	
▲ 3	public static final	int COMPONENT_HIDDEN = 103	
▲ 3	public static final	int COMPONENT_LAST = 103	
▲ 3	public static final	int COMPONENT_MOVED = 100	
▲ 3	public static final	int COMPONENT_RESIZED = 101	
▲ 3	public static final	int COMPONENT_SHOWN = 102	
▲	public static final	int **FOCUS_FIRST** = 1004	
▲	public static final	int **FOCUS_GAINED** = 1004	
▲	public static final	int **FOCUS_LAST** = 1005	
▲	public static final	int **FOCUS_LOST** = 1005	
*	public	**FocusEvent** (java.awt.Component source, int id)	
*	public	**FocusEvent** (java.awt.Component source, int id, boolean temporary)	
1.4 *	public	**FocusEvent** (java.awt.Component source, int id, boolean temporary, java.awt.Component opposite)	
3	public	java.awt.Component getComponent ()	ε810,813,1011
1.4	public	java.awt.Component **getOppositeComponent** ()	ε617
1	public	Object getSource ()	ε618,644,886,565,568
	public	boolean **isTemporary** ()	ε616,618
3	public	**String paramString** ()	
1	protected transient	Object source	

FocusListener
java.awt.event
ε738,743,745,746,752

1.1 *FocusListener*——————————————*java.util.EventListener*

	public	void **focusGained** (FocusEvent e)	ε649,616,617,618
	public	void **focusLost** (FocusEvent e)	ε649,616,617,618

FocusManager

			FocusManager		javax.swing

```
Object
1.4 ○  └java.awt.KeyboardFocusManager 1 - - - - - - - - java.awt.KeyEventDispatcher , java.awt.KeyEventPostProcessor
1.4        └java.awt.DefaultKeyboardFocusManager 2
1.2 ○         └FocusManager⌄
```

	1	*51 inherited members from java.awt.KeyboardFocusManager not shown*			
1.4	2	protected synchronized ...void	dequeueKeyEvents (long after, java.awt.Component untilFocused)		
D △		public static ....void	**disableSwingFocusManager** ()		
1.4	2	protected synchronized ...void	discardKeyEvents (java.awt.Component comp)		
1.4	2	public.................. boolean	dispatchEvent (java.awt.AWTEvent e)		
1.4	2	public.................. boolean	dispatchKeyEvent (java.awt.event.KeyEvent e)		ε636
1.4	2	public......................void	downFocusCycle (java.awt.Container aContainer)		
1.4	2	protected synchronized ...void	enqueueKeyEvents (long after, java.awt.Component untilFocused)		
▲		public static final ....String	**FOCUS_MANAGER_CLASS_PROPERTY** = "FocusManagerClassName"		
✳		public............................	**FocusManager** ()		
1.4	2	public......................void	focusNextComponent (java.awt.Component aComponent)		
1.4	2	public......................void	focusPreviousComponent (java.awt.Component aComponent)		
△		public static ....FocusManager	**getCurrentManager** ()		
D △		public static .... boolean	**isFocusManagerEnabled** ()		
1.4	2	public.................. boolean	postProcessKeyEvent (java.awt.event.KeyEvent e)		
1.4	2	public......................void	processKeyEvent (java.awt.Component focusedComponent, java.awt.event.KeyEvent e)		
△		public static ....void	**setCurrentManager** (FocusManager aFocusManager) throws SecurityException		
1.4	2	public......................void	upFocusCycle (java.awt.Component aComponent)		

			FocusTraversalPolicy		java.awt

```
Object
1.4 ○  └FocusTraversalPolicy⌄
```

✳	public..........................	**FocusTraversalPolicy** ()	
○	public abstract .... Component	**getComponentAfter** (Container focusCycleRoot, Component aComponent)	
			ε615
○	public abstract .... Component	**getComponentBefore** (Container focusCycleRoot, Component aComponent)	
			ε615
○	public abstract .... Component	**getDefaultComponent** (Container focusCycleRoot)	ε615
○	public abstract .... Component	**getFirstComponent** (Container focusCycleRoot)	
	public.............. Component	**getInitialComponent** (Window window)	
○	public abstract .... Component	**getLastComponent** (Container focusCycleRoot)	

			Font		java.awt

```
Object 1                                                                    ε654,870
└Font - - - - - - - - - - - - - - - - - - - - - - - - - - - - - java.io.Serializable⌄
```

▲	public static final ....int	**BOLD** = 1	
1.2	public................. boolean	**canDisplay** (char c)	
1.2	public.......................int	**canDisplayUpTo** (String str)	
1.2	public.......................int	**canDisplayUpTo** (char[] text, int start, int limit)	
1.2	public.......................int	**canDisplayUpTo** (*java.text.CharacterIterator* iter, int start, int limit)	
1.2 ▲	public static final ....int	**CENTER_BASELINE** = 1	
1.3 △	public static .... Font	**createFont** (int fontFormat, java.io.InputStream fontStream) throws FontFormatException, java.io.IOException	
1.2	public.......................... .... java.awt.font.GlyphVector	**createGlyphVector** (java.awt.font.FontRenderContext frc, int[] glyphCodes)	
1.2	public.......................... .... java.awt.font.GlyphVector	**createGlyphVector** (java.awt.font.FontRenderContext frc, String str)	
1.2	public.......................... .... java.awt.font.GlyphVector	**createGlyphVector** (java.awt.font.FontRenderContext frc, char[] chars)	
1.2	public.......................... .... java.awt.font.GlyphVector	**createGlyphVector** (java.awt.font.FontRenderContext frc, *java.text.CharacterIterator* ci)	
1.1 △	public static .... Font	**decode** (String str)	
1.2	public......................Font	**deriveFont** (float size)	
1.2	public......................Font	**deriveFont** (int style)	
1.2	public......................Font	**deriveFont** (java.awt.geom.AffineTransform trans)	
1.2	public......................Font	**deriveFont** (*java.util.Map* attributes)	

Class *Interface* —extends - - -implements ○ abstract ● final △ static ▲ static final ✳ constructor x x—inherited x **x**—declared **x x**—overridden
εn—examples of usage ⌄—has subclass package—see other volume

1.2		public	Font	**deriveFont** (int style, java.awt.geom.AffineTransform trans)
1.2		public	Font	**deriveFont** (int style, float size)
	1	public	**boolean**	**equals** (Object obj)
	1	protected	**void**	**finalize** () throws Throwable
1.2	✱	public		**Font** (*java.util.Map* attributes)
	✱	public		**Font** (String name, int style, int size) ε591,593
1.2		public	*java.util.Map*	**getAttributes** ()
1.2		public	java.text₂	**getAvailableAttributes** ()
		.AttributedCharacterIterator₂		
		.Attribute[]		
1.2		public	byte	**getBaselineFor** (char c)
		public	String	**getFamily** () ε652
1.2		public	String	**getFamily** (java.util.Locale l)
1.2	△	public static	Font	**getFont** (String nm)
1.2	△	public static	Font	**getFont** (*java.util.Map* attributes)
	△	public static	Font	**getFont** (String nm, Font font)
1.2		public	String	**getFontName** ()
1.2		public	String	**getFontName** (java.util.Locale l)
1.2		public	float	**getItalicAngle** ()
1.2		public		**getLineMetrics** (String str, java.awt.font.FontRenderContext frc)
		java.awt.font.LineMetrics		
1.2		public		**getLineMetrics** (char[] chars, int beginIndex, int limit,
		java.awt.font.LineMetrics		java.awt.font.FontRenderContext frc)
1.2		public		**getLineMetrics** (String str, int beginIndex, int limit,
		java.awt.font.LineMetrics		java.awt.font.FontRenderContext frc)
1.2		public		**getLineMetrics** (*java.text.CharacterIterator* ci, int beginIndex, int limit,
		java.awt.font.LineMetrics		java.awt.font.FontRenderContext frc)
1.2		public		**getMaxCharBounds** (java.awt.font.FontRenderContext frc)
		. java.awt.geom.Rectangle2D		
1.2		public	int	**getMissingGlyphCode** ()
		public	String	**getName** () ε652
1.2		public	int	**getNumGlyphs** ()
D		public	*java.awt.peer.FontPeer*	**getPeer** ()
1.2		public	String	**getPSName** ()
		public	int	**getSize** ()
1.2		public	float	**getSize2D** ()
1.2		public		**getStringBounds** (String str, java.awt.font.FontRenderContext frc)
		. java.awt.geom.Rectangle2D		
1.2		public		**getStringBounds** (char[] chars, int beginIndex, int limit,
		. java.awt.geom.Rectangle2D		java.awt.font.FontRenderContext frc)
1.2		public		**getStringBounds** (String str, int beginIndex, int limit,
		. java.awt.geom.Rectangle2D		java.awt.font.FontRenderContext frc)
1.2		public		**getStringBounds** (*java.text.CharacterIterator* ci, int beginIndex, int limit,
		. java.awt.geom.Rectangle2D		java.awt.font.FontRenderContext frc)
		public	int	**getStyle** ()
1.2		public	java₂	**getTransform** ()
		.awt.geom.AffineTransform		
1.2	▲	public static final	int	**HANGING_BASELINE** = 2
	1	public	**int**	**hashCode** ()
1.2		public	boolean	**hasUniformLineMetrics** ()
		public	boolean	**isBold** ()
		public	boolean	**isItalic** ()
		public	boolean	**isPlain** ()
1.4		public	boolean	**isTransformed** ()
	▲	public static final	int	**ITALIC** = 2
1.4	▲	public static final	int	**LAYOUT_LEFT_TO_RIGHT** = 0
1.4	▲	public static final	int	**LAYOUT_NO_LIMIT_CONTEXT** = 4
1.4	▲	public static final	int	**LAYOUT_NO_START_CONTEXT** = 2
1.4	▲	public static final	int	**LAYOUT_RIGHT_TO_LEFT** = 1
1.4		public		**layoutGlyphVector** (java.awt.font.FontRenderContext frc, char[] text, int start,
		.... java.awt.font.GlyphVector		int limit, int flags)
		protected	String	**name**
	▲	public static final	int	**PLAIN** = 0 ε591,593
1.2		protected	float	**pointSize**
1.2	▲	public static final	int	**ROMAN_BASELINE** = 0
		protected	int	**size**
		protected	int	**style**
	1	public	**String**	**toString** ()
1.3	▲	public static final	int	**TRUETYPE_FONT** = 0

FontFormatException

FontFormatException		java.awt

```
        Object
        └Throwable --------------------------- java.io.Serializable⌐
            └Exception
1.3             └FontFormatException
```

*	public..........................	**FontFormatException** (String reason)

F	FontMetrics		java.awt

```
        Object 1
    ○   └FontMetrics ------------------------- java.io.Serializable⌐
```

	public..........................int	**bytesWidth** (byte[] data, int off, int len)	
	public..........................int	**charsWidth** (char[] data, int off, int len)	
	public..........................int	**charWidth** (char ch)	
	public..........................int	**charWidth** (int ch)	
	protected..................Font	**font**	
*	protected......................	**FontMetrics** (Font font)	
	public..........................int	**getAscent** ()	ε591
	public..........................int	**getDescent** ()	
	public..........................Font	**getFont** ()	
	public..........................int	**getHeight** ()	ε593
	public..........................int	**getLeading** ()	
1.2	public.......................... .....java.awt.font.LineMetrics	**getLineMetrics** (String str, Graphics context)	
1.2	public.......................... .....java.awt.font.LineMetrics	**getLineMetrics** (char[] chars, int beginIndex, int limit, Graphics context)	
1.2	public.......................... .....java.awt.font.LineMetrics	**getLineMetrics** (String str, int beginIndex, int limit, Graphics context)	
1.2	public.......................... .....java.awt.font.LineMetrics	**getLineMetrics** (*java.text.CharacterIterator* ci, int beginIndex, int limit, Graphics context)	
	public..........................int	**getMaxAdvance** ()	
	public..........................int	**getMaxAscent** ()	
1.2	public.......................... . java.awt.geom.Rectangle2D	**getMaxCharBounds** (Graphics context)	
D	public..........................int	**getMaxDecent** ()	
	public..........................int	**getMaxDescent** ()	
1.2	public.......................... . java.awt.geom.Rectangle2D	**getStringBounds** (String str, Graphics context)	
1.2	public.......................... . java.awt.geom.Rectangle2D	**getStringBounds** (char[] chars, int beginIndex, int limit, Graphics context)	
1.2	public.......................... . java.awt.geom.Rectangle2D	**getStringBounds** (String str, int beginIndex, int limit, Graphics context)	
1.2	public.......................... . java.awt.geom.Rectangle2D	**getStringBounds** (*java.text.CharacterIterator* ci, int beginIndex, int limit, Graphics context)	
	public..........................int[]	**getWidths** ()	
1.2	public.................boolean	**hasUniformLineMetrics** ()	
	public..........................int	**stringWidth** (String str)	ε593
1	public..................**String**	**toString** ()	

FontPeer		java.awt.peer

1.1	*FontPeer*

- -

FontRenderContext		java.awt.font

```
        Object 1                                                    ε654
1.2     └FontRenderContext
```

1.4	public.................boolean	**equals** (FontRenderContext rhs)
1	public.................**boolean**	**equals** (Object obj)
*	protected......................	**FontRenderContext** ()
*	public..........................	**FontRenderContext** (java.awt.geom.AffineTransform tx, boolean isAntiAliased, boolean usesFractionalMetrics)

Class   *Interface*   —extends   - - -implements   ○ abstract   ● final   △ static   ▲ static final   ✳ constructor   x x—inherited   x **x**—declared   **x x**—overridden
ε*n*—examples of usage   ⌐—has subclass   package—see other volume

```
        public .................... java₂  getTransform ()
        .awt.geom.AffineTransform
  1     public ..................... int  hashCode ()
        public ................ boolean  isAntiAliased ()
        public ................ boolean  usesFractionalMetrics ()
```

FontUIResource   javax.swing.plaf

```
        Object
        └java.awt.Font 1 ----------------------- java.io.Serializable
  1.2     └FontUIResource ---------------------- UIResource
```
ε654,870

```
  1   70 inherited members from java.awt.Font not shown
  *   public ........................  FontUIResource (java.awt.Font font)
  *   public ........................  FontUIResource (String name, int style, int size)
```

FormatConversionProvider   javax.sound.sampled.spi

```
        Object
  1.3 O  └FormatConversionProvider
```

```
  *   public ........................  FormatConversionProvider ()
  O   public abstract ...javax.sound₂  getAudioInputStream (javax.sound.sampled.AudioFormat targetFormat,
        .sampled.AudioInputStream        javax.sound.sampled.AudioInputStream sourceStream)
  O   public abstract ...javax.sound₂  getAudioInputStream (javax.sound.sampled.AudioFormat.Encoding
        .sampled.AudioInputStream        targetEncoding, javax.sound.sampled.AudioInputStream sourceStream)
  O   public abstract ................  getSourceEncodings ()
        ....... javax.sound.sampled₂
        .AudioFormat.Encoding[]
  O   public abstract ................  getTargetEncodings ()
        ....... javax.sound.sampled₂
        .AudioFormat.Encoding[]
  O   public abstract ................  getTargetEncodings (javax.sound.sampled.AudioFormat sourceFormat)
        ....... javax.sound.sampled₂
        .AudioFormat.Encoding[]
  O   public abstract ...javax.sound₂  getTargetFormats (javax.sound.sampled.AudioFormat.Encoding targetEncoding,
        .sampled.AudioFormat[]            javax.sound.sampled.AudioFormat sourceFormat)
      public ................ boolean  isConversionSupported (javax.sound.sampled.AudioFormat targetFormat,
                                         javax.sound.sampled.AudioFormat sourceFormat)
      public ................ boolean  isConversionSupported (javax.sound.sampled.AudioFormat.Encoding
                                         targetEncoding, javax.sound.sampled.AudioFormat sourceFormat)
      public ................ boolean  isSourceEncodingSupported (javax.sound.sampled.AudioFormat.Encoding
                                         sourceEncoding)
      public ................ boolean  isTargetEncodingSupported (javax.sound.sampled.AudioFormat.Encoding
                                         targetEncoding)
```

FormView   javax.swing.text.html

```
        Object
  1.2 O  └javax.swing.text.View 1 ------------------ javax.swing.SwingConstants 3
  1.2       └javax.swing.text.ComponentView 2
  1.2         └FormView ----------------------- java.awt.event.ActionListener 4 (java.util.EventListener)
```

```
  1   44 inherited members from javax.swing.text.View not shown
  3   19 inherited members from javax.swing.SwingConstants not shown
  4   public ...................... void  actionPerformed (java.awt.event.ActionEvent evt)        ε855,644,738,743,745
  2   protected ......................  createComponent ()
        ........ java.awt.Component
  *   public ........................  FormView (javax.swing.text.Element elem)
  2   public ..................... float  getAlignment (int axis)
● 2   public final .....................  getComponent ()
        ........ java.awt.Component
  2   public ..................... float  getMaximumSpan (int axis)
  2   public ..................... float  getMinimumSpan (int axis)
  2   public ..................... float  getPreferredSpan (int axis)
      protected .................. void  imageSubmit (String imageData)
  2   public .......... java.awt.Shape  modelToView (int pos, java.awt.Shape a, javax.swing.text.Position.Bias b)
                                         throws javax.swing.text.BadLocationException
  2   public ...................... void  paint (java.awt.Graphics g, java.awt.Shape a)
```

FormView

D ▲		public static final	String	**RESET** = "Reset"
	2	public	void	setParent (javax.swing.text.View p)
D ▲		public static final	String	**SUBMIT** = "Submit Query"
		protected	void	**submitData** (String data)
	2	public	int	viewToModel (float x, float y, *java.awt.Shape* a, javax.swing.text.Position.Bias[] bias)

FormView.MouseEventListener	protected	javax.swing.text.html

Object
    1.1 ○ └java.awt.event.MouseAdapter[1] - - - - - - - - - - - - *java.awt.event.MouseListener* ↲ (*java.util.EventListener*)
    1.2   └FormView.MouseEventListener

	1	public	void	mouseClicked (java.awt.event.MouseEvent e)	ε646,648,783,967
	1	public	void	mouseEntered (java.awt.event.MouseEvent e)	
✳		protected		**FormView.MouseEventListener** ()	
	1	public	void	mouseExited (java.awt.event.MouseEvent e)	
	1	public	void	mousePressed (java.awt.event.MouseEvent e)	ε602,742,810,1011
	1	public	**void**	**mouseReleased** (java.awt.event.MouseEvent evt)	ε810,1011

Frame	java.awt

Object   ε618,606,733,953,988
  ○ └Component[1] - *java.awt.image.ImageObserver* [4], *MenuContainer*,
                                                java.io.Serializable ↲
    └Container[2]
      └Window[3] - *javax.accessibility.Accessible*
        └Frame ↲

	1	*160 inherited members from Component not shown*			
	2	*52 inherited members from Container not shown*			
	3	*46 inherited members from Window not shown*			
	4	*8 inherited members from java.awt.image.ImageObserver not shown*			
1.1	2	public	void	add (Component comp, Object constraints)	ε559,571,733,601,694
1.1	2	public synchronized	void	addContainerListener (*java.awt.event.ContainerListener* l)	ε573
	3	public	**void**	**addNotify** ()	
1.1	3	public synchronized	void	addWindowListener (*java.awt.event.WindowListener* l)	ε565,566,568,884,905
1.4	3	public synchronized	void	addWindowStateListener (*java.awt.event.WindowStateListener* l)	
					ε569
D ▲		public static final	int	**CROSSHAIR_CURSOR** = 1	
D ▲		public static final	int	**DEFAULT_CURSOR** = 0	
	3	public	void	dispose ()	ε565
D ▲		public static final	int	**E_RESIZE_CURSOR** = 11	
	3	protected	**void**	**finalize** () throws Throwable	
	✳	public		**Frame** () throws HeadlessException	ε561,562,563,565,566
1.3	✳	public		**Frame** (GraphicsConfiguration gc)	ε601,602
	✳	public		**Frame** (String title) throws HeadlessException	ε559,560
1.3	✳	public		**Frame** (String title, GraphicsConfiguration gc)	
1.3	3	public.... javax.accessibility ↲ .**AccessibleContext**		**getAccessibleContext** ()	
	2	public	Component	getComponent (int n)	ε572
1.1	2	public	int	getComponentCount ()	ε572
	2	public	Component[]	getComponents ()	ε572
D		public	int	**getCursorType** ()	
1.4		public synchronized	int	**getExtendedState** ()	ε564
1.2 △		public static	Frame[]	**getFrames** ()	ε567
		public	Image	**getIconImage** ()	
1.4		public	Rectangle	**getMaximizedBounds** ()	
		public	MenuBar	**getMenuBar** ()	
1.1	1	public	Dimension	getSize ()	ε599
1.2		public synchronized	int	**getState** ()	
		public	String	**getTitle** ()	ε567
D ▲		public static final	int	**HAND_CURSOR** = 12	
1.2 ▲		public static final	int	**ICONIFIED** = 1	ε564,569
		public	boolean	**isResizable** ()	ε561
1.4		public	boolean	**isUndecorated** ()	ε562
	1	public	boolean	isVisible ()	ε567
1.4 ▲		public static final	int	**MAXIMIZED_BOTH** = 6	ε564,569
1.4 ▲		public static final	int	**MAXIMIZED_HORIZ** = 2	

Class   *Interface*   —extends   - - -implements   ○ abstract   ● final   △ static   ▲ static final   ✳ constructor   x x—inherited   x **x**—declared   **x x**—overridden
ε*n*—examples of usage   ↲—has subclass   package—see other volume

1.4 ▲		public static final .... int	**MAXIMIZED_VERT** = 4	
D ▲		public static final .... int	**MOVE_CURSOR** = 13	
D ▲		public static final .... int	**N_RESIZE_CURSOR** = 8	
D ▲		public static final .... int	**NE_RESIZE_CURSOR** = 7	
1.2 ▲		public static final .... int	**NORMAL** = 0	
D ▲		public static final .... int	**NW_RESIZE_CURSOR** = 6	
	2	protected .... **String**	**paramString** ()	
	1	public .... **void**	**remove** (MenuComponent m)	
	2	public .... **void**	**removeNotify** ()	
D ▲		public static final .... int	**S_RESIZE_CURSOR** = 9	
D ▲		public static final .... int	**SE_RESIZE_CURSOR** = 5	
D		public ....void	**setCursor** (int cursorType)	
1.4		public synchronized ......void	**setExtendedState** (int state)	ε564
		public synchronized ......void	**setIconImage** (Image image)	ε560
1.1	1	public ....void	setLocation (int x, int y)	ε599
1.4		public synchronized ......void	**setMaximizedBounds** (Rectangle bounds)	ε563
		public ....void	**setMenuBar** (MenuBar mb)	
		public ....void	**setResizable** (boolean resizable)	ε561
1.1	1	public ....void	setSize (int width, int height)	ε559,571
1.2		public synchronized ......void	**setState** (int state)	
		public ....void	**setTitle** (String title)	
1.4		public ....void	**setUndecorated** (boolean undecorated)	ε562
1.1	1	public ....void	setVisible (boolean b)	ε559,565,571
D ▲		public static final .... int	**SW_RESIZE_CURSOR** = 4	
D ▲		public static final .... int	**TEXT_CURSOR** = 2	
D ▲		public static final .... int	**W_RESIZE_CURSOR** = 10	
D ▲		public static final .... int	**WAIT_CURSOR** = 3	

FramePeer   java.awt.peer

FramePeer————————————————— *WindowPeer* [1] (*ContainerPeer* [2] (*ComponentPeer* [3]))

	3	*42 inherited members from ComponentPeer not shown*	
	2	*7 inherited members from ContainerPeer not shown*	
	1	*2 inherited members from WindowPeer not shown*	
1.2		public.........................int	**getState** ()
		public.........................void	**setIconImage** (java.awt.Image im)
1.4		public.........................void	**setMaximizedBounds** (java.awt.Rectangle bounds)
		public.........................void	**setMenuBar** (java.awt.MenuBar mb)
		public.........................void	**setResizable** (boolean resizeable)
1.2		public.........................void	**setState** (int state)
		public.........................void	**setTitle** (String title)

GapContent   javax.swing.text

Object
└ GapVector [1] - *java.io.Serializable*
1.2 └ GapContent - *AbstractDocument.Content* [2]

	1	protected .... **Object**	**allocateArray** (int len)
	2	public .... *Position*	**createPosition** (int offset) throws BadLocationException
*		public	**GapContent** ()
*		public	**GapContent** (int initialLength)
●	1	protected final ....Object	getArray ()
	1	protected .... **int**	**getArrayLength** ()
	2	public ....void	**getChars** (int where, int len, Segment chars) throws BadLocationException
●	1	protected final ....int	getGapEnd ()
●	1	protected final ....int	getGapStart ()
		protected .... java.util.Vector	**getPositionsInRange** (java.util.Vector v, int offset, int length)
	2	public .... String	**getString** (int where, int len) throws BadLocationException
	2	public .... *javax.swing.undo.UndoableEdit*	**insertString** (int where, String str) throws BadLocationException
	2	public ....int	**length** ()
	2	public .... *javax.swing.undo.UndoableEdit*	**remove** (int where, int nitems) throws BadLocationException
	1	protected ....void	replace (int, int, Object, int)
		protected ....void	**resetMarksAtZero** ()
	1	protected ....void	**shiftEnd** (int newSize)
	1	protected ....void	**shiftGap** (int newGapStart)
	1	protected ....void	**shiftGapEndUp** (int newGapEnd)
	1	protected ....void	**shiftGapStartDown** (int newGapStart)
		protected ....void	**updateUndoPositions** (java.util.Vector positions, int offset, int length)

G

Classes

GapVector

GapVector				javax.swing.text

```
Object
└ GapVector ----------------------------- java.io.Serializable
```

○	protected abstract ...... Object	**allocateArray** (int)
✳	public..........................	**GapVector** ()
✳	public..........................	**GapVector** (int)
●	protected final ....Object	**getArray** ()
○	protected abstract ....int	**getArrayLength** ()
●	protected final...............int	**getGapEnd** ()
●	protected final...............int	**getGapStart** ()
	protected ....void	**replace** (int, int, Object, int)
	protected ....void	**shiftEnd** (int)
	protected ....void	**shiftGap** (int)
	protected ....void	**shiftGapEndUp** (int)
	protected ....void	**shiftGapStartDown** (int)

G

GeneralPath		java.awt.geom

```
Object 1
1.2 ● └ GeneralPath -------------------------- java.awt.Shape 2, Cloneable
```

	public.......................void	**append** (*PathIterator* pi, boolean connect)	
	public.......................void	**append** (*java.awt.Shape* s, boolean connect)	
1	public.....................**Object**	**clone** ()	
	public synchronized ....void	**closePath** ()	ε657
2	public.................... boolean	**contains** (Point2D p)	
2	public.................... boolean	**contains** (Rectangle2D r)	
2	public.................... boolean	**contains** (double x, double y)	
2	public.................... boolean	**contains** (double x, double y, double w, double h)	
	public synchronized .... *java.awt.Shape*	**createTransformedShape** (AffineTransform at)	
	public synchronized ....void	**curveTo** (float x1, float y1, float x2, float y2, float x3, float y3)	ε657
✳	public..........................	**GeneralPath** ()	ε657
✳	public..........................	**GeneralPath** (int rule)	
✳	public..........................	**GeneralPath** (*java.awt.Shape* s)	
✳	public..........................	**GeneralPath** (int rule, int initialCapacity)	
2	public...... java.awt.Rectangle	**getBounds** ()	
2	public synchronized Rectangle2D	**getBounds2D** ()	
	public synchronized ...Point2D	**getCurrentPoint** ()	
2	public............... *PathIterator*	**getPathIterator** (AffineTransform at)	
2	public............... *PathIterator*	**getPathIterator** (AffineTransform at, double flatness)	
	public synchronized ....int	**getWindingRule** ()	
2	public................. boolean	**intersects** (Rectangle2D r)	
2	public................. boolean	**intersects** (double x, double y, double w, double h)	
	public synchronized ....void	**lineTo** (float x, float y)	ε657
	public synchronized ......void	**moveTo** (float x, float y)	ε657
	public synchronized ....void	**quadTo** (float x1, float y1, float x2, float y2)	ε657
	public synchronized ....void	**reset** ()	
	public.......................void	**setWindingRule** (int rule)	
	public.......................void	**transform** (AffineTransform at)	
▲	public static final ....int	**WIND_EVEN_ODD** = 0	
▲	public static final ....int	**WIND_NON_ZERO** = 1	

GlyphJustificationInfo		java.awt.font

```
Object
1.2 ● └ GlyphJustificationInfo
```

✳	public..........................	**GlyphJustificationInfo** (float weight, boolean growAbsorb, int growPriority, float growLeftLimit, float growRightLimit, boolean shrinkAbsorb, int shrinkPriority, float shrinkLeftLimit, float shrinkRightLimit)
●	public final .... boolean	**growAbsorb**
●	public final ....float	**growLeftLimit**
●	public final ....int	**growPriority**
●	public final ....float	**growRightLimit**

Class *Interface* —extends - - -implements ○ abstract ● final △ static ▲ static final ✳ constructor x x—inherited x **x**—declared **x x**—overridden
ε*n*—examples of usage └—has subclass package—see other volume

▲	public static final	int	**PRIORITY_INTERCHAR** = 2
▲	public static final	int	**PRIORITY_KASHIDA** = 0
▲	public static final	int	**PRIORITY_NONE** = 3
▲	public static final	int	**PRIORITY_WHITESPACE** = 1
●	public final	boolean	**shrinkAbsorb**
●	public final	float	**shrinkLeftLimit**
●	public final	int	**shrinkPriority**
●	public final	float	**shrinkRightLimit**
●	public final	float	**weight**

GlyphMetrics   java.awt.font

G

Object
1.2 ● └GlyphMetrics

▲	public static final	byte	**COMBINING** = 2
▲	public static final	byte	**COMPONENT** = 3
	public	float	**getAdvance** ()
1.4	public	float	**getAdvanceX** ()
1.4	public	float	**getAdvanceY** ()
	public		**getBounds2D** ()
		. java.awt.geom.Rectangle2D	
	public	float	**getLSB** ()
	public	float	**getRSB** ()
	public	int	**getType** ()
*	public		**GlyphMetrics** (float advance, java.awt.geom.Rectangle2D bounds, byte glyphType)
1.4 *	public		**GlyphMetrics** (boolean horizontal, float advanceX, float advanceY, java.awt.geom.Rectangle2D bounds, byte glyphType)
	public	boolean	**isCombining** ()
	public	boolean	**isComponent** ()
	public	boolean	**isLigature** ()
	public	boolean	**isStandard** ()
	public	boolean	**isWhitespace** ()
▲	public static final	byte	**LIGATURE** = 1
▲	public static final	byte	**STANDARD** = 0
▲	public static final	byte	**WHITESPACE** = 4

GlyphVector   java.awt.font

Object
1.2 ○ └GlyphVector - *Cloneable*

○	public abstract	boolean	**equals** (GlyphVector set)
1.4 ▲	public static final	int	**FLAG_COMPLEX_GLYPHS** = 8
1.4 ▲	public static final	int	**FLAG_HAS_POSITION_ADJUSTMENTS** = 2
1.4 ▲	public static final	int	**FLAG_HAS_TRANSFORMS** = 1
1.4 ▲	public static final	int	**FLAG_MASK** = 15
1.4 ▲	public static final	int	**FLAG_RUN_RTL** = 4
○	public abstract	java.awt.Font	**getFont** ()
○	public abstract		**getFontRenderContext** ()
		FontRenderContext	
1.4	public	int	**getGlyphCharIndex** (int glyphIndex)
1.4	public	int[]	**getGlyphCharIndices** (int beginGlyphIndex, int numEntries, int[] codeReturn)
○	public abstract	int	**getGlyphCode** (int glyphIndex)
○	public abstract	int[]	**getGlyphCodes** (int beginGlyphIndex, int numEntries, int[] codeReturn)
○	public abstract		**getGlyphJustificationInfo** (int glyphIndex)
		GlyphJustificationInfo	
○	public abstract	*java.awt.Shape*	**getGlyphLogicalBounds** (int glyphIndex)
○	public abstract	GlyphMetrics	**getGlyphMetrics** (int glyphIndex)
○	public abstract	*java.awt.Shape*	**getGlyphOutline** (int glyphIndex)
1.4	public	*java.awt.Shape*	**getGlyphOutline** (int glyphIndex, float x, float y)
1.4	public	java.awt.Rectangle	**getGlyphPixelBounds** (int index, FontRenderContext renderFRC, float x, float y)
○	public abstract		**getGlyphPosition** (int glyphIndex)
		java.awt.geom.Point2D	
○	public abstract	float[]	**getGlyphPositions** (int beginGlyphIndex, int numEntries, float[] positionReturn)
○	public abstract	java.	**getGlyphTransform** (int glyphIndex)
		.awt.geom.AffineTransform	
○	public abstract	*java.awt.Shape*	**getGlyphVisualBounds** (int glyphIndex)
1.4	public	int	**getLayoutFlags** ()
○	public abstract		**getLogicalBounds** ()
		. java.awt.geom.Rectangle2D	
○	public abstract	int	**getNumGlyphs** ()

535

GlyphVector

○	public abstract	*java.awt.Shape*	**getOutline** ()
○	public abstract	*java.awt.Shape*	**getOutline** (float x, float y)
1.4	public......	java.awt.Rectangle	**getPixelBounds** (FontRenderContext renderFRC, float x, float y)
○	public abstract..............		**getVisualBounds** ()
	. java.awt.geom.Rectangle2D		
✳	public........................		**GlyphVector** ()
○	public abstract ....void		**performDefaultLayout** ()
○	public abstract ....void		**setGlyphPosition** (int glyphIndex, java.awt.geom.Point2D newPos)
○	public abstract ....void		**setGlyphTransform** (int glyphIndex, java.awt.geom.AffineTransform newTX)

GlyphView
`javax.swing.text`

Object [1]
1.2 ○ └View [2] - *javax.swing.SwingConstants* [3]
1.3   └GlyphView - *TabableView* [4], *Cloneable*

2	*38 inherited members from View not shown*		
3	*19 inherited members from javax.swing.SwingConstants not shown*		
2	public.....................	**View**	**breakView** (int axis, int p0, float pos, float len)
2	public.....................	**void**	**changedUpdate** (*javax.swing.event.DocumentEvent* e, *java.awt.Shape* a, *ViewFactory* f)
	protected ....void		**checkPainter** ()
● 1	protected final..........	**Object**	**clone** ()
2	public.....................	**View**	**createFragment** (int p0, int p1)
2	public.....................	**float**	**getAlignment** (int axis)
	public...........java.awt.Color		**getBackground** ()
2	public.....................	**int**	**getBreakWeight** (int axis, float pos, float len)
2	public.....................	**int**	**getEndOffset** ()
	public...........java.awt.Font		**getFont** ()
	public...........java.awt.Color		**getForeground** ()
	public GlyphView.GlyphPainter		**getGlyphPainter** ()
2	public.....................	**int**	**getNextVisualPositionFrom** (int pos, Position.Bias b, *java.awt.Shape* a, int direction, Position.Bias[] biasRet) throws BadLocationException
4	public.....................float		**getPartialSpan** (int p0, int p1)
2	public.....................	**float**	**getPreferredSpan** (int axis)
2	public.....................	**int**	**getStartOffset** ()
4	public.....................float		**getTabbedSpan** (float x, *TabExpander* e)
	public............*TabExpander*		**getTabExpander** ()
	public............... Segment		**getText** (int p0, int p1)
✳	public.....................		**GlyphView** (*Element* elem)
2	public.....................	**void**	**insertUpdate** (*javax.swing.event.DocumentEvent* e, *java.awt.Shape* a, *ViewFactory* f)
	public................. boolean		**isStrikeThrough** ()
	public................. boolean		**isSubscript** ()
	public................. boolean		**isSuperscript** ()
	public................. boolean		**isUnderline** ()
2	public.........	***java.awt.Shape***	**modelToView** (int pos, *java.awt.Shape* a, Position.Bias b) throws BadLocationException
2	public.....................	**void**	**paint** (java.awt.Graphics g, *java.awt.Shape* a)
2	public.....................	**void**	**removeUpdate** (*javax.swing.event.DocumentEvent* e, *java.awt.Shape* a, *ViewFactory* f)
	public.....................void		**setGlyphPainter** (GlyphView.GlyphPainter p)
2	public.....................	**int**	**viewToModel** (float x, float y, *java.awt.Shape* a, Position.Bias[] biasReturn)

GlyphView.GlyphPainter
`javax.swing.text`

Object
1.3 ○ └GlyphView.GlyphPainter

○	public abstract ....float		**getAscent** (GlyphView v)
○	public abstract ....int		**getBoundedPosition** (GlyphView v, int p0, float x, float len)
○	public abstract ....float		**getDescent** (GlyphView v)
○	public abstract ....float		**getHeight** (GlyphView v)
	public.....................int		**getNextVisualPositionFrom** (GlyphView v, int pos, Position.Bias b, *java.awt.Shape* a, int direction, Position.Bias[] biasRet) throws BadLocationException
	public GlyphView.GlyphPainter		**getPainter** (GlyphView v, int p0, int p1)
○	public abstract ....float		**getSpan** (GlyphView v, int p0, int p1, *TabExpander* e, float x)
✳	public.....................		**GlyphView.GlyphPainter** ()

Class   *Interface* —extends   - - -implements   ○ abstract   ● final   △ static   ▲ static final   ✳ constructor   x x—inherited   x **x**—declared   **x x**—overridden
εn—examples of usage   —has subclass   package—see other volume

○	public abstract *java.awt.Shape*	**modelToView** (GlyphView v, int pos, Position.Bias bias, *java.awt.Shape* a) throws BadLocationException
○	public abstract .... void	**paint** (GlyphView v, java.awt.Graphics g, *java.awt.Shape* a, int p0, int p1)
○	public abstract .... int	**viewToModel** (GlyphView v, float x, float y, *java.awt.Shape* a, Position.Bias[] biasReturn)

GradientPaint   java.awt

Object
1.2   └ GradientPaint - *Paint* [1] (*Transparency* [2])

▲	2	public static final .... int	BITMASK = 2	ε666,667
	1	public .... *PaintContext*	**createContext** (java.awt.image.ColorModel cm, Rectangle deviceBounds, java.awt.geom.Rectangle2D userBounds, java.awt.geom.AffineTransform xform, RenderingHints hints)	
		public .... Color	**getColor1** ()	
		public .... Color	**getColor2** ()	
		public .. java.awt.geom.Point2D	**getPoint1** ()	
		public .. java.awt.geom.Point2D	**getPoint2** ()	
	2	public .... int	**getTransparency** ()	
*		public	**GradientPaint** (java.awt.geom.Point2D pt1, Color color1, java.awt.geom.Point2D pt2, Color color2)	
*		public	**GradientPaint** (java.awt.geom.Point2D pt1, Color color1, java.awt.geom.Point2D pt2, Color color2, boolean cyclic)	
*		public	**GradientPaint** (float x1, float y1, Color color1, float x2, float y2, Color color2)	ε583
*		public	**GradientPaint** (float x1, float y1, Color color1, float x2, float y2, Color color2, boolean cyclic)	ε583
		public .... boolean	**isCyclic** ()	
▲	2	public static final .... int	OPAQUE = 1	ε666,667
▲	2	public static final .... int	TRANSLUCENT = 3	ε666

GraphicAttribute   java.awt.font

Object
1.2 ○   └ GraphicAttribute

▲	public static final .... int	**BOTTOM_ALIGNMENT** = -2
▲	public static final .... int	**CENTER_BASELINE** = 1
○	public abstract .... void	**draw** (java.awt.Graphics2D graphics, float x, float y)
○	public abstract .... float	**getAdvance** ()
●	public final .... int	**getAlignment** ()
○	public abstract .... float	**getAscent** ()
	public java.awt.geom.Rectangle2D	**getBounds** ()
○	public abstract .... float	**getDescent** ()
	public ... GlyphJustificationInfo	**getJustificationInfo** ()
*	protected	**GraphicAttribute** (int alignment)
▲	public static final .... int	**HANGING_BASELINE** = 2
▲ ▶	public static final .... int	**ROMAN_BASELINE** = 0
▲	public static final .... int	**TOP_ALIGNMENT** = -1

Graphics   java.awt

                                         ε575,576,577,578,579

Object [1]
○   └ Graphics

○	public abstract .... void	**clearRect** (int x, int y, int width, int height)	
○	public abstract .... void	**clipRect** (int x, int y, int width, int height)	
○	public abstract .... void	**copyArea** (int x, int y, int width, int height, int dx, int dy)	
○	public abstract .... Graphics	**create** ()	
	public .... Graphics	**create** (int x, int y, int width, int height)	
○	public abstract .... void	**dispose** ()	ε602,667,674
	public .... void	**draw3DRect** (int x, int y, int width, int height, boolean raised)	
○	public abstract .... void	**drawArc** (int x, int y, int width, int height, int startAngle, int arcAngle)	ε586
	public .... void	**drawBytes** (byte[] data, int offset, int length, int x, int y)	
	public .... void	**drawChars** (char[] data, int offset, int length, int x, int y)	
○	public abstract .... boolean	**drawImage** (Image img, int x, int y, *java.awt.image.ImageObserver* observer)	ε581,595,660,667,668

G

Graphics

	O	public abstract .... boolean	**drawImage** (Image img, int x, int y, Color bgcolor, *java.awt.image.ImageObserver* observer)	
	O	public abstract .... boolean	**drawImage** (Image img, int x, int y, int width, int height, *java.awt.image.ImageObserver* observer)	
	O	public abstract .... boolean	**drawImage** (Image img, int x, int y, int width, int height, Color bgcolor, *java.awt.image.ImageObserver* observer)	
1.1	O	public abstract .... boolean	**drawImage** (Image img, int dx1, int dy1, int dx2, int dy2, int sx1, int sy1, int sx2, int sy2, *java.awt.image.ImageObserver* observer)	
1.1	O	public abstract .... boolean	**drawImage** (Image img, int dx1, int dy1, int dx2, int dy2, int sx1, int sy1, int sx2, int sy2, Color bgcolor, *java.awt.image.ImageObserver* observer)	
	O	public abstract ....void	**drawLine** (int x1, int y1, int x2, int y2)	ε586
	O	public abstract ....void	**drawOval** (int x, int y, int width, int height)	ε586,575
		public.....................void	**drawPolygon** (Polygon p)	ε586
	O	public abstract ....void	**drawPolygon** (int[] xPoints, int[] yPoints, int nPoints)	
1.1	O	public abstract ....void	**drawPolyline** (int[] xPoints, int[] yPoints, int nPoints)	
		public.....................void	**drawRect** (int x, int y, int width, int height)	ε586
	O	public abstract ....void	**drawRoundRect** (int x, int y, int width, int height, int arcWidth, int arcHeight)	ε586
	O	public abstract ....void	**drawString** (String str, int x, int y)	ε591
1.2	O	public abstract ....void	**drawString** (*java.text.AttributedCharacterIterator* iterator, int x, int y)	
		public.....................void	**fill3DRect** (int x, int y, int width, int height, boolean raised)	
	O	public abstract ....void	**fillArc** (int x, int y, int width, int height, int startAngle, int arcAngle) ε587,590	
	O	public abstract ....void	**fillOval** (int x, int y, int width, int height)	ε587,695
		public.....................void	**fillPolygon** (Polygon p)	ε587
	O	public abstract ....void	**fillPolygon** (int[] xPoints, int[] yPoints, int nPoints)	
	O	public abstract ....void	**fillRect** (int x, int y, int width, int height)	ε602,878,879,881,929
	O	public abstract ....void	**fillRoundRect** (int x, int y, int width, int height, int arcWidth, int arcHeight)	ε587
	1	public.................... **void**	**finalize** ()	
1.1	O	public abstract .... *Shape*	**getClip** ()	
1.1	O	public abstract ...... Rectangle	**getClipBounds** ()	
1.2		public............... Rectangle	**getClipBounds** (Rectangle r)	
D		public............... Rectangle	**getClipRect** ()	
	O	public abstract ..... Color	**getColor** ()	
	O	public abstract .... Font	**getFont** ()	
		public............. FontMetrics	**getFontMetrics** ()	ε591
	O	public abstract .... FontMetrics	**getFontMetrics** (Font f)	
*		protected .... **Graphics** ()		
1.2		public................. boolean	**hitClip** (int x, int y, int width, int height)	
1.1	O	public abstract ....void	**setClip** (*Shape* clip)	ε578
1.1	O	public abstract ....void	**setClip** (int x, int y, int width, int height)	
	O	public abstract ....void	**setColor** (Color c)	ε602,878,879,881,929
	O	public abstract ....void	**setFont** (Font font)	ε591
	O	public abstract ....void	**setPaintMode** ()	
	O	public abstract ....void	**setXORMode** (Color c1)	
	1	public................. **String**	**toString** ()	
	O	public abstract ....void	**translate** (int x, int y)	

Graphics2D

		java.awt

		Object ε575,576,577,578,579
	O	└Graphics [1]
1.2	O	└Graphics2D

	1	*29 inherited members from Graphics not shown*		
	O	public abstract ....void	**addRenderingHints** (*java.util*.Map hints)	
	O	public abstract ....void	**clip** (*Shape* s)	
	O 1	public abstract ....void	dispose ()	ε669,674,680,695,602
	O	public abstract ....void	**draw** (*Shape* s)	ε589
	1	public.................... **void**	**draw3DRect** (int x, int y, int width, int height, boolean raised)	
	O 1	public abstract ....void	drawArc (int x, int y, int width, int height, int startAngle, int arcAngle)	ε586
	O	public abstract ....void	**drawGlyphVector** (java.awt.font.GlyphVector g, float x, float y)	
	O	public abstract .... boolean	**drawImage** (Image img, java.awt.geom.AffineTransform xform, *java.awt.image.ImageObserver* obs)	ε596
	O 1	public abstract .... boolean	drawImage (Image img, int x, int y, *java.awt.image.ImageObserver* observer)	ε578,667,674,680,581
	O	public abstract ....void	**drawImage** (java.awt.image.BufferedImage img, java.awt.image.BufferedImageOp op, int x, int y)	

Class *Interface* —extends - - -implements O abstract ● final △ static ▲ static final ✳ constructor x x—inherited x **x**—declared **x x**—overridden
εn—examples of usage ˳—has subclass package—see other volume

O	1	public abstract............void	drawLine (int x1, int y1, int x2, int y2)		ε586
O	1	public abstract............void	drawOval (int x, int y, int width, int height)		ε586,575
	1	public......................void	drawPolygon (Polygon p)		ε586
	1	public......................void	drawRect (int x, int y, int width, int height)		ε586
O		public abstract............void	**drawRenderableImage** (*java.awt.image.renderable.RenderableImage* img, java.awt.geom.AffineTransform xform)		
O		public abstract............void	**drawRenderedImage** (*java.awt.image.RenderedImage* img, java.awt.geom.AffineTransform xform)		
O	1	public abstract............void	drawRoundRect (int x, int y, int width, int height, int arcWidth, int arcHeight)		ε586
O	1	public abstract............ **void**	**drawString** (String str, int x, int y)		ε591
O		public abstract............void	**drawString** (String s, float x, float y)		ε592
O	1	public abstract............ **void**	**drawString** (*java.text.AttributedCharacterIterator* iterator, int x, int y)		
O		public abstract............void	**drawString** (*java.text.AttributedCharacterIterator* iterator, float x, float y)		
O		public abstract............void	**fill** (*Shape* s)		ε589,669
	1	public...................... **void**	**fill3DRect** (int x, int y, int width, int height, boolean raised)		
O	1	public abstract............void	fillArc (int x, int y, int width, int height, int startAngle, int arcAngle)		ε587,590
O	1	public abstract............void	fillOval (int x, int y, int width, int height)		ε587,695
	1	public......................void	fillPolygon (Polygon p)		ε587
O	1	public abstract............void	fillRect (int x, int y, int width, int height)		ε587,695,602,878,879
O	1	public abstract............void	fillRoundRect (int x, int y, int width, int height, int arcWidth, int arcHeight)		ε587
O		public abstract.......... Color	**getBackground** ()		
O		public abstract..... *Composite*	**getComposite** ()		
O		public abstract................ GraphicsConfiguration	**getDeviceConfiguration** ()		ε666,674
	1	public.............. FontMetrics	getFontMetrics ()		ε593,591
O		public abstract.......java.awt.font.FontRenderContext	**getFontRenderContext** ()		ε653,654,655
O		public abstract............ *Paint*	**getPaint** ()		
O		public abstract.......... Object	**getRenderingHint** (RenderingHints.Key hintKey)		
O		public abstract RenderingHints	**getRenderingHints** ()		ε577
O		public abstract.......... *Stroke*	**getStroke** ()		
O		public abstract.......... java.awt.geom.AffineTransform	**getTransform** ()		
*		protected......................	**Graphics2D** ()		
O		public abstract........ boolean	**hit** (Rectangle rect, *Shape* s, boolean onStroke)		
O		public abstract............void	**rotate** (double theta)		
O		public abstract............void	**rotate** (double theta, double x, double y)		
O		public abstract............void	**scale** (double sx, double sy)		
O		public abstract............void	**setBackground** (Color color)		
O	1	public abstract............void	setClip (*Shape* clip)		ε578
O	1	public abstract............void	setColor (Color c)		ε582,589,590,669,695
O		public abstract............void	**setComposite** (*Composite* comp)		ε576,669
O		public abstract............void	**setPaint** (*Paint* paint)		ε580,583
O		public abstract............void	**setRenderingHint** (RenderingHints.Key hintKey, Object hintValue)		ε577
O		public abstract............void	**setRenderingHints** (*java.util.Map* hints)		
O		public abstract............void	**setStroke** (*Stroke* s)		ε579
O		public abstract............void	**setTransform** (java.awt.geom.AffineTransform Tx)		ε592
O		public abstract............void	**shear** (double shx, double shy)		
O		public abstract............void	**transform** (java.awt.geom.AffineTransform Tx)		
O		public abstract............void	**translate** (double tx, double ty)		ε681
O	1	public abstract............ **void**	**translate** (int x, int y)		

G

Classes

	GraphicsConfigTemplate		java.awt

1.2 O	Object └GraphicsConfigTemplate ----------------- *java.io.Serializable*	
O	public abstract................ GraphicsConfiguration	**getBestConfiguration** (GraphicsConfiguration[] gc)
*	public......................	**GraphicsConfigTemplate** ()
O	public abstract........ boolean	**isGraphicsConfigSupported** (GraphicsConfiguration gc)
▲	public static final.............int	**PREFERRED** = 2
▲	public static final.............int	**REQUIRED** = 1
▲	public static final.............int	**UNNECESSARY** = 3

GraphicsConfiguration

Object
└GraphicsConfiguration

1.2 ○	Object └GraphicsConfiguration	
○	public abstract .... java .awt.image.BufferedImage	**createCompatibleImage** (int width, int height)
○	public abstract .... java .awt.image.BufferedImage	**createCompatibleImage** (int width, int height, int transparency) ε666,667
1.4 ○	public abstract .... java .awt.image.VolatileImage	**createCompatibleVolatileImage** (int width, int height) ε673,674
1.4	public .... java .awt.image.VolatileImage	**createCompatibleVolatileImage** (int width, int height, ImageCapabilities caps) throws AWTException
1.3 ○	public abstract ...... Rectangle	**getBounds** ()
1.4	public ....BufferCapabilities	**getBufferCapabilities** () ε602
○	public abstract .... java.awt.image.ColorModel	**getColorModel** ()
○	public abstract .... java.awt.image.ColorModel	**getColorModel** (int transparency)
○	public abstract .... java .awt.geom.AffineTransform	**getDefaultTransform** ()
○	public abstract .... GraphicsDevice	**getDevice** ()
1.4	public ...... ImageCapabilities	**getImageCapabilities** ()
○	public abstract .... java .awt.geom.AffineTransform	**getNormalizingTransform** ()
✳	protected	**GraphicsConfiguration** ()

1.2 ○	Object └GraphicsDevice	
1.4	public ....int	**getAvailableAcceleratedMemory** () ε673
	public .. GraphicsConfiguration	**getBestConfiguration** (GraphicsConfigTemplate gct)
○	public abstract .... GraphicsConfiguration[]	**getConfigurations** ()
○	public abstract .... GraphicsConfiguration	**getDefaultConfiguration** () ε601,602,666,667,673
1.4	public ....DisplayMode	**getDisplayMode** () ε598,604,605
1.4	public ....DisplayMode[]	**getDisplayModes** () ε603
1.4	public .... Window	**getFullScreenWindow** () ε605
○	public abstract ....String	**getIDstring** ()
○	public abstract ....int	**getType** ()
✳	protected	**GraphicsDevice** ()
1.4	public .... boolean	**isDisplayChangeSupported** () ε605
1.4	public .... boolean	**isFullScreenSupported** () ε601
1.4	public ....void	**setDisplayMode** (DisplayMode dm) ε605
1.4	public ....void	**setFullScreenWindow** (Window w) ε601,602,605
▲	public static final ....int	**TYPE_IMAGE_BUFFER** = 2
▲	public static final ....int	**TYPE_PRINTER** = 1
▲	public static final ....int	**TYPE_RASTER_SCREEN** = 0

1.2 ○	Object └GraphicsEnvironment	
○	public abstract Graphics2D	**createGraphics** (java.awt.image.BufferedImage img)
○	public abstract ....Font[]	**getAllFonts** () ε652
○	public abstract .... String[]	**getAvailableFontFamilyNames** () ε651
○	public abstract .... String[]	**getAvailableFontFamilyNames** (java.util.Locale l)
1.4	public ....Point	**getCenterPoint** () throws HeadlessException
○	public abstract .... GraphicsDevice	**getDefaultScreenDevice** () throws HeadlessException ε601,602,603,605,666
△	public static synchronized .... GraphicsEnvironment	**getLocalGraphicsEnvironment** () ε598,600,601,602,603
1.4	public .... Rectangle	**getMaximumWindowBounds** () throws HeadlessException

Class   *Interface*   —extends   - - -implements   ○ abstract   ● final   △ static   ▲ static final   ✳ constructor   x x—inherited   x **x**—declared   **x x**—overridden
ε*n*—examples of usage   ⌐—has subclass   package—see other volume

o	public abstract . . . . GraphicsDevice[]	**getScreenDevices** () throws HeadlessException	ε598,600,604,673
*	protected	**GraphicsEnvironment** ()	
1.4 △	public static . . . . boolean	**isHeadless** ()	
1.4	public . . . . boolean	**isHeadlessInstance** ()	

GrayFilter javax.swing

Object   ε665
  └java.awt.image.ImageFilter[1] - - - - - - - - - - - - - - *java.awt.image.ImageConsumer* [3], *Cloneable*˅
     └java.awt.image.RGBImageFilter[2]
1.2   └GrayFilter

G

3	*9 inherited members from java.awt.image.ImageConsumer not shown*		
2	protected . . . . boolean	canFilterIndexColorModel	
1	public . . . . Object	clone ()	
1	protected . . . . *java.awt*₂ *.image.ImageConsumer*	consumer	
△	public static . . . java.awt.Image	**createDisabledImage** (java.awt.Image i)	ε597
2	public . . . . java.awt₂ *.image.IndexColorModel*	filterIndexColorModel (java.awt.image.IndexColorModel icm)	
2	public . . . . **int**	**filterRGB** (int x, int y, int rgb)	ε665
2	public . . . . void	filterRGBPixels (int x, int y, int w, int h, int[] pixels, int off, int scansize)	
1	public . . . . java.awt.image.ImageFilter	getFilterInstance (*java.awt.image.ImageConsumer* ic)	
*	public	**GrayFilter** (boolean b, int p)	
1	public . . . . void	imageComplete (int status)	
2	protected . . . . java.awt.image.ColorModel	newmodel	
2	protected . . . . java.awt.image.ColorModel	origmodel	
1	public . . . . void	resendTopDownLeftRight (*java.awt.image.ImageProducer* ip)	
2	public . . . . void	setColorModel (java.awt.image.ColorModel model)	
1	public . . . . void	setDimensions (int width, int height)	
1	public . . . . void	setHints (int hints)	
2	public . . . . void	setPixels (int x, int y, int w, int h, java.awt.image.ColorModel model, int[] pixels, int off, int scansize)	
2	public . . . . void	setPixels (int x, int y, int w, int h, java.awt.image.ColorModel model, byte[] pixels, int off, int scansize)	
1	public . . . . void	setProperties (java.util.Hashtable props)	
2	public . . . . void	substituteColorModel (java.awt.image.ColorModel oldcm, java.awt.image.ColorModel newcm)	

GridBagConstraints java.awt

Object[1]
└GridBagConstraints - *Cloneable*˅, *java.io.Serializable*˅

Classes

	public . . . . int	**anchor**	ε629
▲	public static final . . . . int	**BOTH** = 1	ε628
▲	public static final . . . . int	**CENTER** = 10	ε629
1	public . . . . **Object**	**clone** ()	
▲	public static final . . . . int	**EAST** = 13	ε629
▲	public . . . . int	**fill**	ε628
1.4 ▲	public static final . . . . int	**FIRST_LINE_END** = 24	
1.4 ▲	public static final . . . . int	**FIRST_LINE_START** = 23	
*	public	**GridBagConstraints** ()	ε622,623,627,628,629
1.2 *	public	**GridBagConstraints** (int gridx, int gridy, int gridwidth, int gridheight, double weightx, double weighty, int anchor, int fill, Insets insets, int ipadx, int ipady)	
	public . . . . int	**gridheight**	
	public . . . . int	**gridwidth**	
	public . . . . int	**gridx**	ε622,623,627
	public . . . . int	**gridy**	ε622,623,627
▲	public static final . . . . int	**HORIZONTAL** = 2	ε628
	public . . . . Insets	**insets**	ε630
	public . . . . int	**ipadx**	ε631
	public . . . . int	**ipady**	ε631
1.4 ▲	public static final . . . . int	**LAST_LINE_END** = 26	
1.4 ▲	public static final . . . . int	**LAST_LINE_START** = 25	
1.4 ▲	public static final . . . . int	**LINE_END** = 22	
1.4 ▲	public static final . . . . int	**LINE_START** = 21	

GridBagConstraints

▲	public static final	int	**NONE** = 0	ε628
▲	public static final	int	**NORTH** = 11	ε629
▲	public static final	int	**NORTHEAST** = 12	ε629
▲	public static final	int	**NORTHWEST** = 18	ε629
1.4 ▲	public static final	int	**PAGE_END** = 20	
1.4 ▲	public static final	int	**PAGE_START** = 19	
▲	public static final	int	**RELATIVE** = -1	
▲	public static final	int	**REMAINDER** = 0	
▲	public static final	int	**SOUTH** = 15	ε629
▲	public static final	int	**SOUTHEAST** = 14	ε629
▲	public static final	int	**SOUTHWEST** = 16	ε629
▲	public static final	int	**VERTICAL** = 3	ε628
	public	double	**weightx**	ε627
	public	double	**weighty**	ε627
▲	public static final	int	**WEST** = 17	ε629

G

GridBagLayout   java.awt

Object [1]
└ GridBagLayout - *LayoutManager2* [2] (*LayoutManager* [3]), *java.io.Serializable*

1.1	[2] public	void	**addLayoutComponent** (Component comp, Object constraints)	
	[3] public	void	**addLayoutComponent** (String name, Component comp)	
	protected	void	**AdjustForGravity** (GridBagConstraints constraints, Rectangle r)	
1.4	protected	void	**adjustForGravity** (GridBagConstraints constraints, Rectangle r)	
	protected	void	**ArrangeGrid** (Container parent)	
1.4	protected	void	**arrangeGrid** (Container parent)	
	public	double[]	**columnWeights**	ε625,626
	public	int[]	**columnWidths**	ε632
	protected	java.util.Hashtable	**comptable**	
	protected	GridBagConstraints	**defaultConstraints**	
	public	GridBagConstraints	**getConstraints** (Component comp)	
1.1	[2] public	float	**getLayoutAlignmentX** (Container parent)	
1.1	[2] public	float	**getLayoutAlignmentY** (Container parent)	
	public	int[][]	**getLayoutDimensions** ()	ε624
1.4	protected	java.awt.GridBagLayoutInfo	**getLayoutInfo** (Container parent, int sizeflag)	
	protected	java.awt.GridBagLayoutInfo	**GetLayoutInfo** (Container parent, int sizeflag)	
	public	Point	**getLayoutOrigin** ()	
	public	double[][]	**getLayoutWeights** ()	ε625
1.4	protected	Dimension	**getMinSize** (Container parent, java.awt.GridBagLayoutInfo info)	
	protected	Dimension	**GetMinSize** (Container parent, java.awt.GridBagLayoutInfo info)	
✳	public		**GridBagLayout** ()	ε622,624,625,626,627
1.1	[2] public	void	**invalidateLayout** (Container target)	
	[3] public	void	**layoutContainer** (Container parent)	ε624,625
	protected	java.awt.GridBagLayoutInfo	**layoutInfo**	
	public	Point	**location** (int x, int y)	
	protected	GridBagConstraints	**lookupConstraints** (Component comp)	
▲	protected static final	int	**MAXGRIDSIZE**	
1.1	[2] public	Dimension	**maximumLayoutSize** (Container target)	
	[3] public	Dimension	**minimumLayoutSize** (Container parent)	
▲	protected static final	int	**MINSIZE**	
	[3] public	Dimension	**preferredLayoutSize** (Container parent)	
▲	protected static final	int	**PREFERREDSIZE**	
	[3] public	void	**removeLayoutComponent** (Component comp)	
	public	int[]	**rowHeights**	ε632
	public	double[]	**rowWeights**	ε625,626
	public	void	**setConstraints** (Component comp, GridBagConstraints constraints)	ε622,623,627,628
	[1] public	String	**toString** ()	

GridLayout   java.awt

Object [1]
└ GridLayout - *LayoutManager* [2], *java.io.Serializable*

Class *Interface* —extends - - -implements ○ abstract ● final △ static ▲ static final ✳ constructor x x—inherited x **x**—declared **x x**—overridden
ε*n*—examples of usage ˌ—has subclass package—see other volume

542

	2	public......................void	**addLayoutComponent** (String name, Component comp)	
1.1		public.........................int	**getColumns** ()	
1.1		public.........................int	**getHgap** ()	
1.1		public.........................int	**getRows** ()	
1.1		public.........................int	**getVgap** ()	
1.1	*	public............................	**GridLayout** ()	
	*	public............................	**GridLayout** (int rows, int cols)	ε853,883
	*	public............................	**GridLayout** (int rows, int cols, int hgap, int vgap)	
	2	public......................void	**layoutContainer** (Container parent)	ε624,625
	2	public...............Dimension	**minimumLayoutSize** (Container parent)	
	2	public...............Dimension	**preferredLayoutSize** (Container parent)	
	2	public......................void	**removeLayoutComponent** (Component comp)	
1.1		public......................void	**setColumns** (int cols)	
1.1		public......................void	**setHgap** (int hgap)	
1.1		public......................void	**setRows** (int rows)	
1.1		public......................void	**setVgap** (int vgap)	
	1	public..................**String**	**toString** ()	

HashAttributeSet — javax.print.attribute

Object[1]
└ HashAttributeSet ---------------------- AttributeSet [2], *java.io.Serializable*

1.4				
	2	public................. boolean	**add** (*Attribute* attribute)	ε710,711,712,703,715
	2	public................. boolean	**addAll** (*AttributeSet* attributes)	
	2	public......................void	**clear** ()	
	2	public................. boolean	**containsKey** (Class category)	
	2	public................. boolean	**containsValue** (*Attribute* attribute)	
	1	public................**boolean**	**equals** (Object object)	
	2	public................ *Attribute*	**get** (Class category)	
	*	public............................	**HashAttributeSet** ()	ε703
	*	protected.........................	**HashAttributeSet** (Class interfaceName)	
	*	public............................	**HashAttributeSet** (*Attribute* attribute)	
	*	public............................	**HashAttributeSet** (*Attribute[]* attributes)	
	*	public............................	**HashAttributeSet** (*AttributeSet* attributes)	
	*	protected.........................	**HashAttributeSet** (*Attribute* attribute, Class interfaceName)	
	*	protected.........................	**HashAttributeSet** (*Attribute[]* attributes, Class interfaceName)	
	*	protected.........................	**HashAttributeSet** (*AttributeSet* attributes, Class interfaceName)	
	1	public......................**int**	**hashCode** ()	
	2	public................. boolean	**isEmpty** ()	
	2	public................. boolean	**remove** (Class category)	
	2	public................. boolean	**remove** (*Attribute* attribute)	
	2	public......................int	**size** ()	
	2	public............... *Attribute[]*	**toArray** ()	ε706

HashDocAttributeSet — javax.print.attribute

Object
└ HashAttributeSet[1] ---------------------- AttributeSet , *java.io.Serializable*
   └ HashDocAttributeSet ------------------ DocAttributeSet (AttributeSet)

1.4				
1.4				
	1	public................. boolean	add (*Attribute* attribute)	ε710,711,712,703,715
	1	public................. boolean	addAll (*AttributeSet* attributes)	
	1	public......................void	clear ()	
	1	public................. boolean	containsKey (Class category)	
	1	public................. boolean	containsValue (*Attribute* attribute)	
	1	public................. boolean	equals (Object object)	
	1	public................ *Attribute*	get (Class category)	
	1	public......................int	hashCode ()	
	*	public............................	**HashDocAttributeSet** ()	
	*	public............................	**HashDocAttributeSet** (*DocAttribute* attribute)	
	*	public............................	**HashDocAttributeSet** (*DocAttribute[]* attributes)	
	*	public............................	**HashDocAttributeSet** (*DocAttributeSet* attributes)	
	1	public................. boolean	isEmpty ()	
	1	public................. boolean	remove (Class category)	
	1	public................. boolean	remove (*Attribute* attribute)	
	1	public......................int	size ()	
	1	public............... *Attribute[]*	toArray ()	ε706

H

Classes

HashPrintJobAttributeSet

			javax.print.attribute

Object
1.4 └HashAttributeSet [1] - AttributeSet ˌ, java.io.Serializable ˌ
1.4   └HashPrintJobAttributeSet - - - - - - - - - - - - - - PrintJobAttributeSet (AttributeSet)

	1	public	boolean	add (Attribute attribute)	ε710,711,712,703,715
	1	public	boolean	addAll (AttributeSet attributes)	
	1	public	void	clear ()	
	1	public	boolean	containsKey (Class category)	
	1	public	boolean	containsValue (Attribute attribute)	
	1	public	boolean	equals (Object object)	
	1	public	Attribute	get (Class category)	
	1	public	int	hashCode ()	
*		public		**HashPrintJobAttributeSet** ()	
*		public		**HashPrintJobAttributeSet** (PrintJobAttribute attribute)	
*		public		**HashPrintJobAttributeSet** (PrintJobAttribute[] attributes)	
*		public		**HashPrintJobAttributeSet** (PrintJobAttributeSet attributes)	ε715
	1	public	boolean	isEmpty ()	
	1	public	boolean	remove (Class category)	
	1	public	boolean	remove (Attribute attribute)	
	1	public	int	size ()	
	1	public	Attribute[]	toArray ()	ε706

HashPrintRequestAttributeSet

			javax.print.attribute

Object
1.4 └HashAttributeSet [1] - AttributeSet ˌ, java.io.Serializable ˌ
1.4   └HashPrintRequestAttributeSet - - - - - - - - - - - PrintRequestAttributeSet (AttributeSet)

	1	public	boolean	add (Attribute attribute)	ε710,711,712,703,715
	1	public	boolean	addAll (AttributeSet attributes)	
	1	public	void	clear ()	
	1	public	boolean	containsKey (Class category)	
	1	public	boolean	containsValue (Attribute attribute)	
	1	public	boolean	equals (Object object)	
	1	public	Attribute	get (Class category)	
	1	public	int	hashCode ()	
*		public		**HashPrintRequestAttributeSet** ()	ε710,711,712
*		public		**HashPrintRequestAttributeSet** (PrintRequestAttribute attribute)	
*		public		**HashPrintRequestAttributeSet** (PrintRequestAttribute[] attributes)	
*		public		**HashPrintRequestAttributeSet** (PrintRequestAttributeSet attributes)	
	1	public	boolean	isEmpty ()	
	1	public	boolean	remove (Class category)	
	1	public	boolean	remove (Attribute attribute)	
	1	public	int	size ()	
	1	public	Attribute[]	toArray ()	ε706

HashPrintServiceAttributeSet

			javax.print.attribute

Object
1.4 └HashAttributeSet [1] - AttributeSet ˌ, java.io.Serializable ˌ
1.4   └HashPrintServiceAttributeSet - - - - - - - - - - - PrintServiceAttributeSet (AttributeSet)

	1	public	boolean	add (Attribute attribute)	ε710,711,712,703,715
	1	public	boolean	addAll (AttributeSet attributes)	
	1	public	void	clear ()	
	1	public	boolean	containsKey (Class category)	
	1	public	boolean	containsValue (Attribute attribute)	
	1	public	boolean	equals (Object object)	
	1	public	Attribute	get (Class category)	
	1	public	int	hashCode ()	
*		public		**HashPrintServiceAttributeSet** ()	
*		public		**HashPrintServiceAttributeSet** (PrintServiceAttribute attribute)	
*		public		**HashPrintServiceAttributeSet** (PrintServiceAttribute[] attributes)	
*		public		**HashPrintServiceAttributeSet** (PrintServiceAttributeSet attributes)	
	1	public	boolean	isEmpty ()	
	1	public	boolean	remove (Class category)	

```
 1   public................. boolean remove (Attribute attribute)
 1   public........................int size ()
 1   public.............. Attribute[] toArray ()                                    ε706
```

HeadlessException	java.awt

ε600,667,673,905

```
     Object
     └ Throwable - - - - - - - - - - - - - - - - - - - - - - - - - java.io.Serializable
         └ Exception
             └ RuntimeException
1.2              └ UnsupportedOperationException
1.4                  └ HeadlessException
```

```
 *   public......................... HeadlessException ()
 *   public......................... HeadlessException (String msg)
```

HierarchyBoundsAdapter	java.awt.event

```
     Object
1.3 ○ └ HierarchyBoundsAdapter - - - - - - - - - - - - - - - - HierarchyBoundsListener 1 (java.util.EventListener)
```

```
 1   public......................void ancestorMoved (HierarchyEvent e)
 1   public......................void ancestorResized (HierarchyEvent e)
 *   public......................... HierarchyBoundsAdapter ()
```

HierarchyBoundsListener	java.awt.event

ε738,743,745,746,752

```
1.3   HierarchyBoundsListener————————————— java.util.EventListener
```

```
     public......................void ancestorMoved (HierarchyEvent e)
     public......................void ancestorResized (HierarchyEvent e)
```

HierarchyEvent	java.awt.event

ε640,641,643,649,566

```
     Object
1.1  └ java.util.EventObject 1 - - - - - - - - - - - - - - - - - - java.io.Serializable
1.1 ○    └ java.awt.AWTEvent 2
1.3          └ HierarchyEvent
```

```
 2   27 inherited members from java.awt.AWTEvent not shown
 ▲   public static final.............int ANCESTOR_MOVED = 1401
 ▲   public static final.............int ANCESTOR_RESIZED = 1402
 ▲   public static final.............int DISPLAYABILITY_CHANGED = 2
     public.... java.awt.Component getChanged ()
     public........java.awt.Container getChangedParent ()
     public.................. long getChangeFlags ()
     public.... java.awt.Component getComponent ()
 1   public....................Object getSource ()                      ε644,886,565,568,570
 ▲   public static final.............int HIERARCHY_CHANGED = 1400
 ▲   public static final.............int HIERARCHY_FIRST = 1400
 ▲   public static final.............int HIERARCHY_LAST = 1402
 *   public......................... HierarchyEvent (java.awt.Component source, int id, java.awt.Component changed,
                                        java.awt.Container changedParent)
 *   public......................... HierarchyEvent (java.awt.Component source, int id, java.awt.Component changed,
                                        java.awt.Container changedParent, long changeFlags)
 2   public.................. String paramString ()
 ▲   public static final.............int PARENT_CHANGED = 1
 ▲   public static final.............int SHOWING_CHANGED = 4
 1   protected transient...... Object source
```

HierarchyListener	java.awt.event

ε738,743,745,746,752

```
1.3   HierarchyListener————————————————— java.util.EventListener
```

```
     public......................void hierarchyChanged (HierarchyEvent e)
```

Highlighter

			javax.swing.text

1.2   *Highlighter*

public....................Object	**addHighlight** (int p0, int p1, *Highlighter.HighlightPainter* p)	
	throws BadLocationException	ε1006
public.......................void	**changeHighlight** (Object tag, int p0, int p1) throws BadLocationException	
public.......................void	**deinstall** (JTextComponent c)	
public... *Highlighter.Highlight[]*	**getHighlights** ()	ε1006
public.......................void	**install** (JTextComponent c)	
public.......................void	**paint** (java.awt.Graphics g)	
public.......................void	**removeAllHighlights** ()	
public.......................void	**removeHighlight** (Object tag)	ε1006

Highlighter.Highlight

		javax.swing.text

1.2   *Highlighter.Highlight*

public...........................int	**getEndOffset** ()	
public...........................	**getPainter** ()	ε1006
.. *Highlighter.HighlightPainter*		
public...........................int	**getStartOffset** ()	

Highlighter.HighlightPainter

		javax.swing.text

1.2   *Highlighter.HighlightPainter*   ε1006

public.......................void	**paint** (java.awt.Graphics g, int p0, int p1, *java.awt.Shape* bounds,	
	JTextComponent c)	

HTML

		javax.swing.text.html

     Object
1.2   └HTML

△	public static .. HTML.Attribute[]	**getAllAttributeKeys** ()
△	public static .... HTML.Tag[]	**getAllTags** ()
△	public static ....HTML.Attribute	**getAttributeKey** (String attName)
△	public static ....int	**getIntegerAttributeValue** (*javax.swing.text.AttributeSet* attr, HTML.Attribute key,
		int def)
△	public static .... HTML.Tag	**getTag** (String tagName)
✳	public...........................	**HTML** ()
▲	public static final ....String	**NULL_ATTRIBUTE_VALUE** = "#DEFAULT"

HTML.Attribute

		javax.swing.text.html

     Object[1]
1.2 ●   └HTML.Attribute

▲	public static final ....HTML.Attribute	**ACTION**
▲	public static final ....HTML.Attribute	**ALIGN**
▲	public static final ....HTML.Attribute	**ALINK**
▲	public static final ....HTML.Attribute	**ALT**
▲	public static final ....HTML.Attribute	**ARCHIVE**
▲	public static final ....HTML.Attribute	**BACKGROUND**
▲	public static final ....HTML.Attribute	**BGCOLOR**
▲	public static final ....HTML.Attribute	**BORDER**
▲	public static final ....HTML.Attribute	**CELLPADDING**
▲	public static final ....HTML.Attribute	**CELLSPACING**
▲	public static final ....HTML.Attribute	**CHECKED**
▲	public static final ....HTML.Attribute	**CLASS**
▲	public static final ....HTML.Attribute	**CLASSID**
▲	public static final ....HTML.Attribute	**CLEAR**
▲	public static final ....HTML.Attribute	**CODE**
▲	public static final ....HTML.Attribute	**CODEBASE**
▲	public static final ....HTML.Attribute	**CODETYPE**
▲	public static final ....HTML.Attribute	**COLOR**
▲	public static final ....HTML.Attribute	**COLS**

Class   *Interface*   —extends   - - -implements   ○ abstract   ● final   △ static   ▲ static final   ✳ constructor   x x—inherited   x **x**—declared   **x x**—overridden
εn—examples of usage   ⌐—has subclass   package—see other volume

▲	public static final .HTML.Attribute	**COLSPAN**
▲	public static final .HTML.Attribute	**COMMENT**
▲	public static final .HTML.Attribute	**COMPACT**
▲	public static final .HTML.Attribute	**CONTENT**
▲	public static final .HTML.Attribute	**COORDS**
▲	public static final .HTML.Attribute	**DATA**
▲	public static final .HTML.Attribute	**DECLARE**
▲	public static final .HTML.Attribute	**DIR**
▲	public static final .HTML.Attribute	**DUMMY**
▲	public static final .HTML.Attribute	**ENCTYPE**
▲	public static final .HTML.Attribute	**ENDTAG**
▲	public static final .HTML.Attribute	**FACE**
▲	public static final .HTML.Attribute	**FRAMEBORDER**
▲	public static final .HTML.Attribute	**HALIGN**
▲	public static final .HTML.Attribute	**HEIGHT**
▲	public static final .HTML.Attribute	**HREF**
▲	public static final .HTML.Attribute	**HSPACE**
▲	public static final .HTML.Attribute	**HTTPEQUIV**
▲	public static final .HTML.Attribute	**ID**
▲	public static final .HTML.Attribute	**ISMAP**
▲	public static final .HTML.Attribute	**LANG**
▲	public static final .HTML.Attribute	**LANGUAGE**
▲	public static final .HTML.Attribute	**LINK**
▲	public static final .HTML.Attribute	**LOWSRC**
▲	public static final .HTML.Attribute	**MARGINHEIGHT**
▲	public static final .HTML.Attribute	**MARGINWIDTH**
▲	public static final .HTML.Attribute	**MAXLENGTH**
▲	public static final .HTML.Attribute	**METHOD**
▲	public static final .HTML.Attribute	**MULTIPLE**
▲	public static final .HTML.Attribute	**N**
▲	public static final .HTML.Attribute	**NAME**
▲	public static final .HTML.Attribute	**NOHREF**
▲	public static final .HTML.Attribute	**NORESIZE**
▲	public static final .HTML.Attribute	**NOSHADE**
▲	public static final .HTML.Attribute	**NOWRAP**
▲	public static final .HTML.Attribute	**PROMPT**
▲	public static final .HTML.Attribute	**REL**
▲	public static final .HTML.Attribute	**REV**
▲	public static final .HTML.Attribute	**ROWS**
▲	public static final .HTML.Attribute	**ROWSPAN**
▲	public static final .HTML.Attribute	**SCROLLING**
▲	public static final .HTML.Attribute	**SELECTED**
▲	public static final .HTML.Attribute	**SHAPE**
▲	public static final .HTML.Attribute	**SHAPES**
▲	public static final .HTML.Attribute	**SIZE**
▲	public static final .HTML.Attribute	**SRC**
▲	public static final .HTML.Attribute	**STANDBY**
▲	public static final .HTML.Attribute	**START**
▲	public static final .HTML.Attribute	**STYLE**
▲	public static final .HTML.Attribute	**TARGET**
▲	public static final .HTML.Attribute	**TEXT**
▲	public static final .HTML.Attribute	**TITLE**
1	public. . . . . **String**	**toString** ()
▲	public static final .HTML.Attribute	**TYPE**
▲	public static final .HTML.Attribute	**USEMAP**
▲	public static final .HTML.Attribute	**VALIGN**
▲	public static final .HTML.Attribute	**VALUE**
▲	public static final .HTML.Attribute	**VALUETYPE**
▲	public static final .HTML.Attribute	**VERSION**
▲	public static final .HTML.Attribute	**VLINK**
▲	public static final .HTML.Attribute	**VSPACE**
▲	public static final .HTML.Attribute	**WIDTH**

ε1017

H

Classes

HTML.Tag		javax.swing.text.html

Object[1]
1.2 └HTML.Tag

▲	public static final . . . . HTML.Tag	**A**	ε1017
▲	public static final . . . . HTML.Tag	**ADDRESS**	
▲	public static final . . . . HTML.Tag	**APPLET**	
▲	public static final . . . . HTML.Tag	**AREA**	
▲	public static final . . . . HTML.Tag	**B**	

HTML.Tag

▲	public static final	HTML.Tag	**BASE**
▲	public static final	HTML.Tag	**BASEFONT**
▲	public static final	HTML.Tag	**BIG**
▲	public static final	HTML.Tag	**BLOCKQUOTE**
▲	public static final	HTML.Tag	**BODY**
▲	public static final	HTML.Tag	**BR**
	public	boolean	**breaksFlow** ()
▲	public static final	HTML.Tag	**CAPTION**
▲	public static final	HTML.Tag	**CENTER**
▲	public static final	HTML.Tag	**CITE**
▲	public static final	HTML.Tag	**CODE**
▲	public static final	HTML.Tag	**COMMENT**
▲	public static final	HTML.Tag	**CONTENT**
▲	public static final	HTML.Tag	**DD**
▲	public static final	HTML.Tag	**DFN**
▲	public static final	HTML.Tag	**DIR**
▲	public static final	HTML.Tag	**DIV**
▲	public static final	HTML.Tag	**DL**
▲	public static final	HTML.Tag	**DT**
▲	public static final	HTML.Tag	**EM**
▲	public static final	HTML.Tag	**FONT**
▲	public static final	HTML.Tag	**FORM**
▲	public static final	HTML.Tag	**FRAME**
▲	public static final	HTML.Tag	**FRAMESET**
▲	public static final	HTML.Tag	**H1**
▲	public static final	HTML.Tag	**H2**
▲	public static final	HTML.Tag	**H3**
▲	public static final	HTML.Tag	**H4**
▲	public static final	HTML.Tag	**H5**
▲	public static final	HTML.Tag	**H6**
▲	public static final	HTML.Tag	**HEAD**
▲	public static final	HTML.Tag	**HR**
▲	public static final	HTML.Tag	**HTML**
▲	public static final	HTML.Tag	**I**
▲	public static final	HTML.Tag	**IMG**
▲	public static final	HTML.Tag	**IMPLIED**
▲	public static final	HTML.Tag	**INPUT**
	public	boolean	**isBlock** ()
▲	public static final	HTML.Tag	**ISINDEX**
	public	boolean	**isPreformatted** ()
▲	public static final	HTML.Tag	**KBD**
▲	public static final	HTML.Tag	**LI**
▲	public static final	HTML.Tag	**LINK**
▲	public static final	HTML.Tag	**MAP**
▲	public static final	HTML.Tag	**MENU**
▲	public static final	HTML.Tag	**META**
▲	public static final	HTML.Tag	**NOFRAMES**
▲	public static final	HTML.Tag	**OBJECT**
▲	public static final	HTML.Tag	**OL**
▲	public static final	HTML.Tag	**OPTION**
▲	public static final	HTML.Tag	**P**
▲	public static final	HTML.Tag	**PARAM**
▲	public static final	HTML.Tag	**PRE**
▲	public static final	HTML.Tag	**S**
▲	public static final	HTML.Tag	**SAMP**
▲	public static final	HTML.Tag	**SCRIPT**
▲	public static final	HTML.Tag	**SELECT**
▲	public static final	HTML.Tag	**SMALL**
1.3 ▲	public static final	HTML.Tag	**SPAN**
▲	public static final	HTML.Tag	**STRIKE**
▲	public static final	HTML.Tag	**STRONG**
▲	public static final	HTML.Tag	**STYLE**
▲	public static final	HTML.Tag	**SUB**
▲	public static final	HTML.Tag	**SUP**
▲	public static final	HTML.Tag	**TABLE**
1.3 ✳	public		**HTML.Tag** ()
✳	protected		**HTML.Tag** (String id)
✳	protected		**HTML.Tag** (String id, boolean causesBreak, boolean isBlock)
▲	public static final	HTML.Tag	**TD**
▲	public static final	HTML.Tag	**TEXTAREA**
▲	public static final	HTML.Tag	**TH**

Class   *Interface*   —extends   - - -implements   ○ abstract   ● final   △ static   ▲ static final   ✳ constructor   x x—inherited   x **x**—declared   **x x**—overridden
εn—examples of usage   ˌ—has subclass   package—see other volume

▲		public static final .... HTML.Tag	**TITLE**
	1	public.................... **String toString** ()	
▲		public static final .... HTML.Tag	**TR**
▲		public static final .... HTML.Tag	**TT**
▲		public static final .... HTML.Tag	**U**
▲		public static final .... HTML.Tag	**UL**
▲		public static final .... HTML.Tag	**VAR**

HTML.UnknownTag
javax.swing.text.html

Object[1]
1.2　└HTML.Tag[2]
1.2　　└HTML.UnknownTag - - - - - - - - - - - - - - - - - - - *java.io.Serializable*

	2	*80 inherited members from HTML.Tag not shown*	
	1	public................. **boolean equals** (Object obj)	
	1	public..................... **int hashCode** ()	
✳		public.......................... **HTML.UnknownTag** (String id)	

HTMLDocument
javax.swing.text.html

Object
1.2 ○　└javax.swing.text.AbstractDocument[1] - - - - - - - *javax.swing.text.Document*, *java.io.Serializable*
1.2　　　└javax.swing.text.DefaultStyledDocument[2] - - *javax.swing.text.StyledDocument* (*javax.swing.text.Document*[3])
1.2　　　　└HTMLDocument

	1	*43 inherited members from javax.swing.text.AbstractDocument not shown*		
	2	public......................void addDocumentListener (*javax.swing.event.DocumentListener* listener)		ε1016
▲		public static final .... String **AdditionalComments** = "AdditionalComments"		
	2	public....*javax.swing.text.Style* addStyle (String nm, *javax.swing.text.Style* parent)		ε989,991,992
	2	protected .... javax.swing.text buffer .DefaultStyledDocument .ElementBuffer		
▲	2	public static final ....int BUFFER_SIZE_DEFAULT = 4096		
	2	protected .... **void create** (javax.swing.text.DefaultStyledDocument.ElementSpec[] data)		
	1	protected .... **createBranchElement** (*javax.swing.text.Element* parent, ... *javax.swing.text.Element* *javax.swing.text.AttributeSet* a)		
	2	protected .... javax.swing **createDefaultRoot** () .text.AbstractDocument .AbstractElement		
	1	protected .... **createLeafElement** (*javax.swing.text.Element* parent, ... *javax.swing.text.Element* *javax.swing.text.AttributeSet* a, int p0, int p1)		
	1	protected .... **void fireChangedUpdate** (*javax.swing.event.DocumentEvent* e)		
	1	protected .... **void fireUndoableEditUpdate** (javax.swing.event.UndoableEditEvent e)		
	2	public...........java.awt.Color getBackground (*javax.swing.text.AttributeSet* attr)		
		public............. java.net.URL **getBase** ()		
	2	public................... getCharacterElement (int pos) ..... *javax.swing.text.Element*		
	2	public................... getDefaultRootElement () ..... *javax.swing.text.Element*		ε984,990,1013
1.3		public.......................... **getElement** (String id) ..... *javax.swing.text.Element*		
1.3		public.......................... **getElement** (*javax.swing.text.Element* e, Object attribute, Object value) ..... *javax.swing.text.Element*		
	2	public...........java.awt.Font getFont (*javax.swing.text.AttributeSet* attr)		
	2	public...........java.awt.Color getForeground (*javax.swing.text.AttributeSet* attr)		
		public.HTMLDocument.Iterator **getIterator** (HTML.Tag t)		ε1017
	2	public....*javax.swing.text.Style* getLogicalStyle (int p)		
	2	public.......................... getParagraphElement (int pos) ..... *javax.swing.text.Element*		
1.3		public... HTMLEditorKit.Parser **getParser** ()		
		public................. boolean **getPreservesUnknownTags** ()		ε1018
		public......... HTMLEditorKit **getReader** (int pos) .ParserCallback		
		public......... HTMLEditorKit **getReader** (int pos, int popDepth, int pushDepth, HTML.Tag insertTag) .ParserCallback		
	2	public....*javax.swing.text.Style* getStyle (String nm)		ε1007,1008,1009,1011,1013
	2	public....*java.util.Enumeration* getStyleNames ()		ε1009,1011
		public.................StyleSheet **getStyleSheet** ()		
		public..........................int **getTokenThreshold** ()		

H

Classes

HTMLDocument

✳		public		**HTMLDocument** ()	ε1018
✳		public		**HTMLDocument** (StyleSheet styles)	
✳		public		**HTMLDocument** (*javax.swing.text.AbstractDocument.Content* c, StyleSheet styles)	
	2	protected	**void**	**insert** (int offset, javax.swing.text.DefaultStyledDocument.ElementSpec[] data)	
				throws javax.swing.text.BadLocationException	
1.3		public	void	**insertAfterEnd** (*javax.swing.text.Element* elem, String htmlText)	
				throws javax.swing.text.BadLocationException, java.io.IOException	
1.3		public	void	**insertAfterStart** (*javax.swing.text.Element* elem, String htmlText)	
				throws javax.swing.text.BadLocationException, java.io.IOException	
1.3		public	void	**insertBeforeEnd** (*javax.swing.text.Element* elem, String htmlText)	
				throws javax.swing.text.BadLocationException, java.io.IOException	
1.3		public	void	**insertBeforeStart** (*javax.swing.text.Element* elem, String htmlText)	
				throws javax.swing.text.BadLocationException, java.io.IOException	
	2	protected	**void**	**insertUpdate** (javax.swing.text.AbstractDocument.DefaultDocumentEvent chng, *javax.swing.text.AttributeSet* attr)	
		public	void	**processHTMLFrameHyperlinkEvent** (HTMLFrameHyperlinkEvent e)	
	2	public	void	removeDocumentListener (*javax.swing.event.DocumentListener* listener)	
	2	public	void	removeStyle (String nm)	
	2	protected	void	removeUpdate (javax.swing.text.AbstractDocument.DefaultDocumentEvent chng)	
		public	void	**setBase** (java.net.URL u)	
	2	public	void	setCharacterAttributes (int offset, int length, *javax.swing.text.AttributeSet* s, boolean replace)	ε1007,1013
1.3		public	void	**setInnerHTML** (*javax.swing.text.Element* elem, String htmlText)	
				throws javax.swing.text.BadLocationException, java.io.IOException	
	2	public	void	setLogicalStyle (int pos, *javax.swing.text.Style* s)	
1.3		public	void	**setOuterHTML** (*javax.swing.text.Element* elem, String htmlText)	
				throws javax.swing.text.BadLocationException, java.io.IOException	
	2	public	**void**	**setParagraphAttributes** (int offset, int length, *javax.swing.text.AttributeSet* s, boolean replace)	ε1007,1013
1.3		public	void	**setParser** (HTMLEditorKit.Parser parser)	
		public	void	**setPreservesUnknownTags** (boolean preservesTags)	
		public	void	**setTokenThreshold** (int n)	
▲	3	public static final	String	StreamDescriptionProperty = "stream"	
	2	protected	void	styleChanged (*javax.swing.text.Style* style)	
▲	3	public static final	String	TitleProperty = "title"	

HTMLDocument.BlockElement   javax.swing.text.html

```
     Object
1.2 O └javax.swing.text.AbstractDocument₂ - - - - - - - javax.swing.text.Element, javax.swing.text.MutableAttributeSet,
            │.AbstractElement¹                          (javax.swing.text.AttributeSet³), java.io.Serializable,
            │                                           javax.swing.tree.TreeNode,
1.2         └javax.swing.text.AbstractDocument₂
            │.BranchElement²
1.2         └HTMLDocument.BlockElement
```

	1	public	void	addAttribute (Object name, Object value)	
	1	public	void	addAttributes (*javax.swing.text.AttributeSet* attr)	
✳		public		**HTMLDocument.BlockElement** (*javax.swing.text.Element* parent, *javax.swing.text.AttributeSet* a)	
	2	public	java.util.*Enumeration*	children ()	ε1023,1024,1028,1029
	1	public	boolean	containsAttribute (Object name, Object value)	
	1	public	boolean	containsAttributes (*javax.swing.text.AttributeSet* attrs)	
	1	public	*javax.swing.text.AttributeSet*	copyAttributes ()	
	1	public	void	dump (java.io.PrintStream psOut, int indentAmount)	
	1	protected	void	finalize () throws Throwable	
	2	public	boolean	getAllowsChildren ()	
	1	public	Object	getAttribute (Object attrName)	ε1010,1013,1017
	1	public	int	getAttributeCount ()	ε1010
	1	public	java.util.*Enumeration*	getAttributeNames ()	ε1010
	1	public	*javax.swing.text.AttributeSet*	getAttributes ()	ε1013
	1	public	*javax.swing.tree.TreeNode*	getChildAt (int childIndex)	
	1	public	int	getChildCount ()	ε1023,1024,1025,1028,1029
	1	public	*javax.swing.text.Document*	getDocument ()	

Class   *Interface* —extends - - -implements ○ abstract ● final △ static ▲ static final ✳ constructor x x—inherited x **x**—declared **x x**—overridden
ε*n*—examples of usage ,—has subclass package—see other volume

2	public		getElement (int index)	ε984,990,1013
	..... javax.swing.text.Element			
2	public	int	getElementCount ()	ε984,990,1013
2	public	int	getElementIndex (int offset)	
2	public	int	getEndOffset ()	ε984,990,1013
1	public	int	getIndex (*javax.swing.tree.TreeNode* node)	
2	public	**String**	**getName** ()	
1	public		getParent ()	ε1027
	... javax.swing.tree.TreeNode			
1	public		getParentElement ()	
	..... javax.swing.text.Element			
1	public	***javax₂***	**getResolveParent** ()	
	.swing.text.AttributeSet			
2	public	int	getStartOffset ()	ε984,990,1013
1	public	boolean	isDefined (Object attrName)	
1	public	boolean	isEqual (*javax.swing.text.AttributeSet* attr)	
2	public	boolean	isLeaf ()	ε984
▲ 3	public static final	Object	NameAttribute	
2	public		positionToElement (int pos)	
	..... javax.swing.text.Element			
1	public	void	removeAttribute (Object name)	
1	public	void	removeAttributes (*java.util.Enumeration* names)	
1	public	void	removeAttributes (*javax.swing.text.AttributeSet* attrs)	
2	public	void	replace (int offset, int length, *javax.swing.text.Element[]* elems)	
▲ 3	public static final	Object	ResolveAttribute	
1	public	void	setResolveParent (*javax.swing.text.AttributeSet* parent)	
2	public	String	toString ()	

H

HTMLDocument.HTMLReader — javax.swing.text.html

	Object	
1.2	└HTMLEditorKit.ParserCallback [1]	
1.2	└HTMLDocument.HTMLReader	

	protected	void	**addContent** (char[] data, int offs, int length)
	protected	void	**addContent** (char[] data, int offs, int length, boolean generateImpliedPIfNecessary)
	protected	void	**addSpecialElement** (HTML.Tag t, *javax.swing.text.MutableAttributeSet* a)
	protected	void	**blockClose** (HTML.Tag t)
	protected	void	**blockOpen** (HTML.Tag t, *javax.swing.text.MutableAttributeSet* attr)
	protected	*javax.swing₂*	**charAttr**
	.text.MutableAttributeSet		
1	public	**void**	**flush** () throws javax.swing.text.BadLocationException
1	public	**void**	**handleComment** (char[] data, int pos)
1.3 1	public	**void**	**handleEndOfLineString** (String eol)
1	public	**void**	**handleEndTag** (HTML.Tag t, int pos)
1	public	void	handleError (String errorMsg, int pos)
1	public	**void**	**handleSimpleTag** (HTML.Tag t, *javax.swing.text.MutableAttributeSet* a, int pos)
1	public	**void**	**handleStartTag** (HTML.Tag t, *javax.swing.text.MutableAttributeSet* a, int pos)
1	public	**void**	**handleText** (char[] data, int pos)
*	public		**HTMLDocument.HTMLReader** (int offset)
*	public		**HTMLDocument.HTMLReader** (int offset, int popDepth, int pushDepth, HTML.Tag insertTag)
1.3 ▲ 1	public static final	Object	IMPLIED
	protected	*java.util.*Vector	**parseBuffer**
	protected	void	**popCharacterStyle** ()
	protected	void	**preContent** (char[] data)
	protected	void	**pushCharacterStyle** ()
	protected	void	**registerTag** (HTML.Tag t, HTMLDocument.HTMLReader.TagAction a)
	protected	void	**textAreaContent** (char[] data)

Classes

HTMLDocument.HTMLReader.BlockAction — javax.swing.text.html

	Object	
1.2	└HTMLDocument.HTMLReader.TagAction [1]	
1.2	└HTMLDocument.HTMLReader₂	
	.BlockAction	

*	public		**HTMLDocument.HTMLReader.BlockAction** ()
1	public	**void**	**end** (HTML.Tag t)
1	public	**void**	**start** (HTML.Tag t, *javax.swing.text.MutableAttributeSet* attr)

	HTMLDocument.HTMLReader.CharacterAction		javax.swing.text.html

Object
1.2 └HTMLDocument.HTMLReader.TagAction [1]
1.2 └HTMLDocument.HTMLReader [2]
.CharacterAction

❋	public.........................	**HTMLDocument.HTMLReader.CharacterAction** ()
1	public....................	**void end** (HTML.Tag t)
1	public....................	**void start** (HTML.Tag t, *javax.swing.text.MutableAttributeSet* attr)

H

	HTMLDocument.HTMLReader.FormAction		javax.swing.text.html

Object
1.2 └HTMLDocument.HTMLReader.TagAction [1]
1.2 └HTMLDocument.HTMLReader [2]
│ .SpecialAction [2]
1.2 └HTMLDocument.HTMLReader [2]
.FormAction

1	public....................	**void end** (HTML.Tag t)
❋	public.........................	**HTMLDocument.HTMLReader.FormAction** ()
2	public....................	**void start** (HTML.Tag t, *javax.swing.text.MutableAttributeSet* attr)

	HTMLDocument.HTMLReader.HiddenAction		javax.swing.text.html

Object
1.2 └HTMLDocument.HTMLReader.TagAction [1]
1.2 └HTMLDocument.HTMLReader [2]
.HiddenAction

1	public....................	**void end** (HTML.Tag t)
❋	public.........................	**HTMLDocument.HTMLReader.HiddenAction** ()
1	public....................	**void start** (HTML.Tag t, *javax.swing.text.MutableAttributeSet* a)

	HTMLDocument.HTMLReader.IsindexAction		javax.swing.text.html

Object
1.2 └HTMLDocument.HTMLReader.TagAction [1]
1.2 └HTMLDocument.HTMLReader [2]
.IsindexAction

1	public....................void end (HTML.Tag t)
❋	public.........................	**HTMLDocument.HTMLReader.IsindexAction** ()
1	public....................	**void start** (HTML.Tag t, *javax.swing.text.MutableAttributeSet* a)

	HTMLDocument.HTMLReader.ParagraphAction		javax.swing.text.html

Object
1.2 └HTMLDocument.HTMLReader.TagAction
1.2 └HTMLDocument.HTMLReader [2]
│ .BlockAction [1]
1.2 └HTMLDocument.HTMLReader [2]
.ParagraphAction

1	public....................	**void end** (HTML.Tag t)
❋	public.........................	**HTMLDocument.HTMLReader.ParagraphAction** ()
1	public....................	**void start** (HTML.Tag t, *javax.swing.text.MutableAttributeSet* a)

Class *Interface* —extends - - -implements ○ abstract ● final △ static ▲ static final ❋ constructor x x—inherited x **x**—declared **x x**—overridden
εn—examples of usage .—has subclass package—see other volume

HTMLDocument.HTMLReader.PreAction		javax.swing.text.html

```
        Object
1.2     └HTMLDocument.HTMLReader.TagAction
1.2       └HTMLDocument.HTMLReader₂
          │ .BlockAction¹
1.2         └HTMLDocument.HTMLReader.PreAction
```

1	public	**void end** (HTML.Tag t)	
∗	public	**HTMLDocument.HTMLReader.PreAction** ()	
1	public	**void start** (HTML.Tag t, *javax.swing.text.MutableAttributeSet* attr)	

HTMLDocument.HTMLReader.SpecialAction		javax.swing.text.html

```
        Object
1.2     └HTMLDocument.HTMLReader.TagAction¹
1.2       └HTMLDocument.HTMLReader₂
            .SpecialAction
```

1	public	void end (HTML.Tag t)
∗	public	**HTMLDocument.HTMLReader.SpecialAction** ()
1	public	**void start** (HTML.Tag t, *javax.swing.text.MutableAttributeSet* a)

HTMLDocument.HTMLReader.TagAction		javax.swing.text.html

```
        Object
1.2     └HTMLDocument.HTMLReader.TagAction
```

	public	void **end** (HTML.Tag t)
	public	void **start** (HTML.Tag t, *javax.swing.text.MutableAttributeSet* a)
∗	public	**HTMLDocument.HTMLReader.TagAction** ()

HTMLDocument.Iterator		javax.swing.text.html

```
        Object
1.2 ○   └HTMLDocument.Iterator
```

○	public abstract	**getAttributes** ()	ε1017
	javax.swing.text.AttributeSet		
○	public abstract int	**getEndOffset** ()	
○	public abstract int	**getStartOffset** ()	
○	public abstract HTML.Tag	**getTag** ()	
○	public abstract boolean	**isValid** ()	ε1017
∗	public	**HTMLDocument.Iterator** ()	
○	public abstract void	**next** ()	ε1017

HTMLDocument.RunElement		javax.swing.text.html

```
        Object
1.2 ○   └javax.swing.text.AbstractDocument₂ - - - - - - - - javax.swing.text.Element, javax.swing.text.MutableAttributeSet
          .AbstractElement¹                               (javax.swing.text.AttributeSet ³), java.io.Serializable,
                                                          javax.swing.tree.TreeNode
1.2       └javax.swing.text.AbstractDocument₂
          │ .LeafElement²
1.2         └HTMLDocument.RunElement
```

1	public void	addAttribute (Object name, Object value)	
1	public void	addAttributes (*javax.swing.text.AttributeSet* attr)	
2	public *java.util.Enumeration*	children ()	ε1023,1024,1028,1029
1	public boolean	containsAttribute (Object name, Object value)	
1	public boolean	containsAttributes (*javax.swing.text.AttributeSet* attrs)	
1	public	copyAttributes ()	
	javax.swing.text.AttributeSet		
1	public void	dump (java.io.PrintStream psOut, int indentAmount)	
1	protected void	finalize () throws Throwable	
2	public boolean	getAllowsChildren ()	
1	public Object	getAttribute (Object attrName)	ε1010,1013,1017
1	public int	getAttributeCount ()	ε1010
1	public *java.util.Enumeration*	getAttributeNames ()	ε1010

H

Classes

553

HTMLDocument.RunElement

	1	public.......................... . *javax.swing.text.AttributeSet*	getAttributes ()	ε1013
	1	public.......................... ... *javax.swing.tree.TreeNode*	getChildAt (int childIndex)	
	1	public.........................int	getChildCount ()	ε1023,1024,1025,1028,1029
	1	public.......................... .. *javax.swing.text.Document*	getDocument ()	
	2	public.......................... ..... *javax.swing.text.Element*	getElement (int index)	ε984,990,1013
	2	public.........................int	getElementCount ()	ε984,990,1013
	2	public.........................int	getElementIndex (int pos)	
	2	public.........................int	getEndOffset ()	ε984,990,1013
	1	public.........................int	getIndex (*javax.swing.tree.TreeNode* node)	
	2	public................**String**	**getName** ()	
	1	public.......................... ..... *javax.swing.tree.TreeNode*	getParent ()	ε1027
	1	public.......................... ..... *javax.swing.text.Element*	getParentElement ()	
	1	public.................***javax***₂ **.swing.text.AttributeSet**	**getResolveParent** ()	
	2	public.........................int	getStartOffset ()	ε984,990,1013
	1	public..............boolean	isDefined (Object attrName)	
	1	public..............boolean	isEqual (*javax.swing.text.AttributeSet* attr)	
	2	public..............boolean	isLeaf ()	ε984
▲	3	public static final........Object	NameAttribute	
	1	public..............void	removeAttribute (Object name)	
	1	public..............void	removeAttributes (*java.util.Enumeration* names)	
	1	public..............void	removeAttributes (*javax.swing.text.AttributeSet* attrs)	
▲	3	public static final........Object	ResolveAttribute	
✳		public..........................	**HTMLDocument.RunElement** (*javax.swing.text.Element* parent, *javax.swing.text.AttributeSet* a, int offs0, int offs1)	
	1	public..............void	setResolveParent (*javax.swing.text.AttributeSet* parent)	
	2	public................String	toString ()	

HTMLEditorKit

javax.swing.text.html

```
     Object
1.2 ○ └javax.swing.text.EditorKit --------------- Cloneable ˅, java.io.Serializable ˅
1.2     └javax.swing.text.DefaultEditorKit 1
1.2       └javax.swing.text.StyledEditorKit 2
1.2         └HTMLEditorKit ------------------ javax.accessibility.Accessible 3
```

	1	*50 inherited members from javax.swing.text.DefaultEditorKit not shown*		
▲		public static final........String	**BOLD_ACTION** = "html-bold-action"	
	2	public................**Object**	**clone** ()	
▲		public static final........String	**COLOR_ACTION** = "html-color-action"	
	2	public.......................... . ***javax.swing.text.Document***	**createDefaultDocument** ()	ε1017
	2	protected.................**void**	**createInputAttributes** (*javax.swing.text.Element* element, *javax.swing.text.MutableAttributeSet* set)	
▲		public static final........String	**DEFAULT_CSS** = "default.css"	
	2	public....................**void**	**deinstall** (javax.swing.JEditorPane c)	
▲		public static final........String	**FONT_CHANGE_BIGGER** = "html-font-bigger"	
▲		public static final........String	**FONT_CHANGE_SMALLER** = "html-font-smaller"	
1.4	3	public......javax.accessibility₂ .AccessibleContext	**getAccessibleContext** ()	ε687
	2	public... ***javax.swing.Action[]***	**getActions** ()	
	2	public.......................... ..... *javax.swing.text.Element*	getCharacterAttributeRun ()	
	1	public....................**String**	**getContentType** ()	
1.3		public..........java.awt.Cursor	**getDefaultCursor** ()	
	2	public............***javax.swing*₂ .text.MutableAttributeSet**	**getInputAttributes** ()	
1.3		public..........java.awt.Cursor	**getLinkCursor** ()	
		protected...................... .... HTMLEditorKit.Parser	**getParser** ()	
		public................StyleSheet	**getStyleSheet** ()	
	2	public................***javax*₂ .swing.text.ViewFactory**	**getViewFactory** ()	

Class *Interface* —extends - - -implements ○ abstract ● final △ static ▲ static final ✳ constructor x x—inherited x **x**—declared **x x**—overridden
ε*n*—examples of usage ˅—has subclass package—see other volume

*	public	....		**HTMLEditorKit** () ε1017,1018
▲	public static final	.... String		**IMG_ALIGN_BOTTOM** = "html-image-align-bottom"
▲	public static final	.... String		**IMG_ALIGN_MIDDLE** = "html-image-align-middle"
▲	public static final	.... String		**IMG_ALIGN_TOP** = "html-image-align-top"
▲	public static final	.... String		**IMG_BORDER** = "html-image-border"
	public	.... void		**insertHTML** (HTMLDocument doc, int offset, String html, int popDepth, int pushDepth, HTML.Tag insertTag) throws javax.swing.text.BadLocationException, java.io.IOException
2	public	.... **void**		**install** (javax.swing.JEditorPane c)
▲	public static final	.... String		**ITALIC_ACTION** = "html-italic-action"
▲	public static final	.... String		**LOGICAL_STYLE_ACTION** = "html-logical-style-action"
▲	public static final	.... String		**PARA_INDENT_LEFT** = "html-para-indent-left"
▲	public static final	.... String		**PARA_INDENT_RIGHT** = "html-para-indent-right"
1	public	.... **void**		**read** (java.io.Reader in, *javax.swing.text.Document* doc, int pos) throws java.io.IOException, javax.swing.text.BadLocationException ε1017,1018
1.3	public	.... void		**setDefaultCursor** (java.awt.Cursor cursor)
1.3	public	.... void		**setLinkCursor** (java.awt.Cursor cursor)
	public	.... void		**setStyleSheet** (StyleSheet s)
1	public	.... **void**		**write** (java.io.Writer out, *javax.swing.text.Document* doc, int pos, int len) throws java.io.IOException, javax.swing.text.BadLocationException

---

HTMLEditorKit.HTMLFactory · javax.swing.text.html

```
        Object
1.2     └HTMLEditorKit.HTMLFactory - - - - - - - - - - - - - javax.swing.text.ViewFactory 1
```

1	public .... javax.swing.text.View	**create** (*javax.swing.text.Element* elem)
*	public	**HTMLEditorKit.HTMLFactory** ()

HTMLEditorKit.HTMLTextAction · javax.swing.text.html

```
        Object
1.2 ○   └javax.swing.AbstractAction 1 - - - - - - - - - - - - - javax.swing.Action 4 (java.awt.event.ActionListener 5
                                                        (java.util.EventListener)), Cloneable , java.io.Serializable 
1.2 ○     └javax.swing.text.TextAction 2
1.2 ○       └javax.swing.text.StyledEditorKit
               .StyledTextAction 3
1.2 ○         └HTMLEditorKit.HTMLTextAction 
```

1	*12 inherited members from javax.swing.AbstractAction not shown*		
2	*3 inherited members from javax.swing.text.TextAction not shown*		
3	*5 inherited members from javax.swing.text.StyledEditorKit.StyledTextAction not shown*		
4	*8 inherited members from javax.swing.Action not shown*		
○ 5	public abstract .... void	actionPerformed (java.awt.event.ActionEvent e)	ε855,644,738,743,745
	protected .... int	**elementCountToTag** (HTMLDocument doc, int offset, HTML.Tag tag)	
	protected .... javax.swing.text.Element	**findElementMatchingTag** (HTMLDocument doc, int offset, HTML.Tag tag)	
	protected .... javax.swing.text.Element[]	**getElementsAt** (HTMLDocument doc, int offset)	
	protected ..... HTMLDocument	**getHTMLDocument** (javax.swing.JEditorPane e)	
	protected .... HTMLEditorKit	**getHTMLEditorKit** (javax.swing.JEditorPane e)	
*	public	**HTMLEditorKit.HTMLTextAction** (String name)	

HTMLEditorKit.InsertHTMLTextAction · javax.swing.text.html

```
        Object
1.2 ○   └javax.swing.AbstractAction 1 - - - - - - - - - - - - - javax.swing.Action 5 (java.awt.event.ActionListener 6
                                                        (java.util.EventListener)), Cloneable , java.io.Serializable 
1.2 ○     └javax.swing.text.TextAction 2
1.2 ○       └javax.swing.text.StyledEditorKit
               .StyledTextAction 3
1.2 ○         └HTMLEditorKit.HTMLTextAction 4
1.2           └HTMLEditorKit
                 .InsertHTMLTextAction
```

1	*12 inherited members from javax.swing.AbstractAction not shown*
2	*3 inherited members from javax.swing.text.TextAction not shown*
3	*5 inherited members from javax.swing.text.StyledEditorKit.StyledTextAction not shown*
4	*5 inherited members from HTMLEditorKit.HTMLTextAction not shown*

H

Classes

HTMLEditorKit.InsertHTMLTextAction

5		*8 inherited members from javax.swing.Action not shown*	
6	public	void	**actionPerformed** (java.awt.event.ActionEvent ae)	ε855,644,738,743,745
	protected	HTML.Tag	**addTag**
	protected	HTML.Tag	**alternateAddTag**
	protected	HTML.Tag	**alternateParentTag**
	protected	String	**html**
1.3	protected	void	**insertAtBoundary** (javax.swing.JEditorPane editor, HTMLDocument doc, int offset, *javax.swing.text.Element* insertElement, String html, HTML.Tag parentTag, HTML.Tag addTag)
D	protected	void	**insertAtBoundry** (javax.swing.JEditorPane editor, HTMLDocument doc, int offset, *javax.swing.text.Element* insertElement, String html, HTML.Tag parentTag, HTML.Tag addTag)
	protected	void	**insertHTML** (javax.swing.JEditorPane editor, HTMLDocument doc, int offset, String html, int popDepth, int pushDepth, HTML.Tag addTag)
✳	public		**HTMLEditorKit.InsertHTMLTextAction** (String name, String html, HTML.Tag parentTag, HTML.Tag addTag)
✳	public		**HTMLEditorKit.InsertHTMLTextAction** (String name, String html, HTML.Tag parentTag, HTML.Tag addTag, HTML.Tag alternateParentTag, HTML.Tag alternateAddTag)
	protected	HTML.Tag	**parentTag**

HTMLEditorKit.LinkController   javax.swing.text.html

Object
 └─java.awt.event.MouseAdapter [1] - - - - - - - - - - - *java.awt.event.MouseListener* (*java.util.EventListener*)
 1.1 ○
 1.2   └─HTMLEditorKit.LinkController - - - - - - - - - - - *java.awt.event.MouseMotionListener* [2] (*java.util.EventListener*),
                                                                java.io.Serializable

	protected	void	**activateLink** (int pos, javax.swing.JEditorPane editor)	
✳	public		**HTMLEditorKit.LinkController** ()	
1	public	**void**	**mouseClicked** (java.awt.event.MouseEvent e)	ε646,648,783,967
1.3	2	public	void	**mouseDragged** (java.awt.event.MouseEvent e)	ε647
1	public	void	mouseEntered (java.awt.event.MouseEvent e)	
1	public	void	mouseExited (java.awt.event.MouseEvent e)	
1.3	2	public	void	**mouseMoved** (java.awt.event.MouseEvent e)	ε647,937
1	public	void	mousePressed (java.awt.event.MouseEvent e)	ε602,742,810,1011
1	public	void	mouseReleased (java.awt.event.MouseEvent e)	ε810,1011

HTMLEditorKit.Parser   javax.swing.text.html

Object
 1.2 ○   └─HTMLEditorKit.Parser

○	public abstract	void	**parse** (java.io.Reader r, HTMLEditorKit.ParserCallback cb, boolean ignoreCharSet) throws java.io.IOException
✳	public		**HTMLEditorKit.Parser** ()

HTMLEditorKit.ParserCallback   javax.swing.text.html

Object
 1.2   └─HTMLEditorKit.ParserCallback

	public	void	**flush** () throws javax.swing.text.BadLocationException	
	public	void	**handleComment** (char[] data, int pos)	
1.3	public	void	**handleEndOfLineString** (String eol)	
	public	void	**handleEndTag** (HTML.Tag t, int pos)	
	public	void	**handleError** (String errorMsg, int pos)	
	public	void	**handleSimpleTag** (HTML.Tag t, *javax.swing.text.MutableAttributeSet* a, int pos)	
	public	void	**handleStartTag** (HTML.Tag t, *javax.swing.text.MutableAttributeSet* a, int pos)	
	public	void	**handleText** (char[] data, int pos)	
1.3 ▲	public static final	Object	**IMPLIED**	
✳	public		**HTMLEditorKit.ParserCallback** ()	ε1018

		HTMLFrameHyperlinkEvent	javax.swing.text.html

ε640,641,643,649,566

```
        Object
1.1     └ java.util.EventObject 1 - - - - - - - - - - - - - - - - - - -  java.io.Serializable ↵
1.2       └ javax.swing.event.HyperlinkEvent 2
1.2         └ HTMLFrameHyperlinkEvent
```

2	public . . . . String	getDescription ()	
2	public . . . . . . javax.swing.event 2 .HyperlinkEvent.EventType	getEventType ()	ε886
1	public . . . . Object	getSource ()	ε644,886,565,568,570
1.4 2	public . . . . javax.swing.text.Element	getSourceElement ()	
	public . . . . String	**getTarget** ()	
2	public . . . . java.net.URL	getURL ()	ε886
*	public	**HTMLFrameHyperlinkEvent** (Object source, javax.swing.event.HyperlinkEvent 2 .EventType type, java.net.URL targetURL, String targetFrame)	
*	public	**HTMLFrameHyperlinkEvent** (Object source, javax.swing.event 2 .HyperlinkEvent.EventType type, java.net.URL targetURL, javax.swing.text.Element sourceElement, String targetFrame)	
*	public	**HTMLFrameHyperlinkEvent** (Object source, javax.swing.event.HyperlinkEvent 2 .EventType type, java.net.URL targetURL, String desc, String targetFrame)	
*	public	**HTMLFrameHyperlinkEvent** (Object source, javax.swing.event 2 .HyperlinkEvent.EventType type, java.net.URL targetURL, String desc, javax.swing.text.Element sourceElement, String targetFrame)	
1	protected transient . . . . . . Object	source	
1	public . . . . String	toString ()	

		HTMLWriter	javax.swing.text.html

```
        Object
1.2 ○   └ javax.swing.text.AbstractWriter 1
1.2       └ HTMLWriter
```

1	*26 inherited members from javax.swing.text.AbstractWriter not shown*		
	protected . . . . void	**closeOutUnwantedEmbeddedTags** (javax.swing.text.AttributeSet attr) throws java.io.IOException	
	protected . . . . void	**comment** (javax.swing.text.Element elem) throws javax.swing.text 2 .BadLocationException, java.io.IOException	
	protected . . . . void	**emptyTag** (javax.swing.text.Element elem) throws javax.swing.text.BadLocationException, java.io.IOException	
	protected . . . . void	**endTag** (javax.swing.text.Element elem) throws java.io.IOException	
*	public	**HTMLWriter** (java.io.Writer w, HTMLDocument doc)	
*	public	**HTMLWriter** (java.io.Writer w, HTMLDocument doc, int pos, int len)	
	protected . . . . boolean	**isBlockTag** (javax.swing.text.AttributeSet attr)	
	protected . . . . boolean	**matchNameAttribute** (javax.swing.text.AttributeSet attr, HTML.Tag tag)	
1.3 1	protected . . . . **void**	**output** (char[] chars, int start, int length) throws java.io.IOException	
	protected . . . . void	**selectContent** (javax.swing.text.AttributeSet attr) throws java.io.IOException	
	protected . . . . void	**startTag** (javax.swing.text.Element elem) throws java.io.IOException, javax.swing.text.BadLocationException	
	protected . . . . boolean	**synthesizedElement** (javax.swing.text.Element elem)	
1	protected . . . . **void**	**text** (javax.swing.text.Element elem) throws javax.swing.text.BadLocationException, java.io.IOException	
	protected . . . . void	**textAreaContent** (javax.swing.text.AttributeSet attr) throws javax.swing.text.BadLocationException, java.io.IOException	
1	public . . . . **void**	**write** () throws java.io.IOException, javax.swing.text.BadLocationException	
1	protected . . . . **void**	**writeAttributes** (javax.swing.text.AttributeSet attr) throws java.io.IOException	
	protected . . . . void	**writeEmbeddedTags** (javax.swing.text.AttributeSet attr) throws java.io.IOException	
1.3 1	protected . . . . **void**	**writeLineSeparator** () throws java.io.IOException	
	protected . . . . void	**writeOption** (Option option) throws java.io.IOException	

		HyperlinkEvent	javax.swing.event

ε640,641,643,649,566

```
        Object
1.1     └ java.util.EventObject 1 - - - - - - - - - - - - - - - - - - -  java.io.Serializable ↵
1.2       └ HyperlinkEvent ↵
```

	public . . . . String	**getDescription** ()	
	public . . . . HyperlinkEvent.EventType	**getEventType** ()	ε886

H

Classes

557

HyperlinkEvent

1.4	1	public.............................Object	**getSource** ()	ε886,644,565,568,570
		public............................ ..... *javax.swing.text.Element*	**getSourceElement** ()	
		public.............java.net.URL	**getURL** ()	ε886
	*	public............................	**HyperlinkEvent** (Object source, HyperlinkEvent.EventType type, java.net.URL u)	
	*	public............................	**HyperlinkEvent** (Object source, HyperlinkEvent.EventType type, java.net.URL u, String desc)	
1.4	*	public............................	**HyperlinkEvent** (Object source, HyperlinkEvent.EventType type, java.net.URL u, String desc, *javax.swing.text.Element* sourceElement)	
	1	protected transient......Object	source	
	1	public....................String	**toString** ()	

H

HyperlinkEvent.EventType
javax.swing.event

Object [1]
1.2 ● └HyperlinkEvent.EventType

▲	public static final............... ... HyperlinkEvent.EventType	**ACTIVATED**	ε886
▲	public static final............... ... HyperlinkEvent.EventType	**ENTERED**	
▲	public static final............... ... HyperlinkEvent.EventType	**EXITED**	
1	public.................... **String**	**toString** ()	

HyperlinkListener
javax.swing.event

1.2	*HyperlinkListener*────────────────── *java.util.EventListener*		ε738,743,745,746,752
	public......................void	**hyperlinkUpdate** (HyperlinkEvent e)	ε886

ICC_ColorSpace
java.awt.color

Object
1.2 O └ColorSpace [1] - - - - - - - - - - - - - - - - - - - *java.io.Serializable*
1.2   └ICC_ColorSpace

	1	*35 inherited members from ColorSpace not shown*	
	1	public................... **float[] fromCIEXYZ** (float[] colorvalue)	
	1	public................... **float[] fromRGB** (float[] rgbvalue)	
1.4	1	public................... **float getMaxValue** (int component)	
1.4	1	public................... **float getMinValue** (int component)	
		public............ICC_Profile **getProfile** ()	
*		public................... **ICC_ColorSpace** (ICC_Profile profile)	
	1	public................... **float[] toCIEXYZ** (float[] colorvalue)	
	1	public................... **float[] toRGB** (float[] colorvalue)	

ICC_Profile
java.awt.color

Object [1]
1.2 └ICC_Profile - *java.io.Serializable*

▲	public static final.............int	**CLASS_ABSTRACT** = 5
▲	public static final.............int	**CLASS_COLORSPACECONVERSION** = 4
▲	public static final.............int	**CLASS_DEVICELINK** = 3
▲	public static final.............int	**CLASS_DISPLAY** = 1
▲	public static final.............int	**CLASS_INPUT** = 0
▲	public static final.............int	**CLASS_NAMEDCOLOR** = 6
▲	public static final.............int	**CLASS_OUTPUT** = 2
	1	protected.................. **void finalize** ()
		public.......................int	**getColorSpaceType** ()
		public....................byte[]	**getData** ()
		public....................byte[]	**getData** (int tagSignature)
△		public static ....ICC_Profile	**getInstance** (byte[] data)
△		public static ....ICC_Profile	**getInstance** (int cspace)
△		public static ....ICC_Profile	**getInstance** (java.io.InputStream s) throws java.io.IOException

---

△	public static .... ICC_Profile	**getInstance** (String fileName) throws java.io.IOException
	public.........................int	**getMajorVersion** ()
	public.........................int	**getMinorVersion** ()
	public.........................int	**getNumComponents** ()
	public.........................int	**getPCSType** ()
	public.........................int	**getProfileClass** ()
▲	public static final ....int	**icAbsoluteColorimetric** = 3
▲	public static final ....int	**icCurveCount** = 8
▲	public static final ....int	**icCurveData** = 12
▲	public static final ....int	**icHdrAttributes** = 56
▲	public static final ....int	**icHdrCmmId** = 4
▲	public static final ....int	**icHdrColorSpace** = 16
▲	public static final ....int	**icHdrCreator** = 80
▲	public static final ....int	**icHdrDate** = 24
▲	public static final ....int	**icHdrDeviceClass** = 12
▲	public static final ....int	**icHdrFlags** = 44
▲	public static final ....int	**icHdrIlluminant** = 68
▲	public static final ....int	**icHdrMagic** = 36
▲	public static final ....int	**icHdrManufacturer** = 48
▲	public static final ....int	**icHdrModel** = 52
▲	public static final ....int	**icHdrPcs** = 20
▲	public static final ....int	**icHdrPlatform** = 40
▲	public static final ....int	**icHdrRenderingIntent** = 64
▲	public static final ....int	**icHdrSize** = 0
▲	public static final ....int	**icHdrVersion** = 8
▲	public static final ....int	**icPerceptual** = 0
▲	public static final ....int	**icRelativeColorimetric** = 1
▲	public static final ....int	**icSaturation** = 2
▲	public static final ....int	**icSigAbstractClass** = 1633842036
▲	public static final ....int	**icSigAToB0Tag** = 1093812784
▲	public static final ....int	**icSigAToB1Tag** = 1093812785
▲	public static final ....int	**icSigAToB2Tag** = 1093812786
▲	public static final ....int	**icSigBlueColorantTag** = 1649957210
▲	public static final ....int	**icSigBlueTRCTag** = 1649693251
▲	public static final ....int	**icSigBToA0Tag** = 1110589744
▲	public static final ....int	**icSigBToA1Tag** = 1110589745
▲	public static final ....int	**icSigBToA2Tag** = 1110589746
▲	public static final ....int	**icSigCalibrationDateTimeTag** = 1667329140
▲	public static final ....int	**icSigCharTargetTag** = 1952543335
1.3 ▲	public static final ....int	**icSigChromaticityTag** = 1667789421
▲	public static final ....int	**icSigCmyData** = 1129142560
▲	public static final ....int	**icSigCmykData** = 1129142603
▲	public static final ....int	**icSigColorSpaceClass** = 1936744803
▲	public static final ....int	**icSigCopyrightTag** = 1668313716
1.3 ▲	public static final ....int	**icSigCrdInfoTag** = 1668441193
▲	public static final ....int	**icSigDeviceMfgDescTag** = 1684893284
▲	public static final ....int	**icSigDeviceModelDescTag** = 1684890724
1.3 ▲	public static final ....int	**icSigDeviceSettingsTag** = 1684371059
▲	public static final ....int	**icSigDisplayClass** = 1835955314
▲	public static final ....int	**icSigGamutTag** = 1734438260
▲	public static final ....int	**icSigGrayData** = 1196573017
▲	public static final ....int	**icSigGrayTRCTag** = 1800688195
▲	public static final ....int	**icSigGreenColorantTag** = 1733843290
▲	public static final ....int	**icSigGreenTRCTag** = 1733579331
▲	public static final ....int	**icSigHead** = 1751474532
▲	public static final ....int	**icSigHlsData** = 1212961568
▲	public static final ....int	**icSigHsvData** = 1213421088
▲	public static final ....int	**icSigInputClass** = 1935896178
▲	public static final ....int	**icSigLabData** = 1281450528
▲	public static final ....int	**icSigLinkClass** = 1818848875
▲	public static final ....int	**icSigLuminanceTag** = 1819635049
▲	public static final ....int	**icSigLuvData** = 1282766368
▲	public static final ....int	**icSigMeasurementTag** = 1835360627
▲	public static final ....int	**icSigMediaBlackPointTag** = 1651208308
▲	public static final ....int	**icSigMediaWhitePointTag** = 2004119668
▲	public static final ....int	**icSigNamedColor2Tag** = 1852009522
▲	public static final ....int	**icSigNamedColorClass** = 1852662636
▲	public static final ....int	**icSigOutputClass** = 1886549106
1.3 ▲	public static final ....int	**icSigOutputResponseTag** = 1919251312
▲	public static final ....int	**icSigPreview0Tag** = 1886545200
▲	public static final ....int	**icSigPreview1Tag** = 1886545201
▲	public static final ....int	**icSigPreview2Tag** = 1886545202
▲	public static final ....int	**icSigProfileDescriptionTag** = 1684370275
▲	public static final ....int	**icSigProfileSequenceDescTag** = 1886610801

I

Classes

ICC_Profile

▲	public static final	int	**icSigPs2CRD0Tag**	= 1886610480
▲	public static final	int	**icSigPs2CRD1Tag**	= 1886610481
▲	public static final	int	**icSigPs2CRD2Tag**	= 1886610482
▲	public static final	int	**icSigPs2CRD3Tag**	= 1886610483
▲	public static final	int	**icSigPs2CSATag**	= 1886597747
▲	public static final	int	**icSigPs2RenderingIntentTag**	= 1886597737
▲	public static final	int	**icSigRedColorantTag**	= 1918392666
▲	public static final	int	**icSigRedTRCTag**	= 1918128707
▲	public static final	int	**icSigRgbData**	= 1380401696
▲	public static final	int	**icSigScreeningDescTag**	= 1935897188
▲	public static final	int	**icSigScreeningTag**	= 1935897198
▲	public static final	int	**icSigSpace2CLR**	= 843271250
▲	public static final	int	**icSigSpace3CLR**	= 860048466
▲	public static final	int	**icSigSpace4CLR**	= 876825682
▲	public static final	int	**icSigSpace5CLR**	= 893602898
▲	public static final	int	**icSigSpace6CLR**	= 910380114
▲	public static final	int	**icSigSpace7CLR**	= 927157330
▲	public static final	int	**icSigSpace8CLR**	= 943934546
▲	public static final	int	**icSigSpace9CLR**	= 960711762
▲	public static final	int	**icSigSpaceACLR**	= 1094929490
▲	public static final	int	**icSigSpaceBCLR**	= 1111706706
▲	public static final	int	**icSigSpaceCCLR**	= 1128483922
▲	public static final	int	**icSigSpaceDCLR**	= 1145261138
▲	public static final	int	**icSigSpaceECLR**	= 1162038354
▲	public static final	int	**icSigSpaceFCLR**	= 1178815570
▲	public static final	int	**icSigTechnologyTag**	= 1952801640
▲	public static final	int	**icSigUcrBgTag**	= 1650877472
▲	public static final	int	**icSigViewingCondDescTag**	= 1987405156
▲	public static final	int	**icSigViewingConditionsTag**	= 1986618743
▲	public static final	int	**icSigXYZData**	= 1482250784
▲	public static final	int	**icSigYCbCrData**	= 1497588338
▲	public static final	int	**icSigYxyData**	= 1501067552
▲	public static final	int	**icTagReserved**	= 4
▲	public static final	int	**icTagType**	= 0
▲	public static final	int	**icXYZNumberX**	= 8
1.3	protected	Object	**readResolve** () throws java.io.ObjectStreamException	
	public	void	**setData** (int tagSignature, byte[] tagData)	
	public	void	**write** (java.io.OutputStream s) throws java.io.IOException	
	public	void	**write** (String fileName) throws java.io.IOException	

ICC_ProfileGray
java.awt.color

Object
| 1.2 | └ICC_Profile[1] - *java.io.Serializable* |
| 1.2 | └ICC_ProfileGray |

1	*127 inherited members from ICC_Profile not shown*		
	public	float	**getGamma** ()
	public	float[]	**getMediaWhitePoint** ()
	public	short[]	**getTRC** ()

ICC_ProfileRGB
java.awt.color

Object
| 1.2 | └ICC_Profile[1] - *java.io.Serializable* |
| 1.2 | └ICC_ProfileRGB |

	1	*127 inherited members from ICC_Profile not shown*		
▲	public static final	int	**BLUECOMPONENT**	= 2
	public	float	**getGamma** (int component)	
	public	float[][]	**getMatrix** ()	
	public	float[]	**getMediaWhitePoint** ()	
	public	short[]	**getTRC** (int component)	
▲	public static final	int	**GREENCOMPONENT**	= 1
▲	public static final	int	**REDCOMPONENT**	= 0

Icon
javax.swing

1.2	*Icon*	ε740,746,750,751,755

```
public...........................int getIconHeight ()
public...........................int getIconWidth ()
public.........................void paintIcon (java.awt.Component c, java.awt.Graphics g, int x, int y)
                                                                                    ε595
```

IconUIResource
javax.swing.plaf

```
         Object
1.2      └ IconUIResource - - - - - - - - - - - - - - - - - - - - - - javax.swing.Icon 1, UIResource, java.io.Serializable
```

```
    1  public...........................int getIconHeight ()
    1  public...........................int getIconWidth ()
 *     public.............................. IconUIResource (javax.swing.Icon delegate)
    1  public.........................void paintIcon (java.awt.Component c, java.awt.Graphics g, int x, int y)
                                                                                    ε595
```

IconView
javax.swing.text

```
         Object
1.2  ○   └ View 1 - - - - - - - - - - - - - - - - - - - - - - - - - - javax.swing.SwingConstants 2
1.2      └ IconView
```

```
    1  47 inherited members from View not shown
    2  19 inherited members from javax.swing.SwingConstants not shown
    1  public..................... float getAlignment (int axis)
    1  public..................... float getPreferredSpan (int axis)
 *     public............................ IconView (Element elem)
    1  public........... java.awt.Shape modelToView (int pos, java.awt.Shape a, Position.Bias b)
                                            throws BadLocationException
    1  public..................... void paint (java.awt.Graphics g, java.awt.Shape a)
    1  public..................... int viewToModel (float x, float y, java.awt.Shape a, Position.Bias[] bias)
```

IIOByteBuffer
javax.imageio.stream

```
         Object
1.4      └ IIOByteBuffer
```

```
       public.....................byte[] getData ()
       public........................int getLength ()
       public........................int getOffset ()
 *     public.............................. IIOByteBuffer (byte[] data, int offset, int length)
       public.........................void setData (byte[] data)
       public.........................void setLength (int length)
       public.........................void setOffset (int offset)
```

IIOException
javax.imageio

```
         Object
         └ Throwable - - - - - - - - - - - - - - - - - - - - - - - - - java.io.Serializable
           └ Exception
             └ java.io.IOException
1.4            └ IIOException
```

```
 *     public........................... IIOException (String message)
 *     public........................... IIOException (String message, Throwable cause)
```

IIOImage
javax.imageio

```
         Object
1.4      └ IIOImage
```

```
       public...........java.imageio getMetadata ()
                 .metadata.IIOMetadata
       public.........................int getNumThumbnails ()
```

IIOImage

	public...java.awt.image.Raster	**getRaster** ()	
	public...............*java.awt*₂	**getRenderedImage** ()	
	.image.RenderedImage		
	public................... java₂	**getThumbnail** (int index)	
	.awt.image.BufferedImage		
	public.............*java.util.List*	**getThumbnails** ()	
	public................ boolean	**hasRaster** ()	
*	public..........................	**IIOImage** (java.awt.image.Raster raster, *java.util.List* thumbnails,	
		javax.imageio.metadata.IIOMetadata metadata)	
*	public.......................	**IIOImage** (*java.awt.image.RenderedImage* image, *java.util.List* thumbnails,	
		javax.imageio.metadata.IIOMetadata metadata)	*ε*699
	protected.............*java.awt*₂	**image**	
	.image.RenderedImage		
	protected.......javax.imageio₂	**metadata**	
	.metadata.IIOMetadata		
	protected..........................	**raster**	
	........java.awt.image.Raster		
	public.....................void	**setMetadata** (javax.imageio.metadata.IIOMetadata metadata)	
	public.....................void	**setRaster** (java.awt.image.Raster raster)	
	public.....................void	**setRenderedImage** (*java.awt.image.RenderedImage* image)	
	public.....................void	**setThumbnails** (*java.util.List* thumbnails)	
	protected..........*java.util.List*	**thumbnails**	

IIOInvalidTreeException   javax.imageio.metadata

```
Object
└ Throwable - - - - - - - - - - - - - - - - - - - - - - - - java.io.Serializable ⌐
   └ Exception
      └ java.io.IOException
1.4       └ javax.imageio.IIOException
1.4          └ IIOInvalidTreeException
```

*	public..... *org.w3c.dom.Node*	**getOffendingNode** ()	
*	public..........................	**IIOInvalidTreeException** (String message, *org.w3c.dom.Node* offendingNode)	
*	public..........................	**IIOInvalidTreeException** (String message, Throwable cause,	
		org.w3c.dom.Node offendingNode)	
	protected . *org.w3c.dom.Node*	**offendingNode**	

IIOMetadata   javax.imageio.metadata

```
     Object
1.4 ○ └ IIOMetadata
```

	public................. boolean	**activateController** ()	
	protected......................	**controller**	
	........*IIOMetadataController*		
	protected......................	**defaultController**	
	........*IIOMetadataController*		
	protected.............. String[]	**extraMetadataFormatClassNames**	
	protected.............. String[]	**extraMetadataFormatNames**	
○	public abstract................	**getAsTree** (String formatName)	
	.... *org.w3c.dom.Node*		
	public... *IIOMetadataController*	**getController** ()	
	public... *IIOMetadataController*	**getDefaultController** ()	
	public................. String[]	**getExtraMetadataFormatNames** ()	
	public...... *IIOMetadataFormat*	**getMetadataFormat** (String formatName)	
	public................. String[]	**getMetadataFormatNames** ()	
	public.................. String	**getNativeMetadataFormatName** ()	
	protected ... IIOMetadataNode	**getStandardChromaNode** ()	
	protected ... IIOMetadataNode	**getStandardCompressionNode** ()	
	protected ... IIOMetadataNode	**getStandardDataNode** ()	
	protected ... IIOMetadataNode	**getStandardDimensionNode** ()	
	protected ... IIOMetadataNode	**getStandardDocumentNode** ()	
	protected ... IIOMetadataNode	**getStandardTextNode** ()	
	protected ... IIOMetadataNode	**getStandardTileNode** ()	
	protected ... IIOMetadataNode	**getStandardTransparencyNode** ()	
●	protected final................	**getStandardTree** ()	
	.... IIOMetadataNode		

Class *Interface* —extends - - -implements ○ abstract ● final △ static ▲ static final ✻ constructor x x—inherited x **x**—declared **x x**—overridden
εn—examples of usage ⌐—has subclass package—see other volume

	public	boolean	**hasController** ()
*	protected		**IIOMetadata** ()
*	protected		**IIOMetadata** (boolean standardMetadataFormatSupported, String nativeMetadataFormatName, String nativeMetadataFormatClassName, String[] extraMetadataFormatNames, String[] extraMetadataFormatClassNames)
○	public abstract	boolean	**isReadOnly** ()
	public	boolean	**isStandardMetadataFormatSupported** ()
○	public abstract	void	**mergeTree** (String formatName, *org.w3c.dom*.Node root) throws IIOInvalidTreeException
	protected	String	**nativeMetadataFormatClassName**
	protected	String	**nativeMetadataFormatName**
○	public abstract	void	**reset** ()
	public	void	**setController** (*IIOMetadataController* controller)
	public	void	**setFromTree** (String formatName, *org.w3c.dom*.Node root) throws IIOInvalidTreeException
	protected	boolean	**standardFormatSupported**

IIOMetadataController   javax.imageio.metadata

1.4	*IIOMetadataController*		
	public	boolean	**activate** (IIOMetadata metadata)

IIOMetadataFormat   javax.imageio.metadata

1.4	*IIOMetadataFormat*		
	public	boolean	**canNodeAppear** (String elementName, javax.imageio.ImageTypeSpecifier imageType)
▲	public static final	int	**CHILD_POLICY_ALL** = 1
▲	public static final	int	**CHILD_POLICY_CHOICE** = 3
▲	public static final	int	**CHILD_POLICY_EMPTY** = 0
▲	public static final	int	**CHILD_POLICY_MAX** = 5
▲	public static final	int	**CHILD_POLICY_REPEAT** = 5
▲	public static final	int	**CHILD_POLICY_SEQUENCE** = 4
▲	public static final	int	**CHILD_POLICY_SOME** = 2
▲	public static final	int	**DATATYPE_BOOLEAN** = 1
▲	public static final	int	**DATATYPE_DOUBLE** = 4
▲	public static final	int	**DATATYPE_FLOAT** = 3
▲	public static final	int	**DATATYPE_INTEGER** = 2
▲	public static final	int	**DATATYPE_STRING** = 0
	public	int	**getAttributeDataType** (String elementName, String attrName)
	public	String	**getAttributeDefaultValue** (String elementName, String attrName)
	public	String	**getAttributeDescription** (String elementName, String attrName, java.util.Locale locale)
	public	String[]	**getAttributeEnumerations** (String elementName, String attrName)
	public	int	**getAttributeListMaxLength** (String elementName, String attrName)
	public	int	**getAttributeListMinLength** (String elementName, String attrName)
	public	String	**getAttributeMaxValue** (String elementName, String attrName)
	public	String	**getAttributeMinValue** (String elementName, String attrName)
	public	String[]	**getAttributeNames** (String elementName)
	public	int	**getAttributeValueType** (String elementName, String attrName)
	public	String[]	**getChildNames** (String elementName)
	public	int	**getChildPolicy** (String elementName)
	public	String	**getElementDescription** (String elementName, java.util.Locale locale)
	public	int	**getElementMaxChildren** (String elementName)
	public	int	**getElementMinChildren** (String elementName)
	public	int	**getObjectArrayMaxLength** (String elementName)
	public	int	**getObjectArrayMinLength** (String elementName)
	public	Class	**getObjectClass** (String elementName)
	public	Object	**getObjectDefaultValue** (String elementName)
	public	Object[]	**getObjectEnumerations** (String elementName)
	public	*Comparable*	**getObjectMaxValue** (String elementName)
	public	*Comparable*	**getObjectMinValue** (String elementName)
	public	int	**getObjectValueType** (String elementName)
	public	String	**getRootName** ()
	public	boolean	**isAttributeRequired** (String elementName, String attrName)
▲	public static final	int	**VALUE_ARBITRARY** = 1
▲	public static final	int	**VALUE_ENUMERATION** = 16
▲	public static final	int	**VALUE_LIST** = 32
▲	public static final	int	**VALUE_NONE** = 0
▲	public static final	int	**VALUE_RANGE** = 2

I

Classes

IIOMetadataFormat

▲	public static final............int	**VALUE_RANGE_MAX_INCLUSIVE** = 10
▲	public static final............int	**VALUE_RANGE_MAX_INCLUSIVE_MASK** = 8
▲	public static final............int	**VALUE_RANGE_MIN_INCLUSIVE** = 6
▲	public static final............int	**VALUE_RANGE_MIN_INCLUSIVE_MASK** = 4
▲	public static final............int	**VALUE_RANGE_MIN_MAX_INCLUSIVE** = 14

IIOMetadataFormatImpl   javax.imageio.metadata

```
      Object
1.4 ○  └─ IIOMetadataFormatImpl - - - - - - - - - - - - - - - - IIOMetadataFormat 1
```

	1	*22 inherited members from IIOMetadataFormat not shown*	
		protected....................void	**addAttribute** (String elementName, String attrName, int dataType, boolean required, String defaultValue)
		protected....................void	**addAttribute** (String elementName, String attrName, int dataType, boolean required, int listMinLength, int listMaxLength)
		protected....................void	**addAttribute** (String elementName, String attrName, int dataType, boolean required, String defaultValue, *java.util*.List enumeratedValues)
		protected....................void	**addAttribute** (String elementName, String attrName, int dataType, boolean required, String defaultValue, String minValue, String maxValue, boolean minInclusive, boolean maxInclusive)
		protected....................void	**addBooleanAttribute** (String elementName, String attrName, boolean hasDefaultValue, boolean defaultValue)
		protected....................void	**addChildElement** (String elementName, String parentName)
		protected....................void	**addElement** (String elementName, String parentName, int childPolicy)
		protected....................void	**addElement** (String elementName, String parentName, int minChildren, int maxChildren)
		protected....................void	**addObjectValue** (String elementName, Class classType, int arrayMinLength, int arrayMaxLength)
		protected....................void	**addObjectValue** (String elementName, Class classType, boolean required, Object defaultValue)
		protected....................void	**addObjectValue** (String elementName, Class classType, boolean required, Object defaultValue, *java.util*.List enumeratedValues)
		protected....................void	**addObjectValue** (String elementName, Class classType, Object defaultValue, *Comparable* minValue, *Comparable* maxValue, boolean minInclusive, boolean maxInclusive)
○	1	public abstract........ boolean	**canNodeAppear** (String elementName, javax.imageio.ImageTypeSpecifier imageType)
	1	public.......................int	**getAttributeDataType** (String elementName, String attrName)
	1	public......................String	**getAttributeDefaultValue** (String elementName, String attrName)
	1	public......................String	**getAttributeDescription** (String elementName, String attrName, java.util.Locale locale)
	1	public.....................String[]	**getAttributeEnumerations** (String elementName, String attrName)
	1	public.......................int	**getAttributeListMaxLength** (String elementName, String attrName)
	1	public.......................int	**getAttributeListMinLength** (String elementName, String attrName)
	1	public......................String	**getAttributeMaxValue** (String elementName, String attrName)
	1	public......................String	**getAttributeMinValue** (String elementName, String attrName)
	1	public.....................String[]	**getAttributeNames** (String elementName)
	1	public.......................int	**getAttributeValueType** (String elementName, String attrName)
	1	public.....................String[]	**getChildNames** (String elementName)
	1	public.......................int	**getChildPolicy** (String elementName)
	1	public......................String	**getElementDescription** (String elementName, java.util.Locale locale)
	1	public.......................int	**getElementMaxChildren** (String elementName)
	1	public.......................int	**getElementMinChildren** (String elementName)
	1	public.......................int	**getObjectArrayMaxLength** (String elementName)
	1	public.......................int	**getObjectArrayMinLength** (String elementName)
	1	public......................Class	**getObjectClass** (String elementName)
	1	public.....................Object	**getObjectDefaultValue** (String elementName)
	1	public....................Object[]	**getObjectEnumerations** (String elementName)
	1	public................*Comparable*	**getObjectMaxValue** (String elementName)
	1	public................*Comparable*	**getObjectMinValue** (String elementName)
	1	public.......................int	**getObjectValueType** (String elementName)
		protected.................String	**getResourceBaseName** ()
	1	public......................String	**getRootName** ()
△		public static.................... *IIOMetadataFormat*	**getStandardFormatInstance** ()
＊		public........................	**IIOMetadataFormatImpl** (String rootName, int childPolicy)
＊		public........................	**IIOMetadataFormatImpl** (String rootName, int minChildren, int maxChildren)
	1	public................. boolean	**isAttributeRequired** (String elementName, String attrName)

Class   *Interface*   —extends   - - -implements   ○ abstract   ● final   △ static   ▲ static final   ＊ constructor   x x—inherited   x **x**—declared   **x x**—overridden
∈n—examples of usage   ⌐has subclass   package—see other volume

protected	...................void	**removeAttribute**	(String elementName, String attrName)
protected	...................void	**removeElement**	(String elementName)
protected	...................void	**removeObjectValue**	(String elementName)
protected	...................void	**setResourceBaseName**	(String resourceBaseName)
▲ public static final	.........String	**standardMetadataFormatName**	= "javax_imageio_1.0"

IIOMetadataNode
javax.imageio.metadata

Object
  └ IIOMetadataNode - *org.w3c.dom.Element* [1] (*org.w3c.dom.Node* [2]),
                                          org.w3c.dom.NodeList [3]

1.4 (left margin)

2	*12 inherited members from org.w3c.dom.Node not shown*			
2	public.....	*org.w3c.dom.Node*	**appendChild**	(*org.w3c.dom.Node* newChild)
2	public.....	*org.w3c.dom.Node*	**cloneNode**	(boolean deep)
1	public....................	String	**getAttribute**	(String name)
1	public........	*org.w3c.dom.Attr*	**getAttributeNode**	(String name)
1	public........	*org.w3c.dom.Attr*	**getAttributeNodeNS**	(String namespaceURI, String localName)
1	public....................	String	**getAttributeNS**	(String namespaceURI, String localName)
2	public....................	*org* *.w3c.dom.NamedNodeMap*	**getAttributes**	()
2	public..	*org.w3c.dom.NodeList*	**getChildNodes**	()
1	public..	*org.w3c.dom.NodeList*	**getElementsByTagName**	(String name)
1	public..	*org.w3c.dom.NodeList*	**getElementsByTagNameNS**	(String namespaceURI, String localName)
2	public..	*org.w3c.dom.Node*	**getFirstChild**	()
2	public.....	*org.w3c.dom.Node*	**getLastChild**	()
3	public.....................int		**getLength**	()
2	public....................	String	**getLocalName**	()
2	public....................	String	**getNamespaceURI**	() throws org.w3c.dom.DOMException
2	public.....	*org.w3c.dom.Node*	**getNextSibling**	()
2	public....................	String	**getNodeName**	()
2	public.....................short		**getNodeType**	()
2	public....................	String	**getNodeValue**	() throws org.w3c.dom.DOMException
2	public..	*org.w3c.dom.Document*	**getOwnerDocument**	()
2	public.....	*org.w3c.dom.Node*	**getParentNode**	()
2	public....................	String	**getPrefix**	()
2	public.....	*org.w3c.dom.Node*	**getPreviousSibling**	()
1	public....................	String	**getTagName**	()
	public....................	Object	**getUserObject**	()
1	public.....................boolean		**hasAttribute**	(String name)
1	public.....................boolean		**hasAttributeNS**	(String namespaceURI, String localName)
2	public.....................boolean		**hasAttributes**	()
2	public.....................boolean		**hasChildNodes**	()
✱	public.....................		**IIOMetadataNode**	()
✱	public.....................		**IIOMetadataNode**	(String nodeName)
2	public.....	*org.w3c.dom.Node*	**insertBefore**	(*org.w3c.dom.Node* newChild, *org.w3c.dom.Node* refChild)
2	public.....................boolean		**isSupported**	(String feature, String version)
3	public.....	*org.w3c.dom.Node*	**item**	(int index)
2	public.....................void		**normalize**	()
1	public.....................void		**removeAttribute**	(String name)
1	public.....	*org.w3c.dom.Attr*	**removeAttributeNode**	(*org.w3c.dom.Attr* oldAttr)
1	public.....................void		**removeAttributeNS**	(String namespaceURI, String localName)
2	public.....	*org.w3c.dom.Node*	**removeChild**	(*org.w3c.dom.Node* oldChild)
2	public.....	*org.w3c.dom.Node*	**replaceChild**	(*org.w3c.dom.Node* newChild, *org.w3c.dom.Node* oldChild)
1	public.....................void		**setAttribute**	(String name, String value)
1	public........	*org.w3c.dom.Attr*	**setAttributeNode**	(*org.w3c.dom.Attr* newAttr) throws org.w3c.dom.DOMException
1	public........	*org.w3c.dom.Attr*	**setAttributeNodeNS**	(*org.w3c.dom.Attr* newAttr)
1	public.....................void		**setAttributeNS**	(String namespaceURI, String qualifiedName, String value)
2	public.....................void		**setNodeValue**	(String nodeValue) throws org.w3c.dom.DOMException
2	public.....................void		**setPrefix**	(String prefix)
	public.....................void		**setUserObject**	(Object userObject)

IIOParam
javax.imageio

Object
  └ IIOParam

1.4 ○ (left margin)

public..................	boolean	**activateController**	()
protected..	*IIOParamController*	**controller**	
protected..	*IIOParamController*	**defaultController**	
protected........	java.awt.Point	**destinationOffset**	

IIOParam

protected .	ImageTypeSpecifier	**destinationType**
public	IIOParamController	**getController** ()
public	IIOParamController	**getDefaultController** ()
public	java.awt.Point	**getDestinationOffset** ()
public	ImageTypeSpecifier	**getDestinationType** ()
public	int[]	**getSourceBands** ()
public	java.awt.Rectangle	**getSourceRegion** ()
public	int	**getSourceXSubsampling** ()
public	int	**getSourceYSubsampling** ()
public	int	**getSubsamplingXOffset** ()
public	int	**getSubsamplingYOffset** ()
public	boolean	**hasController** ()
* protected		**IIOParam** ()
public	void	**setController** (*IIOParamController* controller)
public	void	**setDestinationOffset** (java.awt.Point destinationOffset)
public	void	**setDestinationType** (ImageTypeSpecifier destinationType)
public	void	**setSourceBands** (int[] sourceBands)
public	void	**setSourceRegion** (java.awt.Rectangle sourceRegion)
public	void	**setSourceSubsampling** (int sourceXSubsampling, int sourceYSubsampling, int subsamplingXOffset, int subsamplingYOffset)
protected	int[]	**sourceBands**
protected	java.awt.Rectangle	**sourceRegion**
protected	int	**sourceXSubsampling**
protected	int	**sourceYSubsampling**
protected	int	**subsamplingXOffset**
protected	int	**subsamplingYOffset**

IIOParamController   javax.imageio

1.4	*IIOParamController*
public	boolean **activate** (IIOParam param)

IIOReadProgressListener   javax.imageio.event

1.4	*IIOReadProgressListener* ———— *java.util.EventListener*	ε738,743,745,746,752

public void	**imageComplete** (javax.imageio.ImageReader source)
public void	**imageProgress** (javax.imageio.ImageReader source, float percentageDone)
public void	**imageStarted** (javax.imageio.ImageReader source, int imageIndex)
public void	**readAborted** (javax.imageio.ImageReader source)
public void	**sequenceComplete** (javax.imageio.ImageReader source)
public void	**sequenceStarted** (javax.imageio.ImageReader source, int minIndex)
public void	**thumbnailComplete** (javax.imageio.ImageReader source)
public void	**thumbnailProgress** (javax.imageio.ImageReader source, float percentageDone)
public void	**thumbnailStarted** (javax.imageio.ImageReader source, int imageIndex, int thumbnailIndex)

IIOReadUpdateListener   javax.imageio.event

1.4	*IIOReadUpdateListener* ———— *java.util.EventListener*	ε738,743,745,746,752

public void	**imageUpdate** (javax.imageio.ImageReader source, java.awt.image.BufferedImage theImage, int minX, int minY, int width, int height, int periodX, int periodY, int[] bands)
public void	**passComplete** (javax.imageio.ImageReader source, java.awt.image.BufferedImage theImage)
public void	**passStarted** (javax.imageio.ImageReader source, java.awt.image.BufferedImage theImage, int pass, int minPass, int maxPass, int minX, int minY, int periodX, int periodY, int[] bands)
public void	**thumbnailPassComplete** (javax.imageio.ImageReader source, java.awt.image.BufferedImage theThumbnail)
public void	**thumbnailPassStarted** (javax.imageio.ImageReader source, java.awt.image.BufferedImage theThumbnail, int pass, int minPass, int maxPass, int minX, int minY, int periodX, int periodY, int[] bands)
public void	**thumbnailUpdate** (javax.imageio.ImageReader source, java.awt.image.BufferedImage theThumbnail, int minX, int minY, int width, int height, int periodX, int periodY, int[] bands)

Class   *Interface* —extends - - -implements ○ abstract ● final △ static ▲ static final ✳ constructor x x—inherited x **x**—declared **x x**—overridden
ε*n*—examples of usage ⌐—has subclass package—see other volume

566

IIOReadWarningListener		javax.imageio.event

1.4	*IIOReadWarningListener*————————— *java.util.EventListener*	ε738,743,745,746,752

public......................void **warningOccurred** (javax.imageio.ImageReader source, String warning)

IIORegistry	javax.imageio.spi

Object
1.4 └ ServiceRegistry[1]
1.4 ●   └ IIORegistry

	1	public.................. boolean	contains (Object provider)
	1	public........................void	deregisterAll ()
	1	public........................void	deregisterAll (Class category)
	1	public........................void	deregisterServiceProvider (Object provider)
	1	public.................. boolean	deregisterServiceProvider (Object provider, Class category)
	1	public........................void	finalize () throws Throwable
	1	public.......... *java.util.Iterator*	getCategories ()
△		public static ....IIORegistry	**getDefaultInstance** ()
	1	public.................... Object	getServiceProviderByClass (Class providerClass)
	1	public.......... *java.util.Iterator*	getServiceProviders (Class category, boolean useOrdering)
	1	public.......... *java.util.Iterator*	getServiceProviders (Class category, *ServiceRegistry.Filter* filter, boolean useOrdering)
△	1	public static ... *java.util.Iterator*	lookupProviders (Class providerClass)
△	1	public static ... *java.util.Iterator*	lookupProviders (Class providerClass, ClassLoader loader)
		public........................void	**registerApplicationClasspathSpis** ()
	1	public........................void	registerServiceProvider (Object provider)
	1	public.................. boolean	registerServiceProvider (Object provider, Class category)
	1	public........................void	registerServiceProviders (*java.util.Iterator* providers)
	1	public.................. boolean	setOrdering (Class category, Object firstProvider, Object secondProvider)
	1	public.................. boolean	unsetOrdering (Class category, Object firstProvider, Object secondProvider)

IIOServiceProvider	javax.imageio.spi

Object
1.4 ○ └ IIOServiceProvider - *RegisterableService*[1]

○	public abstract ....String	**getDescription** (java.util.Locale locale)
	public....................String	**getVendorName** ()
	public....................String	**getVersion** ()
✳	public........................	**IIOServiceProvider** ()
✳	public........................	**IIOServiceProvider** (String vendorName, String version)
1	public........................void	**onDeregistration** (ServiceRegistry registry, Class category)
1	public........................void	**onRegistration** (ServiceRegistry registry, Class category)
	protected ....String	**vendorName**
	protected ....String	**version**

IIOWriteProgressListener		javax.imageio.event

1.4	*IIOWriteProgressListener*——————————— *java.util.EventListener*	ε738,743,745,746,752

public......................void **imageComplete** (javax.imageio.ImageWriter source)
public......................void **imageProgress** (javax.imageio.ImageWriter source, float percentageDone)
public......................void **imageStarted** (javax.imageio.ImageWriter source, int imageIndex)
public......................void **thumbnailComplete** (javax.imageio.ImageWriter source)
public......................void **thumbnailProgress** (javax.imageio.ImageWriter source, float percentageDone)
public......................void **thumbnailStarted** (javax.imageio.ImageWriter source, int imageIndex, int thumbnailIndex)
public......................void **writeAborted** (javax.imageio.ImageWriter source)

IIOWriteWarningListener		javax.imageio.event

1.4	*IIOWriteWarningListener*——————————— *java.util.EventListener*	ε738,743,745,746,752

public......................void **warningOccurred** (javax.imageio.ImageWriter source, int imageIndex, String warning)

IllegalComponentStateException

IllegalComponentStateException	java.awt

```
        Object
        └Throwable  - - - - - - - - - - - - - - - - - - - - - - - - - - -  java.io.Serializable
          └Exception
            └RuntimeException
1.1         └IllegalStateException
1.1           └IllegalComponentStateException
```

✳	public	**IllegalComponentStateException** ()
✳	public	**IllegalComponentStateException** (String s)

IllegalPathStateException	java.awt.geom

```
        Object
        └Throwable  - - - - - - - - - - - - - - - - - - - - - - - - - - -  java.io.Serializable
          └Exception
            └RuntimeException
1.2         └IllegalPathStateException
```

✳	public	**IllegalPathStateException** ()
✳	public	**IllegalPathStateException** (String s)

Image	java.awt

```
        Object                                                    ε560,581,597,638,660
   ○    └Image
```

○	public abstract . . . . void	**flush** ()	ε673,674
○	public abstract . . . . Graphics	**getGraphics** ()	
○	public abstract . . . . int	**getHeight** (*java.awt.image.ImageObserver* observer)	ε594,667,671,674,675
○	public abstract . . . . Object	**getProperty** (String name, *java.awt.image.ImageObserver* observer)	
1.1	public . . . . Image	**getScaledInstance** (int width, int height, int hints)	
○	public abstract . . . . *java*₂ *.awt.image.ImageProducer*	**getSource** ()	ε664,665
○	public abstract . . . . int	**getWidth** (*java.awt.image.ImageObserver* observer)	ε594,667,671,674,675
✳	public	**Image** ()	
1.1 ▲	public static final . . . . int	**SCALE_AREA_AVERAGING** = 16	
1.1 ▲	public static final . . . . int	**SCALE_DEFAULT** = 1	
1.1 ▲	public static final . . . . int	**SCALE_FAST** = 2	
1.1 ▲	public static final . . . . int	**SCALE_REPLICATE** = 8	
1.1 ▲	public static final . . . . int	**SCALE_SMOOTH** = 4	
▲	public static final . . . . Object	**UndefinedProperty**	

ImageCapabilities	java.awt

```
        Object¹
1.4     └ImageCapabilities  - - - - - - - - - - - - - - - - - - - - -  Cloneable
```

	1	public . . . . **Object**	**clone** ()
✳		public	**ImageCapabilities** (boolean accelerated)
		public . . . . boolean	**isAccelerated** ()
		public . . . . boolean	**isTrueVolatile** ()

ImageConsumer	java.awt.image

```
        ImageConsumer
- - - - - - - - - - - - - - - - - - - - - - - - - - - - - - - - - - - - - - - - - - - - - - - - - -
```

▲	public static final . . . . int	**COMPLETESCANLINES** = 4
▲	public static final . . . . int	**IMAGEABORTED** = 4
	public . . . . void	**imageComplete** (int status)
▲	public static final . . . . int	**IMAGEERROR** = 1
▲	public static final . . . . int	**RANDOMPIXELORDER** = 1
	public . . . . void	**setColorModel** (ColorModel model)
	public . . . . void	**setDimensions** (int width, int height)
	public . . . . void	**setHints** (int hintflags)

Class   *Interface*   —extends   - - -implements   ○ abstract   ● final   △ static   ▲ static final   ✳ constructor   x x—inherited   x **x**—declared   **x x**—overridden
ε*n*—examples of usage   —has subclass   package—see other volume

	public	.void	**setPixels** (int x, int y, int w, int h, ColorModel model, byte[] pixels, int off, int scansize)
	public	.void	**setPixels** (int x, int y, int w, int h, ColorModel model, int[] pixels, int off, int scansize)
	public	.void	**setProperties** (java.util.Hashtable props)
▲	public static final	int	**SINGLEFRAME** = 16
▲	public static final	int	**SINGLEFRAMEDONE** = 2
▲	public static final	int	**SINGLEPASS** = 8
▲	public static final	int	**STATICIMAGEDONE** = 3
▲	public static final	int	**TOPDOWNLEFTRIGHT** = 2

ImageFilter
java.awt.image

Object[1]
└ ImageFilter - *ImageConsumer*[2], *Cloneable*

ε665

	2	*9 inherited members from ImageConsumer not shown*		
	1	public	**Object clone** ()	
		protected	*ImageConsumer* **consumer**	
		public	ImageFilter **getFilterInstance** (*ImageConsumer* ic)	
	2	public	.void **imageComplete** (int status)	
*		public	**ImageFilter** ()	
		public	.void **resendTopDownLeftRight** (*ImageProducer* ip)	
	2	public	.void **setColorModel** (ColorModel model)	
	2	public	.void **setDimensions** (int width, int height)	
	2	public	.void **setHints** (int hints)	
	2	public	.void **setPixels** (int x, int y, int w, int h, ColorModel model, byte[] pixels, int off, int scansize)	
	2	public	.void **setPixels** (int x, int y, int w, int h, ColorModel model, int[] pixels, int off, int scansize)	
	2	public	.void **setProperties** (java.util.Hashtable props)	

ImageGraphicAttribute
java.awt.font

Object[1]
1.2 ○ └ GraphicAttribute[2]
1.2 ●   └ ImageGraphicAttribute

▲	2	public static final	int BOTTOM_ALIGNMENT = -2
▲	2	public static final	int CENTER_BASELINE = 1
	2	public	**void draw** (java.awt.Graphics2D graphics, float x, float y)
		public	boolean **equals** (ImageGraphicAttribute rhs)
	1	public	**boolean equals** (Object rhs)
	2	public	**float getAdvance** ()
●	2	public final	int **getAlignment** ()
	2	public	**float getAscent** ()
	2	public	**java** **getBounds** ()
		.awt.geom.Rectangle2D	
	2	public	**float getDescent** ()
	2	public	GlyphJustificationInfo getJustificationInfo ()
▲	2	public static final	int HANGING_BASELINE = 2
	1	public	**int hashCode** ()
*		public	**ImageGraphicAttribute** (java.awt.Image image, int alignment)
*		public	**ImageGraphicAttribute** (java.awt.Image image, int alignment, float originX, float originY)
▲	2	public static final	int ROMAN_BASELINE = 0
▲	2	public static final	int TOP_ALIGNMENT = -1

ImageIcon
javax.swing

Object[1]
1.2 └ ImageIcon - *Icon*[2], *java.io.Serializable*, *javax.accessibility.Accessible*[3]

▲		protected static final	**component**	
		java.awt.Component		
1.3	3	public java.accessibility	**getAccessibleContext** ()	ε687
		.AccessibleContext		
		public	String **getDescription** ()	
	2	public	int **getIconHeight** ()	
	2	public	int **getIconWidth** ()	
		public	java.awt.Image **getImage** ()	ε581,594,597,663,665
		public	int **getImageLoadStatus** ()	
		public	*java* **getImageObserver** ()	
		.awt.image.ImageObserver		
*		public	**ImageIcon** ()	

ImageIcon

✳	public		**ImageIcon** (byte[] imageData)	
✳	public		**ImageIcon** (java.awt.Image image)	ε751,597,667,694
✳	public		**ImageIcon** (String filename)	ε740,746,750,751,755
✳	public		**ImageIcon** (java.net.URL location)	
✳	public		**ImageIcon** (byte[] imageData, String description)	
✳	public		**ImageIcon** (java.awt.Image image, String description)	ε902
✳	public		**ImageIcon** (String filename, String description)	
✳	public		**ImageIcon** (java.net.URL location, String description)	
	protected	void	**loadImage** (java.awt.Image image)	
2	public synchronized	void	**paintIcon** (java.awt.Component c, java.awt.Graphics g, int x, int y)	
				ε595
	public	void	**setDescription** (String description)	ε689
	public	void	**setImage** (java.awt.Image image)	
	public	void	**setImageObserver** (*java.awt.image.ImageObserver* observer)	
1	public	String	**toString** ()	
▲	protected static final		**tracker**	
	...... java.awt.MediaTracker			

I

1.4	*ImageInputStream* —————————— *java.io.DataInput* [1]			
	public	void	**close** () throws java.io.IOException	ε698
	public	void	**flush** () throws java.io.IOException	ε699
	public	void	**flushBefore** (long pos) throws java.io.IOException	
	public	int	**getBitOffset** () throws java.io.IOException	
	public	java.nio.ByteOrder	**getByteOrder** ()	
	public	long	**getFlushedPosition** ()	
	public	long	**getStreamPosition** () throws java.io.IOException	
	public	boolean	**isCached** ()	
	public	boolean	**isCachedFile** ()	
	public	boolean	**isCachedMemory** ()	
	public	long	**length** () throws java.io.IOException	
	public	void	**mark** ()	
	public	int	**read** () throws java.io.IOException	
	public	int	**read** (byte[] b) throws java.io.IOException	
	public	int	**read** (byte[] b, int off, int len) throws java.io.IOException	
	public	int	**readBit** () throws java.io.IOException	
	public	long	**readBits** (int numBits) throws java.io.IOException	
1	public	boolean	**readBoolean** () throws java.io.IOException	
1	public	byte	**readByte** () throws java.io.IOException	
	public	void	**readBytes** (IIOByteBuffer buf, int len) throws java.io.IOException	
1	public	char	**readChar** () throws java.io.IOException	
1	public	double	**readDouble** () throws java.io.IOException	
1	public	float	**readFloat** () throws java.io.IOException	
1	public	void	**readFully** (byte[] b) throws java.io.IOException	
1	public	void	**readFully** (byte[] b, int off, int len) throws java.io.IOException	
	public	void	**readFully** (char[] c, int off, int len) throws java.io.IOException	
	public	void	**readFully** (double[] d, int off, int len) throws java.io.IOException	
	public	void	**readFully** (float[] f, int off, int len) throws java.io.IOException	
	public	void	**readFully** (int[] i, int off, int len) throws java.io.IOException	
	public	void	**readFully** (long[] l, int off, int len) throws java.io.IOException	
	public	void	**readFully** (short[] s, int off, int len) throws java.io.IOException	
1	public	int	**readInt** () throws java.io.IOException	
1	public	String	**readLine** () throws java.io.IOException	
1	public	long	**readLong** () throws java.io.IOException	
1	public	short	**readShort** () throws java.io.IOException	
1	public	int	**readUnsignedByte** () throws java.io.IOException	
	public	long	**readUnsignedInt** () throws java.io.IOException	
1	public	int	**readUnsignedShort** () throws java.io.IOException	
1	public	String	**readUTF** () throws java.io.IOException	
	public	void	**reset** () throws java.io.IOException	
	public	void	**seek** (long pos) throws java.io.IOException	
	public	void	**setBitOffset** (int bitOffset) throws java.io.IOException	
	public	void	**setByteOrder** (java.nio.ByteOrder byteOrder)	
1	public	int	**skipBytes** (int n) throws java.io.IOException	
	public	long	**skipBytes** (long n) throws java.io.IOException	

Class   *Interface*   —extends   - - -implements   ○ abstract   ● final   △ static   ▲ static final   ✳ constructor   x x—inherited   x **x**—declared   **x x**—overridden
ε*n*—examples of usage   ⌐—has subclass   package—see other volume

570

ImageInputStreamImpl

Object [1]
1.4 ○ └ImageInputStreamImpl------------------- *ImageInputStream* [2] (*java.io.DataInput*)

	protected	int	**bitOffset**	
	protected .. java.nio.ByteOrder	**byteOrder**	
●	protected final	void	**checkClosed** () throws java.io.IOException	
2	public	void	**close** () throws java.io.IOException	ε698,699
1	protected	**void**	**finalize** () throws Throwable	
2	public	void	**flush** () throws java.io.IOException	ε699
2	public	void	**flushBefore** (long pos) throws java.io.IOException	
	protected	long	**flushedPos**	
2	public	int	**getBitOffset** () throws java.io.IOException	
2	public	java.nio.ByteOrder	**getByteOrder** ()	
2	public	long	**getFlushedPosition** ()	
2	public	long	**getStreamPosition** () throws java.io.IOException	
*	public		**ImageInputStreamImpl** ()	
2	public	boolean	**isCached** ()	
2	public	boolean	**isCachedFile** ()	
2	public	boolean	**isCachedMemory** ()	
2	public	long	**length** ()	
2	public	void	**mark** ()	
○ 2	public abstract	int	**read** () throws java.io.IOException	
2	public	int	**read** (byte[] b) throws java.io.IOException	
○ 2	public abstract	int	**read** (byte[] b, int off, int len) throws java.io.IOException	
2	public	int	**readBit** () throws java.io.IOException	
2	public	long	**readBits** (int numBits) throws java.io.IOException	
2	public	boolean	**readBoolean** () throws java.io.IOException	
2	public	byte	**readByte** () throws java.io.IOException	
2	public	void	**readBytes** (IIOByteBuffer buf, int len) throws java.io.IOException	
2	public	char	**readChar** () throws java.io.IOException	
2	public	double	**readDouble** () throws java.io.IOException	
2	public	float	**readFloat** () throws java.io.IOException	
2	public	void	**readFully** (byte[] b) throws java.io.IOException	
2	public	void	**readFully** (byte[] b, int off, int len) throws java.io.IOException	
2	public	void	**readFully** (char[] c, int off, int len) throws java.io.IOException	
2	public	void	**readFully** (double[] d, int off, int len) throws java.io.IOException	
2	public	void	**readFully** (float[] f, int off, int len) throws java.io.IOException	
2	public	void	**readFully** (int[] i, int off, int len) throws java.io.IOException	
2	public	void	**readFully** (long[] l, int off, int len) throws java.io.IOException	
2	public	void	**readFully** (short[] s, int off, int len) throws java.io.IOException	
2	public	int	**readInt** () throws java.io.IOException	
2	public	String	**readLine** () throws java.io.IOException	
2	public	long	**readLong** () throws java.io.IOException	
2	public	short	**readShort** () throws java.io.IOException	
2	public	int	**readUnsignedByte** () throws java.io.IOException	
2	public	long	**readUnsignedInt** () throws java.io.IOException	
2	public	int	**readUnsignedShort** () throws java.io.IOException	
2	public	String	**readUTF** () throws java.io.IOException	
2	public	void	**reset** () throws java.io.IOException	
2	public	void	**seek** (long pos) throws java.io.IOException	
2	public	void	**setBitOffset** (int bitOffset) throws java.io.IOException	
2	public	void	**setByteOrder** (java.nio.ByteOrder byteOrder)	
2	public	int	**skipBytes** (int n) throws java.io.IOException	
2	public	long	**skipBytes** (long n) throws java.io.IOException	
	protected	long	**streamPos**	

ImageInputStreamSpi

Object
1.4 ○ └IIOServiceProvider [1] -------------------- *RegisterableService*
1.4 ○   └ImageInputStreamSpi

	public	boolean	**canUseCacheFile** ()
	public	*javax.imageio* [2] *.stream.ImageInputStream*	**createInputStreamInstance** (Object input) throws java.io.IOException
○	public abstract	*javax.imageio* [2] *.stream.ImageInputStream*	**createInputStreamInstance** (Object input, boolean useCache, java.io.File cacheDir) throws java.io.IOException
○ 1	public abstract	String	getDescription (java.util.Locale locale)
	public	Class	**getInputClass** ()

ImageInputStreamSpi

	1	public.....................String	getVendorName ()
	1	public.....................String	getVersion ()
✳		protected......................	**ImageInputStreamSpi** ()
✳		public..........................	**ImageInputStreamSpi** (String vendorName, String version, Class inputClass)
		protected.................Class	**inputClass**
		public...............boolean	**needsCacheFile** ()
	1	public..................void	onDeregistration (ServiceRegistry registry, Class category)
	1	public..................void	onRegistration (ServiceRegistry registry, Class category)
	1	protected.................String	vendorName
	1	protected.................String	version

ImageIO   javax.imageio

Object
└ImageIO

1.4 ●

△	public static ....*javax.imageio.* ⊃ *.stream.ImageInputStream*	**createImageInputStream** (Object input) throws java.io.IOException ε698
△	public static ....*javax.imageio.* ⊃ *.stream.ImageOutputStream*	**createImageOutputStream** (Object output) throws java.io.IOException ε699
△	public static .... java.io.File	**getCacheDirectory** ()
△	public static ..... ImageReader	**getImageReader** (ImageWriter writer)
△	public static ...*java.util.Iterator*	**getImageReaders** (Object input) ε698
△	public static ...*java.util.Iterator*	**getImageReadersByFormatName** (String formatName) ε697
△	public static ...*java.util.Iterator*	**getImageReadersByMIMEType** (String MIMEType) ε697
△	public static ...*java.util.Iterator*	**getImageReadersBySuffix** (String fileSuffix) ε697
△	public static ...*java.util.Iterator*	**getImageTranscoders** (ImageReader reader, ImageWriter writer)
△	public static ...... ImageWriter	**getImageWriter** (ImageReader reader)
△	public static ...*java.util.Iterator*	**getImageWriters** (ImageTypeSpecifier type, String formatName)
△	public static ...*java.util.Iterator*	**getImageWritersByFormatName** (String formatName) ε697,699
△	public static ...*java.util.Iterator*	**getImageWritersByMIMEType** (String MIMEType) ε697
△	public static ...*java.util.Iterator*	**getImageWritersBySuffix** (String fileSuffix) ε697
△	public static ....String[]	**getReaderFormatNames** () ε696
△	public static ....String[]	**getReaderMIMETypes** () ε696
△	public static ....boolean	**getUseCache** ()
△	public static ....String[]	**getWriterFormatNames** () ε696
△	public static ....String[]	**getWriterMIMETypes** () ε696
△	public static ....java ⊃ .awt.image.BufferedImage	**read** (java.io.File input) throws java.io.IOException ε694,699
△	public static ....java ⊃ .awt.image.BufferedImage	**read** (java.io.InputStream input) throws java.io.IOException ε694
△	public static ....java ⊃ .awt.image.BufferedImage	**read** (java.net.URL input) throws java.io.IOException ε694
△	public static ....java ⊃ .awt.image.BufferedImage	**read** (*javax.imageio.stream.ImageInputStream* stream) throws java.io.IOException
△	public static ....void	**scanForPlugins** ()
△	public static ....void	**setCacheDirectory** (java.io.File cacheDirectory)
△	public static ....void	**setUseCache** (boolean useCache)
△	public static ....boolean	**write** (*java.awt.image.RenderedImage* im, String formatName, *javax.imageio.stream.ImageOutputStream* output) throws java.io.IOException
△	public static ....boolean	**write** (*java.awt.image.RenderedImage* im, String formatName, java.io.File output) throws java.io.IOException ε695
△	public static ....boolean	**write** (*java.awt.image.RenderedImage* im, String formatName, java.io.OutputStream output) throws java.io.IOException

---

ImageObserver   java.awt.image

ImageObserver

▲	public static final.............int	**ABORT** = 128
▲	public static final.............int	**ALLBITS** = 32
▲	public static final.............int	**ERROR** = 64
▲	public static final.............int	**FRAMEBITS** = 16
▲	public static final.............int	**HEIGHT** = 2
	public.................. boolean	**imageUpdate** (java.awt.Image img, int infoflags, int x, int y, int width, int height)
▲	public static final.............int	**PROPERTIES** = 4
▲	public static final.............int	**SOMEBITS** = 8

Class   *Interface*   —extends   - - -implements   ○ abstract   ● final   △ static   ▲ static final   ✳ constructor   x x—inherited   x **x**—declared   **x x**—overridden
ε*n*—examples of usage   ⌐—has subclass   package—see other volume

▲   public static final . . . . int **WIDTH** = 1

ImageOutputStream

javax.imageio.stream

1.4   *ImageOutputStream*───────────────── *ImageInputStream* [1] (*java.io.DataInput*), *java.io.DataOutput* [2]

1	*42 inherited members from ImageInputStream not shown*			
1	public . . . . void	close () throws java.io.IOException		ε699,698
1	public . . . . void	flush () throws java.io.IOException		ε699
1	public . . . . void	**flushBefore** (long pos) throws java.io.IOException	
2	public . . . . void	**write** (byte[] b) throws java.io.IOException	
2	public . . . . void	**write** (int b) throws java.io.IOException	
2	public . . . . void	**write** (byte[] b, int off, int len) throws java.io.IOException	
	public . . . . void	**writeBit** (int bit) throws java.io.IOException	
	public . . . . void	**writeBits** (long bits, int numBits) throws java.io.IOException	
2	public . . . . void	**writeBoolean** (boolean v) throws java.io.IOException	
2	public . . . . void	**writeByte** (int v) throws java.io.IOException	
2	public . . . . void	**writeBytes** (String s) throws java.io.IOException	
2	public . . . . void	**writeChar** (int v) throws java.io.IOException	
2	public . . . . void	**writeChars** (String s) throws java.io.IOException	
	public . . . . void	**writeChars** (char[] c, int off, int len) throws java.io.IOException	
2	public . . . . void	**writeDouble** (double v) throws java.io.IOException	
	public . . . . void	**writeDoubles** (double[] d, int off, int len) throws java.io.IOException	
2	public . . . . void	**writeFloat** (float v) throws java.io.IOException	
	public . . . . void	**writeFloats** (float[] f, int off, int len) throws java.io.IOException	
2	public . . . . void	**writeInt** (int v) throws java.io.IOException	
	public . . . . void	**writeInts** (int[] i, int off, int len) throws java.io.IOException	
2	public . . . . void	**writeLong** (long v) throws java.io.IOException	
	public . . . . void	**writeLongs** (long[] l, int off, int len) throws java.io.IOException	
2	public . . . . void	**writeShort** (int v) throws java.io.IOException	
	public . . . . void	**writeShorts** (short[] s, int off, int len) throws java.io.IOException	
2	public . . . . void	**writeUTF** (String s) throws java.io.IOException	

ImageOutputStreamImpl

javax.imageio.stream

Object
1.4 ○   └─ImageInputStreamImpl [1] - - - - - - - - - - - - - - - - - *ImageInputStream* (*java.io.DataInput*)
1.4 ○   └─ImageOutputStreamImpl - - - - - - - - - - - - - - *ImageOutputStream* [2] (*ImageInputStream* (*java.io.DataInput*), *java.io.DataOutput*)

1	*51 inherited members from ImageInputStreamImpl not shown*		
●	protected final . . . . void	**flushBits** () throws java.io.IOException	
✳	public	**ImageOutputStreamImpl** ()	
2	public . . . . void	**write** (byte[] b) throws java.io.IOException	
○ 2	public abstract . . . . void	**write** (int b) throws java.io.IOException	
○ 2	public abstract . . . . void	**write** (byte[] b, int off, int len) throws java.io.IOException	
2	public . . . . void	**writeBit** (int bit) throws java.io.IOException	
2	public . . . . void	**writeBits** (long bits, int numBits) throws java.io.IOException	
2	public . . . . void	**writeBoolean** (boolean v) throws java.io.IOException	
2	public . . . . void	**writeByte** (int v) throws java.io.IOException	
2	public . . . . void	**writeBytes** (String s) throws java.io.IOException	
2	public . . . . void	**writeChar** (int v) throws java.io.IOException	
2	public . . . . void	**writeChars** (String s) throws java.io.IOException	
2	public . . . . void	**writeChars** (char[] c, int off, int len) throws java.io.IOException	
2	public . . . . void	**writeDouble** (double v) throws java.io.IOException	
2	public . . . . void	**writeDoubles** (double[] d, int off, int len) throws java.io.IOException	
2	public . . . . void	**writeFloat** (float v) throws java.io.IOException	
2	public . . . . void	**writeFloats** (float[] f, int off, int len) throws java.io.IOException	
2	public . . . . void	**writeInt** (int v) throws java.io.IOException	
2	public . . . . void	**writeInts** (int[] i, int off, int len) throws java.io.IOException	
2	public . . . . void	**writeLong** (long v) throws java.io.IOException	
2	public . . . . void	**writeLongs** (long[] l, int off, int len) throws java.io.IOException	
2	public . . . . void	**writeShort** (int v) throws java.io.IOException	
2	public . . . . void	**writeShorts** (short[] s, int off, int len) throws java.io.IOException	
2	public . . . . void	**writeUTF** (String s) throws java.io.IOException	

I

Classes

ImageOutputStreamSpi

				javax.imageio.spi

```
         Object
1.4 O    └IIOServiceProvider 1 - - - - - - - - - - - - - - - - - - -  RegisterableService
1.4 O        └ImageOutputStreamSpi
```

	public .... boolean	**canUseCacheFile** ()		
	public .... *javax.imageio* ₂ .*stream.ImageOutputStream*	**createOutputStreamInstance** (Object output) throws java.io.IOException		
O	public abstract . *javax.imageio* ₂ .*stream.ImageOutputStream*	**createOutputStreamInstance** (Object output, boolean useCache, java.io.File cacheDir) throws java.io.IOException		
O 1	public abstract .... String	getDescription (java.util.Locale locale)		
	public .... Class	**getOutputClass** ()		
1	public .... String	getVendorName ()		
1	public .... String	getVersion ()		
*	protected	**ImageOutputStreamSpi** ()		
*	public	**ImageOutputStreamSpi** (String vendorName, String version, Class outputClass)		
	public .... boolean	**needsCacheFile** ()		
1	public ....void	onDeregistration (ServiceRegistry registry, Class category)		
1	public ....void	onRegistration (ServiceRegistry registry, Class category)		
	protected .... Class	**outputClass**		
1	protected .... String	vendorName		
1	protected .... String	version		

ImageProducer

				java.awt.image

```
     ImageProducer
```

public .... void	**addConsumer** (*ImageConsumer* ic)	
public .... boolean	**isConsumer** (*ImageConsumer* ic)	
public .... void	**removeConsumer** (*ImageConsumer* ic)	
public .... void	**requestTopDownLeftRightResend** (*ImageConsumer* ic)	
public .... void	**startProduction** (*ImageConsumer* ic)	

ImageReader

				javax.imageio

```
         Object
1.4 O    └ImageReader
```

	public synchronized .... void	**abort** ()
	protected synchronized .... boolean	**abortRequested** ()
	public .... void	**addIIOReadProgressListener** (*javax.imageio.event.IIOReadProgressListener* listener)
	public .... void	**addIIOReadUpdateListener** (*javax.imageio.event.IIOReadUpdateListener* listener)
	public .... void	**addIIOReadWarningListener** (*javax.imageio.event.IIOReadWarningListener* listener)
	protected ..... java.util.Locale[]	**availableLocales**
	public .... boolean	**canReadRaster** ()
△	protected static .... void	**checkReadParamBandSettings** (ImageReadParam param, int numSrcBands, int numDstBands)
	protected synchronized ... void	**clearAbortRequest** ()
△	protected static .... void	**computeRegions** (ImageReadParam param, int srcWidth, int srcHeight, java.awt.image.BufferedImage image, java.awt.Rectangle srcRegion, java.awt.Rectangle destRegion)
	public .... void	**dispose** ()
	public .... float	**getAspectRatio** (int imageIndex) throws java.io.IOException
	public .... java.util.Locale[]	**getAvailableLocales** ()
	public .... ImageReadParam	**getDefaultReadParam** ()
△	protected static .... java₂ .awt.image.BufferedImage	**getDestination** (ImageReadParam param, *java.util.*Iterator imageTypes, int width, int height) throws IIOException
	public .... String	**getFormatName** () throws java.io.IOException ε698
O	public abstract ....int	**getHeight** (int imageIndex) throws java.io.IOException
O	public abstract . javax.imageio ₂ .metadata.IIOMetadata	**getImageMetadata** (int imageIndex) throws java.io.IOException
	public .... javax.imageio ₂ .metadata.IIOMetadata	**getImageMetadata** (int imageIndex, String formatName, *java.util.*Set nodeNames) throws java.io.IOException
O	public abstract *java.util.*Iterator	**getImageTypes** (int imageIndex) throws java.io.IOException

Class *Interface* —extends - - -implements O abstract ● final △ static ▲ static final ✳ constructor x x—inherited x **x**—declared **x x**—overridden
ε*n*—examples of usage ₎—has subclass package—see other volume

public	Object	**getInput** ()
public	java.util.Locale	**getLocale** ()
public	int	**getMinIndex** ()
○ public abstract	int	**getNumImages** (boolean allowSearch) throws java.io.IOException
public	int	**getNumThumbnails** (int imageIndex) throws java.io.IOException
public	javax.imageio⌇ .spi.ImageReaderSpi	**getOriginatingProvider** ()
public	ImageTypeSpecifier	**getRawImageType** (int imageIndex) throws java.io.IOException
△ protected static java.awt.Rectangle		**getSourceRegion** (ImageReadParam param, int srcWidth, int srcHeight)
○ public abstract .javax.imageio⌇ .metadata.IIOMetadata		**getStreamMetadata** () throws java.io.IOException
public	javax.imageio⌇ .metadata.IIOMetadata	**getStreamMetadata** (String formatName, *java.util.Set* nodeNames) throws java.io.IOException
public	int	**getThumbnailHeight** (int imageIndex, int thumbnailIndex) throws java.io.IOException
public	int	**getThumbnailWidth** (int imageIndex, int thumbnailIndex) throws java.io.IOException
public	int	**getTileGridXOffset** (int imageIndex) throws java.io.IOException
public	int	**getTileGridYOffset** (int imageIndex) throws java.io.IOException
public	int	**getTileHeight** (int imageIndex) throws java.io.IOException
public	int	**getTileWidth** (int imageIndex) throws java.io.IOException
○ public abstract	int	**getWidth** (int imageIndex) throws java.io.IOException
public	boolean	**hasThumbnails** (int imageIndex) throws java.io.IOException
protected	boolean	**ignoreMetadata**
＊ protected		**ImageReader** (javax.imageio.spi.ImageReaderSpi originatingProvider)
protected	Object	**input**
public	boolean	**isIgnoringMetadata** ()
public	boolean	**isImageTiled** (int imageIndex) throws java.io.IOException
public	boolean	**isRandomAccessEasy** (int imageIndex) throws java.io.IOException
public	boolean	**isSeekForwardOnly** ()
protected	java.util.Locale	**locale**
protected	int	**minIndex**
protected	javax.imageio⌇ .spi.ImageReaderSpi	**originatingProvider**
protected	void	**processImageComplete** ()
protected	void	**processImageProgress** (float percentageDone)
protected	void	**processImageStarted** (int imageIndex)
protected	void	**processImageUpdate** (java.awt.image.BufferedImage theImage, int minX, int minY, int width, int height, int periodX, int periodY, int[] bands)
protected	void	**processPassComplete** (java.awt.image.BufferedImage theImage)
protected	void	**processPassStarted** (java.awt.image.BufferedImage theImage, int pass, int minPass, int maxPass, int minX, int minY, int periodX, int periodY, int[] bands)
protected	void	**processReadAborted** ()
protected	void	**processSequenceComplete** ()
protected	void	**processSequenceStarted** (int minIndex)
protected	void	**processThumbnailComplete** ()
protected	void	**processThumbnailPassComplete** (java.awt.image.BufferedImage theThumbnail)
protected	void	**processThumbnailPassStarted** (java.awt.image.BufferedImage theThumbnail, int pass, int minPass, int maxPass, int minX, int minY, int periodX, int periodY, int[] bands)
protected	void	**processThumbnailProgress** (float percentageDone)
protected	void	**processThumbnailStarted** (int imageIndex, int thumbnailIndex)
protected	void	**processThumbnailUpdate** (java.awt.image.BufferedImage theThumbnail, int minX, int minY, int width, int height, int periodX, int periodY, int[] bands)
protected	void	**processWarningOccurred** (String warning)
protected	void	**processWarningOccurred** (String baseName, String keyword)
protected	*java.util.List*	**progressListeners**
public	java⌇ .awt.image.BufferedImage	**read** (int imageIndex) throws java.io.IOException
○ public abstract	java⌇ .awt.image.BufferedImage	**read** (int imageIndex, ImageReadParam param) throws java.io.IOException
public	*java.util.Iterator*	**readAll** (*java.util.Iterator* params) throws java.io.IOException
public	IIOImage	**readAll** (int imageIndex, ImageReadParam param) throws java.io.IOException
public	*java.awt⌇ .image.RenderedImage*	**readAsRenderedImage** (int imageIndex, ImageReadParam param) throws java.io.IOException
public	boolean	**readerSupportsThumbnails** ()
public	java.awt.image.Raster	**readRaster** (int imageIndex, ImageReadParam param) throws java.io.IOException
public	java⌇ .awt.image.BufferedImage	**readThumbnail** (int imageIndex, int thumbnailIndex) throws java.io.IOException
public	java⌇ .awt.image.BufferedImage	**readTile** (int imageIndex, int tileX, int tileY) throws java.io.IOException

I

Classes

ImageReader

public	...java.awt.image.Raster	**readTileRaster** (int imageIndex, int tileX, int tileY) throws java.io.IOException
public	......................void	**removeAllIIOReadProgressListeners** ()
public	......................void	**removeAllIIOReadUpdateListeners** ()
public	......................void	**removeAllIIOReadWarningListeners** ()
public	......................void	**removeIIOReadProgressListener** (*javax.imageio.event.IIOReadProgressListener* listener)
public	......................void	**removeIIOReadUpdateListener** (*javax.imageio.event.IIOReadUpdateListener* listener)
public	......................void	**removeIIOReadWarningListener** (*javax.imageio.event.IIOReadWarningListener* listener)
public	......................void	**reset** ()
protected	.............boolean	**seekForwardOnly**
public	......................void	**setInput** (Object input)
public	......................void	**setInput** (Object input, boolean seekForwardOnly)
public	......................void	**setInput** (Object input, boolean seekForwardOnly, boolear ignoreMetadata)
public	......................void	**setLocale** (java.util.Locale locale)
protected	.........*java.util.List*	**updateListeners**
protected	.........*java.util.List*	**warningListeners**
protected	.........*java.util.List*	**warningLocales**

ImageReaderSpi | javax.imageio.spi

Object
1.4 ○ └IIOServiceProvider[1] - *RegisterableService*
1.4 ○   └ImageReaderWriterSpi[2]
1.4 ○   └ImageReaderSpi

	2	*26 inherited members from ImageReaderWriterSpi not shown*
○	public abstract	.... boolean	**canDecodeInput** (Object source) throws java.io.IOException
	public	....	**createReaderInstance** () throws java.io.IOException
		. javax.imageio.ImageReader
○	public abstract	....	**createReaderInstance** (Object extension) throws java.io.IOException
		. javax.imageio.ImageReader
○ 1	public abstract	..........String	getDescription (java.util.Locale locale)
	public	.... String[]	**getImageWriterSpiNames** ()
	public	.... Class[]	**getInputTypes** ()
1	public	.... String	getVendorName ()
1	public	.... String	getVersion ()
*	protected	....	**ImageReaderSpi** ()
*	public	....	**ImageReaderSpi** (String vendorName, String version, String[] names, String[] suffixes, String[] MIMETypes, String readerClassName, Class[] inputTypes, String[] writerSpiNames, boolean supportsStandardStreamMetadataFormat, String nativeStreamMetadataFormatName, String nativeStreamMetadataFormatClassName, String[] extraStreamMetadataFormatNames, String[] extraStreamMetadataFormatClassNames, boolean supportsStandardImageMetadataFormat, String nativeImageMetadataFormatName, String nativeImageMetadataFormatClassName, String[] extraImageMetadataFormatNames, String[] extraImageMetadataFormatClassNames)
	protected	.... Class[]	**inputTypes**
	public	.... boolean	**isOwnReader** (javax.imageio.ImageReader reader)
1	public	.......................void	onDeregistration (ServiceRegistry registry, Class category)
1	public	.......................void	onRegistration (ServiceRegistry registry, Class category)
▲	public static final	.... Class[]	**STANDARD_INPUT_TYPE**
1	protected	................String	vendorName
1	protected	................String	version
	protected	.... String[]	**writerSpiNames**

ImageReaderWriterSpi | javax.imageio.spi

Object
1.4 ○ └IIOServiceProvider[1] - *RegisterableService*
1.4 ○   └ImageReaderWriterSpi↲

protected	.... String[]	**extraImageMetadataFormatClassNames**
protected	.... String[]	**extraImageMetadataFormatNames**

Class   *Interface*   —extends   - - -implements   ○ abstract   ● final   △ static   ▲ static final   * constructor   x x—inherited   x **x**—declared   **x x**—overridden
εn—examples of usage   ↲—has subclass   package—see other volume

		protected .... String[]	**extraStreamMetadataFormatClassNames**
		protected .... String[]	**extraStreamMetadataFormatNames**
○	1	public abstract .... String	getDescription (java.util.Locale locale)
	1	public .... String[]	**getExtraImageMetadataFormatNames** ()
		public .... String[]	**getExtraStreamMetadataFormatNames** ()
		public .... String[]	**getFileSuffixes** ()
		public .... String[]	**getFormatNames** ()
		public	**getImageMetadataFormat** (String formatName)
		.... *javax.imageio.metadata*⟩	
		.IIOMetadataFormat	
		public .... String[]	**getMIMETypes** ()
		public .... String	**getNativeImageMetadataFormatName** ()
		public .... String	**getNativeStreamMetadataFormatName** ()
		public .... String	**getPluginClassName** ()
		public	**getStreamMetadataFormat** (String formatName)
		.... *javax.imageio.metadata*⟩	
		.IIOMetadataFormat	
	1	public .... String	getVendorName ()
	1	public .... String	getVersion ()
*		public	**ImageReaderWriterSpi** ()
*		public	**ImageReaderWriterSpi** (String vendorName, String version, String[] names,
			String[] suffixes, String[] MIMETypes, String pluginClassName,
			boolean supportsStandardStreamMetadataFormat,
			String nativeStreamMetadataFormatName, String
			nativeStreamMetadataFormatClassName, String[]
			extraStreamMetadataFormatNames, String[] extraStreamMetadataFormatClassNames,
			boolean supportsStandardImageMetadataFormat,
			String nativeImageMetadataFormatName, String
			nativeImageMetadataFormatClassName, String[]
			extraImageMetadataFormatNames, String[] extraImageMetadataFormatClassNames)
		public .... boolean	**isStandardImageMetadataFormatSupported** ()
		public .... boolean	**isStandardStreamMetadataFormatSupported** ()
		protected .... String[]	**MIMETypes**
		protected .... String[]	**names**
		protected .... String	**nativeImageMetadataFormatClassName**
		protected .... String	**nativeImageMetadataFormatName**
		protected .... String	**nativeStreamMetadataFormatClassName**
		protected .... String	**nativeStreamMetadataFormatName**
	1	public .... void	onDeregistration (ServiceRegistry registry, Class category)
	1	public .... void	onRegistration (ServiceRegistry registry, Class category)
		protected .... String	**pluginClassName**
		protected .... String[]	**suffixes**
		protected .... boolean	**supportsStandardImageMetadataFormat**
		protected .... boolean	**supportsStandardStreamMetadataFormat**
	1	protected .... String	vendorName
	1	protected .... String	version

ImageReadParam			javax.imageio
		Object	
1.4	○	└ IIOParam[1]	
1.4		└ ImageReadParam⌄	
	1	*27 inherited members from IIOParam not shown*	
		protected .... boolean	**canSetSourceRenderSize**
		public .... boolean	**canSetSourceRenderSize** ()
		protected .... java⟩	**destination**
		.awt.image.BufferedImage	
		protected .... int[]	**destinationBands**
		public .... java⟩	**getDestination** ()
		.awt.image.BufferedImage	
		public .... int[]	**getDestinationBands** ()
		public .... int	**getSourceMaxProgressivePass** ()
		public .... int	**getSourceMinProgressivePass** ()
		public .... int	**getSourceNumProgressivePasses** ()
		public ...... java.awt.Dimension	**getSourceRenderSize** ()
*		public	**ImageReadParam** ()
		protected .... int	**minProgressivePass**
		protected .... int	**numProgressivePasses**
		public .... void	**setDestination** (java.awt.image.BufferedImage destination)
		public .... void	**setDestinationBands** (int[] destinationBands)
	1	public .... **void**	**setDestinationType** (ImageTypeSpecifier destinationType)

ImageReadParam

public	void	**setSourceProgressivePasses** (int minPass, int numPasses)
public	void	**setSourceRenderSize** (java.awt.Dimension size) throws UnsupportedOperationException
protected	java.awt.Dimension	**sourceRenderSize**

ImageTranscoder — javax.imageio

1.4 *ImageTranscoder*

public	javax.imageio .metadata.IIOMetadata	**convertImageMetadata** (javax.imageio.metadata.IIOMetadata inData, ImageTypeSpecifier imageType, ImageWriteParam param)
public	javax.imageio .metadata.IIOMetadata	**convertStreamMetadata** (javax.imageio.metadata.IIOMetadata inData, ImageWriteParam param)

ImageTranscoderSpi — javax.imageio.spi

```
Object
  └ IIOServiceProvider ¹ - - - - - - - - - - - - - - - - - - - - RegisterableService
      └ ImageTranscoderSpi
```
1.4 ○
1.4 ○

○	public abstract	javax .imageio.ImageTranscoder	**createTranscoderInstance** ()
○ 1	public abstract	String	getDescription (java.util.Locale locale)
○	public abstract	String	**getReaderServiceProviderName** ()
1	public	String	getVendorName ()
1	public	String	getVersion ()
○	public abstract	String	**getWriterServiceProviderName** ()
*	protected		**ImageTranscoderSpi** ()
*	public		**ImageTranscoderSpi** (String vendorName, String version)
1	public	void	onDeregistration (ServiceRegistry registry, Class category)
1	public	void	onRegistration (ServiceRegistry registry, Class category)
1	protected	String	vendorName
1	protected	String	version

ImageTypeSpecifier — javax.imageio

```
Object ¹
  └ ImageTypeSpecifier
```
1.4

	protected	java.awt.image.ColorModel	**colorModel**
△	public static	ImageTypeSpecifier	**createBanded** (java.awt.color.ColorSpace colorSpace, int[] bankIndices, int[] bandOffsets, int dataType, boolean hasAlpha, boolean isAlphaPremultiplied)
	public	java.awt.image.BufferedImage	**createBufferedImage** (int width, int height)
△	public static	ImageTypeSpecifier	**createFromBufferedImageType** (int bufferedImageType)
△	public static	ImageTypeSpecifier	**createFromRenderedImage** (*java.awt.image.RenderedImage* image)
△	public static	ImageTypeSpecifier	**createGrayscale** (int bits, int dataType, boolean isSigned)
△	public static	ImageTypeSpecifier	**createGrayscale** (int bits, int dataType, boolean isSigned, boolean isAlphaPremultiplied)
△	public static	ImageTypeSpecifier	**createIndexed** (byte[] redLUT, byte[] greenLUT, byte[] blueLUT, byte[] alphaLUT, int bits, int dataType)
△	public static	ImageTypeSpecifier	**createInterleaved** (java.awt.color.ColorSpace colorSpace, int[] bandOffsets, int dataType, boolean hasAlpha, boolean isAlphaPremultiplied)
△	public static	ImageTypeSpecifier	**createPacked** (java.awt.color.ColorSpace colorSpace, int redMask, int greenMask, int blueMask, int alphaMask, int transferType, boolean isAlphaPremultiplied)
1	public	boolean	**equals** (Object o)
	public	int	**getBitsPerBand** (int band)
	public	int	**getBufferedImageType** ()
	public	java.awt.image.ColorModel	**getColorModel** ()
	public	int	**getNumBands** ()
	public	int	**getNumComponents** ()

```
public.................... java₂  getSampleModel ()
         .awt.image.SampleModel
public.................... java₂  getSampleModel (int width, int height)
         .awt.image.SampleModel
*  public.........................  ImageTypeSpecifier (java.awt.image.RenderedImage image)
*  public.........................  ImageTypeSpecifier (java.awt.image.ColorModel colorModel,
                                       java.awt.image.SampleModel sampleModel)
   protected ............... java₂  sampleModel
            .awt.image.SampleModel
```

ImageView

```
      Object
1.2 O └java.swing.text.View 1 ------------------ javax.swing.SwingConstants 2
1.4    └ImageView
```

```
1  42 inherited members from javax.swing.text.View not shown
2  19 inherited members from javax.swing.SwingConstants not shown
1  public.................... void  changedUpdate (javax.swing.event.DocumentEvent e, java.awt.Shape a,
                                      javax.swing.text.ViewFactory f)
1  public.................... float  getAlignment (int axis)
   public.................... String  getAltText ()
1  public.................... javax₂  getAttributes ()
         .swing.text.AttributeSet
   public......... java.awt.Image  getImage ()
   public............. java.net.URL  getImageURL ()
   public......... javax.swing.Icon  getLoadingImageIcon ()
   public................. boolean  getLoadsSynchronously ()
   public......... javax.swing.Icon  getNoImageIcon ()
1  public.................... float  getPreferredSpan (int axis)
   protected ...........StyleSheet  getStyleSheet ()
1  public.................... String  getToolTipText (float x, float y, java.awt.Shape allocation)
*  public.........................  ImageView (javax.swing.text.Element elem)
1  public......... java.awt.Shape  modelToView (int pos, java.awt.Shape a, javax.swing.text.Position.Bias b)
                                     throws javax.swing.text.BadLocationException
1  public.................... void  paint (java.awt.Graphics g, java.awt.Shape a)
   public....................void  setLoadsSynchronously (boolean newValue)
1  public.................... void  setParent (javax.swing.text.View parent)
   protected ..................void  setPropertiesFromAttributes ()
1  public.................... void  setSize (float width, float height)
1  public.................... int  viewToModel (float x, float y, java.awt.Shape a, javax.swing.text.Position.Bias[] bias)
```

ImageWriteParam

```
      Object
1.4 O └IIOParam 1
1.4    └ImageWriteParam
```

```
1  28 inherited members from IIOParam not shown
   protected ............. boolean  canOffsetTiles
   public................. boolean  canOffsetTiles ()
   public................. boolean  canWriteCompressed ()
   protected ............. boolean  canWriteCompressed
   protected ............. boolean  canWriteProgressive
   public................. boolean  canWriteProgressive ()
   public................. boolean  canWriteTiles ()
   protected ............. boolean  canWriteTiles
   protected ..................int  compressionMode
   protected ..................float  compressionQuality
   protected ...............String  compressionType
   protected ............. String[]  compressionTypes
   public......................float  getBitRate (float quality)
   public......................int  getCompressionMode ()
   public......................float  getCompressionQuality ()
   public................. String[]  getCompressionQualityDescriptions ()
   public................. float[]  getCompressionQualityValues ()
   public.................String  getCompressionType ()
   public................. String[]  getCompressionTypes ()
   public......... java.util.Locale  getLocale ()
   public.................String  getLocalizedCompressionTypeName ()
   public.... java.awt.Dimension[]  getPreferredTileSizes ()
```

ImageWriteParam

	public	int	**getProgressiveMode** ()
	public	int	**getTileGridXOffset** ()
	public	int	**getTileGridYOffset** ()
	public	int	**getTileHeight** ()
	public	int	**getTileWidth** ()
	public	int	**getTilingMode** ()
＊	protected		**ImageWriteParam** ()
＊	public		**ImageWriteParam** (*java.util.*Locale locale)
	public	boolean	**isCompressionLossless** ()
	protected	java.util.Locale	**locale**
▲	public static final	int	**MODE_COPY_FROM_METADATA** = 3
▲	public static final	int	**MODE_DEFAULT** = 1
▲	public static final	int	**MODE_DISABLED** = 0
▲	public static final	int	**MODE_EXPLICIT** = 2 ε699
	protected java.awt.Dimension[]		**preferredTileSizes**
	protected	int	**progressiveMode**
	public	void	**setCompressionMode** (int mode) ε699
	public	void	**setCompressionQuality** (float quality) ε699
	public	void	**setCompressionType** (String compressionType)
	public	void	**setProgressiveMode** (int mode)
	public	void	**setTiling** (int tileWidth, int tileHeight, int tileGridXOffset, int tileGridYOffset)
	public	void	**setTilingMode** (int mode)
	protected	int	**tileGridXOffset**
	protected	int	**tileGridYOffset**
	protected	int	**tileHeight**
	protected	int	**tileWidth**
	protected	int	**tilingMode**
	protected	boolean	**tilingSet**
	public	void	**unsetCompression** ()
	public	void	**unsetTiling** ()

ImageWriter   javax.imageio

Object
1.4 ○ └ImageWriter - *ImageTranscoder [1]*

	public synchronized	void	**abort** ()
	protected synchronized boolean		**abortRequested** ()
	public	void	**addIIOWriteProgressListener** (*javax.imageio.event.IIOWriteProgressListener* listener)
	public	void	**addIIOWriteWarningListener** (*javax.imageio.event.IIOWriteWarningListener* listener)
	protected	java.util.Locale[]	**availableLocales**
	public	boolean	**canInsertEmpty** (int imageIndex) throws java.io.IOException
	public	boolean	**canInsertImage** (int imageIndex) throws java.io.IOException
	public	boolean	**canRemoveImage** (int imageIndex) throws java.io.IOException
	public	boolean	**canReplaceImageMetadata** (int imageIndex) throws java.io.IOException
	public	boolean	**canReplacePixels** (int imageIndex) throws java.io.IOException
	public	boolean	**canReplaceStreamMetadata** () throws java.io.IOException
	public	boolean	**canWriteEmpty** () throws java.io.IOException
	public	boolean	**canWriteRasters** ()
	public	boolean	**canWriteSequence** ()
	protected synchronized	void	**clearAbortRequest** ()
○ 1	public abstract .javax.imageio.metadata.IIOMetadata		**convertImageMetadata** (javax.imageio.metadata.IIOMetadata inData, ImageTypeSpecifier imageType, ImageWriteParam param)
○ 1	public abstract .javax.imageio.metadata.IIOMetadata		**convertStreamMetadata** (javax.imageio.metadata.IIOMetadata inData, ImageWriteParam param)
	public	void	**dispose** () ε699
	public	void	**endInsertEmpty** () throws java.io.IOException
	public	void	**endReplacePixels** () throws java.io.IOException
	public	void	**endWriteEmpty** () throws java.io.IOException
	public	void	**endWriteSequence** () throws java.io.IOException
	public	java.util.Locale[]	**getAvailableLocales** ()
○	public abstract .javax.imageio.metadata.IIOMetadata		**getDefaultImageMetadata** (ImageTypeSpecifier imageType, ImageWriteParam param)
○	public abstract .javax.imageio.metadata.IIOMetadata		**getDefaultStreamMetadata** (ImageWriteParam param)
	public	ImageWriteParam	**getDefaultWriteParam** ()

public	java.util.Locale	**getLocale** ()
public	int	**getNumThumbnailsSupported** (ImageTypeSpecifier imageType, ImageWriteParam param, javax.imageio.metadata.IIOMetadata streamMetadata, javax.imageio.metadata.IIOMetadata imageMetadata)
public	javax₂ .imageio.spi.ImageWriterSpi	**getOriginatingProvider** ()
public	Object	**getOutput** ()
public	java.awt.Dimension[]	**getPreferredThumbnailSizes** (ImageTypeSpecifier imageType, ImageWriteParam param, javax.imageio.metadata.IIOMetadata streamMetadata, javax.imageio.metadata.IIOMetadata imageMetadata)

*

protected		**ImageWriter** (javax.imageio.spi.ImageWriterSpi originatingProvider)
protected	java.util.Locale	**locale**
protected	javax₂ .imageio.spi.ImageWriterSpi	**originatingProvider**
protected	Object	**output**
public	void	**prepareInsertEmpty** (int imageIndex, ImageTypeSpecifier imageType, int width, int height, javax.imageio.metadata.IIOMetadata imageMetadata, *java.util.List* thumbnails, ImageWriteParam param) throws java.io.IOException
public	void	**prepareReplacePixels** (int imageIndex, java.awt.Rectangle region) throws java.io.IOException
public	void	**prepareWriteEmpty** (javax.imageio.metadata.IIOMetadata streamMetadata, ImageTypeSpecifier imageType, int width, int height, javax.imageio.metadata.IIOMetadata imageMetadata, *java.util.List* thumbnails, ImageWriteParam param) throws java.io.IOException
public	void	**prepareWriteSequence** (javax.imageio.metadata.IIOMetadata streamMetadata) throws java.io.IOException
protected	void	**processImageComplete** ()
protected	void	**processImageProgress** (float percentageDone)
protected	void	**processImageStarted** (int imageIndex)
protected	void	**processThumbnailComplete** ()
protected	void	**processThumbnailProgress** (float percentageDone)
protected	void	**processThumbnailStarted** (int imageIndex, int thumbnailIndex)
protected	void	**processWarningOccurred** (int imageIndex, String warning)
protected	void	**processWarningOccurred** (int imageIndex, String baseName, String keyword)
protected	void	**processWriteAborted** ()
protected	*java.util.List*	**progressListeners**
public	void	**removeAllIIOWriteProgressListeners** ()
public	void	**removeAllIIOWriteWarningListeners** ()
public	void	**removeIIOWriteProgressListener** (*javax.imageio.event.IIOWriteProgressListener* listener)
public	void	**removeIIOWriteWarningListener** (*javax.imageio.event.IIOWriteWarningListener* listener)
public	void	**removeImage** (int imageIndex) throws java.io.IOException
public	void	**replaceImageMetadata** (int imageIndex, javax.imageio.metadata.IIOMetadata imageMetadata) throws java.io.IOException
public	void	**replacePixels** (java.awt.image.Raster raster, ImageWriteParam param) throws java.io.IOException
public	void	**replacePixels** (*java.awt.image.RenderedImage* image, ImageWriteParam param) throws java.io.IOException
public	void	**replaceStreamMetadata** (javax.imageio.metadata.IIOMetadata streamMetadata) throws java.io.IOException
public	void	**reset** ()
public	void	**setLocale** (java.util.Locale locale)
public	void	**setOutput** (Object output) ε699
protected	*java.util.List*	**warningListeners**
protected	*java.util.List*	**warningLocales**
public	void	**write** (*java.awt.image.RenderedImage* image) throws java.io.IOException
public	void	**write** (IIOImage image) throws java.io.IOException
public abstract	void	**write** (javax.imageio.metadata.IIOMetadata streamMetadata, IIOImage image, ImageWriteParam param) throws java.io.IOException ε699
public	void	**writeInsert** (int imageIndex, IIOImage image, ImageWriteParam param) throws java.io.IOException
public	void	**writeToSequence** (IIOImage image, ImageWriteParam param) throws java.io.IOException

I

Classes

ImageWriterSpi

		ImageWriterSpi	javax.imageio.spi

```
        Object
1.4 ○   └IIOServiceProvider1 - - - - - - - - - - - - - - - - - - - - RegisterableService
1.4 ○      └ImageReaderWriterSpi2
1.4 ○         └ImageWriterSpi
```

	2	*26 inherited members from ImageReaderWriterSpi not shown*	
		public................. boolean	**canEncodeImage** (*java.awt.image.RenderedImage* im)
○		public abstract .... boolean	**canEncodeImage** (javax.imageio.ImageTypeSpecifier type)
		public.......................... ...javax.imageio.ImageWriter	**createWriterInstance** () throws java.io.IOException
○		public abstract ....javax.imageio.ImageWriter	**createWriterInstance** (Object extension) throws java.io.IOException
○	1	public abstract ....String	getDescription (java.util.Locale locale)
		public..................... String[]	**getImageReaderSpiNames** ()
		public.................... Class[]	**getOutputTypes** ()
	1	public....................String	getVendorName ()
	1	public....................String	getVersion ()
✳		protected	**ImageWriterSpi** ()
✳		public.........................	**ImageWriterSpi** (String vendorName, String version, String[] names, String[] suffixes, String[] MIMETypes, String writerClassName, Class[] outputTypes, String[] readerSpiNames, boolean supportsStandardStreamMetadataFormat, String nativeStreamMetadataFormatName, String nativeStreamMetadataFormatClassName, String[] extraStreamMetadataFormatNames, String[] extraStreamMetadataFormatClassNames, boolean supportsStandardImageMetadataFormat, String nativeImageMetadataFormatName, String nativeImageMetadataFormatClassName, String[] extraImageMetadataFormatNames, String[] extraImageMetadataFormatClassNames)
		public .... boolean	**isFormatLossless** ()
		public .... boolean	**isOwnWriter** (javax.imageio.ImageWriter writer)
	1	public.......................void	onDeregistration (ServiceRegistry registry, Class category)
	1	public.......................void	onRegistration (ServiceRegistry registry, Class category)
		protected .... Class[]	**outputTypes**
		protected .... String[]	**readerSpiNames**
▲		public static final .... Class[]	**STANDARD_OUTPUT_TYPE**
	1	protected ....String	vendorName
	1	protected ....String	version

		ImagingOpException	java.awt.image

```
        Object
        └Throwable - - - - - - - - - - - - - - - - - - - - - - - - - - - java.io.Serializable⌐
           └Exception
              └RuntimeException
1.2              └ImagingOpException
```

✳	public.........................	**ImagingOpException** (String s)	

		IndexColorModel	java.awt.image
			ε660,662,668

```
        Object
○       └ColorModel1 - - - - - - - - - - - - - - - - - - - - - - - - - java.awt.Transparency⌐2
           └IndexColorModel
```

	1	*25 inherited members from ColorModel not shown*		
1.2 ▲	2	public static final.............int	BITMASK = 2	ε666,667
1.2		public...........BufferedImage	**convertToIntDiscrete** (Raster raster, boolean forceARGB)	
1.2	1	public........... SampleModel	**createCompatibleSampleModel** (int w, int h)	
1.2	1	public...........WritableRaster	**createCompatibleWritableRaster** (int w, int h)	
	1	public..................... **void**	**finalize** ()	
●	1	public final .... **int**	**getAlpha** (int pixel)	
●		public final ....void	**getAlphas** (byte[] a)	
●	1	public final .... **int**	**getBlue** (int pixel)	
●		public final ....void	**getBlues** (byte[] b)	

Class   *Interface*   —extends   - - -implements   ○ abstract   ● final   △ static   ▲ static final   ✳ constructor   x x—inherited   x **x**—declared   **x x**—overridden
ε*n*—examples of usage   ⌐—has subclass   package—see other volume

I

1.2	1	public	**int[] getComponents** (int pixel, int[] components, int offset)	
1.2	1	public	**int[] getComponents** (Object pixel, int[] components, int offset)	
1.2	1	public	**int[] getComponentSize** ()	
1.2	1	public	**int getDataElement** (int[] components, int offset)	
1.2		public synchronized	**Object getDataElements** (int rgb, Object pixel)	
1.2		public	**Object getDataElements** (int[] components, int offset, Object pixel)	
●	1	public final	**int getGreen** (int pixel)	
●		public final	**void getGreens** (byte[] g)	
●		public final	**int getMapSize** ()	ε663
●	1	public final	**int getRed** (int pixel)	
●		public final	**void getReds** (byte[] r)	
●	1	public final	**int getRGB** (int pixel)	
1.2 ●		public final	**void getRGBs** (int[] rgb)	
1.2	1	public	**int getTransparency** ()	
●		public final	**int getTransparentPixel** ()	ε663
1.3		public	java.math.BigInteger **getValidPixels** ()	
*		public	**IndexColorModel** (int bits, int size, byte[] cmap, int start, boolean hasalpha)	
*		public	**IndexColorModel** (int bits, int size, byte[] r, byte[] g, byte[] b) ε660	
*		public	**IndexColorModel** (int bits, int size, byte[] r, byte[] g, byte[] b, byte[] a)	
*		public	**IndexColorModel** (int bits, int size, byte[] r, byte[] g, byte[] b, int trans)	
1.3 *		public	**IndexColorModel** (int bits, int size, int[] cmap, int start, int transferType, java.math.BigInteger validBits)	
*		public	**IndexColorModel** (int bits, int size, byte[] cmap, int start, boolean hasalpha, int trans)	
1.2 *		public	**IndexColorModel** (int bits, int size, int[] cmap, int start, boolean hasalpha, int trans, int transferType)	
1.2	1	public	**boolean isCompatibleRaster** (Raster raster)	
1.2	1	public	**boolean isCompatibleSampleModel** (SampleModel sm)	
1.3		public	boolean **isValid** ()	
1.3		public	boolean **isValid** (int pixel)	
1.2 ▲	2	public static final	int OPAQUE = 1	ε666,667
	1	public	**String toString** ()	
1.2 ▲	2	public static final	int TRANSLUCENT = 3	ε666

InlineView

javax.swing.text.html

```
      Object
1.2 ○  └javax.swing.text.View¹ ------------------- javax.swing.SwingConstants⁴
1.3      └javax.swing.text.GlyphView² ------------ javax.swing.text.TabableView, Cloneable
1.2        └javax.swing.text.LabelView³
1.2          └InlineView
```

	1	*37 inherited members from javax.swing.text.View not shown*	
	4	*19 inherited members from javax.swing.SwingConstants not shown*	
	2	public ... javax.swing.text.View	breakView (int axis, int p0, float pos, float len)
	3	public	**void changedUpdate** (*javax.swing.event.DocumentEvent* e, *java.awt.Shape* a, *javax.swing.text.ViewFactory* f)
1.3	2	protected	void checkPainter ()
●	2	protected final	Object clone ()
	2	public ... javax.swing.text.View	createFragment (int p0, int p1)
	2	public	float getAlignment (int axis)
	1	public	**javax .swing.text.AttributeSet getAttributes** ()
1.3	3	public	java.awt.Color getBackground ()
	2	public	**int getBreakWeight** (int axis, float pos, float len)
	2	public	int getEndOffset ()
	3	public	java.awt.Font getFont ()
1.3	3	public	java.awt.Color getForeground ()
1.3	2	public	javax.swing.text .GlyphView.GlyphPainter getGlyphPainter ()
	2	public	int getNextVisualPositionFrom (int pos, javax.swing.text.Position.Bias b, *java.awt.Shape* a, int direction, javax.swing.text.Position.Bias[] biasRet) throws javax.swing.text.BadLocationException
	2	public	float getPartialSpan (int p0, int p1)
	2	public	float getPreferredSpan (int axis)
	2	public	int getStartOffset ()
		protected	StyleSheet **getStyleSheet** ()
	2	public	float getTabbedSpan (float x, *javax.swing.text.TabExpander* e)
1.3	2	public	javax .swing.text.TabExpander getTabExpander ()
1.3	2	public .... javax.swing.text.Segment	getText (int p0, int p1)

Classes

InlineView

*		public	....	**InlineView** (*javax.swing.text.Element* elem)
	2	public	........................void	insertUpdate (*javax.swing.event.DocumentEvent* e, *java.awt.Shape* a, *javax.swing.text.ViewFactory* f)
1.3	3	public	.... boolean	isStrikeThrough ()
1.3	3	public	.... boolean	isSubscript ()
1.3	3	public	.... boolean	isSuperscript ()
1.3	3	public	.... boolean	isUnderline ()
	2	public	.... *java.awt.Shape*	modelToView (int pos, *java.awt.Shape* a, javax.swing.text.Position.Bias b) throws javax.swing.text.BadLocationException
	2	public	........................void	paint (java.awt.Graphics g, *java.awt.Shape* a)
	2	public	........................void	removeUpdate (*javax.swing.event.DocumentEvent* e, *java.awt.Shape* a, *javax.swing.text.ViewFactory* f)
1.3	2	public	........................void	setGlyphPainter (javax.swing.text.GlyphView.GlyphPainter p)
	3	protected	.... **void**	**setPropertiesFromAttributes** ()
	3	protected	................void	setStrikeThrough (boolean s)
	3	protected	................void	setSubscript (boolean s)
	3	protected	................void	setSuperscript (boolean s)
	3	protected	................void	setUnderline (boolean u)
	2	public	........................int	viewToModel (float x, float y, *java.awt.Shape* a, javax.swing.text.Position.Bias[] biasReturn)

InputContext

java.awt.im

Object
 └InputContext *(1.2)*

		public	........................void	**dispatchEvent** (java.awt.AWTEvent event)
		public	........................void	**dispose** ()
		public	........................void	**endComposition** ()
		public	........................Object	**getInputMethodControlObject** ()
	△	public static	...... InputContext	**getInstance** ()
1.3		public	.... java.util.Locale	**getLocale** ()
	*	protected	....	**InputContext** ()
1.3		public	.... boolean	**isCompositionEnabled** ()
1.3		public	........................void	**reconvert** ()
		public	........................void	**removeNotify** (java.awt.Component client)
		public	.... boolean	**selectInputMethod** (java.util.Locale locale)
		public	........................void	**setCharacterSubsets** (Character.Subset[] subsets)
1.3		public	........................void	**setCompositionEnabled** (boolean enable)

InputEvent

java.awt.event
ε640,641,643,649,566

Object
 └ java.util.EventObject[1] - - - - - - - - - - - - - - - - - - - *java.io.Serializable* ⌄   *(1.1)*
   └ java.awt.AWTEvent[2]   *(1.1 ○)*
     └ ComponentEvent[3]   *(1.1)*
       └ InputEvent ⌄   *(1.1 ○)*

	2		*25 inherited members from java.awt.AWTEvent not shown*		
1.4 ▲		public static final	............int	**ALT_DOWN_MASK** = 512	ε859
1.4 ▲		public static final	............int	**ALT_GRAPH_DOWN_MASK** = 8192	
1.2 ▲		public static final	............int	**ALT_GRAPH_MASK** = 32	
▲		public static final	............int	**ALT_MASK** = 8	ε859
1.4 ▲		public static final	............int	**BUTTON1_DOWN_MASK** = 1024	ε859
▲		public static final	............int	**BUTTON1_MASK** = 16	ε646,635,859
1.4 ▲		public static final	............int	**BUTTON2_DOWN_MASK** = 2048	ε859
▲		public static final	............int	**BUTTON2_MASK** = 8	ε646,859
1.4 ▲		public static final	............int	**BUTTON3_DOWN_MASK** = 4096	ε859
▲		public static final	............int	**BUTTON3_MASK** = 4	ε646,859
▲	3	public static final	............int	COMPONENT_FIRST = 100	
▲	3	public static final	............int	COMPONENT_HIDDEN = 103	
▲	3	public static final	............int	COMPONENT_LAST = 103	
▲	3	public static final	............int	COMPONENT_MOVED = 100	
▲	3	public static final	............int	COMPONENT_RESIZED = 101	
▲	3	public static final	............int	COMPONENT_SHOWN = 102	
	2	public	.... **void**	**consume** ()	ε1004
1.4 ▲		public static final	............int	**CTRL_DOWN_MASK** = 128	ε859
▲		public static final	............int	**CTRL_MASK** = 2	ε859

Class   *Interface*   —extends   - - -implements   ○ abstract   ● final   △ static   ▲ static final   * constructor   x x—inherited   x **x**—declared   **x x**—overridden
ε*n*—examples of usage   ⌄—has subclass   package—see other volume

	3	public.... java.awt.Component	getComponent ()		ε810,813,1011
		public.................................int	**getModifiers** ()		ε646
1.4		public.........................int	**getModifiersEx** ()		
1.4 △		public static ....String	**getModifiersExText** (int modifiers)		
	1	public.................... Object	getSource ()		ε644,886,565,568,570
		public..................... long	**getWhen** ()		
		public................... boolean	**isAltDown** ()		
1.2		public................... boolean	**isAltGraphDown** ()		
	2	public................. **boolean**	**isConsumed** ()		
		public................... boolean	**isControlDown** ()		
		public................... boolean	**isMetaDown** ()		
		public................... boolean	**isShiftDown** ()		
1.4 ▲		public static final ....int	**META_DOWN_MASK** = 256		ε859
▲		public static final ....int	**META_MASK** = 4		ε859
	3	public.....................String	paramString ()		
1.4 ▲		public static final ....int	**SHIFT_DOWN_MASK** = 64		ε859
▲		public static final ....int	**SHIFT_MASK** = 1		ε859
	1	protected transient...... Object	source		

InputMap — javax.swing

Object ε870
└InputMap ---------------------------- *java.io.Serializable* (1.3)

	public............. KeyStroke[]	**allKeys** ()		ε860
	public.......................void	**clear** ()		
	public..................... Object	**get** (KeyStroke keyStroke)		ε860
	public.................InputMap	**getParent** ()		ε860,862
*	public.................	**InputMap** ()		ε863
	public............. KeyStroke[]	**keys** ()		ε860,862
	public.......................void	**put** (KeyStroke keyStroke, Object actionMapKey)		ε857,858,861,863,937
	public.......................void	**remove** (KeyStroke key)		
	public.......................void	**setParent** (InputMap map)		ε863
	public.........................int	**size** ()		

InputMapUIResource — javax.swing.plaf

Object ε870
└javax.swing.InputMap[1] ----------------- *java.io.Serializable* (1.3)
  └InputMapUIResource ---------------- *UIResource* (1.3)

1	public. javax.swing.KeyStroke[]	allKeys ()		ε860
1	public.....................void	clear ()		
1	public..................Object	get (javax.swing.KeyStroke keyStroke)		ε860
1	public... javax.swing.InputMap	getParent ()		ε860,862
*	public.........................	**InputMapUIResource** ()		
1	public. javax.swing.KeyStroke[]	keys ()		ε860,862
1	public.....................void	put (javax.swing.KeyStroke keyStroke, Object actionMapKey)		ε857,858,861,863,937
1	public.....................void	remove (javax.swing.KeyStroke key)		
1	public.....................void	setParent (javax.swing.InputMap map)		ε863
1	public.........................int	size ()		

InputMethod — java.awt.im.spi

InputMethod (1.3)

public......................void	**activate** ()	
public......................void	**deactivate** (boolean isTemporary)	
public......................void	**dispatchEvent** (java.awt.AWTEvent event)	
public......................void	**dispose** ()	
public......................void	**endComposition** ()	
public................. Object	**getControlObject** ()	
public.......... java.util.Locale	**getLocale** ()	
public......................void	**hideWindows** ()	
public................. boolean	**isCompositionEnabled** ()	
public......................void	**notifyClientWindowChange** (java.awt.Rectangle bounds)	
public......................void	**reconvert** ()	
public......................void	**removeNotify** ()	
public......................void	**setCharacterSubsets** (Character.Subset[] subsets)	
public......................void	**setCompositionEnabled** (boolean enable)	
public......................void	**setInputMethodContext** (*InputMethodContext* context)	

I

Classes

InputMethod

	public	boolean	**setLocale** (java.util.Locale locale)

1.3   *InputMethodContext*————————————*java.awt.im.InputMethodRequests* [1]

1	public	*java.text.-* *AttributedCharacterIterator*	cancelLatestCommittedText (java.text.AttributedCharacterIterator.Attribute[] attributes)
1.4	public	javax.swing.JFrame	**createInputMethodJFrame** (String title, boolean attachToInputContext)
	public	java.awt.Window	**createInputMethodWindow** (String title, boolean attachToInputContext)
	public	void	**dispatchInputMethodEvent** (int id, *java.text.AttributedCharacterIterator* text, int committedCharacterCount, java.awt.font.TextHitInfo caret, java.awt.font.TextHitInfo visiblePosition)
	public	void	**enableClientWindowNotification** (*InputMethod* inputMethod, boolean enable)
1	public	*java.text.-* *AttributedCharacterIterator*	getCommittedText (int beginIndex, int endIndex, java.text.₂ .AttributedCharacterIterator.Attribute[] attributes)
1	public	int	getCommittedTextLength ()
1	public	int	getInsertPositionOffset ()
1	public . java.awt.font.TextHitInfo		getLocationOffset (int x, int y)
1	public	*java.text.-* *AttributedCharacterIterator*	getSelectedText (java.text.AttributedCharacterIterator.Attribute[] attributes)
1	public	java.awt.Rectangle	getTextLocation (java.awt.font.TextHitInfo offset)

1.3   *InputMethodDescriptor*

	public	*InputMethod*	**createInputMethod** () throws Exception
	public	java.util.Locale[]	**getAvailableLocales** () throws java.awt.AWTException
	public	String	**getInputMethodDisplayName** (java.util.Locale inputLocale, java.util.Locale displayLanguage)
	public	java.awt.Image	**getInputMethodIcon** (java.util.Locale inputLocale)
	public	boolean	**hasDynamicLocaleList** ()

                                                      ε640,641,643,649,566

Object

1.1   └ java.util.EventObject[1] - - - - - - - - - - - - - - - - - - *java.io.Serializable*

1.1 ○   └ java.awt.AWTEvent[2]

1.2   └ InputMethodEvent

2	*25 inherited members from java.awt.AWTEvent not shown*			
▲	public static final	int	**CARET_POSITION_CHANGED** = 1101	
2	public	void	**consume** ()	ε1004
	public . java.awt.font.TextHitInfo		**getCaret** ()	
	public	int	**getCommittedCharacterCount** ()	
1	public	Object	getSource ()	ε644,886,565,568,570
	public	*java.text.-* *AttributedCharacterIterator*	**getText** ()	
	public . java.awt.font.TextHitInfo		**getVisiblePosition** ()	
1.4	public	long	**getWhen** ()	
▲	public static final	int	**INPUT_METHOD_FIRST** = 1100	
▲	public static final	int	**INPUT_METHOD_LAST** = 1101	
▲	public static final	int	**INPUT_METHOD_TEXT_CHANGED** = 1100	
*	public		**InputMethodEvent** (java.awt.Component source, int id, java.awt.font.TextHitInfo caret, java.awt.font.TextHitInfo visiblePosition)	
*	public		**InputMethodEvent** (java.awt.Component source, int id, *java.text.AttributedCharacterIterator* text, int committedCharacterCount, java.awt.font.TextHitInfo caret, java.awt.font.TextHitInfo visiblePosition)	
1.4 *	public		**InputMethodEvent** (java.awt.Component source, int id, long when, *java.text.AttributedCharacterIterator* text, int committedCharacterCount, java.awt.font.TextHitInfo caret, java.awt.font.TextHitInfo visiblePosition)	
2	public	boolean	**isConsumed** ()	
2	public	String	**paramString** ()	
1	protected transient	Object	source	

InputMethodHighlight

java.awt.im

Object
1.2 └InputMethodHighlight

▲	public static final ....int	**CONVERTED_TEXT** = 1
	public ....int	**getState** ()
1.3	public .... *java.util.Map*	**getStyle** ()
	public ....int	**getVariation** ()
*	public	**InputMethodHighlight** (boolean selected, int state)
*	public	**InputMethodHighlight** (boolean selected, int state, int variation)
1.3 *	public	**InputMethodHighlight** (boolean selected, int state, int variation, *java.util.Map* style)
	public .... boolean	**isSelected** ()
▲	public static final ....int	**RAW_TEXT** = 0
▲	public static final .... InputMethodHighlight	**SELECTED_CONVERTED_TEXT_HIGHLIGHT**
▲	public static final .... InputMethodHighlight	**SELECTED_RAW_TEXT_HIGHLIGHT**
▲	public static final .... InputMethodHighlight	**UNSELECTED_CONVERTED_TEXT_HIGHLIGHT**
▲	public static final .... InputMethodHighlight	**UNSELECTED_RAW_TEXT_HIGHLIGHT**

InputMethodListener

java.awt.event

ε738,743,745,746,752

1.2 *InputMethodListener*————————————*java.util.EventListener*

	public ....void	**caretPositionChanged** (InputMethodEvent event)
	public ....void	**inputMethodTextChanged** (InputMethodEvent event)

InputMethodRequests

java.awt.im

1.2 *InputMethodRequests*

	public .... *java.text.-* *AttributedCharacterIterator*	**cancelLatestCommittedText** (java.text.AttributedCharacterIterator.Attribute[] attributes)
	public .... *java.text.-* *AttributedCharacterIterator*	**getCommittedText** (int beginIndex, int endIndex, java.text▷ .AttributedCharacterIterator.Attribute[] attributes)
	public ....int	**getCommittedTextLength** ()
	public ....int	**getInsertPositionOffset** ()
	public . java.awt.font.TextHitInfo	**getLocationOffset** (int x, int y)
	public .... *java.text.-* *AttributedCharacterIterator*	**getSelectedText** (java.text.AttributedCharacterIterator.Attribute[] attributes)
	public ...... java.awt.Rectangle	**getTextLocation** (java.awt.font.TextHitInfo offset)

InputSubset

java.awt.im

Object
1.2 └Character.Subset [1]
1.2 ● └InputSubset

●	1	public final .... boolean	equals (Object obj)
1.3 ▲		public static final .. InputSubset	**FULLWIDTH_DIGITS**
1.3 ▲		public static final .. InputSubset	**FULLWIDTH_LATIN**
▲		public static final .. InputSubset	**HALFWIDTH_KATAKANA**
▲		public static final .. InputSubset	**HANJA**
●	1	public final ....int	hashCode ()
▲		public static final .. InputSubset	**KANJI**
▲		public static final .. InputSubset	**LATIN**
▲		public static final .. InputSubset	**LATIN_DIGITS**
▲		public static final .. InputSubset	**SIMPLIFIED_HANZI**
●	1	public final .... String	toString ()
▲		public static final .. InputSubset	**TRADITIONAL_HANZI**

InputVerifier

javax.swing

Object
1.3 ○ └InputVerifier

I

Classes

587

InputVerifier

*	public		**InputVerifier** ()
	public	boolean	**shouldYieldFocus** (JComponent input)
○	public abstract	boolean	**verify** (JComponent input)

Insets　　　　　　　　　　　　　　　　　　　　　　　java.awt

Object [1]　　　　　　　　　　　　　　　　　　　　　　　　　ε870
└Insets - *Cloneable*, *java.io.Serializable*

	public	int	**bottom**	
1	public	**Object**	**clone** ()	
1	public	**boolean**	**equals** (Object obj)	
1	public	**int**	**hashCode** ()	
*	public		**Insets** (int top, int left, int bottom, int right)	ε630,790,816
	public	int	**left**	
	public	int	**right**	
	public	int	**top**	
1	public	**String**	**toString** ()	

InsetsUIResource　　　　　　　　　　　　　　　　　javax.swing.plaf

Object　　　　　　　　　　　　　　　　　　　　　　　　　ε870
└java.awt.Insets [1] - *Cloneable*, *java.io.Serializable*
　1.2　　└InsetsUIResource - - - - - - - - - - - - - - - - - - - *UIResource*

1	public	int	bottom
1	public	Object	clone ()
1	public	boolean	equals (Object obj)
1	public	int	hashCode ()
*	public		**InsetsUIResource** (int top, int left, int bottom, int right)
1	public	int	left
1	public	int	right
1	public	int	top
1	public	String	toString ()

Instrument　　　　　　　　　　　　　　　　　　　javax.sound.midi

Object
1.3 ○　└SoundbankResource [1]
1.3 ○　　└Instrument

○	1	public abstract	Object	getData ()
	1	public	Class	getDataClass ()
	1	public	String	getName ()
		public	Patch	**getPatch** ()
	1	public	*Soundbank*	getSoundbank ()
*		protected		**Instrument** (*Soundbank* soundbank, Patch patch, String name, Class dataClass)

IntegerSyntax　　　　　　　　　　　　　　　　　javax.print.attribute

Object [1]
1.4 ○　└IntegerSyntax - *java.io.Serializable*, *Cloneable*

1	public	**boolean**	**equals** (Object object)
	public	int	**getValue** ()
1	public	**int**	**hashCode** ()
*	protected		**IntegerSyntax** (int value)
*	protected		**IntegerSyntax** (int value, int lowerBound, int upperBound)
1	public	**String**	**toString** ()

InternalFrameAdapter　　　　　　　　　　　　　　javax.swing.event

Object
1.2 ○　└InternalFrameAdapter - - - - - - - - - - - - - - - - - - - *InternalFrameListener* [1] (*java.util.EventListener*)

Class　*Interface*　—extends　- - -implements　○ abstract　● final　△ static　▲ static final　✳ constructor　x x—inherited　x **x**—declared　**x x**—overridden
ε*n*—examples of usage　－has subclass　package—see other volume

588

1	public.......................void	**internalFrameActivated** (InternalFrameEvent e)
*	public.........................	**InternalFrameAdapter** ()
1	public.......................void	**internalFrameClosed** (InternalFrameEvent e)
1	public.......................void	**internalFrameClosing** (InternalFrameEvent e)
1	public.......................void	**internalFrameDeactivated** (InternalFrameEvent e)
1	public.......................void	**internalFrameDeiconified** (InternalFrameEvent e)
1	public.......................void	**internalFrameIconified** (InternalFrameEvent e)
1	public.......................void	**internalFrameOpened** (InternalFrameEvent e)

InternalFrameEvent
javax.swing.event

ε640,641,643,649,566

Object
1.1 └ java.util.EventObject¹ - - - - - - - - - - - - - - - - - - java.io.Serializable
1.1 O └ java.awt.AWTEvent²
1.2 └ InternalFrameEvent

2	*27 inherited members from java.awt.AWTEvent not shown*	
1.3	public...........................	**getInternalFrame** ()
	.. javax.swing.JInternalFrame	
1	public....................Object	getSource ()
▲	public static final ....int	**INTERNAL_FRAME_ACTIVATED** = 25554
▲	public static final ....int	**INTERNAL_FRAME_CLOSED** = 25551
▲	public static final ....int	**INTERNAL_FRAME_CLOSING** = 25550
▲	public static final ....int	**INTERNAL_FRAME_DEACTIVATED** = 25555
▲	public static final ....int	**INTERNAL_FRAME_DEICONIFIED** = 25553
▲	public static final ....int	**INTERNAL_FRAME_FIRST** = 25549
▲	public static final ....int	**INTERNAL_FRAME_ICONIFIED** = 25552
▲	public static final ....int	**INTERNAL_FRAME_LAST** = 25555
▲	public static final ....int	**INTERNAL_FRAME_OPENED** = 25549
*	public.........................	**InternalFrameEvent** (javax.swing.JInternalFrame source, int id)
2	public....................**String**	**paramString** ()
1	protected transient......Object	source

ε644,886,565,568,570

InternalFrameFocusTraversalPolicy
javax.swing

Object
1.4 O └ java.awt.FocusTraversalPolicy¹
1.4 O └ InternalFrameFocusTraversalPolicy

O 1	public abstract	getComponentAfter (java.awt.Container focusCycleRoot,
	.... java.awt.Component	java.awt.Component aComponent)
O 1	public abstract	getComponentBefore (java.awt.Container focusCycleRoot,
	.... java.awt.Component	java.awt.Component aComponent)
O 1	public abstract	getDefaultComponent (java.awt.Container focusCycleRoot)
	.... java.awt.Component	
O 1	public abstract	getFirstComponent (java.awt.Container focusCycleRoot)
	.... java.awt.Component	
1	public.... java.awt.Component	getInitialComponent (java.awt.Window window)
	public.... java.awt.Component	**getInitialComponent** (JInternalFrame frame)
O 1	public abstract	getLastComponent (java.awt.Container focusCycleRoot)
	.... java.awt.Component	
*	public.........................	**InternalFrameFocusTraversalPolicy** ()

ε615
ε615
ε615

InternalFrameListener
javax.swing.event

ε738,743,745,746,752

1.2 *InternalFrameListener* ———————————— *java.util.EventListener*

	public.......................void	**internalFrameActivated** (InternalFrameEvent e)
	public.......................void	**internalFrameClosed** (InternalFrameEvent e)
	public.......................void	**internalFrameClosing** (InternalFrameEvent e)
	public.......................void	**internalFrameDeactivated** (InternalFrameEvent e)
	public.......................void	**internalFrameDeiconified** (InternalFrameEvent e)
	public.......................void	**internalFrameIconified** (InternalFrameEvent e)
	public.......................void	**internalFrameOpened** (InternalFrameEvent e)

I

Classes

InternalFrameUI

					javax.swing.plaf

InternalFrameUI

```
       Object
1.2 ○  └ComponentUI 1
1.2 ○     └InternalFrameUI
```

	1	*11 inherited members from ComponentUI not shown*
✳		public......................... **InternalFrameUI** ()

InternationalFormatter   javax.swing.text

```
       Object
1.4 ○  └java.swing.JFormattedTextField 2 - - - - - - - - - java.io.Serializable
       |    .AbstractFormatter 1
1.4         └DefaultFormatter 2 - - - - - - - - - - - - - - - - - - Cloneable
1.4            └InternationalFormatter
```

	2	public................**Object** **clone** () throws CloneNotSupportedException
	1	protected........................ getActions ()
		.... ***javax.swing.Action[]***
	2	public.................. boolean getAllowsInvalid ()
	2	public.................. boolean getCommitsOnValidEdit ()
	2	protected...... DocumentFilter getDocumentFilter ()
		public.. java.text.Format.Field[] **getFields** (int offset)
		public......... java.text.Format **getFormat** ()
	1	protected................ javax 2 getFormattedTextField ()
		.swing.JFormattedTextField
		public............. *Comparable* **getMaximum** ()
		public............. *Comparable* **getMinimum** ()
	2	protected...... NavigationFilter getNavigationFilter ()
	2	public.................. boolean getOverwriteMode ()
	2	public.................. Class getValueClass ()
	2	public..................... **void install** (javax.swing.JFormattedTextField ftf)
✳	2	public............................. **InternationalFormatter** ()
✳		public............................. **InternationalFormatter** (java.text.Format format)
	1	protected ....void invalidEdit ()
	2	public...................void setAllowsInvalid (boolean allowsInvalid)
	2	public...................void setCommitsOnValidEdit (boolean commit)
	1	protected ....void setEditValid (boolean valid)
		public...................void **setFormat** (java.text.Format format)
		public...................void **setMaximum** (*Comparable* max)
		public...................void **setMinimum** (*Comparable* minimum)
	2	public...................void setOverwriteMode (boolean overwriteMode)
	2	public...................void setValueClass (Class valueClass)
	2	public...............**Object** **stringToValue** (String text) throws java.text.ParseException
	1	public...................void uninstall ()
	2	public..................... **String** **valueToString** (Object value) throws java.text.ParseException

ε995 appears on the setValueClass row.

InvalidDnDOperationException   java.awt.dnd

```
       Object
       └Throwable - - - - - - - - - - - - - - - - - - - - - - - - - - java.io.Serializable
          └Exception
             └RuntimeException
1.1             └IllegalStateException
1.2                └InvalidDnDOperationException
```

✳	public......................... **InvalidDnDOperationException** ()
✳	public......................... **InvalidDnDOperationException** (String msg)

InvalidMidiDataException   javax.sound.midi

ε716,717,718

```
       Object
       └Throwable - - - - - - - - - - - - - - - - - - - - - - - - - - java.io.Serializable
          └Exception
1.3          └InvalidMidiDataException
```

Class *Interface* —extends - - -implements ○ abstract ● final △ static ▲ static final ✳ constructor x x—inherited x **x**—declared **x x**—overridden
εn—examples of usage —has subclass package—see other volume

✳	public	**InvalidMidiDataException** ()
✳	public	**InvalidMidiDataException** (String message)

InvocationEvent — java.awt.event

ε640,641,643,649,566

```
      Object
1.1   └ java.util.EventObject¹ ------------------- java.io.Serializable⌐
1.1 ○   └ java.awt.AWTEvent²
1.2       └ InvocationEvent ------------------- java.awt.ActiveEvent³
```

	2	*27 inherited members from java.awt.AWTEvent not shown*		
		protected .... boolean	**catchExceptions**	
	3	public .... void	**dispatch** ()	
		public .... Exception	**getException** ()	
	1	public .... Object	getSource ()	ε644,886,565,568,570
1.4		public .... long	**getWhen** ()	
▲		public static final .... int	**INVOCATION_DEFAULT** = 1200	
▲		public static final .... int	**INVOCATION_FIRST** = 1200	
▲		public static final .... int	**INVOCATION_LAST** = 1200	
✳		public	**InvocationEvent** (Object source, *Runnable* runnable)	
✳		public	**InvocationEvent** (Object source, *Runnable* runnable, Object notifier, boolean catchExceptions)	
✳		protected	**InvocationEvent** (Object source, int id, *Runnable* runnable, Object notifier, boolean catchExceptions)	
		protected .... Object	**notifier**	
	2	public .... String	**paramString** ()	
		protected .... *Runnable*	**runnable**	
	1	protected transient ...... Object	source	

ItemEvent — java.awt.event

ε640,641,643,649,566

```
      Object
1.1   └ java.util.EventObject¹ ------------------- java.io.Serializable⌐
1.1 ○   └ java.awt.AWTEvent²
1.1       └ ItemEvent
```

	2	*27 inherited members from java.awt.AWTEvent not shown*		
▲		public static final .... int	**DESELECTED** = 2	ε650,765
		public .... Object	**getItem** ()	ε765
		public . *java.awt.ItemSelectable*	**getItemSelectable** ()	
	1	public .... Object	getSource ()	ε765,644,886,565,568
		public .... int	**getStateChange** ()	ε765
▲		public static final .... int	**ITEM_FIRST** = 701	
▲		public static final .... int	**ITEM_LAST** = 701	
▲		public static final .... int	**ITEM_STATE_CHANGED** = 701	ε650
✳		public	**ItemEvent** (*java.awt.ItemSelectable* source, int id, Object item, int stateChange)	ε650
	2	public .... String	**paramString** ()	
▲		public static final .... int	**SELECTED** = 1	ε650,765
	1	protected transient ...... Object	source	

ItemListener — java.awt.event

ε738,743,745,746,752

```
1.1   ItemListener———————————————— java.util.EventListener⌐
```

	public .... void	**itemStateChanged** (ItemEvent e)	ε650,765

ItemSelectable — java.awt

ε769

```
1.1   ItemSelectable⌐
```

public .... void	**addItemListener** (*java.awt.event.ItemListener* l)	ε650
public .... Object[]	**getSelectedObjects** ()	ε650
public .... void	**removeItemListener** (*java.awt.event.ItemListener* l)	ε650

JApplet

JApplet	javax.swing

```
        Object
  ○     └─java.awt.Component¹ - - - - - - - - - - - - - - - - - - java.awt.image.ImageObserver⁵, java.awt.MenuContainer,
                                                              java.io.Serializable ˬ
           └─java.awt.Container²
              └─java.awt.Panel³ - - - - - - - - - - - - - - - - - javax.accessibility.Accessible
                 └─java.applet.Applet⁴
  1.2              └─JApplet - - - - - - - - - - - - - - - - - - - RootPaneContainer⁶
```

	1	*173 inherited members from java.awt.Component not shown*		
	2	*61 inherited members from java.awt.Container not shown*		
	5	*8 inherited members from java.awt.image.ImageObserver not shown*		
		protected . . javax.accessibility₂ **accessibleContext**		
		.AccessibleContext		
	2	protected . . . . **void** **addImpl** (java.awt.Component comp, Object constraints, int index)		
	3	public . . . . .void addNotify ()		
		protected . . . . JRootPane **createRootPane** ()		
	4	public . . . . .void destroy ()		ε551
	4	public . . . . **javax.accessibility₂ getAccessibleContext** ()		
		.AccessibleContext		
	4	public . . . . getAppletContext ()		
		. . . *java.applet.AppletContext*		
	4	public . . . . .String getAppletInfo ()		
	4	public . . . *java.applet.AudioClip* getAudioClip (java.net.URL url)		
	4	public . . . *java.applet.AudioClip* getAudioClip (java.net.URL url, String name)		
	4	public . . . . java.net.URL getCodeBase ()		
	6	public . . . . . . .java.awt.Container **getContentPane** ()		ε732,733,816,841,887
	4	public . . . . java.net.URL getDocumentBase ()		
	6	public . . . java.awt.Component **getGlassPane** ()		
	4	public . . . . java.awt.Image getImage (java.net.URL url)		
	4	public . . . . java.awt.Image getImage (java.net.URL url, String name)		
		public . . . . JMenuBar **getJMenuBar** ()		
	6	public . . . . JLayeredPane **getLayeredPane** ()		
	4	public . . . . java.util.Locale getLocale ()		
	4	public . . . . .String getParameter (String name)		ε552
	4	public . . . . String[][] getParameterInfo ()		
	6	public . . . . JRootPane **getRootPane** ()		
	4	public . . . . .void init ()		ε551,555,557,558
	4	public . . . . boolean isActive ()		
		protected . . . . boolean **isRootPaneCheckingEnabled** ()		
✳		public . . . . : **JApplet** () throws java.awt.HeadlessException		
▲	4	public static final . . . . newAudioClip (java.net.URL url)		ε556
		. . . . *java.applet.AudioClip*		
	2	protected . . . . **String** **paramString** ()		
	4	public . . . . .void play (java.net.URL url)		
	4	public . . . . .void play (java.net.URL url, String name)		
	2	public . . . . **void** **remove** (java.awt.Component comp)		ε831
	4	public . . . . .void resize (java.awt.Dimension d)		
	4	public . . . . .void resize (int width, int height)		
		protected . . . . JRootPane **rootPane**		
		protected . . . . boolean **rootPaneCheckingEnabled**		
	6	public . . . . .void **setContentPane** (java.awt.Container contentPane)		
	6	public . . . . .void **setGlassPane** (java.awt.Component glassPane)		
		public . . . . .void **setJMenuBar** (JMenuBar menuBar)		
	6	public . . . . .void **setLayeredPane** (JLayeredPane layeredPane)		
	2	public . . . . **void** **setLayout** (*java.awt.LayoutManager* manager)		ε613,622,624,625,627
		protected . . . . .void **setRootPane** (JRootPane root)		
		protected . . . . .void **setRootPaneCheckingEnabled** (boolean enabled)		
●	4	public final . . . . .void setStub (*java.applet.AppletStub* stub)		
	4	public . . . . .void showStatus (String msg)		ε554
	4	public . . . . .void start ()		ε551,558
	4	public . . . . .void stop ()		ε551,558
	2	public . . . . **void** **update** (java.awt.Graphics g)		

Class *Interface* —extends - - -implements ○ abstract ● final △ static ▲ static final ✳ constructor x x—inherited x **x**—declared **x x**—overridden
εn—examples of usage ˬ—has subclass package —see other volume

592

JButton — javax.swing

```
                    Object                                              ε45
        O    └─java.awt.Component 1 ------------------ java.awt.image.ImageObserver 5, java.awt.MenuContainer,
                                                       java.io.Serializable،

                      └─java.awt.Container 2
   1.2  O              └─JComponent 3
   1.2  O                └─AbstractButton 4 ------------------ java.awt.ItemSelectable،, SwingConstants 6
   1.2                    └─JButton، ---------------------- javax.accessibility.Accessible
```

	1	*139 inherited members from java.awt.Component not shown*			
	2	*49 inherited members from java.awt.Container not shown*			
	3	*134 inherited members from JComponent not shown*			
	4	*88 inherited members from AbstractButton not shown*			
	6	*19 inherited members from SwingConstants not shown*			
	5	*8 inherited members from java.awt.image.ImageObserver not shown*			
	4	public	void	**addActionListener** (*java.awt.event.ActionListener* l)	ε705,808,810,644
1.3	4	protected	**void configurePropertiesFromAction** (*Action* a)		
	3	public....	**javax.accessibility₂ .AccessibleContext**	**getAccessibleContext** ()	ε688
1.3 ●	3	public final	ActionMap	**getActionMap** ()	ε857,620,621
	1	public	java.awt.Color	getBackground ()	ε883
1.4	2	public	*java.util.Set*	getFocusTraversalKeys (int id)	ε610
1.4	4	public	int	getIconTextGap ()	ε749
1.3 ●	3	public final	InputMap	**getInputMap** (int condition)	ε857,620,621
	3	public	java.awt.Point	getToolTipLocation (java.awt.event.MouseEvent event)	ε844
	3	public	**String**	**getUIClassID** ()	
		public	boolean	**isDefaultButton** ()	
		public	boolean	**isDefaultCapable** ()	
1.4	1	public	boolean	isFocusOwner ()	ε606
✳		public		**JButton** ()	
✳		public		**JButton** (String text)	ε732,743,816,843,844
1.3 ✳		public		**JButton** (*Action* a)	ε745,746,816,855,857
✳		public		**JButton** (*Icon* icon)	ε688
✳		public		**JButton** (String text, *Icon* icon)	
	4	protected	**String**	**paramString** ()	
	3	public	**void**	**removeNotify** ()	
1.3	4	public	void	setAction (*Action* a)	ε883
	3	public	void	setBackground (java.awt.Color bg)	ε883
	1	public	void	setBounds (int x, int y, int width, int height)	ε854
		public	void	**setDefaultCapable** (boolean defaultCapable)	
	4	public	void	setDisabledIcon (*Icon* disabledIcon)	ε750,755
	4	public	void	setEnabled (boolean b)	ε750
1.4	2	public	void	setFocusTraversalKeys (int id, *java.util.Set* keystrokes)	ε610
	4	public	void	setHorizontalAlignment (int alignment)	ε748
	4	public	void	setHorizontalTextPosition (int textPosition)	ε747
	4	public	void	setIcon (*Icon* defaultIcon)	ε746,755
1.4	4	public	void	setIconTextGap (int iconTextGap)	ε749
	4	public	void	setMargin (java.awt.Insets m)	ε816
	4	public	void	setMnemonic (char mnemonic)	ε690,691
	4	public	void	setPressedIcon (*Icon* pressedIcon)	ε751,755
	4	public	void	setRolloverIcon (*Icon* rolloverIcon)	ε751,755
	4	public	void	setText (String text)	ε744,745,816,754
	3	public	void	setToolTipText (String text)	ε843,844,848,849,688
	4	public	void	setVerticalAlignment (int alignment)	ε748
	4	public	void	setVerticalTextPosition (int textPosition)	ε747
	4	public	**void**	**updateUI** ()	

JCheckBox — javax.swing

```
                    Object                                              ε45
        O    └─java.awt.Component 1 ------------------ java.awt.image.ImageObserver 6, java.awt.MenuContainer,
                                                       java.io.Serializable،

                      └─java.awt.Container 2
   1.2  O              └─JComponent 3
   1.2  O                └─AbstractButton 4 ------------------ java.awt.ItemSelectable،, SwingConstants 7
   1.2                    └─JToggleButton 5 ------------------ javax.accessibility.Accessible
   1.2                      └─JCheckBox
```

	1	*142 inherited members from java.awt.Component not shown*
	2	*51 inherited members from java.awt.Container not shown*

J

Classes

JCheckBox

1.3	▲	public static final .... String	**BORDER_PAINTED_FLAT_CHANGED_PROPERTY**	= "borderPaintedFlat"	
1.3	4	protected .... **void**	**configurePropertiesFromAction** (*Action* a)		
1.3	4	protected .... ***java.beans***_2 ***.PropertyChangeListener***	**createActionPropertyChangeListener** (*Action* a)		
	5	public .... **javax.accessibility**_2 **.AccessibleContext**	**getAccessibleContext** ()		
	4	public .... String	getText ()		ε754,813
	5	public .... **String**	**getUIClassID** ()		
1.3		public .... boolean	**isBorderPaintedFlat** ()		
	4	public .... boolean	isSelected ()		ε752,753
	✳	public	**JCheckBox** ()		
	✳	public	**JCheckBox** (String text)		ε690
1.3	✳	public	**JCheckBox** (*Action* a)		ε752
	✳	public	**JCheckBox** (*Icon* icon)		
	✳	public	**JCheckBox** (String text, *Icon* icon)		
	✳	public	**JCheckBox** (String text, boolean selected)		
	✳	public	**JCheckBox** (*Icon* icon, boolean selected)		
	✳	public	**JCheckBox** (String text, *Icon* icon, boolean selected)		
	5	protected .... **String**	**paramString** ()		
1.3		public .... void	**setBorderPaintedFlat** (boolean b)		
	4	public .... void	setDisabledIcon (*Icon* disabledIcon)		ε755,750
	4	public .... void	setDisabledSelectedIcon (*Icon* disabledSelectedIcon)		ε755
	4	public .... void	setIcon (*Icon* defaultIcon)		ε755,746
	4	public .... void	setMnemonic (char mnemonic)		ε690,691
	4	public .... void	setPressedIcon (*Icon* pressedIcon)		ε755,751
	4	public .... void	setRolloverIcon (*Icon* rolloverIcon)		ε755,751
	4	public .... void	setSelected (boolean b)		ε753
	4	public .... void	setSelectedIcon (*Icon* selectedIcon)		ε755
	4	public .... void	setText (String text)		ε754,744,745,816
	5	public .... **void**	**updateUI** ()		

JCheckBoxMenuItem — javax.swing

	Object	ε45
○	└java.awt.Component[1] - - - - - - - - - - - - - - - - java.awt.image.ImageObserver [6], java.awt.MenuContainer, java.io.Serializable	
	└java.awt.Container[2]	
1.2 ○	└JComponent[3]	
1.2 ○	└AbstractButton[4] - - - - - - - - - - - - - - - - java.awt.ItemSelectable, SwingConstants [7]	
1.2	└JMenuItem[5] - - - - - - - - - - - - - - - - javax.accessibility.Accessible, MenuElement	
1.2	└JCheckBoxMenuItem	

	5	public .... **javax.accessibility**_2 **.AccessibleContext**	**getAccessibleContext** ()	
	4	public .... **Object[]**	**getSelectedObjects** ()	ε650
		public .... boolean	**getState** ()	
	5	public .... **String**	**getUIClassID** ()	
	✳	public	**JCheckBoxMenuItem** ()	
	✳	public	**JCheckBoxMenuItem** (String text)	
1.3	✳	public	**JCheckBoxMenuItem** (*Action* a)	
	✳	public	**JCheckBoxMenuItem** (*Icon* icon)	
	✳	public	**JCheckBoxMenuItem** (String text, boolean b)	
	✳	public	**JCheckBoxMenuItem** (String text, *Icon* icon)	
	✳	public	**JCheckBoxMenuItem** (String text, *Icon* icon, boolean b)	
	5	protected .... **String**	**paramString** ()	
		public synchronized .... void	**setState** (boolean b)	

Class   *Interface*   —extends   - - -implements   ○ abstract   ● final   △ static   ▲ static final   ✳ constructor   x x—inherited   x **x**—declared   **x x**—overridden
εn—examples of usage   ⌐—has subclass   package—see other volume

JColorChooser — javax.swing

```
        Object
   ○    └java.awt.Component¹ - - - - - - - - - - - - - - - - - -  java.awt.image.ImageObserver⁴, java.awt.MenuContainer,
                                                                   java.io.Serializable↲
          └java.awt.Container²
1.2 ○       └JComponent³
1.2           └JColorChooser - - - - - - - - - - - - - - - - - -  javax.accessibility.Accessible
```

1	143 inherited members from java.awt.Component not shown	
2	51 inherited members from java.awt.Container not shown	
3	142 inherited members from JComponent not shown	
4	8 inherited members from java.awt.image.ImageObserver not shown	

3	protected **javax.accessibility**↲ **.AccessibleContext**	**accessibleContext**	
	public......................void	**addChooserPanel** (javax.swing.colorchooser.AbstractColorChooserPanel panel)	ε883
▲	public static final.........String	**CHOOSER_PANELS_PROPERTY** = "chooserPanels"	
△	public static ....JDialog	**createDialog** (java.awt.Component c, String title, boolean modal, JColorChooser chooserPane, java.awt.event.ActionListener okListener, java.awt.event.ActionListener cancelListener) throws java.awt.HeadlessException	ε876,884
3	public.... **javax.accessibility**↲ **.AccessibleContext**	**getAccessibleContext** ()	
	public.............javax.swing↲ .colorchooser.Abstract- ColorChooserPanel[]	**getChooserPanels** ()	ε880,881,882
	public.......java.awt.Color	**getColor** ()	ε877,878,879,881,884
1.4	public................. boolean	**getDragEnabled** ()	
	public............JComponent	**getPreviewPanel** ()	
	public.................... ...javax.swing.colorchooser↲ .ColorSelectionModel	**getSelectionModel** ()	ε878,879,881,885
	public................. javax↲ .swing.plaf.ColorChooserUI	**getUI** ()	
3	public.................. **String**	**getUIClassID** ()	
✳	public..........................	**JColorChooser** ()	ε877,878,879,880,881
✳	public..........................	**JColorChooser** (java.awt.Color initialColor)	ε876
✳	public..........................	**JColorChooser** (*javax.swing.colorchooser.ColorSelectionModel* model)	
3	protected .... **String**	**paramString** ()	
▲	public static final.........String	**PREVIEW_PANEL_PROPERTY** = "previewPanel"	
	public.......................... ...javax.swing.colorchooser.- AbstractColorChooserPanel	**removeChooserPanel** (javax.swing.colorchooser.AbstractColorChooserPanel panel)	ε881
▲	public static final.........String	**SELECTION_MODEL_PROPERTY** = "selectionModel"	
	public......................void	**setChooserPanels** (javax.swing.colorchooser.AbstractColorChooserPanel[] panels)	ε882
	public......................void	**setColor** (int c)	
	public......................void	**setColor** (java.awt.Color color)	ε877
	public......................void	**setColor** (int r, int g, int b)	
1.4	public......................void	**setDragEnabled** (boolean b)	
	public......................void	**setPreviewPanel** (JComponent preview)	ε878,879
	public......................void	**setSelectionModel** (*javax.swing.colorchooser.ColorSelectionModel* newModel)	
	public......................void	**setUI** (javax.swing.plaf.ColorChooserUI ui)	
△	public static .....java.awt.Color	**showDialog** (java.awt.Component component, String title, java.awt.Color initialColor) throws java.awt.HeadlessException	ε876
3	public...................... **void**	**updateUI** ()	

JComboBox — javax.swing

```
        Object
   ○    └java.awt.Component¹ - - - - - - - - - - - - - - - - - -  java.awt.image.ImageObserver⁴, java.awt.MenuContainer,
                                                                   java.io.Serializable↲
          └java.awt.Container²
1.2 ○       └JComponent³
1.2           └JComboBox - - - - - - - - - - - - - - - - - - - -  java.awt.ItemSelectable↲⁵, javax.swing.event.ListDataListener⁶
                                                                   (java.util.EventListener), java.awt.event.ActionListener↲⁷
                                                                   (java.util.EventListener), javax.accessibility.Accessible
```

	1		*142 inherited members from java.awt.Component not shown*	
	2		*51 inherited members from java.awt.Container not shown*	
	3		*138 inherited members from JComponent not shown*	
	4		*8 inherited members from java.awt.image.ImageObserver not shown*	
		protected .... String	**actionCommand**	
	7	public .... void	**actionPerformed** (java.awt.event.ActionEvent e)	ε855,644,738,743,745
		public .... void	**addActionListener** (*java.awt.event.ActionListener* l)	ε766
		public .... void	**addItem** (Object anObject)	ε759
	5	public .... void	**addItemListener** (*java.awt.event.ItemListener* aListener)	ε765,650
	1	public synchronized ...... void	addKeyListener (*java.awt.event.KeyListener* l)	ε762,763
1.4		public .... void	**addPopupMenuListener** (*javax.swing.event.PopupMenuListener* l)	
				ε767
		public .... void	**configureEditor** (*ComboBoxEditor* anEditor, Object anItem)	
1.3		protected .... void	**configurePropertiesFromAction** (*Action* a)	
	6	public .... void	**contentsChanged** (javax.swing.event.ListDataEvent e)	ε785
1.3		protected .... java.beans₂	**createActionPropertyChangeListener** (*Action* a)	
		.PropertyChangeListener		
		protected .... *JComboBox*₂	**createDefaultKeySelectionManager** ()	
		.KeySelectionManager		
		protected .... *ComboBoxModel*	**dataModel**	
		protected .... *ComboBoxEditor*	**editor**	
		protected .... void	**fireActionEvent** ()	
		protected .... void	**fireItemStateChanged** (java.awt.event.ItemEvent e)	
1.4		public .... void	**firePopupMenuCanceled** ()	
1.4		public .... void	**firePopupMenuWillBecomeInvisible** ()	
1.4		public .... void	**firePopupMenuWillBecomeVisible** ()	
	3	public .... **javax.accessibility**₂	**getAccessibleContext** ()	
		.AccessibleContext		
1.3		public .... *Action*	**getAction** ()	
		public .... String	**getActionCommand** ()	
1.4		public .... *java*₂	**getActionListeners** ()	
		.awt.event.ActionListener[]		
		public .... *ComboBoxEditor*	**getEditor** ()	
		public .... Object	**getItemAt** (int index)	ε758
		public .... int	**getItemCount** ()	ε758,759
1.4		public	**getItemListeners** ()	
		java.awt.event.ItemListener[]		
		public .... *JComboBox*₂	**getKeySelectionManager** ()	ε763
		.KeySelectionManager		
		public .... int	**getMaximumRowCount** ()	ε764
	3	public ...... java.awt.Dimension	getMinimumSize ()	ε816
		public .... *ComboBoxModel*	**getModel** ()	ε763
1.4		public .... *javax.swing*₂	**getPopupMenuListeners** ()	
		.event.PopupMenuListener[]		
1.4		public .... Object	**getPrototypeDisplayValue** ()	
		public .... *ListCellRenderer*	**getRenderer** ()	
		public .... int	**getSelectedIndex** ()	ε763
		public .... Object	**getSelectedItem** ()	ε757,766
	5	public .... Object[]	**getSelectedObjects** ()	ε650
		public .... *javax*₂	**getUI** ()	
		.swing.plaf.ComboBoxUI		
	3	public .... **String**	**getUIClassID** ()	
		public .... void	**hidePopup** ()	
		public .... void	**insertItemAt** (Object anObject, int index)	ε759
		protected .... void	**installAncestorListener** ()	
	6	public .... void	**intervalAdded** (javax.swing.event.ListDataEvent e)	ε785
	6	public .... void	**intervalRemoved** (javax.swing.event.ListDataEvent e)	ε785
		protected .... boolean	**isEditable**	
		public .... boolean	**isEditable** ()	
		public .... boolean	**isLightWeightPopupEnabled** ()	
		public .... boolean	**isPopupVisible** ()	ε761
*		public	**JComboBox** ()	
*		public	**JComboBox** (Object[] items)	ε756,757,758,759,760
*		public	**JComboBox** (java.util.Vector items)	
*		public	**JComboBox** (*ComboBoxModel* aModel)	
		protected .... *JComboBox*₂	**keySelectionManager**	
		.KeySelectionManager		
		protected .... boolean	**lightWeightPopupEnabled**	
		protected .... int	**maximumRowCount**	
	3	protected .... **String**	**paramString** ()	

3	public	void	**processKeyEvent** (java.awt.event.KeyEvent e)	
	public	void	**removeActionListener** (*java.awt.event.ActionListener* l)	
	public	void	**removeAllItems** ()	ε759
	public	void	**removeItem** (Object anObject)	
	public	void	**removeItemAt** (int anIndex)	ε759
5	public	void	**removeItemListener** (*java.awt.event.ItemListener* aListener)	ε650
1.4	public	void	**removePopupMenuListener** (*javax.swing.event.PopupMenuListener* l)	
	protected	*ListCellRenderer*	**renderer**	
	protected	void	**selectedItemChanged** ()	
	protected	Object	**selectedItemReminder**	
	public	boolean	**selectWithKeyChar** (char keyChar)	
1.3	public	void	**setAction** (*Action* a)	
	public	void	**setActionCommand** (String aCommand)	
3	public	void	setBackground (java.awt.Color bg)	ε959
	public	void	**setEditable** (boolean aFlag)	ε756,757,765,766,767
	public	void	**setEditor** (*ComboBoxEditor* anEditor)	
3	public	void	**setEnabled** (boolean b)	
	public	void	**setKeySelectionManager** (*JComboBox.KeySelectionManager* aManager)	
				ε760
	public	void	**setLightWeightPopupEnabled** (boolean aFlag)	
	public	void	**setMaximumRowCount** (int count)	ε764
3	public	void	setMaximumSize (java.awt.Dimension maximumSize)	ε816
	public	void	**setModel** (*ComboBoxModel* aModel)	
	public	void	**setPopupVisible** (boolean v)	
1.4	public	void	**setPrototypeDisplayValue** (Object prototypeDisplayValue)	ε816
	public	void	**setRenderer** (*ListCellRenderer* aRenderer)	
	public	void	**setSelectedIndex** (int anIndex)	
	public	void	**setSelectedItem** (Object anObject)	ε757
	public	void	**setUI** (javax.swing.plaf.ComboBoxUI ui)	
	public	void	**showPopup** ()	ε762,763
3	public	void	**updateUI** ()	

JComboBox.KeySelectionManager		javax.swing

1.2	*JComboBox.KeySelectionManager*			
	public	int	**selectionForKey** (char aKey, *ComboBoxModel* aModel)	ε760,763

JComponent	javax.swing

ε733,953,640,641,606

Object
   ○ └java.awt.Component[1] - - - - - - - - - - - - - - - - - - - *java.awt.image.ImageObserver* [3], *java.awt.MenuContainer*,
                                                    java.io.Serializable
      └java.awt.Container[2]
1.2 ○   └JComponent

1	*140 inherited members from java.awt.Component not shown*		
2	*51 inherited members from java.awt.Container not shown*		
3	*8 inherited members from java.awt.image.ImageObserver not shown*		
	protected	javax.accessibility .AccessibleContext	**accessibleContext**
	public	void	**addAncestorListener** (*javax.swing.event.AncestorListener* listener)
1	public synchronized	void	addFocusListener (*java.awt.event.FocusListener* l) ε616,617,649
2	public	void	**addNotify** ()
2	public synchronized	void	**addPropertyChangeListener** (*java.beans.PropertyChangeListener* listener)
2	public synchronized	void	**addPropertyChangeListener** (String propertyName, *java.beans.PropertyChangeListener* listener)
	public synchronized	void	**addVetoableChangeListener** (*java.beans.VetoableChangeListener* listener)
	public	void	**computeVisibleRect** (java.awt.Rectangle visibleRect)
1	public	boolean	**contains** (int x, int y)
	public	JToolTip	**createToolTip** ()
1	public	void	**disable** ()
1	public	void	**enable** ()
1	public	void	**firePropertyChange** (String propertyName, boolean oldValue, boolean newValue)
	public	void	**firePropertyChange** (String propertyName, char oldValue, char newValue)
1	public	void	**firePropertyChange** (String propertyName, int oldValue, int newValue)
	public	void	**firePropertyChange** (String propertyName, long oldValue, long newValue)
	public	void	**firePropertyChange** (String propertyName, byte oldValue, byte newValue)
1	protected	void	**firePropertyChange** (String propertyName, Object oldValue, Object newValue)
	public	void	**firePropertyChange** (String propertyName, double oldValue, double newValue)
	public	void	**firePropertyChange** (String propertyName, float oldValue, float newValue)
	public	void	**firePropertyChange** (String propertyName, short oldValue, short newValue)

J

Classes

JComponent

		protected . . . . void	**fireVetoableChange** (String propertyName, Object oldValue, Object newValue) throws java.beans.PropertyVetoException	
	1	public. . . . . **javax.accessibility₂ .AccessibleContext**	**getAccessibleContext** ()	
		public. . . . . *java₂ .awt.event.ActionListener*	**getActionForKeyStroke** (KeyStroke aKeyStroke)	
1.3 ●		public final . . . . ActionMap	**getActionMap** ()	ε856
	2	public. . . . . **float**	**getAlignmentX** ()	
	2	public. . . . . **float**	**getAlignmentY** ()	
1.4		public. . . . . *javax.swing₂ .event.AncestorListener[]*	**getAncestorListeners** ()	
		public. . . . . boolean	**getAutoscrolls** ()	
		public. . . . . *. . . javax.swing.border.Border*	**getBorder** ()	
	1	public. . . . . **java.awt.Rectangle**	**getBounds** (java.awt.Rectangle rv)	
●		public final . . . . Object	**getClientProperty** (Object key)	
		protected . . . java.awt.Graphics	**getComponentGraphics** (java.awt.Graphics g)	
		public. . . . . int	**getConditionForKeyStroke** (KeyStroke aKeyStroke)	
		public. . . . . int	**getDebugGraphicsOptions** ()	
1.4 △		public static . . . java.util.Locale	**getDefaultLocale** ()	
	1	public. . . . . . **java.awt.Graphics**	**getGraphics** ()	
	1	public. **int**	**getHeight** ()	
1.3 ●		public final . . . . InputMap	**getInputMap** ()	
1.3 ●		public final . . . . InputMap	**getInputMap** (int condition)	ε862
1.3		public. . . . . InputVerifier	**getInputVerifier** ()	
	2	public. . . . . **java.awt.Insets**	**getInsets** ()	
		public. . . . . java.awt.Insets	**getInsets** (java.awt.Insets insets)	
1.3	2	public. . . . . *. . . . **java.util.EventListener[]***	**getListeners** (Class listenerType)	
	1	public. . . . . java.awt.Point	getLocation ()	ε865
	1	public. . . . . **java.awt.Point**	**getLocation** (java.awt.Point rv)	
	2	public. . . . **java.awt.Dimension**	**getMaximumSize** ()	
	2	public. . . . **java.awt.Dimension**	**getMinimumSize** ()	
D		public. . . . java.awt.Component	**getNextFocusableComponent** ()	
	2	public. . . . **java.awt.Dimension**	**getPreferredSize** ()	
1.4	1	public synchronized . . . . *. . . . . **java.beans.- PropertyChangeListener[]***	**getPropertyChangeListeners** ()	
1.4	1	public synchronized . . . . *. . . . . **java.beans.- PropertyChangeListener[]***	**getPropertyChangeListeners** (String propertyName)	
		public. . . . . KeyStroke[]	**getRegisteredKeyStrokes** ()	
		public. . . . . JRootPane	**getRootPane** ()	
	1	public. . . . **java.awt.Dimension**	**getSize** (java.awt.Dimension rv)	
		public. . . . . java.awt.Point	**getToolTipLocation** (java.awt.event.MouseEvent event)	
		public. . . . . String	**getToolTipText** ()	
		public. . . . . String	**getToolTipText** (java.awt.event.MouseEvent event)	
		public. . . . . . . java.awt.Container	**getTopLevelAncestor** ()	
1.4		public. . . . . TransferHandler	**getTransferHandler** ()	ε742
		public. . . . . String	**getUIClassID** ()	
1.3		public. . . . . boolean	**getVerifyInputWhenFocusTarget** ()	
1.4		public synchronized . . . . *. . . . . **java.beans.- VetoableChangeListener[]***	**getVetoableChangeListeners** ()	
		public. . . . . . java.awt.Rectangle	**getVisibleRect** ()	
	1	public. **int**	**getWidth** ()	
	1	public. **int**	**getX** ()	
	1	public. **int**	**getY** ()	
		public. . . . . void	**grabFocus** ()	
	1	public. . . . . **boolean**	**isDoubleBuffered** ()	
△		public static . . . . boolean	**isLightweightComponent** (java.awt.Component c)	
D		public. . . . . boolean	**isManagingFocus** ()	
1.3		public. . . . . boolean	**isMaximumSizeSet** ()	
1.3		public. . . . . boolean	**isMinimumSizeSet** ()	
	1	public. . . . . **boolean**	**isOpaque** ()	
		public. . . . . boolean	**isOptimizedDrawingEnabled** ()	
		public. . . . . boolean	**isPaintingTile** ()	
1.3		public. . . . . boolean	**isPreferredSizeSet** ()	
		public. . . . . boolean	**isRequestFocusEnabled** ()	
		public. . . . . boolean	**isValidateRoot** ()	

*	public		**JComponent** ()	
	protected	javax.swing₂.event.EventListenerList	**listenerList**	
2	public	**void**	**paint** (java.awt.Graphics g)	ε575,878,879,881,899
	protected	void	**paintBorder** (java.awt.Graphics g)	
	protected	void	**paintChildren** (java.awt.Graphics g)	
	protected	void	**paintComponent** (java.awt.Graphics g)	
	public	void	**paintImmediately** (java.awt.Rectangle r)	
	public	void	**paintImmediately** (int x, int y, int w, int h)	
2	protected	**String**	**paramString** ()	
2	public	**void**	**print** (java.awt.Graphics g)	
1	public	**void**	**printAll** (java.awt.Graphics g)	
1.3	protected	void	**printBorder** (java.awt.Graphics g)	
1.3	protected	void	**printChildren** (java.awt.Graphics g)	
1.3	protected	void	**printComponent** (java.awt.Graphics g)	
	protected	void	**processComponentKeyEvent** (java.awt.event.KeyEvent e)	
1.3	protected	boolean	**processKeyBinding** (KeyStroke ks, java.awt.event.KeyEvent e, int condition, boolean pressed)	
1	protected	**void**	**processKeyEvent** (java.awt.event.KeyEvent e)	
1	protected	**void**	**processMouseMotionEvent** (java.awt.event.MouseEvent e)	
●	public final	void	**putClientProperty** (Object key, Object value)	
	public	void	**registerKeyboardAction** (*java.awt.event.ActionListener* anAction, KeyStroke aKeyStroke, int aCondition)	
	public	void	**registerKeyboardAction** (*java.awt.event.ActionListener* anAction, String aCommand, KeyStroke aKeyStroke, int aCondition)	
	public	void	**removeAncestorListener** (*javax.swing.event.AncestorListener* listener)	
2	public	**void**	**removeNotify** ()	
1	public synchronized	**void**	**removePropertyChangeListener** (*java.beans.PropertyChangeListener* listener)	
1	public synchronized	**void**	**removePropertyChangeListener** (String propertyName, *java.beans.PropertyChangeListener* listener)	
	public synchronized	void	**removeVetoableChangeListener** (*java.beans.VetoableChangeListener* listener)	
	public	void	**repaint** (java.awt.Rectangle r)	
1	public	**void**	**repaint** (long tm, int x, int y, int width, int height)	
D	public	boolean	**requestDefaultFocus** ()	
1	public	**void**	**requestFocus** ()	
1.4 1	public	**boolean**	**requestFocus** (boolean temporary)	
1.4 1	public	**boolean**	**requestFocusInWindow** ()	
1.4 1	protected	**boolean**	**requestFocusInWindow** (boolean temporary)	
	public	void	**resetKeyboardActions** ()	
1	public	**void**	**reshape** (int x, int y, int w, int h)	
	public	void	**revalidate** ()	
	public	void	**scrollRectToVisible** (java.awt.Rectangle aRect)	
1.3 ●	public final	void	**setActionMap** (ActionMap am)	
	public	void	**setAlignmentX** (float alignmentX)	
	public	void	**setAlignmentY** (float alignmentY)	
	public	void	**setAutoscrolls** (boolean autoscrolls)	
1	public	**void**	**setBackground** (java.awt.Color bg)	
	public	void	**setBorder** (*javax.swing.border.Border* border)	
	public	void	**setDebugGraphicsOptions** (int debugOptions)	
1.4 △	public static	void	**setDefaultLocale** (java.util.Locale l)	
	public	void	**setDoubleBuffered** (boolean aFlag)	
1	public	**void**	**setEnabled** (boolean enabled)	
1.4 1	public	void	**setFocusable** (boolean focusable)	ε607
2	public	**void**	**setFont** (java.awt.Font font)	
1	public	**void**	**setForeground** (java.awt.Color fg)	
1.3 ●	public final	void	**setInputMap** (int condition, InputMap map)	
1.3	public	void	**setInputVerifier** (InputVerifier inputVerifier)	
	public	void	**setMaximumSize** (java.awt.Dimension maximumSize)	
	public	void	**setMinimumSize** (java.awt.Dimension minimumSize)	
D	public	void	**setNextFocusableComponent** (java.awt.Component aComponent)	
	public	void	**setOpaque** (boolean isOpaque)	
	public	void	**setPreferredSize** (java.awt.Dimension preferredSize)	
	public	void	**setRequestFocusEnabled** (boolean requestFocusEnabled)	
	public	void	**setToolTipText** (String text)	ε938
1.4	public	void	**setTransferHandler** (TransferHandler newHandler)	
	protected	void	**setUI** (javax.swing.plaf.ComponentUI newUI)	
1.3	public	void	**setVerifyInputWhenFocusTarget** (boolean verifyInputWhenFocusTarget)	
1	public	**void**	**setVisible** (boolean aFlag)	
▲	public static final	String	**TOOL_TIP_TEXT_KEY** = "ToolTipText"	
	protected transient	javax₂.swing.plaf.ComponentUI	**ui**	
▲	public static final	int	**UNDEFINED_CONDITION** = -1	
	public	void	**unregisterKeyboardAction** (KeyStroke aKeyStroke)	

J

Classes

JComponent

2	public	**void**	**update** (java.awt.Graphics g)	
	public	void	**updateUI** ()	
▲	public static final	int	**WHEN_ANCESTOR_OF_FOCUSED_COMPONENT** = 1	ε860,862,621
▲	public static final	int	**WHEN_FOCUSED** = 0	ε857,860,861,862,863
▲	public static final	int	**WHEN_IN_FOCUSED_WINDOW** = 2	ε860,862,620

JComponent.AccessibleJComponent.AccessibleContainerHandler   protecte   javax.swing

Object
1.2   └─JComponent.AccessibleJComponent₂ - - - - - - *java.awt.event.ContainerListener* [1] (*java.util.EventListener*)
          .AccessibleContainerHandler

✳	protected		**JComponent.AccessibleJComponent.AccessibleContainerHandler** ()	
1	public	void	**componentAdded** (java.awt.event.ContainerEvent e)	ε573
1	public	void	**componentRemoved** (java.awt.event.ContainerEvent e)	ε573

JComponent.AccessibleJComponent.AccessibleFocusHandler   protecte   javax.swing

Object
1.3   └─JComponent.AccessibleJComponent₂ - - - - - - *java.awt.event.FocusListener* [1] (*java.util.EventListener*)
          .AccessibleFocusHandler

✳	protected		**JComponent.AccessibleJComponent.AccessibleFocusHandler** ()	
1	public	void	**focusGained** (java.awt.event.FocusEvent event)	ε649,616,617,618
1	public	void	**focusLost** (java.awt.event.FocusEvent event)	ε649,616,617,618

JDesktopPane   javax.swing

Object
  ○   └─*java.awt.Component* [1] - - - - - - - - - - - - - - - - - - *java.awt.image.ImageObserver* [5], *java.awt.MenuContainer*,
                                                         java.io.Serializable
        └─*java.awt.Container* [2]
1.2 ○   └─JComponent [3]
1.2   └─*JLayeredPane* [4] - - - - - - - - - - - - - - - - - - *javax.accessibility.Accessible*
1.2   └─JDesktopPane

	1	*143 inherited members from java.awt.Component not shown*		
	2	*48 inherited members from java.awt.Container not shown*		
	3	*140 inherited members from JComponent not shown*		
	4	*29 inherited members from JLayeredPane not shown*		
	5	*8 inherited members from java.awt.image.ImageObserver not shown*		
	2	public.... java.awt.Component	add (java.awt.Component comp)	ε841,571,575,581,590
	4	public.... **javax.accessibility₂ .AccessibleContext**	**getAccessibleContext** ()	
		public	JInternalFrame[]	**getAllFrames** ()	ε842
		public	JInternalFrame[]	**getAllFramesInLayer** (int layer)	
		public	*DesktopManager*	**getDesktopManager** ()	
1.3		public	int	**getDragMode** ()	
1.3		public	JInternalFrame	**getSelectedFrame** ()	
		public	javax₂ .swing.plaf.DesktopPaneUI	**getUI** ()	
	3	public	**String**	**getUIClassID** ()	
	3	public	**boolean**	**isOpaque** ()	
✳		public		**JDesktopPane** ()	ε841
1.3 △		public static	int	**LIVE_DRAG_MODE**	
1.3 △		public static	int	**OUTLINE_DRAG_MODE**	
	4	protected	**String**	**paramString** ()	
		public	void	**setDesktopManager** (*DesktopManager* d)	
1.3		public	void	**setDragMode** (int dragMode)	
1.3		public	void	**setSelectedFrame** (JInternalFrame f)	
		public	void	**setUI** (javax.swing.plaf.DesktopPaneUI ui)	
	3	public	**void**	**updateUI** ()	

Class   *Interface*   —extends   - - -implements   ○ abstract   ● final   △ static   ▲ static final   ✳ constructor   x x—inherited   x **x**—declared   **x x**—overridden
ε*n*—examples of usage   ⌐—has subclass   package—see other volume

JDialog		javax.swing

```
       Object                                                              ε606,618,733,953,988
  o    └─java.awt.Component¹ ------------------- java.awt.image.ImageObserver⁵, java.awt.MenuContainer,
                                                            java.io.Serializable
           └─java.awt.Container²
               └─java.awt.Window³ ------------------ javax.accessibility.Accessible
                   └─java.awt.Dialog⁴
1.2                    └─JDialog --------------------- WindowConstants⁶, RootPaneContainer⁷
```

	1	*165 inherited members from java.awt.Component not shown*		
	2	*54 inherited members from java.awt.Container not shown*		
	3	*45 inherited members from java.awt.Window not shown*		
	6	*4 inherited members from WindowConstants not shown*		
	5	*8 inherited members from java.awt.image.ImageObserver not shown*		
		protected .. javax.accessibility.₂	**accessibleContext**	
		.AccessibleContext		
	2	protected . . . . **void**	**addImpl** (java.awt.Component comp, Object constraints, int index)	
	4	public. . . . . .void	addNotify ()	
	3	public synchronized . . . . . . .void	addWindowListener (*java.awt.event.WindowListener* l)	ε884,905,565,566,568
		protected . . . . JRootPane	**createRootPane** ()	
		protected . . . . .void	**dialogInit** ()	
	4	public. . . . . .void	dispose ()	ε565
	4	public. . . . **javax.accessibility**₂	**getAccessibleContext** ()	
		.AccessibleContext		
	7	public . . . . . . .java.awt.Container	**getContentPane** ()	ε732,733,816,841,887
		public. . . . . .int	**getDefaultCloseOperation** ()	
	7	public. . . . java.awt.Component	**getGlassPane** ()	
		public. . . . . JMenuBar	**getJMenuBar** ()	
	7	public. . . . . JLayeredPane	**getLayeredPane** ()	
	7	public. . . . . JRootPane	**getRootPane** ()	
	4	public. . . . . String	getTitle ()	
	4	public. . . . . .void	hide ()	
1.4 △		public static . . . . boolean	**isDefaultLookAndFeelDecorated** ()	
	4	public. . . . . boolean	isModal ()	
	4	public. . . . . boolean	isResizable ()	
		protected . . . . boolean	**isRootPaneCheckingEnabled** ()	
1.4	4	public. . . . . boolean	isUndecorated ()	
*		public.	**JDialog** () throws java.awt.HeadlessException	
*		public.	**JDialog** (java.awt.Dialog owner) throws java.awt.HeadlessException	
*		public.	**JDialog** (java.awt.Frame owner) throws java.awt.HeadlessException	
*		public.	**JDialog** (java.awt.Dialog owner, String title) throws java.awt.HeadlessException	
*		public.	**JDialog** (java.awt.Dialog owner, boolean modal) throws java.awt.HeadlessException	
*		public.	**JDialog** (java.awt.Frame owner, String title) throws java.awt.HeadlessException	
*		public.	**JDialog** (java.awt.Frame owner, boolean modal) throws java.awt.HeadlessException	
*		public.	**JDialog** (java.awt.Dialog owner, String title, boolean modal)	
			throws java.awt.HeadlessException	
*		public.	**JDialog** (java.awt.Frame owner, String title, boolean modal)	
			throws java.awt.HeadlessException	
1.4 *		public.	**JDialog** (java.awt.Dialog owner, String title, boolean modal,	
			java.awt.GraphicsConfiguration gc) throws java.awt.HeadlessException	
1.4 *		public.	**JDialog** (java.awt.Frame owner, String title, boolean modal,	
			java.awt.GraphicsConfiguration gc)	
	4	protected . . . . **String**	**paramString** ()	
	3	protected . . . . **void**	**processWindowEvent** (java.awt.event.WindowEvent e)	
	2	public. **void**	**remove** (java.awt.Component comp)	ε831
		protected . . . . JRootPane	**rootPane**	
		protected . . . . boolean	**rootPaneCheckingEnabled**	
	7	public. .void	**setContentPane** (java.awt.Container contentPane)	
		public. .void	**setDefaultCloseOperation** (int operation)	
1.4 △		public static . . . . .void	**setDefaultLookAndFeelDecorated** (boolean defaultLookAndFeelDecorated)	
	7	public. .void	**setGlassPane** (java.awt.Component glassPane)	
		public. .void	**setJMenuBar** (JMenuBar menu)	
	7	public. .void	**setLayeredPane** (JLayeredPane layeredPane)	
	2	public. **void**	**setLayout** (*java.awt.LayoutManager* manager)	ε613,622,624,625,627
	4	public. .void	setModal (boolean b)	
	4	public. .void	setResizable (boolean resizable)	
		protected . . . . .void	**setRootPane** (JRootPane root)	
		protected . . . . .void	**setRootPaneCheckingEnabled** (boolean enabled)	
	4	public. .void	setTitle (String title)	
1.4	4	public. .void	setUndecorated (boolean undecorated)	
	1	public. .void	setVisible (boolean b)	ε876,905
	4	public. .void	show ()	ε905,618

	2	public . . . . **void update** (java.awt.Graphics g)	

JEditorPane
javax.swing

	Object	ε861
○	└java.awt.Component[1] - - - - - - - - - - - - - - - - - - - *java.awt.image.ImageObserver* [5], *java.awt.MenuContainer*, *java.io.Serializable*	
	└java.awt.Container[2]	
1.2 ○	└JComponent[3]	
1.2 ○	└javax.swing.text.JTextComponent[4] - - - - *Scrollable, javax.accessibility.Accessible*	
1.2	└JEditorPane	

	1	*139 inherited members from java.awt.Component not shown*	
	2	*51 inherited members from java.awt.Container not shown*	
	3	*140 inherited members from JComponent not shown*	
	4	*66 inherited members from javax.swing.text.JTextComponent not shown*	
	5	*8 inherited members from java.awt.image.ImageObserver not shown*	
		public synchronized . . . . void **addHyperlinkListener** (*javax.swing.event.HyperlinkListener* listener)	
			ε886
		protected . . . . **createDefaultEditorKit** ()	
		. . . . . javax.swing.text.EditorKit	
△		public static . . . . **createEditorKitForContentType** (String type)	
		. . . . . javax.swing.text.EditorKit	
		public . . . . void **fireHyperlinkUpdate** (javax.swing.event.HyperlinkEvent e)	
	4	public . . . . **javax.accessibility** ₂ **getAccessibleContext** ()	
		.AccessibleContext	
●		public final . . . . String **getContentType** ()	
		public . . . . **getEditorKit** ()	
		. . . . . javax.swing.text.EditorKit	
1.3 △		public static . . . . String **getEditorKitClassNameForContentType** (String type)	
		public . . . . **getEditorKitForContentType** (String type)	
		. . . . . javax.swing.text.EditorKit	
1.4		public synchronized . . . . **getHyperlinkListeners** ()	
		. . . . *javax.swing* ₂	
		.event.HyperlinkListener[]	
		public . . . . java.net.URL **getPage** ()	
	3	public . . . . **java.awt.Dimension getPreferredSize** ()	
	4	public . . . . **boolean getScrollableTracksViewportHeight** ()	
	4	public . . . . **boolean getScrollableTracksViewportWidth** ()	
		protected . . java.io.InputStream **getStream** (java.net.URL page) throws java.io.IOException	
	4	public . . . . **String getText** ()	ε953,957,968,1006,618
	3	public . . . . **String getUIClassID** ()	
✳		public . . . . **JEditorPane** ()	
✳		public . . . . **JEditorPane** (String url) throws java.io.IOException	ε886,994
✳		public . . . . **JEditorPane** (java.net.URL initialPage) throws java.io.IOException	
✳		public . . . . **JEditorPane** (String type, String text)	
	4	protected . . . . **String paramString** ()	
		public . . . . void **read** (java.io.InputStream in, Object desc) throws java.io.IOException	
△		public static . . . . void **registerEditorKitForContentType** (String type, String classname)	
△		public static . . . . void **registerEditorKitForContentType** (String type, String classname, ClassLoader loader)	
		public synchronized . . . . void **removeHyperlinkListener** (*javax.swing.event.HyperlinkListener* listener)	
	4	public . . . . **void replaceSelection** (String content)	ε1000,1002
		public . . . . void **scrollToReference** (String reference)	
●		public final . . . . void **setContentType** (String type)	
	4	public . . . . void setEditable (boolean b)	ε886,994,788,988
		public . . . . void **setEditorKit** (javax.swing.text.EditorKit kit)	
		public . . . . void **setEditorKitForContentType** (String type, javax.swing.text.EditorKit k)	
		public . . . . void **setPage** (String url) throws java.io.IOException	
		public . . . . void **setPage** (java.net.URL page) throws java.io.IOException	ε886
	4	public . . . . **void setText** (String t)	ε953,957,1016

Class *Interface* —extends - - -implements ○ abstract ● final △ static ▲ static final ✳ constructor x x—inherited x **x**—declared **x x**—overridden
ε*n*—examples of usage ⌐—has subclass package—see other volume

602

JEditorPane.JEditorPaneAccessibleHypertextSupport.HTMLLink			javax.swing

Object
1.2 ○ └─javax.accessibility.AccessibleHyperlink[1] - - - - - *javax.accessibility.AccessibleAction*
1.2   └─JEditorPane₂
         .JEditorPaneAccessibleHypertextSupport₂
         .HTMLLink

1	public	**boolean**	**doAccessibleAction** (int i)
1	public	**Object**	**getAccessibleActionAnchor** (int i)
1	public	**int**	**getAccessibleActionCount** ()
1	public	**String**	**getAccessibleActionDescription** (int i)
1	public	**Object**	**getAccessibleActionObject** (int i)
1	public	**int**	**getEndIndex** ()
1	public	**int**	**getStartIndex** ()
*	public		**JEditorPane.JEditorPaneAccessibleHypertextSupport.HTMLLink**
			(*javax.swing.text.Element* e)
1	public	**boolean**	**isValid** ()

JFileChooser			javax.swing

Object
○ └─java.awt.Component[1] - - - - - - - - - - - - - - - - - - - *java.awt.image.ImageObserver* [4], *java.awt.MenuContainer*,
                                          java.io.Serializable
      └─java.awt.Container[2]
1.2 ○   └─JComponent[3]
1.2   └─JFileChooser - - - - - - - - - - - - - - - - - - - *javax.accessibility.Accessible*

	1	*143 inherited members from java.awt.Component not shown*	
	2	*51 inherited members from java.awt.Container not shown*	
	3	*141 inherited members from JComponent not shown*	
	4	*8 inherited members from java.awt.image.ImageObserver not shown*	
	public	boolean	**accept** (java.io.File f)
1.3 ▲	public static final	String	**ACCEPT_ALL_FILE_FILTER_USED_CHANGED_PROPERTY**
			= "acceptAllFileFilterUsedChanged"
	3 protected **javax.accessibility**₂	**accessibleContext**	
	.**AccessibleContext**		
▲	public static final	String	**ACCESSORY_CHANGED_PROPERTY** = "AccessoryChangedProperty"
	public	void	**addActionListener** (*java.awt.event.ActionListener* l)
	public	void	**addChoosableFileFilter** (javax.swing.filechooser.FileFilter filter) ε889
	3 public synchronized	void	addPropertyChangeListener (*java.beans.PropertyChangeListener* listener)
			ε899,900,903,904
▲	public static final	String	**APPROVE_BUTTON_MNEMONIC_CHANGED_PROPERTY**
			= "ApproveButtonMnemonicChangedProperty"
▲	public static final	String	**APPROVE_BUTTON_TEXT_CHANGED_PROPERTY**
			= "ApproveButtonTextChangedProperty"
▲	public static final	String	**APPROVE_BUTTON_TOOL_TIP_TEXT_CHANGED_PROPERTY**
			= "ApproveButtonToolTipTextChangedProperty"
▲	public static final	int	**APPROVE_OPTION** = 0 ε890
▲	public static final	String	**APPROVE_SELECTION** = "ApproveSelection"
	public	void	**approveSelection** ()
▲	public static final	int	**CANCEL_OPTION** = 1 ε890
▲	public static final	String	**CANCEL_SELECTION** = "CancelSelection"
	public	void	**cancelSelection** ()
	public	void	**changeToParentDirectory** ()
▲	public static final	String	**CHOOSABLE_FILE_FILTER_CHANGED_PROPERTY**
			= "ChoosableFileFilterChangedProperty"
1.3 ▲	public static final	String	**CONTROL_BUTTONS_ARE_SHOWN_CHANGED_PROPERTY**
			= "ControlButtonsAreShownChangedProperty"
1.4	protected	JDialog	**createDialog** (java.awt.Component parent) throws java.awt.HeadlessException
			ε905
▲	public static final	int	**CUSTOM_DIALOG** = 2
▲	public static final	String	**DIALOG_TITLE_CHANGED_PROPERTY** = "DialogTitleChangedProperty"
▲	public static final	String	**DIALOG_TYPE_CHANGED_PROPERTY** = "DialogTypeChangedProperty"
▲	public static final	int	**DIRECTORIES_ONLY** = 1 ε888
▲	public static final	String	**DIRECTORY_CHANGED_PROPERTY** = "directoryChanged"
	public	void	**ensureFileIsVisible** (java.io.File f)
▲	public static final	int	**ERROR_OPTION** = -1 ε890
▲	public static final	String	**FILE_FILTER_CHANGED_PROPERTY** = "fileFilterChanged"
▲	public static final	String	**FILE_HIDING_CHANGED_PROPERTY** = "FileHidingChanged"
▲	public static final	String	**FILE_SELECTION_MODE_CHANGED_PROPERTY** = "fileSelectionChanged"
▲	public static final	String	**FILE_SYSTEM_VIEW_CHANGED_PROPERTY** = "FileSystemViewChanged"

J

Classes

JFileChooser

▲		public static final .... String	**FILE_VIEW_CHANGED_PROPERTY** = "fileViewChanged"	
▲		public static final .... int	**FILES_AND_DIRECTORIES** = 2	
▲		public static final .... int	**FILES_ONLY** = 0	
		protected .... void	**fireActionPerformed** (String command)	
		public .... javax ₂ .swing.filechooser.FileFilter	**getAcceptAllFileFilter** ()	
	3	public .... **javax.accessibility** ₂ **.AccessibleContext**	**getAccessibleContext** ()	
		public .... JComponent	**getAccessory** ()	
1.4		public .... java ₂ .awt.event.ActionListener[]	**getActionListeners** ()	
		public .... int	**getApproveButtonMnemonic** ()	
		public .... String	**getApproveButtonText** ()	
		public .... String	**getApproveButtonToolTipText** ()	
		public .... javax ₂ .swing.filechooser.FileFilter[]	**getChoosableFileFilters** ()	
1.3		public .... boolean	**getControlButtonsAreShown** ()	
		public .... java.io.File	**getCurrentDirectory** ()	ε891,900,904
		public .... String	**getDescription** (java.io.File f)	
		public .... String	**getDialogTitle** ()	
		public .... int	**getDialogType** ()	
1.4		public .... boolean	**getDragEnabled** ()	
		public .... javax ₂ .swing.filechooser.FileFilter	**getFileFilter** ()	
		public .... int	**getFileSelectionMode** ()	
		public .... javax.swing ₂ .filechooser.FileSystemView	**getFileSystemView** ()	ε897
		public .... javax ₂ .swing.filechooser.FileView	**getFileView** ()	
		public .... Icon	**getIcon** (java.io.File f)	ε901
		public .... String	**getName** (java.io.File f)	
		public .... java.io.File	**getSelectedFile** ()	ε887,889,892,903
		public .... java.io.File[]	**getSelectedFiles** ()	ε895,903
		public .... String	**getTypeDescription** (java.io.File f)	ε893
		public .... javax ₂ .swing.plaf.FileChooserUI	**getUI** ()	
1.3	3	public .... **String**	**getUIClassID** ()	
		public .... boolean	**isAcceptAllFileFilterUsed** ()	
		public .... boolean	**isDirectorySelectionEnabled** ()	
		public .... boolean	**isFileHidingEnabled** ()	ε896
		public .... boolean	**isFileSelectionEnabled** ()	
		public .... boolean	**isMultiSelectionEnabled** ()	
		public .... boolean	**isTraversable** (java.io.File f)	
✳		public	**JFileChooser** ()	ε887,890,891,892,893
✳		public	**JFileChooser** (java.io.File currentDirectory)	ε887,888,889
✳		public	**JFileChooser** (String currentDirectoryPath)	
✳		public	**JFileChooser** (javax.swing.filechooser.FileSystemView fsv)	
✳		public	**JFileChooser** (java.io.File currentDirectory, javax.swing.filechooser.FileSystemView fsv)	
✳		public	**JFileChooser** (String currentDirectoryPath, javax.swing.filechooser.FileSystemView fsv)	
▲		public static final .... String	**MULTI_SELECTION_ENABLED_CHANGED_PROPERTY** = "MultiSelectionEnabledChangedProperty"	
▲		public static final .... int	**OPEN_DIALOG** = 0	
	3	protected .... **String**	**paramString** ()	
		public .... void	**removeActionListener** (java.awt.event.ActionListener l)	
		public .... boolean	**removeChoosableFileFilter** (javax.swing.filechooser.FileFilter f)	
		public .... void	**rescanCurrentDirectory** ()	
		public .... void	**resetChoosableFileFilters** ()	
▲		public static final .... int	**SAVE_DIALOG** = 1	ε905
▲		public static final .... String	**SELECTED_FILE_CHANGED_PROPERTY** = "SelectedFileChangedProperty"	ε903
▲		public static final .... String	**SELECTED_FILES_CHANGED_PROPERTY** = "SelectedFilesChangedProperty"	
1.3		public .... void	**setAcceptAllFileFilterUsed** (boolean b)	
		public .... void	**setAccessory** (JComponent newAccessory)	ε899
		public .... void	**setApproveButtonMnemonic** (char mnemonic)	ε898
		public .... void	**setApproveButtonMnemonic** (int mnemonic)	
		public .... void	**setApproveButtonText** (String approveButtonText)	ε898
		public .... void	**setApproveButtonToolTipText** (String toolTipText)	ε898
1.3		public .... void	**setControlButtonsAreShown** (boolean b)	

	public	void **setCurrentDirectory** (java.io.File dir)	ε891
	public	void **setDialogTitle** (String dialogTitle)	ε900
	public	void **setDialogType** (int dialogType)	
1.4	public	void **setDragEnabled** (boolean b)	
	public	void **setFileFilter** (javax.swing.filechooser.FileFilter filter)	
	public	void **setFileHidingEnabled** (boolean b)	ε896
	public	void **setFileSelectionMode** (int mode)	ε888
	public	void **setFileSystemView** (javax.swing.filechooser.FileSystemView fsv)	
	public	void **setFileView** (javax.swing.filechooser.FileView fileView)	
	public	void **setMultiSelectionEnabled** (boolean b)	ε895
	public	void **setSelectedFile** (java.io.File file)	ε892
	public	void **setSelectedFiles** (java.io.File[] selectedFiles)	
	protected	void **setup** (javax.swing.filechooser.FileSystemView view)	
	public	int **showDialog** (java.awt.Component parent, String approveButtonText) throws java.awt.HeadlessException	
	public	int **showOpenDialog** (java.awt.Component parent) throws java.awt.HeadlessException	ε887,889,890,891,892
	public	int **showSaveDialog** (java.awt.Component parent) throws java.awt.HeadlessException	ε887
3	public	**void updateUI** ()	

JFormattedTextField   javax.swing

ε861

```
      Object
  ○   └java.awt.Component 1 - - - - - - - - - - - - - - - - - - - java.awt.image.ImageObserver 6, java.awt.MenuContainer,
                                                    java.io.Serializable
          └java.awt.Container 2
1.2 ○        └JComponent 3
1.2 ○          └javax.swing.text.JTextComponent 4 - - - - Scrollable, javax.accessibility.Accessible
1.2              └JTextField 5 - - - - - - - - - - - - - - - - - - SwingConstants 7
1.4                └JFormattedTextField
```

1	*138 inherited members from java.awt.Component not shown*		
2	*51 inherited members from java.awt.Container not shown*		
3	*136 inherited members from JComponent not shown*		
4	*68 inherited members from javax.swing.text.JTextComponent not shown*		
5	*26 inherited members from JTextField not shown*		
7	*19 inherited members from SwingConstants not shown*		
6	*8 inherited members from java.awt.image.ImageObserver not shown*		
▲	public static final	int **COMMIT** = 0	
▲	public static final	int **COMMIT_OR_REVERT** = 1	
	public	void **commitEdit** () throws java.text.ParseException	
5	public	*Action[]* **getActions** ()	
	public	int **getFocusLostBehavior** ()	
	public	JFormattedTextField₂ .AbstractFormatter **getFormatter** ()	ε996
	public	JFormattedTextField₂ .AbstractFormatterFactory **getFormatterFactory** ()	ε787
5	public	**String getUIClassID** ()	
	public	Object **getValue** ()	ε995,996
	protected	void **invalidEdit** ()	
	public	boolean **isEditValid** ()	
*	public	**JFormattedTextField** ()	
*	public	**JFormattedTextField** (Object value)	ε995,996
*	public	**JFormattedTextField** (java.text.Format format)	ε995,996
*	public	**JFormattedTextField** (JFormattedTextField.AbstractFormatter formatter)	ε997
*	public	**JFormattedTextField** (JFormattedTextField.AbstractFormatterFactory factory)	
*	public	**JFormattedTextField** (JFormattedTextField.AbstractFormatterFactory factory, Object currentValue)	
▲	public static final	int **PERSIST** = 3	
1	protected	void **processFocusEvent** (java.awt.event.FocusEvent e)	
▲	public static final	int **REVERT** = 2	
3	public	void setBackground (java.awt.Color bg)	ε788
5	public	**void setDocument** (javax.swing.text.Document doc)	ε975,977,1008
4	public	void **setEditable** (boolean b)	ε788,886,988,994
	public	void **setFocusLostBehavior** (int behavior)	
	protected	void **setFormatter** (JFormattedTextField.AbstractFormatter format)	
	public	void **setFormatterFactory** (JFormattedTextField.AbstractFormatterFactory tf)	ε995
4	public	void setMargin (java.awt.Insets m)	ε790

J

Classes

605

JFormattedTextField

JFormattedTextField.AbstractFormatter			javax.swing

Object [1]
1.4 ○ └JFormattedTextField.AbstractFormatter ⌐ - - - - - *java.io.Serializable* ⌐

*	public		**JFormattedTextField.AbstractFormatter** ()
1	protected	**Object**	**clone** () throws CloneNotSupportedException
	protected	*Action[]*	**getActions** ()
	protected	javax⌐ swing.text.DocumentFilter	**getDocumentFilter** ()
	protected	JFormattedTextField	**getFormattedTextField** ()
	protected	javax⌐ swing.text.NavigationFilter	**getNavigationFilter** ()
	public	void	**install** (JFormattedTextField ftf)
	protected	void	**invalidEdit** ()
	protected	void	**setEditValid** (boolean valid)
○	public abstract	Object	**stringToValue** (String text) throws java.text.ParseException
	public	void	**uninstall** ()
○	public abstract	String	**valueToString** (Object value) throws java.text.ParseException

---

JFormattedTextField.AbstractFormatterFactory			javax.swing

Object
1.4 ○ └JFormattedTextField⌐
.AbstractFormatterFactory⌐

*	public		**JFormattedTextField.AbstractFormatterFactory** ()
○	public abstract JFormattedTextField⌐ .AbstractFormatter		**getFormatter** (JFormattedTextField tf)

JFrame			javax.swing

Object   ε988,606,618,733,953
○ └java.awt.Component [1] - - - - - - - - - - - - - - - - - - - *java.awt.image.ImageObserver* [5], *java.awt.MenuContainer*,
                                               java.io.Serializable ⌐
   └java.awt.Container [2]
      └java.awt.Window [3] - - - - - - - - - - - - - - - - - - *javax.accessibility.Accessible*
         └java.awt.Frame [4]
1.2   └JFrame - *WindowConstants* [6], *RootPaneContainer* [7]

1	*159 inherited members from java.awt.Component not shown*			
2	*53 inherited members from java.awt.Container not shown*			
3	*46 inherited members from java.awt.Window not shown*			
4	*42 inherited members from java.awt.Frame not shown*			
5	*8 inherited members from java.awt.image.ImageObserver not shown*			
	protected	javax.accessibility⌐ .AccessibleContext	**accessibleContext**	
2	protected	**void**	**addImpl** (java.awt.Component comp, Object constraints, int index)	
1	public synchronized	void	addKeyListener (*java.awt.event.KeyListener* l)	ε643,645
1	public synchronized	void	addMouseListener (*java.awt.event.MouseListener* l)	ε646,648
1	public synchronized	void	addMouseMotionListener (*java.awt.event.MouseMotionListener* l)	ε647
1	public	java.awt.Image	createImage (int width, int height)	ε666
	protected	JRootPane	**createRootPane** ()	
▲ 6	public static final	int	DISPOSE_ON_CLOSE = 2	
▲ 6	public static final	int	DO_NOTHING_ON_CLOSE = 0	
1.3 ▲ 6	public static final	int	**EXIT_ON_CLOSE** = 3	ε735
	protected	void	**frameInit** ()	ε734
4	public	**javax.accessibility⌐ .AccessibleContext**	**getAccessibleContext** ()	
7	public	java.awt.Container	**getContentPane** ()	ε732,733,816,841,887
	public	int	**getDefaultCloseOperation** ()	ε734,735
7	public	java.awt.Component	**getGlassPane** ()	
	public	JMenuBar	**getJMenuBar** ()	

Class   *Interface*   —extends   - - -implements   ○ abstract   ● final   △ static   ▲ static final   * constructor   x x—inherited   x **x**—declared   **x x**—overridden
εn—examples of usage   ⌐—has subclass   package—see other volume

```
      7 public ........... JLayeredPane  getLayeredPane ()
      7 public .............. JRootPane  getRootPane ()
  ▲   6 public static final ............. int  HIDE_ON_CLOSE = 1
1.4 △   public static ......... boolean  isDefaultLookAndFeelDecorated ()
        protected ............. boolean  isRootPaneCheckingEnabled ()
  *     public ...................  JFrame () throws java.awt.HeadlessException        ε732,734,735,816,841
1.3 *   public ...................  JFrame (java.awt.GraphicsConfiguration gc)
  *     public ...................  JFrame (String title) throws java.awt.HeadlessException   ε733
1.3 *   public ...................  JFrame (String title, java.awt.GraphicsConfiguration gc)
      3 public ..................... void  pack ()                                      ε816,887,901,957,971
      4 protected .............. String  paramString ()
      3 protected ................ void  processWindowEvent (java.awt.event.WindowEvent e)
      2 public .................... void  remove (java.awt.Component comp)              ε831
        protected .......... JRootPane  rootPane
        protected ............. boolean  rootPaneCheckingEnabled
      7 public .....................void  setContentPane (java.awt.Container contentPane)
        public .....................void  setDefaultCloseOperation (int operation)      ε734,735
1.4 △   public static .............. void  setDefaultLookAndFeelDecorated (boolean defaultLookAndFeelDecorated)
1.4   3 public .....................void  setFocusableWindowState (boolean focusableWindowState)  ε608
      7 public .....................void  setGlassPane (java.awt.Component glassPane)
        public .....................void  setJMenuBar (JMenuBar menubar)                ε808,857
      7 public .....................void  setLayeredPane (JLayeredPane layeredPane)
      2 public .................... void  setLayout (java.awt.LayoutManager manager)     ε613,622,624,625,627
        protected .................void  setRootPane (JRootPane root)
        protected .................void  setRootPaneCheckingEnabled (boolean enabled)
      1 public .....................void  setSize (int width, int height)               ε732,733,841,994,575
      1 public .....................void  setVisible (boolean b)                        ε732,733,738,816,841
      2 public .................... void  update (java.awt.Graphics g)
```

JInternalFrame   javax.swing

```
        Object
  ○     └─java.awt.Component 1 ------------------- java.awt.image.ImageObserver 4, java.awt.MenuContainer,
                                                   java.io.Serializable
          └─java.awt.Container 2
1.2 ○       └─JComponent 3
1.2           └─JInternalFrame ------------------- javax.accessibility.Accessible, WindowConstants 5,
                                                   RootPaneContainer 6
```

```
      1 139 inherited members from java.awt.Component not shown
      2 46 inherited members from java.awt.Container not shown
      3 139 inherited members from JComponent not shown
      5 4 inherited members from WindowConstants not shown
      4 8 inherited members from java.awt.image.ImageObserver not shown
      2 protected ................. void  addImpl (java.awt.Component comp, Object constraints, int index)
        public ....................void  addInternalFrameListener (javax.swing.event.InternalFrameListener l)
        protected ............. boolean  closable
  ▲     public static final ........ String  CONTENT_PANE_PROPERTY = "contentPane"
        protected ...... JRootPane  createRootPane ()
        protected ..... JInternalFrame.  desktopIcon
                .JDesktopIcon
        public .....................void  dispose ()
1.3     public .....................void  doDefaultCloseAction ()
        protected .................void  fireInternalFrameEvent (int id)
  ▲     public static final ........ String  FRAME_ICON_PROPERTY = "frameIcon"
        protected ............. Icon  frameIcon
      3 public .... javax.accessibility.  getAccessibleContext ()
          .AccessibleContext
      6 public ....... java.awt.Container  getContentPane ()                            ε841,732,733,816,887
        public ......................int  getDefaultCloseOperation ()
        public ......... JInternalFrame.  getDesktopIcon ()
          .JDesktopIcon
        public .......... JDesktopPane  getDesktopPane ()
1.4 ● 1 public final java.awt.Container  getFocusCycleRootAncestor ()
1.3     public .... java.awt.Component  getFocusOwner ()
        public .................... Icon  getFrameIcon ()
      6 public .... java.awt.Component  getGlassPane ()
1.4     public .... javax.swing.event.  getInternalFrameListeners ()
          .InternalFrameListener[]
        public .......... JMenuBar  getJMenuBar ()
        public ......................int  getLayer ()
      6 public ........... JLayeredPane  getLayeredPane ()
```

JInternalFrame

D	public	JMenuBar	**getMenuBar** ()	
1.4	public	java.awt.Component	**getMostRecentFocusOwner** ()	
1.3	public	java.awt.Rectangle	**getNormalBounds** ()	
3	public	**JRootPane**	**getRootPane** ()	
	public	String	**getTitle** ()	ε842
	public	javax.swing.plaf.InternalFrameUI	**getUI** ()	
3	public	**String**	**getUIClassID** ()	
•	public final	String	**getWarningString** ()	
▲	public static final	String	**GLASS_PANE_PROPERTY** = "glassPane"	
	protected	boolean	**iconable**	
▲	public static final	String	**IS_CLOSED_PROPERTY** = "closed"	
▲	public static final	String	**IS_ICON_PROPERTY** = "icon"	
▲	public static final	String	**IS_MAXIMUM_PROPERTY** = "maximum"	
▲	public static final	String	**IS_SELECTED_PROPERTY** = "selected"	
	public	boolean	**isClosable** ()	ε842
	protected	boolean	**isClosed**	
	public	boolean	**isClosed** ()	
1.4 • 2	public final	**boolean**	**isFocusCycleRoot** ()	
	protected	boolean	**isIcon**	
	public	boolean	**isIcon** ()	ε842
	public	boolean	**isIconifiable** ()	ε842
	public	boolean	**isMaximizable** ()	ε842
	protected	boolean	**isMaximum**	
	public	boolean	**isMaximum** ()	
	public	boolean	**isResizable** ()	ε842
	protected	boolean	**isRootPaneCheckingEnabled** ()	
	protected	boolean	**isSelected**	
	public	boolean	**isSelected** ()	ε842
1	public	boolean	isVisible ()	ε842
*	public		**JInternalFrame** ()	
*	public		**JInternalFrame** (String title)	
*	public		**JInternalFrame** (String title, boolean resizable)	
*	public		**JInternalFrame** (String title, boolean resizable, boolean closable)	
*	public		**JInternalFrame** (String title, boolean resizable, boolean closable, boolean maximizable)	
*	public		**JInternalFrame** (String title, boolean resizable, boolean closable, boolean maximizable, boolean iconifiable)	ε841
▲	public static final	String	**LAYERED_PANE_PROPERTY** = "layeredPane"	
	protected	boolean	**maximizable**	
▲	public static final	String	**MENU_BAR_PROPERTY** = "JMenuBar"	
	public	void	**moveToBack** ()	
	public	void	**moveToFront** ()	
	public	void	**pack** ()	
3	protected	**void**	**paintComponent** (java.awt.Graphics g)	
3	protected	**String**	**paramString** ()	
2	public	**void**	**remove** (java.awt.Component comp)	ε831
	public	void	**removeInternalFrameListener** (*javax.swing.event.InternalFrameListener* l)	
3	public	**void**	**reshape** (int x, int y, int width, int height)	
	protected	boolean	**resizable**	
1.3	public	void	**restoreSubcomponentFocus** ()	
▲	public static final	String	**ROOT_PANE_PROPERTY** = "rootPane"	
	protected	JRootPane	**rootPane**	
	protected	boolean	**rootPaneCheckingEnabled**	
	public	void	**setClosable** (boolean b)	
	public	void	**setClosed** (boolean b) throws java.beans.PropertyVetoException	
6	public	void	**setContentPane** (java.awt.Container c)	
	public	void	**setDefaultCloseOperation** (int operation)	
	public	void	**setDesktopIcon** (JInternalFrame.JDesktopIcon d)	
1.4 • 2	public final	**void**	**setFocusCycleRoot** (boolean focusCycleRoot)	
	public	void	**setFrameIcon** (*Icon* icon)	
6	public	void	**setGlassPane** (java.awt.Component glass)	
	public	void	**setIcon** (boolean b) throws java.beans.PropertyVetoException	
	public	void	**setIconifiable** (boolean b)	
	public	void	**setJMenuBar** (JMenuBar m)	
1.3	public	void	**setLayer** (int layer)	
	public	void	**setLayer** (Integer layer)	
6	public	void	**setLayeredPane** (JLayeredPane layered)	
2	public	**void**	**setLayout** (*java.awt.LayoutManager* manager)	ε613,622,624,625,627
	public	void	**setMaximizable** (boolean b)	
	public	void	**setMaximum** (boolean b) throws java.beans.PropertyVetoException	

J

D	public	....	void	**setMenuBar** (JMenuBar m)	
1.3	public	....	void	**setNormalBounds** (java.awt.Rectangle r)	
	public	....	void	**setResizable** (boolean b)	
	protected	....	void	**setRootPane** (JRootPane root)	
	protected	....	void	**setRootPaneCheckingEnabled** (boolean enabled)	
	public	....	void	**setSelected** (boolean selected) throws java.beans.PropertyVetoException	
1	public	....	void	setSize (int width, int height)	ε841
	public	....	void	**setTitle** (String title)	
	public	....	void	**setUI** (javax.swing.plaf.InternalFrameUI ui)	
3	public	....	void	setVisible (boolean aFlag)	ε841
1	public	....	**void**	**show** ()	
	protected	....	String	**title**	
▲	public static final	....	String	**TITLE_PROPERTY** = "title"	
	public	....	void	**toBack** ()	
	public	....	void	**toFront** ()	
3	public	....	**void**	**updateUI** ()	

JInternalFrame.JDesktopIcon javax.swing

```
Object
 └java.awt.Component¹ - - - - - - - - - - - - - - - - - - - java.awt.image.ImageObserver⁴, java.awt.MenuContainer,
                                                            java.io.Serializable⌟
     └java.awt.Container²
        └JComponent³
           └JInternalFrame.JDesktopIcon - - - - - - - javax.accessibility.Accessible
```

1	*143 inherited members from java.awt.Component not shown*			
2	*51 inherited members from java.awt.Container not shown*			
3	*144 inherited members from JComponent not shown*			
4	*8 inherited members from java.awt.image.ImageObserver not shown*			
3	public....	**javax.accessibility⌟** **.AccessibleContext**	**getAccessibleContext** ()	
	public	.... JDesktopPane	**getDesktopPane** ()	
	public	.... JInternalFrame	**getInternalFrame** ()	
	public	.... javax⌟ .swing.plaf.DesktopIconUI	**getUI** ()	
3	public	.... **String**	**getUIClassID** ()	
*	public	....	**JInternalFrame.JDesktopIcon** (JInternalFrame f)	
	public	.... void	**setInternalFrame** (JInternalFrame f)	
	public	.... void	**setUI** (javax.swing.plaf.DesktopIconUI ui)	
3	public	.... **void**	**updateUI** ()	

JLabel javax.swing

```
Object
 └java.awt.Component¹ - - - - - - - - - - - - - - - - - - - java.awt.image.ImageObserver⁴, java.awt.MenuContainer,
                                                            java.io.Serializable⌟
     └java.awt.Container²
        └JComponent³
           └JLabel⌟ - - - - - - - - - - - - - - - - - - - - SwingConstants⁵, javax.accessibility.Accessible
```

1	*141 inherited members from java.awt.Component not shown*			
2	*50 inherited members from java.awt.Container not shown*			
3	*138 inherited members from JComponent not shown*			
5	*14 inherited members from SwingConstants not shown*			
4	*8 inherited members from java.awt.image.ImageObserver not shown*			
1	public synchronized	.... void	addMouseListener (*java.awt.event.MouseListener* l)	ε742,810
▲ 5	public static final	.... int	BOTTOM = 3	ε739,747,748,834
▲ 5	public static final	.... int	CENTER = 0	ε739,740,933,934,747
	protected	.... int	**checkHorizontalKey** (int key, String message)	
	protected	.... int	**checkVerticalKey** (int key, String message)	
3	protected	.... void	firePropertyChange (String propertyName, Object oldValue, Object newValue)	ε928,936
3	public	.... void	firePropertyChange (String propertyName, boolean oldValue, boolean newValue)	ε928,936
3	public....	**javax.accessibility⌟** **.AccessibleContext**	**getAccessibleContext** ()	
	public	.... *Icon*	**getDisabledIcon** ()	
	public	.... int	**getDisplayedMnemonic** ()	
1.4	public	.... int	**getDisplayedMnemonicIndex** ()	

JLabel

		public	int	**getHorizontalAlignment** ()	
		public	int	**getHorizontalTextPosition** ()	
		public	*Icon*	**getIcon** ()	
		public	int	**getIconTextGap** ()	
		public	java.awt.Component	**getLabelFor** ()	
		public	String	**getText** ()	
		public	javax.swing.plaf.LabelUI	**getUI** ()	
	3	public	**String**	**getUIClassID** ()	
		public	int	**getVerticalAlignment** ()	
		public	int	**getVerticalTextPosition** ()	
	1	public	**boolean**	**imageUpdate** (java.awt.Image img, int infoflags, int x, int y, int w, int h)	
*		public		**JLabel** ()	
*		public		**JLabel** (String text)	ε739,740,741,742,901
*		public		**JLabel** (*Icon* image)	ε740,798,694
*		public		**JLabel** (String text, int horizontalAlignment)	ε739
*		public		**JLabel** (*Icon* image, int horizontalAlignment)	
*		public		**JLabel** (String text, *Icon* icon, int horizontalAlignment)	ε739,740
		protected	java.awt.Component	**labelFor**	
▲	5	public static final	int	LEFT = 2	ε739,747,748,834,981
	3	protected	**String**	**paramString** ()	
	3	public	void	revalidate ()	ε928,936
▲	5	public static final	int	RIGHT = 4	ε739,747,748,981
	3	public	void	setBorder (*javax.swing.border.Border* border)	ε873,874,875
		public	void	**setDisabledIcon** (*Icon* disabledIcon)	
		public	void	**setDisplayedMnemonic** (char aChar)	ε692
		public	void	**setDisplayedMnemonic** (int key)	ε741
1.4		public	void	**setDisplayedMnemonicIndex** (int index) throws IllegalArgumentException	
		public	void	**setHorizontalAlignment** (int alignment)	
		public	void	**setHorizontalTextPosition** (int textPosition)	
		public	void	**setIcon** (*Icon* icon)	ε740,901
		public	void	**setIconTextGap** (int iconTextGap)	
		public	void	**setLabelFor** (java.awt.Component c)	ε692,741
		public	void	**setText** (String text)	
1.4	3	public	void	setTransferHandler (TransferHandler newHandler)	ε742
		public	void	**setUI** (javax.swing.plaf.LabelUI ui)	
		public	void	**setVerticalAlignment** (int alignment)	ε739
		public	void	**setVerticalTextPosition** (int textPosition)	
▲	5	public static final	int	TOP = 1	ε739,747,748,828
	3	public	**void**	**updateUI** ()	
	2	public	void	validate ()	ε928,936,601,674

JLayeredPane   javax.swing

```
         Object
    O    └─java.awt.Component 1 - - - - - - - - - - - - - - - - - - java.awt.image.ImageObserver 4, java.awt.MenuContainer,
                                                                    java.io.Serializable
            └─java.awt.Container 2
    1.2 O      └─JComponent 3
    1.2           └─JLayeredPane - - - - - - - - - - - - - - - - - javax.accessibility.Accessible
```

	1	*143 inherited members from java.awt.Component not shown*			
	2	*49 inherited members from java.awt.Container not shown*			
	3	*143 inherited members from JComponent not shown*			
	4	*8 inherited members from java.awt.image.ImageObserver not shown*			
	2	protected	**void**	**addImpl** (java.awt.Component comp, Object constraints, int index)	
▲		public static final	Integer	**DEFAULT_LAYER** = new Integer(0)	
▲		public static final	Integer	**DRAG_LAYER** = new Integer(400)	
▲		public static final	Integer	**FRAME_CONTENT_LAYER** = new Integer(-30000)	
	3	public	**javax.accessibility .AccessibleContext**	**getAccessibleContext** ()	
		public	int	**getComponentCountInLayer** (int layer)	
		public	java.awt.Component[]	**getComponentsInLayer** (int layer)	
		protected	java.util.Hashtable	**getComponentToLayer** ()	
		public	int	**getIndexOf** (java.awt.Component c)	
		public	int	**getLayer** (java.awt.Component c)	
△		public static	int	**getLayer** (JComponent c)	
△		public static	JLayeredPane	**getLayeredPaneAbove** (java.awt.Component c)	
		protected	Integer	**getObjectForLayer** (int layer)	
		public	int	**getPosition** (java.awt.Component c)	

Class *Interface* —extends - - -implements ○ abstract ● final △ static ▲ static final * constructor x x—inherited x **x**—declared **x x**—overridden
ε*n*—examples of usage ˌ—has subclass package—see other volume

	public	int	**highestLayer** ()	
	protected	int	**insertIndexForLayer** (int layer, int position)	
3	public	**boolean**	**isOptimizedDrawingEnabled** ()	
∗	public		**JLayeredPane** ()	
▲	public static final	String	**LAYER_PROPERTY** = "layeredContainerLayer"	
	public	int	**lowestLayer** ()	
▲	public static final	Integer	**MODAL_LAYER** = new Integer(200)	
	public	void	**moveToBack** (java.awt.Component c)	
	public	void	**moveToFront** (java.awt.Component c)	
3	public	**void**	**paint** (java.awt.Graphics g)	
▲	public static final	Integer	**PALETTE_LAYER** = new Integer(100)	
3	protected	**String**	**paramString** ()	
▲	public static final	Integer	**POPUP_LAYER** = new Integer(300)	
△	public static	void	**putLayer** (JComponent c, int layer)	
2	public	**void**	**remove** (int index)	ε831,832
	public	void	**setLayer** (java.awt.Component c, int layer)	
	public	void	**setLayer** (java.awt.Component c, int layer, int position)	
	public	void	**setPosition** (java.awt.Component c, int position)	

J

JList			javax.swing

```
Object
 └java.awt.Component¹ ------------------- java.awt.image.ImageObserver⁴, java.awt.MenuContainer,
                                            java.io.Serializable⌐
      └java.awt.Container²
         └JComponent³
            └JList ----------------------- Scrollable⁵, javax.accessibility.Accessible
```

1.2 ○
1.2

1	*142 inherited members from java.awt.Component not shown*			
2	*51 inherited members from java.awt.Container not shown*			
3	*142 inherited members from JComponent not shown*			
4	*8 inherited members from java.awt.image.ImageObserver not shown*			
	public	void	**addListSelectionListener** (*javax.swing.event.ListSelectionListener* listener)	ε784
1	public synchronized	void	addMouseListener (*java.awt.event.MouseListener* l)	ε783
	public	void	**addSelectionInterval** (int anchor, int lead)	ε780
	public	void	**clearSelection** ()	ε780
	protected	*ListSelectionModel*	**createSelectionModel** ()	
	public	void	**ensureIndexIsVisible** (int index)	
	protected	void	**fireSelectionValueChanged** (int firstIndex, int lastIndex, boolean isAdjusting)	
3	public	**javax.accessibility**⌐ **.AccessibleContext**	**getAccessibleContext** ()	
	public	int	**getAnchorSelectionIndex** ()	
	public	java.awt.Rectangle	**getCellBounds** (int index0, int index1)	
	public	*ListCellRenderer*	**getCellRenderer** ()	
1.4	public	boolean	**getDragEnabled** ()	
	public	int	**getFirstVisibleIndex** ()	ε777
	public	int	**getFixedCellHeight** ()	
	public	int	**getFixedCellWidth** ()	
	public	int	**getLastVisibleIndex** ()	ε777
1.4	public	int	**getLayoutOrientation** ()	ε782
	public	int	**getLeadSelectionIndex** ()	
1.4	public	*javax.swing*⌐ *.event.ListSelectionListener[]*	**getListSelectionListeners** ()	
	public	int	**getMaxSelectionIndex** ()	ε779
	public	int	**getMinSelectionIndex** ()	
	public	*ListModel*	**getModel** ()	ε777,778,779,780,785
1.4	public	int	**getNextMatch** (String prefix, int startIndex, javax.swing.text.Position.Bias bias)	ε777
5	public	java.awt.Dimension	**getPreferredScrollableViewportSize** ()	ε949
	public	Object	**getPrototypeCellValue** ()	
5	public	int	**getScrollableBlockIncrement** (java.awt.Rectangle visibleRect, int orientation, int direction)	
5	public	boolean	**getScrollableTracksViewportHeight** ()	
5	public	boolean	**getScrollableTracksViewportWidth** ()	
5	public	int	**getScrollableUnitIncrement** (java.awt.Rectangle visibleRect, int orientation, int direction)	
	public	int	**getSelectedIndex** ()	ε779
	public	int[]	**getSelectedIndices** ()	ε779
	public	Object	**getSelectedValue** ()	ε779
	public	Object[]	**getSelectedValues** ()	ε779,784
	public	java.awt.Color	**getSelectionBackground** ()	

Classes

JList

	public	java.awt.Color	**getSelectionForeground** ()	
	public	int	**getSelectionMode** ()	ε781
	public	*ListSelectionModel*	**getSelectionModel** ()	
3	public	**String**	**getToolTipText** (java.awt.event.MouseEvent event)	ε776
	public	javax.swing.plaf.ListUI	**getUI** ()	
3	public	**String**	**getUIClassID** ()	
	public	boolean	**getValueIsAdjusting** ()	
	public	int	**getVisibleRowCount** ()	ε777
1.4 ▲	public static final	int	**HORIZONTAL_WRAP** = 2	ε782
	public	java.awt.Point	**indexToLocation** (int index)	
	public	boolean	**isSelectedIndex** (int index)	ε779
	public	boolean	**isSelectionEmpty** ()	ε779
✳	public		**JList** ()	ε820
✳	public		**JList** (Object[] listData)	ε774,775,776,777,780
✳	public		**JList** (java.util.Vector listData)	
✳	public		**JList** (*ListModel* dataModel)	ε778
	public	int	**locationToIndex** (java.awt.Point location)	ε783
3	protected	**String**	**paramString** ()	
	public	void	**removeListSelectionListener** (*javax.swing.event.ListSelectionListener* listener)	
	public	void	**removeSelectionInterval** (int index0, int index1)	ε780
	public	void	**setCellRenderer** (*ListCellRenderer* cellRenderer)	
1.4	public	void	**setDragEnabled** (boolean b)	
	public	void	**setFixedCellHeight** (int height)	ε775
	public	void	**setFixedCellWidth** (int width)	ε775
1.4	public	void	**setLayoutOrientation** (int layoutOrientation)	ε782
	public	void	**setListData** (Object[] listData)	
	public	void	**setListData** (java.util.Vector listData)	
	public	void	**setModel** (*ListModel* model)	
	public	void	**setPrototypeCellValue** (Object prototypeCellValue)	ε775
	public	void	**setSelectedIndex** (int index)	
	public	void	**setSelectedIndices** (int[] indices)	
	public	void	**setSelectedValue** (Object anObject, boolean shouldScroll)	ε780
	public	void	**setSelectionBackground** (java.awt.Color selectionBackground)	
	public	void	**setSelectionForeground** (java.awt.Color selectionForeground)	
	public	void	**setSelectionInterval** (int anchor, int lead)	ε780
	public	void	**setSelectionMode** (int selectionMode)	ε781
	public	void	**setSelectionModel** (*ListSelectionModel* selectionModel)	
	public	void	**setUI** (javax.swing.plaf.ListUI ui)	
	public	void	**setValueIsAdjusting** (boolean b)	
	public	void	**setVisibleRowCount** (int visibleRowCount)	ε782
3	public	**void**	**updateUI** ()	
1.4 ▲	public static final	int	**VERTICAL** = 0	
1.4 ▲	public static final	int	**VERTICAL_WRAP** = 1	ε782

JMenu
javax.swing

```
      Object                                                                    ε45
   ○  └java.awt.Component¹ - - - - - - - - - - - - - - - java.awt.image.ImageObserver⁶, java.awt.MenuContainer,
                                                          java.io.Serializable
         └java.awt.Container²
1.2 ○      └JComponent³
1.2 ○        └AbstractButton⁴ - - - - - - - - - - - - - - java.awt.ItemSelectable, SwingConstants⁷
1.2          └JMenuItem⁵ - - - - - - - - - - - - - - - javax.accessibility.Accessible, MenuElement
1.2            └JMenu
```

1	141 inherited members from java.awt.Component not shown			
2	45 inherited members from java.awt.Container not shown			
3	140 inherited members from JComponent not shown			
4	96 inherited members from AbstractButton not shown			
7	19 inherited members from SwingConstants not shown			
6	8 inherited members from java.awt.image.ImageObserver not shown			
2	public	**java.awt.Component**	**add** (java.awt.Component c)	ε809,571,575,581,590
	public	JMenuItem	**add** (String s)	
	public	JMenuItem	**add** (*Action* a)	ε811
	public	JMenuItem	**add** (JMenuItem menuItem)	ε808,809,812,857,1011
2	public	**java.awt.Component**	**add** (java.awt.Component c, int index)	
5	public	void	addMenuDragMouseListener (*javax.swing.event.MenuDragMouseListener* l)	
5	public	void	addMenuKeyListener (*javax.swing.event.MenuKeyListener* l)	
	public	void	**addMenuListener** (*javax.swing.event.MenuListener* l)	

Class *Interface* —extends - - -implements ○ abstract ● final △ static ▲ static final ✳ constructor x x—inherited x **x**—declared **x x**—overridden
ε*n*—examples of usage ‿—has subclass package—see other volume

		public	.... void	**addSeparator** ()	
1.4	2	public	.... **void**	**applyComponentOrientation** (java.awt.ComponentOrientation o)	
1.3	5	protected	.... **void**	**configurePropertiesFromAction** (*Action* a)	
		protected	.... *java.beans* ⊋ *.PropertyChangeListener*	**createActionChangeListener** (JMenuItem b)	
1.3		protected	.... JMenuItem	**createActionComponent** (*Action* a)	
1.3	5	protected	*java.beans* ⊋ *.PropertyChangeListener*	createActionPropertyChangeListener (*Action* a)	
		protected	.. JMenu.WinListener	**createWinListener** (JPopupMenu p)	
	4	public	.... **void**	**doClick** (int pressTime)	
		protected	.... void	**fireMenuCanceled** ()	
		protected	.... void	**fireMenuDeselected** ()	
	5	protected	.... void	fireMenuDragMouseDragged (javax.swing.event.MenuDragMouseEvent event)	
	5	protected	.... void	fireMenuDragMouseEntered (javax.swing.event.MenuDragMouseEvent event)	
	5	protected	.... void	fireMenuDragMouseExited (javax.swing.event.MenuDragMouseEvent event)	
	5	protected	.... void	fireMenuDragMouseReleased (javax.swing.event.MenuDragMouseEvent event)	
	5	protected	.... void	fireMenuKeyPressed (javax.swing.event.MenuKeyEvent event)	
	5	protected	.... void	fireMenuKeyReleased (javax.swing.event.MenuKeyEvent event)	
	5	protected	.... void	fireMenuKeyTyped (javax.swing.event.MenuKeyEvent event)	
		protected	.... void	**fireMenuSelected** ()	
	5	public	.... KeyStroke	getAccelerator ()	
	5	public	.... **javax.accessibility** ⊋ **.AccessibleContext**	**getAccessibleContext** ()	
	5	public	... **java.awt.Component**	**getComponent** ()	ε813
		public	.... int	**getDelay** ()	
		public	.... JMenuItem	**getItem** (int pos)	
		public	.... int	**getItemCount** ()	
		public	.... java.awt.Component	**getMenuComponent** (int n)	
		public	.... int	**getMenuComponentCount** ()	
		public	... java.awt.Component[]	**getMenuComponents** ()	
1.4	5	public	...... *javax.swing.event* ⊋ *.MenuDragMouseListener[]*	getMenuDragMouseListeners ()	
1.4	5	public	.... *javax.swing* ⊋ *.event.MenuKeyListener[]*	getMenuKeyListeners ()	
1.4		public	.... *javax* ⊋ *.swing.event.MenuListener[]*	**getMenuListeners** ()	
		public	.... JPopupMenu	**getPopupMenu** ()	ε812
1.3		protected	.... java.awt.Point	**getPopupMenuOrigin** ()	
	5	public	.... ***MenuElement[]***	**getSubElements** ()	
	5	public	.... **String**	**getUIClassID** ()	
	5	protected	.... void	init (String text, *Icon* icon)	
		public	.... void	**insert** (String s, int pos)	
		public	.... JMenuItem	**insert** (*Action* a, int pos)	
		public	.... JMenuItem	**insert** (JMenuItem mi, int pos)	
		public	.... void	**insertSeparator** (int index)	
	5	public	.... boolean	isArmed ()	
		public	.... boolean	**isMenuComponent** (java.awt.Component c)	
		public	.... boolean	**isPopupMenuVisible** ()	
	4	public	.... **boolean**	**isSelected** ()	ε752,753
		public	.... boolean	**isTearOff** ()	
		public	.... boolean	**isTopLevelMenu** ()	
	*	public	....	**JMenu** ()	ε808,809,811,812,857
	*	public	....	**JMenu** (String s)	
1.3	*	public	....	**JMenu** (*Action* a)	
	*	public	....	**JMenu** (String s, boolean b)	
	5	public	.... **void**	**menuSelectionChanged** (boolean isIncluded)	ε814
	5	protected	.... **String**	**paramString** ()	
		protected	.. JMenu.WinListener	**popupListener**	
	3	protected	.... **void**	**processKeyEvent** (java.awt.event.KeyEvent evt)	
	5	public	.... void	processKeyEvent (java.awt.event.KeyEvent e, *MenuElement[]* path, MenuSelectionManager manager)	
	5	public	.... void	processMenuDragMouseEvent (javax.swing.event.MenuDragMouseEvent e)	
	5	public	.... void	processMenuKeyEvent (javax.swing.event.MenuKeyEvent e)	
	5	public	.... void	processMouseEvent (java.awt.event.MouseEvent e, *MenuElement[]* path, MenuSelectionManager manager)	
	2	public	.... **void**	**remove** (int pos)	ε831,832
	2	public	.... **void**	**remove** (java.awt.Component c)	ε831
		public	.... void	**remove** (JMenuItem item)	
	2	public	.... **void**	**removeAll** ()	ε831
	5	public	.... void	removeMenuDragMouseListener (*javax.swing.event.MenuDragMouseListener* l)	
	5	public	.... void	removeMenuKeyListener (*javax.swing.event.MenuKeyListener* l)	
		public	.... void	**removeMenuListener** (*javax.swing.event.MenuListener* l)	
	5	public	.... **void**	**setAccelerator** (KeyStroke keyStroke)	ε693

J

Classes

JMenu

5	public	void	setArmed (boolean b)	
1	public	**void**	**setComponentOrientation** (java.awt.ComponentOrientation o)	
	public	void	**setDelay** (int d)	
5	public	void	setEnabled (boolean b)	ε750
	public	void	**setMenuLocation** (int x, int y)	
4	public	void	setMnemonic (char mnemonic)	ε691,690
4	public	**void**	**setModel** (*ButtonModel* newModel)	
	public	void	**setPopupMenuVisible** (boolean b)	
4	public	**void**	**setSelected** (boolean b)	ε753
5	public	void	setUI (javax.swing.plaf.MenuItemUI ui)	
5	public	**void**	**updateUI** ()	

JMenu.WinListener	protected	javax.swing

Object
- 1.1 ○ └java.awt.event.WindowAdapter[1] - - - - - - - - - - *java.awt.event.WindowListener* (*java.util.EventListener*),
  java.awt.event.WindowStateListener (*java.util.EventListener*),
  java.awt.event.WindowFocusListener (*java.util.EventListener*)
- 1.2 └JMenu.WinListener - - - - - - - - - - - - - - - - - - *java.io.Serializable*

	1	public	void	windowActivated (java.awt.event.WindowEvent e)	
	1	public	void	windowClosed (java.awt.event.WindowEvent e)	ε568
	1	public	**void**	**windowClosing** (java.awt.event.WindowEvent e)	ε565,566,568,884,905
	1	public	void	windowDeactivated (java.awt.event.WindowEvent e)	
	1	public	void	windowDeiconified (java.awt.event.WindowEvent e)	
1.4	1	public	void	windowGainedFocus (java.awt.event.WindowEvent e)	
	1	public	void	windowIconified (java.awt.event.WindowEvent e)	
1.4	1	public	void	windowLostFocus (java.awt.event.WindowEvent e)	
	1	public	void	windowOpened (java.awt.event.WindowEvent e)	ε568
1.4	1	public	void	windowStateChanged (java.awt.event.WindowEvent e)	ε569
	✳	public		**JMenu.WinListener** (JPopupMenu p)	

JMenuBar	javax.swing

Object
- ○ └java.awt.Component[1] - - - - - - - - - - - - - - - - - - *java.awt.image.ImageObserver*[4], *java.awt.MenuContainer*,
  java.io.Serializable
- └java.awt.Container[2]
- 1.2 ○ └JComponent[3]
- 1.2 └JMenuBar - *javax.accessibility.Accessible, MenuElement*[5]

	1	*143 inherited members from java.awt.Component not shown*			
	2	*51 inherited members from java.awt.Container not shown*			
	3	*139 inherited members from JComponent not shown*			
	4	*8 inherited members from java.awt.image.ImageObserver not shown*			
		public	JMenu	**add** (JMenu c)	ε808,809,812,857
	3	public	**void**	**addNotify** ()	
	3	public	**javax.accessibility₂ .AccessibleContext**	**getAccessibleContext** ()	
D	5	public	java.awt.Component	**getComponent** ()	ε813
		public	java.awt.Component	**getComponentAtIndex** (int i)	
		public	int	**getComponentIndex** (java.awt.Component c)	
		public	JMenu	**getHelpMenu** ()	
		public	java.awt.Insets	**getMargin** ()	
		public	JMenu	**getMenu** (int index)	
		public	int	**getMenuCount** ()	
		public	*SingleSelectionModel*	**getSelectionModel** ()	
	5	public	*MenuElement[]*	**getSubElements** ()	
		public	. javax.swing.plaf.MenuBarUI	**getUI** ()	
	3	public	**String**	**getUIClassID** ()	
		public	boolean	**isBorderPainted** ()	
		public	boolean	**isSelected** ()	
✳		public		**JMenuBar** ()	
	5	public	void	**menuSelectionChanged** (boolean isIncluded)	ε808,857
	3	protected	**void**	**paintBorder** (java.awt.Graphics g)	ε814
	3	protected	**String**	**paramString** ()	

Class   *Interface*   —extends   - - -implements   ○ abstract   ● final   △ static   ▲ static final   ✳ constructor   x x—inherited   x **x**—declared   **x x**—overridden
ε*n*—examples of usage   ‿—has subclass   package—see other volume

1.3	3	protected . . . . **boolean**	**processKeyBinding** (KeyStroke ks, java.awt.event.KeyEvent e, int condition, boolean pressed)	
	5	public . . . . void	**processKeyEvent** (java.awt.event.KeyEvent e, *MenuElement[]* path, MenuSelectionManager manager)	
	5	public . . . . void	**processMouseEvent** (java.awt.event.MouseEvent event, *MenuElement[]* path, MenuSelectionManager manager)	
	3	public . . . . **void**	**removeNotify** ()	
		public . . . . void	**setBorderPainted** (boolean b)	
		public . . . . void	**setHelpMenu** (JMenu menu)	
		public . . . . void	**setMargin** (java.awt.Insets m)	
		public . . . . void	**setSelected** (java.awt.Component sel)	
		public . . . . void	**setSelectionModel** (*SingleSelectionModel* model)	
		public . . . . void	**setUI** (javax.swing.plaf.MenuBarUI ui)	
	3	public . . . . **void**	**updateUI** ()	

JMenuItem   javax.swing

ε45

```
Object
 └─java.awt.Component¹ ------------------- java.awt.image.ImageObserver⁵, java.awt.MenuContainer,
                                            java.io.Serializable
       └─java.awt.Container²
            └─JComponent³
                 └─AbstractButton⁴ ------------------ java.awt.ItemSelectable, SwingConstants⁶
                      └─JMenuItem ------------------- javax.accessibility.Accessible, MenuElement⁷
```

	1	*142 inherited members from java.awt.Component not shown*		
	2	*51 inherited members from java.awt.Container not shown*		
	3	*141 inherited members from JComponent not shown*		
	4	*99 inherited members from AbstractButton not shown*		
	6	*19 inherited members from SwingConstants not shown*		
	5	*8 inherited members from java.awt.image.ImageObserver not shown*		
	4	public . . . . void	addActionListener (*java.awt.event.ActionListener* l)	ε808,810,644,705
		public . . . . void	**addMenuDragMouseListener** (*javax.swing.event.MenuDragMouseListener* l)	
		public . . . . void	**addMenuKeyListener** (*javax.swing.event.MenuKeyListener* l)	
1.3	4	protected . . . . **void**	**configurePropertiesFromAction** (*Action* a)	
1.3	4	protected . . . . **java.beans** **.PropertyChangeListener**	**createActionPropertyChangeListener** (*Action* a)	
		protected . . . . void	**fireMenuDragMouseDragged** (javax.swing.event.MenuDragMouseEvent event)	
		protected . . . . void	**fireMenuDragMouseEntered** (javax.swing.event.MenuDragMouseEvent event)	
		protected . . . . void	**fireMenuDragMouseExited** (javax.swing.event.MenuDragMouseEvent event)	
		protected . . . . void	**fireMenuDragMouseReleased** (javax.swing.event.MenuDragMouseEvent event)	
		protected . . . . void	**fireMenuKeyPressed** (javax.swing.event.MenuKeyEvent event)	
		protected . . . . void	**fireMenuKeyReleased** (javax.swing.event.MenuKeyEvent event)	
		protected . . . . void	**fireMenuKeyTyped** (javax.swing.event.MenuKeyEvent event)	
		public . . . . KeyStroke	**getAccelerator** ()	
	3	public . . . . **javax.accessibility** **.AccessibleContext**	**getAccessibleContext** ()	
	7	public . . . . java.awt.Component	**getComponent** ()	ε813
1.4		public . . . . . . *javax.swing.event* *.MenuDragMouseListener[]*	**getMenuDragMouseListeners** ()	
1.4		public . . . . *javax.swing* *.event.MenuKeyListener[]*	**getMenuKeyListeners** ()	
	7	public . . . . *MenuElement[]*	**getSubElements** ()	
	4	public . . . . String	getText ()	ε813,754
	3	public . . . . **String**	**getUIClassID** ()	
	4	protected . . . . **void**	**init** (String text, *Icon* icon)	
		public . . . . boolean	**isArmed** ()	
*		public . . . . **JMenuItem** ()		
*		public	**JMenuItem** (String text)	ε808,809,810,812,814
1.3 *		public	**JMenuItem** (*Action* a)	ε857,1011
*		public	**JMenuItem** (*Icon* icon)	
*		public	**JMenuItem** (String text, int mnemonic)	
*		public	**JMenuItem** (String text, *Icon* icon)	
	7	public . . . . void	**menuSelectionChanged** (boolean isIncluded)	ε814
	4	protected . . . . **String**	**paramString** ()	
	7	public . . . . void	**processKeyEvent** (java.awt.event.KeyEvent e, *MenuElement[]* path, MenuSelectionManager manager)	
		public . . . . void	**processMenuDragMouseEvent** (javax.swing.event.MenuDragMouseEvent e)	
		public . . . . void	**processMenuKeyEvent** (javax.swing.event.MenuKeyEvent e)	
	7	public . . . . void	**processMouseEvent** (java.awt.event.MouseEvent e, *MenuElement[]* path, MenuSelectionManager manager)	
		public . . . . void	**removeMenuDragMouseListener** (*javax.swing.event.MenuDragMouseListener* l)	

J

Classes

JMenuItem

	public	void	**removeMenuKeyListener** (*javax.swing.event.MenuKeyListener* l)	
	public	void	**setAccelerator** (KeyStroke keyStroke)	ε693
	public	void	**setArmed** (boolean b)	
4	public	**void**	**setEnabled** (boolean b)	ε750
	public	void	**setUI** (javax.swing.plaf.MenuItemUI ui)	
4	public	**void**	**updateUI** ()	

JobAttributes   java.awt

Object[1]
1.3 ● └JobAttributes - *Cloneable*

1	public	**Object**	**clone** ()
1	public	**boolean**	**equals** (Object obj)
	public	int	**getCopies** ()
	public	JobAttributes.	**getDefaultSelection** ()
		.DefaultSelectionType	
	public	JobAttributes.	**getDestination** ()
		.DestinationType	
	public		**getDialog** ()
		.... JobAttributes.DialogType	
	public	String	**getFileName** ()
	public	int	**getFromPage** ()
	public	int	**getMaxPage** ()
	public	int	**getMinPage** ()
	public	JobAttributes.Multiple-	**getMultipleDocumentHandling** ()
		DocumentHandlingType	
	public	int[][]	**getPageRanges** ()
	public	String	**getPrinter** ()
	public JobAttributes.SidesType	**getSides** ()
	public	int	**getToPage** ()
1	public	**int**	**hashCode** ()
＊	public		**JobAttributes** ()
＊	public		**JobAttributes** (JobAttributes obj)
＊	public		**JobAttributes** (int copies, JobAttributes.DefaultSelectionType defaultSelection, JobAttributes.DestinationType destination, JobAttributes.DialogType dialog, String fileName, int maxPage, int minPage, JobAttributes.MultipleDocumentHandlingType multipleDocumentHandling, int[][] pageRanges, String printer, JobAttributes.SidesType sides)
	public	void	**set** (JobAttributes obj)
	public	void	**setCopies** (int copies)
	public	void	**setCopiesToDefault** ()
	public	void	**setDefaultSelection** (JobAttributes.DefaultSelectionType defaultSelection)
	public	void	**setDestination** (JobAttributes.DestinationType destination)
	public	void	**setDialog** (JobAttributes.DialogType dialog)
	public	void	**setFileName** (String fileName)
	public	void	**setFromPage** (int fromPage)
	public	void	**setMaxPage** (int maxPage)
	public	void	**setMinPage** (int minPage)
	public	void	**setMultipleDocumentHandling** (JobAttributes.MultipleDocumentHandlingType multipleDocumentHandling)
	public	void	**setMultipleDocumentHandlingToDefault** ()
	public	void	**setPageRanges** (int[][] pageRanges)
	public	void	**setPrinter** (String printer)
	public	void	**setSides** (JobAttributes.SidesType sides)
	public	void	**setSidesToDefault** ()
	public	void	**setToPage** (int toPage)
1	public	**String**	**toString** ()

JobAttributes.DefaultSelectionType   java.awt

Object
1.4 └AttributeValue[1]
1.3 ● └JobAttributes.DefaultSelectionType

▲	public static final	**ALL**	
	.... JobAttributes ͻ		
	.DefaultSelectionType		
1	public.........................int	hashCode ()	
▲	public static final	**RANGE**	
	.... JobAttributes ͻ		
	.DefaultSelectionType		
▲	public static final	**SELECTION**	
	.... JobAttributes ͻ		
	.DefaultSelectionType		
1	public....................String	toString ()	

JobAttributes.DestinationType   java.awt

Object
  └ AttributeValue [1]   (1.4)
    └ JobAttributes.DestinationType   (1.3 ●)

▲	public static final	**FILE**
	.... JobAttributes ͻ	
	.DestinationType	
1	public.........................int	hashCode ()
▲	public static final	**PRINTER**
	.... JobAttributes ͻ	
	.DestinationType	
1	public....................String	toString ()

JobAttributes.DialogType   java.awt

Object
  └ AttributeValue [1]   (1.4)
    └ JobAttributes.DialogType   (1.3 ●)

▲	public static final	**COMMON**
	.... JobAttributes.DialogType	
1	public.........................int	hashCode ()
▲	public static final	**NATIVE**
	.... JobAttributes.DialogType	
▲	public static final	**NONE**
	.... JobAttributes.DialogType	
1	public....................String	toString ()

JobAttributes.MultipleDocumentHandlingType   java.awt

Object
  └ AttributeValue [1]   (1.4)
    └ JobAttributes ͻ   (1.3 ●)
      .MultipleDocumentHandlingType

1	public.........................int	hashCode ()
▲	public static final	**SEPARATE_DOCUMENTS_COLLATED_COPIES**
	.... JobAttributes.Multiple-DocumentHandlingType	
▲	public static final	**SEPARATE_DOCUMENTS_UNCOLLATED_COPIES**
	.... JobAttributes.Multiple-DocumentHandlingType	
1	public....................String	toString ()

JobAttributes.SidesType   java.awt

Object
  └ AttributeValue [1]   (1.4)
    └ JobAttributes.SidesType   (1.3 ●)

1	public.........................int	hashCode ()
▲	public static final	**ONE_SIDED**
	..... JobAttributes.SidesType	
1	public....................String	toString ()

JobAttributes.SidesType

▲   public static final ....   **TWO_SIDED_LONG_EDGE**
       ..... JobAttributes.SidesType
▲   public static final ....   **TWO_SIDED_SHORT_EDGE**
       ..... JobAttributes.SidesType

JobHoldUntil   javax.print.attribute.standard

Object
1.4 ○   └─*javax.print.attribute.DateTimeSyntax*[1] ------- *java.io.Serializable*ˍ, *Cloneable*ˍ
1.4 ●   └─JobHoldUntil ---------------------- *javax.print.attribute.PrintRequestAttribute*
                                   (*javax.print.attribute.Attribute*[2] (*java.io.Serializable*)),
                                   javax.print.attribute.PrintJobAttribute
                                   (*javax.print.attribute.Attribute*[2] (*java.io.Serializable*))

    1   public .... **boolean** **equals** (Object object)
● 2   public final .... Class **getCategory** ()   *ε707*
● 2   public final .... String **getName** ()   *ε706,707,708*
    1   public .... java.util.Date getValue ()
    1   public .... int hashCode ()
✳   public .... **JobHoldUntil** (java.util.Date dateTime)
    1   public .... String toString ()

JobImpressions   javax.print.attribute.standard

Object
1.4 ○   └─*javax.print.attribute.IntegerSyntax*[1] --------- *java.io.Serializable*ˍ, *Cloneable*ˍ
1.4 ●   └─JobImpressions --------------------- *javax.print.attribute.PrintRequestAttribute*
                                     (*javax.print.attribute.Attribute*[2] (*java.io.Serializable*)),
                                     javax.print.attribute.PrintJobAttribute
                                     (*javax.print.attribute.Attribute*[2] (*java.io.Serializable*))

    1   public .... **boolean** **equals** (Object object)
● 2   public final .... Class **getCategory** ()   *ε707*
● 2   public final .... String **getName** ()   *ε706,707,708*
    1   public .... int getValue ()
    1   public .... int hashCode ()
✳   public .... **JobImpressions** (int value)
    1   public .... String toString ()

JobImpressionsCompleted   javax.print.attribute.standard

Object
1.4 ○   └─*javax.print.attribute.IntegerSyntax*[1] --------- *java.io.Serializable*ˍ, *Cloneable*ˍ
1.4 ●   └─JobImpressionsCompleted -------------- *javax.print.attribute.PrintJobAttribute* (*javax.print.attribute.Attribute*[2]
                                     (*java.io.Serializable*))

    1   public .... **boolean** **equals** (Object object)
● 2   public final .... Class **getCategory** ()   *ε707*
● 2   public final .... String **getName** ()   *ε706,707,708*
    1   public .... int getValue ()
    1   public .... int hashCode ()
✳   public .... **JobImpressionsCompleted** (int value)
    1   public .... String toString ()

JobImpressionsSupported   javax.print.attribute.standard

Object
1.4 ○   └─*javax.print.attribute.SetOfIntegerSyntax*[1] ---- *java.io.Serializable*ˍ, *Cloneable*ˍ
1.4 ●   └─JobImpressionsSupported ------------- *javax.print.attribute.SupportedValuesAttribute*
                                     (*javax.print.attribute.Attribute*[2] (*java.io.Serializable*))

    1   public .... boolean contains (int x)
    1   public .... boolean contains (javax.print.attribute.IntegerSyntax attribute)
    1   public .... **boolean** **equals** (Object object)
● 2   public final .... Class **getCategory** ()   *ε707*

Class   *Interface*   —extends   - - -implements   ○ abstract   ● final   △ static   ▲ static final   ✳ constructor   x x—inherited   x **x**—declared   **x x**—overridden
εn—examples of usage   ˍ—has subclass   package—see other volume

1	public	int[][]	getMembers ()	
● 2	public final	String	**getName** ()	ε706,707,708
1	public	int	hashCode ()	
*	public		**JobImpressionsSupported** (int lowerBound, int upperBound)	
1	public	int	next (int x)	
1	public	String	toString ()	

JobKOctets
javax.print.attribute.standard

Object
1.4 ○ └─javax.print.attribute.IntegerSyntax[1] - - - - - - - - *java.io.Serializable⌄, Cloneable⌄*
1.4 ●   └─JobKOctets - *javax.print.attribute.PrintRequestAttribute*
                       (javax.print.attribute.Attribute[2] (java.io.Serializable)),
                       javax.print.attribute.PrintJobAttribute
                       (javax.print.attribute.Attribute[2] (java.io.Serializable))

1	public	**boolean**	**equals** (Object object)	
● 2	public final	Class	**getCategory** ()	ε707
● 2	public final	String	**getName** ()	ε706,707,708
1	public	int	getValue ()	
1	public	int	hashCode ()	
*	public		**JobKOctets** (int value)	
1	public	String	toString ()	

JobKOctetsProcessed
javax.print.attribute.standard

Object
1.4 ○ └─javax.print.attribute.IntegerSyntax[1] - - - - - - - - *java.io.Serializable⌄, Cloneable⌄*
1.4 ●   └─JobKOctetsProcessed - - - - - - - - - - - - - - - - *javax.print.attribute.PrintJobAttribute (javax.print.attribute.Attribute[2]*
                       (java.io.Serializable))

1	public	**boolean**	**equals** (Object object)	
● 2	public final	Class	**getCategory** ()	ε707
● 2	public final	String	**getName** ()	ε706,707,708
1	public	int	getValue ()	
1	public	int	hashCode ()	
*	public		**JobKOctetsProcessed** (int value)	
1	public	String	toString ()	

JobKOctetsSupported
javax.print.attribute.standard

Object
1.4 ○ └─javax.print.attribute.SetOfIntegerSyntax[1] - - - - *java.io.Serializable⌄, Cloneable⌄*
1.4 ●   └─JobKOctetsSupported - - - - - - - - - - - - - - - - *javax.print.attribute.SupportedValuesAttribute*
                       (javax.print.attribute.Attribute[2] (java.io.Serializable))

1	public	boolean	contains (int x)	
1	public	boolean	contains (javax.print.attribute.IntegerSyntax attribute)	
1	public	**boolean**	**equals** (Object object)	
● 2	public final	Class	**getCategory** ()	ε707
1	public	int[][]	getMembers ()	
● 2	public final	String	**getName** ()	ε706,707,708
1	public	int	hashCode ()	
*	public		**JobKOctetsSupported** (int lowerBound, int upperBound)	
1	public	int	next (int x)	
1	public	String	toString ()	

JobMediaSheets
javax.print.attribute.standard

Object
1.4 ○ └─javax.print.attribute.IntegerSyntax[1] - - - - - - - - *java.io.Serializable⌄, Cloneable⌄*
1.4 ●   └─JobMediaSheets - - - - - - - - - - - - - - - - - - - *javax.print.attribute.PrintRequestAttribute*
                       (javax.print.attribute.Attribute[2] (java.io.Serializable)),
                       javax.print.attribute.PrintJobAttribute
                       (javax.print.attribute.Attribute[2] (java.io.Serializable))

1	public	**boolean**	**equals** (Object object)	
● 2	public final	Class	**getCategory** ()	ε707

J

Classes

JobMediaSheets

●	2	public final ....String	**getName** ()	ε706,707,708
	1	public........................int	getValue ()	
	1	public........................int	hashCode ()	
✳		public....................	**JobMediaSheets** (int value)	
	1	public....................String	toString ()	

JobMediaSheetsCompleted javax.print.attribute.standard

Object
1.4 ○ └─*javax.print.attribute.IntegerSyntax*[1] ---------- *java.io.Serializable*ˌ, *Cloneable*ˌ
1.4 ●   └─JobMediaSheetsCompleted ------------- *javax.print.attribute.PrintJobAttribute (javax.print.attribute.Attribute*[2]
                     (*java.io.Serializable*))

	1	public.................**boolean**	**equals** (Object object)	
●	2	public final ....Class	**getCategory** ()	ε707
●	2	public final ....String	**getName** ()	ε706,707,708
	1	public........................int	getValue ()	
	1	public........................int	hashCode ()	
✳		public....................	**JobMediaSheetsCompleted** (int value)	ε715
	1	public....................String	toString ()	

JobMediaSheetsSupported javax.print.attribute.standard

Object
1.4 ○ └─*javax.print.attribute.SetOfIntegerSyntax*[1] ---- *java.io.Serializable*ˌ, *Cloneable*ˌ
1.4 ●   └─JobMediaSheetsSupported ------------- *javax.print.attribute.SupportedValuesAttribute*
                     (*javax.print.attribute.Attribute*[2] (*java.io.Serializable*))

	1	public.................. boolean	contains (int x)
	1	public.................. boolean	contains (javax.print.attribute.IntegerSyntax attribute)
	1	public.................**boolean**	**equals** (Object object)
●	2	public final ....Class	**getCategory** ()
	1	public....................int[][]	getMembers ()
●	2	public final ....String	**getName** ()
	1	public........................int	hashCode ()
✳		public....................	**JobMediaSheetsSupported** (int lowerBound, int upperBound)
	1	public........................int	next (int x)
	1	public....................String	toString ()

(ε707 and ε706,707,708 appear to the right of getCategory and getName respectively)

JobMessageFromOperator javax.print.attribute.standard

Object
1.4 ○ └─*javax.print.attribute.TextSyntax*[1] ----------- *java.io.Serializable*ˌ, *Cloneable*ˌ
1.4 ●   └─JobMessageFromOperator ------------- *javax.print.attribute.PrintJobAttribute (javax.print.attribute.Attribute*[2]
                     (*java.io.Serializable*))

	1	public.................**boolean**	**equals** (Object object)	
●	2	public final ....Class	**getCategory** ()	ε707
	1	public.......... java.util.Locale	getLocale ()	
●	2	public final ....String	**getName** ()	ε706,707,708
	1	public....................String	getValue ()	
	1	public........................int	hashCode ()	
✳		public....................	**JobMessageFromOperator** (String message, java.util.Locale locale)	
	1	public....................String	toString ()	

JobName javax.print.attribute.standard

Object
1.4 ○ └─*javax.print.attribute.TextSyntax*[1] ----------- *java.io.Serializable*ˌ, *Cloneable*ˌ
1.4 ●   └─JobName -------------------------- *javax.print.attribute.PrintRequestAttribute*
                 (*javax.print.attribute.Attribute*[2] (*java.io.Serializable*)),
                 javax.print.attribute.PrintJobAttribute
                 (*javax.print.attribute.Attribute*[2] (*java.io.Serializable*))

Class   *Interface*   —extends   - - -implements   ○ abstract   ● final   △ static   ▲ static final   ✳ constructor   x x—inherited   x **x**—declared   **x x**—overridden
εn—examples of usage   ˌ—has subclass   package—see other volume

620

		public	**boolean**	**equals** (Object object)	
●	2	public final	Class	**getCategory** ()	ε707
	1	public	java.util.Locale	getLocale ()	
●	2	public final	String	**getName** ()	ε706,707,708
	1	public	String	getValue ()	
	1	public	int	hashCode ()	
✳		public		**JobName** (String jobName, java.util.Locale locale)	
	1	public	String	toString ()	

JobOriginatingUserName   javax.print.attribute.standard

Object
　└ javax.print.attribute.TextSyntax[1] - - - - - - - - - - - *java.io.Serializable*‿, *Cloneable*‿   (1.4 ○)
　　└ JobOriginatingUserName - - - - - - - - - - - - - - *javax.print.attribute.PrintJobAttribute (javax.print.attribute.Attribute[2]*   (1.4 ●)
　　　　　　　　　　　　　　　　　　　　　　　　(*java.io.Serializable*))

		public	**boolean**	**equals** (Object object)	
●	2	public final	Class	**getCategory** ()	ε707
	1	public	java.util.Locale	getLocale ()	
●	2	public final	String	**getName** ()	ε706,707,708
	1	public	String	getValue ()	
	1	public	int	hashCode ()	
✳		public		**JobOriginatingUserName** (String userName, java.util.Locale locale)	
	1	public	String	toString ()	

JobPriority   javax.print.attribute.standard

Object
　└ javax.print.attribute.IntegerSyntax[1] - - - - - - - - *java.io.Serializable*‿, *Cloneable*‿   (1.4 ○)
　　└ JobPriority - *javax.print.attribute.PrintRequestAttribute*   (1.4 ●)
　　　　　　　　　　　　　　　　　　(*javax.print.attribute.Attribute[2]* (*java.io.Serializable*)),
　　　　　　　　　　　　　　　　　　javax.print.attribute.PrintJobAttribute
　　　　　　　　　　　　　　　　　　(*javax.print.attribute.Attribute[2]* (*java.io.Serializable*))

		public	**boolean**	**equals** (Object object)	
●	2	public final	Class	**getCategory** ()	ε707
●	2	public final	String	**getName** ()	ε706,707,708
	1	public	int	getValue ()	
	1	public	int	hashCode ()	
✳		public		**JobPriority** (int value)	
	1	public	String	toString ()	

JobPrioritySupported   javax.print.attribute.standard

Object
　└ javax.print.attribute.IntegerSyntax[1] - - - - - - - - *java.io.Serializable*‿, *Cloneable*‿   (1.4 ○)
　　└ JobPrioritySupported - - - - - - - - - - - - - - - - *javax.print.attribute.SupportedValuesAttribute*   (1.4 ●)
　　　　　　　　　　　　　　　　　　(*javax.print.attribute.Attribute[2]* (*java.io.Serializable*))

		public	**boolean**	**equals** (Object object)	
●	2	public final	Class	**getCategory** ()	ε707
●	2	public final	String	**getName** ()	ε706,707,708
	1	public	int	getValue ()	
	1	public	int	hashCode ()	
✳		public		**JobPrioritySupported** (int value)	
	1	public	String	toString ()	

JobSheets   javax.print.attribute.standard

Object
　└ javax.print.attribute.EnumSyntax[1] - - - - - - - - - *java.io.Serializable*‿, *Cloneable*‿   (1.4 ○)
　　└ JobSheets - *javax.print.attribute.PrintRequestAttribute*   (1.4)
　　　　　　　　　　　　　　　　　　(*javax.print.attribute.Attribute[2]* (*java.io.Serializable*)),
　　　　　　　　　　　　　　　　　　javax.print.attribute.PrintJobAttribute
　　　　　　　　　　　　　　　　　　(*javax.print.attribute.Attribute[2]* (*java.io.Serializable*))

		public	Object	clone ()	
●	2	public final	Class	**getCategory** ()	ε707

J

Classes

JobSheets

	1	protected ....**javax.print**₂ .attribute.EnumSyntax[]	**getEnumValueTable** ()	
●	2	public final ....String	**getName** ()	ε706,707,708
	1	protected ....int	getOffset ()	
	1	protected ....**String[]**	**getStringTable** ()	
	1	public.........................int	getValue ()	
	1	public.........................int	hashCode ()	
✳		protected	**JobSheets** (int value)	
▲		public static final ....JobSheets	**NONE**	
	1	protected ....Object	readResolve () throws java.io.ObjectStreamException	
▲		public static final ....JobSheets	**STANDARD**	
	1	public....................String	toString ()	

JobState

javax.print.attribute.standard

```
    Object
1.4 ○  └─javax.print.attribute.EnumSyntax¹ --------- java.io.Serializable., Cloneable.
1.4         └─JobState ------------------------------ javax.print.attribute.PrintJobAttribute (javax.print.attribute.Attribute²
                                                     (java.io.Serializable))
```

▲		public static final ..... JobState	**ABORTED**	
▲		public static final ..... JobState	**CANCELED**	
	1	public....................Object	clone ()	
▲		public static final ..... JobState	**COMPLETED**	
●	2	public final ....Class	**getCategory** ()	ε707
	1	protected ....**javax.print**₂ .attribute.EnumSyntax[]	**getEnumValueTable** ()	
●	2	public final ....String	**getName** ()	ε706,707,708
	1	protected ....int	getOffset ()	
	1	protected ....**String[]**	**getStringTable** ()	
	1	public.........................int	getValue ()	
	1	public.........................int	hashCode ()	
✳		protected	**JobState** (int value)	
▲		public static final ..... JobState	**PENDING**	
▲		public static final ..... JobState	**PENDING_HELD**	
▲		public static final ..... JobState	**PROCESSING**	
▲		public static final ..... JobState	**PROCESSING_STOPPED**	
	1	protected ....Object	readResolve () throws java.io.ObjectStreamException	
	1	public....................String	toString ()	
▲		public static final ..... JobState	**UNKNOWN**	

JobStateReason

javax.print.attribute.standard

```
    Object
1.4 ○  └─javax.print.attribute.EnumSyntax¹ --------- java.io.Serializable., Cloneable.
1.4         └─JobStateReason -------------------- javax.print.attribute.Attribute.² (java.io.Serializable)
```

▲		public static final ....JobStateReason	**ABORTED_BY_SYSTEM**	
	1	public................................Object	clone ()	
▲		public static final ....JobStateReason	**COMPRESSION_ERROR**	
▲		public static final ....JobStateReason	**DOCUMENT_ACCESS_ERROR**	
▲		public static final ....JobStateReason	**DOCUMENT_FORMAT_ERROR**	
●	2	public final ....Class	**getCategory** ()	ε707
	1	protected .... **javax.print.attribute.EnumSyntax[]**	**getEnumValueTable** ()	
●	2	public final ....String	**getName** ()	ε706,707,708
	1	protected ....int	getOffset ()	
	1	protected ....**String[]**	**getStringTable** ()	
	1	public..................................int	getValue ()	
	1	public..................................int	hashCode ()	
▲		public static final ....JobStateReason	**JOB_CANCELED_AT_DEVICE**	
▲		public static final ....JobStateReason	**JOB_CANCELED_BY_OPERATOR**	
▲		public static final ....JobStateReason	**JOB_CANCELED_BY_USER**	
▲		public static final ....JobStateReason	**JOB_COMPLETED_SUCCESSFULLY**	
▲		public static final ....JobStateReason	**JOB_COMPLETED_WITH_ERRORS**	
▲		public static final ....JobStateReason	**JOB_COMPLETED_WITH_WARNINGS**	
▲		public static final ....JobStateReason	**JOB_DATA_INSUFFICIENT**	
▲		public static final ....JobStateReason	**JOB_HOLD_UNTIL_SPECIFIED**	
▲		public static final ....JobStateReason	**JOB_INCOMING**	

Class   *Interface*   —extends   - - -implements   ○ abstract   ● final   △ static   ▲ static final   ✳ constructor   x x—inherited   x **x**—declared   **x x**—overridden
ε*n*—examples of usage   .—has subclass   package—see other volume

▲	public static final	JobStateReason	**JOB_INTERPRETING**
▲	public static final	JobStateReason	**JOB_OUTGOING**
▲	public static final	JobStateReason	**JOB_PRINTING**
▲	public static final	JobStateReason	**JOB_QUEUED**
▲	public static final	JobStateReason	**JOB_QUEUED_FOR_MARKER**
▲	public static final	JobStateReason	**JOB_RESTARTABLE**
▲	public static final	JobStateReason	**JOB_TRANSFORMING**
*	protected		**JobStateReason** (int value)
▲	public static final	JobStateReason	**PRINTER_STOPPED**
▲	public static final	JobStateReason	**PRINTER_STOPPED_PARTLY**
▲	public static final	JobStateReason	**PROCESSING_TO_STOP_POINT**
▲	public static final	JobStateReason	**QUEUED_IN_DEVICE**
1	protected	Object	readResolve () throws java.io.ObjectStreamException
▲	public static final	JobStateReason	**RESOURCES_ARE_NOT_READY**
▲	public static final	JobStateReason	**SERVICE_OFF_LINE**
▲	public static final	JobStateReason	**SUBMISSION_INTERRUPTED**
1	public	String	toString ()
▲	public static final	JobStateReason	**UNSUPPORTED_COMPRESSION**
▲	public static final	JobStateReason	**UNSUPPORTED_DOCUMENT_FORMAT**

J

JobStateReasons   javax.print.attribute.standard

```
Object
1.2 ○  └ java.util.AbstractCollection 1 --------------- java.util.Collection ⌐
1.2 ○     └ java.util.AbstractSet 2 ---------------- java.util.Set ⌐ ( java.util.Collection)
1.2        └ java.util.HashSet 3 ----------------- Cloneable ⌐, java.io.Serializable ⌐
1.4 ●         └ JobStateReasons ---------------- javax.print.attribute.PrintJobAttribute ( javax.print.attribute.Attribute 4
                                                      ( java.io.Serializable))
```

	3	public	**boolean**	**add** (Object o)
	1	public	boolean	addAll (java.util.Collection c)
	3	public	void	clear ()
	3	public	Object	clone ()
	3	public	boolean	contains (Object o)
	1	public	boolean	containsAll (java.util.Collection c)
	2	public	boolean	equals (Object o)
●	4	public final	Class	**getCategory** ()	ε707
●	4	public final	String	**getName** ()	ε706,707,708
	2	public	int	hashCode ()
	3	public	boolean	isEmpty ()
	3	public	java.util.Iterator	iterator ()
*		public		**JobStateReasons** ()
*		public		**JobStateReasons** (int initialCapacity)
*		public		**JobStateReasons** (java.util.Collection collection)
*		public		**JobStateReasons** (int initialCapacity, float loadFactor)
	3	public	boolean	remove (Object o)
	2	public	boolean	removeAll (java.util.Collection c)
	1	public	boolean	retainAll (java.util.Collection c)
	3	public	int	size ()
	1	public	Object[]	toArray ()
	1	public	Object[]	toArray (Object[] a)
	1	public	String	toString ()

Classes

JOptionPane   javax.swing

```
Object
○  └ java.awt.Component 1 ------------------ java.awt.image.ImageObserver 4, java.awt.MenuContainer,
                                                java.io.Serializable ⌐
    └ java.awt.Container 2
1.2 ○     └ JComponent 3
1.2        └ JOptionPane -------------------- javax.accessibility.Accessible
```

1	*143 inherited members from java.awt.Component not shown*	
2	*51 inherited members from java.awt.Container not shown*	
3	*143 inherited members from JComponent not shown*	
4	*8 inherited members from java.awt.image.ImageObserver not shown*	
▲	public static final .... int **CANCEL_OPTION** = 2	
▲	public static final .... int **CLOSED_OPTION** = -1	
	public .... JDialog **createDialog** (java.awt.Component parentComponent, String title)	
	throws java.awt.HeadlessException	ε618

JOptionPane

	public	JInternalFrame	**createInternalFrame** (java.awt.Component parentComponent, String title)
▲	public static final	int	**DEFAULT_OPTION** = -1
▲	public static final	int	**ERROR_MESSAGE** = 0
3	public	**javax.accessibility.** ͻ **.AccessibleContext**	**getAccessibleContext** ()
△	public static	JDesktopPane	**getDesktopPaneForComponent** (java.awt.Component parentComponent)
△	public static	java.awt.Frame	**getFrameForComponent** (java.awt.Component parentComponent) throws java.awt.HeadlessException
	public	*Icon*	**getIcon** ()
	public	Object	**getInitialSelectionValue** ()
	public	Object	**getInitialValue** ()
	public	Object	**getInputValue** ()
	public	int	**getMaxCharactersPerLineCount** ()
	public	Object	**getMessage** ()
	public	int	**getMessageType** ()
	public	Object[]	**getOptions** ()
	public	int	**getOptionType** ()
△	public static	java.awt.Frame	**getRootFrame** () throws java.awt.HeadlessException
	public	Object[]	**getSelectionValues** ()
	public	javax. ͻ .swing.plaf.OptionPaneUI	**getUI** ()
3	public	**String**	**getUIClassID** ()
	public	Object	**getValue** ()
	public	boolean	**getWantsInput** ()
	protected transient	*Icon*	**icon**
▲	public static final	String	**ICON_PROPERTY** = "icon"
▲	public static final	int	**INFORMATION_MESSAGE** = 1
▲	public static final	String	**INITIAL_SELECTION_VALUE_PROPERTY** = "initialSelectionValue"
▲	public static final	String	**INITIAL_VALUE_PROPERTY** = "initialValue"
	protected transient	Object	**initialSelectionValue**
	protected transient	Object	**initialValue**
▲	public static final	String	**INPUT_VALUE_PROPERTY** = "inputValue"
	protected transient	Object	**inputValue**
✳	public		**JOptionPane** ()
✳	public		**JOptionPane** (Object message)
✳	public		**JOptionPane** (Object message, int messageType)
✳	public		**JOptionPane** (Object message, int messageType, int optionType)
✳	public		**JOptionPane** (Object message, int messageType, int optionType, *Icon* icon)
✳	public		**JOptionPane** (Object message, int messageType, int optionType, *Icon* icon, Object[] options)
✳	public		**JOptionPane** (Object message, int messageType, int optionType, *Icon* icon, Object[] options, Object initialValue)
	protected transient	Object	**message**
▲	public static final	String	**MESSAGE_PROPERTY** = "message"
▲	public static final	String	**MESSAGE_TYPE_PROPERTY** = "messageType"
	protected	int	**messageType**
▲	public static final	int	**NO_OPTION** = 1
▲	public static final	int	**OK_CANCEL_OPTION** = 2
▲	public static final	int	**OK_OPTION** = 0
▲	public static final	String	**OPTION_TYPE_PROPERTY** = "optionType"
	protected transient	Object[]	**options**
▲	public static final	String	**OPTIONS_PROPERTY** = "options"
	protected	int	**optionType**
3	protected	**String**	**paramString** ()
▲	public static final	int	**PLAIN_MESSAGE** = -1
▲	public static final	int	**QUESTION_MESSAGE** = 3
	public	void	**selectInitialValue** ()
▲	public static final	String	**SELECTION_VALUES_PROPERTY** = "selectionValues"
	protected transient	Object[]	**selectionValues**
	public	void	**setIcon** (*Icon* newIcon)
	public	void	**setInitialSelectionValue** (Object newValue)
	public	void	**setInitialValue** (Object newInitialValue)
	public	void	**setInputValue** (Object newValue)
	public	void	**setMessage** (Object newMessage)
	public	void	**setMessageType** (int newType)
	public	void	**setOptions** (Object[] newOptions)
	public	void	**setOptionType** (int newType)
△	public static	void	**setRootFrame** (java.awt.Frame newRootFrame)
	public	void	**setSelectionValues** (Object[] newValues)
	public	void	**setUI** (javax.swing.plaf.OptionPaneUI ui)

ε618
ε618

ε618

ε737

J

	public	void	**setValue** (Object newValue)
	public	void	**setWantsInput** (boolean newValue)
△	public static	int	**showConfirmDialog** (java.awt.Component parentComponent, Object message) throws java.awt.HeadlessException *ε737*
△	public static	int	**showConfirmDialog** (java.awt.Component parentComponent, Object message, String title, int optionType) throws java.awt.HeadlessException
△	public static	int	**showConfirmDialog** (java.awt.Component parentComponent, Object message, String title, int optionType, int messageType) throws java.awt.HeadlessException
△	public static	int	**showConfirmDialog** (java.awt.Component parentComponent, Object message, String title, int optionType, int messageType, *Icon* icon) throws java.awt.HeadlessException
△	public static	String	**showInputDialog** (Object message) throws java.awt.HeadlessException
△	public static	String	**showInputDialog** (java.awt.Component parentComponent, Object message) throws java.awt.HeadlessException *ε737*
1.4 △	public static	String	**showInputDialog** (Object message, Object initialSelectionValue)
1.4 △	public static	String	**showInputDialog** (java.awt.Component parentComponent, Object message, Object initialSelectionValue)
△	public static	String	**showInputDialog** (java.awt.Component parentComponent, Object message, String title, int messageType) throws java.awt.HeadlessException
△	public static	Object	**showInputDialog** (java.awt.Component parentComponent, Object message, String title, int messageType, *Icon* icon, Object[] selectionValues, Object initialSelectionValue) throws java.awt.HeadlessException
△	public static	int	**showInternalConfirmDialog** (java.awt.Component parentComponent, Object message)
△	public static	int	**showInternalConfirmDialog** (java.awt.Component parentComponent, Object message, String title, int optionType)
△	public static	int	**showInternalConfirmDialog** (java.awt.Component parentComponent, Object message, String title, int optionType, int messageType)
△	public static	int	**showInternalConfirmDialog** (java.awt.Component parentComponent, Object message, String title, int optionType, int messageType, *Icon* icon)
△	public static	String	**showInternalInputDialog** (java.awt.Component parentComponent, Object message)
△	public static	String	**showInternalInputDialog** (java.awt.Component parentComponent, Object message, String title, int messageType)
△	public static	Object	**showInternalInputDialog** (java.awt.Component parentComponent, Object message, String title, int messageType, *Icon* icon, Object[] selectionValues, Object initialSelectionValue)
△	public static	void	**showInternalMessageDialog** (java.awt.Component parentComponent, Object message)
△	public static	void	**showInternalMessageDialog** (java.awt.Component parentComponent, Object message, String title, int messageType)
△	public static	void	**showInternalMessageDialog** (java.awt.Component parentComponent, Object message, String title, int messageType, *Icon* icon)
△	public static	int	**showInternalOptionDialog** (java.awt.Component parentComponent, Object message, String title, int optionType, int messageType, *Icon* icon, Object[] options, Object initialValue)
△	public static	void	**showMessageDialog** (java.awt.Component parentComponent, Object message) throws java.awt.HeadlessException *ε737*
△	public static	void	**showMessageDialog** (java.awt.Component parentComponent, Object message, String title, int messageType) throws java.awt.HeadlessException
△	public static	void	**showMessageDialog** (java.awt.Component parentComponent, Object message, String title, int messageType, *Icon* icon) throws java.awt.HeadlessException
△	public static	int	**showOptionDialog** (java.awt.Component parentComponent, Object message, String title, int optionType, int messageType, *Icon* icon, Object[] options, Object initialValue) throws java.awt.HeadlessException
▲	public static final	Object	**UNINITIALIZED_VALUE**
3	public	void	**updateUI** ()
	protected transient	Object	**value**
▲	public static final	String	**VALUE_PROPERTY** = "value"
▲	public static final	String	**WANTS_INPUT_PROPERTY** = "wantsInput"
	protected	boolean	**wantsInput**
▲	public static final	int	**WARNING_MESSAGE** = 2
▲	public static final	int	**YES_NO_CANCEL_OPTION** = 1
▲	public static final	int	**YES_NO_OPTION** = 0
▲	public static final	int	**YES_OPTION** = 0 *ε737*

J

Classes

JPanel

		JPanel		javax.swing

```
        Object                                                              ε791
   ○    └java.awt.Component 1 - - - - - - - - - - - - - - - - - - - java.awt.image.ImageObserver 4, java.awt.MenuContainer,
                                                                    java.io.Serializable
          └java.awt.Container 2
1.2 ○       └JComponent 3
1.2           └JPanel - - - - - - - - - - - - - - - - - - - - - - - javax.accessibility.Accessible
```

	1	*143 inherited members from java.awt.Component not shown*
	2	*50 inherited members from java.awt.Container not shown*
	3	*142 inherited members from JComponent not shown*
	4	*8 inherited members from java.awt.image.ImageObserver not shown*

```
     2  public.... java.awt.Component add (java.awt.Component comp)              ε852,853,854,571,575
     3  public.... javax.accessibility getAccessibleContext ()
                   .AccessibleContext
1.4     public javax.swing.plaf.PanelUI getUI ()
     3  public.................. String getUIClassID ()
  *     public.......................... JPanel ()                             ε828,871,879
  *     public.......................... JPanel (boolean isDoubleBuffered)
  *     public.......................... JPanel (java.awt.LayoutManager layout)   ε852,853,854
  *     public.......................... JPanel (java.awt.LayoutManager layout, boolean isDoubleBuffered)
     3  public.................void paint (java.awt.Graphics g)                ε596,666
     3  protected .............. String paramString ()
1.4     public.................void setUI (javax.swing.plaf.PanelUI ui)
     3  public.................. void updateUI ()
```

		JPasswordField		javax.swing

```
        Object                                                              ε861
   ○    └java.awt.Component 1 - - - - - - - - - - - - - - - - - - - java.awt.image.ImageObserver 6, java.awt.MenuContainer,
                                                                    java.io.Serializable
          └java.awt.Container 2
1.2 ○       └JComponent 3
1.2 ○         └javax.swing.text.JTextComponent 4 - - - - Scrollable, javax.accessibility.Accessible
1.2             └JTextField 5 - - - - - - - - - - - - - - - - - - - SwingConstants 7
1.2               └JPasswordField
```

	1	*139 inherited members from java.awt.Component not shown*
	2	*51 inherited members from java.awt.Container not shown*
	3	*137 inherited members from JComponent not shown*
	4	*66 inherited members from javax.swing.text.JTextComponent not shown*
	5	*25 inherited members from JTextField not shown*
	7	*19 inherited members from SwingConstants not shown*
	6	*8 inherited members from java.awt.image.ImageObserver not shown*

```
     5  public synchronized .......void addActionListener (java.awt.event.ActionListener l)   ε980,979
     4  public.................. void copy ()
     4  public.................. void cut ()
        public.................. boolean echoCharIsSet ()
     5  public.... javax.accessibility getAccessibleContext ()
                   .AccessibleContext
        public.................. char getEchoChar ()
        public.................char[] getPassword ()
D    4  public.................. String getText ()                           ε953,957,968,1006,618
D    4  public.................. String getText (int offs, int len) throws javax.swing.text.BadLocationException
                                                                            ε968,984,990,998
     5  public.................. String getUIClassID ()
  *     public.......................... JPasswordField ()
  *     public.......................... JPasswordField (int columns)
  *     public.......................... JPasswordField (String text)          ε980
  *     public.......................... JPasswordField (String text, int columns)
  *     public.......................... JPasswordField (javax.swing.text.Document doc, String txt, int columns)
     5  protected .............. String paramString ()
        public.................void setEchoChar (char c)                     ε980
```

Class   *Interface*   —extends   - - -implements   ○ abstract   ● final   △ static   ▲ static final   ✳ constructor   x x—inherited   x **x**—declared   **x x**—overridden
ε*n*—examples of usage   —has subclass   package—see other volume

JPEGHuffmanTable   javax.imageio.plugins.jpeg

Object[1]
1.4   └JPEGHuffmanTable

	public	short[]	**getLengths** ()
	public	short[]	**getValues** ()
✱	public		**JPEGHuffmanTable** (short[] lengths, short[] values)
▲	public static final		**StdACChrominance**
	..........JPEGHuffmanTable		
▲	public static final		**StdACLuminance**
	..........JPEGHuffmanTable		
▲	public static final		**StdDCChrominance**
	..........JPEGHuffmanTable		
▲	public static final		**StdDCLuminance**
	..........JPEGHuffmanTable		
1	public	String	**toString** ()

J

JPEGImageReadParam   javax.imageio.plugins.jpeg

Object
1.4 ○   └javax.imageio.IIOParam[1]
1.4   └javax.imageio.ImageReadParam[2]
1.4   └JPEGImageReadParam

1	*27 inherited members from javax.imageio.IIOParam not shown*		
	public	boolean	**areTablesSet** ()
2	public	boolean	canSetSourceRenderSize ()
2	protected	boolean	canSetSourceRenderSize ()
2	protected	java₂	destination
	.awt.image.BufferedImage		
2	protected	int[]	destinationBands
	public	JPEGHuffmanTable[]	**getACHuffmanTables** ()
	public	JPEGHuffmanTable[]	**getDCHuffmanTables** ()
2	public	java₂	getDestination ()
	.awt.image.BufferedImage		
2	public	int[]	getDestinationBands ()
	public	JPEGQTable[]	**getQTables** ()
2	public	int	getSourceMaxProgressivePass ()
2	public	int	getSourceMinProgressivePass ()
2	public	int	getSourceNumProgressivePasses ()
2	public	java.awt.Dimension	getSourceRenderSize ()
✱	public		**JPEGImageReadParam** ()
2	protected	int	minProgressivePass
2	protected	int	numProgressivePasses
	public	void	**setDecodeTables** (JPEGQTable[] qTables, JPEGHuffmanTable[] DCHuffmanTables, JPEGHuffmanTable[] ACHuffmanTables)
2	public	void	setDestination (java.awt.image.BufferedImage destination)
2	public	void	setDestinationBands (int[] destinationBands)
2	public	void	setDestinationType (javax.imageio.ImageTypeSpecifier destinationType)
2	public	void	setSourceProgressivePasses (int minPass, int numPasses)
2	public	void	setSourceRenderSize (java.awt.Dimension size) throws UnsupportedOperationException
2	protected :	java.awt.Dimension	sourceRenderSize
	public	void	**unsetDecodeTables** ()

JPEGImageWriteParam   javax.imageio.plugins.jpeg

Object
1.4 ○   └javax.imageio.IIOParam[1]
1.4   └javax.imageio.ImageWriteParam[2]
1.4   └JPEGImageWriteParam

1	*28 inherited members from javax.imageio.IIOParam not shown*		
2	*45 inherited members from javax.imageio.ImageWriteParam not shown*		
	public	boolean	**areTablesSet** ()
	public	JPEGHuffmanTable[]	**getACHuffmanTables** ()
2	public	String[]	**getCompressionQualityDescriptions** ()
2	public	float[]	**getCompressionQualityValues** ()
	public	JPEGHuffmanTable[]	**getDCHuffmanTables** ()
	public	boolean	**getOptimizeHuffmanTables** ()

Classes

JPEGImageWriteParam

	public	JPEGQTable[]	**getQTables** ()		
2	public	**boolean**	**isCompressionLossless** ()		
✶	public		**JPEGImageWriteParam** (java.util.Locale locale)		
2	public	void	setCompressionQuality (float quality)		ε699,699
	public	void	**setEncodeTables** (JPEGQTable[] qTables, JPEGHuffmanTable[] DCHuffmanTables, JPEGHuffmanTable[] ACHuffmanTables)		
	public	void	**setOptimizeHuffmanTables** (boolean optimize)		
2	public	**void**	**unsetCompression** ()		
	public	void	**unsetEncodeTables** ()		

JPEGQTable
javax.imageio.plugins.jpeg

Object[1]
  └JPEGQTable

1.4

	public	JPEGQTable	**getScaledInstance** (float scaleFactor, boolean forceBaseline)	
	public	int[]	**getTable** ()	
✶	public		**JPEGQTable** (int[] table)	
▲	public static final .	JPEGQTable	**K1Div2Luminance**	
▲	public static final .	JPEGQTable	**K1Luminance**	
▲	public static final .	JPEGQTable	**K2Chrominance**	
▲	public static final .	JPEGQTable	**K2Div2Chrominance**	
1	public	**String**	**toString** ()	

JPopupMenu
javax.swing

Object
  └java.awt.Component[1] - - - - - - - - - - - - - - - - - - *java.awt.image.ImageObserver*[4], *java.awt.MenuContainer*,
                                                              java.io.Serializable

  └java.awt.Container[2]
1.2 ○   └JComponent[3]
1.2   └JPopupMenu - - - - - - - - - - - - - - - - - *javax.accessibility.Accessible*, *MenuElement*[5]

	1	*140 inherited members from java.awt.Component not shown*				
	2	*50 inherited members from java.awt.Container not shown*				
	3	*140 inherited members from JComponent not shown*				
	4	*8 inherited members from java.awt.image.ImageObserver not shown*				
		public	JMenuItem	**add** (String s)		
		public	JMenuItem	**add** (*Action* a)		
		public	JMenuItem	**add** (JMenuItem menuItem)		ε810,811,1011
		public	void	**addPopupMenuListener** (*javax.swing.event.PopupMenuListener* l)		
		public	void	**addSeparator** ()		
		protected	*java.beans* .*PropertyChangeListener*	**createActionChangeListener** (JMenuItem b)		
1.3		protected	JMenuItem	**createActionComponent** (*Action* a)		
		protected	void	**firePopupMenuCanceled** ()		
		protected	void	**firePopupMenuWillBecomeInvisible** ()		
		protected	void	**firePopupMenuWillBecomeVisible** ()		
	3	public	*javax.accessibility* .**AccessibleContext**	**getAccessibleContext** ()		
	5	public	java.awt.Component	**getComponent** ()		ε813
D		public	java.awt.Component	**getComponentAtIndex** (int i)		
		public	int	**getComponentIndex** (java.awt.Component c)		
△		public static	boolean	**getDefaultLightWeightPopupEnabled** ()		ε812
		public	java.awt.Component	**getInvoker** ()		
		public	String	**getLabel** ()		
		public	java.awt.Insets	**getMargin** ()		
1.4		public	*javax.swing* .*event.PopupMenuListener[]*	**getPopupMenuListeners** ()		
		public	*SingleSelectionModel*	**getSelectionModel** ()		
	5	public	*MenuElement[]*	**getSubElements** ()		
		public	javax .swing.plaf.PopupMenuUI	**getUI** ()		
	3	public	**String**	**getUIClassID** ()		
		public	void	**insert** (java.awt.Component component, int index)		
		public	void	**insert** (*Action* a, int index)		
		public	boolean	**isBorderPainted** ()		
		public	boolean	**isLightWeightPopupEnabled** ()		ε812

Class *Interface* —extends - - -implements ○ abstract ● final △ static ▲ static final ✶ constructor x x—inherited x **x**—declared **x x**—overridden
ε*n*—examples of usage ˌ—has subclass package—see other volume

1.3		public	boolean	**isPopupTrigger** (java.awt.event.MouseEvent e)	
	1	public	**boolean**	**isVisible** ()	
✱		public		**JPopupMenu** ()	ε810,811,812,1011
✱		public		**JPopupMenu** (String label)	
	5	public	void	**menuSelectionChanged** (boolean isIncluded)	ε814
		public	void	**pack** ()	
	3	protected	**void**	**paintBorder** (java.awt.Graphics g)	
	3	protected	**String**	**paramString** ()	
	1	protected	**void**	**processFocusEvent** (java.awt.event.FocusEvent evt)	
	3	protected	**void**	**processKeyEvent** (java.awt.event.KeyEvent evt)	
	5	public	void	**processKeyEvent** (java.awt.event.KeyEvent e, *MenuElement[]* path, MenuSelectionManager manager)	
	5	public	void	**processMouseEvent** (java.awt.event.MouseEvent event, *MenuElement[]* path, MenuSelectionManager manager)	
	2	public	**void**	**remove** (int pos)	ε831,832
		public	void	**removePopupMenuListener** (*javax.swing.event.PopupMenuListener* l)	
		public	void	**setBorderPainted** (boolean b)	
△		public static	void	**setDefaultLightWeightPopupEnabled** (boolean aFlag)	ε812
		public	void	**setInvoker** (java.awt.Component invoker)	
		public	void	**setLabel** (String label)	
		public	void	**setLightWeightPopupEnabled** (boolean aFlag)	ε812
	1	public	**void**	**setLocation** (int x, int y)	
		public	void	**setPopupSize** (java.awt.Dimension d)	
		public	void	**setPopupSize** (int width, int height)	
		public	void	**setSelected** (java.awt.Component sel)	
		public	void	**setSelectionModel** (*SingleSelectionModel* model)	
		public	void	**setUI** (javax.swing.plaf.PopupMenuUI ui)	
	3	public	**void**	**setVisible** (boolean b)	
		public	void	**show** (java.awt.Component invoker, int x, int y)	ε810,1011
	3	public	**void**	**updateUI** ()	

JPopupMenu.Separator   javax.swing

```
Object
○ └─java.awt.Component¹ - - - - - - - - - - - - - - - - - - java.awt.image.ImageObserver ⁵, java.awt.MenuContainer,
                                                            java.io.Serializable
        └─java.awt.Container²
1.2 ○     └─JComponent³
1.2        └─JSeparator⁴ - - - - - - - - - - - - - - - - - - - - SwingConstants ⁶, javax.accessibility.Accessible
1.2          └─JPopupMenu.Separator
```

	1	*143 inherited members from java.awt.Component not shown*		
	2	*51 inherited members from java.awt.Container not shown*		
	3	*143 inherited members from JComponent not shown*		
	6	*19 inherited members from SwingConstants not shown*		
	5	*8 inherited members from java.awt.image.ImageObserver not shown*		
	4	public	javax.accessibility. .AccessibleContext	getAccessibleContext ()
	4	public	int	getOrientation ()
	4	public	javax.swing.plaf.SeparatorUI	getUI ()
	4	public	**String**	**getUIClassID** ()
	4	protected	String	paramString ()
✱	4	public		**JPopupMenu.Separator** ()
	4	public	void	setOrientation (int orientation)
	4	public	void	setUI (javax.swing.plaf.SeparatorUI ui)
	4	public	void	updateUI ()

JProgressBar   javax.swing

```
Object
○ └─java.awt.Component¹ - - - - - - - - - - - - - - - - - - java.awt.image.ImageObserver ⁴, java.awt.MenuContainer,
                                                            java.io.Serializable
        └─java.awt.Container²
1.2 ○     └─JComponent³
1.2        └─JProgressBar - - - - - - - - - - - - - - - - - - - SwingConstants ⁵, javax.accessibility.Accessible
```

1	*143 inherited members from java.awt.Component not shown*	
2	*51 inherited members from java.awt.Container not shown*	
3	*142 inherited members from JComponent not shown*	

JProgressBar

	public	void	**addChangeListener** (*javax.swing.event.ChangeListener* l)	ε805
	protected transient	javax. .swing.event.ChangeEvent ♪	**changeEvent**	
	protected	*javax.swing* ♪ *.event.ChangeListener*	**changeListener**	
	protected	*javax.swing* ♪ *.event.ChangeListener*	**createChangeListener** ()	
	protected	void	**fireStateChanged** ()	
3	public	**javax.accessibility** ♪ **.AccessibleContext**	**getAccessibleContext** ()	
1.4	public	*javax.swing* ♪ *.event.ChangeListener[]*	**getChangeListeners** ()	
	public	int	**getMaximum** ()	ε803,805
	public	int	**getMinimum** ()	ε803,805
	public	*BoundedRangeModel*	**getModel** ()	ε803
	public	int	**getOrientation** ()	
	public	double	**getPercentComplete** ()	
	public	String	**getString** ()	
	public	javax ♪ .swing.plaf.ProgressBarUI	**getUI** ()	
3	public	**String**	**getUIClassID** ()	
	public	int	**getValue** ()	ε803,805
	public	boolean	**isBorderPainted** ()	
1.4	public	boolean	**isIndeterminate** ()	
	public	boolean	**isStringPainted** ()	
✱	public		**JProgressBar** ()	
✱	public		**JProgressBar** (int orient)	
✱	public		**JProgressBar** (*BoundedRangeModel* newModel)	
✱	public		**JProgressBar** (int min, int max)	ε801,802,804,805
✱	public		**JProgressBar** (int orient, int min, int max)	ε801
	protected	*BoundedRangeModel*	**model**	
	protected	int	**orientation**	
	protected	boolean	**paintBorder**	
3	protected	**void**	**paintBorder** (java.awt.Graphics g)	
	protected	boolean	**paintString**	
3	protected	**String**	**paramString** ()	
	protected	String	**progressString**	
	public	void	**removeChangeListener** (*javax.swing.event.ChangeListener* l)	
	public	void	**setBorderPainted** (boolean b)	
1.4	public	void	**setIndeterminate** (boolean newValue)	ε802
	public	void	**setMaximum** (int n)	ε803
	public	void	**setMinimum** (int n)	ε803
	public	void	**setModel** (*BoundedRangeModel* newModel)	
	public	void	**setOrientation** (int newOrientation)	
	public	void	**setString** (String s)	
	public	void	**setStringPainted** (boolean b)	ε804
	public	void	**setUI** (javax.swing.plaf.ProgressBarUI ui)	
	public	void	**setValue** (int n)	ε802,803
3	public	**void**	**updateUI** ()	
▲ 5	public static final	int	VERTICAL = 1	ε801,794,796,816

JRadioButton

javax.swing

Class *Interface* —extends - - -implements ○ abstract ● final △ static ▲ static final ✱ constructor x x—inherited x **x**—declared **x x**—overridden
ε*n*—examples of usage .—has subclass   package—see other volume

	7	*19 inherited members from SwingConstants not shown*		
	6	*8 inherited members from java.awt.image.ImageObserver not shown*		
1.3	4	protected . . . . **void**	**configurePropertiesFromAction** (*Action* a)	
1.3	4	protected . . . . **java.beans**₂	**createActionPropertyChangeListener** (*Action* a)	
		.PropertyChangeListener		
	5	public . . . . **javax.accessibility**₂	**getAccessibleContext** ()	
		.AccessibleContext		
	4	public . . . . *ButtonModel*	getModel ()	ε769,770,771
	5	public . . . . **String**	**getUIClassID** ()	
✱		public	**JRadioButton** ()	
✱		public	**JRadioButton** (String text)	
1.3 ✱		public	**JRadioButton** (*Action* a)	ε768
✱		public	**JRadioButton** (*Icon* icon)	
✱		public	**JRadioButton** (String text, boolean selected)	
✱		public	**JRadioButton** (String text, *Icon* icon)	
✱		public	**JRadioButton** (*Icon* icon, boolean selected)	
✱		public	**JRadioButton** (String text, *Icon* icon, boolean selected)	
	5	protected . . . . **String**	**paramString** ()	
	5	public . . . . **void**	**updateUI** ()	

JRadioButtonMenuItem

```
  Object                                                              ε45
○ └java.awt.Component¹ - - - - - - - - - - - - - - - - - - - java.awt.image.ImageObserver⁶, java.awt.MenuContainer,
                                                     java.io.Serializable⌄
      └java.awt.Container²
1.2 ○   └JComponent³
1.2 ○     └AbstractButton⁴ - - - - - - - - - - - - - - - - - - - java.awt.ItemSelectable⌄, SwingConstants⁷
1.2       └JMenuItem⁵ - - - - - - - - - - - - - - - - - - - javax.accessibility.Accessible, MenuElement
1.2         └JRadioButtonMenuItem
```

	1	*142 inherited members from java.awt.Component not shown*	
	2	*51 inherited members from java.awt.Container not shown*	
	3	*141 inherited members from JComponent not shown*	
	4	*101 inherited members from AbstractButton not shown*	
	5	*30 inherited members from JMenuItem not shown*	
	7	*19 inherited members from SwingConstants not shown*	
	6	*8 inherited members from java.awt.image.ImageObserver not shown*	
	5	public . . . . **javax.accessibility**₂	**getAccessibleContext** ()
		.AccessibleContext	
	5	public . . . . **String**	**getUIClassID** ()
✱		public	**JRadioButtonMenuItem** ()
✱		public	**JRadioButtonMenuItem** (String text)
1.3 ✱		public	**JRadioButtonMenuItem** (*Action* a)
✱		public	**JRadioButtonMenuItem** (*Icon* icon)
✱		public	**JRadioButtonMenuItem** (String text, boolean selected)
✱		public	**JRadioButtonMenuItem** (String text, *Icon* icon)
✱		public	**JRadioButtonMenuItem** (*Icon* icon, boolean selected)
✱		public	**JRadioButtonMenuItem** (String text, *Icon* icon, boolean selected)
	5	protected . . . . **String**	**paramString** ()

JRootPane

```
  Object
○ └java.awt.Component¹ - - - - - - - - - - - - - - - - - - - java.awt.image.ImageObserver⁴, java.awt.MenuContainer,
                                                     java.io.Serializable⌄
      └java.awt.Container²
1.2 ○   └JComponent³
1.2       └JRootPane - - - - - - - - - - - - - - - - - - - - javax.accessibility.Accessible
```

	1	*143 inherited members from java.awt.Component not shown*	
	2	*50 inherited members from java.awt.Container not shown*	
	3	*139 inherited members from JComponent not shown*	
	4	*8 inherited members from java.awt.image.ImageObserver not shown*	
	2	protected . . . . **void**	**addImpl** (java.awt.Component comp, Object constraints, int index)
	3	public . . . . **void**	**addNotify** ()
1.4 ▲		public static final . . . . int	**COLOR_CHOOSER_DIALOG** = 5
		protected . . . java.awt.Container	**contentPane**
		protected . . . java.awt.Container	**createContentPane** ()
		protected java.awt.Component	**createGlassPane** ()

JRootPane

	protected . . . . JLayeredPane	**createLayeredPane** ()
	protected	**createRootLayout** ()
	. . . . . *java.awt.LayoutManager*	
	protected . . . . JButton	**defaultButton**
D	protected . . . . javax.swing₂	**defaultPressAction**
	.JRootPane.DefaultAction	
D	protected . . . . javax.swing₂	**defaultReleaseAction**
	.JRootPane.DefaultAction	
1.4 ▲	public static final . . . . .int	**ERROR_DIALOG** = 4
1.4 ▲	public static final . . . . .int	**FILE_CHOOSER_DIALOG** = 6
1.4 ▲	public static final . . . . .int	**FRAME** = 1
3	public . . . . **javax.accessibility₂**	**getAccessibleContext** ()
	.AccessibleContext	
	public . . . . . . .java.awt.Container	**getContentPane** ()
	public . . . . JButton	**getDefaultButton** ()
	public . . . . java.awt.Component	**getGlassPane** ()
	public . . . . JMenuBar	**getJMenuBar** ()
	public . . . . JLayeredPane	**getLayeredPane** ()
D	public . . . . JMenuBar	**getMenuBar** ()
1.3	public.	**getUI** ()
	.javax.swing.plaf.RootPaneUI	
3	public . . . . **String**	**getUIClassID** ()
1.4	public. .int	**getWindowDecorationStyle** ()
	protected java.awt.Component	**glassPane**
1.4 ▲	public static final . . . . .int	**INFORMATION_DIALOG** = 3
3	public. . . . . **boolean**	**isOptimizedDrawingEnabled** ()
3	public. . . . . **boolean**	**isValidateRoot** ()
✳	public.	**JRootPane** ()
	protected . . . . JLayeredPane	**layeredPane**
	protected . . . . JMenuBar	**menuBar**
1.4 ▲	public static final . . . . .int	**NONE** = 0
3	protected . . . . **String**	**paramString** ()
1.4 ▲	public static final . . . . .int	**PLAIN_DIALOG** = 2
1.4 ▲	public static final . . . . .int	**QUESTION_DIALOG** = 7
3	public. . . . . **void**	**removeNotify** ()
	public. . . . . .void	**setContentPane** (java.awt.Container content)
	public. . . . . .void	**setDefaultButton** (JButton defaultButton)
	public. . . . . .void	**setGlassPane** (java.awt.Component glass)
	public. . . . . .void	**setJMenuBar** (JMenuBar menu)
	public. . . . . .void	**setLayeredPane** (JLayeredPane layered)
D	public. . . . . .void	**setMenuBar** (JMenuBar menu)
1.3	public. . . . . .void	**setUI** (javax.swing.plaf.RootPaneUI ui)
1.4	public. . . . . .void	**setWindowDecorationStyle** (int windowDecorationStyle)
3	public. . . . . **void**	**updateUI** ()
1.4 ▲	public static final . . . . .int	**WARNING_DIALOG** = 8

JRootPane.RootLayout		protected	javax.swing

Object
1.2 └─JRootPane.RootLayout - - - - - - - - - - - - - - - - - - *java.awt.LayoutManager2* [1] (*java.awt.LayoutManager* [2]),
java.io.Serializable

1	public. . . . . .void	**addLayoutComponent** (java.awt.Component comp, Object constraints)
2	public. . . . . .void	**addLayoutComponent** (String name, java.awt.Component comp)
1	public. . . . . .float	**getLayoutAlignmentX** (java.awt.Container target)
1	public. . . . . .float	**getLayoutAlignmentY** (java.awt.Container target)
1	public. . . . . .void	**invalidateLayout** (java.awt.Container target)
2	public. . . . . .void	**layoutContainer** (java.awt.Container parent) ε624,625
1	public . . . . . .java.awt.Dimension	**maximumLayoutSize** (java.awt.Container target)
2	public . . . . . .java.awt.Dimension	**minimumLayoutSize** (java.awt.Container parent)
2	public . . . . . .java.awt.Dimension	**preferredLayoutSize** (java.awt.Container parent)
2	public. . . . . .void	**removeLayoutComponent** (java.awt.Component comp)
✳	protected	**JRootPane.RootLayout** ()

JScrollBar				javax.swing

```
        Object
   ○    └─java.awt.Component¹ ------------------- java.awt.image.ImageObserver⁴, java.awt.MenuContainer,
                                                        java.io.Serializable
             └─java.awt.Container²
1.2 ○          └─JComponent³
1.2               └─JScrollBar ------------------- java.awt.Adjustable⁵, javax.accessibility.Accessible
```

	1	*143 inherited members from java.awt.Component not shown*		
	2	*51 inherited members from java.awt.Container not shown*		
	3	*140 inherited members from JComponent not shown*		
	4	*8 inherited members from java.awt.image.ImageObserver not shown*		
	5	public.........................void	**addAdjustmentListener** (*java.awt.event.AdjustmentListener* l)	ε822
		protected.....................int	**blockIncrement**	
		protected...................void	**fireAdjustmentValueChanged** (int id, int type, int value)	
	3	public.... **javax.accessibility** ₂ **.AccessibleContext**	**getAccessibleContext** ()	
1.4		public.................*java.awt* ₂ *.event.AdjustmentListener[]*	**getAdjustmentListeners** ()	
	5	public.........................int	**getBlockIncrement** ()	
		public.........................int	**getBlockIncrement** (int direction)	
	5	public.........................int	**getMaximum** ()	
	3	public.... **java.awt.Dimension**	**getMaximumSize** ()	
	5	public.........................int	**getMinimum** ()	
	3	public.... **java.awt.Dimension**	**getMinimumSize** ()	
		public... *BoundedRangeModel*	**getModel** ()	
	5	public.........................int	**getOrientation** ()	ε822
		public.......................... . javax.swing.plaf.ScrollBarUI	**getUI** ()	
	3	public.................. **String**	**getUIClassID** ()	
	5	public.........................int	**getUnitIncrement** ()	
		public.........................int	**getUnitIncrement** (int direction)	
	5	public.........................int	**getValue** ()	
		public................. boolean	**getValueIsAdjusting** ()	
	5	public.........................int	**getVisibleAmount** ()	
▲	5	public static final ....int	HORIZONTAL = 0	ε822
✳		public..........................	**JScrollBar** ()	
✳		public..........................	**JScrollBar** (int orientation)	
✳		public..........................	**JScrollBar** (int orientation, int value, int extent, int min, int max)	
		protected...................... .... *BoundedRangeModel*	**model**	
1.4 ▲	5	public static final ....int	NO_ORIENTATION = 2	
		protected.....................int	**orientation**	
	3	protected............... **String**	**paramString** ()	
	5	public.........................void	**removeAdjustmentListener** (*java.awt.event.AdjustmentListener* l)	
	5	public.........................void	**setBlockIncrement** (int blockIncrement)	
	3	public...................... **void**	**setEnabled** (boolean x)	
	5	public.........................void	**setMaximum** (int maximum)	
	5	public.........................void	**setMinimum** (int minimum)	
		public.........................void	**setModel** (*BoundedRangeModel* newModel)	
		public.........................void	**setOrientation** (int orientation)	
1.4		public.........................void	**setUI** (javax.swing.plaf.ScrollBarUI ui)	
	5	public.........................void	**setUnitIncrement** (int unitIncrement)	
	5	public.........................void	**setValue** (int value)	
		public.........................void	**setValueIsAdjusting** (boolean b)	
		public.........................void	**setValues** (int newValue, int newExtent, int newMin, int newMax)	
	5	public.........................void	**setVisibleAmount** (int extent)	
		protected.....................int	**unitIncrement**	
	3	public...................... **void**	**updateUI** ()	
▲	5	public static final ....int	VERTICAL = 1	

JScrollPane				javax.swing

```
        Object
   ○    └─java.awt.Component¹ ------------------- java.awt.image.ImageObserver⁴, java.awt.MenuContainer,
                                                        java.io.Serializable
             └─java.awt.Container²
1.2 ○          └─JComponent³
1.2               └─JScrollPane ------------------- ScrollPaneConstants⁵, javax.accessibility.Accessible
```

J

Classes

JScrollPane

			Type	Member	
		protected	JViewport	**columnHeader**	
		public	JScrollBar	**createHorizontalScrollBar** ()	
		public	JScrollBar	**createVerticalScrollBar** ()	
		protected	JViewport	**createViewport** ()	
	3	public	**javax.accessibility₂ .AccessibleContext**	**getAccessibleContext** ()	
		public	JViewport	**getColumnHeader** ()	
		public	java.awt.Component	**getCorner** (String key)	
		public	JScrollBar	**getHorizontalScrollBar** ()	ε822
		public	int	**getHorizontalScrollBarPolicy** ()	ε821
		public	JViewport	**getRowHeader** ()	
		public	**javax₂ .swing.plaf.ScrollPaneUI**	**getUI** ()	
	3	public	**String**	**getUIClassID** ()	
		public	JScrollBar	**getVerticalScrollBar** ()	ε822
		public	int	**getVerticalScrollBarPolicy** ()	ε821
		public	JViewport	**getViewport** ()	
		public	*... javax.swing.border.Border*	**getViewportBorder** ()	
		public	java.awt.Rectangle	**getViewportBorderBounds** ()	
▲	5	public static final	int	HORIZONTAL_SCROLLBAR_ALWAYS = 32	ε821
▲	5	public static final	int	HORIZONTAL_SCROLLBAR_NEVER = 31	ε821
		protected	JScrollBar	**horizontalScrollBar**	
		protected	int	**horizontalScrollBarPolicy**	
	3	public	**boolean**	**isValidateRoot** ()	
1.4		public	boolean	**isWheelScrollingEnabled** ()	
*		public		**JScrollPane** ()	
*		public		**JScrollPane** (java.awt.Component view)	ε774,782,820,821,822
*		public		**JScrollPane** (int vsbPolicy, int hsbPolicy)	
*		public		**JScrollPane** (java.awt.Component view, int vsbPolicy, int hsbPolicy)	
		protected java.awt.Component		**lowerLeft**	
		protected java.awt.Component		**lowerRight**	
	3	protected	**String**	**paramString** ()	
		protected	JViewport	**rowHeader**	
		public	void	**setColumnHeader** (JViewport columnHeader)	
		public	void	**setColumnHeaderView** (java.awt.Component view)	
	1	public	**void**	**setComponentOrientation** (java.awt.ComponentOrientation co)	
		public	void	**setCorner** (String key, java.awt.Component corner)	
		public	void	**setHorizontalScrollBar** (JScrollBar horizontalScrollBar)	
		public	void	**setHorizontalScrollBarPolicy** (int policy)	ε821
	2	public	**void**	**setLayout** (*java.awt.LayoutManager* layout)	ε613,622,624,625,627
		public	void	**setRowHeader** (JViewport rowHeader)	
		public	void	**setRowHeaderView** (java.awt.Component view)	
		public	void	**setUI** (javax.swing.plaf.ScrollPaneUI ui)	
		public	void	**setVerticalScrollBar** (JScrollBar verticalScrollBar)	
		public	void	**setVerticalScrollBarPolicy** (int policy)	ε821
		public	void	**setViewport** (JViewport viewport)	
		public	void	**setViewportBorder** (*javax.swing.border.Border* viewportBorder)	
		public	void	**setViewportView** (java.awt.Component view)	
1.4		public	void	**setWheelScrollingEnabled** (boolean handleWheel)	
	3	public	**void**	**updateUI** ()	
		protected java.awt.Component		**upperLeft**	
		protected java.awt.Component		**upperRight**	
▲	5	public static final	int	VERTICAL_SCROLLBAR_ALWAYS = 22	ε821
▲	5	public static final	int	VERTICAL_SCROLLBAR_NEVER = 21	ε821
		protected	JScrollBar	**verticalScrollBar**	
		protected	int	**verticalScrollBarPolicy**	
		protected	JViewport	**viewport**	

J

Class   *Interface*   —extends   - - -implements   ○ abstract   ● final   △ static   ▲ static final   ✳ constructor   x x—inherited   x **x**—declared   **x x**—overridden
ε*n*—examples of usage   ↳—has subclass   package—see other volume

634

JScrollPane.ScrollBar | protected | javax.swing

```
        Object
    ○   └java.awt.Component 1 - - - - - - - - - - - - - - - - - - java.awt.image.ImageObserver 5, java.awt.MenuContainer,
                                                              java.io.Serializable
            └java.awt.Container 2
1.2 ○         └JComponent 3
1.2             └JScrollBar 4 - - - - - - - - - - - - - - - - - - - - java.awt.Adjustable 6, javax.accessibility.Accessible
1.2               └JScrollPane.ScrollBar - - - - - - - - - - - javax.swing.plaf.UIResource
```

	1	*143 inherited members from java.awt.Component not shown*			
	2	*51 inherited members from java.awt.Container not shown*			
	3	*140 inherited members from JComponent not shown*			
	4	*34 inherited members from JScrollBar not shown*			
	5	*8 inherited members from java.awt.image.ImageObserver not shown*			
	4	public	**int** **getBlockIncrement** (int direction)		
	4	public	**int** **getUnitIncrement** (int direction)		
▲	6	public static final	int HORIZONTAL = 0	ε822	
1.4 ▲	6	public static final	int NO_ORIENTATION = 2		
*		public	**JScrollPane.ScrollBar** (int orientation)		
	4	public	**void** **setBlockIncrement** (int blockIncrement)		
	4	public	**void** **setUnitIncrement** (int unitIncrement)		
▲	6	public static final	int VERTICAL = 1		

JSeparator | javax.swing

```
        Object
    ○   └java.awt.Component 1 - - - - - - - - - - - - - - - - - - java.awt.image.ImageObserver 4, java.awt.MenuContainer,
                                                              java.io.Serializable
            └java.awt.Container 2
1.2 ○         └JComponent 3
1.2             └JSeparator - - - - - - - - - - - - - - - - - - - SwingConstants 5, javax.accessibility.Accessible
```

	1	*143 inherited members from java.awt.Component not shown*		
	2	*51 inherited members from java.awt.Container not shown*		
	3	*143 inherited members from JComponent not shown*		
	5	*19 inherited members from SwingConstants not shown*		
	4	*8 inherited members from java.awt.image.ImageObserver not shown*		
	3	public.... **javax.accessibility** **getAccessibleContext** ()	
		.AccessibleContext		
		public.............................int	**getOrientation** ()	
		public.............................	**getUI** ()	
		javax.swing.plaf.SeparatorUI		
	3	public.................... **String**	**getUIClassID** ()	
*		public.............................	**JSeparator** ()	ε809
*		public.............................	**JSeparator** (int orientation)	
	3	protected .... **String**	**paramString** ()	
		public.....................void	**setOrientation** (int orientation)	
		public.....................void	**setUI** (javax.swing.plaf.SeparatorUI ui)	
	3	public..................... **void**	**updateUI** ()	

JSlider | javax.swing

```
        Object
    ○   └java.awt.Component 1 - - - - - - - - - - - - - - - - - - java.awt.image.ImageObserver 4, java.awt.MenuContainer,
                                                              java.io.Serializable
            └java.awt.Container 2
1.2 ○         └JComponent 3
1.2             └JSlider - - - - - - - - - - - - - - - - - - - - - SwingConstants 5, javax.accessibility.Accessible
```

	1	*143 inherited members from java.awt.Component not shown*	
	2	*51 inherited members from java.awt.Container not shown*	
	3	*143 inherited members from JComponent not shown*	
	5	*18 inherited members from SwingConstants not shown*	
	4	*8 inherited members from java.awt.image.ImageObserver not shown*	
		public.....................void **addChangeListener** (javax.swing.event.ChangeListener l)	ε800
		protected transient...... javax **changeEvent**	
		.swing.event.ChangeEvent	
		protected .... javax.swing **changeListener**	
		.event.ChangeListener	

J

Classes

JSlider

	protected . . . . *javax.swing* `createChangeListener ()`		
	.event.ChangeListener		
	public . . . . java.util.Hashtable	**createStandardLabels** (int increment)	
	public . . . . java.util.Hashtable	**createStandardLabels** (int increment, int start)	
	protected . . . . .void	**fireStateChanged** ()	
3	public . . . . . **javax.accessibility**	**getAccessibleContext** ()	
	.AccessibleContext		
1.4	public . . . . *javax.swing*	**getChangeListeners** ()	
	.event.ChangeListener[]		
	public . . . . int	**getExtent** ()	ε795
	public . . . . boolean	**getInverted** ()	
	public . . . . java.util.Dictionary	**getLabelTable** ()	ε798
	public . . . . int	**getMajorTickSpacing** ()	
	public . . . . int	**getMaximum** ()	ε795,798
	public . . . . int	**getMinimum** ()	ε795,798
	public . . . . int	**getMinorTickSpacing** ()	
	public . . . *BoundedRangeModel*	**getModel** ()	ε795
	public . . . . int	**getOrientation** ()	
	public . . . . boolean	**getPaintLabels** ()	ε798
	public . . . . boolean	**getPaintTicks** ()	ε797
	public . . . . boolean	**getPaintTrack** ()	
	public . . . . boolean	**getSnapToTicks** ()	ε799
	public	**getUI** ()	
	. . . . . javax.swing.plaf.SliderUI		
3	public . . . . **String**	**getUIClassID** ()	
	public . . . . int	**getValue** ()	ε795,799,800
	public . . . . boolean	**getValueIsAdjusting** ()	ε800
✳	public	**JSlider** ()	ε794,796,797,798,799
✳	public	**JSlider** (int orientation)	ε794
✳	public	**JSlider** (*BoundedRangeModel* brm)	
✳	public	**JSlider** (int min, int max)	ε794
✳	public	**JSlider** (int min, int max, int value)	ε794
✳	public	**JSlider** (int orientation, int min, int max, int value)	ε794
	protected . . . . int	**majorTickSpacing**	
	protected . . . . int	**minorTickSpacing**	
	protected . . . . int	**orientation**	
3	protected . . . . **String**	**paramString** ()	
	public . . . . .void	**removeChangeListener** (*javax.swing.event.ChangeListener* l)	
	public . . . . .void	**setExtent** (int extent)	ε794,795
	public . . . . .void	**setInverted** (boolean b)	ε796
	public . . . . .void	**setLabelTable** (java.util.Dictionary labels)	ε798
	public . . . . .void	**setMajorTickSpacing** (int n)	ε797,798,799
	public . . . . .void	**setMaximum** (int maximum)	ε795
	public . . . . .void	**setMinimum** (int minimum)	ε795
	public . . . . .void	**setMinorTickSpacing** (int n)	ε797,799
	public . . . . .void	**setModel** (*BoundedRangeModel* newModel)	
	public . . . . .void	**setOrientation** (int orientation)	ε796
	public . . . . .void	**setPaintLabels** (boolean b)	ε798
	public . . . . .void	**setPaintTicks** (boolean b)	ε797,799
	public . . . . .void	**setPaintTrack** (boolean b)	ε794
	public . . . . .void	**setSnapToTicks** (boolean b)	ε799
	public . . . . .void	**setUI** (javax.swing.plaf.SliderUI ui)	
	public . . . . .void	**setValue** (int n)	ε795,799
	public . . . . .void	**setValueIsAdjusting** (boolean b)	
	protected	**sliderModel**	
	. . . . *BoundedRangeModel*		
	protected . . . . boolean	**snapToTicks**	
	protected .void	**updateLabelUIs** ()	
3	public . . . . **void**	**updateUI** ()	
▲ 5	public static final . . . . int	**VERTICAL** = 1	ε794,796,801,816

J

```
        Object
  o     └java.awt.Component¹ - - - - - - - - - - - - - - - - - - java.awt.image.ImageObserver⁴, java.awt.MenuContainer,
                                                                java.io.Serializable┘

           └java.awt.Container²
1.2 o         └JComponent³
1.4             └JSpinner
```

1	*143 inherited members from java.awt.Component not shown*	
2	*51 inherited members from java.awt.Container not shown*	
3	*145 inherited members from JComponent not shown*	
4	*8 inherited members from java.awt.image.ImageObserver not shown*	

	public	void	**addChangeListener** (*javax.swing.event.ChangeListener* listener)	ε791,793
	public	void	**commitEdit** () throws java.text.ParseException	
	protected	JComponent	**createEditor** (*SpinnerModel* model)	
	protected	void	**fireStateChanged** ()	
	public	*javax.swing.event.ChangeListener[]*	**getChangeListeners** ()	
	public	JComponent	**getEditor** ()	ε787,788,790
	public	*SpinnerModel*	**getModel** ()	
	public	Object	**getNextValue** ()	
	public	Object	**getPreviousValue** ()	
	public	*javax.swing.plaf.SpinnerUI*	**getUI** ()	
3	public	**String**	**getUIClassID** ()	
	public	Object	**getValue** ()	ε791,793,960
*	public		**JSpinner** ()	ε786,788,789,790,793
*	public		**JSpinner** (*SpinnerModel* model)	ε786,787,789,792
	public	void	**removeChangeListener** (*javax.swing.event.ChangeListener* listener)	
	public	void	**setEditor** (JComponent editor)	
	public	void	**setModel** (*SpinnerModel* model)	ε960
	public	void	**setUI** (javax.swing.plaf.SpinnerUI ui)	
	public	void	**setValue** (Object value)	ε786,788,791,793,960
3	public	**void**	**updateUI** ()	

J

```
        Object
  o     └java.awt.Component¹ - - - - - - - - - - - - - - - - - - java.awt.image.ImageObserver⁶, java.awt.MenuContainer,
                                                                java.io.Serializable┘

           └java.awt.Container²
1.2 o         └JComponent³
1.2             └JPanel⁴ - - - - - - - - - - - - - - - - - - - - javax.accessibility.Accessible
1.4               └JSpinner.DefaultEditor⁵ - - - - - - - - - - javax.swing.event.ChangeListener (java.util.EventListener),
                                                               java.beans.PropertyChangeListener (java.util.EventListener),
                                                               java.awt.LayoutManager┘

                     └JSpinner.DateEditor
1.4
```

1	*143 inherited members from java.awt.Component not shown*	
2	*51 inherited members from java.awt.Container not shown*	
3	*143 inherited members from JComponent not shown*	
6	*8 inherited members from java.awt.image.ImageObserver not shown*	

5	public	void	addLayoutComponent (String name, java.awt.Component child)	
5	public	void	commitEdit () throws java.text.ParseException	
*	public		**JSpinner.DateEditor** (JSpinner spinner)	
*	public		**JSpinner.DateEditor** (JSpinner spinner, String dateFormatPattern)	
5	public	void	dismiss (JSpinner spinner)	
4	public	javax.accessibility.AccessibleContext	getAccessibleContext ()	
	public	java.text.SimpleDateFormat	**getFormat** ()	
	public	SpinnerDateModel	**getModel** ()	
5	public	JSpinner	getSpinner ()	
5	public	JFormattedTextField	getTextField ()	ε787,788,790
4	public	javax.swing.plaf.PanelUI	getUI ()	
4	public	String	getUIClassID ()	
5	public	void	layoutContainer (java.awt.Container parent)	ε624,625
5	public	java.awt.Dimension	minimumLayoutSize (java.awt.Container parent)	
4	protected	String	paramString ()	

Classes

JSpinner.DateEditor

5	public	java.awt.Dimension	preferredLayoutSize (java.awt.Container parent)
5	public	void	propertyChange (java.beans.PropertyChangeEvent e)
5	public	void	removeLayoutComponent (java.awt.Component child)
4	public	void	setUI (javax.swing.plaf.PanelUI ui)
5	public	void	stateChanged (javax.swing.event.ChangeEvent e)
4	public	void	updateUI ()

ε791,793,800,805,815 (aligned with stateChanged)

JSpinner.DefaultEditor   javax.swing

```
Object
 └─java.awt.Component 1 - - - - - - - - - - - - - - - - - java.awt.image.ImageObserver 5, java.awt.MenuContainer,
                                                          java.io.Serializable
       └─java.awt.Container 2
1.2 ○      └─JComponent 3
1.2          └─JPanel 4 - - - - - - - - - - - - - - - - - javax.accessibility.Accessible
1.4             └─JSpinner.DefaultEditor - - - - - - - - - javax.swing.event.ChangeListener 6 (java.util.EventListener),
                                                          java.beans.PropertyChangeListener 7 (java.util.EventListener),
                                                          java.awt.LayoutManager 8
```

1			*143 inherited members from java.awt.Component not shown*	
2			*51 inherited members from java.awt.Container not shown*	
3			*143 inherited members from JComponent not shown*	
5			*8 inherited members from java.awt.image.ImageObserver not shown*	
8	public	void	**addLayoutComponent** (String name, java.awt.Component child)	
	public	void	**commitEdit** () throws java.text.ParseException	
*	public		**JSpinner.DefaultEditor** (JSpinner spinner)	
	public	void	**dismiss** (JSpinner spinner)	
4	public	javax.accessibility .AccessibleContext	getAccessibleContext ()	
	public	JSpinner	**getSpinner** ()	
	public	JFormattedTextField	**getTextField** ()	ε787,788,790
4	public javax.swing.plaf.PanelUI		getUI ()	
4	public	String	getUIClassID ()	
8	public	void	**layoutContainer** (java.awt.Container parent)	ε624,625
8	public	java.awt.Dimension	**minimumLayoutSize** (java.awt.Container parent)	
4	protected	String	paramString ()	
8	public	java.awt.Dimension	**preferredLayoutSize** (java.awt.Container parent)	
7	public	void	**propertyChange** (java.beans.PropertyChangeEvent e)	
8	public	void	**removeLayoutComponent** (java.awt.Component child)	
4	public	void	setUI (javax.swing.plaf.PanelUI ui)	
6	public	void	**stateChanged** (javax.swing.event.ChangeEvent e)	ε791,793,800,805,815
4	public	void	updateUI ()	

JSpinner.ListEditor   javax.swing

```
Object
 └─java.awt.Component 1 - - - - - - - - - - - - - - - - - java.awt.image.ImageObserver 6, java.awt.MenuContainer,
                                                          java.io.Serializable
       └─java.awt.Container 2
1.2 ○      └─JComponent 3
1.2          └─JPanel 4 - - - - - - - - - - - - - - - - - javax.accessibility.Accessible
1.4             └─JSpinner.DefaultEditor 5 - - - - - - - - javax.swing.event.ChangeListener (java.util.EventListener),
                                                          java.beans.PropertyChangeListener (java.util.EventListener),
                                                          java.awt.LayoutManager
1.4                 └─JSpinner.ListEditor
```

1			*143 inherited members from java.awt.Component not shown*
2			*51 inherited members from java.awt.Container not shown*
3			*143 inherited members from JComponent not shown*
6			*8 inherited members from java.awt.image.ImageObserver not shown*
5	public	void	addLayoutComponent (String name, java.awt.Component child)
5	public	void	commitEdit () throws java.text.ParseException
5	public	void	dismiss (JSpinner spinner)
4	public	javax.accessibility .AccessibleContext	getAccessibleContext ()
	public	SpinnerListModel	**getModel** ()

Class   *Interface*   —extends   - - -implements   ○ abstract   ● final   △ static   ▲ static final   ✱ constructor   x x—inherited   x **x**—declared   **x x**—overridden
εn—examples of usage   ˅—has subclass   package—see other volume

5	public	JSpinner	getSpinner ()	
5	public	JFormattedTextField	getTextField ()	ε787,788,790
4	public javax.swing.plaf.PanelUI		getUI ()	
4	public	String	getUIClassID ()	
5	public	void	layoutContainer (java.awt.Container parent)	ε624,625
*	public		**JSpinner.ListEditor** (JSpinner spinner)	
5	public	java.awt.Dimension	minimumLayoutSize (java.awt.Container parent)	
4	protected	String	paramString ()	
5	public	java.awt.Dimension	preferredLayoutSize (java.awt.Container parent)	
5	public	void	propertyChange (java.beans.PropertyChangeEvent e)	
5	public	void	removeLayoutComponent (java.awt.Component child)	
4	public	void	setUI (javax.swing.plaf.PanelUI ui)	
5	public	void	stateChanged (javax.swing.event.ChangeEvent e)	ε791,793,800,805,815
4	public	void	updateUI ()	

JSpinner.NumberEditor — javax.swing

J

```
Object
 └java.awt.Component¹ ------------------- java.awt.image.ImageObserver⁶, java.awt.MenuContainer,
                                          java.io.Serializable
     └java.awt.Container²
1.2      └JComponent³
1.2          └JPanel⁴ ------------------------ javax.accessibility.Accessible
1.4              └JSpinner.DefaultEditor⁵ ---------- javax.swing.event.ChangeListener (java.util.EventListener),
                                                     java.beans.PropertyChangeListener (java.util.EventListener),
                                                     java.awt.LayoutManager
1.4                  └JSpinner.NumberEditor
```

1	*143 inherited members from java.awt.Component not shown*			
2	*51 inherited members from java.awt.Container not shown*			
3	*143 inherited members from JComponent not shown*			
6	*8 inherited members from java.awt.image.ImageObserver not shown*			
5	public	void	addLayoutComponent (String name, java.awt.Component child)	
5	public	void	commitEdit () throws java.text.ParseException	
5	public	void	dismiss (JSpinner spinner)	
4	public	javax.accessibility. .AccessibleContext	getAccessibleContext ()	
	public	java.text.DecimalFormat	**getFormat** ()	
	public	SpinnerNumberModel	**getModel** ()	
5	public	JSpinner	getSpinner ()	
5	public	JFormattedTextField	getTextField ()	ε787,788,790
4	public javax.swing.plaf.PanelUI		getUI ()	
4	public	String	getUIClassID ()	
5	public	void	layoutContainer (java.awt.Container parent)	ε624,625
5	public	java.awt.Dimension	minimumLayoutSize (java.awt.Container parent)	
*	public		**JSpinner.NumberEditor** (JSpinner spinner)	
*	public		**JSpinner.NumberEditor** (JSpinner spinner, String decimalFormatPattern)	
4	protected	String	paramString ()	
5	public	java.awt.Dimension	preferredLayoutSize (java.awt.Container parent)	
5	public	void	propertyChange (java.beans.PropertyChangeEvent e)	
5	public	void	removeLayoutComponent (java.awt.Component child)	
4	public	void	setUI (javax.swing.plaf.PanelUI ui)	
5	public	void	stateChanged (javax.swing.event.ChangeEvent e)	ε791,793,800,805,815
4	public	void	updateUI ()	

JSplitPane — javax.swing

```
Object
 └java.awt.Component¹ ------------------- java.awt.image.ImageObserver⁴, java.awt.MenuContainer,
                                          java.io.Serializable
     └java.awt.Container²
1.2      └JComponent³
1.2          └JSplitPane --------------------- javax.accessibility.Accessible
```

1	*142 inherited members from java.awt.Component not shown*			
2	*46 inherited members from java.awt.Container not shown*			
3	*141 inherited members from JComponent not shown*			
4	*8 inherited members from java.awt.image.ImageObserver not shown*			
2	public	java.awt.Component	add (java.awt.Component comp)	ε963,571,575,581,590
2	protected	**void**	**addImpl** (java.awt.Component comp, Object constraints, int index)	

JSplitPane

Class *Interface* —extends - - -implements ○ abstract ● final △ static ▲ static final ✱ constructor x x—inherited x **x**—declared **x x**—overridden
ε*n*—examples of usage ⸱—has subclass package—see other volume

640

J

JTabbedPane	javax.swing

```
     Object
  ○  └java.awt.Component¹ - - - - - - - - - - - - - - - - - -  java.awt.image.ImageObserver ⁴, java.awt.MenuContainer,
                                                                  java.io.Serializable ⌐
         └java.awt.Container²
1.2  ○     └JComponent³
1.2         └JTabbedPane - - - - - - - - - - - - - - - -  javax.accessibility.Accessible, SwingConstants ⁵
```

	1	*143 inherited members from java.awt.Component not shown*		
	2	*43 inherited members from java.awt.Container not shown*		
	3	*140 inherited members from JComponent not shown*		
	5	*16 inherited members from SwingConstants not shown*		
	4	*8 inherited members from java.awt.image.ImageObserver not shown*		
	2	public... **java.awt.Component**	**add** (java.awt.Component component)	ε830,571,575,581,590
	2	public............ **void**	**add** (java.awt.Component component, Object constraints)	ε733,559,571,601,694
	2	public... **java.awt.Component**	**add** (java.awt.Component component, int index)	
	2	public... **java.awt.Component**	**add** (String title, java.awt.Component component)	
	2	public............ **void**	**add** (java.awt.Component component, Object constraints, int index)	
		public....................void	**addChangeListener** (*javax.swing.event.ChangeListener* l)	ε840
		public....................void	**addTab** (String title, java.awt.Component component)	ε828,830,835,836,837
		public....................void	**addTab** (String title, *Icon* icon, java.awt.Component component)	ε830
		public....................void	**addTab** (String title, *Icon* icon, java.awt.Component component, String tip)	ε830,836
▲	5	public static final ....int	BOTTOM = 3	ε834,739,747,748
		protected transient...... javax **swing.event.ChangeEvent**	**changeEvent**	
		protected......... *javax.swing* **.event.ChangeListener**	**changeListener**	
		protected......... *javax.swing* **.event.ChangeListener**	**createChangeListener** ()	
		protected....................void	**fireStateChanged** ()	
	3	public.... **javax.accessibility .AccessibleContext**	**getAccessibleContext** ()	
		public.............java.awt.Color	**getBackgroundAt** (int index)	ε832
		public...... java.awt.Rectangle	**getBoundsAt** (int index)	
1.4		public............. *javax.swing* **.event.ChangeListener[]**	**getChangeListeners** ()	
		public.... java.awt.Component	**getComponentAt** (int index)	ε832,833
		public..................... *Icon*	**getDisabledIconAt** (int index)	ε832
1.4		public..........................int	**getDisplayedMnemonicIndexAt** (int tabIndex)	ε832
		public.............java.awt.Color	**getForegroundAt** (int index)	ε832
		public..................... *Icon*	**getIconAt** (int index)	ε832,833
1.4		public..........................int	**getMnemonicAt** (int tabIndex)	ε832,833
		public... *SingleSelectionModel*	**getModel** ()	
		public..... java.awt.Component	**getSelectedComponent** ()	
		public..........................int	**getSelectedIndex** ()	ε829,840
		public..........................int	**getTabCount** ()	ε829,831,832,833,835
1.4		public..........................int	**getTabLayoutPolicy** ()	ε839
		public..........................int	**getTabPlacement** ()	ε834
		public..........................int	**getTabRunCount** ()	ε839
		public.......................String	**getTitleAt** (int index)	ε832,833
	3	public.......................**String**	**getToolTipText** (java.awt.event.MouseEvent event)	
1.3		public.......................String	**getToolTipTextAt** (int index)	ε832,833,836
		public...................... javax **.swing.plaf.TabbedPaneUI**	**getUI** ()	
	3	public.......................**String**	**getUIClassID** ()	
1.4		public..........................int	**indexAtLocation** (int x, int y)	
		public..........................int	**indexOfComponent** (java.awt.Component component)	ε833
		public..........................int	**indexOfTab** (String title)	ε833
		public..........................int	**indexOfTab** (*Icon* icon)	ε833
		public....................void	**insertTab** (String title, *Icon* icon, java.awt.Component component, String tip, int index)	ε830,832
		public.................. boolean	**isEnabledAt** (int index)	ε832,833,835
*		public..........................	**JTabbedPane** ()	ε828,830,834,835,836
*		public..........................	**JTabbedPane** (int tabPlacement)	ε834
1.4 *		public..........................	**JTabbedPane** (int tabPlacement, int tabLayoutPolicy)	
▲	5	public static final ....int	LEFT = 2	ε834,739,747,748,981
		protected...................... *SingleSelectionModel*	**model**	
	3	protected.............. **String**	**paramString** ()	
	2	public.................... **void**	**remove** (int index)	ε831,832
	2	public.................... **void**	**remove** (java.awt.Component component)	ε831

JTabbedPane

	2	public	**void**	**removeAll** ()	ε831
		public	void	**removeChangeListener** (*javax.swing.event.ChangeListener* l)	
		public	void	**removeTabAt** (int index)	
1.4 ▲		public static final	int	**SCROLL_TAB_LAYOUT** = 1	ε839
	3	public	void	setBackground (java.awt.Color bg)	ε837
		public	void	**setBackgroundAt** (int index, java.awt.Color background)	ε832,837
		public	void	**setComponentAt** (int index, java.awt.Component component)	
		public	void	**setDisabledIconAt** (int index, *Icon* disabledIcon)	ε832
1.4		public	void	**setDisplayedMnemonicIndexAt** (int tabIndex, int mnemonicIndex)	
					ε832
		public	void	**setEnabledAt** (int index, boolean enabled)	ε832,835
	3	public	void	setForeground (java.awt.Color fg)	ε837
		public	void	**setForegroundAt** (int index, java.awt.Color foreground)	ε832,837
		public	void	**setIconAt** (int index, *Icon* icon)	
1.4		public	void	**setMnemonicAt** (int tabIndex, int mnemonic)	ε832,838
		public	void	**setModel** (*SingleSelectionModel* model)	
		public	void	**setSelectedComponent** (java.awt.Component c)	
		public	void	**setSelectedIndex** (int index)	ε829
1.4		public	void	**setTabLayoutPolicy** (int tabLayoutPolicy)	ε839
		public	void	**setTabPlacement** (int tabPlacement)	ε834
		public	void	**setTitleAt** (int index, String title)	
1.3		public	void	**setToolTipTextAt** (int index, String toolTipText)	ε836
		public	void	**setUI** (javax.swing.plaf.TabbedPaneUI ui)	
		protected	int	**tabPlacement**	
▲	5	public static final	int	TOP = 1	ε828,739,747,748
	3	public	**void**	**updateUI** ()	
1.4 ▲		public static final	int	**WRAP_TAB_LAYOUT** = 0	

JTabbedPane.ModelListener	protected	javax.swing

Object

1.2	└JTabbedPane.ModelListener ------------- *javax.swing.event.ChangeListener* [1] (*java.util.EventListener*), *java.io.Serializable*

*		protected	**JTabbedPane.ModelListener** ()	
	1	public	void	**stateChanged** (javax.swing.event.ChangeEvent e)	ε791,793,800,805,815

JTable	javax.swing

Object

○	└java.awt.Component [1] ------------------ *java.awt.image.ImageObserver* [4], *java.awt.MenuContainer*, *java.io.Serializable*
	└java.awt.Container [2]
1.2 ○	└JComponent [3]
1.2	└JTable ----------------------- *javax.swing.event.TableModelListener* [5] (*java.util.EventListener*), *Scrollable* [6], *javax.swing.event.TableColumnModelListener* [7] (*java.util.EventListener*), *javax.swing.event* *.ListSelectionListener* [8] (*java.util.EventListener*), *javax.swing.event.CellEditorListener* [9] (*java.util.EventListener*), *javax.accessibility.Accessible*

	1	*139 inherited members from java.awt.Component not shown*
	3	*138 inherited members from JComponent not shown*
	4	*8 inherited members from java.awt.image.ImageObserver not shown*
	2	public.... java.awt.Component	add (java.awt.Component comp)	ε571,575,581,590,610
	2	public	void	add (java.awt.Component comp, Object constraints)	ε733,559,571,601,694
	2	public.... java.awt.Component	add (java.awt.Component comp, int index)	
	2	public.... java.awt.Component	add (String name, java.awt.Component comp)	
	2	public	void	add (java.awt.Component comp, Object constraints, int index)	
		public	void	**addColumn** (javax.swing.table.TableColumn aColumn)	ε920
		public	void	**addColumnSelectionInterval** (int index0, int index1)	ε941
	2	public synchronized	void	addContainerListener (*java.awt.event.ContainerListener* l)	ε573
	2	protected	void	addImpl (java.awt.Component comp, Object constraints, int index)	
	3	public	**void**	**addNotify** ()	
		public	void	**addRowSelectionInterval** (int index0, int index1)	ε941
1.4	2	public	void	applyComponentOrientation (java.awt.ComponentOrientation o)	
1.4	2	public	boolean	areFocusTraversalKeysSet (int id)	

Class *Interface* —extends - - -implements ○ abstract ● final △ static ▲ static final ✳ constructor x x—inherited x **x**—declared **x x**—overridden
ε*n*—examples of usage ˎ—has subclass package—see other volume

J

Classes

JTable

	public	String	**getColumnName** (int column)	
	public	boolean	**getColumnSelectionAllowed** ()	ε942,964
2	public	java.awt.Component	getComponent (int n)	ε572
2	public	java.awt.Component	getComponentAt (java.awt.Point p)	
2	public	java.awt.Component	getComponentAt (int x, int y)	
2	public	int	getComponentCount ()	ε572
2	public	java.awt.Component[]	getComponents ()	ε572
1.4	2	public synchronized . *java.awt*. *.event.ContainerListener[]*	getContainerListeners ()	
	public	*javax*. *.swing.table.TableCellEditor*	**getDefaultEditor** (Class columnClass)	ε927
	public	*javax.swing*. *.table.TableCellRenderer*	**getDefaultRenderer** (Class columnClass)	ε927
1.4		public	boolean	**getDragEnabled** ()	
	public	int	**getEditingColumn** ()	
	public	int	**getEditingRow** ()	
	public	java.awt.Component	**getEditorComponent** ()	
1.4	2	public	*java.util*.*Set*	getFocusTraversalKeys (int id)	ε610
1.4	2	public	*java*. *.awt.FocusTraversalPolicy*	getFocusTraversalPolicy ()	ε615
1	public	java.awt.Color	getForeground ()	ε959
	public	java.awt.Color	**getGridColor** ()	
	public	java.awt.Dimension	**getIntercellSpacing** ()	ε952
2	public	*java.awt.LayoutManager*	getLayout ()	
	public	*javax*. *.swing.table.TableModel*	**getModel** ()	ε920,922,926,930,950
1	public	java.awt.Container	getParent ()	ε946,947,948
6	public	java.awt.Dimension	**getPreferredScrollableViewportSize** ()	ε949
3	public	java.awt.Dimension	getPreferredSize ()	ε949
	public	int	**getRowCount** ()	ε907,912,913,950
	public	int	**getRowHeight** ()	ε913,952
1.3	public	int	**getRowHeight** (int row)	ε913
	public	int	**getRowMargin** ()	
	public	boolean	**getRowSelectionAllowed** ()	ε942,964
6	public	int	**getScrollableBlockIncrement** (java.awt.Rectangle visibleRect, int orientation, int direction)	
6	public	boolean	**getScrollableTracksViewportHeight** ()	
6	public	boolean	**getScrollableTracksViewportWidth** ()	
6	public	int	**getScrollableUnitIncrement** (java.awt.Rectangle visibleRect, int orientation, int direction)	
	public	int	**getSelectedColumn** ()	ε942
	public	int	**getSelectedColumnCount** ()	
	public	int[]	**getSelectedColumns** ()	ε942
	public	int	**getSelectedRow** ()	ε942
	public	int	**getSelectedRowCount** ()	
	public	int[]	**getSelectedRows** ()	ε942
	public	java.awt.Color	**getSelectionBackground** ()	ε959
	public	java.awt.Color	**getSelectionForeground** ()	ε959
	public	*ListSelectionModel*	**getSelectionModel** ()	ε940,942,944,957,964
	public	boolean	**getShowHorizontalLines** ()	
	public	boolean	**getShowVerticalLines** ()	
1.4	public	boolean	**getSurrendersFocusOnKeystroke** ()	
	public	*javax*. *.swing.table.JTableHeader*	**getTableHeader** ()	ε924,925,931,932,933
3	public	**String**	**getToolTipText** (java.awt.event.MouseEvent event)	
	public	javax.swing.plaf.TableUI	**getUI** ()	
3	public	**String**	**getUIClassID** ()	
	public	Object	**getValueAt** (int row, int column)	ε926,950,957
	protected	java.awt.Color	**gridColor**	
	protected	void	**initializeLocalVars** ()	
2	public	void	invalidate ()	
2	public	boolean	isAncestorOf (java.awt.Component c)	
	public	boolean	**isCellEditable** (int row, int column)	ε958
	public	boolean	**isCellSelected** (int row, int column)	ε942
	public	boolean	**isColumnSelected** (int column)	
	public	boolean	**isEditing** ()	
1.4	2	public	boolean	isFocusCycleRoot ()	
1.4	2	public	boolean	isFocusCycleRoot (java.awt.Container container)	
1.4	2	public	boolean	isFocusTraversalPolicySet ()	
	public	boolean	**isRowSelected** (int row)	
✳	public		**JTable** ()	ε914,920,922,927,928

Class *Interface* —extends - - -implements ○ abstract ● final △ static ▲ static final ✳ constructor x x—inherited x **x**—declared **x x**—overridden
ε*n*—examples of usage ◡—has subclass package—see other volume

∗		public...........................	**JTable** (*javax.swing.table.TableModel* dm)	ε908,909,910,911,912
∗		public...........................	**JTable** (int numRows, int numColumns)	ε906,913,917,919,921
∗		public...........................	**JTable** (Object[][] rowData, Object[] columnNames)	ε906
∗		public...........................	**JTable** (java.util.Vector rowData, java.util.Vector columnNames)	ε906
∗		public...........................	**JTable** (*javax.swing.table.TableModel* dm, *javax.swing.table.TableColumnModel* cm)	
∗		public...........................	**JTable** (*javax.swing.table.TableModel* dm, *javax.swing.table.TableColumnModel* cm, *ListSelectionModel* sm)	
	2	public.....................void	list (java.io.PrintStream out, int indent)	
	2	public.....................void	list (java.io.PrintWriter out, int indent)	
		public.....................void	**moveColumn** (int column, int targetColumn)	ε921,923,924
	2	public.....................void	paintComponents (java.awt.Graphics g)	
	3	protected...............**String**	**paramString** ()	
		protected .. java.awt.Dimension	**preferredViewportSize**	
		public.... java.awt.Component	**prepareEditor** (*javax.swing.table.TableCellEditor* editor, int row, int column)	
		public.... java.awt.Component	**prepareRenderer** (*javax.swing.table.TableCellRenderer* renderer, int row, int column)	ε914,938,913
	2	public.....................void	printComponents (java.awt.Graphics g)	
	2	protected ....void	processContainerEvent (java.awt.event.ContainerEvent e)	
	2	protected ....void	processEvent (java.awt.AWTEvent e)	
1.3	3	protected ....**boolean**	**processKeyBinding** (KeyStroke ks, java.awt.event.KeyEvent e, int condition, boolean pressed)	
	2	public.....................void	remove (int index)	ε831,832
	2	public.....................void	remove (java.awt.Component comp)	ε831
	2	public.....................void	removeAll ()	ε831
		public.....................void	**removeColumn** (javax.swing.table.TableColumn aColumn)	ε922
		public.....................void	**removeColumnSelectionInterval** (int index0, int index1)	ε941
	2	public synchronized ....void	removeContainerListener (*java.awt.event.ContainerListener* l)	
		public.....................void	**removeEditor** ()	
	3	public .... **void**	**removeNotify** ()	
		public.....................void	**removeRowSelectionInterval** (int index0, int index1)	ε941
		protected ....void	**resizeAndRepaint** ()	
		public......................int	**rowAtPoint** (java.awt.Point point)	
		protected ....int	**rowHeight**	
		protected ....int	**rowMargin**	
		protected .... boolean	**rowSelectionAllowed**	
		public.....................void	**selectAll** ()	ε941
		protected ....java.awt.Color	**selectionBackground**	
		protected ....java.awt.Color	**selectionForeground**	
		protected .. *ListSelectionModel*	**selectionModel**	
		public.....................void	**setAutoCreateColumnsFromModel** (boolean autoCreateColumnsFromModel)	ε920,921,922,961,962
		public.....................void	**setAutoResizeMode** (int mode)	ε917,918,945,949,950
		public.....................void	**setCellEditor** (*javax.swing.table.TableCellEditor* anEditor)	
		public.....................void	**setCellSelectionEnabled** (boolean cellSelectionEnabled)	ε943
		public.....................void	**setColumnModel** (*javax.swing.table.TableColumnModel* columnModel)	
		public.....................void	**setColumnSelectionAllowed** (boolean columnSelectionAllowed)	ε939,941,956
		public.....................void	**setColumnSelectionInterval** (int index0, int index1)	ε941
		public.....................void	**setDefaultEditor** (Class columnClass, *javax.swing.table.TableCellEditor* editor)	
		public.....................void	**setDefaultRenderer** (Class columnClass, *javax.swing.table.TableCellRenderer* renderer)	ε929
1.4		public.....................void	**setDragEnabled** (boolean b)	
		public.....................void	**setEditingColumn** (int aColumn)	
		public.....................void	**setEditingRow** (int aRow)	ε943
1.4	1	public.....................void	setFocusable (boolean focusable)	
1.4	2	public.....................void	setFocusCycleRoot (boolean focusCycleRoot)	
1.4	2	public.....................void	setFocusTraversalKeys (int id, *java.util.Set* keystrokes)	ε610
1.4	2	public.....................void	setFocusTraversalPolicy (java.awt.FocusTraversalPolicy policy)	
		public.....................void	**setGridColor** (java.awt.Color gridColor)	ε951
		public.....................void	**setIntercellSpacing** (java.awt.Dimension intercellSpacing)	ε952
	2	public.....................void	setLayout (java.awt.LayoutManager mgr)	ε613,622,624,625,627
		public.....................void	**setModel** (*javax.swing.table.TableModel* dataModel)	ε922
		public.....................void	**setPreferredScrollableViewportSize** (java.awt.Dimension size)	
		public.....................void	**setRowHeight** (int rowHeight)	ε952,913
1.3		public.....................void	**setRowHeight** (int row, int rowHeight)	ε913
		public.....................void	**setRowMargin** (int rowMargin)	
		public.....................void	**setRowSelectionAllowed** (boolean rowSelectionAllowed)	ε939,941,956
		public.....................void	**setRowSelectionInterval** (int index0, int index1)	ε941
		public.....................void	**setSelectionBackground** (java.awt.Color selectionBackground)	
		public.....................void	**setSelectionForeground** (java.awt.Color selectionForeground)	
		public.....................void	**setSelectionMode** (int selectionMode)	ε940,941,942
		public.....................void	**setSelectionModel** (*ListSelectionModel* newModel)	
		public.....................void	**setShowGrid** (boolean showGrid)	ε951

JTable

		public	void	**setShowHorizontalLines** (boolean showHorizontalLines)	ε951
		public	void	**setShowVerticalLines** (boolean showVerticalLines)	ε951
1.4		public	void	**setSurrendersFocusOnKeystroke** (boolean surrendersFocusOnKeystroke)	
		public	void	**setTableHeader** (javax.swing.table.JTableHeader tableHeader) ε935	
		public	void	**setUI** (javax.swing.plaf.TableUI ui)	
		public	void	**setValueAt** (Object aValue, int row, int column)	ε926,957
		protected	boolean	**showHorizontalLines**	
		protected	boolean	**showVerticalLines**	
D		public	void	**sizeColumnsToFit** (boolean lastColumnOnly)	
		public	void	**sizeColumnsToFit** (int resizingColumn)	
	5	public	void	**tableChanged** (javax.swing.event.TableModelEvent e)	ε957,965
		protected	javax.swing.table.JTableHeader	**tableHeader**	
1.4	2	public	void	transferFocusBackward ()	
1.4	2	public	void	transferFocusDownCycle ()	
1.3		protected	void	**unconfigureEnclosingScrollPane** ()	
	3	public	**void**	**updateUI** ()	
	2	public	void	validate ()	ε601,674,928,936
	2	protected	void	validateTree ()	
	8	public	void	**valueChanged** (javax.swing.event.ListSelectionEvent e)	ε784,957,964

JTable.AccessibleJTable.AccessibleJTableModelChange   protected   javax.swing

```
      Object
1.3   └JTable.AccessibleJTable ͻ ---------------- javax.accessibility.AccessibleTableModelChange ¹
        .AccessibleJTableModelChange
```

*		protected		**JTable.AccessibleJTable.AccessibleJTableModelChange**	
				(int type, int firstRow, int lastRow, int firstColumn, int lastColumn)	
▲	1	public static final	int	DELETE = -1	
		protected	int	**firstColumn**	
		protected	int	**firstRow**	
	1	public	int	**getFirstColumn** ()	
	1	public	int	**getFirstRow** ()	
	1	public	int	**getLastColumn** ()	
	1	public	int	**getLastRow** ()	
	1	public	int	**getType** ()	
▲	1	public static final	int	INSERT = 1	
		protected	int	**lastColumn**	
		protected	int	**lastRow**	
		protected	int	**type**	
▲	1	public static final	int	UPDATE = 0	

JTableHeader   javax.swing.table

```
      Object                                                              ε931
  ○   └java.awt.Component¹ ------------------ java.awt.image.ImageObserver⁴, java.awt.MenuContainer,
                                              java.io.Serializable ͻ
          └java.awt.Container²
1.2  ○       └javax.swing.JComponent³
1.2           └JTableHeader -------------------- javax.swing.event.TableColumnModelListener⁵
                                      (java.util.EventListener), javax.accessibility.Accessible
```

	1	*138 inherited members from java.awt.Component not shown*			
	2	*51 inherited members from java.awt.Container not shown*			
	3	*141 inherited members from javax.swing.JComponent not shown*			
	4	*8 inherited members from java.awt.image.ImageObserver not shown*			
	1	public synchronized	void	addMouseListener (*java.awt.event.MouseListener* l)	ε967
	1	public synchronized	void	addMouseMotionListener (*java.awt.event.MouseMotionListener* l)	
					ε937
	5	public	void	**columnAdded** (javax.swing.event.TableColumnModelEvent e)	ε966
		public	int	**columnAtPoint** (java.awt.Point point)	
	5	public	void	**columnMarginChanged** (javax.swing.event.ChangeEvent e)	ε966
		protected	*TableColumnModel*	**columnModel**	
	5	public	void	**columnMoved** (javax.swing.event.TableColumnModelEvent e)	ε966
	5	public	void	**columnRemoved** (javax.swing.event.TableColumnModelEvent e)	
					ε966

Class *Interface* —extends - - -implements ○ abstract ● final △ static ▲ static final ✳ constructor x x—inherited x **x**—declared **x x**—overridden
εn—examples of usage ͻ—has subclass package—see other volume

	5	public	void	**columnSelectionChanged** (javax.swing.event.ListSelectionEvent e)	ε966
		protected	TableColumnModel	**createDefaultColumnModel** ()	
1.3		protected	TableCellRenderer	**createDefaultRenderer** ()	
		protected transient		**draggedColumn**	
			TableColumn		
		protected transient	int	**draggedDistance**	
	3	public	**javax.accessibility**	**getAccessibleContext** ()	
			.AccessibleContext		
	1	public	java.awt.Color	getBackground ()	ε933,934
		public	TableColumnModel	**getColumnModel** ()	ε933
1.3		public	TableCellRenderer	**getDefaultRenderer** ()	ε950
		public	TableColumn	**getDraggedColumn** ()	
		public	int	**getDraggedDistance** ()	
	1	public	java.awt.Font	getFont ()	ε933,934
	1	public	java.awt.Color	getForeground ()	ε933,934
		public	java.awt.Rectangle	**getHeaderRect** (int column)	ε967
		public	boolean	**getReorderingAllowed** ()	
		public	boolean	**getResizingAllowed** ()	
		public	TableColumn	**getResizingColumn** ()	
		public	javax.swing.JTable	**getTable** ()	ε937,967
	3	public	**String**	getToolTipText (java.awt.event.MouseEvent event)	
		public	javax	**getUI** ()	
			.swing.plaf.TableHeaderUI		
	3	public	**String**	getUIClassID ()	
		public	boolean	**getUpdateTableInRealTime** ()	
		protected	void	**initializeLocalVars** ()	
**		public		**JTableHeader** ()	
**		public		**JTableHeader** (TableColumnModel cm)	
	3	protected	**String**	paramString ()	
		protected	boolean	**reorderingAllowed**	
		public	void	**resizeAndRepaint** ()	ε932
		protected	boolean	**resizingAllowed**	
		protected transient		**resizingColumn**	
			TableColumn		
		public	void	**setColumnModel** (TableColumnModel columnModel)	
1.3		public	void	**setDefaultRenderer** (TableCellRenderer defaultRenderer)	
		public	void	**setDraggedColumn** (TableColumn aColumn)	
		public	void	**setDraggedDistance** (int distance)	
		public	void	**setReorderingAllowed** (boolean reorderingAllowed)	ε924
		public	void	**setResizingAllowed** (boolean resizingAllowed)	ε925
		public	void	**setResizingColumn** (TableColumn aColumn)	
		public	void	**setTable** (javax.swing.JTable table)	
	3	public	void	setToolTipText (String text)	ε937
		public	void	**setUI** (javax.swing.plaf.TableHeaderUI ui)	
		public	void	**setUpdateTableInRealTime** (boolean flag)	
		protected	javax.swing.JTable	**table**	
		protected	boolean	**updateTableInRealTime**	
	3	public	**void**	**updateUI** ()	

JTextArea				javax.swing

ε861

Object
  └─java.awt.Component[1] - - - - - - - - - - - - - - - - - - - java.awt.image.ImageObserver[5], java.awt.MenuContainer,
                                                                   java.io.Serializable

    └─java.awt.Container[2]

1.2   └─JComponent[3]

1.2   └─javax.swing.text.JTextComponent[4] - - - - Scrollable, javax.accessibility.Accessible

1.2   └─JTextArea

1 *139 inherited members from java.awt.Component not shown*
2 *51 inherited members from java.awt.Container not shown*
3 *134 inherited members from JComponent not shown*
4 *65 inherited members from javax.swing.text.JTextComponent not shown*
5 *8 inherited members from java.awt.image.ImageObserver not shown*

		public	void	**append** (String str)	ε983
		protected		**createDefaultModel** ()	
			javax.swing.text.Document		
	4	public	**javax.accessibility**	**getAccessibleContext** ()	
			.AccessibleContext		
1.3 ●	3	public final	ActionMap	getActionMap ()	ε858,861,986,1002,1034
		public	int	**getColumns** ()	

JTextArea

	protected . . . . int	**getColumnWidth** ()	
	4	public	getDocument ()	ε984,1006,1034,968,969
		. . *javax.swing.text.Document*	
1.3 ●	3	public final . . . . InputMap	getInputMap ()	ε858,1002,1034
1.3 ●	3	public final . . . . InputMap	getInputMap (int condition)	ε860,861,863
	4	public	getKeymap ()	ε1001,1005,856,862
		. . . . *javax.swing.text.Keymap*	
		public . . . . int	**getLineCount** ()	
		public . . . . int	**getLineEndOffset** (int line) throws javax.swing.text.BadLocationException	
		public . . . . int	**getLineOfOffset** (int offset) throws javax.swing.text.BadLocationException	
		public . . . . int	**getLineStartOffset** (int line) throws javax.swing.text.BadLocationException	
		public . . . . boolean	**getLineWrap** ()	
	4	public . . . . **java.awt.Dimension**	**getPreferredScrollableViewportSize** ()	ε949
	3	public . . . . **java.awt.Dimension**	**getPreferredSize** ()	
		protected . . . . int	**getRowHeight** ()	
		public . . . . int	**getRows** ()	
	4	public . . . . boolean	**getScrollableTracksViewportWidth** ()	
	4	public . . . . int	**getScrollableUnitIncrement** (java.awt.Rectangle visibleRect, int orientation, int direction)	
		public . . . . int	**getTabSize** ()	ε985
	4	public . . . . String	getText (int offs, int len) throws javax.swing.text.BadLocationException	
				ε984,968,990,998
	3	public . . . . **String**	**getUIClassID** ()	
		public . . . . boolean	**getWrapStyleWord** ()	
		public . . . . void	**insert** (String str, int pos)	ε983
*		public	**JTextArea** ()	ε733,820,821,822,841
*		public	**JTextArea** (String text)	ε968,983,984
*		public	**JTextArea** (*javax.swing.text.Document* doc)	
*		public	**JTextArea** (int rows, int columns)	
*		public	**JTextArea** (String text, int rows, int columns)	
*		public	**JTextArea** (*javax.swing.text.Document* doc, String text, int rows, int columns)	
	4	protected . . . . **String**	**paramString** ()	
		public . . . . void	**replaceRange** (String str, int start, int end)	ε983
1.3 ●	3	public final . . . . void	setActionMap (ActionMap am)	ε861
		public . . . . void	**setColumns** (int columns)	ε988
	4	public . . . . void	setEditable (boolean b)	ε988,788,886,994
	3	public . . . . **void**	**setFont** (java.awt.Font f)	
1.3 ●	3	public final . . . . void	setInputMap (int condition, InputMap map)	ε861,863
		public . . . . void	**setLineWrap** (boolean wrap)	ε987
		public . . . . void	**setRows** (int rows)	ε988
		public . . . . void	**setTabSize** (int size)	ε985
		public . . . . void	**setWrapStyleWord** (boolean word)	ε987

JTextComponent

javax.swing.text

Object   ε861

○ └ java.awt.Component [1] - - - - - - - - - - - - - - - - - - - *java.awt.image.ImageObserver* [4], *java.awt.MenuContainer*, *java.io.Serializable*

　　└ java.awt.Container [2]

1.2 ○ 　　　└ javax.swing.JComponent [3]

1.2 ○ 　　　　└ JTextComponent - - - - - - - - - - - - - - - *javax.swing.Scrollable* [5], *javax.accessibility.Accessible*

1	*139 inherited members from java.awt.Component not shown*	
2	*51 inherited members from java.awt.Container not shown*	
3	*141 inherited members from javax.swing.JComponent not shown*	
4	*8 inherited members from java.awt.image.ImageObserver not shown*	

	public . . . . void	**addCaretListener** (*javax.swing.event.CaretListener* listener)	ε1015
1	public . . . . **void**	**addInputMethodListener** (*java.awt.event.InputMethodListener* l)	
△	public static . . . . *Keymap*	**addKeymap** (String nm, *Keymap* parent)	
	public . . . . void	**copy** ()	
	public . . . . void	**cut** ()	
▲	public static final . . . . String	**DEFAULT_KEYMAP** = "default"	
	protected . . . . void	**fireCaretUpdate** (javax.swing.event.CaretEvent e)	
▲	public static final . . . . String	**FOCUS_ACCELERATOR_KEY** = "focusAcceleratorKey"	
	3	public . . . . **javax.accessibility**	**getAccessibleContext** ()
		.AccessibleContext	
	public . . . . . *javax.swing.Action[]*	**getActions** ()	
	public . . . . *Caret*	**getCaret** ()	
	public . . . . java.awt.Color	**getCaretColor** ()	ε999

Class   *Interface*   —extends   - - -implements   ○ abstract   ● final   △ static   ▲ static final   ✳ constructor   x x—inherited   x **x**—declared   **x x**—overridden
ε*n*—examples of usage   ↲—has subclass   package—see other volume

1.4	public	javax₂ .swing.event.CaretListener[]	**getCaretListeners** ()	
	public	int	**getCaretPosition** ()	ε972,998,1002,1003,1004
	public	java.awt.Color	**getDisabledTextColor** ()	
	public	*Document*	**getDocument** ()	ε968,969,970,971,972
1.4	public	boolean	**getDragEnabled** ()	
	public	char	**getFocusAccelerator** ()	
	public	*Highlighter*	**getHighlighter** ()	ε1006
1	public	***java.awt.im₂ .InputMethodRequests***	**getInputMethodRequests** ()	
	public	*Keymap*	**getKeymap** ()	ε1001,856,862
△	public static	*Keymap*	**getKeymap** (String nm)	
	public	java.awt.Insets	**getMargin** ()	
1.4	public	NavigationFilter	**getNavigationFilter** ()	
5	public	java.awt.Dimension	**getPreferredScrollableViewportSize** ()	ε949
5	public	int	**getScrollableBlockIncrement** (java.awt.Rectangle visibleRect, int orientation, int direction)	
5	public	boolean	**getScrollableTracksViewportHeight** ()	
5	public	boolean	**getScrollableTracksViewportWidth** ()	
5	public	int	**getScrollableUnitIncrement** (java.awt.Rectangle visibleRect, int orientation, int direction)	
	public	String	**getSelectedText** ()	ε1000,1002
	public	java.awt.Color	**getSelectedTextColor** ()	
	public	java.awt.Color	**getSelectionColor** ()	
	public	int	**getSelectionEnd** ()	ε1002
	public	int	**getSelectionStart** ()	ε972,1002
	public	String	**getText** ()	ε968,618
	public	String	**getText** (int offs, int len) throws BadLocationException	ε968,998
3	public	**String**	**getToolTipText** (java.awt.event.MouseEvent event)	
	public	javax.swing.plaf.TextUI	**getUI** ()	ε978
	public	boolean	**isEditable** ()	
*	public		**JTextComponent** ()	
△	public static	void	**loadKeymap** (*Keymap* map, JTextComponent.KeyBinding[] bindings, *javax.swing.Action[]* actions)	
	public	java.awt.Rectangle	**modelToView** (int pos) throws BadLocationException	
	public	void	**moveCaretPosition** (int pos)	ε998,1002
3	protected	**String**	**paramString** ()	
	public	void	**paste** ()	
1	protected	**void**	**processInputMethodEvent** (java.awt.event.InputMethodEvent e)	
	public	void	**read** (java.io.Reader in, Object desc) throws java.io.IOException	
	public	void	**removeCaretListener** (*javax.swing.event.CaretListener* listener)	
△	public static	*Keymap*	**removeKeymap** (String nm)	
3	public	**void**	**removeNotify** ()	
	public	void	**replaceSelection** (String content)	ε1000,1002
3	public	void	requestFocus ()	ε618
	public	void	**select** (int selectionStart, int selectionEnd)	ε1000,1002
	public	void	**selectAll** ()	
	public	void	**setCaret** (*Caret* c)	
	public	void	**setCaretColor** (java.awt.Color c)	ε998
	public	void	**setCaretPosition** (int position)	
1	public	**void**	**setComponentOrientation** (java.awt.ComponentOrientation o)	
	public	void	**setDisabledTextColor** (java.awt.Color c)	
	public	void	**setDocument** (*Document* doc)	ε975,977
1.4	public	void	**setDragEnabled** (boolean b)	ε976
	public	void	**setEditable** (boolean b)	ε788,886,988,994
	public	void	**setFocusAccelerator** (char aKey)	
	public	void	**setHighlighter** (*Highlighter* h)	
	public	void	**setKeymap** (*Keymap* map)	
	public	void	**setMargin** (java.awt.Insets m)	ε790
1.4	public	void	**setNavigationFilter** (NavigationFilter filter)	
	public	void	**setSelectedTextColor** (java.awt.Color c)	ε1000
	public	void	**setSelectionColor** (java.awt.Color c)	ε1000
	public	void	**setSelectionEnd** (int selectionEnd)	ε972,1000,618
	public	void	**setSelectionStart** (int selectionStart)	ε972,1000,618
	public	void	**setText** (String t)	ε1016
	public	void	**setUI** (javax.swing.plaf.TextUI ui)	
3	public	**void**	**updateUI** ()	
	public	int	**viewToModel** (java.awt.Point pt)	
	public	void	**write** (java.io.Writer out) throws java.io.IOException	

J

Classes

JTextComponent.KeyBinding

		javax.swing.text

Object
   └JTextComponent.KeyBinding   ε870

1.2

	public....................String	**actionName**
	public.. javax.swing.KeyStroke	**key**
✳	public..........................	**JTextComponent.KeyBinding** (javax.swing.KeyStroke key, String actionName)

JTextField

		javax.swing

Object   ε861
   └java.awt.Component [1] - - - - - - - - - - - - - - - - - *java.awt.image.ImageObserver* [5], *java.awt.MenuContainer*,
                                                     java.io.Serializable
     └java.awt.Container [2]

1.2 O   └JComponent [3]
1.2 O   └javax.swing.text.JTextComponent [4] - - - - *Scrollable, javax.accessibility.Accessible*
1.2   └JTextField - *SwingConstants* [6]

	1	*137 inherited members from java.awt.Component not shown*
	2	*51 inherited members from java.awt.Container not shown*
	3	*135 inherited members from JComponent not shown*
	4	*68 inherited members from javax.swing.text.JTextComponent not shown*
	6	*16 inherited members from SwingConstants not shown*
	5	*8 inherited members from java.awt.image.ImageObserver not shown*

		public synchronized ......void	**addActionListener** (*java.awt.event.ActionListener* l)	ε979
	1	public synchronized ......void	addFocusListener (*java.awt.event.FocusListener* l)	ε618
	1	public synchronized ......void	addKeyListener (*java.awt.event.KeyListener* l)	ε1004
▲	6	public static final.............int	CENTER = 0	ε981,739,740,747,748
1.3		protected ....void	**configurePropertiesFromAction** (*Action* a)	
1.3		protected .... *java.beans*	**createActionPropertyChangeListener** (*Action* a)	
		.*PropertyChangeListener*		
		protected	**createDefaultModel** ()	
		.. *javax.swing.text.Document*		
		protected ....void	**fireActionPerformed** ()	
	4	public.... **javax.accessibility**	**getAccessibleContext** ()	
		.AccessibleContext		
1.3		public................... *Action*	**getAction** ()	
1.4		public synchronized ..... *java*	**getActionListeners** ()	
		.*awt.event.ActionListener[]*		
1.3 ●	3	public final .... ActionMap	getActionMap ()	ε857,1003,612
	4	public.... ***Action[]***	**getActions** ()	
		public.....................int	**getColumns** ()	
		protected ....int	**getColumnWidth** ()	
		public.....................int	**getHorizontalAlignment** ()	
		public... *BoundedRangeModel*	**getHorizontalVisibility** ()	
1.3 ●	3	public final ....InputMap	getInputMap (int condition)	ε857,1003,612
	3	public.... **java.awt.Dimension**	**getPreferredSize** ()	
		public.....................int	**getScrollOffset** ()	
	4	public....................String	getText ()	ε953,957,968,1006,618
	3	public.............. **String**	**getUIClassID** ()	
	3	public.............. **boolean**	**isValidateRoot** ()	
✳		public..............	**JTextField** ()	ε857,953,957,975,1003
✳		public..............	**JTextField** (int columns)	ε741,1003,1004,618
✳		public..............	**JTextField** (String text)	ε970,979,981
✳		public..............	**JTextField** (String text, int columns)	ε979
✳		public..............	**JTextField** (*javax.swing.text.Document* doc, String text, int columns)	
▲	6	public static final.............int	LEFT = 2	ε981,739,747,748,834
▲		public static final........String	**notifyAction** = "notify-field-accept"	
	4	protected .... **String**	**paramString** ()	
		public...................void	**postActionEvent** ()	
		public synchronized ......void	**removeActionListener** (*java.awt.event.ActionListener* l)	
▲	6	public static final.............int	RIGHT = 4	ε981,739,747,748
	3	public.............. **void**	scrollRectToVisible (java.awt.Rectangle r)	
1.3		public...................void	**setAction** (*Action* a)	ε957
		public...................void	**setActionCommand** (String command)	
		public...................void	**setColumns** (int columns)	
	4	public.............. **void**	setDocument (*javax.swing.text.Document* doc)	ε975,977,1008
	3	public.............. **void**	setFont (java.awt.Font f)	

Class   *Interface*   —extends   - - -implements   O abstract   ● final   △ static   ▲ static final   ✳ constructor   x x—inherited   x **x**—declared   **x x**—overridden
εn—examples of usage   —has subclass   package—see other volume

J

public......................void	**setHorizontalAlignment** (int alignment)		ε981
public......................void	**setScrollOffset** (int scrollOffset)		
4 public......................void	setText (String t)		ε953,957,1016

    ε861

      Object

○   └java.awt.Component[1] - - - - - - - - - - - - - - - - - - *java.awt.image.ImageObserver*[6], *java.awt.MenuContainer*,
                                  java.io.Serializable⌐

       └java.awt.Container[2]

1.2 ○   └JComponent[3]

1.2 ○   └javax.swing.text.JTextComponent[4] - - - - *Scrollable*, *javax.accessibility.Accessible*

1.2   └JEditorPane[5]

1.2   └JTextPane

---

   1   *138 inherited members from java.awt.Component not shown*
   2   *51 inherited members from java.awt.Container not shown*
   3   *140 inherited members from JComponent not shown*
   4   *64 inherited members from javax.swing.text.JTextComponent not shown*
   5   *24 inherited members from JEditorPane not shown*
   6   *8 inherited members from java.awt.image.ImageObserver not shown*

1	public synchronized ....void	addMouseListener (*java.awt.event.MouseListener* l)	ε1011
	public....*javax.swing.text.Style*	**addStyle** (String nm, *javax.swing.text.Style* parent)	ε1007,1008,1011,1012,1013
5	protected...................... **javax.swing.text.EditorKit**	**createDefaultEditorKit** ()	
	public............................ . *javax.swing.text.AttributeSet*	**getCharacterAttributes** ()	
4	public............................ .. *javax.swing.text.Document*	getDocument ()	ε989,990,991,992,1006
	public............. *javax.swing*⌐ .*text.MutableAttributeSet*	**getInputAttributes** ()	
	public....*javax.swing.text.Style*	**getLogicalStyle** ()	ε993,1012
	public............................ . *javax.swing.text.AttributeSet*	**getParagraphAttributes** ()	
	public....*javax.swing.text.Style*	**getStyle** (String nm)	ε1007,1008,1009,1011,1013
	public............. *javax*⌐ .*swing.text.StyledDocument*	**getStyledDocument** ()	ε1007,1013
●	protected final........... *javax*⌐ .*swing.text.StyledEditorKit*	**getStyledEditorKit** ()	
5	public...................String	getText ()	ε1006,953,957,968,618
4	public...................String	getText (int offs, int len) throws javax.swing.text.BadLocationException	ε990,968,984,998
5	public................... **String**	**getUIClassID** ()	
	public......................void	**insertComponent** (java.awt.Component c)	
	public......................void	**insertIcon** (*Icon* g)	
*	public......................	**JTextPane** ()	ε969,978,989,990,991
*	public......................	**JTextPane** (*javax.swing.text.StyledDocument* doc)	
5	protected .... **String**	**paramString** ()	
	public......................void	**removeStyle** (String nm)	
5	public...................... **void**	**replaceSelection** (String content)	ε1000,1002
	public......................void	**setCharacterAttributes** (*javax.swing.text.AttributeSet* attr, boolean replace)	ε1011,1013
4	public...................... **void**	**setDocument** (*javax.swing.text.Document* doc)	ε1008,975,977
● 5	public final .... **void**	**setEditorKit** (javax.swing.text.EditorKit kit)	
	public......................void	**setLogicalStyle** (*javax.swing.text.Style* s)	ε993,1011,1012
	public......................void	**setParagraphAttributes** (*javax.swing.text.AttributeSet* attr, boolean replace)	ε1011,1012,1013
	public......................void	**setStyledDocument** (*javax.swing.text.StyledDocument* doc)	

    ε45

      Object

○   └java.awt.Component[1] - - - - - - - - - - - - - - - - - - *java.awt.image.ImageObserver*[5], *java.awt.MenuContainer*,
                                    java.io.Serializable⌐

       └java.awt.Container[2]

1.2 ○   └JComponent[3]

1.2 ○   └AbstractButton[4] - - - - - - - - - - - - - - - - - - *java.awt.ItemSelectable*⌐, *SwingConstants*[6]

1.2   └JToggleButton⌐ - - - - - - - - - - - - - - - - - - *javax.accessibility.Accessible*

J

Classes

JToggleButton

	1	*142 inherited members from java.awt.Component not shown*			
	2	*51 inherited members from java.awt.Container not shown*			
	3	*141 inherited members from JComponent not shown*			
	4	*103 inherited members from AbstractButton not shown*			
	6	*19 inherited members from SwingConstants not shown*			
	5	*8 inherited members from java.awt.image.ImageObserver not shown*			
	3	public....	**javax.accessibility** **.AccessibleContext**	**getAccessibleContext** ()	
	3	public..................	**String**	**getUIClassID** ()	
*		public......................		**JToggleButton** ()	
*		public......................		**JToggleButton** (String text)	
1.3 *		public......................		**JToggleButton** (*Action* a)	ε816
*		public......................		**JToggleButton** (*Icon* icon)	
*		public......................		**JToggleButton** (String text, *Icon* icon)	
*		public......................		**JToggleButton** (String text, boolean selected)	
*		public......................		**JToggleButton** (*Icon* icon, boolean selected)	
*		public......................		**JToggleButton** (String text, *Icon* icon, boolean selected)	
	4	protected	**String**	**paramString** ()	
	4	public......................	void	setMargin (java.awt.Insets m)	ε816
	4	public......................	void	setText (String text)	ε816,744,745,754
	4	public......................	**void**	**updateUI** ()	

JToggleButton.ToggleButtonModel javax.swing

Object
1.2	└ DefaultButtonModel [1] - *ButtonModel (java.awt.ItemSelectable)*, *java.io.Serializable*
1.2	└ JToggleButton.ToggleButtonModel

	1	*38 inherited members from DefaultButtonModel not shown*		
	1	public.................	**boolean**	**isSelected** ()
	1	public.................	**void**	**setPressed** (boolean b)
	1	public.................	**void**	**setSelected** (boolean b)
*		public........................		**JToggleButton.ToggleButtonModel** ()

JToolBar javax.swing

Object
○	└ java.awt.Component [1] - - - - - - - - - - - - - - - - - - - *java.awt.image.ImageObserver* [4], *java.awt.MenuContainer*,
	java.io.Serializable
	└ java.awt.Container [2]
1.2 ○	└ JComponent [3]
1.2	└ JToolBar - *SwingConstants* [5], *javax.accessibility.Accessible*

	1	*143 inherited members from java.awt.Component not shown*			
	2	*48 inherited members from java.awt.Container not shown*			
	3	*141 inherited members from JComponent not shown*			
	5	*17 inherited members from SwingConstants not shown*			
	4	*8 inherited members from java.awt.image.ImageObserver not shown*			
	2	public.... java.awt.Component		add (java.awt.Component comp)	ε816,571,575,581,590
		public.................. JButton		**add** (*Action* a)	
	2	protected	**void**	**addImpl** (java.awt.Component comp, Object constraints, int index)	
	3	public synchronized .... void		addPropertyChangeListener (*java.beans.PropertyChangeListener* listener)	ε817
		public........................void		**addSeparator** ()	
		public........................void		**addSeparator** (java.awt.Dimension size)	
		protected......... *java.beans. .PropertyChangeListener*		**createActionChangeListener** (JButton b)	
1.3		protected .... JButton		**createActionComponent** (*Action* a)	
	3	public.... **javax.accessibility** **.AccessibleContext**		**getAccessibleContext** ()	
		public.... java.awt.Component		**getComponentAtIndex** (int i)	
		public........................int		**getComponentIndex** (java.awt.Component c)	
		public......... java.awt.Insets		**getMargin** ()	
		public........................int		**getOrientation** ()	ε816
		public........................ *... javax.swing.plaf.ToolBarUI*		**getUI** ()	
	3	public..................	**String**	**getUIClassID** ()	
▲	5	public static final ....int		HORIZONTAL = 0	ε817

Class *Interface* —extends - - -implements ○ abstract ● final △ static ▲ static final * constructor x x—inherited x **x**—declared **x x**—overridden
ε*n*—examples of usage ⌣—has subclass package—see other volume

652

	public	boolean	**isBorderPainted** ()	
	public	boolean	**isFloatable** ()	ε818
1.4	public	boolean	**isRollover** ()	ε819
✳	public		**JToolBar** ()	ε816,817,818,819
✳	public		**JToolBar** (int orientation)	
1.3 ✳	public		**JToolBar** (String name)	
1.3 ✳	public		**JToolBar** (String name, int orientation)	ε816
3	protected	**void**	**paintBorder** (java.awt.Graphics g)	
3	protected	**String**	**paramString** ()	
	public	void	**setBorderPainted** (boolean b)	
	public	void	**setFloatable** (boolean b)	ε818
2	public	**void**	**setLayout** (*java.awt.LayoutManager* mgr)	ε613,622,624,625,627
	public	void	**setMargin** (java.awt.Insets m)	
	public	void	**setOrientation** (int o)	
1.4	public	void	**setRollover** (boolean rollover)	ε819
	public	void	**setUI** (javax.swing.plaf.ToolBarUI ui)	
3	public	**void**	**updateUI** ()	
▲ 5	public static final	int	VERTICAL = 1	ε816,794,796,801

J

```
Object
 └java.awt.Component 1 ------------------- java.awt.image.ImageObserver 5, java.awt.MenuContainer,
                                           java.io.Serializable
    └java.awt.Container 2
       └JComponent 3
          └JSeparator 4 ------------------- SwingConstants 6, javax.accessibility.Accessible
             └JToolBar.Separator
```

- 1.2 ○
- 1.2
- 1.2

1	*143 inherited members from java.awt.Component not shown*		
2	*51 inherited members from java.awt.Container not shown*		
3	*140 inherited members from JComponent not shown*		
6	*19 inherited members from SwingConstants not shown*		
5	*8 inherited members from java.awt.image.ImageObserver not shown*		
4	public	javax.accessibility.AccessibleContext	getAccessibleContext ()
3	public	**java.awt.Dimension**	**getMaximumSize** ()
3	public	**java.awt.Dimension**	**getMinimumSize** ()
4	public	int	getOrientation ()
3	public	**java.awt.Dimension**	**getPreferredSize** ()
	public	java.awt.Dimension	**getSeparatorSize** ()
4	public	javax.swing.plaf.SeparatorUI	getUI ()
4	public	**String**	**getUIClassID** ()
4	protected	String	paramString ()
✳	public		**JToolBar.Separator** ()
✳	public		**JToolBar.Separator** (java.awt.Dimension size)
4	public	void	setOrientation (int orientation)
	public	void	**setSeparatorSize** (java.awt.Dimension size)
4	public	void	setUI (javax.swing.plaf.SeparatorUI ui)
4	public	void	updateUI ()

Classes

```
Object
 └java.awt.Component 1 ------------------- java.awt.image.ImageObserver 4, java.awt.MenuContainer,
                                           java.io.Serializable
    └java.awt.Container 2
       └JComponent 3
          └JToolTip ------------------- javax.accessibility.Accessible
```

- 1.2 ○
- 1.2

1	*143 inherited members from java.awt.Component not shown*		
2	*51 inherited members from java.awt.Container not shown*		
3	*143 inherited members from JComponent not shown*		
4	*8 inherited members from java.awt.image.ImageObserver not shown*		
3	public	**javax.accessibility.AccessibleContext**	**getAccessibleContext** ()
	public	JComponent	**getComponent** ()
	public	String	**getTipText** ()
	public	javax.swing.plaf.ToolTipUI	**getUI** ()

JToolTip

3	public	**String**	**getUIClassID** ()
∗	public		**JToolTip** ()
3	protected	**String**	**paramString** ()
	public	void	**setComponent** (JComponent c)
	public	void	**setTipText** (String tipText)
3	public	**void**	**updateUI** ()

JTree   javax.swing

Object
 └─*java.awt.Component*[1] - - - - - - - - - - - - - - - - - - *java.awt.image.ImageObserver* [4], *java.awt.MenuContainer*,
                                                                   java.io.Serializable
     └─*java.awt.Container*[2]
1.2 ○   └─*JComponent*[3]
1.2   └─JTree - *Scrollable* [5], *javax.accessibility.Accessible*

	1	*143 inherited members from java.awt.Component not shown*		
	3	*142 inherited members from JComponent not shown*		
	4	*8 inherited members from java.awt.image.ImageObserver not shown*		
	2	public.... java.awt.Component	add (java.awt.Component comp)	ε571,575,581,590,610
	2	public void	add (java.awt.Component comp, Object constraints)	ε733,559,571,601,694
	2	public.... java.awt.Component	add (java.awt.Component comp, int index)	
	2	public.... java.awt.Component	add (String name, java.awt.Component comp)	
	2	public void	add (java.awt.Component comp, Object constraints, int index)	
	2	public synchronized void	addContainerListener (*java.awt.event.ContainerListener* l)	ε573
	2	protected void	addImpl (java.awt.Component comp, Object constraints, int index)	
		public void	**addSelectionInterval** (int index0, int index1)	
		public void	**addSelectionPath** (javax.swing.tree.TreePath path)	
		public void	**addSelectionPaths** (javax.swing.tree.TreePath[] paths)	
		public void	**addSelectionRow** (int row)	
		public void	**addSelectionRows** (int[] rows)	
		public void	**addTreeExpansionListener** (*javax.swing.event.TreeExpansionListener* tel)	
				ε1032
		public void	**addTreeSelectionListener** (*javax.swing.event.TreeSelectionListener* tsl)	
				ε1033
		public void	**addTreeWillExpandListener** (*javax.swing.event.TreeWillExpandListener* tel)	
				ε1032
1.3 ▲		public static final String	**ANCHOR_SELECTION_PATH_PROPERTY** = "anchorSelectionPath"	
1.4	2	public void	applyComponentOrientation (java.awt.ComponentOrientation o)	
1.4	2	public boolean	areFocusTraversalKeysSet (int id)	
		public void	**cancelEditing** ()	
▲		public static final String	**CELL_EDITOR_PROPERTY** = "cellEditor"	
▲		public static final String	**CELL_RENDERER_PROPERTY** = "cellRenderer"	
		protected transient *javax* [2]	**cellEditor**	
		.swing.tree.TreeCellEditor		
		protected transient *javax* [2]	**cellRenderer**	
		.swing.tree.TreeCellRenderer		
		public void	**clearSelection** ()	
		protected void	**clearToggledPaths** ()	
		public void	**collapsePath** (javax.swing.tree.TreePath path)	ε1029
		public void	**collapseRow** (int row)	
		public String	**convertValueToText** (Object value, boolean selected, boolean expanded, boolean leaf, int row, boolean hasFocus)	
△		protected static	**createTreeModel** (Object value)	
		.. javax.swing.tree.TreeModel		
		protected *javax.swing* [2]	**createTreeModelListener** ()	
		.event.TreeModelListener		
	2	public void	doLayout ()	
		protected boolean	**editable**	
▲		public static final String	**EDITABLE_PROPERTY** = "editable"	
		public void	**expandPath** (javax.swing.tree.TreePath path)	ε1029
		public void	**expandRow** (int row)	
1.3 ▲		public static final String	**EXPANDS_SELECTED_PATHS_PROPERTY** = "expandsSelectedPaths"	
	2	public.... java.awt.Component	findComponentAt (java.awt.Point p)	
	2	public.... java.awt.Component	findComponentAt (int x, int y)	
		public void	**fireTreeCollapsed** (javax.swing.tree.TreePath path)	
		public void	**fireTreeExpanded** (javax.swing.tree.TreePath path)	
		public void	**fireTreeWillCollapse** (javax.swing.tree.TreePath path) throws javax.swing.tree.ExpandVetoException	

Class   *Interface*   —extends   - - -implements   ○ abstract   ● final   △ static   ▲ static final   ∗ constructor   x x—inherited   x **x**—declared   **x x**—overridden
ε*n*—examples of usage   ˌ—has subclass   package—see other volume

JTree

	public	boolean	**getShowsRootHandles** ()
1.3	public	int	**getToggleClickCount** ()
3	public	**String**	**getToolTipText** (java.awt.event.MouseEvent event)
1.4	public	*javax.swing.event₂ .TreeExpansionListener[]*	**getTreeExpansionListeners** ()
1.4	public	*javax.swing.event₂ .TreeSelectionListener[]*	**getTreeSelectionListeners** ()
1.4	public	*javax.swing.event.- TreeWillExpandListener[]*	**getTreeWillExpandListeners** ()
	public	javax.swing.plaf.TreeUI	**getUI** ()
3	public	**String**	**getUIClassID** ()
	public	int	**getVisibleRowCount** ()
	public	boolean	**hasBeenExpanded** (javax.swing.tree.TreePath path)
2	public	void	invalidate ()
▲	public static final	String	**INVOKES_STOP_CELL_EDITING_PROPERTY** = "invokesStopCellEditing"
	protected	boolean	**invokesStopCellEditing**
2	public	boolean	isAncestorOf (java.awt.Component c)
	public	boolean	**isCollapsed** (int row)
	public	boolean	**isCollapsed** (javax.swing.tree.TreePath path)
	public	boolean	**isEditable** ()
	public	boolean	**isEditing** ()
	public	boolean	**isExpanded** (int row)
	public	boolean	**isExpanded** (javax.swing.tree.TreePath path)
	public	boolean	**isFixedRowHeight** ()
1.4 2	public	boolean	isFocusCycleRoot ()
1.4 2	public	boolean	isFocusCycleRoot (java.awt.Container container)
1.4 2	public	boolean	isFocusTraversalPolicySet ()
	public	boolean	**isLargeModel** ()
	public	boolean	**isPathEditable** (javax.swing.tree.TreePath path)
	public	boolean	**isPathSelected** (javax.swing.tree.TreePath path)
	public	boolean	**isRootVisible** ()
	public	boolean	**isRowSelected** (int row)
	public	boolean	**isSelectionEmpty** ()
	public	boolean	**isVisible** (javax.swing.tree.TreePath path) — ε1023,1028
*	public		**JTree** () — ε1020,1021,1022,1023,1024
*	public		**JTree** (Object[] value)
*	public		**JTree** (java.util.Hashtable value)
*	public		**JTree** (java.util.Vector value)
*	public		**JTree** (*javax.swing.tree.TreeModel* newModel)
*	public		**JTree** (*javax.swing.tree.TreeNode* root) — ε1019
*	public		**JTree** (*javax.swing.tree.TreeNode* root, boolean asksAllowsChildren)
▲	public static final	String	**LARGE_MODEL_PROPERTY** = "largeModel"
	protected	boolean	**largeModel**
1.3 ▲	public static final	String	**LEAD_SELECTION_PATH_PROPERTY** = "leadSelectionPath"
2	public	void	list (java.io.PrintStream out, int indent)
2	public	void	list (java.io.PrintWriter out, int indent)
	public	void	**makeVisible** (javax.swing.tree.TreePath path)
2	public	void	paintComponents (java.awt.Graphics g)
3	protected	**String**	**paramString** ()
2	public	void	printComponents (java.awt.Graphics g)
2	protected	void	processContainerEvent (java.awt.event.ContainerEvent e)
2	protected	void	processEvent (java.awt.AWTEvent e)
2	public	void	remove (int index) — ε831,832
2	public	void	remove (java.awt.Component comp) — ε831
2	public	void	removeAll () — ε831
2	public synchronized	void	removeContainerListener (*java.awt.event.ContainerListener* l)
1.3	protected	boolean	**removeDescendantSelectedPaths** (javax.swing.tree.TreePath path, boolean includePath)
	protected	void	**removeDescendantToggledPaths** (*java.util.Enumeration* toRemove)
	public	void	**removeSelectionInterval** (int index0, int index1)
	public	void	**removeSelectionPath** (javax.swing.tree.TreePath path)
	public	void	**removeSelectionPaths** (javax.swing.tree.TreePath[] paths)
	public	void	**removeSelectionRow** (int row)
	public	void	**removeSelectionRows** (int[] rows)
	public	void	**removeTreeExpansionListener** (*javax.swing.event.TreeExpansionListener* tel)
	public	void	**removeTreeSelectionListener** (*javax.swing.event.TreeSelectionListener* tsl)
	public	void	**removeTreeWillExpandListener** (*javax.swing.event.TreeWillExpandListener* tel)
▲	public static final	String	**ROOT_VISIBLE_PROPERTY** = "rootVisible"
	protected	boolean	**rootVisible**
▲	public static final	String	**ROW_HEIGHT_PROPERTY** = "rowHeight"
	protected	int	**rowHeight**

---

	public	void	**scrollPathToVisible** (javax.swing.tree.TreePath path)	
	public	void	**scrollRowToVisible** (int row)	
▲	public static final	String	**SCROLLS_ON_EXPAND_PROPERTY** = "scrollsOnExpand"	
	protected	boolean	**scrollsOnExpand**	
▲	public static final	String	**SELECTION_MODEL_PROPERTY** = "selectionModel"	
	protected transient	*javax.swingↄ* *.tree.TreeSelectionModel*	**selectionModel**	
	protected transient	JTreeↄ *.TreeSelectionRedirector*	**selectionRedirector**	
1.3	public	void	**setAnchorSelectionPath** (javax.swing.tree.TreePath newPath)	
	public	void	**setCellEditor** (*javax.swing.tree.TreeCellEditor* cellEditor)	
	public	void	**setCellRenderer** (*javax.swing.tree.TreeCellRenderer* x)	
1.4	public	void	**setDragEnabled** (boolean b)	
	public	void	**setEditable** (boolean flag)	
	protected	void	**setExpandedState** (javax.swing.tree.TreePath path, boolean state)	ε1030
1.3	public	void	**setExpandsSelectedPaths** (boolean newValue)	
1.4 2	public	void	setFocusCycleRoot (boolean focusCycleRoot)	
1.4 2	public	void	setFocusTraversalKeys (int id, *java.util*.Set keystrokes)	ε610
1.4 2	public	void	setFocusTraversalPolicy (java.awt.FocusTraversalPolicy policy)	
	public	void	**setInvokesStopCellEditing** (boolean newValue)	
	public	void	**setLargeModel** (boolean newValue)	
2	public	void	setLayout (*java.awt.LayoutManager* mgr)	ε613,622,624,625,627
1.3	public	void	**setLeadSelectionPath** (javax.swing.tree.TreePath newPath)	
	public	void	**setModel** (*javax.swing.tree.TreeModel* newModel)	
	public	void	**setRootVisible** (boolean rootVisible)	
	public	void	**setRowHeight** (int rowHeight)	ε1031
	public	void	**setScrollsOnExpand** (boolean newValue)	
	public	void	**setSelectionInterval** (int index0, int index1)	
	public	void	**setSelectionModel** (*javax.swing.tree.TreeSelectionModel* selectionModel)	
	public	void	**setSelectionPath** (javax.swing.tree.TreePath path)	
	public	void	**setSelectionPaths** (javax.swing.tree.TreePath[] paths)	
	public	void	**setSelectionRow** (int row)	
	public	void	**setSelectionRows** (int[] rows)	
	public	void	**setShowsRootHandles** (boolean newValue)	
1.3	public	void	**setToggleClickCount** (int clickCount)	
	public	void	**setUI** (javax.swing.plaf.TreeUI ui)	
	public	void	**setVisibleRowCount** (int newCount)	
▲	public static final	String	**SHOWS_ROOT_HANDLES_PROPERTY** = "showsRootHandles"	
	protected	boolean	**showsRootHandles**	
	public	void	**startEditingAtPath** (javax.swing.tree.TreePath path)	
	public	boolean	**stopEditing** ()	
1.3 ▲	public static final	String	**TOGGLE_CLICK_COUNT_PROPERTY** = "toggleClickCount"	
	protected	int	**toggleClickCount**	
1.4 2	public	void	transferFocusBackward ()	
1.4 2	public	void	transferFocusDownCycle ()	
▲	public static final	String	**TREE_MODEL_PROPERTY** = "model"	
	public	void	**treeDidChange** ()	
	protected transient	*.. javax.swing.tree. TreeModel*	**treeModel**	
	protected transient	*javax.swingↄ* *.event. TreeModelListener*	**treeModelListener**	
3	public	**void**	**updateUI** ()	
2	public	void	validate ()	ε601,674,928,936
2	protected	void	validateTree ()	
▲	public static final	String	**VISIBLE_ROW_COUNT_PROPERTY** = "visibleRowCount"	
	protected	int	**visibleRowCount**	

JTree.DynamicUtilTreeNode `javax.swing`

```
Object
1.2  └javax.swing.tree.DefaultMutableTreeNode 1 -- Cloneable., javax.swing.tree.MutableTreeNode
                                 (javax.swing.tree. TreeNode), java.io.Serializable.
1.2        └JTree.DynamicUtilTreeNode
```

1	*52 inherited members from javax.swing.tree.DefaultMutableTreeNode not shown*		
1	public.. *java.util.Enumeration*	**children** ()	ε1023,1024,1028,1029
	protected	Object	**childValue**
△	public static	void	**createChildren** (javax.swing.tree.DefaultMutableTreeNode parent, Object children)
*	public		**JTree.DynamicUtilTreeNode** (Object value, Object children)

JTree.DynamicUtilTreeNode

1	public	**getChildAt** (int index)	
	. *javax.swing.tree.TreeNode*		
1	public int	**getChildCount** ()	ε1023,1024,1025,1028,1029
	protected boolean	**hasChildren**	
1	public **boolean**	**isLeaf** ()	
	protected void	**loadChildren** ()	
	protected boolean	**loadedChildren**	

JTree.EmptySelectionModel   protected   javax.swing

Object
1.2 └javax.swing.tree.DefaultTreeSelectionModel[1] - *Cloneable*, *java.io.Serializable*, *javax.swing.tree*
                                            . *TreeSelectionModel* [2]
1.2   └JTree.EmptySelectionModel

	1	*47 inherited members from javax.swing.tree.DefaultTreeSelectionModel not shown*		
	1	public void	**addSelectionPaths** (javax.swing.tree.TreePath[] paths)	
▲	2	public static final int	CONTIGUOUS_TREE_SELECTION = 2	ε1022
▲	2	public static final int	DISCONTIGUOUS_TREE_SELECTION = 4	ε1022
✳		protected	**JTree.EmptySelectionModel** ()	
	1	public void	**removeSelectionPaths** (javax.swing.tree.TreePath[] paths)	
	1	public void	**setSelectionPaths** (javax.swing.tree.TreePath[] pPaths)	
▲		protected static final	**sharedInstance**	
		. JTree.EmptySelectionModel		
△		public static	**sharedInstance** ()	
		. JTree.EmptySelectionModel		
▲	2	public static final int	SINGLE_TREE_SELECTION = 1	ε1022

JTree.TreeModelHandler   protected   javax.swing

Object
1.2 └JTree.TreeModelHandler - - - - - - - - - - - - - - - - - *javax.swing.event.TreeModelListener* [1] (*java.util.EventListener*)

✳	protected	**JTree.TreeModelHandler** ()	
1	public void	**treeNodesChanged** (javax.swing.event.TreeModelEvent e)	
1	public void	**treeNodesInserted** (javax.swing.event.TreeModelEvent e)	
1	public void	**treeNodesRemoved** (javax.swing.event.TreeModelEvent e)	
1	public void	**treeStructureChanged** (javax.swing.event.TreeModelEvent e)	

JTree.TreeSelectionRedirector   protected   javax.swing

Object
1.2 └JTree.TreeSelectionRedirector - - - - - - - - - - - - *java.io.Serializable*, *javax.swing.event.TreeSelectionListener* [1]
                                                    (*java.util.EventListener*)

✳	protected	**JTree.TreeSelectionRedirector** ()	
1	public void	**valueChanged** (javax.swing.event.TreeSelectionEvent e)	ε1033

JViewport   javax.swing

Object
○ └java.awt.Component[1] - - - - - - - - - - - - - - - - - - *java.awt.image.ImageObserver* [4], *java.awt.MenuContainer*,
                                                    java.io.Serializable
      └java.awt.Container[2]
1.2 ○   └JComponent[3]
1.2   └JViewport - *javax.accessibility.Accessible*

	1	*143 inherited members from java.awt.Component not shown*	
	2	*49 inherited members from java.awt.Container not shown*	
	3	*134 inherited members from JComponent not shown*	
	4	*8 inherited members from java.awt.image.ImageObserver not shown*	
		public void	**addChangeListener** (*javax.swing.event.ChangeListener* l)
D	2	protected **void**	**addImpl** (java.awt.Component child, Object constraints, int index)
		protected boolean	**backingStore**
1.3 ▲		public static final int	**BACKINGSTORE_SCROLL_MODE** = 2

Class   *Interface* —extends - - -implements ○ abstract ● final △ static ▲ static final ✳ constructor x x—inherited x **x**—declared **x x**—overridden
ε*n*—examples of usage —has subclass package—see other volume

	protected transient............ .... java.awt.Image	**backingStoreImage**		
1.3 ▲	public static final ....int	**BLIT_SCROLL_MODE** = 1		
	protected .... boolean	**computeBlit** (int dx, int dy, java.awt.Point blitFrom, java.awt.Point blitTo, java.awt.Dimension blitSize, java.awt.Rectangle blitPaint)		
	protected .... *java.awt.LayoutManager*	**createLayoutManager** ()		
	protected ....JViewport.ViewListener	**createViewListener** ()		
3	protected .... **void**	**firePropertyChange** (String propertyName, Object oldValue, Object newValue)		
	protected ....void	**fireStateChanged** ()		
3	public.... **javax.accessibility** ₂ **.AccessibleContext**	**getAccessibleContext** ()		
1.4	public...... *javax.swing* ₂ *.event.ChangeListener[]*	**getChangeListeners** ()		
	public......java.awt.Dimension	**getExtentSize** ()		*ε*946
● 3	public final .... **java.awt.Insets**	**getInsets** ()		
● 3	public final .... **java.awt.Insets**	**getInsets** (java.awt.Insets insets)		
1.3	public........................int	**getScrollMode** ()		
1.3	public.......................... ..javax.swing.plaf.ViewportUI	**getUI** ()		
3	public.................... **String**	**getUIClassID** ()		
	public.... java.awt.Component	**getView** ()		
	public........... java.awt.Point	**getViewPosition** ()		*ε*946,947
	public...... java.awt.Rectangle	**getViewRect** ()		*ε*948
	public......java.awt.Dimension	**getViewSize** ()		
D	public................. boolean	**isBackingStoreEnabled** ()		
3	public.................... **boolean**	**isOptimizedDrawingEnabled** ()		
	protected .... boolean	**isViewSizeSet**		
✳	public..........................	**JViewport** ()		
	protected .... java.awt.Point	**lastPaintPosition**		
3	public.................... **void**	**paint** (java.awt.Graphics g)		
3	protected .... **String**	**paramString** ()		
2	public.................... **void**	**remove** (java.awt.Component child)		*ε*831
	public.....................void	**removeChangeListener** (*javax.swing.event.ChangeListener* l)		
3	public.................... **void**	**repaint** (long tm, int x, int y, int w, int h)		
3	public.................... **void**	**reshape** (int x, int y, int w, int h)		
3	public.................... **void**	**scrollRectToVisible** (java.awt.Rectangle contentRect)		*ε*947,948
	protected .... boolean	**scrollUnderway**		
D	public.....................void	**setBackingStoreEnabled** (boolean enabled)		
● 3	public final .... **void**	**setBorder** (*javax.swing.border.Border* border)		
	public.....................void	**setExtentSize** (java.awt.Dimension newExtent)		
1.3	public.....................void	**setScrollMode** (int mode)		
1.3	public.....................void	**setUI** (javax.swing.plaf.ViewportUI ui)		
	public.....................void	**setView** (java.awt.Component view)		
	public.....................void	**setViewPosition** (java.awt.Point p)		
	public.....................void	**setViewSize** (java.awt.Dimension newSize)		
1.3 ▲	public static final ....int	**SIMPLE_SCROLL_MODE** = 0		
	public......java.awt.Dimension	**toViewCoordinates** (java.awt.Dimension size)		
	public........... java.awt.Point	**toViewCoordinates** (java.awt.Point p)		
3	public.................... **void**	**updateUI** ()		

J

Classes

JViewport.ViewListener		protected	javax.swing

Object
└java.awt.event.ComponentAdapter[1] - - - - - - - - *java.awt.event.ComponentListener* (*java.util.EventListener*)
     1.1 ○
     1.2 └JViewport.ViewListener - - - - - - - - - - - - - - - - *java.io.Serializable*

1	public.....................void	componentHidden (java.awt.event.ComponentEvent e)		*ε*570
1	public.....................void	componentMoved (java.awt.event.ComponentEvent e)		*ε*570
1	public.................... **void**	**componentResized** (java.awt.event.ComponentEvent e)		*ε*570
1	public.....................void	componentShown (java.awt.event.ComponentEvent e)		*ε*570
✳	protected	**JViewport.ViewListener** ()		

JWindow

JWindow			javax.swing

```
          Object                                                    ε606,618,733,953,988
  ○       └java.awt.Component¹ ------------------ java.awt.image.ImageObserver⁴, java.awt.MenuContainer,
                                                          java.io.Serializable ⌄
             └java.awt.Container²
                └java.awt.Window³ ----------------- javax.accessibility.Accessible
  1.2          └JWindow -------------------- RootPaneContainer⁵
```

	1		*166 inherited members from java.awt.Component not shown*		
	2		*54 inherited members from java.awt.Container not shown*		
	3		*51 inherited members from java.awt.Window not shown*		
	4		*8 inherited members from java.awt.image.ImageObserver not shown*		
		protected .. javax.accessibility ⌄ .AccessibleContext	**accessibleContext**		
	2	protected .... **void**	**addImpl** (java.awt.Component comp, Object constraints, int index)		
		protected .... JRootPane	**createRootPane** ()		
	3	public.... **javax.accessibility** ⌄ **.AccessibleContext**	**getAccessibleContext** ()		
	5	public.......java.awt.Container	**getContentPane** ()	ε732,733,816,841,887
	5	public.... java.awt.Component	**getGlassPane** ()	
	5	public........... JLayeredPane	**getLayeredPane** ()	
	5	public........... JRootPane	**getRootPane** ()	
		protected .... boolean	**isRootPaneCheckingEnabled** ()	
✳		public...................	**JWindow** ()	
✳		public......................	**JWindow** (java.awt.Frame owner)	
1.3 ✳		public......................	**JWindow** (java.awt.GraphicsConfiguration gc)	
✳		public......................	**JWindow** (java.awt.Window owner)	
1.3 ✳		public......................	**JWindow** (java.awt.Window owner, java.awt.GraphicsConfiguration gc)	
	2	protected .... **String**	**paramString** ()	
	2	public................... **void**	**remove** (java.awt.Component comp)	ε831
		protected .... JRootPane	**rootPane**	
		protected .... boolean	**rootPaneCheckingEnabled**	
	5	public...................void	**setContentPane** (java.awt.Container contentPane)	
	5	public...................void	**setGlassPane** (java.awt.Component glassPane)	
	5	public...................void	**setLayeredPane** (JLayeredPane layeredPane)	
	2	public................... **void**	**setLayout** (*java.awt.LayoutManager* manager)	ε613,622,624,625,627
		protected ....void	**setRootPane** (JRootPane root)	
		protected ....void	**setRootPaneCheckingEnabled** (boolean enabled)	
	2	public................... **void**	**update** (java.awt.Graphics g)	
		protected ....void	**windowInit** ()	

Kernel		java.awt.image

```
          Object¹
  1.2     └Kernel ------------------------------- Cloneable ⌄
```

	1	public....................**Object**	**clone** ()	
●		public final ....int	**getHeight** ()	
●		public final ....float[]	**getKernelData** (float[] data)	
●		public final ....int	**getWidth** ()	
●		public final ....int	**getXOrigin** ()	
●		public final ....int	**getYOrigin** ()	
✳		public..........................	**Kernel** (int width, int height, float[] data)	ε677,678,679

KeyAdapter		java.awt.event

```
          Object
  1.1 ○    └KeyAdapter ⌄ ------------------------- KeyListener¹ (java.util.EventListener)
```

✳		public..........................	**KeyAdapter** ()	ε643
	1	public.....................void	**keyPressed** (KeyEvent e)	ε643,645,762,763
	1	public.....................void	**keyReleased** (KeyEvent e)	
	1	public.....................void	**keyTyped** (KeyEvent e)	ε1004

Class   *Interface*   —extends   - - -implements   ○ abstract   ● final   △ static   ▲ static final   ✳ constructor   x x—inherited   x **x**—declared   **x x**—overridden
ε*n*—examples of usage   ⌄—has subclass   package—see other volume

KeyboardFocusManager			java.awt

Object

1.4 ○　└KeyboardFocusManager　- - - - - - - - - - - - - - - - - *KeyEventDispatcher* [1], *KeyEventPostProcessor* [2]

```
        public......................void  addKeyEventDispatcher (KeyEventDispatcher dispatcher)              ε636
        public......................void  addKeyEventPostProcessor (KeyEventPostProcessor processor)
        public......................void  addPropertyChangeListener (java.beans.PropertyChangeListener listener)
                                                                                                     ε609
        public......................void  addPropertyChangeListener (String propertyName,
                                           java.beans.PropertyChangeListener listener)
        public......................void  addVetoableChangeListener (java.beans.VetoableChangeListener listener)
                                                                                                     ε609
        public......................void  addVetoableChangeListener (String propertyName,
                                           java.beans.VetoableChangeListener listener)
   ▲    public static final .............int  BACKWARD_TRAVERSAL_KEYS = 1                               ε611
        public......................void  clearGlobalFocusOwner ()                                      ε619
   ○    protected abstract .........void  dequeueKeyEvents (long after, Component untilFocused)
   ○    protected abstract .........void  discardKeyEvents (Component comp)
   ○    public abstract ........ boolean  dispatchEvent (AWTEvent e)
   ○  1 public abstract ........ boolean  dispatchKeyEvent (java.awt.event.KeyEvent e)                  ε636
   ▲    public static final .............int  DOWN_CYCLE_TRAVERSAL_KEYS = 3
   ●    public final .................void  downFocusCycle ()
   ○    public abstract ............void  downFocusCycle (Container aContainer)
   ○    protected abstract .........void  enqueueKeyEvents (long after, Component untilFocused)
        protected ..................void  firePropertyChange (String propertyName, Object oldValue, Object newValue)
        protected ..................void  fireVetoableChange (String propertyName, Object oldValue, Object newValue)
                                           throws java.beans.PropertyVetoException
   ●    public final .................void  focusNextComponent ()
   ○    public abstract ............void  focusNextComponent (Component aComponent)
   ●    public final .................void  focusPreviousComponent ()
   ○    public abstract ............void  focusPreviousComponent (Component aComponent)
   ▲    public static final .............int  FORWARD_TRAVERSAL_KEYS = 0                                 ε610,611
        public................ Window  getActiveWindow ()
        public.............. Container  getCurrentFocusCycleRoot ()
   △    public static ..................  getCurrentKeyboardFocusManager ()                             ε606,609,611,615,619
        .....KeyboardFocusManager
        public............... java.util.Set  getDefaultFocusTraversalKeys (int id)                        ε611
        public synchronized .......  getDefaultFocusTraversalPolicy ()
        ........ FocusTraversalPolicy
        public............... Window  getFocusedWindow ()                                                ε606
        public.............. Component  getFocusOwner ()                                                  ε606,615
        protected ............ Window  getGlobalActiveWindow () throws SecurityException
        protected ........... Container  getGlobalCurrentFocusCycleRoot () throws SecurityException
        protected .......... Window  getGlobalFocusedWindow () throws SecurityException
        protected .......... Component  getGlobalFocusOwner () throws SecurityException
        protected .......... Component  getGlobalPermanentFocusOwner () throws SecurityException
        protected synchronized .......  getKeyEventDispatchers ()
        ................. java.util.List
        protected .......... java.util.List  getKeyEventPostProcessors ()
        public.............. Component  getPermanentFocusOwner ()
        public synchronized ..........  getPropertyChangeListeners ()
        ................. java.beans.-
        PropertyChangeListener[]
        public synchronized ..........  getPropertyChangeListeners (String propertyName)
        ................. java.beans.-
        PropertyChangeListener[]
        public synchronized ..........  getVetoableChangeListeners ()
        ................. java.beans.-
        VetoableChangeListener[]
        public synchronized ..........  getVetoableChangeListeners (String propertyName)
        ................. java.beans.-
        VetoableChangeListener[]
   *    public......................  KeyboardFocusManager ()
   ○  2 public abstract ........ boolean  postProcessKeyEvent (java.awt.event.KeyEvent e)
   ○    public abstract ............void  processKeyEvent (Component focusedComponent, java.awt.event.KeyEvent e)
   ●    public final .................void  redispatchEvent (Component target, AWTEvent e)
        public......................void  removeKeyEventDispatcher (KeyEventDispatcher dispatcher)
        public......................void  removeKeyEventPostProcessor (KeyEventPostProcessor processor)
        public......................void  removePropertyChangeListener (java.beans.PropertyChangeListener listener)
        public......................void  removePropertyChangeListener (String propertyName,
                                           java.beans.PropertyChangeListener listener)
```

K

Classes

KeyboardFocusManager

	public	void	**removeVetoableChangeListener** (*java.beans.VetoableChangeListener* listener)
	public	void	**removeVetoableChangeListener** (String propertyName, *java.beans.VetoableChangeListener* listener)
△	public static synchronized	void	**setCurrentKeyboardFocusManager** (KeyboardFocusManager newManager) throws SecurityException
	public	void	**setDefaultFocusTraversalKeys** (int id, *java.util.Set* keystrokes) ε611
	public	void	**setDefaultFocusTraversalPolicy** (FocusTraversalPolicy defaultPolicy)
	protected	void	**setGlobalActiveWindow** (Window activeWindow)
	public	void	**setGlobalCurrentFocusCycleRoot** (Container newFocusCycleRoot)
	protected	void	**setGlobalFocusedWindow** (Window focusedWindow)
	protected	void	**setGlobalFocusOwner** (Component focusOwner)
	protected	void	**setGlobalPermanentFocusOwner** (Component permanentFocusOwner)
▲	public static final	int	**UP_CYCLE_TRAVERSAL_KEYS** = 2
●	public final	void	**upFocusCycle** ()
○	public abstract	void	**upFocusCycle** (Component aComponent)

KeyEvent java.awt.event

	Object	ε643,640,641,649,566
1.1	└ java.util.EventObject [1] - *java.io.Serializable*	
1.1 ○	└ java.awt.AWTEvent [2]	
1.1	└ ComponentEvent [3]	
1.1 ○	└ InputEvent [4]	
1.1	└ KeyEvent	

▲	2	public static final	long	ACTION_EVENT_MASK = 128	
▲	2	public static final	long	ADJUSTMENT_EVENT_MASK = 256	
1.4 ▲	4	public static final	int	ALT_DOWN_MASK = 512	ε859
1.4 ▲	4	public static final	int	ALT_GRAPH_DOWN_MASK = 8192	
1.2 ▲	4	public static final	int	ALT_GRAPH_MASK = 32	
▲	4	public static final	int	ALT_MASK = 8	ε859
1.4 ▲	4	public static final	int	BUTTON1_DOWN_MASK = 1024	ε859
▲	4	public static final	int	BUTTON1_MASK = 16	ε646,635,859
1.4 ▲	4	public static final	int	BUTTON2_DOWN_MASK = 2048	ε859
▲	4	public static final	int	BUTTON2_MASK = 8	ε646,859
1.4 ▲	4	public static final	int	BUTTON3_DOWN_MASK = 4096	ε859
▲	4	public static final	int	BUTTON3_MASK = 4	ε646,859
▲		public static final	char	**CHAR_UNDEFINED** = '?'	ε762
▲	2	public static final	long	COMPONENT_EVENT_MASK = 1	
▲	3	public static final	int	COMPONENT_FIRST = 100	
▲	3	public static final	int	COMPONENT_HIDDEN = 103	
▲	3	public static final	int	COMPONENT_LAST = 103	
▲	3	public static final	int	COMPONENT_MOVED = 100	
▲	3	public static final	int	COMPONENT_RESIZED = 101	
▲	3	public static final	int	COMPONENT_SHOWN = 102	
	4	public	void	consume ()	ε1004
	2	protected	boolean	consumed	
▲	2	public static final	long	CONTAINER_EVENT_MASK = 2	
1.4 ▲	4	public static final	int	CTRL_DOWN_MASK = 128	ε859
▲	4	public static final	int	CTRL_MASK = 2	ε859
▲	2	public static final	long	FOCUS_EVENT_MASK = 4	
	3	public	java.awt.Component	getComponent ()	ε810,813,1011
	2	public	int	getID ()	ε636,1001
		public	char	**getKeyChar** ()	ε645,636,762,763,1004
		public	int	**getKeyCode** ()	ε645
1.4		public	int	**getKeyLocation** ()	
△		public static	String	**getKeyModifiersText** (int modifiers)	
△		public static	String	**getKeyText** (int keyCode)	
	4	public	int	getModifiers ()	ε646
1.4	4	public	int	getModifiersEx ()	
1.4 △	4	public static	String	getModifiersExText (int modifiers)	
	1	public	Object	getSource ()	ε762,763,1003,1004,644
	4	public	long	getWhen ()	
1.3 ▲	2	public static final	long	HIERARCHY_BOUNDS_EVENT_MASK = 65536	
1.3 ▲	2	public static final	long	HIERARCHY_EVENT_MASK = 32768	
	2	protected	int	id	
1.2 ▲	2	public static final	long	INPUT_METHOD_EVENT_MASK = 2048	
1.3 ▲	2	public static final	long	INVOCATION_EVENT_MASK = 16384	
		public	boolean	**isActionKey** ()	

Class *Interface* —extends - - -implements ○ abstract ● final △ static ▲ static final ✳ constructor x x—inherited x **x**—declared **x x**—overridden
ε*n*—examples of usage ↲—has subclass package—see other volume

		4	public	boolean	isAltDown ()	
1.2		4	public	boolean	isAltGraphDown ()	
		4	public	boolean	isConsumed ()	
		4	public	boolean	isControlDown ()	
		4	public	boolean	isMetaDown ()	
		4	public	boolean	isShiftDown ()	
	▲	2	public static final	long	ITEM_EVENT_MASK = 512	
	▲	2	public static final	long	KEY_EVENT_MASK = 8	
	▲		public static final	int	**KEY_FIRST** = 400	
	▲		public static final	int	**KEY_LAST** = 402	
1.4	▲		public static final	int	**KEY_LOCATION_LEFT** = 2	
1.4	▲		public static final	int	**KEY_LOCATION_NUMPAD** = 4	
1.4	▲		public static final	int	**KEY_LOCATION_RIGHT** = 3	
1.4	▲		public static final	int	**KEY_LOCATION_STANDARD** = 1	
1.4	▲		public static final	int	**KEY_LOCATION_UNKNOWN** = 0	
	▲		public static final	int	**KEY_PRESSED** = 401	ε859
	▲		public static final	int	**KEY_RELEASED** = 402	ε859
	▲		public static final	int	**KEY_TYPED** = 400	ε636,859,862
	✳		public		**KeyEvent** (java.awt.Component source, int id, long when, int modifiers, int keyCode)	
	✳		public		**KeyEvent** (java.awt.Component source, int id, long when, int modifiers, int keyCode, char keyChar)	
1.4	✳		public		**KeyEvent** (java.awt.Component source, int id, long when, int modifiers, int keyCode, char keyChar, int keyLocation)	
1.4	▲	4	public static final	int	META_DOWN_MASK = 256	ε859
	▲	4	public static final	int	META_MASK = 4	ε859
	▲	2	public static final	long	MOUSE_EVENT_MASK = 16	
	▲	2	public static final	long	MOUSE_MOTION_EVENT_MASK = 32	
1.4	▲	2	public static final	long	MOUSE_WHEEL_EVENT_MASK = 131072	
1.3	▲	2	public static final	long	PAINT_EVENT_MASK = 8192	
		3	public	String	**paramString** ()	
	▲	2	public static final	int	RESERVED_ID_MAX = 1999	
			public	void	**setKeyChar** (char keyChar)	ε636
			public	void	**setKeyCode** (int keyCode)	
			public	void	**setModifiers** (int modifiers)	
1.4		2	public	void	setSource (Object newSource)	
1.4	▲	4	public static final	int	SHIFT_DOWN_MASK = 64	ε859
	▲	4	public static final	int	SHIFT_MASK = 1	ε693,859
		1	protected transient	Object	source	
	▲	2	public static final	long	TEXT_EVENT_MASK = 1024	
		2	public	String	toString ()	
	▲		public static final	int	**VK_0** = 48	ε859
	▲		public static final	int	**VK_1** = 49	
	▲		public static final	int	**VK_2** = 50	
	▲		public static final	int	**VK_3** = 51	
	▲		public static final	int	**VK_4** = 52	
	▲		public static final	int	**VK_5** = 53	
	▲		public static final	int	**VK_6** = 54	
	▲		public static final	int	**VK_7** = 55	
	▲		public static final	int	**VK_8** = 56	
	▲		public static final	int	**VK_9** = 57	ε859
	▲		public static final	int	**VK_A** = 65	ε635,855,859
	▲		public static final	int	**VK_ACCEPT** = 30	ε859
	▲		public static final	int	**VK_ADD** = 107	ε859
1.2	▲		public static final	int	**VK_AGAIN** = 65481	ε859
1.2	▲		public static final	int	**VK_ALL_CANDIDATES** = 256	ε859
1.2	▲		public static final	int	**VK_ALPHANUMERIC** = 240	ε859
	▲		public static final	int	**VK_ALT** = 18	ε859
1.2	▲		public static final	int	**VK_ALT_GRAPH** = 65406	ε859
1.2	▲		public static final	int	**VK_AMPERSAND** = 150	ε859
1.2	▲		public static final	int	**VK_ASTERISK** = 151	ε859
1.2	▲		public static final	int	**VK_AT** = 512	ε859
	▲		public static final	int	**VK_B** = 66	
	▲		public static final	int	**VK_BACK_QUOTE** = 192	ε859
	▲		public static final	int	**VK_BACK_SLASH** = 92	ε859
	▲		public static final	int	**VK_BACK_SPACE** = 8	ε859
1.2	▲		public static final	int	**VK_BRACELEFT** = 161	ε859
1.2	▲		public static final	int	**VK_BRACERIGHT** = 162	ε859
	▲		public static final	int	**VK_C** = 67	
	▲		public static final	int	**VK_CANCEL** = 3	ε859
	▲		public static final	int	**VK_CAPS_LOCK** = 20	ε859
1.2	▲		public static final	int	**VK_CIRCUMFLEX** = 514	ε859
	▲		public static final	int	**VK_CLEAR** = 12	ε859
	▲		public static final	int	**VK_CLOSE_BRACKET** = 93	ε859
1.2	▲		public static final	int	**VK_CODE_INPUT** = 258	ε859

KeyEvent

1.2 ▲	public static final .... int	**VK_COLON** = 513		ε859
▲	public static final .... int	**VK_COMMA** = 44		ε859
1.2 ▲	public static final .... int	**VK_COMPOSE** = 65312		ε859
▲	public static final .... int	**VK_CONTROL** = 17		ε859
▲	public static final .... int	**VK_CONVERT** = 28		ε859
1.2 ▲	public static final .... int	**VK_COPY** = 65485		ε859
1.2 ▲	public static final .... int	**VK_CUT** = 65489		ε859
▲	public static final .... int	**VK_D** = 68		
1.2 ▲	public static final .... int	**VK_DEAD_ABOVEDOT** = 134		ε859
1.2 ▲	public static final .... int	**VK_DEAD_ABOVERING** = 136		ε859
1.2 ▲	public static final .... int	**VK_DEAD_ACUTE** = 129		ε859
1.2 ▲	public static final .... int	**VK_DEAD_BREVE** = 133		ε859
1.2 ▲	public static final .... int	**VK_DEAD_CARON** = 138		ε859
1.2 ▲	public static final .... int	**VK_DEAD_CEDILLA** = 139		ε859
1.2 ▲	public static final .... int	**VK_DEAD_CIRCUMFLEX** = 130		ε859
1.2 ▲	public static final .... int	**VK_DEAD_DIAERESIS** = 135		ε859
1.2 ▲	public static final .... int	**VK_DEAD_DOUBLEACUTE** = 137		ε859
1.2 ▲	public static final .... int	**VK_DEAD_GRAVE** = 128		ε859
1.2 ▲	public static final .... int	**VK_DEAD_IOTA** = 141		ε859
1.2 ▲	public static final .... int	**VK_DEAD_MACRON** = 132		ε859
1.2 ▲	public static final .... int	**VK_DEAD_OGONEK** = 140		ε859
1.2 ▲	public static final .... int	**VK_DEAD_SEMIVOICED_SOUND** = 143		ε859
1.2 ▲	public static final .... int	**VK_DEAD_TILDE** = 131		ε859
1.2 ▲	public static final .... int	**VK_DEAD_VOICED_SOUND** = 142		ε859
▲	public static final .... int	**VK_DECIMAL** = 110		ε859
▲	public static final .... int	**VK_DELETE** = 127		ε859
▲	public static final .... int	**VK_DIVIDE** = 111		ε859
1.2 ▲	public static final .... int	**VK_DOLLAR** = 515		ε859
▲	public static final .... int	**VK_DOWN** = 40		ε859
▲	public static final .... int	**VK_E** = 69		
▲	public static final .... int	**VK_END** = 35		ε859
▲	public static final .... int	**VK_ENTER** = 10		ε859
▲	public static final .... int	**VK_EQUALS** = 61		ε859
▲	public static final .... int	**VK_ESCAPE** = 27		ε859
1.2 ▲	public static final .... int	**VK_EURO_SIGN** = 516		ε859
1.2 ▲	public static final .... int	**VK_EXCLAMATION_MARK** = 517		ε859
▲	public static final .... int	**VK_F** = 70		
▲	public static final .... int	**VK_F1** = 112		ε859
▲	public static final .... int	**VK_F10** = 121		ε859
▲	public static final .... int	**VK_F11** = 122		ε859
▲	public static final .... int	**VK_F12** = 123		ε859
1.2 ▲	public static final .... int	**VK_F13** = 61440		ε859
1.2 ▲	public static final .... int	**VK_F14** = 61441		ε859
1.2 ▲	public static final .... int	**VK_F15** = 61442		ε859
1.2 ▲	public static final .... int	**VK_F16** = 61443		ε859
1.2 ▲	public static final .... int	**VK_F17** = 61444		ε859
1.2 ▲	public static final .... int	**VK_F18** = 61445		ε859
1.2 ▲	public static final .... int	**VK_F19** = 61446		ε859
▲	public static final .... int	**VK_F2** = 113		ε859
1.2 ▲	public static final .... int	**VK_F20** = 61447		ε859
1.2 ▲	public static final .... int	**VK_F21** = 61448		ε859
1.2 ▲	public static final .... int	**VK_F22** = 61449		ε859
1.2 ▲	public static final .... int	**VK_F23** = 61450		ε859
1.2 ▲	public static final .... int	**VK_F24** = 61451		ε859
▲	public static final .... int	**VK_F3** = 114		ε859
▲	public static final .... int	**VK_F4** = 115		ε859
▲	public static final .... int	**VK_F5** = 116		ε859
▲	public static final .... int	**VK_F6** = 117		ε859
▲	public static final .... int	**VK_F7** = 118		ε859
▲	public static final .... int	**VK_F8** = 119		ε859
▲	public static final .... int	**VK_F9** = 120		ε859
▲	public static final .... int	**VK_FINAL** = 24		ε859
1.2 ▲	public static final .... int	**VK_FIND** = 65488		ε859
1.2 ▲	public static final .... int	**VK_FULL_WIDTH** = 243		ε859
▲	public static final .... int	**VK_G** = 71		
1.2 ▲	public static final .... int	**VK_GREATER** = 160		ε859
▲	public static final .... int	**VK_H** = 72		
1.2 ▲	public static final .... int	**VK_HALF_WIDTH** = 244		ε859
▲	public static final .... int	**VK_HELP** = 156		ε859
1.2 ▲	public static final .... int	**VK_HIRAGANA** = 242		ε859
▲	public static final .... int	**VK_HOME** = 36		ε645,859

K

Class *Interface* —extends - - -implements ○ abstract ● final △ static ▲ static final ✳ constructor x x—inherited x **x**—declared **x x**—overridden
ε*n*—examples of usage ⌐—has subclass package—see other volume

K

Classes

KeyEvent

1.2 ▲	public static final	int	**VK_UNDO** = 65483		ε859
▲	public static final	int	**VK_UP** = 38		ε859
▲	public static final	int	**VK_V** = 86		
▲	public static final	int	**VK_W** = 87		
▲	public static final	int	**VK_X** = 88		
▲	public static final	int	**VK_Y** = 89		
▲	public static final	int	**VK_Z** = 90		ε859
▲ 2	public static final	long	WINDOW_EVENT_MASK = 64		
1.4 ▲ 2	public static final	long	WINDOW_FOCUS_EVENT_MASK = 524288		
1.4 ▲ 2	public static final	long	WINDOW_STATE_EVENT_MASK = 262144		

KeyEventDispatcher			java.awt
1.4	*KeyEventDispatcher*		
	public	boolean	**dispatchKeyEvent** (java.awt.event.KeyEvent e)	ε636

KeyEventPostProcessor			java.awt
1.4	*KeyEventPostProcessor*		
	public	boolean	**postProcessKeyEvent** (java.awt.event.KeyEvent e)	

KeyListener			java.awt.event
1.1	*KeyListener* ——————————— *java.util.EventListener*		ε738,743,745,746,752
	public	void	**keyPressed** (KeyEvent e)	ε643,645,762,763
	public	void	**keyReleased** (KeyEvent e)	
	public	void	**keyTyped** (KeyEvent e)	ε1004

Keymap			javax.swing.text
1.2	*Keymap*		
	public	void	**addActionForKeyStroke** (javax.swing.KeyStroke key, *javax.swing.Action* a)	
	public	*javax.swing.Action*	**getAction** (javax.swing.KeyStroke key)	ε1005
	public	*javax.swing.Action[]*	**getBoundActions** ()	ε856
	public	javax.swing.KeyStroke[]	**getBoundKeyStrokes** ()	ε1005
	public	*javax.swing.Action*	**getDefaultAction** ()	ε1001,1005,856,862
	public	javax.swing.KeyStroke[]	**getKeyStrokesForAction** (*javax.swing.Action* a)	
	public	String	**getName** ()	
	public	*Keymap*	**getResolveParent** ()	ε1001,1005,856,862
	public	boolean	**isLocallyDefined** (javax.swing.KeyStroke key)	ε862
	public	void	**removeBindings** ()	
	public	void	**removeKeyStrokeBinding** (javax.swing.KeyStroke keys)	
	public	void	**setDefaultAction** (*javax.swing.Action* a)	ε1001
	public	void	**setResolveParent** (*Keymap* parent)	

KeyStroke			javax.swing
	Object		ε860
1.4	└java.awt.AWTKeyStroke [1] - - - - - - - - - - - - - - *java.io.Serializable*		
1.2	└KeyStroke		
● 1	public final	boolean	equals (Object anObject)	ε862
1.4 △ 1	public static		getAWTKeyStroke (char keyChar)	
		java.awt.AWTKeyStroke		
1.4 △ 1	public static		getAWTKeyStroke (String s)	
		java.awt.AWTKeyStroke		
1.4 △ 1	public static		getAWTKeyStroke (int keyCode, int modifiers)	
		java.awt.AWTKeyStroke		
1.4 △ 1	public static		getAWTKeyStroke (Character keyChar, int modifiers)	
		java.awt.AWTKeyStroke		
1.4 △ 1	public static		getAWTKeyStroke (int keyCode, int modifiers, boolean onKeyRelease)	
		java.awt.AWTKeyStroke		

Class *Interface* —extends - - -implements ○ abstract ● final △ static ▲ static final ✳ constructor x x—inherited x **x**—declared **x x**—overridden
ε*n*—examples of usage ⌄—has subclass package—see other volume

1.4 △	1	public static	getAWTKeyStrokeForEvent (java.awt.event.KeyEvent anEvent)	
		...... java.awt.AWTKeyStroke		
1.4 ●	1	public final .... char	getKeyChar ()	ε859
1.4 ●	1	public final ....int	getKeyCode ()	ε859
1.4 ●	1	public final ....int	getKeyEventType ()	ε859,862
△		public static .... KeyStroke	**getKeyStroke** (char keyChar)	ε858
△		public static .... KeyStroke	**getKeyStroke** (String s)	ε855,857,858,861,862
D △		public static .... KeyStroke	**getKeyStroke** (char keyChar, boolean onKeyRelease)	
△		public static .... KeyStroke	**getKeyStroke** (int keyCode, int modifiers)	ε693
1.3 △		public static .... KeyStroke	**getKeyStroke** (Character keyChar, int modifiers)	ε862,1003,612
△		public static .... KeyStroke	**getKeyStroke** (int keyCode, int modifiers, boolean onKeyRelease)	
△		public static .... KeyStroke	**getKeyStrokeForEvent** (java.awt.event.KeyEvent anEvent)	
1.4 ●	1	public final ....int	getModifiers ()	ε859
	1	public........................int	hashCode ()	
1.4 ●	1	public final .... boolean	isOnKeyRelease ()	
1.4	1	protected ....Object	readResolve () throws java.io.ObjectStreamException	
1.4 △	1	protected static ....void	registerSubclass (Class subclass)	
	1	public....................String	toString ()	

Label — java.awt

```
Object
 └Component 1 - - - - - - - - - - - - - - - - - - - - - - - - - java.awt.image.ImageObserver 2, MenuContainer,
                                                java.io.Serializable
    └Label - - - - - - - - - - - - - - - - - - - - - - - - - javax.accessibility.Accessible
```

	1	*208 inherited members from Component not shown*		
	2	*8 inherited members from java.awt.image.ImageObserver not shown*		
	1	public..................... **void**	**addNotify** ()	
		public static final ....int	**CENTER** = 1	
1.3	1	public.... **javax.accessibility**	**getAccessibleContext** ()	
		.AccessibleContext		
		public........................int	**getAlignment** ()	
		public.....................String	**getText** ()	
∗		public...........................	**Label** () throws HeadlessException	
∗		public...........................	**Label** (String text) throws HeadlessException	
∗		public...........................	**Label** (String text, int alignment) throws HeadlessException	
▲		public static final ....int	**LEFT** = 0	
	1	protected .... **String**	**paramString** ()	
▲		public static final ....int	**RIGHT** = 2	
		public synchronized ....void	**setAlignment** (int alignment)	
		public.....................void	**setText** (String text)	

LabelPeer — java.awt.peer

```
LabelPeer—————————————————————ComponentPeer 1
```

	1	*42 inherited members from ComponentPeer not shown*	
		public.....................void	**setAlignment** (int alignment)
		public.....................void	**setText** (String label)

LabelUI — javax.swing.plaf

```
Object
 └ComponentUI 1
    └LabelUI
```

1.2 ○			
1.2 ○			
	1	*11 inherited members from ComponentUI not shown*	
∗		public........................	**LabelUI** ()

LabelView — javax.swing.text

```
Object
 └View 1 - - - - - - - - - - - - - - - - - - - - - - - - - - javax.swing.SwingConstants 3
    └GlyphView 2 - - - - - - - - - - - - - - - - - - - - - - TabableView, Cloneable
       └LabelView
```

1.2 ○		
1.3		
1.2		
	1	*38 inherited members from View not shown*
	3	*19 inherited members from javax.swing.SwingConstants not shown*

LabelView

LayeredHighlighter
javax.swing.text

LayeredHighlighter.LayerPainter
javax.swing.text

Class *Interface* —extends - - -implements ○ abstract ● final △ static ▲ static final ✳ constructor x x—inherited x **x**—declared **x x**—overridden
ε*n*—examples of usage ⌐—has subclass package—see other volume

668

○   public abstract *java.awt.Shape* **paintLayer** (java.awt.Graphics g, int p0, int p1, *java.awt.Shape* viewBounds,
                JTextComponent editor, View view)

LayoutFocusTraversalPolicy	javax.swing

Object
1.4 ○   └java.awt.FocusTraversalPolicy[1]
1.4 ○   └InternalFrameFocusTraversalPolicy[2]
1.4   └SortingFocusTraversalPolicy[3]
1.4   └LayoutFocusTraversalPolicy - - - - - - - - *java.io.Serializable*

3	protected ....**boolean**	**accept** (java.awt.Component aComponent)	
3	protected *java.util.Comparator*	getComparator ()	
3	public... **java.awt.Component**	**getComponentAfter** (java.awt.Container focusCycleRoot, java.awt.Component aComponent)	ε615
3	public... **java.awt.Component**	**getComponentBefore** (java.awt.Container focusCycleRoot, java.awt.Component aComponent)	ε615
3	public.... java.awt.Component	getDefaultComponent (java.awt.Container focusCycleRoot)	ε615
3	public... **java.awt.Component**	**getFirstComponent** (java.awt.Container focusCycleRoot)	
3	public................. boolean	getImplicitDownCycleTraversal ()	
1	public.... java.awt.Component	getInitialComponent (java.awt.Window window)	
2	public.... java.awt.Component	getInitialComponent (JInternalFrame frame)	
3	public... **java.awt.Component**	**getLastComponent** (java.awt.Container focusCycleRoot)	
*	public.........................	**LayoutFocusTraversalPolicy** ()	
3	protected ....void	setComparator (*java.util.Comparator* comparator)	
3	public......................void	setImplicitDownCycleTraversal (boolean implicitDownCycleTraversal)	

LayoutManager	java.awt

LayoutManager

public......................void	**addLayoutComponent** (String name, Component comp)	
public......................void	**layoutContainer** (Container parent)	ε624,625
public................Dimension	**minimumLayoutSize** (Container parent)	
public................Dimension	**preferredLayoutSize** (Container parent)	
public......................void	**removeLayoutComponent** (Component comp)	

LayoutManager2	java.awt

1.1   *LayoutManager2* ——————————— *LayoutManager*[1]

	public......................void	**addLayoutComponent** (Component comp, Object constraints)	
1	public......................void	addLayoutComponent (String name, Component comp)	
	public.......................float	**getLayoutAlignmentX** (Container target)	
	public.......................float	**getLayoutAlignmentY** (Container target)	
	public......................void	**invalidateLayout** (Container target)	
1	public......................void	layoutContainer (Container parent)	ε624,625
	public................Dimension	**maximumLayoutSize** (Container target)	
1	public................Dimension	minimumLayoutSize (Container parent)	
1	public................Dimension	preferredLayoutSize (Container parent)	
1	public......................void	removeLayoutComponent (Component comp)	

LayoutQueue	javax.swing.text

Object
1.3   └LayoutQueue

	public synchronized ....void	**addTask** (*Runnable* task)
△	public static ..... LayoutQueue	**getDefaultQueue** ()
*	public.........................	**LayoutQueue** ()
△	public static ....void	**setDefaultQueue** (LayoutQueue q)
	protected synchronized	**waitForWork** ()
	.....................*Runnable*	

LightweightPeer

LightweightPeer			java.awt.peer

LightweightPeer————————————————*ComponentPeer*¸ ¹

- -
>   *1 42 inherited members from ComponentPeer not shown*

Line	javax.sound.sampled

1.3 *Line*¸

public......................void	**addLineListener** (*LineListener* listener)	*ε*731
public......................void	**close** ()	
public................. Control	**getControl** (Control.Type control)	*ε*730
public.................Control[]	**getControls** ()	
public.................Line.Info	**getLineInfo** ()	
public................. boolean	**isControlSupported** (Control.Type control)	
public................. boolean	**isOpen** ()	
public......................void	**open** () throws LineUnavailableException	
public......................void	**removeLineListener** (*LineListener* listener)	

Line.Info	javax.sound.sampled

Object¹
1.3 └Line.Info¸

	public.................... Class	**getLineClass** ()
*	public........................	**Line.Info** (Class lineClass)
	public................ boolean	**matches** (Line.Info info)
1	public.................. **String**	**toString** ()

Line2D	java.awt.geom

Object¹
1.2 ○ └Line2D¸ - *java.awt.Shape*², Cloneable¸

	1	public...................**Object**	**clone** ()
	2	public................. boolean	**contains** (Point2D p)
	2	public................. boolean	**contains** (Rectangle2D r)
	2	public................. boolean	**contains** (double x, double y)
	2	public................. boolean	**contains** (double x, double y, double w, double h)
	2	public...... java.awt.Rectangle	**getBounds** ()
○	2	public abstract ... Rectangle2D	getBounds2D ()
○		public abstract Point2D	**getP1** ()
○		public abstract Point2D	**getP2** ()
	2	public.............. *PathIterator*	**getPathIterator** (AffineTransform at)
	2	public.............. *PathIterator*	**getPathIterator** (AffineTransform at, double flatness)
○		public abstract ....double	**getX1** ()
○		public abstract ....double	**getX2** ()
○		public abstract ....double	**getY1** ()
○		public abstract ....double	**getY2** ()
	2	public................. boolean	**intersects** (Rectangle2D r)
	2	public................. boolean	**intersects** (double x, double y, double w, double h)
		public................. boolean	**intersectsLine** (Line2D l)
		public................. boolean	**intersectsLine** (double X1, double Y1, double X2, double Y2)
*		protected	**Line2D** ()
△		public static .... boolean	**linesIntersect** (double X1, double Y1, double X2, double Y2, double X3, double Y3, double X4, double Y4)
		public...................double	**ptLineDist** (Point2D pt)
		public...................double	**ptLineDist** (double PX, double PY)
△		public static ....double	**ptLineDist** (double X1, double Y1, double X2, double Y2, double PX, double PY)
		public...................double	**ptLineDistSq** (Point2D pt)
		public...................double	**ptLineDistSq** (double PX, double PY)
△		public static ....double	**ptLineDistSq** (double X1, double Y1, double X2, double Y2, double PX, double PY)
		public...................double	**ptSegDist** (Point2D pt)
		public...................double	**ptSegDist** (double PX, double PY)
△		public static ....double	**ptSegDist** (double X1, double Y1, double X2, double Y2, double PX, double PY)
		public...................double	**ptSegDistSq** (Point2D pt)
		public...................double	**ptSegDistSq** (double PX, double PY)
△		public static ....double	**ptSegDistSq** (double X1, double Y1, double X2, double Y2, double PX, double PY)

Class   *Interface*   —extends   - - -implements   ○ abstract   ● final   △ static   ▲ static final   ✳ constructor   x x—inherited   x **x**—declared   **x x**—overridden
εn—examples of usage   ¸—has subclass   package —see other volume

	public	int	**relativeCCW** (Point2D p)
	public	int	**relativeCCW** (double PX, double PY)
△	public static	int	**relativeCCW** (double X1, double Y1, double X2, double Y2, double PX, double PY)
	public	void	**setLine** (Line2D l)
	public	void	**setLine** (Point2D p1, Point2D p2)
○	public abstract	void	**setLine** (double X1, double Y1, double X2, double Y2)

Line2D.Double   java.awt.geom

Object
1.2 ○ └─Line2D[1] - *java.awt.Shape*[2], *Cloneable*⌄
1.2 └─Line2D.Double

	1	*30 inherited members from Line2D not shown*		
*		public		**Line2D.Double** ()
*		public		**Line2D.Double** (Point2D p1, Point2D p2)
*		public		**Line2D.Double** (double X1, double Y1, double X2, double Y2)
	2	public	Rectangle2D	**getBounds2D** ()
	1	public	**Point2D**	**getP1** ()
	1	public	**Point2D**	**getP2** ()
	1	public	**double**	**getX1** ()
	1	public	**double**	**getX2** ()
	1	public	**double**	**getY1** ()
	1	public	**double**	**getY2** ()
	1	public	**void**	**setLine** (double X1, double Y1, double X2, double Y2)
		public	double	**x1**
		public	double	**x2**
		public	double	**y1**
		public	double	**y2**

Line2D.Float   java.awt.geom

Object
1.2 ○ └─Line2D[1] - *java.awt.Shape*[2], *Cloneable*⌄
1.2 └─Line2D.Float

	1	*30 inherited members from Line2D not shown*			
*		public		**Line2D.Float** ()	
*		public		**Line2D.Float** (Point2D p1, Point2D p2)	
*		public		**Line2D.Float** (float X1, float Y1, float X2, float Y2)	ε656
	2	public	Rectangle2D	**getBounds2D** ()	
	1	public	**Point2D**	**getP1** ()	
	1	public	**Point2D**	**getP2** ()	
	1	public	**double**	**getX1** ()	
	1	public	**double**	**getX2** ()	
	1	public	**double**	**getY1** ()	
	1	public	**double**	**getY2** ()	
	1	public	**void**	**setLine** (double X1, double Y1, double X2, double Y2)	
		public	void	**setLine** (float X1, float Y1, float X2, float Y2)	
		public	float	**x1**	
		public	float	**x2**	
		public	float	**y1**	
		public	float	**y2**	

LineBorder   javax.swing.border
ε873

Object
1.2 ○ └─AbstractBorder[1] - *Border*, *java.io.Serializable*⌄
1.2 └─LineBorder⌄

△		public static	*Border*	**createBlackLineBorder** ()
△		public static	*Border*	**createGrayLineBorder** ()
	1	public	**java.awt.Insets**	**getBorderInsets** (java.awt.Component c)
	1	public	**java.awt.Insets**	**getBorderInsets** (java.awt.Component c, java.awt.Insets insets)
	1	public	java.awt.Rectangle	getInteriorRectangle (java.awt.Component c, int x, int y, int width, int height)
△	1	public static		getInteriorRectangle (java.awt.Component c, *Border* b, int x, int y, int width,
			java.awt.Rectangle	int height)
		public	java.awt.Color	**getLineColor** ()
1.3		public	boolean	**getRoundedCorners** ()
		public	int	**getThickness** ()

L

Classes

LineBorder

1	public	**boolean**	**isBorderOpaque** ()
*	public		**LineBorder** (java.awt.Color color)
*	public		**LineBorder** (java.awt.Color color, int thickness)
1.3 *	public		**LineBorder** (java.awt.Color color, int thickness, boolean roundedCorners)
	protected	java.awt.Color	**lineColor**
1	public	**void**	**paintBorder** (java.awt.Component c, java.awt.Graphics g, int x, int y, int width, int height)
	protected	boolean	**roundedCorners**
	protected	int	**thickness**

LineBreakMeasurer   java.awt.font

Object
1.2 ● └LineBreakMeasurer

	public	void	**deleteChar** (*java.text.AttributedCharacterIterator* newParagraph, int deletePos)	
	public	int	**getPosition** ()	ε653
	public	void	**insertChar** (*java.text.AttributedCharacterIterator* newParagraph, int insertPos)	
*	public		**LineBreakMeasurer** (*java.text.AttributedCharacterIterator* text, FontRenderContext frc)	ε653
*	public		**LineBreakMeasurer** (*java.text.AttributedCharacterIterator* text, java.text.BreakIterator breakIter, FontRenderContext frc)	
	public	TextLayout	**nextLayout** (float wrappingWidth)	ε653
	public	TextLayout	**nextLayout** (float wrappingWidth, int offsetLimit, boolean requireNextWord)	
	public	int	**nextOffset** (float wrappingWidth)	
	public	int	**nextOffset** (float wrappingWidth, int offsetLimit, boolean requireNextWord)	
	public	void	**setPosition** (int newPosition)	

LineEvent   javax.sound.sampled

Object   ε640,641,643,649,566
1.1 └ java.util.EventObject[1] - - - - - - - - - - - - - - - - - - - *java.io.Serializable*
1.3   └LineEvent

●	public final	long	**getFramePosition** ()	
●	public final	*Line*	**getLine** ()	
1	public	Object	getSource ()	ε644,886,565,568,570
●	public final	LineEvent.Type	**getType** ()	ε731
*	public		**LineEvent** (*Line* line, LineEvent.Type type, long position)	
1	protected transient	Object	source	
1	public	**String**	**toString** ()	

LineEvent.Type   javax.sound.sampled

Object[1]
1.3 └LineEvent.Type

▲	public static final		**CLOSE**	
		LineEvent.Type		
● 1	public final	**boolean**	**equals** (Object obj)	
● 1	public final	**int**	**hashCode** ()	
▲	public static final		**OPEN**	
		LineEvent.Type		
▲	public static final		**START**	
		LineEvent.Type		
▲	public static final		**STOP**	ε731
		LineEvent.Type		
1	public	**String**	**toString** ()	
*	protected		**LineEvent.Type** (String name)	

LineListener   javax.sound.sampled

1.3	*LineListener*	———————	*java.util.EventListener*	ε738,743,745,746,752
	public	void	**update** (LineEvent event)	ε731

Class *Interface* —extends - - -implements ○ abstract ● final △ static ▲ static final ✱ constructor x x—inherited x **x**—declared **x x**—overridden
ε*n*—examples of usage ⌐—has subclass package—see other volume

LineMetrics	java.awt.font

```
      Object
1.2 ○  └LineMetrics
```

○	public abstract .... float	**getAscent** ()
○	public abstract .... int	**getBaselineIndex** ()
○	public abstract .... float[]	**getBaselineOffsets** ()
○	public abstract .... float	**getDescent** ()
○	public abstract .... float	**getHeight** ()
○	public abstract .... float	**getLeading** ()
○	public abstract .... int	**getNumChars** ()
○	public abstract .... float	**getStrikethroughOffset** ()
○	public abstract .... float	**getStrikethroughThickness** ()
○	public abstract .... float	**getUnderlineOffset** ()
○	public abstract .... float	**getUnderlineThickness** ()
✳	public	**LineMetrics** ()

LineUnavailableException	javax.sound.sampled
	ε723,724

```
      Object
      └Throwable ------------------------- java.io.Serializable
        └Exception
1.3       └LineUnavailableException
```

✳	public	**LineUnavailableException** ()
✳	public	**LineUnavailableException** (String message)

L

List❶	java.awt

```
      Object
○    └Component¹ ------------------------- java.awt.image.ImageObserver², MenuContainer,
                                           java.io.Serializable
          └List ------------------------- ItemSelectable³, javax.accessibility.Accessible
```

	1	*201 inherited members from Component not shown*		
	2	*8 inherited members from java.awt.image.ImageObserver not shown*		
1.1		public .... void	**add** (String item)	
1.1		public .... void	**add** (String item, int index)	
1.1		public synchronized .... void	**addActionListener** (*java.awt.event.ActionListener* l)	
D		public .... void	**addItem** (String item)	
D		public synchronized .... void	**addItem** (String item, int index)	
1.1	3	public synchronized .... void	**addItemListener** (*java.awt.event.ItemListener* l)	ε650,765
	1	public .... **void**	**addNotify** ()	
D		public .... boolean	**allowsMultipleSelections** ()	
D		public synchronized .... void	**clear** ()	
D		public .... int	**countItems** ()	
D		public .... void	**delItem** (int position)	
D		public synchronized ...... void	**delItems** (int start, int end)	
		public synchronized ...... void	**deselect** (int index)	
1.3	1	public.... **javax.accessibility .AccessibleContext**	**getAccessibleContext** ()	
1.4		public synchronized ..... *java.awt.event.ActionListener[]*	**getActionListeners** ()	
		public .... String	**getItem** (int index)	
1.1		public .... int	**getItemCount** ()	
1.4		public synchronized .... *java.awt.event.ItemListener[]*	**getItemListeners** ()	
1.1		public ... String[]	**getItems** ()	
1.3	1	public...... *java.util.EventListener[]*	**getListeners** (Class listenerType)	
1.1	1	public.............. **Dimension**	**getMinimumSize** ()	
1.1		public.............. Dimension	**getMinimumSize** (int rows)	
1.1	1	public.............. **Dimension**	**getPreferredSize** ()	
1.1		public.............. Dimension	**getPreferredSize** (int rows)	
		public .... int	**getRows** ()	
		public synchronized .... int	**getSelectedIndex** ()	
		public synchronized ...... int[]	**getSelectedIndexes** ()	
		public synchronized ..... String	**getSelectedItem** ()	
		public synchronized ... String[]	**getSelectedItems** ()	
1.1	3	public................. Object[]	**getSelectedObjects** ()	ε650

List❶

		public.........................int	**getVisibleIndex** ()	
1.1		public................. boolean	**isIndexSelected** (int index)	
1.1		public................. boolean	**isMultipleMode** ()	
D		public................. boolean	**isSelected** (int index)	
	✳	public.............................	**List** () throws HeadlessException	
1.1	✳	public.............................	**List** (int rows) throws HeadlessException	
	✳	public.............................	**List** (int rows, boolean multipleMode) throws HeadlessException	
		public synchronized ....void	**makeVisible** (int index)	
D	1	public................**Dimension**	**minimumSize** ()	
D		public................Dimension	**minimumSize** (int rows)	
	1	protected .... **String**	**paramString** ()	
D	1	public................**Dimension**	**preferredSize** ()	
D		public................Dimension	**preferredSize** (int rows)	
1.1		protected ....void	**processActionEvent** (java.awt.event.ActionEvent e)	
1.1	1	protected .... **void**	**processEvent** (AWTEvent e)	
1.1		protected ....void	**processItemEvent** (java.awt.event.ItemEvent e)	
1.1		public....................void	**remove** (int position)	
1.1		public synchronized ......void	**remove** (String item)	
1.1		public synchronized .....void	**removeActionListener** (*java.awt.event.ActionListener* l)	
1.1		public....................void	**removeAll** ()	
1.1	3	public synchronized .....void	**removeItemListener** (*java.awt.event.ItemListener* l)	ε650
	1	public.................... **void**	**removeNotify** ()	
		public synchronized .....void	**replaceItem** (String newValue, int index)	
		public....................void	**select** (int index)	
1.1		public....................void	**setMultipleMode** (boolean b)	
D		public synchronized ....void	**setMultipleSelections** (boolean b)	

ListCellRenderer javax.swing

1.2	*ListCellRenderer*

public.... java.awt.Component	**getListCellRendererComponent** (JList list, Object value, int index, boolean isSelected, boolean cellHasFocus)

ListDataEvent javax.swing.event

Object   ε640,641,643,649,566

1.1   └ java.util.EventObject¹ - - - - - - - - - - - - - - - - - - - *java.io.Serializable*

1.2   └─ListDataEvent

▲		public static final.............int	**CONTENTS_CHANGED** = 0	
		public........................int	**getIndex0** ()	ε785
		public........................int	**getIndex1** ()	ε785
	1	public................. Object	getSource ()	ε785,644,886,565,568
		public........................int	**getType** ()	
▲		public static final.............int	**INTERVAL_ADDED** = 1	
▲		public static final.............int	**INTERVAL_REMOVED** = 2	
✳		public.............................	**ListDataEvent** (Object source, int type, int index0, int index1)	
	1	protected transient...... Object	source	
	1	public................. **String**	**toString** ()	

ListDataListener javax.swing.event

1.2	*ListDataListener*————————————————*java.util.EventListener* ε738,743,745,746,752

public....................void	**contentsChanged** (ListDataEvent e)	ε785
public....................void	**intervalAdded** (ListDataEvent e)	ε785
public....................void	**intervalRemoved** (ListDataEvent e)	ε785

ListModel javax.swing

1.2	*ListModel*

public....................void	**addListDataListener** (*javax.swing.event.ListDataListener* l)	ε785
public................ Object	**getElementAt** (int index)	ε776,777,779
public........................int	**getSize** ()	ε777,778,780
public....................void	**removeListDataListener** (*javax.swing.event.ListDataListener* l)	

Class   *Interface*   —extends   - - -implements   ○ abstract   ● final   △ static   ▲ static final   ✳ constructor   x x—inherited   x **x**—declared   **x x**—overridden
ε*n*—examples of usage   ˅—has subclass   package—see other volume

ListPeer			java.awt.peer	

	ListPeer─────────────────────── ComponentPeer ˬ 1	
	1 42 inherited members from ComponentPeer not shown	
1.1	public......................void **add** (String item, int index)	
	public......................void **addItem** (String item, int index)	
	public......................void **clear** ()	
	public......................void **delItems** (int start, int end)	
	public......................void **deselect** (int index)	
1.1	public......java.awt.Dimension **getMinimumSize** (int rows)	
1.1	public......java.awt.Dimension **getPreferredSize** (int rows)	
	public......................int[] **getSelectedIndexes** ()	
	public......................void **makeVisible** (int index)	
	public......java.awt.Dimension **minimumSize** (int v)	
	public......java.awt.Dimension **preferredSize** (int v)	
1.1	public......................void **removeAll** ()	
	public......................void **select** (int index)	
1.1	public......................void **setMultipleMode** (boolean b)	
	public......................void **setMultipleSelections** (boolean v)	

ListSelectionEvent			javax.swing.event	
			ε957,966,640,641,643	

	Object	
1.1	└ java.util.EventObject¹ - - - - - - - - - - - - - - - - - - - *java.io.Serializable* ˬ	
1.2	└─ListSelectionEvent	
	public......................int **getFirstIndex** ()	ε964
	public......................int **getLastIndex** ()	ε964
1	public......................Object getSource ()	ε784,964,644,886,565
	public................boolean **getValueIsAdjusting** ()	ε784,964
*	public.......................... **ListSelectionEvent** (Object source, int firstIndex, int lastIndex, boolean isAdjusting)	
1	protected transient......Object source	
1	public.................. **String toString** ()	

ListSelectionListener			javax.swing.event	

1.2	*ListSelectionListener──────────── java.util.EventListener* ˬ	ε738,743,745,746,752
	public......................void **valueChanged** (ListSelectionEvent e)	ε784,957,964

ListSelectionModel			javax.swing	

1.2	*ListSelectionModel*	
	public......................void **addListSelectionListener** (*javax.swing.event.ListSelectionListener* x)	
		ε957,964
	public......................void **addSelectionInterval** (int index0, int index1)	
	public......................void **clearSelection** ()	
	public......................int **getAnchorSelectionIndex** ()	ε944,957
	public......................int **getLeadSelectionIndex** ()	
	public......................int **getMaxSelectionIndex** ()	ε942
	public......................int **getMinSelectionIndex** ()	
	public......................int **getSelectionMode** ()	ε940
	public................boolean **getValueIsAdjusting** ()	
	public......................void **insertIndexInterval** (int index, int length, boolean before)	
	public................boolean **isSelectedIndex** (int index)	
	public................boolean **isSelectionEmpty** ()	
▲	public static final............int **MULTIPLE_INTERVAL_SELECTION** = 2	ε940,941,942
	public......................void **removeIndexInterval** (int index0, int index1)	
	public......................void **removeListSelectionListener** (*javax.swing.event.ListSelectionListener* x)	
	public......................void **removeSelectionInterval** (int index0, int index1)	
	public......................void **setAnchorSelectionIndex** (int index)	
	public......................void **setLeadSelectionIndex** (int index)	
	public......................void **setSelectionInterval** (int index0, int index1)	
	public......................void **setSelectionMode** (int selectionMode)	
	public......................void **setValueIsAdjusting** (boolean valueIsAdjusting)	
▲	public static final............int **SINGLE_INTERVAL_SELECTION** = 1	ε940,942
▲	public static final............int **SINGLE_SELECTION** = 0	ε940,942

L

Classes

675

ListUI

			javax.swing.plaf

		Object	
1.2	○	└ComponentUI[1]	
1.2	○	└ListUI⌄	

	1	*11 inherited members from ComponentUI not shown*	
○		public abstract . . . . java.awt.Rectangle	**getCellBounds** (javax.swing.JList list, int index1, int index2)
○		public abstract . . java.awt.Point	**indexToLocation** (javax.swing.JList list, int index)
✳		public	**ListUI** ()
○		public abstract . . . . int	**locationToIndex** (javax.swing.JList list, java.awt.Point location)

ListView

			javax.swing.text.html

		Object	
1.2	○	└javax.swing.text.View[1] - - - - - - - - - - - - - - - - - - - *javax.swing.SwingConstants[5]*	
1.2	○	└javax.swing.text.CompositeView[2]	
1.2		└javax.swing.text.BoxView[3]	
1.2		└BlockView[4]	
1.2		└ListView	

L

	1	*31 inherited members from javax.swing.text.View not shown*
	2	*17 inherited members from javax.swing.text.CompositeView not shown*
	3	*25 inherited members from javax.swing.text.BoxView not shown*
	5	*19 inherited members from javax.swing.text.SwingConstants not shown*
	4	protected . . . . javax.swing.SizeRequirements calculateMajorAxisRequirements (int axis, javax.swing.SizeRequirements r)
	4	protected . . . . javax.swing.SizeRequirements calculateMinorAxisRequirements (int axis, javax.swing.SizeRequirements r)
	4	public . . . . void changedUpdate (*javax.swing.event.DocumentEvent* changes, *java.awt.Shape* a, *javax.swing.text.ViewFactory* f)
	4	public . . . . **float** **getAlignment** (int axis)
	4	public . . . . *javax.swing.text.AttributeSet* getAttributes ()
	4	public . . . . float getMaximumSpan (int axis)
	4	public . . . . float getMinimumSpan (int axis)
	4	public . . . . float getPreferredSpan (int axis)
	4	public . . . . int getResizeWeight (int axis)
	4	protected . . . . StyleSheet getStyleSheet ()
	4	protected . . . . void layoutMinorAxis (int targetSpan, int axis, int[] offsets, int[] spans)
✳		public . . . . **ListView** (*javax.swing.text.Element* elem)
	4	public . . . . **void** **paint** (java.awt.Graphics g, *java.awt.Shape* allocation)
	3	protected . . . . **void** **paintChild** (java.awt.Graphics g, java.awt.Rectangle alloc, int index)
	4	public . . . . void setParent (javax.swing.text.View parent)
	4	protected . . . . **void** **setPropertiesFromAttributes** ()

LookAndFeel

			javax.swing

| | | Object[1] | ε867 |
| 1.2 | ○ | └LookAndFeel⌄ | |

		public . . . . UIDefaults	**getDefaults** ()
○		public abstract . . . . String	**getDescription** ()
1.4	△	public static . . . . Object	**getDesktopPropertyValue** (String systemPropertyName, Object fallbackValue)
○		public abstract . . . . String	**getID** ()
○		public abstract . . . . String	**getName** ()
1.4		public . . . . boolean	**getSupportsWindowDecorations** ()
		public . . . . void	**initialize** ()
△		public static . . . . void	**installBorder** (JComponent c, String defaultBorderName)
△		public static . . . . void	**installColors** (JComponent c, String defaultBgName, String defaultFgName)
△		public static . . . . void	**installColorsAndFont** (JComponent c, String defaultBgName, String defaultFgName, String defaultFontName)
○		public abstract . . . . boolean	**isNativeLookAndFeel** ()
○		public abstract . . . . boolean	**isSupportedLookAndFeel** ()
1.3	△	public static . . . . void	**loadKeyBindings** (InputMap retMap, Object[] keys)
✳		public	**LookAndFeel** ()

Class *Interface* —extends - - -implements ○ abstract ● final △ static ▲ static final ✳ constructor x x—inherited x **x**—declared **x x**—overridden
εn—examples of usage ⌄—has subclass package—see other volume

1.3 △	public static .... ComponentInputMap	**makeComponentInputMap** (JComponent c, Object[] keys)	
△	public static .... Object	**makeIcon** (Class baseClass, String gifFile)	
1.3 △	public static .... InputMap	**makeInputMap** (Object[] keys)	
△	public static ...... javax.swing₂ .text.JTextComponent₂ .KeyBinding[]	**makeKeyBindings** (Object[] keyBindingList)	
1.4	public.....................void	**provideErrorFeedback** (java.awt.Component component)	
1	public.................. **String**	**toString** ()	
	public.....................void	**uninitialize** ()	
△	public static ....void	**uninstallBorder** (JComponent c)	

LookupOp
java.awt.image

Object
1.2 └LookupOp - *BufferedImageOp* [1], *RasterOp* [2]

1	public........... BufferedImage	**createCompatibleDestImage** (BufferedImage src, ColorModel destCM)	
2	public........... WritableRaster	**createCompatibleDestRaster** (Raster src)	
● 1	public final ..... BufferedImage	**filter** (BufferedImage src, BufferedImage dst)	ε672,675,676,677,678
● 2	public final ..... WritableRaster	**filter** (Raster src, WritableRaster dst)	
● 1	public final java.awt.geom.Rectangle2D	**getBounds2D** (BufferedImage src)	
● 2	public final java.awt.geom.Rectangle2D	**getBounds2D** (Raster src)	
● 1	public final java.awt.geom.Point2D	**getPoint2D** (java.awt.geom.Point2D srcPt, java.awt.geom.Point2D dstPt)	
● 1	public final .... java.awt.RenderingHints	**getRenderingHints** ()	
●	public final .... LookupTable	**getTable** ()	
*	public..........................	**LookupOp** (LookupTable lookup, java.awt.RenderingHints hints)	

LookupTable
java.awt.image

Object
1.2 ○ └LookupTable␣

	public.........................int	**getNumComponents** ()	
	public.........................int	**getOffset** ()	
○	public abstract .... int[]	**lookupPixel** (int[] src, int[] dest)	
*	protected	**LookupTable** (int offset, int numComponents)	

MaskFormatter
javax.swing.text

Object
1.4 ○ └javax.swing.JFormattedTextField₂ - - - - - - - - - - *java.io.Serializable*␣
    │ .AbstractFormatter [1]
1.4 └DefaultFormatter [2] - *Cloneable*␣
1.4 └MaskFormatter

2	public...................Object	clone () throws CloneNotSupportedException	
1	protected . *javax.swing.Action[]*	getActions ()	
2	public.................. boolean	getAllowsInvalid ()	
2	public.................. boolean	getCommitsOnValidEdit ()	
2	protected ...... DocumentFilter	getDocumentFilter ()	
1	protected .... javax₂ .swing.JFormattedTextField	getFormattedTextField ()	
	public................... String	**getInvalidCharacters** ()	
	public................... String	**getMask** ()	
2	protected ...... NavigationFilter	getNavigationFilter ()	
2	public.................. boolean	getOverwriteMode ()	
	public................... String	**getPlaceholder** ()	
	public...................... char	**getPlaceholderCharacter** ()	
	public................... String	**getValidCharacters** ()	
2	public..................... Class	getValueClass ()	
	public.................. boolean	**getValueContainsLiteralCharacters** ()	
2	public.................... **void**	**install** (javax.swing.JFormattedTextField ftf)	
1	protected ....void	invalidEdit ()	
*	public..........................	**MaskFormatter** ()	
*	public..........................	**MaskFormatter** (String mask) throws java.text.ParseException ε997	

MaskFormatter

2	public	void	setAllowsInvalid (boolean allowsInvalid)	
2	public	void	setCommitsOnValidEdit (boolean commit)	
1	protected	void	setEditValid (boolean valid)	
	public	void	**setInvalidCharacters** (String invalidCharacters)	
	public	void	**setMask** (String mask) throws java.text.ParseException	
2	public	void	setOverwriteMode (boolean overwriteMode)	
	public	void	**setPlaceholder** (String placeholder)	
	public	void	**setPlaceholderCharacter** (char placeholder)	ε997
	public	void	**setValidCharacters** (String validCharacters)	
2	public	void	setValueClass (Class valueClass)	ε995
	public	void	**setValueContainsLiteralCharacters** (boolean containsLiteralChars)	
2	public	**Object**	**stringToValue** (String value) throws java.text.ParseException	
1	public	void	uninstall ()	
2	public	**String**	**valueToString** (Object value) throws java.text.ParseException	

MatteBorder

javax.swing.border

		Object	ε873
1.2	○	└AbstractBorder[1] - *Border*, *java.io.Serializable*	
1.2		└EmptyBorder[2]	
1.2		└MatteBorder	

2	protected	int	bottom	
	protected	java.awt.Color	**color**	
1.3	2	public	**java.awt.Insets**	**getBorderInsets** ()
	2	public	**java.awt.Insets**	**getBorderInsets** (java.awt.Component c)
	2	public	**java.awt.Insets**	**getBorderInsets** (java.awt.Component c, java.awt.Insets insets)
	1	public	java.awt.Rectangle	getInteriorRectangle (java.awt.Component c, int x, int y, int width, int height)
△	1	public static	java.awt.Rectangle	getInteriorRectangle (java.awt.Component c, *Border* b, int x, int y, int width, int height)
1.3		public	java.awt.Color	**getMatteColor** ()
1.3		public	*javax.swing.Icon*	**getTileIcon** ()
	2	public	**boolean**	**isBorderOpaque** ()
	2	protected	int	left
	*	public	**MatteBorder**	(*javax.swing.Icon* tileIcon)
1.3	*	public	**MatteBorder**	(java.awt.Insets borderInsets, java.awt.Color matteColor)
1.3	*	public	**MatteBorder**	(java.awt.Insets borderInsets, *javax.swing.Icon* tileIcon)
	*	public	**MatteBorder**	(int top, int left, int bottom, int right, java.awt.Color matteColor)
	*	public	**MatteBorder**	(int top, int left, int bottom, int right, *javax.swing.Icon* tileIcon)
	2	public	**void**	**paintBorder** (java.awt.Component c, java.awt.Graphics g, int x, int y, int width, int height)
	2	protected	int	right
		protected	*javax.swing.Icon*	**tileIcon**
	2	protected	int	top

Media

javax.print.attribute.standard

		Object[1]	
1.4	○	└javax.print.attribute.EnumSyntax[2] - - - - - - - - - *java.io.Serializable*, *Cloneable*
1.4	○	└Media - *javax.print.attribute.DocAttribute* (*javax.print.attribute.Attribute*[3] (*java.io.Serializable*)), *javax.print.attribute.PrintRequestAttribute* (*javax.print.attribute.Attribute*[3] (*java.io.Serializable*)), *javax.print.attribute.PrintJobAttribute* (*javax.print.attribute.Attribute*[3] (*java.io.Serializable*))

	2	public	Object	clone ()	
	1	public	**boolean**	**equals** (Object object)	
●	3	public final	Class	**getCategory** ()	ε707
	2	protected	javax.print.attribute.EnumSyntax[]	getEnumValueTable ()	
●	3	public final	String	**getName** ()	ε706,707,708
	2	protected	int	getOffset ()	
	2	protected	String[]	getStringTable ()	
	2	public	int	getValue ()	
	2	public	int	hashCode ()	
*		protected		**Media** (int value)	
	2	protected	Object	readResolve () throws java.io.ObjectStreamException	

Class *Interface* —extends - - -implements ○ abstract ● final △ static ▲ static final ✳ constructor x x—inherited x **x**—declared **x x**—overridden
ε*n*—examples of usage ‿—has subclass package—see other volume

2	public	String	toString ()	

MediaName

Object
```
1.4 ○    └─javax.print.attribute.EnumSyntax¹ --------- java.io.Serializable⌄, Cloneable⌄
1.4 ○        └─Media² ------------------------- javax.print.attribute.DocAttribute (javax.print.attribute.Attribute
                                                (java.io.Serializable)), javax.print.attribute.PrintRequestAttribute
                                                (javax.print.attribute.Attribute (java.io.Serializable)),
                                                javax.print.attribute.PrintJobAttribute
                                                (javax.print.attribute.Attribute (java.io.Serializable))
1.4             └─MediaName -------------------- javax.print.attribute.Attribute⌄ (java.io.Serializable)
```

	1	public	Object	clone ()	
	2	public	boolean	equals (Object object)	
●	2	public final	Class	getCategory ()	ε707
	1	protected	**javax.print.attribute.EnumSyntax[]**	**getEnumValueTable ()**	
●	2	public final	String	getName ()	ε706,707,708
	1	protected	int	getOffset ()	
	1	protected	**String[]**	**getStringTable ()**	
	1	public	int	getValue ()	
	1	public	int	hashCode ()	
▲		public static final	MediaName	**ISO_A4_TRANSPARENT**	
▲		public static final	MediaName	**ISO_A4_WHITE**	
✳		protected		**MediaName** (int value)	
▲		public static final	MediaName	**NA_LETTER_TRANSPARENT**	
▲		public static final	MediaName	**NA_LETTER_WHITE**	
	1	protected	Object	readResolve () throws java.io.ObjectStreamException	
	1	public	String	toString ()	

MediaPrintableArea

Object¹
```
1.4 ●    └─MediaPrintableArea -------------------- javax.print.attribute.DocAttribute (javax.print.attribute.Attribute²
                                                (java.io.Serializable)), javax.print.attribute.PrintRequestAttribute
                                                (javax.print.attribute.Attribute² (java.io.Serializable)),
                                                javax.print.attribute.PrintJobAttribute
                                                (javax.print.attribute.Attribute² (java.io.Serializable))
```

●	1	public	**boolean**	**equals** (Object object)	
●	2	public final	Class	**getCategory** ()	ε707
		public	float	**getHeight** (int units)	
●	2	public final	String	**getName** ()	ε706,707,708
		public	float[]	**getPrintableArea** (int units)	
		public	float	**getWidth** (int units)	
		public	float	**getX** (int units)	
		public	float	**getY** (int units)	
	1	public	**int**	**hashCode** ()	
▲		public static final	int	**INCH** = 25400	
✳		public		**MediaPrintableArea** (float x, float y, float w, float h, int units)	
✳		public		**MediaPrintableArea** (int x, int y, int w, int h, int units)	
▲		public static final	int	**MM** = 1000	
	1	public	**String**	**toString** ()	
		public	String	**toString** (int units, String unitsName)	

MediaSize

Object
```
1.4 ○    └─javax.print.attribute.Size2DSyntax¹ --------- java.io.Serializable⌄, Cloneable⌄
1.4         └─MediaSize ------------------------- javax.print.attribute.Attribute⌄² (java.io.Serializable)
```

	1	public	**boolean**	**equals** (Object object)	
△		public static	MediaSizeName	**findMedia** (float x, float y, int units)	
●	2	public final	Class	**getCategory** ()	ε707
△		public static	MediaSize	**getMediaSizeForName** (MediaSizeName media)	
		public	MediaSizeName	**getMediaSizeName** ()	
●	2	public final	String	**getName** ()	ε706,707,708
	1	public	float[]	getSize (int units)	

MediaSize

	1	public.......................float	getX (int units)
	1	protected.....................int	getXMicrometers ()
	1	public.......................float	getY (int units)
	1	protected.....................int	getYMicrometers ()
	1	public..........................int	hashCode ()
▲	1	public static final.............int	INCH = 25400
*		public..........................	**MediaSize** (float x, float y, int units)
*		public..........................	**MediaSize** (int x, int y, int units)
*		public..........................	**MediaSize** (float x, float y, int units, MediaSizeName media)
*		public..........................	**MediaSize** (int x, int y, int units, MediaSizeName media)
▲	1	public static final.............int	MM = 1000
	1	public....................String	toString ()
	1	public....................String	toString (int units, String unitsName)

MediaSize.Engineering javax.print.attribute.standard

Object
1.4 ● └ MediaSize.Engineering

▲	public static final .... MediaSize **A**
▲	public static final .... MediaSize **B**
▲	public static final .... MediaSize **C**
▲	public static final .... MediaSize **D**
▲	public static final .... MediaSize **E**

M

MediaSize.ISO javax.print.attribute.standard

Object
1.4 ● └ MediaSize.ISO

▲	public static final .... MediaSize **A0**
▲	public static final .... MediaSize **A1**
▲	public static final .... MediaSize **A10**
▲	public static final .... MediaSize **A2**
▲	public static final .... MediaSize **A3**
▲	public static final .... MediaSize **A4**
▲	public static final .... MediaSize **A5**
▲	public static final .... MediaSize **A6**
▲	public static final .... MediaSize **A7**
▲	public static final .... MediaSize **A8**
▲	public static final .... MediaSize **A9**
▲	public static final .... MediaSize **B0**
▲	public static final .... MediaSize **B1**
▲	public static final .... MediaSize **B10**
▲	public static final .... MediaSize **B2**
▲	public static final .... MediaSize **B3**
▲	public static final .... MediaSize **B4**
▲	public static final .... MediaSize **B5**
▲	public static final .... MediaSize **B6**
▲	public static final .... MediaSize **B7**
▲	public static final .... MediaSize **B8**
▲	public static final .... MediaSize **B9**
▲	public static final .... MediaSize **C3**
▲	public static final .... MediaSize **C4**
▲	public static final .... MediaSize **C5**
▲	public static final .... MediaSize **C6**
▲	public static final .... MediaSize **DESIGNATED_LONG**

MediaSize.JIS javax.print.attribute.standard

Object
1.4 ● └ MediaSize.JIS

▲	public static final .... MediaSize **B0**
▲	public static final .... MediaSize **B1**
▲	public static final .... MediaSize **B10**
▲	public static final .... MediaSize **B2**
▲	public static final .... MediaSize **B3**

Class   *Interface*   —extends   - - -implements   ○ abstract   ● final   △ static   ▲ static final   * constructor   x x—inherited   x **x**—declared   **x x**—overridden
εn—examples of usage   └ has subclass   package—see other volume

▲ public static final ....MediaSize **B4**
▲ public static final ....MediaSize **B5**
▲ public static final ....MediaSize **B6**
▲ public static final ....MediaSize **B7**
▲ public static final ....MediaSize **B8**
▲ public static final ....MediaSize **B9**
▲ public static final ....MediaSize **CHOU_1**
▲ public static final ....MediaSize **CHOU_2**
▲ public static final ....MediaSize **CHOU_3**
▲ public static final ....MediaSize **CHOU_30**
▲ public static final ....MediaSize **CHOU_4**
▲ public static final ....MediaSize **CHOU_40**
▲ public static final ....MediaSize **KAKU_0**
▲ public static final ....MediaSize **KAKU_1**
▲ public static final ....MediaSize **KAKU_2**
▲ public static final ....MediaSize **KAKU_20**
▲ public static final ....MediaSize **KAKU_3**
▲ public static final ....MediaSize **KAKU_4**
▲ public static final ....MediaSize **KAKU_5**
▲ public static final ....MediaSize **KAKU_6**
▲ public static final ....MediaSize **KAKU_7**
▲ public static final ....MediaSize **KAKU_8**
▲ public static final ....MediaSize **KAKU_A4**
▲ public static final ....MediaSize **YOU_1**
▲ public static final ....MediaSize **YOU_2**
▲ public static final ....MediaSize **YOU_3**
▲ public static final ....MediaSize **YOU_4**
▲ public static final ....MediaSize **YOU_5**
▲ public static final ....MediaSize **YOU_6**
▲ public static final ....MediaSize **YOU_7**

MediaSize.NA   javax.print.attribute.standard

Object
1.4 ● └MediaSize.NA

▲ public static final ....MediaSize **LEGAL**
▲ public static final ....MediaSize **LETTER**
▲ public static final ....MediaSize **NA_10x13_ENVELOPE**
▲ public static final ....MediaSize **NA_10x14_ENVELOPE**
▲ public static final ....MediaSize **NA_10X15_ENVELOPE**
▲ public static final ....MediaSize **NA_5X7**
▲ public static final ....MediaSize **NA_6X9_ENVELOPE**
▲ public static final ....MediaSize **NA_7X9_ENVELOPE**
▲ public static final ....MediaSize **NA_8X10**
▲ public static final ....MediaSize **NA_9x11_ENVELOPE**
▲ public static final ....MediaSize **NA_9x12_ENVELOPE**
▲ public static final ....MediaSize **NA_NUMBER_10_ENVELOPE**
▲ public static final ....MediaSize **NA_NUMBER_11_ENVELOPE**
▲ public static final ....MediaSize **NA_NUMBER_12_ENVELOPE**
▲ public static final ....MediaSize **NA_NUMBER_14_ENVELOPE**
▲ public static final ....MediaSize **NA_NUMBER_9_ENVELOPE**

MediaSize.Other   javax.print.attribute.standard

Object
1.4 ● └MediaSize.Other

▲ public static final ....MediaSize **EXECUTIVE**
▲ public static final ....MediaSize **FOLIO**
▲ public static final ....MediaSize **INVOICE**
▲ public static final ....MediaSize **ITALY_ENVELOPE**
▲ public static final ....MediaSize **JAPANESE_DOUBLE_POSTCARD**
▲ public static final ....MediaSize **JAPANESE_POSTCARD**
▲ public static final ....MediaSize **LEDGER**
▲ public static final ....MediaSize **MONARCH_ENVELOPE**
▲ public static final ....MediaSize **PERSONAL_ENVELOPE**
▲ public static final ....MediaSize **QUARTO**

M

Classes

MediaSizeName

Object
1.4 ○ └─*javax.print.attribute.EnumSyntax*[1] --------- *java.io.Serializable*, *Cloneable*
1.4 ○ 　└─*Media*[2] -------------------------- *javax.print.attribute.DocAttribute* (*javax.print.attribute.Attribute*
　　　　　　　　　　　　　　　　　　　　　　　　(*java.io.Serializable*)), *javax.print.attribute.PrintRequestAttribute*
　　　　　　　　　　　　　　　　　　　　　　　　(*javax.print.attribute.Attribute* (*java.io.Serializable*)),
　　　　　　　　　　　　　　　　　　　　　　　　javax.print.attribute.PrintJobAttribute
　　　　　　　　　　　　　　　　　　　　　　　　(*javax.print.attribute.Attribute* (*java.io.Serializable*))
1.4 　└─MediaSizeName

▲		public static final	MediaSizeName	**A**
▲		public static final	MediaSizeName	**B**
▲		public static final	MediaSizeName	**C**
	1	public	Object	clone ()
▲		public static final	MediaSizeName	**D**
▲		public static final	MediaSizeName	**E**
	2	public	boolean	equals (Object object)
▲		public static final	MediaSizeName	**EXECUTIVE**
▲		public static final	MediaSizeName	**FOLIO**
●	2	public final	Class	getCategory () ε707
	1	protected	**javax.print.attribute.EnumSyntax[]**	**getEnumValueTable** ()
●	2	public final	String	getName () ε706,707,708
	1	protected	int	getOffset ()
	1	protected	**String[]**	**getStringTable** ()
	1	public	int	getValue ()
	1	public	int	hashCode ()
▲		public static final	MediaSizeName	**INVOICE**
▲		public static final	MediaSizeName	**ISO_A0**
▲		public static final	MediaSizeName	**ISO_A1**
▲		public static final	MediaSizeName	**ISO_A10**
▲		public static final	MediaSizeName	**ISO_A2**
▲		public static final	MediaSizeName	**ISO_A3**
▲		public static final	MediaSizeName	**ISO_A4**
▲		public static final	MediaSizeName	**ISO_A5**
▲		public static final	MediaSizeName	**ISO_A6**
▲		public static final	MediaSizeName	**ISO_A7**
▲		public static final	MediaSizeName	**ISO_A8**
▲		public static final	MediaSizeName	**ISO_A9**
▲		public static final	MediaSizeName	**ISO_B0**
▲		public static final	MediaSizeName	**ISO_B1**
▲		public static final	MediaSizeName	**ISO_B10**
▲		public static final	MediaSizeName	**ISO_B2**
▲		public static final	MediaSizeName	**ISO_B3**
▲		public static final	MediaSizeName	**ISO_B4**
▲		public static final	MediaSizeName	**ISO_B5**
▲		public static final	MediaSizeName	**ISO_B6**
▲		public static final	MediaSizeName	**ISO_B7**
▲		public static final	MediaSizeName	**ISO_B8**
▲		public static final	MediaSizeName	**ISO_B9**
▲		public static final	MediaSizeName	**ISO_C0**
▲		public static final	MediaSizeName	**ISO_C1**
▲		public static final	MediaSizeName	**ISO_C2**
▲		public static final	MediaSizeName	**ISO_C3**
▲		public static final	MediaSizeName	**ISO_C4**
▲		public static final	MediaSizeName	**ISO_C5**
▲		public static final	MediaSizeName	**ISO_C6**
▲		public static final	MediaSizeName	**ISO_DESIGNATED_LONG**
▲		public static final	MediaSizeName	**ITALY_ENVELOPE**
▲		public static final	MediaSizeName	**JAPANESE_DOUBLE_POSTCARD**
▲		public static final	MediaSizeName	**JAPANESE_POSTCARD**
▲		public static final	MediaSizeName	**JIS_B0**
▲		public static final	MediaSizeName	**JIS_B1**
▲		public static final	MediaSizeName	**JIS_B10**
▲		public static final	MediaSizeName	**JIS_B2**
▲		public static final	MediaSizeName	**JIS_B3**
▲		public static final	MediaSizeName	**JIS_B4**
▲		public static final	MediaSizeName	**JIS_B5**
▲		public static final	MediaSizeName	**JIS_B6**
▲		public static final	MediaSizeName	**JIS_B7**

Class *Interface* —extends - - -implements ○ abstract ● final △ static ▲ static final ✳ constructor x x—inherited x **x**—declared **x x**—overridden
ε*n*—examples of usage ₎—has subclass ▨package—see other volume
682

▲	public static final	MediaSizeName	**JIS_B8**
▲	public static final	MediaSizeName	**JIS_B9**
▲	public static final	MediaSizeName	**LEDGER**
✳	protected		**MediaSizeName** (int value)
▲	public static final	MediaSizeName	**MONARCH_ENVELOPE**
▲	public static final	MediaSizeName	**NA_10X13_ENVELOPE**
▲	public static final	MediaSizeName	**NA_10X14_ENVELOPE**
▲	public static final	MediaSizeName	**NA_10X15_ENVELOPE**
▲	public static final	MediaSizeName	**NA_5X7**
▲	public static final	MediaSizeName	**NA_6X9_ENVELOPE**
▲	public static final	MediaSizeName	**NA_7X9_ENVELOPE**
▲	public static final	MediaSizeName	**NA_8X10**
▲	public static final	MediaSizeName	**NA_9X11_ENVELOPE**
▲	public static final	MediaSizeName	**NA_9X12_ENVELOPE**
▲	public static final	MediaSizeName	**NA_LEGAL**
▲	public static final	MediaSizeName	**NA_LETTER**
▲	public static final	MediaSizeName	**NA_NUMBER_10_ENVELOPE**
▲	public static final	MediaSizeName	**NA_NUMBER_11_ENVELOPE**
▲	public static final	MediaSizeName	**NA_NUMBER_12_ENVELOPE**
▲	public static final	MediaSizeName	**NA_NUMBER_14_ENVELOPE**
▲	public static final	MediaSizeName	**NA_NUMBER_9_ENVELOPE**
▲	public static final	MediaSizeName	**PERSONAL_ENVELOPE**
▲	public static final	MediaSizeName	**QUARTO**
1	protected	Object	readResolve () throws java.io.ObjectStreamException
▲	public static final	MediaSizeName	**TABLOID**
1	public	String	toString ()

M

MediaTracker

```
Object
 └ MediaTracker - - - - - - - - - - - - - - - - - - - - - - - - - java.io.Serializable⌄
```

▲	public static final	int	**ABORTED** = 2
	public	void	**addImage** (Image image, int id)
	public synchronized	void	**addImage** (Image image, int id, int w, int h)
	public	boolean	**checkAll** ()
	public	boolean	**checkAll** (boolean load)
	public	boolean	**checkID** (int id)
	public	boolean	**checkID** (int id, boolean load)
▲	public static final	int	**COMPLETE** = 8
▲	public static final	int	**ERRORED** = 4
	public synchronized	Object[]	**getErrorsAny** ()
	public synchronized	Object[]	**getErrorsID** (int id)
	public synchronized	boolean	**isErrorAny** ()
	public synchronized	boolean	**isErrorID** (int id)
▲	public static final	int	**LOADING** = 1
✳	public		**MediaTracker** (Component comp)
1.1	public synchronized	void	**removeImage** (Image image)
1.1	public synchronized	void	**removeImage** (Image image, int id)
1.1	public synchronized	void	**removeImage** (Image image, int id, int width, int height)
	public	int	**statusAll** (boolean load)
	public	int	**statusID** (int id, boolean load)
	public	void	**waitForAll** () throws InterruptedException
	public synchronized	boolean	**waitForAll** (long ms) throws InterruptedException
	public	void	**waitForID** (int id) throws InterruptedException
	public synchronized	boolean	**waitForID** (int id, long ms) throws InterruptedException

Classes

MediaTray

```
Object
 └ javax.print.attribute.EnumSyntax¹ - - - - - - - - - java.io.Serializable⌄, Cloneable⌄
    └ Media² - - - - - - - - - - - - - - - - - - - - - - - - javax.print.attribute.DocAttribute (javax.print.attribute.Attribute
                                                           (java.io.Serializable)), javax.print.attribute.PrintRequestAttribute
                                                           (javax.print.attribute.Attribute (java.io.Serializable)),
                                                           javax.print.attribute.PrintJobAttribute
                                                           (javax.print.attribute.Attribute (java.io.Serializable))
       └ MediaTray - - - - - - - - - - - - - - - - - - - - javax.print.attribute.Attribute⌄ (java.io.Serializable)
```
(1.4 ○, 1.4 ○, 1.4)

▲	public static final	MediaTray	**BOTTOM**
1	public	Object	clone ()
▲	public static final	MediaTray	**ENVELOPE**

683

MediaTray

	2	public .... boolean	equals (Object object)	
●	2	public final .... Class	getCategory ()	ε707
	1	protected .... **javax.print**	**getEnumValueTable ()**	
		.attribute.EnumSyntax[]		
●	2	public final .... String	getName ()	ε706,707,708
	1	protected .... int	getOffset ()	
	1	protected .... **String[]**	**getStringTable ()**	
	1	public .... int	getValue ()	
	1	public .... int	hashCode ()	
▲		public static final .... MediaTray	**LARGE_CAPACITY**	
▲		public static final .... MediaTray	**MAIN**	
▲		public static final .... MediaTray	**MANUAL**	
✻		protected	**MediaTray** (int value)	
▲		public static final .... MediaTray	**MIDDLE**	
	1	protected .... Object	readResolve () throws java.io.ObjectStreamException	
▲		public static final .... MediaTray	**SIDE**	
▲		public static final .... MediaTray	**TOP**	
	1	public .... String	toString ()	

MemoryCacheImageInputStream — javax.imageio.stream

```
        Object
1.4 ○   └─ImageInputStreamImpl 1 ----------------- ImageInputStream ˌ (java.io.DataInput)
1.4        └─MemoryCacheImageInputStream
```

	1	*44 inherited members from ImageInputStreamImpl not shown*		
	1	public .... **void**	**close** () throws java.io.IOException	ε698,699
	1	public .... **void**	**flushBefore** (long pos) throws java.io.IOException	
	1	public .... **boolean**	**isCached** ()	
	1	public .... **boolean**	**isCachedFile** ()	
	1	public .... **boolean**	**isCachedMemory** ()	
✻		public	**MemoryCacheImageInputStream** (java.io.InputStream stream)	
	1	public .... **int**	**read** () throws java.io.IOException	
	1	public .... **int**	**read** (byte[] b, int off, int len) throws java.io.IOException	

MemoryCacheImageOutputStream — javax.imageio.stream

```
        Object
1.4 ○   └─ImageInputStreamImpl 1 ----------------- ImageInputStream ˌ (java.io.DataInput)
1.4 ○     └─ImageOutputStreamImpl 2 -------------- ImageOutputStream (ImageInputStream (java.io.DataInput),
                                                                      java.io.DataOutput)
1.4          └─MemoryCacheImageOutputStream
```

	1	*43 inherited members from ImageInputStreamImpl not shown*		
	1	public .... **void**	**close** () throws java.io.IOException	ε698,699
	1	public .... **void**	**flushBefore** (long pos) throws java.io.IOException	
●	2	protected final .... void	flushBits () throws java.io.IOException	
	1	public .... **boolean**	**isCached** ()	
	1	public .... **boolean**	**isCachedFile** ()	
	1	public .... **boolean**	**isCachedMemory** ()	
	1	public .... **long**	**length** ()	
✻		public	**MemoryCacheImageOutputStream** (java.io.OutputStream stream)	
	1	public .... **int**	**read** () throws java.io.IOException	
	1	public .... **int**	**read** (byte[] b, int off, int len) throws java.io.IOException	
	2	public .... void	write (byte[] b) throws java.io.IOException	
	2	public .... **void**	**write** (int b) throws java.io.IOException	
	2	public .... **void**	**write** (byte[] b, int off, int len) throws java.io.IOException	
	2	public .... void	writeBit (int bit) throws java.io.IOException	
	2	public .... void	writeBits (long bits, int numBits) throws java.io.IOException	
	2	public .... void	writeBoolean (boolean v) throws java.io.IOException	
	2	public .... void	writeByte (int v) throws java.io.IOException	
	2	public .... void	writeBytes (String s) throws java.io.IOException	
	2	public .... void	writeChar (int v) throws java.io.IOException	
	2	public .... void	writeChars (String s) throws java.io.IOException	
	2	public .... void	writeChars (char[] c, int off, int len) throws java.io.IOException	
	2	public .... void	writeDouble (double v) throws java.io.IOException	
	2	public .... void	writeDoubles (double[] d, int off, int len) throws java.io.IOException	

Class *Interface* —extends - - -implements ○ abstract ● final △ static ▲ static final ✻ constructor x x—inherited x **x**—declared **x x**—overridden
ε*n*—examples of usage ˌ—has subclass package—see other volume

684

	2	public	void	writeFloat (float v) throws java.io.IOException
	2	public	void	writeFloats (float[] f, int off, int len) throws java.io.IOException
	2	public	void	writeInt (int v) throws java.io.IOException
	2	public	void	writeInts (int[] i, int off, int len) throws java.io.IOException
	2	public	void	writeLong (long v) throws java.io.IOException
	2	public	void	writeLongs (long[] l, int off, int len) throws java.io.IOException
	2	public	void	writeShort (int v) throws java.io.IOException
	2	public	void	writeShorts (short[] s, int off, int len) throws java.io.IOException
	2	public	void	writeUTF (String s) throws java.io.IOException

---

MemoryImageSource   java.awt.image

Object
└MemoryImageSource - - - - - - - - - - - - - - - - - - - *ImageProducer* [1]

	1	public synchronized	void	**addConsumer** (*ImageConsumer* ic)
	1	public synchronized	boolean	**isConsumer** (*ImageConsumer* ic)
*		public		**MemoryImageSource** (int w, int h, int[] pix, int off, int scan)
*		public		**MemoryImageSource** (int w, int h, ColorModel cm, byte[] pix, int off, int scan)
				ε660
*		public		**MemoryImageSource** (int w, int h, int[] pix, int off, int scan, java.util.Hashtable props)
*		public		**MemoryImageSource** (int w, int h, ColorModel cm, int[] pix, int off, int scan)
*		public		**MemoryImageSource** (int w, int h, ColorModel cm, byte[] pix, int off, int scan, java.util.Hashtable props)
*		public		**MemoryImageSource** (int w, int h, ColorModel cm, int[] pix, int off, int scan, java.util.Hashtable props)
1.1		public	void	**newPixels** ()
1.1		public synchronized	void	**newPixels** (byte[] newpix, ColorModel newmodel, int offset, int scansize)
1.1		public synchronized	void	**newPixels** (int x, int y, int w, int h)
1.1		public synchronized	void	**newPixels** (int[] newpix, ColorModel newmodel, int offset, int scansize)
1.1		public synchronized	void	**newPixels** (int x, int y, int w, int h, boolean framenotify)
	1	public synchronized	void	**removeConsumer** (*ImageConsumer* ic)
	1	public	void	**requestTopDownLeftRightResend** (*ImageConsumer* ic)
1.1		public synchronized	void	**setAnimated** (boolean animated)
1.1		public synchronized	void	**setFullBufferUpdates** (boolean fullbuffers)
	1	public	void	**startProduction** (*ImageConsumer* ic)

Menu   java.awt

Object
○ └MenuComponent [1] - *java.io.Serializable*
   └MenuItem [2] - *javax.accessibility.Accessible*
     └Menu - *MenuContainer* [3]

		public	MenuItem	**add** (MenuItem mi)
		public	void	**add** (String label)
1.1	2	public synchronized	void	addActionListener (*java.awt.event.ActionListener* l)
	2	public	**void**	**addNotify** ()
		public	void	**addSeparator** ()
D		public	int	**countItems** ()
1.1	2	public	void	deleteShortcut ()
1.1 ●	2	protected final	void	disableEvents (long eventsToDisable)
1.1 ●	1	public final	void	dispatchEvent (AWTEvent e)
1.1 ●	2	protected final	void	enableEvents (long eventsToEnable)
1.3	2	public.... **javax.accessibility .AccessibleContext**		**getAccessibleContext** ()
1.1	2	public	String	getActionCommand ()
1.4	2	public synchronized ..... *java .awt.event.ActionListener[]*		getActionListeners ()
	1	public	Font	getFont ()
		public	MenuItem	**getItem** (int index)
1.1		public	int	**getItemCount** ()
	2	public	String	getLabel ()
1.3	2	public. *java.util.EventListener[]*		getListeners (Class listenerType)
1.1	1	public	String	getName ()
	1	public	*MenuContainer*	getParent ()
1.1	2	public	MenuShortcut	getShortcut ()
1.2 ●	1	protected final	Object	getTreeLock ()
1.1		public	void	**insert** (MenuItem menuitem, int index)
1.1		public	void	**insert** (String label, int index)

Menu

1.1		public	void	**insertSeparator** (int index)
	2	public	boolean	isEnabled ()
		public	boolean	**isTearOff** ()
1.1	✳	public		**Menu** () throws HeadlessException
	✳	public		**Menu** (String label) throws HeadlessException
	✳	public		**Menu** (String label, boolean tearOff) throws HeadlessException
	2	public	**String**	**paramString** ()
1.1	2	protected	void	processActionEvent (java.awt.event.ActionEvent e)
1.1	2	protected	void	processEvent (AWTEvent e)
		public	void	**remove** (int index)
	3	public	void	**remove** (MenuComponent item)
1.1	2	public synchronized	void	removeActionListener (*java.awt.event.ActionListener* l)
1.1		public	void	**removeAll** ()
	1	public	**void**	**removeNotify** ()
1.1	2	public	void	setActionCommand (String command)
1.1	2	public synchronized	void	setEnabled (boolean b)
	1	public	void	setFont (Font f)
	2	public synchronized	void	setLabel (String label)
1.1	1	public	void	setName (String name)
1.1	2	public	void	setShortcut (MenuShortcut s)
	1	public	String	toString ()

MenuBar   java.awt

```
      Object
  ○   └ MenuComponent¹ - - - - - - - - - - - - - - - - - -  java.io.Serializable
          └ MenuBar - - - - - - - - - - - - - - - - - - - - MenuContainer², javax.accessibility.Accessible
```

		public	Menu	**add** (Menu m)
		public	void	**addNotify** ()
D		public	int	**countMenus** ()
1.1		public	void	**deleteShortcut** (MenuShortcut s)
1.1	● 1	public final	void	dispatchEvent (AWTEvent e)
1.3	1	public.... **javax.accessibility .AccessibleContext**		**getAccessibleContext** ()
	1	public	Font	getFont ()
		public	Menu	**getHelpMenu** ()
		public	Menu	**getMenu** (int i)
1.1		public	int	**getMenuCount** ()
1.1	1	public	String	getName ()
	1	public	*MenuContainer*	getParent ()
1.1		public	MenuItem	**getShortcutMenuItem** (MenuShortcut s)
1.2	● 1	protected final	Object	getTreeLock ()
	✳	public		**MenuBar** () throws HeadlessException
	1	protected	String	paramString ()
1.1	1	protected	void	processEvent (AWTEvent e)
		public	void	**remove** (int index)
	2	public	void	**remove** (MenuComponent m)
	1	public	**void**	**removeNotify** ()
	1	public	void	setFont (Font f)
		public	void	**setHelpMenu** (Menu m)
1.1	1	public	void	setName (String name)
1.1		public synchronized *java.util*.Enumeration	**shortcuts** ()
	1	public	String	toString ()

MenuBarPeer   java.awt.peer

```
      MenuBarPeer ─────────────────────── MenuComponentPeer ¹
```

	1	*1 inherited members from MenuComponentPeer not shown*		
		public	void	**addHelpMenu** (java.awt.Menu m)
		public	void	**addMenu** (java.awt.Menu m)
		public	void	**delMenu** (int index)

Class   *Interface*   —extends   - - -implements   ○ abstract   ● final   △ static   ▲ static final   ✳ constructor   x x—inherited   x **x**—declared   **x x**—overridden
εn—examples of usage   ˶—has subclass   package—see other volume

MenuBarUI

		javax.swing.plaf

```
       Object
1.2 ○    └ComponentUI 1
1.2 ○      └MenuBarUI ⌄
```

      1 *11 inherited members from ComponentUI not shown*
   ✳ public.......................... **MenuBarUI** ()

MenuComponent

		java.awt

```
       Object 1
   ○   └MenuComponent ⌄ ---------------------- java.io.Serializable ⌄
```

1.1 ●	public final ....void	**dispatchEvent** (AWTEvent e)
1.3	public......javax.accessibility ₂ .AccessibleContext	**getAccessibleContext** ()
	public.................... Font	**getFont** ()
1.1	public....................String	**getName** ()
	public.......... MenuContainer	**getParent** ()
D	public...........java.awt ₂ .peer.MenuComponentPeer	**getPeer** ()
1.2 ●	protected final..........Object	**getTreeLock** ()
✳	public..........................	**MenuComponent** () throws HeadlessException
	protected ....String	**paramString** ()
D	public.................. boolean	**postEvent** (Event evt)
1.1	protected ....void	**processEvent** (AWTEvent e)
	public.......................void	**removeNotify** ()
	public.......................void	**setFont** (Font f)
1.1	public.......................void	**setName** (String name)
1	public.................. **String**	**toString** ()

MenuComponentPeer

		java.awt.peer

```
       MenuComponentPeer ⌄
```

      public.......................void **dispose** ()

MenuContainer

		java.awt

```
       MenuContainer
```

	public.................... Font	**getFont** ()
D	public.................. boolean	**postEvent** (Event evt)
	public.......................void	**remove** (MenuComponent comp)

MenuDragMouseEvent

		javax.swing.event
		ε640,641,643,649,566

```
       Object
1.1    └ java.util.EventObject 1 -------------------- java.io.Serializable ⌄
1.1 ○    └java.awt.AWTEvent 2
1.1        └java.awt.event.ComponentEvent 3
1.1 ○        └java.awt.event.InputEvent 4
1.1            └java.awt.event.MouseEvent 5
1.2              └MenuDragMouseEvent
```

      2 *25 inherited members from java.awt.AWTEvent not shown*
      4 *27 inherited members from java.awt.event.InputEvent not shown*

1.4 ▲ 5	public static final.............int	BUTTON1 = 1
1.4 ▲ 5	public static final.............int	BUTTON2 = 2
1.4 ▲ 5	public static final.............int	BUTTON3 = 3
▲ 3	public static final.............int	COMPONENT_FIRST = 100
▲ 3	public static final.............int	COMPONENT_HIDDEN = 103
▲ 3	public static final.............int	COMPONENT_LAST = 103
▲ 3	public static final.............int	COMPONENT_MOVED = 100
▲ 3	public static final.............int	COMPONENT_RESIZED = 101
▲ 3	public static final.............int	COMPONENT_SHOWN = 102
1.4 5	public.........................int	getButton ()
5	public.........................int	getClickCount ()
3	public.... java.awt.Component	getComponent ()

ε648,783,955,960
ε810,813,1011

M

Classes

MenuDragMouseEvent

		public............. javax.swing	₂	**getMenuSelectionManager** ()	
		.MenuSelectionManager			
1.4 △	5	public static .... String		getMouseModifiersText (int modifiers)	
		public...........................		**getPath** ()	
		.. *javax.swing.MenuElement[]*			
	5	public............ java.awt.Point		getPoint ()	ε646,647,776,783
	1	public.................... Object		getSource ()	ε644,886,565,568,570
	5	public...................... int		getX ()	ε810,937,967,1011
	5	public...................... int		getY ()	ε810,967,1011
	5	public................. boolean		isPopupTrigger ()	ε810,1011
✻		public...........................		**MenuDragMouseEvent** (java.awt.Component source, int id, long when,	
				int modifiers, int x, int y, int clickCount, boolean popupTrigger,	
				javax.swing.MenuElement[] p, javax.swing.MenuSelectionManager m)	
▲	5	public static final .... int		MOUSE_CLICKED = 500	
▲	5	public static final .... int		MOUSE_DRAGGED = 506	
▲	5	public static final .... int		MOUSE_ENTERED = 504	
▲	5	public static final .... int		MOUSE_EXITED = 505	
▲	5	public static final .... int		MOUSE_FIRST = 500	
▲	5	public static final .... int		MOUSE_LAST = 507	
▲	5	public static final .... int		MOUSE_MOVED = 503	
▲	5	public static final .... int		MOUSE_PRESSED = 501	
▲	5	public static final .... int		MOUSE_RELEASED = 502	
1.4 ▲	5	public static final .... int		MOUSE_WHEEL = 507	
1.4 ▲	5	public static final .... int		NOBUTTON = 0	
	5	public..................... String		paramString ()	
	1	protected transient...... Object		source	
	5	public synchronized ....void		translatePoint (int x, int y)	

MenuDragMouseListener
javax.swing.event

1.2	*MenuDragMouseListener*————————————*java.util.EventListener*⌐		ε738,743,745,746,752
	public.......................void	**menuDragMouseDragged** (MenuDragMouseEvent e)	
	public.......................void	**menuDragMouseEntered** (MenuDragMouseEvent e)	
	public.......................void	**menuDragMouseExited** (MenuDragMouseEvent e)	
	public.......................void	**menuDragMouseReleased** (MenuDragMouseEvent e)	

MenuElement
javax.swing

1.2	*MenuElement*		ε815
	public.... java.awt.Component	**getComponent** ()	ε813
	public.......... *MenuElement[]*	**getSubElements** ()	
	public.......................void	**menuSelectionChanged** (boolean isIncluded)	ε814
	public.......................void	**processKeyEvent** (java.awt.event.KeyEvent event, *MenuElement[]* path,	
		MenuSelectionManager manager)	
	public.......................void	**processMouseEvent** (java.awt.event.MouseEvent event, *MenuElement[]* path,	
		MenuSelectionManager manager)	

MenuEvent
javax.swing.event

		Object	ε640,641,643,649,566
1.1		└ java.util.EventObject ¹ - - - - - - - - - - - - - - - - - - - *java.io.Serializable* ⌐	
1.2		└ MenuEvent	
✻	1	public..................... Object	getSource ()	ε644,886,565,568,570
		public...........................	**MenuEvent** (Object source)	
	1	protected transient...... Object	source	
	1	public..................... String	toString ()	

MenuItem
java.awt

	Object	
○	└ MenuComponent ¹ - *java.io.Serializable* ⌐	
	└ MenuItem ⌐ - *javax.accessibility.Accessible*	

Class   *Interface*   —extends   - - -implements   ○ abstract   ● final   △ static   ▲ static final   ✻ constructor   x x—inherited   x **x**—declared   **x x**—overridden
ε*n*—examples of usage   ⌐—has subclass   package—see other volume

1.1		public synchronized ....void	**addActionListener** (*java.awt.event.ActionListener* l)
		public......................void	**addNotify** ()
1.1		public......................void	**deleteShortcut** ()
D		public synchronized ....void	**disable** ()
1.1 ●		protected final..............void	**disableEvents** (long eventsToDisable)
1.1 ●	1	public final ....void	dispatchEvent (AWTEvent e)
D		public synchronized ....void	**enable** ()
D		public......................void	**enable** (boolean b)
1.1 ●		protected final..............void	**enableEvents** (long eventsToEnable)
1.3	1	public.... **javax.accessibility** **.AccessibleContext**	**getAccessibleContext** ()
1.1		public......................String	**getActionCommand** ()
1.4		public synchronized ..... *java* *.awt.event.ActionListener[]*	**getActionListeners** ()
	1	public...................... Font	getFont ()
		public......................String	**getLabel** ()
1.3		public. *java.util.EventListener[]*	**getListeners** (Class listenerType)
1.1	1	public......................String	getName ()
	1	public.......... *MenuContainer*	getParent ()
1.1		public............MenuShortcut	**getShortcut** ()
1.2 ●	1	protected final...........Object	getTreeLock ()
		public................. boolean	**isEnabled** ()
1.1 *		public.........................	**MenuItem** () throws HeadlessException
*		public.........................	**MenuItem** (String label) throws HeadlessException
1.1 *		public.........................	**MenuItem** (String label, MenuShortcut s) throws HeadlessException
	1	public.................... **String**	**paramString** ()
1.1		protected ....void	**processActionEvent** (java.awt.event.ActionEvent e)
1.1	1	protected .... **void**	**processEvent** (AWTEvent e)
1.1		public synchronized ....void	**removeActionListener** (*java.awt.event.ActionListener* l)
	1	public......................void	removeNotify ()
1.1		public......................void	**setActionCommand** (String command)
1.1		public synchronized ....void	**setEnabled** (boolean b)
	1	public......................void	setFont (Font f)
		public synchronized ....void	**setLabel** (String label)
1.1	1	public......................void	setName (String name)
1.1		public......................void	**setShortcut** (MenuShortcut s)
	1	public....................String	toString ()

MenuItemPeer			java.awt.peer

MenuItemPeer ————————————————MenuComponentPeer 1

	1	*1 inherited members from MenuComponentPeer not shown*	
		public......................void	**disable** ()
		public......................void	**enable** ()
1.1		public......................void	**setEnabled** (boolean b)
		public......................void	**setLabel** (String label)

MenuItemUI			javax.swing.plaf

Object

1.2 ○	└ ComponentUI 1	
1.2 ○	└ ButtonUI	
1.2 ○	└ MenuItemUI	

	1	*11 inherited members from ComponentUI not shown*	
*		public.........................	**MenuItemUI** ()

MenuKeyEvent			javax.swing.event
			ε640,641,643,649,566

Object

1.1	└ java.util.EventObject 1 - - - - - - - - - - - - - - - - - - *java.io.Serializable*	
1.1 ○	└ java.awt.AWTEvent 2	
1.1	└ java.awt.event.ComponentEvent 3	
1.1 ○	└ java.awt.event.InputEvent 4	
1.1	└ java.awt.event.KeyEvent 5	
1.2	└ MenuKeyEvent	

	2	*25 inherited members from java.awt.AWTEvent not shown*
	4	*27 inherited members from java.awt.event.InputEvent not shown*

MenuKeyEvent

	5	*207 inherited members from java.awt.event.KeyEvent not shown*		
▲	3	public static final.............int	COMPONENT_FIRST = 100	
▲	3	public static final.............int	COMPONENT_HIDDEN = 103	
▲	3	public static final.............int	COMPONENT_LAST = 103	
▲	3	public static final.............int	COMPONENT_MOVED = 100	
▲	3	public static final.............int	COMPONENT_RESIZED = 101	
▲	3	public static final.............int	COMPONENT_SHOWN = 102	
	3	public.... java.awt.Component	getComponent ()	ε810,813,1011
		public...............javax.swing ﹍ .MenuSelectionManager	**getMenuSelectionManager** ()	
		public.......................... .. *javax.swing.MenuElement[]*	**getPath** ()	
	1	public...................Object	getSource ()	ε644,886,565,568,570
*		public........................	**MenuKeyEvent** (java.awt.Component source, int id, long when, int modifiers, int keyCode, char keyChar, *javax.swing.MenuElement[]* p, javax.swing.MenuSelectionManager m)	
	1	protected transient......Object	source	

MenuKeyListener
javax.swing.event

1.2	*MenuKeyListener*————————————————*java.util.EventListener* ﹍		ε738,743,745,746,752
	public.......................void	**menuKeyPressed** (MenuKeyEvent e)	
	public.......................void	**menuKeyReleased** (MenuKeyEvent e)	
	public.......................void	**menuKeyTyped** (MenuKeyEvent e)	

MenuListener
javax.swing.event

1.2	*MenuListener*————————————————*java.util.EventListener* ﹍		ε738,743,745,746,752
	public.......................void	**menuCanceled** (MenuEvent e)	
	public.......................void	**menuDeselected** (MenuEvent e)	
	public.......................void	**menuSelected** (MenuEvent e)	

MenuPeer
java.awt.peer

	MenuPeer ﹍ ————————————————*MenuItemPeer* ﹍ [1] (*MenuComponentPeer* [2])		
1	*4 inherited members from MenuItemPeer not shown*		
2	*1 inherited members from MenuComponentPeer not shown*		
	public.......................void	**addItem** (java.awt.MenuItem item)	
	public.......................void	**addSeparator** ()	
	public.......................void	**delItem** (int index)	

MenuSelectionManager
javax.swing

1.2	Object └MenuSelectionManager		
	public.......................void	**addChangeListener** (*javax.swing.event.ChangeListener* l)	ε815
	protected transient...... javax ﹍ .swing.event.ChangeEvent	**changeEvent**	
	public.......................void	**clearSelectedPath** ()	
	public.... java.awt.Component	**componentForPoint** (java.awt.Component source, java.awt.Point sourcePoint)	
△	public static .... MenuSelectionManager	**defaultManager** ()	ε813,815
	protected ....void	**fireStateChanged** ()	
1.4	public............. *javax.swing* ﹍ *.event.ChangeListener[]*	**getChangeListeners** ()	
	public.......... *MenuElement[]*	**getSelectedPath** ()	ε813,815
	public................. boolean	**isComponentPartOfCurrentMenu** (java.awt.Component c)	
	protected .... javax.swing ﹍ .event.EventListenerList	**listenerList**	
*	public........................	**MenuSelectionManager** ()	
	public.......................void	**processKeyEvent** (java.awt.event.KeyEvent e)	
	public.......................void	**processMouseEvent** (java.awt.event.MouseEvent event)	
	public.......................void	**removeChangeListener** (*javax.swing.event.ChangeListener* l)	

Class   *Interface*   —extends   - - -implements   ○ abstract   ● final   △ static   ▲ static final   ✻ constructor   x x—inherited   x **x**—declared   **x x**—overridden
ε*n*—examples of usage   ﹍—has subclass   package—see other volume

public.......................void **setSelectedPath** (*MenuElement[]* path)

MenuShortcut
java.awt

Object[1]
1.1 └MenuShortcut ------------------------ *java.io.Serializable*

	public.................. boolean	**equals** (MenuShortcut s)
1	public.................. **boolean**	**equals** (Object obj)
	public.......................int	**getKey** ()
1	public........................ **int**	**hashCode** ()
*	public....................	**MenuShortcut** (int key)
*	public....................	**MenuShortcut** (int key, boolean useShiftModifier)
	protected ....String	**paramString** ()
1	public.................... **String**	**toString** ()
	public.................. boolean	**usesShiftModifier** ()

MetaEventListener
javax.sound.midi

1.3 *MetaEventListener*————————— *java.util.EventListener*   *ε738,743,745,746,752*

public.......................void **meta** (MetaMessage meta)   *ε722*

MetaMessage
javax.sound.midi

Object
1.3 ○ └MidiMessage[1] ------------------------ *Cloneable*
1.3   └MetaMessage

1	public.................... **Object**	**clone** ()	
1	protected ....byte[]	data	
	public.....................byte[]	**getData** ()	
1	public.......................int	getLength ()	
1	public.....................byte[]	getMessage ()	
1	public.......................int	getStatus ()	
	public.......................int	**getType** ()	*ε722*
1	protected ....int	length	
▲	public static final ....int	**META** = 255	
*	public....................	**MetaMessage** ()	
*	protected	**MetaMessage** (byte[] data)	
1	protected ....void	setMessage (byte[] data, int length) throws InvalidMidiDataException	
	public.......................void	**setMessage** (int type, byte[] data, int length) throws InvalidMidiDataException	

MidiChannel
javax.sound.midi

1.3 *MidiChannel*

public.......................void	**allNotesOff** ()	
public.......................void	**allSoundOff** ()	
public.......................void	**controlChange** (int controller, int value)	*ε721*
public.......................int	**getChannelPressure** ()	
public.......................int	**getController** (int controller)	
public.................. boolean	**getMono** ()	
public.................. boolean	**getMute** ()	
public.................. boolean	**getOmni** ()	
public.......................int	**getPitchBend** ()	
public.......................int	**getPolyPressure** (int noteNumber)	
public.......................int	**getProgram** ()	
public.................. boolean	**getSolo** ()	
public.................. boolean	**localControl** (boolean on)	
public.......................void	**noteOff** (int noteNumber)	
public.......................void	**noteOff** (int noteNumber, int velocity)	
public.......................void	**noteOn** (int noteNumber, int velocity)	
public.......................void	**programChange** (int program)	
public.......................void	**programChange** (int bank, int program)	
public.......................void	**resetAllControllers** ()	
public.......................void	**setChannelPressure** (int pressure)	
public.......................void	**setMono** (boolean on)	
public.......................void	**setMute** (boolean mute)	
public.......................void	**setOmni** (boolean on)	

MidiChannel

public	void	**setPitchBend** (int bend)
public	void	**setPolyPressure** (int noteNumber, int pressure)
public	void	**setSolo** (boolean soloState)

MidiDevice
javax.sound.midi

1.3   *MidiDevice*

public	void	**close** ()
public	MidiDevice.Info	**getDeviceInfo** ()
public	int	**getMaxReceivers** ()
public	int	**getMaxTransmitters** ()
public	long	**getMicrosecondPosition** ()	ε720
public	*Receiver*	**getReceiver** () throws MidiUnavailableException
public	*Transmitter*	**getTransmitter** () throws MidiUnavailableException
public	boolean	**isOpen** ()
public	void	**open** () throws MidiUnavailableException	ε716,717

MidiDevice.Info
javax.sound.midi

Object[1]
    └ MidiDevice.Info
1.3

●	1	public final	**boolean**	**equals** (Object obj)
●		public final	String	**getDescription** ()
●		public final	String	**getName** ()
●		public final	String	**getVendor** ()
●		public final	String	**getVersion** ()
●	1	public final	**int**	**hashCode** ()
*		protected		**MidiDevice.Info** (String name, String vendor, String description, String version)
●	1	public final	**String**	**toString** ()

MidiDeviceProvider
javax.sound.midi.spi

Object
    └ MidiDeviceProvider
1.3 ○

○	public abstract *javax.sound.midi.MidiDevice*	**getDevice** (javax.sound.midi.MidiDevice.Info info)
○	public abstract *javax.sound .midi.MidiDevice.Info[]*	**getDeviceInfo** ()
	public	boolean	**isDeviceSupported** (javax.sound.midi.MidiDevice.Info info)
*	public	**MidiDeviceProvider** ()

MidiEvent
javax.sound.midi

Object
    └ MidiEvent
1.3

public	MidiMessage	**getMessage** ()
public	long	**getTick** ()
* public		**MidiEvent** (MidiMessage message, long tick)
public	void	**setTick** (long tick)

MidiFileFormat
javax.sound.midi

Object
    └ MidiFileFormat
1.3

protected	int	**byteLength**
protected	float	**divisionType**
public	int	**getByteLength** ()
public	float	**getDivisionType** ()
public	long	**getMicrosecondLength** ()
public	int	**getResolution** ()
public	int	**getType** ()	ε718

Class   *Interface*   —extends   - - -implements   ○ abstract   ● final   △ static   ▲ static final   * constructor   x x—inherited   x **x**—declared   **x x**—overridden
ε*n*—examples of usage   ˌ—has subclass   package—see other volume

*	protected . . . . long	**microsecondLength**	
	public.	**MidiFileFormat** (int type, float divisionType, int resolution, int bytes, long microseconds)	
	protected . . . . .int	**resolution**	
	protected . . . . .int	**type**	
▲	public static final . . . . .int	**UNKNOWN_LENGTH** = -1	

MidiFileReader

javax.sound.midi.spi

Object
1.3 O └MidiFileReader

O	public abstract . . . . javax**₂** .sound.midi.MidiFileFormat	**getMidiFileFormat** (java.io.File file) throws javax.sound.midi**₂** .InvalidMidiDataException, java.io.IOException
O	public abstract . . . . javax**₂** .sound.midi.MidiFileFormat	**getMidiFileFormat** (java.io.InputStream stream) throws javax.sound.midi.InvalidMidiDataException, java.io.IOException
O	public abstract . . . . javax**₂** .sound.midi.MidiFileFormat	**getMidiFileFormat** (java.net.URL url) throws javax.sound.midi**₂** .InvalidMidiDataException, java.io.IOException
O	public abstract . . . . javax.sound.midi.Sequence	**getSequence** (java.io.File file) throws javax.sound.midi.InvalidMidiDataException, java.io.IOException
O	public abstract . . . . javax.sound.midi.Sequence	**getSequence** (java.io.InputStream stream) throws javax.sound.midi.InvalidMidiDataException, java.io.IOException
O	public abstract . . . . javax.sound.midi.Sequence	**getSequence** (java.net.URL url) throws javax.sound.midi.InvalidMidiDataException, java.io.IOException
*	public.	**MidiFileReader** ()

M

MidiFileWriter

javax.sound.midi.spi

Object
1.3 O └MidiFileWriter

O	public abstract . . . . int[]	**getMidiFileTypes** ()
O	public abstract . . . . int[]	**getMidiFileTypes** (javax.sound.midi.Sequence sequence)
	public. . . . . boolean	**isFileTypeSupported** (int fileType)
	public. . . . . boolean	**isFileTypeSupported** (int fileType, javax.sound.midi.Sequence sequence)
*	public.	**MidiFileWriter** ()
O	public abstract . . . . .int	**write** (javax.sound.midi.Sequence in, int fileType, java.io.File out) throws java.io.IOException
O	public abstract . . . . .int	**write** (javax.sound.midi.Sequence in, int fileType, java.io.OutputStream out) throws java.io.IOException

---

MidiMessage

javax.sound.midi

Object[1]
1.3 O └MidiMessage. - *Cloneable*.

O	1	public abstract . . . .**Object**	**clone** ()
		protected . . . . byte[]	**data**
		public. . . . . .int	**getLength** ()
		public. . . . . byte[]	**getMessage** ()
		public. . . . . .int	**getStatus** ()
		protected . . . . .int	**length**
*		protected	**MidiMessage** (byte[] data)
		protected . . . . .void	**setMessage** (byte[] data, int length) throws InvalidMidiDataException

---

MidiSystem

javax.sound.midi

Object
1.3 └MidiSystem

△	public static . . . . *MidiDevice*	**getMidiDevice** (MidiDevice.Info info) throws MidiUnavailableException
△	public static . MidiDevice.Info[]	**getMidiDeviceInfo** ()
△	public static . . . . MidiFileFormat	**getMidiFileFormat** (java.io.File file) throws InvalidMidiDataException, java.io.IOException *ε718*
△	public static . . . . MidiFileFormat	**getMidiFileFormat** (java.io.InputStream stream) throws InvalidMidiDataException, java.io.IOException
△	public static . . . . MidiFileFormat	**getMidiFileFormat** (java.net.URL url) throws InvalidMidiDataException, java.io.IOException *ε718*

Classes

MidiSystem

△	public static	int[]	**getMidiFileTypes** ()
△	public static	int[]	**getMidiFileTypes** (Sequence sequence)
△	public static	*Receiver*	**getReceiver** () throws MidiUnavailableException
△	public static	Sequence	**getSequence** (java.io.File file) throws InvalidMidiDataException, java.io.IOException *ε*716
△	public static	Sequence	**getSequence** (java.io.InputStream stream) throws InvalidMidiDataException, java.io.IOException
△	public static	Sequence	**getSequence** (java.net.URL url) throws InvalidMidiDataException, java.io.IOException *ε*716
△	public static	*Sequencer*	**getSequencer** () throws MidiUnavailableException *ε*716,717
△	public static	*Soundbank*	**getSoundbank** (java.io.File file) throws InvalidMidiDataException, java.io.IOException
△	public static	*Soundbank*	**getSoundbank** (java.io.InputStream stream) throws InvalidMidiDataException, java.io.IOException
△	public static	*Soundbank*	**getSoundbank** (java.net.URL url) throws InvalidMidiDataException, java.io.IOException
△	public static	*Synthesizer*	**getSynthesizer** () throws MidiUnavailableException
△	public static	*Transmitter*	**getTransmitter** () throws MidiUnavailableException
△	public static	boolean	**isFileTypeSupported** (int fileType)
△	public static	boolean	**isFileTypeSupported** (int fileType, Sequence sequence)
△	public static	int	**write** (Sequence in, int type, java.io.File out) throws java.io.IOException
△	public static	int	**write** (Sequence in, int fileType, java.io.OutputStream out) throws java.io.IOException

M

MidiUnavailableException | javax.sound.midi

```
Object                                                             ε716,717
└Throwable - - - - - - - - - - - - - - - - - - - - - - - - java.io.Serializable
   └Exception
1.3    └MidiUnavailableException
```

✳	public	**MidiUnavailableException** ()
✳	public	**MidiUnavailableException** (String message)

MimeTypeParseException | java.awt.datatransfer

```
Object
└Throwable - - - - - - - - - - - - - - - - - - - - - - - - java.io.Serializable
   └Exception
1.3    └MimeTypeParseException
```

✳	public	**MimeTypeParseException** ()
✳	public	**MimeTypeParseException** (String s)

MinimalHTMLWriter | javax.swing.text.html

```
        Object
1.2 ○   └javax.swing.text.AbstractWriter 1
1.2       └MinimalHTMLWriter
```

	1	*28 inherited members from javax.swing.text.AbstractWriter not shown*	
		protected ... void	**endFontTag** () throws java.io.IOException
		protected ... boolean	**inFontTag** ()
		protected ... boolean	**isText** (*javax.swing.text.Element* elem)
✳		public	**MinimalHTMLWriter** (*java.io.Writer* w, *javax.swing.text.StyledDocument* doc)
✳		public	**MinimalHTMLWriter** (*java.io.Writer* w, *javax.swing.text.StyledDocument* doc, int pos, int len)
		protected ... void	**startFontTag** (String style) throws java.io.IOException
	1	protected ... **void**	**text** (*javax.swing.text.Element* elem) throws java.io.IOException, javax.swing.text.BadLocationException
	1	public ... **void**	**write** () throws java.io.IOException, javax.swing.text.BadLocationException
	1	protected ... **void**	**writeAttributes** (*javax.swing.text.AttributeSet* attr) throws java.io.IOException
		protected ... void	**writeBody** () throws java.io.IOException, javax.swing.text.BadLocationException
		protected ... void	**writeComponent** (*javax.swing.text.Element* elem) throws java.io.IOException
		protected ... void	**writeContent** (*javax.swing.text.Element* elem, boolean needsIndenting) throws java.io.IOException, javax.swing.text.BadLocationException

---

Class *Interface* —extends - - -implements ○ abstract ● final △ static ▲ static final ✳ constructor x x—inherited x **x**—declared **x x**—overridden
εn—examples of usage ⌐has subclass package—see other volume

protected .... void **writeEndParagraph** () throws java.io.IOException
protected .... void **writeEndTag** (String endTag) throws java.io.IOException
protected .... void **writeHeader** () throws java.io.IOException
protected .... void **writeHTMLTags** (*javax.swing.text.AttributeSet* attr) throws java.io.IOException
protected .... void **writeImage** (*javax.swing.text.Element* elem) throws java.io.IOException
protected .... void **writeLeaf** (*javax.swing.text.Element* elem) throws java.io.IOException
protected .... void **writeNonHTMLAttributes** (*javax.swing.text.AttributeSet* attr)
     throws java.io.IOException
protected .... void **writeStartParagraph** (*javax.swing.text.Element* elem) throws java.io.IOException
protected .... void **writeStartTag** (String tag) throws java.io.IOException
protected .... void **writeStyles** () throws java.io.IOException

---

Mixer   javax.sound.sampled

1.3   *Mixer* ———————————————— *Line* [1]

1	public	void	addLineListener (*LineListener* listener)	ε731
1	public	void	close ()	
1	public	Control	getControl (Control.Type control)	ε730
1	public	Control[]	getControls ()	
	public	*Line*	**getLine** (Line.Info info) throws LineUnavailableException	
1	public	Line.Info	getLineInfo ()	
	public	int	**getMaxLines** (Line.Info info)	
	public	Mixer.Info	**getMixerInfo** ()	
	public	Line.Info[]	**getSourceLineInfo** ()	
	public	Line.Info[]	**getSourceLineInfo** (Line.Info info)	
	public	*Line[]*	**getSourceLines** ()	
	public	Line.Info[]	**getTargetLineInfo** ()	
	public	Line.Info[]	**getTargetLineInfo** (Line.Info info)	
	public	*Line[]*	**getTargetLines** ()	
1	public	boolean	isControlSupported (Control.Type control)	
	public	boolean	**isLineSupported** (Line.Info info)	
1	public	boolean	isOpen ()	
	public	boolean	**isSynchronizationSupported** (*Line[]* lines, boolean maintainSync)	
1	public	void	open () throws LineUnavailableException	
1	public	void	removeLineListener (*LineListener* listener)	
	public	void	**synchronize** (*Line[]* lines, boolean maintainSync)	
	public	void	**unsynchronize** (*Line[]* lines)	

Mixer.Info   javax.sound.sampled

  Object [1]
1.3   └─Mixer.Info

● 1	public final	**boolean**	**equals** (Object obj)
●	public final	String	**getDescription** ()
●	public final	String	**getName** ()
●	public final	String	**getVendor** ()
●	public final	String	**getVersion** ()
● 1	public final	**int**	**hashCode** ()
*	protected		**Mixer.Info** (String name, String vendor, String description, String version)
● 1	public final	**String**	**toString** ()

MixerProvider   javax.sound.sampled.spi

  Object
1.3 ○   └─MixerProvider

○	public abstract	**getMixer** (javax.sound.sampled.Mixer.Info info)
	.. *javax.sound.sampled.Mixer*	
○	public abstract .... javax [2]	**getMixerInfo** ()
	.sound.sampled.Mixer.Info[]	
	public .... boolean	**isMixerSupported** (javax.sound.sampled.Mixer.Info info)
*	public	**MixerProvider** ()

MouseAdapter   java.awt.event

  Object
1.1 ○   └─MouseAdapter ----------------------- *MouseListener* [1] (*java.util.EventListener*)

MouseAdapter

✱		public........................	**MouseAdapter** ()	ε602,742,783,810,1011
	1	public....................void	**mouseClicked** (MouseEvent e)	ε646,648,783,967
	1	public....................void	**mouseEntered** (MouseEvent e)	
	1	public....................void	**mouseExited** (MouseEvent e)	
	1	public....................void	**mousePressed** (MouseEvent e)	ε602,742,810,1011
	1	public....................void	**mouseReleased** (MouseEvent e)	ε810,1011

MouseDragGestureRecognizer
java.awt.dnd

Object
1.2 ○ └DragGestureRecognizer[1] - - - - - - - - - - - - - - - - *java.io.Serializable*
1.2 ○   └MouseDragGestureRecognizer - - - - - - - - - *java.awt.event.MouseListener*[2] (*java.util.EventListener*),
                                      java.awt.event.MouseMotionListener[3] (*java.util.EventListener*)

	1	public synchronized ....void	addDragGestureListener (*DragGestureListener* dgl)	
			throws java.util.TooManyListenersException	
	1	protected synchronized ...void	appendEvent (java.awt.event.InputEvent awtie)	
	1	protected java.awt.Component	component	
	1	protected transient............. ....*DragGestureListener*	dragGestureListener	
	1	protected ....DragSource	dragSource	
	1	protected ....java.util.ArrayList	events	
	1	protected synchronized ...void	fireDragGestureRecognized (int dragAction, java.awt.Point p)	
	1	public synchronized ....java.awt.Component	getComponent ()	
	1	public.............DragSource	getDragSource ()	
	1	public synchronized ....int	getSourceActions ()	
	1	public.......................... ....java.awt.event.InputEvent	getTriggerEvent ()	
	2	public....................void	**mouseClicked** (java.awt.event.MouseEvent e)	ε646,648,783,967
	3	public....................void	**mouseDragged** (java.awt.event.MouseEvent e)	ε647
✱		protected......................	**MouseDragGestureRecognizer** (DragSource ds)	
✱		protected......................	**MouseDragGestureRecognizer** (DragSource ds, java.awt.Component c)	
✱		protected......................	**MouseDragGestureRecognizer** (DragSource ds, java.awt.Component c, int act)	
✱		protected......................	**MouseDragGestureRecognizer** (DragSource ds, java.awt.Component c, int act, *DragGestureListener* dgl)	
	2	public....................void	**mouseEntered** (java.awt.event.MouseEvent e)	
	2	public....................void	**mouseExited** (java.awt.event.MouseEvent e)	
	3	public....................void	**mouseMoved** (java.awt.event.MouseEvent e)	ε647,937
	2	public....................void	**mousePressed** (java.awt.event.MouseEvent e)	ε602,742,810,1011
	2	public....................void	**mouseReleased** (java.awt.event.MouseEvent e)	ε810,1011
	1	protected ....**void**	**registerListeners** ()	
	1	public synchronized ....void	removeDragGestureListener (*DragGestureListener* dgl)	
	1	public....................void	resetRecognizer ()	
	1	public synchronized ....void	setComponent (java.awt.Component c)	
	1	public synchronized ....void	setSourceActions (int actions)	
	1	protected ....int	sourceActions	
	1	protected ....**void**	**unregisterListeners** ()	

MouseEvent
java.awt.event

Object   ε602,844,640,641,643
1.1   └ java.util.EventObject[1] - - - - - - - - - - - - - - - - - - - *java.io.Serializable*
1.1 ○   └java.awt.AWTEvent[2]
1.1   └ComponentEvent[3]
1.1 ○   └ InputEvent[4]
1.1   └MouseEvent

	2	*25 inherited members from java.awt.AWTEvent not shown*		
	4	*26 inherited members from InputEvent not shown*		
1.4 ▲		public static final.............int	**BUTTON1** = 1	
1.4 ▲		public static final.............int	**BUTTON2** = 2	
1.4 ▲		public static final.............int	**BUTTON3** = 3	
▲	3	public static final.............int	COMPONENT_FIRST = 100	
▲	3	public static final.............int	COMPONENT_HIDDEN = 103	
▲	3	public static final.............int	COMPONENT_LAST = 103	
▲	3	public static final.............int	COMPONENT_MOVED = 100	

Class   *Interface*   —extends   - - -implements   ○ abstract   ● final   △ static   ▲ static final   ✱ constructor   x x—inherited   x **x**—declared   **x x**—overridden
ε*n*—examples of usage   —has subclass   package—see other volume

▲	3	public static final ....int	**COMPONENT_RESIZED** = 101	
▲	3	public static final ....int	**COMPONENT_SHOWN** = 102	
1.4		public........................int	**getButton** ()	
		public........................int	**getClickCount** ()	ε648,783,955,960
	3	public.... java.awt.Component	getComponent ()	ε810,813,1011
	4	public........................int	getModifiers ()	ε646
1.4 △		public static ....String	**getMouseModifiersText** (int modifiers)	
		public...........java.awt.Point	**getPoint** ()	ε646,647,776,783
	1	public........................Object	getSource ()	ε742,783,937,967,644
		public........................int	**getX** ()	ε810,937,967,1011
		public........................int	**getY** ()	ε810,967,1011
		public.................. boolean	**isPopupTrigger** ()	ε810,1011
▲		public static final ....int	**MOUSE_CLICKED** = 500	
▲		public static final ....int	**MOUSE_DRAGGED** = 506	
▲		public static final ....int	**MOUSE_ENTERED** = 504	
▲		public static final ....int	**MOUSE_EXITED** = 505	
▲		public static final ....int	**MOUSE_FIRST** = 500	
▲		public static final ....int	**MOUSE_LAST** = 507	
▲		public static final ....int	**MOUSE_MOVED** = 503	
▲		public static final ....int	**MOUSE_PRESSED** = 501	
▲		public static final ....int	**MOUSE_RELEASED** = 502	
1.4 ▲		public static final ....int	**MOUSE_WHEEL** = 507	
*		public........................	**MouseEvent** (java.awt.Component source, int id, long when, int modifiers, int x, int y, int clickCount, boolean popupTrigger)	
1.4 *		public........................	**MouseEvent** (java.awt.Component source, int id, long when, int modifiers, int x, int y, int clickCount, boolean popupTrigger, int button)	
1.4 ▲		public static final ....int	**NOBUTTON** = 0	
	3	public................. **String**	**paramString** ()	
	1	protected transient......Object	source	
		public synchronized ....void	**translatePoint** (int x, int y)	

MouseInputAdapter — javax.swing.event

Object
└MouseInputAdapter ˵ - *MouseInputListener* (*java.awt.event.MouseListener* [1]
(*java.util.EventListener*), *java.awt.event.MouseMotionListener* [2]
(*java.util.EventListener*))

	1	public........................void	**mouseClicked** (java.awt.event.MouseEvent e)	ε646,648,783,967
	2	public........................void	**mouseDragged** (java.awt.event.MouseEvent e)	ε647
	1	public........................void	**mouseEntered** (java.awt.event.MouseEvent e)	
	1	public........................void	**mouseExited** (java.awt.event.MouseEvent e)	
*		public........................	**MouseInputAdapter** ()	
	2	public........................void	**mouseMoved** (java.awt.event.MouseEvent e)	ε647,937
	1	public........................void	**mousePressed** (java.awt.event.MouseEvent e)	ε602,742,810,1011
	1	public........................void	**mouseReleased** (java.awt.event.MouseEvent e)	ε810,1011

MouseInputListener — javax.swing.event

1.2	*MouseInputListener*————————————*java.awt.event.MouseListener* ˎ [1]	ε738,743,745,746,752
	(*java.util.EventListener*),	
	java.awt.event.MouseMotionListener ˎ [2]	
	(*java.util.EventListener*)	

	1	public........................void	mouseClicked (java.awt.event.MouseEvent e)	ε646,648,783,967
	2	public........................void	mouseDragged (java.awt.event.MouseEvent e)	ε647
	1	public........................void	mouseEntered (java.awt.event.MouseEvent e)	
	1	public........................void	mouseExited (java.awt.event.MouseEvent e)	
	2	public........................void	mouseMoved (java.awt.event.MouseEvent e)	ε647,937
	1	public........................void	mousePressed (java.awt.event.MouseEvent e)	ε602,742,810,1011
	1	public........................void	mouseReleased (java.awt.event.MouseEvent e)	ε810,1011

MouseListener — java.awt.event

1.1	*MouseListener* ˎ————————————*java.util.EventListener* ˎ	ε738,743,745,746,752

public........................void	**mouseClicked** (MouseEvent e)	ε646,648,783,967
public........................void	**mouseEntered** (MouseEvent e)	
public........................void	**mouseExited** (MouseEvent e)	
public........................void	**mousePressed** (MouseEvent e)	ε602,742,810,1011

M

Classes

MouseListener

public......................void **mouseReleased** (MouseEvent e)		ε810,1011

MouseMotionAdapter | java.awt.event

Object
1.1 ○ └─MouseMotionAdapter ------------------- *MouseMotionListener* [1] (*java.util.EventListener*)

	1	public......................void **mouseDragged** (MouseEvent e)	ε647
✳		public...................... **MouseMotionAdapter** ()	
	1	public......................void **mouseMoved** (MouseEvent e)	ε647,937

MouseMotionListener | java.awt.event

1.1 *MouseMotionListener* ─────────────── *java.util.EventListener* ε738,743,745,746,752

public......................void **mouseDragged** (MouseEvent e)		ε647
public......................void **mouseMoved** (MouseEvent e)		ε647,937

MouseWheelEvent | java.awt.event

Object ε640,641,643,649,566
1.1 └─ java.util.EventObject [1] ------------------- *java.io.Serializable*
1.1 ○   └─java.awt.AWTEvent [2]
1.1   └─ComponentEvent [3]
1.1 ○   └─InputEvent [4]
1.1   └─MouseEvent [5]
1.4   └─MouseWheelEvent

	2	*25 inherited members from java.awt.AWTEvent not shown*		
	4	*27 inherited members from InputEvent not shown*		
▲	5	public static final.............int BUTTON1 = 1		
▲	5	public static final.............int BUTTON2 = 2		
▲	5	public static final.............int BUTTON3 = 3		
▲	3	public static final.............int COMPONENT_FIRST = 100		
▲	3	public static final.............int COMPONENT_HIDDEN = 103		
▲	3	public static final.............int COMPONENT_LAST = 103		
▲	3	public static final.............int COMPONENT_MOVED = 100		
▲	3	public static final.............int COMPONENT_RESIZED = 101		
▲	3	public static final.............int COMPONENT_SHOWN = 102		
	5	public......................int getButton ()		
	5	public......................int getClickCount ()	ε648,783,955,960	
	3	public.... java.awt.Component getComponent ()	ε810,813,1011	
△	5	public static ....String getMouseModifiersText (int modifiers)		
	5	public............java.awt.Point getPoint ()	ε646,647,776,783	
		public......................int **getScrollAmount** ()		
		public......................int **getScrollType** ()		
	1	public......................Object getSource ()	ε644,886,565,568,570	
		public......................int **getUnitsToScroll** ()		
		public......................int **getWheelRotation** ()		
	5	public......................int getX ()	ε810,937,967,1011	
	5	public......................int getY ()	ε810,967,1011	
	5	public...............boolean isPopupTrigger ()	ε810,1011	
▲	5	public static final.............int MOUSE_CLICKED = 500		
▲	5	public static final.............int MOUSE_DRAGGED = 506		
▲	5	public static final.............int MOUSE_ENTERED = 504		
▲	5	public static final.............int MOUSE_EXITED = 505		
▲	5	public static final.............int MOUSE_FIRST = 500		
▲	5	public static final.............int MOUSE_LAST = 507		
▲	5	public static final.............int MOUSE_MOVED = 503		
▲	5	public static final.............int MOUSE_PRESSED = 501		
▲	5	public static final.............int MOUSE_RELEASED = 502		
▲	5	public static final.............int MOUSE_WHEEL = 507		
✳		public...................... **MouseWheelEvent** (java.awt.Component source, int id, long when, int modifiers, int x, int y, int clickCount, boolean popupTrigger, int scrollType, int scrollAmount, int wheelRotation)		
▲	5	public static final.............int NOBUTTON = 0		
	5	public................... **String paramString** ()		
	1	protected transient......Object source		

5	public synchronized ....void	translatePoint (int x, int y)	
▲	public static final ....int	**WHEEL_BLOCK_SCROLL** = 1	
▲	public static final ....int	**WHEEL_UNIT_SCROLL** = 0	

MouseWheelListener java.awt.event

1.4	*MouseWheelListener* ——————————— *java.util.EventListener*	ε738,743,745,746,752
	public......................void **mouseWheelMoved** (MouseWheelEvent e)	

MultiDoc javax.print

1.4	*MultiDoc*	
	public...................... *Doc* **getDoc** () throws java.io.IOException	
	public................. *MultiDoc* **next** () throws java.io.IOException	

MultiDocPrintJob javax.print

1.4	*MultiDocPrintJob* ——————————— *DocPrintJob* [1]	
1	public......................void	addPrintJobAttributeListener (*javax.print.event.PrintJobAttributeListener* listener,
		javax.print.attribute.PrintJobAttributeSet attributes) ε715
1	public......................void	addPrintJobListener (*javax.print.event.PrintJobListener* listener) ε714
1	public..... *javax.print.attribute₂*	getAttributes () ε715
	.PrintJobAttributeSet	
1	public............. *PrintService*	getPrintService ()
1	public......................void	print (*Doc* doc, *javax.print.attribute.PrintRequestAttributeSet* attributes)
		throws PrintException ε700,702,710,711,712
	public......................void	**print** (*MultiDoc* multiDoc, *javax.print.attribute.PrintRequestAttributeSet* attributes)
		throws PrintException
1	public......................void	removePrintJobAttributeListener (*javax.print.event.PrintJobAttributeListener* listener)
1	public......................void	removePrintJobListener (*javax.print.event.PrintJobListener* listener)

MultiDocPrintService javax.print

1.4	*MultiDocPrintService* ——————————— *PrintService* [1]	ε703
1	public......................void	addPrintServiceAttributeListener (*javax.print.event.PrintServiceAttributeListener*
		listener) ε713
	public........ *MultiDocPrintJob*	**createMultiDocPrintJob** ()
1	public............. *DocPrintJob*	createPrintJob () ε700,701,702,705,714
1	public.................. boolean	equals (Object obj)
1	public..... *javax.print.attribute₂*	getAttribute (Class category)
	.PrintServiceAttribute	
1	public..... *javax.print.attribute₂*	getAttributes () ε706
	.PrintServiceAttributeSet	
1	public.................... Object	getDefaultAttributeValue (Class category) ε707,708
1	public.................... String	getName () ε706,707,708
1	public........ ServiceUIFactory	getServiceUIFactory ()
1	public................ Class[]	getSupportedAttributeCategories () ε707
1	public.................... Object	getSupportedAttributeValues (Class category, DocFlavor flavor,
		javax.print.attribute.AttributeSet attributes) ε709,707
1	public.......... DocFlavor[]	getSupportedDocFlavors ()
1	public...................... *javax₂*	getUnsupportedAttributes (DocFlavor flavor, *javax.print.attribute.AttributeSet*
	.print.attribute.AttributeSet	attributes)
1	public......................int	hashCode ()
1	public.................. boolean	isAttributeCategorySupported (Class category)
1	public.................. boolean	isAttributeValueSupported (*javax.print.attribute.Attribute* attrval, DocFlavor flavor,
		javax.print.attribute.AttributeSet attributes)
1	public.................. boolean	isDocFlavorSupported (DocFlavor flavor)
1	public......................void	removePrintServiceAttributeListener (*javax.print.event.PrintServiceAttributeListener*
		listener)

MultiPixelPackedSampleModel java.awt.image

	Object [1]	ε668
1.2 ○	└SampleModel [2]	
1.2	└MultiPixelPackedSampleModel	

MultiPixelPackedSampleModel

2			*30 inherited members from SampleModel not shown*
2	public	**SampleModel**	**createCompatibleSampleModel** (int w, int h)
2	public	**DataBuffer**	**createDataBuffer** ()
2	public	**SampleModel**	**createSubsetSampleModel** (int[] bands)
1	public	**boolean**	**equals** (Object o)
	public	int	**getBitOffset** (int x)
	public	int	**getDataBitOffset** ()
2	public	**Object**	**getDataElements** (int x, int y, Object obj, DataBuffer data)
2	public	**int**	**getNumDataElements** ()
	public	int	**getOffset** (int x, int y)
2	public	**int[]**	**getPixel** (int x, int y, int[] iArray, DataBuffer data)
	public	int	**getPixelBitStride** ()
2	public	**int**	**getSample** (int x, int y, int b, DataBuffer data)
2	public	**int[]**	**getSampleSize** ()
2	public	**int**	**getSampleSize** (int band)
	public	int	**getScanlineStride** ()
2	public	**int**	**getTransferType** ()
1	public	**int**	**hashCode** ()
*	public		**MultiPixelPackedSampleModel** (int dataType, int w, int h, int numberOfBits)
*	public		**MultiPixelPackedSampleModel** (int dataType, int w, int h, int numberOfBits, int scanlineStride, int dataBitOffset)
2	public	**void**	**setDataElements** (int x, int y, Object obj, DataBuffer data)
2	public	**void**	**setPixel** (int x, int y, int[] iArray, DataBuffer data)
2	public	**void**	**setSample** (int x, int y, int b, int s, DataBuffer data)

M

MultipleDocumentHandling · javax.print.attribute.standard

```
Object
 └javax.print.attribute.EnumSyntax¹ ----------- java.io.Serializable, Cloneable
     └MultipleDocumentHandling ------------- javax.print.attribute.PrintRequestAttribute
                                             (javax.print.attribute.Attribute² (java.io.Serializable)),
                                             javax.print.attribute.PrintJobAttribute
                                             (javax.print.attribute.Attribute² (java.io.Serializable))
```

	1	public	Object	clone ()
●	2	public final	Class	**getCategory** ()	ε707
	1	protected	**javax.print** **.attribute.EnumSyntax[]**	**getEnumValueTable** ()
●	2	public final	String	**getName** ()	ε706,707,708
	1	protected	int	getOffset ()
	1	protected	**String[]**	**getStringTable** ()
	1	public	int	getValue ()
	1	public	int	hashCode ()
*		protected		**MultipleDocumentHandling** (int value)
	1	protected	Object	readResolve () throws java.io.ObjectStreamException
▲		public static final	.. MultipleDocumentHandling	**SEPARATE_DOCUMENTS_COLLATED_COPIES**
▲		public static final	.. MultipleDocumentHandling	**SEPARATE_DOCUMENTS_UNCOLLATED_COPIES**
▲		public static final	.. MultipleDocumentHandling	**SINGLE_DOCUMENT**
▲		public static final	.. MultipleDocumentHandling	**SINGLE_DOCUMENT_NEW_SHEET**
	1	public	String	toString ()

MultipleMaster · java.awt.font

1.2	*MultipleMaster*	
public	java.awt.Font	**deriveMMFont** (float[] axes)
public	java.awt.Font	**deriveMMFont** (float[] glyphWidths, float avgStemWidth, float typicalCapHeight, float typicalXHeight, float italicAngle)
public	float[]	**getDesignAxisDefaults** ()
public	String[]	**getDesignAxisNames** ()
public	float[]	**getDesignAxisRanges** ()
public	int	**getNumDesignAxes** ()

Class   *Interface*   —extends   - - -implements   ○ abstract   ● final   △ static   ▲ static final   ✳ constructor   x x—inherited   x **x**—declared   **x x**—overridden
εn—examples of usage   ⌄—has subclass   package—see other volume

MutableAttributeSet

					javax.swing.text
1.2		MutableAttributeSet ————————————— AttributeSet, [1]			ε975,989,991,992,993

	public	void	**addAttribute** (Object name, Object value)	
	public	void	**addAttributes** (*AttributeSet* attributes)	
1	public	boolean	containsAttribute (Object name, Object value)	
1	public	boolean	containsAttributes (*AttributeSet* attributes)	
1	public	*AttributeSet*	copyAttributes ()	
1	public	Object	getAttribute (Object key)	ε1010,1013,1017
1	public	int	getAttributeCount ()	ε1010
1	public	*java.util.Enumeration*	getAttributeNames ()	ε1010
1	public	*AttributeSet*	getResolveParent ()	
1	public	boolean	isDefined (Object attrName)	
1	public	boolean	isEqual (*AttributeSet* attr)	
▲ 1	public static final	Object	NameAttribute	
	public	void	**removeAttribute** (Object name)	
	public	void	**removeAttributes** (*java.util*.Enumeration names)	
	public	void	**removeAttributes** (*AttributeSet* attributes)	
▲ 1	public static final	Object	ResolveAttribute	
	public	void	**setResolveParent** (*AttributeSet* parent)	

MutableComboBoxModel

					javax.swing
1.2		MutableComboBoxModel ————————————— ComboBoxModel, [1] (ListModel [2])			

	public	void	**addElement** (Object obj)	
2	public	void	addListDataListener (*javax.swing.event.ListDataListener* l)	ε785
2	public	Object	getElementAt (int index)	ε760,776,777,779,785
1	public	Object	getSelectedItem ()	ε760
2	public	int	getSize ()	ε760,777,778,780
	public	void	**insertElementAt** (Object obj, int index)	
	public	void	**removeElement** (Object obj)	
	public	void	**removeElementAt** (int index)	
2	public	void	removeListDataListener (*javax.swing.event.ListDataListener* l)	
1	public	void	setSelectedItem (Object anItem)	

MutableTreeNode

					javax.swing.tree
1.2		MutableTreeNode ————————————— TreeNode, [1]			ε1026

1	public	*java.util*.Enumeration	children ()	ε1023,1024,1028,1029
1	public	boolean	getAllowsChildren ()	
1	public	*TreeNode*	getChildAt (int childIndex)	
1	public	int	getChildCount ()	ε1025,1023,1024,1028,1029
1	public	int	getIndex (*TreeNode* node)	
1	public	*TreeNode*	getParent ()	ε1027
	public	void	**insert** (*MutableTreeNode* child, int index)	
1	public	boolean	isLeaf ()	
	public	void	**remove** (int index)	
	public	void	**remove** (*MutableTreeNode* node)	
	public	void	**removeFromParent** ()	
	public	void	**setParent** (*MutableTreeNode* newParent)	
	public	void	**setUserObject** (Object object)	

NavigationFilter

			javax.swing.text
1.4		Object └NavigationFilter	

	public	int	**getNextVisualPositionFrom** (JTextComponent text, int pos, Position.Bias bias, int direction, Position.Bias[] biasRet) throws BadLocationException	
	public	void	**moveDot** (NavigationFilter.FilterBypass fb, int dot, Position.Bias bias)	
*	public		**NavigationFilter** ()	
	public	void	**setDot** (NavigationFilter.FilterBypass fb, int dot, Position.Bias bias)	

NavigationFilter.FilterBypass

			javax.swing.text
1.4 ○		Object └NavigationFilter.FilterBypass	

NavigationFilter.FilterBypass

✳	public		**NavigationFilter.FilterBypass** ()
○	public abstract	*Caret*	**getCaret** ()
○	public abstract	void	**moveDot** (int dot, Position.Bias bias)
○	public abstract	void	**setDot** (int dot, Position.Bias bias)

NoninvertibleTransformException `java.awt.geom`

```
Object
 └Throwable ---------------------------- java.io.Serializable.
   └Exception
     └NoninvertibleTransformException
```
1.2

✳	public	**NoninvertibleTransformException** (String s)

NumberFormatter `javax.swing.text`

```
Object
 └javax.swing.JFormattedTextField. ---------- java.io.Serializable.
   .AbstractFormatter 1
    └DefaultFormatter 2 -------------------- Cloneable.
      └InternationalFormatter 3
        └NumberFormatter
```
1.4 ○
1.4
1.4
1.4

	3	public	Object	clone () throws CloneNotSupportedException
	3	protected . *javax.swing.Action[]*	getActions ()	
	2	public	boolean	getAllowsInvalid ()
	2	public	boolean	getCommitsOnValidEdit ()
	2	protected	DocumentFilter	getDocumentFilter ()
	3	public . . java.text.Format.Field[]	getFields (int offset)	
	3	public	java.text.Format	getFormat ()
	1	protected	javax.	getFormattedTextField ()
		.swing.JFormattedTextField		
	3	public	*Comparable*	getMaximum ()
	3	public	*Comparable*	getMinimum ()
	2	protected	NavigationFilter	getNavigationFilter ()
	2	public	boolean	getOverwriteMode ()
	2	public	Class	getValueClass ()
	3	public	void	install (javax.swing.JFormattedTextField ftf)
	1	protected	void	invalidEdit ()
✳		public		**NumberFormatter** ()
✳		public		**NumberFormatter** (java.text.NumberFormat format) ε995
	2	public	void	setAllowsInvalid (boolean allowsInvalid)
	2	public	void	setCommitsOnValidEdit (boolean commit)
	1	protected	void	setEditValid (boolean valid)
	3	public	**void**	**setFormat** (java.text.Format format)
	3	public	void	setMaximum (*Comparable* max)
	3	public	void	setMinimum (*Comparable* minimum)
	2	public	void	setOverwriteMode (boolean overwriteMode)
	2	public	void	setValueClass (Class valueClass) ε995
	3	public	Object	stringToValue (String text) throws java.text.ParseException
	1	public	void	uninstall ()
	3	public	String	valueToString (Object value) throws java.text.ParseException

---

NumberOfDocuments `javax.print.attribute.standard`

```
Object
 └javax.print.attribute.IntegerSyntax 1 -------- java.io.Serializable., Cloneable.
   └NumberOfDocuments ----------------- javax.print.attribute.PrintJobAttribute (javax.print.attribute.Attribute 2
                                                       (java.io.Serializable))
```
1.4 ○
1.4 ●

		1	public	**boolean**	**equals** (Object object)
●	2	public final	Class	**getCategory** ()	ε707
●	2	public final	String	**getName** ()	ε706,707,708
		1	public	int	getValue ()
		1	public	int	hashCode ()
✳			public		**NumberOfDocuments** (int value)

Class *Interface* —extends - - -implements ○ abstract ● final △ static ▲ static final ✳ constructor x x—inherited x **x**—declared **x x**—overridden
ε*n*—examples of usage .—has subclass package—see other volume

	1	public	String	toString ()	

NumberOfInterveningJobs javax.print.attribute.standard

Object
1.4 ○ └─javax.print.attribute.IntegerSyntax[1] - - - - - - - - *java.io.Serializable* , *Cloneable*
1.4 ●   └─NumberOfInterveningJobs - - - - - - - - - - - - - *javax.print.attribute.PrintJobAttribute (javax.print.attribute.Attribute[2]*
                                                        (java.io.Serializable))

	1	public	**boolean**	**equals** (Object object)	
●	2	public final	Class	**getCategory** ()	ε707
●	2	public final	String	**getName** ()	ε706,707,708
	1	public	int	getValue ()	
	1	public	int	hashCode ()	
✳		public		**NumberOfInterveningJobs** (int value)	
	1	public	String	toString ()	

NumberUp javax.print.attribute.standard

Object
1.4 ○ └─javax.print.attribute.IntegerSyntax[1] - - - - - - - - *java.io.Serializable* , *Cloneable*
1.4 ●   └─NumberUp - *javax.print.attribute.DocAttribute (javax.print.attribute.Attribute[2]*
                                                  (java.io.Serializable)), javax.print.attribute.PrintRequestAttribute
                                                  (javax.print.attribute.Attribute[2] (java.io.Serializable)),
                                                  javax.print.attribute.PrintJobAttribute
                                                  (javax.print.attribute.Attribute[2] (java.io.Serializable))

	1	public	**boolean**	**equals** (Object object)	
●	2	public final	Class	**getCategory** ()	ε707
●	2	public final	String	**getName** ()	ε706,707,708
	1	public	int	getValue ()	
	1	public	int	hashCode ()	
✳		public		**NumberUp** (int value)	
	1	public	String	toString ()	

N

NumberUpSupported javax.print.attribute.standard

Object
1.4 ○ └─javax.print.attribute.SetOfIntegerSyntax[1] - - - - *java.io.Serializable* , *Cloneable*
1.4 ●   └─NumberUpSupported - - - - - - - - - - - - - - - - - *javax.print.attribute.SupportedValuesAttribute*
                                                  (javax.print.attribute.Attribute[2] (java.io.Serializable))

	1	public	boolean	contains (int x)	
	1	public	boolean	contains (javax.print.attribute.IntegerSyntax attribute)	
	1	public	**boolean**	**equals** (Object object)	
●	2	public final	Class	**getCategory** ()	ε707
	1	public	int[][]	getMembers ()	
●	2	public final	String	**getName** ()	ε706,707,708
	1	public	int	hashCode ()	
	1	public	int	next (int x)	
✳		public		**NumberUpSupported** (int member)	
✳		public		**NumberUpSupported** (int[][] members)	
✳		public		**NumberUpSupported** (int lowerBound, int upperBound)	
	1	public	String	toString ()	

Classes

NumericShaper java.awt.font

Object[1]
1.4 ● └─NumericShaper - *java.io.Serializable*

▲		public static final	int	**ALL_RANGES** = 524287
▲		public static final	int	**ARABIC** = 2
▲		public static final	int	**BENGALI** = 16
▲		public static final	int	**DEVANAGARI** = 8
▲		public static final	int	**EASTERN_ARABIC** = 4
	1	public	**boolean**	**equals** (Object o)
▲		public static final	int	**ETHIOPIC** = 65536
▲		public static final	int	**EUROPEAN** = 1

NumericShaper

△	public static ... NumericShaper	**getContextualShaper** (int ranges)	
△	public static ... NumericShaper	**getContextualShaper** (int ranges, int defaultContext)	
	public............................int	**getRanges** ()	
△	public static ... NumericShaper	**getShaper** (int singleRange)	
▲	public static final.............int	**GUJARATI** = 64	
▲	public static final.............int	**GURMUKHI** = 32	
1	public.......................**int**	**hashCode** ()	
	public.................. boolean	**isContextual** ()	
▲	public static final.............int	**KANNADA** = 1024	
▲	public static final.............int	**KHMER** = 131072	
▲	public static final.............int	**LAO** = 8192	
▲	public static final.............int	**MALAYALAM** = 2048	
▲	public static final.............int	**MONGOLIAN** = 262144	
▲	public static final.............int	**MYANMAR** = 32768	
▲	public static final.............int	**ORIYA** = 128	
	public............................void	**shape** (char[] text, int start, int count)	
	public............................void	**shape** (char[] text, int start, int count, int context)	
▲	public static final.............int	**TAMIL** = 256	
▲	public static final.............int	**TELUGU** = 512	
▲	public static final.............int	**THAI** = 4096	
▲	public static final.............int	**TIBETAN** = 16384	
1	public.................. **String**	**toString** ()	

ObjectView   javax.swing.text.html

Object
  └javax.swing.text.View [1] - - - - - - - - - - - - - - - - - - - *javax.swing.SwingConstants* [3]
    └javax.swing.text.ComponentView [2]
      └ObjectView

1.2 ○
1.2
1.2

1	*44 inherited members from javax.swing.text.View not shown*		
3	*19 inherited members from javax.swing.SwingConstants not shown*		
2	protected .... **createComponent** ()		
	.... **java.awt.Component**		
2	public............................float	getAlignment (int axis)	
● 2	public final	getComponent ()	
	.... java.awt.Component		
2	public............................float	getMaximumSpan (int axis)	
2	public............................float	getMinimumSpan (int axis)	
2	public............................float	getPreferredSpan (int axis)	
2	public.......... *java.awt.Shape*	modelToView (int pos, *java.awt.Shape* a, javax.swing.text.Position.Bias b)	
		throws javax.swing.text.BadLocationException	
✳	public..........................	**ObjectView** (*javax.swing.text.Element* elem)	
2	public............................void	paint (java.awt.Graphics g, *java.awt.Shape* a)	
2	public............................void	setParent (javax.swing.text.View p)	
2	public............................int	viewToModel (float x, float y, *java.awt.Shape* a, javax.swing.text.Position.Bias[] bias)	

OpenType   java.awt.font

1.2   *OpenType*
- -

	public....................byte[]	**getFontTable** (int sfntTag)	
	public....................byte[]	**getFontTable** (String strSfntTag)	
	public....................byte[]	**getFontTable** (int sfntTag, int offset, int count)	
	public....................byte[]	**getFontTable** (String strSfntTag, int offset, int count)	
	public............................int	**getFontTableSize** (int sfntTag)	
	public............................int	**getFontTableSize** (String strSfntTag)	
	public............................int	**getVersion** ()	
▲	public static final.............int	**TAG_ACNT** = 1633906292	
▲	public static final.............int	**TAG_AVAR** = 1635148146	
▲	public static final.............int	**TAG_BASE** = 1111577413	
▲	public static final.............int	**TAG_BDAT** = 1650745716	
▲	public static final.............int	**TAG_BLOC** = 1651273571	
▲	public static final.............int	**TAG_BSLN** = 1651731566	
▲	public static final.............int	**TAG_CFF** = 1128678944	
▲	public static final.............int	**TAG_CMAP** = 1668112752	
▲	public static final.............int	**TAG_CVAR** = 1668702578	
▲	public static final.............int	**TAG_CVT** = 1668707360	
▲	public static final.............int	**TAG_DSIG** = 1146308935	

Class   *Interface*   —extends   - - -implements   ○ abstract   ● final   △ static   ▲ static final   ✳ constructor   x x—inherited   x **x**—declared   **x x**—overridden
ε *n*—examples of usage   ⌐—has subclass   package—see other volume

▲	public static final	int	**TAG_EBDT**	= 1161970772
▲	public static final	int	**TAG_EBLC**	= 1161972803
▲	public static final	int	**TAG_EBSC**	= 1161974595
▲	public static final	int	**TAG_FDSC**	= 1717859171
▲	public static final	int	**TAG_FEAT**	= 1717920116
▲	public static final	int	**TAG_FMTX**	= 1718449272
▲	public static final	int	**TAG_FPGM**	= 1718642541
▲	public static final	int	**TAG_FVAR**	= 1719034226
▲	public static final	int	**TAG_GASP**	= 1734439792
▲	public static final	int	**TAG_GDEF**	= 1195656518
▲	public static final	int	**TAG_GLYF**	= 1735162214
▲	public static final	int	**TAG_GPOS**	= 1196445523
▲	public static final	int	**TAG_GSUB**	= 1196643650
▲	public static final	int	**TAG_GVAR**	= 1735811442
▲	public static final	int	**TAG_HDMX**	= 1751412088
▲	public static final	int	**TAG_HEAD**	= 1751474532
▲	public static final	int	**TAG_HHEA**	= 1751672161
▲	public static final	int	**TAG_HMTX**	= 1752003704
▲	public static final	int	**TAG_JSTF**	= 1246975046
▲	public static final	int	**TAG_JUST**	= 1786082164
▲	public static final	int	**TAG_KERN**	= 1801810542
▲	public static final	int	**TAG_LCAR**	= 1818452338
▲	public static final	int	**TAG_LOCA**	= 1819239265
▲	public static final	int	**TAG_LTSH**	= 1280594760
▲	public static final	int	**TAG_MAXP**	= 1835104368
▲	public static final	int	**TAG_MMFX**	= 1296909912
▲	public static final	int	**TAG_MMSD**	= 1296913220
▲	public static final	int	**TAG_MORT**	= 1836020340
▲	public static final	int	**TAG_NAME**	= 1851878757
▲	public static final	int	**TAG_OPBD**	= 1836020340
▲	public static final	int	**TAG_OS2**	= 1330851634
▲	public static final	int	**TAG_PCLT**	= 1346587732
▲	public static final	int	**TAG_POST**	= 1886352244
▲	public static final	int	**TAG_PREP**	= 1886545264
▲	public static final	int	**TAG_PROP**	= 1886547824
▲	public static final	int	**TAG_TRAK**	= 1953653099
▲	public static final	int	**TAG_TYP1**	= 1954115633
▲	public static final	int	**TAG_VDMX**	= 1447316824
▲	public static final	int	**TAG_VHEA**	= 1986553185
▲	public static final	int	**TAG_VMTX**	= 1986884728

O

Option

Object [1]
1.2 └─Option

public	*. javax.swing.text.AttributeSet*	**getAttributes** ()
public	String	**getLabel** ()
public	String	**getValue** ()
public	boolean	**isSelected** ()
* public		**Option** (*javax.swing.text.AttributeSet* attr)
public	void	**setLabel** (String label)
protected	void	**setSelection** (boolean state)
[1] public	**String**	**toString** ()

Classes

OptionPaneUI

Object
1.2 ○ └─ComponentUI [1]
1.2 ○   └─OptionPaneUI

[1] *11 inherited members from ComponentUI not shown*
○ public abstract .... boolean **containsCustomComponents** (javax.swing.JOptionPane op)
* public .... **OptionPaneUI** ()
○ public abstract ....void **selectInitialValue** (javax.swing.JOptionPane op)

OrientationRequested

OrientationRequested		javax.print.attribute.standard

Object
1.4 ○ └javax.print.attribute.EnumSyntax [1] - - - - - - - - - *java.io.Serializable*‿, *Cloneable*‿
1.4 ● └OrientationRequested - - - - - - - - - - - - - - - - *javax.print.attribute.DocAttribute (javax.print.attribute.Attribute [2]*
(*java.io.Serializable*)), *javax.print.attribute.PrintRequestAttribute*
(*javax.print.attribute.Attribute [2]* (*java.io.Serializable*)),
javax.print.attribute.PrintJobAttribute
(*javax.print.attribute.Attribute [2]* (*java.io.Serializable*))

	1	public................Object	clone ()		
●	2	public final..............Class	**getCategory** ()		ε707
	1	protected.........**javax.print**‚ **.attribute.EnumSyntax[]**	getEnumValueTable ()		
●	2	public final..............String	**getName** ()		ε706,707,708
	1	protected..................**int**	**getOffset** ()		
	1	protected..........**String[]**	**getStringTable** ()		
	1	public........................int	getValue ()		
	1	public........................int	hashCode ()		
▲		public static final............. ....OrientationRequested	**LANDSCAPE**		ε710
✳		protected.....................	**OrientationRequested** (int value)		
▲		public static final.............. ....OrientationRequested	**PORTRAIT**		ε710
	1	protected...............Object	readResolve () throws java.io.ObjectStreamException		
▲		public static final.............. ....OrientationRequested	**REVERSE_LANDSCAPE**		
▲		public static final.............. ....OrientationRequested	**REVERSE_PORTRAIT**		
	1	public...................String	toString ()		

OutputDeviceAssigned		javax.print.attribute.standard

Object
1.4 ○ └javax.print.attribute.TextSyntax [1] - - - - - - - - - - - *java.io.Serializable*‿, *Cloneable*‿
1.4 ● └OutputDeviceAssigned - - - - - - - - - - - - - - - - *javax.print.attribute.PrintJobAttribute (javax.print.attribute.Attribute [2]*
(*java.io.Serializable*))

	1	public................**boolean**	**equals** (Object object)	
●	2	public final..............Class	**getCategory** ()	ε707
	1	public..........java.util.Locale	getLocale ()	
●	2	public final..............String	**getName** ()	ε706,707,708
	1	public...................String	getValue ()	
	1	public........................int	hashCode ()	
✳		public........................	**OutputDeviceAssigned** (String deviceName, java.util.Locale locale)	
	1	public...................String	toString ()	

OverlayLayout		javax.swing

Object
1.2 └OverlayLayout - *java.awt.LayoutManager2 [1]* (*java.awt.LayoutManager [2]*),
java.io.Serializable‿

	1	public........................void	**addLayoutComponent** (java.awt.Component comp, Object constraints)	
	2	public........................void	**addLayoutComponent** (String name, java.awt.Component comp)	
	1	public........................float	**getLayoutAlignmentX** (java.awt.Container target)	
	1	public........................float	**getLayoutAlignmentY** (java.awt.Container target)	
	1	public........................void	**invalidateLayout** (java.awt.Container target)	
	2	public........................void	**layoutContainer** (java.awt.Container target)	ε624,625
	1	public......java.awt.Dimension	**maximumLayoutSize** (java.awt.Container target)	
	2	public......java.awt.Dimension	**minimumLayoutSize** (java.awt.Container target)	
✳		public........................	**OverlayLayout** (java.awt.Container target)	
	2	public......java.awt.Dimension	**preferredLayoutSize** (java.awt.Container target)	
	2	public........................void	**removeLayoutComponent** (java.awt.Component comp)	

PackedColorModel
java.awt.image

ε660,662,668

```
        Object
   ○    └ColorModel¹ ------------------------- java.awt.Transparency ˎ²
1.2 ○       └PackedColorModel ˎ
```

	1	*39 inherited members from ColorModel not shown*	
▲	2	public static final . . . . int	**BITMASK** = 2	ε666,667
	1	public . . . . **SampleModel**	**createCompatibleSampleModel** (int w, int h)
	1	public . . . . **boolean**	**equals** (Object obj)
	1	public . . . . **WritableRaster**	**getAlphaRaster** (WritableRaster raster)
●		public final . . . . int	**getMask** (int index)
●		public final . . . . int[]	**getMasks** ()
	1	public . . . . **boolean**	**isCompatibleSampleModel** (SampleModel sm)
▲	2	public static final . . . . int	**OPAQUE** = 1	ε666,667
∗		public	**PackedColorModel** (java.awt.color.ColorSpace space, int bits, int[] colorMaskArray, int alphaMask, boolean isAlphaPremultiplied, int trans, int transferType)
∗		public	**PackedColorModel** (java.awt.color.ColorSpace space, int bits, int rmask, int gmask, int bmask, int amask, boolean isAlphaPremultiplied, int trans, int transferType)
▲	2	public static final . . . . int	**TRANSLUCENT** = 3	ε666

Pageable
java.awt.print

```
1.2     Pageable
```

	public . . . . int	**getNumberOfPages** ()
	public . . . . PageFormat	**getPageFormat** (int pageIndex) throws IndexOutOfBoundsException
	public . . . . *Printable*	**getPrintable** (int pageIndex) throws IndexOutOfBoundsException
▲	public static final . . . . int	**UNKNOWN_NUMBER_OF_PAGES** = -1

PageAttributes
java.awt

```
        Object¹
1.3 ●   └PageAttributes ------------------------- Cloneable ˎ
```

	1	public . . . . **Object**	**clone** ()
	1	public . . . . **boolean**	**equals** (Object obj)
		public . . . . PageAttributes.ColorType	**getColor** ()
		public . . . . PageAttributes.MediaType	**getMedia** ()
		public . . . . PageAttributes ˎ .OrientationRequestedType	**getOrientationRequested** ()
		public . . . . PageAttributes.OriginType	**getOrigin** ()
		public . . . . int[]	**getPrinterResolution** ()
		public . . . . PageAttributes ˎ .PrintQualityType	**getPrintQuality** ()
	1	public . . . . **int**	**hashCode** ()
∗		public	**PageAttributes** ()
∗		public	**PageAttributes** (PageAttributes obj)
∗		public	**PageAttributes** (PageAttributes.ColorType color, PageAttributes.MediaType media, PageAttributes.OrientationRequestedType orientationRequested, PageAttributes.OriginType origin, PageAttributes.PrintQualityType printQuality, int[] printerResolution)
		public . . . . void	**set** (PageAttributes obj)
		public . . . . void	**setColor** (PageAttributes.ColorType color)
		public . . . . void	**setMedia** (PageAttributes.MediaType media)
		public . . . . void	**setMediaToDefault** ()
		public . . . . void	**setOrientationRequested** (int orientationRequested)
		public . . . . void	**setOrientationRequested** (PageAttributes.OrientationRequestedType orientationRequested)
		public . . . . void	**setOrientationRequestedToDefault** ()
		public . . . . void	**setOrigin** (PageAttributes.OriginType origin)
		public . . . . void	**setPrinterResolution** (int printerResolution)
		public . . . . void	**setPrinterResolution** (int[] printerResolution)
		public . . . . void	**setPrinterResolutionToDefault** ()
		public . . . . void	**setPrintQuality** (int printQuality)
		public . . . . void	**setPrintQuality** (PageAttributes.PrintQualityType printQuality)
		public . . . . void	**setPrintQualityToDefault** ()
	1	public . . . . **String**	**toString** ()

P

Classes

PageAttributes.ColorType		java.awt

```
        Object
1.4     └AttributeValue 1
1.3 ●       └PageAttributes.ColorType
```

▲	public static final	**COLOR**
	. . . . PageAttributes.ColorType	
1	public . . . . int	hashCode ()
▲	public static final	**MONOCHROME**
	. . . . PageAttributes.ColorType	
1	public . . . . String	toString ()

PageAttributes.MediaType		java.awt

```
        Object
1.4     └AttributeValue 1
1.3 ●       └PageAttributes.MediaType
```

▲	public static final . . . . PageAttributes.MediaType	**A**
▲	public static final . . . . PageAttributes.MediaType	**A0**
▲	public static final . . . . PageAttributes.MediaType	**A1**
▲	public static final . . . . PageAttributes.MediaType	**A10**
▲	public static final . . . . PageAttributes.MediaType	**A2**
▲	public static final . . . . PageAttributes.MediaType	**A3**
▲	public static final . . . . PageAttributes.MediaType	**A4**
▲	public static final . . . . PageAttributes.MediaType	**A5**
▲	public static final . . . . PageAttributes.MediaType	**A6**
▲	public static final . . . . PageAttributes.MediaType	**A7**
▲	public static final . . . . PageAttributes.MediaType	**A8**
▲	public static final . . . . PageAttributes.MediaType	**A9**
▲	public static final . . . . PageAttributes.MediaType	**B**
▲	public static final . . . . PageAttributes.MediaType	**B0**
▲	public static final . . . . PageAttributes.MediaType	**B1**
▲	public static final . . . . PageAttributes.MediaType	**B10**
▲	public static final . . . . PageAttributes.MediaType	**B2**
▲	public static final . . . . PageAttributes.MediaType	**B3**
▲	public static final . . . . PageAttributes.MediaType	**B4**
▲	public static final . . . . PageAttributes.MediaType	**B5**
▲	public static final . . . . PageAttributes.MediaType	**B6**
▲	public static final . . . . PageAttributes.MediaType	**B7**
▲	public static final . . . . PageAttributes.MediaType	**B8**
▲	public static final . . . . PageAttributes.MediaType	**B9**
▲	public static final . . . . PageAttributes.MediaType	**C**
▲	public static final . . . . PageAttributes.MediaType	**C0**
▲	public static final . . . . PageAttributes.MediaType	**C1**
▲	public static final . . . . PageAttributes.MediaType	**C10**
▲	public static final . . . . PageAttributes.MediaType	**C2**
▲	public static final . . . . PageAttributes.MediaType	**C3**
▲	public static final . . . . PageAttributes.MediaType	**C4**
▲	public static final . . . . PageAttributes.MediaType	**C5**
▲	public static final . . . . PageAttributes.MediaType	**C6**
▲	public static final . . . . PageAttributes.MediaType	**C7**
▲	public static final . . . . PageAttributes.MediaType	**C8**
▲	public static final . . . . PageAttributes.MediaType	**C9**
▲	public static final . . . . PageAttributes.MediaType	**D**
▲	public static final . . . . PageAttributes.MediaType	**E**
▲	public static final . . . . PageAttributes.MediaType	**ENV_10**
▲	public static final . . . . PageAttributes.MediaType	**ENV_10X13**
▲	public static final . . . . PageAttributes.MediaType	**ENV_10X14**
▲	public static final . . . . PageAttributes.MediaType	**ENV_10X15**
▲	public static final . . . . PageAttributes.MediaType	**ENV_11**
▲	public static final . . . . PageAttributes.MediaType	**ENV_12**
▲	public static final . . . . PageAttributes.MediaType	**ENV_14**
▲	public static final . . . . PageAttributes.MediaType	**ENV_6X9**
▲	public static final . . . . PageAttributes.MediaType	**ENV_7X9**
▲	public static final . . . . PageAttributes.MediaType	**ENV_9**
▲	public static final . . . . PageAttributes.MediaType	**ENV_9X11**
▲	public static final . . . . PageAttributes.MediaType	**ENV_9X12**
▲	public static final . . . . PageAttributes.MediaType	**ENV_INVITE**

P

Class   *Interface*   —extends   - - -implements   ○ abstract   ● final   △ static   ▲ static final   ✳ constructor   x x—inherited   x **x**—declared   **x x**—overridden
ε*n*—examples of usage   ‿—has subclass   package—see other volume

708

▲	public static final	PageAttributes.MediaType	**ENV_ITALY**
▲	public static final	PageAttributes.MediaType	**ENV_MONARCH**
▲	public static final	PageAttributes.MediaType	**ENV_PERSONAL**
▲	public static final	PageAttributes.MediaType	**EXECUTIVE**
▲	public static final	PageAttributes.MediaType	**FOLIO**
1	public	int	hashCode ()
▲	public static final	PageAttributes.MediaType	**INVITE**
▲	public static final	PageAttributes.MediaType	**INVITE_ENVELOPE**
▲	public static final	PageAttributes.MediaType	**INVOICE**
▲	public static final	PageAttributes.MediaType	**ISO_2A0**
▲	public static final	PageAttributes.MediaType	**ISO_4A0**
▲	public static final	PageAttributes.MediaType	**ISO_A0**
▲	public static final	PageAttributes.MediaType	**ISO_A1**
▲	public static final	PageAttributes.MediaType	**ISO_A10**
▲	public static final	PageAttributes.MediaType	**ISO_A2**
▲	public static final	PageAttributes.MediaType	**ISO_A3**
▲	public static final	PageAttributes.MediaType	**ISO_A4**
▲	public static final	PageAttributes.MediaType	**ISO_A5**
▲	public static final	PageAttributes.MediaType	**ISO_A6**
▲	public static final	PageAttributes.MediaType	**ISO_A7**
▲	public static final	PageAttributes.MediaType	**ISO_A8**
▲	public static final	PageAttributes.MediaType	**ISO_A9**
▲	public static final	PageAttributes.MediaType	**ISO_B0**
▲	public static final	PageAttributes.MediaType	**ISO_B1**
▲	public static final	PageAttributes.MediaType	**ISO_B10**
▲	public static final	PageAttributes.MediaType	**ISO_B2**
▲	public static final	PageAttributes.MediaType	**ISO_B3**
▲	public static final	PageAttributes.MediaType	**ISO_B4**
▲	public static final	PageAttributes.MediaType	**ISO_B4_ENVELOPE**
▲	public static final	PageAttributes.MediaType	**ISO_B5**
▲	public static final	PageAttributes.MediaType	**ISO_B5_ENVELOPE**
▲	public static final	PageAttributes.MediaType	**ISO_B6**
▲	public static final	PageAttributes.MediaType	**ISO_B7**
▲	public static final	PageAttributes.MediaType	**ISO_B8**
▲	public static final	PageAttributes.MediaType	**ISO_B9**
▲	public static final	PageAttributes.MediaType	**ISO_C0**
▲	public static final	PageAttributes.MediaType	**ISO_C0_ENVELOPE**
▲	public static final	PageAttributes.MediaType	**ISO_C1**
▲	public static final	PageAttributes.MediaType	**ISO_C10**
▲	public static final	PageAttributes.MediaType	**ISO_C10_ENVELOPE**
▲	public static final	PageAttributes.MediaType	**ISO_C1_ENVELOPE**
▲	public static final	PageAttributes.MediaType	**ISO_C2**
▲	public static final	PageAttributes.MediaType	**ISO_C2_ENVELOPE**
▲	public static final	PageAttributes.MediaType	**ISO_C3**
▲	public static final	PageAttributes.MediaType	**ISO_C3_ENVELOPE**
▲	public static final	PageAttributes.MediaType	**ISO_C4**
▲	public static final	PageAttributes.MediaType	**ISO_C4_ENVELOPE**
▲	public static final	PageAttributes.MediaType	**ISO_C5**
▲	public static final	PageAttributes.MediaType	**ISO_C5_ENVELOPE**
▲	public static final	PageAttributes.MediaType	**ISO_C6**
▲	public static final	PageAttributes.MediaType	**ISO_C6_ENVELOPE**
▲	public static final	PageAttributes.MediaType	**ISO_C7**
▲	public static final	PageAttributes.MediaType	**ISO_C7_ENVELOPE**
▲	public static final	PageAttributes.MediaType	**ISO_C8**
▲	public static final	PageAttributes.MediaType	**ISO_C8_ENVELOPE**
▲	public static final	PageAttributes.MediaType	**ISO_C9**
▲	public static final	PageAttributes.MediaType	**ISO_C9_ENVELOPE**
▲	public static final	PageAttributes.MediaType	**ISO_DESIGNATED_LONG**
▲	public static final	PageAttributes.MediaType	**ISO_DESIGNATED_LONG_ENVELOPE**
▲	public static final	PageAttributes.MediaType	**ITALY**
▲	public static final	PageAttributes.MediaType	**ITALY_ENVELOPE**
▲	public static final	PageAttributes.MediaType	**JIS_B0**
▲	public static final	PageAttributes.MediaType	**JIS_B1**
▲	public static final	PageAttributes.MediaType	**JIS_B10**
▲	public static final	PageAttributes.MediaType	**JIS_B2**
▲	public static final	PageAttributes.MediaType	**JIS_B3**
▲	public static final	PageAttributes.MediaType	**JIS_B4**
▲	public static final	PageAttributes.MediaType	**JIS_B5**
▲	public static final	PageAttributes.MediaType	**JIS_B6**
▲	public static final	PageAttributes.MediaType	**JIS_B7**
▲	public static final	PageAttributes.MediaType	**JIS_B8**
▲	public static final	PageAttributes.MediaType	**JIS_B9**
▲	public static final	PageAttributes.MediaType	**LEDGER**
▲	public static final	PageAttributes.MediaType	**LEGAL**

P

Classes

709

PageAttributes.MediaType

▲	public static final	PageAttributes.MediaType	**LETTER**
▲	public static final	PageAttributes.MediaType	**MONARCH**
▲	public static final	PageAttributes.MediaType	**MONARCH_ENVELOPE**
▲	public static final	PageAttributes.MediaType	**NA_10X13_ENVELOPE**
▲	public static final	PageAttributes.MediaType	**NA_10X14_ENVELOPE**
▲	public static final	PageAttributes.MediaType	**NA_10X15_ENVELOPE**
▲	public static final	PageAttributes.MediaType	**NA_6X9_ENVELOPE**
▲	public static final	PageAttributes.MediaType	**NA_7X9_ENVELOPE**
▲	public static final	PageAttributes.MediaType	**NA_9X11_ENVELOPE**
▲	public static final	PageAttributes.MediaType	**NA_9X12_ENVELOPE**
▲	public static final	PageAttributes.MediaType	**NA_LEGAL**
▲	public static final	PageAttributes.MediaType	**NA_LETTER**
▲	public static final	PageAttributes.MediaType	**NA_NUMBER_10_ENVELOPE**
▲	public static final	PageAttributes.MediaType	**NA_NUMBER_11_ENVELOPE**
▲	public static final	PageAttributes.MediaType	**NA_NUMBER_12_ENVELOPE**
▲	public static final	PageAttributes.MediaType	**NA_NUMBER_14_ENVELOPE**
▲	public static final	PageAttributes.MediaType	**NA_NUMBER_9_ENVELOPE**
▲	public static final	PageAttributes.MediaType	**NOTE**
▲	public static final	PageAttributes.MediaType	**PERSONAL**
▲	public static final	PageAttributes.MediaType	**PERSONAL_ENVELOPE**
▲	public static final	PageAttributes.MediaType	**QUARTO**
▲	public static final	PageAttributes.MediaType	**STATEMENT**
▲	public static final	PageAttributes.MediaType	**TABLOID**
1	public	String	toString ()

PageAttributes.OrientationRequestedType `java.awt`

```
      Object
1.4   └ AttributeValue 1
1.3 ● └ PageAttributes.OrientationRequestedType
```

1	public	int	hashCode ()
▲	public static final		**LANDSCAPE**
	PageAttributes ₂ .OrientationRequestedType		
▲	public static final		**PORTRAIT**
	PageAttributes ₂ .OrientationRequestedType		
1	public	String	toString ()

PageAttributes.OriginType `java.awt`

```
      Object
1.4   └ AttributeValue 1
1.3 ● └ PageAttributes.OriginType
```

1	public	int	hashCode ()
▲	public static final		**PHYSICAL**
	PageAttributes.OriginType		
▲	public static final		**PRINTABLE**
	PageAttributes.OriginType		
1	public	String	toString ()

PageAttributes.PrintQualityType `java.awt`

```
      Object
1.4   └ AttributeValue 1
1.3 ● └ PageAttributes.PrintQualityType
```

▲	public static final		**DRAFT**
	PageAttributes ₂ .PrintQualityType		
1	public	int	hashCode ()
▲	public static final		**HIGH**
	PageAttributes ₂ .PrintQualityType		

Class *Interface* —extends - - -implements ○ abstract ● final △ static ▲ static final ✳ constructor x x—inherited x **x**—declared **x x**—overridden
εn—examples of usage ˳—has subclass `package`—see other volume

▲ public static final .... **NORMAL**
............PageAttributes₂
.PrintQualityType
1 public .... String toString ()

PageFormat		java.awt.print

Object[1]
1.2 └ PageFormat - *Cloneable* ⌄
ε686

1 public .... **Object clone** ()
public .... double **getHeight** () ε682
public .... double **getImageableHeight** () ε682
public .... double **getImageableWidth** () ε682
public .... double **getImageableX** () ε681,682
public .... double **getImageableY** () ε681,682
public .... double[] **getMatrix** ()
public .... int **getOrientation** ()
public .... Paper **getPaper** ()
public .... double **getWidth** () ε682
▲ public static final .... int **LANDSCAPE** = 0 ε683,684,685
✳ public .... **PageFormat** ()
▲ public static final .... int **PORTRAIT** = 1 ε683,684
▲ public static final .... int **REVERSE_LANDSCAPE** = 2
public .... void **setOrientation** (int orientation) throws IllegalArgumentException ε683,684,685
public .... void **setPaper** (Paper paper)

PageRanges		javax.print.attribute.standard

Object
1.4 ○ └ javax.print.attribute.SetOfIntegerSyntax[1] - - - - *java.io.Serializable* ⌄, *Cloneable* ⌄
1.4 ● └ PageRanges - *javax.print.attribute.DocAttribute* (*javax.print.attribute.Attribute*[2]
(*java.io.Serializable*)), *javax.print.attribute.PrintRequestAttribute*
(*javax.print.attribute.Attribute*[2] (*java.io.Serializable*)),
javax.print.attribute.PrintJobAttribute
(*javax.print.attribute.Attribute*[2] (*java.io.Serializable*))

1 public .... boolean **contains** (int x)
1 public .... boolean **contains** (javax.print.attribute.IntegerSyntax attribute)
1 public .... **boolean equals** (Object object)
● 2 public final .... Class **getCategory** () ε707
1 public .... int[][] getMembers ()
● 2 public final .... String **getName** () ε706,707,708
1 public .... int hashCode ()
1 public .... int next (int x)
✳ public .... **PageRanges** (int member)
✳ public .... **PageRanges** (int[][] members)
✳ public .... **PageRanges** (String members)
✳ public .... **PageRanges** (int lowerBound, int upperBound)
1 public .... String toString ()

PagesPerMinute		javax.print.attribute.standard

Object
1.4 ○ └ javax.print.attribute.IntegerSyntax[1] - - - - - - - - - *java.io.Serializable* ⌄, *Cloneable* ⌄
1.4 ● └ PagesPerMinute - *javax.print.attribute.PrintServiceAttribute*
(*javax.print.attribute.Attribute*[2] (*java.io.Serializable*))

1 public .... **boolean equals** (Object object) ε707
● 2 public final .... Class **getCategory** () ε706,707,708
● 2 public final .... String **getName** ()
1 public .... int getValue ()
1 public .... int hashCode ()
✳ public .... **PagesPerMinute** (int value)
1 public .... String toString ()

P

Classes

PagesPerMinuteColor

PagesPerMinuteColor

javax.print.attribute.standard

```
          Object
1.4 ○     └ javax.print.attribute.IntegerSyntax 1 - - - - - - - - ·   java.io.Serializable ˎ, Cloneable ˎ
1.4 ●         └ PagesPerMinuteColor - - - - - - - - - - - - - - - - -   javax.print.attribute.PrintServiceAttribute
                                                                      (javax.print.attribute.Attribute 2 ( java.io.Serializable ))
```

	1	public.................**boolean**	**equals** (Object object)	
●	2	public final ....Class	**getCategory** ()	ε707
●	2	public final ....String	**getName** ()	ε706,707,708
	1	public.........................int	getValue ()	
	1	public.........................int	hashCode ()	
*		public.........................	**PagesPerMinuteColor** (int value)	
	1	public.....................String	toString ()	

Paint

java.awt

```
1.2       Paint ———————————————————— Transparency ˎ 1
```

▲	1	public static final.............int	BITMASK = 2	ε666,667
		public............. PaintContext	**createContext** (java.awt.image.ColorModel cm, Rectangle deviceBounds,	
			java.awt.geom.Rectangle2D userBounds, java.awt.geom.AffineTransform xform,	
			RenderingHints hints)	
	1	public.........................int	getTransparency ()	
▲	1	public static final.............int	OPAQUE = 1	ε666,667
▲	1	public static final.............int	TRANSLUCENT = 3	ε666

PaintContext

java.awt

```
1.2       PaintContext
```

	public.......................void	**dispose** ()
	public............................	**getColorModel** ()
	.. java.awt.image.ColorModel	
	public...java.awt.image.Raster	**getRaster** (int x, int y, int w, int h)

PaintEvent

java.awt.event

```
          Object                                                                     ε640,641,643,649,566
1.1       └ java.util.EventObject 1 - - - - - - - - - - - - - - - - - - - -   java.io.Serializable ˎ
1.1 ○        └ java.awt.AWTEvent 2
1.1              └ ComponentEvent 3
1.1                  └ PaintEvent
```

	2	*27 inherited members from java.awt.AWTEvent not shown*		
▲	3	public static final.............int	COMPONENT_FIRST = 100	
▲	3	public static final.............int	COMPONENT_HIDDEN = 103	
▲	3	public static final.............int	COMPONENT_LAST = 103	
▲	3	public static final.............int	COMPONENT_MOVED = 100	
▲	3	public static final.............int	COMPONENT_RESIZED = 101	
▲	3	public static final.............int	COMPONENT_SHOWN = 102	
	3	public.... java.awt.Component	getComponent ()	ε810,813,1011
	1	public...................Object	getSource ()	ε644,886,565,568,570
		public...... java.awt.Rectangle	**getUpdateRect** ()	
▲		public static final.............int	**PAINT** = 800	
▲		public static final.............int	**PAINT_FIRST** = 800	
▲		public static final.............int	**PAINT_LAST** = 801	
*		public.........................	**PaintEvent** (java.awt.Component source, int id, java.awt.Rectangle updateRect)	
	3	public.....................**String**	**paramString** ()	
		public......................void	**setUpdateRect** (java.awt.Rectangle updateRect)	
	1	protected transient......Object	source	
▲		public static final.............int	**UPDATE** = 801	

Class *Interface* —extends - - -implements ○ abstract ● final △ static ▲ static final * constructor x x—inherited x **x**—declared **x x**—overridden
ε*n*—examples of usage ˎ—has subclass package—see other volume

Panel · java.awt

ε606,618,733,953,988

```
Object
 └Component¹ ------------------------- java.awt.image.ImageObserver ³, MenuContainer,
                                        java.io.Serializable
     └Container²
        └Panel ------------------------- javax.accessibility.Accessible
```

	1	*176 inherited members from Component not shown*		
	2	*65 inherited members from Container not shown*		
	3	*8 inherited members from java.awt.image.ImageObserver not shown*		
	2	public............. Component	add (Component comp)	ε571,575,581,590,610
	2	public.................... **void**	**addNotify** ()	
1.3	1	public.... **javax.accessibility**₂ **.AccessibleContext**	**getAccessibleContext** ()	
*		public.........................	**Panel** ()	ε571
1.1 *		public.........................	**Panel** (*LayoutManager* layout)	ε571

PanelPeer · java.awt.peer

```
PanelPeer——————————————ContainerPeer ¹ (ComponentPeer ²)
```

- 2 *42 inherited members from ComponentPeer not shown*
- 1 *7 inherited members from ContainerPeer not shown*

PanelUI · javax.swing.plaf

```
     Object
1.2 ○ └ComponentUI¹
1.2 ○   └PanelUI
```

	1	*11 inherited members from ComponentUI not shown*	
*		public.........................	**PanelUI** ()

Paper · java.awt.print

```
     Object¹
1.2  └Paper ------------------------------- Cloneable
```

	1	public.................. **Object**	**clone** ()
		public...................double	**getHeight** ()
		public...................double	**getImageableHeight** ()
		public...................double	**getImageableWidth** ()
		public...................double	**getImageableX** ()
		public...................double	**getImageableY** ()
		public...................double	**getWidth** ()
*		public.........................	**Paper** ()
		public...................void	**setImageableArea** (double x, double y, double width, double height)
		public...................void	**setSize** (double width, double height)

ParagraphView❶ · javax.swing.text.html

```
     Object
1.2 ○ └javax.swing.text.View¹ ------------------ javax.swing.SwingConstants ⁶
1.2 ○   └javax.swing.text.CompositeView²
1.2      └javax.swing.text.BoxView³
1.3 ○       └javax.swing.text.FlowView⁴
1.2          └javax.swing.text.ParagraphView⁵ --- javax.swing.text.TabExpander
1.2             └ParagraphView
```

	1	*28 inherited members from javax.swing.text.View not shown*	
	2	*14 inherited members from javax.swing.text.CompositeView not shown*	
	3	*27 inherited members from javax.swing.text.BoxView not shown*	
	6	*19 inherited members from javax.swing.SwingConstants not shown*	
	5	protected.................void	adjustRow (javax.swing.text.ParagraphView.Row r, int desiredSpan, int x)
	5	public....javax.swing.text.View	breakView (int axis, float len, *java.awt.Shape* a)
	4	protected............... **javax**₂ **.swing.SizeRequirements**	**calculateMinorAxisRequirements** (int axis, javax.swing.SizeRequirements r)

ParagraphView ❶

	5	public	void	changedUpdate (*javax.swing.event.DocumentEvent* changes, *java.awt.Shape* a, *javax.swing.text.ViewFactory* f)
1.3	5	protected	createRow ()
			.... javax.swing.text.View	
	5	protected	int	findOffsetToCharactersInString (char[] string, int start)
	5	protected	int	firstLineIndent
	5	protected	boolean	flipEastAndWestAtEnds (int position, javax.swing.text.Position.Bias bias)
	5	public	float	getAlignment (int axis)
	1	public	***javax*** ₂	**getAttributes** ()
		.swing.text.AttributeSet		
	5	public	int	getBreakWeight (int axis, float len)
	5	protected	int	getClosestPositionTo (int pos, javax.swing.text.Position.Bias b, *java.awt.Shape* a, int direction, javax.swing.text.Position.Bias[] biasRet, int rowIndex, int x) throws javax.swing.text.BadLocationException
1.3	4	public	int	getFlowAxis ()
1.3	5	public	int	getFlowSpan (int index)
1.3	5	public	int	getFlowStart (int index)
	5	protected	getLayoutView (int index)
			.... javax.swing.text.View	
	5	protected	int	getLayoutViewCount ()
	3	public	**float**	**getMaximumSpan** (int axis)
	3	public	**float**	**getMinimumSpan** (int axis)
	5	protected	int	getNextNorthSouthVisualPositionFrom (int pos, javax.swing.text.Position.Bias b, *java.awt.Shape* a, int direction, javax.swing.text.Position.Bias[] biasRet) throws javax.swing.text.BadLocationException
	5	protected	float	getPartialSize (int startOffset, int endOffset)
	3	public	**float**	**getPreferredSpan** (int axis)
		protected	StyleSheet	**getStyleSheet** ()
	5	protected	float	getTabBase ()
	5	protected	getTabSet ()
			...... javax.swing.text.TabSet	
	4	protected	int	getViewIndexAtPosition (int pos)
	4	public	void	insertUpdate (*javax.swing.event.DocumentEvent* changes, *java.awt.Shape* a, *javax.swing.text.ViewFactory* f)
	1	public	**boolean**	**isVisible** ()
	4	protected	void	layout (int width, int height)
1.3	4	protected	layoutPool
			.... javax.swing.text.View	
1.3	4	protected	int	layoutSpan
	4	protected	void	loadChildren (*javax.swing.text.ViewFactory* f)
	5	public	float	nextTabStop (float x, int tabOffset)
	5	public	**void**	**paint** (java.awt.Graphics g, *java.awt.Shape* a)
✳		public		**ParagraphView** (*javax.swing.text.Element* elem)
	4	public	void	removeUpdate (*javax.swing.event.DocumentEvent* changes, *java.awt.Shape* a, *javax.swing.text.ViewFactory* f)
	5	protected	void	setFirstLineIndent (float fi)
	5	protected	void	setJustification (int j)
	5	protected	void	setLineSpacing (float ls)
	2	public	**void**	**setParent** (javax.swing.text.View parent)
	5	protected	**void**	**setPropertiesFromAttributes** ()
1.3	4	protected	javax.swing ₂	strategy
		.text.FlowView.FlowStrategy		

ParagraphView ❷

javax.swing.text

```
       Object
1.2 ○  └View 1 - - - - - - - - - - - - - - - - - - - - - - - - - - - - javax.swing.SwingConstants 5
1.2 ○    └CompositeView 2
1.2        └BoxView 3
1.3 ○        └FlowView 4
1.2            └ParagraphView ‿ - - - - - - - - - - - - - - TabExpander 6
```

1 *30 inherited members from View not shown*
2 *15 inherited members from CompositeView not shown*
3 *30 inherited members from BoxView not shown*
5 *19 inherited members from javax.swing.SwingConstants not shown*

protected	void	**adjustRow** (javax.swing.text.ParagraphView.Row r, int desiredSpan, int x)
public	View	**breakView** (int axis, float len, *java.awt.Shape* a)

Class   *Interface*   —extends   - - -implements   ○ abstract   ● final   △ static   ▲ static final   ✳ constructor   x x—inherited   x **x**—declared   **x x**—overridden
εn—examples of usage   ‿—has subclass   package—see other volume

	4	protected	javax₂ .swing.SizeRequirements	**calculateMinorAxisRequirements** (int axis, javax.swing.SizeRequirements r)
	4	public	**void**	**changedUpdate** (*javax.swing.event.DocumentEvent* changes, *java.awt.Shape* a, *ViewFactory* f)
1.3	4	protected	**View**	**createRow** ()
		protected	int	**findOffsetToCharactersInString** (char[] string, int start)
		protected	int	**firstLineIndent**
	3	protected	**boolean**	**flipEastAndWestAtEnds** (int position, Position.Bias bias)
	3	public	**float**	**getAlignment** (int axis)
		public	int	**getBreakWeight** (int axis, float len)
		protected	int	**getClosestPositionTo** (int pos, Position.Bias b, java.awt.Shape a, int direction, Position.Bias[] biasRet, int rowIndex, int x) throws BadLocationException
1.3	4	public	int	getFlowAxis ()
1.3	4	public	**int**	**getFlowSpan** (int index)
1.3	4	public	**int**	**getFlowStart** (int index)
		protected	View	**getLayoutView** (int index)
		protected	int	**getLayoutViewCount** ()
	2	protected	**int**	**getNextNorthSouthVisualPositionFrom** (int pos, Position.Bias b, *java.awt.Shape* a, int direction, Position.Bias[] biasRet) throws BadLocationException
		protected	float	**getPartialSize** (int startOffset, int endOffset)
		protected	float	**getTabBase** ()
		protected	TabSet	**getTabSet** ()
	4	protected	int	getViewIndexAtPosition (int pos)
	4	public	void	**insertUpdate** (*javax.swing.event.DocumentEvent* changes, *java.awt.Shape* a, *ViewFactory* f)
	4	protected	void	**layout** (int width, int height)
1.3	4	protected	View	layoutPool
1.3	4	protected	int	layoutSpan
	4	protected	void	loadChildren (*ViewFactory* f)
	6	public	float	**nextTabStop** (float x, int tabOffset)
	3	public	**void**	**paint** (java.awt.Graphics g, *java.awt.Shape* a)
*		public		**ParagraphView** (*Element* elem)
	4	public	void	**removeUpdate** (*javax.swing.event.DocumentEvent* changes, *java.awt.Shape* a, *ViewFactory* f)
		protected	void	**setFirstLineIndent** (float fi)
		protected	void	**setJustification** (int j)
		protected	void	**setLineSpacing** (float ls)
		protected	void	**setPropertiesFromAttributes** ()
1.3	4	protected	FlowView.FlowStrategy	strategy

ParameterBlock			java.awt.image.renderable

Object[1]

1.2 └─ParameterBlock - *Cloneable*˯, *java.io.Serializable*˯

	public	ParameterBlock	**add** (byte b)
	public	ParameterBlock	**add** (char c)
	public	ParameterBlock	**add** (double d)
	public	ParameterBlock	**add** (float f)
	public	ParameterBlock	**add** (int i)
	public	ParameterBlock	**add** (Object obj)
	public	ParameterBlock	**add** (long l)
	public	ParameterBlock	**add** (short s)
	public	ParameterBlock	**addSource** (Object source)
1	public	**Object**	**clone** ()
	public	byte	**getByteParameter** (int index)
	public	char	**getCharParameter** (int index)
	public	double	**getDoubleParameter** (int index)
	public	float	**getFloatParameter** (int index)
	public	int	**getIntParameter** (int index)
	public	long	**getLongParameter** (int index)
	public	int	**getNumParameters** ()
	public	int	**getNumSources** ()
	public	Object	**getObjectParameter** (int index)
	public	Class[]	**getParamClasses** ()
	public	java.util.Vector	**getParameters** ()
	public	*RenderableImage*	**getRenderableSource** (int index)
	public	java.awt₂ .image.RenderedImage	**getRenderedSource** (int index)
	public	short	**getShortParameter** (int index)
	public	Object	**getSource** (int index)

ParameterBlock

	public	java.util.Vector	**getSources** ()
✱	public		**ParameterBlock** ()
✱	public		**ParameterBlock** (java.util.Vector sources)
✱	public		**ParameterBlock** (java.util.Vector sources, java.util.Vector parameters)
	protected	java.util.Vector	**parameters**
	public	void	**removeParameters** ()
	public	void	**removeSources** ()
	public	ParameterBlock	**set** (byte b, int index)
	public	ParameterBlock	**set** (char c, int index)
	public	ParameterBlock	**set** (double d, int index)
	public	ParameterBlock	**set** (float f, int index)
	public	ParameterBlock	**set** (int i, int index)
	public	ParameterBlock	**set** (Object obj, int index)
	public	ParameterBlock	**set** (long l, int index)
	public	ParameterBlock	**set** (short s, int index)
	public	void	**setParameters** (java.util.Vector parameters)
	public	ParameterBlock	**setSource** (Object source, int index)
	public	void	**setSources** (java.util.Vector sources)
	public	Object	**shallowClone** ()
	protected	java.util.Vector	**sources**

Parser ❶
javax.swing.text.html.parser

Object
1.2 └─Parser - DTDConstants [1]

	1	*35 inherited members from DTDConstants not shown*	
	protected	DTD	**dtd**
	protected	void	**endTag** (boolean omitted)
	protected	void	**error** (String err)
	protected	void	**error** (String err, String arg1)
	protected	void	**error** (String err, String arg1, String arg2)
	protected	void	**error** (String err, String arg1, String arg2, String arg3)
	protected	void	**flushAttributes** ()
	protected	javax.swing .text.SimpleAttributeSet	**getAttributes** ()
	protected	int	**getCurrentLine** ()
	protected	int	**getCurrentPos** ()
	protected	void	**handleComment** (char[] text)
	protected	void	**handleEmptyTag** (TagElement tag) throws javax.swing.text .ChangedCharSetException
	protected	void	**handleEndTag** (TagElement tag)
	protected	void	**handleEOFInComment** ()
	protected	void	**handleError** (int ln, String msg)
	protected	void	**handleStartTag** (TagElement tag)
	protected	void	**handleText** (char[] text)
	protected	void	**handleTitle** (char[] text)
	protected	TagElement	**makeTag** (Element elem)
	protected	TagElement	**makeTag** (Element elem, boolean fictional)
	protected	void	**markFirstTime** (Element elem)
	public synchronized	void	**parse** (java.io.Reader in) throws java.io.IOException
	public	String	**parseDTDMarkup** () throws java.io.IOException
	protected	boolean	**parseMarkupDeclarations** (StringBuffer strBuff) throws java.io.IOException
✱	public		**Parser** (DTD dtd)
	protected	void	**startTag** (TagElement tag) throws javax.swing.text.ChangedCharSetException
	protected	boolean	**strict**

ParserDelegator
javax.swing.text.html.parser

Object
1.2 ○ └─javax.swing.text.html.HTMLEditorKit.Parser [1]
1.2   └─ParserDelegator - java.io.Serializable

△	protected static	DTD	**createDTD** (DTD dtd, String name)
	1 public	void	**parse** (java.io.Reader r, javax.swing.text.html.HTMLEditorKit.ParserCallback cb, boolean ignoreCharSet) throws java.io.IOException
✱	public		**ParserDelegator** ()
△	protected static	void	**setDefaultDTD** ()

Class *Interface* —extends - - -implements ○ abstract ● final △ static ▲ static final ✱ constructor x x—inherited x **x**—declared x x—overridden
ε*n*—examples of usage ˷—has subclass package—see other volume

		PasswordView	javax.swing.text

```
         Object
1.2  ○   └─View 1 ------------------------------- javax.swing.SwingConstants 4
1.2       └─PlainView 2 ------------------------- TabExpander
1.2         └─FieldView 3
1.2           └─PasswordView
```

	1	*43 inherited members from View not shown*	
	4	*19 inherited members from javax.swing.SwingConstants not shown*	
	3	protected ...... *java.awt.Shape*	adjustAllocation (*java.awt.Shape* a)
	2	public .... void	changedUpdate (*javax.swing.event.DocumentEvent* changes, *java.awt.Shape* a, *ViewFactory* f)
1.4	2	protected .... void	damageLineRange (int line0, int line1, *java.awt.Shape* a, java.awt.Component host)
		protected .... int	**drawEchoCharacter** (java.awt.Graphics g, int x, int y, char c)
	2	protected .... void	drawLine (int lineIndex, java.awt.Graphics g, int x, int y)
	2	protected .... **int drawSelectedText** (java.awt.Graphics g, int x, int y, int p0, int p1) throws BadLocationException	
	2	protected .... **int drawUnselectedText** (java.awt.Graphics g, int x, int y, int p0, int p1) throws BadLocationException	
	3	protected java.awt.FontMetrics	getFontMetrics ()
●	2	protected final .... Segment	getLineBuffer ()
	3	public .... **float getPreferredSpan** (int axis)	
	3	public .... int	getResizeWeight (int axis)
	2	protected .... int	getTabSize ()
	3	public .... void	insertUpdate (*javax.swing.event.DocumentEvent* changes, *java.awt.Shape* a, *ViewFactory* f)
1.4	2	protected .. java.awt.Rectangle	lineToRect (*java.awt.Shape* a, int line)
	2	protected java.awt.FontMetrics	metrics
	3	public .... ***java.awt.Shape* modelToView** (int pos, *java.awt.Shape* a, Position.Bias b) throws BadLocationException	
	2	public .... float	nextTabStop (float x, int tabOffset)
	3	public .... void	paint (java.awt.Graphics g, *java.awt.Shape* a)
✳		public .... **PasswordView** (*Element* elem)	
	3	public .... void	removeUpdate (*javax.swing.event.DocumentEvent* changes, *java.awt.Shape* a, *ViewFactory* f)
	2	public .... void	setSize (float width, float height)
1.4	2	protected .... void	updateDamage (*javax.swing.event.DocumentEvent* changes, *java.awt.Shape* a, *ViewFactory* f)
1.4	2	protected .... void	updateMetrics ()
	3	public .... **int viewToModel** (float fx, float fy, *java.awt.Shape* a, Position.Bias[] bias)	

		Patch	javax.sound.midi

```
         Object
1.3      └─Patch
```

	public .... int	**getBank** ()
	public .... int	**getProgram** ()
✳	public	**Patch** (int bank, int program)

		PathIterator	java.awt.geom

```
1.2      PathIterator
```

	public .... int	**currentSegment** (double[] coords)
	public .... int	**currentSegment** (float[] coords)
	public .... int	**getWindingRule** ()
	public .... boolean	**isDone** ()
	public .... void	**next** ()
▲	public static final .... int	**SEG_CLOSE** = 4
▲	public static final .... int	**SEG_CUBICTO** = 3
▲	public static final .... int	**SEG_LINETO** = 1
▲	public static final .... int	**SEG_MOVETO** = 0
▲	public static final .... int	**SEG_QUADTO** = 2
▲	public static final .... int	**WIND_EVEN_ODD** = 0
▲	public static final .... int	**WIND_NON_ZERO** = 1

P

Classes

PDLOverrideSupported

		PDLOverrideSupported		javax.print.attribute.standard	

Object
1.4 ○ └ javax.print.attribute.EnumSyntax[1] - - - - - - - - - - *java.io.Serializable*, *Cloneable*
1.4   └ PDLOverrideSupported - - - - - - - - - - - - - - - - *javax.print.attribute.PrintServiceAttribute*
            (*javax.print.attribute.Attribute*[2] (*java.io.Serializable*))

▲		public static final	**ATTEMPTED**		
		. . . . . PDLOverrideSupported			
	1	public . . . . Object	clone ()		
●	2	public final . . . . Class	**getCategory** ()	ε707	
	1	protected . . . . **javax.print**₂	**getEnumValueTable** ()		
		.attribute.EnumSyntax[]			
●	2	public final . . . . String	**getName** ()	ε706,707,708	
	1	protected . . . . int	getOffset ()		
	1	protected . . . . **String[]**	**getStringTable** ()		
	1	public . . . . int	getValue ()		
	1	public . . . . int	hashCode ()		
▲		public static final	**NOT_ATTEMPTED**		
		. . . . . PDLOverrideSupported			
✳		protected	**PDLOverrideSupported** (int value)		
	1	protected . . . . Object	readResolve () throws java.io.ObjectStreamException		
	1	public . . . . String	toString ()		

		PixelGrabber		java.awt.image

Object
└ PixelGrabber - *ImageConsumer* [1]

	1	*9 inherited members from ImageConsumer not shown*			
1.1		public synchronized . . . . void	**abortGrabbing** ()		
1.1		public synchronized	**getColorModel** ()	ε661,662	
		. . . . ColorModel			
1.1		public synchronized . . . . int	**getHeight** ()		
1.1		public synchronized . . . . Object	**getPixels** ()		
1.1		public synchronized . . . . int	**getStatus** ()		
1.1		public synchronized . . . . int	**getWidth** ()		
		public . . . . boolean	**grabPixels** () throws InterruptedException	ε661,662	
		public synchronized . . boolean	**grabPixels** (long ms) throws InterruptedException		
	1	public synchronized . . . . void	**imageComplete** (int status)		
1.1	✳	public	**PixelGrabber** (java.awt.Image img, int x, int y, int w, int h, boolean forceRGB)		
				ε661,662	
	✳	public	**PixelGrabber** (java.awt.Image img, int x, int y, int w, int h, int[] pix, int off, int scansize)		
	✳	public	**PixelGrabber** (*ImageProducer* ip, int x, int y, int w, int h, int[] pix, int off, int scansize)		
	1	public . . . . void	**setColorModel** (ColorModel model)		
	1	public . . . . void	**setDimensions** (int width, int height)		
	1	public . . . . void	**setHints** (int hints)		
	1	public . . . . void	**setPixels** (int srcX, int srcY, int srcW, int srcH, ColorModel model, int[] pixels, int srcOff, int srcScan)		
	1	public . . . . void	**setPixels** (int srcX, int srcY, int srcW, int srcH, ColorModel model, byte[] pixels, int srcOff, int srcScan)		
	1	public . . . . void	**setProperties** (java.util.Hashtable props)		
1.1		public synchronized . . . . void	**startGrabbing** ()		
		public synchronized . . . . int	**status** ()		

		PixelInterleavedSampleModel		java.awt.image

Object   ε668
1.2 ○ └ SampleModel[1]
1.2   └ ComponentSampleModel[2]
1.2   └ PixelInterleavedSampleModel

	2	*31 inherited members from ComponentSampleModel not shown*		
	2	public . . . . **SampleModel**	**createCompatibleSampleModel** (int w, int h)	
	2	public . . . . **SampleModel**	**createSubsetSampleModel** (int[] bands)	
	1	protected . . . . int	dataType	
	1	public . . . . Object	getDataElements (int x, int y, int w, int h, Object obj, DataBuffer data)	
●	1	public final . . . . int	getDataType ()	

Class *Interface* —extends - - -implements ○ abstract ● final △ static ▲ static final ✳ constructor x x—inherited x **x**—declared **x x**—overridden
ε*n*—examples of usage ‿—has subclass package—see other volume

●	1	public final .... int	getHeight ()
●	1	public final .... int	getNumBands ()
	1	public .... float[]	getPixel (int x, int y, float[] fArray, DataBuffer data)
	1	public .... double[]	getPixel (int x, int y, double[] dArray, DataBuffer data)
	1	public .... float[]	getPixels (int x, int y, int w, int h, float[] fArray, DataBuffer data)
	1	public .... double[]	getPixels (int x, int y, int w, int h, double[] dArray, DataBuffer data)
	1	public .... float[]	getSamples (int x, int y, int w, int h, int b, float[] fArray, DataBuffer data)
	1	public .... double[]	getSamples (int x, int y, int w, int h, int b, double[] dArray, DataBuffer data)
	1	public .... int	getTransferType ()
●	1	public final .... int	getWidth ()
	2	public .... **int hashCode** ()
	1	protected .... int	height
*		public	**PixelInterleavedSampleModel** (int dataType, int w, int h, int pixelStride, int scanlineStride, int[] bandOffsets)
	1	public .... void	setDataElements (int x, int y, int w, int h, Object obj, DataBuffer data)
	1	public .... void	setPixel (int x, int y, float[] fArray, DataBuffer data)
	1	public .... void	setPixel (int x, int y, double[] dArray, DataBuffer data)
	1	public .... void	setPixels (int x, int y, int w, int h, float[] fArray, DataBuffer data)
	1	public .... void	setPixels (int x, int y, int w, int h, double[] dArray, DataBuffer data)
	1	public .... void	setSamples (int x, int y, int w, int h, int b, float[] fArray, DataBuffer data)
	1	public .... void	setSamples (int x, int y, int w, int h, int b, double[] dArray, DataBuffer data)
	1	protected .... int	width

PlainDocument javax.swing.text

```
      Object
1.2 O └ AbstractDocument¹ -------------------- Document‚², java.io.Serializable‚
1.2       └ PlainDocument
```

	1	*48 inherited members from AbstractDocument not shown*	
		protected . AbstractDocument‚ .AbstractElement	**createDefaultRoot** ()
	1	public .... ***Element***	**getDefaultRootElement** () ε984,990,1013
	1	public .... ***Element***	**getParagraphElement** (int pos)
	1	public .... **void**	**insertString** (int offs, String str, *AttributeSet* a) throws BadLocationException ε975,970,989,991,992
	1	protected .... **void**	**insertUpdate** (AbstractDocument.DefaultDocumentEvent chng, *AttributeSet* attr)
▲		public .... String	**lineLimitAttribute** = "lineLimit"
*		public	**PlainDocument** ()
*		public	**PlainDocument** (*AbstractDocument.Content* c)
	1	protected .... **void**	**removeUpdate** (AbstractDocument.DefaultDocumentEvent chng)
▲	2	public static final .... String	StreamDescriptionProperty = "stream"
▲		public static final .... String	**tabSizeAttribute** = "tabSize"
▲	2	public static final .... String	TitleProperty = "title"

PlainView javax.swing.text

```
      Object
1.2 O └ View¹ ----------------------------- javax.swing.SwingConstants²
1.2       └ PlainView‚ -------------------------- TabExpander³
```

	1	*44 inherited members from View not shown*	
	2	*19 inherited members from javax.swing.SwingConstants not shown*	
	1	public .... **void**	**changedUpdate** (*javax.swing.event.DocumentEvent* changes, *java.awt.Shape* a, *ViewFactory* f)
1.4		protected .... void	**damageLineRange** (int line0, int line1, *java.awt.Shape* a, java.awt.Component host)
		protected .... void	**drawLine** (int lineIndex, java.awt.Graphics g, int x, int y)
		protected .... int	**drawSelectedText** (java.awt.Graphics g, int x, int y, int p0, int p1) throws BadLocationException
		protected .... int	**drawUnselectedText** (java.awt.Graphics g, int x, int y, int p0, int p1) throws BadLocationException
●		protected final .... Segment	**getLineBuffer** ()
	1	public .... **float**	**getPreferredSpan** (int axis)
		protected .... int	**getTabSize** ()
	1	public .... **void**	**insertUpdate** (*javax.swing.event.DocumentEvent* changes, *java.awt.Shape* a, *ViewFactory* f)
1.4		protected .. java.awt.Rectangle	**lineToRect** (*java.awt.Shape* a, int line)
		protected java.awt.FontMetrics	**metrics**
	1	public .... ***java.awt.Shape***	**modelToView** (int pos, *java.awt.Shape* a, Position.Bias b) throws BadLocationException
	3	public .... float	**nextTabStop** (float x, int tabOffset)

P

Classes

PlainView

1	public	**void**	**paint** (java.awt.Graphics g, *java.awt.Shape* a)
✳	public		**PlainView** (*Element* elem)
1	public	**void**	**removeUpdate** (*javax.swing.event.DocumentEvent* changes, *java.awt.Shape* a, *ViewFactory* f)
1	public	**void**	**setSize** (float width, float height)
1.4	protected	void	**updateDamage** (*javax.swing.event.DocumentEvent* changes, *java.awt.Shape* a, *ViewFactory* f)
1.4	protected	void	**updateMetrics** ()
1	public	**int**	**viewToModel** (float fx, float fy, *java.awt.Shape* a, Position.Bias[] bias)

Point   java.awt

Object[1]
 └─java.awt.geom.Point2D[2] - - - - - - - - - - - - - - - - - *Cloneable*
1.2 ○   └─Point - *java.io.Serializable*

ε570,117

	2	public	Object	clone ()
1.2	2	public	double	distance (java.awt.geom.Point2D pt)
1.2	2	public	double	distance (double PX, double PY)
1.2 △	2	public static	double	distance (double X1, double Y1, double X2, double Y2)
1.2	2	public	double	distanceSq (java.awt.geom.Point2D pt)
1.2	2	public	double	distanceSq (double PX, double PY)
1.2 △	2	public static	double	distanceSq (double X1, double Y1, double X2, double Y2)
	2	public	**boolean**	**equals** (Object obj)
1.1		public	Point	**getLocation** ()
1.2	2	public	**double**	**getX** ()
1.2	2	public	**double**	**getY** ()
	2	public	int	hashCode ()
		public	**void**	**move** (int x, int y)
1.1 ✳		public		**Point** ()
1.1 ✳		public		**Point** (Point p)
✳		public		**Point** (int x, int y)
1.2	2	public	void	setLocation (java.awt.geom.Point2D p)
1.1		public	void	**setLocation** (Point p)
1.2	2	public	**void**	**setLocation** (double x, double y)
1.1		public	void	**setLocation** (int x, int y)
1		public	**String**	**toString** ()
		public	void	**translate** (int dx, int dy)
		public	int	**x**
		public	int	**y**

ε865
ε844

ε946,947
ε946,947

Point2D   java.awt.geom

Object[1]
1.2 ○ └─Point2D - *Cloneable*

ε570,117

	1	public	**Object**	**clone** ()
		public	double	**distance** (Point2D pt)
		public	double	**distance** (double PX, double PY)
△		public static	double	**distance** (double X1, double Y1, double X2, double Y2)
		public	double	**distanceSq** (Point2D pt)
		public	double	**distanceSq** (double PX, double PY)
△		public static	double	**distanceSq** (double X1, double Y1, double X2, double Y2)
	1	public	**boolean**	**equals** (Object obj)
○		public abstract	double	**getX** ()
○		public abstract	double	**getY** ()
	1	public	**int**	**hashCode** ()
✳		protected		**Point2D** ()
		public	void	**setLocation** (Point2D p)
○		public abstract	void	**setLocation** (double x, double y)

Point2D.Double   java.awt.geom

Object[1]
1.2 ○ └─Point2D[2] - *Cloneable*
1.2   └─Point2D.Double

ε570,117

Class *Interface* —extends - - -implements ○ abstract ● final △ static ▲ static final ✳ constructor x x—inherited x **x**—declared **x x**—overridden
ε*n*—examples of usage ⌄—has subclass package—see other volume

	2	public....................	Object	clone ()
	2	public....................	double	distance (Point2D pt)
	2	public....................	double	distance (double PX, double PY)
△	2	public static	double	distance (double X1, double Y1, double X2, double Y2)
	2	public....................	double	distanceSq (Point2D pt)
	2	public....................	double	distanceSq (double PX, double PY)
△	2	public static	double	distanceSq (double X1, double Y1, double X2, double Y2)
✳		public........................		**Point2D.Double** ()
✳		public........................		**Point2D.Double** (double x, double y)
	2	public....................	boolean	equals (Object obj)
	2	public....................	**double**	**getX** ()
	2	public....................	**double**	**getY** ()
	2	public....................	int	hashCode ()
	2	public....................	void	setLocation (Point2D p)
	2	public....................	**void**	**setLocation** (double x, double y)
	1	public....................	**String**	**toString** ()
		public....................	double	**x**
		public....................	double	**y**

Point2D.Float

java.awt.geom

Object [1]
```
1.2 ○  └Point2D [2] ---------------------------- Cloneable
1.2       └Point2D.Float
```

ε570,117

	2	public....................	Object	clone ()
	2	public....................	double	distance (Point2D pt)
	2	public....................	double	distance (double PX, double PY)
△	2	public static	double	distance (double X1, double Y1, double X2, double Y2)
	2	public....................	double	distanceSq (Point2D pt)
	2	public....................	double	distanceSq (double PX, double PY)
△	2	public static	double	distanceSq (double X1, double Y1, double X2, double Y2)
	2	public....................	boolean	equals (Object obj)
✳		public........................		**Point2D.Float** ()
✳		public........................		**Point2D.Float** (float x, float y)
	2	public....................	**double**	**getX** ()
	2	public....................	**double**	**getY** ()
	2	public....................	int	hashCode ()
	2	public....................	void	setLocation (Point2D p)
	2	public....................	**void**	**setLocation** (double x, double y)
		public....................	void	**setLocation** (float x, float y)
	1	public....................	**String**	**toString** ()
		public....................	float	**x**
		public....................	float	**y**

Polygon

java.awt

Object
```
└Polygon ---------------------------- Shape [1], java.io.Serializable
```

ε586,587

		public....................	void	**addPoint** (int x, int y)
1.1		protected	Rectangle	**bounds**
1.2	1	public....................	boolean	**contains** (java.awt.geom.Point2D p)
1.2	1	public....................	boolean	**contains** (java.awt.geom.Rectangle2D r)
1.1		public....................	boolean	**contains** (Point p)
1.2	1	public....................	boolean	**contains** (double x, double y)
1.1		public....................	boolean	**contains** (int x, int y)
1.2	1	public....................	boolean	**contains** (double x, double y, double w, double h)
D		public....................	Rectangle	**getBoundingBox** ()
1.1	1	public....................	Rectangle	**getBounds** ()
1.2	1	public....................	. java.awt.geom.Rectangle2D	**getBounds2D** ()
1.2	1	public........................ ...java.awt.geom.PathIterator		**getPathIterator** (java.awt.geom.AffineTransform at)
1.2	1	public........................ ...java.awt.geom.PathIterator		**getPathIterator** (java.awt.geom.AffineTransform at, double flatness)
D		public....................	boolean	**inside** (int x, int y)
1.2	1	public....................	boolean	**intersects** (java.awt.geom.Rectangle2D r)
1.2	1	public....................	boolean	**intersects** (double x, double y, double w, double h)
1.4		public....................	void	**invalidate** ()
		public....................	int	**npoints**

Polygon

✳	public		**Polygon** ()	ε586,587
✳	public		**Polygon** (int[] xpoints, int[] ypoints, int npoints)	
1.4	public	void	**reset** ()	
1.1	public	void	**translate** (int deltaX, int deltaY)	
	public	int[]	**xpoints**	
	public	int[]	**ypoints**	

Popup
javax.swing

Object
  1.4 └Popup

	public	void	**hide** ()
✳	protected		**Popup** ()
✳	protected		**Popup** (java.awt.Component owner, java.awt.Component contents, int x, int y)
	public	void	**show** ()

PopupFactory
javax.swing

Object
  1.4 └PopupFactory

	public	Popup	**getPopup** (java.awt.Component owner, java.awt.Component contents, int x, int y) throws IllegalArgumentException
△	public static	PopupFactory	**getSharedInstance** ()
✳	public		**PopupFactory** ()
△	public static	void	**setSharedInstance** (PopupFactory factory)

PopupMenu
java.awt

Object
  ○ └MenuComponent [1] - *java.io.Serializable*
      └MenuItem [2] - *javax.accessibility.Accessible*
         └Menu [3] - *MenuContainer*
  1.1   └PopupMenu

	3	public	MenuItem	add (MenuItem mi)
	3	public	void	add (String label)
	2	public synchronized	void	addActionListener (*java.awt.event.ActionListener* l)
	3	public	**void**	**addNotify** ()
	3	public	void	addSeparator ()
	2	public	void	deleteShortcut ()
●	2	protected final	void	disableEvents (long eventsToDisable)
●	1	public final	void	dispatchEvent (AWTEvent e)
●	2	protected final	void	enableEvents (long eventsToEnable)
1.3	3	public	**javax.accessibility.AccessibleContext**	**getAccessibleContext** ()
	2	public	String	getActionCommand ()
1.4	2	public synchronized	*java.awt.event.ActionListener[]*	getActionListeners ()
	1	public	Font	getFont ()
	3	public	MenuItem	getItem (int index)
	3	public	int	getItemCount ()
	2	public	String	getLabel ()
1.3	2	public	*java.util.EventListener[]*	getListeners (Class listenerType)
	1	public	String	getName ()
	1	public	*MenuContainer*	getParent ()
	2	public	MenuShortcut	getShortcut ()
1.2 ●	1	protected final	Object	getTreeLock ()
	3	public	void	insert (MenuItem menuitem, int index)
	3	public	void	insert (String label, int index)
	3	public	void	insertSeparator (int index)
	2	public	boolean	isEnabled ()
	3	public	boolean	isTearOff ()
	3	public	String	paramString ()
✳		public		**PopupMenu** () throws HeadlessException
✳		public		**PopupMenu** (String label) throws HeadlessException

---

Class *Interface* —extends - - -implements ○ abstract ● final △ static ▲ static final ✳ constructor x x—inherited x **x**—declared **x x**—overridden
ε*n*—examples of usage ˯—has subclass package—see other volume

2	protected	. . . . .void	processActionEvent (java.awt.event.ActionEvent e)
2	protected	. . . . .void	processEvent (AWTEvent e)
3	public	. . . . .void	remove (int index)
3	public	. . . . .void	remove (MenuComponent item)
2	public synchronized	. . . . . . .void	removeActionListener (*java.awt.event.ActionListener* l)
3	public	. . . . .void	removeAll ()
3	public	. . . . .void	removeNotify ()
2	public	. . . . .void	setActionCommand (String command)
2	public synchronized	. . . . . . .void	setEnabled (boolean b)
1	public	. . . . .void	setFont (Font f)
2	public synchronized	. . . . . . .void	setLabel (String label)
1	public	. . . . .void	setName (String name)
2	public	. . . . .void	setShortcut (MenuShortcut s)
	public	. . . . .void	**show** (Component origin, int x, int y)
1	public	. . . . .String	toString ()

PopupMenuEvent | javax.swing.event

Object
1.1 └ java.util.EventObject [1] - - - - - - - - - - - - - - - - - - - *java.io.Serializable*
1.2 └ PopupMenuEvent

ε640,641,643,649,566

1	public	. . . . .Object	getSource ()
*	public	. . . .	**PopupMenuEvent** (Object source)
1	protected transient	. . . . . .Object	source
1	public	. . . . .String	toString ()

ε767,644,886,565,568

PopupMenuListener | javax.swing.event

1.2 *PopupMenuListener*────────────────── *java.util.EventListener*

ε738,743,745,746,752

	public	. . . . .void	**popupMenuCanceled** (PopupMenuEvent e)	ε767
	public	. . . . .void	**popupMenuWillBecomeInvisible** (PopupMenuEvent e)	ε767
	public	. . . . .void	**popupMenuWillBecomeVisible** (PopupMenuEvent e)	ε767

PopupMenuPeer | java.awt.peer

1.1 *PopupMenuPeer*──────────────── *MenuPeer* [1] (*MenuItemPeer* [2] (*MenuComponentPeer* [3]))

2	*4 inherited members from MenuItemPeer not shown*	
1	*3 inherited members from MenuPeer not shown*	
3	*1 inherited members from MenuComponentPeer not shown*	
	public . . . . .void	**show** (java.awt.Event e)

PopupMenuUI | javax.swing.plaf

Object
1.2 ○ └ ComponentUI [1]
1.2 ○ └ PopupMenuUI

	1	*11 inherited members from ComponentUI not shown*	
1.4	public . . . . . . javax.swing.Popup	**getPopup** (javax.swing.JPopupMenu popup, int x, int y)
1.3	public . . . . boolean	**isPopupTrigger** (java.awt.event.MouseEvent e)
*	public	**PopupMenuUI** ()

Port | javax.sound.sampled

1.3 *Port*────────────────────────── *Line* [1]

1	public	. . . . .void	addLineListener (*LineListener* listener)	ε731
1	public	. . . . .void	close ()	
1	public	. . . . Control	getControl (Control.Type control)	ε730
1	public	. . . . .Control[]	getControls ()	
1	public	. . . . Line.Info	getLineInfo ()	
1	public	. . . . boolean	isControlSupported (Control.Type control)	
1	public	. . . . boolean	isOpen ()	
1	public	. . . . .void	open () throws LineUnavailableException	
1	public	. . . . .void	removeLineListener (*LineListener* listener)	

P

Classes

Port.Info

Port.Info				javax.sound.sampled

```
          Object 1
1.3         └ Line.Info 2
1.3            └ Port.Info
```

▲		public static final . . . . . . Port.Info	**COMPACT_DISC**	
●	1	public final . . . . **boolean**	**equals** (Object obj)	
	2	public. . . . . Class	getLineClass ()	
		public. . . . . String	**getName** ()	
●	1	public final . . . . **int**	**hashCode** ()	
▲		public static final . . . . . Port.Info	**HEADPHONE**	
✳		public.	**Port.Info** (Class lineClass, String name, boolean isSource)	
		public. . . . . boolean	**isSource** ()	
▲		public static final . . . . . Port.Info	**LINE_IN**	
▲		public static final . . . . . Port.Info	**LINE_OUT**	
	2	public. . . . . **boolean**	**matches** (Line.Info info)	
▲		public static final . . . . . Port.Info	**MICROPHONE**	
▲		public static final . . . . . Port.Info	**SPEAKER**	
●	2	public final . . . . **String**	**toString** ()	

Position				javax.swing.text

```
1.2      Position
```

	public. . . . . int	**getOffset** ()	ε974

Position.Bias				javax.swing.text

```
          Object 1
1.2 ●       └ Position.Bias
```

▲		public static final . Position.Bias	**Backward**	ε777,1024
▲		public static final . Position.Bias	**Forward**	ε777,1024,1025,1026
	1	public. . . . . **String**	**toString** ()	

PresentationDirection				javax.print.attribute.standard

```
          Object
1.4 ○       └ javax.print.attribute.EnumSyntax 1 - - - - - - - - - java.io.Serializable ˬ, Cloneable ˬ
1.4 ●          └ PresentationDirection - - - - - - - - - - - - - - - java.print.attribute.PrintJobAttribute (javax.print.attribute.Attribute 2
                                                                     (java.io.Serializable)), javax.print.attribute.PrintRequestAttribute
                                                                     (javax.print.attribute.Attribute 2 (java.io.Serializable))
```

	1	public. . . . . Object	clone ()	
●	2	public final . . . . Class	**getCategory** ()	ε707
	1	protected . . . . **javax.print₂** **.attribute.EnumSyntax[]**	**getEnumValueTable** ()	
●	2	public final . . . . String	**getName** ()	ε706,707,708
	1	protected. . . . . int	getOffset ()	
	1	protected . . . . **String[]**	**getStringTable** ()	
	1	public. . . . . int	getValue ()	
	1	public. . . . . int	hashCode ()	
	1	protected. . . . . Object	readResolve () throws java.io.ObjectStreamException	
▲		public static final . . . . PresentationDirection	**TOBOTTOM_TOLEFT**	
▲		public static final . . . . PresentationDirection	**TOBOTTOM_TORIGHT**	
▲		public static final . . . . PresentationDirection	**TOLEFT_TOBOTTOM**	
▲		public static final . . . . PresentationDirection	**TOLEFT_TOTOP**	
▲		public static final . . . . PresentationDirection	**TORIGHT_TOBOTTOM**	
▲		public static final . . . . PresentationDirection	**TORIGHT_TOTOP**	
	1	public. . . . . String	toString ()	

Class *Interface* —extends - - -implements ○ abstract ● final △ static ▲ static final ✳ constructor x x—inherited x **x**—declared **x x**—overridden
ε*n*—examples of usage ˬ—has subclass package—see other volume

▲	public static final . . . . **TOTOP_TOLEFT**	
	. . . . PresentationDirection	
▲	public static final . . . . **TOTOP_TORIGHT**	
	. . . . PresentationDirection	

Printable   java.awt.print

1.2	*Printable*	
▲	public static final . . . . int **NO_SUCH_PAGE** = 1	ε681,682
▲	public static final . . . . int **PAGE_EXISTS** = 0	ε681,684
	public . . . . int **print** (java.awt.Graphics graphics, PageFormat pageFormat, int pageIndex)	
	throws PrinterException	ε681,682,683,684,686

PrinterAbortException   java.awt.print

Object   ε705
└Throwable - *java.io.Serializable*˅
   └Exception
1.2   └PrinterException
1.2   └PrinterAbortException

*	public . . . . **PrinterAbortException** ()	
*	public . . . . **PrinterAbortException** (String msg)	

PrinterException   java.awt.print

Object   ε681,683,684,686
└Throwable - *java.io.Serializable*˅
   └Exception
1.2   └PrinterException˅

*	public . . . . **PrinterException** ()	
*	public . . . . **PrinterException** (String msg)	

PrinterGraphics   java.awt.print

1.2	*PrinterGraphics*	
	public . . . . PrinterJob **getPrinterJob** ()	

PrinterInfo   javax.print.attribute.standard

Object
1.4 ○   └javax.print.attribute.TextSyntax[1] - - - - - - - - - - - *java.io.Serializable*˅, *Cloneable*˅
1.4 ●   └PrinterInfo - *javax.print.attribute.PrintServiceAttribute*
                               (*javax.print.attribute.Attribute*[2] (*java.io.Serializable*))

	1	public . . . . **boolean equals** (Object object)	
●	2	public final . . . . Class **getCategory** ()	ε707
	1	public . . . . java.util.Locale getLocale ()	
●	2	public final . . . . String **getName** ()	ε706,707,708
	1	public . . . . String getValue ()	
	1	public . . . . int hashCode ()	
*		public . . . . **PrinterInfo** (String info, java.util.Locale locale)	
	1	public . . . . String toString ()	

PrinterIOException   java.awt.print

Object
└Throwable[1] - *java.io.Serializable*˅
   └Exception
1.2   └PrinterException
1.2   └PrinterIOException

1.4	1	public . . . . **Throwable getCause** ()
		public . . . . . java.io.IOException **getIOException** ()

PrinterIOException

✱	public........................	**PrinterIOException** (java.io.IOException exception)

PrinterIsAcceptingJobs javax.print.attribute.standard

Object
- 1.4 ○ └javax.print.attribute.EnumSyntax[1] - - - - - - - - - java.io.Serializable, Cloneable
- 1.4 ● └PrinterIsAcceptingJobs - - - - - - - - - - - - - - - - javax.print.attribute.PrintServiceAttribute
  (javax.print.attribute.Attribute[2] (java.io.Serializable))

▲		public static final..............	**ACCEPTING_JOBS**	
		...... PrinterIsAcceptingJobs		
	1	public...................Object	clone ()	
●	2	public final ....Class	**getCategory** ()	ε707
	1	protected.........**javax.print**₂	**getEnumValueTable** ()	
		.attribute.EnumSyntax[]		
●	2	public final ....String	**getName** ()	ε706,707,708
	1	protected...............int	getOffset ()	
	1	protected............. **String[]**	getStringTable ()	
	1	public.......................int	getValue ()	
	1	public.......................int	hashCode ()	
▲		public static final..............	**NOT_ACCEPTING_JOBS**	
		...... PrinterIsAcceptingJobs		
✱		protected.....................	**PrinterIsAcceptingJobs** (int value)	
	1	protected...............Object	readResolve () throws java.io.ObjectStreamException	
	1	public...................String	toString ()	

PrinterJob java.awt.print

Object
- 1.2 ○ └PrinterJob

○	public abstract.............void	**cancel** ()	
	public............PageFormat	**defaultPage** ()	ε681,683,684,685,686
○	public abstract ....PageFormat	**defaultPage** (PageFormat page)	
○	public abstract..............int	**getCopies** ()	
○	public abstract ....String	**getJobName** ()	
△	public static .... PrinterJob	**getPrinterJob** ()	ε681,683,684,685,686
1.4	public.. javax.print.PrintService	**getPrintService** ()	
○	public abstract ....String	**getUserName** ()	
○	public abstract .... boolean	**isCancelled** ()	
1.4 △	public static	**lookupPrintServices** ()	
	..... javax.print.PrintService[]		
1.4 △	public static .... javax.print.-	**lookupStreamPrintServices** (String mimeType)	
	StreamPrintServiceFactory[]		
○	public abstract ....PageFormat	**pageDialog** (PageFormat page) throws java.awt.HeadlessException	
			ε685
1.4	public.............PageFormat	**pageDialog** (javax.print.attribute.PrintRequestAttributeSet attributes)	
		throws java.awt.HeadlessException	
○	public abstract.............void	**print** () throws PrinterException	ε681,682,683,684,686
1.4	public....................void	**print** (javax.print.attribute.PrintRequestAttributeSet attributes)	
		throws PrinterException	
○	public abstract .... boolean	**printDialog** () throws java.awt.HeadlessException	ε686
1.4	public.................. boolean	**printDialog** (javax.print.attribute.PrintRequestAttributeSet attributes)	
		throws java.awt.HeadlessException	
✱	public............................	**PrinterJob** ()	
○	public abstract.............void	**setCopies** (int copies)	
○	public abstract.............void	**setJobName** (String jobName)	
○	public abstract.............void	**setPageable** (Pageable document) throws NullPointerException ε684	
○	public abstract.............void	**setPrintable** (Printable painter)	
○	public abstract.............void	**setPrintable** (Printable painter, PageFormat format)	ε681,683,686
1.4	public.......................void	**setPrintService** (javax.print.PrintService service) throws PrinterException	
○	public abstract ....PageFormat	**validatePage** (PageFormat page)	

Class *Interface* —extends - - -implements ○ abstract ● final △ static ▲ static final ✱ constructor x x—inherited x **x**—declared **x x**—overridden
ε*n*—examples of usage ⌐—has subclass package —see other volume

PrinterLocation

javax.print.attribute.standard

```
      Object
1.4 ○  └ javax.print.attribute.TextSyntax¹ - - - - - - - - - - - java.io.Serializable⌐, Cloneable⌐
1.4 ●     └ PrinterLocation - - - - - - - - - - - - - - - - - - - - javax.print.attribute.PrintServiceAttribute
                                           (javax.print.attribute.Attribute² (java.io.Serializable))
```

	1	public.................**boolean**	**equals** (Object object)	
●	2	public final ....Class	**getCategory** ()	ε707
	1	public.......... java.util.Locale	getLocale ()	
●	2	public final ....String	**getName** ()	ε706,707,708
	1	public....................String	getValue ()	
	1	public.......................int	hashCode ()	
*		public..........................	**PrinterLocation** (String location, java.util.Locale locale)	
	1	public...................String	toString ()	

PrinterMakeAndModel

javax.print.attribute.standard

```
      Object
1.4 ○  └ javax.print.attribute.TextSyntax¹ - - - - - - - - - - - java.io.Serializable⌐, Cloneable⌐
1.4 ●     └ PrinterMakeAndModel - - - - - - - - - - - - - - - - - javax.print.attribute.PrintServiceAttribute
                                           (javax.print.attribute.Attribute² (java.io.Serializable))
```

	1	public.................**boolean**	**equals** (Object object)	
●	2	public final ....Class	**getCategory** ()	ε707
	1	public.......... java.util.Locale	getLocale ()	
●	2	public final ....String	**getName** ()	ε706,707,708
	1	public....................String	getValue ()	
	1	public.......................int	hashCode ()	
*		public..........................	**PrinterMakeAndModel** (String makeAndModel, java.util.Locale locale)	
	1	public...................String	toString ()	

PrinterMessageFromOperator

javax.print.attribute.standard

```
      Object
1.4 ○  └ javax.print.attribute.TextSyntax¹ - - - - - - - - - - - java.io.Serializable⌐, Cloneable⌐
1.4 ●     └ PrinterMessageFromOperator - - - - - - - - - - javax.print.attribute.PrintServiceAttribute
                                           (javax.print.attribute.Attribute² (java.io.Serializable))
```

	1	public.................**boolean**	**equals** (Object object)	
●	2	public final ....Class	**getCategory** ()	ε707
	1	public.......... java.util.Locale	getLocale ()	
●	2	public final ....String	**getName** ()	ε706,707,708
	1	public....................String	getValue ()	
	1	public.......................int	hashCode ()	
*		public..........................	**PrinterMessageFromOperator** (String message, java.util.Locale locale)	
	1	public...................String	toString ()	

PrinterMoreInfo

javax.print.attribute.standard

```
      Object
1.4 ○  └ javax.print.attribute.URISyntax¹ - - - - - - - - - - - java.io.Serializable⌐, Cloneable⌐
1.4 ●     └ PrinterMoreInfo - - - - - - - - - - - - - - - - - - - - javax.print.attribute.PrintServiceAttribute
                                           (javax.print.attribute.Attribute² (java.io.Serializable))
```

	1	public.................**boolean**	**equals** (Object object)	
●	2	public final ....Class	**getCategory** ()	ε707
●	2	public final ....String	**getName** ()	ε706,707,708
	1	public............ java.net.URI	getURI ()	
	1	public.......................int	hashCode ()	
*		public..........................	**PrinterMoreInfo** (java.net.URI uri)	
	1	public...................String	toString ()	

P

Classes

PrinterMoreInfoManufacturer

		PrinterMoreInfoManufacturer		javax.print.attribute.standard

Object
- 1.4 ○ └─ *javax.print.attribute.URISyntax*[1] - - - - - - - - - - - *java.io.Serializable*, *Cloneable*,
- 1.4 ●   └─ PrinterMoreInfoManufacturer - - - - - - - - - - - *javax.print.attribute.PrintServiceAttribute*
     (*javax.print.attribute.Attribute*[2] (*java.io.Serializable*))

	1	public................**boolean** **equals** (Object object)	
●	2	public final .... Class **getCategory** ()	ε707
●	2	public final .... String **getName** ()	ε706,707,708
	1	public............... java.net.URI getURI ()	
	1	public..................int hashCode ()	
✳		public................... **PrinterMoreInfoManufacturer** (java.net.URI uri)	
	1	public................... String toString ()	

		PrinterName		javax.print.attribute.standard

Object
- 1.4 ○ └─ *javax.print.attribute.TextSyntax*[1] - - - - - - - - - - - *java.io.Serializable*, *Cloneable*,
- 1.4 ●   └─ PrinterName - *javax.print.attribute.PrintServiceAttribute*
     (*javax.print.attribute.Attribute*[2] (*java.io.Serializable*))

	1	public................**boolean** **equals** (Object object)	
●	2	public final .... Class **getCategory** ()	ε707
	1	public.......... java.util.Locale getLocale ()	
●	2	public final .... String **getName** ()	ε706,707,708
	1	public................... String getValue ()	
	1	public..................int hashCode ()	
✳		public................... **PrinterName** (String printerName, java.util.Locale locale)	ε703
	1	public................... String toString ()	

		PrinterResolution		javax.print.attribute.standard

Object
- 1.4 ○ └─ *javax.print.attribute.ResolutionSyntax*[1] - - - - - - *java.io.Serializable*, *Cloneable*,
- 1.4 ●   └─ PrinterResolution - *javax.print.attribute.DocAttribute* (*javax.print.attribute.Attribute*[2]
     (*java.io.Serializable*)), *javax.print.attribute.PrintRequestAttribute*
     (*javax.print.attribute.Attribute*[2] (*java.io.Serializable*)),
     javax.print.attribute.PrintJobAttribute
     (*javax.print.attribute.Attribute*[2] (*java.io.Serializable*))

▲	1	public static final ....int DPCM = 254	
▲	1	public static final ....int DPI = 100	
	1	public................**boolean** **equals** (Object object)	
●	2	public final .... Class **getCategory** ()	ε707
	1	public....................int getCrossFeedResolution (int units)	
	1	protected....................int getCrossFeedResolutionDphi ()	
	1	public....................int getFeedResolution (int units)	
	1	protected....................int getFeedResolutionDphi ()	
●	2	public final .... String **getName** ()	ε706,707,708
	1	public................... int[] getResolution (int units)	
	1	public....................int hashCode ()	
	1	public................... boolean lessThanOrEquals (javax.print.attribute.ResolutionSyntax other)	
✳		public................... **PrinterResolution** (int crossFeedResolution, int feedResolution, int units)	
	1	public................... String toString ()	
	1	public................... String toString (int units, String unitsName)	

		PrinterState		javax.print.attribute.standard

Object
- 1.4 ○ └─ *javax.print.attribute.EnumSyntax*[1] - - - - - - - - - - *java.io.Serializable*, *Cloneable*,
- 1.4 ●   └─ PrinterState - *javax.print.attribute.PrintServiceAttribute*
     (*javax.print.attribute.Attribute*[2] (*java.io.Serializable*))

	1	public................... Object clone ()	
●	2	public final .... Class **getCategory** ()	ε707

Class   *Interface*   —extends   - - -implements   ○ abstract   ● final   △ static   ▲ static final   ✳ constructor   x x—inherited   x **x**—declared   **x x**—overridden
ε*n*—examples of usage   ⌐—has subclass   package—see other volume

1	protected	**javax.print**₂ **.attribute.EnumSyntax[]**	**getEnumValueTable** ()	
● 2	public final	String	**getName** ()	ε706,707,708
1	protected	int	getOffset ()	
1	protected	**String[]**	**getStringTable** ()	
1	public	int	getValue ()	
1	public	int	hashCode ()	
▲	public static final	PrinterState	**IDLE**	
✱	protected		**PrinterState** (int value)	
▲	public static final	PrinterState	**PROCESSING**	
1	protected	Object	readResolve () throws java.io.ObjectStreamException	
▲	public static final	PrinterState	**STOPPED**	
1	public	String	toString ()	
▲	public static final	PrinterState	**UNKNOWN**	

PrinterStateReason	javax.print.attribute.standard

Object
1.4 ○ └javax.print.attribute.EnumSyntax[1] - - - - - - - - - *java.io.Serializable*˳, *Cloneable*˳
1.4 └PrinterStateReason - - - - - - - - - - - - - - - - - - *javax.print.attribute.Attribute*˳ [2] (*java.io.Serializable*)

P

1	public	Object	clone ()	
▲	public static final	PrinterStateReason	**CONNECTING_TO_DEVICE**	
▲	public static final	PrinterStateReason	**COVER_OPEN**	
▲	public static final	PrinterStateReason	**DEVELOPER_EMPTY**	
▲	public static final	PrinterStateReason	**DEVELOPER_LOW**	
▲	public static final	PrinterStateReason	**DOOR_OPEN**	
▲	public static final	PrinterStateReason	**FUSER_OVER_TEMP**	
▲	public static final	PrinterStateReason	**FUSER_UNDER_TEMP**	
● 2	public final	Class	**getCategory** ()	ε707
1	protected	**javax.print.attribute.EnumSyntax[]**	**getEnumValueTable** ()	
● 2	public final	String	**getName** ()	ε706,707,708
1	protected	int	getOffset ()	
1	protected	**String[]**	**getStringTable** ()	
1	public	int	getValue ()	
1	public	int	hashCode ()	
▲	public static final	PrinterStateReason	**INPUT_TRAY_MISSING**	
▲	public static final	PrinterStateReason	**INTERLOCK_OPEN**	
▲	public static final	PrinterStateReason	**INTERPRETER_RESOURCE_UNAVAILABLE**	
▲	public static final	PrinterStateReason	**MARKER_SUPPLY_EMPTY**	
▲	public static final	PrinterStateReason	**MARKER_SUPPLY_LOW**	
▲	public static final	PrinterStateReason	**MARKER_WASTE_ALMOST_FULL**	
▲	public static final	PrinterStateReason	**MARKER_WASTE_FULL**	
▲	public static final	PrinterStateReason	**MEDIA_EMPTY**	
▲	public static final	PrinterStateReason	**MEDIA_JAM**	
▲	public static final	PrinterStateReason	**MEDIA_LOW**	
▲	public static final	PrinterStateReason	**MEDIA_NEEDED**	
▲	public static final	PrinterStateReason	**MOVING_TO_PAUSED**	
▲	public static final	PrinterStateReason	**OPC_LIFE_OVER**	
▲	public static final	PrinterStateReason	**OPC_NEAR_EOL**	
▲	public static final	PrinterStateReason	**OTHER**	
▲	public static final	PrinterStateReason	**OUTPUT_AREA_ALMOST_FULL**	
▲	public static final	PrinterStateReason	**OUTPUT_AREA_FULL**	
▲	public static final	PrinterStateReason	**OUTPUT_TRAY_MISSING**	
▲	public static final	PrinterStateReason	**PAUSED**	
✱	protected		**PrinterStateReason** (int value)	
1	protected	Object	readResolve () throws java.io.ObjectStreamException	
▲	public static final	PrinterStateReason	**SHUTDOWN**	
▲	public static final	PrinterStateReason	**SPOOL_AREA_FULL**	
▲	public static final	PrinterStateReason	**STOPPED_PARTLY**	
▲	public static final	PrinterStateReason	**STOPPING**	
▲	public static final	PrinterStateReason	**TIMED_OUT**	
▲	public static final	PrinterStateReason	**TONER_EMPTY**	
▲	public static final	PrinterStateReason	**TONER_LOW**	
1	public	String	toString ()	

Classes

PrinterStateReasons

PrinterStateReasons				javax.print.attribute.standard

```
        Object
1.2 ○   └ java.util.AbstractMap¹ ----------------- java.util.Map˷
1.2      └ java.util.HashMap² ------------------- Cloneable˷, java.io.Serializable˷
1.4 ●       └ PrinterStateReasons --------------- javax.print.attribute.PrintServiceAttribute
                                                  (javax.print.attribute.Attribute³ (java.io.Serializable))
```

	2	public	void	clear ()	
	2	public	Object	clone ()	
	2	public	boolean	containsKey (Object key)	
	2	public	boolean	containsValue (Object value)	ε577
	2	public	java.util.Set	entrySet ()	
	1	public	boolean	equals (Object o)	
	2	public	Object	get (Object key)	
●	3	public final	Class	**getCategory** ()	ε707
●	3	public final	String	**getName** ()	ε706,707,708
	1	public	int	hashCode ()	
	2	public	boolean	isEmpty ()	
	2	public	java.util.Set	keySet ()	ε870
✳		public		**PrinterStateReasons** ()	
✳		public		**PrinterStateReasons** (int initialCapacity)	
✳		public		**PrinterStateReasons** (java.util.Map map)	
✳		public		**PrinterStateReasons** (int initialCapacity, float loadFactor)	
		public	java.util.Set	**printerStateReasonSet** (Severity severity)	
	2	public	**Object**	**put** (Object reason, Object severity)	
	2	public	void	putAll (java.util.Map t)	
	2	public	Object	remove (Object key)	
	2	public	int	size ()	
	1	public	String	toString ()	
	2	public	java.util.Collection	values ()	

PrinterURI				javax.print.attribute.standard

```
        Object
1.4 ○   └ javax.print.attribute.URISyntax¹ ----------- java.io.Serializable˷, Cloneable˷
1.4 ●    └ PrinterURI ------------------------- javax.print.attribute.PrintServiceAttribute
                                                (javax.print.attribute.Attribute² (java.io.Serializable))
```

	1	public	**boolean**	**equals** (Object object)	
●	2	public final	Class	**getCategory** ()	ε707
●	2	public final	String	**getName** ()	ε706,707,708
	1	public	java.net.URI	getURI ()	
	1	public	int	hashCode ()	
✳		public		**PrinterURI** (java.net.URI uri)	
	1	public	String	toString ()	

PrintEvent				javax.print.event
				ε640,641,643,649,566

```
        Object
1.1   └ java.util.EventObject¹ ------------------ java.io.Serializable˷
1.4    └ PrintEvent˷
```

	1	public	Object	getSource ()	ε644,886,565,568,570
✳		public		**PrintEvent** (Object source)	
	1	protected transient	Object	source	
	1	public	**String**	**toString** ()	

PrintException				javax.print
				ε700,701,702,710,711

```
        Object
      └ Throwable¹ ------------------------- java.io.Serializable˷
       └ Exception
1.4     └ PrintException
```

Class *Interface* —extends - - -implements ○ abstract ● final △ static ▲ static final ✳ constructor x x—inherited x **x**—declared **x x**—overridden
εn—examples of usage ˷—has subclass package—see other volume

730

1	public...............Throwable	getCause ()	ε705
*	public........................	**PrintException** ()	
*	public........................	**PrintException** (Exception e)	
*	public........................	**PrintException** (String s)	
*	public........................	**PrintException** (String s, Exception e)	

PrintGraphics — java.awt

1.1	*PrintGraphics*
	public.................PrintJob **getPrintJob** ()

PrintJob — java.awt

1.1 ○ Object [1]
　　└PrintJob

○	public abstract............void	**end** ()
1	public..................... **void**	**finalize** ()
○	public abstract.......Graphics	**getGraphics** ()
○	public abstract.....Dimension	**getPageDimension** ()
○	public abstract..............int	**getPageResolution** ()
○	public abstract.......boolean	**lastPageFirst** ()
*	public........................	**PrintJob** ()

PrintJobAdapter — javax.print.event

1.4 ○ Object
　　└PrintJobAdapter ----------------------- *PrintJobListener* [1]

1	public.....................void	**printDataTransferCompleted** (PrintJobEvent pje)	ε714
*	public........................	**PrintJobAdapter** ()	
1	public.....................void	**printJobCanceled** (PrintJobEvent pje)	ε714
1	public.....................void	**printJobCompleted** (PrintJobEvent pje)	ε714
1	public.....................void	**printJobFailed** (PrintJobEvent pje)	ε714
1	public.....................void	**printJobNoMoreEvents** (PrintJobEvent pje)	ε714
1	public.....................void	**printJobRequiresAttention** (PrintJobEvent pje)	ε714

PrintJobAttribute — javax.print.attribute

1.4 *PrintJobAttribute*————————————*Attribute* [1] (*java.io.Serializable*)

1	public.....................Class	getCategory ()	ε707
1	public.....................String	getName ()	ε706,707,708

PrintJobAttributeEvent — javax.print.event

ε640,641,643,649,566

1.1 Object
　　└java.util.EventObject [1] ------------------- *java.io.Serializable*
1.4 　　└PrintEvent [2]
1.4 　　　└PrintJobAttributeEvent

	public.....*javax.print.attribute.*	**getAttributes** ()	
	.PrintJobAttributeSet		
	public. *javax.print.DocPrintJob*	**getPrintJob** ()	
1	public..................Object	getSource ()	ε644,886,565,568,570
*	public........................	**PrintJobAttributeEvent** (*javax.print.DocPrintJob* source,	
		javax.print.attribute.PrintJobAttributeSet attributes)	
1	protected transient......Object	source	
2	public.....................String	toString ()	

PrintJobAttributeListener — javax.print.event

1.4	*PrintJobAttributeListener*
	public.......................void **attributeUpdate** (PrintJobAttributeEvent pjae)

P

Classes

PrintJobAttributeSet

	javax.print.attribute

1.4	*PrintJobAttributeSet*————————————*AttributeSet* ‿ [1]

1	public	boolean	**add** (*Attribute* attribute)	ε715,710,711,712,703
1	public	boolean	**addAll** (*AttributeSet* attributes)	
1	public	void	clear ()	
1	public	boolean	containsKey (Class category)	
1	public	boolean	containsValue (*Attribute* attribute)	
1	public	boolean	equals (Object object)	
1	public	*Attribute*	get (Class category)	
1	public	int	hashCode ()	
1	public	boolean	isEmpty ()	
1	public	boolean	remove (Class category)	
1	public	boolean	remove (*Attribute* attribute)	
1	public	int	size ()	
1	public	*Attribute[]*	toArray ()	ε706

PrintJobEvent

	javax.print.event

	Object	ε640,641,643,649,566
1.1	└ java.util.EventObject [1] - - - - - - - - - - - - - - - - - - *java.io.Serializable* ‿	
1.4	└ PrintEvent [2]	
1.4	└ PrintJobEvent	

▲	public static final	int	**DATA_TRANSFER_COMPLETE** = 106	
	public	int	**getPrintEventType** ()	
	public	*javax.print.DocPrintJob*	**getPrintJob** ()	
1	public	Object	getSource ()	ε644,886,565,568,570
▲	public static final	int	**JOB_CANCELED** = 101	
▲	public static final	int	**JOB_COMPLETE** = 102	
▲	public static final	int	**JOB_FAILED** = 103	
▲	public static final	int	**NO_MORE_EVENTS** = 105	
✳	public		**PrintJobEvent** (*javax.print.DocPrintJob* source, int reason)	
▲	public static final	int	**REQUIRES_ATTENTION** = 104	
1	protected transient	Object	source	
2	public	String	toString ()	

PrintJobListener

	javax.print.event

1.4	*PrintJobListener*

	public	void	**printDataTransferCompleted** (PrintJobEvent pje)	ε714
	public	void	**printJobCanceled** (PrintJobEvent pje)	ε714
	public	void	**printJobCompleted** (PrintJobEvent pje)	ε714
	public	void	**printJobFailed** (PrintJobEvent pje)	ε714
	public	void	**printJobNoMoreEvents** (PrintJobEvent pje)	ε714
	public	void	**printJobRequiresAttention** (PrintJobEvent pje)	ε714

PrintQuality

	javax.print.attribute.standard

	Object	
1.4 ○	└ javax.print.attribute.EnumSyntax [1] - - - - - - - - - *java.io.Serializable* ‿, *Cloneable* ‿	
1.4	└ PrintQuality - *javax.print.attribute.DocAttribute* (*javax.print.attribute.Attribute* [2]	
		(*java.io.Serializable*)), *javax.print.attribute.PrintRequestAttribute*
		(*javax.print.attribute.Attribute* [2] (*java.io.Serializable*)),
		javax.print.attribute.PrintJobAttribute
		(*javax.print.attribute.Attribute* [2] (*java.io.Serializable*))

1	public	Object	clone ()	
▲	public static final	PrintQuality	**DRAFT**	
● 2	public final	Class	**getCategory** ()	ε707
1	protected	*javax.print* ₂ **.attribute.EnumSyntax[]**	getEnumValueTable ()	
● 2	public final	String	**getName** ()	ε706,707,708
1	protected	int	getOffset ()	
1	protected	**String[]**	getStringTable ()	

Class *Interface* —extends - - -implements ○ abstract ● final △ static ▲ static final ✳ constructor x x—inherited x **x**—declared **x x**—overridden
εn—examples of usage ‿—has subclass package—see other volume

1	public	int	getValue ()	
1	public	int	hashCode ()	
▲	public static final...PrintQuality		**HIGH**	
▲	public static final...PrintQuality		**NORMAL**	
*	protected		**PrintQuality** (int value)	
1	protected	Object	readResolve () throws java.io.ObjectStreamException	
1	public	String	toString ()	

PrintRequestAttribute — javax.print.attribute

1.4   *PrintRequestAttribute*————————*Attribute* ,[1] (*java.io.Serializable*)

1	public	Class	getCategory ()	ε707
1	public	String	getName ()	ε706,707,708

PrintRequestAttributeSet — javax.print.attribute

1.4   *PrintRequestAttributeSet*————————*AttributeSet* ,[1]

1	public	boolean	**add** (*Attribute* attribute)	ε710,711,712,715,703
1	public	boolean	**addAll** (*AttributeSet* attributes)	
1	public	void	clear ()	
1	public	boolean	containsKey (Class category)	
1	public	boolean	containsValue (*Attribute* attribute)	
1	public	boolean	equals (Object object)	
1	public	*Attribute*	get (Class category)	
1	public	int	hashCode ()	
1	public	boolean	isEmpty ()	
1	public	boolean	remove (Class category)	
1	public	boolean	remove (*Attribute* attribute)	
1	public	int	size ()	
1	public	*Attribute[]*	toArray ()	ε706

PrintService — javax.print

1.4   *PrintService* ,   ε703

	public	void	**addPrintServiceAttributeListener** (*javax.print.event.PrintServiceAttributeListener* listener) ε713
	public	*DocPrintJob*	**createPrintJob** () ε700,702,705,714,715
	public	boolean	**equals** (Object obj)
	public	*javax.print.attribute* ₂ .PrintServiceAttribute	**getAttribute** (Class category)
	public	*javax.print.attribute* ₂ .PrintServiceAttributeSet	**getAttributes** () ε706
	public	Object	**getDefaultAttributeValue** (Class category) ε707,708
	public	String	**getName** () ε706,707,708
	public	ServiceUIFactory	**getServiceUIFactory** ()
	public	Class[]	**getSupportedAttributeCategories** () ε707
	public	Object	**getSupportedAttributeValues** (Class category, DocFlavor flavor, *javax.print.attribute.AttributeSet* attributes) ε709,707
	public	DocFlavor[]	**getSupportedDocFlavors** ()
	public	*javax* ₂ .print.attribute.AttributeSet	**getUnsupportedAttributes** (DocFlavor flavor, *javax.print.attribute.AttributeSet* attributes)
	public	int	**hashCode** ()
	public	boolean	**isAttributeCategorySupported** (Class category)
	public	boolean	**isAttributeValueSupported** (*javax.print.attribute.Attribute* attrval, DocFlavor flavor, *javax.print.attribute.AttributeSet* attributes)
	public	boolean	**isDocFlavorSupported** (DocFlavor flavor)
	public	void	**removePrintServiceAttributeListener** (*javax.print.event* ₂ .PrintServiceAttributeListener listener)

PrintServiceAttribute — javax.print.attribute

1.4   *PrintServiceAttribute*————————*Attribute* ,[1] (*java.io.Serializable*)

1	public	Class	getCategory ()	ε707
1	public	String	getName ()	ε706,707,708

PrintServiceAttributeEvent

PrintServiceAttributeEvent
javax.print.event

```
                Object                                                              ε640,641,643,649,566
1.1             └ java.util.EventObject 1 - - - - - - - - - - - - - - - - - - - java.io.Serializable
1.4                 └ PrintEvent 2
1.4                     └ PrintServiceAttributeEvent
```

	public.....*javax.print.attribute*	**getAttributes** ()
	.*PrintServiceAttributeSet*	
	public.. *javax.print.PrintService*	**getPrintService** ()
1	public....................Object	getSource ()
*	public........................	**PrintServiceAttributeEvent** (*javax.print.PrintService* source,
		javax.print.attribute.PrintServiceAttributeSet attributes)
1	protected transient......Object	source
2	public....................String	toString ()

ε644,886,565,568,570

PrintServiceAttributeListener
javax.print.event

```
1.4    PrintServiceAttributeListener
```

	public.....................void	**attributeUpdate** (PrintServiceAttributeEvent psae)

PrintServiceAttributeSet
javax.print.attribute

```
1.4    PrintServiceAttributeSet─────────────AttributeSet 1
```

1	public............... boolean	**add** (*Attribute* attribute)	ε710,711,712,703,715
1	public............... boolean	**addAll** (*AttributeSet* attributes)	
1	public.....................void	clear ()	
1	public............... boolean	containsKey (Class category)	
1	public............... boolean	containsValue (*Attribute* attribute)	
1	public............... boolean	equals (Object object)	
1	public............... *Attribute*	get (Class category)	
1	public.......................int	hashCode ()	
1	public............... boolean	isEmpty ()	
1	public............... boolean	remove (Class category)	
1	public............... boolean	remove (*Attribute* attribute)	
1	public.......................int	size ()	
1	public............... *Attribute[]*	toArray ()	ε706

PrintServiceLookup
javax.print

```
       Object
1.4 ○  └ PrintServiceLookup
```

○	public abstract .... *PrintService*	**getDefaultPrintService** ()	
○	public abstract.................	**getMultiDocPrintServices** (DocFlavor[] flavors, *javax.print.attribute.AttributeSet*	
	.......*MultiDocPrintService[]*	attributes)	
○	public abstract .. *PrintService[]*	**getPrintServices** ()	
○	public abstract .. *PrintService[]*	**getPrintServices** (DocFlavor flavor, *javax.print.attribute.AttributeSet* attributes)	
▲	public static final .. *PrintService*	**lookupDefaultPrintService** ()	ε700,703
▲	public static final...............	**lookupMultiDocPrintServices** (DocFlavor[] flavors,	
	.......*MultiDocPrintService[]*	*javax.print.attribute.AttributeSet* attributes)	
▲	public static final *PrintService[]*	**lookupPrintServices** (DocFlavor flavor, *javax.print.attribute.AttributeSet* attributes)	
			ε703,713
*	public........................	**PrintServiceLookup** ()	
△	public static .... boolean	**registerService** (*PrintService* service)	
△	public static .... boolean	**registerServiceProvider** (PrintServiceLookup sp)	

ProfileDataException
java.awt.color

```
       Object
       └ Throwable - - - - - - - - - - - - - - - - - - - - - - - - - java.io.Serializable
           └ Exception
               └ RuntimeException
1.2                └ ProfileDataException
```

Class *Interface* —extends - - -implements ○ abstract ● final △ static ▲ static final ✳ constructor x x—inherited x **x**—declared **x x**—overridden
ε*n*—examples of usage ˌ—has subclass package—see other volume

＊ public . . . . **ProfileDataException** (String s)

ProgressBarUI | javax.swing.plaf

Object
1.2 ○ └ComponentUI[1]
1.2 ○   └ProgressBarUI

  1 *11 inherited members from ComponentUI not shown*
＊ public . . . . **ProgressBarUI** ()

ProgressMonitor | javax.swing

Object
1.2 └ProgressMonitor

public . . . . void **close** ()	
public . . . . int **getMaximum** ()	
public . . . . int **getMillisToDecideToPopup** ()	ε807
public . . . . int **getMillisToPopup** ()	ε807
public . . . . int **getMinimum** ()	
public . . . . String **getNote** ()	
public . . . . boolean **isCanceled** ()	ε806

＊ public . . . . **ProgressMonitor** (java.awt.Component parentComponent, Object message, String note, int min, int max) ε806

public . . . . void **setMaximum** (int m)	
public . . . . void **setMillisToDecideToPopup** (int millisToDecideToPopup)	ε807
public . . . . void **setMillisToPopup** (int millisToPopup)	ε807
public . . . . void **setMinimum** (int m)	
public . . . . void **setNote** (String note)	ε806
public . . . . void **setProgress** (int nv)	ε806

ProgressMonitorInputStream | javax.swing

Object
○ └ java.io.InputStream
  └ java.io.FilterInputStream[1]
1.2   └ProgressMonitorInputStream

1 public . . . . int available () throws java.io.IOException
1 public . . . . **void close** () throws java.io.IOException
  public . . . . ProgressMonitor **getProgressMonitor** ()
1 protected . . java.io.InputStream in
1 public synchronized . . . . void mark (int readlimit)
1 public . . . . boolean markSupported ()
＊ public . . . . **ProgressMonitorInputStream** (java.awt.Component parentComponent, Object message, java.io.InputStream in)
1 public . . . . **int read** () throws java.io.IOException
1 public . . . . **int read** (byte[] b) throws java.io.IOException
1 public . . . . **int read** (byte[] b, int off, int len) throws java.io.IOException ε724
1 public synchronized . . . . . . **void reset** () throws java.io.IOException
1 public . . . . **long skip** (long n) throws java.io.IOException

---

QuadCurve2D | java.awt.geom

Object[1]
1.2 ○ └QuadCurve2D - *java.awt.Shape*[2], *Cloneable*

1 public . . . .**Object clone** ()
2 public . . . . boolean **contains** (Point2D p)
2 public . . . . boolean **contains** (Rectangle2D r)
2 public . . . . boolean **contains** (double x, double y)
2 public . . . . boolean **contains** (double x, double y, double w, double h)
2 public . . . . . . java.awt.Rectangle **getBounds** ()
○ 2 public abstract . . . Rectangle2D getBounds2D ()
○ public abstract . . . . Point2D **getCtrlPt** ()
○ public abstract . . . . double **getCtrlX** ()
○ public abstract . . . . double **getCtrlY** ()
  public . . . . double **getFlatness** ()

QuadCurve2D

△	public static	double	**getFlatness** (double[] coords, int offset)
△	public static	double	**getFlatness** (double x1, double y1, double ctrlx, double ctrly, double x2, double y2)
	public	double	**getFlatnessSq** ()
△	public static	double	**getFlatnessSq** (double[] coords, int offset)
△	public static	double	**getFlatnessSq** (double x1, double y1, double ctrlx, double ctrly, double x2, double y2)
○	public abstract	Point2D	**getP1** ()
○	public abstract	Point2D	**getP2** ()
2	public	PathIterator	**getPathIterator** (AffineTransform at)
2	public	PathIterator	**getPathIterator** (AffineTransform at, double flatness)
○	public abstract	double	**getX1** ()
○	public abstract	double	**getX2** ()
○	public abstract	double	**getY1** ()
○	public abstract	double	**getY2** ()
2	public	boolean	**intersects** (Rectangle2D r)
2	public	boolean	**intersects** (double x, double y, double w, double h)
*	protected		**QuadCurve2D** ()
	public	void	**setCurve** (QuadCurve2D c)
	public	void	**setCurve** (double[] coords, int offset)
	public	void	**setCurve** (Point2D[] pts, int offset)
	public	void	**setCurve** (Point2D p1, Point2D cp, Point2D p2)
○	public abstract	void	**setCurve** (double x1, double y1, double ctrlx, double ctrly, double x2, double y2)
△	public static	int	**solveQuadratic** (double[] eqn)
1.3 △	public static	int	**solveQuadratic** (double[] eqn, double[] res)
	public	void	**subdivide** (QuadCurve2D left, QuadCurve2D right)
△	public static	void	**subdivide** (QuadCurve2D src, QuadCurve2D left, QuadCurve2D right)
△	public static	void	**subdivide** (double[] src, int srcoff, double[] left, int leftoff, double[] right, int rightoff)

Q

QuadCurve2D.Double   java.awt.geom

```
Object
 └QuadCurve2D¹ - - - - - - - - - - - - - - - - - - - - - - - java.awt.Shape², Cloneable
    └QuadCurve2D.Double
```

1	*25 inherited members from QuadCurve2D not shown*		
	public	double	**ctrlx**
	public	double	**ctrly**
*	public		**QuadCurve2D.Double** ()
*	public		**QuadCurve2D.Double** (double x1, double y1, double ctrlx, double ctrly, double x2, double y2)
2	public	Rectangle2D	**getBounds2D** ()
1	public	**Point2D**	**getCtrlPt** ()
1	public	**double**	**getCtrlX** ()
1	public	**double**	**getCtrlY** ()
1	public	**Point2D**	**getP1** ()
1	public	**Point2D**	**getP2** ()
1	public	**double**	**getX1** ()
1	public	**double**	**getX2** ()
1	public	**double**	**getY1** ()
1	public	**double**	**getY2** ()
1	public	**void**	**setCurve** (double x1, double y1, double ctrlx, double ctrly, double x2, double y2)
	public	double	**x1**
	public	double	**x2**
	public	double	**y1**
	public	double	**y2**

QuadCurve2D.Float   java.awt.geom

```
Object
 └QuadCurve2D¹ - - - - - - - - - - - - - - - - - - - - - - - java.awt.Shape², Cloneable
    └QuadCurve2D.Float
```

1	*25 inherited members from QuadCurve2D not shown*		
	public	float	**ctrlx**
	public	float	**ctrly**
*	public		**QuadCurve2D.Float** ()
*	public		**QuadCurve2D.Float** (float x1, float y1, float ctrlx, float ctrly, float x2, float y2)
2	public	Rectangle2D	**getBounds2D** ()
1	public	**Point2D**	**getCtrlPt** ()

Class *Interface* —extends - - -implements ○ abstract ● final △ static ▲ static final * constructor x x—inherited x **x**—declared **x x**—overridden
εn—examples of usage ⌐—has subclass package—see other volume

1	public	double	**getCtrlX** ()	
1	public	double	**getCtrlY** ()	
1	public	**Point2D**	**getP1** ()	
1	public	**Point2D**	**getP2** ()	
1	public	double	**getX1** ()	
1	public	double	**getX2** ()	
1	public	double	**getY1** ()	
1	public	double	**getY2** ()	
1	public	void	**setCurve** (double x1, double y1, double ctrlx, double ctrly, double x2, double y2)	
	public	void	**setCurve** (float x1, float y1, float ctrlx, float ctrly, float x2, float y2)	
	public	float	**x1**	
	public	float	**x2**	
	public	float	**y1**	
	public	float	**y2**	

QueuedJobCount

javax.print.attribute.standard

Object
1.4 ○ └ javax.print.attribute.IntegerSyntax[1] -------- *java.io.Serializable, Cloneable*
1.4 ● └ QueuedJobCount ------------------ *javax.print.attribute.PrintServiceAttribute*
(*javax.print.attribute.Attribute*[2] (*java.io.Serializable*))

1	public	boolean	**equals** (Object object)		
● 2	public final	Class	**getCategory** ()		ε707
● 2	public final	String	**getName** ()		ε706,707,708
1	public	int	getValue ()		
1	public	int	hashCode ()		
*	public		**QueuedJobCount** (int value)		
1	public	String	toString ()		

Raster

java.awt.image

ε668

Object
1.2 └ Raster

△	public static	WritableRaster	**createBandedRaster** (int dataType, int w, int h, int bands, java.awt.Point location)	
△	public static	WritableRaster	**createBandedRaster** (int dataType, int w, int h, int scanlineStride, int[] bankIndices, int[] bandOffsets, java.awt.Point location)	
	public static	WritableRaster	**createBandedRaster** (DataBuffer dataBuffer, int w, int h, int scanlineStride, int[] bankIndices, int[] bandOffsets, java.awt.Point location)	
	public	Raster	**createChild** (int parentX, int parentY, int width, int height, int childMinX, int childMinY, int[] bandList)	
	public	WritableRaster	**createCompatibleWritableRaster** ()	
	public	WritableRaster	**createCompatibleWritableRaster** (java.awt.Rectangle rect)	
	public	WritableRaster	**createCompatibleWritableRaster** (int w, int h)	
	public	WritableRaster	**createCompatibleWritableRaster** (int x, int y, int w, int h)	
△	public static	WritableRaster	**createInterleavedRaster** (int dataType, int w, int h, int bands, java.awt.Point location)	
△	public static	WritableRaster	**createInterleavedRaster** (int dataType, int w, int h, int scanlineStride, int pixelStride, int[] bandOffsets, java.awt.Point location)	
△	public static	WritableRaster	**createInterleavedRaster** (DataBuffer dataBuffer, int w, int h, int scanlineStride, int pixelStride, int[] bandOffsets, java.awt.Point location)	
△	public static	WritableRaster	**createPackedRaster** (int dataType, int w, int h, int[] bandMasks, java.awt.Point location)	
△	public static	WritableRaster	**createPackedRaster** (DataBuffer dataBuffer, int w, int h, int bitsPerPixel, java.awt.Point location)	
△	public static	WritableRaster	**createPackedRaster** (int dataType, int w, int h, int bands, int bitsPerBand, java.awt.Point location)	
△	public static	WritableRaster	**createPackedRaster** (DataBuffer dataBuffer, int w, int h, int scanlineStride, int[] bandMasks, java.awt.Point location)	
△	public static	Raster	**createRaster** (SampleModel sm, DataBuffer db, java.awt.Point location)	
	public	Raster	**createTranslatedChild** (int childMinX, int childMinY)	
△	public static	WritableRaster	**createWritableRaster** (SampleModel sm, java.awt.Point location)	
△	public static	WritableRaster	**createWritableRaster** (SampleModel sm, DataBuffer db, java.awt.Point location)	
				ε668
	protected	DataBuffer	**dataBuffer**	
	public	java.awt.Rectangle	**getBounds** ()	
	public	DataBuffer	**getDataBuffer** ()	
	public	Object	**getDataElements** (int x, int y, Object outData)	
	public	Object	**getDataElements** (int x, int y, int w, int h, Object outData)	
●	public final	int	**getHeight** ()	
●	public final	int	**getMinX** ()	

Raster

●	public final	........................int	**getMinY** ()
●	public final	........................int	**getNumBands** ()
●	public final	........................int	**getNumDataElements** ()
	public	........................Raster	**getParent** ()
	public	........................float[]	**getPixel** (int x, int y, float[] fArray)
	public	........................int[]	**getPixel** (int x, int y, int[] iArray)
	public	........................double[]	**getPixel** (int x, int y, double[] dArray)
	public	........................int[]	**getPixels** (int x, int y, int w, int h, int[] iArray)
	public	........................double[]	**getPixels** (int x, int y, int w, int h, double[] dArray)
	public	........................float[]	**getPixels** (int x, int y, int w, int h, float[] fArray)
	public	........................int	**getSample** (int x, int y, int b)
	public	........................double	**getSampleDouble** (int x, int y, int b)
	public	........................float	**getSampleFloat** (int x, int y, int b)
	public	........................SampleModel	**getSampleModel** ()
●	public final	........................int	**getSampleModelTranslateX** ()
●	public final	........................int	**getSampleModelTranslateY** ()
	public	........................int[]	**getSamples** (int x, int y, int w, int h, int b, int[] iArray)
	public	........................float[]	**getSamples** (int x, int y, int w, int h, int b, float[] fArray)
	public	........................double[]	**getSamples** (int x, int y, int w, int h, int b, double[] dArray)
●	public final	........................int	**getTransferType** ()
●	public final	........................int	**getWidth** ()
	protected	........................int	**height**
	protected	........................int	**minX**
	protected	........................int	**minY**
	protected	........................int	**numBands**
	protected	........................int	**numDataElements**
	protected	........................Raster	**parent**
✳	protected	....	**Raster** (SampleModel sampleModel, java.awt.Point origin)
✳	protected	....	**Raster** (SampleModel sampleModel, DataBuffer dataBuffer, java.awt.Point origin)
✳	protected	....	**Raster** (SampleModel sampleModel, DataBuffer dataBuffer, java.awt.Rectangle aRegion, java.awt.Point sampleModelTranslate, Raster parent)
	protected	........................SampleModel	**sampleModel**
	protected	........................int	**sampleModelTranslateX**
	protected	........................int	**sampleModelTranslateY**
	protected	........................int	**width**

RasterFormatException
java.awt.image

```
Object
└ Throwable - - - - - - - - - - - - - - - - - - - - - - - - - - - java.io.Serializable ⌣
   └ Exception
      └ RuntimeException
         └ RasterFormatException
```
1.2

✳	public	**RasterFormatException** (String s)

RasterOp
java.awt.image

1.2   *RasterOp*

public	........................WritableRaster	**createCompatibleDestRaster** (Raster src)
public	........................WritableRaster	**filter** (Raster src, WritableRaster dest)
public	.... java.awt.geom.Rectangle2D	**getBounds2D** (Raster src)
public	.. java.awt.geom.Point2D	**getPoint2D** (java.awt.geom.Point2D srcPt, java.awt.geom.Point2D dstPt)
public	java.awt.RenderingHints	**getRenderingHints** ()

Receiver
javax.sound.midi

1.3   *Receiver*

public	........................void	**close** ()
public	........................void	**send** (MidiMessage message, long timeStamp)

Class   *Interface*   —extends   - - -implements   ○ abstract   ● final   △ static   ▲ static final   ✳ constructor   x x—inherited   x **x**—declared   **x x**—overridden
εn—examples of usage   ⌣—has subclass   package—see other volume

Rectangle					java.awt

```
          Object 1                                                              ε572
1.2 O     └java.awt.geom.RectangularShape 2 --------- Shape, Cloneable‚
1.2 O       └java.awt.geom.Rectangle2D 3
              └Rectangle‚ ----------------------- java.io.Serializable‚
```

1.2		3	public ....void	add (java.awt.geom.Point2D pt)	
1.2		3	public ....void	add (java.awt.geom.Rectangle2D r)	
			public ....void	**add** (Point pt)	
			public ....void	**add** (Rectangle r)	
1.2		3	public ....void	add (double newx, double newy)	
			public ....void	**add** (int newx, int newy)	
		2	public ....Object	clone ()	
1.2		2	public .... boolean	contains (java.awt.geom.Point2D p)	
1.2		2	public .... boolean	contains (java.awt.geom.Rectangle2D r)	
1.1			public .... boolean	**contains** (Point p)	
1.2			public .... boolean	**contains** (Rectangle r)	ε946
1.2		3	public .... boolean	contains (double x, double y)	
1.1			public .... boolean	**contains** (int x, int y)	ε967
1.2		3	public .... boolean	contains (double x, double y, double w, double h)	
1.2		3	public .... boolean	**contains** (int X, int Y, int W, int H)	
1.2		3	public .... **java‚** .awt.geom.Rectangle2D	**createIntersection** (java.awt.geom.Rectangle2D r)	
1.2		3	public .... **java‚** .awt.geom.Rectangle2D	**createUnion** (java.awt.geom.Rectangle2D r)	
		3	public .... **boolean**	**equals** (Object obj)	
1.1		2	public .... **Rectangle**	**getBounds** ()	
1.2		3	public .... **java‚** .awt.geom.Rectangle2D	**getBounds2D** ()	
1.2		2	public ....double	getCenterX ()	
1.2		2	public ....double	getCenterY ()	
1.2		2	public ... java.awt.geom.Rectangle2D	getFrame ()	
1.2		2	public .... **double**	**getHeight** ()	
1.1			public ....Point	**getLocation** ()	
1.2		2	public ....double	getMaxX ()	
1.2		2	public ....double	getMaxY ()	
1.2		2	public ....double	getMinX ()	
1.2		2	public ....double	getMinY ()	
1.2		3	public ... java.awt.geom.PathIterator	getPathIterator (java.awt.geom.AffineTransform at)	
1.2		3	public ... java.awt.geom.PathIterator	getPathIterator (java.awt.geom.AffineTransform at, double flatness)	
1.1			public ....Dimension	**getSize** ()	
1.2		2	public .... **double**	**getWidth** ()	ε826
1.2		2	public .... **double**	**getX** ()	
1.2		2	public .... **double**	**getY** ()	
			public ....void	**grow** (int h, int v)	ε967
		3	public ....int	hashCode ()	
			public ....int	**height**	ε590,948
D			public .... boolean	**inside** (int X, int Y)	
1.2	△	3	public static ....void	intersect (java.awt.geom.Rectangle2D src1, java.awt.geom.Rectangle2D src2, java.awt.geom.Rectangle2D dest)	
			public .... Rectangle	**intersection** (Rectangle r)	
1.2		2	public .... boolean	intersects (java.awt.geom.Rectangle2D r)	
			public .... boolean	**intersects** (Rectangle r)	
1.2		3	public .... boolean	intersects (double x, double y, double w, double h)	
1.2		3	public .... boolean	intersectsLine (java.awt.geom.Line2D l)	
1.2		3	public .... boolean	intersectsLine (double x1, double y1, double x2, double y2)	
		2	public .... **boolean**	**isEmpty** ()	
D			public ....void	**move** (int x, int y)	
1.2	▲	3	public static final ....int	OUT_BOTTOM = 8	
1.2	▲	3	public static final ....int	OUT_LEFT = 1	
1.2	▲	3	public static final ....int	OUT_RIGHT = 4	
1.2	▲	3	public static final ....int	OUT_TOP = 2	
1.2		3	public ....int	outcode (java.awt.geom.Point2D p)	
1.2		3	public .... **int**	**outcode** (double x, double y)	
	*		public .... **Rectangle**	**Rectangle** ()	
	*		public .... **Rectangle**	**Rectangle** (Dimension d)	ε864,946
	*		public .... **Rectangle**	**Rectangle** (Point p)	
1.1	*		public .... **Rectangle**	**Rectangle** (Rectangle r)	
	*		public .... **Rectangle**	**Rectangle** (int width, int height)	

R

Classes

Rectangle

	✳	public............................		**Rectangle** (Point p, Dimension d)	
	✳	public............................		**Rectangle** (int x, int y, int width, int height)	ε563,580,864
D		public.....................void		**reshape** (int x, int y, int width, int height)	
D		public.....................void		**resize** (int width, int height)	
1.1		public.....................void		**setBounds** (Rectangle r)	
1.1		public.....................void		**setBounds** (int x, int y, int width, int height)	
1.2	2	public.....................void		setFrame (java.awt.geom.Rectangle2D r)	
1.2	2	public.....................void		setFrame (java.awt.geom.Point2D loc, java.awt.geom.Dimension2D size)	
1.2	3	public.....................void		setFrame (double x, double y, double w, double h)	
1.2	2	public.....................void		setFrameFromCenter (java.awt.geom.Point2D center, java.awt.geom.Point2D corner)	
1.2	2	public.....................void		setFrameFromCenter (double centerX, double centerY, double cornerX, double cornerY)	
1.2	2	public.....................void		setFrameFromDiagonal (java.awt.geom.Point2D p1, java.awt.geom.Point2D p2)	
1.2	2	public.....................void		setFrameFromDiagonal (double x1, double y1, double x2, double y2)	
1.1		public.....................void		**setLocation** (Point p)	
1.1		public.....................void		**setLocation** (int x, int y)	ε946,947,948
1.2	3	public.....................void		setRect (java.awt.geom.Rectangle2D r)	
1.2	3	public................**void**		**setRect** (double x, double y, double width, double height)	
1.1		public.....................void		**setSize** (Dimension d)	
1.1		public.....................void		**setSize** (int width, int height)	
	1	public................**String**		**toString** ()	
		public.....................void		**translate** (int x, int y)	ε948
		public...............Rectangle		**union** (Rectangle r)	
1.2 △	3	public static ....void		union (java.awt.geom.Rectangle2D src1, java.awt.geom.Rectangle2D src2, java.awt.geom.Rectangle2D dest)	
		public........................int		**width**	ε590,948,967
		public........................int		**x**	ε590,946,947,948,967
		public........................int		**y**	ε590,946,947,948

R	**Rectangle2D**	java.awt.geom

			Object [1]	ε572
1.2 ○			└RectangularShape [2] - *java.awt.Shape [3]*, *Cloneable*	
1.2 ○			└Rectangle2D	

		public.....................void	**add** (Point2D pt)	
		public.....................void	**add** (Rectangle2D r)	
		public.....................void	**add** (double newx, double newy)	
	2	public.................Object	clone ()	
	2	public............... boolean	contains (Point2D p)	
	2	public............... boolean	contains (Rectangle2D r)	
	3	public............... boolean	**contains** (double x, double y)	
	3	public............... boolean	**contains** (double x, double y, double w, double h)	
○		public abstract ...Rectangle2D	**createIntersection** (Rectangle2D r)	
○		public abstract ...Rectangle2D	**createUnion** (Rectangle2D r)	
	1	public................**boolean**	**equals** (Object obj)	
	2	public...... java.awt.Rectangle	getBounds ()	
	3	public.............Rectangle2D	**getBounds2D** ()	
	2	public...............double	getCenterX ()	
	2	public...............double	getCenterY ()	
	2	public...........Rectangle2D	getFrame ()	
○	2	public abstract ....double	getHeight ()	
	2	public...............double	getMaxX ()	
	2	public...............double	getMaxY ()	
	2	public...............double	getMinX ()	
	2	public...............double	getMinY ()	
	3	public......... *PathIterator*	**getPathIterator** (AffineTransform at)	
	2	public......... *PathIterator*	**getPathIterator** (AffineTransform at, double flatness)	
○	2	public abstract ....double	getWidth ()	ε826
○	2	public abstract ....double	getX ()	
○	2	public abstract ....double	getY ()	
	1	public................**int**	**hashCode** ()	
△		public static ....void	**intersect** (Rectangle2D src1, Rectangle2D src2, Rectangle2D dest)	
	2	public............... boolean	intersects (Rectangle2D r)	
	3	public............... boolean	**intersects** (double x, double y, double w, double h)	
		public............... boolean	**intersectsLine** (Line2D l)	
		public............... boolean	**intersectsLine** (double x1, double y1, double x2, double y2)	
○	2	public abstract .... boolean	isEmpty ()	
▲		public static final ....int	**OUT_BOTTOM** = 8	

Class   *Interface*   —extends   - - -implements   ○ abstract   ● final   △ static   ▲ static final   ✳ constructor   x x—inherited   x **x**—declared   **x x**—overridden
ε*n*—examples of usage   —has subclass   package—see other volume

▲		public static final	.............int	**OUT_LEFT** = 1
▲		public static final	.............int	**OUT_RIGHT** = 4
▲		public static final	.............int	**OUT_TOP** = 2
		public	.............int	**outcode** (Point2D p)
○		public abstract	.............int	**outcode** (double x, double y)
✳		protected	....	**Rectangle2D** ()
	2	public	.............void	setFrame (Rectangle2D r)
	2	public	.............void	setFrame (Point2D loc, Dimension2D size)
	2	public	.............**void setFrame** (double x, double y, double w, double h)
	2	public	.............void	setFrameFromCenter (Point2D center, Point2D corner)
	2	public	.............void	setFrameFromCenter (double centerX, double centerY, double cornerX, double cornerY)
	2	public	.............void	setFrameFromDiagonal (Point2D p1, Point2D p2)
	2	public	.............void	setFrameFromDiagonal (double x1, double y1, double x2, double y2)
		public	.............**void setRect** (Rectangle2D r)
○		public abstract	.............**void setRect** (double x, double y, double w, double h)
△		public static	.............void	**union** (Rectangle2D src1, Rectangle2D src2, Rectangle2D dest)

Rectangle2D.Double
java.awt.geom

ε572

		Object[1]
1.2	○	└─RectangularShape[2] - *java.awt.Shape, Cloneable*
1.2	○	└─Rectangle2D[3]
1.2		└─Rectangle2D.Double

	3	public	.............void	add (Point2D pt)
	3	public	.............void	add (Rectangle2D r)
	3	public	.............void	add (double newx, double newy)
	2	public	.............Object	clone ()
	2	public	.............boolean	contains (Point2D p)
	2	public	.............boolean	contains (Rectangle2D r)
	3	public	.............boolean	contains (double x, double y)
	3	public	.............boolean	contains (double x, double y, double w, double h)
	3	public	.............**Rectangle2D createIntersection** (Rectangle2D r)
	3	public	.............**Rectangle2D createUnion** (Rectangle2D r)
✳		public	....	**Rectangle2D.Double** ()
✳		public	....	**Rectangle2D.Double** (double x, double y, double w, double h)
	3	public	.............boolean	equals (Object obj)
	2	public	.............java.awt.Rectangle	getBounds ()
	3	public	.............**Rectangle2D getBounds2D** ()
	2	public	.............double	getCenterX ()
	2	public	.............double	getCenterY ()
	2	public	.............Rectangle2D	getFrame ()
	2	public	.............**double getHeight** ()
	2	public	.............double	getMaxX ()
	2	public	.............double	getMaxY ()
	2	public	.............double	getMinX ()
	2	public	.............double	getMinY ()
	3	public	.............*PathIterator*	getPathIterator (AffineTransform at)
	3	public	.............*PathIterator*	getPathIterator (AffineTransform at, double flatness)
	2	public	.............**double getWidth** ()
	2	public	.............**double getX** ()
	2	public	.............**double getY** ()
	3	public	.............int	hashCode ()
		public	.............double	**height**
△	3	public static	.............void	intersect (Rectangle2D src1, Rectangle2D src2, Rectangle2D dest)
	2	public	.............boolean	intersects (Rectangle2D r)
	3	public	.............boolean	intersects (double x, double y, double w, double h)
	3	public	.............boolean	intersectsLine (Line2D l)
	3	public	.............boolean	intersectsLine (double x1, double y1, double x2, double y2)
	2	public	.............**boolean isEmpty** ()
▲	3	public static final	.............int	OUT_BOTTOM = 8
▲	3	public static final	.............int	OUT_LEFT = 1
▲	3	public static final	.............int	OUT_RIGHT = 4
▲	3	public static final	.............int	OUT_TOP = 2
	3	public	.............int	outcode (Point2D p)
	3	public	.............**int outcode** (double x, double y)
	2	public	.............void	setFrame (Rectangle2D r)
	2	public	.............void	setFrame (Point2D loc, Dimension2D size)
	3	public	.............void	setFrame (double x, double y, double w, double h)
	3	public	.............void	setFrameFromCenter (Point2D center, Point2D corner)
	2	public	.............void	setFrameFromCenter (double centerX, double centerY, double cornerX, double cornerY)

ε826

R

Classes

Rectangle2D.Double

```
   2  public......................void  setFrameFromDiagonal (Point2D p1, Point2D p2)
   2  public......................void  setFrameFromDiagonal (double x1, double y1, double x2, double y2)
   3  public......................void  setRect (Rectangle2D r)
   3  public......................void  setRect (double x, double y, double w, double h)
   1  public....................String  toString ()
△  3  public static ..............void  union (Rectangle2D src1, Rectangle2D src2, Rectangle2D dest)
      public....................double  width
      public....................double  x
      public....................double  y
```

Rectangle2D.Float   java.awt.geom

```
                                              Object 1                                      ε572
1.2 ○     └ RectangularShape 2 - - - - - - - - - - - - - - - - - - - - java.awt.Shape, Cloneable ⌄
1.2 ○         └ Rectangle2D 3
1.2             └ Rectangle2D.Float
```

```
   3  public......................void  add (Point2D pt)
   3  public......................void  add (Rectangle2D r)
   3  public......................void  add (double newx, double newy)
   2  public....................Object  clone ()
   2  public...................boolean  contains (Point2D p)
   2  public...................boolean  contains (Rectangle2D r)
   3  public...................boolean  contains (double x, double y)
   3  public...................boolean  contains (double x, double y, double w, double h)
   3  public............Rectangle2D  createIntersection (Rectangle2D r)
   3  public............Rectangle2D  createUnion (Rectangle2D r)
   3  public...................boolean  equals (Object obj)
✳     public............Rectangle2D.Float ()
✳     public............Rectangle2D.Float (float x, float y, float w, float h)        ε656,660,668,669
   2  public...... java.awt.Rectangle  getBounds ()
   3  public............Rectangle2D  getBounds2D ()
   2  public....................double  getCenterX ()
   2  public....................double  getCenterY ()
   2  public...............Rectangle2D  getFrame ()
   2  public....................double  getHeight ()
   2  public....................double  getMaxX ()
   2  public....................double  getMaxY ()
   2  public....................double  getMinX ()
   2  public....................double  getMinY ()
   3  public...............PathIterator  getPathIterator (AffineTransform at)
   3  public...............PathIterator  getPathIterator (AffineTransform at, double flatness)
   2  public....................double  getWidth ()                                      ε826
   2  public....................double  getX ()
   2  public....................double  getY ()
   3  public.......................int  hashCode ()
      public......................float  height                                         ε660,668
△  3  public static ..............void  intersect (Rectangle2D src1, Rectangle2D src2, Rectangle2D dest)
   2  public...................boolean  intersects (Rectangle2D r)
   3  public...................boolean  intersects (double x, double y, double w, double h)
   3  public...................boolean  intersectsLine (Line2D l)
   3  public...................boolean  intersectsLine (double x1, double y1, double x2, double y2)
   2  public...................boolean  isEmpty ()
▲  3  public static final .........int  OUT_BOTTOM  = 8
▲  3  public static final .........int  OUT_LEFT  = 1
▲  3  public static final .........int  OUT_RIGHT  = 4
▲  3  public static final .........int  OUT_TOP  = 2
   3  public.......................int  outcode (Point2D p)
   3  public.......................int  outcode (double x, double y)
   2  public......................void  setFrame (Rectangle2D r)
   2  public......................void  setFrame (Point2D loc, Dimension2D size)
   3  public......................void  setFrame (double x, double y, double w, double h)
   2  public......................void  setFrameFromCenter (Point2D center, Point2D corner)
   2  public......................void  setFrameFromCenter (double centerX, double centerY, double cornerX,
                                          double cornerY)
   2  public......................void  setFrameFromDiagonal (Point2D p1, Point2D p2)
   2  public......................void  setFrameFromDiagonal (double x1, double y1, double x2, double y2)
   3  public......................void  setRect (Rectangle2D r)
   3  public......................void  setRect (double x, double y, double w, double h)
      public......................void  setRect (float x, float y, float w, float h)
```

Class   *Interface*   —extends   - - -implements   ○ abstract   ● final   △ static   ▲ static final   ✳ constructor   x x—inherited   x **x**—declared   **x x**—overridden
ε*n*—examples of usage   ⌄—has subclass   package—see other volume

1	public	String	**toString** ()		
△ 3	public static	void	union (Rectangle2D src1, Rectangle2D src2, Rectangle2D dest)		
	public	float	**width**		ε660,668
	public	float	**x**		ε660,668
	public	float	**y**		ε660,668

RectangularShape

java.awt.geom

ε572

Object [1]
1.2 ○ └ RectangularShape - *java.awt.Shape* [2], *Cloneable*

	1	public	**Object**	**clone** ()	
	2	public	boolean	**contains** (Point2D p)	
	2	public	boolean	**contains** (Rectangle2D r)	
○	2	public abstract	boolean	contains (double x, double y)	
○	2	public abstract	boolean	contains (double x, double y, double w, double h)	
	2	public	java.awt.Rectangle	**getBounds** ()	
○	2	public abstract	Rectangle2D	getBounds2D ()	
		public	double	**getCenterX** ()	
		public	double	**getCenterY** ()	
		public	Rectangle2D	**getFrame** ()	
○		public abstract	double	**getHeight** ()	
		public	double	**getMaxX** ()	
		public	double	**getMaxY** ()	
		public	double	**getMinX** ()	
		public	double	**getMinY** ()	
○	2	public abstract	*PathIterator*	getPathIterator (AffineTransform at)	
	2	public	*PathIterator*	**getPathIterator** (AffineTransform at, double flatness)	
○		public abstract	double	**getWidth** ()	ε826
○		public abstract	double	**getX** ()	
○		public abstract	double	**getY** ()	
	2	public	boolean	**intersects** (Rectangle2D r)	
○	2	public abstract	boolean	intersects (double x, double y, double w, double h)	
○		public abstract	boolean	**isEmpty** ()	
*		protected		**RectangularShape** ()	
		public	void	**setFrame** (Rectangle2D r)	
		public	void	**setFrame** (Point2D loc, Dimension2D size)	
○		public abstract	void	**setFrame** (double x, double y, double w, double h)	
		public	void	**setFrameFromCenter** (Point2D center, Point2D corner)	
		public	void	**setFrameFromCenter** (double centerX, double centerY, double cornerX, double cornerY)	
		public	void	**setFrameFromDiagonal** (Point2D p1, Point2D p2)	
		public	void	**setFrameFromDiagonal** (double x1, double y1, double x2, double y2)	

ReferenceUriSchemesSupported

javax.print.attribute.standard

Object
1.4 ○ └ javax.print.attribute.EnumSyntax [1] - - - - - - - - - *java.io.Serializable*, *Cloneable*
1.4 └ ReferenceUriSchemesSupported - - - - - - - - *javax.print.attribute.Attribute* [2] (*java.io.Serializable*)

	1	public	Object	clone ()	
▲		public static final	Reference-UriSchemesSupported	**FILE**	
▲		public static final	Reference-UriSchemesSupported	**FTP**	
●	2	public final	Class	**getCategory** ()	ε707
	1	protected	**javax.print.attribute.EnumSyntax[]**	getEnumValueTable ()	
●	2	public final	String	**getName** ()	ε706,707,708
	1	protected	int	getOffset ()	
	1	protected	**String[]**	**getStringTable** ()	
	1	public	int	getValue ()	
▲		public static final	Reference-UriSchemesSupported	**GOPHER**	
	1	public	int	hashCode ()	
▲		public static final	Reference-UriSchemesSupported	**HTTP**	
▲		public static final	Reference-UriSchemesSupported	**HTTPS**	
▲		public static final	Reference-UriSchemesSupported	**NEWS**	

R

Classes

ReferenceUriSchemesSupported

▲	public static final ... Reference-UriSchemesSupported	**NNTP**	
1	protected .... Object	readResolve () throws java.io.ObjectStreamException	
✶	protected	**ReferenceUriSchemesSupported** (int value)	
1	public .... String	toString ()	
▲	public static final ... Reference-UriSchemesSupported	**WAIS**	

RegisterableService

javax.imageio.spi

1.4   *RegisterableService*

public .... void	**onDeregistration** (ServiceRegistry registry, Class category)
public .... void	**onRegistration** (ServiceRegistry registry, Class category)

RenderableImage

java.awt.image.renderable

1.2   *RenderableImage*

public .... *java.awt.image.RenderedImage*	**createDefaultRendering** ()
public .... *java.awt.image.RenderedImage*	**createRendering** (RenderContext renderContext)
public .... *java.awt.image.RenderedImage*	**createScaledRendering** (int w, int h, java.awt.RenderingHints hints)
public .... float	**getHeight** ()
public .... float	**getMinX** ()
public .... float	**getMinY** ()
public .... Object	**getProperty** (String name)
public .... String[]	**getPropertyNames** ()
public .... java.util.Vector	**getSources** ()
public .... float	**getWidth** ()
▲ public static final .... String	**HINTS_OBSERVED** = "HINTS_OBSERVED"
public .... boolean	**isDynamic** ()

RenderableImageOp

java.awt.image.renderable

Object
  └RenderableImageOp - *RenderableImage 1*

1.2

1	public .... *java.awt.image.RenderedImage*	**createDefaultRendering** ()	
1	public .... *java.awt.image.RenderedImage*	**createRendering** (RenderContext renderContext)	
1	public .... *java.awt.image.RenderedImage*	**createScaledRendering** (int w, int h, java.awt.RenderingHints hints)	
1	public .... float	**getHeight** ()	
1	public .... float	**getMinX** ()	
1	public .... float	**getMinY** ()	
	public .... ParameterBlock	**getParameterBlock** ()	
1	public .... Object	**getProperty** (String name)	
1	public .... String[]	**getPropertyNames** ()	
1	public .... java.util.Vector	**getSources** ()	
1	public .... float	**getWidth** ()	
▲ 1	public static final .... String	HINTS_OBSERVED = "HINTS_OBSERVED"	
1	public .... boolean	**isDynamic** ()	
✶	public	**RenderableImageOp** (*ContextualRenderedImageFactory* CRIF, ParameterBlock paramBlock)	
	public .... ParameterBlock	**setParameterBlock** (ParameterBlock paramBlock)	

RenderableImageProducer

java.awt.image.renderable

Object
  └RenderableImageProducer - - - - - - - - - - - - - - *java.awt.image.ImageProducer 1*, *Runnable 2*

1.2

1	public synchronized .... void	**addConsumer** (*java.awt.image.ImageConsumer* ic)	
1	public synchronized .. boolean	**isConsumer** (*java.awt.image.ImageConsumer* ic)	

Class   *Interface*   —extends   - - -implements   ○ abstract   ● final   △ static   ▲ static final   ✶ constructor   x x—inherited   x **x**—declared   **x x**—overridden
εn—examples of usage   ⌐—has subclass   package—see other volume

*	1	public synchronized ....void	**removeConsumer** (*java.awt.image.ImageConsumer* ic)
		public............................	**RenderableImageProducer** (*RenderableImage* rdblImage, RenderContext rc)
	1	public.............................void	**requestTopDownLeftRightResend** (*java.awt.image.ImageConsumer* ic)
	2	public.............................void	**run** ()
		public synchronized ......void	**setRenderContext** (RenderContext rc)
	1	public synchronized ......void	**startProduction** (*java.awt.image.ImageConsumer* ic)

RenderContext   java.awt.image.renderable

Object[1]

1.2   └RenderContext ----------------------- *Cloneable*

	1	public...................**Object**	**clone** ()
1.3		public.........................void	**concatenateTransform** (java.awt.geom.AffineTransform modTransform)
D		public.........................void	**concetenateTransform** (java.awt.geom.AffineTransform modTransform)
		public......... *java.awt.Shape*	**getAreaOfInterest** ()
		public java.awt.RenderingHints	**getRenderingHints** ()
		public....................java.	**getTransform** ()
		.awt.geom.AffineTransform	
1.3		public.........................void	**preConcatenateTransform** (java.awt.geom.AffineTransform modTransform)
D		public.........................void	**preConcetenateTransform** (java.awt.geom.AffineTransform modTransform)
*		public............................	**RenderContext** (java.awt.geom.AffineTransform usr2dev)
*		public............................	**RenderContext** (java.awt.geom.AffineTransform usr2dev, *java.awt.Shape* aoi)
*		public............................	**RenderContext** (java.awt.geom.AffineTransform usr2dev, java.awt.RenderingHints hints)
*		public............................	**RenderContext** (java.awt.geom.AffineTransform usr2dev, *java.awt.Shape* aoi, java.awt.RenderingHints hints)
		public.........................void	**setAreaOfInterest** (*java.awt.Shape* newAoi)
		public.........................void	**setRenderingHints** (java.awt.RenderingHints hints)
		public.........................void	**setTransform** (java.awt.geom.AffineTransform newTransform)

RenderedImage   java.awt.image

ε695,699

1.2   *RenderedImage*

public.......... WritableRaster	**copyData** (WritableRaster raster)	
public............... ColorModel	**getColorModel** ()	ε661,662
public................... Raster	**getData** ()	
public................... Raster	**getData** (java.awt.Rectangle rect)	
public.........................int	**getHeight** ()	ε672
public.........................int	**getMinTileX** ()	
public.........................int	**getMinTileY** ()	
public.........................int	**getMinX** ()	
public.........................int	**getMinY** ()	
public.........................int	**getNumXTiles** ()	
public.........................int	**getNumYTiles** ()	
public...................Object	**getProperty** (String name)	
public.................. String[]	**getPropertyNames** ()	
public............SampleModel	**getSampleModel** ()	
public........... java.util.Vector	**getSources** ()	
public................... Raster	**getTile** (int tileX, int tileY)	
public.........................int	**getTileGridXOffset** ()	
public.........................int	**getTileGridYOffset** ()	
public.........................int	**getTileHeight** ()	
public.........................int	**getTileWidth** ()	
public.........................int	**getWidth** ()	ε672

RenderedImageFactory   java.awt.image.renderable

1.2   *RenderedImageFactory*

public................ *java.awt.*	**create** (ParameterBlock paramBlock, java.awt.RenderingHints hints)
.image.RenderedImage	

Renderer   javax.swing

1.2   *Renderer*

public.... java.awt.Component	**getComponent** ()
public.........................void	**setValue** (Object aValue, boolean isSelected)

R

Classes

RenderingHints

Object [1]

1.2   └RenderingHints - *java.util.Map* [2], *Cloneable*

		public	void	**add** (RenderingHints hints)	
	2	public	void	**clear** ()	
	1	public	**Object**	**clone** ()	
	2	public	boolean	**containsKey** (Object key)	
	2	public	boolean	**containsValue** (Object value)	ε577
	2	public	*java.util.Set*	**entrySet** ()	
	1	public	**boolean**	**equals** (Object o)	
	2	public	Object	**get** (Object key)	
	1	public	**int**	**hashCode** ()	
	2	public	boolean	**isEmpty** ()	
▲		public static final RenderingHints.Key		**KEY_ALPHA_INTERPOLATION**	
▲		public static final RenderingHints.Key		**KEY_ANTIALIASING**	ε577
▲		public static final RenderingHints.Key		**KEY_COLOR_RENDERING**	
▲		public static final RenderingHints.Key		**KEY_DITHERING**	
▲		public static final RenderingHints.Key		**KEY_FRACTIONALMETRICS**	
▲		public static final RenderingHints.Key		**KEY_INTERPOLATION**	
▲		public static final RenderingHints.Key		**KEY_RENDERING**	
1.3 ▲		public static final RenderingHints.Key		**KEY_STROKE_CONTROL**	
▲		public static final RenderingHints.Key		**KEY_TEXT_ANTIALIASING**	ε577
	2	public	*java.util.Set*	**keySet** ()	ε870
	2	public	Object	**put** (Object key, Object value)	
	2	public	void	**putAll** (*java.util.Map* m)	
	2	public	Object	**remove** (Object key)	
✳		public		**RenderingHints** (*java.util.Map* init)	
✳		public		**RenderingHints** (RenderingHints.Key key, Object value)	
	2	public	int	**size** ()	
	1	public	**String**	**toString** ()	
▲		public static final	Object	**VALUE_ALPHA_INTERPOLATION_DEFAULT**	
▲		public static final	Object	**VALUE_ALPHA_INTERPOLATION_QUALITY**	
▲		public static final	Object	**VALUE_ALPHA_INTERPOLATION_SPEED**	
▲		public static final	Object	**VALUE_ANTIALIAS_DEFAULT**	
▲		public static final	Object	**VALUE_ANTIALIAS_OFF**	ε577
▲		public static final	Object	**VALUE_ANTIALIAS_ON**	ε577
▲		public static final	Object	**VALUE_COLOR_RENDER_DEFAULT**	
▲		public static final	Object	**VALUE_COLOR_RENDER_QUALITY**	
▲		public static final	Object	**VALUE_COLOR_RENDER_SPEED**	
▲		public static final	Object	**VALUE_DITHER_DEFAULT**	
▲		public static final	Object	**VALUE_DITHER_DISABLE**	
▲		public static final	Object	**VALUE_DITHER_ENABLE**	
▲		public static final	Object	**VALUE_FRACTIONALMETRICS_DEFAULT**	
▲		public static final	Object	**VALUE_FRACTIONALMETRICS_OFF**	
▲		public static final	Object	**VALUE_FRACTIONALMETRICS_ON**	
▲		public static final	Object	**VALUE_INTERPOLATION_BICUBIC**	
▲		public static final	Object	**VALUE_INTERPOLATION_BILINEAR**	
▲		public static final	Object	**VALUE_INTERPOLATION_NEAREST_NEIGHBOR**	
▲		public static final	Object	**VALUE_RENDER_DEFAULT**	
▲		public static final	Object	**VALUE_RENDER_QUALITY**	
▲		public static final	Object	**VALUE_RENDER_SPEED**	
1.3 ▲		public static final	Object	**VALUE_STROKE_DEFAULT**	
1.3 ▲		public static final	Object	**VALUE_STROKE_NORMALIZE**	
1.3 ▲		public static final	Object	**VALUE_STROKE_PURE**	
▲		public static final	Object	**VALUE_TEXT_ANTIALIAS_DEFAULT**	
▲		public static final	Object	**VALUE_TEXT_ANTIALIAS_OFF**	ε577
▲		public static final	Object	**VALUE_TEXT_ANTIALIAS_ON**	ε577
	2	public	*java.util.Collection*	**values** ()	

R

Class   *Interface*   —extends   - - -implements   ○ abstract   ● final   △ static   ▲ static final   ✳ constructor   x x—inherited   x **x**—declared   **x x**—overridden
εn—examples of usage   ⌄—has subclass   package —see other volume

RenderingHints.Key
java.awt

Object [1]
└ RenderingHints.Key

1.2 ○

●	1	public final .... **boolean**	**equals** (Object o)
●	1	public final .... **int**	**hashCode** ()
●		protected final................int	**intKey** ()
○		public abstract .... boolean	**isCompatibleValue** (Object val)
✳		protected	**RenderingHints.Key** (int privatekey)

RepaintManager
javax.swing

Object [1]
└ RepaintManager

1.2

		public synchronized ....void	**addDirtyRegion** (JComponent c, int x, int y, int w, int h)
		public synchronized ....void	**addInvalidComponent** (JComponent invalidComponent)
△		public static .. RepaintManager	**currentManager** (java.awt.Component c)
△		public static .. RepaintManager	**currentManager** (JComponent c)
		public...... java.awt.Rectangle	**getDirtyRegion** (JComponent aComponent)
		public...... java.awt.Dimension	**getDoubleBufferMaximumSize** ()
		public.......... java.awt.Image	**getOffscreenBuffer** (java.awt.Component c, int proposedWidth, int proposedHeight)
1.4		public.......... java.awt.Image	**getVolatileOffscreenBuffer** (java.awt.Component c, int proposedWidth, int proposedHeight)
		public................... boolean	**isCompletelyDirty** (JComponent aComponent)
		public................... boolean	**isDoubleBufferingEnabled** ()
		public...................void	**markCompletelyClean** (JComponent aComponent)
		public...................void	**markCompletelyDirty** (JComponent aComponent)
		public...................void	**paintDirtyRegions** ()
		public synchronized ....void	**removeInvalidComponent** (JComponent component)
✳		public...................	**RepaintManager** ()
△		public static ....void	**setCurrentManager** (RepaintManager aRepaintManager)
		public...................void	**setDoubleBufferingEnabled** (boolean aFlag)
		public...................void	**setDoubleBufferMaximumSize** (java.awt.Dimension d)
	1	public synchronized .... **String**	**toString** ()
		public...................void	**validateInvalidComponents** ()

R

ReplicateScaleFilter
java.awt.image

ε665

Object
└ ImageFilter [1] - ImageConsumer [2], Cloneable
  └ ReplicateScaleFilter

1.1

	2	*9 inherited members from ImageConsumer not shown*	
	1	public................... Object	clone ()
	1	protected ..... *ImageConsumer*	consumer
		protected ....int	**destHeight**
		protected ....int	**destWidth**
	1	public............... ImageFilter	getFilterInstance (*ImageConsumer* ic)
	1	public...................void	imageComplete (int status)
		protected .... Object	**outpixbuf**
✳		public...................	**ReplicateScaleFilter** (int width, int height)
	1	public...................void	resendTopDownLeftRight (*ImageProducer* ip)
	1	public...................void	setColorModel (ColorModel model)
	1	public................... **void**	**setDimensions** (int w, int h)
	1	public...................void	setHints (int hints)
	1	public................... **void**	**setPixels** (int x, int y, int w, int h, ColorModel model, byte[] pixels, int off, int scansize)
	1	public................... **void**	**setPixels** (int x, int y, int w, int h, ColorModel model, int[] pixels, int off, int scansize)
	1	public................... **void**	**setProperties** (java.util.Hashtable props)
		protected .... int[]	**srccols**
		protected ....int	**srcHeight**
		protected .... int[]	**srcrows**
		protected ....int	**srcWidth**

Classes

747

RequestingUserName

RequestingUserName				javax.print.attribute.standard

Object
1.4 ○ └─javax.print.attribute.TextSyntax [1] - - - - - - - - - - - *java.io.Serializable* ˎ *Cloneable* ˎ
1.4 ●   └─RequestingUserName - - - - - - - - - - - - - - - - - *javax.print.attribute.PrintRequestAttribute*
                                               (*javax.print.attribute.Attribute* [2] (*java.io.Serializable*))

●	1	public	**boolean**	**equals** (Object object)	
●	2	public final	Class	**getCategory** ()	ε707
	1	public	java.util.Locale	getLocale ()	
●	2	public final	String	**getName** ()	ε706,707,708
	1	public	String	getValue ()	
	1	public	int	hashCode ()	
✳		public		**RequestingUserName** (String userName, java.util.Locale locale)	
	1	public	String	toString ()	

RescaleOp	java.awt.image

Object
1.2 └─RescaleOp - *BufferedImageOp* [1], *RasterOp* [2]

	1	public	BufferedImage	**createCompatibleDestImage** (BufferedImage src, ColorModel destCM)	
	2	public	WritableRaster	**createCompatibleDestRaster** (Raster src)	
●	1	public final	BufferedImage	**filter** (BufferedImage src, BufferedImage dst)	ε680,672,675,676,677
●	2	public final	WritableRaster	**filter** (Raster src, WritableRaster dst)	
●	1	public final . java.awt.geom.Rectangle2D		**getBounds2D** (BufferedImage src)	
●	2	public final . java.awt.geom.Rectangle2D		**getBounds2D** (Raster src)	
●		public final	int	**getNumFactors** ()	
●		public final	float[]	**getOffsets** (float[] offsets)	
●	1	public final java.awt.geom.Point2D		**getPoint2D** (java.awt.geom.Point2D srcPt, java.awt.geom.Point2D dstPt)	
●	1	public final . . . . . java.awt.RenderingHints		**getRenderingHints** ()	
●		public final	float[]	**getScaleFactors** (float[] scaleFactors)	
✳		public		**RescaleOp** (float scaleFactor, float offset, java.awt.RenderingHints hints)	ε680
✳		public		**RescaleOp** (float[] scaleFactors, float[] offsets, java.awt.RenderingHints hints)	

ResolutionSyntax	javax.print.attribute

Object [1]
1.4 ○ └─ResolutionSyntax ˎ - *java.io.Serializable* ˎ *Cloneable* ˎ

▲		public static final	int	**DPCM** = 254
▲		public static final	int	**DPI** = 100
	1	public	**boolean**	**equals** (Object object)
		public	int	**getCrossFeedResolution** (int units)
		protected	int	**getCrossFeedResolutionDphi** ()
		public	int	**getFeedResolution** (int units)
		protected	int	**getFeedResolutionDphi** ()
		public	int[]	**getResolution** (int units)
	1	public	**int**	**hashCode** ()
		public	boolean	**lessThanOrEquals** (ResolutionSyntax other)
✳		public		**ResolutionSyntax** (int crossFeedResolution, int feedResolution, int units)
	1	public	**String**	**toString** ()
		public	String	**toString** (int units, String unitsName)

ReverbType	javax.sound.sampled

Object [1]
1.3 └─ReverbType

●	1	public final	**boolean**	**equals** (Object obj)
●		public final	int	**getDecayTime** ()
●		public final	int	**getEarlyReflectionDelay** ()

Class   *Interface*   —extends   - - -implements   ○ abstract   ● final   △ static   ▲ static final   ✳ constructor   x x—inherited   x **x**—declared   **x x**—overridden
ε*n*—examples of usage   ˎ—has subclass   package—see other volume

●		public final	................float	**getEarlyReflectionIntensity** ()
●		public final	...................int	**getLateReflectionDelay** ()
●		public final	................float	**getLateReflectionIntensity** ()
●	1	public final	.... **int**	**hashCode** ()
*		protected	....	**ReverbType** (String name, int earlyReflectionDelay, float earlyReflectionIntensity, int lateReflectionDelay, float lateReflectionIntensity, int decayTime)
●	1	public final	.... **String**	**toString** ()

RGBImageFilter   java.awt.image

ε665

```
Object
└ImageFilter¹ - - - - - - - - - - - - - - - - - - - - - - - - - ImageConsumer², Cloneable˩
   └RGBImageFilter˩
```

	2	*9 inherited members from ImageConsumer not shown*			
		protected	.... boolean	**canFilterIndexColorModel**	
	1	public	....................Object	clone ()	
	1	protected	.....*ImageConsumer*	consumer	
		public	.... IndexColorModel	**filterIndexColorModel** (IndexColorModel icm)	
○		public abstract	...............int	**filterRGB** (int x, int y, int rgb)	ε665
		public	....................void	**filterRGBPixels** (int x, int y, int w, int h, int[] pixels, int off, int scansize)	
	1	public	...............ImageFilter	getFilterInstance (*ImageConsumer* ic)	
	1	public	....................void	imageComplete (int status)	
		protected	.... ColorModel	**newmodel**	
		protected	.... ColorModel	**origmodel**	
	1	public	....................void	resendTopDownLeftRight (*ImageProducer* ip)	
*		public	....	**RGBImageFilter** ()	
	1	public	.... **void**	**setColorModel** (ColorModel model)	
	1	public	....................void	setDimensions (int width, int height)	
	1	public	....................void	setHints (int hints)	
	1	public	.... **void**	**setPixels** (int x, int y, int w, int h, ColorModel model, int[] pixels, int off, int scansize)	
	1	public	.... **void**	**setPixels** (int x, int y, int w, int h, ColorModel model, byte[] pixels, int off, int scansize)	
	1	public	....................void	setProperties (java.util.Hashtable props)	
		public	....................void	**substituteColorModel** (ColorModel oldcm, ColorModel newcm)	

R

Robot   java.awt

```
Object¹
└Robot
```
1.3

		public synchronized	..... java .awt.image.BufferedImage	**createScreenCapture** (Rectangle screenRect)	ε864
		public synchronized	.......void	**delay** (int ms)	
		public synchronized	.........int	**getAutoDelay** ()	
		public synchronized	..... Color	**getPixelColor** (int x, int y)	
		public synchronized	.. boolean	**isAutoWaitForIdle** ()	
		public synchronized	......void	**keyPress** (int keycode)	ε635
		public synchronized	......void	**keyRelease** (int keycode)	ε635
		public synchronized	......void	**mouseMove** (int x, int y)	ε634
		public synchronized	......void	**mousePress** (int buttons)	ε635
		public synchronized	......void	**mouseRelease** (int buttons)	ε635
1.4		public synchronized	......void	**mouseWheel** (int wheelAmt)	
	*	public	....	**Robot** () throws AWTException	ε634,635,864
	*	public	....	**Robot** (GraphicsDevice screen) throws AWTException	
		public synchronized	......void	**setAutoDelay** (int ms)	
		public synchronized	......void	**setAutoWaitForIdle** (boolean isOn)	
	1	public synchronized	.... **String**	**toString** ()	
		public synchronized	.......void	**waitForIdle** ()	

Classes

RobotPeer   java.awt.peer

1.3   *RobotPeer*

public	...................int	**getRGBPixel** (int x, int y)
public	...................int[]	**getRGBPixels** (java.awt.Rectangle bounds)
public	...................void	**keyPress** (int keycode)
public	...................void	**keyRelease** (int keycode)
public	...................void	**mouseMove** (int x, int y)
public	...................void	**mousePress** (int buttons)
public	...................void	**mouseRelease** (int buttons)

1.4   public.....................void **mouseWheel** (int wheelAmt)

RootPaneContainer   javax.swing

1.2   *RootPaneContainer*

public.......java.awt.Container **getContentPane** ()		ε732,733,816,841,887

public.......java.awt.Container **getContentPane** ()
public.... java.awt.Component **getGlassPane** ()
public.............. JLayeredPane **getLayeredPane** ()
public.............. JRootPane **getRootPane** ()
public.....................void **setContentPane** (java.awt.Container contentPane)
public.....................void **setGlassPane** (java.awt.Component glassPane)
public.....................void **setLayeredPane** (JLayeredPane layeredPane)

RootPaneUI   javax.swing.plaf

     Object
1.2 O   └ ComponentUI [1]
1.3 O   └ RootPaneUI

    [1] *11 inherited members from ComponentUI not shown*
*   public........................ **RootPaneUI** ()

RoundRectangle2D   java.awt.geom

     Object   ε572
1.2 O   └ RectangularShape [1] - - - - - - - - - - - - - - - - - - - *java.awt.Shape* [2], *Cloneable*
1.2 O   └ RoundRectangle2D

	[1]	public....................Object	clone ()
	[1]	public.................. boolean	contains (Point2D p)
	[1]	public.................. boolean	contains (Rectangle2D r)
	[2]	public.................. boolean	**contains** (double x, double y)
	[2]	public.................. boolean	**contains** (double x, double y, double w, double h)
O		public abstract..........double	**getArcHeight** ()
O		public abstract..........double	**getArcWidth** ()
	[1]	public...... java.awt.Rectangle	getBounds ()
O	[2]	public abstract ...Rectangle2D	getBounds2D ()
	[1]	public....................double	getCenterX ()
	[1]	public....................double	getCenterY ()
	[1]	public............. Rectangle2D	getFrame ()
O	[1]	public abstract ....double	getHeight ()
	[1]	public....................double	getMaxX ()
	[1]	public....................double	getMaxY ()
	[1]	public....................double	getMinX ()
	[1]	public....................double	getMinY ()
	[2]	public.............. *PathIterator*	**getPathIterator** (AffineTransform at)
	[1]	public.............. *PathIterator*	getPathIterator (AffineTransform at, double flatness)
O	[1]	public abstract..........double	getWidth ()
O	[1]	public abstract..........double	getX ()
O	[1]	public abstract..........double	getY ()
	[1]	public.................. boolean	intersects (Rectangle2D r)
	[2]	public.................. boolean	**intersects** (double x, double y, double w, double h)
O	[1]	public abstract .... boolean	isEmpty ()
*		protected......................	**RoundRectangle2D** ()
	[1]	public....................void	setFrame (Rectangle2D r)
	[1]	public....................void	setFrame (Point2D loc, Dimension2D size)
	[1]	public.......... **void setFrame**	(double x, double y, double w, double h)
	[1]	public....................void	setFrameFromCenter (Point2D center, Point2D corner)
	[1]	public....................void	setFrameFromCenter (double centerX, double centerY, double cornerX, double cornerY)
	[1]	public....................void	setFrameFromDiagonal (Point2D p1, Point2D p2)
	[1]	public....................void	setFrameFromDiagonal (double x1, double y1, double x2, double y2)
		public....................void	**setRoundRect** (RoundRectangle2D rr)
O		public abstract ....void	**setRoundRect** (double x, double y, double w, double h, double arcWidth, double arcHeight)

ε826 (appears to the right of getWidth/getX/getY rows)

Class   *Interface*   —extends   - - -implements   O abstract   ● final   △ static   ▲ static final   * constructor   x x—inherited   x **x**—declared   **x x**—overridden
ε*n*—examples of usage   ⌐—has subclass   package—see other volume

		RoundRectangle2D.Double	java.awt.geom

ε572

```
        Object
1.2 ○   └ RectangularShape 1 -------------------- java.awt.Shape 3, Cloneable ⌐
1.2 ○       └ RoundRectangle2D 2
1.2           └ RoundRectangle2D.Double
```

	public..................double	**archeight**	
	public..................double	**arcwidth**	
1	public..................Object	clone ()	
1	public.................boolean	contains (Point2D p)	
1	public.................boolean	contains (Rectangle2D r)	
2	public.................boolean	contains (double x, double y)	
2	public.................boolean	contains (double x, double y, double w, double h)	
∗	public.........................	**RoundRectangle2D.Double** ()	
∗	public.........................	**RoundRectangle2D.Double** (double x, double y, double w, double h, double arcw, double arch)	
2	public............... **double**	**getArcHeight** ()	
2	public............... **double**	**getArcWidth** ()	
1	public...... java.awt.Rectangle	getBounds ()	
3	public............Rectangle2D	**getBounds2D** ()	
1	public..................double	getCenterX ()	
1	public..................double	getCenterY ()	
1	public...........Rectangle2D	getFrame ()	
1	public........... **double**	**getHeight** ()	
1	public..................double	getMaxX ()	
1	public..................double	getMaxY ()	
1	public..................double	getMinX ()	
1	public..................double	getMinY ()	
2	public............*PathIterator*	getPathIterator (AffineTransform at)	
1	public............*PathIterator*	getPathIterator (AffineTransform at, double flatness)	ε826
1	public........... **double**	**getWidth** ()	
1	public........... **double**	**getX** ()	
1	public........... **double**	**getY** ()	
	public..................double	**height**	
1	public.................boolean	intersects (Rectangle2D r)	
2	public.................boolean	intersects (double x, double y, double w, double h)	
1	public........... **boolean**	**isEmpty** ()	
1	public..................void	setFrame (Rectangle2D r)	
1	public..................void	setFrame (Point2D loc, Dimension2D size)	
2	public..................void	setFrame (double x, double y, double w, double h)	
1	public..................void	setFrameFromCenter (Point2D center, Point2D corner)	
1	public..................void	setFrameFromCenter (double centerX, double centerY, double cornerX, double cornerY)	
1	public..................void	setFrameFromDiagonal (Point2D p1, Point2D p2)	
1	public..................void	setFrameFromDiagonal (double x1, double y1, double x2, double y2)	
2	public........... **void**	**setRoundRect** (RoundRectangle2D rr)	
2	public........... **void**	**setRoundRect** (double x, double y, double w, double h, double arcw, double arch)	
	public..................double	**width**	
	public..................double	**x**	
	public..................double	**y**	

		RoundRectangle2D.Float	java.awt.geom

ε572

```
        Object
1.2 ○   └ RectangularShape 1 -------------------- java.awt.Shape 3, Cloneable ⌐
1.2 ○       └ RoundRectangle2D 2
1.2           └ RoundRectangle2D.Float
```

	public.....................float	**archeight**	
	public.....................float	**arcwidth**	
1	public..................Object	clone ()	
1	public.................boolean	contains (Point2D p)	
1	public.................boolean	contains (Rectangle2D r)	
2	public.................boolean	contains (double x, double y)	
2	public.................boolean	contains (double x, double y, double w, double h)	
∗	public.........................	**RoundRectangle2D.Float** ()	
∗	public.........................	**RoundRectangle2D.Float** (float x, float y, float w, float h, float arcw, float arch)	
			ε656
2	public........... **double**	**getArcHeight** ()	
2	public........... **double**	**getArcWidth** ()	
1	public...... java.awt.Rectangle	getBounds ()	

R

RoundRectangle2D.Float

3	public	Rectangle2D	**getBounds2D** ()		
1	public	double	getCenterX ()		
1	public	double	getCenterY ()		
1	public	Rectangle2D	getFrame ()		
1	public	**double**	**getHeight** ()		
1	public	double	getMaxX ()		
1	public	double	getMaxY ()		
1	public	double	getMinX ()		
1	public	double	getMinY ()		
2	public	*PathIterator*	getPathIterator (AffineTransform at)		
1	public	*PathIterator*	getPathIterator (AffineTransform at, double flatness)		
1	public	**double**	**getWidth** ()		ε826
1	public	**double**	**getX** ()		
1	public	**double**	**getY** ()		
	public	float	**height**		
1	public	boolean	intersects (Rectangle2D r)		
2	public	boolean	intersects (double x, double y, double w, double h)		
1	public	**boolean**	**isEmpty** ()		
1	public	void	setFrame (Rectangle2D r)		
1	public	void	setFrame (Point2D loc, Dimension2D size)		
2	public	void	setFrame (double x, double y, double w, double h)		
1	public	void	setFrameFromCenter (Point2D center, Point2D corner)		
1	public	void	setFrameFromCenter (double centerX, double centerY, double cornerX, double cornerY)		
1	public	void	setFrameFromDiagonal (Point2D p1, Point2D p2)		
1	public	void	setFrameFromDiagonal (double x1, double y1, double x2, double y2)		
2	public	**void**	**setRoundRect** (RoundRectangle2D rr)		
2	public	**void**	**setRoundRect** (double x, double y, double w, double h, double arcw, double arch)		
	public	void	**setRoundRect** (float x, float y, float w, float h, float arcw, float arch)		
	public	float	**width**		
	public	float	**x**		
	public	float	**y**		

R

RowMapper
javax.swing.tree

1.2	*RowMapper*		
	public	int[]	**getRowsForPaths** (TreePath[] path)

RTFEditorKit
javax.swing.text.rtf

```
      Object
1.2 O └ javax.swing.text.EditorKit - - - - - - - - - - - - - - - - - Cloneable , java.io.Serializable
1.2        └ javax.swing.text.DefaultEditorKit 1
1.2           └ javax.swing.text.StyledEditorKit 2
1.2              └ RTFEditorKit
```

1	*48 inherited members from javax.swing.text.DefaultEditorKit not shown*				
2	public	Object	clone ()		
2	public		createDefaultDocument ()		ε1017
	.. javax.swing.text.Document				
2	protected	void	createInputAttributes (*javax.swing.text.Element* element, *javax.swing.text.MutableAttributeSet* set)		
2	public	void	deinstall (javax.swing.JEditorPane c)		
2	public	*javax.swing.Action[]*	getActions ()		
2	public		getCharacterAttributeRun ()		
	..... javax.swing.text.Element				
1	public	**String**	**getContentType** ()		
2	public	*javax.swing .text.MutableAttributeSet*	getInputAttributes ()		
2	public	*javax.swing.text.ViewFactory*	getViewFactory ()		
2	public	void	install (javax.swing.JEditorPane c)		
1	public	**void**	**read** (java.io.InputStream in, *javax.swing.text.Document* doc, int pos) throws java.io.IOException, javax.swing.text.BadLocationException		
1	public	**void**	**read** (java.io.Reader in, *javax.swing.text.Document* doc, int pos) throws java.io.IOException, javax.swing.text.BadLocationException ε1017,1018		
✳	public		**RTFEditorKit** ()		

Class *Interface* —extends - - -implements ○ abstract ● final △ static ▲ static final ✳ constructor x x—inherited x **x**—declared **x x**—overridden
ε*n*—examples of usage —has subclass package—see other volume

1	public	**void write** (java.io.OutputStream out, *javax.swing.text.Document* doc, int pos, int len)	
		throws java.io.IOException, javax.swing.text.BadLocationException	
1	public	**void write** (java.io.Writer out, *javax.swing.text.Document* doc, int pos, int len)	
		throws java.io.IOException, javax.swing.text.BadLocationException	

SampleModel   java.awt.image

Object
  └SampleModel   ε668

1.2 ○

○	public abstract .. SampleModel	**createCompatibleSampleModel** (int w, int h)
○	public abstract ..... DataBuffer	**createDataBuffer** ()
○	public abstract .. SampleModel	**createSubsetSampleModel** (int[] bands)
	protected .... int	**dataType**
○	public abstract .... Object	**getDataElements** (int x, int y, Object obj, DataBuffer data)
	public .... Object	**getDataElements** (int x, int y, int w, int h, Object obj, DataBuffer data)
●	public final .... int	**getDataType** ()
●	public final .... int	**getHeight** ()
●	public final .... int	**getNumBands** ()
○	public abstract .... int	**getNumDataElements** ()
	public .... float[]	**getPixel** (int x, int y, float[] fArray, DataBuffer data)
	public .... double[]	**getPixel** (int x, int y, double[] dArray, DataBuffer data)
	public .... int[]	**getPixel** (int x, int y, int[] iArray, DataBuffer data)
	public .... double[]	**getPixels** (int x, int y, int w, int h, double[] dArray, DataBuffer data)
	public .... int[]	**getPixels** (int x, int y, int w, int h, int[] iArray, DataBuffer data)
	public .... float[]	**getPixels** (int x, int y, int w, int h, float[] fArray, DataBuffer data)
○	public abstract .... int	**getSample** (int x, int y, int b, DataBuffer data)
	public .... double	**getSampleDouble** (int x, int y, int b, DataBuffer data)
	public .... float	**getSampleFloat** (int x, int y, int b, DataBuffer data)
	public .... int[]	**getSamples** (int x, int y, int w, int h, int b, int[] iArray, DataBuffer data)
	public .... float[]	**getSamples** (int x, int y, int w, int h, int b, float[] fArray, DataBuffer data)
	public .... double[]	**getSamples** (int x, int y, int w, int h, int b, double[] dArray, DataBuffer data)
○	public abstract .... int[]	**getSampleSize** ()
○	public abstract .... int	**getSampleSize** (int band)
	public .... int	**getTransferType** ()
●	public final .... int	**getWidth** ()
	protected .... int	**height**
	protected .... int	**numBands**
*	public	**SampleModel** (int dataType, int w, int h, int numBands)
○	public abstract .... void	**setDataElements** (int x, int y, Object obj, DataBuffer data)
	public .... void	**setDataElements** (int x, int y, int w, int h, Object obj, DataBuffer data)
	public .... void	**setPixel** (int x, int y, float[] fArray, DataBuffer data)
	public .... void	**setPixel** (int x, int y, int[] iArray, DataBuffer data)
	public .... void	**setPixel** (int x, int y, double[] dArray, DataBuffer data)
	public .... void	**setPixels** (int x, int y, int w, int h, double[] dArray, DataBuffer data)
	public .... void	**setPixels** (int x, int y, int w, int h, float[] fArray, DataBuffer data)
	public .... void	**setPixels** (int x, int y, int w, int h, int[] iArray, DataBuffer data)
	public .... void	**setSample** (int x, int y, int b, double s, DataBuffer data)
○	public abstract .... void	**setSample** (int x, int y, int b, int s, DataBuffer data)
	public .... void	**setSample** (int x, int y, int b, float s, DataBuffer data)
	public .... void	**setSamples** (int x, int y, int w, int h, int b, float[] fArray, DataBuffer data)
	public .... void	**setSamples** (int x, int y, int w, int h, int b, double[] dArray, DataBuffer data)
	public .... void	**setSamples** (int x, int y, int w, int h, int b, int[] iArray, DataBuffer data)
	protected .... int	**width**

S

Classes

Scrollable   javax.swing

1.2 *Scrollable*

	public ...... java.awt.Dimension	**getPreferredScrollableViewportSize** ()	ε949
	public .... int	**getScrollableBlockIncrement** (java.awt.Rectangle visibleRect, int orientation, int direction)
	public .... boolean	**getScrollableTracksViewportHeight** ()
	public .... boolean	**getScrollableTracksViewportWidth** ()
	public .... int	**getScrollableUnitIncrement** (java.awt.Rectangle visibleRect, int orientation, int direction)

Scrollbar

Scrollbar　　　　　　　　　　　　　　　　　　　　　　　　　　　　　　　　java.awt

```
      Object
○     └Component¹ - - - - - - - - - - - - - - - - - - - - - - - java.awt.image.ImageObserver ², MenuContainer,
                                                    java.io.Serializable
           └Scrollbar - - - - - - - - - - - - - - - - - - - - Adjustable ³, javax.accessibility.Accessible
```

	1	*206 inherited members from Component not shown*	
	2	*8 inherited members from java.awt.image.ImageObserver not shown*	
1.1	3	public synchronized ....void **addAdjustmentListener** (*java.awt.event.AdjustmentListener* l)	ε822
1	1	public.....................**void addNotify** ()	
1.3	1	public.... **javax.accessibility₂ getAccessibleContext** ()	
		.AccessibleContext	
1.4		public synchronized . *java.awt₂* **getAdjustmentListeners** ()	
		.event.AdjustmentListener[]	
1.1	3	public.........................int **getBlockIncrement** ()	
D		public.........................int **getLineIncrement** ()	
1.3	1	public......................... **getListeners** (Class listenerType)	
		.... *java.util.EventListener[]*	
	3	public.........................int **getMaximum** ()	
	3	public.........................int **getMinimum** ()	
	3	public.........................int **getOrientation** ()	ε822
D		public.........................int **getPageIncrement** ()	
1.1	3	public.........................int **getUnitIncrement** ()	
	3	public.........................int **getValue** ()	
1.4		public.................. boolean **getValueIsAdjusting** ()	
D		public.........................int **getVisible** ()	
1.1	3	public.........................int **getVisibleAmount** ()	
▲	3	public static final ....int **HORIZONTAL** = 0	ε822
1.4 ▲	3	public static final ....int NO_ORIENTATION = 2	
	1	protected .... **String paramString** ()	
1.1		protected ....void **processAdjustmentEvent** (java.awt.event.AdjustmentEvent e)	
1.1	1	protected .... **void processEvent** (AWTEvent e)	
1.1	3	public synchronized ....void **removeAdjustmentListener** (*java.awt.event.AdjustmentListener* l)	
✳		public.......................... **Scrollbar** () throws HeadlessException	
✳		public.......................... **Scrollbar** (int orientation) throws HeadlessException	
✳		public.......................... **Scrollbar** (int orientation, int value, int visible, int minimum, int maximum)	
		throws HeadlessException	
1.1	3	public.........................void **setBlockIncrement** (int v)	
D		public synchronized ....void **setLineIncrement** (int v)	
1.1	3	public.........................void **setMaximum** (int newMaximum)	
1.1	3	public.........................void **setMinimum** (int newMinimum)	
1.1		public.........................void **setOrientation** (int orientation)	
D		public synchronized ....void **setPageIncrement** (int v)	
1.1	3	public.........................void **setUnitIncrement** (int v)	
	3	public.........................void **setValue** (int newValue)	
1.4		public.........................void **setValueIsAdjusting** (boolean b)	
		public.........................void **setValues** (int value, int visible, int minimum, int maximum)	
1.1	3	public.........................void **setVisibleAmount** (int newAmount)	
▲	3	public static final ....int **VERTICAL** = 1	

ScrollbarPeer　　　　　　　　　　　　　　　　　　　　　　　　　　　　　java.awt.peer

```
      ScrollbarPeer———————————————————ComponentPeer 1
```

	1	*42 inherited members from ComponentPeer not shown*
		public.........................void **setLineIncrement** (int l)
		public.........................void **setPageIncrement** (int l)
		public.........................void **setValues** (int value, int visible, int minimum, int maximum)

ScrollBarUI　　　　　　　　　　　　　　　　　　　　　　　　　　　　　javax.swing.plaf

```
      Object
1.2 ○ └ComponentUI¹
1.2 ○    └ScrollBarUI
```

	1	*11 inherited members from ComponentUI not shown*
✳		public.......................... **ScrollBarUI** ()

Class　*Interface*　—extends　- - -implements　○ abstract　● final　△ static　▲ static final　✳ constructor　x x—inherited　x **x**—declared　**x x**—overridden
ε*n*—examples of usage　˛—has subclass　package—see other volume

ScrollPane		java.awt

ε606,618,733,953,988

```
Object
 └─Component 1 ------------------------- java.awt.image.ImageObserver 3, MenuContainer,
                                          java.io.Serializable
        └─Container 2
           └─ScrollPane ----------------------- javax.accessibility.Accessible
```

	1		*175 inherited members from Component not shown*
	2		*60 inherited members from Container not shown*
	3		*8 inherited members from java.awt.image.ImageObserver not shown*
●	2	protected final .... **void**	**addImpl** (Component comp, Object constraints, int index)
	2	public .... **void**	**addNotify** ()
	2	public .... **void**	**doLayout** ()
1.4		protected .... boolean	**eventTypeEnabled** (int type)
1.3	1	public .... **javax.accessibility** ₂ .AccessibleContext	**getAccessibleContext** ()
		public .... *Adjustable*	**getHAdjustable** ()
		public .... int	**getHScrollbarHeight** ()
		public .... int	**getScrollbarDisplayPolicy** ()
		public .... Point	**getScrollPosition** ()
		public .... *Adjustable*	**getVAdjustable** ()
		public .... Dimension	**getViewportSize** ()
		public .... int	**getVScrollbarWidth** ()
1.4		public .... boolean	**isWheelScrollingEnabled** ()
D	2	public .... **void**	**layout** ()
	2	public .... **String**	**paramString** ()
	2	public .... **void**	**printComponents** (Graphics g)
1.4	1	protected .... **void**	**processMouseWheelEvent** (java.awt.event.MouseWheelEvent e)
▲		public static final .... int	**SCROLLBARS_ALWAYS** = 1
▲		public static final .... int	**SCROLLBARS_AS_NEEDED** = 0
▲		public static final .... int	**SCROLLBARS_NEVER** = 2
*		public	**ScrollPane** () throws HeadlessException
*		public	**ScrollPane** (int scrollbarDisplayPolicy) throws HeadlessException
●	2	public final .... **void**	**setLayout** (*LayoutManager* mgr) ε613,622,624,625,627
		public .... void	**setScrollPosition** (Point p)
		public .... void	**setScrollPosition** (int x, int y)
1.4		public .... void	**setWheelScrollingEnabled** (boolean handleWheel)

ScrollPaneAdjustable	java.awt

```
Object 1
1.4  └─ScrollPaneAdjustable ------------------- Adjustable 2, java.io.Serializable
```

	2	public synchronized .... void	**addAdjustmentListener** (java.awt.event.AdjustmentListener l) ε822
		public synchronized . java.awt ₂ .event.AdjustmentListener[]	**getAdjustmentListeners** ()
	2	public .... int	**getBlockIncrement** ()
	2	public .... int	**getMaximum** ()
	2	public .... int	**getMinimum** ()
	2	public .... int	**getOrientation** () ε822
	2	public .... int	**getUnitIncrement** ()
	2	public .... int	**getValue** ()
		public .... boolean	**getValueIsAdjusting** ()
	2	public .... int	**getVisibleAmount** ()
▲	2	public static final .... int	HORIZONTAL = 0 ε822
▲	2	public static final .... int	NO_ORIENTATION = 2
		public .... String	**paramString** ()
	2	public synchronized .... void	**removeAdjustmentListener** (java.awt.event.AdjustmentListener l)
	2	public synchronized ...... void	**setBlockIncrement** (int b)
	2	public .... void	**setMaximum** (int max)
	2	public .... void	**setMinimum** (int min)
	2	public synchronized ...... void	**setUnitIncrement** (int u)
	2	public .... void	**setValue** (int v)
		public .... void	**setValueIsAdjusting** (boolean b)
	2	public .... void	**setVisibleAmount** (int v)
	1	public .... **String**	**toString** ()
▲	2	public static final .... int	VERTICAL = 1

S

Classes

755

ScrollPaneConstants

ScrollPaneConstants			javax.swing

1.2			*ScrollPaneConstants*
▲	public static final	String	**COLUMN_HEADER** = "COLUMN_HEADER"
▲	public static final	String	**HORIZONTAL_SCROLLBAR** = "HORIZONTAL_SCROLLBAR"
▲	public static final	int	**HORIZONTAL_SCROLLBAR_ALWAYS** = 32 ε821
▲	public static final	int	**HORIZONTAL_SCROLLBAR_AS_NEEDED** = 30
▲	public static final	int	**HORIZONTAL_SCROLLBAR_NEVER** = 31 ε821
▲	public static final	String	**HORIZONTAL_SCROLLBAR_POLICY** = "HORIZONTAL_SCROLLBAR_POLICY"
1.3 ▲	public static final	String	**LOWER_LEADING_CORNER** = "LOWER_LEADING_CORNER"
▲	public static final	String	**LOWER_LEFT_CORNER** = "LOWER_LEFT_CORNER"
▲	public static final	String	**LOWER_RIGHT_CORNER** = "LOWER_RIGHT_CORNER"
1.3 ▲	public static final	String	**LOWER_TRAILING_CORNER** = "LOWER_TRAILING_CORNER"
▲	public static final	String	**ROW_HEADER** = "ROW_HEADER"
1.3 ▲	public static final	String	**UPPER_LEADING_CORNER** = "UPPER_LEADING_CORNER"
▲	public static final	String	**UPPER_LEFT_CORNER** = "UPPER_LEFT_CORNER"
▲	public static final	String	**UPPER_RIGHT_CORNER** = "UPPER_RIGHT_CORNER"
1.3 ▲	public static final	String	**UPPER_TRAILING_CORNER** = "UPPER_TRAILING_CORNER"
▲	public static final	String	**VERTICAL_SCROLLBAR** = "VERTICAL_SCROLLBAR"
▲	public static final	int	**VERTICAL_SCROLLBAR_ALWAYS** = 22
▲	public static final	int	**VERTICAL_SCROLLBAR_AS_NEEDED** = 20
▲	public static final	int	**VERTICAL_SCROLLBAR_NEVER** = 21 ε821
▲	public static final	String	**VERTICAL_SCROLLBAR_POLICY** = "VERTICAL_SCROLLBAR_POLICY"
▲	public static final	String	**VIEWPORT** = "VIEWPORT"

ScrollPaneLayout			javax.swing

1.2		Object

└ ScrollPaneLayout - *java.awt.LayoutManager* [1], *ScrollPaneConstants* [2],
                                                       java.io.Serializable

	2	*21 inherited members from ScrollPaneConstants not shown*	
	1	public .... void	**addLayoutComponent** (String s, java.awt.Component c)
		protected java.awt.Component	**addSingletonComponent** (java.awt.Component oldC, java.awt.Component newC)
		protected .... JViewport	**colHead**
		public .... JViewport	**getColumnHeader** ()
		public .... java.awt.Component	**getCorner** (String key)
		public .... JScrollBar	**getHorizontalScrollBar** ()
		public .... int	**getHorizontalScrollBarPolicy** ()
		public .... JViewport	**getRowHeader** ()
		public .... JScrollBar	**getVerticalScrollBar** ()
		public .... int	**getVerticalScrollBarPolicy** ()
		public .... JViewport	**getViewport** ()
D		public ...... java.awt.Rectangle	**getViewportBorderBounds** (JScrollPane scrollpane)
		protected .... JScrollBar	**hsb**
		protected .... int	**hsbPolicy**
	1	public .... void	**layoutContainer** (java.awt.Container parent) ε624,625
		protected java.awt.Component	**lowerLeft**
		protected java.awt.Component	**lowerRight**
	1	public ...... java.awt.Dimension	**minimumLayoutSize** (java.awt.Container parent)
	1	public ...... java.awt.Dimension	**preferredLayoutSize** (java.awt.Container parent)
	1	public .... void	**removeLayoutComponent** (java.awt.Component c)
		protected .... JViewport	**rowHead**
*		public	**ScrollPaneLayout** ()
		public .... void	**setHorizontalScrollBarPolicy** (int x)
		public .... void	**setVerticalScrollBarPolicy** (int x)
		public .... void	**syncWithScrollPane** (JScrollPane sp)
		protected java.awt.Component	**upperLeft**
		protected java.awt.Component	**upperRight**
		protected .... JViewport	**viewport**
		protected .... JScrollBar	**vsb**
		protected .... int	**vsbPolicy**

Class   *Interface*   —extends   - - -implements   ○ abstract   ● final   △ static   ▲ static final   ✳ constructor   x x—inherited   x **x**—declared   **x x**—overridden
ε*n*—examples of usage   ‿—has subclass   package—see other volume

756

ScrollPaneLayout.UIResource	javax.swing

	Object	
1.2	└ScrollPaneLayout[1] - *java.awt.LayoutManager*, *ScrollPaneConstants*[2],	
	java.io.Serializable	
1.2	└ScrollPaneLayout.UIResource - - - - - - - - - - *javax.swing.plaf.UIResource*	

1	*29 inherited members from ScrollPaneLayout not shown*
2	*21 inherited members from ScrollPaneConstants not shown*
*	public.......................... **ScrollPaneLayout.UIResource** ()

ScrollPanePeer	java.awt.peer

1.1	*ScrollPanePeer*——————————————*ContainerPeer*, [1] (*ComponentPeer* [2])

2	*42 inherited members from ComponentPeer not shown*
1	*7 inherited members from ContainerPeer not shown*
	public.......................void **childResized** (int w, int h)
	public..........................int **getHScrollbarHeight** ()
	public..........................int **getVScrollbarWidth** ()
	public.......................void **setScrollPosition** (int x, int y)
	public.......................void **setUnitIncrement** (*java.awt.Adjustable* adj, int u)
	public.......................void **setValue** (*java.awt.Adjustable* adj, int v)

ScrollPaneUI	javax.swing.plaf

	Object	
1.2 ○	└ComponentUI[1]	
1.2 ○	└ScrollPaneUI	

1	*11 inherited members from ComponentUI not shown*
*	public.......................... **ScrollPaneUI** ()

Segment	javax.swing.text

	Object[1]	
1.2	└Segment - *Cloneable*, *java.text.CharacterIterator*, [2] (*Cloneable*)	

		public.....................char[] **array**	ε969
	1	public.....................**Object** **clone** ()	
		public..........................int **count**	ε969
1.3	2	public..................... char **current** ()	
▲	2	public static final .... char DONE = '?'	
1.3	2	public..................... char **first** ()	ε969
1.3	2	public..........................int **getBeginIndex** ()	
1.3	2	public..........................int **getEndIndex** ()	
1.3	2	public..........................int **getIndex** ()	
1.4		public................... boolean **isPartialReturn** ()	
1.3	2	public..................... char **last** ()	
1.3	2	public..................... char **next** ()	ε969
		public..........................int **offset**	ε969
1.3	2	public..................... char **previous** ()	
*		public................... **Segment** ()	ε969
*		public................... **Segment** (char[] array, int offset, int count)	
1.3	2	public..................... char **setIndex** (int position)	
1.4		public.......................void **setPartialReturn** (boolean p)	ε969
	1	public................... **String** **toString** ()	

SeparatorUI	javax.swing.plaf

	Object	
1.2 ○	└ComponentUI[1]	
1.2 ○	└SeparatorUI	

1	*11 inherited members from ComponentUI not shown*
*	public.......................... **SeparatorUI** ()

S

Classes

Sequence

		Sequence		javax.sound.midi
		Object		ε716
1.3		└Sequence		

	public	Track	**createTrack** ()	
	public	boolean	**deleteTrack** (Track track)	
	protected	float	**divisionType**	
	public	float	**getDivisionType** ()	
	public	long	**getMicrosecondLength** ()	
	public	Patch[]	**getPatchList** ()	
	public	int	**getResolution** ()	
	public	long	**getTickLength** ()	
	public	Track[]	**getTracks** ()	
▲	public static final	float	**PPQ** = 0.0	
	protected	int	**resolution**	
✳	public		**Sequence** (float divisionType, int resolution) throws InvalidMidiDataException	
✳	public		**Sequence** (float divisionType, int resolution, int numTracks) throws InvalidMidiDataException	
▲	public static final	float	**SMPTE_24** = 24.0	
▲	public static final	float	**SMPTE_25** = 25.0	
▲	public static final	float	**SMPTE_30** = 30.0	
▲	public static final	float	**SMPTE_30DROP** = 29.97	
	protected	java.util.Vector	**tracks**	

		Sequencer		javax.sound.midi
1.3		Sequencer————————————MidiDevice [1]		

	public	int[]	**addControllerEventListener** (*ControllerEventListener* listener, int[] controllers)	
	public	boolean	**addMetaEventListener** (*MetaEventListener* listener)	ε722
[1]	public	void	close ()	
[1]	public	MidiDevice.Info	getDeviceInfo ()	
	public	Sequencer.SyncMode	**getMasterSyncMode** ()	
	public	Sequencer.SyncMode[]	**getMasterSyncModes** ()	
[1]	public	int	getMaxReceivers ()	
[1]	public	int	getMaxTransmitters ()	
	public	long	**getMicrosecondLength** ()	ε719
[1]	public	long	**getMicrosecondPosition** ()	ε720
[1]	public	*Receiver*	getReceiver () throws MidiUnavailableException	
	public	Sequence	**getSequence** ()	
	public	Sequencer.SyncMode	**getSlaveSyncMode** ()	
	public	Sequencer.SyncMode[]	**getSlaveSyncModes** ()	
	public	float	**getTempoFactor** ()	
	public	float	**getTempoInBPM** ()	
	public	float	**getTempoInMPQ** ()	
	public	long	**getTickLength** ()	
	public	long	**getTickPosition** ()	
	public	boolean	**getTrackMute** (int track)	
	public	boolean	**getTrackSolo** (int track)	
[1]	public	*Transmitter*	getTransmitter () throws MidiUnavailableException	
[1]	public	boolean	isOpen ()	
	public	boolean	**isRecording** ()	
	public	boolean	**isRunning** ()	
[1]	public	void	open () throws MidiUnavailableException	ε716,717
	public	void	**recordDisable** (Track track)	
	public	void	**recordEnable** (Track track, int channel)	
	public	int[]	**removeControllerEventListener** (*ControllerEventListener* listener, int[] controllers)	
	public	void	**removeMetaEventListener** (*MetaEventListener* listener)	
	public	void	**setMasterSyncMode** (Sequencer.SyncMode sync)	
	public	void	**setMicrosecondPosition** (long microseconds)	
	public	void	**setSequence** (java.io.InputStream stream) throws java.io.IOException, InvalidMidiDataException	ε717
	public	void	**setSequence** (Sequence sequence) throws InvalidMidiDataException	ε716
	public	void	**setSlaveSyncMode** (Sequencer.SyncMode sync)	
	public	void	**setTempoFactor** (float factor)	
	public	void	**setTempoInBPM** (float bpm)	
	public	void	**setTempoInMPQ** (float mpq)	
	public	void	**setTickPosition** (long tick)	

S

Class   *Interface*   —extends   - - -implements   ○ abstract   ● final   △ static   ▲ static final   ✳ constructor   x x—inherited   x **x**—declared   **x x**—overridden
ε*n*—examples of usage   ┌—has subclass   package —see other volume

public.....................void	**setTrackMute** (int track, boolean mute)	
public.....................void	**setTrackSolo** (int track, boolean solo)	
public.....................void	**start** ()	*ε*716,717
public.....................void	**startRecording** ()	
public.....................void	**stop** ()	
public.....................void	**stopRecording** ()	

Sequencer.SyncMode   javax.sound.midi

Object[1]
1.3   └ Sequencer.SyncMode

● 1	public final .... **boolean**	**equals** (Object obj)
● 1	public final .... **int**	**hashCode** ()
▲	public static final.............. ....Sequencer.SyncMode	**INTERNAL_CLOCK**
▲	public static final.............. ....Sequencer.SyncMode	**MIDI_SYNC**
▲	public static final.............. ....Sequencer.SyncMode	**MIDI_TIME_CODE**
▲	public static final.............. ....Sequencer.SyncMode	**NO_SYNC**
*	protected....................	**Sequencer.SyncMode** (String name)
● 1	public final .... **String**	**toString** ()

ServiceRegistry   javax.imageio.spi

Object[1]
1.4   └ ServiceRegistry

	public................. boolean	**contains** (Object provider)
	public.....................void	**deregisterAll** ()
	public.....................void	**deregisterAll** (Class category)
	public.....................void	**deregisterServiceProvider** (Object provider)
	public................. boolean	**deregisterServiceProvider** (Object provider, Class category)
1	public..................... **void**	**finalize** () throws Throwable
	public.........*java.util*.Iterator	**getCategories** ()
	public...................Object	**getServiceProviderByClass** (Class providerClass)
	public.........*java.util*.Iterator	**getServiceProviders** (Class category, boolean useOrdering)
	public.........*java.util*.Iterator	**getServiceProviders** (Class category, *ServiceRegistry.Filter* filter, boolean useOrdering)
△	public static ... *java.util*.Iterator	**lookupProviders** (Class providerClass)
△	public static ... *java.util*.Iterator	**lookupProviders** (Class providerClass, ClassLoader loader)
	public.....................void	**registerServiceProvider** (Object provider)
	public................. boolean	**registerServiceProvider** (Object provider, Class category)
	public.....................void	**registerServiceProviders** (*java.util*.Iterator providers)
*	public......................	**ServiceRegistry** (*java.util*.Iterator categories)
	public................. boolean	**setOrdering** (Class category, Object firstProvider, Object secondProvider)
	public................. boolean	**unsetOrdering** (Class category, Object firstProvider, Object secondProvider)

ServiceRegistry.Filter   javax.imageio.spi

1.4   *ServiceRegistry.Filter*

	public................. boolean	**filter** (Object provider)

ServiceUI   javax.print

Object
1.4   └ ServiceUI

△	public static .... *PrintService*	**printDialog** (java.awt.GraphicsConfiguration gc, int x, int y, *PrintService[]* services, *PrintService* defaultService, DocFlavor flavor, *javax.print.attribute* .*PrintRequestAttributeSet* attributes) throws java.awt.HeadlessException
*	public......................	**ServiceUI** ()

S

Classes

ServiceUIFactory

		ServiceUIFactory	javax.print

Object
1.4 O └ ServiceUIFactory

▲	public static final	int	**ABOUT_UIROLE** = 1
▲	public static final	int	**ADMIN_UIROLE** = 2
▲	public static final	String	**DIALOG_UI** = "java.awt.Dialog"
O	public abstract	Object	**getUI** (int role, String ui)
O	public abstract	String[]	**getUIClassNamesForRole** (int role)
▲	public static final	String	**JCOMPONENT_UI** = "javax.swing.JComponent"
▲	public static final	String	**JDIALOG_UI** = "javax.swing.JDialog"
▲	public static final	int	**MAIN_UIROLE** = 3
▲	public static final	String	**PANEL_UI** = "java.awt.Panel"
▲	public static final	int	**RESERVED_UIROLE** = 99
✳	public		**ServiceUIFactory** ()

	SetOfIntegerSyntax		javax.print.attribute

Object [1]
1.4 O └ SetOfIntegerSyntax - *java.io.Serializable*, *Cloneable*

	public	boolean	**contains** (int x)
	public	boolean	**contains** (IntegerSyntax attribute)
1	public	**boolean**	**equals** (Object object)
	public	int[][]	**getMembers** ()
1	public	**int**	**hashCode** ()
	public	int	**next** (int x)
✳	protected		**SetOfIntegerSyntax** (int member)
✳	protected		**SetOfIntegerSyntax** (int[][] members)
✳	protected		**SetOfIntegerSyntax** (String members)
✳	protected		**SetOfIntegerSyntax** (int lowerBound, int upperBound)
1	public	**String**	**toString** ()

	Severity		javax.print.attribute.standard

Object
1.4 O └ javax.print.attribute.EnumSyntax [1] - - - - - - - - - *java.io.Serializable*, *Cloneable*
1.4 ● └ Severity - *javax.print.attribute.Attribute* [2] (*java.io.Serializable*)

	1	public	Object	clone ()
▲		public static final	Severity	**ERROR**
●	2	public final	Class	**getCategory** ()	ε707
	1	protected	**javax.print** [2] **.attribute.EnumSyntax[]**	**getEnumValueTable** ()
●	2	public final	String	**getName** ()	ε706,707,708
	1	protected	int	getOffset ()
	1	protected	**String[]**	**getStringTable** ()
	1	public	int	getValue ()
	1	public	int	hashCode ()
	1	protected	Object	readResolve () throws java.io.ObjectStreamException
▲		public static final	Severity	**REPORT**
✳		protected		**Severity** (int value)
	1	public	String	toString ()
▲		public static final	Severity	**WARNING**

	Shape		java.awt

1.1 *Shape* ε578,588,656,659

1.2	public	boolean	**contains** (java.awt.geom.Point2D p)
1.2	public	boolean	**contains** (java.awt.geom.Rectangle2D r)
1.2	public	boolean	**contains** (double x, double y)
1.2	public	boolean	**contains** (double x, double y, double w, double h)
	public	Rectangle	**getBounds** ()
1.2	public	. java.awt.geom.Rectangle2D	**getBounds2D** ()

Class *Interface* —extends - - -implements O abstract ● final △ static ▲ static final ✳ constructor x x—inherited x **x**—declared **x x**—overridden
ε*n*—examples of usage ‿—has subclass package—see other volume

1.2	public	**getPathIterator** (java.awt.geom.AffineTransform at)	
	...*java.awt.geom.PathIterator*		
1.2	public	**getPathIterator** (java.awt.geom.AffineTransform at, double flatness)	
	...*java.awt.geom.PathIterator*		
1.2	public .... boolean	**intersects** (java.awt.geom.Rectangle2D r)	
1.2	public .... boolean	**intersects** (double x, double y, double w, double h)	

ShapeGraphicAttribute `java.awt.font`

Object[1]
1.2 ○ └GraphicAttribute[2]
1.2 ● └ShapeGraphicAttribute

▲ 2	public static final ....int	BOTTOM_ALIGNMENT = -2	
▲ 2	public static final ....int	CENTER_BASELINE = 1	
2	public .... **void**	**draw** (java.awt.Graphics2D graphics, float x, float y)	
	public .... boolean	**equals** (ShapeGraphicAttribute rhs)	
1	public ....**boolean**	**equals** (Object rhs)	
▲	public static final ..... boolean	**FILL** = false	
2	public .... **float**	**getAdvance** ()	
● 2	public final ....int	getAlignment ()	
2	public .... **float**	**getAscent** ()	
2	public .... **java**₂	**getBounds** ()	
	.awt.geom.Rectangle2D		
2	public .... **float**	**getDescent** ()	
2	public... GlyphJustificationInfo	getJustificationInfo ()	
▲ 2	public static final ....int	HANGING_BASELINE = 2	
1	public .... **int**	**hashCode** ()	
▲ 2	public static final ....int	ROMAN_BASELINE = 0	
✳	public	**ShapeGraphicAttribute** (*java.awt.Shape* shape, int alignment, boolean stroke)	
▲	public static final ..... boolean	**STROKE** = true	
▲ 2	public static final ....int	TOP_ALIGNMENT = -1	

SheetCollate `javax.print.attribute.standard`

Object
1.4 ○ └javax.print.attribute.EnumSyntax[1] --------- *java.io.Serializable*, *Cloneable*
1.4 ● └SheetCollate ---------------------- *javax.print.attribute.DocAttribute (javax.print.attribute.Attribute[2]*
   (*java.io.Serializable*)), *javax.print.attribute.PrintRequestAttribute*
   (*javax.print.attribute.Attribute[2]* (*java.io.Serializable*)),
   javax.print.attribute.PrintJobAttribute
   (*javax.print.attribute.Attribute[2]* (*java.io.Serializable*))

1	public .... Object	clone ()	
▲	public static final . SheetCollate	**COLLATED**	
● 2	public final .... Class	**getCategory** ()	ε707
1	protected .... **javax.print**₂	**getEnumValueTable** ()	
	.attribute.EnumSyntax[]		
● 2	public final .... String	**getName** ()	ε706,707,708
1	protected ....int	getOffset ()	
1	protected .... **String[]**	**getStringTable** ()	
1	public ....int	getValue ()	
1	public ....int	hashCode ()	
1	protected .... Object	readResolve () throws java.io.ObjectStreamException	
✳	protected	**SheetCollate** (int value)	
1	public .... String	toString ()	
▲	public static final . SheetCollate	**UNCOLLATED**	

ShortLookupTable `java.awt.image`

Object
1.2 ○ └LookupTable[1]
1.2 └ShortLookupTable

1	public ....int	getNumComponents ()	
1	public ....int	getOffset ()	
●	public final .... short[][]	**getTable** ()	
1	public ....**int[]**	**lookupPixel** (int[] src, int[] dst)	
	public .... short[]	**lookupPixel** (short[] src, short[] dst)	
✳	public	**ShortLookupTable** (int offset, short[] data)	

ShortLookupTable

✱	public	**ShortLookupTable** (int offset, short[][] data)	

ShortMessage `javax.sound.midi`

```
Object
1.3 ○   └─MidiMessage ¹ ------------------------- Cloneable ⌄
1.3         └─ShortMessage
```

▲	public static final	int	**ACTIVE_SENSING** = 254
▲	public static final	int	**CHANNEL_PRESSURE** = 208
1	public	**Object**	**clone** ()
▲	public static final	int	**CONTINUE** = 251
▲	public static final	int	**CONTROL_CHANGE** = 176
1	protected	byte[]	data
▲	public static final	int	**END_OF_EXCLUSIVE** = 247
	public	int	**getChannel** ()
	public	int	**getCommand** ()
	public	int	**getData1** ()
	public	int	**getData2** ()
●	protected final	int	**getDataLength** (int status) throws InvalidMidiDataException
1	public	int	getLength ()
1	public	byte[]	getMessage ()
1	public	int	getStatus ()
1	protected	int	length
▲	public static final	int	**MIDI_TIME_CODE** = 241
▲	public static final	int	**NOTE_OFF** = 128
▲	public static final	int	**NOTE_ON** = 144
▲	public static final	int	**PITCH_BEND** = 224
▲	public static final	int	**POLY_PRESSURE** = 160
▲	public static final	int	**PROGRAM_CHANGE** = 192
	public	void	**setMessage** (int status) throws InvalidMidiDataException
1	protected	void	setMessage (byte[] data, int length) throws InvalidMidiDataException
	public	void	**setMessage** (int status, int data1, int data2) throws InvalidMidiDataException
	public	void	**setMessage** (int command, int channel, int data1, int data2) throws InvalidMidiDataException
✱	public		**ShortMessage** ()
✱	protected		**ShortMessage** (byte[] data)
▲	public static final	int	**SONG_POSITION_POINTER** = 242
▲	public static final	int	**SONG_SELECT** = 243
▲	public static final	int	**START** = 250
▲	public static final	int	**STOP** = 252
▲	public static final	int	**SYSTEM_RESET** = 255
▲	public static final	int	**TIMING_CLOCK** = 248
▲	public static final	int	**TUNE_REQUEST** = 246

Sides `javax.print.attribute.standard`

```
Object
1.4 ○   └─javax.print.attribute.EnumSyntax ¹ --------- java.io.Serializable ⌄, Cloneable ⌄
1.4 ●       └─Sides ------------------------------- javax.print.attribute.DocAttribute (javax.print.attribute.Attribute ²
                                                   (java.io.Serializable)), javax.print.attribute.PrintRequestAttribute
                                                   (javax.print.attribute.Attribute ² (java.io.Serializable)),
                                                   javax.print.attribute.PrintJobAttribute
                                                   (javax.print.attribute.Attribute ² (java.io.Serializable))
```

1	public	Object	clone ()	
▲	public static final	Sides	**DUPLEX**	
● 2	public final	Class	**getCategory** ()	ε707
1	protected	**javax.print ⌄ .attribute.EnumSyntax[]**	**getEnumValueTable** ()	
● 2	public final	String	**getName** ()	ε706,707,708
1	protected	int	getOffset ()	
1	protected	**String[]**	**getStringTable** ()	
1	public	int	getValue ()	
1	public	int	hashCode ()	
▲	public static final	Sides	**ONE_SIDED**	
1	protected	Object	readResolve () throws java.io.ObjectStreamException	
✱	protected		**Sides** (int value)	

Class *Interface* —extends - - -implements ○ abstract ● final △ static ▲ static final ✱ constructor   x x—inherited   x **x**—declared   **x x**—overridden
ε*n*—examples of usage ⌄—has subclass package—see other volume

1	public	String	**toString** ()
▲	public static final	Sides	**TUMBLE**
▲	public static final	Sides	**TWO_SIDED_LONG_EDGE**
▲	public static final	Sides	**TWO_SIDED_SHORT_EDGE**

SimpleAttributeSet   javax.swing.text

Object[1]
1.2 └ SimpleAttributeSet - *MutableAttributeSet*[2] (*AttributeSet*[3]), *java.io.Serializable*,
                                                                  Cloneable

2	public	void	**addAttribute** (Object name, Object value)
2	public	void	**addAttributes** (*AttributeSet* attributes)
1	public	**Object**	**clone** ()
3	public	boolean	**containsAttribute** (Object name, Object value)
3	public	boolean	**containsAttributes** (*AttributeSet* attributes)
3	public	*AttributeSet*	**copyAttributes** ()
▲	public static final	*AttributeSet*	**EMPTY**
1	public	**boolean**	**equals** (Object obj)
3	public	Object	**getAttribute** (Object name) ε1017,1010,1013
3	public	int	**getAttributeCount** () ε1010
3	public	*java.util.Enumeration*	**getAttributeNames** () ε1010
3	public	*AttributeSet*	**getResolveParent** ()
1	public	**int**	**hashCode** ()
3	public	boolean	**isDefined** (Object attrName)
	public	boolean	**isEmpty** ()
3	public	boolean	**isEqual** (*AttributeSet* attr)
▲ 3	public static final	Object	NameAttribute
2	public	void	**removeAttribute** (Object name)
2	public	void	**removeAttributes** (*java.util.Enumeration* names)
2	public	void	**removeAttributes** (*AttributeSet* attributes)
▲ 3	public static final	Object	ResolveAttribute
2	public	void	**setResolveParent** (*AttributeSet* parent)
*	public		**SimpleAttributeSet** ()
*	public		**SimpleAttributeSet** (*AttributeSet* source)
1	public	**String**	**toString** ()

SimpleDoc   javax.print

Object
1.4 ● └ SimpleDoc - *Doc*[1]

1	public	*javax.print.attribute.DocAttributeSet*	**getAttributes** ()
1	public	DocFlavor	**getDocFlavor** ()
1	public	Object	**getPrintData** () throws java.io.IOException
1	public	java.io.Reader	**getReaderForText** () throws java.io.IOException
1	public	java.io.InputStream	**getStreamForBytes** () throws java.io.IOException
*	public		**SimpleDoc** (Object printData, DocFlavor flavor, *javax.print.attribute.DocAttributeSet* attributes) ε700,701,702,705

SinglePixelPackedSampleModel   java.awt.image
ε668

Object[1]
1.2 ○ └ SampleModel[2]
1.2   └ SinglePixelPackedSampleModel

2	*27 inherited members from SampleModel not shown*		
2	public	**SampleModel**	**createCompatibleSampleModel** (int w, int h)
2	public	**DataBuffer**	**createDataBuffer** ()
2	public	**SampleModel**	**createSubsetSampleModel** (int[] bands)
1	public	**boolean**	**equals** (Object o)
	public	int[]	**getBitMasks** ()
	public	int[]	**getBitOffsets** ()
2	public	**Object**	**getDataElements** (int x, int y, Object obj, DataBuffer data)
2	public	**int**	**getNumDataElements** ()
	public	int	**getOffset** (int x, int y)
2	public	**int[]**	**getPixel** (int x, int y, int[] iArray, DataBuffer data)
2	public	**int[]**	**getPixels** (int x, int y, int w, int h, int[] iArray, DataBuffer data)
2	public	**int**	**getSample** (int x, int y, int b, DataBuffer data)

SinglePixelPackedSampleModel

	2	public	int[]	**getSamples** (int x, int y, int w, int h, int b, int[] iArray, DataBuffer data)
	2	public	int[]	**getSampleSize** ()
	2	public	int	**getSampleSize** (int band)
		public	int	**getScanlineStride** ()
	1	public	int	**hashCode** ()
	2	public	void	**setDataElements** (int x, int y, Object obj, DataBuffer data)
	2	public	void	**setPixel** (int x, int y, int[] iArray, DataBuffer data)
	2	public	void	**setPixels** (int x, int y, int w, int h, int[] iArray, DataBuffer data)
	2	public	void	**setSample** (int x, int y, int b, int s, DataBuffer data)
	2	public	void	**setSamples** (int x, int y, int w, int h, int b, int[] iArray, DataBuffer data)
✳		public		**SinglePixelPackedSampleModel** (int dataType, int w, int h, int[] bitMasks)
				ε668
✳		public		**SinglePixelPackedSampleModel** (int dataType, int w, int h, int scanlineStride, int[] bitMasks)

SingleSelectionModel   javax.swing

1.2   *SingleSelectionModel*

public	void	**addChangeListener** (*javax.swing.event.ChangeListener* listener)
public	void	**clearSelection** ()
public	int	**getSelectedIndex** ()
public	boolean	**isSelected** ()
public	void	**removeChangeListener** (*javax.swing.event.ChangeListener* listener)
public	void	**setSelectedIndex** (int index)

Size2DSyntax   javax.print.attribute

Object[1]
1.4 ○   └ Size2DSyntax ------------------------------- *java.io.Serializable*, *Cloneable*

	1	public	boolean	**equals** (Object object)
		public	float[]	**getSize** (int units)
		public	float	**getX** (int units)
		protected	int	**getXMicrometers** ()
		public	float	**getY** (int units)
		protected	int	**getYMicrometers** ()
	1	public	int	**hashCode** ()
▲		public static final	int	**INCH** = 25400
▲		public static final	int	**MM** = 1000
✳		protected		**Size2DSyntax** (float x, float y, int units)
✳		protected		**Size2DSyntax** (int x, int y, int units)
	1	public	String	**toString** ()
		public	String	**toString** (int units, String unitsName)

SizeRequirements   javax.swing

Object[1]
1.2   └ SizeRequirements ---------------------- *java.io.Serializable*

△		public static	int[]	**adjustSizes** (int delta, SizeRequirements[] children)
		public	float	**alignment**
△		public static	void	**calculateAlignedPositions** (int allocated, SizeRequirements total, SizeRequirements[] children, int[] offsets, int[] spans)
1.4 △		public static	void	**calculateAlignedPositions** (int allocated, SizeRequirements total, SizeRequirements[] children, int[] offsets, int[] spans, boolean normal)
△		public static	void	**calculateTiledPositions** (int allocated, SizeRequirements total, SizeRequirements[] children, int[] offsets, int[] spans)
1.4 △		public static	void	**calculateTiledPositions** (int allocated, SizeRequirements total, SizeRequirements[] children, int[] offsets, int[] spans, boolean forward)
△		public static SizeRequirements		**getAlignedSizeRequirements** (SizeRequirements[] children)
△		public static SizeRequirements		**getTiledSizeRequirements** (SizeRequirements[] children)
		public	int	**maximum**
		public	int	**minimum**
		public	int	**preferred**
✳		public		**SizeRequirements** ()
✳		public		**SizeRequirements** (int min, int pref, int max, float a)

1	public.................... **String toString** ()	

SizeSequence

```
Object
1.3   └SizeSequence
```

	public.......................int	**getIndex** (int position)	
	public.......................int	**getPosition** (int index)	
	public.......................int	**getSize** (int index)	
	public.......................int[]	**getSizes** ()	
	public.......................void	**insertEntries** (int start, int length, int value)	
	public.......................void	**removeEntries** (int start, int length)	
	public.......................void	**setSize** (int index, int size)	
	public.......................void	**setSizes** (int[] sizes)	
*	public.........................	**SizeSequence** ()	
*	public.........................	**SizeSequence** (int numEntries)	
*	public.........................	**SizeSequence** (int[] sizes)	
*	public.........................	**SizeSequence** (int numEntries, int value)	

SliderUI

```
      Object
1.2 O └ComponentUI¹
1.2 O   └SliderUI
```

1	*11 inherited members from ComponentUI not shown*	
*	public.......................... **SliderUI** ()	

SoftBevelBorder

ε873

```
      Object
1.2 O └AbstractBorder¹ ----------------------- Border, java.io.Serializable
1.2       └BevelBorder²
1.2         └SoftBevelBorder
```

	2	protected ....int	bevelType
	2	public.......................int	getBevelType ()
	2	public.......... **java.awt.Insets**	**getBorderInsets** (java.awt.Component c)
	2	public.......... **java.awt.Insets**	**getBorderInsets** (java.awt.Component c, java.awt.Insets insets)
1.3	2	public..........java.awt.Color	getHighlightInnerColor ()
	2	public..........java.awt.Color	getHighlightInnerColor (java.awt.Component c)
1.3	2	public..........java.awt.Color	getHighlightOuterColor ()
	2	public..........java.awt.Color	getHighlightOuterColor (java.awt.Component c)
	1	public...... java.awt.Rectangle	getInteriorRectangle (java.awt.Component c, int x, int y, int width, int height)
△	1	public static .... java.awt.Rectangle	getInteriorRectangle (java.awt.Component c, *Border* b, int x, int y, int width, int height)
1.3	2	public..........java.awt.Color	getShadowInnerColor ()
	2	public..........java.awt.Color	getShadowInnerColor (java.awt.Component c)
1.3	2	public..........java.awt.Color	getShadowOuterColor ()
	2	public..........java.awt.Color	getShadowOuterColor (java.awt.Component c)
	2	protected ....java.awt.Color	highlightInner
	2	protected ....java.awt.Color	highlightOuter
	2	public..................... **boolean**	**isBorderOpaque** ()
▲	2	public static final ....int	LOWERED = 1
	2	public..................... **void**	**paintBorder** (java.awt.Component c, java.awt.Graphics g, int x, int y, int width, int height)
	2	protected ....void	paintLoweredBevel (java.awt.Component c, java.awt.Graphics g, int x, int y, int width, int height)
	2	protected ....void	paintRaisedBevel (java.awt.Component c, java.awt.Graphics g, int x, int y, int width, int height)
▲	2	public static final ....int	RAISED = 0
	2	protected ....java.awt.Color	shadowInner
	2	protected ....java.awt.Color	shadowOuter
*		public..........................	**SoftBevelBorder** (int bevelType)
*		public..........................	**SoftBevelBorder** (int bevelType, java.awt.Color highlight, java.awt.Color shadow)
*		public..........................	**SoftBevelBorder** (int bevelType, java.awt.Color highlightOuterColor, java.awt.Color highlightInnerColor, java.awt.Color shadowOuterColor, java.awt.Color shadowInnerColor)

S

Classes

SortingFocusTraversalPolicy

SortingFocusTraversalPolicy			javax.swing

Object
1.4 ○ └java.awt.FocusTraversalPolicy [1]
1.4 ○   └InternalFrameFocusTraversalPolicy [2]
1.4   └SortingFocusTraversalPolicy ⌄

	protected .... boolean	**accept** (java.awt.Component aComponent)	
	protected *java.util.Comparator*	**getComparator** ()	
1	public... **java.awt.Component**	**getComponentAfter** (java.awt.Container focusCycleRoot,	
		java.awt.Component aComponent)	ε615
1	public... **java.awt.Component**	**getComponentBefore** (java.awt.Container focusCycleRoot,	
		java.awt.Component aComponent)	ε615
1	public... **java.awt.Component**	**getDefaultComponent** (java.awt.Container focusCycleRoot)	ε615
1	public... **java.awt.Component**	**getFirstComponent** (java.awt.Container focusCycleRoot)	
	public............... boolean	**getImplicitDownCycleTraversal** ()	
1	public.... java.awt.Component	getInitialComponent (java.awt.Window window)	
2	public.... java.awt.Component	getInitialComponent (JInternalFrame frame)	
1	public... **java.awt.Component**	**getLastComponent** (java.awt.Container focusCycleRoot)	
	protected.................void	**setComparator** (*java.util.Comparator* comparator)	
	public.....................void	**setImplicitDownCycleTraversal** (boolean implicitDownCycleTraversal)	
✱	protected	**SortingFocusTraversalPolicy** ()	
✱	public..........................	**SortingFocusTraversalPolicy** (*java.util.Comparator* comparator)	

Soundbank		javax.sound.midi

1.3   *Soundbank*

public...................String	**getDescription** ()
public..............Instrument	**getInstrument** (Patch patch)
public...............Instrument[]	**getInstruments** ()
public...................String	**getName** ()
public.. SoundbankResource[]	**getResources** ()
public...................String	**getVendor** ()
public...................String	**getVersion** ()

SoundbankReader	javax.sound.midi.spi

Object
1.3 ○ └SoundbankReader

○	public abstract	**getSoundbank** (java.io.File file) throws javax.sound.midi.InvalidMidiDataException,
	javax.sound.midi.Soundbank	java.io.IOException
○	public abstract	**getSoundbank** (java.io.InputStream stream) throws
	javax.sound.midi.Soundbank	javax.sound.midi.InvalidMidiDataException, java.io.IOException
○	public abstract	**getSoundbank** (java.net.URL url) throws javax.sound.midi[2]
	javax.sound.midi.Soundbank	.InvalidMidiDataException, java.io.IOException
✱	public..........................	**SoundbankReader** ()

SoundbankResource	javax.sound.midi

Object
1.3 ○ └SoundbankResource ⌄

○	public abstract .... Object	**getData** ()
	public...................Class	**getDataClass** ()
	public...................String	**getName** ()
	public...............*Soundbank*	**getSoundbank** ()
✱	protected	**SoundbankResource** (*Soundbank* soundBank, String name, Class dataClass)

SourceDataLine	javax.sound.sampled

1.3   *SourceDataLine*────────────────── *DataLine* ⌄ [1] (*Line* [2])

2	public.......................void	addLineListener (*LineListener* listener)	ε731
1	public.......................int	available ()	

Class   *Interface*   —extends   - - -implements   ○ abstract   ● final   △ static   ▲ static final   ✱ constructor   x x—inherited   x **x**—declared   **x x**—overridden
ε*n*—examples of usage   ⌄—has subclass   package—see other volume

2	public	void	close ()
1	public	void	drain ()
1	public	void	flush ()
1	public	int	getBufferSize ()
2	public	Control	getControl (Control.Type control)
2	public	Control[]	getControls ()
1	public	AudioFormat	getFormat ()
1	public	int	getFramePosition ()
1	public	float	getLevel ()
2	public	Line.Info	getLineInfo ()
1	public	long	getMicrosecondPosition ()
1	public	boolean	isActive ()
2	public	boolean	isControlSupported (Control.Type control)
1	public	boolean	isOpen ()
1	public	boolean	isRunning ()
2	public	void	open () throws LineUnavailableException
	public	void	**open** (AudioFormat format) throws LineUnavailableException
	public	void	**open** (AudioFormat format, int bufferSize) throws LineUnavailableException
2	public	void	removeLineListener (*LineListener* listener)
1	public	void	start ()
1	public	void	stop ()
	public	int	**write** (byte[] b, int off, int len)

Right-column references:
- close / *ε*724
- getBufferSize / *ε*724,728
- getControl / *ε*730
- getFormat / *ε*728
- getMicrosecondPosition / *ε*729
- open / *ε*724
- removeLineListener / *ε*724,723,725
- start / *ε*724
- stop / *ε*724
- write / *ε*724

SpinnerDateModel

javax.swing

```
Object
1.4 O └─AbstractSpinnerModel 1 ------------------ SpinnerModel 2
1.4    └─SpinnerDateModel -------------------- java.io.Serializable
```

1	public	void	addChangeListener (*javax.swing.event.ChangeListener* l)
1	protected	void	fireStateChanged ()
	public	int	**getCalendarField** ()
1	public	*javax.swing.event.ChangeListener[]*	getChangeListeners ()
	public	java.util.Date	**getDate** ()
	public	*Comparable*	**getEnd** ()
1	public	*java.util.EventListener[]*	getListeners (Class listenerType)
2	public	Object	**getNextValue** ()
2	public	Object	**getPreviousValue** ()
	public	*Comparable*	**getStart** ()
2	public	Object	**getValue** ()
1	protected	*javax.swing.event.EventListenerList*	listenerList
1	public	void	removeChangeListener (*javax.swing.event.ChangeListener* l)
	public	void	**setCalendarField** (int calendarField)
	public	void	**setEnd** (*Comparable* end)
	public	void	**setStart** (*Comparable* start)
2	public	void	**setValue** (Object value)
*	public		**SpinnerDateModel** ()
*	public		**SpinnerDateModel** (java.util.Date value, *Comparable* start, *Comparable* end, int calendarField)

Right-column references:
- getNextValue / *ε*792
- getPreviousValue / *ε*792
- SpinnerDateModel () / *ε*786
- SpinnerDateModel (...) / *ε*787

SpinnerListModel

javax.swing

```
Object
1.4 O └─AbstractSpinnerModel 1 ------------------ SpinnerModel 2
1.4    └─SpinnerListModel -------------------- java.io.Serializable
```

1	public	void	addChangeListener (*javax.swing.event.ChangeListener* l)
1	protected	void	fireStateChanged ()
1	public	*javax.swing.event.ChangeListener[]*	getChangeListeners ()
	public	java.util.List	**getList** ()
1	public	*java.util.EventListener[]*	getListeners (Class listenerType)
2	public	Object	**getNextValue** ()
2	public	Object	**getPreviousValue** ()
2	public	Object	**getValue** ()
1	protected	*javax.swing.event.EventListenerList*	listenerList
1	public	void	removeChangeListener (*javax.swing.event.ChangeListener* l)
	public	void	**setList** (*java.util.List* list)

Right-column references:
- getNextValue / *ε*792
- getPreviousValue / *ε*792

SpinnerListModel

	2	public......................void	**setValue** (Object elt)
*		public...........................	**SpinnerListModel** ()
*		public...........................	**SpinnerListModel** (Object[] values)
*		public...........................	**SpinnerListModel** (*java.util.List* values)

ε786,791
ε960

SpinnerModel `javax.swing`

1.4	*SpinnerModel*	ε789

public......................void	**addChangeListener** (*javax.swing.event.ChangeListener* I)
public......................Object	**getNextValue** ()
public......................Object	**getPreviousValue** ()
public......................Object	**getValue** ()
public......................void	**removeChangeListener** (*javax.swing.event.ChangeListener* I)
public......................void	**setValue** (Object value)

ε792
ε792

SpinnerNumberModel `javax.swing`

Object
 └AbstractSpinnerModel[1] ----------------- *SpinnerModel*[2]   1.4 ○
  └SpinnerNumberModel ----------------- *java.io.Serializable*   1.4

	1	public....................void	addChangeListener (*javax.swing.event.ChangeListener* I)
	1	protected...................void	fireStateChanged ()
	1	public........... *javax.swing* ⊇	getChangeListeners ()
		.event.ChangeListener[]	
	1	public. *java.util.EventListener[]*	getListeners (Class listenerType)
		public........... *Comparable*	**getMaximum** ()
		public........... *Comparable*	**getMinimum** ()
	2	public....................Object	**getNextValue** ()
		public............... Number	**getNumber** ()
	2	public....................Object	**getPreviousValue** ()
		public............... Number	**getStepSize** ()
	2	public....................Object	**getValue** ()
	1	protected......... *javax.swing* ⊇	listenerList
		.event.EventListenerList	
	1	public....................void	removeChangeListener (*javax.swing.event.ChangeListener* I)
		public....................void	**setMaximum** (*Comparable* maximum)
		public....................void	**setMinimum** (*Comparable* minimum)
		public....................void	**setStepSize** (Number stepSize)
	2	public....................void	**setValue** (Object value)
*		public...........................	**SpinnerNumberModel** ()
*		public...........................	**SpinnerNumberModel** (double value, double minimum, double maximum, double stepSize)
*		public...........................	**SpinnerNumberModel** (int value, int minimum, int maximum, int stepSize)
*		public...........................	**SpinnerNumberModel** (Number value, *Comparable* minimum, *Comparable* maximum, Number stepSize)

ε792
ε792

ε789

SpinnerUI `javax.swing.plaf`

Object
 └ComponentUI[1]   1.2 ○
  └SpinnerUI   1.4 ○

	1	*11 inherited members from ComponentUI not shown*	
*		public...........................	**SpinnerUI** ()

SplitPaneUI `javax.swing.plaf`

Object
 └ComponentUI[1]   1.2 ○
  └SplitPaneUI   1.2 ○

	1	*11 inherited members from ComponentUI not shown*	
○		public abstract.............void	**finishedPaintingChildren** (javax.swing.JSplitPane jc, java.awt.Graphics g)

Class *Interface* —extends - - -implements ○ abstract ● final △ static ▲ static final ✳ constructor x x—inherited x **x**—declared **x x**—overridden
ε*n*—examples of usage ˌ—has subclass package—see other volume

768

○	public abstract	int	**getDividerLocation** (javax.swing.JSplitPane jc)
○	public abstract	int	**getMaximumDividerLocation** (javax.swing.JSplitPane jc)
○	public abstract	int	**getMinimumDividerLocation** (javax.swing.JSplitPane jc)
○	public abstract	void	**resetToPreferredSizes** (javax.swing.JSplitPane jc)
○	public abstract	void	**setDividerLocation** (javax.swing.JSplitPane jc, int location)
✱	public		**SplitPaneUI** ()

Spring — javax.swing

Object
1.4 ○ └Spring

△	public static	Spring	**constant** (int pref)
△	public static	Spring	**constant** (int min, int pref, int max)
○	public abstract	int	**getMaximumValue** ()
○	public abstract	int	**getMinimumValue** ()
○	public abstract	int	**getPreferredValue** ()
○	public abstract	int	**getValue** ()
△	public static	Spring	**max** (Spring s1, Spring s2)
△	public static	Spring	**minus** (Spring s)
○	public abstract	void	**setValue** (int value)
✱	protected		**Spring** ()
△	public static	Spring	**sum** (Spring s1, Spring s2)
▲	public static final	int	**UNSET** = -2147483648

SpringLayout — javax.swing

Object
1.4 └SpringLayout - *java.awt.LayoutManager2* [1] (*java.awt.LayoutManager* [2])

1	public	void	**addLayoutComponent** (java.awt.Component component, Object constraints)	
2	public	void	**addLayoutComponent** (String name, java.awt.Component c)	
▲	public static final	String	**EAST** = "East"	
	public	Spring	**getConstraint** (String edgeName, java.awt.Component c)	
	public	SpringLayout.Constraints	**getConstraints** (java.awt.Component c)	
1	public	float	**getLayoutAlignmentX** (java.awt.Container p)	
1	public	float	**getLayoutAlignmentY** (java.awt.Container p)	
1	public	void	**invalidateLayout** (java.awt.Container p)	
2	public	void	**layoutContainer** (java.awt.Container parent)	ε624,625
1	public	java.awt.Dimension	**maximumLayoutSize** (java.awt.Container parent)	
2	public	java.awt.Dimension	**minimumLayoutSize** (java.awt.Container parent)	
▲	public static final	String	**NORTH** = "North"	
2	public	java.awt.Dimension	**preferredLayoutSize** (java.awt.Container parent)	
	public	void	**putConstraint** (String e1, java.awt.Component c1, Spring s, String e2, java.awt.Component c2)	
	public	void	**putConstraint** (String e1, java.awt.Component c1, int pad, String e2, java.awt.Component c2)	
2	public	void	**removeLayoutComponent** (java.awt.Component c)	
▲	public static final	String	**SOUTH** = "South"	
✱	public		**SpringLayout** ()	
▲	public static final	String	**WEST** = "West"	

SpringLayout.Constraints — javax.swing

Object
1.4 └SpringLayout.Constraints

✱	public		**SpringLayout.Constraints** ()
✱	public		**SpringLayout.Constraints** (Spring x, Spring y)
✱	public		**SpringLayout.Constraints** (Spring x, Spring y, Spring width, Spring height)
	public	Spring	**getConstraint** (String edgeName)
	public	Spring	**getHeight** ()
	public	Spring	**getWidth** ()
	public	Spring	**getX** ()
	public	Spring	**getY** ()
	public	void	**setConstraint** (String edgeName, Spring s)
	public	void	**setHeight** (Spring height)
	public	void	**setWidth** (Spring width)
	public	void	**setX** (Spring x)

S

Classes

	public	.....void	**setY** (Spring y)	

StateEdit
`javax.swing.undo`

Object
1.2 └AbstractUndoableEdit[1] - - - - - - - - - - - - - - - - - - *UndoableEdit*, *java.io.Serializable*⌄
1.2 └StateEdit

	1	public	boolean	addEdit (*UndoableEdit* anEdit)	ε1034
	1	public	boolean	canRedo ()	ε1034
	1	public	boolean	canUndo ()	ε1034
	1	public	void	die ()	ε1034
		public	void	**end** ()	
	1	public	**String**	**getPresentationName** ()	
	1	public	String	getRedoPresentationName ()	
	1	public	String	getUndoPresentationName ()	
		protected	void	**init** (*StateEditable* anObject, String name)	
	1	public	boolean	isSignificant ()	
		protected	*StateEditable*	**object**	
		protected	java.util.Hashtable	**postState**	
		protected	java.util.Hashtable	**preState**	
▲		protected static final	String	**RCSID**	
	1	public	**void**	**redo** ()	ε1034
▲	1	protected static final	String	RedoName	
		protected	void	**removeRedundantState** ()	
	1	public	boolean	replaceEdit (*UndoableEdit* anEdit)	
*		public	**StateEdit**	**StateEdit** (*StateEditable* anObject)	
*		public	**StateEdit**	**StateEdit** (*StateEditable* anObject, String name)	
	1	public	String	toString ()	
	1	public	**void**	**undo** ()	ε1034
▲	1	protected static final	String	UndoName	
		protected	String	**undoRedoName**	

S

StateEditable
`javax.swing.undo`

1.2 *StateEditable*

▲	public static final	String	**RCSID**	= "$Id: StateEditable.java,v 1.2 1997/09/08 19:39:08 marklin Exp $"
	public	void	**restoreState** (java.util.Hashtable state)	
	public	void	**storeState** (java.util.Hashtable state)	

StreamPrintService
`javax.print`

Object ε704
1.4 ○ └StreamPrintService - *PrintService*⌄[1]

○	1	public abstract	void	addPrintServiceAttributeListener (*javax.print.event.PrintServiceAttributeListener* listener)	ε713
○	1	public abstract	*DocPrintJob*	createPrintJob ()	ε701,700,702,705,714
		public	void	**dispose** ()	
○	1	public abstract	*javax.print.attribute*⌄.*PrintServiceAttribute*	getAttribute (Class category)	
○	1	public abstract	*javax.print.attribute*⌄.*PrintServiceAttributeSet*	getAttributes ()	ε706
○	1	public abstract	Object	getDefaultAttributeValue (Class category)	ε707,708
○	1	public abstract	String	getName ()	ε706,707,708
○		public abstract	String	**getOutputFormat** ()	
		public	java.io.OutputStream	**getOutputStream** ()	
○	1	public abstract	ServiceUIFactory	getServiceUIFactory ()	
○	1	public abstract	Class[]	getSupportedAttributeCategories ()	ε707
○	1	public abstract	Object	getSupportedAttributeValues (Class category, DocFlavor flavor, *javax.print.attribute.AttributeSet* attributes)	ε709,707
○	1	public abstract	DocFlavor[]	getSupportedDocFlavors ()	
○	1	public abstract	*javax*⌄.*print.attribute.AttributeSet*	getUnsupportedAttributes (DocFlavor flavor, *javax.print.attribute.AttributeSet* attributes)	

Class *Interface* —extends - - -implements ○ abstract ● final △ static ▲ static final ✳ constructor x x—inherited x **x**—declared **x x**—overridden
ε*n*—examples of usage ⌄—has subclass package—see other volume

O	1	public abstract .... boolean	isAttributeCategorySupported (Class category)
O	1	public abstract .... boolean	isAttributeValueSupported (*javax.print.attribute.Attribute* attrval, DocFlavor flavor, *javax.print.attribute.AttributeSet* attributes)
		public .... boolean	**isDisposed** ()
O	1	public abstract .... boolean	isDocFlavorSupported (DocFlavor flavor)
O	1	public abstract .... void	removePrintServiceAttributeListener (*javax.print.event.PrintServiceAttributeListener* listener)
*		protected	**StreamPrintService** (java.io.OutputStream out)

StreamPrintServiceFactory | javax.print

Object
1.4 O └─StreamPrintServiceFactory

O		public abstract .... String	**getOutputFormat** ()	
O		public abstract .... StreamPrintService	**getPrintService** (java.io.OutputStream out)	ε701,704
O		public abstract .... DocFlavor[]	**getSupportedDocFlavors** ()	
△		public static .... StreamPrintServiceFactory[]	**lookupStreamPrintServiceFactories** (DocFlavor flavor, String outputMimeType)	ε701,704
*		public	**StreamPrintServiceFactory** ()	

StringContent | javax.swing.text

Object
1.2 ● └─StringContent - *AbstractDocument.Content* [1], *java.io.Serializable*

1	public .... *Position*	**createPosition** (int offset) throws BadLocationException
1	public .... void	**getChars** (int where, int len, Segment chars) throws BadLocationException
	protected .... java.util.Vector	**getPositionsInRange** (java.util.Vector v, int offset, int length)
1	public .... String	**getString** (int where, int len) throws BadLocationException
1	public .... *javax₂ .swing.undo.UndoableEdit*	**insertString** (int where, String str) throws BadLocationException
1	public .... int	**length** ()
1	public .... *javax₂ .swing.undo.UndoableEdit*	**remove** (int where, int nitems) throws BadLocationException
*	public	**StringContent** ()
*	public	**StringContent** (int initialLength)
	protected .... void	**updateUndoPositions** (java.util.Vector positions)

StringSelection | java.awt.datatransfer

Object
1.1 └─StringSelection - *Transferable* [1], *ClipboardOwner* [2]

1	public .... Object	**getTransferData** (DataFlavor flavor) throws UnsupportedFlavorException, java.io.IOException	ε637,638,642
1	public .... DataFlavor[]	**getTransferDataFlavors** ()	ε638
1	public .... boolean	**isDataFlavorSupported** (DataFlavor flavor)	ε637,638,642
2	public .... void	**lostOwnership** (Clipboard clipboard, *Transferable* contents)	ε639
*	public	**StringSelection** (String data)	ε637,639,640

Stroke | java.awt

Stroke
1.2

public .... *Shape*	**createStrokedShape** (*Shape* p)	ε588

Style | javax.swing.text

Style ──────────────────────── *MutableAttributeSet*, [1] (*AttributeSet* [2]) ε989,991,992,993,1007
1.2

1	public .... void	addAttribute (Object name, Object value)	
1	public .... void	addAttributes (*AttributeSet* attributes)	
	public .... void	**addChangeListener** (*javax.swing.event.ChangeListener* l)	ε1013
2	public .... boolean	containsAttribute (Object name, Object value)	
2	public .... boolean	containsAttributes (*AttributeSet* attributes)	
2	public .... *AttributeSet*	copyAttributes ()	

S

Classes

771

Style

	2	public	Object	getAttribute (Object key)	ε1010,1013,1017
	2	public	int	getAttributeCount ()	ε1010
	2	public	*java.util.Enumeration*	getAttributeNames ()	ε1010
		public	String	**getName** ()	ε1013
	2	public	*AttributeSet*	getResolveParent ()	
	2	public	boolean	isDefined (Object attrName)	
	2	public	boolean	isEqual (*AttributeSet* attr)	
▲	2	public static final	Object	NameAttribute	
	1	public	void	removeAttribute (Object name)	
	1	public	void	removeAttributes (*java.util.Enumeration* names)	
	1	public	void	removeAttributes (*AttributeSet* attributes)	
		public	void	**removeChangeListener** (*javax.swing.event.ChangeListener* l)	
▲	2	public static final	Object	ResolveAttribute	
	1	public	void	setResolveParent (*AttributeSet* parent)	

StyleConstants javax.swing.text

Object [1]
1.2 └StyleConstants

▲	public static final	int	**ALIGN_CENTER** = 1	
▲	public static final	int	**ALIGN_JUSTIFIED** = 3	
▲	public static final	int	**ALIGN_LEFT** = 0	
▲	public static final	int	**ALIGN_RIGHT** = 2	
▲	public static final	Object	**Alignment**	
▲	public static final	Object	**Background**	
▲	public static final	Object	**BidiLevel**	
▲	public static final	Object	**Bold**	
▲	public static final	Object	**ComponentAttribute**	
▲	public static final	String	**ComponentElementName** = "component"	
▲	public static final	Object	**ComposedTextAttribute**	
▲	public static final	Object	**FirstLineIndent**	
▲	public static final	Object	**FontFamily**	
▲	public static final	Object	**FontSize**	
▲	public static final	Object	**Foreground**	ε1014
△	public static	int	**getAlignment** (*AttributeSet* a)	
△	public static	java.awt.Color	**getBackground** (*AttributeSet* a)	
△	public static	int	**getBidiLevel** (*AttributeSet* a)	
△	public static	java.awt.Component	**getComponent** (*AttributeSet* a)	
△	public static	float	**getFirstLineIndent** (*AttributeSet* a)	
△	public static	String	**getFontFamily** (*AttributeSet* a)	
△	public static	int	**getFontSize** (*AttributeSet* a)	
△	public static	java.awt.Color	**getForeground** (*AttributeSet* a)	
△	public static	*javax.swing.Icon*	**getIcon** (*AttributeSet* a)	
△	public static	float	**getLeftIndent** (*AttributeSet* a)	
△	public static	float	**getLineSpacing** (*AttributeSet* a)	
△	public static	float	**getRightIndent** (*AttributeSet* a)	
△	public static	float	**getSpaceAbove** (*AttributeSet* a)	
△	public static	float	**getSpaceBelow** (*AttributeSet* a)	
△	public static	TabSet	**getTabSet** (*AttributeSet* a)	
▲	public static final	Object	**IconAttribute**	
▲	public static final	String	**IconElementName** = "icon"	
△	public static	boolean	**isBold** (*AttributeSet* a)	
△	public static	boolean	**isItalic** (*AttributeSet* a)	
△	public static	boolean	**isStrikeThrough** (*AttributeSet* a)	
△	public static	boolean	**isSubscript** (*AttributeSet* a)	
△	public static	boolean	**isSuperscript** (*AttributeSet* a)	
△	public static	boolean	**isUnderline** (*AttributeSet* a)	
▲	public static final	Object	**Italic**	ε1014
▲	public static final	Object	**LeftIndent**	
▲	public static final	Object	**LineSpacing**	ε1014
▲	public static final	Object	**ModelAttribute**	
▲	public static final	Object	**NameAttribute**	ε1010,1013
▲	public static final	Object	**Orientation**	
▲	public static final	Object	**ResolveAttribute**	ε1010
▲	public static final	Object	**RightIndent**	
△	public static	void	**setAlignment** (*MutableAttributeSet* a, int align)	
△	public static	void	**setBackground** (*MutableAttributeSet* a, java.awt.Color fg)	ε989
△	public static	void	**setBidiLevel** (*MutableAttributeSet* a, int o)	

Class   *Interface*   —extends   - - -implements   O abstract   ● final   △ static   ▲ static final   ✱ constructor   x x—inherited   x **x**—declared   **x x**—overridden
εn—examples of usage   ‿—has subclass   package—see other volume

△	public static	void	**setBold** (*MutableAttributeSet* a, boolean b)	ε989,1007,1008,1011,1012
△	public static	void	**setComponent** (*MutableAttributeSet* a, java.awt.Component c)	ε992
△	public static	void	**setFirstLineIndent** (*MutableAttributeSet* a, float i)	
△	public static	void	**setFontFamily** (*MutableAttributeSet* a, String fam)	ε989
△	public static	void	**setFontSize** (*MutableAttributeSet* a, int s)	ε989,1007,1011
△	public static	void	**setForeground** (*MutableAttributeSet* a, java.awt.Color fg)	ε989,1007,1008,1011,1012
△	public static	void	**setIcon** (*MutableAttributeSet* a, *javax.swing.Icon* c)	ε991
△	public static	void	**setItalic** (*MutableAttributeSet* a, boolean b)	ε989,1007,1011
△	public static	void	**setLeftIndent** (*MutableAttributeSet* a, float i)	
△	public static	void	**setLineSpacing** (*MutableAttributeSet* a, float i)	
△	public static	void	**setRightIndent** (*MutableAttributeSet* a, float i)	
△	public static	void	**setSpaceAbove** (*MutableAttributeSet* a, float i)	
△	public static	void	**setSpaceBelow** (*MutableAttributeSet* a, float i)	
△	public static	void	**setStrikeThrough** (*MutableAttributeSet* a, boolean b)	
△	public static	void	**setSubscript** (*MutableAttributeSet* a, boolean b)	
△	public static	void	**setSuperscript** (*MutableAttributeSet* a, boolean b)	
△	public static	void	**setTabSet** (*MutableAttributeSet* a, TabSet tabs)	ε993
△	public static	void	**setUnderline** (*MutableAttributeSet* a, boolean b)	ε1007,1011,1012,1013
▲	public static final	Object	**SpaceAbove**	
▲	public static final	Object	**SpaceBelow**	
▲	public static final	Object	**StrikeThrough**	
▲	public static final	Object	**Subscript**	
▲	public static final	Object	**Superscript**	
▲	public static final	Object	**TabSet**	
▲ 1	public	String	**toString** ()	
▲	public static final	Object	**Underline**	

StyleConstants.CharacterConstants · javax.swing.text

Object
- 1.2 └StyleConstants [1]
- 1.2 　└StyleConstants.CharacterConstants - - - - - - *AttributeSet.CharacterAttribute*

	1	*64 inherited members from StyleConstants not shown*		
▲	1	public static final	**Object Background**	
▲	1	public static final	**Object BidiLevel**	
▲	1	public static final	**Object Bold**	
▲	1	public static final	**Object ComponentAttribute**	
▲		public static final	Object **Family**	
▲	1	public static final	**Object Foreground**	ε1014
▲	1	public static final	**Object IconAttribute**	
▲	1	public static final	**Object Italic**	ε1014
▲		public static final	Object **Size**	
▲	1	public static final	**Object StrikeThrough**	
▲	1	public static final	**Object Subscript**	
▲	1	public static final	**Object Superscript**	
▲	1	public static final	**Object Underline**	

StyleConstants.ColorConstants · javax.swing.text

Object
- 1.2 └StyleConstants [1]
- 1.2 　└StyleConstants.ColorConstants - - - - - - - - - *AttributeSet.ColorAttribute*, *AttributeSet.CharacterAttribute*

	1	*73 inherited members from StyleConstants not shown*		
▲	1	public static final	**Object Background**	
▲	1	public static final	**Object Foreground**	ε1014

StyleConstants.FontConstants · javax.swing.text

Object
- 1.2 └StyleConstants [1]
- 1.2 　└StyleConstants.FontConstants - - - - - - - - - - *AttributeSet.FontAttribute*, *AttributeSet.CharacterAttribute*

	1	*73 inherited members from StyleConstants not shown*		
▲	1	public static final	**Object Bold**	
▲		public static final	Object **Family**	
▲	1	public static final	**Object Italic**	ε1014
▲		public static final	Object **Size**	

StyleConstants.ParagraphConstants

StyleConstants.ParagraphConstants	javax.swing.text

```
        Object
1.2     └StyleConstants 1
1.2         └StyleConstants.ParagraphConstants - - - - - - AttributeSet.ParagraphAttribute
```

	1	*66 inherited members from StyleConstants not shown*	
▲	1	public static final . . . .**Object Alignment**	
▲	1	public static final . . . .**Object FirstLineIndent**	
▲	1	public static final . . . .**Object LeftIndent**	
▲	1	public static final . . . .**Object LineSpacing**	ε1014
▲	1	public static final . . . .**Object Orientation**	
▲	1	public static final . . . .**Object RightIndent**	
▲	1	public static final . . . .**Object SpaceAbove**	
▲	1	public static final . . . .**Object SpaceBelow**	
▲	1	public static final . . . .**Object TabSet**	

StyleContext	javax.swing.text

```
        Object 1
1.2     └StyleContext - - - - - - - - - - - - - - - - - - - - - - - - - java.io.Serializable , AbstractDocument.AttributeContext 2
```

	2	public synchronized . . . . **addAttribute** (*AttributeSet* old, Object name, Object value)
		. . . . *AttributeSet*
	2	public synchronized . . . . **addAttributes** (*AttributeSet* old, *AttributeSet* attr)
		. . . . *AttributeSet*
		public . . . . .void **addChangeListener** (*javax.swing.event.ChangeListener* l)
		public . . . .*Style* **addStyle** (String nm, *Style* parent)
		protected . *MutableAttributeSet* **createLargeAttributeSet** (*AttributeSet* a)
		protected . . . . StyleContext 2 **createSmallAttributeSet** (*AttributeSet* a)
		.SmallAttributeSet
▲		public static final . . . . .String **DEFAULT_STYLE** = "default"
		public . . . . .java.awt.Color **getBackground** (*AttributeSet* attr)
1.4		public . . . .*javax.swing* 2 **getChangeListeners** ()
		.*event.ChangeListener[]*
		protected . . . . .int **getCompressionThreshold** ()
▲		public static final . StyleContext **getDefaultStyleContext** ()
	2	public . . . . *AttributeSet* **getEmptySet** ()
		public . . . . .java.awt.Font **getFont** (*AttributeSet* attr)
		public . . . . .java.awt.Font **getFont** (String family, int style, int size)
		public . . . . java.awt.FontMetrics **getFontMetrics** (java.awt.Font f)
		public . . . . .java.awt.Color **getForeground** (*AttributeSet* attr)
△		public static . . . . .Object **getStaticAttribute** (Object key)
△		public static . . . . .Object **getStaticAttributeKey** (Object key)
		public . . . .*Style* **getStyle** (String nm)
		public . . . . *java.util.Enumeration* **getStyleNames** ()
		public . . . . .void **readAttributes** (java.io.ObjectInputStream in, *MutableAttributeSet* a)
		throws ClassNotFoundException, java.io.IOException
△		public static . . . . .void **readAttributeSet** (java.io.ObjectInputStream in, *MutableAttributeSet* a)
		throws ClassNotFoundException, java.io.IOException
	2	public . . . . .void **reclaim** (*AttributeSet* a)
△		public static . . . . .void **registerStaticAttributeKey** (Object key)
	2	public synchronized . . . . **removeAttribute** (*AttributeSet* old, Object name)
		. . . . *AttributeSet*
	2	public synchronized . . . . **removeAttributes** (*AttributeSet* old, *java.util.Enumeration* names)
		. . . . *AttributeSet*
	2	public synchronized . . . . **removeAttributes** (*AttributeSet* old, *AttributeSet* attrs)
		. . . . *AttributeSet*
		public . . . . .void **removeChangeListener** (*javax.swing.event.ChangeListener* l)
		public . . . . .void **removeStyle** (String nm)
*		public . . . . **StyleContext** ()
	1	public . . . . **String** **toString** ()
		public . . . . .void **writeAttributes** (java.io.ObjectOutputStream out, *AttributeSet* a)
		throws java.io.IOException
△		public static . . . . .void **writeAttributeSet** (java.io.ObjectOutputStream out, *AttributeSet* a)
		throws java.io.IOException

ε1008 appears beside **StyleContext** ()

S

Class *Interface* —extends - - -implements ○ abstract ● final △ static ▲ static final ✳ constructor x x—inherited x **x**—declared **x x**—overridden
εn—examples of usage .—has subclass package—see other volume

		Object [1]		
1.2		└─StyleContext.NamedStyle - - - - - - - - - - - - - - - *Style* [2] (*MutableAttributeSet* [3] (*AttributeSet* [4])), *java.io.Serializable* ˅		

	3	public . . . . void	**addAttribute** (Object name, Object value)	
	3	public . . . . void	**addAttributes** (*AttributeSet* attr)	
	2	public . . . . void	**addChangeListener** (*javax.swing.event.ChangeListener* l)	ε1013
		protected transient . . . . . . javax ˅ .swing.event.ChangeEvent	**changeEvent**	
	4	public . . . . boolean	**containsAttribute** (Object name, Object value)	
	4	public . . . . boolean	**containsAttributes** (*AttributeSet* attrs)	
	4	public . . . . *AttributeSet*	**copyAttributes** ()	
		protected . . . . void	**fireStateChanged** ()	
	4	public . . . . Object	**getAttribute** (Object attrName)	ε1010,1013,1017
	4	public . . . . int	**getAttributeCount** ()	ε1010
	4	public . . . . *java.util.Enumeration*	**getAttributeNames** ()	ε1010
1.4		public . . . . *javax.swing* ˅ .event.ChangeListener[]	**getChangeListeners** ()	
1.3		public . *java.util.EventListener[]*	**getListeners** (Class listenerType)	
	2	public . . . . String	**getName** ()	ε1013
	4	public . . . . *AttributeSet*	**getResolveParent** ()	
	4	public . . . . boolean	**isDefined** (Object attrName)	
	4	public . . . . boolean	**isEqual** (*AttributeSet* attr)	
		protected . . . . javax.swing ˅ .event.EventListenerList	**listenerList**	
▲	4	public static final . . . . Object	NameAttribute	
*		public	**StyleContext.NamedStyle** ()	
*		public	**StyleContext.NamedStyle** (*Style* parent)	
*		public	**StyleContext.NamedStyle** (String name, *Style* parent)	
	3	public . . . . void	**removeAttribute** (Object name)	
	3	public . . . . void	**removeAttributes** (*java.util.Enumeration* names)	
	3	public . . . . void	**removeAttributes** (*AttributeSet* attrs)	
	2	public . . . . void	**removeChangeListener** (*javax.swing.event.ChangeListener* l)	
▲	4	public static final . . . . Object	ResolveAttribute	
		public . . . . void	**setName** (String name)	
	3	public . . . . void	**setResolveParent** (*AttributeSet* parent)	
	1	public . . . . String	**toString** ()	

		Object [1]		
1.2		└─StyleContext.SmallAttributeSet - - - - - - - - - - - *AttributeSet* ˅ [2]		

	1	public . . . . **Object**	**clone** ()	
	2	public . . . . boolean	**containsAttribute** (Object name, Object value)	
	2	public . . . . boolean	**containsAttributes** (*AttributeSet* attrs)	
	2	public . . . . *AttributeSet*	**copyAttributes** ()	
	1	public . . . . **boolean**	**equals** (Object obj)	
	2	public . . . . Object	**getAttribute** (Object key)	ε1010,1013,1017
	2	public . . . . int	**getAttributeCount** ()	ε1010
	2	public . . . . *java.util.Enumeration*	**getAttributeNames** ()	ε1010
	2	public . . . . *AttributeSet*	**getResolveParent** ()	
	1	public . . . . **int**	**hashCode** ()	
	2	public . . . . boolean	**isDefined** (Object key)	
	2	public . . . . boolean	**isEqual** (*AttributeSet* attr)	
▲	2	public static final . . . . Object	NameAttribute	
▲	2	public static final . . . . Object	ResolveAttribute	
*		public	**StyleContext.SmallAttributeSet** (Object[] attributes)	
*		public	**StyleContext.SmallAttributeSet** (*AttributeSet* attrs)	
	1	public . . . . **String**	**toString** ()	

1.2		*StyledDocument* ──────────────── *Document* ˅ [1]		
	1	public . . . . void	addDocumentListener (*javax.swing.event.DocumentListener* listener)	ε1016
		public . . . . *Style*	**addStyle** (String nm, *Style* parent)	ε989,991,992
	1	public . . . . void	addUndoableEditListener (*javax.swing.event.UndoableEditListener* listener)	ε1034

S

Classes

StyledDocument

1	public	*Position*	createPosition (int offs) throws BadLocationException	ε974
	public	java.awt.Color	**getBackground** (*AttributeSet* attr)	
	public	*Element*	**getCharacterElement** (int pos)	
1	public	*Element*	getDefaultRootElement ()	ε984,990,1013
1	public	*Position*	getEndPosition ()	
	public	java.awt.Font	**getFont** (*AttributeSet* attr)	
	public	java.awt.Color	**getForeground** (*AttributeSet* attr)	
1	public	int	getLength ()	ε989,991,992,1006,968
	public	*Style*	**getLogicalStyle** (int p)	
	public	*Element*	**getParagraphElement** (int pos)	
1	public	Object	getProperty (Object key)	
1	public	*Element[]*	getRootElements ()	
1	public	*Position*	getStartPosition ()	
	public	*Style*	**getStyle** (String nm)	ε1007,1008,1009,1011,1013
1	public	String	getText (int offset, int length) throws BadLocationException	ε1006,971,972,973,1002
1	public	void	getText (int offset, int length, Segment txt) throws BadLocationException	
				ε969
1	public	void	insertString (int offset, String str, *AttributeSet* a) throws BadLocationException	
				ε989,991,992,975,970
1	public	void	putProperty (Object key, Object value)	
1	public	void	remove (int offs, int len) throws BadLocationException	ε970,1002
1	public	void	removeDocumentListener (*javax.swing.event.DocumentListener* listener)	
	public	void	**removeStyle** (String nm)	
1	public	void	removeUndoableEditListener (*javax.swing.event.UndoableEditListener* listener)	
1	public	void	render (*Runnable* r)	ε971
	public	void	**setCharacterAttributes** (int offset, int length, *AttributeSet* s, boolean replace)	
				ε1007,1013
	public	void	**setLogicalStyle** (int pos, *Style* s)	
	public	void	**setParagraphAttributes** (int offset, int length, *AttributeSet* s, boolean replace)	
				ε1007,1013
▲ *1*	public static final	String	StreamDescriptionProperty = "stream"	
▲ *1*	public static final	String	TitleProperty = "title"	

StyledEditorKit | javax.swing.text

```
Object
1.2 ○  └EditorKit 1 - - - - - - - - - - - - - - - - - - - - - - - - - - - - Cloneable , java.io.Serializable
1.2        └DefaultEditorKit 2
1.2            └StyledEditorKit
```

2	*53 inherited members from DefaultEditorKit not shown*			
1	public	**Object**	**clone** ()	
2	public	***Document***	**createDefaultDocument** ()	ε1017
	protected	void	**createInputAttributes** (*Element* element, *MutableAttributeSet* set)	
1	public	**void**	**deinstall** (javax.swing.JEditorPane c)	
2	public	***javax.swing.Action[]***	**getActions** ()	
	public	*Element*	**getCharacterAttributeRun** ()	
	public	*MutableAttributeSet*	**getInputAttributes** ()	
2	public	***ViewFactory***	**getViewFactory** ()	
1	public	**void**	**install** (javax.swing.JEditorPane c)	
✳	public		**StyledEditorKit** ()	

StyledEditorKit.AlignmentAction | javax.swing.text

```
Object
1.2 ○  └javax.swing.AbstractAction 1 - - - - - - - - - - - - - javax.swing.Action 4 (java.awt.event.ActionListener 5
                                                           (java.util.EventListener)), Cloneable , java.io.Serializable
1.2 ○      └TextAction 2
1.2 ○          └StyledEditorKit.StyledTextAction 3
1.2              └StyledEditorKit.AlignmentAction
```

1	*12 inherited members from javax.swing.AbstractAction not shown*			
2	*3 inherited members from TextAction not shown*			
3	*5 inherited members from StyledEditorKit.StyledTextAction not shown*			
4	*8 inherited members from javax.swing.Action not shown*			
5	public	void	**actionPerformed** (java.awt.event.ActionEvent e)	ε855,644,738,743,745
✳	public		**StyledEditorKit.AlignmentAction** (String nm, int a)	

Class   *Interface*   —extends   - - -implements   ○ abstract   ● final   △ static   ▲ static final   ✳ constructor   x x—inherited   x **x**—declared   **x x**—overridden
εη—examples of usage   —has subclass   package—see other volume

StyledEditorKit.BoldAction	javax.swing.text

Object
1.2 ○ └─javax.swing.AbstractAction [1] - - - - - - - - - - - - - - *javax.swing.Action* [4] (*java.awt.event.ActionListener* [5]
(*java.util.EventListener*)), *Cloneable*, *java.io.Serializable*

1.2 ○   └─TextAction [2]
1.2 ○   └─StyledEditorKit.StyledTextAction [3]
1.2   └─StyledEditorKit.BoldAction

  1 *12 inherited members from javax.swing.AbstractAction not shown*
  2 *3 inherited members from TextAction not shown*
  3 *5 inherited members from StyledEditorKit.StyledTextAction not shown*
  4 *8 inherited members from javax.swing.Action not shown*
  5 public . . . . void **actionPerformed** (java.awt.event.ActionEvent e)   ε855,644,738,743,745
  * public . . . . **StyledEditorKit.BoldAction** ()

StyledEditorKit.FontFamilyAction	javax.swing.text

Object
1.2 ○ └─javax.swing.AbstractAction [1] - - - - - - - - - - - - - - *javax.swing.Action* [4] (*java.awt.event.ActionListener* [5]
(*java.util.EventListener*)), *Cloneable*, *java.io.Serializable*

1.2 ○   └─TextAction [2]
1.2 ○   └─StyledEditorKit.StyledTextAction [3]
1.2   └─StyledEditorKit.FontFamilyAction

  1 *12 inherited members from javax.swing.AbstractAction not shown*
  2 *3 inherited members from TextAction not shown*
  3 *5 inherited members from StyledEditorKit.StyledTextAction not shown*
  4 *8 inherited members from javax.swing.Action not shown*
  5 public . . . . void **actionPerformed** (java.awt.event.ActionEvent e)   ε855,644,738,743,745
  * public . . . . **StyledEditorKit.FontFamilyAction** (String nm, String family)

S

StyledEditorKit.FontSizeAction	javax.swing.text

Object
1.2 ○ └─javax.swing.AbstractAction [1] - - - - - - - - - - - - - - *javax.swing.Action* [4] (*java.awt.event.ActionListener* [5]
(*java.util.EventListener*)), *Cloneable*, *java.io.Serializable*

1.2 ○   └─TextAction [2]
1.2 ○   └─StyledEditorKit.StyledTextAction [3]
1.2   └─StyledEditorKit.FontSizeAction

  1 *12 inherited members from javax.swing.AbstractAction not shown*
  2 *3 inherited members from TextAction not shown*
  3 *5 inherited members from StyledEditorKit.StyledTextAction not shown*
  4 *8 inherited members from javax.swing.Action not shown*
  5 public . . . . void **actionPerformed** (java.awt.event.ActionEvent e)   ε855,644,738,743,745
  * public . . . . **StyledEditorKit.FontSizeAction** (String nm, int size)

Classes

StyledEditorKit.ForegroundAction	javax.swing.text

Object
1.2 ○ └─javax.swing.AbstractAction [1] - - - - - - - - - - - - - - *javax.swing.Action* [4] (*java.awt.event.ActionListener* [5]
(*java.util.EventListener*)), *Cloneable*, *java.io.Serializable*

1.2 ○   └─TextAction [2]
1.2 ○   └─StyledEditorKit.StyledTextAction [3]
1.2   └─StyledEditorKit.ForegroundAction

  1 *12 inherited members from javax.swing.AbstractAction not shown*
  2 *3 inherited members from TextAction not shown*
  3 *5 inherited members from StyledEditorKit.StyledTextAction not shown*
  4 *8 inherited members from javax.swing.Action not shown*
  5 public . . . . void **actionPerformed** (java.awt.event.ActionEvent e)   ε855,644,738,743,745
  * public . . . . **StyledEditorKit.ForegroundAction** (String nm, java.awt.Color fg)

StyledEditorKit.ItalicAction — javax.swing.text

```
     Object
1.2 ○ └javax.swing.AbstractAction 1 --------------- javax.swing.Action 4 (java.awt.event.ActionListener 5
        |                                            (java.util.EventListener)), Cloneable, java.io.Serializable
1.2 ○   └TextAction 2
1.2 ○     └StyledEditorKit.StyledTextAction 3
1.2         └StyledEditorKit.ItalicAction
```

1 *12 inherited members from javax.swing.AbstractAction not shown*
2 *3 inherited members from TextAction not shown*
3 *5 inherited members from StyledEditorKit.StyledTextAction not shown*
4 *8 inherited members from javax.swing.Action not shown*
5 public........................void **actionPerformed** (java.awt.event.ActionEvent e) — ε855,644,738,743,745
* public........................... **StyledEditorKit.ItalicAction** ()

StyledEditorKit.StyledTextAction — javax.swing.text

```
     Object
1.2 ○ └javax.swing.AbstractAction 1 --------------- javax.swing.Action 3 (java.awt.event.ActionListener 4
        |                                            (java.util.EventListener)), Cloneable, java.io.Serializable
1.2 ○   └TextAction 2
1.2 ○     └StyledEditorKit.StyledTextAction
```

1 *12 inherited members from javax.swing.AbstractAction not shown*
2 *3 inherited members from TextAction not shown*
3 *8 inherited members from javax.swing.Action not shown*
○ 4 public abstract.............void actionPerformed (java.awt.event.ActionEvent e) — ε1011,855,644,738,743
● protected final.................. **getEditor** (java.awt.event.ActionEvent e)
..... javax.swing.JEditorPane
● protected final.................. **getStyledDocument** (javax.swing.JEditorPane e)
.... *StyledDocument*
● protected final.. StyledEditorKit **getStyledEditorKit** (javax.swing.JEditorPane e)
● protected final.............void **setCharacterAttributes** (javax.swing.JEditorPane editor, *AttributeSet* attr, boolean replace)
● protected final.............void **setParagraphAttributes** (javax.swing.JEditorPane editor, *AttributeSet* attr, boolean replace)
* public........................... **StyledEditorKit.StyledTextAction** (String nm)

StyledEditorKit.UnderlineAction — javax.swing.text

```
     Object
1.2 ○ └javax.swing.AbstractAction 1 --------------- javax.swing.Action 4 (java.awt.event.ActionListener 5
        |                                            (java.util.EventListener)), Cloneable, java.io.Serializable
1.2 ○   └TextAction 2
1.2 ○     └StyledEditorKit.StyledTextAction 3
1.2         └StyledEditorKit.UnderlineAction
```

1 *12 inherited members from javax.swing.AbstractAction not shown*
2 *3 inherited members from TextAction not shown*
3 *5 inherited members from StyledEditorKit.StyledTextAction not shown*
4 *8 inherited members from javax.swing.Action not shown*
5 public........................void **actionPerformed** (java.awt.event.ActionEvent e) — ε855,644,738,743,745
* public........................... **StyledEditorKit.UnderlineAction** ()

StyleSheet — javax.swing.text.html

```
     Object
1.2   └javax.swing.text.StyleContext 1 ------------- java.io.Serializable, javax.swing.text.AbstractDocument
        |                                             .AttributeContext
1.2     └StyleSheet
```

1 public.................... ***javax.swing.text.AttributeSet*** **addAttribute** (*javax.swing.text.AttributeSet* old, Object key, Object value)
1 public.................... ***javax.swing.text.AttributeSet*** **addAttributes** (*javax.swing.text.AttributeSet* old, *javax.swing.text.AttributeSet* attr)

Class *Interface* —extends ---implements ○ abstract ● final △ static ▲ static final * constructor x x—inherited x **x**—declared **x x**—overridden
εn—examples of usage ˬ—has subclass package—see other volume

	1	public......................void	addChangeListener (*javax.swing.event.ChangeListener* l)
1.3		public......................void	**addCSSAttribute** (*javax.swing.text.MutableAttributeSet* attr, CSS.Attribute key, String value)
1.3		public.................. boolean	**addCSSAttributeFromHTML** (*javax.swing.text.MutableAttributeSet* attr, CSS.Attribute key, String value)
		public......................void	**addRule** (String rule)
	1	public....*javax.swing.text.Style*	addStyle (String nm, *javax.swing.text.Style* parent)
1.3		public......................void	**addStyleSheet** (StyleSheet ss)
	1	protected........ ***javax.swing*** ***.text.MutableAttributeSet***	**createLargeAttributeSet** (*javax.swing.text.AttributeSet* a)
	1	protected........ **javax** **.swing.text.StyleContext** **.SmallAttributeSet**	**createSmallAttributeSet** (*javax.swing.text.AttributeSet* a)
▲	1	public static final........ String	DEFAULT_STYLE = "default"
	1	public............**java.awt.Color**	**getBackground** (*javax.swing.text.AttributeSet* a)
1.3		public............ java.net.URL	**getBase** ()
		public... StyleSheet.BoxPainter	**getBoxPainter** (*javax.swing.text.AttributeSet* a)
1.4	1	public............ *javax.swing* *.event.ChangeListener[]*	getChangeListeners ()
	1	protected....................int	getCompressionThreshold ()
		public.......................... . *javax.swing.text.AttributeSet*	**getDeclaration** (String decl)
▲	1	public static final........ javax .swing.text.StyleContext	getDefaultStyleContext ()
	1	public.......................... . *javax.swing.text.AttributeSet*	getEmptySet ()
	1	public............**java.awt.Font**	**getFont** (*javax.swing.text.AttributeSet* a)
	1	public............java.awt.Font	getFont (String family, int style, int size)
	1	public.... java.awt.FontMetrics	getFontMetrics (java.awt.Font f)
	1	public............**java.awt.Color**	**getForeground** (*javax.swing.text.AttributeSet* a)
△		public static ....int	**getIndexOfSize** (float pt)
		public... StyleSheet.ListPainter	**getListPainter** (*javax.swing.text.AttributeSet* a)
		public....................float	**getPointSize** (int index)
		public....................float	**getPointSize** (String size)
		public....*javax.swing.text.Style*	**getRule** (String selector)
		public....*javax.swing.text.Style*	**getRule** (HTML.Tag t, *javax.swing.text.Element* e)
△	1	public static .... Object	getStaticAttribute (Object key)
△	1	public static .... Object	getStaticAttributeKey (Object key)
	1	public....*javax.swing.text.Style*	getStyle (String nm)
	1	public.... *java.util.Enumeration*	getStyleNames ()
1.3		public..............StyleSheet[]	**getStyleSheets** ()
		public.......................... . *javax.swing.text.AttributeSet*	**getViewAttributes** (javax.swing.text.View v)
1.3		public......................void	**importStyleSheet** (java.net.URL url)
		public......................void	**loadRules** (java.io.Reader in, java.net.URL ref) throws java.io.IOException
	1	public......................void	readAttributes (java.io.ObjectInputStream in, *javax.swing.text.MutableAttributeSet* a) throws ClassNotFoundException, java.io.IOException
△	1	public static ....void	readAttributeSet (java.io.ObjectInputStream in, *javax.swing.text.MutableAttributeSet* a) throws ClassNotFoundException, java.io.IOException
	1	public......................void	reclaim (*javax.swing.text.AttributeSet* a)
△	1	public static ....void	registerStaticAttributeKey (Object key)
	1	public.......................***javax*** **.swing.text.AttributeSet**	**removeAttribute** (*javax.swing.text.AttributeSet* old, Object key)
	1	public.......................***javax*** **.swing.text.AttributeSet**	**removeAttributes** (*javax.swing.text.AttributeSet* old, *java.util.Enumeration* names)
	1	public.......................***javax*** **.swing.text.AttributeSet**	**removeAttributes** (*javax.swing.text.AttributeSet* old, *javax.swing.text.AttributeSet* attrs)
	1	public......................void	removeChangeListener (*javax.swing.event.ChangeListener* l)
	1	public...................... **void**	**removeStyle** (String nm)
1.3		public......................void	**removeStyleSheet** (StyleSheet ss)
1.3		public......................void	**setBase** (java.net.URL base)
		public......................void	**setBaseFontSize** (int sz)
		public......................void	**setBaseFontSize** (String size)
		public............java.awt.Color	**stringToColor** (String string)
∗		public..........................	**StyleSheet** ()
	1	public...................... String	toString ()
		public.......................... . *javax.swing.text.AttributeSet*	**translateHTMLToCSS** (*javax.swing.text.AttributeSet* htmlAttrSet)
	1	public......................void	writeAttributes (java.io.ObjectOutputStream out, *javax.swing.text.AttributeSet* a) throws java.io.IOException
△	1	public static ....void	writeAttributeSet (java.io.ObjectOutputStream out, *javax.swing.text.AttributeSet* a) throws java.io.IOException

S

Classes

StyleSheet.BoxPainter	javax.swing.text.html

```
       Object
1.2    └StyleSheet.BoxPainter - - - - - - - - - - - - - - - - - - - java.io.Serializable
```

public......................float **getInset** (int side, javax.swing.text.View v)
public........................void **paint** (java.awt.Graphics g, float x, float y, float w, float h, javax.swing.text.View v)

StyleSheet.ListPainter	javax.swing.text.html

```
       Object
1.2    └StyleSheet.ListPainter - - - - - - - - - - - - - - - - - - - java.io.Serializable
```

public........................void **paint** (java.awt.Graphics g, float x, float y, float w, float h, javax.swing.text.View v,
int item)

SupportedValuesAttribute	javax.print.attribute

```
1.4    SupportedValuesAttribute ─────────────────── Attribute 1 (java.io.Serializable)
```

1	public....................Class getCategory ()	ε707
1	public....................String getName ()	ε706,707,708

SwingConstants	javax.swing

```
1.2    SwingConstants
```

▲	public static final............int	**BOTTOM** = 3	ε747,748
▲	public static final............int	**CENTER** = 0	ε747,748
▲	public static final............int	**EAST** = 3	
▲	public static final............int	**HORIZONTAL** = 0	ε817
▲	public static final............int	**LEADING** = 10	
▲	public static final............int	**LEFT** = 2	ε747,748
1.4 ▲	public static final............int	**NEXT** = 12	
▲	public static final............int	**NORTH** = 1	
▲	public static final............int	**NORTH_EAST** = 2	
▲	public static final............int	**NORTH_WEST** = 8	
1.4 ▲	public static final............int	**PREVIOUS** = 13	
▲	public static final............int	**RIGHT** = 4	ε747,748
▲	public static final............int	**SOUTH** = 5	
▲	public static final............int	**SOUTH_EAST** = 4	
▲	public static final............int	**SOUTH_WEST** = 6	
▲	public static final............int	**TOP** = 1	ε747,748
▲	public static final............int	**TRAILING** = 11	
▲	public static final............int	**VERTICAL** = 1	ε794,796,801,816
▲	public static final............int	**WEST** = 7	

SwingPropertyChangeSupport	javax.swing.event

```
       Object
1.1    └java.beans.PropertyChangeSupport 1 - - - - - - java.io.Serializable
1.2 ●    └SwingPropertyChangeSupport
```

1	public synchronized ...... **void addPropertyChangeListener** (*java.beans.PropertyChangeListener* listener)	
1	public synchronized ...... **void addPropertyChangeListener** (String propertyName,	
	java.beans.PropertyChangeListener listener)	
1	public........................ **void firePropertyChange** (java.beans.PropertyChangeEvent evt)	
1	public........................ **void firePropertyChange** (String propertyName, Object oldValue, Object newValue)	
1	public........................void firePropertyChange (String propertyName, int oldValue, int newValue)	
1	public........................void firePropertyChange (String propertyName, boolean oldValue, boolean newValue)	
1.4	1 public synchronized .... **getPropertyChangeListeners** ()	
	.... *java.beans.-*	
	PropertyChangeListener[]	
1.4	1 public synchronized .... **getPropertyChangeListeners** (String propertyName)	
	.... *java.beans.-*	
	PropertyChangeListener[]	
1	public synchronized .. **boolean hasListeners** (String propertyName)	

Class *Interface* —extends - - -implements ○ abstract ● final △ static ▲ static final ✳ constructor x x—inherited x **x**—declared **x x**—overridden
ε*n*—examples of usage ˎ—has subclass package—see other volume

S

1	public synchronized	**void**	**removePropertyChangeListener** (*java.beans.PropertyChangeListener* listener)
1	public synchronized	**void**	**removePropertyChangeListener** (String propertyName, *java.beans.PropertyChangeListener* listener)
*	public.........................		**SwingPropertyChangeSupport** (Object sourceBean)

SwingUtilities javax.swing

```
         Object
1.2      └─SwingUtilities - - - - - - - - - - - - - - - - - - - - - - - - SwingConstants ¹
```

	1	*19 inherited members from SwingConstants not shown*		
1.4 △		public static .... java.awt.Rectangle	**calculateInnerArea** (JComponent c, java.awt.Rectangle r)	
△		public static .... java.awt.Rectangle[]	**computeDifference** (java.awt.Rectangle rectA, java.awt.Rectangle rectB)	
△		public static .... java.awt.Rectangle	**computeIntersection** (int x, int y, int width, int height, java.awt.Rectangle dest)	
△		public static ....int	**computeStringWidth** (java.awt.FontMetrics fm, String str)	
△		public static .... java.awt.Rectangle	**computeUnion** (int x, int y, int width, int height, java.awt.Rectangle dest)	
△		public static .... java.awt.event.MouseEvent	**convertMouseEvent** (java.awt.Component source, java.awt.event.MouseEvent sourceEvent, java.awt.Component destination)	
△		public static ..... java.awt.Point	**convertPoint** (java.awt.Component source, java.awt.Point aPoint, java.awt.Component destination)	
△		public static ..... java.awt.Point	**convertPoint** (java.awt.Component source, int x, int y, java.awt.Component destination)	
△		public static ....void	**convertPointFromScreen** (java.awt.Point p, java.awt.Component c)	ε865
△		public static ....void	**convertPointToScreen** (java.awt.Point p, java.awt.Component c)	ε865
△		public static .... java.awt.Rectangle	**convertRectangle** (java.awt.Component source, java.awt.Rectangle aRectangle, java.awt.Component destination)	
D △		public static .... java.awt.Component	**findFocusOwner** (java.awt.Component c)	
△		public static .... *javax ₂ .accessibility.Accessible*	**getAccessibleAt** (java.awt.Component c, java.awt.Point p)	
△		public static .... *javax ₂ .accessibility.Accessible*	**getAccessibleChild** (java.awt.Component c, int i)	
△		public static ....int	**getAccessibleChildrenCount** (java.awt.Component c)	
△		public static ....int	**getAccessibleIndexInParent** (java.awt.Component c)	
△		public static .... javax.accessibility ₂ .AccessibleStateSet	**getAccessibleStateSet** (java.awt.Component c)	
△		public static java.awt.Container	**getAncestorNamed** (String name, java.awt.Component comp)	
△		public static java.awt.Container	**getAncestorOfClass** (Class c, java.awt.Component comp)	
△		public static .... java.awt.Component	**getDeepestComponentAt** (java.awt.Component parent, int x, int y)	
△		public static .... java.awt.Rectangle	**getLocalBounds** (java.awt.Component aComponent)	
△		public static .... java.awt.Component	**getRoot** (java.awt.Component c)	ε738
△		public static .... JRootPane	**getRootPane** (java.awt.Component c)	
1.3 △		public static .... ActionMap	**getUIActionMap** (JComponent component)	
1.3 △		public static ....InputMap	**getUIInputMap** (JComponent component, int condition)	
1.3 △		public static .. java.awt.Window	**getWindowAncestor** (java.awt.Component c)	
△		public static ....void	**invokeAndWait** (*Runnable* doRun) throws InterruptedException, java.lang.reflect.InvocationTargetException	
△		public static ....void	**invokeLater** (*Runnable* doRun)	
△		public static .... boolean	**isDescendingFrom** (java.awt.Component a, java.awt.Component b)	
△		public static .... boolean	**isEventDispatchThread** ()	
△		public static .... boolean	**isLeftMouseButton** (java.awt.event.MouseEvent anEvent)	
△		public static .... boolean	**isMiddleMouseButton** (java.awt.event.MouseEvent anEvent)	
▲		public static final ...... boolean	**isRectangleContainingRectangle** (java.awt.Rectangle a, java.awt.Rectangle b)	
△		public static .... boolean	**isRightMouseButton** (java.awt.event.MouseEvent anEvent)	
△		public static ....String	**layoutCompoundLabel** (java.awt.FontMetrics fm, String text, *Icon* icon, int verticalAlignment, int horizontalAlignment, int verticalTextPosition, int horizontalTextPosition, java.awt.Rectangle viewR, java.awt.Rectangle iconR, java.awt.Rectangle textR, int textIconGap)	
△		public static ....String	**layoutCompoundLabel** (JComponent c, java.awt.FontMetrics fm, String text, *Icon* icon, int verticalAlignment, int horizontalAlignment, int verticalTextPosition, int horizontalTextPosition, java.awt.Rectangle viewR, java.awt.Rectangle iconR, java.awt.Rectangle textR, int textIconGap)	

S

Classes

SwingUtilities

Synthesizer   javax.sound.midi

1.3   *Synthesizer*————————————————— *MidiDevice* [1]

1	public .... void	close ()	
	public .... Instrument[]	**getAvailableInstruments** ()	
	public .... *MidiChannel[]*	**getChannels** ()	ε721
	public .... *Soundbank*	**getDefaultSoundbank** ()	
1	public .... MidiDevice.Info	getDeviceInfo ()	
	public .... long	**getLatency** ()	
	public .... Instrument[]	**getLoadedInstruments** ()	
	public .... int	**getMaxPolyphony** ()	
1	public .... int	getMaxReceivers ()	
1	public .... int	getMaxTransmitters ()	
1	public .... long	getMicrosecondPosition ()	ε720
1	public .... *Receiver*	getReceiver () throws MidiUnavailableException	
1	public .... *Transmitter*	getTransmitter () throws MidiUnavailableException	
	public .... VoiceStatus[]	**getVoiceStatus** ()	
1	public .... boolean	isOpen ()	
	public .... boolean	**isSoundbankSupported** (*Soundbank* soundbank)	
	public .... boolean	**loadAllInstruments** (*Soundbank* soundbank)	
	public .... boolean	**loadInstrument** (Instrument instrument)	
	public .... boolean	**loadInstruments** (*Soundbank* soundbank, Patch[] patchList)	
1	public .... void	open () throws MidiUnavailableException	ε716,717
	public .... boolean	**remapInstrument** (Instrument from, Instrument to)	
	public .... void	**unloadAllInstruments** (*Soundbank* soundbank)	
	public .... void	**unloadInstrument** (Instrument instrument)	
	public .... void	**unloadInstruments** (*Soundbank* soundbank, Patch[] patchList)	

SysexMessage   javax.sound.midi

Object
  └MidiMessage [1] - *Cloneable*
1.3 ○
1.3   └SysexMessage

1	public .... **Object clone** ()	
1	protected .... byte[] data	
	public .... byte[] **getData** ()	
1	public .... int getLength ()	
1	public .... byte[] getMessage ()	
1	public .... int getStatus ()	
1	protected .... int length	
1	public .... **void setMessage** (byte[] data, int length) throws InvalidMidiDataException	
	public .... void **setMessage** (int status, byte[] data, int length) throws InvalidMidiDataException	
▲	public static final .... int **SPECIAL_SYSTEM_EXCLUSIVE** = 247	
✳	public .... **SysexMessage** ()	
✳	protected .... **SysexMessage** (byte[] data)	
▲	public static final .... int **SYSTEM_EXCLUSIVE** = 240	

SystemColor   java.awt

Object   ε584,791,832,870,878
  └Color [1] - *Paint* (*Transparency* [2]), *java.io.Serializable*
1.1 ●   └SystemColor

Class *Interface* —extends - - -implements ○ abstract ● final △ static ▲ static final ✳ constructor x x—inherited x **x**—declared **x x**—overridden
ε*n*—examples of usage —has subclass package—see other volume

	1	*49 inherited members from Color not shown*		
▲		public static final .... int	**ACTIVE_CAPTION** = 1	
▲		public static final .... int	**ACTIVE_CAPTION_BORDER** = 3	
▲		public static final .... int	**ACTIVE_CAPTION_TEXT** = 2	
▲		public static final . SystemColor	**activeCaption**	
▲		public static final . SystemColor	**activeCaptionBorder**	
▲		public static final . SystemColor	**activeCaptionText**	
1.2 ▲	2	public static final .... int	BITMASK = 2	ε666,667
▲		public static final . SystemColor	**control**	
▲		public static final .... int	**CONTROL** = 17	
▲		public static final .... int	**CONTROL_DK_SHADOW** = 22	
▲		public static final .... int	**CONTROL_HIGHLIGHT** = 19	
▲		public static final .... int	**CONTROL_LT_HIGHLIGHT** = 20	
▲		public static final .... int	**CONTROL_SHADOW** = 21	
▲		public static final .... int	**CONTROL_TEXT** = 18	
▲		public static final . SystemColor	**controlDkShadow**	
▲		public static final . SystemColor	**controlHighlight**	
▲		public static final . SystemColor	**controlLtHighlight**	
▲		public static final . SystemColor	**controlShadow**	
▲		public static final . SystemColor	**controlText**	
1.2	1	public .... ***PaintContext***	**createContext** (java.awt.image.ColorModel cm, Rectangle r, java.awt.geom ⏎ .Rectangle2D r2d, java.awt.geom.AffineTransform xform, RenderingHints hints)	
▲		public static final . SystemColor	**desktop**	
▲		public static final .... int	**DESKTOP** = 0	
	1	public .... **int**	**getRGB** ()	
▲		public static final .... int	**INACTIVE_CAPTION** = 4	
▲		public static final .... int	**INACTIVE_CAPTION_BORDER** = 6	
▲		public static final .... int	**INACTIVE_CAPTION_TEXT** = 5	
▲		public static final . SystemColor	**inactiveCaption**	
▲		public static final . SystemColor	**inactiveCaptionBorder**	
▲		public static final . SystemColor	**inactiveCaptionText**	
▲		public static final . SystemColor	**info**	
▲		public static final .... int	**INFO** = 24	
▲		public static final .... int	**INFO_TEXT** = 25	
▲		public static final . SystemColor	**infoText**	
▲		public static final . SystemColor	**menu**	
▲		public static final .... int	**MENU** = 10	
▲		public static final .... int	**MENU_TEXT** = 11	
▲		public static final . SystemColor	**menuText**	
▲		public static final .... int	**NUM_COLORS** = 26	
1.2 ▲	2	public static final .... int	OPAQUE = 1	ε666,667
▲		public static final . SystemColor	**scrollbar**	
▲		public static final .... int	**SCROLLBAR** = 23	
▲		public static final . SystemColor	**text**	
▲		public static final .... int	**TEXT** = 12	
▲		public static final .... int	**TEXT_HIGHLIGHT** = 14	
▲		public static final .... int	**TEXT_HIGHLIGHT_TEXT** = 15	
▲		public static final .... int	**TEXT_INACTIVE_TEXT** = 16	
▲		public static final .... int	**TEXT_TEXT** = 13	
▲		public static final . SystemColor	**textHighlight**	
▲		public static final . SystemColor	**textHighlightText**	
▲		public static final . SystemColor	**textInactiveText**	
▲		public static final . SystemColor	**textText**	
	1	public .... **String**	**toString** ()	
1.2 ▲	2	public static final .... int	TRANSLUCENT = 3	ε666
▲		public static final . SystemColor	**window**	
▲		public static final .... int	**WINDOW** = 7	
▲		public static final .... int	**WINDOW_BORDER** = 8	
▲		public static final .... int	**WINDOW_TEXT** = 9	
▲		public static final . SystemColor	**windowBorder**	
▲		public static final . SystemColor	**windowText**	

S

Classes

SystemFlavorMap	java.awt.datatransfer

```
      Object
1.2 ● └ SystemFlavorMap --------------------- FlavorMap 1, FlavorTable 2 (FlavorMap 1)
```

1.4		public synchronized .... void	**addFlavorForUnencodedNative** (String nat, DataFlavor flav)
1.4		public synchronized .... void	**addUnencodedNativeForFlavor** (DataFlavor flav, String nat)
△		public static .... DataFlavor	**decodeDataFlavor** (String nat) throws ClassNotFoundException
△		public static .... String	**decodeJavaMIMEType** (String nat)
△		public static .... String	**encodeDataFlavor** (DataFlavor flav)
△		public static .... String	**encodeJavaMIMEType** (String mimeType)

SystemFlavorMap

	△	public static ....FlavorMap	**getDefaultFlavorMap** ()	
1.4	2	public synchronized	**getFlavorsForNative** (String nat)	
		.................java.util.List		
	1	public synchronized	**getFlavorsForNatives** (String[] natives)	
		.................java.util.Map		
1.4	2	public synchronized	**getNativesForFlavor** (DataFlavor flav)	
		.................java.util.List		
	1	public synchronized	**getNativesForFlavors** (DataFlavor[] flavors)	
		.................java.util.Map		
	△	public static .... boolean	**isJavaMIMEType** (String str)	
1.4		public synchronized ....void	**setFlavorsForNative** (String nat, DataFlavor[] flavors)	
1.4		public synchronized ....void	**setNativesForFlavor** (DataFlavor flav, String[] natives)	

TabableView   javax.swing.text

1.2	*TabableView*
	public.....................float **getPartialSpan** (int p0, int p1)
	public.....................float **getTabbedSpan** (float x, *TabExpander* e)

TabbedPaneUI   javax.swing.plaf

		Object
1.2	○	└ComponentUI [1]
1.2	○	└TabbedPaneUI
	1	*11 inherited members from ComponentUI not shown*
	○	public abstract .... **getTabBounds** (javax.swing.JTabbedPane pane, int index)
		.... java.awt.Rectangle
	○	public abstract ....int **getTabRunCount** (javax.swing.JTabbedPane pane)
	✳	public......................... **TabbedPaneUI** ()
	○	public abstract ....int **tabForCoordinate** (javax.swing.JTabbedPane pane, int x, int y)

TabExpander   javax.swing.text

1.2	*TabExpander*
	public.....................float **nextTabStop** (float x, int tabOffset)

TableCellEditor   javax.swing.table

1.2		*TableCellEditor*————————————————————*javax.swing.CellEditor* [1]	
	1	public.....................void addCellEditorListener (*javax.swing.event.CellEditorListener* l)	
	1	public.....................void cancelCellEditing ()	ε956
	1	public.................Object getCellEditorValue ()	ε953,954,960
		public.... java.awt.Component **getTableCellEditorComponent** (javax.swing.JTable table, Object value,	
		boolean isSelected, int row, int column)	ε953,960
	1	public................ boolean isCellEditable (java.util.EventObject anEvent)	ε955,960
	1	public.....................void removeCellEditorListener (*javax.swing.event.CellEditorListener* l)	
	1	public................ boolean shouldSelectCell (java.util.EventObject anEvent)	
	1	public................ boolean stopCellEditing ()	ε954,956

TableCellRenderer   javax.swing.table

1.2	*TableCellRenderer* ε913,914,933,934,938
	public.... java.awt.Component **getTableCellRendererComponent** (javax.swing.JTable table, Object value,
	boolean isSelected, boolean hasFocus, int row, int column) ε928,929,936,950,959

TableColumn   javax.swing.table

	Object ε937
1.2	└TableColumn - *java.io.Serializable*

Class   *Interface*   ——extends   - - -implements   ○ abstract   ● final   △ static   ▲ static final   ✳ constructor   x x—inherited   x **x**—declared   **x x**—overridden
εn—examples of usage   —has subclass   package—see other volume

	public synchronized ....void	**addPropertyChangeListener** (*java.beans.PropertyChangeListener* listener)	
▲	public static final........String	**CELL_RENDERER_PROPERTY** = "cellRenderer"	
	protected ....*TableCellEditor*	**cellEditor**	
	protected ... *TableCellRenderer*	**cellRenderer**	
▲	public static final.........String	**COLUMN_WIDTH_PROPERTY** = "columWidth"	
	protected ... *TableCellRenderer*	**createDefaultHeaderRenderer** ()	
D	public......................void	**disableResizedPosting** ()	
D	public......................void	**enableResizedPosting** ()	
	public..........*TableCellEditor*	**getCellEditor** ()	
	public...... *TableCellRenderer*	**getCellRenderer** ()	
	public...... *TableCellRenderer*	**getHeaderRenderer** ()	ε950
	public....................Object	**getHeaderValue** ()	ε950
	public....................Object	**getIdentifier** ()	
	public.......................int	**getMaxWidth** ()	
	public.......................int	**getMinWidth** ()	
	public.......................int	**getModelIndex** ()	ε915,916,922,927
	public.......................int	**getPreferredWidth** ()	
1.4	public synchronized .... *java.beans.- PropertyChangeListener[]*	**getPropertyChangeListeners** ()	
	public.................. boolean	**getResizable** ()	
	public.......................int	**getWidth** ()	
▲	public static final........String	**HEADER_RENDERER_PROPERTY** = "headerRenderer"	
▲	public static final........String	**HEADER_VALUE_PROPERTY** = "headerValue"	
	protected ... *TableCellRenderer*	**headerRenderer**	
	protected ....Object	**headerValue**	
	protected ....Object	**identifier**	
	protected .... boolean	**isResizable**	
	protected ....int	**maxWidth**	
	protected ....int	**minWidth**	
	protected ....int	**modelIndex**	
	public synchronized ....void	**removePropertyChangeListener** (*java.beans.PropertyChangeListener* listener)	
D	protected transient...........int	**resizedPostingDisableCount**	
	public......................void	**setCellEditor** (*TableCellEditor* cellEditor)	ε927,953,959,960
	public......................void	**setCellRenderer** (*TableCellRenderer* cellRenderer)	ε927,928,959,960
	public......................void	**setHeaderRenderer** (*TableCellRenderer* headerRenderer)	ε933,934,936
	public......................void	**setHeaderValue** (Object headerValue)	ε920,932,933,934
	public......................void	**setIdentifier** (Object identifier)	
	public......................void	**setMaxWidth** (int maxWidth)	ε919
	public......................void	**setMinWidth** (int minWidth)	ε919
	public......................void	**setModelIndex** (int modelIndex)	ε922
	public......................void	**setPreferredWidth** (int preferredWidth)	ε917,919,950
	public......................void	**setResizable** (boolean isResizable)	
	public......................void	**setWidth** (int width)	
	public......................void	**sizeWidthToFit** ()	
∗	public......................	**TableColumn** ()	
∗	public......................	**TableColumn** (int modelIndex)	ε920
∗	public......................	**TableColumn** (int modelIndex, int width)	
∗	public......................	**TableColumn** (int modelIndex, int width, *TableCellRenderer* cellRenderer, *TableCellEditor* cellEditor)	
	protected ....int	**width**	

TableColumnModel

1.2   *TableColumnModel*

public......................void	**addColumn** (TableColumn aColumn)	
public......................void	**addColumnModelListener** (*javax.swing.event.TableColumnModelListener* x)	ε966
public............. TableColumn	**getColumn** (int columnIndex)	ε915,916,917,919,922
public.......................int	**getColumnCount** ()	
public.......................int	**getColumnIndex** (Object columnIdentifier)	
public.......................int	**getColumnIndexAtX** (int xPosition)	ε937,967
public.......................int	**getColumnMargin** ()	
public.... *java.util.Enumeration*	**getColumns** ()	ε916,922,927
public.................. boolean	**getColumnSelectionAllowed** ()	
public...................int	**getSelectedColumnCount** ()	
public....................int[]	**getSelectedColumns** ()	
public......... *javax.swing.ListSelectionModel*	**getSelectionModel** ()	ε942,944,957,964
public.......................int	**getTotalColumnWidth** ()	
public......................void	**moveColumn** (int columnIndex, int newIndex)	

T

TableColumnModel

public	void	**removeColumn** (TableColumn column)	ε963
public	void	**removeColumnModelListener** (*javax.swing.event.TableColumnModelListener* x)	
public	void	**setColumnMargin** (int newMargin)	
public	void	**setColumnSelectionAllowed** (boolean flag)	
public	void	**setSelectionModel** (*javax.swing.ListSelectionModel* newModel)	

TableColumnModelEvent
javax.swing.event

Object   ε640,641,643,649,566
1.1 └ java.util.EventObject[1] - - - - - - - - - - - - - - - - - - - *java.io.Serializable*
1.2   └ TableColumnModelEvent

	protected	int	**fromIndex**	
	public	int	**getFromIndex** ()	ε966
1	public	Object	getSource ()	ε644,886,565,568,570
	public	int	**getToIndex** ()	ε966
1	protected transient	Object	source	
*	public		**TableColumnModelEvent** (*javax.swing.table.TableColumnModel* source, int from, int to)	
	protected	int	**toIndex**	
1	public	String	toString ()	

TableColumnModelListener
javax.swing.event

1.2 *TableColumnModelListener*————————————*java.util.EventListener*   ε738,743,745,746,752

public	void	**columnAdded** (TableColumnModelEvent e)	ε966
public	void	**columnMarginChanged** (ChangeEvent e)	ε966
public	void	**columnMoved** (TableColumnModelEvent e)	ε966
public	void	**columnRemoved** (TableColumnModelEvent e)	ε966
public	void	**columnSelectionChanged** (ListSelectionEvent e)	ε966

TableHeaderUI
javax.swing.plaf

Object
1.2 ○ └ ComponentUI[1]
1.2 ○   └ TableHeaderUI

1	*11 inherited members from ComponentUI not shown*		
*	public		**TableHeaderUI** ()

TableModel
javax.swing.table

1.2 *TableModel*   ε950,958

public	void	**addTableModelListener** (*javax.swing.event.TableModelListener* l)	
			ε957,965
public	Class	**getColumnClass** (int columnIndex)	ε927,929
public	int	**getColumnCount** ()	ε920,921
public	String	**getColumnName** (int columnIndex)	
public	int	**getRowCount** ()	ε911,909,910,962
public	Object	**getValueAt** (int rowIndex, int columnIndex)	ε926
public	boolean	**isCellEditable** (int rowIndex, int columnIndex)	ε958
public	void	**removeTableModelListener** (*javax.swing.event.TableModelListener* l)	
public	void	**setValueAt** (Object aValue, int rowIndex, int columnIndex)	ε926

TableModelEvent
javax.swing.event

Object   ε640,641,643,649,566
1.1 └ java.util.EventObject[1] - - - - - - - - - - - - - - - - - - - *java.io.Serializable*
1.2   └ TableModelEvent

▲	public static final	int	**ALL_COLUMNS** = -1	ε957,965
	protected	int	**column**	
▲	public static final	int	**DELETE** = -1	ε965
	protected	int	**firstRow**	
	public	int	**getColumn** ()	ε957,965

Class *Interface* —extends - - -implements ○ abstract ● final △ static ▲ static final ✱ constructor x x—inherited x **x**—declared **x x**—overridden
ε*n*—examples of usage ⌐has subclass package—see other volume

	public	int	**getFirstRow** ()	ε957,965
	public	int	**getLastRow** ()	ε957,965
1	public	Object	getSource ()	ε644,886,565,568,570
	public	int	**getType** ()	ε965
▲	public static final	int	**HEADER_ROW** = -1	ε957,965
▲	public static final	int	**INSERT** = 1	ε965
	protected	int	**lastRow**	
1	protected transient	Object	source	
*	public		**TableModelEvent** (*javax.swing.table.TableModel* source)	
*	public		**TableModelEvent** (*javax.swing.table.TableModel* source, int row)	
*	public		**TableModelEvent** (*javax.swing.table.TableModel* source, int firstRow, int lastRow)	
*	public		**TableModelEvent** (*javax.swing.table.TableModel* source, int firstRow, int lastRow, int column)	
*	public		**TableModelEvent** (*javax.swing.table.TableModel* source, int firstRow, int lastRow, int column, int type)	
1	public	String	toString ()	
	protected	int	**type**	
▲	public static final	int	**UPDATE** = 0	ε965

TableModelListener   javax.swing.event

1.2	*TableModelListener* ——————— *java.util.EventListener*			ε738,743,745,746,752
	public	void	**tableChanged** (TableModelEvent e)	ε957,965

TableUI   javax.swing.plaf

```
      Object
1.2 ○  └ComponentUI 1
1.2 ○    └TableUI
```

1	*11 inherited members from ComponentUI not shown*		
*	public		**TableUI** ()

TableView   javax.swing.text

```
      Object
1.2 ○  └View 1 - - - - - - - - - - - - - - - - - - - - - - - - - - javax.swing.SwingConstants 4
1.2 ○    └CompositeView 2
1.2        └BoxView 3
1.2 ○        └TableView
```

	1	*33 inherited members from View not shown*		
	2	*17 inherited members from CompositeView not shown*		
	3	*31 inherited members from BoxView not shown*		
	4	*19 inherited members from javax.swing.SwingConstants not shown*		
	3	protected	javax₂.swing.SizeRequirements	**calculateMinorAxisRequirements** (int axis, javax.swing.SizeRequirements r)
D		protected	TableView.TableCell	**createTableCell** (*Element* elem)
		protected	TableView.TableRow	**createTableRow** (*Element* elem)
1.3	3	protected	void	**forwardUpdate** (*javax.swing.event.DocumentEvent.ElementChange* ec, *javax.swing.event.DocumentEvent* e, *java.awt.Shape* a, *ViewFactory* f)
	2	protected	View	**getViewAtPosition** (int pos, java.awt.Rectangle a)
		protected	void	**layoutColumns** (int targetSpan, int[] offsets, int[] spans, javax.swing.SizeRequirements[] reqs)
	3	protected	void	**layoutMinorAxis** (int targetSpan, int axis, int[] offsets, int[] spans)
	3	public	void	**replace** (int offset, int length, View[] views)
*		public		**TableView** (*Element* elem)

TableView.TableCell   javax.swing.text

```
      Object
1.2 ○  └View 1 - - - - - - - - - - - - - - - - - - - - - - - - - - javax.swing.SwingConstants 4
1.2 ○    └CompositeView 2
1.2        └BoxView 3
D            └TableView.TableCell - - - - - - - - - - - - - - - javax.swing.text.TableView.GridCell
```

1	*33 inherited members from View not shown*
2	*18 inherited members from CompositeView not shown*

T

Classes

787

TableView.TableCell

TableView.TableRow   javax.swing.text

```
        Object
 1.2 ○   └View¹ - - - - - - - - - - - - - - - - - - - - - - - - javax.swing.SwingConstants ⁴
 1.2 ○     └CompositeView²
 1.2        └BoxView³
 1.2          └TableView.TableRow
```

TabSet   javax.swing.text

```
        Object¹
 1.2     └TabSet - - - - - - - - - - - - - - - - - - - - - - - - java.io.Serializable
```

TabStop   javax.swing.text

```
        Object¹
 1.2     └TabStop - - - - - - - - - - - - - - - - - - - - - - - - java.io.Serializable
```

Class   *Interface*   —extends   - - -implements   ○ abstract   ● final   △ static   ▲ static final   ✳ constructor   x x—inherited   x **x**—declared   **x x**—overridden
εn—examples of usage   ⌣—has subclass   package—see other volume

788

TagElement	javax.swing.text.html.parser

Object
1.2 └─TagElement

public	boolean	**breaksFlow** ()
public	boolean	**fictional** ()
public	Element	**getElement** ()
public	javax.2	**getHTMLTag** ()
	.swing.text.html.HTML.Tag	
public	boolean	**isPreformatted** ()
* public		**TagElement** (Element elem)
* public		**TagElement** (Element elem, boolean fictional)

TargetDataLine	javax.sound.sampled

1.3 *TargetDataLine*────────────────*DataLine* [1] (*Line* [2])

2	public	void	addLineListener (*LineListener* listener)	ε731
1	public	int	available ()	
2	public	void	close ()	
1	public	void	drain ()	ε724
1	public	void	flush ()	
1	public	int	getBufferSize ()	ε724,728
2	public	Control	getControl (Control.Type control)	ε730
2	public	Control[]	getControls ()	
1	public	AudioFormat	getFormat ()	ε728
1	public	int	getFramePosition ()	
1	public	float	getLevel ()	
2	public	Line.Info	getLineInfo ()	
1	public	long	getMicrosecondPosition ()	ε729
1	public	boolean	isActive ()	
2	public	boolean	isControlSupported (Control.Type control)	
2	public	boolean	isOpen ()	
1	public	boolean	isRunning ()	
2	public	void	open () throws LineUnavailableException	
	public	void	**open** (AudioFormat format) throws LineUnavailableException	
	public	void	**open** (AudioFormat format, int bufferSize) throws LineUnavailableException	
	public	int	**read** (byte[] b, int off, int len)	
2	public	void	removeLineListener (*LineListener* listener)	
1	public	void	start ()	ε723,724,725
1	public	void	stop ()	ε724

TextAction	javax.swing.text

Object
1.2 ○ └─javax.swing.AbstractAction [1] - - - - - - - - - - - - - *javax.swing.Action* [2] (*java.awt.event.ActionListener* [3]
　　　　　　　　　　　　　　　　　(*java.util.EventListener*)), *Cloneable*, java.io.Serializable
1.2 ○ 　　└─TextAction

1	*12 inherited members from javax.swing.AbstractAction not shown*		
2	*8 inherited members from javax.swing.Action not shown*		
○ 3	public abstract	void	actionPerformed (java.awt.event.ActionEvent e)	ε972,1002,1011,855,644
▲	public static final		**augmentList** (*javax.swing.Action[]* list1, *javax.swing.Action[]* list2)	
		javax.swing.Action[]		
●	protected final		**getFocusedComponent** ()	
		JTextComponent		
●	protected final		**getTextComponent** (java.awt.event.ActionEvent e)	
		JTextComponent		
*	public		**TextAction** (String name)	ε972,1002

TextArea	java.awt

Object
○ └─Component [1] - *java.awt.image.ImageObserver* [3], *MenuContainer*,
　　　　　　　　　　　　　　　　　　　java.io.Serializable
　　└─TextComponent [2] - - - - - - - - - - - - - - - - - - - *javax.accessibility.Accessible*
　　　└─TextArea

T

TextArea

	1		*198 inherited members from Component not shown*
	3		*8 inherited members from java.awt.image.ImageObserver not shown*
	2	public..................... **void**	**addNotify** ()
1.1	2	public synchronized ....void	addTextListener (*java.awt.event.TextListener* l)
1.1		public..........................void	**append** (String str)
D		public synchronized ....void	**appendText** (String str)
1.2	2	public..........................void	enableInputMethods (boolean enable)
1.3	2	public.... **javax.accessibility** ₂ **.AccessibleContext**	**getAccessibleContext** ()
	2	public.................. Color	getBackground ()
1.1	2	public synchronized ....int	getCaretPosition ()
		public..........................int	**getColumns** ()
1.3	2	public . *java.util*.EventListener[]	getListeners (Class listenerType)
1.1	1	public.............. **Dimension**	**getMinimumSize** ()
1.1		public..............Dimension	**getMinimumSize** (int rows, int columns)
1.1	1	public.............. **Dimension**	**getPreferredSize** ()
1.1		public..............Dimension	**getPreferredSize** (int rows, int columns)
		public..........................int	**getRows** ()
1.1		public..........................int	**getScrollbarVisibility** ()
	2	public synchronized ..... String	getSelectedText ()
	2	public synchronized ....int	getSelectionEnd ()
	2	public synchronized ....int	getSelectionStart ()
	2	public synchronized ..... String	getText ()
1.4	2	public synchronized .... *java.awt.event.TextListener[]*	getTextListeners ()
1.1		public..........................void	**insert** (String str, int pos)
D		public synchronized ....void	**insertText** (String str, int pos)
	2	public.................. boolean	isEditable ()
D	1	public.............. **Dimension**	**minimumSize** ()
D		public..............Dimension	**minimumSize** (int rows, int columns)
	2	protected .... **String**	**paramString** ()
D	1	public.............. **Dimension**	**preferredSize** ()
D		public..............Dimension	**preferredSize** (int rows, int columns)
1.1	2	protected ....void	processEvent (AWTEvent e)
1.1	2	protected ....void	processTextEvent (java.awt.event.TextEvent e)
	2	public..........................void	removeNotify ()
1.1	2	public synchronized ....void	removeTextListener (*java.awt.event.TextListener* l)
1.1		public..........................void	**replaceRange** (String str, int start, int end)
D		public synchronized ....void	**replaceText** (String str, int start, int end)
1.1 ▲		public static final ....int	**SCROLLBARS_BOTH** = 0
1.1 ▲		public static final ....int	**SCROLLBARS_HORIZONTAL_ONLY** = 2
1.1 ▲		public static final ....int	**SCROLLBARS_NONE** = 3
1.1 ▲		public static final ....int	**SCROLLBARS_VERTICAL_ONLY** = 1
	2	public synchronized ....void	select (int selectionStart, int selectionEnd)
	2	public synchronized ......void	selectAll ()
	2	public..........................void	setBackground (Color c)
1.1	2	public synchronized ....void	setCaretPosition (int position)
1.1		public..........................void	**setColumns** (int columns)
	2	public synchronized ....void	setEditable (boolean b)
1.1		public..........................void	**setRows** (int rows)
1.1	2	public synchronized ....void	setSelectionEnd (int selectionEnd)
1.1	2	public synchronized ....void	setSelectionStart (int selectionStart)
	2	public synchronized ....void	setText (String t)
*		public..........................	**TextArea** () throws HeadlessException ε559,571
*		public..........................	**TextArea** (String text) throws HeadlessException
*		public..........................	**TextArea** (int rows, int columns) throws HeadlessException
*		public..........................	**TextArea** (String text, int rows, int columns) throws HeadlessException
1.1 *		public..........................	**TextArea** (String text, int rows, int columns, int scrollbars) throws HeadlessException
1.1	2	protected transient............. .. *java.awt.event.TextListener*	textListener

---

TextAreaPeer 　　　　　　　　　　　　　　　　　　　　　　　　　java.awt.peer

TextAreaPeer————————————— *TextComponentPeer* 〟[1] (*ComponentPeer* [2])

	2		*42 inherited members from ComponentPeer not shown*
	1		*11 inherited members from TextComponentPeer not shown*
1.1		public......java.awt.Dimension	**getMinimumSize** (int rows, int columns)
1.1		public......java.awt.Dimension	**getPreferredSize** (int rows, int columns)
1.1		public..........................void	**insert** (String text, int pos)

Class *Interface* —extends - - -implements ○ abstract ● final △ static ▲ static final ✳ constructor x x—inherited x **x**—declared **x x**—overridden
ε*n*—examples of usage 〟—has subclass package—see other volume

	public	void	**insertText** (String txt, int pos)
	public	java.awt.Dimension	**minimumSize** (int rows, int cols)
	public	java.awt.Dimension	**preferredSize** (int rows, int cols)
1.1	public	void	**replaceRange** (String text, int start, int end)
	public	void	**replaceText** (String txt, int start, int end)

TextAttribute · java.awt.font

Object
1.2 └ java.text.AttributedCharacterIterator ⟂ - - - - - - - *java.io.Serializable* ⌐
　　　└ .Attribute [1]
1.2 ● 　　└ TextAttribute

▲		public static final . TextAttribute	**BACKGROUND**	ε655
▲		public static final . TextAttribute	**BIDI_EMBEDDING**	
▲		public static final . TextAttribute	**CHAR_REPLACEMENT**	
●	1	public final .... boolean	equals (Object obj)	
▲		public static final . TextAttribute	**FAMILY**	
▲		public static final . TextAttribute	**FONT**	ε655
▲		public static final . TextAttribute	**FOREGROUND**	
	1	protected .... String	getName ()	
●	1	public final .... int	hashCode ()	
▲		public static final . TextAttribute	**INPUT_METHOD_HIGHLIGHT**	
▲	1	public static final .... java.text ⟂	INPUT_METHOD_SEGMENT	
		.AttributedCharacterIterator ⟂		
		.Attribute		
1.3 ▲		public static final . TextAttribute	**INPUT_METHOD_UNDERLINE**	
▲		public static final . TextAttribute	**JUSTIFICATION**	
▲		public static final .... Float	**JUSTIFICATION_FULL** = new Float(1.0)	
▲		public static final .... Float	**JUSTIFICATION_NONE** = new Float(0.0)	
▲	1	public static final .... java.text ⟂	LANGUAGE	
		.AttributedCharacterIterator ⟂		
		.Attribute		
1.4 ▲		public static final . TextAttribute	**NUMERIC_SHAPING**	
▲		public static final . TextAttribute	**POSTURE**	
▲		public static final .... Float	**POSTURE_OBLIQUE** = new Float(0.2)	
▲		public static final .... Float	**POSTURE_REGULAR** = new Float(0.0)	
▲	1	public static final .... java.text ⟂	READING	
		.AttributedCharacterIterator ⟂		
		.Attribute		
	1	protected .... **Object**	**readResolve** () throws java.io.InvalidObjectException	
▲		public static final . TextAttribute	**RUN_DIRECTION**	
▲		public static final ...... Boolean	**RUN_DIRECTION_LTR** = new Boolean(false)	
▲		public static final ...... Boolean	**RUN_DIRECTION_RTL** = new Boolean(true)	
▲		public static final . TextAttribute	**SIZE**	
▲		public static final . TextAttribute	**STRIKETHROUGH**	
▲		public static final ...... Boolean	**STRIKETHROUGH_ON** = new Boolean(true)	
▲		public static final . TextAttribute	**SUPERSCRIPT**	
▲		public static final .... Integer	**SUPERSCRIPT_SUB** = new Integer(-1)	
▲		public static final .... Integer	**SUPERSCRIPT_SUPER** = new Integer(1)	
▲		public static final . TextAttribute	**SWAP_COLORS**	
▲		public static final ...... Boolean	**SWAP_COLORS_ON** = new Boolean(true)	
*		protected	**TextAttribute** (String name)	
	1	public .... String	toString ()	
▲		public static final . TextAttribute	**TRANSFORM**	
▲		public static final . TextAttribute	**UNDERLINE**	
1.3 ▲		public static final .... Integer	**UNDERLINE_LOW_DASHED** = new Integer(5)	
1.3 ▲		public static final .... Integer	**UNDERLINE_LOW_DOTTED** = new Integer(3)	
1.3 ▲		public static final .... Integer	**UNDERLINE_LOW_GRAY** = new Integer(4)	
1.3 ▲		public static final .... Integer	**UNDERLINE_LOW_ONE_PIXEL** = new Integer(1)	
1.3 ▲		public static final .... Integer	**UNDERLINE_LOW_TWO_PIXEL** = new Integer(2)	
▲		public static final .... Integer	**UNDERLINE_ON** = new Integer(0)	
▲		public static final . TextAttribute	**WEIGHT**	
▲		public static final .... Float	**WEIGHT_BOLD** = new Float(2.0)	
▲		public static final .... Float	**WEIGHT_DEMIBOLD** = new Float(1.75)	
▲		public static final .... Float	**WEIGHT_DEMILIGHT** = new Float(0.875)	
▲		public static final .... Float	**WEIGHT_EXTRA_LIGHT** = new Float(0.5)	
▲		public static final .... Float	**WEIGHT_EXTRABOLD** = new Float(2.5)	
▲		public static final .... Float	**WEIGHT_HEAVY** = new Float(2.25)	
▲		public static final .... Float	**WEIGHT_LIGHT** = new Float(0.75)	
▲		public static final .... Float	**WEIGHT_MEDIUM** = new Float(1.5)	
▲		public static final .... Float	**WEIGHT_REGULAR** = new Float(1.0)	
▲		public static final .... Float	**WEIGHT_SEMIBOLD** = new Float(1.25)	

T

Classes

TextAttribute

▲	public static final	Float	**WEIGHT_ULTRABOLD** = new Float(2.75)
▲	public static final .	TextAttribute	**WIDTH**
▲	public static final	Float	**WIDTH_CONDENSED** = new Float(0.75)
▲	public static final	Float	**WIDTH_EXTENDED** = new Float(1.5)
▲	public static final	Float	**WIDTH_REGULAR** = new Float(1.0)
▲	public static final	Float	**WIDTH_SEMI_CONDENSED** = new Float(0.875)
▲	public static final	Float	**WIDTH_SEMI_EXTENDED** = new Float(1.25)

TextComponent   java.awt

```
     Object
  ○  └─Component¹ ------------------- java.awt.image.ImageObserver², MenuContainer,
                                      java.io.Serializable
         └─TextComponent ----------------- javax.accessibility.Accessible
```

	1		*202 inherited members from Component not shown*
	2		*8 inherited members from java.awt.image.ImageObserver not shown*
	1	public .... **void**	**addNotify** ()
1.1		public synchronized ...... void	**addTextListener** (*java.awt.event.TextListener* l)
1.2	1	public .... **void**	**enableInputMethods** (boolean enable)
1.3	1	public.... **javax.accessibility**₂ **.AccessibleContext**	**getAccessibleContext** ()
	1	public .... **Color**	**getBackground** ()
1.1		public synchronized ....int	**getCaretPosition** ()
1.3	1	public......................... .... ***java.util.EventListener[]***	**getListeners** (Class listenerType)
		public synchronized .....String	**getSelectedText** ()
		public synchronized ....int	**getSelectionEnd** ()
		public synchronized ....int	**getSelectionStart** ()
		public synchronized .....String	**getText** ()
1.4		public synchronized .... *java.awt.event.TextListener[]*	**getTextListeners** ()
		public................. boolean	**isEditable** ()
	1	protected .... **String**	**paramString** ()
1.1	1	protected .... **void**	**processEvent** (AWTEvent e)
1.1		protected ....void	**processTextEvent** (java.awt.event.TextEvent e)
	1	public.................. **void**	**removeNotify** ()
1.1		public synchronized ....void	**removeTextListener** (*java.awt.event.TextListener* l)
		public synchronized ....void	**select** (int selectionStart, int selectionEnd)
		public synchronized ....void	**selectAll** ()
	1	public.................... **void**	**setBackground** (Color c)
1.1		public synchronized ....void	**setCaretPosition** (int position)
		public synchronized ....void	**setEditable** (boolean b)
1.1		public synchronized ....void	**setSelectionEnd** (int selectionEnd)
1.1		public synchronized ....void	**setSelectionStart** (int selectionStart)
		public synchronized ....void	**setText** (String t)
1.1		protected transient............. .. *java.awt.event.TextListener*	**textListener**

TextComponentPeer   java.awt.peer

```
     TextComponentPeer ─────────────── ComponentPeer ¹
```

	1		*42 inherited members from ComponentPeer not shown*
1.3		public..................... long	**filterEvents** (long mask)
1.1		public...........................int	**getCaretPosition** ()
1.3		public...... java.awt.Rectangle	**getCharacterBounds** (int i)
1.3		public...........................int	**getIndexAtPoint** (int x, int y)
		public...........................int	**getSelectionEnd** ()
		public...........................int	**getSelectionStart** ()
		public....................String	**getText** ()
		public.....................void	**select** (int selStart, int selEnd)
1.1		public.....................void	**setCaretPosition** (int pos)
		public.....................void	**setEditable** (boolean editable)
		public.....................void	**setText** (String l)

Class *Interface* —extends - - -implements ○ abstract ● final △ static ▲ static final ✳ constructor x x—inherited x **x**—declared **x x**—overridden
ε*n*—examples of usage ‿—has subclass package—see other volume

	TextEvent		java.awt.event

ε640,641,643,649,566

```
       Object
1.1    └ java.util.EventObject 1 - - - - - - - - - - - - - - - - - - - java.io.Serializable
1.1 ○    └ java.awt.AWTEvent 2
1.1        └ TextEvent
```

	2	*27 inherited members from java.awt.AWTEvent not shown*	
	1	public.................Object getSource ()	ε644,886,565,568,570
	2	public................. **String paramString** ()	
	1	protected transient......Object source	
▲		public static final............int **TEXT_FIRST** = 900	
▲		public static final............int **TEXT_LAST** = 900	
▲		public static final............int **TEXT_VALUE_CHANGED** = 900	
✳		public......................... **TextEvent** (Object source, int id)	

	TextField		java.awt

```
       Object
○    └ Component 1 - - - - - - - - - - - - - - - - - - - - - - - - java.awt.image.ImageObserver 3, MenuContainer,
                                                                  java.io.Serializable
         └ TextComponent 2 - - - - - - - - - - - - - - - - - - - - javax.accessibility.Accessible
           └ TextField
```

	1	*198 inherited members from Component not shown*
	3	*8 inherited members from java.awt.image.ImageObserver not shown*
1.1		public synchronized ....void **addActionListener** (*java.awt.event.ActionListener* l)
	2	public..................... **void addNotify** ()
1.1	2	public synchronized ....void addTextListener (*java.awt.event.TextListener* l)
		public.................. boolean **echoCharIsSet** ()
1.2	2	public.....................void enableInputMethods (boolean enable)
1.3	2	public.... **javax.accessibility .AccessibleContext getAccessibleContext** ()
1.4		public synchronized ..... *java .awt.event.ActionListener[]* **getActionListeners** ()
	2	public..................... Color getBackground ()
1.1	2	public synchronized ....int getCaretPosition ()
		public.......................int **getColumns** ()
		public..................... char **getEchoChar** ()
1.3	2	public......................... **getListeners** (Class listenerType) .... *java.util.EventListener[]*
1.1	1	public.............. **Dimension getMinimumSize** ()
1.1		public................Dimension **getMinimumSize** (int columns)
1.1	1	public.............. **Dimension getPreferredSize** ()
1.1		public................Dimension **getPreferredSize** (int columns)
	2	public synchronized ..... String getSelectedText ()
	2	public synchronized ....int getSelectionEnd ()
	2	public synchronized ....int getSelectionStart ()
	2	public synchronized ..... String getText ()
1.4	2	public synchronized .... getTextListeners () . *java.awt.event.TextListener[]*
	2	public.................. boolean isEditable ()
D	1	public.............. **Dimension minimumSize** ()
D		public................Dimension **minimumSize** (int columns)
	2	protected .... **String paramString** ()
D	1	public.............. **Dimension preferredSize** ()
D		public................Dimension **preferredSize** (int columns)
1.1		protected ....void **processActionEvent** (java.awt.event.ActionEvent e)
1.1	2	protected .... **void processEvent** (AWTEvent e)
1.1	2	protected ....void processTextEvent (java.awt.event.TextEvent e)
1.1		public synchronized ....void **removeActionListener** (*java.awt.event.ActionListener* l)
	2	public...................void removeNotify ()
1.1	2	public synchronized ....void removeTextListener (*java.awt.event.TextListener* l)
	2	public synchronized ....void select (int selectionStart, int selectionEnd)
	2	public synchronized ....void selectAll ()
	2	public...................void setBackground (Color c)
1.1	2	public synchronized ....void setCaretPosition (int position)
1.1		public synchronized ....void **setColumns** (int columns)
1.1		public...................void **setEchoChar** (char c)
D		public...................void **setEchoCharacter** (char c)
	2	public synchronized ....void setEditable (boolean b)
1.1	2	public synchronized ....void setSelectionEnd (int selectionEnd)

T

Classes

TextField

1.1	2	public synchronized ....void	setSelectionStart (int selectionStart)
	2	public........................ **void**	**setText** (String t)
✳		public........................	**TextField** () throws HeadlessException
✳		public........................	**TextField** (int columns) throws HeadlessException
✳		public........................	**TextField** (String text) throws HeadlessException
✳		public........................	**TextField** (String text, int columns) throws HeadlessException
1.1	2	protected transient.............	textListener
		.. *java.awt.event.TextListener*	

TextFieldPeer — java.awt.peer

TextFieldPeer———————————————— *TextComponentPeer* [1] (*ComponentPeer* [2])

- -

	2	*42 inherited members from ComponentPeer not shown*
	1	*11 inherited members from TextComponentPeer not shown*
1.1	public......java.awt.Dimension	**getMinimumSize** (int columns)
1.1	public......java.awt.Dimension	**getPreferredSize** (int columns)
	public......java.awt.Dimension	**minimumSize** (int cols)
	public......java.awt.Dimension	**preferredSize** (int cols)
1.1	public........................void	**setEchoChar** (char echoChar)
	public........................void	**setEchoCharacter** (char c)

- -

TextHitInfo — java.awt.font

Object [1]
└─TextHitInfo

1.2 ●			
△	public static ....TextHitInfo	**afterOffset** (int offset)
△	public static ....TextHitInfo	**beforeOffset** (int offset)
	public.................. boolean	**equals** (TextHitInfo hitInfo)
1	public.................... **boolean**	**equals** (Object obj)
	public..........................int	**getCharIndex** ()
	public..........................int	**getInsertionIndex** ()
	public..............TextHitInfo	**getOffsetHit** (int delta)
	public..............TextHitInfo	**getOtherHit** ()
1	public........................ **int**	**hashCode** ()
	public.................. boolean	**isLeadingEdge** ()
△	public static ....TextHitInfo	**leading** (int charIndex)
1	public........................ **String**	**toString** ()
△	public static ....TextHitInfo	**trailing** (int charIndex)

TextLayout — java.awt.font

Object [1]
└─TextLayout - *Cloneable*

1.2 ●			
▲	1	protected ....**Object**	**clone** ()
		public static final	**DEFAULT_CARET_POLICY**
		.......TextLayout.CaretPolicy	
		public........................void	**draw** (java.awt.Graphics2D g2, float x, float y) *ε*653,655
		public.................. boolean	**equals** (TextLayout rhs)
	1	public.................... **boolean**	**equals** (Object obj)
		public........................float	**getAdvance** ()
		public........................float	**getAscent** () *ε*653
		public........................ byte	**getBaseline** ()
		public........................float[]	**getBaselineOffsets** ()
		public.......... *java.awt.Shape*	**getBlackBoxBounds** (int firstEndpoint, int secondEndpoint)
		public........................	**getBounds** ()
		. java.awt.geom.Rectangle2D	
		public........................float[]	**getCaretInfo** (TextHitInfo hit)
		public........................float[]	**getCaretInfo** (TextHitInfo hit, java.awt.geom.Rectangle2D bounds)
		public.......... *java.awt.Shape*	**getCaretShape** (TextHitInfo hit)
		public.......... *java.awt.Shape*	**getCaretShape** (TextHitInfo hit, java.awt.geom.Rectangle2D bounds)
		public........*java.awt.Shape[]*	**getCaretShapes** (int offset)
		public........*java.awt.Shape[]*	**getCaretShapes** (int offset, java.awt.geom.Rectangle2D bounds)
		public........*java.awt.Shape[]*	**getCaretShapes** (int offset, java.awt.geom.Rectangle2D bounds,
			TextLayout.CaretPolicy policy)
		public........................int	**getCharacterCount** ()

Class   *Interface*   —extends   - - -implements   ○ abstract   ● final   △ static   ▲ static final   ✳ constructor   x x—inherited   x **x**—declared   **x x**—overridden
εn—examples of usage   ⌄—has subclass   package—see other volume

public	byte	**getCharacterLevel** (int index)	
public	float	**getDescent** ()	ε653
public	TextLayout	**getJustifiedLayout** (float justificationWidth)	
public	float	**getLeading** ()	ε653
public	*java.awt.Shape*	**getLogicalHighlightShape** (int firstEndpoint, int secondEndpoint)	
public	*java.awt.Shape*	**getLogicalHighlightShape** (int firstEndpoint, int secondEndpoint, java.awt.geom.Rectangle2D bounds)	
public	int[]	**getLogicalRangesForVisualSelection** (TextHitInfo firstEndpoint, TextHitInfo secondEndpoint)	
public	TextHitInfo	**getNextLeftHit** (int offset)	
public	TextHitInfo	**getNextLeftHit** (TextHitInfo hit)	
public	TextHitInfo	**getNextLeftHit** (int offset, TextLayout.CaretPolicy policy)	
public	TextHitInfo	**getNextRightHit** (int offset)	
public	TextHitInfo	**getNextRightHit** (TextHitInfo hit)	
public	TextHitInfo	**getNextRightHit** (int offset, TextLayout.CaretPolicy policy)	
public	*java.awt.Shape*	**getOutline** (java.awt.geom.AffineTransform tx)	ε654
public	float	**getVisibleAdvance** ()	
public	*java.awt.Shape*	**getVisualHighlightShape** (TextHitInfo firstEndpoint, TextHitInfo secondEndpoint)	
public	*java.awt.Shape*	**getVisualHighlightShape** (TextHitInfo firstEndpoint, TextHitInfo secondEndpoint, java.awt.geom.Rectangle2D bounds)	
public	TextHitInfo	**getVisualOtherHit** (TextHitInfo hit)	
protected	void	**handleJustify** (float justificationWidth)	
1 public	**int**	**hashCode** ()	
public	TextHitInfo	**hitTestChar** (float x, float y)	
public	TextHitInfo	**hitTestChar** (float x, float y, java.awt.geom.Rectangle2D bounds)	
public	boolean	**isLeftToRight** ()	
public	boolean	**isVertical** ()	
* public		**TextLayout** (*java.text.AttributedCharacterIterator* text, FontRenderContext frc)	ε655
* public		**TextLayout** (String string, java.awt.Font font, FontRenderContext frc)	ε654
* public		**TextLayout** (String string, *java.util.Map* attributes, FontRenderContext frc)	
1 public	**String**	**toString** ()	

TextLayout.CaretPolicy — java.awt.font

Object
└ TextLayout.CaretPolicy

1.2

* public		**TextLayout.CaretPolicy** ()
public	TextHitInfo	**getStrongCaret** (TextHitInfo hit1, TextHitInfo hit2, TextLayout layout)

TextListener — java.awt.event

1.1 *TextListener* ──────────── *java.util.EventListener* ╌   ε738,743,745,746,752

public	void	**textValueChanged** (TextEvent e)

TextMeasurer — java.awt.font

Object [1]
└ TextMeasurer ╌╌╌╌╌╌╌╌╌╌╌ *Cloneable* ╌

1.3 ●

1 protected	**Object**	**clone** ()
public	void	**deleteChar** (*java.text.AttributedCharacterIterator* newParagraph, int deletePos)
public	float	**getAdvanceBetween** (int start, int limit)
public	TextLayout	**getLayout** (int start, int limit)
public	int	**getLineBreakIndex** (int start, float maxAdvance)
public	void	**insertChar** (*java.text.AttributedCharacterIterator* newParagraph, int insertPos)
* public		**TextMeasurer** (*java.text.AttributedCharacterIterator* text, FontRenderContext frc)

TextSyntax — javax.print.attribute

Object [1]
└ TextSyntax ╌╌╌╌╌╌╌╌╌╌╌ *java.io.Serializable* ╌, *Cloneable* ╌

1.4 ○

1 public	**boolean**	**equals** (Object object)
public	java.util.Locale	**getLocale** ()
public	String	**getValue** ()
1 public	**int**	**hashCode** ()

T

Classes

TextSyntax

*	protected	**TextSyntax** (String value, java.util.Locale locale)	
1	public	**String toString** ()	

```
        Object
1.2 ○   └ComponentUI 1
1.2 ○     └TextUI
```

1		*11 inherited members from ComponentUI not shown*	
○	public abstract .... void	**damageRange** (javax.swing.text.JTextComponent t, int p0, int p1)	
○	public abstract .... void	**damageRange** (javax.swing.text.JTextComponent t, int p0, int p1, javax.swing.text.Position.Bias firstBias, javax.swing.text.Position.Bias secondBias)	
○	public abstract ..... javax.swing.text.EditorKit	**getEditorKit** (javax.swing.text.JTextComponent t)	
○	public abstract .... int	**getNextVisualPositionFrom** (javax.swing.text.JTextComponent t, int pos, javax.swing.text.Position.Bias b, int direction, javax.swing.text.Position.Bias[] biasRet) throws javax.swing.text.BadLocationException	
○	public abstract .... javax.swing.text.View	**getRootView** (javax.swing.text.JTextComponent t)	ε978
1.4	public .... String	**getToolTipText** (javax.swing.text.JTextComponent t, java.awt.Point pt)	
○	public abstract .... java.awt.Rectangle	**modelToView** (javax.swing.text.JTextComponent t, int pos) throws javax.swing.text.BadLocationException	
○	public abstract .... java.awt.Rectangle	**modelToView** (javax.swing.text.JTextComponent t, int pos, javax.swing.text.Position.Bias bias) throws javax.swing.text.BadLocationException	
*	public	**TextUI** ()	
○	public abstract .... int	**viewToModel** (javax.swing.text.JTextComponent t, java.awt.Point pt)	
○	public abstract .... int	**viewToModel** (javax.swing.text.JTextComponent t, java.awt.Point pt, javax.swing.text.Position.Bias[] biasReturn)	

```
        Object
1.2     └TexturePaint - - - - - - - - - - - - - - - - - - - - - - - - - - - Paint 1 (Transparency 2)
```

▲ 2	public static final .... int	BITMASK = 2	ε666,667
1	public .... *PaintContext*	**createContext** (java.awt.image.ColorModel cm, Rectangle deviceBounds, java.awt.geom.Rectangle2D userBounds, java.awt.geom.AffineTransform xform, RenderingHints hints)	
	public ... java.awt.geom.Rectangle2D	**getAnchorRect** ()	
	public ... java.awt.image.BufferedImage	**getImage** ()	
2	public .... int	**getTransparency** ()	
▲ 2	public static final .... int	OPAQUE = 1	ε666,667
*	public	**TexturePaint** (java.awt.image.BufferedImage txtr, java.awt.geom.Rectangle2D anchor)	ε580
▲ 2	public static final .... int	TRANSLUCENT = 3	ε666

```
1.2     TileObserver
```

	public .... void	**tileUpdate** (*WritableRenderedImage* source, int tileX, int tileY, boolean willBeWritable)	

```
        Object
1.2     └Timer - - - - - - - - - - - - - - - - - - - - - - - - - - - java.io.Serializable
```

	public .... void	**addActionListener** (*java.awt.event.ActionListener* listener)	
	protected .... void	**fireActionPerformed** (java.awt.event.ActionEvent e)	
1.4	public ... java.awt.event.ActionListener[]	**getActionListeners** ()	
	public .... int	**getDelay** ()	

Class *Interface* —extends - - -implements ○ abstract ● final △ static ▲ static final ✳ constructor x x—inherited x **x**—declared **x x**—overridden
ε*n*—examples of usage   —has subclass   package—see other volume

	public	int	**getInitialDelay** ()
1.3	public . *java.util.EventListener[]*	**getListeners** (Class listenerType)
△	public static	boolean	**getLogTimers** ()
	public	boolean	**isCoalesce** ()
	public	boolean	**isRepeats** ()
	public	boolean	**isRunning** ()
	protected	javax.swing❷	**listenerList**
	.event.EventListenerList		
	public	void	**removeActionListener** (*java.awt.event.ActionListener* listener)
	public	void	**restart** ()
	public	void	**setCoalesce** (boolean flag)
	public	void	**setDelay** (int delay)
	public	void	**setInitialDelay** (int initialDelay)
△	public static	void	**setLogTimers** (boolean flag)
	public	void	**setRepeats** (boolean flag)
	public	void	**start** ()
	public	void	**stop** ()
✳	public		**Timer** (int delay, *java.awt.event.ActionListener* listener)

TitledBorder		javax.swing.border

ε873

	Object
1.2 ○	└ AbstractBorder[1] - *Border*, *java.io.Serializable* ┘
1.2	└ TitledBorder ┘

▲	public static final	int	**ABOVE_BOTTOM** = 4
▲	public static final	int	**ABOVE_TOP** = 1
▲	public static final	int	**BELOW_BOTTOM** = 6
▲	public static final	int	**BELOW_TOP** = 3
	protected	*Border*	**border**
▲	public static final	int	**BOTTOM** = 5
▲	public static final	int	**CENTER** = 2
▲	public static final	int	**DEFAULT_JUSTIFICATION** = 0
▲	public static final	int	**DEFAULT_POSITION** = 0
▲	protected static final	int	**EDGE_SPACING**
	public	*Border*	**getBorder** ()
1	public	**java.awt.Insets**	**getBorderInsets** (java.awt.Component c)
1	public	**java.awt.Insets**	**getBorderInsets** (java.awt.Component c, java.awt.Insets insets)
	protected	java.awt.Font	**getFont** (java.awt.Component c)
1	public	java.awt.Rectangle	getInteriorRectangle (java.awt.Component c, int x, int y, int width, int height)
△ 1	public static		getInteriorRectangle (java.awt.Component c, *Border* b, int x, int y, int width,
	java.awt.Rectangle		int height)
	public	java.awt.Dimension	**getMinimumSize** (java.awt.Component c)
	public	String	**getTitle** ()
	public	java.awt.Color	**getTitleColor** ()
	public	java.awt.Font	**getTitleFont** ()
	public	int	**getTitleJustification** ()
	public	int	**getTitlePosition** ()
1	public	**boolean**	**isBorderOpaque** ()
1.3 ▲	public static final	int	**LEADING** = 4
▲	public static final	int	**LEFT** = 1
1	public	**void**	**paintBorder** (java.awt.Component c, java.awt.Graphics g, int x, int y, int width,
			int height)
▲	public static final	int	**RIGHT** = 3
	public	void	**setBorder** (*Border* border)
	public	void	**setTitle** (String title)
	public	void	**setTitleColor** (java.awt.Color titleColor)
	public	void	**setTitleFont** (java.awt.Font titleFont)
	public	void	**setTitleJustification** (int titleJustification)
	public	void	**setTitlePosition** (int titlePosition)
▲	protected static final	int	**TEXT_INSET_H**
▲	protected static final	int	**TEXT_SPACING**
	protected	String	**title**
	protected	java.awt.Color	**titleColor**
✳	public		**TitledBorder** (String title)
✳	public		**TitledBorder** (*Border* border)
✳	public		**TitledBorder** (*Border* border, String title)
✳	public		**TitledBorder** (*Border* border, String title, int titleJustification, int titlePosition)
✳	public		**TitledBorder** (*Border* border, String title, int titleJustification, int titlePosition,
			java.awt.Font titleFont)
✳	public		**TitledBorder** (*Border* border, String title, int titleJustification, int titlePosition,
			java.awt.Font titleFont, java.awt.Color titleColor)
	protected	java.awt.Font	**titleFont**

ε874

ε874

ε874
ε874

T

Classes

TitledBorder

	protected .... int	**titleJustification**	
	protected .... int	**titlePosition**	
▲	public static final .... int	**TOP** = 2	
1.3 ▲	public static final .... int	**TRAILING** = 5	

ToolBarUI   javax.swing.plaf

Object
  └ ComponentUI [1]
    └ ToolBarUI

1.2 ○		
1.2 ○		

[1] *11 inherited members from ComponentUI not shown*

| * | public .... | **ToolBarUI** () |

Toolkit   java.awt

Object
  └ Toolkit

○			

1.2	public .... void	**addAWTEventListener** (*java.awt.event.AWTEventListener* listener, long eventMask)
1.2	public synchronized .... void	**addPropertyChangeListener** (String name, *java.beans.PropertyChangeListener* pcl)
1.1 ○	public abstract .... void	**beep** ()
○	public abstract .... int	**checkImage** (Image image, int width, int height, *java.awt.image.ImageObserver* observer)
○	protected abstract .... *java.awt.peer.ButtonPeer*	**createButton** (Button target) throws HeadlessException
○	protected abstract .... *... java.awt.peer.CanvasPeer*	**createCanvas** (Canvas target)
○	protected abstract .... *java.awt.peer.CheckboxPeer*	**createCheckbox** (Checkbox target) throws HeadlessException
○	protected abstract .... *................ java.awt.peer₂ .CheckboxMenuItemPeer*	**createCheckboxMenuItem** (CheckboxMenuItem target) throws HeadlessException
○	protected abstract .... *.... java.awt.peer.ChoicePeer*	**createChoice** (Choice target) throws HeadlessException
1.1	protected .... *java₂ .awt.peer.LightweightPeer*	**createComponent** (Component target)
1.2	public .... Cursor	**createCustomCursor** (Image cursor, Point hotSpot, String name) throws IndexOutOfBoundsException, HeadlessException
○	protected abstract .... *.... java.awt.peer.DialogPeer*	**createDialog** (Dialog target) throws HeadlessException
1.2	public .... java.awt.dnd₂ .DragGestureRecognizer	**createDragGestureRecognizer** (Class abstractRecognizerClass, java.awt.dnd.DragSource ds, Component c, int srcActions, *java.awt.dnd.DragGestureListener* dgl)
1.2 ○	public abstract .... *.......... java.awt.dnd.peer₂ .DragSourceContextPeer*	**createDragSourceContextPeer** (java.awt.dnd.DragGestureEvent dge) throws java.awt.dnd.InvalidDnDOperationException
○	protected abstract .... *.java.awt.peer.FileDialogPeer*	**createFileDialog** (FileDialog target) throws HeadlessException
○	protected abstract .... *.....java.awt.peer.FramePeer*	**createFrame** (Frame target) throws HeadlessException
1.1	public .... Image	**createImage** (byte[] imagedata)
○	public abstract .... Image	**createImage** (*java.awt.image.ImageProducer* producer) ε660,665,670
1.2 ○	public abstract .... Image	**createImage** (String filename)
1.2 ○	public abstract .... Image	**createImage** (java.net.URL url) ε137
1.1 ○	public abstract .... Image	**createImage** (byte[] imagedata, int imageoffset, int imagelength)
○	protected abstract .... *..... java.awt.peer.LabelPeer*	**createLabel** (Label target) throws HeadlessException
○	protected abstract .... *........ java.awt.peer.ListPeer*	**createList** (List target) throws HeadlessException
○	protected abstract .... *..... java.awt.peer.MenuPeer*	**createMenu** (Menu target) throws HeadlessException
○	protected abstract .... *.java.awt.peer.MenuBarPeer*	**createMenuBar** (MenuBar target) throws HeadlessException
○	protected abstract .... *.java.awt.peer.MenuItemPeer*	**createMenuItem** (MenuItem target) throws HeadlessException

---

		Modifiers / Return type	Method
	○	protected abstract .... *java.awt.peer.PanelPeer*	**createPanel** (Panel target)
1.1	○	protected abstract .... *java₂ .awt.peer.PopupMenuPeer*	**createPopupMenu** (PopupMenu target) throws HeadlessException
	○	protected abstract .... *java.awt.peer.ScrollbarPeer*	**createScrollbar** (Scrollbar target) throws HeadlessException
1.1	○	protected abstract .... *java₂ .awt.peer.ScrollPanePeer*	**createScrollPane** (ScrollPane target) throws HeadlessException
	○	protected abstract .... *java.awt.peer.TextAreaPeer*	**createTextArea** (TextArea target) throws HeadlessException
	○	protected abstract .... *java.awt.peer.TextFieldPeer*	**createTextField** (TextField target) throws HeadlessException
	○	protected abstract .... *java.awt.peer.WindowPeer*	**createWindow** (Window target) throws HeadlessException
1.2	●	protected final.... *java.util.Map*	**desktopProperties**
1.2	●	protected final.... java.beans₂ .PropertyChangeSupport	**desktopPropsSupport**
1.4		public................ *java.awt₂ .event.AWTEventListener[]*	**getAWTEventListeners** ()
1.4		public................ *java.awt₂ .event.AWTEventListener[]*	**getAWTEventListeners** (long eventMask)
1.2		public...............Dimension	**getBestCursorSize** (int preferredWidth, int preferredHeight) throws HeadlessException
	○	public abstract................ .. java.awt.image.ColorModel	**getColorModel** () throws HeadlessException
	△	public static synchronized .... Toolkit	**getDefaultToolkit** () ε560,594,598,599,637
1.2	●	public final synchronized ....Object	**getDesktopProperty** (String propertyName)
D	○	public abstract .... String[]	**getFontList** ()
D	○	public abstract .... FontMetrics	**getFontMetrics** (Font font)
D	○	protected abstract ....*java.awt.peer.FontPeer*	**getFontPeer** (String name, int style)
	○	public abstract .... Image	**getImage** (String filename) ε560,594
	○	public abstract .... Image	**getImage** (java.net.URL url)
1.3		public.................. boolean	**getLockingKeyState** (int keyCode) throws UnsupportedOperationException
1.2		public...........................int	**getMaximumCursorColors** () throws HeadlessException
1.1		public...........................int	**getMenuShortcutKeyMask** () throws HeadlessException
1.1	△	protected static ..... Container	**getNativeContainer** (Component c)
1.1	○	public abstract .... PrintJob	**getPrintJob** (Frame frame, String jobtitle, java.util.Properties props)
1.3		public.................. PrintJob	**getPrintJob** (Frame frame, String jobtitle, JobAttributes jobAttributes, PageAttributes pageAttributes)
1.1	△	public static ....String	**getProperty** (String key, String defaultValue)
1.4		public............. java.beans.- PropertyChangeListener[]	**getPropertyChangeListeners** ()
1.4		public synchronized .... java.beans.- PropertyChangeListener[]	**getPropertyChangeListeners** (String propertyName)
1.4		public....................Insets	**getScreenInsets** (GraphicsConfiguration gc) throws HeadlessException
	○	public abstract ....int	**getScreenResolution** () throws HeadlessException
	○	public abstract ......Dimension	**getScreenSize** () throws HeadlessException ε598,599,864
1.1	○	public abstract .... java₂ .awt.datatransfer.Clipboard	**getSystemClipboard** () throws HeadlessException ε637,638,639
1.1	●	public final ....EventQueue	**getSystemEventQueue** ()
1.1	○	protected abstract EventQueue	**getSystemEventQueueImpl** ()
1.4		public..................... java₂ .awt.datatransfer.Clipboard	**getSystemSelection** () throws HeadlessException
1.2		protected ....void	**initializeDesktopProperties** ()
1.4		public.................. boolean	**isDynamicLayoutActive** () throws HeadlessException
1.4		protected .... boolean	**isDynamicLayoutSet** () throws HeadlessException
1.4		public.................. boolean	**isFrameStateSupported** (int state) throws HeadlessException
1.2		protected ....Object	**lazilyLoadDesktopProperty** (String name)
1.1		protected ....void	**loadSystemColors** (int[] systemColors) throws HeadlessException
1.3	○	public abstract ... *java.util.Map*	**mapInputMethodHighlight** (java.awt.im.InputMethodHighlight highlight) throws HeadlessException
	○	public abstract .... boolean	**prepareImage** (Image image, int width, int height, *java.awt.image.ImageObserver* observer)
1.2		public........................void	**removeAWTEventListener** (*java.awt.event.AWTEventListener* listener)
1.2		public synchronized ....void	**removePropertyChangeListener** (String name, java.beans₂ .PropertyChangeListener pcl)
1.2	●	protected final..............void	**setDesktopProperty** (String name, Object newValue)
1.4		public.......................void	**setDynamicLayout** (boolean dynamic) throws HeadlessException

T

Classes

Toolkit

ToolTipManager   javax.swing

Object
- 1.1 O └java.awt.event.MouseAdapter [1] ----------- *java.awt.event.MouseListener* (*java.util.EventListener*)
- 1.2 └ToolTipManager --------------------- *java.awt.event.MouseMotionListener* [2] (*java.util.EventListener*)

	public	int	**getDismissDelay** ()	ε847
	public	int	**getInitialDelay** ()	ε846
	public	int	**getReshowDelay** ()	
	protected	boolean	**heavyWeightPopupEnabled**	
	public	boolean	**isEnabled** ()	
	public	boolean	**isLightWeightPopupEnabled** ()	
	protected	boolean	**lightWeightPopupEnabled**	
1	public	void	mouseClicked (java.awt.event.MouseEvent e)	ε646,648,783,967
2	public	void	**mouseDragged** (java.awt.event.MouseEvent event)	ε647
1	public	**void**	**mouseEntered** (java.awt.event.MouseEvent event)	
1	public	**void**	**mouseExited** (java.awt.event.MouseEvent event)	
2	public	void	**mouseMoved** (java.awt.event.MouseEvent event)	ε647,937
1	public	**void**	**mousePressed** (java.awt.event.MouseEvent event)	ε602,742,810,1011
1	public	void	mouseReleased (java.awt.event.MouseEvent e)	ε810,1011
	public	void	**registerComponent** (JComponent component)	
	public	void	**setDismissDelay** (int milliseconds)	ε847
	public	void	**setEnabled** (boolean flag)	ε845
	public	void	**setInitialDelay** (int milliseconds)	ε846
	public	void	**setLightWeightPopupEnabled** (boolean aFlag)	
	public	void	**setReshowDelay** (int milliseconds)	
△	public static ..	ToolTipManager	**sharedInstance** ()	ε845,846,847
	public	void	**unregisterComponent** (JComponent component)	

ToolTipManager.insideTimerAction   protected   javax.swing

Object
- 1.2 └ToolTipManager.insideTimerAction -------- *java.awt.event.ActionListener* [1] (*java.util.EventListener*)

1	public	void	**actionPerformed** (java.awt.event.ActionEvent e)	ε855,644,738,743,745
✳	protected		**ToolTipManager.insideTimerAction** ()	

ToolTipManager.outsideTimerAction   protected   javax.swing

Object
- 1.2 └ToolTipManager.outsideTimerAction ------- *java.awt.event.ActionListener* [1] (*java.util.EventListener*)

1	public	void	**actionPerformed** (java.awt.event.ActionEvent e)	ε855,644,738,743,745
✳	protected		**ToolTipManager.outsideTimerAction** ()	

ToolTipManager.stillInsideTimerAction   protected   javax.swing

Object
- 1.2 └ToolTipManager.stillInsideTimerAction ------ *java.awt.event.ActionListener* [1] (*java.util.EventListener*)

1	public	void	**actionPerformed** (java.awt.event.ActionEvent e)	ε855,644,738,743,745
✳	protected		**ToolTipManager.stillInsideTimerAction** ()	

ToolTipUI   javax.swing.plaf

Object
- 1.2 O └ComponentUI [1]
- 1.2 O └ToolTipUI

Class *Interface* —extends - - -implements O abstract ● final △ static ▲ static final ✳ constructor x x—inherited x **x**—declared **x x**—overridden
εn—examples of usage —has subclass package—see other volume

T

* public.......................... **ToolTipUI** ()

Track · javax.sound.midi

Object
1.3 └─Track

public	boolean	**add** (MidiEvent event)
protected	java.util.Vector	**events**
public	MidiEvent	**get** (int index) throws ArrayIndexOutOfBoundsException
public	boolean	**remove** (MidiEvent event)
public	int	**size** ()
public	long	**ticks** ()

Transferable · java.awt.datatransfer

1.1 *Transferable* ε639,640

public	Object	**getTransferData** (DataFlavor flavor) throws UnsupportedFlavorException, java.io.IOException	ε637,638,642
public	DataFlavor[]	**getTransferDataFlavors** ()	ε638
public	boolean	**isDataFlavorSupported** (DataFlavor flavor)	ε637,638,642

TransferHandler · javax.swing

Object
1.4 └─TransferHandler - *java.io.Serializable*

	public	boolean	**canImport** (JComponent comp, java.awt.datatransfer.DataFlavor[] transferFlavors) ε742
▲	public static final	int	**COPY** = 1
▲	public static final	int	**COPY_OR_MOVE** = 3
	protected	java.awt.datatransfer.Transferable	**createTransferable** (JComponent c)
	public	void	**exportAsDrag** (JComponent comp, java.awt.event.InputEvent e, int action) ε742
	protected	void	**exportDone** (JComponent source, *java.awt.datatransfer.Transferable* data, int action)
	public	void	**exportToClipboard** (JComponent comp, java.awt.datatransfer.Clipboard clip, int action)
△	public static	Action	**getCopyAction** ()
△	public static	Action	**getCutAction** ()
△	public static	Action	**getPasteAction** ()
	public	int	**getSourceActions** (JComponent c)
	public	Icon	**getVisualRepresentation** (*java.awt.datatransfer.Transferable* t)
	public	boolean	**importData** (JComponent comp, *java.awt.datatransfer.Transferable* t)
▲	public static final	int	**MOVE** = 2
▲	public static final	int	**NONE** = 0
*	protected		**TransferHandler** ()
*	public		**TransferHandler** (String property) ε742

TransformAttribute · java.awt.font

Object
1.2 ● └─TransformAttribute - *java.io.Serializable*

	public	java.awt.geom.AffineTransform	**getTransform** ()
1.4	public	boolean	**isIdentity** ()
*	public		**TransformAttribute** (java.awt.geom.AffineTransform transform)

Transmitter · javax.sound.midi

1.3 *Transmitter*

public	void	**close** ()
public	Receiver	**getReceiver** ()
public	void	**setReceiver** (*Receiver* receiver)

Transparency
java.awt

1.2	*Transparency*	
▲	public static final .... int **BITMASK** = 2	ε666,667
	public........................ int **getTransparency** ()	
▲	public static final .... int **OPAQUE** = 1	ε666,667
▲	public static final .... int **TRANSLUCENT** = 3	ε666

TreeCellEditor
javax.swing.tree

1.2	*TreeCellEditor*————————————*javax.swing.CellEditor* [1]	
1	public .... void addCellEditorListener (*javax.swing.event.CellEditorListener* l)	
1	public .... void cancelCellEditing ()	ε956
1	public .... Object getCellEditorValue ()	ε953,954,960
	public .... java.awt.Component **getTreeCellEditorComponent** (javax.swing.JTree tree, Object value, boolean isSelected, boolean expanded, boolean leaf, int row)	
1	public .... boolean isCellEditable (java.util.EventObject anEvent)	ε955,960
	public .... void removeCellEditorListener (*javax.swing.event.CellEditorListener* l)	
1	public .... boolean shouldSelectCell (java.util.EventObject anEvent)	
1	public .... boolean stopCellEditing ()	ε954,956

TreeCellRenderer
javax.swing.tree

1.2	*TreeCellRenderer*	
	public .... java.awt.Component **getTreeCellRendererComponent** (javax.swing.JTree tree, Object value, boolean selected, boolean expanded, boolean leaf, int row, boolean hasFocus)	

TreeExpansionEvent
javax.swing.event

	Object	ε640,641,643,649,566
1.1	└ java.util.EventObject [1] - - - - - - - - - - - - - - - - - *java.io.Serializable*	
1.2	└ TreeExpansionEvent	
	public .... **getPath** ()	ε1032
	.... javax.swing.tree.TreePath	
1	public .... Object getSource ()	ε1032,644,886,565,568
	protected .... **path**	
	.... javax.swing.tree.TreePath	
1	protected transient ...... Object source	
1	public .... String toString ()	
*	public .... **TreeExpansionEvent** (Object source, javax.swing.tree.TreePath path)	

TreeExpansionListener
javax.swing.event

1.2	*TreeExpansionListener*————————————*java.util.EventListener*	ε738,743,745,746,752
	public .... void **treeCollapsed** (TreeExpansionEvent event)	ε1032
	public .... void **treeExpanded** (TreeExpansionEvent event)	ε1032

TreeModel
javax.swing.tree

1.2	*TreeModel*	
	public .... void **addTreeModelListener** (*javax.swing.event.TreeModelListener* l)	
	public .... Object **getChild** (Object parent, int index)	
	public .... int **getChildCount** (Object parent)	
	public .... int **getIndexOfChild** (Object parent, Object child)	
	public .... Object **getRoot** ()	ε1023,1024,1028,1029
	public .... boolean **isLeaf** (Object node)	
	public .... void **removeTreeModelListener** (*javax.swing.event.TreeModelListener* l)	
	public .... void **valueForPathChanged** (TreePath path, Object newValue)	

Class *Interface* —extends - - -implements ○ abstract ● final △ static ▲ static final ✳ constructor x x—inherited x **x**—declared **x x**—overridden
ε*n*—examples of usage ⌣—has subclass package—see other volume

TreeModelEvent

					javax.swing.event

ε640,641,643,649,566

```
         Object
1.1      └ java.util.EventObject 1 - - - - - - - - - - - - - - - - - - - java.io.Serializable
1.2           └ TreeModelEvent
```

	protected . . . . int[]	**childIndices**	
	protected . . . . Object[]	**children**	
	public . . . . int[]	**getChildIndices** ()	
	public . . . . Object[]	**getChildren** ()	
	public . . . . Object[]	**getPath** ()	
1	public . . . . Object	getSource ()	ε644,886,565,568,570
	public	**getTreePath** ()	
	. . . . javax.swing.tree.TreePath		
	protected	**path**	
	. . . . javax.swing.tree.TreePath		
1	protected transient . . . . . . Object	source	
1	public . . . . **String**	**toString** ()	
*	public	**TreeModelEvent** (Object source, Object[] path)	
*	public	**TreeModelEvent** (Object source, javax.swing.tree.TreePath path)	
*	public	**TreeModelEvent** (Object source, javax.swing.tree.TreePath path, int[] childIndices,	
		Object[] children)	
*	public	**TreeModelEvent** (Object source, Object[] path, int[] childIndices, Object[] children)	

TreeModelListener

					javax.swing.event

ε738,743,745,746,752

```
1.2      TreeModelListener ───────────────────── java.util.EventListener
```

public . . . . void	**treeNodesChanged** (TreeModelEvent e)	
public . . . . void	**treeNodesInserted** (TreeModelEvent e)	
public . . . . void	**treeNodesRemoved** (TreeModelEvent e)	
public . . . . void	**treeStructureChanged** (TreeModelEvent e)	

TreeNode

					javax.swing.tree

ε1026

```
1.2      TreeNode
```

public . . . . *java.util.Enumeration*	**children** ()	ε1023,1024,1028,1029
public . . . . boolean	**getAllowsChildren** ()	
public . . . . *TreeNode*	**getChildAt** (int childIndex)	
public . . . . int	**getChildCount** ()	ε1023,1024,1028,1029
public . . . . int	**getIndex** (*TreeNode* node)	
public . . . . *TreeNode*	**getParent** ()	ε1027
public . . . . boolean	**isLeaf** ()	

TreePath

					javax.swing.tree

ε1030,1032

```
         Object 1
1.2      └ TreePath - - - - - - - - - - - - - - - - - - - - - - - - - - java.io.Serializable
```

1	public . . . . **boolean**	**equals** (Object o)	
	public . . . . Object	**getLastPathComponent** ()	ε1023,1024,1025,1026,1028
	public . . . . TreePath	**getParentPath** ()	
	public . . . . Object[]	**getPath** ()	
	public . . . . Object	**getPathComponent** (int element)	
	public . . . . int	**getPathCount** ()	
1	public . . . . **int**	**hashCode** ()	
	public . . . . boolean	**isDescendant** (TreePath aTreePath)	
	public . . . . TreePath	**pathByAddingChild** (Object child)	ε1023,1024,1028,1029
1	public . . . . **String**	**toString** ()	
*	protected	**TreePath** ()	
*	public	**TreePath** (Object singlePath)	ε1023,1024,1028,1029
*	public	**TreePath** (Object[] path)	ε1027
*	protected	**TreePath** (Object[] path, int length)	
*	protected	**TreePath** (TreePath parent, Object lastElement)	

TreeSelectionEvent

TreeSelectionEvent	javax.swing.event

Object
1.1 └ *java.util.EventObject* [1] - - - - - - - - - - - - - - - - - - - *java.io.Serializable* ⌄ ε640,641,643,649,566
1.2 └ TreeSelectionEvent

	protected . . . . boolean[]	**areNew**	
	public . . . . Object	**cloneWithSource** (Object newSource)	
	public	**getNewLeadSelectionPath** ()	
	. . . . javax.swing.tree.TreePath		
	public	**getOldLeadSelectionPath** ()	
	. . . . javax.swing.tree.TreePath		
	public	**getPath** ()	
	. . . . javax.swing.tree.TreePath		
	public	**getPaths** ()	ε1033
	. . javax.swing.tree.TreePath[]		
1	public . . . . Object	getSource ()	ε644,886,565,568,570
	public . . . . boolean	**isAddedPath** ()	
1.3	public . . . . boolean	**isAddedPath** (int index)	ε1033
	public . . . . boolean	**isAddedPath** (javax.swing.tree.TreePath path)	
	protected	**newLeadSelectionPath**	
	. . . . javax.swing.tree.TreePath		
	protected	**oldLeadSelectionPath**	
	. . . . javax.swing.tree.TreePath		
	protected	**paths**	
	. . javax.swing.tree.TreePath[]		
1	protected transient . . . . . . Object	source	
1	public . . . . String	toString ()	
*	public	**TreeSelectionEvent** (Object source, javax.swing.tree.TreePath[] paths, boolean[] areNew, javax.swing.tree.TreePath oldLeadSelectionPath, javax.swing.tree.TreePath newLeadSelectionPath)	
*	public	**TreeSelectionEvent** (Object source, javax.swing.tree.TreePath path, boolean isNew, javax.swing.tree.TreePath oldLeadSelectionPath, javax.swing.tree.TreePath newLeadSelectionPath)	

T

TreeSelectionListener	javax.swing.event

1.2	*TreeSelectionListener*	*java.util.EventListener* ⌄	ε738,743,745,746,752
	public . . . . void	**valueChanged** (TreeSelectionEvent e)	ε1033

TreeSelectionModel	javax.swing.tree

1.2	*TreeSelectionModel*		
	public . . . . void	**addPropertyChangeListener** (*java.beans.PropertyChangeListener* listener)	
	public . . . . void	**addSelectionPath** (TreePath path)	
	public . . . . void	**addSelectionPaths** (TreePath[] paths)	
	public . . . . void	**addTreeSelectionListener** (*javax.swing.event.TreeSelectionListener* x)	
	public . . . . void	**clearSelection** ()	
▲	public static final . . . . int	**CONTIGUOUS_TREE_SELECTION** = 2	ε1022
▲	public static final . . . . int	**DISCONTIGUOUS_TREE_SELECTION** = 4	ε1022
	public . . . . TreePath	**getLeadSelectionPath** ()	
	public . . . . int	**getLeadSelectionRow** ()	
	public . . . . int	**getMaxSelectionRow** ()	
	public . . . . int	**getMinSelectionRow** ()	
	public . . . . RowMapper	**getRowMapper** ()	
	public . . . . int	**getSelectionCount** ()	
	public . . . . int	**getSelectionMode** ()	
	public . . . . TreePath	**getSelectionPath** ()	
	public . . . . TreePath[]	**getSelectionPaths** ()	
	public . . . . int[]	**getSelectionRows** ()	
	public . . . . boolean	**isPathSelected** (TreePath path)	
	public . . . . boolean	**isRowSelected** (int row)	
	public . . . . boolean	**isSelectionEmpty** ()	
	public . . . . void	**removePropertyChangeListener** (*java.beans.PropertyChangeListener* listener)	
	public . . . . void	**removeSelectionPath** (TreePath path)	
	public . . . . void	**removeSelectionPaths** (TreePath[] paths)	
	public . . . . void	**removeTreeSelectionListener** (*javax.swing.event.TreeSelectionListener* x)	

public	void	**resetRowSelection** ()	
public	void	**setRowMapper** (*RowMapper* newMapper)	
public	void	**setSelectionMode** (int mode)	ε1022
public	void	**setSelectionPath** (TreePath path)	
public	void	**setSelectionPaths** (TreePath[] paths)	
▲ public static final	int	**SINGLE_TREE_SELECTION** = 1	ε1022

TreeUI javax.swing.plaf

```
Object
1.2 ○  └ComponentUI¹
1.2 ○    └TreeUI
```

	1	*11 inherited members from ComponentUI not shown*
○	public abstract ....void	**cancelEditing** (javax.swing.JTree tree)
○	public abstract ...... javax.swing.tree.TreePath	**getClosestPathForLocation** (javax.swing.JTree tree, int x, int y)
○	public abstract ...... javax.swing.tree.TreePath	**getEditingPath** (javax.swing.JTree tree)
○	public abstract ...... java.awt.Rectangle	**getPathBounds** (javax.swing.JTree tree, javax.swing.tree.TreePath path)
○	public abstract ...... javax.swing.tree.TreePath	**getPathForRow** (javax.swing.JTree tree, int row)
○	public abstract ....int	**getRowCount** (javax.swing.JTree tree)
○	public abstract ....int	**getRowForPath** (javax.swing.JTree tree, javax.swing.tree.TreePath path)
○	public abstract ....boolean	**isEditing** (javax.swing.JTree tree)
○	public abstract ....void	**startEditingAtPath** (javax.swing.JTree tree, javax.swing.tree.TreePath path)
○	public abstract ....boolean	**stopEditing** (javax.swing.JTree tree)
∗	public	**TreeUI** ()

TreeWillExpandListener javax.swing.event

ε738,743,745,746,752

```
1.2   TreeWillExpandListener————————java.util.EventListener
```

public	void	**treeWillCollapse** (TreeExpansionEvent event) throws javax.swing.tree.ExpandVetoException	ε1032
public	void	**treeWillExpand** (TreeExpansionEvent event) throws javax.swing.tree.ExpandVetoException	ε1032

U

UIDefaults javax.swing

```
Object
○  └java.util.Dictionary
     └java.util.Hashtable¹ - - - - - - - - - - - - - - - - - java.util.Map, Cloneable, java.io.Serializable
1.2    └UIDefaults
```

	public synchronized ......void	**addPropertyChangeListener** (*java.beans.PropertyChangeListener* listener)	
1.4	public synchronized ......void	**addResourceBundle** (String bundleName)	
1	public synchronized ......void	clear ()	
1	public synchronized ....Object	clone ()	
1	public synchronized .. boolean	contains (Object value)	
1	public synchronized .. boolean	containsKey (Object key)	
1	public .... boolean	containsValue (Object value)	ε577
1	public synchronized .... java.util.Enumeration	elements ()	
1	public .... java.util.Set	entrySet ()	
1	public synchronized .. boolean	equals (Object o)	
	protected ....void	**firePropertyChange** (String propertyName, Object oldValue, Object newValue)	ε870
1	public ....**Object**	**get** (Object key)	
1.4	public .... Object	**get** (Object key, java.util.Locale l)	ε870
1.4	public .... boolean	**getBoolean** (Object key)	
1.4	public .... boolean	**getBoolean** (Object key, java.util.Locale l)	ε870
	public ...... javax.swing.border.Border	**getBorder** (Object key)	
1.4	public ...... javax.swing.border.Border	**getBorder** (Object key, java.util.Locale l)	
	public .... java.awt.Color	**getColor** (Object key)	ε870
1.4	public .... java.awt.Color	**getColor** (Object key, java.util.Locale l)	
	public .... java.util.Locale	**getDefaultLocale** ()	
	public ...... java.awt.Dimension	**getDimension** (Object key)	ε870
1.4	public ...... java.awt.Dimension	**getDimension** (Object key, java.util.Locale l)	

Classes

UIDefaults

		public	java.awt.Font	**getFont** (Object key)	ε870
1.4		public	java.awt.Font	**getFont** (Object key, java.util.Locale l)	
		public	*Icon*	**getIcon** (Object key)	ε870
1.4		public	*Icon*	**getIcon** (Object key, java.util.Locale l)	
		public	java.awt.Insets	**getInsets** (Object key)	ε870
1.4		public	java.awt.Insets	**getInsets** (Object key, java.util.Locale l)	
		public	int	**getInt** (Object key)	ε870
1.4		public	int	**getInt** (Object key, java.util.Locale l)	
1.4		public synchronized *java.beans.-PropertyChangeListener[]*		**getPropertyChangeListeners** ()	
		public	String	**getString** (Object key)	ε870
1.4		public	String	**getString** (Object key, java.util.Locale l)	
		public	javax.swing.plaf.ComponentUI	**getUI** (JComponent target)	
		public	Class	**getUIClass** (String uiClassID)	
		public	Class	**getUIClass** (String uiClassID, ClassLoader uiClassLoader)	
		protected	void	**getUIError** (String msg)	
	1	public synchronized	int	hashCode ()	
	1	public synchronized	boolean	isEmpty ()	
	1	public synchronized *java.util.Enumeration*		keys ()	
	1	public	*java.util.Set*	keySet ()	ε870
	1	public	**Object**	**put** (Object key, Object value)	
	1	public synchronized	void	putAll (*java.util.Map* t)	
		public	void	**putDefaults** (Object[] keyValueList)	
	1	protected	void	rehash ()	
	1	public synchronized	Object	remove (Object key)	
		public synchronized	void	**removePropertyChangeListener** (java.beans.*PropertyChangeListener* listener)	
1.4		public synchronized	void	**removeResourceBundle** (String bundleName)	
1.4		public	void	**setDefaultLocale** (java.util.Locale l)	
	1	public synchronized	int	size ()	
	1	public synchronized	String	toString ()	
✳		public		**UIDefaults** ()	
✳		public		**UIDefaults** (Object[] keyValueList)	
	1	public	*java.util.Collection*	values ()	

U

UIDefaults.ActiveValue | javax.swing

1.2	*UIDefaults.ActiveValue*

public	Object **createValue** (UIDefaults table)	ε872

UIDefaults.LazyInputMap | javax.swing

Object
└UIDefaults.LazyInputMap ---------------- *UIDefaults.LazyValue* [1]

1.3

	1	public	Object **createValue** (UIDefaults table)	ε871
✳		public	**UIDefaults.LazyInputMap** (Object[] bindings)

UIDefaults.LazyValue | javax.swing

1.2	*UIDefaults.LazyValue*

public	Object **createValue** (UIDefaults table)	ε871

UIDefaults.ProxyLazyValue | javax.swing

Object
└UIDefaults.ProxyLazyValue -------------- *UIDefaults.LazyValue* [1]

1.3

	1	public	Object **createValue** (UIDefaults table)	ε871
✳		public	**UIDefaults.ProxyLazyValue** (String c)
✳		public	**UIDefaults.ProxyLazyValue** (String c, String m)
✳		public	**UIDefaults.ProxyLazyValue** (String c, Object[] o)

Class *Interface* —extends - - -implements ○ abstract ● final △ static ▲ static final ✳ constructor x x—inherited x **x**—declared **x x**—overridden
εn—examples of usage ⌐—has subclass package—see other volume

*	public	. . . .	**UIDefaults.ProxyLazyValue** (String c, String m, Object[] o)	

UIManager				javax.swing

```
       Object
1.2    └─UIManager - - - - - - - - - - - - - - - - - - - - - - - - - - - - java.io.Serializable
```

△	public static	. . . . void	**addAuxiliaryLookAndFeel** (LookAndFeel laf)	
△	public static	. . . . void	**addPropertyChangeListener** (*java.beans.PropertyChangeListener* listener)	
△	public static	. . . . Object	**get** (Object key)	ε871,872
1.4 △	public static	. . . . Object	**get** (Object key, java.util.Locale l)	
△	public static	. . . LookAndFeel[]	**getAuxiliaryLookAndFeels** ()	
1.4 △	public static	. . . . boolean	**getBoolean** (Object key)	
1.4 △	public static	. . . . boolean	**getBoolean** (Object key, java.util.Locale l)	
△	public static	. . . . *javax.swing.border.Border*	**getBorder** (Object key)	ε933,934
1.4 △	public static	. . . . *javax.swing.border.Border*	**getBorder** (Object key, java.util.Locale l)	
△	public static	. . . . . java.awt.Color	**getColor** (Object key)	
1.4 △	public static	. . . . . java.awt.Color	**getColor** (Object key, java.util.Locale l)	
△	public static	. . . . String	**getCrossPlatformLookAndFeelClassName** ()	ε868
△	public static	. . . . UIDefaults	**getDefaults** ()	
△	public static	. . . . java.awt.Dimension	**getDimension** (Object key)	
1.4 △	public static	. . . . java.awt.Dimension	**getDimension** (Object key, java.util.Locale l)	
△	public static	. . . . . . java.awt.Font	**getFont** (Object key)	
1.4 △	public static	. . . . . . java.awt.Font	**getFont** (Object key, java.util.Locale l)	
△	public static	. . . . *Icon*	**getIcon** (Object key)	
1.4 △	public static	. . . . *Icon*	**getIcon** (Object key, java.util.Locale l)	
△	public static	. . . . java.awt.Insets	**getInsets** (Object key)	
1.4 △	public static	. . . . java.awt.Insets	**getInsets** (Object key, java.util.Locale l)	
△	public static	. . . . UIManager .LookAndFeelInfo[]	**getInstalledLookAndFeels** ()	ε866
△	public static	. . . . int	**getInt** (Object key)	
1.4 △	public static	. . . . int	**getInt** (Object key, java.util.Locale l)	
△	public static	. . . . . . LookAndFeel	**getLookAndFeel** ()	ε867
△	public static	. . . . UIDefaults	**getLookAndFeelDefaults** ()	ε870
1.4 △	public static	. . . . . . *java.beans.- PropertyChangeListener[]*	**getPropertyChangeListeners** ()	
△	public static	. . . . String	**getString** (Object key)	
1.4 △	public static	. . . . String	**getString** (Object key, java.util.Locale l)	
△	public static	. . . . String	**getSystemLookAndFeelClassName** ()	ε868
△	public static	. . . . javax .swing.plaf.ComponentUI	**getUI** (JComponent target)	
△	public static	. . . . void	**installLookAndFeel** (UIManager.LookAndFeelInfo info)	
△	public static	. . . . void	**installLookAndFeel** (String name, String className)	
△	public static	. . . . Object	**put** (Object key, Object value)	ε806,871,872,1020
△	public static	. . . . boolean	**removeAuxiliaryLookAndFeel** (LookAndFeel laf)	
△	public static	. . . . void	**removePropertyChangeListener** (*java.beans.PropertyChangeListener* listener)	
△	public static	. . . . void	**setInstalledLookAndFeels** (UIManager.LookAndFeelInfo[] infos) throws SecurityException	
△	public static	. . . . void	**setLookAndFeel** (String className) throws ClassNotFoundException, InstantiationException, IllegalAccessException, UnsupportedLookAndFeelException	ε867,868
△	public static	. . . . void	**setLookAndFeel** (LookAndFeel newLookAndFeel) throws UnsupportedLookAndFeelException	
*	public	. . . .	**UIManager** ()	

UIManager.LookAndFeelInfo			javax.swing

```
       Object[1]
1.2    └─UIManager.LookAndFeelInfo
```

	public	. . . . String	**getClassName** ()	ε866
	public	. . . . String	**getName** ()	ε866
*	public	. . . .	**UIManager.LookAndFeelInfo** (String name, String className)	
1	public	. . . . **String**	**toString** ()	

U

Classes

807

UIResource	javax.swing.plaf
1.2	*UIResource*

UndoableEdit	javax.swing.undo
1.2	*UndoableEdit*

public............... boolean	**addEdit** (*UndoableEdit* anEdit)	ε1034
public............... boolean	**canRedo** ()	ε1034
public............... boolean	**canUndo** ()	ε1034
public.................... void	**die** ()	
public.................... String	**getPresentationName** ()	
public.................... String	**getRedoPresentationName** ()	
public.................... String	**getUndoPresentationName** ()	
public............... boolean	**isSignificant** ()	
public.................... void	**redo** () throws CannotRedoException	ε1034
public............... boolean	**replaceEdit** (*UndoableEdit* anEdit)	
public.................... void	**undo** () throws CannotUndoException	ε1034

UndoableEditEvent	javax.swing.event

Object
 └ java.util.EventObject [1] - - - - - - - - - - - - - - - - - *java.io.Serializable*
     └ UndoableEditEvent

1.1
1.2

ε640,641,643,649,566

public............... *javax*$_2$	**getEdit** ()	ε1034
.*swing.undo.UndoableEdit*		
1 public................ Object	getSource ()	ε644,886,565,568,570
1 protected transient...... Object	source	
1 public................ String	toString ()	
* public....................	**UndoableEditEvent** (Object source, *javax.swing.undo.UndoableEdit* edit)	

UndoableEditListener	javax.swing.event
1.2	*UndoableEditListener* ——————— *java.util.EventListener* ε738,743,745,746,752

public.................... void	**undoableEditHappened** (UndoableEditEvent e)	ε1034

UndoableEditSupport	javax.swing.undo

Object [1]
 └ UndoableEditSupport

1.2

protected.................... void	**_postEdit** (*UndoableEdit* e)	
public synchronized .... void	**addUndoableEditListener** (*javax.swing.event.UndoableEditListener* l)	
public synchronized .... void	**beginUpdate** ()	
protected .... CompoundEdit	**compoundEdit**	
protected .... CompoundEdit	**createCompoundEdit** ()	
public synchronized .... void	**endUpdate** ()	
1.4 public synchronized	**getUndoableEditListeners** ()	
.... *javax.swing.event*$_2$		
.*UndoableEditListener[]*		
public.......................... int	**getUpdateLevel** ()	
protected .... java.util.Vector	**listeners**	
public synchronized .... void	**postEdit** (*UndoableEdit* e)	
protected .... Object	**realSource**	
public synchronized .... void	**removeUndoableEditListener** (*javax.swing.event.UndoableEditListener* l)	
1 public.................... **String**	**toString** ()	
* public..........................	**UndoableEditSupport** ()	
* public..........................	**UndoableEditSupport** (Object r)	
protected .... int	**updateLevel**	

Class *Interface* —extends - - -implements ○ abstract ● final △ static ▲ static final ✳ constructor x x—inherited x **x**—declared **x x**—overridden
ε*n*—examples of usage ⌄—has subclass package—see other volume

		UndoManager		javax.swing.undo

```
        Object
1.2     └ AbstractUndoableEdit 1 - - - - - - - - - - - - - - - - - -  UndoableEdit, java.io.Serializable ˏ
1.2        └ CompoundEdit 2
1.2           └ UndoManager - - - - - - - - - - - - - - - - - -  javax.swing.event.UndoableEditListener 3 (java.util.EventListener)
```

2	public synchronized .. **boolean**	**addEdit** (*UndoableEdit* anEdit)		ε1034
2	public synchronized .. **boolean**	**canRedo** ()		ε1034
2	public synchronized .. **boolean**	**canUndo** ()		ε1034
	public synchronized .. boolean	**canUndoOrRedo** ()		
2	public.......................void	die ()		
	public synchronized ....void	**discardAllEdits** ()		
2	protected .... java.util.Vector	edits		
	protected........ *UndoableEdit*	**editToBeRedone** ()		
	protected........ *UndoableEdit*	**editToBeUndone** ()		
2	public synchronized ...... **void**	**end** ()		
	public synchronized ....int	**getLimit** ()		
2	public....................String	getPresentationName ()		
2	public synchronized .... **String**	**getRedoPresentationName** ()		
	public synchronized .....String	**getUndoOrRedoPresentationName** ()		
2	public synchronized .... **String**	**getUndoPresentationName** ()		
2	public.................. boolean	isInProgress ()		
2	public.................. boolean	isSignificant ()		
2	protected........ *UndoableEdit*	lastEdit ()		
2	public synchronized ...... **void**	**redo** () throws CannotRedoException		ε1034
▲ 1	protected static final .....String	RedoName		
	protected ....void	**redoTo** (*UndoableEdit* edit) throws CannotRedoException		
1	public.................. boolean	replaceEdit (*UndoableEdit* anEdit)		
	public synchronized ....void	**setLimit** (int l)		
2	public.................... **String**	**toString** ()		
	protected ....void	**trimEdits** (int from, int to)		
	protected ....void	**trimForLimit** ()		
2	public synchronized ...... **void**	**undo** () throws CannotUndoException		ε1034
3	public.....................void	**undoableEditHappened** (javax.swing.event.UndoableEditEvent e)		ε1034
✳	public.........................	**UndoManager** ()		ε1034
▲ 1	protected static final .....String	UndoName		
	public synchronized ....void	**undoOrRedo** () throws CannotRedoException, CannotUndoException		
	protected ....void	**undoTo** (*UndoableEdit* edit) throws CannotUndoException		

		UnmodifiableSetException		javax.print.attribute

```
        Object
        └ Throwable - - - - - - - - - - - - - - - - - - - - - - - - - -  java.io.Serializable ˏ
           └ Exception
              └ RuntimeException
1.4              └ UnmodifiableSetException
```

✳	public.........................	**UnmodifiableSetException** ()	
✳	public.........................	**UnmodifiableSetException** (String message)	

		UnsupportedAudioFileException		javax.sound.sampled

ε723,724,726,727

```
        Object
        └ Throwable - - - - - - - - - - - - - - - - - - - - - - - - - -  java.io.Serializable ˏ
           └ Exception
1.3           └ UnsupportedAudioFileException
```

✳	public.........................	**UnsupportedAudioFileException** ()	
✳	public.........................	**UnsupportedAudioFileException** (String message)	

		UnsupportedFlavorException		java.awt.datatransfer

ε637,642

```
        Object
        └ Throwable - - - - - - - - - - - - - - - - - - - - - - - - - -  java.io.Serializable ˏ
           └ Exception
1.1           └ UnsupportedFlavorException
```

U

Classes

UnsupportedFlavorException

✳	public............................	**UnsupportedFlavorException** (DataFlavor flavor)	ε638

UnsupportedLookAndFeelException	javax.swing

```
       Object                                              ε867,868
       └Throwable - - - - - - - - - - - - - - - - - - - - - - - - - - java.io.Serializable
         └Exception
1.2       └UnsupportedLookAndFeelException
```

✳	public............................	**UnsupportedLookAndFeelException** (String s)

URIException	javax.print

```
1.4    URIException
```

	public............................int	**getReason** ()
	public............. java.net.URI	**getUnsupportedURI** ()
▲	public static final............int	**URIInaccessible** = 1
▲	public static final............int	**URIOtherProblem** = -1
▲	public static final............int	**URISchemeNotSupported** = 2

URISyntax	javax.print.attribute

```
       Object¹
1.4 ○  └URISyntax - - - - - - - - - - - - - - - - - - - - - - - - - - java.io.Serializable, Cloneable
```

1	public................**boolean**	**equals** (Object object)	
	public............. java.net.URI	**getURI** ()	
1	public......................**int**	**hashCode** ()	
1	public................**String**	**toString** ()	
✳	protected	**URISyntax** (java.net.URI uri)	

U

Utilities	javax.swing.text

```
       Object
1.2    └Utilities
```

▲	public static final............int	**drawTabbedText** (Segment s, int x, int y, java.awt.Graphics g, *TabExpander* e, int startOffset)
▲	public static final............int	**getBreakLocation** (Segment s, java.awt.FontMetrics metrics, int x0, int x, *TabExpander* e, int startOffset)
▲	public static final............int	**getNextWord** (JTextComponent c, int offs) throws BadLocationException ε972
▲	public static final...... *Element*	**getParagraphElement** (JTextComponent c, int offs)
▲	public static final............int	**getPositionAbove** (JTextComponent c, int offs, int x) throws BadLocationException
▲	public static final............int	**getPositionBelow** (JTextComponent c, int offs, int x) throws BadLocationException
▲	public static final............int	**getPreviousWord** (JTextComponent c, int offs) throws BadLocationException ε972
▲	public static final............int	**getRowEnd** (JTextComponent c, int offs) throws BadLocationException ε973
▲	public static final............int	**getRowStart** (JTextComponent c, int offs) throws BadLocationException
▲	public static final............int	**getTabbedTextOffset** (Segment s, java.awt.FontMetrics metrics, int x0, int x, *TabExpander* e, int startOffset)
▲	public static final............int	**getTabbedTextOffset** (Segment s, java.awt.FontMetrics metrics, int x0, int x, *TabExpander* e, int startOffset, boolean round)
▲	public static final............int	**getTabbedTextWidth** (Segment s, java.awt.FontMetrics metrics, int x, *TabExpander* e, int startOffset)
▲	public static final............int	**getWordEnd** (JTextComponent c, int offs) throws BadLocationException ε972
▲	public static final............int	**getWordStart** (JTextComponent c, int offs) throws BadLocationException ε972
✳	public............................	**Utilities** ()

Class   *Interface*   —extends   - - -implements   ○ abstract   ● final   △ static   ▲ static final   ✳ constructor   x x—inherited   x **x**—declared   **x x**—overridden
ε*n*—examples of usage   ,—has subclass   package—see other volume

Object
1.2 ○ └AbstractLayoutCache [1] - - - - - - - - - - - - - - - - - *RowMapper*
1.2   └VariableHeightLayoutCache

1	public.....	**java.awt.Rectangle**	**getBounds** (TreePath path, java.awt.Rectangle placeIn)
1	public.................	**boolean**	**getExpandedState** (TreePath path)
1	public.................	*TreeModel*	getModel ()
1	public.. AbstractLayoutCache ⌇ .NodeDimensions		getNodeDimensions ()
1	protected ..	java.awt.Rectangle	getNodeDimensions (Object value, int row, int depth, boolean expanded, java.awt.Rectangle placeIn)
1	public.................	**TreePath**	**getPathClosestTo** (int x, int y)
1	public.................	**TreePath**	**getPathForRow** (int row)
1	public.................	**int**	**getPreferredHeight** ()
1	public.................	**int**	**getPreferredWidth** (java.awt.Rectangle bounds)
1	public.................	**int**	**getRowCount** ()
1	public.................	**int**	**getRowForPath** (TreePath path)
1	public.................	int	getRowHeight ()
1	public.................	int[]	getRowsForPaths (TreePath[] paths)
1	public.....	*TreeSelectionModel*	getSelectionModel ()
1	public.................	**int**	**getVisibleChildCount** (TreePath path)
1	public..	*java.util.Enumeration*	**getVisiblePathsFrom** (TreePath path)
1	public.................	**void**	**invalidatePathBounds** (TreePath path)
1	public.................	**void**	**invalidateSizes** ()
1	public.................	**boolean**	**isExpanded** (TreePath path)
1	protected	boolean	isFixedRowHeight ()
1	public.................	boolean	isRootVisible ()
1	protected .... AbstractLayoutCache ⌇ .NodeDimensions		nodeDimensions
1	protected	boolean	rootVisible
1	protected	int	rowHeight
1	public.................	**void**	**setExpandedState** (TreePath path, boolean isExpanded)
1	public.................	**void**	**setModel** (*TreeModel* newModel)
1	public.................	**void**	**setNodeDimensions** (AbstractLayoutCache.NodeDimensions nd)
1	public.................	**void**	**setRootVisible** (boolean rootVisible)
1	public.................	**void**	**setRowHeight** (int rowHeight)
1	public.................	void	setSelectionModel (*TreeSelectionModel* newLSM)
1	protected	*TreeModel*	treeModel
1	public.................	**void**	**treeNodesChanged** (javax.swing.event.TreeModelEvent e)
1	public.................	**void**	**treeNodesInserted** (javax.swing.event.TreeModelEvent e)
1	public.................	**void**	**treeNodesRemoved** (javax.swing.event.TreeModelEvent e)
1	protected .	*TreeSelectionModel*	treeSelectionModel
1	public.................	**void**	**treeStructureChanged** (javax.swing.event.TreeModelEvent e)
*	public.................		**VariableHeightLayoutCache** ()

Object
1.2 ○ └View ‿ - *javax.swing.SwingConstants* [1]

1	*19 inherited members from javax.swing.SwingConstants not shown*		
1.3	public.....................	void	**append** (View v)
▲	public static final	int	**BadBreakWeight** = 0
	public.................	View	**breakView** (int axis, int offset, float pos, float len)
	public.....................	void	**changedUpdate** (*javax.swing.event.DocumentEvent* e, *java.awt.Shape* a, *ViewFactory* f)
	public.....................	View	**createFragment** (int p0, int p1)
▲	public static final	int	**ExcellentBreakWeight** = 2000
▲	public static final	int	**ForcedBreakWeight** = 3000
1.3	protected	void	**forwardUpdate** (*javax.swing.event.DocumentEvent.ElementChange* ec, *javax.swing.event.DocumentEvent* e, *java.awt.Shape* a, *ViewFactory* f)
1.3	protected	void	**forwardUpdateToView** (View v, *javax.swing.event.DocumentEvent* e, *java.awt.Shape* a, *ViewFactory* f)
	public.....................	float	**getAlignment** (int axis)
	public.............	*AttributeSet*	**getAttributes** ()
	public.................	int	**getBreakWeight** (int axis, float pos, float len)
	public..........	*java.awt.Shape*	**getChildAllocation** (int index, *java.awt.Shape* a)
	public.......	java.awt.Container	**getContainer** ()
	public..............	*Document*	**getDocument** ()

811

View

	public	*Element*	**getElement** ()
	public	int	**getEndOffset** ()
1.3	public	java.awt.Graphics	**getGraphics** ()
	public	float	**getMaximumSpan** (int axis)
	public	float	**getMinimumSpan** (int axis)
	public	int	**getNextVisualPositionFrom** (int pos, Position.Bias b, *java.awt.Shape* a, int direction, Position.Bias[] biasRet) throws BadLocationException
	public	View	**getParent** ()
○	public abstract	float	**getPreferredSpan** (int axis)
	public	int	**getResizeWeight** (int axis)
	public	int	**getStartOffset** ()
1.4	public	String	**getToolTipText** (float x, float y, *java.awt.Shape* allocation)
	public	View	**getView** (int n) ε978
	public	int	**getViewCount** () ε978
	public	*ViewFactory*	**getViewFactory** ()
1.3	public	int	**getViewIndex** (int pos, Position.Bias b)
1.4	public	int	**getViewIndex** (float x, float y, *java.awt.Shape* allocation)
▲	public static final	int	**GoodBreakWeight** = 1000
1.3	public	void	**insert** (int offs, View v)
	public	void	**insertUpdate** (*javax.swing.event.DocumentEvent* e, *java.awt.Shape* a, *ViewFactory* f)
	public	boolean	**isVisible** ()
D	public	*java.awt.Shape*	**modelToView** (int pos, *java.awt.Shape* a) throws BadLocationException
○	public abstract	*java.awt.Shape*	**modelToView** (int pos, *java.awt.Shape* a, Position.Bias b) throws BadLocationException
	public	*java.awt.Shape*	**modelToView** (int p0, Position.Bias b0, int p1, Position.Bias b1, *java.awt.Shape* a) throws BadLocationException
○	public abstract	void	**paint** (java.awt.Graphics g, *java.awt.Shape* allocation)
	public	void	**preferenceChanged** (View child, boolean width, boolean height)
1.3	public	void	**remove** (int i)
1.3	public	void	**removeAll** ()
	public	void	**removeUpdate** (*javax.swing.event.DocumentEvent* e, *java.awt.Shape* a, *ViewFactory* f)
1.3	public	void	**replace** (int offset, int length, View[] views)
	public	void	**setParent** (View parent)
	public	void	**setSize** (float width, float height)
1.3	protected	boolean	**updateChildren** (*javax.swing.event.DocumentEvent.ElementChange* ec, *javax.swing.event.DocumentEvent* e, *ViewFactory* f)
1.3	protected	void	**updateLayout** (*javax.swing.event.DocumentEvent.ElementChange* ec, *javax.swing.event.DocumentEvent* e, *java.awt.Shape* a)
✳	public		**View** (*Element* elem)
D	public	int	**viewToModel** (float x, float y, *java.awt.Shape* a)
○	public abstract	int	**viewToModel** (float x, float y, *java.awt.Shape* a, Position.Bias[] biasReturn)
▲	public static final	int	**X_AXIS** = 0
▲	public static final	int	**Y_AXIS** = 1

ViewFactory   javax.swing.text

1.2	*ViewFactory*		
	public	View	**create** (*Element* elem)

ViewportLayout   javax.swing

Object
└ ViewportLayout - *java.awt.LayoutManager* ˌ[1], *java.io.Serializable* ˌ

1	public	void	**addLayoutComponent** (String name, java.awt.Component c)
1	public	void	**layoutContainer** (java.awt.Container parent) ε624,625
1	public	java.awt.Dimension	**minimumLayoutSize** (java.awt.Container parent)
1	public	java.awt.Dimension	**preferredLayoutSize** (java.awt.Container parent)
1	public	void	**removeLayoutComponent** (java.awt.Component c)
✳	public		**ViewportLayout** ()

Class *Interface* —extends - - -implements ○ abstract ● final △ static ▲ static final ✳ constructor x x—inherited x **x**—declared **x x**—overridden
ε*n*—examples of usage ˌ—has subclass package—see other volume

ViewportUI
javax.swing.plaf

```
     Object
1.2 ○ └ ComponentUI 1
1.2 ○    └ ViewportUI
```

	1	*11 inherited members from ComponentUI not shown*		
∗		public.........................	**ViewportUI** ()	

VoiceStatus
javax.sound.midi

```
     Object
1.3  └ VoiceStatus
```

	public................. boolean	**active**	
	public.......................int	**bank**	
	public.......................int	**channel**	
	public.......................int	**note**	
	public.......................int	**program**	
∗	public.........................	**VoiceStatus** ()	
	public.......................int	**volume**	

VolatileImage
java.awt.image

ε560,581,597,638,660

```
     Object
○    └ java.awt.Image 1
1.4 ○    └ VolatileImage
```

○		public abstract........ boolean	**contentsLost** ()	ε674
○		public abstract................	**createGraphics** ()	ε674
		.... java.awt.Graphics2D		
	1	public.................... **void**	**flush** ()	ε673,674
○		public abstract................	**getCapabilities** ()	
		.. java.awt.ImageCapabilities		
	1	public...... **java.awt.Graphics**	**getGraphics** ()	
○		public abstract...............int	**getHeight** ()	
○	1	public abstract...............int	getHeight (*ImageObserver* observer)	ε674,594,667,671,675
○	1	public abstract..........Object	getProperty (String name, *ImageObserver* observer)	
	1	public......... java.awt.Image	getScaledInstance (int width, int height, int hints)	
○		public abstract . BufferedImage	**getSnapshot** ()	
	1	public......... **ImageProducer**	**getSource** ()	ε664,665,670
○		public abstract...............int	**getWidth** ()	
○	1	public abstract...............int	getWidth (*ImageObserver* observer)	ε674,594,667,671,675
▲		public static final.............int	**IMAGE_INCOMPATIBLE** = 2	ε674
▲		public static final.............int	**IMAGE_OK** = 0	ε674
▲		public static final.............int	**IMAGE_RESTORED** = 1	ε674
▲	1	public static final.............int	SCALE_AREA_AVERAGING = 16	
▲	1	public static final.............int	SCALE_DEFAULT = 1	
▲	1	public static final.............int	SCALE_FAST = 2	
▲	1	public static final.............int	SCALE_REPLICATE = 8	
▲	1	public static final.............int	SCALE_SMOOTH = 4	
▲	1	public static final........Object	UndefinedProperty	
○		public abstract...............int	**validate** (java.awt.GraphicsConfiguration gc)	ε674
∗		public.........................	**VolatileImage** ()	

Window
java.awt

ε606,618,733,953,988

```
     Object 1
○    └ Component 2 - - - - - - - - - - - - - - - - - - - - - - - - - - - java.awt.image.ImageObserver 4, MenuContainer,
                                                         java.io.Serializable
        └ Container 3
           └ Window - - - - - - - - - - - - - - - - - - - - - - - javax.accessibility.Accessible
```

	2	*162 inherited members from Component not shown*		
	3	*57 inherited members from Container not shown*		
	4	*8 inherited members from java.awt.image.ImageObserver not shown*		
1.1	3	public......................void	add (Component comp, Object constraints)	ε601,733,559,571,694
1.1	2	public synchronized ....void	addMouseListener (*java.awt.event.MouseListener* l)	ε602
	3	public.................... **void**	**addNotify** ()	
1.2	3	public.................... **void**	**addPropertyChangeListener** (*java.beans.PropertyChangeListener* listener)	

W

Classes

Window

Ver.		#	Modifiers / Return	Method	Ref.
1.2		3	public ... **void**	**addPropertyChangeListener** (String propertyName, *java.beans.PropertyChangeListener* listener)	
1.4			public synchronized ... void	**addWindowFocusListener** (*java.awt.event.WindowFocusListener* l)	
1.1			public synchronized ... void	**addWindowListener** (*java.awt.event.WindowListener* l)	ε565,566,568,884,905
1.4			public synchronized ... void	**addWindowStateListener** (*java.awt.event.WindowStateListener* l)	ε569
D			public ... void	**applyResourceBundle** (String rbName)	
D			public ... void	**applyResourceBundle** (*java.util*.ResourceBundle rb)	
1.4			public ... void	**createBufferStrategy** (int numBuffers)	ε602
1.4			public ... void	**createBufferStrategy** (int numBuffers, BufferCapabilities caps) throws AWTException	
			public ... void	**dispose** ()	ε565
		1	protected ... **void**	**finalize** () throws Throwable	
1.3		2	public .... **javax.accessibility .AccessibleContext**	**getAccessibleContext** ()	
1.4			public ... java .awt.image.BufferStrategy	**getBufferStrategy** ()	ε602
1.4			public ... boolean	**getFocusableWindowState** ()	
1.4	●	2	public final ... **Container**	**getFocusCycleRootAncestor** ()	
1.1			public ... Component	**getFocusOwner** ()	
1.4		3	public ... *java.util*.**Set**	**getFocusTraversalKeys** (int id)	ε610
1.3		2	public **GraphicsConfiguration**	**getGraphicsConfiguration** ()	
1.2		2	public ... int	getHeight ()	ε602
1.2		2	public ... **java.awt.im.InputContext**	**getInputContext** ()	
1.3		3	public ... *java*.*util*.***EventListener[]***	**getListeners** (Class listenerType)	
1.1		2	public ... *java*.*util*.**Locale**	**getLocale** ()	
1.4			public ... Component	**getMostRecentFocusOwner** ()	
1.2			public ... Window[]	**getOwnedWindows** ()	
1.2			public ... Window	**getOwner** ()	
		2	public ... **Toolkit**	**getToolkit** ()	
	●		public final ... String	**getWarningString** ()	
1.2		2	public ... int	getWidth ()	ε602
1.4			public synchronized ... *java.awt.event .WindowFocusListener[]*	**getWindowFocusListeners** ()	
1.4			public synchronized . *java.awt .event.WindowListener[]*	**getWindowListeners** ()	
1.4			public synchronized ... *java.awt.event .WindowStateListener[]*	**getWindowStateListeners** ()	
		2	public ... **void**	hide ()	
1.4			public ... boolean	**isActive** ()	
1.4	●		public final ... boolean	**isFocusableWindow** ()	
1.4	●	3	public final ... **boolean**	**isFocusCycleRoot** ()	
1.4			public ... boolean	**isFocused** ()	
		2	public ... **boolean**	**isShowing** ()	
			public ... void	**pack** ()	ε816,887,901,957,971
D		2	public ... **boolean**	postEvent (Event e)	
1.1		3	protected ... **void**	**processEvent** (AWTEvent e)	
1.1			protected ... void	**processWindowEvent** (java.awt.event.WindowEvent e)	
1.4			protected ... void	**processWindowFocusEvent** (java.awt.event.WindowEvent e)	
1.4			protected ... void	**processWindowStateEvent** (java.awt.event.WindowEvent e)	
1.4			public synchronized ... void	**removeWindowFocusListener** (*java.awt.event.WindowFocusListener* l)	
1.1			public synchronized ... void	**removeWindowListener** (*java.awt.event.WindowListener* l)	
1.4			public synchronized ... void	**removeWindowStateListener** (*java.awt.event.WindowStateListener* l)	
		2	public ... void	requestFocus ()	ε602
1.1		2	public ... **void**	**setCursor** (Cursor cursor)	
1.4			public ... void	**setFocusableWindowState** (boolean focusableWindowState)	ε608
1.4	●	3	public final ... **void**	**setFocusCycleRoot** (boolean focusCycleRoot)	
1.4			public ... void	**setLocationRelativeTo** (Component c)	
		2	public ... **void**	**show** ()	ε905,618
			public ... void	**toBack** ()	
			public ... void	**toFront** ()	
		3	public ... void	validate ()	ε601,674,928,936
	✳		public ...	**Window** (Frame owner)	ε601,602
1.2	✳		public ...	**Window** (Window owner)	
1.3	✳		public ...	**Window** (Window owner, GraphicsConfiguration gc)	

W

Class *Interface* —extends - - -implements ○ abstract ● final △ static ▲ static final ✳ constructor x x—inherited x **x**—declared **x x**—overridden
εn—examples of usage ‿—has subclass package—see other volume

WindowAdapter				java.awt.event

```
        Object
1.1 ○   └WindowAdapter ---------------------- WindowListener ¹ (java.util.EventListener), WindowStateListener ²
                                              (java.util.EventListener), WindowFocusListener ³
                                              (java.util.EventListener)
```

	1	public ....void	**windowActivated** (WindowEvent e)	
*		public	**WindowAdapter** ()	ε565,566,568,569,884
	1	public ....void	**windowClosed** (WindowEvent e)	ε568
	1	public ....void	**windowClosing** (WindowEvent e)	ε565,566,568,884,905
	1	public ....void	**windowDeactivated** (WindowEvent e)	
	1	public ....void	**windowDeiconified** (WindowEvent e)	
1.4	3	public ....void	**windowGainedFocus** (WindowEvent e)	
	1	public ....void	**windowIconified** (WindowEvent e)	
1.4	3	public ....void	**windowLostFocus** (WindowEvent e)	
	1	public ....void	**windowOpened** (WindowEvent e)	ε568
1.4	2	public ....void	**windowStateChanged** (WindowEvent e)	ε569

WindowConstants				javax.swing

```
1.2     WindowConstants
```

▲	public static final ....int	**DISPOSE_ON_CLOSE** = 2	
▲	public static final ....int	**DO_NOTHING_ON_CLOSE** = 0	ε735
1.4 ▲	public static final ....int	**EXIT_ON_CLOSE** = 3	ε734
▲	public static final ....int	**HIDE_ON_CLOSE** = 1	

WindowEvent				java.awt.event
				ε566,884,905,640,641

```
        Object
1.1     └ java.util.EventObject ¹ -------------------- java.io.Serializable
1.1 ○     └ java.awt.AWTEvent ²
1.1         └ ComponentEvent ³
1.1           └ WindowEvent
```

	2	*27 inherited members from java.awt.AWTEvent not shown*		
▲	3	public static final ....int	COMPONENT_FIRST = 100	
▲	3	public static final ....int	COMPONENT_HIDDEN = 103	
▲	3	public static final ....int	COMPONENT_LAST = 103	
▲	3	public static final ....int	COMPONENT_MOVED = 100	
▲	3	public static final ....int	COMPONENT_RESIZED = 101	
▲	3	public static final ....int	COMPONENT_SHOWN = 102	
	3	public .... java.awt.Component	getComponent ()	ε810,813,1011
1.4		public ....int	**getNewState** ()	ε569
1.4		public ....int	**getOldState** ()	ε569
1.4		public ....java.awt.Window	**getOppositeWindow** ()	
	1	public ....Object	getSource ()	ε565,568,644,886,570
		public ....java.awt.Window	**getWindow** ()	
	3	public .... **String**	**paramString** ()	
	1	protected transient...... Object	source	
▲		public static final ....int	**WINDOW_ACTIVATED** = 205	
▲		public static final ....int	**WINDOW_CLOSED** = 202	
▲		public static final ....int	**WINDOW_CLOSING** = 201	
▲		public static final ....int	**WINDOW_DEACTIVATED** = 206	
▲		public static final ....int	**WINDOW_DEICONIFIED** = 204	
▲		public static final ....int	**WINDOW_FIRST** = 200	
1.4 ▲		public static final ....int	**WINDOW_GAINED_FOCUS** = 207	
▲		public static final ....int	**WINDOW_ICONIFIED** = 203	
▲		public static final ....int	**WINDOW_LAST** = 209	
1.4 ▲		public static final ....int	**WINDOW_LOST_FOCUS** = 208	
▲		public static final ....int	**WINDOW_OPENED** = 200	
1.4 ▲		public static final ....int	**WINDOW_STATE_CHANGED** = 209	
*		public	**WindowEvent** (java.awt.Window source, int id)	
1.4 *		public	**WindowEvent** (java.awt.Window source, int id, java.awt.Window opposite)	
1.4 *		public	**WindowEvent** (java.awt.Window source, int id, int oldState, int newState)	
1.4 *		public	**WindowEvent** (java.awt.Window source, int id, java.awt.Window opposite, int oldState, int newState)	

W

Classes

WindowFocusListener — java.awt.event

1.4	*WindowFocusListener*————————————*java.util.EventListener*	ε738,743,745,746,752
	public.......................void **windowGainedFocus** (WindowEvent e)	
	public.......................void **windowLostFocus** (WindowEvent e)	

WindowListener — java.awt.event

1.1	*WindowListener*————————————*java.util.EventListener*	ε568,738,743,745,746
	public.......................void **windowActivated** (WindowEvent e)	
	public.......................void **windowClosed** (WindowEvent e)	ε568
	public.......................void **windowClosing** (WindowEvent e)	ε565,566,568,884,905
	public.......................void **windowDeactivated** (WindowEvent e)	
	public.......................void **windowDeiconified** (WindowEvent e)	
	public.......................void **windowIconified** (WindowEvent e)	
	public.......................void **windowOpened** (WindowEvent e)	ε568

WindowPeer — java.awt.peer

	WindowPeer————————————*ContainerPeer* [1] (*ComponentPeer* [2])
2	*42 inherited members from ComponentPeer not shown*
1	*7 inherited members from ContainerPeer not shown*
	public.......................void **toBack** ()
	public.......................void **toFront** ()

WindowStateListener — java.awt.event

1.4	*WindowStateListener*————————————*java.util.EventListener*	ε569,738,743,745,746
	public.......................void **windowStateChanged** (WindowEvent e)	ε569

WrappedPlainView — javax.swing.text

```
Object
 └View¹ - - - - - - - - - - - - - - - - - - - - - - - - - - - javax.swing.SwingConstants⁴
  └CompositeView²
   └BoxView³
    └WrappedPlainView - - - - - - - - - - - - - TabExpander⁵
```

1.2 O		
1.2 O		
1.2		
1.2		
1	*30 inherited members from View not shown*	
2	*17 inherited members from CompositeView not shown*	
3	*30 inherited members from BoxView not shown*	
4	*19 inherited members from javax.swing.SwingConstants not shown*	
	protected.....................int **calculateBreakPosition** (int p0, int p1)	
1	public.......................**void changedUpdate** (*javax.swing.event.DocumentEvent* e, *java.awt.Shape* a, *ViewFactory* f)	
	protected.....................void **drawLine** (int p0, int p1, java.awt.Graphics g, int x, int y)	
	protected.....................int **drawSelectedText** (java.awt.Graphics g, int x, int y, int p0, int p1) throws BadLocationException	
	protected.....................int **drawUnselectedText** (java.awt.Graphics g, int x, int y, int p0, int p1) throws BadLocationException	
●	protected final........ Segment **getLineBuffer** ()	
3	public.......................**float getMaximumSpan** (int axis)	
3	public.......................**float getMinimumSpan** (int axis)	
3	public.......................**float getPreferredSpan** (int axis)	
	protected.....................int **getTabSize** ()	
1	public.......................**void insertUpdate** (*javax.swing.event.DocumentEvent* e, *java.awt.Shape* a, *ViewFactory* f)	
2	protected.................**void loadChildren** (*ViewFactory* f)	
5	public.......................float **nextTabStop** (float x, int tabOffset)	
3	public.......................**void paint** (java.awt.Graphics g, *java.awt.Shape* a)	
1	public.......................**void removeUpdate** (*javax.swing.event.DocumentEvent* e, *java.awt.Shape* a, *ViewFactory* f)	
3	public.......................**void setSize** (float width, float height)	
✳	public....................... **WrappedPlainView** (*Element* elem)	

Class   *Interface*   —extends   - - -implements   O abstract   ● final   △ static   ▲ static final   ✳ constructor   x x—inherited   x **x**—declared   **x x**—overridden
ε*n*—examples of usage   ˏ—has subclass   package—see other volume

*	public . . . . **WrappedPlainView** (*Element* elem, boolean wordWrap)	

WritableRaster		java.awt.image

	Object	ε668
1.2	└Raster[1]	
1.2	└WritableRaster	

1	*57 inherited members from Raster not shown*	
	public . . . . WritableRaster **createWritableChild** (int parentX, int parentY, int w, int h, int childMinX, int childMinY, int[] bandList)	
	public . . . . WritableRaster **createWritableTranslatedChild** (int childMinX, int childMinY)	
	public . . . . WritableRaster **getWritableParent** ()	
	public . . . . void **setDataElements** (int x, int y, Raster inRaster)	
	public . . . . void **setDataElements** (int x, int y, Object inData)	
	public . . . . void **setDataElements** (int x, int y, int w, int h, Object inData)	
	public . . . . void **setPixel** (int x, int y, int[] iArray)	
	public . . . . void **setPixel** (int x, int y, double[] dArray)	
	public . . . . void **setPixel** (int x, int y, float[] fArray)	
	public . . . . void **setPixels** (int x, int y, int w, int h, int[] iArray)	
	public . . . . void **setPixels** (int x, int y, int w, int h, double[] dArray)	
	public . . . . void **setPixels** (int x, int y, int w, int h, float[] fArray)	
	public . . . . void **setRect** (Raster srcRaster)	
	public . . . . void **setRect** (int dx, int dy, Raster srcRaster)	
	public . . . . void **setSample** (int x, int y, int b, float s)	
	public . . . . void **setSample** (int x, int y, int b, int s)	
	public . . . . void **setSample** (int x, int y, int b, double s)	
	public . . . . void **setSamples** (int x, int y, int w, int h, int b, float[] fArray)	
	public . . . . void **setSamples** (int x, int y, int w, int h, int b, double[] dArray)	
	public . . . . void **setSamples** (int x, int y, int w, int h, int b, int[] iArray)	
*	protected . . . . **WritableRaster** (SampleModel sampleModel, java.awt.Point origin)	
*	protected . . . . **WritableRaster** (SampleModel sampleModel, DataBuffer dataBuffer, java.awt.Point origin)	
*	protected . . . . **WritableRaster** (SampleModel sampleModel, DataBuffer dataBuffer, java.awt .Rectangle aRegion, java.awt.Point sampleModelTranslate, WritableRaster parent)	

WritableRenderedImage		java.awt.image

1.2	*WritableRenderedImage* ——————— *RenderedImage* [1]	ε695,699
	public . . . . void **addTileObserver** (*TileObserver* to)	
1	public . . . . WritableRaster copyData (WritableRaster raster)	
1	public . . . . ColorModel getColorModel ()	ε661,662
1	public . . . . Raster getData ()	
1	public . . . . Raster getData (java.awt.Rectangle rect)	
1	public . . . . int getHeight ()	ε672
1	public . . . . int getMinTileX ()	
1	public . . . . int getMinTileY ()	
1	public . . . . int getMinX ()	
1	public . . . . int getMinY ()	
1	public . . . . int getNumXTiles ()	
1	public . . . . int getNumYTiles ()	
1	public . . . . Object getProperty (String name)	
1	public . . . . String[] getPropertyNames ()	
1	public . . . . SampleModel getSampleModel ()	
1	public . . . . java.util.Vector getSources ()	
1	public . . . . Raster getTile (int tileX, int tileY)	
1	public . . . . int getTileGridXOffset ()	
1	public . . . . int getTileGridYOffset ()	
1	public . . . . int getTileHeight ()	
1	public . . . . int getTileWidth ()	
1	public . . . . int getWidth ()	ε672
	public . . . . WritableRaster **getWritableTile** (int tileX, int tileY)	
	public . . . . java.awt.Point[] **getWritableTileIndices** ()	
	public . . . . boolean **hasTileWriters** ()	
	public . . . . boolean **isTileWritable** (int tileX, int tileY)	
	public . . . . void **releaseWritableTile** (int tileX, int tileY)	
	public . . . . void **removeTileObserver** (*TileObserver* to)	
	public . . . . void **setData** (Raster r)	

ZoneView

ZoneView		javax.swing.text

```
        Object
1.2 ○    └View 1 - - - - - - - - - - - - - - - - - - - - - - - - - - - - javax.swing.SwingConstants 4
1.2 ○       └CompositeView 2
1.2          └BoxView 3
1.3             └ZoneView
```

	1	*30 inherited members from View not shown*	
	2	*16 inherited members from CompositeView not shown*	
	3	*35 inherited members from BoxView not shown*	
	4	*19 inherited members from javax.swing.SwingConstants not shown*	
		protected . . . . View	**createZone** (int p0, int p1)
		public . . . . int	**getMaximumZoneSize** ()
		public . . . . int	**getMaxZonesLoaded** ()
	2	protected . . . . **int**	**getViewIndexAtPosition** (int pos)
	1	public . . . . **void**	**insertUpdate** (*javax.swing.event.DocumentEvent* changes, *java.awt.Shape* a, *ViewFactory* f)
		protected . . . . boolean	**isZoneLoaded** (View zone)
	2	protected . . . . **void**	**loadChildren** (*ViewFactory* f)
	1	public . . . . **void**	**removeUpdate** (*javax.swing.event.DocumentEvent* changes, *java.awt.Shape* a, *ViewFactory* f)
		public . . . . void	**setMaximumZoneSize** (int size)
		public . . . . void	**setMaxZonesLoaded** (int mzl)
		protected . . . . void	**unloadZone** (View zone)
	1	protected . . . . **boolean**	**updateChildren** (*javax.swing.event.DocumentEvent.ElementChange* ec, *javax.swing.event.DocumentEvent* e, *ViewFactory* f)
*		public	**ZoneView** (*Element* elem, int axis)
		protected . . . . void	**zoneWasLoaded** (View zone)

Class *Interface* —extends - - -implements ○ abstract ● final △ static ▲ static final ✳ constructor x x—inherited x **x**—declared **x x**—overridden
εn—examples of usage ⌐—has subclass package—see other volume

Part 3
TOPICS

This part contains information about each major release of the Java APIs.

Contents

Statistics

Packages	8	**Members**	2125
		Fields	261
Classes and Interfaces	212	static	3
Classes	172	static final	167
abstract	21	protected	50
final	20	Constructors	319
Interfaces	40	protected	6
		Methods	1545
		abstract	102
		static	149
		final	140
		static final	1
		protected	78

Packages

Package	Classes	Members	Interfaces	Members
java.applet	1	22	3	16
java.awt	44	732	2	8
java.awt.image	9	94	3	30
java.awt.peer	0	0	22	84
java.io	28	310	3	30
java.lang	62	504	2	1
java.net	16	145	3	3
java.util	12	143	2	3

Exceptions and Errors

This is a complete listing of all the exceptions and errors in this version of Java. The "*" indicates a checked exception or error; these must be declared in the throws clause.

java.lang	AbstractMethodError	java.lang	IllegalMonitorStateException
java.lang	ArithmeticException	java.lang	IllegalThreadStateException
java.lang	ArrayIndexOutOfBoundsException	java.lang	IncompatibleClassChangeError
java.lang	ArrayStoreException	java.lang	IndexOutOfBoundsException
java.awt	AWTError	java.lang	InstantiationError
java.awt	*AWTException	java.lang	*InstantiationException
java.lang	ClassCastException	java.lang	InternalError
java.lang	ClassCircularityError	java.lang	*InterruptedException
java.lang	ClassFormatError	java.io	*InterruptedIOException
java.lang	*ClassNotFoundException	java.io	*IOException
java.lang	*CloneNotSupportedException	java.lang	LinkageError
java.util	EmptyStackException	java.net	*MalformedURLException
java.io	*EOFException	java.lang	NegativeArraySizeException
java.lang	Error	java.lang	NoClassDefFoundError
java.lang	*Exception	java.util	NoSuchElementException
java.io	*FileNotFoundException	java.lang	NoSuchFieldError
java.lang	IllegalAccessError	java.lang	NoSuchMethodError
java.lang	*IllegalAccessException	java.lang	*NoSuchMethodException
java.lang	IllegalArgumentException	java.lang	NullPointerException

java.lang	NumberFormatException	java.lang	*Throwable
java.lang	OutOfMemoryError	java.lang	UnknownError
java.net	*ProtocolException	java.net	*UnknownHostException
java.lang	RuntimeException	java.net	*UnknownServiceException
java.lang	SecurityException	java.lang	UnsatisfiedLinkError
java.net	*SocketException	java.io	*UTFDataFormatException
java.lang	StackOverflowError	java.lang	VerifyError
java.lang	StringIndexOutOfBoundsException	java.lang	VirtualMachineError
java.lang	ThreadDeath		

Statistics

Packages 23	

Classes and Interfaces 504	
Classes 391	
abstract 58	
final 38	
Interfaces 113	

Members 5478	
Fields 926	
static 4	
final 2	
static final 764	
protected 111	
Constructors 701	
protected 43	
Methods 3851	
abstract 202	
static 360	
final 207	
static final 24	
protected 191	

Packages

New	Package	Classes	Members	Interfaces	Members
	java.applet	1	1	3	0
	java.awt	54	16	7	0
•	java.awt.datatransfer	4	0	2	0
•	java.awt.event	19	4	11	0
	java.awt.image	11	3	3	1
	java.awt.peer	0	0	27	0
•	java.beans	17	2	6	2
	java.io	61	5	8	0
	java.lang	67	8	2	0
•	java.lang.reflect	6	0	1	0
•	java.math	2	3	0	0
	java.net	22	1	4	0
•	java.rmi	18	1	1	0
•	java.rmi.dgc	2	0	1	0
•	java.rmi.registry	1	0	2	0
•	java.rmi.server	16	1	7	0
•	java.security	21	1	5	1
•	java.security.acl	3	0	5	1
•	java.security.interfaces	0	0	5	0
•	java.sql	9	1	8	7
•	java.text	18	3	1	0
	java.util	23	1	3	0
•	java.util.zip	16	1	1	0

Topics

New Classes in Existing Packages

java.awt
Adjustable, AWTEvent, AWTEventMulticaster, Cursor, EventQueue, IllegalComponentStateException, *ItemSelectable*, *LayoutManager2*, MenuShortcut, PopupMenu, *PrintGraphics*, PrintJob, ScrollPane, *Shape*, SystemColor

java.awt.image
AreaAveragingScaleFilter, ReplicateScaleFilter

java.awt.peer
ActiveEvent, *FontPeer*, *LightweightPeer*,
PopupMenuPeer, *ScrollPanePeer*
java.io
BufferedReader, BufferedWriter, CharArrayReader,
CharArrayWriter, CharConversionException,
Externalizable, FileReader, FileWriter, FilterReader,
FilterWriter, InputStreamReader, InvalidClassException,
InvalidObjectException, LineNumberReader,
NotActiveException, NotSerializableException,
ObjectInput, ObjectInputStream, *ObjectInputValidation*,
ObjectOutput, ObjectOutputStream, ObjectStreamClass,
ObjectStreamException, OptionalDataException,
OutputStreamWriter, PipedReader, PipedWriter,
PrintWriter, PushbackReader, Reader, *Serializable*,
StreamCorruptedException, StringReader, StringWriter,

SyncFailedException, UnsupportedEncodingException,
WriteAbortedException, Writer
java.lang
Byte, ExceptionInInitializerError, IllegalStateException,
NoSuchFieldException, Short, Void
java.net
BindException, ConnectException,
DatagramSocketImpl, *FileNameMap*,
HttpURLConnection, MulticastSocket,
NoRouteToHostException
java.util
Calendar, *EventListener*, EventObject,
GregorianCalendar, ListResourceBundle, Locale,
MissingResourceException, PropertyResourceBundle,
ResourceBundle, SimpleTimeZone, TimeZone,
TooManyListenersException

New Members in Existing Classes

java.awt
  Component
    list( )
  Container
    processEvent( )

  Menu
    getItemCount( )
java.lang
  Character
    MATH_SYMBOL, UPPERCASE_LETTER

Removed Classes

java.lang
  Win32Process

Removed Members

java.awt.peer
  ComponentPeer
    handleEvent( ), nextFocus( )
  FramePeer
    setCursor( )
  ScrollbarPeer
    setValue( )

java.io
  PushbackInputStream
    pushBack
java.lang
  SecurityManager
    checkPropertyAccess( )
java.net
  DatagramSocket
    finalize( )

Modified Classes and Members

These tables show all the classes and members whose signatures were modified from the previous version.
"+" indicates an added keyword; "-" indicates a removed keyword.

Class Modifier Changes

java.awt
  Color   - final

Class Modifier Changes

java.net

ServerSocket, Socket	- final

Implements Changes

java.awt

BorderLayout, CardLayout, GridBagLayout	- java.awt.LayoutManager, + java.awt.LayoutManager2, + java.io.Serializable
Checkbox, CheckboxMenuItem, Choice, List	+ java.awt.ItemSelectable
CheckboxGroup, Color, Dimension, Event, FlowLayout, Font, FontMetrics, GridBagConstraints, GridLayout, Insets, MediaTracker, MenuComponent, Point	+ java.io.Serializable
Component	+ java.awt.MenuContainer, + java.io.Serializable
Polygon, Rectangle	+ java.awt.Shape, + java.io.Serializable
Scrollbar	+ java.awt.Adjustable

java.io

File	+ java.io.Serializable

java.lang

Boolean, Character, Class, Number, String, StringBuffer, Throwable	+ java.io.Serializable

java.net

InetAddress, URL	+ java.io.Serializable
SocketImpl	+ java.net.SocketOptions

java.util

BitSet, Hashtable, Random, Vector	+ java.io.Serializable
Date	+ java.io.Serializable, + java.lang.Cloneable

Member Modifier Changes

java.awt

MediaTracker checkAll( )	- synchronized

Newly Deprecated Classes

java.io
LineNumberInputStream, StringBufferInputStream

Newly Deprecated Members

java.awt
BorderLayout
addLayoutComponent( )
CardLayout
addLayoutComponent( )
CheckboxGroup
getCurrent( ), setCurrent( )
Choice
countItems( )
Component
action( ), bounds( ), deliverEvent( ), disable( ),
enable( ), getPeer( ), gotFocus( ), handleEvent( ),
hide( ), inside( ), keyDown( ), keyUp( ), layout( ),
locate( ), location( ), lostFocus( ), minimumSize( ),
mouseDown( ), mouseDrag( ), mouseEnter( ),
mouseExit( ), mouseMove( ), mouseUp( ), move( ),
nextFocus( ), postEvent( ), preferredSize( ),
reshape( ), resize( ), show( ), size( )
Container
countComponents( ), deliverEvent( ), insets( ),
layout( ), locate( ), minimumSize( ), preferredSize( )
FontMetrics
getMaxDecent( )
Frame
getCursorType( ), setCursor( )
Graphics
getClipRect( )
List
allowsMultipleSelections( ), clear( ), countItems( ),
delItems( ), isSelected( ), minimumSize( ),
preferredSize( ), setMultipleSelections( )
Menu
countItems( )

MenuBar
    countMenus( )
MenuComponent
    getPeer( ), postEvent( )
MenuContainer
    postEvent( )
MenuItem
    disable( ), enable( )
Polygon
    getBoundingBox( ), inside( )
Rectangle
    inside( ), move( ), reshape( ), resize( )
ScrollPane
    layout( )
Scrollbar
    getLineIncrement( ), getPageIncrement( ),
    getVisible( ), setLineIncrement( ),
    setPageIncrement( )
TextArea
    appendText( ), insertText( ), minimumSize( ),
    preferredSize( ), replaceText( )
TextField
    minimumSize( ), preferredSize( ), setEchoCharacter( )
Window
    postEvent( )
java.awt.event
KeyEvent
    setModifiers( )
java.io
ByteArrayOutputStream
    toString( )

DataInputStream
    readLine( )
PrintStream
    PrintStream( )
StreamTokenizer
    StreamTokenizer( )
java.lang
Character
    isJavaLetter( ), isJavaLetterOrDigit( ), isSpace( )
ClassLoader
    defineClass( )
Runtime
    getLocalizedInputStream( ),
    getLocalizedOutputStream( )
String
    getBytes( ), String( )
System
    getenv( )
java.net
Socket
    Socket( )
java.util
Date
    Date( ), getDate( ), getDay( ), getHours( ),
    getMinutes( ), getMonth( ), getSeconds( ),
    getTimezoneOffset( ), getYear( ), parse( ),
    setDate( ), setHours( ), setMinutes( ), setMonth( ),
    setSeconds( ), setYear( ), toGMTString( ),
    toLocaleString( ), UTC( )

Statistics

Packages 60

Classes and Interfaces 1781
  Classes 1462
    abstract 206
      abstract protected 1
    final 173
    protected 125
      abstract protected 1
  Interfaces 319

Members 20935
  Fields 3538
    static 22
    final 31
    static final 2346
    protected 972
  Constructors 2337
    protected 232
  Methods 15060
    abstract 915
    static 1126
    final 417
    static final 55
    protected 1672

Packages

New	Package	Classes	Members	Interfaces	Members
	java.applet	1	24	3	16
	java.awt	67	1666	14	57
•	java.awt.color	7	180	0	0
	java.awt.datatransfer	5	56	3	6
•	java.awt.dnd	17	182	4	13
	java.awt.event	21	376	13	32
•	java.awt.font	14	224	2	64
•	java.awt.geom	32	645	1	12
•	java.awt.im	3	27	1	7
	java.awt.image	40	685	8	70
•	java.awt.image.renderable	4	80	3	19
	java.awt.peer	0	0	26	123
•	java.awt.print	7	57	3	8
	java.beans	17	140	8	38
•	java.beans.beancontext	12	156	11	32
	java.io	66	680	10	73
	java.lang	75	815	3	2
•	java.lang.ref	5	15	0	0
	java.lang.reflect	8	104	1	5
	java.math	2	91	0	0
	java.net	29	320	5	14
	java.rmi	19	46	1	0
•	java.rmi.activation	12	70	4	16
	java.rmi.dgc	2	8	1	2
	java.rmi.registry	1	7	2	8
	java.rmi.server	16	85	9	30
	java.security	54	369	8	20
	java.security.acl	3	3	5	27
•	java.security.cert	13	94	1	4
	java.security.interfaces	0	0	8	20
•	java.security.spec	11	40	2	0
	java.sql	10	107	16	550
	java.text	21	361	2	20

Java 1.2
Packages

New	Package	Classes	Members	Interfaces	Members
	java.util	39	697	13	103
•	java.util.jar	8	77	0	0
	java.util.zip	16	156	1	4
•	javax.accessibility	7	136	7	59
•	javax.swing	158	3436	23	175
•	javax.swing.border	9	135	1	3
•	javax.swing.colorchooser	3	22	1	4
•	javax.swing.event	23	140	23	60
•	javax.swing.filechooser	3	20	0	0
•	javax.swing.plaf	42	123	1	0
•	javax.swing.plaf.basic	184	1926	1	8
•	javax.swing.plaf.metal	61	531	0	0
•	javax.swing.plaf.multi	29	443	0	0
•	javax.swing.table	9	238	4	30
•	javax.swing.text	75	1036	21	121
•	javax.swing.text.html	41	483	0	0
•	javax.swing.text.html.parser	9	142	1	35
•	javax.swing.text.rtf	1	7	0	0
•	javax.swing.tree	13	319	7	54
•	javax.swing.undo	7	84	2	14
•	org.omg.CORBA	76	607	29	109
•	org.omg.CORBA.DynAnyPackage	4	8	0	0
•	org.omg.CORBA.ORBPackage	2	4	0	0
•	org.omg.CORBA.TypeCodePackage	2	4	0	0
•	org.omg.CORBA.portable	7	129	4	6
•	org.omg.CosNaming	22	142	2	13
•	org.omg.CosNaming₂ .NamingContextPackage	18	91	0	0

New Classes in Existing Packages

java.awt
  ActiveEvent, AlphaComposite, AWTPermission,
  BasicStroke, ComponentOrientation, *Composite*,
  CompositeContext, GradientPaint, Graphics2D,
  GraphicsConfigTemplate, GraphicsConfiguration,
  GraphicsDevice, GraphicsEnvironment, *Paint*,
  PaintContext, RenderingHints, RenderingHints.Key,
  Stroke, TexturePaint, *Transparency*

java.awt.datatransfer
  FlavorMap, SystemFlavorMap

java.awt.event
  AWTEventListener, InputMethodEvent,
  InputMethodListener, InvocationEvent

java.awt.image
  AffineTransformOp, BandCombineOp,
  BandedSampleModel, BufferedImage,
  BufferedImageFilter, *BufferedImageOp*,
  ByteLookupTable, ColorConvertOp,
  ComponentColorModel, ComponentSampleModel,
  ConvolveOp, DataBuffer, DataBufferByte,
  DataBufferInt, DataBufferShort, DataBufferUShort,
  ImagingOpException, Kernel, LookupOp,
  LookupTable, MultiPixelPackedSampleModel,
  PackedColorModel, PixelInterleavedSampleModel,
  Raster, RasterFormatException, *RasterOp*,
  RenderedImage, RescaleOp, SampleModel,
  ShortLookupTable, SinglePixelPackedSampleModel,
  TileObserver, WritableRaster, *WritableRenderedImage*

java.beans
  AppletInitializer, *DesignMode*

java.io
  FileFilter, FilePermission, ObjectInputStream.GetField,
  ObjectOutputStream.PutField, *ObjectStreamConstants*,
  ObjectStreamField, SerializablePermission

java.lang
  Character.Subset, Character.UnicodeBlock,
  Comparable, InheritableThreadLocal,
  Package, RuntimePermission, ThreadLocal,
  UnsupportedClassVersionError,
  UnsupportedOperationException

java.lang.reflect
  AccessibleObject, ReflectPermission

java.net
  Authenticator, JarURLConnection, NetPermission,
  PasswordAuthentication, *SocketOptions*,
  SocketPermission, URLClassLoader, URLDecoder

java.rmi
  MarshalledObject

java.rmi.server
  RMIClientSocketFactory, *RMIServerSocketFactory*

java.security
  AccessControlContext, AccessControlException,
  AccessController, AlgorithmParameterGenerator,
  AlgorithmParameterGeneratorSpi,
  AlgorithmParameters, AlgorithmParametersSpi,
  AllPermission, BasicPermission, CodeSource,

GeneralSecurityException, *Guard*, GuardedObject, InvalidAlgorithmParameterException, KeyFactory, KeyFactorySpi, KeyPairGeneratorSpi, KeyStore, KeyStoreException, KeyStoreSpi, MessageDigestSpi, Permission, PermissionCollection, Permissions, Policy, *PrivilegedAction*, PrivilegedActionException, *PrivilegedExceptionAction*, ProtectionDomain, SecureClassLoader, SecureRandomSpi, SecurityPermission, SignatureSpi, SignedObject, UnrecoverableKeyException, UnresolvedPermission

java.security.interfaces
RSAPrivateCrtKey, *RSAPrivateKey*, *RSAPublicKey*

java.sql
Array, BatchUpdateException, *Blob*, *Clob*, *Ref*, *SQLData*, *SQLInput*, *SQLOutput*, *Struct*

java.text
Annotation, *AttributedCharacterIterator*, AttributedCharacterIterator.Attribute, AttributedString

java.util
AbstractCollection, AbstractList, AbstractMap, AbstractSequentialList, AbstractSet, ArrayList, Arrays, *Collection*, Collections, *Comparator*, ConcurrentModificationException, HashMap, HashSet, *Iterator*, LinkedList, *List*, *ListIterator*, *Map*, *Map.Entry*, PropertyPermission, *Set*, *SortedMap*, *SortedSet*, TreeMap, TreeSet, WeakHashMap

New Members in Existing Classes

java.applet
Applet
   newAudioClip( )

java.awt
AWTEvent
   finalize( ), INPUT_METHOD_EVENT_MASK
AWTEventMulticaster
   add( ), caretPositionChanged( ), inputMethodTextChanged( ), remove( )
BorderLayout
   AFTER_LAST_LINE, AFTER_LINE_ENDS, BEFORE_FIRST_LINE, BEFORE_LINE_BEGINS
Canvas
   Canvas( )
Color
   Color( ), createContext( ), getAlpha( ), getColorComponents( ), getColorSpace( ), getComponents( ), getRGBColorComponents( ), getRGBComponents( ), getTransparency( )
Component
   addInputMethodListener( ), addPropertyChangeListener( ), coalesceEvents( ), enableInputMethods( ), firePropertyChange( ), getBounds( ), getComponentOrientation( ), getDropTarget( ), getHeight( ), getInputContext( ), getInputMethodRequests( ), getLocation( ), getSize( ), getWidth( ), getX( ), getY( ), hasFocus( ), isDisplayable( ), isDoubleBuffered( ), isLightweight( ), isOpaque( ), processInputMethodEvent( ), removeInputMethodListener( ), removePropertyChangeListener( ), setComponentOrientation( ), setDropTarget( )
Container
   findComponentAt( ), setFont( )
Cursor
   Cursor( ), CUSTOM_CURSOR, getName( ), getSystemCustomCursor( ), name, toString( )
Dialog
   Dialog( )
Dimension
   getHeight( ), getWidth( ), setSize( )
EventQueue
   dispatchEvent( ), invokeAndWait( ), invokeLater( ), isDispatchThread( ), pop( ), push( )
FlowLayout
   LEADING, TRAILING

Font
   canDisplay( ), canDisplayUpTo( ), CENTER_BASELINE, createGlyphVector( ), deriveFont( ), finalize( ), Font( ), getAttributes( ), getAvailableAttributes( ), getBaselineFor( ), getFamily( ), getFont( ), getFontName( ), getItalicAngle( ), getLineMetrics( ), getMaxCharBounds( ), getMissingGlyphCode( ), getNumGlyphs( ), getPSName( ), getSize2D( ), getStringBounds( ), getTransform( ), HANGING_BASELINE, hasUniformLineMetrics( ), pointSize, ROMAN_BASELINE
FontMetrics
   getLineMetrics( ), getMaxCharBounds( ), getStringBounds( ), hasUniformLineMetrics( )
Frame
   finalize( ), getFrames( ), getState( ), ICONIFIED, NORMAL, removeNotify( ), setState( )
Graphics
   drawString( ), getClipBounds( ), hitClip( )
GridBagConstraints
   GridBagConstraints( )
MenuComponent
   getTreeLock( )
MenuShortcut
   equals( ), hashCode( )
Point
   getX( ), getY( ), setLocation( )
Polygon
   contains( ), getBounds2D( ), getPathIterator( ), intersects( )
Rectangle
   contains( ), createIntersection( ), createUnion( ), getBounds2D( ), getHeight( ), getWidth( ), getX( ), getY( ), outcode( ), setRect( )
Shape
   contains( ), getBounds2D( ), getPathIterator( ), intersects( )
SystemColor
   createContext( )
TextField
   setText( )
Toolkit
   addAWTEventListener( ), addPropertyChangeListener( ), createCustomCursor( ),

createDragGestureRecognizer( ),
createDragSourceContextPeer( ),
createImage( ), desktopProperties,
desktopPropsSupport, getBestCursorSize( ),
getDesktopProperty( ), getMaximumCursorColors( ),
initializeDesktopProperties( ),
lazilyLoadDesktopProperty( ),
removeAWTEventListener( ),
removePropertyChangeListener( ),
setDesktopProperty( )

Window
applyResourceBundle( ), finalize( ),
getInputContext( ), getOwnedWindows( ),
getOwner( ), Window( )

java.awt.datatransfer

DataFlavor
clone( ), DataFlavor( ), equals( ),
getParameter( ), getPrimaryType( ),
getSubType( ), isFlavorJavaFileListType( ),
isFlavorRemoteObjectType( ),
isFlavorSerializedObjectType( ),
isMimeTypeSerializedObject( ),
isRepresentationClassInputStream( ),
isRepresentationClassRemote( ),
isRepresentationClassSerializable( ),
javaFileListFlavor, javaJVMLocalObjectMimeType,
javaRemoteObjectMimeType,
javaSerializedObjectMimeType, readExternal( ),
tryToLoadClass( ), writeExternal( )

java.awt.event

InputEvent
ALT_GRAPH_MASK, isAltGraphDown( )
KeyEvent
VK_AGAIN, VK_ALL_CANDIDATES,
VK_ALPHANUMERIC, VK_ALT_GRAPH,
VK_AMPERSAND, VK_ASTERISK, VK_AT,
VK_BRACELEFT, VK_BRACERIGHT,
VK_CIRCUMFLEX, VK_CODE_INPUT,
VK_COLON, VK_COMPOSE, VK_COPY, VK_CUT,
VK_DEAD_ABOVEDOT, VK_DEAD_ABOVERING,
VK_DEAD_ACUTE, VK_DEAD_BREVE,
VK_DEAD_CARON, VK_DEAD_CEDILLA,
VK_DEAD_CIRCUMFLEX, VK_DEAD_DIAERESIS,
VK_DEAD_DOUBLEACUTE,
VK_DEAD_GRAVE, VK_DEAD_IOTA,
VK_DEAD_MACRON, VK_DEAD_OGONEK,
VK_DEAD_SEMIVOICED_SOUND,
VK_DEAD_TILDE, VK_DEAD_VOICED_SOUND,
VK_DOLLAR, VK_EURO_SIGN,
VK_EXCLAMATION_MARK, VK_F13, VK_F14,
VK_F15, VK_F16, VK_F17, VK_F18, VK_F19,
VK_F20, VK_F21, VK_F22, VK_F23, VK_F24,
VK_FIND, VK_FULL_WIDTH, VK_GREATER,
VK_HALF_WIDTH, VK_HIRAGANA,
VK_INVERTED_EXCLAMATION_MARK,
VK_JAPANESE_HIRAGANA,
VK_JAPANESE_KATAKANA,
VK_JAPANESE_ROMAN, VK_KATAKANA,
VK_KP_DOWN, VK_KP_LEFT,
VK_KP_RIGHT, VK_KP_UP,
VK_LEFT_PARENTHESIS, VK_LESS, VK_MINUS,
VK_NUMBER_SIGN, VK_PASTE, VK_PLUS,
VK_PREVIOUS_CANDIDATE, VK_PROPS,
VK_QUOTEDBL, VK_RIGHT_PARENTHESIS,
VK_ROMAN_CHARACTERS, VK_STOP,
VK_UNDERSCORE, VK_UNDO

java.awt.image

ColorModel
coerceData( ), ColorModel( ),
createCompatibleSampleModel( ),
createCompatibleWritableRaster( ), equals( ),
getAlpha( ), getAlphaRaster( ), getBlue( ),
getColorSpace( ), getComponents( ),
getComponentSize( ), getDataElement( ),
getDataElements( ), getGreen( ),
getNormalizedComponents( ),
getNumColorComponents( ), getNumComponents( ),
getRed( ), getRGB( ), getTransparency( ),
getUnnormalizedComponents( ), hasAlpha( ),
isAlphaPremultiplied( ), isCompatibleRaster( ),
isCompatibleSampleModel( ), toString( ),
transferType
DirectColorModel
coerceData( ), createCompatibleWritableRaster( ),
DirectColorModel( ), getAlpha( ), getBlue( ),
getComponents( ), getDataElement( ),
getDataElements( ), getGreen( ), getRed( ),
getRGB( ), isCompatibleRaster( ), toString( )
IndexColorModel
convertToIntDiscrete( ),
createCompatibleSampleModel( ),
createCompatibleWritableRaster( ), finalize( ),
getComponents( ), getComponentSize( ),
getDataElement( ), getDataElements( ),
getRGBs( ), getTransparency( ), IndexColorModel( ),
isCompatibleRaster( ), isCompatibleSampleModel( ),
toString( )

java.awt.peer

FramePeer
getState( ), setState( )
WindowPeer
CONSUME_EVENT, FOCUS_NEXT,
FOCUS_PREVIOUS, handleFocusTraversalEvent( ),
IGNORE_EVENT

java.beans

Beans
instantiate( )
FeatureDescriptor
isPreferred( ), setPreferred( )
IndexedPropertyDescriptor
setIndexedReadMethod( ), setIndexedWriteMethod( )
Introspector
flushCaches( ), flushFromCaches( ),
getBeanInfo( ), IGNORE_ALL_BEANINFO,
IGNORE_IMMEDIATE_BEANINFO,
USE_ALL_BEANINFO
PropertyChangeSupport
addPropertyChangeListener( ), firePropertyChange( ),
hasListeners( ), removePropertyChangeListener( )
PropertyDescriptor
setReadMethod( ), setWriteMethod( )
VetoableChangeSupport
addVetoableChangeListener( ),
fireVetoableChange( ), hasListeners( ),
removeVetoableChangeListener( )

java.io

BufferedInputStream
close( )
ByteArrayInputStream
close( )
ByteArrayOutputStream
close( )

File
    compareTo( ), createNewFile( ), createTempFile( ),
    deleteOnExit( ), getAbsoluteFile( ),
    getCanonicalFile( ), getParentFile( ), isHidden( ),
    listFiles( ), listRoots( ), setLastModified( ),
    setReadOnly( ), toURL( )
ObjectInputStream
    ObjectInputStream( ), readFields( ),
    readObjectOverride( )
ObjectOutputStream
    ObjectOutputStream( ), putFields( ),
    useProtocolVersion( ), writeFields( ),
    writeObjectOverride( )
ObjectStreamClass
    getField( ), getFields( ), NO_FIELDS
PipedReader
    read( ), ready( )
PipedWriter
    write( )
PrintWriter
    out
PushbackInputStream
    close( ), skip( )
PushbackReader
    mark( ), reset( )
RandomAccessFile
    setLength( )
Serializable
    serialVersionUID

java.lang
Byte
    compareTo( )
Character
    compareTo( )
Class
    forName( ), getPackage( ), getProtectionDomain( )
ClassLoader
    ClassLoader( ), defineClass( ), definePackage( ),
    findClass( ), findLibrary( ), findResource( ),
    findResources( ), getPackage( ),
    getPackages( ), getParent( ), getResources( ),
    getSystemClassLoader( ), getSystemResources( )
ClassNotFoundException
    ClassNotFoundException( ), getException( ),
    printStackTrace( )
Double
    compareTo( ), parseDouble( )
ExceptionInInitializerError
    printStackTrace( )
Float
    compareTo( ), parseFloat( )
Integer
    compareTo( )
Long
    compareTo( ), decode( )
Math
    toDegrees( ), toRadians( )
SecurityManager
    checkPermission( )
Short
    compareTo( )
String
    CASE_INSENSITIVE_ORDER, compareTo( ),
    compareToIgnoreCase( )

StringBuffer
    delete( ), deleteCharAt( ), insert( ), replace( ),
    substring( )
System
    mapLibraryName( ), setProperty( )
Thread
    getContextClassLoader( ), setContextClassLoader( )
ThreadGroup
    interrupt( )
java.lang.reflect
InvocationTargetException
    printStackTrace( )
Modifier
    isStrict( ), STRICT
java.math
BigDecimal
    compareTo( ), unscaledValue( )
BigInteger
    compareTo( ), ONE, ZERO
java.net
DatagramPacket
    DatagramPacket( ), getOffset( ), setData( )
DatagramSocket
    connect( ), disconnect( ), getInetAddress( ),
    getPort( ), getReceiveBufferSize( ),
    getSendBufferSize( ), setReceiveBufferSize( ),
    setSendBufferSize( )
DatagramSocketImpl
    getTimeToLive( ), setTimeToLive( )
HttpURLConnection
    getErrorStream( ), getPermission( )
MulticastSocket
    getTimeToLive( ), setTimeToLive( )
Socket
    getReceiveBufferSize( ), getSendBufferSize( ),
    setReceiveBufferSize( ), setSendBufferSize( )
URL
    URL( )
URLConnection
    getFileNameMap( ), getPermission( ),
    setFileNameMap( )
java.rmi
RemoteException
    printStackTrace( )
java.rmi.registry
LocateRegistry
    createRegistry( ), getRegistry( )
java.rmi.server
ObjID
    ACTIVATOR_ID
RMIClassLoader
    getClassAnnotation( ), loadClass( )
RMISocketFactory
    getDefaultSocketFactory( )
RemoteObject
    getRef( ), toStub( )
RemoteRef
    invoke( ), serialVersionUID
ServerCloneException
    printStackTrace( )
ServerRef
    serialVersionUID
UnicastRemoteObject
    exportObject( ), unexportObject( ),
    UnicastRemoteObject( )

Topics

java.security
Key
serialVersionUID
KeyPairGenerator
genKeyPair( ), getProvider( ), initialize( )
MessageDigest
digest( ), getDigestLength( ), getProvider( )
PrivateKey
serialVersionUID
Provider
clear( ), entrySet( ), keySet( ), load( ), put( ), putAll( ),
remove( ), values( )
PublicKey
serialVersionUID
SecureRandom
generateSeed( ), getInstance( ), getProvider( ),
SecureRandom( )
Signature
getProvider( ), initSign( ), setParameter( ), sign( )

java.security.interfaces
DSAPrivateKey
serialVersionUID
DSAPublicKey
serialVersionUID

java.sql
CallableStatement
getArray( ), getBigDecimal( ), getBlob( ), getClob( ),
getDate( ), getObject( ), getRef( ), getTime( ),
getTimestamp( ), registerOutParameter( )
Connection
createStatement( ), getTypeMap( ), prepareCall( ),
prepareStatement( ), setTypeMap( )
DatabaseMetaData
deletesAreDetected( ), getConnection( ),
getUDTs( ), insertsAreDetected( ),
othersDeletesAreVisible( ), othersInsertsAreVisible( ),
othersUpdatesAreVisible( ),
ownDeletesAreVisible( ), ownInsertsAreVisible( ),
ownUpdatesAreVisible( ), supportsBatchUpdates( ),
supportsResultSetConcurrency( ),
supportsResultSetType( ), updatesAreDetected( )
DriverManager
getLogWriter( ), setLogWriter( )
PreparedStatement
addBatch( ), getMetaData( ), setArray( ), setBlob( ),
setCharacterStream( ), setClob( ), setDate( ),
setNull( ), setRef( ), setTime( ), setTimestamp( )
ResultSet
absolute( ), afterLast( ), beforeFirst( ),
cancelRowUpdates( ), CONCUR_READ_ONLY,
CONCUR_UPDATABLE, deleteRow( ),
FETCH_FORWARD, FETCH_REVERSE,
FETCH_UNKNOWN, first( ), getArray( ),
getBigDecimal( ), getBlob( ), getCharacterStream( ),
getClob( ), getConcurrency( ), getDate( ),
getFetchDirection( ), getFetchSize( ), getObject( ),
getRef( ), getRow( ), getStatement( ), getTime( ),
getTimestamp( ), getType( ), insertRow( ),
isAfterLast( ), isBeforeFirst( ), isFirst( ), isLast( ),
last( ), moveToCurrentRow( ), moveToInsertRow( ),
previous( ), refreshRow( ), relative( ), rowDeleted( ),
rowInserted( ), rowUpdated( ), setFetchDirection( ),
setFetchSize( ), TYPE_FORWARD_ONLY,
TYPE_SCROLL_INSENSITIVE,
TYPE_SCROLL_SENSITIVE, updateAsciiStream( ),
updateBigDecimal( ), updateBinaryStream( ),

updateBoolean( ), updateByte( ), updateBytes( ),
updateCharacterStream( ), updateDate( ),
updateDouble( ), updateFloat( ), updateInt( ),
updateLong( ), updateNull( ), updateObject( ),
updateRow( ), updateShort( ), updateString( ),
updateTime( ), updateTimestamp( )
ResultSetMetaData
getColumnClassName( )
Statement
addBatch( ), clearBatch( ), executeBatch( ),
getConnection( ), getFetchDirection( ),
getFetchSize( ), getResultSetConcurrency( ),
getResultSetType( ), setFetchDirection( ),
setFetchSize( )
Timestamp
equals( )
Types
ARRAY, BLOB, CLOB, DISTINCT, JAVA_OBJECT,
REF, STRUCT

java.text
BreakIterator
isBoundary( ), preceding( )
CollationElementIterator
getMaxExpansion( ), getOffset( ), previous( ),
setOffset( ), setText( )
CollationKey
compareTo( )
Collator
compare( )
DecimalFormat
setMaximumFractionDigits( ),
setMaximumIntegerDigits( ),
setMinimumFractionDigits( ),
setMinimumIntegerDigits( )
DecimalFormatSymbols
getCurrencySymbol( ),
getInternationalCurrencySymbol( ),
getMonetaryDecimalSeparator( ),
setCurrencySymbol( ),
setInternationalCurrencySymbol( ),
setMonetaryDecimalSeparator( )
FieldPosition
equals( ), hashCode( ), setBeginIndex( ),
setEndIndex( ), toString( )
ParsePosition
equals( ), getErrorIndex( ), hashCode( ),
setErrorIndex( ), toString( )
RuleBasedCollator
getCollationElementIterator( )
SimpleDateFormat
get2DigitYearStart( ), set2DigitYearStart( )
StringCharacterIterator
setText( )

java.util
BitSet
andNot( ), length( )
Calendar
getActualMaximum( ), getActualMinimum( ),
hashCode( ), roll( ), toString( )
Date
clone( ), compareTo( )
GregorianCalendar
getActualMaximum( ), getActualMinimum( ), roll( )
Hashtable
containsValue( ), entrySet( ), equals( ), hashCode( ),
Hashtable( ), keySet( ), putAll( ), values( )

Locale
    getAvailableLocales( ), getISOCountries( ),
    getISOLanguages( )
Properties
    setProperty( ), store( )
Random
    nextBoolean( ), nextInt( )
ResourceBundle
    getBundle( ), getLocale( )
SimpleTimeZone
    getDSTSavings( ), hasSameRules( ),
    setDSTSavings( ), setEndRule( ), setStartRule( ),
    SimpleTimeZone( ), toString( )
TimeZone
    getDisplayName( ), hasSameRules( ), LONG,
    SHORT

Vector
    add( ), addAll( ), clear( ), containsAll( ), equals( ),
    get( ), hashCode( ), remove( ), removeAll( ),
    removeRange( ), retainAll( ), set( ), subList( ),
    toArray( ), Vector( )
java.util.zip
InflaterInputStream
    available( ), close( )
ZipEntry
    clone( ), hashCode( ), setCompressedSize( ),
    ZipEntry( )
ZipFile
    size( )
ZipInputStream
    available( ), createZipEntry( )

Removed Classes

java.awt.peer
    ActiveEvent

Removed Members

java.awt
Frame
    dispose( )
Point
    hashCode( )
Rectangle
    hashCode( )
java.rmi
RMISecurityManager
    checkAccept( ), checkAccess( ),
    checkAwtEventQueueAccess( ), checkConnect( ),
    checkCreateClassLoader( ), checkDelete( ),
    checkExec( ), checkExit( ), checkLink( ),
    checkListen( ), checkMemberAccess( ),
    checkMulticast( ), checkPackageDefinition( ),
    checkPrintJobAccess( ), checkPropertiesAccess( ),
    checkPropertyAccess( ), checkRead( ),

    checkSecurityAccess( ), checkSetFactory( ),
    checkSystemClipboardAccess( ),
    checkTopLevelWindow( ), checkWrite( ),
    getSecurityContext( )
java.security
KeyPairGenerator
    generateKeyPair( )
MessageDigest
    engineDigest( ), engineReset( ), engineUpdate( )
Signature
    engineGetParameter( ), engineInitSign( ),
    engineInitVerify( ), engineSetParameter( ),
    engineSign( ), engineUpdate( ), engineVerify( )
java.util
GregorianCalendar
    after( ), before( )

Modified Classes and Members

These tables show all the classes and members whose signatures were modified from the previous version.
"+" indicates an added keyword; "-" indicates a removed keyword.

Class Modifier Changes

java.awt
    Container   - abstract
java.lang
    SecurityManager   - abstract

Topics

833

Class Modifier Changes

java.util
    BitSet   - final

Extends Changes

java.awt
    Dimension   - java.lang.Object,
                                              + java.awt.geom.Dimension2D
    Point   - java.lang.Object, + java.awt.geom.Point2D
    Rectangle   - java.lang.Object,
                                              + java.awt.geom.Rectangle2D

java.awt.image
    DirectColorModel   - java.awt.image.ColorModel,
                                              + java.awt.image.PackedColorModel

java.lang.reflect
    Constructor, Field, Method   - java.lang.Object,
                                            + java.lang.reflect.AccessibleObject

java.security
    DigestException, KeyException, NoSuchAlgorithmException,   - java.lang.Exception,
       NoSuchProviderException, SignatureException   + java.security.GeneralSecurityException
    KeyPairGenerator   - java.lang.Object,
                                            + java.security.KeyPairGeneratorSpi
    MessageDigest   - java.lang.Object,
                                            + java.security.MessageDigestSpi
    Signature   - java.lang.Object,
                                            + java.security.SignatureSpi

java.util
    Vector   - java.lang.Object, + java.util.AbstractList

Implements Changes

java.awt
    AWTEventMulticaster   + java.awt.event.InputMethodListener
    Color   + java.awt.Paint

java.awt.datatransfer
    DataFlavor   + java.io.Externalizable,
                                            + java.lang.Cloneable

java.awt.image
    ColorModel   + java.awt.Transparency

java.io
    File   + java.lang.Comparable

java.lang
    Byte, Character, Double, Float, Integer, Long, Short, String   + java.lang.Comparable

java.math
    BigDecimal, BigInteger   + java.lang.Comparable

java.rmi.server
    RMISocketFactory   + java.rmi.server.RMIClientSocketFactory,
                                          + java.rmi.server
                                            .RMIServerSocketFactory

java.security
    KeyPair   + java.io.Serializable

java.text
    BreakIterator   - java.io.Serializable
    CollationKey   + java.lang.Comparable
    Collator   - java.io.Serializable, + java.util.Comparator

java.util
    Date   + java.lang.Comparable
    Hashtable   + java.util.Map
    Vector   + java.util.List

Implements Changes

java.util.zip
    ZipEntry | + java.lang.Cloneable

Member Modifier Changes

java.awt
  Button
    setLabel( ) | - synchronized
  Checkbox
    setLabel( ) | - synchronized
  Choice
    addItem( ), insert( ), remove( ), removeAll( ) | - synchronized
    select( ) | + synchronized
  Container
    Container( ) | - protected, + public
  Dialog
    setResizable( ) | - synchronized
  Frame
    setResizable( ) | - synchronized
  Label
    setText( ) | - synchronized

java.beans
  Introspector
    getBeanInfoSearchPath( ), setBeanInfoSearchPath( ) | + synchronized
  PropertyEditorManager
    findEditor( ), getEditorSearchPath( ), setEditorSearchPath( ) | + synchronized

java.io
  File
    isAbsolute( ) | - native
  FileDescriptor
    valid( ) | - native
  ObjectInputStream
    defaultReadObject( ), enableResolveObject( ) | - final
  ObjectOutputStream
    defaultWriteObject( ), enableReplaceObject( ) | - final
  PipedOutputStream
    connect( ) | + synchronized
  PipedReader
    read( ) | + synchronized
  PipedWriter
    connect( ), flush( ) | + synchronized
  StringWriter
    StringWriter( ) | - protected, + public

java.lang
  Class
    forName( ), getClassLoader( ), newInstance( ) | - native
    getDeclaringClass( ) | + native
  ClassLoader
    findLoadedClass( ) | + native
    getSystemResource( ), getSystemResourceAsStream( ) | - final
    loadClass( ) | - abstract, + synchronized

java.lang.reflect
  Constructor
    getModifiers( ) | - native
  Field
    getModifiers( ) | - native
  Method
    getModifiers( ) | - native

Topics

Member Modifier Changes

java.lang
  Runtime
    load( ), loadLibrary( )   - synchronized
    runFinalization( )   - native
  SecurityManager
    SecurityManager( )   - protected, + public
    classLoaderDepth( ), currentClassLoader( )   - native
  System
    setSecurityManager( )   + synchronized
  Thread
    checkAccess( )   + final

java.net
  InetAddress
    getLocalHost( )   + synchronized
  MulticastSocket
    send( )   - synchronized
  URL
    hashCode( )   + synchronized

java.rmi
  RMISecurityManager
    checkPackageAccess( )   - synchronized

java.rmi.server
  RMISocketFactory
    getFailureHandler( ), getSocketFactory( ), setFailureHandler( ),   + synchronized
      setSocketFactory( )

java.security
  KeyPairGenerator
    initialize( )   - abstract

java.sql
  DriverManager
    deregisterDriver( ), getDriver( ), getDrivers( ), println( ),   + synchronized
      setLogStream( )

java.util
  Calendar
    after( ), before( ), equals( )   - abstract
  GregorianCalendar
    hashCode( )   - synchronized
  Vector
    addElement( ), capacity( ), contains( ), copyInto( ), elementAt( ),   - final
      ensureCapacity( ), firstElement( ), indexOf( ), insertElementAt( ),
      isEmpty( ), lastElement( ), lastIndexOf( ), removeAllElements( ),
      removeElement( ), removeElementAt( ), setElementAt( ), setSize( ),
      size( ), toString( ), trimToSize( )
    elements( )   - final, - synchronized

java.util.zip
  Adler32
    update( )   - native
  CRC32
    update( )   - native
  Deflater
    deflate( ), end( ), getAdler( ), getTotalIn( ), getTotalOut( ), reset( ),   - native
      setDictionary( )

Member Modifier Changes

Inflater
    end( ), getAdler( ), getTotalIn( ), getTotalOut( ), inflate( ), reset( ),   - native
        setDictionary( )

Throws Changes

java.io
  FileOutputStream
    FileOutputStream( )   - java.io.IOException,
                  + java.io.FileNotFoundException

  RandomAccessFile
    RandomAccessFile( )   - java.io.IOException,
                  + java.io.FileNotFoundException

  StringReader
    ready( )   + java.io.IOException
  StringWriter
    close( )   + java.io.IOException

java.lang
  ClassLoader
    defineClass( )   + java.lang.ClassFormatError

java.math
  BigDecimal
    BigDecimal( ), valueOf( )   - java.lang.NumberFormatException
    divide( ), setScale( )   - java.lang.ArithmeticException,
                  - java.lang.IllegalArgumentException

  BigInteger
    BigInteger( )   - java.lang.NumberFormatException
    BigInteger( )   - java.lang.IllegalArgumentException
    add( ), clearBit( ), divide( ), divideAndRemainder( ), flipBit( ),   - java.lang.ArithmeticException
        modInverse( ), pow( ), remainder( ), setBit( ), testBit( )

java.rmi
  Naming
    bind( ), list( ), lookup( ), rebind( ), unbind( )   - java.rmi.UnknownHostException

java.rmi.registry
  LocateRegistry
    getRegistry( )   - java.rmi.UnknownHostException

Newly Deprecated Classes

java.rmi
  RMISecurityException, ServerRuntimeException
java.rmi.registry
  RegistryHandler
java.rmi.server
  LoaderHandler, LogStream, Operation,
  RemoteCall, *Skeleton*, SkeletonMismatchException,
  SkeletonNotFoundException

java.security
  Certificate, Identity, IdentityScope, Signer
javax.swing.text
  DefaultTextUI
org.omg.CORBA
  Principal, PrincipalHolder

Newly Deprecated Members

java.awt
  Font
    getPeer( )
  Frame
    CROSSHAIR_CURSOR, DEFAULT_CURSOR,
    E_RESIZE_CURSOR, HAND_CURSOR,
    MOVE_CURSOR, N_RESIZE_CURSOR,
    NE_RESIZE_CURSOR, NW_RESIZE_CURSOR,
    S_RESIZE_CURSOR, SE_RESIZE_CURSOR,
    SW_RESIZE_CURSOR, TEXT_CURSOR,
    W_RESIZE_CURSOR, WAIT_CURSOR
  List
    addItem( ), delItem( )

Topics

Toolkit
getFontList( ), getFontMetrics( ), getFontPeer( )
java.awt.datatransfer
DataFlavor
normalizeMimeType( ),
normalizeMimeTypeParameter( )
java.io
ObjectInputStream
readLine( )
java.lang
Runtime
runFinalizersOnExit( )
SecurityManager
classDepth( ), classLoaderDepth( ),
currentClassLoader( ), currentLoadedClass( ),
getInCheck( ), inCheck, inClass( ), inClassLoader( )
System
runFinalizersOnExit( )
Thread
countStackFrames( ), resume( ), stop( ), suspend( )
ThreadGroup
allowThreadSuspension( ), resume( ), stop( ),
suspend( )
java.net
DatagramSocketImpl
getTTL( ), setTTL( )
MulticastSocket
getTTL( ), setTTL( )
java.rmi
RMISecurityException
RMISecurityException( )
ServerRuntimeException
ServerRuntimeException( )
java.rmi.registry
RegistryHandler
registryImpl( ), registryStub( )
java.rmi.server
LoaderHandler
getSecurityContext( ), loadClass( )
LogStream
getDefaultStream( ), getOutputStream( ),
log( ), parseLevel( ), setDefaultStream( ),
setOutputStream( ), toString( ), write( )
Operation
getOperation( ), Operation( ), toString( )
RMIClassLoader
getSecurityContext( ), loadClass( )
RemoteCall
done( ), executeCall( ), getInputStream( ),
getOutputStream( ), getResultStream( ),
releaseInputStream( ), releaseOutputStream( )
RemoteRef
done( ), invoke( ), newCall( )
RemoteStub
setRef( )
Skeleton
dispatch( ), getOperations( )
SkeletonMismatchException
SkeletonMismatchException( )

java.security
Security
getAlgorithmProperty( )
Signature
getParameter( ), setParameter( )
SignatureSpi
engineGetParameter( ), engineSetParameter( )
java.sql
CallableStatement
getBigDecimal( )
Date
Date( ), getHours( ), getMinutes( ), getSeconds( ),
setHours( ), setMinutes( ), setSeconds( )
DriverManager
getLogStream( ), setLogStream( )
PreparedStatement
setUnicodeStream( )
ResultSet
getBigDecimal( ), getUnicodeStream( )
Time
getDate( ), getDay( ), getMonth( ), getYear( ),
setDate( ), setMonth( ), setYear( )
Timestamp
Timestamp( )
java.util
Properties
save( )
javax.swing
AbstractButton
getLabel( ), setLabel( )
JInternalFrame
getMenuBar( ), setMenuBar( )
JPasswordField
getText( )
JRootPane
getMenuBar( ), setMenuBar( )
JTable
createScrollPaneForTable( ), sizeColumnsToFit( )
KeyStroke
getKeyStroke( )
ScrollPaneLayout
getViewportBorderBounds( )
ToolTipManager
setLightWeightPopupEnabled( )
javax.swing.text
View
modelToView( ), viewToModel( )
org.omg.CORBA
Any
extract_Principal( ), insert_Principal( )
ORB
create_recursive_sequence_tc( ), get_current( )
Principal
name( )
ServerRequest
except( ), op_name( ), params( ), result( )
org.omg.CORBA.portable
InputStream
read_Principal( )
OutputStream
write_Principal( )

Exceptions and Errors

This is a complete listing of all the exceptions and errors in this version of Java. The "*" indicates a checked exception or error; these must be declared in the throws clause.

java.lang	AbstractMethodError		java.lang	ExceptionInInitializerError
java.security	AccessControlException		javax.swing.tree	*ExpandVetoException
java.rmi	*AccessException		java.rmi.server	*ExportException
java.security.acl	*AclNotFoundException		java.io	*FileNotFoundException
java.rmi.activation	*ActivateFailedException		org.omg.CORBA	FREE_MEM
java.rmi.activation	*ActivationException		java.security	*GeneralSecurityException
org.omg.CosNaming 2 .NamingContextPackage	*AlreadyBound		java.lang	IllegalAccessError
			java.lang	*IllegalAccessException
java.rmi	*AlreadyBoundException		java.lang	IllegalArgumentException
org.omg.CORBA.portable	*ApplicationException		java.awt	IllegalComponentStateException
java.lang	ArithmeticException		java.lang	IllegalMonitorStateException
java.lang	ArrayIndexOutOfBoundsException		java.awt.geom	IllegalPathStateException
java.lang	ArrayStoreException		java.lang	IllegalStateException
java.awt	AWTError		java.lang	IllegalThreadStateException
java.awt	*AWTException		java.awt.image	ImagingOpException
org.omg.CORBA	BAD_CONTEXT		org.omg.CORBA	IMP_LIMIT
org.omg.CORBA	BAD_INV_ORDER		java.lang	IncompatibleClassChangeError
org.omg.CORBA	BAD_OPERATION		org.omg.CORBA 2 .ORBPackage	*InconsistentTypeCode
org.omg.CORBA	BAD_PARAM			
org.omg.CORBA	BAD_TYPECODE		java.lang	IndexOutOfBoundsException
org.omg.CORBA 2 .TypeCodePackage	*BadKind		org.omg.CORBA	INITIALIZE
			java.lang	InstantiationError
javax.swing.text	*BadLocationException		java.lang	*InstantiationException
java.sql	*BatchUpdateException		org.omg.CORBA	INTERNAL
java.net	*BindException		java.lang	InternalError
org.omg.CORBA 2	*Bounds		java.lang	*InterruptedException
org.omg.CORBA 2 .TypeCodePackage	*Bounds		java.io	*InterruptedIOException
			org.omg.CORBA	INTF_REPOS
org.omg.CosNaming 2 .NamingContextPackage	*CannotProceed		java.beans	*IntrospectionException
			org.omg.CORBA	INV_FLAG
javax.swing.undo	CannotRedoException		org.omg.CORBA	INV_IDENT
javax.swing.undo	CannotUndoException		org.omg.CORBA	INV_OBJREF
java.security.cert	*CertificateEncodingException		org.omg.CORBA	INV_POLICY
java.security.cert	*CertificateException		org.omg.CORBA 2 .DynAnyPackage	*Invalid
java.security.cert	*CertificateExpiredException			
java.security.cert	*CertificateNotYetValidException		org.omg.CORBA	INVALID_TRANSACTION
java.security.cert	*CertificateParsingException		java.security	*InvalidAlgorithmParameterException
javax.swing.text	*ChangedCharSetException		java.io	*InvalidClassException
java.io	*CharConversionException		java.awt.dnd	InvalidDnDOperationException
java.lang	ClassCastException		java.security	*InvalidKeyException
java.lang	ClassCircularityError		java.security.spec	*InvalidKeySpecException
java.lang	ClassFormatError		org.omg.CORBA 2 .ORBPackage	*InvalidName
java.lang	*ClassNotFoundException			
java.lang	*CloneNotSupportedException		org.omg.CosNaming 2 .NamingContextPackage	*InvalidName
java.awt.color	CMMException			
org.omg.CORBA	COMM_FAILURE		java.io	*InvalidObjectException
java.util	ConcurrentModificationException		java.security	InvalidParameterException
java.net	*ConnectException		java.security.spec	*InvalidParameterSpecException
java.rmi	*ConnectException		org.omg.CORBA 2 .DynAnyPackage	*InvalidSeq
java.rmi	*ConnectIOException			
java.security.cert	*CRLException		org.omg.CORBA 2 .DynAnyPackage	*InvalidValue
org.omg.CORBA	DATA_CONVERSION			
java.util.zip	*DataFormatException		java.lang.reflect	*InvocationTargetException
java.sql	*DataTruncation		java.io	*IOException
java.security	*DigestException		java.util.jar	*JarException
java.util	EmptyStackException		java.security	*KeyException
java.io	*EOFException		java.security	*KeyManagementException
java.lang	Error		java.security	*KeyStoreException
java.lang	*Exception		java.security.acl	*LastOwnerException

Package	Exception/Error	Package	Exception/Error
java.lang	LinkageError	java.lang	RuntimeException
java.net	*MalformedURLException	java.lang	SecurityException
org.omg.CORBA	MARSHAL	java.rmi.server	*ServerCloneException
java.rmi	*MarshalException	java.rmi	*ServerError
java.util	MissingResourceException	java.rmi	*ServerException
java.lang	NegativeArraySizeException	java.rmi.server	*ServerNotActiveException
org.omg.CORBA	NO_IMPLEMENT	java.rmi	*ServerRuntimeException
org.omg.CORBA	NO_MEMORY	java.security	*SignatureException
org.omg.CORBA	NO_PERMISSION	java.rmi.server	*SkeletonMismatchException
org.omg.CORBA	NO_RESOURCES	java.rmi.server	*SkeletonNotFoundException
org.omg.CORBA	NO_RESPONSE	java.net	*SocketException
java.lang	NoClassDefFoundError	java.rmi.server	*SocketSecurityException
java.awt.geom	*NoninvertibleTransformException	java.sql	*SQLException
java.net	*NoRouteToHostException	java.sql	*SQLWarning
java.security	*NoSuchAlgorithmException	java.lang	StackOverflowError
java.util	NoSuchElementException	java.io	*StreamCorruptedException
java.lang	NoSuchFieldError	java.lang	StringIndexOutOfBoundsException
java.lang	*NoSuchFieldException	java.rmi	*StubNotFoundException
java.lang	NoSuchMethodError	java.io	*SyncFailedException
java.lang	*NoSuchMethodException	org.omg.CORBA	SystemException
java.rmi	*NoSuchObjectException	java.lang	ThreadDeath
java.security	*NoSuchProviderException	java.lang	*Throwable
java.io	*NotActiveException	java.util	*TooManyListenersException
java.rmi	*NotBoundException	org.omg.CORBA	TRANSACTION_REQUIRED
org.omg.CosNaming.NamingContextPackage	*NotEmpty	org.omg.CORBA	TRANSACTION_ROLLEDBACK
		org.omg.CORBA	TRANSIENT
org.omg.CosNaming.NamingContextPackage	*NotFound	org.omg.CORBA.DynAnyPackage	*TypeMismatch
java.security.acl	*NotOwnerException	java.rmi	*UnexpectedException
java.io	*NotSerializableException	org.omg.CORBA	UNKNOWN
java.lang	NullPointerException	java.lang	UnknownError
java.lang	NumberFormatException	java.rmi.activation	*UnknownGroupException
org.omg.CORBA	OBJ_ADAPTER	java.rmi	*UnknownHostException
org.omg.CORBA	OBJECT_NOT_EXIST	java.net	*UnknownHostException
java.io	*ObjectStreamException	java.rmi.activation	*UnknownObjectException
java.io	*OptionalDataException	java.net	*UnknownServiceException
java.lang	OutOfMemoryError	org.omg.CORBA	*UnknownUserException
java.text	*ParseException	java.rmi	*UnmarshalException
org.omg.CORBA	PERSIST_STORE	java.security	*UnrecoverableKeyException
org.omg.CORBA	*PolicyError	java.lang	UnsatisfiedLinkError
java.awt.print	*PrinterAbortException	java.lang	UnsupportedClassVersionError
java.awt.print	*PrinterException	java.io	*UnsupportedEncodingException
java.awt.print	*PrinterIOException	java.awt.datatransfer	*UnsupportedFlavorException
java.security	*PrivilegedActionException	javax.swing	*UnsupportedLookAndFeelException
java.awt.color	ProfileDataException	java.lang	UnsupportedOperationException
java.beans	*PropertyVetoException	org.omg.CORBA	*UserException
java.net	*ProtocolException	java.io	*UTFDataFormatException
java.security	ProviderException	java.lang	VerifyError
java.awt.image	RasterFormatException	java.lang	VirtualMachineError
org.omg.CORBA.portable	*RemarshalException	java.io	*WriteAbortedException
java.rmi	*RemoteException	org.omg.CORBA	*WrongTransaction
java.rmi	RMISecurityException	java.util.zip	*ZipException

Statistics

Packages	77

Classes and Interfaces	2130
Classes	1730
abstract	261
abstract protected	3
final	221
protected	157
abstract protected	3
Interfaces	400

Members	23901
Fields	4006
static	24
final	27
static final	2713
protected	1050
Constructors	2737
protected	299
Methods	17158
abstract	968
static	1496
final	460
static final	57
protected	1803

Packages

New	Package	Classes	Members	Interfaces	Members
	java.applet	2	28	3	16
	java.awt	108	2253	14	57
	java.awt.color	7	185	0	0
	java.awt.datatransfer	6	66	3	6
	java.awt.dnd	17	182	4	13
	java.awt.event	23	397	15	35
	java.awt.font	15	236	2	64
	java.awt.geom	32	647	1	12
	java.awt.im	3	35	1	7
•	java.awt.im.spi	0	0	3	24
	java.awt.image	40	699	8	70
	java.awt.image.renderable	4	82	3	19
	java.awt.peer	0	0	27	136
	java.awt.print	7	57	3	8
	java.beans	17	140	8	38
	java.beans.beancontext	12	156	11	32
	java.io	66	684	10	74
	java.lang	76	858	3	2
	java.lang.ref	5	15	0	0
	java.lang.reflect	10	116	2	6
	java.math	2	91	0	0
	java.net	29	347	6	16
	java.rmi	19	45	1	0
	java.rmi.activation	12	70	4	16
	java.rmi.dgc	2	8	1	2
	java.rmi.registry	1	7	2	8
	java.rmi.server	16	86	9	30
	java.security	54	376	9	21
	java.security.acl	3	3	5	27
	java.security.cert	14	97	1	4
	java.security.interfaces	0	0	9	19
	java.security.spec	12	45	2	0
	java.sql	11	109	16	550

New	Package	Classes	Members	Interfaces	Members
	java.text	21	361	2	20
	java.util	41	715	13	103
	java.util.jar	8	83	0	0
	java.util.zip	16	160	1	4
	javax.accessibility	9	179	10	93
•	javax.naming	36	243	5	64
•	javax.naming.directory	15	120	3	55
•	javax.naming.event	2	19	5	16
•	javax.naming.ldap	4	20	7	22
•	javax.naming.spi	4	26	8	9
•	javax.rmi	1	6	0	0
•	javax.rmi.CORBA	3	21	5	38
•	javax.sound.midi	17	150	9	101
•	javax.sound.midi.spi	4	22	0	0
•	javax.sound.sampled	26	199	8	50
•	javax.sound.sampled.spi	4	29	0	0
	javax.swing	168	3443	23	182
	javax.swing.border	9	152	1	3
	javax.swing.colorchooser	3	22	1	4
	javax.swing.event	23	143	23	60
	javax.swing.filechooser	3	20	0	0
	javax.swing.plaf	46	128	1	0
	javax.swing.plaf.basic	187	1968	1	8
	javax.swing.plaf.metal	67	573	0	0
	javax.swing.plaf.multi	29	443	0	0
	javax.swing.table	9	251	4	30
	javax.swing.text	84	1202	21	121
	javax.swing.text.html	41	533	0	0
	javax.swing.text.html.parser	9	142	1	35
	javax.swing.text.rtf	1	7	0	0
	javax.swing.tree	13	336	7	54
	javax.swing.undo	7	84	2	14
•	javax.transaction	3	6	0	0
	org.omg.CORBA	129	969	38	176
	org.omg.CORBA.DynAnyPackage	4	8	0	0
	org.omg.CORBA.ORBPackage	2	4	0	0
	org.omg.CORBA.TypeCodePackage	2	4	0	0
	org.omg.CORBA.portable	9	133	9	11
•	org.omg.CORBA_2_3	1	6	0	0
•	org.omg.CORBA_2_3.portable	4	18	0	0
	org.omg.CosNaming	22	142	4	13
	org.omg.CosNaming₂.NamingContextPackage	18	91	0	0
•	org.omg.SendingContext	0	0	2	0
•	org.omg.stub.java.rmi	1	2	0	0

New Classes in Existing Packages

java.applet
Applet.AccessibleApplet
java.awt
Button.AccessibleAWTButton, Canvas₂
.AccessibleAWTCanvas, Checkbox₂
.AccessibleAWTCheckbox, CheckboxMenuItem₂
.AccessibleAWTCheckboxMenuItem,
Choice.AccessibleAWTChoice,
Component.AccessibleAWTComponent,
Component.AccessibleAWTComponent₂

.AccessibleAWTComponentHandler,
Component.AccessibleAWTComponent₂
.AccessibleAWTFocusHandler, Container₂
.AccessibleAWTContainer, Container₂
.AccessibleAWTContainer.AccessibleContainerHandler,
Dialog.AccessibleAWTDialog, FontFormatException,
Frame.AccessibleAWTFrame, JobAttributes,
JobAttributes.DefaultSelectionType, JobAttributes₂
.DestinationType, JobAttributes.DialogType,
JobAttributes.MultipleDocumentHandlingType,

JobAttributes.SidesType, Label.AccessibleAWTLabel, List.AccessibleAWTList, List.AccessibleAWTList₂ .AccessibleAWTListChild, Menu.AccessibleAWTMenu, MenuBar.AccessibleAWTMenuBar, MenuComponent₂ .AccessibleAWTMenuComponent, MenuItem₂ .AccessibleAWTMenuItem, PageAttributes, PageAttributes.ColorType, PageAttributes₂ .MediaType, PageAttributes.OrientationRequestedType, PageAttributes.OriginType, PageAttributes₂ .PrintQualityType, Panel.AccessibleAWTPanel, PopupMenu.AccessibleAWTPopupMenu, Robot, Scrollbar.AccessibleAWTScrollBar, ScrollPane.AccessibleAWTScrollPane, TextArea₂ .AccessibleAWTTextArea, TextComponent₂ .AccessibleAWTTextComponent, TextField₂ .AccessibleAWTTextField, Window₂ .AccessibleAWTWindow

java.awt.datatransfer
MimeTypeParseException

java.awt.event
HierarchyBoundsAdapter, *HierarchyBoundsListener*, HierarchyEvent, *HierarchyListener*

java.awt.font
TextMeasurer

java.awt.peer
RobotPeer

java.lang
StrictMath

java.lang.reflect
InvocationHandler, Proxy, UndeclaredThrowableException

java.net
DatagramSocketImplFactory

java.security
DomainCombiner

java.security.cert
Certificate.CertificateRep

java.security.interfaces
RSAKey

java.security.spec
RSAKeyGenParameterSpec

java.sql
SQLPermission

java.util
Timer, TimerTask

javax.accessibility
AccessibleIcon, AccessibleRelation, AccessibleRelationSet, *AccessibleTable*, *AccessibleTableModelChange*

javax.swing
AbstractCellEditor, ActionMap, ComponentInputMap, ImageIcon.AccessibleImageIcon, InputMap, InputVerifier, JComponent.AccessibleJComponent₂

.AccessibleFocusHandler, JTable.AccessibleJTable₂ .AccessibleJTableModelChange, SizeSequence, UIDefaults.LazyInputMap, UIDefaults.ProxyLazyValue

javax.swing.plaf
ActionMapUIResource, ComponentInputMapUIResource, InputMapUIResource, RootPaneUI

javax.swing.plaf.basic
BasicDesktopPaneUI.OpenAction, BasicHTML, BasicRootPaneUI

javax.swing.plaf.metal
MetalBorders.OptionDialogBorder, MetalBorders₂ .PaletteBorder, MetalBorders.TableHeaderBorder, MetalBorders.ToggleButtonBorder, MetalIconFactory₂ .PaletteCloseIcon, MetalInternalFrameTitlePane

javax.swing.text
AsyncBoxView, AsyncBoxView.ChildLocator, AsyncBoxView.ChildState, FlowView, FlowView₂ .FlowStrategy, GlyphView, GlyphView.GlyphPainter, LayoutQueue, ZoneView

org.omg.CORBA
_IDLTypeStub, _PolicyStub, AnySeqHelper, AnySeqHolder, BooleanSeqHelper, BooleanSeqHolder, CharSeqHelper, CharSeqHolder, CompletionStatusHelper, CurrentHelper, CurrentHolder, *CurrentOperations*, *CustomMarshal*, *DataInputStream*, *DataOutputStream*, DefinitionKindHelper, *DomainManagerOperations*, DoubleSeqHelper, DoubleSeqHolder, FieldNameHelper, FloatSeqHelper, FloatSeqHolder, IdentifierHelper, IDLTypeHelper, *IDLTypeOperations*, *IRObjectOperations*, LongLongSeqHelper, LongLongSeqHolder, LongSeqHelper, LongSeqHolder, NameValuePairHelper, ObjectHelper, OctetSeqHelper, OctetSeqHolder, *OMGVMCID*, PolicyHelper, PolicyHolder, PolicyListHelper, PolicyListHolder, *PolicyOperations*, PolicyTypeHelper, RepositoryIdHelper, SetOverrideTypeHelper, ShortSeqHelper, ShortSeqHolder, StringValueHelper, StructMemberHelper, ULongLongSeqHelper, ULongLongSeqHolder, ULongSeqHelper, ULongSeqHolder, UnionMemberHelper, UShortSeqHelper, UShortSeqHolder, ValueBaseHelper, ValueBaseHolder, ValueMemberHelper, VersionSpecHelper, VisibilityHelper, WCharSeqHelper, WCharSeqHolder, WStringValueHelper

org.omg.CORBA.portable
BoxedValueHelper, *CustomValue*, IndirectionException, *StreamableValue*, UnknownException, *ValueBase*, *ValueFactory*

org.omg.CosNaming
BindingIteratorOperations, *NamingContextOperations*

New Members in Existing Classes

If a new member overrides an existing member, it is included in this listing.

java.applet
Applet
getAccessibleContext( )

java.awt
AWTEvent
HIERARCHY_BOUNDS_EVENT_MASK, HIERARCHY_EVENT_MASK, INVOCATION₂ _EVENT_MASK, PAINT_EVENT_MASK

Topics

AWTEventMulticaster
    add( ), ancestorMoved( ), ancestorResized( ),
    hierarchyChanged( ), remove( )
Button
    getAccessibleContext( ), getListeners( )
Canvas
    getAccessibleContext( )
Checkbox
    getAccessibleContext( ), getListeners( )
CheckboxMenuItem
    getAccessibleContext( ), getListeners( )
Choice
    getAccessibleContext( ), getListeners( )
Component
    addHierarchyBoundsListener( ),
    addHierarchyListener( ), getAccessibleContext( ),
    getGraphicsConfiguration( ), getListeners( ),
    processHierarchyBoundsEvent( ),
    processHierarchyEvent( ),
    removeHierarchyBoundsListener( ),
    removeHierarchyListener( )
Container
    getListeners( )
Cursor
    finalize( )
Dialog
    dispose( ), getAccessibleContext( ), hide( )
Dimension
    hashCode( )
Font
    createFont( ), TRUETYPE_FONT
Frame
    Frame( ), getAccessibleContext( )
GraphicsConfiguration
    getBounds( )
Insets
    hashCode( )
Label
    getAccessibleContext( )
List
    getAccessibleContext( ), getListeners( )
Menu
    getAccessibleContext( )
MenuBar
    getAccessibleContext( )
MenuComponent
    getAccessibleContext( )
MenuItem
    getAccessibleContext( ), getListeners( )
Panel
    getAccessibleContext( )
PopupMenu
    getAccessibleContext( )
RenderingHints
    KEY_STROKE_CONTROL, VALUE_STROKE$_2$
    _DEFAULT, VALUE_STROKE_NORMALIZE,
    VALUE_STROKE_PURE
ScrollPane
    getAccessibleContext( )
Scrollbar
    getAccessibleContext( ), getListeners( )
TextArea
    getAccessibleContext( )
TextComponent
    getAccessibleContext( ), getBackground( ),
    getListeners( ), setBackground( )

TextField
    getAccessibleContext( ), getListeners( )
Toolkit
    getLockingKeyState( ), getPrintJob( ),
    mapInputMethodHighlight( ), setLockingKeyState( )
Window
    getAccessibleContext( ), getGraphicsConfiguration( ),
    getListeners( ), hide( ), setCursor( ), Window( )
java.awt.color
  ICC_Profile
    icSigChromaticityTag, icSigCrdInfoTag,
    icSigDeviceSettingsTag, icSigOutputResponseTag,
    readResolve( )
java.awt.datatransfer
  DataFlavor
    getDefaultRepresentationClass( ),
    getDefaultRepresentationClassAsString( ),
    getReaderForText( ), getTextPlainUnicodeFlavor( ),
    hashCode( ), match( ), selectBestTextFlavor( ),
    toString( )
java.awt.event
  KeyEvent
    setSource( ), VK_INPUT_METHOD_ON_OFF,
    VK_KANA_LOCK
java.awt.font
  TextAttribute
    INPUT_METHOD_UNDERLINE, UNDERLINE$_2$
    _LOW_DASHED, UNDERLINE_LOW_DOTTED,
    UNDERLINE_LOW_GRAY, UNDERLINE_LOW$_2$
    _ONE_PIXEL, UNDERLINE_LOW_TWO_PIXEL
java.awt.geom
  CubicCurve2D
    solveCubic( )
  QuadCurve2D
    solveQuadratic( )
java.awt.im
  InputContext
    getLocale( ), isCompositionEnabled( ), reconvert( ),
    setCompositionEnabled( )
  InputMethodHighlight
    getStyle( ), InputMethodHighlight( )
  InputSubset
    FULLWIDTH_DIGITS, FULLWIDTH_LATIN
java.awt.image
  BandedSampleModel
    getSampleDouble( ), getSampleFloat( ), setSample( )
  ColorModel
    getTransferType( ), hashCode( )
  ComponentSampleModel
    getSampleDouble( ), getSampleFloat( ), setSample( )
  IndexColorModel
    getValidPixels( ), IndexColorModel( ), isValid( )
java.awt.image.renderable
  RenderContext
    concatenateTransform( ), preConcatenateTransform( )
java.awt.peer
  ChoicePeer
    removeAll( )
  ComponentPeer
    coalescePaintEvent( ), getGraphicsConfiguration( )
  TextComponentPeer
    filterEvents( ), getCharacterBounds( ),
    getIndexAtPoint( )
java.io
  ObjectInputStream
    readClassDescriptor( ), resolveProxyClass( )

ObjectOutputStream
annotateProxyClass( ), writeClassDescriptor( )
ObjectStreamConstants
TC_LONGSTRING, TC_PROXYCLASSDESC
java.lang
Double
doubleToRawLongBits( )
Float
floatToRawIntBits( )
InheritableThreadLocal
get( ), set( )
Runtime
addShutdownHook( ), exec( ), halt( ),
removeShutdownHook( )
java.net
ContentHandler
getContent( )
DatagramSocket
setDatagramSocketImplFactory( )
HttpURLConnection
getHeaderFieldDate( ), getInstanceFollowRedirects( ),
HTTP_NOT_IMPLEMENTED,
instanceFollowRedirects,
setInstanceFollowRedirects( )
Socket
getKeepAlive( ), setKeepAlive( ), shutdownInput( ),
shutdownOutput( )
SocketImpl
shutdownInput( ), shutdownOutput( )
SocketOptions
SO_KEEPALIVE
URL
getAuthority( ), getContent( ), getPath( ), getQuery( ),
getUserInfo( ), set( )
URLConnection
getContent( )
URLStreamHandler
equals( ), getDefaultPort( ), getHostAddress( ),
hashCode( ), hostsEqual( ), sameFile( ), setURL( )
java.rmi.server
RMIClassLoader
getClassLoader( )
java.security
AccessControlContext
AccessControlContext( ), getDomainCombiner( )
KeyPairGenerator
generateKeyPair( )
PrivilegedActionException
toString( )
Security
getProviders( )
Signature
initVerify( )
java.security.cert
Certificate
writeReplace( )
java.util
AbstractSet
removeAll( )
Collections
EMPTY_MAP, singletonList( ), singletonMap( )
WeakHashMap
WeakHashMap( )

java.util.jar
Attributes.Name
EXTENSION_INSTALLATION, EXTENSION_LIST,
EXTENSION_NAME, IMPLEMENTATION_URL,
IMPLEMENTATION_VENDOR_ID
JarFile
JarFile( )
java.util.zip
ZipFile
finalize( ), OPEN_DELETE, OPEN_READ, ZipFile( )
javax.accessibility
AccessibleContext
ACCESSIBLE_ACTION_PROPERTY, ACCESSIBLE↪
_TABLE_CAPTION_CHANGED, ACCESSIBLE↪
_TABLE_COLUMN_DESCRIPTION_CHANGED,
ACCESSIBLE_TABLE_COLUMN_HEADER↪
_CHANGED, ACCESSIBLE_TABLE_MODEL↪
_CHANGED, ACCESSIBLE_TABLE_ROW↪
_DESCRIPTION_CHANGED, ACCESSIBLE↪
_TABLE_ROW_HEADER_CHANGED,
ACCESSIBLE_TABLE_SUMMARY_CHANGED,
getAccessibleIcon( ), getAccessibleRelationSet( ),
getAccessibleTable( )
AccessibleRole
CANVAS, ICON, LIST_ITEM
javax.swing
AbstractAction
getKeys( )
AbstractButton
configurePropertiesFromAction( ),
createActionPropertyChangeListener( ), getAction( ),
imageUpdate( ), isFocusTraversable( ), setAction( )
AbstractButton.AccessibleAbstractButton
getAccessibleIcon( ), getAccessibleRelationSet( ),
getAccessibleText( ), getAfterIndex( ), getAtIndex( ),
getBeforeIndex( ), getCaretPosition( ),
getCharacterAttribute( ), getCharacterBounds( ),
getCharCount( ), getIndexAtPoint( ),
getSelectedText( ), getSelectionEnd( ),
getSelectionStart( )
AbstractListModel
getListeners( )
Action
ACCELERATOR_KEY, ACTION_COMMAND_KEY,
MNEMONIC_KEY
BorderFactory
createEtchedBorder( )
ButtonGroup
getButtonCount( )
DefaultBoundedRangeModel
getListeners( )
DefaultButtonModel
getGroup( ), getListeners( )
DefaultCellEditor.EditorDelegate
shouldSelectCell( )
DefaultListCellRenderer
firePropertyChange( ), repaint( ), revalidate( ),
validate( )
DefaultListSelectionModel
getListeners( )
DefaultSingleSelectionModel
getListeners( )
ImageIcon
getAccessibleContext( ), toString( )
JApplet
remove( )

Topics

JButton
> configurePropertiesFromAction( ), JButton( ),
> removeNotify( )

JCheckBox
> BORDER_PAINTED_FLAT_CHANGED$_2$
> _PROPERTY, configurePropertiesFromAction( ),
> createActionPropertyChangeListener( ),
> isBorderPaintedFlat( ), JCheckBox( ),
> setBorderPaintedFlat( )

JCheckBoxMenuItem
> JCheckBoxMenuItem( )

JComboBox
> configurePropertiesFromAction( ),
> createActionPropertyChangeListener( ), getAction( ),
> setAction( )

JComboBox.AccessibleJComboBox
> addAccessibleSelection( ),
> clearAccessibleSelection( ), getAccessibleChild( ),
> getAccessibleChildrenCount( ),
> getAccessibleSelection( ),
> getAccessibleSelectionCount( ),
> isAccessibleChildSelected( ),
> removeAccessibleSelection( ),
> selectAllAccessibleSelection( )

JComponent
> addPropertyChangeListener( ), disable( ), enable( ),
> getActionMap( ), getInputMap( ), getInputVerifier( ),
> getListeners( ), getVerifyInputWhenFocusTarget( ),
> hide( ), isMaximumSizeSet( ), isMinimumSizeSet( ),
> isPreferredSizeSet( ), print( ), printAll( ),
> printBorder( ), printChildren( ),
> printComponent( ), processKeyBinding( ),
> removePropertyChangeListener( ),
> setActionMap( ), setInputMap( ), setInputVerifier( ),
> setVerifyInputWhenFocusTarget( )

JComponent.AccessibleJComponent
> accessibleFocusHandler

JDesktopPane
> getDragMode( ), getSelectedFrame( ), LIVE_DRAG$_2$
> _MODE, OUTLINE_DRAG_MODE, setDragMode( ),
> setSelectedFrame( )

JDialog
> processKeyEvent( ), remove( )

JEditorPane
> getEditorKitClassNameForContentType( ),
> isFocusCycleRoot( ), processKeyEvent( )

JFileChooser
> ACCEPT_ALL_FILE_FILTER_USED$_2$
> _CHANGED_PROPERTY, CONTROL$_2$
> _BUTTONS_ARE_SHOWN_CHANGED$_2$
> _PROPERTY, getControlButtonsAreShown( ),
> isAcceptAllFileFilterUsed( ),
> setAcceptAllFileFilterUsed( ),
> setControlButtonsAreShown( )

JFrame
> EXIT_ON_CLOSE, JFrame( ), remove( )

JInternalFrame
> doDefaultCloseAction( ), getFocusOwner( ),
> getNormalBounds( ), paintComponent( ), remove( ),
> restoreSubcomponentFocus( ), setLayer( ),
> setNormalBounds( )

JLabel
> imageUpdate( )

JLabel.AccessibleJLabel
> getAccessibleIcon( ), getAccessibleRelationSet( ),
> getAccessibleText( ), getAfterIndex( ), getAtIndex( ),

> getBeforeIndex( ), getCaretPosition( ),
> getCharacterAttribute( ), getCharacterBounds( ),
> getCharCount( ), getIndexAtPoint( ),
> getSelectedText( ), getSelectionEnd( ),
> getSelectionStart( )

JMenu
> add( ), createActionComponent( ),
> getPopupMenuOrigin( ), JMenu( )

JMenuBar
> processKeyBinding( )

JMenuItem
> configurePropertiesFromAction( ),
> createActionPropertyChangeListener( ), JMenuItem( )

JPopupMenu
> createActionComponent( ), isPopupTrigger( ),
> remove( )

JRadioButton
> configurePropertiesFromAction( ),
> createActionPropertyChangeListener( ),
> JRadioButton( )

JRadioButtonMenuItem
> JRadioButtonMenuItem( )

JRootPane
> getUI( ), getUIClassID( ),
> isOptimizedDrawingEnabled( ), setUI( ), updateUI( )

JScrollBar
> isFocusTraversable( )

JScrollPane
> setComponentOrientation( )

JSplitPane
> DIVIDER_LOCATION_PROPERTY,
> getResizeWeight( ), isValidateRoot( ), RESIZE$_2$
> _WEIGHT_PROPERTY, setResizeWeight( )

JTabbedPane
> getToolTipTextAt( ), remove( ), setToolTipTextAt( )

JTable
> changeSelection( ), doLayout( ), getRowHeight( ),
> isFocusTraversable( ), processKeyBinding( ),
> removeNotify( ), setRowHeight( ),
> unconfigureEnclosingScrollPane( )

JTable.AccessibleJTable
> getAccessibleAt( ), getAccessibleCaption( ),
> getAccessibleColumnAtIndex( ),
> getAccessibleColumnCount( ),
> getAccessibleColumnDescription( ),
> getAccessibleColumnExtentAt( ),
> getAccessibleColumnHeader( ),
> getAccessibleIndexAt( ), getAccessibleRowAtIndex( ),
> getAccessibleRowCount( ),
> getAccessibleRowDescription( ),
> getAccessibleRowExtentAt( ),
> getAccessibleRowHeader( ),
> getAccessibleSummary( ), getAccessibleTable( ),
> getSelectedAccessibleColumns( ),
> getSelectedAccessibleRows( ),
> isAccessibleColumnSelected( ),
> isAccessibleRowSelected( ),
> isAccessibleSelected( ), setAccessibleCaption( ),
> setAccessibleColumnDescription( ),
> setAccessibleColumnHeader( ),
> setAccessibleRowDescription( ),
> setAccessibleRowHeader( ),
> setAccessibleSummary( )

JTextArea
> processKeyEvent( )

JTextField
    configurePropertiesFromAction( ),
    createActionPropertyChangeListener( ), getAction( ),
    setAction( )
JToggleButton
    JToggleButton( )
JToolBar
    createActionComponent( ), JToolBar( )
JTree
    ANCHOR_SELECTION_PATH_PROPERTY,
    EXPANDS_SELECTED_PATHS₂
    _PROPERTY, getAnchorSelectionPath( ),
    getExpandsSelectedPaths( ), getToggleClickCount( ),
    LEAD_SELECTION_PATH_PROPERTY,
    removeDescendantSelectedPaths( ),
    setAnchorSelectionPath( ),
    setExpandsSelectedPaths( ),
    setLeadSelectionPath( ), setToggleClickCount( ),
    TOGGLE_CLICK_COUNT_PROPERTY
JViewport
    BACKINGSTORE_SCROLL_MODE, BLIT_SCROLL₂
    _MODE, firePropertyChange( ), getScrollMode( ),
    getUI( ), getUIClassID( ), setScrollMode( ), setUI( ),
    SIMPLE_SCROLL_MODE, updateUI( )
JWindow
    JWindow( ), remove( )
KeyStroke
    getKeyStroke( )
LookAndFeel
    loadKeyBindings( ), makeComponentInputMap( ),
    makeInputMap( )
ScrollPaneConstants
    LOWER_LEADING_CORNER, LOWER_TRAILING₂
    _CORNER, UPPER_LEADING_CORNER,
    UPPER_TRAILING_CORNER
SwingUtilities
    getUIActionMap( ), getUIInputMap( ),
    getWindowAncestor( ), notifyAction( ),
    replaceUIActionMap( ), replaceUIInputMap( )
Timer
    getListeners( )
javax.swing.border
BevelBorder
    getHighlightInnerColor( ), getHighlightOuterColor( ),
    getShadowInnerColor( ), getShadowOuterColor( )
EmptyBorder
    getBorderInsets( )
EtchedBorder
    getHighlightColor( ), getShadowColor( )
LineBorder
    getRoundedCorners( ), LineBorder( )
MatteBorder
    getBorderInsets( ), getMatteColor( ), getTileIcon( ),
    MatteBorder( )
TitledBorder
    LEADING, TRAILING
javax.swing.event
EventListenerList
    getListeners( )
InternalFrameEvent
    getInternalFrame( )
TreeSelectionEvent
    isAddedPath( )
javax.swing.plaf
PopupMenuUI
    isPopupTrigger( )

javax.swing.plaf.basic
BasicBorders
    getButtonBorder( ), getInternalFrameBorder( ),
    getMenuBarBorder( ), getProgressBarBorder( ),
    getRadioButtonBorder( ), getSplitPaneBorder( ),
    getSplitPaneDividerBorder( ), getTextFieldBorder( ),
    getToggleButtonBorder( )
BasicComboBoxRenderer
    getPreferredSize( )
BasicEditorPaneUI
    installKeyboardActions( ), propertyChange( )
BasicInternalFrameTitlePane
    addNotify( ), removeNotify( ), uninstallListeners( )
BasicMenuItemUI
    installComponents( ), uninstallComponents( )
BasicPopupMenuUI
    isPopupTrigger( )
BasicSliderUI
    drawInverted( ), leftToRightCache,
    recalculateIfOrientationChanged( )
BasicSplitPaneDivider
    getBorder( ), getInsets( ), getMinimumSize( ),
    setBorder( )
BasicTextFieldUI
    propertyChange( )
BasicTextUI
    update( )
javax.swing.plaf.metal
MetalBorders
    getButtonBorder( ), getDesktopIconBorder( ),
    getTextBorder( ), getTextFieldBorder( ),
    getToggleButtonBorder( )
MetalFileChooserUI
    addControlButtons( ), createActionMap( ),
    getActionMap( ), getBottomPanel( ),
    getButtonPanel( ), installListeners( ), installUI( ),
    removeControlButtons( ), uninstallComponents( )
MetalIconFactory
    getCheckBoxIcon( )
javax.swing.table
AbstractTableModel
    getListeners( )
DefaultTableCellRenderer
    firePropertyChange( ), repaint( ), revalidate( ),
    validate( )
DefaultTableColumnModel
    getListeners( )
DefaultTableModel
    setColumnCount( ), setRowCount( )
JTableHeader
    createDefaultRenderer( ), getDefaultRenderer( ),
    setDefaultRenderer( )
javax.swing.text
AbstractDocument
    getListeners( )
AbstractWriter
    getCanWrapLines( ), getCurrentLineLength( ),
    getEndOffset( ), getIndentLevel( ),
    getIndentSpace( ), getLineLength( ),
    getLineSeparator( ), getStartOffset( ), getWriter( ),
    isLineEmpty( ), output( ), setCanWrapLines( ),
    setCurrentLineLength( ), setLineSeparator( ), write( ),
    writeLineSeparator( )
BoxView
    forwardUpdate( ), getAxis( ), getChildAllocation( ),
    layoutChanged( ), setAxis( )

Topics

CompositeView
  getViewIndex( )
DefaultCaret
  equals( ), getListeners( )
JTextComponent
  addInputMethodListener( )
LabelView
  getBackground( ), getForeground( ),
  isStrikeThrough( ), isSubscript( ), isSuperscript( ),
  isUnderline( )
ParagraphView
  createRow( ), getFlowSpan( ), getFlowStart( )
Segment
  clone( ), current( ), first( ), getBeginIndex( ),
  getEndIndex( ), getIndex( ), last( ), next( ),
  previous( ), setIndex( )
StyleContext.NamedStyle
  getListeners( )
TableView
  forwardUpdate( ), replace( )
TableView.TableRow
  replace( )
View
  append( ), forwardUpdate( ), forwardUpdateToView( ),
  getGraphics( ), getViewIndex( ), insert( ), remove( ),
  removeAll( ), replace( ), updateChildren( ),
  updateLayout( )

javax.swing.text.html
BlockView
  calculateMajorAxisRequirements( ),
  calculateMinorAxisRequirements( ),
  changedUpdate( ), layoutMinorAxis( ), setParent( )
HTML.Tag
  SPAN, Tag( )
HTMLDocument
  fireChangedUpdate( ), fireUndoableEditUpdate( ),
  getElement( ), getParser( ), insertAfterEnd( ),
  insertAfterStart( ), insertBeforeEnd( ),
  insertBeforeStart( ), setInnerHTML( ),
  setOuterHTML( ), setParagraphAttributes( ),
  setParser( )

HTMLDocument.HTMLReader
  handleEndOfLineString( )
HTMLEditorKit
  getDefaultCursor( ), getInputAttributes( ),
  getLinkCursor( ), setDefaultCursor( ), setLinkCursor( )
HTMLEditorKit.InsertHTMLTextAction
  insertAtBoundary( )
HTMLEditorKit.LinkController
  mouseDragged( ), mouseMoved( )
HTMLEditorKit.ParserCallback
  handleEndOfLineString( ), IMPLIED
HTMLWriter
  output( ), writeLineSeparator( )
InlineView
  changedUpdate( ), getBreakWeight( )
ListView
  setPropertiesFromAttributes( )
ParagraphView
  paint( )
StyleSheet
  addAttribute( ), addAttributes( ), addCSSAttribute( ),
  addCSSAttributeFromHTML( ), addStyleSheet( ),
  createLargeAttributeSet( ), createSmallAttributeSet( ),
  getBase( ), getStyleSheets( ), importStyleSheet( ),
  removeAttribute( ), removeAttributes( ),
  removeStyle( ), removeStyleSheet( ), setBase( )
javax.swing.tree
DefaultTreeCellRenderer
  firePropertyChange( ), hasFocus, repaint( ),
  revalidate( ), validate( )
DefaultTreeModel
  getListeners( )
DefaultTreeSelectionModel
  getListeners( )
VariableHeightLayoutCache
  getPreferredHeight( )
org.omg.CORBA
ORB
  destroy( )

Removed Classes

javax.swing
JPopupMenu.WindowPopup.AccessibleWindowPopup

Removed Members

java.io
  Serializable
    serialVersionUID
java.rmi
  RMISecurityManager
    checkPackageAccess( )
java.security.interfaces
  RSAPrivateKey
    getModulus( )
  RSAPublicKey
    getModulus( )

javax.swing
  Box.AccessibleBox
    addFocusListener( ), contains( ), getAccessibleAt( ),
    getAccessibleChild( ), getAccessibleChildrenCount( ),
    getAccessibleComponent( ),
    getAccessibleIndexInParent( ),
    getAccessibleParent( ), getAccessibleStateSet( ),
    getBackground( ), getBounds( ), getCursor( ),
    getFont( ), getFontMetrics( ), getForeground( ),
    getLocale( ), getLocation( ), getLocationOnScreen( ),
    getSize( ), isEnabled( ), isFocusTraversable( ),
    isShowing( ), isVisible( ), removeFocusListener( ),

requestFocus( ), setBackground( ), setBounds( ),
setCursor( ), setEnabled( ), setFont( ),
setForeground( ), setLocation( ), setSize( ),
setVisible( )

Box.Filler.AccessibleBoxFiller
addFocusListener( ), contains( ), getAccessibleAt( ),
getAccessibleChild( ), getAccessibleChildrenCount( ),
getAccessibleComponent( ),
getAccessibleIndexInParent( ),
getAccessibleParent( ), getAccessibleStateSet( ),
getBackground( ), getBounds( ), getCursor( ),
getFont( ), getFontMetrics( ), getForeground( ),
getLocale( ), getLocation( ), getLocationOnScreen( ),
getSize( ), isEnabled( ), isFocusTraversable( ),
isShowing( ), isVisible( ), removeFocusListener( ),
requestFocus( ), setBackground( ), setBounds( ),
setCursor( ), setEnabled( ), setFont( ),
setForeground( ), setLocation( ), setSize( ),
setVisible( )

CellRendererPane.AccessibleCellRendererPane
addFocusListener( ), contains( ), getAccessibleAt( ),
getAccessibleChild( ), getAccessibleChildrenCount( ),
getAccessibleComponent( ),
getAccessibleIndexInParent( ),
getAccessibleParent( ), getAccessibleStateSet( ),
getBackground( ), getBounds( ), getCursor( ),
getFont( ), getFontMetrics( ), getForeground( ),
getLocale( ), getLocation( ), getLocationOnScreen( ),
getSize( ), isEnabled( ), isFocusTraversable( ),
isShowing( ), isVisible( ), removeFocusListener( ),
requestFocus( ), setBackground( ), setBounds( ),
setCursor( ), setEnabled( ), setFont( ),
setForeground( ), setLocation( ), setSize( ),
setVisible( )

DefaultCellEditor
addCellEditorListener( ), changeEvent,
fireEditingCanceled( ), fireEditingStopped( ),
listenerList, removeCellEditorListener( )

JApplet.AccessibleJApplet
addFocusListener( ), contains( ), getAccessibleAt( ),
getAccessibleChild( ), getAccessibleChildrenCount( ),
getAccessibleComponent( ),
getAccessibleIndexInParent( ),
getAccessibleParent( ), getAccessibleRole( ),
getAccessibleStateSet( ), getBackground( ),
getBounds( ), getCursor( ), getFont( ),
getFontMetrics( ), getForeground( ), getLocale( ),
getLocation( ), getLocationOnScreen( ), getSize( ),
isEnabled( ), isFocusTraversable( ), isShowing( ),
isVisible( ), removeFocusListener( ), requestFocus( ),
setBackground( ), setBounds( ), setCursor( ),
setEnabled( ), setFont( ), setForeground( ),
setLocation( ), setSize( ), setVisible( )

JCheckBoxMenuItem
init( ), updateUI( )

JComponent.AccessibleJComponent
addFocusListener( ), contains( ),
getAccessibleAt( ), getAccessibleComponent( ),
getAccessibleIndexInParent( ),
getAccessibleParent( ), getBackground( ),
getBounds( ), getCursor( ), getFont( ),
getFontMetrics( ), getForeground( ), getLocale( ),
getLocation( ), getLocationOnScreen( ), getSize( ),
isEnabled( ), isFocusTraversable( ), isShowing( ),
isVisible( ), removeFocusListener( ), requestFocus( ),

setBackground( ), setBounds( ), setCursor( ),
setEnabled( ), setFont( ), setForeground( ),
setLocation( ), setSize( ), setVisible( )

JDialog.AccessibleJDialog
addFocusListener( ), contains( ), getAccessibleAt( ),
getAccessibleChild( ), getAccessibleChildrenCount( ),
getAccessibleComponent( ),
getAccessibleIndexInParent( ),
getAccessibleParent( ), getAccessibleRole( ),
getBackground( ), getBounds( ), getCursor( ),
getFont( ), getFontMetrics( ), getForeground( ),
getLocale( ), getLocation( ), getLocationOnScreen( ),
getSize( ), isEnabled( ), isFocusTraversable( ),
isShowing( ), isVisible( ), removeFocusListener( ),
requestFocus( ), setBackground( ), setBounds( ),
setCursor( ), setEnabled( ), setFont( ),
setForeground( ), setLocation( ), setSize( ),
setVisible( )

JFrame.AccessibleJFrame
addFocusListener( ), contains( ), getAccessibleAt( ),
getAccessibleChild( ), getAccessibleChildrenCount( ),
getAccessibleComponent( ),
getAccessibleIndexInParent( ),
getAccessibleParent( ), getAccessibleRole( ),
getBackground( ), getBounds( ), getCursor( ),
getFont( ), getFontMetrics( ), getForeground( ),
getLocale( ), getLocation( ), getLocationOnScreen( ),
getSize( ), isEnabled( ), isFocusTraversable( ),
isShowing( ), isVisible( ), removeFocusListener( ),
requestFocus( ), setBackground( ), setBounds( ),
setCursor( ), setEnabled( ), setFont( ),
setForeground( ), setLocation( ), setSize( ),
setVisible( )

JInternalFrame
getBackground( ), getForeground( ),
setBackground( ), setForeground( ), setVisible( )

JPopupMenu
remove( )

JRadioButtonMenuItem
init( ), updateUI( )

JScrollPane
isOpaque( )

JTable
reshape( )

JTextArea
processComponentKeyEvent( )

JTextPane
getScrollableTracksViewportWidth( )

JToolBar
remove( )

JWindow.AccessibleJWindow
addFocusListener( ), contains( ), getAccessibleAt( ),
getAccessibleChild( ), getAccessibleChildrenCount( ),
getAccessibleComponent( ),
getAccessibleIndexInParent( ),
getAccessibleParent( ), getAccessibleRole( ),
getAccessibleStateSet( ), getBackground( ),
getBounds( ), getCursor( ), getFont( ),
getFontMetrics( ), getForeground( ), getLocale( ),
getLocation( ), getLocationOnScreen( ), getSize( ),
isEnabled( ), isFocusTraversable( ), isShowing( ),
isVisible( ), removeFocusListener( ), requestFocus( ),
setBackground( ), setBounds( ), setCursor( ),
setEnabled( ), setFont( ), setForeground( ),
setLocation( ), setSize( ), setVisible( )

Topics

javax.swing.plaf.basic
   BasicSplitPaneUI.BasicVerticalLayoutManager
      getAvailableSize( ), getInitialLocation( ),
      getPreferredSizeOfComponent( ),
      getSizeOfComponent( ), minimumLayoutSize( ),
      preferredLayoutSize( ), setComponentToSize( )
javax.swing.plaf.metal
   MetalComboBoxUI
      installKeyboardActions( ), uninstallKeyboardActions( )
   MetalInternalFrameUI
      replacePane( )
javax.swing.text
   BoxView
      changedUpdate( ), insertUpdate( ), removeUpdate( )
   CompositeView
      append( ), insert( ), removeAll( )
   DefaultEditorKit
      clone( )
   JTextComponent
      isOpaque( ), processComponentKeyEvent( ),
      setEnabled( ), setOpaque( )
   LabelView
      breakView( ), createFragment( ), getAlignment( ),
      getBreakWeight( ), getNextVisualPositionFrom( ),
      getPreferredSpan( ), insertUpdate( ), modelToView( ),
      paint( ), removeUpdate( ), toString( ), viewToModel( )
   ParagraphView
      calculateMinorAxisRequirements( ),
      getViewAtPosition( ), getViewIndexAtPosition( ),
      insertUpdate( ), layout( ), loadChildren( ),
      removeUpdate( )

   PlainView
      preferenceChanged( )
   TableView
      loadChildren( )
   TableView.TableCell
      getPreferredSpan( )
   TableView.TableRow
      loadChildren( )
javax.swing.text.html
   HTMLWriter
      write( )
   InlineView
      isVisible( )
   ParagraphView
      changedUpdate( )
org.omg.CORBA
   DomainManager
      get_domain_policy( )
   IDLType
      type( )
   IRObject
      def_kind( ), destroy( )
   Policy
      copy( ), destroy( ), policy_type( )
org.omg.CosNaming
   BindingIterator
      destroy( ), next_n( ), next_one( )
   NamingContext
      bind( ), bind_context( ), bind_new_context( ),
      destroy( ), list( ), new_context( ), rebind( ), rebind$_2$
      _context( ), resolve( ), unbind( )

Modified Classes and Members

These tables show all the classes and members whose signatures were modified from the previous version. "+" indicates an added keyword; "-" indicates a removed keyword.

Extends Changes

javax.swing

Box.AccessibleBox, CellRendererPane.AccessibleCellRendererPane, JComponent.AccessibleJComponent	- javax.accessibility.AccessibleContext, + java.awt.Container.AccessibleAWTContainer
Box.Filler.AccessibleBoxFiller	- javax.accessibility.AccessibleContext, + java.awt.Component.AccessibleAWTComponent
DefaultCellEditor	- java.lang.Object, + javax.swing.AbstractCellEditor
JApplet.AccessibleJApplet	- javax.accessibility.AccessibleContext, + java.applet.Applet.AccessibleApplet
JDialog.AccessibleJDialog	- javax.accessibility.AccessibleContext, + java.awt.Dialog.AccessibleAWTDialog
JFrame.AccessibleJFrame	- javax.accessibility.AccessibleContext, + java.awt.Frame.AccessibleAWTFrame
JWindow.AccessibleJWindow	- javax.accessibility.AccessibleContext, + java.awt.Window.AccessibleAWTWindow

javax.swing.text

LabelView	- javax.swing.text.View, + javax.swing.text.GlyphView
ParagraphView	- javax.swing.text.BoxView, + javax.swing.text.FlowView

Implements Changes

java.awt

AWTEventMulticaster	+ java.awt.event.HierarchyBoundsListener, + java.awt.event.HierarchyListener

Implements Changes

Button, Canvas, Checkbox, CheckboxMenuItem, Choice, Label, List, Menu, MenuBar, MenuItem, Panel, Scrollbar, ScrollPane, TextComponent, Window	+ javax.accessibility.Accessible
java.awt.color	
ColorSpace, ICC_Profile	+ java.io.Serializable
java.security.cert	
Certificate	+ java.io.Serializable
java.security.interfaces	
RSAPrivateKey	- java.security.PrivateKey, + java.security.interfaces.RSAKey, + java.security.PrivateKey
RSAPublicKey	- java.security.PublicKey, + java.security.interfaces.RSAKey, + java.security.PublicKey
javax.swing	
AbstractButton.AccessibleAbstractButton, JLabel.AccessibleJLabel	+ javax.accessibility.AccessibleText
DefaultCellEditor	- java.io.Serializable
ImageIcon	+ javax.accessibility.Accessible
JComboBox.AccessibleJComboBox	+ javax.accessibility.AccessibleSelection
JTable.AccessibleJTable	+ javax.accessibility.AccessibleTable
javax.swing.text	
LabelView	+ javax.swing.text.TabableView
Segment	+ java.lang.Cloneable, + java.text.CharacterIterator
javax.swing.text.html	
CSS	+ java.io.Serializable
HTMLEditorKit.LinkController	+ java.awt.event.MouseMotionListener
javax.swing.text.html.parser	
ParserDelegator	+ java.io.Serializable
org.omg.CORBA	
Current	+ org.omg.CORBA.CurrentOperations, + org.omg.CORBA.portable.IDLEntity
DomainManager	+ org.omg.CORBA.DomainManagerOperations, + org.omg.CORBA.portable.IDLEntity
IDLType	- org.omg.CORBA.Object, + org.omg.CORBA.IDLTypeOperations
IRObject	+ org.omg.CORBA.IRObjectOperations
Policy	+ org.omg.CORBA.PolicyOperations, + org.omg.CORBA.portable.IDLEntity
org.omg.CosNaming	
BindingIterator	+ org.omg.CosNaming.BindingIteratorOperations
NamingContext	+ org.omg.CosNaming.NamingContextOperations

Member Modifier Changes

java.awt	
Component	
setCursor( )	- synchronized
java.awt.datatransfer	
StringSelection	
getTransferData( ), getTransferDataFlavors( )	- synchronized
java.awt	
EventQueue	
postEvent( )	- synchronized
Frame	
setCursor( )	- synchronized
GraphicsEnvironment	
getLocalGraphicsEnvironment( )	+ synchronized

Topics

851

Java 1.3
Modified Classes and Members

Member Modifier Changes

java.awt.im
  InputContext
    dispatchEvent( ), endComposition( )   - synchronized

java.awt.image
  IndexColorModel
    getDataElements( )   + synchronized

java.awt
  Scrollbar
    setValues( )   - synchronized
  Toolkit
    setDesktopProperty( )   - synchronized

java.io
  BufferedInputStream
    close( )   - synchronized

java.lang
  Math
    abs( ), max( ), min( ), round( ), toDegrees( ), toRadians( )   + strictfp
    acos( ), asin( ), atan( ), atan2( ), ceil( ), cos( ), exp( ),   - native, + strictfp
      floor( ), IEEEremainder( ), log( ), pow( ), rint( ), sin( ),
      sqrt( ), tan( )
    random( )   - synchronized, + strictfp
  System
    setSecurityManager( )   - synchronized

java.net
  URL
    setURLStreamHandlerFactory( )   - synchronized
  URLConnection
    getFileNameMap( )   + synchronized

java.security
  Provider
    entrySet( )   + synchronized
  Security
    getProvider( ), getProviders( ), insertProviderAt( ),   + synchronized
      removeProvider( )

java.text
  RuleBasedCollator
    compare( ), getCollationKey( )   + synchronized

javax.swing
  AbstractAction
    putValue( ), setEnabled( )   - synchronized
  AbstractButton
    getSelectedObjects( )   - synchronized

javax.swing.filechooser
  FileView
    getDescription( ), getIcon( ), getName( ),   - abstract
      getTypeDescription( ), isTraversable( )

javax.swing
  JCheckBoxMenuItem
    getSelectedObjects( )   - synchronized
  JEditorPane
    getEditorKit( )   - final

javax.swing.plaf.basic
  BasicSliderUI
    MAX_SCROLL, MIN_SCROLL, NEGATIVE_SCROLL,   + static
      POSITIVE_SCROLL

javax.swing.text
  BoxView
    getHeight( ), getOffset( ), getSpan( ), getWidth( )   - final

Member Modifier Changes

CompositeView
    getBottomInset( ), getLeftInset( ), getRightInset( ),   - final
        getTopInset( ), setInsets( ), setParagraphInsets( )
EditorKit
    clone( )   - abstract
LabelView
    getFont( )   - protected, + public
javax.swing
    UIManager
        addPropertyChangeListener( ),   - synchronized
           removePropertyChangeListener( )

Throws Changes

java.io
    FileOutputStream
        FileOutputStream( )   - java.io.IOException, + java.io.FileNotFoundException
    RandomAccessFile
        RandomAccessFile( )   - java.io.IOException, + java.io.FileNotFoundException
java.net
    URLDecoder
        decode( )   - java.lang.Exception
org.omg.CORBA
    TypeCode
        member_visibility( )   - org.omg.CORBA.Bounds,
                         + org.omg.CORBA.TypeCodePackage.Bounds

Newly Deprecated Classes

javax.swing.text
    TableView.TableCell

Newly Deprecated Members

java.awt.datatransfer
    DataFlavor
        equals( ), plainTextFlavor
java.awt.image.renderable
    RenderContext
        concetenateTransform( ), preConcetenateTransform( )
java.net
    HttpURLConnection
        HTTP_SERVER_ERROR
    URLConnection
        getDefaultRequestProperty( ),
        setDefaultRequestProperty( )
    URLStreamHandler
        setURL( )
java.rmi.dgc
    VMID
        isUnique( )
java.sql
    Time
        Time( )
javax.swing
    JComponent
        hide( )

    JMenuBar
        getComponentAtIndex( )
    JPopupMenu
        getComponentAtIndex( )
    JRootPane
        defaultPressAction, defaultReleaseAction
    JViewport
        backingStore, isBackingStoreEnabled( ),
        setBackingStoreEnabled( )
javax.swing.plaf.basic
    BasicDesktopPaneUI
        closeKey, maximizeKey, minimizeKey, navigateKey,
        navigateKey2
    BasicInternalFrameUI
        openMenuKey
    BasicSplitPaneUI
        createKeyboardDownRightListener( ),
        createKeyboardEndListener( ),
        createKeyboardHomeListener( ),
        createKeyboardResizeToggleListener( ),
        createKeyboardUpLeftListener( ),
        dividerResizeToggleKey, downKey,
        endKey, getDividerBorderSize( ),
        homeKey, keyboardDownRightListener,

Topics

keyboardEndListener, keyboardHomeListener,
keyboardResizeToggleListener,
keyboardUpLeftListener, leftKey, rightKey, upKey
BasicTabbedPaneUI
downKey, leftKey, rightKey, upKey
BasicToolBarUI
downKey, leftKey, rightKey, upKey
javax.swing.table
TableColumn
disableResizedPosting( ), enableResizedPosting( ),
resizedPostingDisableCount

javax.swing.text
LabelView
getFontMetrics( )
TableView
createTableCell( )
javax.swing.text.html
FormView
RESET, SUBMIT
HTMLEditorKit.InsertHTMLTextAction
insertAtBoundry( )
org.omg.CORBA
TCKind
TCKind( )

Exceptions and Errors

This is a complete listing of all the exceptions and errors in this version of Java. The "*" indicates a checked exception or error; these must be declared in the throws clause.

java.lang	AbstractMethodError
java.security	AccessControlException
java.rmi	*AccessException
java.security.acl	*AclNotFoundException
java.rmi.activation	*ActivateFailedException
java.rmi.activation	*ActivationException
org.omg.CosNaming₂ .NamingContextPackage	*AlreadyBound
java.rmi	*AlreadyBoundException
org.omg.CORBA.portable	*ApplicationException
java.lang	ArithmeticException
java.lang	ArrayIndexOutOfBoundsException
java.lang	ArrayStoreException
javax.naming.directory	*AttributeInUseException
javax.naming.directory	*AttributeModificationException
javax.naming	*AuthenticationException
javax.naming	*AuthenticationNotSupportedException
java.awt	AWTError
java.awt	*AWTException
org.omg.CORBA	BAD_CONTEXT
org.omg.CORBA	BAD_INV_ORDER
org.omg.CORBA	BAD_OPERATION
org.omg.CORBA	BAD_PARAM
org.omg.CORBA	BAD_TYPECODE
org.omg.CORBA₂ .TypeCodePackage	*BadKind
javax.swing.text	*BadLocationException
java.sql	*BatchUpdateException
java.net	*BindException
org.omg.CORBA	*Bounds
org.omg.CORBA₂ .TypeCodePackage	*Bounds
org.omg.CosNaming₂ .NamingContextPackage	*CannotProceed
javax.naming	*CannotProceedException
javax.swing.undo	CannotRedoException
javax.swing.undo	CannotUndoException
java.security.cert	*CertificateEncodingException
java.security.cert	*CertificateException
java.security.cert	*CertificateExpiredException
java.security.cert	*CertificateNotYetValidException
java.security.cert	*CertificateParsingException
javax.swing.text	*ChangedCharSetException
java.io	*CharConversionException

java.lang	ClassCastException
java.lang	ClassCircularityError
java.lang	ClassFormatError
java.lang	*ClassNotFoundException
java.lang	*CloneNotSupportedException
java.awt.color	CMMException
org.omg.CORBA	COMM_FAILURE
javax.naming	*CommunicationException
java.util	ConcurrentModificationException
javax.naming	*ConfigurationException
java.rmi	*ConnectException
java.net	*ConnectException
java.rmi	*ConnectIOException
javax.naming	*ContextNotEmptyException
java.security.cert	*CRLException
org.omg.CORBA	DATA_CONVERSION
java.util.zip	*DataFormatException
java.sql	*DataTruncation
java.security	*DigestException
java.util	EmptyStackException
java.io	*EOFException
java.lang	Error
java.lang	*Exception
java.lang	ExceptionInInitializerError
javax.swing.tree	*ExpandVetoException
java.rmi.server	*ExportException
java.io	*FileNotFoundException
java.awt	*FontFormatException
org.omg.CORBA	FREE_MEM
java.security	*GeneralSecurityException
java.lang	IllegalAccessError
java.lang	*IllegalAccessException
java.lang	IllegalArgumentException
java.awt	IllegalComponentStateException
java.lang	IllegalMonitorStateException
java.awt.geom	IllegalPathStateException
java.lang	IllegalStateException
java.lang	IllegalThreadStateException
java.awt.image	ImagingOpException
org.omg.CORBA	IMP_LIMIT
java.lang	IncompatibleClassChangeError
org.omg.CORBA₂ .ORBPackage	*InconsistentTypeCode
java.lang	IndexOutOfBoundsException

org.omg.CORBA.portable	IndirectionException		javax.naming	*NamingSecurityException
org.omg.CORBA	INITIALIZE		java.lang	NegativeArraySizeException
java.lang	InstantiationError		org.omg.CORBA	NO_IMPLEMENT
java.lang	*InstantiationException		org.omg.CORBA	NO_MEMORY
javax.naming	*InsufficientResourcesException		org.omg.CORBA	NO_PERMISSION
org.omg.CORBA	INTERNAL		org.omg.CORBA	NO_RESOURCES
java.lang	InternalError		org.omg.CORBA	NO_RESPONSE
java.lang	*InterruptedException		java.lang	NoClassDefFoundError
java.io	*InterruptedIOException		javax.naming	*NoInitialContextException
javax.naming	*InterruptedNamingException		java.awt.geom	*NoninvertibleTransformException
org.omg.CORBA	INTF_REPOS		javax.naming	*NoPermissionException
java.beans	*IntrospectionException		java.net	*NoRouteToHostException
org.omg.CORBA	INV_FLAG		java.security	*NoSuchAlgorithmException
org.omg.CORBA	INV_IDENT		javax.naming.directory	*NoSuchAttributeException
org.omg.CORBA	INV_OBJREF		java.util	NoSuchElementException
org.omg.CORBA	INV_POLICY		java.lang	NoSuchFieldError
org.omg.CORBA⊋ .DynAnyPackage	*Invalid		java.lang	*NoSuchFieldException
			java.lang	NoSuchMethodError
org.omg.CORBA	INVALID_TRANSACTION		java.lang	*NoSuchMethodException
java.security	*InvalidAlgorithmParameterException		java.rmi	*NoSuchObjectException
javax.naming.directory	*InvalidAttributeIdentifierException		java.security	*NoSuchProviderException
javax.naming.directory	*InvalidAttributesException		java.io	*NotActiveException
javax.naming.directory	*InvalidAttributeValueException		java.rmi	*NotBoundException
java.io	*InvalidClassException		javax.naming	*NotContextException
java.awt.dnd	InvalidDnDOperationException		org.omg.CosNaming⊋ .NamingContextPackage	*NotEmpty
java.security	*InvalidKeyException			
java.security.spec	*InvalidKeySpecException		org.omg.CosNaming⊋ .NamingContextPackage	*NotFound
javax.sound.midi	*InvalidMidiDataException			
org.omg.CosNaming⊋ .NamingContextPackage	*InvalidName		java.security.acl	*NotOwnerException
			java.io	*NotSerializableException
org.omg.CORBA⊋ .ORBPackage	*InvalidName		java.lang	NullPointerException
			java.lang	NumberFormatException
javax.naming	*InvalidNameException		org.omg.CORBA	OBJ_ADAPTER
java.io	*InvalidObjectException		org.omg.CORBA	OBJECT_NOT_EXIST
java.security	InvalidParameterException		java.io	*ObjectStreamException
java.security.spec	*InvalidParameterSpecException		javax.naming	*OperationNotSupportedException
javax.naming.directory	*InvalidSearchControlsException		java.io	*OptionalDataException
javax.naming.directory	*InvalidSearchFilterException		java.lang	OutOfMemoryError
org.omg.CORBA⊋ .DynAnyPackage	*InvalidSeq		java.text	*ParseException
			javax.naming	*PartialResultException
javax.transaction	*InvalidTransactionException		org.omg.CORBA	PERSIST_STORE
org.omg.CORBA⊋ .DynAnyPackage	*InvalidValue		org.omg.CORBA	*PolicyError
			java.awt.print	*PrinterAbortException
java.lang.reflect	*InvocationTargetException		java.awt.print	*PrinterException
java.io	*IOException		java.awt.print	*PrinterIOException
java.util.jar	*JarException		java.security	*PrivilegedActionException
java.security	*KeyException		java.awt.color	ProfileDataException
java.security	*KeyManagementException		java.beans	*PropertyVetoException
java.security	*KeyStoreException		java.net	*ProtocolException
java.security.acl	*LastOwnerException		java.security	ProviderException
javax.naming.ldap	*LdapReferralException		java.awt.image	RasterFormatException
javax.naming	*LimitExceededException		javax.naming	*ReferralException
javax.sound.sampled	*LineUnavailableException		org.omg.CORBA.portable	*RemarshalException
java.lang	LinkageError		java.rmi	*RemoteException
javax.naming	*LinkException		java.rmi	RMISecurityException
javax.naming	*LinkLoopException		java.lang	RuntimeException
javax.naming	*MalformedLinkException		javax.naming.directory	*SchemaViolationException
java.net	*MalformedURLException		java.lang	SecurityException
org.omg.CORBA	MARSHAL		java.rmi.server	*ServerCloneException
java.rmi	*MarshalException		java.rmi	*ServerError
javax.sound.midi	*MidiUnavailableException		java.rmi	*ServerException
java.awt.datatransfer	*MimeTypeParseException		java.rmi.server	*ServerNotActiveException
java.util	MissingResourceException		java.rmi	*ServerRuntimeException
javax.naming	*NameAlreadyBoundException		javax.naming	*ServiceUnavailableException
javax.naming	*NameNotFoundException		java.security	*SignatureException
javax.naming	*NamingException		javax.naming	*SizeLimitExceededException

java.rmi.server	*SkeletonMismatchException		org.omg.CORBA	UNKNOWN
java.rmi.server	*SkeletonNotFoundException		java.lang	UnknownError
java.net	*SocketException		org.omg.CORBA.portable	UnknownException
java.rmi.server	*SocketSecurityException		java.rmi.activation	*UnknownGroupException
java.sql	*SQLException		java.rmi	*UnknownHostException
java.sql	*SQLWarning		java.net	*UnknownHostException
java.lang	StackOverflowError		java.rmi.activation	*UnknownObjectException
java.io	*StreamCorruptedException		java.net	*UnknownServiceException
java.lang	StringIndexOutOfBoundsException		org.omg.CORBA	*UnknownUserException
java.rmi	*StubNotFoundException		java.rmi	*UnmarshalException
java.io	*SyncFailedException		java.security	*UnrecoverableKeyException
org.omg.CORBA	SystemException		java.lang	UnsatisfiedLinkError
java.lang	ThreadDeath		javax.sound.sampled	*UnsupportedAudioFileException
java.lang	*Throwable		java.lang	UnsupportedClassVersionError
javax.naming	*TimeLimitExceededException		java.io	*UnsupportedEncodingException
java.util	*TooManyListenersException		java.awt.datatransfer	*UnsupportedFlavorException
org.omg.CORBA	TRANSACTION_REQUIRED		javax.swing	*UnsupportedLookAndFeelException
org.omg.CORBA	TRANSACTION_ROLLEDBACK		java.lang	UnsupportedOperationException
javax.transaction	*TransactionRequiredException		org.omg.CORBA	*UserException
javax.transaction	*TransactionRolledbackException		java.io	*UTFDataFormatException
org.omg.CORBA	TRANSIENT		java.lang	VerifyError
org.omg.CORBA.DynAnyPackage	*TypeMismatch		java.lang	VirtualMachineError
			java.io	*WriteAbortedException
java.lang.reflect	UndeclaredThrowableException		org.omg.CORBA	*WrongTransaction
java.rmi	*UnexpectedException		java.util.zip	*ZipException

Statistics

Packages	136	**Members**		32138
		Fields		5136
Classes and Interfaces	3020	static		23
Classes	2367	final		28
abstract	477	static final		3692
abstract protected	3	protected		1164
final	345	Constructors		3736
protected	162	protected		444
abstract protected	3	Methods		23266
Interfaces	653	abstract		1436
		static		2213
		final		908
		static final		91
		protected		2172

Packages

New	Package	Classes	Members	Interfaces	Members
	java.applet	2	28	3	19
	java.awt	123	2646	16	60
	java.awt.color	7	189	0	0
	java.awt.datatransfer	6	77	4	8
	java.awt.dnd	19	210	5	14
	java.awt.event	25	454	18	39
	java.awt.font	16	286	2	64
	java.awt.geom	32	639	1	12
	java.awt.im	3	35	1	7
	java.awt.im.spi	0	0	3	25
	java.awt.image	44	778	8	70
	java.awt.image.renderable	4	82	3	19
	java.awt.peer	0	0	27	144
	java.awt.print	7	65	3	8
	java.beans	27	212	9	39
	java.beans.beancontext	12	156	11	32
	java.io	66	701	10	74
	java.lang	78	950	4	6
	java.lang.ref	5	15	0	0
	java.lang.reflect	10	112	2	6
	java.math	2	92	0	0
	java.net	38	520	6	21
•	java.nio	14	238	0	0
•	java.nio.channels	31	142	7	9
•	java.nio.channels.spi	5	37	0	0
•	java.nio.charset	11	95	0	0
•	java.nio.charset.spi	1	3	0	0
	java.rmi	19	43	1	0
	java.rmi.activation	12	67	4	16
	java.rmi.dgc	2	8	1	2
	java.rmi.registry	1	7	2	8
	java.rmi.server	17	92	9	30
	java.security	54	392	9	21

Topics

Java 1.4

Packages

New	Package	Classes	Members	Interfaces	Members
	java.security.acl	3	3	5	27
	java.security.cert	36	317	8	20
	java.security.interfaces	0	0	10	26
	java.security.spec	15	59	2	0
	java.sql	11	115	18	697
	java.text	26	441	2	20
	java.util	46	787	14	103
	java.util.jar	8	83	0	0
•	java.util.logging	15	170	1	1
•	java.util.prefs	6	104	3	5
•	java.util.regex	3	38	0	0
	java.util.zip	16	159	1	4
	javax.accessibility	9	187	14	110
•	javax.crypto	22	195	1	0
•	javax.crypto.interfaces	0	0	4	6
•	javax.crypto.spec	12	64	0	0
•	javax.imageio	9	328	2	3
•	javax.imageio.event	0	0	5	24
•	javax.imageio.metadata	4	131	2	49
•	javax.imageio.plugins.jpeg	4	36	0	0
•	javax.imageio.spi	9	102	2	3
•	javax.imageio.stream	9	137	2	68
	javax.naming	36	243	5	64
	javax.naming.directory	15	120	3	55
	javax.naming.event	2	19	5	16
	javax.naming.ldap	6	34	7	22
	javax.naming.spi	4	26	8	9
•	javax.net	2	13	0	0
•	javax.net.ssl	19	125	10	34
•	javax.print	15	126	10	42
•	javax.print.attribute	15	120	11	23
•	javax.print.attribute.standard	74	648	0	0
•	javax.print.event	5	24	3	8
	javax.rmi	1	6	0	0
	javax.rmi.CORBA	3	21	5	38
•	javax.security.auth	7	40	2	4
•	javax.security.auth.callback	8	60	2	1
•	javax.security.auth.kerberos	5	61	0	0
•	javax.security.auth.login	8	29	0	0
•	javax.security.auth.spi	0	0	1	5
•	javax.security.auth.x500	2	19	0	0
•	javax.security.cert	7	32	0	0
	javax.sound.midi	17	150	9	101
	javax.sound.midi.spi	4	22	0	0
	javax.sound.sampled	26	199	8	50
	javax.sound.sampled.spi	4	29	0	0
•	javax.sql	2	4	12	110
	javax.swing	189	3799	24	191
	javax.swing.border	9	153	1	3
	javax.swing.colorchooser	3	25	1	4
	javax.swing.event	23	148	23	60
	javax.swing.filechooser	3	33	0	0
	javax.swing.plaf	47	131	1	0
	javax.swing.plaf.basic	192	2059	1	8
	javax.swing.plaf.metal	68	587	0	0
	javax.swing.plaf.multi	31	474	0	0
	javax.swing.table	9	252	4	30
	javax.swing.text	95	1330	21	121

New	Package	Classes	Members		Interfaces	Members
	javax.swing.text.html	42	557		0	0
	javax.swing.text.html.parser	9	142		1	35
	javax.swing.text.rtf	1	6		0	0
	javax.swing.tree	13	342		7	54
	javax.swing.undo	7	85		2	14
	javax.transaction	3	6		0	0
•	javax.transaction.xa	1	29		2	26
•	javax.xml.parsers	6	63		0	0
•	javax.xml.transform	6	63		6	16
•	javax.xml.transform.dom	2	16		1	1
•	javax.xml.transform.sax	3	29		2	7
•	javax.xml.transform.stream	2	30		0	0
•	org.ietf.jgss	5	76		3	74
	org.omg.CORBA	144	1091		38	176
	org.omg.CORBA.DynAnyPackage	4	8		0	0
	org.omg.CORBA.ORBPackage	2	4		0	0
	org.omg.CORBA.TypeCodePackage	2	4		0	0
	org.omg.CORBA.portable	9	133		9	11
	org.omg.CORBA_2_3	1	6		0	0
	org.omg.CORBA_2_3.portable	4	18		0	0
	org.omg.CosNaming	28	183		6	17
•	org.omg.CosNaming↪ .NamingContextExtPackage	6	36		0	0
	org.omg.CosNaming↪ .NamingContextPackage	18	103		0	0
•	org.omg.Dynamic	1	4		0	0
•	org.omg.DynamicAny	27	598		22	96
•	org.omg.DynamicAny↪ .DynAnyFactoryPackage	2	9		0	0
•	org.omg.DynamicAny.DynAnyPackage	4	18		0	0
•	org.omg.IOP	21	128		14	15
•	org.omg.IOP.CodecFactoryPackage	2	9		0	0
•	org.omg.IOP.CodecPackage	6	27		0	0
•	org.omg.Messaging	1	7		1	1
•	org.omg.PortableInterceptor	5	28		29	67
•	org.omg.PortableInterceptor↪ .ORBInitInfoPackage	5	27		0	0
•	org.omg.PortableServer	19	129		35	58
•	org.omg.PortableServer.CurrentPackage	2	9		0	0
•	org.omg.PortableServer↪ .POAManagerPackage	3	20		0	0
•	org.omg.PortableServer.POAPackage	20	92		0	0
•	org.omg.PortableServer↪ .ServantLocatorPackage	1	6		0	0
•	org.omg.PortableServer.portable	0	0		1	8
	org.omg.SendingContext	0	0		2	0
	org.omg.stub.java.rmi	1	2		0	0
•	org.w3c.dom	1	17		17	111
•	org.xml.sax	6	45		11	70
•	org.xml.sax.ext	0	0		2	11
•	org.xml.sax.helpers	10	159		0	0

New Classes in Existing Packages

Topics

java.awt
AttributeValue, AWTKeyStroke, BufferCapabilities, BufferCapabilities.FlipContents, Component$_2$.BltBufferStrategy, Component.FlipBufferStrategy, ContainerOrderFocusTraversalPolicy, DefaultFocusTraversalPolicy, DefaultKeyboardFocusManager, DisplayMode, FocusTraversalPolicy, HeadlessException, ImageCapabilities, KeyboardFocusManager, *KeyEventDispatcher*, *KeyEventPostProcessor*, ScrollPaneAdjustable

java.awt.datatransfer
FlavorTable

java.awt.dnd
DragSourceAdapter, *DragSourceMotionListener*, DropTargetAdapter

java.awt.event
AWTEventListenerProxy, MouseWheelEvent, *MouseWheelListener*, *WindowFocusListener*, *WindowStateListener*

java.awt.font
NumericShaper

java.awt.image
BufferStrategy, DataBufferDouble, DataBufferFloat, VolatileImage

java.beans
DefaultPersistenceDelegate, Encoder, EventHandler, *ExceptionListener*, Expression, PersistenceDelegate, PropertyChangeListenerProxy, Statement, VetoableChangeListenerProxy, XMLDecoder, XMLEncoder

java.lang
AssertionError, *CharSequence*, StackTraceElement

java.net
Inet4Address, Inet6Address, InetSocketAddress, NetworkInterface, PortUnreachableException, SocketAddress, SocketTimeoutException, URI, URISyntaxException

java.rmi.server
RMIClassLoaderSpi

java.security.cert
CertPath, CertPath.CertPathRep, CertPathBuilder, CertPathBuilderException, *CertPathBuilderResult*, CertPathBuilderSpi, *CertPathParameters*, CertPathValidator, CertPathValidatorException, *CertPathValidatorResult*, CertPathValidatorSpi, *CertSelector*, CertStore, CertStoreException, *CertStoreParameters*, CertStoreSpi, CollectionCertStoreParameters, *CRLSelector*, LDAPCertStoreParameters, PKIXBuilderParameters, PKIXCertPathBuilderResult, PKIXCertPathChecker, PKIXCertPathValidatorResult, PKIXParameters, *PolicyNode*, PolicyQualifierInfo, TrustAnchor, X509CertSelector, X509CRLSelector

java.security.interfaces
RSAMultiPrimePrivateCrtKey

java.security.spec
PSSParameterSpec, RSAMultiPrimePrivateCrtKeySpec, RSAOtherPrimeInfo

java.sql
ParameterMetaData, *Savepoint*

java.text
Bidi, DateFormat.Field, Format.Field, MessageFormat$_2$.Field, NumberFormat.Field

java.util
Currency, EventListenerProxy, IdentityHashMap, LinkedHashMap, LinkedHashSet, *RandomAccess*

javax.accessibility
AccessibleEditableText, *AccessibleExtendedComponent*, *AccessibleExtendedTable*, *AccessibleKeyBinding*

javax.naming.ldap
StartTlsRequest, StartTlsResponse

javax.swing
AbstractSpinnerModel, InternalFrameFocusTraversalPolicy, JFormattedTextField, JFormattedTextField.AbstractFormatter, JFormattedTextField.AbstractFormatterFactory, JSpinner, JSpinner.DateEditor, JSpinner.DefaultEditor, JSpinner.ListEditor, JSpinner.NumberEditor, LayoutFocusTraversalPolicy, Popup, PopupFactory, SortingFocusTraversalPolicy, SpinnerDateModel, SpinnerListModel, *SpinnerModel*, SpinnerNumberModel, Spring, SpringLayout, SpringLayout.Constraints, TransferHandler

javax.swing.plaf
SpinnerUI

javax.swing.plaf.basic
BasicBorders.RolloverButtonBorder, BasicFormattedTextFieldUI, BasicMenuUI$_2$.MouseInputHandler, BasicScrollPaneUI$_2$.MouseWheelHandler, BasicSpinnerUI

javax.swing.plaf.metal
MetalRootPaneUI

javax.swing.plaf.multi
MultiRootPaneUI, MultiSpinnerUI

javax.swing.text
DateFormatter, DefaultFormatter, DefaultFormatterFactory, DocumentFilter, DocumentFilter.FilterBypass, InternationalFormatter, MaskFormatter, NavigationFilter, NavigationFilter$_2$.FilterBypass, NumberFormatter

javax.swing.text.html
ImageView

org.omg.CORBA
LocalObject, ParameterMode, ParameterModeHelper, ParameterModeHolder, PolicyErrorCodeHelper, PolicyErrorHelper, PolicyErrorHolder, StringSeqHelper, StringSeqHolder, UnknownUserExceptionHelper, UnknownUserExceptionHolder, WrongTransactionHelper, WrongTransactionHolder, WStringSeqHelper, WStringSeqHolder

org.omg.CosNaming
_NamingContextExtStub, BindingIteratorPOA, *NamingContextExt*, NamingContextExtHelper, NamingContextExtHolder, *NamingContextExtOperations*, NamingContextExtPOA, NamingContextPOA

New Members in Existing Classes

If a new member overrides an existing member, it is included in this listing.

java.applet

AppletContext
getStream( ), getStreamKeys( ), setStream( )

java.awt

Adjustable
NO_ORIENTATION

AlphaComposite
Dst, DST, DST_ATOP, DstAtop, SRC_ATOP, SrcAtop, Xor, XOR

AWTEvent
MOUSE_WHEEL_EVENT_MASK, setSource( ), WINDOW_FOCUS_EVENT_MASK, WINDOW₂ _STATE_EVENT_MASK

AWTEventMulticaster
add( ), getListeners( ), mouseWheelMoved( ), remove( ), windowGainedFocus( ), windowLostFocus( ), windowStateChanged( )

BorderLayout
LINE_END, LINE_START, PAGE_END, PAGE₂ _START

Button
getActionListeners( )

Canvas
createBufferStrategy( ), getBufferStrategy( ), update( )

Checkbox
getItemListeners( )

CheckboxMenuItem
getItemListeners( )

Choice
getItemListeners( )

Color
BLACK, BLUE, CYAN, DARK_GRAY, GRAY, GREEN, LIGHT_GRAY, MAGENTA, ORANGE, PINK, RED, WHITE, YELLOW

Component
addMouseWheelListener( ), applyComponentOrientation( ), areFocusTraversalKeysSet( ), createVolatileImage( ), firePropertyChange( ), getComponentListeners( ), getFocusCycleRootAncestor( ), getFocusListeners( ), getFocusTraversalKeys( ), getFocusTraversalKeysEnabled( ), getHierarchyBoundsListeners( ), getHierarchyListeners( ), getIgnoreRepaint( ), getInputMethodListeners( ), getKeyListeners( ), getMouseListeners( ), getMouseMotionListeners( ), getMouseWheelListeners( ), getPropertyChangeListeners( ), isBackgroundSet( ), isCursorSet( ), isFocusable( ), isFocusCycleRoot( ), isFocusOwner( ), isFontSet( ), isForegroundSet( ), processMouseWheelEvent( ), removeMouseWheelListener( ), requestFocus( ), requestFocusInWindow( ), setFocusable( ), setFocusTraversalKeys( ), setFocusTraversalKeysEnabled( ), setIgnoreRepaint( ), transferFocusBackward( ), transferFocusUpCycle( )

Container
addPropertyChangeListener( ), applyComponentOrientation( ), areFocusTraversalKeysSet( ), getContainerListeners( ), getFocusTraversalKeys( ), getFocusTraversalPolicy( ), isFocusCycleRoot( ), isFocusTraversalPolicySet( ), setFocusCycleRoot( ), setFocusTraversalKeys( ), setFocusTraversalPolicy( ), transferFocusBackward( ), transferFocusDownCycle( )

Dialog
Dialog( ), isUndecorated( ), setUndecorated( )

EventQueue
getCurrentEvent( ), getMostRecentEventTime( )

Font
isTransformed( ), LAYOUT_LEFT_TO_RIGHT, LAYOUT_NO_LIMIT_CONTEXT, LAYOUT_NO₂ _START_CONTEXT, LAYOUT_RIGHT_TO_LEFT, layoutGlyphVector( )

Frame
getExtendedState( ), getMaximizedBounds( ), isUndecorated( ), MAXIMIZED_BOTH, MAXIMIZED₂ _HORIZ, MAXIMIZED_VERT, setExtendedState( ), setMaximizedBounds( ), setUndecorated( )

GraphicsConfiguration
createCompatibleVolatileImage( ), getBufferCapabilities( ), getImageCapabilities( )

GraphicsDevice
getAvailableAcceleratedMemory( ), getDisplayMode( ), getDisplayModes( ), getFullScreenWindow( ), isDisplayChangeSupported( ), isFullScreenSupported( ), setDisplayMode( ), setFullScreenWindow( )

GraphicsEnvironment
getCenterPoint( ), getMaximumWindowBounds( ), isHeadless( ), isHeadlessInstance( )

GridBagConstraints
FIRST_LINE_END, FIRST_LINE_START, LAST₂ _LINE_END, LAST_LINE_START, LINE_END, LINE_START, PAGE_END, PAGE_START

GridBagLayout
adjustForGravity( ), arrangeGrid( ), getLayoutInfo( ), getMinSize( )

List
getActionListeners( ), getItemListeners( )

MenuItem
getActionListeners( )

Polygon
invalidate( ), reset( )

Robot
mouseWheel( )

Scrollbar
getAdjustmentListeners( ), getValueIsAdjusting( ), setValueIsAdjusting( )

ScrollPane
eventTypeEnabled( ), isWheelScrollingEnabled( ), processMouseWheelEvent( ), setWheelScrollingEnabled( )

TextComponent
addNotify( ), enableInputMethods( ), getTextListeners( )

TextField
getActionListeners( )

Toolkit
getAWTEventListeners( ), getPropertyChangeListeners( ), getScreenInsets( ), getSystemSelection( ), isDynamicLayoutActive( ), isDynamicLayoutSet( ), isFrameStateSupported( ), setDynamicLayout( )

Window
addPropertyChangeListener( ), addWindowFocusListener( ), addWindowStateListener( ), createBufferStrategy( ), getBufferStrategy( ), getFocusableWindowState( ), getFocusCycleRootAncestor( ), getFocusTraversalKeys( ),

Topics

getMostRecentFocusOwner( ),
getWindowFocusListeners( ), getWindowListeners( ),
getWindowStateListeners( ), isActive( ),
isFocusableWindow( ), isFocusCycleRoot( ),
isFocused( ), processWindowFocusEvent( ),
processWindowStateEvent( ),
removeWindowFocusListener( ),
removeWindowStateListener( ),
setFocusableWindowState( ), setFocusCycleRoot( ),
setLocationRelativeTo( )

java.awt.color
 ColorSpace
 getMaxValue( ), getMinValue( )
 ICC_ColorSpace
 getMaxValue( ), getMinValue( )

java.awt.datatransfer
 DataFlavor
 imageFlavor, isFlavorTextType( ),
 isRepresentationClassByteBuffer( ),
 isRepresentationClassCharBuffer( ),
 isRepresentationClassReader( )
 SystemFlavorMap
 addFlavorForUnencodedNative( ),
 addUnencodedNativeForFlavor( ),
 getFlavorsForNative( ), getNativesForFlavor( ),
 setFlavorsForNative( ), setNativesForFlavor( )

java.awt.dnd
 DragGestureEvent
 startDrag( )
 DragSource
 addDragSourceListener( ),
 addDragSourceMotionListener( ),
 getDragSourceListeners( ),
 getDragSourceMotionListeners( ),
 getListeners( ), removeDragSourceListener( ),
 removeDragSourceMotionListener( )
 DragSourceContext
 dragMouseMoved( )
 DragSourceDragEvent
 DragSourceDragEvent( ), getGestureModifiersEx( )
 DragSourceDropEvent
 DragSourceDropEvent( )
 DragSourceEvent
 DragSourceEvent( ), getLocation( ), getX( ), getY( )

java.awt.event
 ActionEvent
 ActionEvent( ), getWhen( )
 AdjustmentEvent
 AdjustmentEvent( ), getValueIsAdjusting( )
 FocusEvent
 FocusEvent( ), getOppositeComponent( )
 InputEvent
 ALT_DOWN_MASK, ALT_GRAPH_DOWN_MASK,
 BUTTON1_DOWN_MASK, BUTTON2_DOWN_
 _MASK, BUTTON3_DOWN_MASK, CTRL_DOWN_
 _MASK, getModifiersEx( ), getModifiersExText( ),
 META_DOWN_MASK, SHIFT_DOWN_MASK
 InputMethodEvent
 getWhen( ), InputMethodEvent( )
 InvocationEvent
 getWhen( )
 KeyEvent
 getKeyLocation( ), KEY_LOCATION_LEFT, KEY_
 _LOCATION_NUMPAD, KEY_LOCATION_RIGHT,
 KEY_LOCATION_STANDARD, KEY_LOCATION_
 _UNKNOWN, KeyEvent( ), VK_SEPARATOR

 MouseEvent
 BUTTON1, BUTTON2, BUTTON3, getButton( ),
 getMouseModifiersText( ), MOUSE_WHEEL,
 MouseEvent( ), NOBUTTON
 WindowAdapter
 windowGainedFocus( ), windowLostFocus( ),
 windowStateChanged( )
 WindowEvent
 getNewState( ), getOldState( ),
 getOppositeWindow( ), WINDOW_GAINED_FOCUS,
 WINDOW_LOST_FOCUS, WINDOW_STATE_
 _CHANGED, WindowEvent( )

java.awt.font
 FontRenderContext
 equals( ), hashCode( )
 GlyphMetrics
 getAdvanceX( ), getAdvanceY( ), GlyphMetrics( )
 GlyphVector
 FLAG_COMPLEX_GLYPHS, FLAG_HAS_
 _POSITION_ADJUSTMENTS, FLAG_HAS_
 _TRANSFORMS, FLAG_MASK, FLAG_RUN_RTL,
 getGlyphCharIndex( ), getGlyphCharIndices( ),
 getGlyphOutline( ), getGlyphPixelBounds( ),
 getLayoutFlags( ), getPixelBounds( )
 TextAttribute
 NUMERIC_SHAPING
 TextMeasurer
 clone( )
 TransformAttribute
 isIdentity( )

java.awt.im.spi
 InputMethodContext
 createInputMethodJFrame( )

java.awt.image
 BandedSampleModel
 hashCode( )
 ColorModel
 getDataElement( ), getDataElements( ),
 getNormalizedComponents( )
 ComponentColorModel
 ComponentColorModel( ), getDataElement( ),
 getDataElements( ), getNormalizedComponents( ),
 getUnnormalizedComponents( )
 ComponentSampleModel
 equals( ), hashCode( )
 MultiPixelPackedSampleModel
 equals( ), hashCode( )
 PixelInterleavedSampleModel
 hashCode( )
 SinglePixelPackedSampleModel
 equals( ), hashCode( )

java.awt.peer
 ComponentPeer
 canDetermineObscurity( ), createBuffers( ),
 createVolatileImage( ), destroyBuffers( ), flip( ),
 getBackBuffer( ), handlesWheelScrolling( ),
 isFocusable( ), isObscured( ), requestFocus( ),
 updateCursorImmediately( )
 ContainerPeer
 beginLayout( ), endLayout( ), isPaintPending( )
 FramePeer
 setMaximizedBounds( )
 RobotPeer
 mouseWheel( )

java.awt.print
    PrinterIOException
        getCause( )
    PrinterJob
        getPrintService( ), lookupPrintServices( ),
        lookupStreamPrintServices( ), pageDialog( ),
        print( ), printDialog( ), setPrintService( )

java.beans
    EventSetDescriptor
        EventSetDescriptor( ), getGetListenerMethod( )
    IndexedPropertyDescriptor
        equals( )
    PropertyChangeSupport
        getPropertyChangeListeners( )
    PropertyDescriptor
        equals( )
    VetoableChangeSupport
        getVetoableChangeListeners( )

java.io
    File
        File( ), toURI( )
    FileInputStream
        getChannel( )
    FileOutputStream
        FileOutputStream( ), getChannel( )
    FileWriter
        FileWriter( )
    InputStreamReader
        InputStreamReader( )
    ObjectInputStream
        readUnshared( )
    ObjectOutputStream
        writeUnshared( )
    ObjectStreamField
        isUnshared( ), ObjectStreamField( )
    OutputStreamWriter
        OutputStreamWriter( )
    PrintStream
        PrintStream( )
    RandomAccessFile
        getChannel( )
    WriteAbortedException
        getCause( )

java.lang
    Boolean
        toString( ), valueOf( )
    Character
        DIRECTIONALITY_ARABIC_NUMBER,
        DIRECTIONALITY_BOUNDARY_NEUTRAL,
        DIRECTIONALITY_COMMON_NUMBER$_2$
        _SEPARATOR, DIRECTIONALITY_EUROPEAN$_2$
        _NUMBER, DIRECTIONALITY_EUROPEAN$_2$
        _NUMBER_SEPARATOR, DIRECTIONALITY$_2$
        _EUROPEAN_NUMBER_TERMINATOR,
        DIRECTIONALITY_LEFT_TO_RIGHT,
        DIRECTIONALITY_LEFT_TO_RIGHT_EMBEDDING,
        DIRECTIONALITY_LEFT_TO_RIGHT_OVERRIDE,
        DIRECTIONALITY_NONSPACING_MARK,
        DIRECTIONALITY_OTHER_NEUTRALS,
        DIRECTIONALITY_PARAGRAPH_SEPARATOR,
        DIRECTIONALITY_POP_DIRECTIONAL$_2$
        _FORMAT, DIRECTIONALITY_RIGHT_TO$_2$
        _LEFT, DIRECTIONALITY_RIGHT_TO_LEFT$_2$
        _ARABIC, DIRECTIONALITY_RIGHT_TO_LEFT$_2$
        _EMBEDDING, DIRECTIONALITY_RIGHT_TO$_2$
        _LEFT_OVERRIDE, DIRECTIONALITY_SEGMENT$_2$
        _SEPARATOR, DIRECTIONALITY_UNDEFINED,
        DIRECTIONALITY_WHITESPACE, FINAL$_2$
        _QUOTE_PUNCTUATION, getDirectionality( ),
        INITIAL_QUOTE_PUNCTUATION, isMirrored( ),
        toString( )
    Character.UnicodeBlock
        BOPOMOFO_EXTENDED, BRAILLE_PATTERNS,
        CHEROKEE, CJK_RADICALS_SUPPLEMENT,
        CJK_UNIFIED_IDEOGRAPHS_EXTENSION_A,
        ETHIOPIC, IDEOGRAPHIC_DESCRIPTION$_2$
        _CHARACTERS, KANGXI_RADICALS, KHMER,
        MONGOLIAN, MYANMAR, OGHAM, RUNIC,
        SINHALA, SYRIAC, THAANA, UNIFIED$_2$
        _CANADIAN_ABORIGINAL_SYLLABICS, YI$_2$
        _RADICALS, YI_SYLLABLES
    Class
        desiredAssertionStatus( )
    ClassLoader
        clearAssertionStatus( ), setClassAssertionStatus( ),
        setDefaultAssertionStatus( ),
        setPackageAssertionStatus( )
    ClassNotFoundException
        getCause( )
    Double
        compare( )
    Error
        Error( )
    Exception
        Exception( )
    ExceptionInInitializerError
        getCause( )
    Float
        compare( )
    Runtime
        availableProcessors( ), maxMemory( )
    RuntimeException
        RuntimeException( )
    String
        contentEquals( ), matches( ), replaceAll( ),
        replaceFirst( ), split( ), subSequence( )
    StringBuffer
        append( ), indexOf( ), lastIndexOf( ), subSequence( )
    Thread
        holdsLock( ), Thread( )
    Throwable
        getCause( ), getStackTrace( ), initCause( ),
        setStackTrace( ), Throwable( )

java.lang.reflect
    InvocationTargetException
        getCause( )
    UndeclaredThrowableException
        getCause( )

java.math
    BigInteger
        probablePrime( )

java.net
    Authenticator
        getRequestingHost( ),
        requestPasswordAuthentication( )
    DatagramPacket
        DatagramPacket( ), getSocketAddress( ),
        setSocketAddress( )
    DatagramSocket
        bind( ), connect( ), DatagramSocket( ),
        getBroadcast( ), getChannel( ),
        getLocalSocketAddress( ),

Topics

getRemoteSocketAddress( ), getReuseAddress( ),
getTrafficClass( ), isBound( ), isClosed( ),
isConnected( ), setBroadcast( ), setReuseAddress( ),
setTrafficClass( )

DatagramSocketImpl
connect( ), disconnect( ), joinGroup( ), leaveGroup( ),
peekData( )

InetAddress
getByAddress( ), getCanonicalHostName( ),
isAnyLocalAddress( ), isLinkLocalAddress( ),
isLoopbackAddress( ), isMCGlobal( ),
isMCLinkLocal( ), isMCNodeLocal( ),
isMCOrgLocal( ), isMCSiteLocal( ),
isSiteLocalAddress( )

MulticastSocket
getLoopbackMode( ), getNetworkInterface( ),
joinGroup( ), leaveGroup( ), MulticastSocket( ),
setLoopbackMode( ), setNetworkInterface( )

ServerSocket
bind( ), getChannel( ), getLocalSocketAddress( ),
getReceiveBufferSize( ), getReuseAddress( ),
isBound( ), isClosed( ), ServerSocket( ),
setReceiveBufferSize( ), setReuseAddress( )

Socket
bind( ), connect( ), getChannel( ),
getLocalSocketAddress( ), getOOBInline( ),
getRemoteSocketAddress( ), getReuseAddress( ),
getTrafficClass( ), isBound( ), isClosed( ),
isConnected( ), isInputShutdown( ),
isOutputShutdown( ), sendUrgentData( ),
setOOBInline( ), setReuseAddress( ),
setTrafficClass( )

SocketImpl
connect( ), sendUrgentData( ), supportsUrgentData( )

SocketOptions
IP_MULTICAST_IF2, IP_MULTICAST_LOOP,
IP_TOS, SO_BROADCAST, SO_OOBINLINE

URL
getDefaultPort( )

URLConnection
addRequestProperty( ), getHeaderFields( ),
getRequestProperties( )

URLDecoder
decode( )

URLEncoder
encode( )

java.rmi
RemoteException
getCause( )

java.rmi.activation
ActivationException
getCause( )

java.rmi.server
RMIClassLoader
getDefaultProviderInstance( ), loadClass( ),
loadProxyClass( )

ServerCloneException
getCause( )

java.security
AlgorithmParameterGenerator
getInstance( )

AlgorithmParameters
getInstance( )

KeyFactory
getInstance( )

KeyPairGenerator
getInstance( )

KeyStore
getInstance( )

MessageDigest
getInstance( )

Policy
getPermissions( ), implies( )

PrivilegedActionException
getCause( )

ProtectionDomain
getClassLoader( ), getPrincipals( ),
ProtectionDomain( )

SecureRandom
getInstance( )

Security
getAlgorithms( )

Signature
getInstance( ), getParameters( ), verify( )

SignatureSpi
engineGetParameters( ), engineVerify( )

java.security.cert
CertificateFactory
generateCertPath( ), getCertPathEncodings( ),
getInstance( )

CertificateFactorySpi
engineGenerateCertPath( ),
engineGetCertPathEncodings( )

X509Certificate
getExtendedKeyUsage( ),
getIssuerAlternativeNames( ),
getIssuerX500Principal( ),
getSubjectAlternativeNames( ),
getSubjectX500Principal( )

X509CRL
getIssuerX500Principal( )

java.sql
Blob
setBinaryStream( ), setBytes( ), truncate( )

CallableStatement
getArray( ), getBigDecimal( ), getBlob( ),
getBoolean( ), getByte( ), getBytes( ), getClob( ),
getDate( ), getDouble( ), getFloat( ), getInt( ),
getLong( ), getObject( ), getRef( ), getShort( ),
getString( ), getTime( ), getTimestamp( ), getURL( ),
registerOutParameter( ), setAsciiStream( ),
setBigDecimal( ), setBinaryStream( ), setBoolean( ),
setByte( ), setBytes( ), setCharacterStream( ),
setDate( ), setDouble( ), setFloat( ), setInt( ),
setLong( ), setNull( ), setObject( ), setShort( ),
setString( ), setTime( ), setTimestamp( ), setURL( )

Clob
setAsciiStream( ), setCharacterStream( ), setString( ),
truncate( )

Connection
createStatement( ), getHoldability( ), prepareCall( ),
prepareStatement( ), releaseSavepoint( ), rollback( ),
setHoldability( ), setSavepoint( )

DatabaseMetaData
attributeNoNulls, attributeNullable,
attributeNullableUnknown, getAttributes( ),
getDatabaseMajorVersion( ),
getDatabaseMinorVersion( ),
getJDBCMajorVersion( ), getJDBCMinorVersion( ),
getResultSetHoldability( ), getSQLStateType( ),
getSuperTables( ), getSuperTypes( ),

locatorsUpdateCopy( ), sqlStateSQL99,
sqlStateXOpen, supportsGetGeneratedKeys( ),
supportsMultipleOpenResults( ),
supportsNamedParameters( ),
supportsResultSetHoldability( ),
supportsSavepoints( ), supportsStatementPooling( )

PreparedStatement
getParameterMetaData( ), setURL( )

Ref
getObject( ), setObject( )

ResultSet
CLOSE_CURSORS_AT_COMMIT, getURL( ),
HOLD_CURSORS_OVER_COMMIT, updateArray( ),
updateBlob( ), updateClob( ), updateRef( )

SQLInput
readURL( )

SQLOutput
writeURL( )

Statement
CLOSE_ALL_RESULTS, CLOSE_CURRENT₂
_RESULT, execute( ), EXECUTE_FAILED,
executeUpdate( ), getGeneratedKeys( ),
getMoreResults( ), getResultSetHoldability( ), KEEP₂
_CURRENT_RESULT, NO_GENERATED_KEYS,
RETURN_GENERATED_KEYS, SUCCESS_NO₂
_INFO

Timestamp
compareTo( ), getTime( ), setTime( )

Types
BOOLEAN, DATALINK

java.text
DecimalFormat
formatToCharacterIterator( ), getCurrency( ),
setCurrency( )
DecimalFormatSymbols
getCurrency( ), setCurrency( )
FieldPosition
FieldPosition( ), getFieldAttribute( )
Format
formatToCharacterIterator( )
MessageFormat
formatToCharacterIterator( ),
getFormatsByArgumentIndex( ),
MessageFormat( ), setFormatByArgumentIndex( ),
setFormatsByArgumentIndex( )
NumberFormat
getCurrency( ), getIntegerInstance( ), setCurrency( )
SimpleDateFormat
formatToCharacterIterator( )

java.util
AbstractMap
clone( )
BitSet
cardinality( ), clear( ), flip( ), get( ), intersects( ),
isEmpty( ), nextClearBit( ), nextSetBit( ), set( )
Collections
indexOfSubList( ), lastIndexOfSubList( ), list( ),
replaceAll( ), rotate( ), swap( )
Locale
Locale( )
SimpleTimeZone
getOffset( ), SimpleTimeZone( ), STANDARD_TIME,
UTC_TIME, WALL_TIME
TimeZone
getDSTSavings( ), getOffset( )

WeakHashMap
containsValue( ), keySet( ), putAll( ), values( )
javax.accessibility
AccessibleContext
ACCESSIBLE_HYPERTEXT_OFFSET,
getAccessibleEditableText( )
AccessibleRole
DATE_EDITOR, FONT_CHOOSER, GROUP_BOX,
HYPERLINK, SPIN_BOX, STATUS_BAR
javax.swing
AbstractAction
getPropertyChangeListeners( )
AbstractButton
getActionListeners( ), getChangeListeners( ),
getDisplayedMnemonicIndex( ), getIconTextGap( ),
getItemListeners( ), getMultiClickThreshhold( ),
setDisplayedMnemonicIndex( ), setIconTextGap( ),
setMultiClickThreshhold( )
AbstractButton.AccessibleAbstractButton
getAccessibleKeyBinding( ), getTitledBorderText( ),
getToolTipText( )
AbstractCellEditor
getCellEditorListeners( )
AbstractListModel
getListDataListeners( )
BoxLayout
LINE_AXIS, PAGE_AXIS
DefaultBoundedRangeModel
getChangeListeners( )
DefaultButtonModel
getActionListeners( ), getChangeListeners( ),
getItemListeners( )
DefaultListSelectionModel
getListSelectionListeners( )
DefaultSingleSelectionModel
getChangeListeners( )
JColorChooser
getDragEnabled( ), setDragEnabled( )
JComboBox
addPopupMenuListener( ),
firePopupMenuCanceled( ),
firePopupMenuWillBecomeInvisible( ),
firePopupMenuWillBecomeVisible( ),
getActionListeners( ), getItemListeners( ),
getPopupMenuListeners( ),
getPrototypeDisplayValue( ),
removePopupMenuListener( ),
setPrototypeDisplayValue( )
JComponent
getAncestorListeners( ), getDefaultLocale( ),
getPropertyChangeListeners( ), getTransferHandler( ),
getVetoableChangeListeners( ), requestFocus( ),
requestFocusInWindow( ), setDefaultLocale( ),
setTransferHandler( )
JComponent.AccessibleJComponent
getAccessibleKeyBinding( ), getTitledBorderText( ),
getToolTipText( )
JDialog
isDefaultLookAndFeelDecorated( ), JDialog( ),
setDefaultLookAndFeelDecorated( )
JEditorPane
getHyperlinkListeners( )
JEditorPane.AccessibleJEditorPaneHTML
getAccessibleAt( ), getAccessibleChild( ),
getAccessibleChildrenCount( )

Topics

865

JFileChooser
createDialog( ), getActionListeners( ),
getDragEnabled( ), setDragEnabled( )
JFrame
isDefaultLookAndFeelDecorated( ),
setDefaultLookAndFeelDecorated( )
JInternalFrame
getFocusCycleRootAncestor( ),
getInternalFrameListeners( ),
getMostRecentFocusOwner( ), isFocusCycleRoot( ),
setFocusCycleRoot( )
JLabel
getDisplayedMnemonicIndex( ),
setDisplayedMnemonicIndex( )
JLabel.AccessibleJLabel
getAccessibleKeyBinding( ), getTitledBorderText( ),
getToolTipText( )
JList
getDragEnabled( ), getLayoutOrientation( ),
getListSelectionListeners( ), getNextMatch( ),
getToolTipText( ), HORIZONTAL_WRAP,
setDragEnabled( ), setLayoutOrientation( ),
VERTICAL, VERTICAL_WRAP
JMenu
applyComponentOrientation( ),
configurePropertiesFromAction( ),
getMenuListeners( ), setComponentOrientation( )
JMenuItem
getMenuDragMouseListeners( ),
getMenuKeyListeners( )
JOptionPane
showInputDialog( )
JPanel
getUI( ), setUI( )
JPopupMenu
getPopupMenuListeners( ), processFocusEvent( ),
processKeyEvent( )
JProgressBar
getChangeListeners( ), isIndeterminate( ),
setIndeterminate( )
JRootPane
COLOR_CHOOSER_DIALOG, ERROR₂
_DIALOG, FILE_CHOOSER_DIALOG, FRAME,
getWindowDecorationStyle( ), INFORMATION₂
_DIALOG, NONE, PLAIN_DIALOG, QUESTION₂
_DIALOG, setWindowDecorationStyle( ), WARNING₂
_DIALOG
JScrollBar
getAdjustmentListeners( ), setUI( )
JScrollPane
isWheelScrollingEnabled( ),
setWheelScrollingEnabled( )
JSlider
getChangeListeners( )
JTabbedPane
getChangeListeners( ),
getDisplayedMnemonicIndexAt( ), getMnemonicAt( ),
getTabLayoutPolicy( ), indexAtLocation( ),
JTabbedPane( ), SCROLL_TAB_LAYOUT,
setDisplayedMnemonicIndexAt( ), setMnemonicAt( ),
setTabLayoutPolicy( ), WRAP_TAB_LAYOUT
JTable
getDragEnabled( ),
getSurrendersFocusOnKeystroke( ),
setDragEnabled( ),
setSurrendersFocusOnKeystroke( )

JTable.AccessibleJTable
getAccessibleColumn( ), getAccessibleIndex( ),
getAccessibleRow( )
JTextField
getActionListeners( ), setDocument( )
JToolBar
isRollover( ), setLayout( ), setRollover( )
JTree
getDragEnabled( ), getNextMatch( ),
getTreeExpansionListeners( ),
getTreeSelectionListeners( ),
getTreeWillExpandListeners( ), setDragEnabled( )
JViewport
getChangeListeners( )
JWindow
update( )
LookAndFeel
getDesktopPropertyValue( ),
getSupportsWindowDecorations( ),
provideErrorFeedback( )
MenuSelectionManager
getChangeListeners( )
RepaintManager
getVolatileOffscreenBuffer( )
SizeRequirements
calculateAlignedPositions( ), calculateTiledPositions( )
SwingConstants
NEXT, PREVIOUS
SwingUtilities
calculateInnerArea( ), processKeyBindings( )
Timer
getActionListeners( )
UIDefaults
addResourceBundle( ), get( ), getBoolean( ),
getBorder( ), getColor( ), getDefaultLocale( ),
getDimension( ), getFont( ), getIcon( ), getInsets( ),
getInt( ), getPropertyChangeListeners( ), getString( ),
removeResourceBundle( ), setDefaultLocale( )
UIManager
get( ), getBoolean( ), getBorder( ), getColor( ),
getDimension( ), getFont( ), getIcon( ), getInsets( ),
getInt( ), getPropertyChangeListeners( ), getString( )
WindowConstants
EXIT_ON_CLOSE
javax.swing.border
SoftBevelBorder
getBorderInsets( )
javax.swing.colorchooser
AbstractColorChooserPanel
getDisplayedMnemonicIndex( ), getMnemonic( )
DefaultColorSelectionModel
getChangeListeners( )
javax.swing.event
HyperlinkEvent
getSourceElement( ), HyperlinkEvent( )
ListDataEvent
toString( )
SwingPropertyChangeSupport
getPropertyChangeListeners( )
javax.swing.filechooser
FileSystemView
createFileSystemRoot( ), getChild( ),
getDefaultDirectory( ), getSystemDisplayName( ),
getSystemIcon( ), getSystemTypeDescription( ),
isComputerNode( ), isDrive( ), isFileSystem( ),

isFileSystemRoot( ), isFloppyDrive( ), isParent( ),
isTraversable( )
javax.swing.plaf
PopupMenuUI
getPopup( )
TextUI
getToolTipText( )
javax.swing.plaf.basic
BasicArrowButton
BasicArrowButton( )
BasicBorders.ButtonBorder
getBorderInsets( )
BasicBorders.FieldBorder
getBorderInsets( )
BasicBorders.MarginBorder
getBorderInsets( )
BasicBorders.MenuBarBorder
getBorderInsets( )
BasicBorders.RadioButtonBorder
getBorderInsets( )
BasicBorders.ToggleButtonBorder
getBorderInsets( )
BasicButtonUI
paintText( )
BasicComboPopup
firePopupMenuCanceled( ),
firePopupMenuWillBecomeInvisible( ),
firePopupMenuWillBecomeVisible( )
BasicDirectoryModel
renameFile( )
BasicFileChooserUI
directoryOpenButtonMnemonic,
directoryOpenButtonText,
directoryOpenButtonToolTipText, getDirectory( ),
isDirectorySelected( ), setDirectory( ),
setDirectorySelected( )
BasicFileChooserUI.DoubleClickListener
mouseEntered( )
BasicGraphicsUtils
drawStringUnderlineCharAt( )
BasicInternalFrameTitlePane
getTitle( ), paintTitleBackground( )
BasicLookAndFeel
createAudioAction( ), getAudioActionMap( ),
playSound( )
BasicMenuItemUI
doClick( ), paintBackground( ), paintText( )
BasicProgressBarUI
getAnimationIndex( ), getBox( ),
incrementAnimationIndex( ), paintDeterminate( ),
paintIndeterminate( ), setAnimationIndex( ),
startAnimationTimer( ), stopAnimationTimer( )
BasicScrollPaneUI
createMouseWheelListener( )
BasicSplitPaneUI.FocusHandler
focusGained( )
BasicTabbedPaneUI
calcRect, getNextTabIndexInRun( ),
getNextTabRun( ), getPreviousTabIndexInRun( ),
getPreviousTabRun( ), getTabBounds( ),
getTextViewForTab( ), installComponents( ),
paintTabArea( ), selectNextTabInRun( ),
selectPreviousTabInRun( ), uninstallComponents( )
BasicTextFieldUI
installUI( )

BasicTextPaneUI
installUI( )
BasicTextUI
getToolTipText( )
BasicToggleButtonUI
getTextShiftOffset( )
BasicToolBarUI
constraintBeforeFloating, createFloatingWindow( ),
createNonRolloverBorder( ), createRolloverBorder( ),
installNonRolloverBorders( ), installNormalBorders( ),
installRolloverBorders( ), isRolloverBorders( ),
setBorderToNonRollover( ), setBorderToNormal( ),
setBorderToRollover( ), setRolloverBorders( )
BasicTreeUI.KeyHandler
keyTyped( )
BasicTreeUI.MouseHandler
mouseDragged( ), mouseMoved( ),
mouseReleased( )
DefaultMenuLayout
preferredLayoutSize( )
javax.swing.plaf.metal
MetalBorders.ButtonBorder
getBorderInsets( )
MetalBorders.Flush3DBorder
getBorderInsets( )
MetalBorders.InternalFrameBorder
getBorderInsets( )
MetalBorders.MenuBarBorder
getBorderInsets( )
MetalBorders.MenuItemBorder
getBorderInsets( )
MetalBorders.OptionDialogBorder
getBorderInsets( )
MetalBorders.PaletteBorder
getBorderInsets( )
MetalBorders.PopupMenuBorder
getBorderInsets( )
MetalBorders.ToolBarBorder
getBorderInsets( )
MetalDesktopIconUI
getMaximumSize( ), getMinimumSize( ),
installListeners( ), uninstallListeners( )
MetalFileChooserUI
createDetailsView( ), createListSelectionListener( ),
setDirectorySelected( )
MetalFileChooserUI.DirectoryComboBoxModel
getDepth( )
MetalInternalFrameTitlePane
addNotify( ), uninstallDefaults( )
MetalInternalFrameUI
installListeners( ), uninstallComponents( ),
uninstallListeners( )
MetalLookAndFeel
getSupportsWindowDecorations( ),
provideErrorFeedback( )
MetalProgressBarUI
paintDeterminate( ), paintIndeterminate( )
MetalToolBarUI
createNonRolloverBorder( ), createRolloverBorder( )
MetalToolTipUI
isAcceleratorHidden( ), uninstallUI( )
javax.swing.plaf.multi
MultiPopupMenuUI
getPopup( ), isPopupTrigger( )
MultiTextUI
getToolTipText( )

Topics

javax.swing.table
AbstractTableModel
getTableModelListeners( )
DefaultTableCellRenderer
isOpaque( )
DefaultTableColumnModel
getColumnModelListeners( )
TableColumn
getPropertyChangeListeners( )
javax.swing.text
AbstractDocument
getDocumentFilter( ), getDocumentListeners( ),
getUndoableEditListeners( ), replace( ),
setDocumentFilter( )
AsyncBoxView
getEstimatedMajorSpan( ), getInsetSpan( ),
getNextVisualPositionFrom( ),
setEstimatedMajorSpan( )
BoxView
isLayoutValid( )
DefaultCaret
getChangeListeners( )
JTextComponent
getCaretListeners( ), getDragEnabled( ),
getNavigationFilter( ), getToolTipText( ),
setComponentOrientation( ), setDragEnabled( ),
setNavigationFilter( )
JTextComponent.AccessibleJTextComponent
cut( ), delete( ), doAccessibleAction( ),
getAccessibleAction( ), getAccessibleActionCount( ),
getAccessibleActionDescription( ),
getAccessibleEditableText( ), getTextRange( ),
insertTextAtIndex( ), paste( ), replaceText( ),
selectText( ), setAttributes( ), setTextContents( )
PasswordView
getPreferredSpan( )
PlainDocument
insertString( )
PlainView
damageLineRange( ), lineToRect( ), setSize( ),
updateDamage( ), updateMetrics( )
Segment
isPartialReturn( ), setPartialReturn( )
StyleContext
getChangeListeners( )
StyleContext.NamedStyle
getChangeListeners( )
View
getToolTipText( ), getViewIndex( )
javax.swing.text.html
BlockView
getMaximumSpan( ), getMinimumSpan( ),
getPreferredSpan( )
FormView
getMaximumSpan( )
HTMLEditorKit
getAccessibleContext( )
javax.swing.tree
DefaultTreeCellEditor
getCellEditorListeners( )
DefaultTreeCellEditor.DefaultTextField
setBorder( )
DefaultTreeCellRenderer
getFont( )
DefaultTreeModel
getTreeModelListeners( )

DefaultTreeSelectionModel
getPropertyChangeListeners( ),
getTreeSelectionListeners( )
javax.swing.undo
UndoableEditSupport
getUndoableEditListeners( )
org.omg.CORBA
Any
extract_Streamable( )
DefinitionKind
_dk_AbstractInterface, dk_AbstractInterface
DynamicImplementation
_ids( )
ServiceDetailHelper
ServiceDetailHelper( )
ServiceInformationHelper
ServiceInformationHelper( )
org.omg.CosNaming
_BindingIteratorStub
_BindingIteratorStub( )
_NamingContextStub
_NamingContextStub( )
BindingHelper
BindingHelper( )
BindingIteratorHelper
BindingIteratorHelper( )
BindingListHelper
BindingListHelper( )
BindingType
BindingType( )
BindingTypeHelper
BindingTypeHelper( )
IstringHelper
IstringHelper( )
NameComponentHelper
NameComponentHelper( )
NameHelper
NameHelper( )
NamingContextHelper
NamingContextHelper( )
org.omg.CosNaming.NamingContextPackage
AlreadyBound
AlreadyBound( )
AlreadyBoundHelper
AlreadyBoundHelper( )
CannotProceed
CannotProceed( )
CannotProceedHelper
CannotProceedHelper( )
InvalidName
InvalidName( )
InvalidNameHelper
InvalidNameHelper( )
NotEmpty
NotEmpty( )
NotEmptyHelper
NotEmptyHelper( )
NotFound
NotFound( )
NotFoundHelper
NotFoundHelper( )
NotFoundReason
NotFoundReason( )
NotFoundReasonHelper
NotFoundReasonHelper( )

Removed Members

java.awt
AWTEvent
finalize( )
java.awt.event
KeyEvent
setSource( )
java.awt.geom
CubicCurve2D
getBounds2D( )
Line2D
getBounds2D( )
QuadCurve2D
getBounds2D( )
RectangularShape
contains( ), getBounds2D( ), getPathIterator( ),
intersects( )
java.awt.peer
ComponentPeer
isFocusTraversable( ), requestFocus( ), setCursor( )
WindowPeer
CONSUME_EVENT, FOCUS_NEXT, FOCUS₂
_PREVIOUS, handleFocusTraversalEvent( ),
IGNORE_EVENT
java.lang
ClassNotFoundException
printStackTrace( )
ExceptionInInitializerError
printStackTrace( )
InheritableThreadLocal
get( ), set( )
java.lang.reflect
InvocationTargetException
printStackTrace( )
UndeclaredThrowableException
printStackTrace( )
java.net
DatagramSocketImpl
getOption( ), setOption( )
SocketImpl
getOption( ), setOption( )
java.rmi
RemoteException
printStackTrace( )
java.rmi.activation
ActivationException
printStackTrace( )
ActivationGroup
newInstance( )
java.rmi.server
ServerCloneException
printStackTrace( )
java.security
PrivilegedActionException
printStackTrace( )
java.security.cert
X509Certificate
getCriticalExtensionOIDs( ), getExtensionValue( ),
getNonCriticalExtensionOIDs( ),
hasUnsupportedCriticalExtension( )

X509CRL
getCriticalExtensionOIDs( ), getExtensionValue( ),
getNonCriticalExtensionOIDs( ),
hasUnsupportedCriticalExtension( )
X509CRLEntry
getCriticalExtensionOIDs( ), getExtensionValue( ),
getNonCriticalExtensionOIDs( ),
hasUnsupportedCriticalExtension( )
java.util.zip
GZIPOutputStream
close( )
javax.swing
AbstractAction
actionPerformed( )
AbstractButton
isFocusTraversable( )
AbstractCellEditor
getCellEditorValue( )
AbstractListModel
getElementAt( ), getSize( )
DefaultFocusManager
focusNextComponent( ), focusPreviousComponent( ),
processKeyEvent( )
FocusManager
focusNextComponent( ), focusPreviousComponent( ),
processKeyEvent( )
JApplet
processKeyEvent( )
JCheckBoxMenuItem
requestFocus( )
JComboBox
isFocusTraversable( )
JComponent
hasFocus( ), hide( ), isFocusCycleRoot( ),
isFocusTraversable( ), processFocusEvent( )
JDialog
processKeyEvent( ), setLocationRelativeTo( )
JEditorPane
isFocusCycleRoot( ), isManagingFocus( ),
processComponentKeyEvent( ), processKeyEvent( )
JFrame
processKeyEvent( )
JMenuBar
isManagingFocus( )
JRadioButtonMenuItem
requestFocus( )
JRootPane
isFocusCycleRoot( )
JScrollBar
isFocusTraversable( )
JSeparator
isFocusTraversable( )
JTable
isFocusTraversable( ), isManagingFocus( )
JTextArea
isManagingFocus( ), processKeyEvent( )
KeyStroke
equals( ), getKeyChar( ), getKeyCode( ),
getModifiers( ), hashCode( ), isOnKeyRelease( ),
toString( )

Topics

869

javax.swing.plaf.basic
　BasicCheckBoxMenuItemUI
　　installDefaults( )
　BasicEditorPaneUI
　　installKeyboardActions( )
　BasicFileChooserUI.BasicFileView
　　isTraversable( )
　BasicInternalFrameTitlePane
　　addNotify( ), removeNotify( )
　BasicRadioButtonMenuItemUI
　　installDefaults( )
　BasicTextFieldUI
　　createCaret( )
　BasicTextPaneUI
　　getEditorKit( )
　BasicToggleButtonUI
　　paintButtonPressed( ), paintFocus( ), paintText( )
javax.swing.plaf.metal
　MetalComboBoxUI
　　configureArrowButton( ), installListeners( ),
　　installUI( ), isFocusTraversable( ),
　　selectNextPossibleValue( ),
　　selectPreviousPossibleValue( ),
　　unconfigureArrowButton( ), uninstallListeners( ),
　　uninstallUI( )
　MetalProgressBarUI
　　paint( )
　MetalTextFieldUI
　　installUI( )
　MetalToolBarUI
　　installNonRolloverBorders( ), installNormalBorders( ),
　　installRolloverBorders( ), isRolloverBorders( ),
　　setBorderToNormal( ), setBorderToRollover( ),
　　setRolloverBorders( )
　MetalToolBarUI.MetalContainerListener
　　componentAdded( ), componentRemoved( )
　MetalToolBarUI.MetalRolloverListener
　　propertyChange( )

javax.swing.table
　AbstractTableModel
　　getColumnCount( ), getRowCount( ), getValueAt( )
javax.swing.text
　ComponentView
　　setSize( )
　IconView
　　setSize( )
　JTextComponent
　　isFocusTraversable( )
　LayeredHighlighter
　　addHighlight( ), changeHighlight( ),
　　deinstall( ), getHighlights( ), install( ), paint( ),
　　removeAllHighlights( ), removeHighlight( )
　LayeredHighlighter.LayerPainter
　　paint( )
javax.swing.text.html
　HTMLFrameHyperlinkEvent
　　getSourceElement( )
javax.swing.text.rtf
　RTFEditorKit
　　clone( )
org.omg.CORBA
　CompletionStatus
　　CompletionStatus( )
org.omg.CosNaming
　_BindingIteratorImplBase
　　destroy( ), next_n( ), next_one( )
　_BindingIteratorStub
　　_BindingIteratorStub( )
　_NamingContextImplBase
　　bind( ), bind_context( ), bind_new_context( ),
　　destroy( ), list( ), new_context( ), rebind( ), rebind₂
　　_context( ), resolve( ), unbind( )
　_NamingContextStub
　　_NamingContextStub( )

Modified Classes and Members

These tables show all the classes and members whose signatures were modified from the previous version. "+" indicates an added keyword; "−" indicates a removed keyword.

Class Modifier Changes

java.net
　InetAddress — − final
org.omg.CORBA
　AnySeqHelper, BooleanSeqHelper, CharSeqHelper, — − final, + abstract
　　DoubleSeqHelper, FloatSeqHelper, LongLongSeqHelper,
　　LongSeqHelper, OctetSeqHelper, ShortSeqHelper,
　　ULongLongSeqHelper, ULongSeqHelper,
　　UShortSeqHelper, WCharSeqHelper
　CompletionStatus, INV_POLICY, WrongTransaction — + final
　DynamicImplementation, Principal — − abstract
　ServiceDetailHelper, ServiceInformationHelper — + abstract
　StringValueHelper, WStringValueHelper — − final
org.omg.CORBA.ORBPackage
　InvalidName — + final

Class Modifier Changes

org.omg.CosNaming

BindingHelper, BindingIteratorHelper, BindingListHelper, BindingTypeHelper, IstringHelper, NameComponentHelper, NameHelper, NamingContextHelper	+ abstract
BindingType	- final

org.omg.CosNaming.NamingContextPackage

AlreadyBoundHelper, CannotProceedHelper, InvalidNameHelper, NotEmptyHelper, NotFoundHelper, NotFoundReasonHelper	+ abstract
NotFoundReason	- final

Extends Changes

javax.swing

Box	- java.awt.Container, + javax.swing.JComponent
Box.Filler	- java.awt.Component, + javax.swing.JComponent
FocusManager	- java.lang.Object, + java.awt.DefaultKeyboardFocusManager
KeyStroke	- java.lang.Object, + java.awt.AWTKeyStroke

javax.swing.plaf.metal

MetalToolBarUI.MetalContainerListener	- java.lang.Object, + javax.swing.plaf.basic ⤸ .BasicToolBarUI.ToolBarContListener
MetalToolBarUI.MetalRolloverListener	- java.lang.Object, + javax.swing.plaf.basic ⤸ .BasicToolBarUI.PropertyListener

Implements Changes

java.awt

AWTEventMulticaster	+ java.awt.event.MouseWheelListener, + java.awt.event.WindowFocusListener, + java.awt.event.WindowStateListener

java.awt.datatransfer

SystemFlavorMap	+ java.awt.datatransfer.FlavorTable

java.awt.dnd

DragGestureRecognizer, DragSource, DropTargetContext	+ java.io.Serializable
DragSourceContext	+ java.awt.dnd.DragSourceMotionListener, + java.io.Serializable

java.awt.event

WindowAdapter	+ java.awt.event.WindowFocusListener, + java.awt.event.WindowStateListener

java.awt.font

TextMeasurer	+ java.lang.Cloneable

java.lang

String, StringBuffer	+ java.lang.CharSequence

java.util

ArrayList, Vector	+ java.util.RandomAccess

javax.swing

AbstractButton.AccessibleAbstractButton, JComponent.AccessibleJComponent, JLabel.AccessibleJLabel	+ javax.accessibility.AccessibleExtendedComponent
JTable.AccessibleJTable	- javax.accessibility.AccessibleTable, + javax.accessibility.AccessibleExtendedTable

javax.swing.plaf.basic

BasicTreeUI.MouseHandler	+ java.awt.event.MouseMotionListener

javax.swing.text

JTextComponent.AccessibleJTextComponent	+ javax.accessibility.AccessibleAction, + javax.accessibility.AccessibleEditableText

Topics

Java 1.4
Modified Classes and Members

Implements Changes

javax.swing.text.html
    HTMLEditorKit   + javax.accessibility.Accessible

Member Modifier Changes

java.awt
  Cursor
    finalize( )   - native
  Dialog
    setTitle( )   - synchronized
java.awt.dnd
  DragGestureRecognizer
    dragGestureListener   + transient
  DragSourceContext
    dragDropEnd( ), dragEnter( ), dragExit( ), dragOver( ),   - synchronized
      dropActionChanged( )
    setCursor( ), updateCurrentCursor( )   + synchronized
  DropTarget
    dropActionChanged( )   + synchronized
    getDefaultActions( ), isActive( ), setDefaultActions( )   - synchronized
  DropTargetContext
    addNotify( ), getTransferable( ), removeNotify( )   - synchronized
  DropTargetContext.TransferableProxy
    getTransferData( ), getTransferDataFlavors( ),   - synchronized
      isDataFlavorSupported( )
java.awt
  EventQueue
    getNextEvent( )   - synchronized
  Frame
    setTitle( )   - synchronized
java.io
  ByteArrayInputStream
    close( )   - synchronized
  ByteArrayOutputStream
    close( )   - native
  FileInputStream
    close( )   - native
  FileOutputStream
    close( )   - native
  ObjectInputStream
    registerValidation( )   - synchronized
java.lang.reflect
  Constructor
    newInstance( )   - native
  Field
    get( ), getBoolean( ), getByte( ), getChar( ), getDouble( ),   - native
      getFloat( ), getInt( ), getLong( ), getShort( ), set( ),
      setBoolean( ), setByte( ), setChar( ), setDouble( ),
      setFloat( ), setInt( ), setLong( ), setShort( )
  Method
    invoke( )   - native
java.lang
  StringBuffer
    capacity( ), length( ), substring( )   + synchronized
  Throwable
    fillInStackTrace( )   + synchronized
java.net
  Socket
    Socket( )   - protected, + public

Member Modifier Changes

   URLConnection
      guessContentTypeFromName( )   - protected, + public

java.sql
   DriverManager
      println( ), setLogWriter( )   - synchronized

java.util
   Calendar
      get( ), set( )   - final
      getInstance( )   - synchronized
      getTimeInMillis( ), setTimeInMillis( )   - protected, + public
   Hashtable
      isEmpty( ), size( )   + synchronized
   Vector
      capacity( ), isEmpty( ), lastIndexOf( ), size( ), subList( )   + synchronized

javax.rmi.CORBA
   Stub
      Stub( )   - protected, + public

javax.swing
   BoxLayout
      getLayoutAlignmentX( ), getLayoutAlignmentY( ),   + synchronized
         invalidateLayout( )

javax.swing.filechooser
   FileSystemView
      getRoots( ), isHiddenFile( ), isRoot( )   - abstract

javax.swing
   JEditorPane
      scrollToReference( )   - protected, + public

javax.swing.text
   AsyncBoxView
      flushRequirementChanges( )   - synchronized
   DefaultHighlighter
      DefaultPainter   + final
   PlainDocument
      PlainDocument( )   - protected, + public

org.omg.CORBA
   Any
      extract_Principal( ), insert_Principal( ), insert_Streamable( )   - abstract
      extract_Value( ), insert_Value( )   + abstract
   DynamicImplementation
      invoke( )   - abstract

org.omg.CORBA.portable
   Delegate
      get_interface_def( )   + abstract
   InputStream
      read_Principal( )   - abstract
   OutputStream
      write_Principal( )   - abstract

org.omg.CORBA
   Principal
      name( )   - abstract
   TypeCode
      concrete_base_type( ), equivalent( ), fixed_digits( ),   + abstract
         fixed_scale( ), get_compact_typecode( ),
         member_visibility( ), type_modifier( )

org.omg.CosNaming
   BindingType
      from_int( )   - final

Topics

Member Modifier Changes

org.omg.CosNaming.NamingContextPackage
  NotFoundReason
    from_int( )   - final

Throws Changes

java.applet
  Applet
    Applet( )   + java.awt.HeadlessException
java.awt
  Button
    Button( )   + java.awt.HeadlessException
  Checkbox
    Checkbox( )   + java.awt.HeadlessException
  CheckboxMenuItem
    CheckboxMenuItem( )   + java.awt.HeadlessException
  Choice
    Choice( )   + java.awt.HeadlessException
  Cursor
    getSystemCustomCursor( )   + java.awt.HeadlessException
java.awt.dnd
  DragSource
    DragSource( )   + java.awt.HeadlessException
  DropTarget
    DropTarget( )   + java.awt.HeadlessException
java.awt
  Frame
    Frame( )   + java.awt.HeadlessException
  GraphicsEnvironment
    getDefaultScreenDevice( ), getScreenDevices( )   + java.awt.HeadlessException
  Label
    Label( )   + java.awt.HeadlessException
  List
    List( )   + java.awt.HeadlessException
  Menu
    Menu( )   + java.awt.HeadlessException
  MenuBar
    MenuBar( )   + java.awt.HeadlessException
  MenuComponent
    MenuComponent( )   + java.awt.HeadlessException
  MenuItem
    MenuItem( )   + java.awt.HeadlessException
  PopupMenu
    PopupMenu( )   + java.awt.HeadlessException
java.awt.print
  PrinterJob
    pageDialog( ), printDialog( )   + java.awt.HeadlessException
java.awt
  Scrollbar
    Scrollbar( )   + java.awt.HeadlessException
  ScrollPane
    ScrollPane( )   + java.awt.HeadlessException
  TextArea
    TextArea( )   + java.awt.HeadlessException
  TextField
    TextField( )   + java.awt.HeadlessException

Throws Changes

Toolkit
    createButton( ), createCheckbox( ),   + java.awt.HeadlessException
        createCheckboxMenuItem( ), createChoice( ),
        createCustomCursor( ), createDialog( ),
        createFileDialog( ), createFrame( ), createLabel( ),
        createList( ), createMenu( ), createMenuBar( ),
        createMenuItem( ), createPopupMenu( ),
        createScrollbar( ), createScrollPane( ),
        createTextArea( ), createTextField( ),
        createWindow( ), getBestCursorSize( ),
        getColorModel( ), getMaximumCursorColors( ),
        getMenuShortcutKeyMask( ), getScreenResolution( ),
        getScreenSize( ), getSystemClipboard( ),
        loadSystemColors( ), mapInputMethodHighlight( )
    getLockingKeyState( ), setLockingKeyState( )   + java.lang.UnsupportedOperationException

java.io
    ObjectInputStream
        ObjectInputStream( )   − java.io.StreamCorruptedException
        defaultReadObject( ), readFields( )   − java.io.NotActiveException
    ObjectInputStream.GetField
        defaulted( ), get( )   − java.lang.IllegalArgumentException
    ObjectInputStream
        readObject( ), readObjectOverride( )   − java.io.OptionalDataException

java.rmi.activation
    ActivationGroup_Stub
        newInstance( )   − java.rmi.RemoteException
                        java.rmi.activation.ActivationException,
                     + java.rmi.activation.ActivationException,
                     + java.rmi.RemoteException

java.util
    ResourceBundle
        getBundle( ), getObject( ), getString( ), getStringArray( ),   − java.util.MissingResourceException
        handleGetObject( )

javax.rmi.CORBA
    Tie
        deactivate( )   + java.rmi.NoSuchObjectException
    Util
        unexportObject( )   + java.rmi.NoSuchObjectException
    UtilDelegate
        unexportObject( )   + java.rmi.NoSuchObjectException

javax.swing
    FocusManager
        setCurrentManager( )   + java.lang.SecurityException
    JApplet
        JApplet( )   + java.awt.HeadlessException
    JColorChooser
        createDialog( ), showDialog( )   + java.awt.HeadlessException
    JDialog
        JDialog( )   + java.awt.HeadlessException
    JFileChooser
        showDialog( ), showOpenDialog( ), showSaveDialog( )   + java.awt.HeadlessException
    JFrame
        JFrame( )   + java.awt.HeadlessException
    JOptionPane
        createDialog( ), getFrameForComponent( ),   + java.awt.HeadlessException
        getRootFrame( ), showConfirmDialog( ),
        showInputDialog( ), showMessageDialog( ),
        showOptionDialog( )

Topics

Throws Changes

org.omg.CORBA
  Any
    insert_fixed( )   + org.omg.CORBA.BAD_INV_ORDER
    insert_Object( )   − org.omg.CORBA.BAD_OPERATION,
                                    + org.omg.CORBA.BAD_PARAM

  CompletionStatus
    from_int( )   − org.omg.CORBA.BAD_PARAM
  DefinitionKind
    from_int( )   − org.omg.CORBA.BAD_PARAM
  SetOverrideType
    from_int( )   − org.omg.CORBA.BAD_PARAM
  TCKind
    from_int( )   − org.omg.CORBA.BAD_PARAM
org.omg.CosNaming
  BindingIteratorHelper
    narrow( )   − org.omg.CORBA.BAD_PARAM
  BindingType
    from_int( )   − org.omg.CORBA.BAD_PARAM
  NamingContextHelper
    narrow( )   − org.omg.CORBA.BAD_PARAM
org.omg.CosNaming.NamingContextPackage
  NotFoundReason
    from_int( )   − org.omg.CORBA.BAD_PARAM

Newly Deprecated Classes

javax.accessibility
  AccessibleResourceBundle
javax.security.auth
  Policy
javax.swing.plaf.metal
  MetalComboBoxUI.MetalComboPopup

org.omg.CORBA
  DynamicImplementation
org.xml.sax
  AttributeList, *DocumentHandler*, HandlerBase, *Parser*
org.xml.sax.helpers
  AttributeListImpl, ParserFactory

Newly Deprecated Members

java.awt
  Component
    isFocusTraversable( )
  ComponentOrientation
    getOrientation( )
  Window
    applyResourceBundle( )
java.io
  ObjectOutputStream.PutField
    write( )
java.lang
  SecurityManager
    checkMulticast( )
java.net
  MulticastSocket
    send( )
  URLDecoder
    decode( )

  URLEncoder
    encode( )
javax.swing
  FocusManager
    disableSwingFocusManager( ),
    isFocusManagerEnabled( )
  JComponent
    getNextFocusableComponent( ),
    isManagingFocus( ), requestDefaultFocus( ),
    setNextFocusableComponent( )
  SwingUtilities
    findFocusOwner( )
javax.swing.plaf.metal
  MetalComboBoxUI
    editablePropertyChanged( ), removeListeners( )
org.omg.CORBA
  DynamicImplementation
    invoke( )

Exceptions and Errors

This is a complete listing of all the exceptions and errors in this version of Java. The "*" indicates a checked exception or error; these must be declared in the throws clause.

java.lang	AbstractMethodError
java.security	AccessControlException
java.rmi	*AccessException
javax.security.auth.login	*AccountExpiredException
java.security.acl	*AclNotFoundException
java.rmi.activation	*ActivateFailedException
java.rmi.activation	*ActivationException
org.omg.PortableServer⊋ .POAPackage	*AdapterAlreadyExists
org.omg.PortableServer⊋ .POAManagerPackage	*AdapterInactive
org.omg.PortableServer⊋ .POAPackage	*AdapterNonExistent
org.omg.CosNaming⊋ .NamingContextPackage	*AlreadyBound
java.rmi	*AlreadyBoundException
java.nio.channels	AlreadyConnectedException
org.omg.CORBA.portable	*ApplicationException
java.lang	ArithmeticException
java.lang	ArrayIndexOutOfBoundsException
java.lang	ArrayStoreException
java.lang	AssertionError
java.nio.channels	AsynchronousCloseException
javax.naming.directory	*AttributeInUseException
javax.naming.directory	*AttributeModificationException
javax.naming	*AuthenticationException
javax.naming	*AuthenticationNotSupportedException
java.awt	AWTError
java.awt	*AWTException
java.util.prefs	*BackingStoreException
org.omg.CORBA	BAD_CONTEXT
org.omg.CORBA	BAD_INV_ORDER
org.omg.CORBA	BAD_OPERATION
org.omg.CORBA	BAD_PARAM
org.omg.CORBA	BAD_TYPECODE
org.omg.CORBA⊋ .TypeCodePackage	*BadKind
javax.swing.text	*BadLocationException
javax.crypto	*BadPaddingException
java.sql	*BatchUpdateException
java.net	*BindException
org.omg.CORBA	*Bounds
org.omg.CORBA⊋ .TypeCodePackage	*Bounds
java.nio	BufferOverflowException
java.nio	BufferUnderflowException
java.nio.channels	CancelledKeyException
org.omg.CosNaming⊋ .NamingContextPackage	*CannotProceed
javax.naming	*CannotProceedException
javax.swing.undo	CannotRedoException
javax.swing.undo	CannotUndoException
java.security.cert	*CertificateEncodingException
javax.security.cert	*CertificateEncodingException
java.security.cert	*CertificateException
javax.security.cert	*CertificateException
java.security.cert	*CertificateExpiredException
javax.security.cert	*CertificateExpiredException
java.security.cert	*CertificateNotYetValidException

javax.security.cert	*CertificateNotYetValidException
java.security.cert	*CertificateParsingException
javax.security.cert	*CertificateParsingException
java.security.cert	*CertPathBuilderException
java.security.cert	*CertPathValidatorException
java.security.cert	*CertStoreException
javax.swing.text	*ChangedCharSetException
java.nio.charset	*CharacterCodingException
java.io	*CharConversionException
java.lang	ClassCastException
java.lang	ClassCircularityError
java.lang	ClassFormatError
java.lang	*ClassNotFoundException
java.lang	*CloneNotSupportedException
java.nio.channels	*ClosedByInterruptException
java.nio.channels	*ClosedChannelException
java.nio.channels	ClosedSelectorException
java.awt.color	CMMException
java.nio.charset	CoderMalfunctionError
org.omg.CORBA	COMM_FAILURE
javax.naming	*CommunicationException
java.util	ConcurrentModificationException
javax.naming	*ConfigurationException
java.net	*ConnectException
java.rmi	*ConnectException
java.rmi	*ConnectIOException
java.nio.channels	ConnectionPendingException
javax.naming	*ContextNotEmptyException
javax.security.auth.login	*CredentialExpiredException
java.security.cert	*CRLException
org.omg.CORBA	DATA_CONVERSION
java.util.zip	*DataFormatException
java.sql	*DataTruncation
javax.security.auth	*DestroyFailedException
java.security	*DigestException
org.w3c.dom	DOMException
org.omg⊋ .PortableInterceptor⊋ .ORBInitInfoPackage	*DuplicateName
java.util	EmptyStackException
java.io	*EOFException
java.lang	Error
java.lang	*Exception
java.lang	ExceptionInInitializerError
javax.crypto	*ExemptionMechanismException
javax.swing.tree	*ExpandVetoException
java.rmi.server	*ExportException
javax.xml.parsers	FactoryConfigurationError
javax.security.auth.login	*FailedLoginException
java.nio.channels	*FileLockInterruptionException
java.io	*FileNotFoundException
java.awt	*FontFormatException
org.omg.IOP⊋ .CodecPackage	*FormatMismatch
org.omg⊋ .PortableInterceptor	*ForwardRequest
org.omg.PortableServer	*ForwardRequest
org.omg.CORBA	FREE_MEM
java.security	*GeneralSecurityException

org.ietf.jgss	*GSSException
java.awt	HeadlessException
javax.imageio	*IIOException
javax.imageio.metadata	*IIOInvalidTreeException
java.lang	IllegalAccessError
java.lang	*IllegalAccessException
java.lang	IllegalArgumentException
java.nio.channels	IllegalBlockingModeException
javax.crypto	*IllegalBlockSizeException
java.nio.charset	IllegalCharsetNameException
java.awt	IllegalComponentStateException
java.lang	IllegalMonitorStateException
java.awt.geom	IllegalPathStateException
java.nio.channels	IllegalSelectorException
java.lang	IllegalStateException
java.lang	IllegalThreadStateException
java.awt.image	ImagingOpException
org.omg.CORBA	IMP_LIMIT
java.lang	IncompatibleClassChangeError
org.omg.CORBA .ORBPackage	*InconsistentTypeCode
org.omg.DynamicAny .DynAnyFactoryPackage	*InconsistentTypeCode
java.lang	IndexOutOfBoundsException
org.omg.CORBA.portable	IndirectionException
org.omg.CORBA	INITIALIZE
java.lang	InstantiationError
java.lang	*InstantiationException
javax.naming	*InsufficientResourcesException
org.omg.CORBA	INTERNAL
java.lang	InternalError
java.lang	*InterruptedException
java.io	*InterruptedIOException
javax.naming	*InterruptedNamingException
org.omg.CORBA	INTF_REPOS
java.beans	*IntrospectionException
org.omg.CORBA	INV_FLAG
org.omg.CORBA	INV_IDENT
org.omg.CORBA	INV_OBJREF
org.omg.CORBA	INV_POLICY
org.omg.CORBA .DynAnyPackage	*Invalid
org.omg.CORBA	INVALID_TRANSACTION
org.omg.CosNaming .NamingContextExtPackage	*InvalidAddress
java.security	*InvalidAlgorithmParameterException
javax.naming.directory	*InvalidAttributeIdentifierException
javax.naming.directory	*InvalidAttributesException
javax.naming.directory	*InvalidAttributeValueException
java.io	*InvalidClassException
java.awt.dnd	InvalidDnDOperationException
java.security	*InvalidKeyException
java.security.spec	*InvalidKeySpecException
java.nio	InvalidMarkException
javax.sound.midi	*InvalidMidiDataException
org.omg.CORBA .ORBPackage	*InvalidName
org.omg.CosNaming .NamingContextPackage	*InvalidName
org.omg .PortableInterceptor .ORBInitInfoPackage	*InvalidName
javax.naming	*InvalidNameException
java.io	*InvalidObjectException
java.security	InvalidParameterException
java.security.spec	*InvalidParameterSpecException

org.omg.PortableServer .POAPackage	*InvalidPolicy
java.util.prefs	*InvalidPreferencesFormatException
javax.naming.directory	*InvalidSearchControlsException
javax.naming.directory	*InvalidSearchFilterException
org.omg.CORBA .DynAnyPackage	*InvalidSeq
org.omg .PortableInterceptor	*InvalidSlot
javax.transaction	*InvalidTransactionException
org.omg.IOP .CodecPackage	*InvalidTypeForEncoding
org.omg.CORBA .DynAnyPackage	*InvalidValue
org.omg.DynamicAny .DynAnyPackage	*InvalidValue
java.lang.reflect	*InvocationTargetException
java.io	*IOException
java.util.jar	*JarException
java.security	*KeyException
java.security	*KeyManagementException
java.security	*KeyStoreException
java.security.acl	*LastOwnerException
javax.naming.ldap	*LdapReferralException
javax.naming	*LimitExceededException
javax.sound.sampled	*LineUnavailableException
java.lang	LinkageError
javax.naming	*LinkException
javax.naming	*LinkLoopException
javax.security.auth.login	*LoginException
java.nio.charset	*MalformedInputException
javax.naming	*MalformedLinkException
java.net	*MalformedURLException
org.omg.CORBA	MARSHAL
java.rmi	*MarshalException
javax.sound.midi	*MidiUnavailableException
java.awt.datatransfer	*MimeTypeParseException
java.util	MissingResourceException
javax.naming	*NameAlreadyBoundException
javax.naming	*NameNotFoundException
javax.naming	*NamingException
javax.naming	*NamingSecurityException
java.lang	NegativeArraySizeException
org.omg.CORBA	NO_IMPLEMENT
org.omg.CORBA	NO_MEMORY
org.omg.CORBA	NO_PERMISSION
org.omg.CORBA	NO_RESOURCES
org.omg.CORBA	NO_RESPONSE
java.lang	NoClassDefFoundError
java.nio.channels	NoConnectionPendingException
org.omg.PortableServer .CurrentPackage	*NoContext
javax.naming	*NoInitialContextException
java.awt.geom	*NoninvertibleTransformException
java.nio.channels	NonReadableChannelException
java.nio.channels	NonWritableChannelException
javax.naming	*NoPermissionException
java.net	*NoRouteToHostException
org.omg.PortableServer .POAPackage	*NoServant
java.security	*NoSuchAlgorithmException
javax.naming.directory	*NoSuchAttributeException
java.util	NoSuchElementException
java.lang	NoSuchFieldError
java.lang	*NoSuchFieldException
java.lang	NoSuchMethodError

Package	Exception/Error
java.lang	*NoSuchMethodException
java.rmi	*NoSuchObjectException
javax.crypto	*NoSuchPaddingException
java.security	*NoSuchProviderException
java.io	*NotActiveException
java.rmi	*NotBoundException
javax.naming	*NotContextException
org.omg.CosNaming.NamingContextPackage	*NotEmpty
org.omg.CosNaming.NamingContextPackage	*NotFound
java.security.acl	*NotOwnerException
java.io	*NotSerializableException
java.nio.channels	NotYetBoundException
java.nio.channels	NotYetConnectedException
java.lang	NullPointerException
java.lang	NumberFormatException
org.omg.CORBA	OBJ_ADAPTER
org.omg.CORBA	OBJECT_NOT_EXIST
org.omg.PortableServer.POAPackage	*ObjectAlreadyActive
org.omg.PortableServer.POAPackage	*ObjectNotActive
java.io	*ObjectStreamException
javax.naming	*OperationNotSupportedException
java.io	*OptionalDataException
java.lang	OutOfMemoryError
java.nio.channels	OverlappingFileLockException
java.text	*ParseException
javax.xml.parsers	*ParserConfigurationException
javax.naming	*PartialResultException
java.util.regex	PatternSyntaxException
org.omg.CORBA	PERSIST_STORE
org.omg.CORBA	*PolicyError
java.net	*PortUnreachableException
java.awt.print	*PrinterAbortException
java.awt.print	*PrinterException
java.awt.print	*PrinterIOException
javax.print	*PrintException
java.security	*PrivilegedActionException
java.awt.color	ProfileDataException
java.beans	*PropertyVetoException
java.net	*ProtocolException
java.security	ProviderException
java.awt.image	RasterFormatException
java.nio	ReadOnlyBufferException
javax.naming	*ReferralException
javax.security.auth	*RefreshFailedException
org.omg.CORBA.portable	*RemarshalException
java.rmi	*RemoteException
java.rmi	RMISecurityException
java.lang	RuntimeException
org.xml.sax	*SAXException
org.xml.sax	*SAXNotRecognizedException
org.xml.sax	*SAXNotSupportedException
org.xml.sax	*SAXParseException
javax.naming.directory	*SchemaViolationException
java.lang	SecurityException
org.omg.PortableServer.POAPackage	*ServantAlreadyActive
org.omg.PortableServer.POAPackage	*ServantNotActive
java.rmi.server	*ServerCloneException
java.rmi	*ServerError
java.rmi	*ServerException
java.rmi.server	*ServerNotActiveException
java.rmi	*ServerRuntimeException
javax.naming	*ServiceUnavailableException
javax.crypto	*ShortBufferException
java.security	*SignatureException
javax.naming	*SizeLimitExceededException
java.rmi.server	*SkeletonMismatchException
java.rmi.server	*SkeletonNotFoundException
java.net	*SocketException
java.rmi.server	*SocketSecurityException
java.net	*SocketTimeoutException
java.sql	*SQLException
java.sql	*SQLWarning
javax.net.ssl	*SSLException
javax.net.ssl	*SSLHandshakeException
javax.net.ssl	*SSLKeyException
javax.net.ssl	*SSLPeerUnverifiedException
javax.net.ssl	*SSLProtocolException
java.lang	StackOverflowError
java.io	*StreamCorruptedException
java.lang	StringIndexOutOfBoundsException
java.rmi	*StubNotFoundException
java.io	*SyncFailedException
org.omg.CORBA	SystemException
java.lang	ThreadDeath
java.lang	*Throwable
javax.naming	*TimeLimitExceededException
java.util	*TooManyListenersException
org.omg.CORBA	TRANSACTION_REQUIRED
org.omg.CORBA	TRANSACTION_ROLLEDBACK
javax.transaction	*TransactionRequiredException
javax.transaction	*TransactionRolledbackException
javax.xml.transform	*TransformerConfigurationException
javax.xml.transform	*TransformerException
javax.xml.transform	TransformerFactoryConfigurationError
org.omg.CORBA	TRANSIENT
org.omg.CORBA.DynAnyPackage	*TypeMismatch
org.omg.DynamicAny.DynAnyPackage	*TypeMismatch
org.omg.IOP.CodecPackage	*TypeMismatch
java.lang.reflect	UndeclaredThrowableException
java.rmi	*UnexpectedException
org.omg.CORBA	UNKNOWN
org.omg.IOP.CodecFactoryPackage	*UnknownEncoding
java.lang	UnknownError
org.omg.CORBA.portable	UnknownException
java.rmi.activation	*UnknownGroupException
java.net	*UnknownHostException
java.rmi	*UnknownHostException
java.rmi.activation	*UnknownObjectException
java.net	*UnknownServiceException
org.omg.CORBA	*UnknownUserException
java.nio.charset	*UnmappableCharacterException
java.rmi	*UnmarshalException
javax.print.attribute	UnmodifiableSetException
java.security	*UnrecoverableKeyException
java.nio.channels	UnresolvedAddressException
java.lang	UnsatisfiedLinkError
java.nio.channels	UnsupportedAddressTypeException
javax.sound.sampled	*UnsupportedAudioFileException
javax.security.auth.callback	*UnsupportedCallbackException
java.nio.charset	UnsupportedCharsetException
java.lang	UnsupportedClassVersionError

Topics

java.io	*UnsupportedEncodingException	java.io	*WriteAbortedException
java.awt.datatransfer	*UnsupportedFlavorException	org.omg.PortableServer⊃ .POAPackage	*WrongAdapter
javax.swing	*UnsupportedLookAndFeelException		
java.lang	UnsupportedOperationException	org.omg.PortableServer⊃ .POAPackage	*WrongPolicy
java.net	*URISyntaxException		
org.omg.CORBA	*UserException	org.omg.CORBA	*WrongTransaction
java.io	*UTFDataFormatException	javax.transaction.xa	*XAException
java.lang	VerifyError	java.util.zip	*ZipException
java.lang	VirtualMachineError		

UI Default Values

This table shows all the UI default values for the three default look and feels - Windows (W), Motif (F), Metal (L). A look and feel (L&F) of '*' means all three look and feels have the same value for the UI default. A type of "keybindings" is of the class javax.swing.text.JTextComponent.KeyBinding[]. All color values are shown in the form *#RRGGBB* where *RR* is red, *GG* is green, and *BB* is blue. For keystrokes, the following abbreviations are used - a (alt), c (ctrl), m (meta), s (shift), b1 (button1), b2 (button2) b3 (button3), t (typed), p (pressed), r (released).

UI Defaults Name	L&F	Type	Value
Application⸗ .useSystemFontSettings	W	Boolean	true
AuditoryCues.allAuditoryCues	*	Object[]	CheckBoxMenuItem.commandSound, InternalFrame.closeSound, InternalFrame.maximizeSound, InternalFrame.minimizeSound, InternalFrame.restoreDownSound, InternalFrame.restoreUpSound, MenuItem.commandSound, OptionPane.errorSound, OptionPane.informationSound, OptionPane.questionSound, OptionPane.warningSound, PopupMenu.popupSound, RadioButtonMenuItem.commandSound
AuditoryCues.cueList	*	Object[]	CheckBoxMenuItem.commandSound, InternalFrame.closeSound, InternalFrame.maximizeSound, InternalFrame.minimizeSound, InternalFrame.restoreDownSound, InternalFrame.restoreUpSound, MenuItem.commandSound, OptionPane.errorSound, OptionPane.informationSound, OptionPane.questionSound, OptionPane.warningSound, PopupMenu.popupSound, RadioButtonMenuItem.commandSound
AuditoryCues.defaultCueList	L	Object[]	OptionPane.errorSound, OptionPane.informationSound, OptionPane.questionSound, OptionPane.warningSound
AuditoryCues.noAuditoryCues	*	Object[]	mute
Button.background	L	Color	#cccccc
	F		#aeb2c3
	W		#d4d0c8
Button.border	*	Border	class=javax.swing.plaf.BorderUIResource$CompoundBorderUIResource
Button.darkShadow	L	Color	#666666
	F		#000000
	W		#404040
Button.dashedRectGapHeight	W	Integer	8
Button.dashedRectGapWidth	W	Integer	10
Button.dashedRectGapX	W	Integer	5
Button.dashedRectGapY	W	Integer	4
Button.disabledForeground	W	Color	#808080
Button.disabledShadow	W	Color	#ffffff
Button.disabledText	L	Color	#999999
Button.focus	L	Color	#9999cc
	W		#000000
Button.focusInputMap	*	InputMap	pSPACE, rSPACE
Button.font	L	Font	name=Dialog, style=BOLD, size=12
	F		name=Dialog, style=PLAIN, size=12
	W		name=Tahoma, style=PLAIN, size=11
Button.foreground	*	Color	#000000
Button.highlight	L	Color	#ffffff
	F		#dcdee5
	W		#ffffff
Button.light	L	Color	#ffffff
	F		#dcdee5
	W		#d4d0c8
Button.margin	L	Insets	left=14, right=14, top=2, bottom=2
	F		left=4, right=4, top=2, bottom=2
	W		left=14, right=14, top=2, bottom=2
Button.select	L	Color	#999999
	F		#9397a5
Button.shadow	L	Color	#999999

UI Defaults Name	L&F	Type	Value
	F		#63656f
	W		#808080
Button.showMnemonics	W	Boolean	false
Button.textIconGap	*	Integer	4
Button.textShiftOffset	L	Integer	0
	F		0
	W		1
ButtonUI	L	String	javax.swing.plaf.metal.MetalButtonUI
	F		com.sun.java.swing.plaf.motif.MotifButtonUI
	W		com.sun.java.swing.plaf.windows.WindowsButtonUI
CheckBox.background	L	Color	#cccccc
	F		#aeb2c3
	W		#d4d0c8
CheckBox.border	*	Border	class=javax.swing.plaf.BorderUIResource$CompoundBorderUIResource
CheckBox.darkShadow	W	Color	#404040
CheckBox.disabledText	L	Color	#999999
CheckBox.focus	L	Color	#9999cc
	F		#b24d7a
	W		#000000
CheckBox.focusInputMap	*	InputMap	pSPACE, rSPACE
CheckBox.font	L	Font	name=Dialog, style=BOLD, size=12
	F		name=Dialog, style=PLAIN, size=12
	W		name=Tahoma, style=PLAIN, size=11
CheckBox.foreground	*	Color	#000000
CheckBox.highlight	W	Color	#ffffff
CheckBox.icon	L	Icon	class=javax.swing.plaf.metal.MetalIconFactory$CheckBoxIcon
	F		class=com.sun.java.swing.plaf.motif.MotifIconFactory$CheckBoxIcon
	W		class=com.sun.java.swing.plaf.windows.WindowsIconFactory$CheckBoxIcon
CheckBox.interiorBackground	W	Color	#ffffff
CheckBox.light	W	Color	#d4d0c8
CheckBox.margin	L	Insets	left=2, right=2, top=2, bottom=2
	F		left=2, right=2, top=2, bottom=6
	W		left=2, right=2, top=2, bottom=2
CheckBox.shadow	W	Color	#808080
CheckBox.textIconGap	L	Integer	4
	F		8
	W		4
CheckBox.textShiftOffset	*	Integer	0
CheckBoxMenuItem ⏎ .acceleratorFont	L	Font	name=Dialog, style=PLAIN, size=10
	F		name=Dialog, style=PLAIN, size=12
	W		name=Dialog, style=PLAIN, size=12
CheckBoxMenuItem ⏎ .acceleratorForeground	L	Color	#666699
	F		#000000
	W		#000000
CheckBoxMenuItem ⏎ .acceleratorSelectionForeground	L	Color	#000000
	F		#fff7e9
	W		#ffffff
CheckBoxMenuItem.arrowIcon	L	Icon	class=javax.swing.plaf.metal.MetalIconFactory$MenuItemArrowIcon
	F		class=com.sun.java.swing.plaf.motif.MotifIconFactory$MenuItemArrowIcon
	W		class=javax.swing.plaf.basic.BasicIconFactory$MenuItemArrowIcon
CheckBoxMenuItem.background	L	Color	#cccccc
	F		#aeb2c3
	W		#d4d0c8
CheckBoxMenuItem.border	L	Border	class=javax.swing.plaf.metal.MetalBorders$MenuItemBorder
	F		class=javax.swing.plaf.BorderUIResource$CompoundBorderUIResource
	W		class=javax.swing.plaf.basic.BasicBorders$MarginBorder
CheckBoxMenuItem ⏎ .borderPainted	L	Boolean	true
	F		false
	W		false
CheckBoxMenuItem.checkIcon	L	Icon	class=javax.swing.plaf.metal.MetalIconFactory$CheckBoxMenuItemIcon

UI Defaults Name	L&F	Type	Value
	F		class=com.sun.java.swing.plaf.motif.MotifIconFactory$CheckBoxIcon
	W		class=javax.swing.plaf.basic.BasicIconFactory$CheckBoxMenuItemIcon
CheckBoxMenuItemↄ .commandSound	L	String	sounds/MenuItemCommand.wav
	W		win.sound.menuCommand
CheckBoxMenuItemↄ .disabledForeground	L	Color	#999999
CheckBoxMenuItem.font	L	Font	name=Dialog, style=BOLD, size=12
	F		name=Dialog, style=PLAIN, size=12
	W		name=Tahoma, style=PLAIN, size=11
CheckBoxMenuItem.foreground	*	Color	#000000
CheckBoxMenuItem.margin	*	Insets	left=2, right=2, top=2, bottom=2
CheckBoxMenuItemↄ .selectionBackground	L	Color	#9999cc
	F		#a5a5a5
	W		#0a246a
CheckBoxMenuItemↄ .selectionForeground	L	Color	#000000
	F		#000000
	W		#ffffff
CheckBoxMenuItemUI	L	String	javax.swing.plaf.basic.BasicCheckBoxMenuItemUI
	F		com.sun.java.swing.plaf.motif.MotifCheckBoxMenuItemUI
	W		javax.swing.plaf.basic.BasicCheckBoxMenuItemUI
CheckBoxUI	L	String	javax.swing.plaf.metal.MetalCheckBoxUI
	F		com.sun.java.swing.plaf.motif.MotifCheckBoxUI
	W		com.sun.java.swing.plaf.windows.WindowsCheckBoxUI
Checkbox.select	L	Color	#999999
ColorChooser.background	L	Color	#cccccc
	F		#aeb2c3
	W		#d4d0c8
ColorChooser.font	*	Font	name=Dialog, style=PLAIN, size=12
ColorChooser.foreground	*	Color	#000000
ColorChooser.rgbBlueMnemonic	*	Integer	66
ColorChooserↄ .rgbGreenMnemonic	*	Integer	78
ColorChooser.rgbRedMnemonic	*	Integer	68
ColorChooserↄ .swatchesDefaultRecentColor	L	Color	#cccccc
	F		#aeb2c3
	W		#d4d0c8
ColorChooserↄ .swatchesRecentSwatchSize	*	Dimension	java.awt.Dimension[width=10,height=10]
ColorChooserↄ .swatchesSwatchSize	*	Dimension	java.awt.Dimension[width=10,height=10]
ColorChooserUI	*	String	javax.swing.plaf.basic.BasicColorChooserUI
ComboBox.ancestorInputMap	L	InputMap	pPAGE_DOWN, pENTER, pPAGE_UP, pSPACE, ab2pDOWN, pDOWN, ab2pKP_UP, pESCAPE, pKP_DOWN, pUP, ab2pUP, pKP_UP, pHOME, ab2pKP_DOWN, pEND
	F		pPAGE_UP, pPAGE_DOWN, pEND, pESCAPE, pHOME, pKP_UP, pKP_DOWN, pUP, pDOWN
	W		pPAGE_UP, pPAGE_DOWN, pEND, pESCAPE, pENTER, pHOME, pKP_UP, pKP_DOWN, pUP, pF4, pDOWN
ComboBox.background	L	Color	#cccccc
	F		#aeb2c3
	W		#ffffff
ComboBox.border	F	Border	class=javax.swing.plaf.BorderUIResource$CompoundBorderUIResource
	W		class=javax.swing.plaf.basic.BasicBorders$FieldBorder
ComboBox.buttonBackground	L	Color	#cccccc
	F		#aeb2c3
	W		#d4d0c8
ComboBox.buttonDarkShadow	L	Color	#666666
	F		#000000
	W		#404040
ComboBox.buttonHighlight	L	Color	#ffffff
	F		#dcdee5

UI Defaults Name	L&F	Type	Value
	W		#ffffff
ComboBox.buttonShadow	L	Color	#999999
	F		#63656f
	W		#808080
ComboBox.control	F	Color	#aeb2c3
ComboBox.controlForeground	F	Color	#000000
ComboBox.disabledBackground	L	Color	#cccccc
	F		#aeb2c3
	W		#d4d0c8
ComboBox.disabledForeground	L	Color	#999999
	F		#808080
	W		#808080
ComboBox.font	L	Font	name=Dialog, style=BOLD, size=12
	F		name=Dialog, style=PLAIN, size=12
	W		name=SansSerif, style=PLAIN, size=12
ComboBox.foreground	*	Color	#000000
ComboBox.listBackground	L	Color	#cccccc
ComboBox.listForeground	L	Color	#000000
ComboBox.selectionBackground	L	Color	#9999cc
	F		#000000
	W		#0a246a
ComboBox.selectionForeground	L	Color	#000000
	F		#fff7e9
	W		#ffffff
ComboBoxUI	L	String	javax.swing.plaf.metal.MetalComboBoxUI
	F		com.sun.java.swing.plaf.motif.MotifComboBoxUI
	W		com.sun.java.swing.plaf.windows.WindowsComboBoxUI
Desktop.ancestorInputMap	L	InputMap	pKP_UP, scab2pF6, spKP_LEFT, spRIGHT, pKP_DOWN, cpF4, pKP_LEFT, pLEFT, cpF5, pKP_RIGHT, pUP, scpF12, cpF6, pESCAPE, cpF7, pRIGHT, cab2pF6, cpF8, pDOWN, spKP_DOWN, spUP, cpF9, cpF10, spKP_RIGHT, spDOWN, cpTAB, cpF12, spKP_UP, spLEFT
	F		pKP_UP, scab2pF6, spKP_LEFT, spRIGHT, pKP_DOWN, cpF4, pKP_LEFT, pLEFT, cpF5, pKP_RIGHT, pUP, scpF12, cpF6, pESCAPE, cpF7, pRIGHT, cab2pF6, cpF8, pDOWN, spKP_DOWN, spUP, cpF9, cpF10, spKP_RIGHT, spDOWN, cpTAB, cpF12, spKP_UP, spLEFT
	W		cab2pF6, cpF6, cpF10, scpF12, cpF5, cpF9, pKP_RIGHT, pDOWN, cpF4, pKP_LEFT, pRIGHT, cpF8, pESCAPE, pKP_DOWN, pUP, cpF12, pKP_UP, cpTAB, pLEFT, cpF7, scab2pF6
Desktop.background	L	Color	#9999cc
	F		#005c5c
	W		#3a6ea5
DesktopIcon.background	L	Color	#cccccc
DesktopIcon.border	L	Border	class=javax.swing.plaf.BorderUIResource$CompoundBorderUIResource
	W		class=javax.swing.plaf.BorderUIResource$CompoundBorderUIResource
DesktopIcon.font	L	Font	name=Dialog, style=BOLD, size=12
DesktopIcon.foreground	L	Color	#000000
DesktopIcon.icon	F	Icon	
DesktopIcon.width	L	Integer	160
	W		160
DesktopIcon.windowBindings	F	Object[]	ESCAPE, hideSystemMenu
DesktopIconUI	L	String	javax.swing.plaf.metal.MetalDesktopIconUI
	F		com.sun.java.swing.plaf.motif.MotifDesktopIconUI
	W		com.sun.java.swing.plaf.windows.WindowsDesktopIconUI
DesktopPaneUI	L	String	javax.swing.plaf.basic.BasicDesktopPaneUI
	F		com.sun.java.swing.plaf.motif.MotifDesktopPaneUI
	W		com.sun.java.swing.plaf.windows.WindowsDesktopPaneUI
DirectoryPaneUI	F	String	com.sun.java.swing.plaf.motif.MotifDirectoryPaneUI
EditorPane.background	*	Color	#ffffff
EditorPane.border	*	Border	class=javax.swing.plaf.basic.BasicBorders$MarginBorder
EditorPane.caretBlinkRate	*	Integer	500
EditorPane.caretForeground	L	Color	#000000
	F		#ff0000
	W		#000000

UI Defaults Name	L&F	Type	Value
EditorPane.focusInputMap	L	InputMap	spUP, cpRIGHT, scpLEFT, spKP_UP, pDOWN, scpT, t, cpLEFT, pCUT, pEND, spPAGE_UP, pKP_UP, pDELETE, cpHOME, spLEFT, cpEND, scpRIGHT, pLEFT, pKP_LEFT, spKP_RIGHT, cpSPACE, cpBACK_SLASH, pENTER, spHOME, pRIGHT, scpPAGE_UP, spDOWN, pPAGE_DOWN, spKP_LEFT, scpO, cpX, scpPAGE_DOWN, cpC, cpKP_RIGHT, spEND, cpKP_LEFT, pHOME, cpV, pKP_DOWN, cpA, spRIGHT, scpEND, pCOPY, scpKP_LEFT, cpT, spKP_DOWN, pTAB, pUP, scpHOME, spPAGE_DOWN, pKP_RIGHT, scpKP_RIGHT, pPAGE_UP, pPASTE
	F		cpT, cpF, pEND, scpO, spINSERT, spRIGHT, pHOME, scpPAGE_UP, pKP_LEFT, pLEFT, spPAGE_DOWN, t, pKP_RIGHT, scpEND, pUP, scpT, cpSPACE, pCOPY, spHOME, pRIGHT, cpSLASH, scpLEFT, cpINSERT, pDOWN, pPASTE, spUP, scpRIGHT, cpEND, cpBACK_SLASH, cpN, cpHOME, spPAGE_UP, pCUT, cpLEFT, spDOWN, cpP, cpB, scpPAGE_DOWN, spEND, cpRIGHT, pDELETE, pTAB, scpHOME, cpD, pPAGE_UP, spDELETE, pENTER, spLEFT, pPAGE_DOWN
	W		cpT, pEND, scpO, spINSERT, spRIGHT, pHOME, cpV, scpPAGE_UP, pKP_LEFT, pLEFT, spPAGE_DOWN, t, cpX, pKP_RIGHT, scpEND, pUP, scpT, cpSPACE, pCOPY, spHOME, pRIGHT, scpLEFT, cpINSERT, pDOWN, pPASTE, spUP, cpEND, scpRIGHT, cpBACK_SLASH, cpHOME, spPAGE_UP, cpA, pCUT, cpLEFT, spDOWN, scpPAGE_DOWN, cpC, spEND, cpRIGHT, pDELETE, scpHOME, pTAB, pPAGE_UP, spDELETE, pENTER, spLEFT, pPAGE_DOWN
EditorPane.font	L	Font	name=Dialog, style=PLAIN, size=12
	F		name=Serif, style=PLAIN, size=12
	W		name=Serif, style=PLAIN, size=12
EditorPane.foreground	*	Color	#000000
EditorPane.inactiveForeground	L	Color	#999999
	F		#808080
	W		#808080
EditorPane.keyBindings	*	keybinding	[pDOWN->caret-up] [pENTER->caret-down] [pPAGE_DOWN->page-up] [pPAGE_UP->page-down] [pTAB->insert-break] [pUP->insert-tab]
EditorPane.margin	*	Insets	left=3, right=3, top=3, bottom=3
EditorPane.selectionBackground	L	Color	#ccccff
	F		#c0c0c0
	W		#0a246a
EditorPane.selectionForeground	L	Color	#000000
	F		#fff7e9
	W		#ffffff
EditorPaneUI	L	String	javax.swing.plaf.basic.BasicEditorPaneUI
	F		com.sun.java.swing.plaf.motif.MotifEditorPaneUI
	W		com.sun.java.swing.plaf.windows.WindowsEditorPaneUI
FileChooser.ancestorInputMap	L	InputMap	pESCAPE, pBACK_SPACE, pENTER
	F		pESCAPE
	W		pESCAPE, pBACK_SPACE, pENTER
FileChooser⟩ .cancelButtonMnemonic	*	Integer	67
FileChooser.detailsViewIcon	L	Icon	class=javax.swing.plaf.metal.MetalIconFactory$FileChooserDetailViewIcon
	F	Object	null
	W	Icon	class=javax.swing.ImageIcon
FileChooser⟩ .directoryOpenButtonMnemonic	*	Integer	79
FileChooser⟩ .enterFileNameLabelMnemonic	F	Integer	78
FileChooser⟩ .fileNameLabelMnemonic	L	Integer	78
	W		78
FileChooser.filesLabelMnemonic	F	Integer	73
FileChooser⟩ .filesOfTypeLabelMnemonic	L	Integer	84
	W		84
FileChooser.filterLabelMnemonic	F	Integer	82
FileChooser⟩ .foldersLabelMnemonic	F	Integer	79
FileChooser⟩ .helpButtonMnemonic	*	Integer	72
FileChooser.homeFolderIcon	L	Icon	class=javax.swing.plaf.metal.MetalIconFactory$FileChooserHomeFolderIcon
	F	Object	null

UI Defaults Name	L&F	Type	Value
	W		class=javax.swing.LookAndFeel$1
FileChooser.listViewIcon	L	Icon	class=javax.swing.plaf.metal.MetalIconFactory$FileChooserListViewIcon
	F	Object	null
	W	Icon	class=javax.swing.ImageIcon
FileChooser⮑ .lookInLabelMnemonic	L	Integer	73
	W		73
FileChooser.newFolderIcon	L	Icon	class=javax.swing.plaf.metal.MetalIconFactory$FileChooserNewFolderIcon
	F	Object	null
	W	Icon	class=javax.swing.ImageIcon
FileChooser⮑ .openButtonMnemonic	*	Integer	79
FileChooser.pathLabelMnemonic	F	Integer	80
FileChooser⮑ .saveButtonMnemonic	*	Integer	83
FileChooser.upFolderIcon	L	Icon	class=javax.swing.plaf.metal.MetalIconFactory$FileChooserUpFolderIcon
	F	Object	null
	W	Icon	class=javax.swing.ImageIcon
FileChooser⮑ .updateButtonMnemonic	*	Integer	85
FileChooserUI	L	String	javax.swing.plaf.metal.MetalFileChooserUI
	F		com.sun.java.swing.plaf.motif.MotifFileChooserUI
	W		com.sun.java.swing.plaf.windows.WindowsFileChooserUI
FileView.computerIcon	L	Icon	class=javax.swing.plaf.metal.MetalIconFactory$TreeComputerIcon
	F	Object	null
	W	Icon	
FileView.directoryIcon	L	Icon	class=javax.swing.plaf.metal.MetalIconFactory$TreeFolderIcon
	F	Object	null
	W	Icon	
FileView.fileIcon	L	Icon	class=javax.swing.plaf.metal.MetalIconFactory$TreeLeafIcon
	F	Object	null
	W	Icon	
FileView.floppyDriveIcon	L	Icon	class=javax.swing.plaf.metal.MetalIconFactory$TreeFloppyDriveIcon
	F	Object	null
	W	Icon	
FileView.hardDriveIcon	L	Icon	class=javax.swing.plaf.metal.MetalIconFactory$TreeHardDriveIcon
	F	Object	null
	W	Icon	
FormattedTextField.background	L	Color	#ffffff
	F		#aeb2c3
	W		#ffffff
FormattedTextField.border	L	Border	class=javax.swing.plaf.BorderUIResource$CompoundBorderUIResource
	F		class=javax.swing.plaf.basic.BasicBorders$FieldBorder
	W		class=javax.swing.plaf.basic.BasicBorders$FieldBorder
FormattedTextField⮑ .caretBlinkRate	*	Integer	500
FormattedTextField⮑ .caretForeground	*	Color	#000000
FormattedTextField⮑ .focusInputMap	*	InputMap	pKP_UP, pEND, scpO, spKP_LEFT, spRIGHT, pKP_DOWN, pHOME, cpV, pKP_LEFT, pLEFT, t, cpX, pKP_RIGHT, pUP, scpKP_RIGHT, pCOPY, spHOME, pESCAPE, pRIGHT, scpLEFT, cpKP_LEFT, pDOWN, cpKP_RIGHT, pPASTE, scpRIGHT, cpBACK_SLASH, cpA, spKP_RIGHT, pCUT, cpLEFT, scpKP_LEFT, cpC, spEND, cpRIGHT, pDELETE, pENTER, spLEFT
FormattedTextField.font	L	Font	name=Dialog, style=PLAIN, size=12
	F		name=SansSerif, style=PLAIN, size=12
	W		name=SansSerif, style=PLAIN, size=12
FormattedTextField.foreground	*	Color	#000000
FormattedTextField⮑ .inactiveBackground	L	Color	#cccccc
	F		#aeb2c3
	W		#d4d0c8
FormattedTextField⮑ .inactiveForeground	L	Color	#999999
	F		#808080
	W		#808080

UI Defaults Name	L&F	Type	Value
FormattedTextField.margin	*	Insets	left=0, right=0, top=0, bottom=0
FormattedTextField⊋ .selectionBackground	L	Color	#ccccff
	F		#000000
	W		#0a246a
FormattedTextField⊋ .selectionForeground	L	Color	#000000
	F		#fff7e9
	W		#ffffff
FormattedTextFieldUI	*	String	javax.swing.plaf.basic.BasicFormattedTextFieldUI
InternalFrame.activeBorderColor	W	Color	#d4d0c8
InternalFrame⊋ .activeTitleBackground	L	Color	#ccccff
	F		#b24d7a
	W		#0a246a
InternalFrame⊋ .activeTitleForeground	L	Color	#000000
	F		#ffffff
	W		#ffffff
InternalFrame.activeTitleGradient	W	Color	#a6caf0
InternalFrame.border	L	Border	class=javax.swing.plaf.metal.MetalBorders$InternalFrameBorder
	F		class=javax.swing.plaf.BorderUIResource$CompoundBorderUIResource
	W		class=javax.swing.plaf.BorderUIResource$CompoundBorderUIResource
InternalFrame.borderColor	L	Color	#cccccc
	F		#aeb2c3
	W		#d4d0c8
InternalFrame⊋ .borderDarkShadow	L	Color	#666666
	F		#000000
	W		#404040
InternalFrame.borderHighlight	L	Color	#ffffff
	F		#dcdee5
	W		#ffffff
InternalFrame.borderLight	L	Color	#ffffff
	F		#dcdee5
	W		#d4d0c8
InternalFrame.borderShadow	L	Color	#999999
	F		#63656f
	W		#808080
InternalFrame.borderWidth	W	Integer	1
InternalFrame.closeIcon	L	Icon	class=javax.swing.plaf.metal.MetalIconFactory$InternalFrameCloseIcon
	F		class=javax.swing.plaf.basic.BasicIconFactory$EmptyFrameIcon
	W		class=com.sun.java.swing.plaf.windows.WindowsIconFactory$CloseIcon
InternalFrame.closeSound	L	String	sounds/FrameClose.wav
	W		win.sound.close
InternalFrame.icon	L	Icon	class=javax.swing.plaf.metal.MetalIconFactory$InternalFrameDefaultMenuIcon
	F	Object	null
	W	Icon	
InternalFrame.iconifyIcon	L	Icon	class=javax.swing.plaf.metal.MetalIconFactory$InternalFrameMinimizeIcon
	F		class=javax.swing.plaf.basic.BasicIconFactory$EmptyFrameIcon
	W		class=com.sun.java.swing.plaf.windows.WindowsIconFactory$IconifyIcon
InternalFrame⊋ .inactiveBorderColor	W	Color	#d4d0c8
InternalFrame⊋ .inactiveTitleBackground	L	Color	#cccccc
	F		#aeb2c3
	W		#808080
InternalFrame⊋ .inactiveTitleForeground	L	Color	#000000
	F		#000000
	W		#d4d0c8
InternalFrame⊋ .inactiveTitleGradient	W	Color	#c0c0c0
InternalFrame.maximizeIcon	L	Icon	class=javax.swing.plaf.metal.MetalIconFactory$InternalFrameMaximizeIcon

Swing
UI Default Values

UI Defaults Name	L&F	Type	Value
	F		class=javax.swing.plaf.basic.BasicIconFactory$EmptyFrameIcon
	W		class=com.sun.java.swing.plaf.windows.WindowsIconFactory$MaximizeIcon
InternalFrame.maximizeSound	L	String	sounds/FrameMaximize.wav
	W		win.sound.maximize
InternalFrame.minimizeIcon	L	Icon	class=javax.swing.plaf.metal.MetalIconFactory$InternalFrameAltMaximizeIcon
	F		class=javax.swing.plaf.basic.BasicIconFactory$EmptyFrameIcon
	W		class=com.sun.java.swing.plaf.windows.WindowsIconFactory$MinimizeIcon
InternalFrame⊋ .minimizeIconBackground	W	Color	#d4d0c8
InternalFrame.minimizeSound	L	String	sounds/FrameMinimize.wav
	W		win.sound.minimize
InternalFrame⊋ .optionDialogBorder	L	Border	class=javax.swing.plaf.metal.MetalBorders$OptionDialogBorder
InternalFrame.paletteBorder	L	Border	class=javax.swing.plaf.metal.MetalBorders$PaletteBorder
InternalFrame.paletteCloseIcon	L	Icon	class=javax.swing.plaf.metal.MetalIconFactory$PaletteCloseIcon
InternalFrame.paletteTitleHeight	L	Integer	11
InternalFrame⊋ .resizeIconHighlight	W	Color	#d4d0c8
InternalFrame.resizeIconShadow	W	Color	#808080
InternalFrame⊋ .restoreDownSound	L	String	sounds/FrameRestoreDown.wav
	W		win.sound.restoreDown
InternalFrame.restoreUpSound	L	String	sounds/FrameRestoreUp.wav
	W		win.sound.restoreUp
InternalFrame.titleFont	L	Font	name=Dialog, style=BOLD, size=12
	F		name=Dialog, style=BOLD, size=12
	W		name=Tahoma, style=BOLD, size=11
InternalFrame.windowBindings	*	Object[]	shift ESCAPE, showSystemMenu, ctrl SPACE, showSystemMenu, ESCAPE, hideSystemMenu
InternalFrameUI	L	String	javax.swing.plaf.metal.MetalInternalFrameUI
	F		com.sun.java.swing.plaf.motif.MotifInternalFrameUI
	W		com.sun.java.swing.plaf.windows.WindowsInternalFrameUI
Label.background	L	Color	#cccccc
	F		#aeb2c3
	W		#d4d0c8
Label.disabledForeground	L	Color	#999999
	F		#ffffff
	W		#808080
Label.disabledShadow	L	Color	#999999
	F		#63656f
	W		#ffffff
Label.font	L	Font	name=Dialog, style=BOLD, size=12
	F		name=Dialog, style=PLAIN, size=12
	W		name=Tahoma, style=PLAIN, size=11
Label.foreground	*	Color	#000000
LabelUI	L	String	javax.swing.plaf.metal.MetalLabelUI
	F		com.sun.java.swing.plaf.motif.MotifLabelUI
	W		com.sun.java.swing.plaf.windows.WindowsLabelUI
List.background	L	Color	#ffffff
	F		#aeb2c3
	W		#ffffff
List.cellRenderer	*	Object	class=javax.swing.DefaultListCellRenderer$UIResource
List.focusCellBorderColor	W	Color	#ffffff
List.focusCellHighlightBorder	L	LineBorder	color=#9999cc, thickness=1, rounded=false
	F		color=#b24d7a, thickness=1, rounded=false
	W		color=#ffffff, thickness=1, rounded=false
List.focusInputMap	L	InputMap	pKP_UP, pEND, spKP_LEFT, spRIGHT, pKP_DOWN, pHOME, cpV, pKP_LEFT, pLEFT, spPAGE_DOWN, cpX, pKP_RIGHT, pUP, pCOPY, spHOME, pRIGHT, cpSLASH, pDOWN, pPASTE, spKP_DOWN, spUP, cpBACK_SLASH, spPAGE_UP, cpA, spKP_RIGHT, pCUT, spDOWN, cpC, spEND, pPAGE_UP, spKP_UP, spLEFT, pPAGE_DOWN

UI Defaults Name	L&F	Type	Value
	F		pKP_UP, pEND, spKP_LEFT, spINSERT, spRIGHT, pKP_DOWN, pHOME, pKP_LEFT, pLEFT, spPAGE_DOWN, pKP_RIGHT, pUP, cpSPACE, pCOPY, spHOME, pRIGHT, cpSLASH, cpINSERT, pDOWN, pPASTE, spKP_DOWN, spUP, cpBACK_SLASH, spPAGE_UP, cpA, spKP_RIGHT, pCUT, spDOWN, spEND, pPAGE_UP, spDELETE, spKP_UP, spLEFT, pPAGE_DOWN
	W		pKP_UP, pEND, spKP_LEFT, spRIGHT, pKP_DOWN, pHOME, cpV, pKP_LEFT, pLEFT, spPAGE_DOWN, cpX, pKP_RIGHT, pUP, cpSPACE, pCOPY, spHOME, pRIGHT, cpSLASH, pDOWN, pPASTE, spKP_DOWN, spUP, cpBACK_SLASH, spPAGE_UP, cpA, spKP_RIGHT, pCUT, spDOWN, cpC, spEND, pPAGE_UP, spKP_UP, spLEFT, pPAGE_DOWN
List.focusInputMap.RightToLeft	*	InputMap	pLEFT, pKP_LEFT, spLEFT, spKP_LEFT, pRIGHT, pKP_RIGHT, spRIGHT, spKP_RIGHT
List.font	L	Font	name=Dialog, style=BOLD, size=12
	F		name=Dialog, style=PLAIN, size=12
	W		name=Tahoma, style=PLAIN, size=11
List.foreground	*	Color	#000000
List.selectionBackground	L	Color	#ccccff
	F		#000000
	W		#0a246a
List.selectionForeground	L	Color	#000000
	F		#fff7e9
	W		#ffffff
ListUI	*	String	javax.swing.plaf.basic.BasicListUI
Menu.acceleratorFont	L	Font	name=Dialog, style=PLAIN, size=10
	F		name=Dialog, style=PLAIN, size=12
	W		name=Dialog, style=PLAIN, size=12
Menu.acceleratorForeground	L	Color	#666699
	F		#000000
	W		#000000
Menu.acceleratorSelectionForeground	L	Color	#000000
	F		#fff7e9
	W		#ffffff
Menu.arrowIcon	L	Icon	class=javax.swing.plaf.metal.MetalIconFactory$MenuArrowIcon
	F		class=com.sun.java.swing.plaf.motif.MotifIconFactory$MenuArrowIcon
	W		class=com.sun.java.swing.plaf.windows.WindowsIconFactory$MenuArrowIcon
Menu.background	L	Color	#cccccc
	F		#aeb2c3
	W		#d4d0c8
Menu.border	L	Border	class=javax.swing.plaf.metal.MetalBorders$MenuItemBorder
	F		class=javax.swing.plaf.BorderUIResource$CompoundBorderUIResource
	W		class=javax.swing.plaf.basic.BasicBorders$MarginBorder
Menu.borderPainted	L	Boolean	true
	F		false
	W		false
Menu.checkIcon	L	Object	null
	F	Icon	class=com.sun.java.swing.plaf.motif.MotifIconFactory$MenuItemCheckIcon
	W		class=javax.swing.plaf.basic.BasicIconFactory$MenuItemCheckIcon
Menu.disabledForeground	L	Color	#999999
Menu.font	L	Font	name=Dialog, style=BOLD, size=12
	F		name=Dialog, style=PLAIN, size=12
	W		name=Tahoma, style=PLAIN, size=11
Menu.foreground	*	Color	#000000
Menu.margin	*	Insets	left=2, right=2, top=2, bottom=2
Menu.menuPopupOffsetX	*	Integer	0
Menu.menuPopupOffsetY	*	Integer	0
Menu.selectionBackground	L	Color	#9999cc
	F		#a5a5a5
	W		#0a246a
Menu.selectionForeground	L	Color	#000000
	F		#000000
	W		#ffffff
Menu.shortcutKeys	L	int[]	8
	F		8, 4
	W		8

Swing

UI Default Values

UI Defaults Name	L&F	Type	Value
Menu.submenuPopupOffsetX	L	Integer	-4
	F		-2
	W		-4
Menu.submenuPopupOffsetY	L	Integer	-3
	F		3
	W		-3
MenuBar.background	L	Color	#cccccc
	F		#aeb2c3
	W		#d4d0c8
MenuBar.border	L	Border	class=javax.swing.plaf.metal.MetalBorders$MenuBarBorder
	F		class=com.sun.java.swing.plaf.motif.MotifBorders$MenuBarBorder
	W		class=javax.swing.plaf.basic.BasicBorders$MenuBarBorder
MenuBar.font	L	Font	name=Dialog, style=BOLD, size=12
	F		name=Dialog, style=PLAIN, size=12
	W		name=Tahoma, style=PLAIN, size=11
MenuBar.foreground	*	Color	#000000
MenuBar.highlight	L	Color	#ffffff
	F		#dcdee5
	W		#ffffff
MenuBar.shadow	L	Color	#999999
	F		#63656f
	W		#808080
MenuBar.windowBindings	*	Object[]	F10, takeFocus
MenuBarUI	L	String	javax.swing.plaf.basic.BasicMenuBarUI
	F		com.sun.java.swing.plaf.motif.MotifMenuBarUI
	W		javax.swing.plaf.basic.BasicMenuBarUI
MenuItem.acceleratorDelimiter	L	String	-
	F		+
	W		+
MenuItem.acceleratorFont	L	Font	name=Dialog, style=PLAIN, size=10
	F		name=Dialog, style=PLAIN, size=12
	W		name=Tahoma, style=PLAIN, size=11
MenuItem.acceleratorForeground	L	Color	#666699
	F		#000000
	W		#000000
MenuItem↩ .acceleratorSelectionForeground	L	Color	#000000
	F		#fff7e9
	W		#ffffff
MenuItem.arrowIcon	L	Icon	class=javax.swing.plaf.metal.MetalIconFactory$MenuItemArrowIcon
	F		class=com.sun.java.swing.plaf.motif.MotifIconFactory$MenuItemArrowIcon
	W		class=com.sun.java.swing.plaf.windows↩ .WindowsIconFactory$MenuItemArrowIcon
MenuItem.background	L	Color	#cccccc
	F		#aeb2c3
	W		#d4d0c8
MenuItem.border	L	Border	class=javax.swing.plaf.metal.MetalBorders$MenuItemBorder
	F		class=javax.swing.plaf.BorderUIResource$CompoundBorderUIResource
	W		class=javax.swing.plaf.basic.BasicBorders$MarginBorder
MenuItem.borderPainted	L	Boolean	true
	F		false
	W		false
MenuItem.checkIcon	L	Object	null
	F	Icon	class=com.sun.java.swing.plaf.motif.MotifIconFactory$MenuItemCheckIcon
	W		class=com.sun.java.swing.plaf.windows↩ .WindowsIconFactory$MenuItemCheckIcon
MenuItem.commandSound	L	String	sounds/MenuItemCommand.wav
	W		win.sound.menuCommand
MenuItem.disabledForeground	L	Color	#999999
	W		#808080
MenuItem.font	L	Font	name=Dialog, style=BOLD, size=12
	F		name=Dialog, style=PLAIN, size=12
	W		name=Tahoma, style=PLAIN, size=11
MenuItem.foreground	*	Color	#000000

UI Defaults Name	L&F	Type	Value
MenuItem.margin	*	Insets	left=2, right=2, top=2, bottom=2
MenuItem.selectionBackground	L	Color	#9999cc
	F		#a5a5a5
	W		#0a246a
MenuItem.selectionForeground	L	Color	#000000
	F		#000000
	W		#ffffff
MenuItemUI	L	String	javax.swing.plaf.basic.BasicMenuItemUI
	F		com.sun.java.swing.plaf.motif.MotifMenuItemUI
	W		com.sun.java.swing.plaf.windows.WindowsMenuItemUI
MenuUI	L	String	javax.swing.plaf.basic.BasicMenuUI
	F		com.sun.java.swing.plaf.motif.MotifMenuUI
	W		com.sun.java.swing.plaf.windows.WindowsMenuUI
OptionPane.background	L	Color	#cccccc
	F		#aeb2c3
	W		#d4d0c8
OptionPane.border	L	EmptyBorder	top=10, left=10, bottom=12, right=10
	F		top=10, left=0, bottom=0, right=0
	W		top=10, left=10, bottom=12, right=10
OptionPane.buttonAreaBorder	L	EmptyBorder	top=6, left=0, bottom=0, right=0
	F		top=10, left=10, bottom=10, right=10
	W		top=6, left=0, bottom=0, right=0
OptionPane⤵ .buttonClickThreshhold	*	Integer	500
OptionPane.errorDialog.border⤵ .background	L	Color	#993333
OptionPane.errorDialog⤵ .titlePane.background	L	Color	#ff9999
OptionPane.errorDialog⤵ .titlePane.foreground	L	Color	#330000
OptionPane.errorDialog⤵ .titlePane.shadow	L	Color	#cc6666
OptionPane.errorIcon	*	Icon	
OptionPane.errorSound	L	String	sounds/OptionPaneError.wav
	W		win.sound.hand
OptionPane.font	L	Font	name=Dialog, style=PLAIN, size=12
	F		name=Dialog, style=PLAIN, size=12
	W		name=Tahoma, style=PLAIN, size=11
OptionPane.foreground	*	Color	#000000
OptionPane.informationIcon	*	Icon	
OptionPane.informationSound	L	String	sounds/OptionPaneInformation.wav
	W		win.sound.asterisk
OptionPane.messageAreaBorder	L	EmptyBorder	top=0, left=0, bottom=0, right=0
	F		top=10, left=10, bottom=12, right=10
	W		top=0, left=0, bottom=0, right=0
OptionPane.messageForeground	*	Color	#000000
OptionPane.minimumSize	*	Dimension	javax.swing.plaf.DimensionUIResource[width=262,height=90]
OptionPane.questionDialog⤵ .border.background	L	Color	#336633
OptionPane.questionDialog⤵ .titlePane.background	L	Color	#99cc99
OptionPane.questionDialog⤵ .titlePane.foreground	L	Color	#003300
OptionPane.questionDialog⤵ .titlePane.shadow	L	Color	#669966
OptionPane.questionIcon	*	Icon	
OptionPane.questionSound	L	String	sounds/OptionPaneQuestion.wav
	W		win.sound.question
OptionPane.warningDialog⤵ .border.background	L	Color	#996633
OptionPane.warningDialog⤵ .titlePane.background	L	Color	#ffcc99
OptionPane.warningDialog⤵ .titlePane.foreground	L	Color	#663300

Topics

UI Defaults Name	L&F	Type	Value
OptionPane.warningDialog₂ .titlePane.shadow	L	Color	#cc9966
OptionPane.warningIcon	*	Icon	
OptionPane.warningSound	L	String	sounds/OptionPaneWarning.wav
	W		win.sound.exclamation
OptionPane.windowBindings	*	Object[]	ESCAPE, close
OptionPaneUI	L	String	javax.swing.plaf.basic.BasicOptionPaneUI
	F		com.sun.java.swing.plaf.motif.MotifOptionPaneUI
	W		javax.swing.plaf.basic.BasicOptionPaneUI
Panel.background	L	Color	#cccccc
	F		#aeb2c3
	W		#d4d0c8
Panel.font	L	Font	name=Dialog, style=PLAIN, size=12
	F		name=Dialog, style=PLAIN, size=12
	W		name=Tahoma, style=PLAIN, size=11
Panel.foreground	*	Color	#000000
PanelUI	*	String	javax.swing.plaf.basic.BasicPanelUI
PasswordField.background	L	Color	#ffffff
	F		#aeb2c3
	W		#ffffff
PasswordField.border	L	Border	class=javax.swing.plaf.BorderUIResource$CompoundBorderUIResource
	F		class=javax.swing.plaf.BorderUIResource$CompoundBorderUIResource
	W		class=javax.swing.plaf.basic.BasicBorders$FieldBorder
PasswordField.caretBlinkRate	*	Integer	500
PasswordField.caretForeground	*	Color	#000000
PasswordField.focusInputMap	L	InputMap	pEND, scpO, spKP_LEFT, spRIGHT, pHOME, cpV, pKP_LEFT, pLEFT, t, cpX, pKP_RIGHT, scpKP_RIGHT, pCOPY, spHOME, pRIGHT, scpLEFT, cpKP_LEFT, cpKP_RIGHT, pPASTE, scpRIGHT, cpBACK_SLASH, cpA, spKP_RIGHT, pCUT, cpLEFT, scpKP_LEFT, cpC, spEND, cpRIGHT, pDELETE, pENTER, spLEFT
	F		cpF, pEND, scpO, spINSERT, spRIGHT, pHOME, pKP_LEFT, pLEFT, t, pKP_RIGHT, pCOPY, spHOME, pRIGHT, cpSLASH, scpLEFT, cpINSERT, pPASTE, scpRIGHT, cpBACK_SLASH, pCUT, cpLEFT, cpB, spEND, cpRIGHT, pDELETE, cpD, spDELETE, pENTER, spLEFT
	W		pEND, scpO, spINSERT, spRIGHT, pHOME, cpV, pKP_LEFT, pLEFT, t, cpX, pKP_RIGHT, pCOPY, spHOME, pRIGHT, scpLEFT, cpINSERT, pPASTE, scpRIGHT, cpBACK_SLASH, cpA, pCUT, cpLEFT, cpC, spEND, cpRIGHT, pDELETE, spDELETE, pENTER, spLEFT
PasswordField.font	L	Font	name=Dialog, style=PLAIN, size=12
	F		name=Monospaced, style=PLAIN, size=12
	W		name=MonoSpaced, style=PLAIN, size=12
PasswordField.foreground	*	Color	#000000
PasswordField₂ .inactiveBackground	L	Color	#cccccc
	F		#aeb2c3
	W		#d4d0c8
PasswordField₂ .inactiveForeground	L	Color	#999999
	F		#808080
	W		#808080
PasswordField.keyBindings	*	keybinding	[pENTER->notify-field-accept]
PasswordField.margin	*	Insets	left=0, right=0, top=0, bottom=0
PasswordField₂ .selectionBackground	L	Color	#ccccff
	F		#000000
	W		#0a246a
PasswordField₂ .selectionForeground	L	Color	#000000
	F		#fff7e9
	W		#ffffff
PasswordFieldUI	L	String	javax.swing.plaf.basic.BasicPasswordFieldUI
	F		com.sun.java.swing.plaf.motif.MotifPasswordFieldUI
	W		com.sun.java.swing.plaf.windows.WindowsPasswordFieldUI
PopupMenu.background	L	Color	#cccccc
	F		#aeb2c3

UI Defaults Name	L&F	Type	Value
	W		#d4d0c8
PopupMenu.border	L	Border	class=javax.swing.plaf.metal.MetalBorders$PopupMenuBorder
	F		class=javax.swing.plaf.BorderUIResource$CompoundBorderUIResource
	W		class=javax.swing.plaf.BorderUIResource$CompoundBorderUIResource
PopupMenu.font	L	Font	name=Dialog, style=PLAIN, size=12
	F		name=Dialog, style=PLAIN, size=12
	W		name=Tahoma, style=PLAIN, size=11
PopupMenu.foreground	*	Color	#000000
PopupMenu.popupSound	L	String	sounds/PopupMenuPopup.wav
	W		win.sound.menuPopup
PopupMenu⟩ .selectedWindowInputMapBindings	L	Object[]	ESCAPE, cancel, DOWN, selectNext, KP_DOWN, selectNext, UP, selectPrevious, KP_UP, selectPrevious, LEFT, selectParent, KP_LEFT, selectParent, RIGHT, selectChild, KP_RIGHT, selectChild, ENTER, return, SPACE, return
	F		ESCAPE, cancel, TAB, cancel, shift TAB, cancel, DOWN, selectNext, KP_DOWN, selectNext, UP, selectPrevious, KP_UP, selectPrevious, LEFT, selectParent, KP_LEFT, selectParent, RIGHT, selectChild, KP_RIGHT, selectChild, ENTER, return, SPACE, return
	W		ESCAPE, cancel, DOWN, selectNext, KP_DOWN, selectNext, UP, selectPrevious, KP_UP, selectPrevious, LEFT, selectParent, KP_LEFT, selectParent, RIGHT, selectChild, KP_RIGHT, selectChild, ENTER, return, SPACE, return
PopupMenu⟩ .selectedWindowInputMapBindings⟩ .RightToLeft	*	Object[]	LEFT, selectChild, KP_LEFT, selectChild, RIGHT, selectParent, KP_RIGHT, selectParent
PopupMenuSeparatorUI	L	String	javax.swing.plaf.metal.MetalPopupMenuSeparatorUI
	F		com.sun.java.swing.plaf.motif.MotifPopupMenuSeparatorUI
	W		javax.swing.plaf.basic.BasicPopupMenuSeparatorUI
PopupMenuUI	L	String	javax.swing.plaf.basic.BasicPopupMenuUI
	F		com.sun.java.swing.plaf.motif.MotifPopupMenuUI
	W		com.sun.java.swing.plaf.windows.WindowsPopupMenuUI
ProgressBar.background	L	Color	#cccccc
	F		#aeb2c3
	W		#d4d0c8
ProgressBar⟩ .backgroundHighlight	L	Color	#cccccc
ProgressBar.border	L	LineBorder	color=#666666, thickness=1, rounded=false
	F	Border	class=com.sun.java.swing.plaf.motif.MotifBorders$BevelBorder
	W		class=javax.swing.plaf.BorderUIResource$CompoundBorderUIResource
ProgressBar.cellLength	L	Integer	1
	F		6
	W		7
ProgressBar.cellSpacing	L	Integer	0
	F		0
	W		2
ProgressBar.cycleTime	*	Integer	3000
ProgressBar.font	L	Font	name=Dialog, style=BOLD, size=12
	F		name=Dialog, style=PLAIN, size=12
	W		name=Tahoma, style=PLAIN, size=11
ProgressBar.foreground	L	Color	#9999cc
	F		#9397a5
	W		#0a246a
ProgressBar.foregroundHighlight	L	Color	#9999cc
ProgressBar.highlight	W	Color	#ffffff
ProgressBar.repaintInterval	*	Integer	50
ProgressBar⟩ .selectionBackground	L	Color	#666699
	F		#000000
	W		#0a246a
ProgressBar⟩ .selectionForeground	L	Color	#cccccc
	F		#aeb2c3
	W		#d4d0c8
ProgressBar.shadow	W	Color	#808080
ProgressBarUI	L	String	javax.swing.plaf.metal.MetalProgressBarUI
	F		com.sun.java.swing.plaf.motif.MotifProgressBarUI

UI Defaults Name	L&F	Type	Value
	W		com.sun.java.swing.plaf.windows.WindowsProgressBarUI
RadioButton.background	L	Color	#cccccc
	F		#aeb2c3
	W		#d4d0c8
RadioButton.border	*	Border	class=javax.swing.plaf.BorderUIResource$CompoundBorderUIResource
RadioButton.darkShadow	L	Color	#666666
	F		#000000
	W		#404040
RadioButton.disabledText	L	Color	#999999
RadioButton.focus	L	Color	#9999cc
	F		#b24d7a
	W		#000000
RadioButton.focusInputMap	*	InputMap	pSPACE, rSPACE
RadioButton.font	L	Font	name=Dialog, style=BOLD, size=12
	F		name=Dialog, style=PLAIN, size=12
	W		name=Tahoma, style=PLAIN, size=11
RadioButton.foreground	*	Color	#000000
RadioButton.highlight	L	Color	#ffffff
	F		#dcdee5
	W		#ffffff
RadioButton.icon	L	Icon	class=javax.swing.plaf.metal.MetalIconFactory$RadioButtonIcon
	F		class=com.sun.java.swing.plaf.motif.MotifIconFactory$RadioButtonIcon
	W		class=com.sun.java.swing.plaf.windows.WindowsIconFactory$RadioButtonIcon
RadioButton.interiorBackground	W	Color	#ffffff
RadioButton.light	L	Color	#ffffff
	F		#dcdee5
	W		#d4d0c8
RadioButton.margin	L	Insets	left=2, right=2, top=2, bottom=2
	F		left=2, right=2, top=2, bottom=6
	W		left=2, right=2, top=2, bottom=2
RadioButton.select	L	Color	#999999
RadioButton.shadow	L	Color	#999999
	F		#63656f
	W		#808080
RadioButton.textIconGap	L	Integer	4
	F		8
	W		4
RadioButton.textShiftOffset	*	Integer	0
RadioButtonMenuItem₂.acceleratorFont	L	Font	name=Dialog, style=PLAIN, size=10
	F		name=Dialog, style=PLAIN, size=12
	W		name=Dialog, style=PLAIN, size=12
RadioButtonMenuItem₂.acceleratorForeground	L	Color	#666699
	F		#000000
	W		#000000
RadioButtonMenuItem₂.acceleratorSelectionForeground	L	Color	#000000
	F		#fff7e9
	W		#ffffff
RadioButtonMenuItem.arrowIcon	L	Icon	class=javax.swing.plaf.metal.MetalIconFactory$MenuItemArrowIcon
	F		class=com.sun.java.swing.plaf.motif.MotifIconFactory$MenuItemArrowIcon
	W		class=javax.swing.plaf.basic.BasicIconFactory$MenuItemArrowIcon
RadioButtonMenuItem₂.background	L	Color	#cccccc
	F		#aeb2c3
	W		#d4d0c8
RadioButtonMenuItem.border	L	Border	class=javax.swing.plaf.metal.MetalBorders$MenuItemBorder
	F		class=javax.swing.plaf.BorderUIResource$CompoundBorderUIResource
	W		class=javax.swing.plaf.basic.BasicBorders$MarginBorder
RadioButtonMenuItem₂.borderPainted	L	Boolean	true
	F		false
	W		false

UI Defaults Name	L&F	Type	Value
RadioButtonMenuItem.checkIcon	L	Icon	class=javax.swing.plaf.metal.MetalIconFactory$RadioButtonMenuItemIcon
	F		class=com.sun.java.swing.plaf.motif.MotifIconFactory$RadioButtonIcon
	W		class=javax.swing.plaf.basic.BasicIconFactory$RadioButtonMenuItemIcon
RadioButtonMenuItem⤸.commandSound	L	String	sounds/MenuItemCommand.wav
	W		win.sound.menuCommand
RadioButtonMenuItem⤸.disabledForeground	L	Color	#999999
	W		#808080
RadioButtonMenuItem.font	L	Font	name=Dialog, style=BOLD, size=12
	F		name=Dialog, style=PLAIN, size=12
	W		name=Tahoma, style=PLAIN, size=11
RadioButtonMenuItem⤸.foreground	*	Color	#000000
RadioButtonMenuItem.margin	*	Insets	left=2, right=2, top=2, bottom=2
RadioButtonMenuItem⤸.selectionBackground	L	Color	#9999cc
	F		#a5a5a5
	W		#0a246a
RadioButtonMenuItem⤸.selectionForeground	L	Color	#000000
	F		#000000
	W		#ffffff
RadioButtonMenuItemUI	L	String	javax.swing.plaf.basic.BasicRadioButtonMenuItemUI
	F		com.sun.java.swing.plaf.motif.MotifRadioButtonMenuItemUI
	W		javax.swing.plaf.basic.BasicRadioButtonMenuItemUI
RadioButtonUI	L	String	javax.swing.plaf.metal.MetalRadioButtonUI
	F		com.sun.java.swing.plaf.motif.MotifRadioButtonUI
	W		com.sun.java.swing.plaf.windows.WindowsRadioButtonUI
RootPane⤸.colorChooserDialogBorder	L	Border	class=javax.swing.plaf.metal.MetalBorders$QuestionDialogBorder
RootPane⤸.defaultButtonWindowKeyBindings	*	Object[]	ENTER, press, released ENTER, release, ctrl ENTER, press, ctrl released ENTER, release
RootPane.errorDialogBorder	L	Border	class=javax.swing.plaf.metal.MetalBorders$ErrorDialogBorder
RootPane⤸.fileChooserDialogBorder	L	Border	class=javax.swing.plaf.metal.MetalBorders$QuestionDialogBorder
RootPane.frameBorder	L	Border	class=javax.swing.plaf.metal.MetalBorders$FrameBorder
RootPane⤸.informationDialogBorder	L	Border	class=javax.swing.plaf.metal.MetalBorders$DialogBorder
RootPane.plainDialogBorder	L	Border	class=javax.swing.plaf.metal.MetalBorders$DialogBorder
RootPane.questionDialogBorder	L	Border	class=javax.swing.plaf.metal.MetalBorders$QuestionDialogBorder
RootPane.warningDialogBorder	L	Border	class=javax.swing.plaf.metal.MetalBorders$WarningDialogBorder
RootPaneUI	L	String	javax.swing.plaf.metal.MetalRootPaneUI
	F		javax.swing.plaf.basic.BasicRootPaneUI
	W		com.sun.java.swing.plaf.windows.WindowsRootPaneUI
ScrollBar⤸.allowsAbsolutePositioning	L	Boolean	true
	F		true
ScrollBar.background	L	Color	#cccccc
	F		#9397a5
	W		#d4d0c8
ScrollBar.border	F	Border	class=com.sun.java.swing.plaf.motif.MotifBorders$BevelBorder
ScrollBar.darkShadow	L	Color	#666666
ScrollBar.focusInputMap	L	InputMap	pPAGE_UP, pPAGE_DOWN, pEND, pHOME, pLEFT, pKP_UP, pKP_DOWN, pUP, pRIGHT, pKP_LEFT, pDOWN, pKP_RIGHT
	F		cpPAGE_DOWN, pPAGE_DOWN, pPAGE_UP, cpPAGE_UP, pKP_RIGHT, pDOWN, pKP_LEFT, pRIGHT, pKP_DOWN, pUP, pKP_UP, pLEFT, pHOME, pEND
	W		cpPAGE_DOWN, pPAGE_DOWN, pPAGE_UP, cpPAGE_UP, pKP_RIGHT, pDOWN, pKP_LEFT, pRIGHT, pKP_DOWN, pUP, pKP_UP, pLEFT, pHOME, pEND
ScrollBar.focusInputMap⤸.RightToLeft	*	InputMap	pRIGHT, pKP_RIGHT, pLEFT, pKP_LEFT
ScrollBar.foreground	L	Color	#cccccc
	F		#aeb2c3

Topics

UI Defaults Name	L&F	Type	Value
	W		#d4d0c8
ScrollBar.highlight	L	Color	#ffffff
ScrollBar.maximumThumbSize	*	Dimension	javax.swing.plaf.DimensionUIResource[width=4096,height=4096]
ScrollBar.minimumThumbSize	*	Dimension	javax.swing.plaf.DimensionUIResource[width=8,height=8]
ScrollBar.shadow	L	Color	#999999
ScrollBar.thumb	L	Color	#9999cc
	F		#aeb2c3
	W		#d4d0c8
ScrollBar.thumbDarkShadow	L	Color	#666666
	F		#000000
	W		#404040
ScrollBar.thumbHighlight	L	Color	#ccccff
	F		#dcdee5
	W		#ffffff
ScrollBar.thumbShadow	L	Color	#666699
	F		#63656f
	W		#808080
ScrollBar.track	L	Color	#cccccc
	F		#9397a5
	W		#ffffff
ScrollBar.trackForeground	W	Color	#d4d0c8
ScrollBar.trackHighlight	L	Color	#666666
	F		#000000
	W		#000000
ScrollBar⤶.trackHighlightForeground	W	Color	#404040
ScrollBar.width	L	Integer	17
	F		16
	W		16
ScrollBarUI	L	String	javax.swing.plaf.metal.MetalScrollBarUI
	F		com.sun.java.swing.plaf.motif.MotifScrollBarUI
	W		com.sun.java.swing.plaf.windows.WindowsScrollBarUI
ScrollPane.ancestorInputMap	*	InputMap	cpPAGE_DOWN, pPAGE_DOWN, pPAGE_UP, cpPAGE_UP, pKP_RIGHT, pDOWN, pKP_LEFT, cpHOME, pRIGHT, pKP_DOWN, pUP, pKP_UP, pLEFT, cpEND
ScrollPane.ancestorInputMap⤶.RightToLeft	*	InputMap	cpPAGE_UP, cpPAGE_DOWN
ScrollPane.background	L	Color	#cccccc
	F		#aeb2c3
	W		#d4d0c8
ScrollPane.border	L	Border	class=javax.swing.plaf.metal.MetalBorders$ScrollPaneBorder
	W		class=javax.swing.plaf.basic.BasicBorders$FieldBorder
ScrollPane.font	L	Font	name=Dialog, style=PLAIN, size=12
	F		name=Dialog, style=PLAIN, size=12
	W		name=Tahoma, style=PLAIN, size=11
ScrollPane.foreground	*	Color	#000000
ScrollPane.viewportBorder	F	Border	class=com.sun.java.swing.plaf.motif.MotifBorders$BevelBorder
ScrollPaneUI	L	String	javax.swing.plaf.metal.MetalScrollPaneUI
	F		com.sun.java.swing.plaf.motif.MotifScrollPaneUI
	W		javax.swing.plaf.basic.BasicScrollPaneUI
Separator.background	L	Color	#ffffff
	F		#dcdee5
	W		#ffffff
Separator.foreground	L	Color	#666699
	F		#63656f
	W		#808080
Separator.highlight	L	Color	#ffffff
	F		#dcdee5
	W		#ffffff
Separator.shadow	L	Color	#999999
	F		#63656f
	W		#808080
SeparatorUI	L	String	javax.swing.plaf.metal.MetalSeparatorUI
	F		com.sun.java.swing.plaf.motif.MotifSeparatorUI
	W		javax.swing.plaf.basic.BasicSeparatorUI

UI Defaults Name	L&F	Type	Value
Slider.background	L	Color	#cccccc
	F		#9397a5
	W		#d4d0c8
Slider.border	F	Border	class=javax.swing.plaf.BorderUIResource$CompoundBorderUIResource
Slider.focus	L	Color	#9999cc
	F		#000000
	W		#404040
Slider.focusInputMap	L	InputMap	cpPAGE_DOWN, pPAGE_DOWN, pPAGE_UP, cpPAGE_UP, pKP_RIGHT, pDOWN, pKP_LEFT, pRIGHT, pKP_DOWN, pUP, pKP_UP, pLEFT, pHOME, pEND
	F		cpPAGE_UP, pEND, pHOME, cpPAGE_DOWN, pLEFT, pKP_UP, pKP_DOWN, pUP, pRIGHT, pKP_LEFT, pDOWN, pKP_RIGHT
	W		pPAGE_UP, pPAGE_DOWN, pEND, pHOME, pLEFT, pKP_UP, pKP_DOWN, pUP, pRIGHT, pKP_LEFT, pDOWN, pKP_RIGHT
Slider.focusInputMap.RightToLeft	*	InputMap	pRIGHT, pKP_RIGHT, pLEFT, pKP_LEFT
Slider.focusInsets	L	Insets	left=0, right=0, top=0, bottom=0
	F		left=0, right=0, top=0, bottom=0
	W		left=2, right=2, top=2, bottom=2
Slider.foreground	L	Color	#9999cc
	F		#aeb2c3
	W		#d4d0c8
Slider.highlight	L	Color	#ffffff
	F		#dcdee5
	W		#ffffff
Slider.horizontalThumbIcon	L	Icon	class=javax.swing.plaf.metal.MetalIconFactory$HorizontalSliderThumbIcon
Slider.majorTickLength	L	Integer	6
Slider.shadow	L	Color	#999999
	F		#63656f
	W		#808080
Slider.trackWidth	L	Integer	7
Slider.verticalThumbIcon	L	Icon	class=javax.swing.plaf.metal.MetalIconFactory$VerticalSliderThumbIcon
SliderUI	L	String	javax.swing.plaf.metal.MetalSliderUI
	F		com.sun.java.swing.plaf.motif.MotifSliderUI
	W		javax.swing.plaf.basic.BasicSliderUI
Spinner.ancestorInputMap	*	InputMap	pUP, pKP_UP, pDOWN, pKP_DOWN
Spinner.arrowButtonSize	*	Dimension	java.awt.Dimension[width=16,height=5]
Spinner.background	L	Color	#cccccc
	F		#aeb2c3
	W		#d4d0c8
Spinner.border	*	Border	class=javax.swing.plaf.BorderUIResource$BevelBorderUIResource
Spinner.font	*	Font	name=MonoSpaced, style=PLAIN, size=12
Spinner.foreground	L	Color	#cccccc
	F		#aeb2c3
	W		#d4d0c8
SpinnerUI	*	String	javax.swing.plaf.basic.BasicSpinnerUI
SplitPane.activeThumb	F	Color	#b24d7a
SplitPane.ancestorInputMap	*	InputMap	pF6, pF8, pEND, pHOME, pKP_UP, pLEFT, pKP_DOWN, pUP, pRIGHT, pKP_LEFT, pDOWN, pKP_RIGHT
SplitPane.background	L	Color	#cccccc
	F		#aeb2c3
	W		#d4d0c8
SplitPane.border	*	Border	class=javax.swing.plaf.basic.BasicBorders$SplitPaneBorder
SplitPane.darkShadow	L	Color	#666666
	F		#000000
	W		#404040
SplitPane.dividerSize	L	Integer	10
	F		20
	W		5
SplitPane.highlight	L	Color	#ffffff
	F		#dcdee5
	W		#d4d0c8
SplitPane.shadow	L	Color	#999999
	F		#63656f
	W		#808080
SplitPaneDivider.border	*	Border	class=javax.swing.plaf.basic.BasicBorders$SplitPaneDividerBorder

Topics

UI Defaults Name	L&F	Type	Value
SplitPaneUI	L	String	javax.swing.plaf.metal.MetalSplitPaneUI
	F		com.sun.java.swing.plaf.motif.MotifSplitPaneUI
	W		com.sun.java.swing.plaf.windows.WindowsSplitPaneUI
TabbedPane.ancestorInputMap	*	InputMap	cpPAGE_DOWN, cpPAGE_UP, cpUP, cpKP_UP
TabbedPane.background	L	Color	#999999
	F		#aeb2c3
	W		#d4d0c8
TabbedPane.contentBorderInsets	L	Insets	left=2, right=3, top=2, bottom=3
	F		left=2, right=2, top=2, bottom=2
	W		left=2, right=3, top=2, bottom=3
TabbedPane.darkShadow	L	Color	#666666
	F		#63656f
	W		#404040
TabbedPane.focus	L	Color	#666699
	F		#b24d7a
	W		#000000
TabbedPane.focusInputMap	*	InputMap	cpDOWN, pKP_UP, pLEFT, cpKP_DOWN, pUP, pKP_DOWN, pKP_LEFT, pRIGHT, pKP_RIGHT, pDOWN
TabbedPane.font	L	Font	name=Dialog, style=BOLD, size=12
	F		name=Dialog, style=PLAIN, size=12
	W		name=Tahoma, style=PLAIN, size=11
TabbedPane.foreground	*	Color	#000000
TabbedPane.highlight	L	Color	#ffffff
	F		#dcdee5
	W		#ffffff
TabbedPane.light	L	Color	#cccccc
	F		#dcdee5
	W		#d4d0c8
TabbedPane.selectHighlight	L	Color	#ffffff
TabbedPane.selected	L	Color	#cccccc
TabbedPane.selectedTabPadInsets	L	Insets	left=2, right=1, top=2, bottom=2
	F		left=0, right=0, top=3, bottom=1
	W		left=2, right=1, top=2, bottom=2
TabbedPane.shadow	L	Color	#999999
	F		#63656f
	W		#808080
TabbedPane.tabAreaBackground	L	Color	#cccccc
TabbedPane.tabAreaInsets	L	Insets	left=2, right=6, top=4, bottom=0
	F		left=2, right=8, top=4, bottom=0
	W		left=2, right=2, top=3, bottom=0
TabbedPane.tabInsets	L	Insets	left=9, right=9, top=0, bottom=1
	F		left=4, right=4, top=3, bottom=3
	W		left=4, right=4, top=0, bottom=1
TabbedPane.tabRunOverlay	*	Integer	2
TabbedPane.textIconGap	*	Integer	4
TabbedPane.unselectedTabBackground	F	Color	#9397a5
TabbedPane.unselectedTabForeground	F	Color	#000000
TabbedPane.unselectedTabHighlight	F	Color	#d2d7eb
TabbedPane.unselectedTabShadow	F	Color	#666973
TabbedPaneUI	L	String	javax.swing.plaf.metal.MetalTabbedPaneUI
	F		com.sun.java.swing.plaf.motif.MotifTabbedPaneUI
	W		javax.swing.plaf.basic.BasicTabbedPaneUI
Table.ancestorInputMap	L	InputMap	pKP_UP, pEND, spKP_LEFT, spRIGHT, pKP_DOWN, pHOME, cpV, scpPAGE_UP, pKP_LEFT, pLEFT, spPAGE_DOWN, cpX, pKP_RIGHT, scpEND, pUP, pCOPY, spENTER, spHOME, pESCAPE, pRIGHT, cpPAGE_UP, pDOWN, cpPAGE_DOWN, pPASTE, spKP_DOWN, spUP, cpEND, cpHOME, spPAGE_UP, pF2, cpA, spKP_RIGHT, pCUT, spDOWN, scpPAGE_DOWN, spTAB, cpC, spEND, scpHOME, pTAB, pPAGE_UP, spKP_UP, pENTER, spLEFT, pPAGE_DOWN

UI Defaults Name	L&F	Type	Value
	F		pKP_UP, pEND, spKP_LEFT, spINSERT, spRIGHT, pKP_DOWN, pHOME, scpPAGE_UP, pKP_LEFT, pLEFT, spPAGE_DOWN, pKP_RIGHT, scpEND, pUP, pCOPY, spENTER, spHOME, pESCAPE, pRIGHT, cpPAGE_UP, cpINSERT, pDOWN, cpPAGE_DOWN, pPASTE, spKP_DOWN, spUP, cpEND, cpHOME, spPAGE_UP, pF2, cpA, spKP_RIGHT, pCUT, spDOWN, scpPAGE_DOWN, spTAB, spEND, scpHOME, pTAB, pPAGE_UP, spDELETE, spKP_UP, pENTER, spLEFT, pPAGE_DOWN
	W		pKP_UP, pEND, spKP_LEFT, spRIGHT, pKP_DOWN, pHOME, cpV, scpPAGE_UP, pKP_LEFT, pLEFT, spPAGE_DOWN, cpX, pKP_RIGHT, scpEND, pUP, pCOPY, spENTER, spHOME, pESCAPE, pRIGHT, cpPAGE_UP, pDOWN, cpPAGE_DOWN, pPASTE, spKP_DOWN, spUP, cpEND, cpHOME, spPAGE_UP, pF2, cpA, spKP_RIGHT, pCUT, spDOWN, scpPAGE_DOWN, spTAB, cpC, spEND, scpHOME, pTAB, pPAGE_UP, spKP_UP, pENTER, spLEFT, pPAGE_DOWN
Table.ancestorInputMap ⊋ .RightToLeft	*	InputMap	cpPAGE_UP, scpPAGE_UP, spLEFT, scpPAGE_DOWN, spKP_RIGHT, cpPAGE_DOWN, pLEFT, spRIGHT, spKP_LEFT, pKP_LEFT, pRIGHT, pKP_RIGHT
Table.background	L	Color	#ffffff
	F		#aeb2c3
	W		#ffffff
Table.darkShadow	W	Color	#404040
Table.focusCellBackground	L	Color	#ffffff
	F		#aeb2c3
	W		#ffffff
Table.focusCellForeground	*	Color	#000000
Table.focusCellHighlightBorder	L	LineBorder	color=#9999cc, thickness=1, rounded=false
	F		color=#b24d7a, thickness=1, rounded=false
	W		color=#ffff00, thickness=1, rounded=false
Table.font	L	Font	name=Dialog, style=PLAIN, size=12
	F		name=Dialog, style=PLAIN, size=12
	W		name=Tahoma, style=PLAIN, size=11
Table.foreground	*	Color	#000000
Table.gridColor	L	Color	#999999
	F		#808080
	W		#808080
Table.highlight	W	Color	#ffffff
Table.light	W	Color	#d4d0c8
Table.scrollPaneBorder	L	Border	class=javax.swing.plaf.metal.MetalBorders$ScrollPaneBorder
	W		class=javax.swing.plaf.BorderUIResource$BevelBorderUIResource
Table.selectionBackground	L	Color	#ccccff
	F		#000000
	W		#0a246a
Table.selectionForeground	L	Color	#000000
	F		#fff7e9
	W		#ffffff
Table.shadow	W	Color	#808080
TableHeader.background	L	Color	#cccccc
	F		#aeb2c3
	W		#d4d0c8
TableHeader.cellBorder	L	Border	class=javax.swing.plaf.metal.MetalBorders$TableHeaderBorder
	F		class=javax.swing.plaf.BorderUIResource$BevelBorderUIResource
	W		class=javax.swing.plaf.BorderUIResource$CompoundBorderUIResource
TableHeader.font	L	Font	name=Dialog, style=PLAIN, size=12
	F		name=Dialog, style=PLAIN, size=12
	W		name=Tahoma, style=PLAIN, size=11
TableHeader.foreground	*	Color	#000000
TableHeaderUI	*	String	javax.swing.plaf.basic.BasicTableHeaderUI
TableUI	*	String	javax.swing.plaf.basic.BasicTableUI
TextArea.background	L	Color	#ffffff
	F		#aeb2c3
	W		#ffffff
TextArea.border	*	Border	class=javax.swing.plaf.basic.BasicBorders$MarginBorder
TextArea.caretBlinkRate	*	Integer	500
TextArea.caretForeground	*	Color	#000000

Topics

UI Defaults Name	L&F	Type	Value
TextArea.focusInputMap	L	InputMap	spUP, cpRIGHT, scpLEFT, spKP_UP, pDOWN, scpT, t, cpLEFT, pCUT, pEND, spPAGE_UP, pKP_UP, pDELETE, cpHOME, spLEFT, cpEND, scpRIGHT, pLEFT, pKP_LEFT, spKP_RIGHT, cpSPACE, cpBACK_SLASH, pENTER, spHOME, pRIGHT, scpPAGE_UP, spDOWN, pPAGE_DOWN, spKP_LEFT, scpO, cpX, scpPAGE_DOWN, cpC, cpKP_RIGHT, spEND, cpKP_LEFT, pHOME, cpV, pKP_DOWN, cpA, spRIGHT, scpEND, pCOPY, scpKP_LEFT, cpT, spKP_DOWN, pTAB, pUP, scpHOME, spPAGE_DOWN, pKP_RIGHT, scpKP_RIGHT, pPAGE_UP, pPASTE
	F		cpT, cpF, pEND, scpO, spINSERT, spRIGHT, pHOME, scpPAGE_UP, pKP_LEFT, pLEFT, spPAGE_DOWN, t, pKP_RIGHT, scpEND, pUP, scpT, cpSPACE, pCOPY, spHOME, pRIGHT, cpSLASH, scpLEFT, cpINSERT, pDOWN, pPASTE, spUP, scpRIGHT, cpEND, cpBACK_SLASH, cpN, cpHOME, spPAGE_UP, pCUT, cpLEFT, spDOWN, cpP, cpB, scpPAGE_DOWN, spEND, cpRIGHT, pDELETE, pTAB, scpHOME, cpD, pPAGE_UP, spDELETE, pENTER, spLEFT, pPAGE_DOWN
	W		cpT, pEND, scpO, spINSERT, spRIGHT, pHOME, cpV, scpPAGE_UP, pKP_LEFT, pLEFT, spPAGE_DOWN, t, cpX, pKP_RIGHT, scpEND, pUP, scpT, cpSPACE, pCOPY, spHOME, pRIGHT, scpLEFT, cpINSERT, pPASTE, spUP, cpEND, scpRIGHT, cpBACK_SLASH, cpHOME, spPAGE_UP, cpA, pCUT, cpLEFT, spDOWN, scpPAGE_DOWN, cpC, spEND, cpRIGHT, pDELETE, scpHOME, pTAB, pPAGE_UP, spDELETE, pENTER, spLEFT, pPAGE_DOWN
TextArea.font	L	Font	name=Dialog, style=PLAIN, size=12
	F		name=Monospaced, style=PLAIN, size=12
	W		name=MonoSpaced, style=PLAIN, size=12
TextArea.foreground	*	Color	#000000
TextArea.inactiveForeground	L	Color	#999999
	F		#808080
	W		#808080
TextArea.keyBindings	*	keybinding	[pDOWN->caret-up] [pENTER->caret-down] [pPAGE_DOWN->page-up] [pPAGE_UP->page-down] [pTAB->insert-break] [pUP->insert-tab]
TextArea.margin	*	Insets	left=0, right=0, top=0, bottom=0
TextArea.selectionBackground	L	Color	#ccccff
	F		#000000
	W		#0a246a
TextArea.selectionForeground	L	Color	#000000
	F		#fff7e9
	W		#ffffff
TextAreaUI	L	String	javax.swing.plaf.basic.BasicTextAreaUI
	F		com.sun.java.swing.plaf.motif.MotifTextAreaUI
	W		com.sun.java.swing.plaf.windows.WindowsTextAreaUI
TextField.background	L	Color	#ffffff
	F		#aeb2c3
	W		#ffffff
TextField.border	L	Border	class=javax.swing.plaf.BorderUIResource$CompoundBorderUIResource
	F		class=javax.swing.plaf.BorderUIResource$CompoundBorderUIResource
	W		class=javax.swing.plaf.basic.BasicBorders$FieldBorder
TextField.caretBlinkRate	*	Integer	500
TextField.caretForeground	*	Color	#000000
TextField.darkShadow	L	Color	#666666
	F		#000000
	W		#404040
TextField.focusInputMap	L	InputMap	pEND, scpO, spKP_LEFT, spRIGHT, pHOME, cpV, pKP_LEFT, pLEFT, t, cpX, pKP_RIGHT, scpKP_RIGHT, pCOPY, spHOME, pRIGHT, scpLEFT, cpKP_LEFT, cpKP_RIGHT, pPASTE, scpRIGHT, cpBACK_SLASH, cpA, spKP_RIGHT, pCUT, cpLEFT, scpKP_LEFT, cpC, spEND, cpRIGHT, pDELETE, pENTER, spLEFT
	F		cpF, pEND, scpO, spINSERT, spRIGHT, pHOME, pKP_LEFT, pLEFT, t, pKP_RIGHT, pCOPY, spHOME, pRIGHT, cpSLASH, scpLEFT, cpINSERT, pPASTE, scpRIGHT, cpBACK_SLASH, pCUT, cpLEFT, cpB, spEND, cpRIGHT, pDELETE, cpD, spDELETE, pENTER, spLEFT
	W		pEND, scpO, spINSERT, spRIGHT, pHOME, cpV, pKP_LEFT, pLEFT, t, cpX, pKP_RIGHT, pCOPY, spHOME, pRIGHT, scpLEFT, cpINSERT, pPASTE, scpRIGHT, cpBACK_SLASH, cpA, pCUT, cpLEFT, cpC, spEND, cpRIGHT, pDELETE, spDELETE, pENTER, spLEFT
TextField.font	L	Font	name=Dialog, style=PLAIN, size=12
	F		name=SansSerif, style=PLAIN, size=12
	W		name=SansSerif, style=PLAIN, size=12

UI Defaults Name	L&F	Type	Value
TextField.foreground	*	Color	#000000
TextField.highlight	L	Color	#ffffff
	F		#dcdee5
	W		#ffffff
TextField.inactiveBackground	L	Color	#cccccc
	F		#aeb2c3
	W		#d4d0c8
TextField.inactiveForeground	L	Color	#999999
	F		#808080
	W		#808080
TextField.keyBindings	*	keybinding	[pENTER->notify-field-accept]
TextField.light	L	Color	#ffffff
	F		#dcdee5
	W		#d4d0c8
TextField.margin	L	Insets	left=0, right=0, top=0, bottom=0
	F		left=0, right=0, top=0, bottom=0
	W		left=1, right=1, top=1, bottom=1
TextField.selectionBackground	L	Color	#ccccff
	F		#000000
	W		#0a246a
TextField.selectionForeground	L	Color	#000000
	F		#fff7e9
	W		#ffffff
TextField.shadow	L	Color	#999999
	F		#63656f
	W		#808080
TextFieldUI	L	String	javax.swing.plaf.metal.MetalTextFieldUI
	F		com.sun.java.swing.plaf.motif.MotifTextFieldUI
	W		com.sun.java.swing.plaf.windows.WindowsTextFieldUI
TextPane.background	*	Color	#ffffff
TextPane.border	*	Border	class=javax.swing.plaf.basic.BasicBorders$MarginBorder
TextPane.caretBlinkRate	*	Integer	500
TextPane.caretForeground	*	Color	#000000
TextPane.focusInputMap	L	InputMap	spUP, cpRIGHT, scpLEFT, spKP_UP, pDOWN, scpT, t, cpLEFT, pCUT, pEND, spPAGE_UP, pKP_UP, pDELETE, cpHOME, spLEFT, cpEND, scpRIGHT, pLEFT, pKP_LEFT, spKP_RIGHT, cpSPACE, cpBACK_SLASH, pENTER, spHOME, pRIGHT, scpPAGE_UP, spDOWN, pPAGE_DOWN, spKP_LEFT, scpO, cpX, scpPAGE_DOWN, cpC, cpKP_RIGHT, spEND, cpKP_LEFT, pHOME, cpV, pKP_DOWN, cpA, spRIGHT, scpEND, pCOPY, scpKP_LEFT, cpT, spKP_DOWN, pTAB, pUP, scpHOME, spPAGE_DOWN, pKP_RIGHT, scpKP_RIGHT, pPAGE_UP, pPASTE
	F		cpT, cpF, pEND, scpO, spINSERT, spRIGHT, pHOME, scpPAGE_UP, pKP_LEFT, pLEFT, spPAGE_DOWN, scpEND, pUP, scpT, cpSPACE, pCOPY, spHOME, pRIGHT, cpSLASH, scpLEFT, cpINSERT, pDOWN, pPASTE, spUP, scpRIGHT, cpEND, cpBACK_SLASH, cpN, cpHOME, spPAGE_UP, pCUT, cpLEFT, spDOWN, cpP, cpB, scpPAGE_DOWN, spEND, cpRIGHT, pDELETE, pTAB, scpHOME, cpD, pPAGE_UP, spDELETE, pENTER, spLEFT, pPAGE_DOWN
	W		cpT, pEND, scpO, spINSERT, spRIGHT, pHOME, cpV, scpPAGE_UP, pKP_LEFT, pLEFT, spPAGE_DOWN, scpEND, pUP, scpT, cpSPACE, pCOPY, spHOME, pRIGHT, scpLEFT, cpINSERT, pDOWN, pPASTE, spUP, cpEND, scpRIGHT, cpBACK_SLASH, cpHOME, spPAGE_UP, cpA, pCUT, cpLEFT, spDOWN, scpPAGE_DOWN, cpC, spEND, cpRIGHT, pDELETE, scpHOME, pTAB, pPAGE_UP, spDELETE, pENTER, spLEFT, pPAGE_DOWN
TextPane.font	L	Font	name=Dialog, style=PLAIN, size=12
	F		name=Serif, style=PLAIN, size=12
	W		name=Serif, style=PLAIN, size=12
TextPane.foreground	*	Color	#000000
TextPane.inactiveForeground	L	Color	#999999
	F		#808080
	W		#808080
TextPane.keyBindings	*	keybinding	[pDOWN->caret-up] [pENTER->caret-down] [pPAGE_DOWN->page-up] [pPAGE_UP->page-down] [pTAB->insert-break] [pUP->insert-tab]
TextPane.margin	*	Insets	left=3, right=3, top=3, bottom=3
TextPane.selectionBackground	L	Color	#ccccff
	F		#c0c0c0

Topics

UI Defaults Name	L&F	Type	Value
TextPane.selectionForeground	W	Color	#0a246a
	L		#000000
	F		#fff7e9
TextPaneUI	W		#ffffff
	L	String	javax.swing.plaf.basic.BasicTextPaneUI
	F		com.sun.java.swing.plaf.motif.MotifTextPaneUI
	W		com.sun.java.swing.plaf.windows.WindowsTextPaneUI
TitledBorder.border	L	LineBorder	color=#999999, thickness=1, rounded=false
	F	Border	class=javax.swing.plaf.BorderUIResource$EtchedBorderUIResource
	W		class=javax.swing.plaf.BorderUIResource$EtchedBorderUIResource
TitledBorder.font	L	Font	name=Dialog, style=BOLD, size=12
	F		name=Dialog, style=PLAIN, size=12
	W		name=Tahoma, style=PLAIN, size=11
TitledBorder.titleColor	*	Color	#000000
ToggleButton.background	L	Color	#cccccc
	F		#aeb2c3
	W		#d4d0c8
ToggleButton.border	*	Border	class=javax.swing.plaf.BorderUIResource$CompoundBorderUIResource
ToggleButton.darkShadow	L	Color	#666666
	F		#000000
	W		#404040
ToggleButton₂.disabledBackground	L	Color	#cccccc
ToggleButton₂.disabledSelectedBackground	L	Color	#999999
ToggleButton₂.disabledSelectedText	L	Color	#666666
ToggleButton.disabledText	L	Color	#999999
ToggleButton.focus	L	Color	#9999cc
	F		#000000
	W		#000000
ToggleButton.focusInputMap	*	InputMap	pSPACE, rSPACE
ToggleButton.font	L	Font	name=Dialog, style=BOLD, size=12
	F		name=Dialog, style=PLAIN, size=12
	W		name=Tahoma, style=PLAIN, size=11
ToggleButton.foreground	*	Color	#000000
ToggleButton.highlight	L	Color	#ffffff
	F		#dcdee5
	W		#ffffff
ToggleButton.light	L	Color	#ffffff
	F		#dcdee5
	W		#d4d0c8
ToggleButton.margin	*	Insets	left=14, right=14, top=2, bottom=2
ToggleButton.select	L	Color	#999999
	F		#9397a5
ToggleButton.shadow	L	Color	#999999
	F		#63656f
	W		#808080
ToggleButton.text	L	Color	#cccccc
ToggleButton.textIconGap	*	Integer	4
ToggleButton.textShiftOffset	L	Integer	0
	F		0
	W		1
ToggleButtonUI	L	String	javax.swing.plaf.metal.MetalToggleButtonUI
	F		com.sun.java.swing.plaf.motif.MotifToggleButtonUI
	W		com.sun.java.swing.plaf.windows.WindowsToggleButtonUI
ToolBar.ancestorInputMap	*	InputMap	pUP, pKP_UP, pDOWN, pKP_DOWN, pLEFT, pKP_LEFT, pRIGHT, pKP_RIGHT
ToolBar.background	L	Color	#cccccc
	F		#aeb2c3
	W		#d4d0c8
ToolBar.border	L	Border	class=javax.swing.plaf.metal.MetalBorders$ToolBarBorder
	F		class=javax.swing.plaf.BorderUIResource$EtchedBorderUIResource
	W		class=com.sun.java.swing.plaf.windows.WindowsBorders$ToolBarBorder
ToolBar.darkShadow	L	Color	#666666

UI Defaults Name	L&F	Type	Value
	F		#000000
	W		#404040
ToolBar.dockingBackground	L	Color	#cccccc
	F		#aeb2c3
	W		#d4d0c8
ToolBar.dockingForeground	L	Color	#666699
	F		#ff0000
	W		#ff0000
ToolBar.floatingBackground	L	Color	#cccccc
	F		#aeb2c3
	W		#d4d0c8
ToolBar.floatingForeground	L	Color	#ccccff
	F		#404040
	W		#404040
ToolBar.font	L	Font	name=Dialog, style=BOLD, size=12
	F		name=Dialog, style=PLAIN, size=12
	W		name=Tahoma, style=PLAIN, size=11
ToolBar.foreground	*	Color	#000000
ToolBar.highlight	L	Color	#ffffff
	F		#dcdee5
	W		#ffffff
ToolBar.light	L	Color	#ffffff
	F		#dcdee5
	W		#d4d0c8
ToolBar.separatorSize	L	Dimension	javax.swing.plaf.DimensionUIResource[width=10,height=10]
	F		javax.swing.plaf.DimensionUIResource[width=10,height=10]
	W		javax.swing.plaf.DimensionUIResource[width=6,height=20]
ToolBar.shadow	L	Color	#999999
	F		#63656f
	W		#808080
ToolBarSeparatorUI	L	String	javax.swing.plaf.basic.BasicToolBarSeparatorUI
	F		javax.swing.plaf.basic.BasicToolBarSeparatorUI
	W		com.sun.java.swing.plaf.windows.WindowsSeparatorUI
ToolBarUI	L	String	javax.swing.plaf.metal.MetalToolBarUI
	F		javax.swing.plaf.basic.BasicToolBarUI
	W		com.sun.java.swing.plaf.windows.WindowsToolBarUI
ToolTip.background	L	Color	#ccccff
	F		#fff7e9
	W		#ffffe1
ToolTip.backgroundInactive	L	Color	#cccccc
ToolTip.border	L	LineBorder	color=#666699, thickness=1, rounded=false
	F	Border	class=com.sun.java.swing.plaf.motif.MotifBorders$BevelBorder
	W	LineBorder	color=#000000, thickness=1, rounded=false
ToolTip.borderInactive	L	LineBorder	color=#666666, thickness=1, rounded=false
ToolTip.font	L	Font	name=Dialog, style=PLAIN, size=12
	F		name=SansSerif, style=PLAIN, size=12
	W		name=Tahoma, style=PLAIN, size=11
ToolTip.foreground	*	Color	#000000
ToolTip.foregroundInactive	L	Color	#666666
ToolTip.hideAccelerator	L	Boolean	false
ToolTipUI	L	String	javax.swing.plaf.metal.MetalToolTipUI
	F		javax.swing.plaf.basic.BasicToolTipUI
	W		javax.swing.plaf.basic.BasicToolTipUI
Tree.ancestorInputMap	*	InputMap	pESCAPE
Tree.background	L	Color	#ffffff
	F		#9397a5
	W		#ffffff
Tree.changeSelectionWithFocus	*	Boolean	true
Tree.closedIcon	L	Icon	class=javax.swing.plaf.metal.MetalIconFactory$TreeFolderIcon
	F		
	W		
Tree.collapsedIcon	L	Icon	class=javax.swing.plaf.metal.MetalIconFactory$TreeControlIcon
	F		class=com.sun.java.swing.plaf.motif.MotifTreeUI$MotifCollapsedIcon
	W		class=com.sun.java.swing.plaf.windows.WindowsTreeUI$CollapsedIcon

UI Defaults Name	L&F	Type	Value
Tree‚ .drawsFocusBorderAroundIcon	L	Boolean	false
	F		true
	W		false
Tree.editorBorder	L	LineBorder	color=#000000, thickness=1, rounded=false
	F	Border	class=com.sun.java.swing.plaf.motif.MotifBorders$FocusBorder
	W	LineBorder	color=#000000, thickness=1, rounded=false
Tree.editorBorderSelectionColor	F	Color	#b24d7a
Tree.expandedIcon	L	Icon	class=javax.swing.plaf.metal.MetalIconFactory$TreeControlIcon
	F		class=com.sun.java.swing.plaf.motif.MotifTreeUI$MotifExpandedIcon
	W		class=com.sun.java.swing.plaf.windows.WindowsTreeUI$ExpandedIcon
Tree.focusInputMap	L	InputMap	pKP_UP, pEND, spSPACE, pKP_DOWN, pHOME, cpV, scpPAGE_UP, pKP_LEFT, pLEFT, spPAGE_DOWN, cpX, pKP_RIGHT, cpKP_UP, pUP, cpSPACE, pCOPY, cpKP_DOWN, spHOME, pRIGHT, cpSLASH, cpPAGE_UP, cpKP_LEFT, pDOWN, cpPAGE_DOWN, cpKP_RIGHT, pPASTE, spKP_DOWN, spUP, cpEND, cpBACK_SLASH, cpHOME, spPAGE_UP, pF2, cpA, pCUT, spDOWN, cpLEFT, scpPAGE_DOWN, cpUP, cpC, spEND, pSPACE, cpRIGHT, pPAGE_UP, cpDOWN, spKP_UP, pPAGE_DOWN
	F		pKP_UP, pEND, spSPACE, spINSERT, pKP_DOWN, pHOME, scpPAGE_UP, pKP_LEFT, pLEFT, spPAGE_DOWN, pKP_RIGHT, pUP, cpSPACE, pCOPY, spHOME, pRIGHT, cpSLASH, cpPAGE_UP, cpINSERT, pDOWN, cpPAGE_DOWN, pPASTE, spKP_DOWN, spUP, cpBACK_SLASH, spPAGE_UP, pF2, cpA, pCUT, spDOWN, scpPAGE_DOWN, spEND, pSPACE, pPAGE_UP, spDELETE, spKP_UP, pPAGE_DOWN
	W		pKP_UP, pEND, spSPACE, pKP_DOWN, pHOME, cpV, scpPAGE_UP, pKP_LEFT, pLEFT, spPAGE_DOWN, cpX, pKP_RIGHT, cpKP_UP, pUP, cpSPACE, pCOPY, cpKP_DOWN, spHOME, pRIGHT, cpSLASH, cpPAGE_UP, cpKP_LEFT, pDOWN, cpPAGE_DOWN, cpKP_RIGHT, pPASTE, spKP_DOWN, spUP, cpEND, cpBACK_SLASH, cpHOME, spPAGE_UP, pF2, cpA, pCUT, spDOWN, cpLEFT, scpPAGE_DOWN, cpUP, cpC, spEND, pSPACE, cpRIGHT, pPAGE_UP, cpDOWN, spKP_UP, pPAGE_DOWN
Tree.focusInputMap.RightToLeft	*	InputMap	pRIGHT, pKP_RIGHT, pLEFT, pKP_LEFT
Tree.font	L	Font	name=Dialog, style=PLAIN, size=12
	F		name=Dialog, style=PLAIN, size=12
	W		name=Tahoma, style=PLAIN, size=11
Tree.foreground	*	Color	#000000
Tree.hash	L	Color	#ccccff
	F		#000000
	W		#808080
Tree.iconBackground	F	Color	#aeb2c3
Tree.iconForeground	F	Color	#63656f
Tree.iconHighlight	F	Color	#dcdee5
Tree.iconShadow	F	Color	#63656f
Tree.leafIcon	L	Icon	class=javax.swing.plaf.metal.MetalIconFactory$TreeLeafIcon
	F		
	W		
Tree.leftChildIndent	*	Integer	7
Tree.line	L	Color	#ccccff
Tree.openIcon	L	Icon	class=javax.swing.plaf.metal.MetalIconFactory$TreeFolderIcon
	F		
	W		
Tree.rightChildIndent	*	Integer	13
Tree.rowHeight	L	Integer	0
	F		18
	W		16
Tree.scrollsOnExpand	*	Boolean	true
Tree.selectionBackground	L	Color	#ccccff
	F		#fff7e9
	W		#0a246a
Tree.selectionBorderColor	L	Color	#9999cc
	F		#b24d7a
	W		#ffff00
Tree.selectionForeground	L	Color	#000000
	F		#000000
	W		#ffffff
Tree.textBackground	L	Color	#ffffff

UI Defaults Name	L&F	Type	Value
	F		#9397a5
	W		#ffffff
Tree.textForeground	*	Color	#000000
TreeUI	L	String	javax.sun.java.swing.plaf.metal.MetalTreeUI
	F		com.sun.java.swing.plaf.motif.MotifTreeUI
	W		com.sun.java.swing.plaf.windows.WindowsTreeUI
Viewport.background	L	Color	#cccccc
	F		#aeb2c3
	W		#d4d0c8
Viewport.font	L	Font	name=Dialog, style=PLAIN, size=12
	F		name=Dialog, style=PLAIN, size=12
	W		name=Tahoma, style=PLAIN, size=11
Viewport.foreground	*	Color	#000000
ViewportUI	*	String	javax.swing.plaf.basic.BasicViewportUI
activeCaption	L	Color	#ccccff
	F		#000080
	W		#0a246a
activeCaptionBorder	L	Color	#9999cc
	F		#b24d7a
	W		#d4d0c8
activeCaptionText	L	Color	#000000
	F		#ffffff
	W		#ffffff
control	L	Color	#cccccc
	F		#aeb2c3
	W		#d4d0c8
controlDkShadow	L	Color	#666666
	F		#000000
	W		#404040
controlHighlight	L	Color	#ffffff
	F		#dcdee5
	W		#d4d0c8
controlLightShadow	F	Color	#9397a5
controlLtHighlight	L	Color	#ffffff
	F		#dcdee5
	W		#ffffff
controlShadow	L	Color	#999999
	F		#63656f
	W		#808080
controlText	*	Color	#000000
desktop	L	Color	#9999cc
	F		#005c5c
	W		#3a6ea5
inactiveCaption	L	Color	#cccccc
	F		#aeb2c3
	W		#808080
inactiveCaptionBorder	L	Color	#999999
	F		#aeb2c3
	W		#d4d0c8
inactiveCaptionText	L	Color	#000000
	F		#000000
	W		#d4d0c8
info	L	Color	#ccccff
	F		#fff7e9
	W		#ffffe1
infoText	*	Color	#000000
menu	L	Color	#cccccc
	F		#aeb2c3
	W		#d4d0c8
menuPressedItemB	W	Color	#000000
menuPressedItemF	W	Color	#000000
menuText	*	Color	#000000
scrollbar	L	Color	#cccccc
	F		#aeb2c3

UI Defaults Name	L&F	Type	Value
	W		#d4d0c8
text	L	Color	#ffffff
	F		#fff7e9
	W		#ffffff
textHighlight	L	Color	#ccccff
	F		#000000
	W		#0a246a
textHighlightText	L	Color	#000000
	F		#fff7e9
	W		#ffffff
textInactiveText	L	Color	#999999
	F		#808080
	W		#808080
textText	*	Color	#000000
window	L	Color	#ffffff
	F		#aeb2c3
	W		#ffffff
windowBorder	L	Color	#cccccc
	F		#aeb2c3
	W		#000000
windowText	*	Color	#000000

Part 4

CROSS-REFERENCE

This part contains a cross-reference of all of the 1.4 Java classes and interfaces of the packages included in this volume. To save space, there are no cross-reference entries for primitive types, constructors, `java.lang.Object`, or `java.lang.String`.

The cross-reference consists of entries and subentries. An entry is displayed in bold type and shows a class, interface, or member name. If the entry is a class or interface, the package containing the class or interface is shown on the right. If the entry is a member name, all classes or interfaces that have a member with that name are listed to the right. Member names are shown in a condensed font to conserve space.

A class or interface may be followed by an up-arrow (ˆ) or a down-arrow (ˌ). The up-arrow inidicates that the class has a superclass other than `Error`, `Exception`, `Object`, or `RuntimeException`. In the case of an interface, it indicates that the interface extends from another interface. The down-arrow indicates that the class has a subclass. In the case of an interface, it indicates that the interface is extended by another interface.

An entry may be followed by subentries that contain more information about that class, interface, or member. For example, the "returned by" subentry for a class lists all members that return an instance of the class. Following is a list of the set of subentries.It's important to note that this cross-reference does not include any overridden methods. For example, if C.m() overrides A.m(), the entry "m" shows A but not C. To discover all classes that inherit m() and possibly implement m(), look up the "A" entry and there you will find all the classes that are descendents of A.

Subentry	Description
descendents	Shows the entire list of descendents (except for the ones that already appear in "subclasses") of this class or interface.
extended by	Shows all interfaces that extend this interface.
fields	Shows all fields of this type.
implemented by	Shows all classes that implement this interface.
passed to	Shows each method and constructor whose parameter list includes at least one parameter of this type.
returned by	Shows all methods that return an object of this type.
subclasses	Shows all subclasses of this class.
thrown by	Shows all methods and constructors that throw this exception.

_postEdit( ): **U**ndoableEditSupport
A: **H**TML.Tag **M**ediaSize.Engineering **M**ediaSizeName^
  PageAttributes.MediaType^
a: **A**WTEventMulticaster
A0: **M**ediaSize.ISO **P**ageAttributes.MediaType^
A1: **M**ediaSize.ISO **P**ageAttributes.MediaType^
A10: **M**ediaSize.ISO **P**ageAttributes.MediaType^
A2: **M**ediaSize.ISO **P**ageAttributes.MediaType^
A3: **M**ediaSize.ISO **P**ageAttributes.MediaType^
A4: **M**ediaSize.ISO **P**ageAttributes.MediaType^
A5: **M**ediaSize.ISO **P**ageAttributes.MediaType^
A6: **M**ediaSize.ISO **P**ageAttributes.MediaType^
A7: **M**ediaSize.ISO **P**ageAttributes.MediaType^
A8: **M**ediaSize.ISO **P**ageAttributes.MediaType^
A9: **M**ediaSize.ISO **P**ageAttributes.MediaType^
ABORT: *ImageObserver*
abort( ): **I**mageReader **I**mageWriter
ABORTED: **J**obState^ **M**ediaTracker
ABORTED_BY_SYSTEM: **J**obStateReason^
abortGrabbing( ): **P**ixelGrabber
abortRequested( ): **I**mageReader **I**mageWriter
ABOUT_UIROLE: **S**erviceUIFactory
ABOVE_BOTTOM: **T**itledBorder̠
ABOVE_TOP: **T**itledBorder̠
AbstractAction̠: javax.swing
 —subclasses: **T**extAction̠
 —descendents: **D**efaultEditorKit.BeepAction^
  DefaultEditorKit.CopyAction^ **D**efaultEditorKit.CutAction^
  DefaultEditorKit.DefaultKeyTypedAction^
  DefaultEditorKit.InsertBreakAction^
  DefaultEditorKit.InsertContentAction^
  DefaultEditorKit.InsertTabAction^
  DefaultEditorKit.PasteAction^
  HTMLEditorKit.HTMLTextAction̠
  HTMLEditorKit.InsertHTMLTextAction^
  StyledEditorKit.AlignmentAction^ **S**tyledEditorKit.BoldAction^
  StyledEditorKit.FontFamilyAction^
  StyledEditorKit.FontSizeAction^
  StyledEditorKit.ForegroundAction^
  StyledEditorKit.ItalicAction^ **S**tyledEditorKit.StyledTextAction̠
  StyledEditorKit.UnderlineAction^
AbstractBorder̠: javax.swing.border
 —subclasses: **B**evelBorder̠ **C**ompoundBorder̠ **E**mptyBorder̠
  EtchedBorder̠ **L**ineBorder̠ **T**itledBorder̠
 —descendents: **B**orderUIResource.BevelBorderUIResource^
  BorderUIResource.CompoundBorderUIResource^
  BorderUIResource.EmptyBorderUIResource^
  BorderUIResource.EtchedBorderUIResource^
  BorderUIResource.LineBorderUIResource^
  BorderUIResource.MatteBorderUIResource^
  BorderUIResource.TitledBorderUIResource^ **M**atteBorder̠
  SoftBevelBorder^
AbstractButton̠: javax.swing
 —subclasses: **J**Button̠ **J**MenuItem̠ **J**ToggleButton̠
 —descendents: **J**CheckBox^ **J**CheckBoxMenuItem̠ **J**Menu^
  JRadioButton^ **J**RadioButtonMenuItem^
 —passed to: **A**bstractButton.AccessibleAbstractButton( )
  ButtonGroup < add( ), remove( ) >
AbstractButton.AccessibleAbstractButton̠: javax.swing
 —subclasses: **J**Button.AccessibleJButton^
  JMenuItem.AccessibleJMenuItem̠
  JToggleButton.AccessibleJToggleButton̠
 —descendents: **J**CheckBox.AccessibleJCheckBox^
  JCheckBoxMenuItem.AccessibleJCheckBoxMenuItem^
  JMenu.AccessibleJMenu^
  JRadioButton.AccessibleJRadioButton^
  JRadioButtonMenuItem.AccessibleJRadioButtonMenuItem^
AbstractButton.ButtonChangeListener: javax.swing
AbstractCellEditor̠: javax.swing
 —subclasses: **D**efaultCellEditor^
AbstractCollection: java.util
 —descendents: **J**obStateReasons^

AbstractColorChooserPanel: javax.swing.colorchooser
 —passed to: **J**ColorChooser^ < addChooserPanel( ),
  removeChooserPanel( ), setChooserPanels( ) >
 —returned
  by: **C**olorChooserComponentFactory.getDefaultChooserPanels( )
  JColorChooser^ < getChooserPanels( ), removeChooserPanel( ) >
AbstractDocument: javax.swing.text
 —subclasses: **D**efaultStyledDocument̠ **P**lainDocument^
 —descendents: **H**TMLDocument^
 —passed to: **A**bstractDocument.AbstractElement( )
  AbstractDocument.BranchElement( )
  AbstractDocument.DefaultDocumentEvent( )
  AbstractDocument.LeafElement( )
AbstractDocument.AbstractElement: javax.swing.text
 —subclasses: **A**bstractDocument.BranchElement̠
  AbstractDocument.LeafElement̠
 —descendents: **D**efaultStyledDocument.SectionElement^
  HTMLDocument.BlockElement^
  HTMLDocument.RunElement^
 —returned by: **D**efaultStyledDocument̠.createDefaultRoot( )
  HTMLDocument^.createDefaultRoot( )
  PlainDocument^.createDefaultRoot( )
AbstractDocument.AttributeContext: javax.swing.text
 —passed to: **A**bstractDocument( )
 —returned by: **A**bstractDocument̠.getAttributeContext( )
 —implemented by: **S**tyleContext̠
AbstractDocument.BranchElement: javax.swing.text
 —subclasses: **D**efaultStyledDocument.SectionElement^
  HTMLDocument.BlockElement^
AbstractDocument.Content: javax.swing.text
 —passed to: **A**bstractDocument( ) **D**efaultStyledDocument( )
  HTMLDocument( ) **P**lainDocument( )
 —returned by: **A**bstractDocument̠.getContent( )
 —implemented by: **G**apContent^ **S**tringContent
AbstractDocument.DefaultDocumentEvent: javax.swing.text
 —passed to: **A**bstractDocument < insertUpdate( ),
  postRemoveUpdate( ), removeUpdate( ) >
  DefaultStyledDocument̠ < insertUpdate( ), removeUpdate( ) >
  DefaultStyledDocument.ElementBuffer < change( ), insert( ),
  remove( ) > **H**TMLDocument^.insertUpdate( ) **P**lainDocument^
  < insertUpdate( ), removeUpdate( ) >
AbstractDocument.ElementEdit^: javax.swing.text
AbstractDocument.LeafElement̠: javax.swing.text
 —subclasses: **H**TMLDocument.RunElement^
AbstractLayoutCache̠: javax.swing.tree
 —subclasses: **F**ixedHeightLayoutCache^
  VariableHeightLayoutCache^
AbstractLayoutCache.NodeDimensions: javax.swing.tree
 —passed to: **A**bstractLayoutCache̠.setNodeDimensions( )
 —returned by: **A**bstractLayoutCache̠.getNodeDimensions( )
 —fields: **A**bstractLayoutCache̠.nodeDimensions
AbstractListModel̠: javax.swing
 —subclasses: **D**efaultComboBoxModel^ **D**efaultListModel^
AbstractMap: java.util
 —descendents: **P**rinterStateReasons^
AbstractSet̠: java.util
 —descendents: **J**obStateReasons^
AbstractSpinnerModel̠: javax.swing
 —subclasses: **S**pinnerDateModel^ **S**pinnerListModel^
  SpinnerNumberModel^
AbstractTableModel̠: javax.swing.table
 —subclasses: **D**efaultTableModel^
AbstractUndoableEdit̠: javax.swing.undo
 —subclasses: **A**bstractDocument.ElementEdit^ **C**ompoundEdit̠
  DefaultStyledDocument.AttributeUndoableEdit^ **S**tateEdit̠
 —descendents: **A**bstractDocument.DefaultDocumentEvent^
  UndoManager^
AbstractWriter̠: javax.swing.text
 —subclasses: **H**TMLWriter^ **M**inimalHTMLWriter^
ACCELERATOR_KEY: *Action*^
accept( ): **C**ontainerOrderFocusTraversalPolicy **F**ileFilter
  JFileChooser^ **S**ortingFocusTraversalPolicy̠

A

—returned by: **A**ctionMap˯.getParent( )
JComponent˯.getActionMap( ) **S**wingUtilities.getUIActionMap( )
ActionMapUIResourceˆ: javax.swing.plaf
actionName: **J**TextComponent.KeyBinding
actionPerformed( ): *ActionListener*˯ **A**WTEventMulticaster
DefaultCellEditor.EditorDelegate **D**efaultTreeCellEditor
DropTarget.DropTargetAutoScroller **F**ormView˯
JComboBox˯ **L**ist.AccessibleAWTList˯
ToolTipManager.insideTimerAction
ToolTipManager.outsideTimerAction
ToolTipManager.stillInsideTimerAction
activate( ): *IIOMetadataController IIOParamController*
InputMethod
activateController( ): *IIOMetadata IIOParam*˯
ACTIVATED: **H**yperlinkEvent.EventType
activateFrame( ): **D**efaultDesktopManager *DesktopManager*
activateLink( ): **H**TMLEditorKit.LinkController˯
active: **V**oiceStatus
ACTIVE: **A**ccessibleState˯
ACTIVE_CAPTION: **S**ystemColor˯
ACTIVE_CAPTION_BORDER: **S**ystemColor˯
ACTIVE_CAPTION_TEXT: **S**ystemColor˯
ACTIVE_SENSING: **S**hortMessage˯
activeCaption: **S**ystemColor˯
activeCaptionBorder: **S**ystemColor˯
activeCaptionText: **S**ystemColor˯
ActiveEvent: java.awt
—implemented by: **I**nvocationEvent˯
add( ): **A**ccessibleRelationSet **A**ccessibleStateSet **A**rea
javax.print.attribute.AttributeSet˯ **A**WTEventMulticaster
ButtonGroup *ChoicePeer*˯ **C**omponent˯ **D**efaultListModel˯
DefaultMutableTreeNode˯ **E**ventListenerList
HashAttributeSet˯ *ListPeer*˯ **M**enu˯ **M**enuBar˯
ParameterBlock **R**ectangle2D˯ **R**enderingHints **T**rack
addAccessibleSelection( ): *AccessibleSelection*
JComboBox.AccessibleJComboBox˯ **J**List.AccessibleJList˯
JMenu.AccessibleJMenu˯ **J**MenuBar.AccessibleJMenuBar˯
JTabbedPane.AccessibleJTabbedPane˯
JTable.AccessibleJTable˯ **J**Tree.AccessibleJTree˯
JTree.AccessibleJTree.AccessibleJTreeNode˯
List.AccessibleAWTList˯
MenuComponent.AccessibleAWTMenuComponent˯
addActionForKeyStroke( ): *Keymap*
addActionListener( ): **A**bstractButton˯ **B**utton˯ *ButtonModel*˯
ComboBoxEditor **D**efaultButtonModel˯ **J**ComboBox˯
JFileChooser˯ **J**TextField˯ java.awt.**L**ist˯ **M**enuItem˯
TextField˯ **T**imer
addAdjustmentListener( ): *Adjustable* **J**ScrollBar˯ *Scrollbar*˯
ScrollPaneAdjustable
addAll( ): **A**ccessibleRelationSet **A**ccessibleStateSet
javax.print.attribute.AttributeSet˯ **H**ashAttributeSet˯
addAncestorListener( ): **J**Component˯
addAttribute( ): **A**bstractDocument.AbstractElement˯
AbstractDocument.AttributeContext **I**IOMetadataFormatImpl˯
MutableAttributeSet˯ **S**impleAttributeSet **S**tyleContext˯
StyleContext.NamedStyle
addAttributes( ): **A**bstractDocument.AbstractElement˯
AbstractDocument.AttributeContext MutableAttributeSet˯
SimpleAttributeSet **S**tyleContext˯ **S**tyleContext.NamedStyle
addAuxiliaryLookAndFeel( ): **U**IManager
addAWTEventListener( ): **T**oolkit
addBooleanAttribute( ): **I**IOMetadataFormatImpl
addCaretListener( ): **J**TextComponent˯
addCellEditorListener( ): **A**bstractCellEditor˯ *CellEditor*˯
DefaultTreeCellEditor
addChangeListener( ): **A**bstractButton˯ **A**bstractSpinnerModel˯
BoundedRangeModel **B**uttonModel˯ **C**aret˯
ColorSelectionModel **D**efaultBoundedRangeModel˯
DefaultButtonModel˯ **D**efaultCaret˯
DefaultColorSelectionModel **D**efaultSingleSelectionModel˯
JProgressBar˯ **J**Slider˯ **J**Spinner˯ **J**TabbedPane˯
JViewport˯ **M**enuSelectionManager *SingleSelectionModel*

SpinnerModel Style˯ **S**tyleContext˯
StyleContext.NamedStyle
addChildElement( ): **I**IOMetadataFormatImpl
addChoosableFileFilter( ): **J**FileChooser˯
addChooserPanel( ): **J**ColorChooser˯
addColumn( ): **D**efaultTableColumnModel **D**efaultTableModel˯
JTable˯ *TableColumnModel*
addColumnModelListener( ): **D**efaultTableColumnModel
TableColumnModel
addColumnSelectionInterval( ): **J**Table˯
addComponentListener( ): **C**omponent˯
addConsumer( ): **F**ilteredImageSource *ImageProducer*
MemoryImageSource **R**enderableImageProducer
addContainerListener( ): **C**ontainer˯
addContent( ): **H**TMLDocument.HTMLReader˯
addControllerEventListener( ): *Sequencer*˯
addCSSAttribute( ): **S**tyleSheet˯
addCSSAttributeFromHTML( ): **S**tyleSheet˯
addDirtyRegion( ): **R**epaintManager
addDocumentListener( ): **A**bstractDocument˯
javax.swing.text.Document˯
addDragGestureListener( ): **D**ragGestureRecognizer˯
addDragSourceListener( ): **D**ragSource **D**ragSourceContext
addDragSourceMotionListener( ): **D**ragSource
addDropTargetListener( ): **D**ropTarget
addEdit( ): **A**bstractUndoableEdit˯ *UndoableEdit*
addElement( ): **D**efaultComboBoxModel˯ **D**efaultListModel˯
IIOMetadataFormatImpl *MutableComboBoxModel*˯
addFlavorForUnencodedNative( ): **S**ystemFlavorMap
addFocusListener( ): *AccessibleComponent*˯
Component˯ **C**omponent.AccessibleAWTComponent˯
JList.AccessibleJList.AccessibleJListChild˯
JTable.AccessibleJTable.AccessibleJTableCell˯
JTableHeader.AccessibleJTableHeader˲
.AccessibleJTableHeaderEntry˯
JTree.AccessibleJTree.AccessibleJTreeNode˯
MenuComponent.AccessibleAWTMenuComponent˯
addHelpMenu( ): *MenuBarPeer*˯
addHierarchyBoundsListener( ): **C**omponent˯
addHierarchyListener( ): **C**omponent˯
addHighlight( ): *Highlighter*
addHyperlinkListener( ): **J**EditorPane˯
addIIOReadProgressListener( ): **I**mageReader
addIIOReadUpdateListener( ): **I**mageReader
addIIOReadWarningListener( ): **I**mageReader
addIIOWriteProgressListener( ): **I**mageWriter
addIIOWriteWarningListener( ): **I**mageWriter
addImage( ): **M**ediaTracker
addImpl( ): **C**ontainer˯
addInputMethodListener( ): **C**omponent˯
addInternal( ): **A**WTEventMulticaster
addInternalFrameListener( ): **J**InternalFrame˯
addInvalidComponent( ): **R**epaintManager
addItem( ): **C**hoice˯ *ChoicePeer*˯ **J**ComboBox˯ java.awt.**L**ist˯
ListPeer˯ *MenuPeer*˯
addItemListener( ): **A**bstractButton˯ **C**heckbox˯
CheckboxMenuItem˯ **C**hoice˯ **D**efaultButtonModel˯
ItemSelectable˯ **J**ComboBox˯ java.awt.**L**ist˯
AdditionalComments: **H**TMLEditorKit
addKeyEventDispatcher( ): **K**eyboardFocusManager˯
addKeyEventPostProcessor( ): **K**eyboardFocusManager˯
addKeyListener( ): **C**omponent˯
addKeymap( ): **J**TextComponent
addLayoutComponent( ): **B**orderLayout **B**oxLayout
CardLayout **F**lowLayout **G**ridBagLayout **G**ridLayout
JRootPane.RootLayout **J**Spinner.DefaultEditor˯
LayoutManager **O**verlayLayout **S**crollPaneLayout˯
SpringLayout **V**iewportLayout
addLineListener( ): *Line*˯
addListDataListener( ): **A**bstractListModel˯ *ListModel*˯
addListSelectionListener( ): **D**efaultListSelectionModel **J**List˯
ListSelectionModel

A

ALL_COLUMNS: TableModelEvent^
ALL_RANGES: NumericShaper
ALLBITS: *ImageObserver*
allKeys(): ActionMap‿ InputMap‿
allNotesOff(): *MidiChannel*
allocateArray(): GapVector
allowsChildren: DefaultMutableTreeNode‿
allowsMultipleSelections(): java.awt.List^
allSoundOff(): *MidiChannel*
AlphaComposite: java.awt
—returned by: AlphaComposite.getInstance()
—fields: AlphaComposite < Clear, Dst, DstAtop, DstIn, DstOut, DstOver, Src, SrcAtop, SrcIn, SrcOut, SrcOver, Xor >
ALT: HTML.Attribute
ALT_DOWN_MASK: InputEvent^
ALT_GRAPH_DOWN_MASK: InputEvent^
ALT_GRAPH_MASK: InputEvent^
ALT_MASK: ActionEvent Event InputEvent^
alternateAddTag: HTMLEditorKit.InsertHTMLTextAction^
alternateParentTag: HTMLEditorKit.InsertHTMLTextAction^
ANCESTOR_ADDED: AncestorEvent^
ANCESTOR_MOVED: AncestorEvent^ HierarchyEvent^
ANCESTOR_REMOVED: AncestorEvent^
ANCESTOR_RESIZED: HierarchyEvent^
ancestorAdded(): *AncestorListener*^
AncestorEvent^: javax.swing.event
—passed to: *AncestorListener*^ < ancestorAdded(), ancestorMoved(), ancestorRemoved() >
AncestorListener^: javax.swing.event
—passed to: JComponent^ < addAncestorListener(), removeAncestorListener() >
—returned by: JComponent^.getAncestorListeners()
ancestorMoved(): *AncestorListener*^ AWTEventMulticaster HierarchyBoundsAdapter *HierarchyBoundsListener*^
ancestorRemoved(): *AncestorListener*^
ancestorResized(): AWTEventMulticaster HierarchyBoundsAdapter *HierarchyBoundsListener*^
anchor: GridBagConstraints
ANCHOR_SELECTION_PATH_PROPERTY: JTree^
ANY: *DTDConstants*
append(): Book GeneralPath JTextArea^ TextArea^ View‿
appendChild(): IIOMetadataNode
appendEvent(): DragGestureRecognizer‿
appendText(): TextArea^
applet: DTD
APPLET: HTML.Tag‿
Applet^: java.applet
—subclasses: JApplet^
—passed to: Applet.AccessibleApplet()
java.beans.*AppletInitializer* < activate(), initialize() >
org.omg.CORBA.ORB < init(), set_parameters() >
—returned by: *AppletContext*.getApplet()
Applet.AccessibleApplet^: java.applet
—subclasses: JApplet.AccessibleJApplet^
AppletContext: java.applet
—returned by: Applet^.getAppletContext()
AppletStub.getAppletContext()
appletResize(): *AppletStub*
AppletStub: java.applet
—passed to: Applet^.setStub()
APPLY_REVERB: BooleanControl.Type^
applyComponentOrientation(): Component‿
applyResourceBundle(): Window^
APPROVE_BUTTON_MNEMONIC_CHANGED_PROPERTY: JFileChooser^
APPROVE_BUTTON_TEXT_CHANGED_PROPERTY: JFileChooser^
APPROVE_BUTTON_TOOL_TIP_TEXT_CHANGED_PROPERTY: JFileChooser^
APPROVE_OPTION: JFileChooser^
APPROVE_SELECTION: JFileChooser^
approveSelection(): JFileChooser^

ARABIC: NumericShaper
Arc2D^: java.awt.geom
—subclasses: Arc2D.Double^ Arc2D.Float^
—passed to: Arc2D^.setArc()
Arc2D.Double^: java.awt.geom
Arc2D.Float^: java.awt.geom
archeight: RoundRectangle2D.Double^ RoundRectangle2D.Float^
ARCHIVE: HTML.Attribute
arcwidth: RoundRectangle2D.Double^ RoundRectangle2D.Float^
AREA: HTML.Tag^
Area: java.awt.geom
—passed to: Area < add(), equals(), exclusiveOr(), intersect(), subtract() >
—returned by: Area.createTransformedArea()
AreaAveragingScaleFilter^: java.awt.image
areFocusTraversalKeysSet(): Component‿
areNew: TreeSelectionEvent^
arePathsContiguous(): DefaultTreeSelectionModel‿
areTablesSet(): JPEGImageReadParam^ JPEGImageWriteParam^
arg: Event
ARMED: AccessibleState^ DefaultButtonModel‿
arrangeGrid(): GridBagLayout
ArrangeGrid(): GridBagLayout
array: Segment
ArrayIndexOutOfBoundsException^: java.lang
—thrown by: Track.get()
ArrayList^: java.util
—fields: DragGestureRecognizer‿.events
asksAllowsChildren: DefaultTreeModel
asksAllowsChildren(): DefaultTreeModel
AsyncBoxView^: javax.swing.text
—passed to: AsyncBoxView.ChildLocator() AsyncBoxView.ChildState()
AsyncBoxView.ChildLocator: javax.swing.text
—fields: AsyncBoxView^.locator
AsyncBoxView.ChildState: javax.swing.text
—passed to: AsyncBoxView < majorRequirementChange(), minorRequirementChange() >
AsyncBoxView.ChildLocator.childChanged()
—returned by: AsyncBoxView^ < createChildState(), getChildState() >
—fields: AsyncBoxView.ChildLocator.lastValidOffset
ATTEMPTED: PDLOverrideSupported^
Attr^: org.w3c.dom
—passed to: IIOMetadataNode < removeAttributeNode(), setAttributeNode(), setAttributeNodeNS() >
—returned by: IIOMetadataNode < getAttributeNode(), getAttributeNodeNS(), removeAttributeNode(), setAttributeNode(), setAttributeNodeNS() >
Attribute^: javax.print.attribute
—extended by: *DocAttribute*^ *PrintJobAttribute*^ *PrintRequestAttribute*^ *PrintServiceAttribute*^ *SupportedValuesAttribute*^
—passed to: javax.print.attribute.*AttributeSet*‿ < add(), containsValue(), remove() >
AttributeSetUtilities.verifyCategoryForValue()
DocAttributeSet^.add() HashAttributeSet‿ < add(), containsValue(), HashAttributeSet(), remove() >
PrintJobAttributeSet^.add() *PrintRequestAttributeSet*^.add()
PrintService‿.isAttributeValueSupported()
PrintServiceAttributeSet^.add()
—returned by: AttributeException.getUnsupportedValues()
javax.print.attribute.*AttributeSet*‿ < get(), toArray() >
AttributeSetUtilities.verifyAttributeValue() HashAttributeSet‿ < get(), toArray() >
—implemented by: JobStateReason^ MediaName^ MediaSize^ MediaTray^ PrinterStateReason^ ReferenceUriSchemesSupported^ Severity^

JobAttributes.MultipleDocumentHandlingType^
JobAttributes.SidesType^ **P**ageAttributes.ColorType^
PageAttributes.MediaType^
PageAttributes.OrientationRequestedType^
PageAttributes.OriginType^ **P**ageAttributes.PrintQualityType^
atts: javax.swing.text.html.parser.**Element**
AU: **A**udioFileFormat.Type
AudioClip: java.applet
—returned by: **A**pplet^ < getAudioClip( ), newAudioClip( ) >
AppletContext.getAudioClip( )
AudioFileFormat: javax.sound.sampled
—returned by: **A**udioFileReader.getAudioFileFormat( )
AudioSystem.getAudioFileFormat( )
AudioFileFormat.Type: javax.sound.sampled
—passed to: **A**udioFileFormat( ) **A**udioFileWriter
< isFileTypeSupported( ), write( ) > **A**udioSystem
< isFileTypeSupported( ), write( ) >
—returned by: **A**udioFileFormat.getType( )
AudioFileWriter.getAudioFileTypes( )
AudioSystem.getAudioFileTypes( )
—fields: **A**udioFileFormat.Type < AIFC, AIFF, AU, SND, WAVE >
AudioFileReader: javax.sound.sampled.spi
AudioFileWriter: javax.sound.sampled.spi
AudioFormat: javax.sound.sampled
—passed to: **A**udioFileFormat( ) **A**udioFormat.matches( )
AudioInputStream( ) **A**udioSystem < getAudioInputStream( ),
getTargetEncodings( ), getTargetFormats( ),
isConversionSupported( ) > *Clip*^.open( ) **D**ataLine.Info^
< DataLine.Info( ), isFormatSupported( ) >
FormatConversionProvider < getAudioInputStream( ),
getTargetEncodings( ), getTargetFormats( ),
isConversionSupported( ) > *SourceDataLine*^.open( )
TargetDataLine^.open( )
—returned by: **A**udioFileFormat.getFormat( )
AudioInputStream^.getFormat( )
AudioSystem.getTargetFormats( )
DataLine^.getFormat( ) **D**ataLine.Info^.getFormats( )
FormatConversionProvider.getTargetFormats( )
—fields: **A**udioInputStream^.format
AudioFormat.Encoding: javax.sound.sampled
—passed to: **A**udioFormat( ) **A**udioSystem
< getAudioInputStream( ), getTargetEncodings( ),
getTargetFormats( ), isConversionSupported( ) >
FormatConversionProvider < getAudioInputStream( ),
getTargetFormats( ), isConversionSupported( ),
isSourceEncodingSupported( ), isTargetEncodingSupported( ) >
—returned by: **A**udioFormat.getEncoding( )
AudioSystem.getTargetEncodings( ) **F**ormatConversionProvider
< getSourceEncodings( ), getTargetEncodings( ) >
—fields: **A**udioFormat.encoding **A**udioFormat.Encoding < ALAW,
PCM_SIGNED, PCM_UNSIGNED, ULAW >
AudioInputStream^: javax.sound.sampled
—passed to: **A**udioFileWriter < getAudioFileTypes( ),
isFileTypeSupported( ), write( ) > **A**udioSystem
< getAudioFileTypes( ), getAudioInputStream( ),
isFileTypeSupported( ), write( ) > *Clip*^.open( )
FormatConversionProvider.getAudioInputStream( )
—returned by: **A**udioFileReader.getAudioInputStream( )
AudioSystem.getAudioInputStream( )
FormatConversionProvider.getAudioInputStream( )
AudioPermission^: javax.sound.sampled
AudioSystem: javax.sound.sampled
augmentList( ): **T**extAction^
AUTO_RESIZE_ALL_COLUMNS: **J**Table^
AUTO_RESIZE_LAST_COLUMN: **J**Table^
AUTO_RESIZE_NEXT_COLUMN: **J**Table^
AUTO_RESIZE_OFF: **J**Table^
AUTO_RESIZE_SUBSEQUENT_COLUMNS: **J**Table^
autoCreateColumnsFromModel: **J**Table^
autoResizeMode: **J**Table^
Autoscroll: java.awt.dnd
autoscroll( ): *Autoscroll*

AUTOSENSE: **D**ocFlavor.BYTE_ARRAY^
DocFlavor.INPUT_STREAM^ **D**ocFlavor.URL^
AUX_RETURN: **F**loatControl.Type^
AUX_SEND: **F**loatControl.Type^
available( ): *DataLine*^
availableLocales: **I**mageReader **I**mageWriter
AWT_COMPONENT: **A**ccessibleRole^
AWTError: java.awt
AWTEvent^: java.awt
—subclasses: **A**ctionEvent^ **A**djustmentEvent^ **A**ncestorEvent^
ComponentEvent^ **H**ierarchyEvent^ **I**nputMethodEvent^
InternalFrameEvent^ **I**nvocationEvent^ **I**temEvent^
TextEvent^
—descendents: **C**ontainerEvent^ **F**ocusEvent^ **I**nputEvent^
KeyEvent^ **M**enuDragMouseEvent^ **M**enuKeyEvent^
MouseEvent^ **M**ouseWheelEvent^ **P**aintEvent^
WindowEvent^
—passed to: *AWTEventListener*^.eventDispatched( )
AWTEventListenerProxy^.eventDispatched( )
Button^.processEvent( ) **C**heckbox^.processEvent( )
CheckboxMenuItem^.processEvent( ) **C**hoice^.processEvent( )
Component < coalesceEvents( ), dispatchEvent( ),
processEvent( ) > *ComponentPeer*.handleEvent( )
Container^.processEvent( ) **E**ventQueue < dispatchEvent( ),
postEvent( ) > **I**nputContext.dispatchEvent( )
InputMethod.dispatchEvent( ) **K**eyboardFocusManager
< dispatchEvent( ), redispatchEvent( ) >
java.awt.**L**ist.processEvent( ) **M**enuComponent
< dispatchEvent( ), processEvent( ) > **M**enuItem^.processEvent( )
Scrollbar^.processEvent( ) **T**extComponent^.processEvent( )
TextField^.processEvent( ) **W**indow^.processEvent( )
—returned by: **C**omponent.coalesceEvents( ) **E**ventQueue
< getCurrentEvent( ), getNextEvent( ), peekEvent( ) >
AWTEventListener^: java.awt.event
—passed to: **A**WTEventListenerProxy( ) **T**oolkit
< addAWTEventListener( ), removeAWTEventListener( ) >
—returned by: **T**oolkit.getAWTEventListeners( )
—implemented by: **A**WTEventListenerProxy^
AWTEventListenerProxy^: java.awt.event
AWTEventMulticaster: java.awt
AWTException: java.awt
—thrown by: **C**anvas^.createBufferStrategy( )
Component.createVolatileImage( )
Component.FlipBufferStrategy^
< Component.FlipBufferStrategy( ), createBuffers( ) >
ComponentPeer.createBuffers( )
Cursor.getSystemCustomCursor( )
GraphicsConfiguration.createCompatibleVolatileImage( )
InputMethodDescriptor.getAvailableLocales( ) **R**obot( )
Window^.createBufferStrategy( )
AWTKeyStroke: java.awt
—subclasses: **K**eyStroke^
—returned by: **A**WTKeyStroke < getAWTKeyStroke( ),
getAWTKeyStrokeForEvent( ) >
AWTPermission^: java.awt
B: HTML.Tag MediaSize.Engineering **M**ediaSizeName^
PageAttributes.MediaType^
b: **A**WTEventMulticaster
B0: **M**ediaSize.ISO **M**ediaSize.JIS **P**ageAttributes.MediaType^
B1: **M**ediaSize.ISO **M**ediaSize.JIS **P**ageAttributes.MediaType^
B10: **M**ediaSize.ISO **M**ediaSize.JIS **P**ageAttributes.MediaType^
B2: **M**ediaSize.ISO **M**ediaSize.JIS **P**ageAttributes.MediaType^
B3: **M**ediaSize.ISO **M**ediaSize.JIS **P**ageAttributes.MediaType^
B4: **M**ediaSize.ISO **M**ediaSize.JIS **P**ageAttributes.MediaType^
B5: **M**ediaSize.ISO **M**ediaSize.JIS **P**ageAttributes.MediaType^
B6: **M**ediaSize.ISO **M**ediaSize.JIS **P**ageAttributes.MediaType^
B7: **M**ediaSize.ISO **M**ediaSize.JIS **P**ageAttributes.MediaType^
B8: **M**ediaSize.ISO **M**ediaSize.JIS **P**ageAttributes.MediaType^
B9: **M**ediaSize.ISO **M**ediaSize.JIS **P**ageAttributes.MediaType^
BACK_SPACE: **E**vent
backBuffers: **C**omponent.BltBufferStrategy^

BACKGROUND: **B**ufferCapabilities.FlipContents^ **C**SS.Attribute
  HTML.Attribute **T**extAttribute^
Background: **S**tyleConstants
BACKGROUND_ATTACHMENT: **C**SS.Attribute
BACKGROUND_COLOR: **C**SS.Attribute
BACKGROUND_IMAGE: **C**SS.Attribute
BACKGROUND_POSITION: **C**SS.Attribute
BACKGROUND_REPEAT: **C**SS.Attribute
backgroundNonSelectionColor: **D**efaultTreeCellRenderer^
backgroundSelectionColor: **D**efaultTreeCellRenderer^
backingStore: **J**Viewport^
BACKINGSTORE_SCROLL_MODE: **J**Viewport^
backingStoreImage: **J**Viewport^
Backward: **P**osition.Bias
BACKWARD_TRAVERSAL_KEYS: **K**eyboardFocusManager
backwardAction: **D**efaultEditorKit^
BAD_LOCATION: **A**bstractDocument
BadBreakWeight: **V**iew
BadLocationException: javax.swing.text
  —thrown by: **A**bstractDocument < createPosition( ),
  getText( ), insertString( ), remove( ), replace( ) >
  ***A**bstractDocument.Content* < createPosition( ),
  getChars( ), getString( ), insertString( ), remove( ) >
  AbstractWriter < getText( ), text( ), write( ) >
  CompositeView^ < getNextEastWestVisualPositionFrom( ),
  getNextNorthSouthVisualPositionFrom( ) >
  DefaultStyledDocument^.insert( ) *javax.swing.text.**D**ocument*
  < createPosition( ), getText( ), insertString( ), remove( ) >
  DocumentFilter < insertString( ), remove( ), replace( ) >
  DocumentFilter.FilterBypass < insertString( ), remove( ),
  replace( ) > **E**ditorKit < read( ), write( ) > **G**apContent^
  < createPosition( ), getChars( ), getString( ),
  insertString( ), remove( ) > **G**lyphView.GlyphPainter
  < getNextVisualPositionFrom( ), modelToView( ) >
  Highlighter < addHighlight( ), changeHighlight( ) >
  HTMLDocument^ < insert( ), insertAfterEnd( ), insertAfterStart( ),
  insertBeforeEnd( ), insertBeforeStart( ), setInnerHTML( ),
  setOuterHTML( ) > **H**TMLEditorKit^.insertHTML( )
  HTMLEditorKit.ParserCallback.flush( ) **H**TMLWriter^
  < comment( ), emptyTag( ), startTag( ), text( ),
  textAreaContent( ), write( ) > **J**TextArea^ < getLineEndOffset( ),
  getLineOfOffset( ), getLineStartOffset( ) > **J**TextComponent^
  < getText( ), modelToView( ) > **M**inimalHTMLWriter^
  < text( ), write( ), writeBody( ), writeContent( ) >
  NavigationFilter.getNextVisualPositionFrom( )
  *javax.swing.text.**P**aragraphView^* < getClosestPositionTo( ),
  getNextNorthSouthVisualPositionFrom( ) > **P**asswordView^
  < drawSelectedText( ), drawUnselectedText( ) > **P**lainView^
  < drawSelectedText( ), drawUnselectedText( ) > **S**tringContent
  < createPosition( ), getChars( ), getString( ), insertString( ),
  remove( ) > **T**extUI^ < getNextVisualPositionFrom( ),
  modelToView( ) > **U**tilities < getNextWord( ), getPositionAbove( ),
  getPositionBelow( ), getPreviousWord( ), getRowEnd( ),
  getRowStart( ), getWordEnd( ), getWordStart( ) > **V**iew
  < getNextVisualPositionFrom( ), modelToView( ) >
  WrappedPlainView^ < drawSelectedText( ),
  drawUnselectedText( ) >
BALANCE: **F**loatControl.Type^
BandCombineOp: java.awt.image
BandedSampleModel^: java.awt.image
bandOffsets: **C**omponentSampleModel^
bank: **V**oiceStatus
bankIndices: **C**omponentSampleModel^
banks: **D**ataBuffer
base: **D**TD
BASE: **H**TML.Tag
BASEFONT: **H**TML.Tag
baselineLayout( ): **B**oxView^
baselineRequirements( ): **B**oxView^
BasicPermission^: java.security
  —subclasses: **A**udioPermission^ **A**WTPermission^
BasicStroke: java.awt

—subclasses: **D**efaultTextUI^
beep( ): **T**oolkit
beepAction: **D**efaultEditorKit^
BEFORE_FIRST_LINE: **B**orderLayout
BEFORE_LINE_BEGINS: **B**orderLayout
beforeOffset( ): **T**extHitInfo
beginAction: **D**efaultEditorKit^
beginDraggingFrame( ): **D**efaultDesktopManager
  DesktopManager
beginLayout( ): *ContainerPeer*^
beginLineAction: **D**efaultEditorKit^
beginParagraphAction: **D**efaultEditorKit^
beginResizingFrame( ): **D**efaultDesktopManager
  DesktopManager
beginUpdate( ): **U**ndoableEditSupport
beginValidate( ): *ContainerPeer*^
beginWordAction: **D**efaultEditorKit^
BELOW_BOTTOM: **T**itledBorder^
BELOW_TOP: **T**itledBorder^
BENGALI: **N**umericShaper
BevelBorder^: javax.swing.border
  —subclasses: **B**orderUIResource.BevelBorderUIResource^
  SoftBevelBorder^
bevelType: **B**evelBorder^
BGCOLOR: **H**TML.Attribute
BIDI_EMBEDDING: **T**extAttribute^
BidiElementName: **A**bstractDocument
BidiLevel: **S**tyleConstants
BIG: **H**TML.Tag
bigEndian: **A**udioFormat
BigInteger^: java.math
  —passed to: **I**ndexColorModel( )
  —returned by: **I**ndexColorModel^.getValidPixels( )
BIND: **F**inishings^
BIT_DEPTH_MULTI: **D**isplayMode
BITMASK: *Transparency*
bitOffset: **I**mageInputStreamImpl
BitSet: java.util
  —passed to: **D**TD.defineElement( )
  —fields: javax.swing.text.html.parser.**E**lement < exclusions,
  inclusions >
BLACK: **C**olor
black: **C**olor
BLIT_SCROLL_MODE: **J**Viewport^
BLOCK_DECREMENT: **A**djustmentEvent^
BLOCK_INCREMENT: **A**djustmentEvent^
blockClose( ): **H**TMLDocument.HTMLReader^
blockIncrement: **J**ScrollBar
blockOpen( ): **H**TMLDocument.HTMLReader^
BLOCKQUOTE: **H**TML.Tag
BlockView^: javax.swing.text.html
  —subclasses: **L**istView^
BLUE: **C**olor
blue: **C**olor
BLUECOMPONENT: **I**CC_ProfileRGB^
body: **D**TD
BODY: **H**TML.Tag
BOLD: **F**ont
Bold: **S**tyleConstants
BOLD_ACTION: **H**TMLEditorKit^
Book: java.awt.print
Boolean: java.lang
  —passed to: **D**efaultDesktopManager.setWasIcon( )
  —returned by: **F**ileSystemView.isTraversable( )
  FileView.isTraversable( )
  —fields: **T**extAttribute^ < RUN_DIRECTION_LTR,
  RUN_DIRECTION_RTL, STRIKETHROUGH_ON,
  SWAP_COLORS_ON >
BooleanControl^: javax.sound.sampled
BooleanControl.Type^: javax.sound.sampled
  —passed to: **B**ooleanControl( )
  —fields: **B**ooleanControl.Type^ < APPLY_REVERB, MUTE >

B

C

CAP_ROUND: **B**asicStroke
CAP_SQUARE: **B**asicStroke
capacity( ): **D**efaultListModel^
caps: **C**omponent.BltBufferStrategy^
   Component.FlipBufferStrategy^
CAPS_LOCK: **E**vent
CAPTION: **H**TML.Tag_
CardLayout: java.awt
Caret: javax.swing.text
  —passed to: **J**TextComponent^.setCaret( )
  —returned by: **E**ditorKit_.createCaret( )
   JTextComponent^.getCaret( )
   NavigationFilter.FilterBypass.getCaret( )
  —implemented by: **D**efaultCaret^
CARET_POSITION_CHANGED: **I**nputMethodEvent^
CaretEvent^: javax.swing.event
  —passed to: *CaretListener*^.caretUpdate( )
   JTextComponent^.fireCaretUpdate( )
   JTextComponent.AccessibleJTextComponent^.caretUpdate( )
CaretListener^: javax.swing.event
  —passed to: **J**TextComponent^ < addCaretListener( ),
  removeCaretListener( ) >
  —returned by: **J**TextComponent^.getCaretListeners( )
  —implemented by: **J**TextComponent.AccessibleJTextComponent^
caretPositionChanged( ): **A**WTEventMulticaster
  *I*nputMethodListener^
caretUpdate( ): *CaretListener*^
  JTextComponent.AccessibleJTextComponent^
catchExceptions: **I**nvocationEvent^
CDATA: *D*TDConstants
CELL_EDITOR_PROPERTY: **J**Tree^
CELL_RENDERER_PROPERTY: **J**Tree^ **T**ableColumn
cellEditor: **J**Table^ **J**Tree^ **T**ableColumn
*CellEditor*_: javax.swing
  —extended by: *T*ableCellEditor^ *T*reeCellEditor^
  —implemented by: **A**bstractCellEditor_
CellEditorListener^: javax.swing.event
  —passed to: **A**bstractCellEditor_ < addCellEditorListener( ),
  removeCellEditorListener( ) > *CellEditor*_ < addCellEditorListener( ),
  removeCellEditorListener( ) > **D**efaultTreeCellEditor
  < addCellEditorListener( ), removeCellEditorListener( ) >
  —returned by: **A**bstractCellEditor_.getCellEditorListeners( )
  DefaultTreeCellEditor.getCellEditorListeners( )
  —implemented by: **J**Table^ **J**Table.AccessibleJTable^
CELLPADDING: **H**TML.Attribute
cellRenderer: **J**Tree^ **T**ableColumn
CellRendererPane^: javax.swing
  —passed to: **C**ellRendererPane.AccessibleCellRendererPane( )
CellRendererPane.AccessibleCellRendererPane^: javax.swing
cellSelectionEnabled: **J**Table^
CELLSPACING: **H**TML.Attribute
CENTER: **B**orderLayout **F**lowLayout **G**ridBagConstraints
  HTML.Tag_ **L**abel^ *SwingConstants* **T**itledBorder^
CENTER_ALIGNMENT: **C**omponent_
CENTER_BASELINE: **F**ont_ **G**raphicAttribute_
CHANGE: **D**ocumentEvent.EventType
change( ): **D**efaultStyledDocument.ElementBuffer
CHANGED: **D**ragSourceContext
ChangedCharSetException^: javax.swing.text
  —thrown by: **D**ocumentParser^.handleEmptyTag( )
  javax.swing.text.html.parser.**P**arser_ < handleEmptyTag( ),
  startTag( ) >
changedUpdate( ): *DocumentListener*^ **F**lowView.FlowStrategy
  JTextComponent.AccessibleJTextComponent^ **V**iew_
changeEvent: **A**bstractButton^ **A**bstractCellEditor_
  DefaultBoundedRangeModel **D**efaultButtonModel_
  DefaultCaret^ **D**efaultColorSelectionModel
  DefaultSingleSelectionModel **D**efaultTableColumnModel
  JProgressBar^ **J**Slider^ **J**TabbedPane^
  MenuSelectionManager **S**tyleContext.NamedStyle
ChangeEvent^: javax.swing.event

  —passed
  to: **A**bstractButton.ButtonChangeListener.stateChanged( )
  CellEditorListener^ < editingCanceled( ),
  editingStopped( ) > *ChangeListener*^.stateChanged( )
  JMenuItem.AccessibleJMenuItem^.stateChanged( )
  JScrollPane.AccessibleJScrollPane^.stateChanged( )
  JSpinner.DefaultEditor^.stateChanged( )
  JTabbedPane.AccessibleJTabbedPane^.stateChanged( )
  JTabbedPane.ModelListener.stateChanged( ) **J**Table^
  < columnMarginChanged( ), editingCanceled( ),
  editingStopped( ) > **J**Table.AccessibleJTable^
  < columnMarginChanged( ), editingCanceled( ),
  editingStopped( ) > **J**TableHeader^.columnMarginChanged( )
  TableColumnModelListener^.columnMarginChanged( )
  —fields: **A**bstractButton^.changeEvent
  AbstractCellEditor_.changeEvent
  DefaultBoundedRangeModel.changeEvent
  DefaultButtonModel_.changeEvent **D**efaultCaret^.changeEvent
  DefaultColorSelectionModel.changeEvent
  DefaultSingleSelectionModel.changeEvent
  DefaultTableColumnModel.changeEvent
  JProgressBar^.changeEvent **J**Slider^.changeEvent
  JTabbedPane^.changeEvent
  MenuSelectionManager.changeEvent
  StyleContext.NamedStyle.changeEvent
changeHighlight( ): *Highlighter*
changeListener: **A**bstractButton^ **J**ProgressBar^ **J**Slider^
  JTabbedPane^
ChangeListener^: javax.swing.event
  —passed to: **A**bstractButton^ < addChangeListener( ),
  removeChangeListener( ) > **A**bstractSpinnerModel_
  < addChangeListener( ), removeChangeListener( ) >
  BoundedRangeModel < addChangeListener( ),
  removeChangeListener( ) > *ButtonModel*^ < addChangeListener( ),
  removeChangeListener( ) > *Caret* < addChangeListener( ),
  removeChangeListener( ) > *ColorSelectionModel*
  < addChangeListener( ), removeChangeListener( ) >
  DefaultBoundedRangeModel < addChangeListener( ),
  removeChangeListener( ) > **D**efaultButtonModel_
  < addChangeListener( ), removeChangeListener( ) >
  DefaultCaret^ < addChangeListener( ), removeChangeListener( ) >
  DefaultColorSelectionModel < addChangeListener( ),
  removeChangeListener( ) > **D**efaultSingleSelectionModel
  < addChangeListener( ), removeChangeListener( ) >
  JProgressBar^ < addChangeListener( ), removeChangeListener( ) >
  JSlider^ < addChangeListener( ), removeChangeListener( ) >
  JSpinner^ < addChangeListener( ), removeChangeListener( ) >
  JTabbedPane^ < addChangeListener( ),
  removeChangeListener( ) > **J**Viewport^ < addChangeListener( ),
  removeChangeListener( ) > **M**enuSelectionManager
  < addChangeListener( ), removeChangeListener( ) >
  SingleSelectionModel < addChangeListener( ),
  removeChangeListener( ) > *SpinnerModel* < addChangeListener( ),
  removeChangeListener( ) > *Style*^ < addChangeListener( ),
  removeChangeListener( ) > **S**tyleContext_ < addChangeListener( ),
  removeChangeListener( ) > **S**tyleContext.NamedStyle
  < addChangeListener( ), removeChangeListener( ) >
  —returned by: **A**bstractButton^
  < createChangeListener( ), getChangeListeners( ) >
  AbstractSpinnerModel_.getChangeListeners( )
  DefaultBoundedRangeModel.getChangeListeners( )
  DefaultButtonModel_.getChangeListeners( )
  DefaultCaret^.getChangeListeners( )
  DefaultColorSelectionModel.getChangeListeners( )
  DefaultSingleSelectionModel.getChangeListeners( )
  JProgressBar^ < createChangeListener( ),
  getChangeListeners( ) > **J**Slider^ < createChangeListener( ),
  getChangeListeners( ) > **J**Spinner^.getChangeListeners( )
  JTabbedPane^ < createChangeListener( ),
  getChangeListeners( ) > **J**Viewport^.getChangeListeners( )
  MenuSelectionManager.getChangeListeners( )

StyleContext⌄.getChangeListeners( )
StyleContext.NamedStyle.getChangeListeners( )
—implemented by: **A**bstractButton.ButtonChangeListener
JMenuItem.AccessibleJMenuItem⌃
JScrollPane.AccessibleJScrollPane⌃ **J**Spinner.DefaultEditor⌃
JTabbedPane.AccessibleJTabbedPane⌃
JTabbedPane.ModelListener
—fields: **A**bstractButton⌃.changeListener
JProgressBar⌃.changeListener **J**Slider⌃.changeListener
JTabbedPane⌃.changeListener
changeSelection( ): **J**Table⌃
changeShape( ): **B**ox.Filler⌃
changeSupport: **A**bstractAction⌄ **D**efaultTreeSelectionModel⌄
changeToParentDirectory( ): **J**FileChooser⌃
changeUpdate( ): **D**efaultStyledDocument.ElementBuffer
channel: **V**oiceStatus
CHANNEL_PRESSURE: **S**hortMessage⌃
channels: **A**udioFormat
CHAR_REPLACEMENT: **T**extAttribute⌃
CHAR_UNDEFINED: **K**eyEvent⌃
CHARACTER: *A*ccessibleText⌄
Character: java.lang
—passed to: **A**WTKeyStroke⌄.getAWTKeyStroke( )
KeyStroke⌃.getKeyStroke( )
Character.Subset⌄: java.lang
—subclasses: **I**nputSubset⌃
—passed to: **I**nputContext.setCharacterSubsets( )
*I*nputMethod.setCharacterSubsets( )
CharacterIterator⌃: java.text
—passed to: **F**ont⌄ < canDisplayUpTo( ), createGlyphVector( ),
getLineMetrics( ), getStringBounds( ) > **F**ontMetrics
< getLineMetrics( ), getStringBounds( ) >
—implemented by: **S**egment
charAttr: **H**TMLDocument.HTMLReader⌃
charsWidth( ): **F**ontMetrics
charWidth( ): **F**ontMetrics
CHECK_BOX: **A**ccessibleRole⌃
checkAll( ): **M**ediaTracker
Checkbox⌃: java.awt
—passed to: **C**heckbox.AccessibleAWTCheckbox( )
CheckboxGroup < setCurrent( ), setSelectedCheckbox( ) >
Toolkit.createCheckbox( )
—returned by: **C**heckboxGroup < getCurrent( ),
getSelectedCheckbox( ) >
Checkbox.AccessibleAWTCheckbox⌃: java.awt
CheckboxGroup: java.awt
—passed to: **C**heckbox⌃ < Checkbox( ), setCheckboxGroup( ) >
CheckboxPeer⌃.setCheckboxGroup( )
—returned by: **C**heckbox⌃.getCheckboxGroup( )
CheckboxMenuItem⌃: java.awt
—passed
to: **C**heckboxMenuItem.AccessibleAWTCheckboxMenuItem( )
Toolkit.createCheckboxMenuItem( )
CheckboxMenuItem.AccessibleAWTCheckboxMenuItem⌃:
java.awt
CheckboxMenuItemPeer⌃: java.awt.peer
—returned by: **T**oolkit.createCheckboxMenuItem( )
CheckboxPeer⌃: java.awt.peer
—returned by: **T**oolkit.createCheckbox( )
checkClosed( ): **I**mageInputStreamImpl⌄
CHECKED: **A**ccessibleState⌄ **H**TML.Attribute
checkHorizontalKey( ): **A**bstractButton⌃ **J**Label⌃
checkID( ): **M**ediaTracker
checkImage( ): **C**omponent⌄ *ComponentPeer*⌄ **T**oolkit
checkPainter( ): **G**lyphView⌃
checkReadParamBandSettings( ): **I**mageReader
checkVerticalKey( ): **A**bstractButton⌃ **J**Label⌃
CHILD_POLICY_ALL: *I*IOMetadataFormat
CHILD_POLICY_CHOICE: *I*IOMetadataFormat
CHILD_POLICY_EMPTY: *I*IOMetadataFormat
CHILD_POLICY_MAX: *I*IOMetadataFormat
CHILD_POLICY_REPEAT: *I*IOMetadataFormat

CHILD_POLICY_SEQUENCE: *I*IOMetadataFormat
CHILD_POLICY_SOME: *I*IOMetadataFormat
childAlloc: **A**syncBoxView.ChildLocator
childAllocation( ): **C**ompositeView⌃
childChanged( ): **A**syncBoxView.ChildLocator
childIndices: **T**reeModelEvent⌃
children: **D**efaultMutableTreeNode⌄ **T**reeModelEvent⌃
children( ): **A**bstractDocument.AbstractElement⌄
DefaultMutableTreeNode⌄ *TreeNode*⌄
childResized( ): *ScrollPanePeer*⌃
childValue: **J**Tree.DynamicUtilTreeNode⌃
Choice⌃: java.awt
—passed to: **C**hoice.AccessibleAWTChoice( )
Toolkit.createChoice( )
Choice.AccessibleAWTChoice⌃: java.awt
ChoicePeer⌃: java.awt.peer
—returned by: **T**oolkit.createChoice( )
CHOOSABLE_FILE_FILTER_CHANGED_PROPERTY:
JFileChooser⌃
CHOOSER_PANELS_PROPERTY: **J**ColorChooser⌃
CHORD: **A**rc2D⌃
CHOU_1: **M**ediaSize.JIS
CHOU_2: **M**ediaSize.JIS
CHOU_3: **M**ediaSize.JIS
CHOU_30: **M**ediaSize.JIS
CHOU_4: **M**ediaSize.JIS
CHOU_40: **M**ediaSize.JIS
Chromaticity⌃: javax.print.attribute.standard
—fields: **C**hromaticity⌃ < COLOR, MONOCHROME >
CITE: **H**TML.Tag⌄
CLASS: **H**TML.Attribute
Class: java.lang
—passed to: **A**bstractDocument⌄.getListeners( )
AbstractListModel⌄.getListeners( )
AbstractSpinnerModel⌄.getListeners( )
AbstractTableModel⌄.getListeners( )
*javax.print.attribute.*AttributeSet⌄ < containsKey( ),
get( ), remove( ) > **A**ttributeSetUtilities
< verifyAttributeCategory( ), verifyAttributeValue( ),
verifyCategoryForValue( ) > **A**WTEventMulticaster.getListeners( )
AWTKeyStroke⌄.registerSubclass( )
Component⌄.getListeners( ) **D**ataFlavor( ) **D**ataLine.Info( )
DefaultBoundedRangeModel.getListeners( )
DefaultButtonModel⌄.getListeners( )
DefaultCaret⌃.getListeners( ) **D**efaultFormatter⌃.setValueClass( )
DefaultListSelectionModel.getListeners( )
DefaultSingleSelectionModel.getListeners( )
DefaultTableColumnModel.getListeners( )
DefaultTreeModel.getListeners( )
DefaultTreeSelectionModel.getListeners( ) **D**ragSource
< createDragGestureRecognizer( ), getListeners( ) >
EventListenerList < add( ), getListenerCount( ),
getListeners( ), remove( ) > **H**ashAttributeSet⌄
< containsKey( ), get( ), HashAttributeSet⌄,
remove( ) > **I**IOMetadataFormatImpl.addObjectValue( )
*I*IOServiceProvider⌄ < onDeregistration( ), onRegistration( ) >
ImageInputStreamSpi( ) **I**mageOutputStreamSpi( )
ImageReaderSpi( ) **I**mageWriterSpi( ) **I**nstrument( ) **J**Table⌃
< getDefaultEditor( ), getDefaultRenderer( ), setDefaultEditor( ),
setDefaultRenderer( ) > **L**ine.Info( ) **L**ookAndFeel.makeIcon( )
MenuItem⌃.getListeners( ) **P**ort.Info( ) *PrintService*⌄
< getAttribute( ), getDefaultAttributeValue( ),
getSupportedAttributeValues( ), isAttributeCategorySupported( ) >
RegisterableService < onDeregistration( ), onRegistration( ) >
ServiceRegistry⌄ < deregisterAll( ), deregisterServiceProvider( ),
getServiceProviderByClass( ), getServiceProviders( ),
lookupProviders( ), registerServiceProvider( ),
setOrdering( ), unsetOrdering( ) > **S**oundbankResource( )
StyleContext.NamedStyle.getListeners( )
SwingUtilities.getAncestorOfClass( ) **T**imer.getListeners( )
Toolkit.createDragGestureRecognizer( )

C

—returned by: **A**bstractTableModel⌄.getColumnClass( )
Attribute^.getCategory( )
*Attribute*Exception.getUnsupportedAttributes( )
AttributeSetUtilities.verifyAttributeCategory( )
Chromaticity^.getCategory( ) **C**olorSupported^.getCategory( )
Compression^.getCategory( ) **C**opies^.getCategory( )
CopiesSupported^.getCategory( ) **D**ataFlavor
< getDefaultRepresentationClass( ), getRepresentationClass( ),
tryToLoadClass( ) > **D**ateTimeAtCompleted^.getCategory( )
DateTimeAtCreation^.getCategory( )
DateTimeAtProcessing^.getCategory( )
DefaultFormatter^.getValueClass( ) **D**estination^.getCategory( )
DocumentName^.getCategory( ) **F**idelity^.getCategory( )
Finishings^.getCategory( ) *IIOMetadataFormat*.getObjectClass( )
IIOMetadataFormatImpl.getObjectClass( )
ImageInputStreamSpi^.getInputClass( )
ImageOutputStreamSpi^.getOutputClass( )
ImageReaderSpi^.getInputTypes( )
ImageWriterSpi^.getOutputTypes( )
JobHoldUntil^.getCategory( ) **J**obImpressions^.getCategory( )
JobImpressionsCompleted^.getCategory( )
JobImpressionsSupported^.getCategory( )
JobKOctets^.getCategory( )
JobKOctetsProcessed^.getCategory( )
JobKOctetsSupported^.getCategory( )
JobMediaSheets^.getCategory( )
JobMediaSheetsCompleted^.getCategory( )
JobMediaSheetsSupported^.getCategory( )
JobMessageFromOperator^.getCategory( )
JobName^.getCategory( )
JobOriginatingUserName^.getCategory( )
JobPriority^.getCategory( ) **J**obPrioritySupported^.getCategory( )
JobSheets^.getCategory( ) **J**obState^.getCategory( )
JobStateReason^.getCategory( )
JobStateReasons^.getCategory( ) **J**Table^.getColumnClass( )
Line.Info⌄.getLineClass( ) **M**edia⌄.getCategory( )
MediaPrintableArea.getCategory( ) **M**ediaSize^.getCategory( )
MultipleDocumentHandling^.getCategory( )
NumberOfDocuments^.getCategory( )
NumberOfInterveningJobs^.getCategory( )
NumberUp^.getCategory( )
NumberUpSupported^.getCategory( )
OrientationRequested^.getCategory( )
OutputDeviceAssigned^.getCategory( )
PageRanges^.getCategory( ) **P**agesPerMinute^.getCategory( )
PagesPerMinuteColor^.getCategory( )
ParameterBlock.getParamClasses( )
PDLOverrideSupported^.getCategory( )
PresentationDirection^.getCategory( ) **P**rinterInfo^.getCategory( )
PrinterIsAcceptingJobs^.getCategory( )
PrinterLocation^.getCategory( )
PrinterMakeAndModel^.getCategory( )
PrinterMessageFromOperator^.getCategory( )
PrinterMoreInfo^.getCategory( )
PrinterMoreInfoManufacturer^.getCategory( )
PrinterName^.getCategory( ) **P**rinterResolution^.getCategory( )
PrinterState^.getCategory( ) **P**rinterStateReason^.getCategory( )
PrinterStateReasons^.getCategory( )
PrinterURI^.getCategory( ) **P**rintQuality^.getCategory( )
PrintService⌄.getSupportedAttributeCategories( )
QueuedJobCount^.getCategory( )
ReferenceUriSchemesSupported^.getCategory( )
RequestingUserName^.getCategory( )
Severity^.getCategory( ) **S**heetCollate^.getCategory( )
Sides^.getCategory( ) **S**oundbankResource⌄.getDataClass( )
TableModel.getColumnClass( ) **U**IDefaults^.getUIClass( )
—fields: **I**mageInputStreamSpi^.inputClass
ImageOutputStreamSpi^.outputClass **I**mageReaderSpi^
< inputTypes, STANDARD_INPUT_TYPE > **I**mageWriterSpi^
< outputTypes, STANDARD_OUTPUT_TYPE >
CLASS_ABSTRACT: ICC_Profile⌄

CLASS_COLORSPACECONVERSION: ICC_Profile⌄
CLASS_DEVICELINK: ICC_Profile⌄
CLASS_DISPLAY: ICC_Profile⌄
CLASS_INPUT: ICC_Profile⌄
CLASS_NAMEDCOLOR: ICC_Profile⌄
CLASS_OUTPUT: ICC_Profile⌄
CLASSID: HTML.Attribute
ClassLoader: java.lang
—passed to: **D**ataFlavor < DataFlavor( ), tryToLoadClass( ) >
JEditorPane^.registerEditorKitForContentType( )
ServiceRegistry⌄.lookupProviders( ) **U**IDefaults^.getUIClass( )
ClassNotFoundException: java.lang
—thrown by: **D**ataFlavor < DataFlavor( ), readExternal( ),
tryToLoadClass( ) > **S**tyleContext⌄ < readAttributes( ),
readAttributeSet( ) > **S**ystemFlavorMap.decodeDataFlavor( )
UIManager.setLookAndFeel( )
Clear: AlphaComposite
CLEAR: **A**lphaComposite **C**SS.Attribute **H**TML.Attribute
clear( ): **A**ccessibleRelationSet **A**ccessibleStateSet
ActionMap⌄ *javax.print.attribute.AttributeSet*
DefaultListModel **H**ashAttributeSet⌄ **I**nputMap⌄
java.awt.List^ *ListPeer*^ **R**enderingHints
clearAbortRequest( ): **I**mageReader **I**mageWriter
clearAccessibleSelection( ): *AccessibleSelection*
JComboBox.AccessibleJComboBox^ **J**List.AccessibleJList^
JMenu.AccessibleJMenu^ **J**MenuBar.AccessibleJMenuBar^
JTabbedPane.AccessibleJTabbedPane^
JTable.AccessibleJTable^ **J**Tree.AccessibleJTree^
JTree.AccessibleJTree.AccessibleJTreeNode^
List.AccessibleAWTList^
MenuComponent.AccessibleAWTMenuComponent^
clearAutoscroll( ): **D**ropTarget
clearGlobalFocusOwner( ): **K**eyboardFocusManager⌄
clearRect( ): **G**raphics⌄
clearSelectedPath( ): **M**enuSelectionManager
clearSelection( ): **D**efaultListSelectionModel
DefaultSingleSelectionModel **D**efaultTreeSelectionModel⌄
JList^ **J**Table^ **J**Tree^ *ListSelectionModel*
SingleSelectionModel *TreeSelectionModel*
clearToggledPaths( ): **J**Tree^
clickCount: **E**vent
clickCountToStart: **D**efaultCellEditor^
Clip^: javax.sound.sampled
clip( ): **G**raphics2D^
Clipboard: java.awt.datatransfer
—passed to: *ClipboardOwner*.lostOwnership( )
StringSelection.lostOwnership( )
TransferHandler.exportToClipboard( )
—returned by: **T**oolkit < getSystemClipboard( ),
getSystemSelection( ) >
ClipboardOwner: java.awt.datatransfer
—passed to: **C**lipboard.setContents( )
—implemented by: **S**tringSelection
—fields: **C**lipboard.owner
clipRect( ): **G**raphics⌄
clone( ): **A**bstractAction **A**ffineTransform **A**rea
BufferCapabilities **C**ubicCurve2D **D**ataFlavor
DefaultListSelectionModel **D**efaultMutableTreeNode⌄
DefaultStyledDocument.ElementBuffer
DefaultTreeSelectionModel⌄ **D**imension2D⌄ **E**ditorKit⌄
ElementIterator **E**numSyntax⌄ **G**eneralPath **G**lyphView^
GridBagConstraints **I**mageCapabilities **I**mageFilter⌄ **I**nsets⌄
JFormattedTextField.AbstractFormatter⌄ **J**obAttributes
Kernel **L**ine2D⌄ **M**idiMessage⌄ **P**ageAttributes
PageFormat **P**aper **P**arameterBlock **P**oint2D⌄
QuadCurve2D⌄ **R**ectangularShape⌄ **R**enderContext
RenderingHints **S**egment **S**impleAttributeSet
StyleContext.SmallAttributeSet **T**extLayout **T**extMeasurer
Cloneable: java.lang
—implemented by: **A**bstractAction⌄ **A**ffineTransform
Area **B**ufferCapabilities **C**ubicCurve2D⌄
DataFlavor **D**ateTimeSyntax⌄ **D**efaultFormatter^

C

C

selectionForeground > **L**ineBorder^.lineColor **M**atteBorder^.color
TitledBorder^.titleColor
COLOR_ACTION: **H**TMLEditorKit^
COLOR_CHOOSER: **A**ccessibleRole^
COLOR_CHOOSER_DIALOG: **J**RootPane^
ColorChooserComponentFactory: javax.swing.colorchooser
ColorChooserUI^: javax.swing.plaf
— passed to: **J**ColorChooser^.setUI( )
— returned by: **J**ColorChooser^.getUI( )
ColorConvertOp: java.awt.image
colorModel: **I**mageTypeSpecifier
ColorModel_: java.awt.image
— subclasses: **C**omponentColorModel^ **I**ndexColorModel^
  PackedColorModel^
— descendents: **D**irectColorModel^
— passed to: **A**ffineTransformOp.createCompatibleDestImage( )
  AlphaComposite.createContext( ) **B**ufferedImage( )
  BufferedImageOp.createCompatibleDestImage( )
  Color_.createContext( )
  ColorConvertOp.createCompatibleDestImage( )
  Composite.createContext( )
  ConvolveOp.createCompatibleDestImage( )
  GradientPaint.createContext( ) *ImageConsumer*
  < setColorModel( ), setPixels( ) > **I**mageFilter_
  < setColorModel( ), setPixels( ) > **I**mageTypeSpecifier( )
  LookupOp.createCompatibleDestImage( ) **M**emoryImageSource
  < MemoryImageSource( ), newPixels( ) >
  Paint^.createContext( ) **P**ixelGrabber < setColorModel( ),
  setPixels( ) > **R**escaleOp.createCompatibleDestImage( )
  RGBImageFilter^.substituteColorModel( )
  TexturePaint.createContext( )
— returned by: **B**ufferedImage^.getColorModel( ) **C**olorModel_
  < coerceData( ), getRGBdefault( ) > **C**omponent_.getColorModel( )
  *ComponentPeer*_.getColorModel( )
  GraphicsConfiguration.getColorModel( )
  ImageTypeSpecifier.getColorModel( )
  PaintContext.getColorModel( ) **P**ixelGrabber.getColorModel( )
  *RenderedImage*_.getColorModel( ) **T**oolkit.getColorModel( )
— fields: **I**mageTypeSpecifier.colorModel **R**GBImageFilter^
  < newmodel, origmodel >
ColorSelectionModel: javax.swing.colorchooser
— passed to: **J**ColorChooser^ < JColorChooser( ),
  setSelectionModel( ) >
— returned
  by: **A**bstractColorChooserPanel^.getColorSelectionModel( )
  JColorChooser^.getSelectionModel( )
— implemented by: **D**efaultColorSelectionModel
ColorSpace_: java.awt.color
— subclasses: **I**CC_ColorSpace^
— passed to: **C**olor_ < Color( ), getColorComponents( ),
  getComponents( ) > **C**olorConvertOp( ) **C**olorModel( )
  ComponentColorModel( ) **D**irectColorModel( )
  ImageTypeSpecifier < createBanded( ), createInterleaved( ),
  createPacked( ) > **P**ackedColorModel( )
— returned by: **C**olor_.getColorSpace( )
  ColorModel_.getColorSpace( ) **C**olorSpace_.getInstance( )
ColorSupported^: javax.print.attribute.standard
— fields: **C**olorSupported^ < NOT_SUPPORTED, SUPPORTED >
ColorUIResource^: javax.swing.plaf
COLS: **H**TML.Attribute
COLSPAN: **H**TML.Attribute
column: **T**ableModelEvent^
COLUMN_HEADER: **A**ccessibleRole^ *ScrollPaneConstants*
COLUMN_WIDTH_PROPERTY: **T**ableColumn
columnAdded( ): **J**Table^ **J**Table.AccessibleJTable^
  JTableHeader^ *TableColumnModelListener*^
columnAtPoint( ): **J**Table^ **J**TableHeader^
columnHeader: **J**ScrollPane
columnIdentifiers: **D**efaultTableModel^
columnMargin: **D**efaultTableColumnModel
columnMarginChanged( ): **J**Table^ **J**Table.AccessibleJTable^
  JTableHeader^ *TableColumnModelListener*^

columnModel: **J**Table^ **J**TableHeader^
columnMoved( ): **J**Table^ **J**Table.AccessibleJTable^
  JTableHeader^ *TableColumnModelListener*^
columnRemoved( ): **J**Table^ **J**Table.AccessibleJTable^
  JTableHeader^ *TableColumnModelListener*^
columnSelectionAllowed: **D**efaultTableColumnModel
columnSelectionChanged( ): **J**Table^
  JTable.AccessibleJTable^ **J**TableHeader^
  TableColumnModelListener^
columnWeights: **G**ridBagLayout
columnWidths: **G**ridBagLayout
COMBINING: **G**lyphMetrics
COMBO_BOX: **A**ccessibleRole^
ComboBoxEditor: javax.swing
— passed to: **J**ComboBox^ < configureEditor( ), setEditor( ) >
— returned by: **J**ComboBox^.getEditor( )
— fields: **J**ComboBox^.editor
ComboBoxModel^: javax.swing
— extended by: *MutableComboBoxModel*^
— passed to: **J**ComboBox^ < JComboBox( ), setModel( ) >
  JComboBox.KeySelectionManager.selectionForKey( )
— returned by: **J**ComboBox^.getModel( )
— fields: **J**ComboBox^.dataModel
ComboBoxUI^: javax.swing.plaf
— passed to: **J**ComboBox^.setUI( )
— returned by: **J**ComboBox^.getUI( )
COMMENT: **H**TML.Attribute **H**TML.Tag_
comment( ): **H**TMLWriter
COMMIT: **J**FormattedTextField^
COMMIT_OR_REVERT: **J**FormattedTextField^
commitEdit( ): **J**FormattedTextField^ **J**Spinner^
  JSpinner.DefaultEditor^
COMMON: **J**obAttributes.DialogType^
COMPACT: **H**TML.Attribute
COMPACT_DISC: **P**ort.Info^
Comparable: java.lang
— passed to: **I**IOMetadataFormatImpl.addObjectValue( )
  InternationalFormatter^ < setMaximum( ), setMinimum( ) >
  SpinnerDateModel^ < setEnd( ), setStart( ),
  SpinnerNumberModel^ < setMaximum( ),
  setMinimum( ), SpinnerNumberModel^) >
— returned by: *IIOMetadataFormat* < getObjectMaxValue( ),
  getObjectMinValue( ) > **I**IOMetadataFormatImpl
  < getObjectMaxValue( ), getObjectMinValue( ) >
  InternationalFormatter^ < getMaximum( ), getMinimum( ) >
  SpinnerDateModel^ < getEnd( ), getStart( ) >
  SpinnerNumberModel^ < getMaximum( ), getMinimum( ) >
Comparator: java.util
— passed to: **S**ortingFocusTraversalPolicy^ < setComparator( ),
  SortingFocusTraversalPolicy( ) >
— returned by: **S**ortingFocusTraversalPolicy^.getComparator( )
compareTabOrder( ): **D**efaultFocusManager^
COMPLETE: **M**ediaTracker
COMPLETED: **J**obState^
COMPLETESCANLINES: *ImageConsumer*
COMPONENT: **G**lyphMetrics
component: **D**ragGestureRecognizer_ **I**mageIcon
Component_: java.awt
— subclasses: **B**utton^ **C**anvas^ **C**heckbox^ **C**hoice^
  Container^ **L**abel^ java.awt.**L**ist^ **S**crollbar^
  TextComponent^
— descendents: **A**bstractButton^
  AbstractColorChooserPanel^ **A**pplet^ **B**ox^ **B**ox.Filler^
  CellRendererPane^ **D**efaultListCellRenderer^
  DefaultListCellRenderer.UIResource^
  DefaultTableCellRenderer^
  DefaultTableCellRenderer.UIResource^
  DefaultTreeCellEditor.DefaultTextField^
  DefaultTreeCellEditor.EditorContainer^
  DefaultTreeCellRenderer^ **D**ialog^ **F**ileDialog^ **F**rame^
  JApplet^ **J**Button^ **J**CheckBox^ **J**CheckBoxMenuItem^
  JColorChooser^ **J**ComboBox^ **J**Component^

JDesktopPane^ JDialog^ JEditorPane^ JFileChooser^
JFormattedTextField^ JFrame^ JInternalFrame^
JInternalFrame.JDesktopIcon^ JLabel^ JLayeredPane^
JList^ JMenu^ JMenuBar^ JMenuItem^ JOptionPane^
JPanel^ JPasswordField^ JPopupMenu^
JPopupMenu.Separator^ JProgressBar^ JRadioButton^
JRadioButtonMenuItem^ JRootPane^ JScrollBar^
JScrollPane^ JScrollPane.ScrollBar^ JSeparator^ JSlider^
JSpinner^ JSpinner.DateEditor^ JSpinner.DefaultEditor^
JSpinner.ListEditor^ JSpinner.NumberEditor^ JSplitPane^
JTabbedPane^ JTable^ JTableHeader^ JTextArea^
JTextComponent^ JTextField^ JTextPane^ JToggleButton^
JToolBar^ JToolBar.Separator^ JToolTip^ JTree^
JViewport^ JWindow^ Panel^ ScrollPane^ TextArea^
TextField^ Window^
—passed to: AbstractBorder. < getBorderInsets( ),
getInteriorRectangle( ), paintBorder( ) > BevelBorder^
< getHighlightInnerColor( ), getHighlightOuterColor( ),
getShadowInnerColor( ), getShadowOuterColor( ),
paintLoweredBevel( ), paintRaisedBevel( ) > Border
< getBorderInsets( ), paintBorder( ) > BorderLayout
< addLayoutComponent( ), removeLayoutComponent( ) >
BorderUIResource < getBorderInsets( ),
paintBorder( ) > BoxLayout < addLayoutComponent( ),
removeLayoutComponent( ) > CardLayout
< addLayoutComponent( ), removeLayoutComponent( ) >
CellRendererPane^ < addImpl( ), paintComponent( ) >
Component.AccessibleAWTComponent( )
Component.BltBufferStrategy( )
Component.FlipBufferStrategy( ) ComponentEvent( )
ComponentPeer_.requestFocus( ) Container^ < add( ),
addImpl( ), isAncestorOf( ), remove( ) > ContainerEvent( )
ContainerOrderFocusTraversalPolicy^.accept( )
DefaultFocusManager^ < compareTabOrder( ),
getComponentAfter( ), getComponentBefore( ) >
DefaultFocusTraversalPolicy^.accept( )
DefaultKeyboardFocusManager^
< dequeueKeyEvents( ), discardKeyEvents( ),
enqueueKeyEvents( ) > DragGestureRecognizer_
< DragGestureRecognizer( ), setComponent( ) >
DragSource < createDefaultDragGestureRecognizer( ),
createDragGestureRecognizer( ) > DropTarget
< createDropTargetAutoScroller( ), DropTarget( ), setComponent( ) >
DropTarget.DropTargetAutoScroller( ) EtchedBorder^
< getHighlightColor( ), getShadowColor( ) > FlowLayout
< addLayoutComponent( ), removeLayoutComponent( ) >
FocusEvent( ) FocusTraversalPolicy
< getComponentAfter( ), getComponentBefore( ) >
GridBagLayout < addLayoutComponent( ), getConstraints( ),
lookupConstraints( ), removeLayoutComponent( ),
setConstraints( ) > GridLayout < addLayoutComponent( ),
removeLayoutComponent( ) > HierarchyEvent( ) Icon.paintIcon( )
IconUIResource.paintIcon( ) ImageIcon.paintIcon( )
InputContext.removeNotify( ) InputMethodEvent( ) JApplet^
< addImpl( ), setGlassPane( ) > JColorChooser^ < createDialog( ),
showDialog( ) > JComponent^ < isLightweightComponent( ),
setNextFocusableComponent( ) > JDialog^ < addImpl( ),
setGlassPane( ) > JFileChooser^ < createDialog( ), showDialog( ),
showOpenDialog( ), showSaveDialog( ) > JFrame^ < addImpl( ),
setGlassPane( ) > JInternalFrame^ < addImpl( ),
setGlassPane( ) > JLabel^.setLabelFor( ) JLayeredPane^
< addImpl( ), getIndexOf( ), getLayer( ), getLayeredPaneAbove( ),
getPosition( ), moveToBack( ), moveToFront( ), setLayer( ),
setPosition( ) > JMenu^.isMenuComponent( )
JMenuBar^ < getComponentIndex( ), setSelected( ) >
JOptionPane^ < createDialog( ), createInternalFrame( ),
getDesktopPaneForComponent( ), getFrameForComponent( ),
showConfirmDialog( ), showInputDialog( ),
showInternalConfirmDialog( ), showInternalInputDialog( ),
showInternalMessageDialog( ), showInternalOptionDialog( ),
showMessageDialog( ), showOptionDialog( ) > JPopupMenu^
< getComponentIndex( ), insert( ), setInvoker( ), setSelected( ),

show( ) > JRootPane^ < addImpl( ), setGlassPane( ) >
JRootPane.RootLayout < addLayoutComponent( ),
removeLayoutComponent( ) > JScrollPane^ < JScrollPane( ),
setColumnHeaderView( ), setCorner( ), setRowHeaderView( ),
setViewportView( ) > JSpinner.DefaultEditor^
< addLayoutComponent( ), removeLayoutComponent( ) >
JSplitPane^ < addImpl( ), JSplitPane( ), setBottomComponent( ),
setLeftComponent( ), setRightComponent( ),
setTopComponent( ) > JTabbedPane^ < addTab( ),
indexOfComponent( ), insertTab( ), setComponentAt( ),
setSelectedComponent( ) > JTextPane^.insertComponent( )
JToolBar^ < addImpl( ), getComponentIndex( ) >
JViewport^ < addImpl( ), setView( ) > JWindow^
< addImpl( ), setGlassPane( ) > KeyboardFocusManager_
< dequeueKeyEvents( ), discardKeyEvents( ), enqueueKeyEvents( ),
focusNextComponent( ), focusPreviousComponent( ),
processKeyEvent( ), redispatchEvent( ), setGlobalFocusOwner( ),
setGlobalPermanentFocusOwner( ), upFocusCycle( ) > KeyEvent( )
LayoutFocusTraversalPolicy^.accept( ) LayoutManager_
< addLayoutComponent( ), removeLayoutComponent( ) >
LayoutManager2^.addLayoutComponent( )
LookAndFeel.provideErrorFeedback( )
MediaTracker( ) MenuDragMouseEvent( )
MenuKeyEvent( ) MenuSelectionManager
< componentForPoint( ), isComponentPartOfCurrentMenu( ) >
MouseDragGestureRecognizer( ) MouseEvent( )
MouseWheelEvent( ) OverlayLayout
< addLayoutComponent( ), removeLayoutComponent( ) >
PaintEvent( ) PlainView^.damageLineRange( ) Popup( )
PopupFactory.getPopup( ) PopupMenu^.show( )
ProgressMonitor( ) ProgressMonitorInputStream( )
RepaintManager < currentManager( ),
getOffscreenBuffer( ), getVolatileOffscreenBuffer( ) >
RootPaneContainer.setGlassPane( ) ScrollPane^.addImpl( )
ScrollPaneLayout < addLayoutComponent( ),
addSingletonComponent( ), removeLayoutComponent( ) >
SortingFocusTraversalPolicy^.accept( ) SpringLayout
< addLayoutComponent( ), getConstraint( ), getConstraints( ),
putConstraint( ), removeLayoutComponent( ) >
StyleConstants_.setComponent( ) SwingUtilities
< convertMouseEvent( ), convertPoint( ),
convertPointFromScreen( ), convertPointToScreen( ),
convertRectangle( ), findComponentAt( ), getAccessibleAt( ),
getAccessibleChild( ), getAccessibleChildrenCount( ),
getAccessibleIndexInParent( ), getAccessibleStateSet( ),
getAncestorNamed( ), getAncestorOfClass( ),
getDeepestComponentAt( ), getLocalBounds( ), getRoot( ),
getRootPane( ), getWindowAncestor( ), isDescendingFrom( ),
paintComponent( ), updateComponentTreeUI( ),
windowForComponent( ) > TitledBorder^ < getFont( ),
getMinimumSize( ) > Toolkit < createComponent( ),
createDragGestureRecognizer( ), getNativeContainer( ) >
ViewportLayout < addLayoutComponent( ),
removeLayoutComponent( ) > Window_.setLocationRelativeTo( )
—returned by: java.beans.beancontext ⊇
.BeanContextChildComponentProxy.getComponent( )
Box^ < createGlue( ), createHorizontalGlue( ),
createHorizontalStrut( ), createRigidArea( ), createVerticalGlue( ),
createVerticalStrut( ) > ComboBoxEditor.getEditorComponent( )
Component_ < getComponentAt( ), locate( ) >
ComponentEvent^.getComponent( ) ComponentView^
< createComponent( ), getComponent( ) > Container^ < add( ),
findComponentAt( ), getComponent( ), getComponents( ) >
ContainerEvent^.getChild( ) DefaultCellEditor^
< getComponent( ), getTableCellEditorComponent( ),
getTreeCellEditorComponent( ) > DefaultFocusManager^
< getComponentAfter( ), getComponentBefore( ),
getFirstComponent( ), getLastComponent( ) >
DefaultListCellRenderer^.getListCellRendererComponent( )
DefaultTableCellRenderer^.getTableCellRendererComponent( )
DefaultTreeCellEditor.getTreeCellEditorComponent( )

DefaultTreeCellRenderer^.getTreeCellRendererComponent( )
DragGestureEvent^.getComponent( )
DragGestureRecognizer.getComponent( )
DragSourceContext.getComponent( )
DropTarget.getComponent( )
DropTargetContext.getComponent( )
FocusEvent^.getOppositeComponent( )
FocusTraversalPolicy < getComponentAfter( ),
getComponentBefore( ), getDefaultComponent( ),
getFirstComponent( ), getInitialComponent( ),
getLastComponent( ) > FormView^.createComponent( )
HierarchyEvent^ < getChanged( ), getComponent( ) >
InternalFrameFocusTraversalPolicy.getInitialComponent( )
JApplet^.getGlassPane( )
JComponent^.getNextFocusableComponent( )
JDialog^.getGlassPane( ) JFrame^.getGlassPane( )
JInternalFrame^ < getFocusOwner( ), getGlassPane( ),
getMostRecentFocusOwner( ) > JLabel^.getLabelFor( )
JLayeredPane^.getComponentsInLayer( ) JMenu^
< getMenuComponent( ), getMenuComponents( ) >
JMenuBar^ < getComponent( ), getComponentAtIndex( ) >
JMenuItem^.getComponent( ) JPopupMenu^ < getComponent( ),
getComponentAtIndex( ), getInvoker( ) > JRootPane^
< createGlassPane( ), getGlassPane( ) > JScrollPane^.getCorner( )
JSplitPane^ < getBottomComponent( ), getLeftComponent( ),
getRightComponent( ), getTopComponent( ) > JTabbedPane^
< getComponentAt( ), getSelectedComponent( ) > JTable^
< getEditorComponent( ), prepareEditor( ), prepareRenderer( ) >
JToolBar^.getComponentAtIndex( ) JViewport^.getView( )
JWindow^.getGlassPane( ) KeyboardFocusManager
< getFocusOwner( ), getGlobalFocusOwner( ),
getGlobalPermanentFocusOwner( ), getPermanentFocusOwner( ) >
ListCellRenderer.getListCellRendererComponent( )
MenuElement.getComponent( )
MenuSelectionManager.componentForPoint( )
ObjectView^.createComponent( )
java.beans.PropertyEditor.getCustomEditor( )
java.beans.PropertyEditorSupport.getCustomEditor( )
Renderer.getComponent( ) RootPaneContainer.getGlassPane( )
ScrollPaneLayout < addSingletonComponent( ), getCorner( ) >
StyleConstants.getComponent( ) SwingUtilities
< findFocusOwner( ), getDeepestComponentAt( ),
getRoot( ) > TableCellEditor^.getTableCellEditorComponent( )
TableCellRenderer.getTableCellRendererComponent( )
TreeCellEditor^.getTreeCellEditorComponent( )
TreeCellRenderer.getTreeCellRendererComponent( ) Window
< getFocusOwner( ), getMostRecentFocusOwner( ) >
—fields: DefaultTreeCellEditor.editingComponent
DragGestureRecognizer.component ImageIcon.component
JLabel^.labelFor JRootPane^.glassPane JScrollPane^
< lowerLeft, lowerRight, upperLeft, upperRight > JSplitPane^
< leftComponent, rightComponent > JTable^.editorComp
ScrollPaneLayout < lowerLeft, lowerRight, upperLeft,
upperRight >
Component.AccessibleAWTComponent^: java.awt
—subclasses: Box.Filler.AccessibleBoxFiller^
Button.AccessibleAWTButton^
Canvas.AccessibleAWTCanvas^
Checkbox.AccessibleAWTCheckbox^
Choice.AccessibleAWTChoice^
Container.AccessibleAWTContainer^
Label.AccessibleAWTLabel^ List.AccessibleAWTList^
List.AccessibleAWTList.AccessibleAWTListChild^
Scrollbar.AccessibleAWTScrollBar^
TextComponent.AccessibleAWTTextComponent^
—descendents: AbstractButton.AccessibleAbstractButton^
Applet.AccessibleApplet^ Box.AccessibleBox^
CellRendererPane.AccessibleCellRendererPane^
Dialog.AccessibleAWTDialog^ Frame.AccessibleAWTFrame^
JApplet.AccessibleJApplet^ JButton.AccessibleJButton^
JCheckBox.AccessibleJCheckBox^

JCheckBoxMenuItem.AccessibleJCheckBoxMenuItem^
JColorChooser.AccessibleJColorChooser^
JComboBox.AccessibleJComboBox^
JComponent.AccessibleJComponent^
JDesktopPane.AccessibleJDesktopPane^
JDialog.AccessibleJDialog^
JEditorPane.AccessibleJEditorPane^
JEditorPane.AccessibleJEditorPaneHTML^
JEditorPane.JEditorPaneAccessibleHypertextSupport^
JFileChooser.AccessibleJFileChooser^
JFrame.AccessibleJFrame^
JInternalFrame.AccessibleJInternalFrame^
JInternalFrame.JDesktopIcon.AccessibleJDesktopIcon^
JLabel.AccessibleJLabel^
JLayeredPane.AccessibleJLayeredPane^
JList.AccessibleJList^ JMenu.AccessibleJMenu^
JMenuBar.AccessibleJMenuBar^
JMenuItem.AccessibleJMenuItem^
JOptionPane.AccessibleJOptionPane^
JPanel.AccessibleJPanel^
JPasswordField.AccessibleJPasswordField^
JPopupMenu.AccessibleJPopupMenu^
JProgressBar.AccessibleJProgressBar^
JRadioButton.AccessibleJRadioButton^
JRadioButtonMenuItem.AccessibleJRadioButtonMenuItem^
JRootPane.AccessibleJRootPane^
JScrollBar.AccessibleJScrollBar^
JScrollPane.AccessibleJScrollPane^
JSeparator.AccessibleJSeparator^
JSlider.AccessibleJSlider^ JSplitPane.AccessibleJSplitPane^
JTabbedPane.AccessibleJTabbedPane^
JTable.AccessibleJTable^
JTableHeader.AccessibleJTableHeader^
JTextArea.AccessibleJTextArea^
JTextComponent.AccessibleJTextComponent^
JTextField.AccessibleJTextField^
JToggleButton.AccessibleJToggleButton^
JToolBar.AccessibleJToolBar^ JToolTip.AccessibleJToolTip^
JTree.AccessibleJTree^ JViewport.AccessibleJViewport^
JWindow.AccessibleJWindow^ Panel.AccessibleAWTPanel^
ScrollPane.AccessibleAWTScrollPane^
TextArea.AccessibleAWTTextArea^
TextField.AccessibleAWTTextField^
Window.AccessibleAWTWindow^
—passed to: Component.AccessibleAWTComponent
.AccessibleAWTComponentHandler( ) Component
.AccessibleAWTComponent.AccessibleAWTFocusHandler( )
Component.AccessibleAWTComponent
.AccessibleAWTComponentHandler: java.awt
Component.AccessibleAWTComponent
.AccessibleAWTFocusHandler: java.awt
Component.BltBufferStrategy^: java.awt
Component.FlipBufferStrategy^: java.awt
COMPONENT_ADDED: ContainerEvent^
COMPONENT_EVENT_MASK: AWTEvent^
COMPONENT_FIRST: ComponentEvent^
COMPONENT_HIDDEN: ComponentEvent^
COMPONENT_LAST: ComponentEvent^
COMPONENT_MOVED: ComponentEvent^
COMPONENT_REMOVED: ContainerEvent^
COMPONENT_RESIZED: ComponentEvent^
COMPONENT_SHOWN: ComponentEvent^
ComponentAdapter: java.awt.event
—subclasses: JViewport.ViewListener^
componentAdded( ): AWTEventMulticaster Container
.AccessibleAWTContainer.AccessibleContainerHandler
ContainerAdapter ContainerListener^ JComponent
.AccessibleJComponent.AccessibleContainerHandler
ComponentAttribute: StyleConstants
ComponentColorModel^: java.awt.image
ComponentElementName: StyleConstants
ComponentEvent^: java.awt.event

Container / Container.AccessibleAWTContainer

—subclasses: **C**ellRendererPane^
DefaultTreeCellEditor.EditorContainer^ **J**Component⌣ **P**anel⌣
ScrollPane^ **W**indow⌣
—descendents: **A**bstractButton⌣ **A**bstractColorChooserPanel^
Applet⌣ **B**ox^ **B**ox.Filler^ **D**efaultListCellRenderer⌣
DefaultListCellRenderer.UIResource^
DefaultTableCellRenderer⌣
DefaultTableCellRenderer.UIResource^
DefaultTreeCellEditor.DefaultTextField^
DefaultTreeCellRenderer^ **D**ialog⌣ **F**ileDialog⌣ **F**rame⌣
JApplet^ **J**Button^ **J**CheckBox^ **J**CheckBoxMenuItem^
JColorChooser^ **J**ComboBox^ **J**DesktopPane^ **J**Dialog^
JEditorPane⌣ **J**FileChooser^ **J**FormattedTextField^ **J**Frame^
JInternalFrame^ **J**InternalFrame.JDesktopIcon^ **J**Label⌣
JLayeredPane⌣ **J**List⌣ **J**Menu^ **J**MenuBar^ **J**MenuItem⌣
JOptionPane^ **J**Panel⌣ **J**PasswordField^ **J**PopupMenu^
JPopupMenu.Separator^ **J**ProgressBar^ **J**RadioButton^
JRadioButtonMenuItem^ **J**RootPane⌣ **J**ScrollBar⌣
JScrollPane^ **J**ScrollPane.ScrollBar^ **J**Separator⌣ **J**Slider^
JSpinner^ **J**Spinner.DateEditor^ **J**Spinner.DefaultEditor⌣
JSpinner.ListEditor^ **J**Spinner.NumberEditor^ **J**SplitPane^
JTabbedPane^ **J**Table^ **J**TableHeader^ **J**TextArea⌣
JTextComponent⌣ **J**TextField^ **J**TextPane^ **J**ToggleButton⌣
JToolBar^ **J**ToolBar.Separator^ **J**ToolTip^ **J**Tree^
JViewport^ **J**Window^
—passed to: **A**ncestorEvent( ) **B**orderLayout
< getLayoutAlignmentX( ), getLayoutAlignmentY( ),
invalidateLayout( ), layoutContainer( ), maximumLayoutSize( ),
minimumLayoutSize( ), preferredLayoutSize( ) > **B**oxLayout
< getLayoutAlignmentX( ), getLayoutAlignmentY( ),
invalidateLayout( ), layoutContainer( ), maximumLayoutSize( ),
minimumLayoutSize( ), preferredLayoutSize( ) > **C**ardLayout
< first( ), getLayoutAlignmentX( ), getLayoutAlignmentY( ),
invalidateLayout( ), last( ), layoutContainer( ),
maximumLayoutSize( ), minimumLayoutSize( ),
next( ), preferredLayoutSize( ), previous( ),
show( ) > **C**ellRendererPane^.paintComponent( )
Component⌣.isFocusCycleRoot( )
Container.AccessibleAWTContainer( )
DefaultFocusManager^ < getComponentAfter( ),
getComponentBefore( ), getFirstComponent( ),
getLastComponent( ) > **F**lowLayout < layoutContainer( ),
minimumLayoutSize( ), preferredLayoutSize( ) >
FocusTraversalPolicy⌣ < getComponentAfter( ),
getComponentBefore( ), getDefaultComponent( ),
getFirstComponent( ), getLastComponent( ) > **G**ridBagLayout
< arrangeGrid( ), ArrangeGrid( ), getLayoutAlignmentX( ),
getLayoutAlignmentY( ), getLayoutInfo( ), GetLayoutInfo( ),
getMinSize( ), GetMinSize( ), invalidateLayout( ),
layoutContainer( ), maximumLayoutSize( ), minimumLayoutSize( ),
preferredLayoutSize( ) > **G**ridLayout < layoutContainer( ),
minimumLayoutSize( ), preferredLayoutSize( ) > **H**ierarchyEvent( )
JApplet^.setContentPane( ) **J**Dialog^.setContentPane( )
JFrame^.setContentPane( ) **J**InternalFrame^.setContentPane( )
JRootPane^.setContentPane( ) **J**RootPane.RootLayout
< getLayoutAlignmentX( ), getLayoutAlignmentY( ),
invalidateLayout( ), layoutContainer( ), maximumLayoutSize( ),
minimumLayoutSize( ), preferredLayoutSize( ) >
JSpinner.DefaultEditor⌣ < layoutContainer( ),
minimumLayoutSize( ), preferredLayoutSize( ) >
JWindow^.setContentPane( ) **K**eyboardFocusManager⌣
< downFocusCycle( ), setGlobalCurrentFocusCycleRoot( ) >
LayoutManager⌣ < layoutContainer( ), minimumLayoutSize( ),
preferredLayoutSize( ) > *LayoutManager2*^
< getLayoutAlignmentX( ), getLayoutAlignmentY( ),
invalidateLayout( ), maximumLayoutSize( ) > **O**verlayLayout
< getLayoutAlignmentX( ), getLayoutAlignmentY( ),
invalidateLayout( ), layoutContainer( ), maximumLayoutSize( ),
minimumLayoutSize( ), OverlayLayout( ), preferredLayoutSize( ) >
RootPaneContainer.setContentPane( ) **S**crollPaneLayout⌣
< layoutContainer( ), minimumLayoutSize( ),
preferredLayoutSize( ) > **S**pringLayout < getLayoutAlignmentX( ),

getLayoutAlignmentY( ), invalidateLayout( ), layoutContainer( ),
maximumLayoutSize( ), minimumLayoutSize( ),
preferredLayoutSize( ) > **S**wingUtilities.paintComponent( )
ViewportLayout < layoutContainer( ), minimumLayoutSize( ),
preferredLayoutSize( ) >
—returned by: **A**ncestorEvent^ < getAncestor( ),
getAncestorParent( ) > *java.beans.beancontext* ⌐
*.**B**eanContextContainerProxy*.getContainer( )
Component⌣ < getFocusCycleRootAncestor( ),
getParent( ) > **C**ontainerEvent^.getContainer( )
DefaultTreeCellEditor.createContainer( )
HierarchyEvent^.getChangedParent( ) **J**Applet^.getContentPane( )
JComponent⌣.getTopLevelAncestor( ) **J**Dialog^.getContentPane( )
JFrame^.getContentPane( ) **J**InternalFrame^.getContentPane( )
JRootPane^ < createContentPane( ),
getContentPane( ) > **J**Window^.getContentPane( )
KeyboardFocusManager⌣ < getCurrentFocusCycleRoot( ),
getGlobalCurrentFocusCycleRoot( ) >
RootPaneContainer.getContentPane( ) **S**wingUtilities
< getAncestorNamed( ), getAncestorOfClass( ) >
Toolkit.getNativeContainer( ) **V**iew⌣.getContainer( )
—fields: **D**efaultTreeCellEditor.editingContainer
JRootPane^.contentPane

Container.AccessibleAWTContainer⌣: java.awt

—subclasses: **B**ox.AccessibleBox^
CellRendererPane.AccessibleCellRendererPane^
JComponent.AccessibleJComponent⌣
Panel.AccessibleAWTPanel⌣
ScrollPane.AccessibleAWTScrollPane^
Window.AccessibleAWTWindow⌣
—descendents: **A**bstractButton.AccessibleAbstractButton⌣
Applet.AccessibleApplet⌣ **D**ialog.AccessibleAWTDialog⌣
Frame.AccessibleAWTFrame⌣
JApplet.AccessibleJApplet⌣ **J**Button.AccessibleJButton^
JCheckBox.AccessibleJCheckBox^
JCheckBoxMenuItem.AccessibleJCheckBoxMenuItem^
JColorChooser.AccessibleJColorChooser^
JComboBox.AccessibleJComboBox^
JDesktopPane.AccessibleJDesktopPane^
JDialog.AccessibleJDialog^
JEditorPane.AccessibleJEditorPane⌣
JEditorPane.AccessibleJEditorPaneHTML^
JEditorPane.JEditorPaneAccessibleHypertextSupport^
JFileChooser.AccessibleJFileChooser^
JFrame.AccessibleJFrame^
JInternalFrame.AccessibleJInternalFrame^
JInternalFrame.JDesktopIcon.AccessibleJDesktopIcon^
JLabel.AccessibleJLabel^
JLayeredPane.AccessibleJLayeredPane^
JList.AccessibleJList^ **J**Menu.AccessibleJMenu^
JMenuBar.AccessibleJMenuBar^
JMenuItem.AccessibleJMenuItem⌣
JOptionPane.AccessibleJOptionPane^
JPanel.AccessibleJPanel^
JPasswordField.AccessibleJPasswordField^
JPopupMenu.AccessibleJPopupMenu^
JProgressBar.AccessibleJProgressBar^
JRadioButton.AccessibleJRadioButton^
JRadioButtonMenuItem.AccessibleJRadioButtonMenuItem^
JRootPane.AccessibleJRootPane^
JScrollBar.AccessibleJScrollBar^
JScrollPane.AccessibleJScrollPane^
JSeparator.AccessibleJSeparator^
JSlider.AccessibleJSlider^ **J**SplitPane.AccessibleJSplitPane^
JTabbedPane.AccessibleJTabbedPane^
JTable.AccessibleJTable^
JTableHeader.AccessibleJTableHeader^
JTextArea.AccessibleJTextArea^
JTextComponent.AccessibleJTextComponent⌣
JTextField.AccessibleJTextField⌣
JToggleButton.AccessibleJToggleButton⌣
JToolBar.AccessibleJToolBar^ **J**ToolTip.AccessibleJToolTip^

C

COPIED: BufferCapabilities.FlipContents^
Copies^: javax.print.attribute.standard
CopiesSupported^: javax.print.attribute.standard
copy: DefaultStyledDocument.AttributeUndoableEdit^
COPY: TransferHandler
copy( ): JTextComponent‿
COPY_OR_MOVE: TransferHandler
copyAction: DefaultEditorKit‿
copyArea( ): Graphics‿
copyAttributes( ): AbstractDocument.AbstractElement‿
  javax.swing.text.AttributeSet‿ SimpleAttributeSet
  StyleContext.NamedStyle StyleContext.SmallAttributeSet
copyData( ): BufferedImage^ *RenderedImage*‿
copyInto( ): DefaultListModel^
count: Segment
countComponents( ): Container‿
countItems( ): Choice^ java.awt.List^ Menu‿
countMenus( ): MenuBar^
COVER: Finishings^
COVER_OPEN: PrinterStateReason^
create( ): DefaultStyledDocument‿ Graphics‿
  HTMLEditorKit.HTMLFactory *RenderedImageFactory*‿
  ViewFactory
createActionChangeListener( ): JMenu^ JPopupMenu^
  JToolBar^
createActionComponent( ): JMenu^ JPopupMenu^ JToolBar^
createActionListener( ): AbstractButton‿
createActionPropertyChangeListener( ): AbstractButton‿
  JComboBox^ JTextField‿
createBackBuffers( ): Component.BltBufferStrategy^
createBanded( ): ImageTypeSpecifier
createBandedRaster( ): Raster‿
createBevelBorder( ): BorderFactory
createBlackLineBorder( ): LineBorder‿
createBranchElement( ): AbstractDocument‿
createBufferedImage( ): ImageTypeSpecifier
createBuffers( ): Component.FlipBufferStrategy^
  ComponentPeer‿
createBufferStrategy( ): Canvas^ Window‿
createButton( ): Toolkit
createCanvas( ): Toolkit
createCaret( ): EditorKit‿
createChangeListener( ): AbstractButton‿ JProgressBar^
  JSlider^ JTabbedPane^
createCheckbox( ): Toolkit
createCheckboxMenuItem( ): Toolkit
createChild( ): Raster‿
createChildren( ): JTree.DynamicUtilTreeNode^
createChildState( ): AsyncBoxView^
createChoice( ): Toolkit
createCompatibleDestImage( ): AffineTransformOp‿
  BufferedImageOp ColorConvertOp ConvolveOp
  LookupOp RescaleOp
createCompatibleDestRaster( ): AffineTransformOp‿
  BandCombineOp ColorConvertOp ConvolveOp
  LookupOp *RasterOp* RescaleOp
createCompatibleImage( ): GraphicsConfiguration
createCompatibleSampleModel( ): ColorModel‿
  SampleModel
createCompatibleVolatileImage( ): GraphicsConfiguration
createCompatibleWritableRaster( ): ColorModel‿ Raster‿
createComponent( ): ComponentView‿ Toolkit
createCompoundBorder( ): BorderFactory
createCompoundEdit( ): UndoableEditSupport
createContainer( ): DefaultTreeCellEditor
createContentPane( ): JRootPane^
createContext( ): AlphaComposite Color‿ *Composite*
  GradientPaint *Paint*^ TexturePaint
createCustomCursor( ): Toolkit
createDataBuffer( ): SampleModel‿
createDefaultColumnModel( ): JTable^ JTableHeader^
createDefaultColumnsFromModel( ): JTable^

createDefaultDataModel( ): JTable^
createDefaultDocument( ): EditorKit^
createDefaultDragGestureRecognizer( ): DragSource
createDefaultEditorKit( ): JEditorPane^
createDefaultEditors( ): JTable^
createDefaultHeaderRenderer( ): TableColumn
createDefaultKeySelectionManager( ): JComboBox^
createDefaultModel( ): JTextArea^ JTextField‿
createDefaultRenderer( ): JTableHeader^
createDefaultRenderers( ): JTable^
createDefaultRendering( ): *RenderableImage*
  RenderableImageOp
createDefaultRoot( ): DefaultStyledDocument‿ PlainDocument^
createDefaultSelectionModel( ): JTable^
createDefaultTableHeader( ): JTable^
createDialog( ): JColorChooser^ JFileChooser^ JOptionPane^
  Toolkit
createDisabledImage( ): GrayFilter
createDragGestureRecognizer( ): DragSource Toolkit
createDragSourceContext( ): DragSource
createDragSourceContextPeer( ): Toolkit
createDropTargetAutoScroller( ): DropTarget
createDropTargetContext( ): DropTarget
createDTD( ): ParserDelegator^
createEditor( ): JSpinner^
createEditorKitForContentType( ): JEditorPane‿
createEmptyBorder( ): BorderFactory
createEtchedBorder( ): BorderFactory
createFileDialog( ): Toolkit
createFileObject( ): FileSystemView
createFileSystemRoot( ): FileSystemView
createFont( ): Font‿
createFragment( ): View‿
createFrame( ): Toolkit
createFromBufferedImageType( ): ImageTypeSpecifier
createFromRenderedImage( ): ImageTypeSpecifier
createGlassPane( ): JRootPane^
createGlue( ): Box^
createGlyphVector( ): Font‿
createGraphics( ): BufferedImage^ GraphicsEnvironment
  VolatileImage^
createGrayLineBorder( ): LineBorder‿
createGrayscale( ): ImageTypeSpecifier
createHorizontalBox( ): Box^
createHorizontalGlue( ): Box^
createHorizontalScrollBar( ): JScrollPane^
createHorizontalStrut( ): Box^
createImage( ): Component‿ *ComponentPeer*‿ Toolkit
createImageInputStream( ): ImageIO
createImageOutputStream( ): ImageIO
createIndexed( ): ImageTypeSpecifier
createInputAttributes( ): StyledEditorKit‿
createInputMethod( ): *InputMethodDescriptor*
createInputMethodJFrame( ): *InputMethodContext*^
createInputMethodWindow( ): *InputMethodContext*^
createInputStreamInstance( ): ImageInputStreamSpi^
createInterleaved( ): ImageTypeSpecifier
createInterleavedRaster( ): Raster‿
createInternalFrame( ): JOptionPane^
createIntersection( ): Rectangle2D‿
createInverse( ): AffineTransform
createItemListener( ): AbstractButton‿
createLabel( ): Toolkit
createLargeAttributeSet( ): StyleContext‿
createLayeredPane( ): JRootPane^
createLayoutManager( ): JViewport^
createLeafElement( ): AbstractDocument‿
createLineBorder( ): BorderFactory
createList( ): Toolkit
createLoweredBevelBorder( ): BorderFactory
createMatteBorder( ): BorderFactory
createMenu( ): Toolkit

C

C

—fields: **C**ursor.predefined **D**ragSource < DefaultCopyDrop, DefaultCopyNoDrop, DefaultLinkDrop, DefaultLinkNoDrop, DefaultMoveDrop, DefaultMoveNoDrop >
curveTo( ): **G**eneralPath
CUSTOM_CURSOR: **C**ursor
CUSTOM_DIALOG: **J**FileChooser^
cut( ): *AccessibleEditableText*^ **J**TextComponent⌐
JTextComponent.AccessibleJTextComponent⌐
cutAction: **D**efaultEditorKit⌐
CYAN: **C**olor⌐
cyan: **C**olor⌐
D: **M**ediaSize.Engineering **M**ediaSizeName^
PageAttributes.MediaType^
damage( ): **D**efaultCaret^
damageLineRange( ): **P**lainView⌐
damageRange( ): **T**extUI^
DARK_GRAY: **C**olor⌐
darker( ): **C**olor⌐
darkGray: **C**olor⌐
data: javax.swing.text.html.parser.**E**lement
javax.swing.text.html.parser.**E**ntity **M**idiMessage⌐
DATA: **H**TML.Attribute
DATA_TRANSFER_COMPLETE: **P**rintJobEvent^
dataBuffer: **R**aster⌐
DataBuffer⌐: java.awt.image
—subclasses: **D**ataBufferByte^ **D**ataBufferDouble^
DataBufferFloat^ **D**ataBufferInt^ **D**ataBufferShort^
DataBufferUShort^
—passed to: **R**aster⌐ < createBandedRaster( ),
createInterleavedRaster( ), createPackedRaster( ), createRaster( ),
createWritableRaster( ), Raster( ) > **S**ampleModel
< getDataElements( ), getPixel( ), getPixels( ), getSample( ),
getSampleDouble( ), getSampleFloat( ), getSamples( ),
setDataElements( ), setPixel( ), setPixels( ), setSample( ),
setSamples( ) > **W**ritableRaster⌐
—returned by: **R**aster⌐.getDataBuffer( )
SampleModel⌐.createDataBuffer( )
—fields: **R**aster⌐.dataBuffer
DataBufferByte^: java.awt.image
DataBufferDouble^: java.awt.image
DataBufferFloat^: java.awt.image
DataBufferInt^: java.awt.image
DataBufferShort^: java.awt.image
DataBufferUShort^: java.awt.image
DataFlavor: java.awt.datatransfer
—passed to: **D**ataFlavor < equals( ), isMimeTypeEqual( ),
match( ), selectBestTextFlavor( ) >
DropTargetContext.isDataFlavorSupported( )
DropTargetContext.TransferableProxy
< getTransferData( ), isDataFlavorSupported( ) >
DropTargetDragEvent^.isDataFlavorSupported( )
DropTargetDropEvent^.isDataFlavorSupported( )
FlavorMap⌐.getNativesForFlavors( )
FlavorTable^.getNativesForFlavor( ) **S**tringSelection
< getTransferData( ), isDataFlavorSupported( ) >
SystemFlavorMap < addFlavorForUnencodedNative( ),
addUnencodedNativeForFlavor( ), encodeDataFlavor( ),
getNativesForFlavor( ), getNativesForFlavors( ),
setFlavorsForNative( ), setNativesForFlavor( ) > *Transferable*
< getTransferData( ), isDataFlavorSupported( ) >
TransferHandler.canImport( ) **U**nsupportedFlavorException( )
—returned by: **D**ataFlavor
< getTextPlainUnicodeFlavor( ), selectBestTextFlavor( ) >
DropTargetContext.getCurrentDataFlavors( )
DropTargetContext.TransferableProxy.getTransferDataFlavors( )
DropTargetDragEvent^.getCurrentDataFlavors( )
DropTargetDropEvent^.getCurrentDataFlavors( )
StringSelection.getTransferDataFlavors( )
SystemFlavorMap.decodeDataFlavor( )
Transferable.getTransferDataFlavors( )
—fields: **D**ataFlavor < imageFlavor, javaFileListFlavor,
plainTextFlavor, stringFlavor >

DataInput⌐: java.io
—extended by: *ImageInputStream*⌐
DataInputStream^: java.io
—passed to: **D**TD.read( )
DataLine⌐: javax.sound.sampled
—extended by: *Clip*^ *SourceDataLine*^ *TargetDataLine*^
DataLine.Info^: javax.sound.sampled
dataModel: **J**ComboBox^ **J**Table^
DataOutput⌐: java.io
—extended by: *ImageOutputStream*⌐
dataType: **D**ataBuffer⌐ **S**ampleModel⌐
DATATYPE_BOOLEAN: **I**IOMetadataFormat
DATATYPE_DOUBLE: **I**IOMetadataFormat
DATATYPE_FLOAT: **I**IOMetadataFormat
DATATYPE_INTEGER: **I**IOMetadataFormat
DATATYPE_STRING: **I**IOMetadataFormat
dataVector: **D**efaultTableModel^
Date: java.util
—passed to: **D**ateTimeAtCompleted( ) **D**ateTimeAtCreation( )
DateTimeAtProcessing( ) **D**ateTimeSyntax( ) **J**obHoldUntil( )
SpinnerDateModel( )
—returned by: **D**ateTimeSyntax⌐.getValue( )
SpinnerDateModel^.getDate( )
DATE_EDITOR: **A**ccessibleRole^
DateFormat^: java.text
—passed to: **D**ateFormatter^ < DateFormatter( ), setFormat( ) >
DateFormatter^: javax.swing.text
DateTimeAtCompleted^: javax.print.attribute.standard
DateTimeAtCreation^: javax.print.attribute.standard
DateTimeAtProcessing^: javax.print.attribute.standard
DateTimeSyntax⌐: javax.print.attribute
—subclasses: **D**ateTimeAtCompleted^ **D**ateTimeAtCreation^
DateTimeAtProcessing^ **J**obHoldUntil^
DD: **H**TML.Tag⌐
deactivate( ): *InputMethod*
deactivateFrame( ): **D**efaultDesktopManager *DesktopManager*
DebugGraphics^: javax.swing
DecimalFormat^: java.text
—returned by: **J**Spinner.NumberEditor^.getFormat( )
DECLARE: **H**TML.Attribute
decode( ): **C**olor **F**ont
decodeDataFlavor( ): **S**ystemFlavorMap
decodeJavaMIMEType( ): **S**ystemFlavorMap
decrIndent( ): **A**bstractWriter⌐
defAttributeList( ): **D**TD
DEFAULT: **A**ction^ **D**ragSourceContext **D**TDConstants
DEFAULT_CARET_POLICY: **T**extLayout
DEFAULT_CSS: **H**TMLEditorKit^
DEFAULT_CURSOR: **C**ursor **F**rame⌐
DEFAULT_JUSTIFICATION: **T**itledBorder⌐
DEFAULT_KEYMAP: **J**TextComponent⌐
DEFAULT_LAYER: **J**LayeredPane⌐
DEFAULT_OPTION: **J**OptionPane⌐
DEFAULT_POSITION: **T**itledBorder⌐
DEFAULT_STYLE: **S**tyleContext⌐
DefaultBoundedRangeModel: javax.swing
defaultButton: **J**RootPane^
DefaultButtonModel^: javax.swing
—subclasses: **J**ToggleButton.ToggleButtonModel^
DefaultCaret^: javax.swing.text
DefaultCellEditor^: javax.swing
—passed to: **D**efaultCellEditor.EditorDelegate( )
DefaultCellEditor.EditorDelegate: javax.swing
—fields: **D**efaultCellEditor^.delegate
DefaultColorSelectionModel: javax.swing.colorchooser
DefaultComboBoxModel^: javax.swing
defaultConstraints: **G**ridBagLayout
defaultController: **I**IOMetadata **I**IOParam⌐
DefaultCopyDrop: **D**ragSource
DefaultCopyNoDrop: **D**ragSource
DefaultDesktopManager: javax.swing
DefaultEditorKit⌐: javax.swing.text

—subclasses: **S**tyledEditorKit˘
—descendants: **H**TMLEditorKit^ **R**TFEditorKit^
DefaultEditorKit.BeepAction^: javax.swing.text
DefaultEditorKit.CopyAction^: javax.swing.text
DefaultEditorKit.CutAction^: javax.swing.text
DefaultEditorKit.DefaultKeyTypedAction^: javax.swing.text
DefaultEditorKit.InsertBreakAction^: javax.swing.text
DefaultEditorKit.InsertContentAction^: javax.swing.text
DefaultEditorKit.InsertTabAction^: javax.swing.text
DefaultEditorKit.PasteAction^: javax.swing.text
defaultEditorsByColumnClass: **J**Table^
DefaultFocusManager^: javax.swing
DefaultFocusTraversalPolicy^: java.awt
DefaultFormatter^: javax.swing.text
—subclasses: **I**nternationalFormatter˘ **M**askFormatter^
—descendants: **D**ateFormatter^ **N**umberFormatter^
DefaultFormatterFactory^: javax.swing.text
DefaultHighlighter^: javax.swing.text
DefaultHighlighter.DefaultHighlightPainter^: javax.swing.text
DefaultKeyboardFocusManager˘: java.awt
—subclasses: **F**ocusManager˘
—descendants: **D**efaultFocusManager^
defaultKeyTypedAction: **D**efaultEditorKit˘
DefaultLinkDrop: **D**ragSource
DefaultLinkNoDrop: **D**ragSource
DefaultListCellRenderer^: javax.swing
—subclasses: **D**efaultListCellRenderer.UIResource^
DefaultListCellRenderer.UIResource^: javax.swing
DefaultListModel^: javax.swing
DefaultListSelectionModel: javax.swing
—fields: **D**efaultTreeSelectionModel˘.listSelectionModel
defaultManager(): **M**enuSelectionManager
DefaultMoveDrop: **D**ragSource
DefaultMoveNoDrop: **D**ragSource
DefaultMutableTreeNode˘: javax.swing.tree
—subclasses: **J**Tree.DynamicUtilTreeNode^
—passed to: **D**efaultMutableTreeNode˘ < getSharedAncestor(),
    isNodeDescendant(), isNodeRelated() >
    JTree.DynamicUtilTreeNode^.createChildren()
—returned by: **D**efaultMutableTreeNode˘ < getFirstLeaf(),
    getLastLeaf(), getNextLeaf(), getNextNode(), getNextSibling(),
    getPreviousLeaf(), getPreviousNode(), getPreviousSibling() >
defaultPage(): **P**rinterJob
DefaultPainter: **D**efaultHighlighter^
defaultPressAction: **J**RootPane^
defaultReleaseAction: **J**RootPane^
defaultRenderersByColumnClass: **J**Table^
DefaultSingleSelectionModel: javax.swing
DefaultStyledDocument^: javax.swing.text
—subclasses: **H**TMLDocument^
—passed to: **D**efaultStyledDocument.ElementBuffer()
    DefaultStyledDocument.SectionElement()
DefaultStyledDocument.AttributeUndoableEdit^:
    javax.swing.text
DefaultStyledDocument.ElementBuffer: javax.swing.text
—fields: **D**efaultStyledDocument˘.buffer
DefaultStyledDocument.ElementSpec: javax.swing.text
—passed to: **D**efaultStyledDocument˘ < create(), insert() >
    DefaultStyledDocument.ElementBuffer < insert(),
    insertUpdate() > **H**TMLDocument^ < create(), insert() >
DefaultStyledDocument.SectionElement^: javax.swing.text
DefaultTableCellRenderer^: javax.swing.table
—subclasses: **D**efaultTableCellRenderer.UIResource^
DefaultTableCellRenderer.UIResource^: javax.swing.table
DefaultTableColumnModel: javax.swing.table
DefaultTableModel^: javax.swing.table
DefaultTextUI: javax.swing.text
DefaultTreeCellEditor: javax.swing.tree
—passed to: **D**efaultTreeCellEditor.DefaultTextField()
    DefaultTreeCellEditor.EditorContainer()
DefaultTreeCellEditor.DefaultTextField^: javax.swing.tree
DefaultTreeCellEditor.EditorContainer^: javax.swing.tree

DefaultTreeCellRenderer^: javax.swing.tree
—passed to: **D**efaultTreeCellEditor()
—fields: **D**efaultTreeCellEditor.renderer
DefaultTreeModel: javax.swing.tree
DefaultTreeSelectionModel˘: javax.swing.tree
—subclasses: **J**Tree.EmptySelectionModel^
defContentModel(): **D**TD
defElement(): **D**TD
defEntity(): **D**TD
defineAttributes(): **D**TD
defineElement(): **D**TD
defineEntity(): **D**TD
DEFLATE: **C**ompression^
deiconifyFrame(): **D**efaultDesktopManager *DesktopManager*
deinstall(): *Caret* **D**efaultCaret^ **E**ditorKit˘ *Highlighter*
delay(): **R**obot
delegate: **D**efaultCellEditor^
DELETE: *AccessibleTableModelChange* **E**vent
    TableModelEvent^
delete(): *AccessibleEditableText*^
    JTextComponent.AccessibleJTextComponent˘
deleteChar(): **L**ineBreakMeasurer **T**extMeasurer
deleteNextCharAction: **D**efaultEditorKit˘
deletePrevCharAction: **D**efaultEditorKit˘
deleteShortcut(): **M**enuBar^ **M**enuItem˘
deleteTrack(): **S**equence
delItem(): java.awt.**L**ist^ *MenuPeer*˘
delItems(): java.awt.**L**ist^ *ListPeer*^
deliverEvent(): **C**omponent
delMenu(): *MenuBarPeer*˘
deltaTransform(): **A**ffineTransform
depth(): **E**lementIterator
depthFirstEnumeration(): **D**efaultMutableTreeNode˘
dequeueKeyEvents(): **K**eyboardFocusManager˘
deregisterAll(): **S**erviceRegistry˘
deregisterServiceProvider(): **S**erviceRegistry˘
deriveFont(): **F**ont
deriveMMFont(): *MultipleMaster*
deselect(): java.awt.**L**ist^ *ListPeer*^
DESELECTED: **I**temEvent^
DESIGNATED_LONG: **M**ediaSize.ISO
DESKTOP: **S**ystemColor
desktop: **S**ystemColor^
DESKTOP_ICON: **A**ccessibleRole^
DESKTOP_PANE: **A**ccessibleRole^
desktopIcon: **J**InternalFrame^
DesktopIconUI: javax.swing.plaf
—passed to: **J**InternalFrame.JDesktopIcon^.setUI()
—returned by: **J**InternalFrame.JDesktopIcon^.getUI()
DesktopManager: javax.swing
—passed to: **J**DesktopPane^.setDesktopManager()
—returned by: **J**DesktopPane^.getDesktopManager()
—implemented by: **D**efaultDesktopManager
DesktopPaneUI^: javax.swing.plaf
—passed to: **J**DesktopPane^.setUI()
—returned by: **J**DesktopPane^.getUI()
desktopProperties: **T**oolkit
desktopPropsSupport: **T**oolkit
destHeight: **R**eplicateScaleFilter˘
destination: **I**mageReadParam˘
Destination: javax.print.attribute.standard
destinationBands: **I**mageReadParam˘
destinationOffset: **I**IOParam˘
destinationType: **I**IOParam˘
destroy(): **A**pplet^
destroyBuffers(): **C**omponent.FlipBufferStrategy^
    ComponentPeer˘
destWidth: **R**eplicateScaleFilter˘
determineOffset(): **D**efaultTreeCellEditor
DEVANAGARI: **N**umericShaper
DEVELOPER_EMPTY: **P**rinterStateReason^
DEVELOPER_LOW: **P**rinterStateReason^

D

DFN: HTML.Tag⌄
DIALOG: AccessibleRole^
Dialog: java.awt
—subclasses: FileDialog^ JDialog^
—passed to: Dialog() Dialog.AccessibleAWTDialog()
　JDialog() Toolkit.createDialog()
Dialog.AccessibleAWTDialog: java.awt
—subclasses: JDialog.AccessibleJDialog^
DIALOG_TITLE_CHANGED_PROPERTY: JFileChooser^
DIALOG_TYPE_CHANGED_PROPERTY: JFileChooser^
DIALOG_UI: ServiceUIFactory
dialogInit(): JDialog^
DialogPeer: java.awt.peer
—extended by: FileDialogPeer^
—returned by: Toolkit.createDialog()
Dictionary: java.util
—descendents: UIDefaults^
—passed to: AbstractDocument⌄.setDocumentProperties()
　JSlider^.setLabelTable()
—returned by: AbstractDocument⌄.getDocumentProperties()
　JSlider^.getLabelTable()
die(): AbstractUndoableEdit⌄ UndoableEdit
Dimension: java.awt
—subclasses: DimensionUIResource^
—passed to: AccessibleComponent⌄.setSize()
　Box^.createRigidArea() Box.Filler^ < Box.Filler(),
　changeShape() > Component⌄ < getSize(), resize(),
　setSize() > Component.AccessibleAWTComponent^.setSize()
　Dimension⌄ < Dimension(), setSize() >
　ImageReadParam^.setSourceRenderSize() JComponent⌄
　< setMaximumSize(), setMinimumSize(), setPreferredSize() >
　JList.AccessibleJList.AccessibleJListChild^.setSize()
　JPopupMenu^.setPopupSize() JTable^
　< setIntercellSpacing(), setPreferredScrollableViewportSize() >
　JTable.AccessibleJTable.AccessibleJTableCell^.setSize()
　JTableHeader.AccessibleJTableHeader⌄
　.AccessibleJTableHeaderEntry^.setSize()
　JToolBar^.addSeparator() JToolBar.Separator^
　< JToolBar.Separator(), setSeparatorSize() >
　JTree.AccessibleJTree.AccessibleJTreeNode^.setSize()
　JViewport^ < computeBlit(), setExtentSize(),
　setViewSize(), toViewCoordinates() >
　MenuComponent.AccessibleAWTMenuComponent^.setSize()
　Rectangle⌄ < Rectangle(), setSize() >
　RepaintManager.setDoubleBufferMaximumSize()
—returned by: AccessibleComponent⌄.getSize() BorderLayout
　< maximumLayoutSize(), minimumLayoutSize(),
　preferredLayoutSize() > BoxLayout < maximumLayoutSize(),
　minimumLayoutSize(), preferredLayoutSize() > CardLayout
　< maximumLayoutSize(), minimumLayoutSize(),
　preferredLayoutSize() > Component⌄ < getMaximumSize(),
　getMinimumSize(), getPreferredSize(), getSize(),
　minimumSize(), preferredSize(), size() >
　Component.AccessibleAWTComponent^.getSize()
　ComponentPeer⌄ < getMinimumSize(), getPreferredSize(),
　minimumSize(), preferredSize() > ComponentUI⌄
　< getMaximumSize(), getMinimumSize(), getPreferredSize() >
　Dimension⌄.getSize() FlowLayout < minimumLayoutSize(),
　preferredLayoutSize() > GridBagLayout
　< getMinSize(), GetMinSize(), maximumLayoutSize(),
　minimumLayoutSize(), preferredLayoutSize() > GridLayout
　< minimumLayoutSize(), preferredLayoutSize() >
　ImageReadParam^.getSourceRenderSize()
　ImageWriteParam^.getPreferredTileSizes()
　ImageWriter.getPreferredThumbnailSizes()
　JList^.getPreferredScrollableViewportSize()
　JList.AccessibleJList.AccessibleJListChild^.getSize()
　JRootPane.RootLayout < maximumLayoutSize(),
　minimumLayoutSize(), preferredLayoutSize() >
　JSpinner.DefaultEditor⌄ < minimumLayoutSize(),
　preferredLayoutSize() > JTable^ < getIntercellSpacing(),

getPreferredScrollableViewportSize() >
　JTable.AccessibleJTable.AccessibleJTableCell^.getSize()
　JTableHeader.AccessibleJTableHeader⌄
　.AccessibleJTableHeaderEntry^.getSize()
　JTextComponent⌄.getPreferredScrollableViewportSize()
　JToolBar.Separator^.getSeparatorSize()
　JTree^.getPreferredScrollableViewportSize()
　JTree.AccessibleJTree.AccessibleJTreeNode^.getSize()
　JViewport^ < getExtentSize(), getViewSize(),
　toViewCoordinates() > LayoutManager⌄
　< minimumLayoutSize(), preferredLayoutSize() >
　LayoutManager2^.maximumLayoutSize() java.awt.List^
　< getMinimumSize(), getPreferredSize(), minimumSize(),
　preferredSize() > ListPeer^ < getMinimumSize(),
　getPreferredSize(), minimumSize(), preferredSize() >
　MenuComponent.AccessibleAWTMenuComponent⌄.getSize()
　OverlayLayout < maximumLayoutSize(),
　minimumLayoutSize(), preferredLayoutSize() >
　PrintJob.getPageDimension() Rectangle⌄.getSize()
　RepaintManager.getDoubleBufferMaximumSize()
　Scrollable.getPreferredScrollableViewportSize()
　ScrollPane^.getViewportSize() ScrollPaneLayout⌄
　< minimumLayoutSize(), preferredLayoutSize() > SpringLayout
　< maximumLayoutSize(), minimumLayoutSize(),
　preferredLayoutSize() > TextArea^ < getMinimumSize(),
　getPreferredSize(), minimumSize(), preferredSize() >
　TextAreaPeer^ < getMinimumSize(), getPreferredSize(),
　minimumSize(), preferredSize() > TextField^
　< getMinimumSize(), getPreferredSize(), minimumSize(),
　preferredSize() > TextFieldPeer^ < getMinimumSize(),
　getPreferredSize(), minimumSize(), preferredSize() >
　TitledBorder⌄.getMinimumSize() Toolkit < getBestCursorSize(),
　getScreenSize() > UIDefaults^.getDimension()
　UIManager.getDimension() ViewportLayout
　< minimumLayoutSize(), preferredLayoutSize() >
—fields: ImageReadParam⌄.sourceRenderSize
　ImageWriteParam⌄.preferredTileSizes
　JTable^.preferredViewportSize
Dimension2D: java.awt.geom
—subclasses: Dimension^
—descendents: DimensionUIResource^
—passed to: Arc2D^.setArc() Dimension2D⌄.setSize()
　RectangularShape⌄.setFrame()
DimensionUIResource^: javax.swing.plaf
DIR: HTML.Attribute HTML.Tag⌄
DirectColorModel^: java.awt.image
DIRECTORIES_ONLY: JFileChooser^
DIRECTORY_CHANGED_PROPERTY: JFileChooser^
DIRECTORY_PANE: AccessibleRole^
disable(): Component⌄ ComponentPeer⌄ MenuItem⌄
　MenuItemPeer⌄
DISABLED_ICON_CHANGED_PROPERTY: AbstractButton⌄
DISABLED_SELECTED_ICON_CHANGED_PROPERTY:
　AbstractButton⌄
disableEvents(): Component⌄ MenuItem⌄
disableResizedPosting(): TableColumn
disableSwingFocusManager(): FocusManager⌄
discardAllEdits(): UndoManager^
discardKeyEvents(): KeyboardFocusManager⌄
DISCONTIGUOUS_TREE_SELECTION: TreeSelectionModel
dismiss(): JSpinner.DefaultEditor⌄
dispatch(): ActiveEvent InvocationEvent^
dispatchEvent(): Component⌄ EventQueue InputContext
　InputMethod KeyboardFocusManager⌄ MenuComponent⌄
dispatchInputMethodEvent(): InputMethodContext^
dispatchKeyEvent(): KeyboardFocusManager⌄
　KeyEventDispatcher
DISPLAY: CSS.Attribute
DISPLAYABILITY_CHANGED: HierarchyEvent^
DisplayMode: java.awt
—passed to: DisplayMode.equals()
　GraphicsDevice.setDisplayMode()

—returned by: **G**raphicsDevice < getDisplayMode( ),
getDisplayModes( ) >
dispose( ): *ComponentPeer*⌄ *CompositeContext* **G**raphics⌄
ImageReader **I**mageWriter **I**nputContext *InputMethod*
JInternalFrame^ *MenuComponentPeer*⌄ **P**aintContext
StreamPrintService **W**indow^
DISPOSE_ON_CLOSE: *WindowConstants*
distance( ): **P**oint2D⌄
distanceSq( ): **P**oint2D⌄
DIV: **H**TML.Tag⌄
DIVIDER: **J**SplitPane^
DIVIDER_LOCATION_PROPERTY: **J**SplitPane^
DIVIDER_SIZE_PROPERTY: **J**SplitPane^
dividerSize: **J**SplitPane^
divisionType: **M**idiFileFormat **S**equence
DL: **H**TML.Tag⌄
DnDConstants: java.awt.dnd
DO_NOTHING_ON_CLOSE: *WindowConstants*
doAccessibleAction( ):
AbstractButton.AccessibleAbstractButton^ *AccessibleAction*
AccessibleHyperlink⌄ **B**utton.AccessibleAWTButton^
Checkbox.AccessibleAWTCheckbox^
Choice.AccessibleAWTChoice^
JComboBox.AccessibleJComboBox^
JTextComponent.AccessibleJTextComponent^
JTree.AccessibleJTree.AccessibleJTreeNode^
MenuItem.AccessibleAWTMenuItem^
Doc: javax.print
—passed to: *DocPrintJob*⌄.print( )
—returned by: *MultiDoc*.getDoc( )
—implemented by: **S**impleDoc
DocAttribute^: javax.print.attribute
—passed to: **H**ashDocAttributeSet( )
—implemented by: **C**hromaticity^ **C**ompression^
DocumentName^ **F**inishings^ **M**edia^ **M**ediaPrintableArea
NumberUp^ **O**rientationRequested^ **P**ageRanges^
PrinterResolution^ **P**rintQuality^ **S**heetCollate^ **S**ides^
DocAttributeSet^: javax.print.attribute
—passed to: **A**ttributeSetUtilities < synchronizedView( ),
unmodifiableView( ) > **H**ashDocAttributeSet( ) **S**impleDoc( )
—returned by: **A**ttributeSetUtilities < synchronizedView( ),
unmodifiableView( ) > *Doc*.getAttributes( )
SimpleDoc.getAttributes( )
—implemented by: **H**ashDocAttributeSet^
DocFlavor⌄: javax.print
—subclasses: **D**ocFlavor.BYTE_ARRAY^
DocFlavor.CHAR_ARRAY^ **D**ocFlavor.INPUT_STREAM^
DocFlavor.READER^ **D**ocFlavor.SERVICE_FORMATTED^
DocFlavor.STRING^ **D**ocFlavor.URL^
—passed to: *PrintService*⌄ < getSupportedAttributeValues( ),
getUnsupportedAttributes( ), isAttributeValueSupported( ),
isDocFlavorSupported( ) > **P**rintServiceLookup
< getMultiDocPrintServices( ), getPrintServices( ),
lookupMultiDocPrintServices( ), lookupPrintServices( ) >
ServiceUI.printDialog( ) **S**impleDoc( )
StreamPrintServiceFactory.lookupStreamPrintServiceFactories( )
—returned by: *Doc*.getDocFlavor( )
FlavorException.getUnsupportedFlavors( )
PrintService⌄.getSupportedDocFlavors( )
SimpleDoc.getDocFlavor( )
StreamPrintServiceFactory.getSupportedDocFlavors( )
DocFlavor.BYTE_ARRAY^: javax.print
—fields: **D**ocFlavor.BYTE_ARRAY^ < AUTOSENSE, GIF, JPEG,
PCL, PDF, PNG, POSTSCRIPT, TEXT_HTML_HOST,
TEXT_HTML_US_ASCII, TEXT_HTML_UTF_16,
TEXT_HTML_UTF_16BE, TEXT_HTML_UTF_16LE,
TEXT_HTML_UTF_8, TEXT_PLAIN_HOST, TEXT_PLAIN_US_ASCII,
TEXT_PLAIN_UTF_16, TEXT_PLAIN_UTF_16BE,
TEXT_PLAIN_UTF_16LE, TEXT_PLAIN_UTF_8 >
DocFlavor.CHAR_ARRAY^: javax.print
—fields: **D**ocFlavor.CHAR_ARRAY^ < TEXT_HTML, TEXT_PLAIN >
DocFlavor.INPUT_STREAM^: javax.print

—fields: **D**ocFlavor.INPUT_STREAM^ < AUTOSENSE, GIF, JPEG,
PCL, PDF, PNG, POSTSCRIPT, TEXT_HTML_HOST,
TEXT_HTML_US_ASCII, TEXT_HTML_UTF_16,
TEXT_HTML_UTF_16BE, TEXT_HTML_UTF_16LE,
TEXT_HTML_UTF_8, TEXT_PLAIN_HOST, TEXT_PLAIN_US_ASCII,
TEXT_PLAIN_UTF_16, TEXT_PLAIN_UTF_16BE,
TEXT_PLAIN_UTF_16LE, TEXT_PLAIN_UTF_8 >
DocFlavor.READER^: javax.print
—fields: **D**ocFlavor.READER^ < TEXT_HTML, TEXT_PLAIN >
DocFlavor.SERVICE_FORMATTED^: javax.print
—fields: **D**ocFlavor.SERVICE_FORMATTED^ < PAGEABLE,
PRINTABLE, RENDERABLE_IMAGE >
DocFlavor.STRING^: javax.print
—fields: **D**ocFlavor.STRING^ < TEXT_HTML, TEXT_PLAIN >
DocFlavor.URL^: javax.print
—fields: **D**ocFlavor.URL^ < AUTOSENSE, GIF, JPEG, PCL, PDF,
PNG, POSTSCRIPT, TEXT_HTML_HOST, TEXT_HTML_US_ASCII,
TEXT_HTML_UTF_16, TEXT_HTML_UTF_16BE,
TEXT_HTML_UTF_16LE, TEXT_HTML_UTF_8, TEXT_PLAIN_HOST,
TEXT_PLAIN_US_ASCII, TEXT_PLAIN_UTF_16,
TEXT_PLAIN_UTF_16BE, TEXT_PLAIN_UTF_16LE,
TEXT_PLAIN_UTF_8 >
doClick( ): **A**bstractButton^
DocPrintJob⌄: javax.print
—extended by: *CancelablePrintJob*^ *MultiDocPrintJob*^
—passed to: **P**rintJobAttributeEvent( ) **P**rintJobEvent( )
—returned by: **P**rintJobAttributeEvent^.getPrintJob( )
PrintJobEvent^.getPrintJob( ) *PrintService*⌄.createPrintJob( )
Document⌄: javax.swing.text
—extended by: *StyledDocument*^
—passed to: **A**bstractWriter( ) **E**ditorKit < read( ), write( ) >
ElementIterator( ) **J**PasswordField( ) **J**TextArea( )
JTextComponent^.setDocument( ) **J**TextField( )
—returned
by: **A**bstractDocument.AbstractElement⌄.getDocument( )
AbstractDocument.DefaultDocumentEvent^.getDocument( )
AbstractWriter⌄.getDocument( ) *DocumentEvent*.getDocument( )
DocumentFilter.FilterBypass.getDocument( )
EditorKit⌄.createDefaultDocument( )
javax.swing.text.Element.getDocument( )
JTextArea^.createDefaultModel( )
JTextComponent^.getDocument( )
JTextField^.createDefaultModel( ) **V**iew⌄.getDocument( )
—implemented by: **A**bstractDocument⌄
Document^: org.w3c.dom
—returned by: **I**IOMetadataNode.getOwnerDocument( )
DOCUMENT_ACCESS_ERROR: **J**obStateReason^
DOCUMENT_FORMAT_ERROR: **J**obStateReason^
DocumentEvent: javax.swing.event
—passed to: **A**bstractDocument⌄ < fireChangedUpdate( ),
fireInsertUpdate( ), fireRemoveUpdate( ) >
AsyncBoxView^.updateLayout( ) **B**oxView^.forwardUpdate( )
DocumentListener^ < changedUpdate( ), insertUpdate( ),
removeUpdate( ) > **F**lowView.FlowStrategy
< changedUpdate( ), insertUpdate( ), removeUpdate( ) >
HTMLDocument^.fireChangedUpdate( )
JTextComponent.AccessibleJTextComponent^
< changedUpdate( ), insertUpdate( ), removeUpdate( ) >
PlainView^.updateDamage( ) **T**ableView^.forwardUpdate( )
View⌄ < changedUpdate( ), forwardUpdate( ), forwardUpdateToView( ),
insertUpdate( ), removeUpdate( ), updateChildren( ),
updateLayout( ) > **Z**oneView^.updateChildren( )
—implemented by: **A**bstractDocument.DefaultDocumentEvent^
DocumentEvent.ElementChange: javax.swing.event
—passed to: **A**syncBoxView^.updateLayout( )
BoxView^.forwardUpdate( ) **T**ableView^.forwardUpdate( ) **V**iew⌄
< forwardUpdate( ), updateChildren( ), updateLayout( ) >
ZoneView^.updateChildren( )
—returned
by: **A**bstractDocument.DefaultDocumentEvent^.getChange( )
DocumentEvent.getChange( )
—implemented by: **A**bstractDocument.ElementEdit^

DocumentEvent.EventType: javax.swing.event
— passed to: **A**bstractDocument.DefaultDocumentEvent( )
— returned
  by: **A**bstractDocument.DefaultDocumentEvent^.getType( )
  *D*ocumentEvent.getType( )
— fields: **D**ocumentEvent.EventType < CHANGE, INSERT, REMOVE >

DocumentFilter: javax.swing.text
— passed to: **A**bstractDocument⌄.setDocumentFilter( )
— returned by: **A**bstractDocument⌄.getDocumentFilter( )
  DefaultFormatter^.getDocumentFilter( )
  JFormattedTextField.AbstractFormatter⌄.getDocumentFilter( )

DocumentFilter.FilterBypass: javax.swing.text
— passed to: **D**ocumentFilter < insertString( ), remove( ), replace( ) >

DocumentListener^: javax.swing.event
— passed to: **A**bstractDocument < addDocumentListener( ), removeDocumentListener( ) > *javax.swing.text.Document*⌄ < addDocumentListener( ), removeDocumentListener( ) >
— returned by: **A**bstractDocument⌄.getDocumentListeners( )
— implemented by: **J**TextComponent.AccessibleJTextComponent⌃

DocumentName: javax.print.attribute.standard

DocumentParser^: javax.swing.text.html.parser

doDefaultCloseAction( ): **J**InternalFrame^

doLayout( ): **C**omponent

DOMException: org.w3c.dom
— thrown by: **I**IOMetadataNode < getNamespaceURI( ), getNodeValue( ), setAttributeNode( ), setNodeValue( ) >

DOOR_OPEN: **P**rinterStateReason^

DOWN: **E**vent

DOWN_CYCLE_TRAVERSAL_KEYS: **K**eyboardFocusManager⌄

downAction: **D**efaultEditorKit⌃

downFocusCycle( ): **K**eyboardFocusManager⌄

DPCM: **R**esolutionSyntax⌄

DPI: **R**esolutionSyntax⌄

DRAFT: **P**ageAttributes.PrintQualityType^ **P**rintQuality^

DRAG_LAYER: **J**LayeredPane^

dragDropEnd( ): **D**ragSourceAdapter **D**ragSourceContext *DragSourceListener*^

dragEnter( ): **D**ragSourceAdapter **D**ragSourceContext *DragSourceListener*^ **D**ropTarget **D**ropTargetAdapter *DropTargetListener*^

dragExit( ): **D**ragSourceAdapter **D**ragSourceContext *DragSourceListener*^ **D**ropTarget **D**ropTargetAdapter *DropTargetListener*^

dragFrame( ): **D**efaultDesktopManager *DesktopManager*

draggedColumn: **J**TableHeader^

draggedDistance: **J**TableHeader^

DragGestureEvent^: java.awt.dnd
— passed to: *DragGestureListener*^.dragGestureRecognized( ) **D**ragSource < createDragSourceContext( ), startDrag( ) > **D**ragSourceContext( ) **T**oolkit.createDragSourceContextPeer( )
— returned by: **D**ragSourceContext.getTrigger( )

dragGestureListener: **D**ragGestureRecognizer⌄

DragGestureListener^: java.awt.dnd
— passed to: **D**ragGestureRecognizer⌄ < addDragGestureListener( ), DragGestureRecognizer( ), removeDragGestureListener( ) > **D**ragSource < createDefaultDragGestureRecognizer( ), createDragGestureRecognizer( ) > **M**ouseDragGestureRecognizer( ) **T**oolkit.createDragGestureRecognizer( )
— fields: **D**ragGestureRecognizer⌄.dragGestureListener

dragGestureRecognized( ): *DragGestureListener*^

DragGestureRecognizer⌄: java.awt.dnd
— subclasses: **M**ouseDragGestureRecognizer^
— passed to: **D**ragGestureEvent( )
— returned
  by: **D**ragGestureEvent^.getSourceAsDragGestureRecognizer( ) **D**ragSource < createDefaultDragGestureRecognizer( ), createDragGestureRecognizer( ) > **T**oolkit.createDragGestureRecognizer( )

dragMouseMoved( ): **D**ragSourceAdapter **D**ragSourceContext *DragSourceMotionListener*^

dragOver( ): **D**ragSourceAdapter **D**ragSourceContext *DragSourceListener*^ **D**ropTarget **D**ropTargetAdapter *DropTargetListener*^

dragSource: **D**ragGestureRecognizer⌄

DragSource: java.awt.dnd
— passed to: **D**ragGestureRecognizer( ) **M**ouseDragGestureRecognizer( ) **T**oolkit.createDragGestureRecognizer( )
— returned by: **D**ragGestureEvent^.getDragSource( ) **D**ragGestureRecognizer⌄.getDragSource( ) **D**ragSource.getDefaultDragSource( ) **D**ragSourceContext.getDragSource( )
— fields: **D**ragGestureRecognizer⌄.dragSource

DragSourceAdapter: java.awt.dnd

DragSourceContext: java.awt.dnd
— passed to: **D**ragSourceDragEvent( ) **D**ragSourceDropEvent( ) **D**ragSourceEvent( )
— returned by: **D**ragSource.createDragSourceContext( ) **D**ragSourceEvent^.getDragSourceContext( )

DragSourceContextPeer: java.awt.dnd.peer
— passed to: **D**ragSource.createDragSourceContext( ) **D**ragSourceContext( )
— returned by: **T**oolkit.createDragSourceContextPeer( )

DragSourceDragEvent^: java.awt.dnd
— passed to: **D**ragSourceAdapter < dragEnter( ), dragMouseMoved( ), dragOver( ), dropActionChanged( ) > **D**ragSourceContext < dragEnter( ), dragMouseMoved( ), dragOver( ), dropActionChanged( ) > *DragSourceListener*^ < dragEnter( ), dragOver( ), dropActionChanged( ) > *DragSourceMotionListener*^.dragMouseMoved( )

DragSourceDropEvent^: java.awt.dnd
— passed to: **D**ragSourceAdapter.dragDropEnd( ) **D**ragSourceContext.dragDropEnd( ) *DragSourceListener*^.dragDropEnd( )

DragSourceEvent^: java.awt.dnd
— subclasses: **D**ragSourceDragEvent^ **D**ragSourceDropEvent^
— passed to: **D**ragSourceAdapter.dragExit( ) **D**ragSourceContext.dragExit( ) *DragSourceListener*^.dragExit( )

DragSourceListener^: java.awt.dnd
— passed to: **D**ragGestureEvent^.startDrag( ) **D**ragSource < addDragSourceListener( ), createDragSourceContext( ), removeDragSourceListener( ), startDrag( ) > **D**ragSourceContext < addDragSourceListener( ), DragSourceContext( ), removeDragSourceListener( ) >
— returned by: **D**ragSource.getDragSourceListeners( )
— implemented by: **D**ragSourceAdapter **D**ragSourceContext

DragSourceMotionListener^: java.awt.dnd
— passed to: **D**ragSource < addDragSourceMotionListener( ), removeDragSourceMotionListener( ) >
— returned by: **D**ragSource.getDragSourceMotionListeners( )
— implemented by: **D**ragSourceAdapter **D**ragSourceContext

drain( ): *DataLine*⌃

draw( ): **G**raphicAttribute⌄ **G**raphics2D^ **T**extLayout

draw3DRect( ): **G**raphics⌄

drawArc( ): **G**raphics⌄

drawBuffer( ): **C**omponent.FlipBufferStrategy^

drawBytes( ): **G**raphics⌄

drawChars( ): **G**raphics⌄

drawEchoCharacter( ): **P**asswordView^

drawGlyphVector( ): **G**raphics2D^

drawImage( ): **G**raphics⌄

drawLine( ): **G**raphics⌄ **P**lainView⌃ **W**rappedPlainView^

drawOval( ): **G**raphics⌄

drawPolygon( ): **G**raphics⌄

drawPolyline( ): **G**raphics⌄

drawRect( ): **G**raphics⌄

drawRenderableImage( ): **G**raphics2D^

drawRenderedImage( ): **G**raphics2D^

drawRoundRect( ): **G**raphics⌄

drawSelectedText( ): **P**lainView⌃ **W**rappedPlainView^

drawString(): Graphics
drawTabbedText(): Utilities
drawUnselectedText(): PlainView^ **W**rappedPlainView^
drawVBuffer: Component.FlipBufferStrategy^
drop(): DropTarget *DropTargetListener*^
dropActionChanged(): DragSourceAdapter
   DragSourceContext *DragSourceListener*^ DropTarget
   DropTargetAdapter *DropTargetListener*^
dropComplete(): DropTargetContext DropTargetDropEvent^
DropTarget: java.awt.dnd
  —passed to: Component.setDropTarget()
  —returned by: Component.getDropTarget()
   DropTargetContext.getDropTarget()
DropTarget.DropTargetAutoScroller: java.awt.dnd
  —returned by: DropTarget.createDropTargetAutoScroller()
DropTargetAdapter: java.awt.dnd
DropTargetContext: java.awt.dnd
  —passed to: DropTargetDragEvent() DropTargetDropEvent()
   DropTargetEvent()
  —returned by: DropTarget
   < createDropTargetContext(), getDropTargetContext() >
   DropTargetEvent.getDropTargetContext()
  —fields: DropTargetEvent.context
DropTargetContext.TransferableProxy: java.awt.dnd
DropTargetContextPeer: java.awt.dnd.peer
  —passed to: DropTargetContext.addNotify()
DropTargetDragEvent^: java.awt.dnd
  —passed to: DropTarget < dragEnter(), dragOver(),
   dropActionChanged() > DropTargetAdapter < dragEnter(),
   dragOver(), dropActionChanged() > *DropTargetListener*^
   < dragEnter(), dragOver(), dropActionChanged() >
DropTargetDropEvent^: java.awt.dnd
  —passed to: DropTarget.drop() *DropTargetListener*^.drop()
DropTargetEvent^: java.awt.dnd
  —subclasses: DropTargetDragEvent^ DropTargetDropEvent^
  —passed to: DropTarget.dragExit() DropTargetAdapter.dragExit()
   DropTargetListener^.dragExit()
DropTargetListener^: java.awt.dnd
  —passed to: DropTarget < addDropTargetListener(), DropTarget(),
   removeDropTargetListener() >
  —implemented by: DropTarget DropTargetAdapter
Dst: AlphaComposite
DST: AlphaComposite
DST_ATOP: AlphaComposite
DST_IN: AlphaComposite
DST_OUT: AlphaComposite
DST_OVER: AlphaComposite
DstAtop: AlphaComposite
DstIn: AlphaComposite
DstOut: AlphaComposite
DstOver: AlphaComposite
DT: HTML.Tag
dtd: javax.swing.text.html.parser.Parser
DTD: javax.swing.text.html.parser
  —passed to: DocumentParser() DTD.putDTDHash()
   javax.swing.text.html.parser.Parser()
   ParserDelegator^.createDTD()
  —returned by: DTD.getDTD() ParserDelegator^.createDTD()
  —fields: javax.swing.text.html.parser.Parser.dtd
DTDConstants: javax.swing.text.html.parser
  —implemented by: javax.swing.text.html.parser.AttributeList
   DTD javax.swing.text.html.parser.Element
   javax.swing.text.html.parser.Entity
   javax.swing.text.html.parser.Parser
DUMMY: HTML.Attribute
dump(): AbstractDocument
  AbstractDocument.AbstractElement
DUPLEX: Sides^
E: MediaSize.Engineering MediaSizeName^
  PageAttributes.MediaType^
E_RESIZE_CURSOR: Cursor Frame^

EAST: BorderLayout GridBagConstraints SpringLayout
  SwingConstants
EASTERN_ARABIC: NumericShaper
echoCharIsSet(): JPasswordField^ TextField^
EDGE_NO_OP: ConvolveOp
EDGE_SPACING: TitledBorder
EDGE_STITCH: Finishings^
EDGE_STITCH_BOTTOM: Finishings^
EDGE_STITCH_LEFT: Finishings^
EDGE_STITCH_RIGHT: Finishings^
EDGE_STITCH_TOP: Finishings^
EDGE_ZERO_FILL: ConvolveOp
editable: JTree^
EDITABLE: AccessibleState^
EDITABLE_PROPERTY: JTree^
editCellAt(): JTable^
editingCanceled(): *CellEditorListener*^ JTable^
  JTable.AccessibleJTable^
editingColumn: JTable^
editingComponent: DefaultTreeCellEditor
editingContainer: DefaultTreeCellEditor
editingIcon: DefaultTreeCellEditor
editingRow: JTable^
editingStopped(): *CellEditorListener*^ JTable^
  JTable.AccessibleJTable^
editor: JComboBox^
editorComp: JTable^
editorComponent: DefaultCellEditor^
EditorContainer(): DefaultTreeCellEditor.EditorContainer^
EditorKit: javax.swing.text
  —subclasses: DefaultEditorKit
  —descendents: HTMLEditorKit^ RTFEditorKit^ StyledEditorKit
  —passed to: JEditorPane < setEditorKit(),
   setEditorKitForContentType() >
  —returned by: JEditorPane < createDefaultEditorKit(),
   createEditorKitForContentType(),
   getEditorKit(), getEditorKitForContentType() >
   JTextPane^.createDefaultEditorKit() TextUI^.getEditorKit()
edits: CompoundEdit
editToBeRedone(): UndoManager^
editToBeUndone(): UndoManager^
element: DefaultStyledDocument.AttributeUndoableEdit^
Element: javax.swing.text
  —passed to: AbstractDocument < createBranchElement(),
   createLeafElement() > AbstractDocument.AbstractElement()
   AbstractDocument.BranchElement
   < AbstractDocument.BranchElement(), replace() >
   AbstractDocument.DefaultDocumentEvent^.getChange()
   AbstractDocument.ElementEdit()
   AbstractDocument.LeafElement() AbstractWriter
   < AbstractWriter(), getText(), inRange(),
   text() > AsyncBoxView() BlockView()
   BoxView() ComponentView() CompositeView()
   DefaultStyledDocument.AttributeUndoableEdit()
   DefaultStyledDocument.ElementBuffer
   < clone(), DefaultStyledDocument.ElementBuffer() >
   DocumentEvent.getChange() ElementIterator()
   FieldView() FlowView() FormView() GlyphView()
   HTMLDocument^ < createBranchElement(), createLeafElement(),
   getElement(), insertAfterEnd(), insertAfterStart(),
   insertBeforeEnd(), insertBeforeStart(), setInnerHTML(),
   setOuterHTML() > HTMLDocument.BlockElement()
   HTMLDocument.RunElement()
   HTMLEditorKit^.createInputAttributes()
   HTMLEditorKit.HTMLFactory.create()
   HTMLEditorKit.InsertHTMLTextAction^ < insertAtBoundary(),
   insertAtBoundry() > HTMLFrameHyperlinkEvent()
   HTMLWriter^ < comment(), emptyTag(), endTag(), startTag(),
   synthesizedElement(), text() > HyperlinkEvent()
   IconView() ImageView() InlineView() JEditorPane
   .JEditorPaneAccessibleHypertextSupport.HTMLLink()
   LabelView() ListView() MinimalHTMLWriter^

E

< isText( ), text( ), writeComponent( ), writeContent( ), writeImage( ), writeLeaf( ), writeStartParagraph( ) > **O**bjectView( ) *javax.swing.text.html.***P**aragraphView( ) *javax.swing.text.***P**aragraphView( ) **P**asswordView( ) **P**lainView( ) **S**tyledEditorKit͡.createInputAttributes( ) **S**tyleSheet^.getRule( ) **T**ableView^ < createTableCell( ), createTableRow( ), TableView( ) > **T**ableView.TableCell( ) **T**ableView.TableRow( ) **V**iew( ) **V**iewFactory.create( ) **W**rappedPlainView( ) **Z**oneView( )
—returned by: **A**bstractDocument͜ < createBranchElement( ), createLeafElement( ), getBidiRootElement( ), getDefaultRootElement( ), getParagraphElement( ), getRootElements( ) > **A**bstractDocument.AbstractElement͜ < getElement( ), getParentElement( ) > **A**bstractDocument.BranchElement^.positionToElement( ) **A**bstractDocument.ElementEdit^ < getChildrenAdded( ), getChildrenRemoved( ), getElement( ) > **D**efaultStyledDocument^.getCharacterElement( ) **D**efaultStyledDocument.ElementBuffer < clone( ), getRootElement( ) > *javax.swing.text.***D**ocument͜ < getDefaultRootElement( ), getRootElements( ) > **D**ocumentEvent.ElementChange < getChildrenAdded( ), getChildrenRemoved( ), getElement( ) > *javax.swing.text.***E**lement < getElement( ), getParentElement( ) > **E**lementIterator < current( ), first( ), next( ), previous( ) > **H**TMLDocument^ < createBranchElement( ), createLeafElement( ), getElement( ) > **H**TMLEditorKit.HTMLTextAction͡ < findElementMatchingTag( ), getElementsAt( ) > **H**yperlinkEvent͡.getSourceElement( ) *StyledDocument^* < getCharacterElement( ), getParagraphElement( ) > **S**tyledEditorKit͡.getCharacterAttributeRun( ) **U**tilities.getParagraphElement( ) **V**iew͜.getElement( )
—implemented by: **A**bstractDocument.AbstractElement͜
—fields: **D**efaultStyledDocument.AttributeUndoableEdit^.element
Element: *javax.swing.text.html.parser*
—passed to: **C**ontentModel( ) *javax.swing.text.html.parser.***P**arser͜ < makeTag( ), markFirstTime( ) > **T**agElement( )
—returned by: **C**ontentModel.first( ) **D**TD < defElement( ), defineElement( ), getElement( ) > **T**agElement.getElement( )
—fields: **D**TD < applet, base, body, head, html, isindex, meta, p, param, pcdata, title >
Element^: `org.w3c.dom`
—implemented by: **I**IOMetadataNode
elementAt( ): **D**efaultListModel^
elementCountToTag( ): **H**TMLEditorKit.HTMLTextAction͡
elementHash: **D**TD
ElementIterator: *javax.swing.text*
—returned by: **A**bstractWriter͜.getElementIterator( )
ElementNameAttribute: **A**bstractDocument͜
elements: **D**TD
elements( ): **D**efaultListModel^
Ellipse2D^: *java.awt.geom*
—subclasses: **E**llipse2D.Double͡ **E**llipse2D.Float^
Ellipse2D.Double͡: *java.awt.geom*
Ellipse2D.Float^: *java.awt.geom*
EM: **H**TML.Tag͜
EMPTY: *DTDConstants* **S**impleAttributeSet
empty( ): **C**ontentModel
EMPTY_ENUMERATION: **D**efaultMutableTreeNode͜
EmptyBorder͡: *javax.swing.border*
—subclasses: **B**orderUIResource.EmptyBorderUIResource^ **M**atteBorder^
—descendents: **B**orderUIResource.MatteBorderUIResource^
EmptyStackException: `java.util`
—thrown by: **E**ventQueue.pop( )
emptyTag( ): **H**TMLWriter^
enable( ): **C**omponent͜ *ComponentPeer͜* **M**enuItem͡ *MenuItemPeer͡*
enableClientWindowNotification( ): *InputMethodContext^*
enabled: **A**bstractAction͜
ENABLED: **A**ccessibleState^ **D**efaultButtonModel͜

enableEvents( ): **C**omponent͜ **M**enuItem͡
enableInputMethods( ): **C**omponent͜
enableResizedPosting( ): **T**ableColumn
encodeDataFlavor( ): **S**ystemFlavorMap
encodeJavaMIMEType( ): **S**ystemFlavorMap
encoding: **A**udioFormat
ENCTYPE: **H**TML.Attribute
END: **E**vent
end( ): **C**ompoundEdit͡ **H**TMLDocument.HTMLReader.TagAction͜ **P**rintJob **S**tateEdit^
END_OF_EXCLUSIVE: **S**hortMessage^
endAction: **D**efaultEditorKit͡
endComposition( ): **I**nputContext *InputMethod*
endDraggingFrame( ): **D**efaultDesktopManager *DesktopManager*
endFontTag( ): **M**inimalHTMLWriter^
endInsertEmpty( ): **I**mageWriter
endLayout( ): *ContainerPeer^*
endLineAction: **D**efaultEditorKit͡
EndOfLineStringProperty: **D**efaultEditorKit͡
endParagraphAction: **D**efaultEditorKit͡
endReplacePixels( ): **I**mageWriter
endResizingFrame( ): **D**efaultDesktopManager *DesktopManager*
ENDTAG: *DTDConstants* **H**TML.Attribute
endTag( ): **H**TMLWriter^ *javax.swing.text.html.parser.***P**arser͜
EndTagType: **D**efaultStyledDocument.ElementSpec
endUpdate( ): **U**ndoableEditSupport
endValidate( ): *ContainerPeer^*
endWordAction: **D**efaultEditorKit͡
endWriteEmpty( ): **I**mageWriter
endWriteSequence( ): **I**mageWriter
enqueueKeyEvents( ): **K**eyboardFocusManager͜
ensureCapacity( ): **D**efaultListModel^
ensureFileIsVisible( ): **F**ileChooserUI^ **J**FileChooser^
ensureIndexIsVisible( ): **J**List^
ENTER: **D**ragSourceContext **E**vent
ENTERED: **H**yperlinkEvent.EventType
ENTITIES: *DTDConstants*
ENTITY: *DTDConstants*
Entity: *javax.swing.text.html.parser*
—returned by: **D**TD < defEntity( ), defineEntity( ), getEntity( ) >
entityHash: **D**TD
entrySet( ): **R**enderingHints
EnumControl^: *javax.sound.sampled*
EnumControl.Type^: *javax.sound.sampled*
—passed to: **E**numControl( )
—fields: **E**numControl.Type^.REVERB
Enumeration: `java.util`
—passed to: **A**bstractDocument.AbstractElement͜.removeAttributes( ) *AbstractDocument.AttributeContext*.removeAttributes( ) **J**Tree^.removeDescendantToggledPaths( ) *MutableAttributeSet͡*.removeAttributes( ) **S**impleAttributeSet.removeAttributes( ) **S**tyleContext͜.removeAttributes( ) **S**tyleContext.NamedStyle.removeAttributes( )
—returned by: **A**bstractDocument.AbstractElement͜ < children( ), getAttributeNames( ) > **A**bstractLayoutCache͜.getVisiblePathsFrom( ) *AppletContext*.getApplets( ) *javax.swing.text.html.parser.***A**ttributeList.getValues( ) *javax.swing.text.***A**ttributeSet͜.getAttributeNames( ) **B**uttonGroup.getElements( ) **D**efaultListModel^.elements( ) **D**efaultMutableTreeNode͜ < breadthFirstEnumeration( ), children( ), depthFirstEnumeration( ), pathFromAncestorEnumeration( ), postorderEnumeration( ), preorderEnumeration( ) > **D**efaultStyledDocument͡.getStyleNames( ) **D**efaultTableColumnModel.getColumns( ) **J**Tree^ < getDescendantToggledPaths( ), getExpandedDescendants( ) >

E

E

EventListenerProxy: java.util
—subclasses: **A**WTEventListenerProxy^
EventObject: java.util
—subclasses: **A**WTEvent^ **C**aretEvent^ **C**hangeEvent^
DragGestureEvent^ **D**ragSourceEvent^ **D**ropTargetEvent^
HyperlinkEvent^ **L**ineEvent^ **L**istDataEvent^
ListSelectionEvent^ **M**enuEvent^ **P**opupMenuEvent^
PrintEvent^ **T**ableColumnModelEvent^ **T**ableModelEvent^
TreeExpansionEvent^ **T**reeModelEvent^
TreeSelectionEvent^ **U**ndoableEditEvent^
—descendents: **A**ctionEvent^ **A**djustmentEvent^
AncestorEvent^ **C**omponentEvent^ **C**ontainerEvent^
DragSourceDragEvent^ **D**ragSourceDropEvent^
DropTargetDragEvent^ **D**ropTargetDropEvent^ **F**ocusEvent^
HierarchyEvent^ **H**TMLFrameHyperlinkEvent^ **I**nputEvent^
InputMethodEvent^ **I**nternalFrameEvent^ **I**nvocationEvent^
ItemEvent^ **K**eyEvent^ **M**enuDragMouseEvent^
MenuKeyEvent^ **M**ouseEvent^ **M**ouseWheelEvent^
PaintEvent^ **P**rintJobAttributeEvent^ **P**rintJobEvent^
PrintServiceAttributeEvent^ **T**extEvent^ **W**indowEvent^
—passed to: **A**bstractCellEditor < isCellEditable( ),
shouldSelectCell( ) > *CellEditor* < isCellEditable( ),
shouldSelectCell( ) > **D**efaultCellEditor.EditorDelegate
< isCellEditable( ), shouldSelectCell( ), startCellEditing( ) >
DefaultTreeCellEditor < canEditImmediately( ), isCellEditable( ),
shouldSelectCell( ), shouldStartEditingTimer( ) >
JTable^.editCellAt( )
EventQueue: java.awt
—passed to: **E**ventQueue.push( )
—returned by: **T**oolkit < getSystemEventQueue( ),
getSystemEventQueueImpl( ) >
events: **D**ragGestureRecognizer^ **T**rack
eventTypeEnabled( ): **S**crollPane^
evt: **E**vent
ExcellentBreakWeight: **V**iew
Exception^: java.lang
—subclasses: **A**WTException **B**adLocationException
ExpandVetoException **F**ontFormatException
InvalidMidiDataException **L**ineUnavailableException
MidiUnavailableException **M**imeTypeParseException
NoninvertibleTransformException **P**rinterException
PrintException **U**nsupportedAudioFileException
UnsupportedFlavorException
UnsupportedLookAndFeelException
—descendents: **C**annotRedoException **C**annotUndoException
ChangedCharSetException^ **C**MMException
HeadlessException^ **I**IOException^ **I**IOInvalidTreeException^
IllegalComponentStateException^ **I**llegalPathStateException
ImagingOpException **I**nvalidDnDOperationException^
PrinterAbortException^ **P**rinterIOException^
ProfileDataException **R**asterFormatException
UnmodifiableSetException
—passed to: **P**rintException( )
—returned by: **I**nvocationEvent^.getException( )
—thrown by: *InputMethodDescriptor*.createInputMethod( )
exclusions: javax.swing.text.html.parser.**E**lement
exclusiveOr( ): **A**rea
EXECUTIVE: **M**ediaSize.Other **M**ediaSizeName^
PageAttributes.MediaType^
EXIT_ON_CLOSE: **J**Frame^ *WindowConstants*
EXITED: **H**yperlinkEvent.EventType
EXPANDABLE: **A**ccessibleState^
EXPANDED: **A**ccessibleState^
expandPath( ): **J**Tree^
expandRow( ): **J**Tree^
EXPANDS_SELECTED_PATHS_PROPERTY: **J**Tree^
ExpandVetoException: javax.swing.tree
—thrown by: **J**Tree^ < fireTreeWillCollapse( ), fireTreeWillExpand( ) >
TreeWillExpandListener^ < treeWillCollapse( ),
treeWillExpand( ) >
exportAsDrag( ): **T**ransferHandler
exportDone( ): **T**ransferHandler

exportToClipboard( ): **T**ransferHandler
extent: **A**rc2D.Double^ **A**rc2D.Float^
Externalizable^: java.io
—implemented by: **D**ataFlavor
extraImageMetadataFormatClassNames:
ImageReaderWriterSpi^
extraImageMetadataFormatNames: **I**mageReaderWriterSpi^
extraMetadataFormatClassNames: **I**IOMetadata
extraMetadataFormatNames: **I**IOMetadata
extraStreamMetadataFormatClassNames:
ImageReaderWriterSpi^
extraStreamMetadataFormatNames: **I**mageReaderWriterSpi^
F1: **E**vent
F10: **E**vent
F11: **E**vent
F12: **E**vent
F2: **E**vent
F3: **E**vent
F4: **E**vent
F5: **E**vent
F6: **E**vent
F7: **E**vent
F8: **E**vent
F9: **E**vent
FACE: **H**TML.Attribute
FAMILY: **T**extAttribute^
Family: **S**tyleConstants.CharacterConstants^
StyleConstants.FontConstants^
fictional( ): **T**agElement
Fidelity^: javax.print.attribute.standard
—fields: **F**idelity^ < FIDELITY_FALSE, FIDELITY_TRUE >
FIDELITY_FALSE: **F**idelity^
FIDELITY_TRUE: **F**idelity^
FieldView^: javax.swing.text
—subclasses: **P**asswordView^
FILE: **J**obAttributes.DestinationType^
ReferenceUriSchemesSupported^
File: java.io
—passed to: **A**udioFileReader < getAudioFileFormat( ),
getAudioInputStream( ) > **A**udioFileWriter.write( )
AudioSystem < getAudioFileFormat( ), getAudioInputStream( ),
write( ) > **F**ileCacheImageInputStream( )
FileCacheImageOutputStream( )
FileChooserUI^.ensureFileIsVisible( ) **F**ileFilter.accept( )
FileImageInputStream( ) **F**ileImageOutputStream( )
FileSystemView < createFileObject( ), createFileSystemRoot( ),
createNewFolder( ), getChild( ), getFiles( ), getParentDirectory( ),
getSystemDisplayName( ), getSystemIcon( ),
getSystemTypeDescription( ), isComputerNode( ),
isDrive( ), isFileSystem( ), isFileSystemRoot( ),
isFloppyDrive( ), isHiddenFile( ), isParent( ), isRoot( ),
isTraversable( ) > **F**ileView < getDescription( ), getIcon( ),
getName( ), getTypeDescription( ), isTraversable( ) >
ImageInputStreamSpi^.createInputStreamInstance( )
ImageIO < read( ), setCacheDirectory( ), write( ) >
ImageOutputStreamSpi^.createOutputStreamInstance( )
JFileChooser^ < accept( ), ensureFileIsVisible( ),
getDescription( ), getIcon( ), getName( ), getTypeDescription( ),
isTraversable( ), **J**FileChooser( ), setCurrentDirectory( ),
setSelectedFile( ), setSelectedFiles( ) > **M**idiFileReader
< getMidiFileFormat( ), getSequence( ) > **M**idiFileWriter.write( )
MidiSystem < getMidiFileFormat( ), getSequence( ),
getSoundbank( ), write( ) > **S**oundbankReader.getSoundbank( )
—returned by: **F**ileSystemView < createFileObject( ),
createFileSystemRoot( ), createNewFolder( ), getChild( ),
getDefaultDirectory( ), getFiles( ), getHomeDirectory( ),
getParentDirectory( ), getRoots( ) > **I**mageIO.getCacheDirectory( )
JFileChooser^ < getCurrentDirectory( ), getSelectedFile( ),
getSelectedFiles( ) >
FILE_CHOOSER: **A**ccessibleRole^
FILE_CHOOSER_DIALOG: **J**RootPane^
FILE_FILTER_CHANGED_PROPERTY: **J**FileChooser^

Class *Interface* ^—has superclass —has subclass package—see other volume

F

fireVetoableChange( ): JComponent⌐
　　KeyboardFocusManager⌐
fireVisibleDataPropertyChange( ): JTree.AccessibleJTree^
first( ): **C**ardLayout **C**ontentModel **E**lementIterator **S**egment
FIRST_LINE_END: **G**ridBagConstraints
FIRST_LINE_START: **G**ridBagConstraints
firstColumn:
　　JTable.AccessibleJTable.AccessibleJTableModelChange
firstElement( ): **D**efaultListModel^
FirstLineIndent: **S**tyleConstants⌐
firstLineIndent: javax.swing.text.**P**aragraphView⌐
firstRow:
　　JTable.AccessibleJTable.AccessibleJTableModelChange
　　TableModelEvent^
FIXED: *DTDConstants*⌐
FixedHeightLayoutCache^: javax.swing.tree
FLAG_COMPLEX_GLYPHS: **G**lyphVector
FLAG_HAS_POSITION_ADJUSTMENTS: **G**lyphVector
FLAG_HAS_TRANSFORMS: **G**lyphVector
FLAG_MASK: **G**lyphVector
FLAG_RUN_RTL: **G**lyphVector
FLASH_OPTION: **D**ebugGraphics^
flashColor( ): **D**ebugGraphics^
flashCount( ): **D**ebugGraphics^
flashTime( ): **D**ebugGraphics^
FlatteningPathIterator: java.awt.geom
FlavorException: javax.print
FlavorMap⌐: java.awt.datatransfer
　—extended by: *FlavorTable*^
　—passed to: **D**ragSource.startDrag( ) **D**ropTarget < DropTarget( ),
　　setFlavorMap( ) >
　—returned by: **D**ragSource.getFlavorMap( )
　　DropTarget.getFlavorMap( )
　　SystemFlavorMap.getDefaultFlavorMap( )
　—implemented by: **S**ystemFlavorMap
FlavorTable^: java.awt.datatransfer
　—implemented by: **S**ystemFlavorMap
flip( ): **C**omponent.FlipBufferStrategy^ *ComponentPeer*⌐
flipEastAndWestAtEnds( ): **C**ompositeView⌐
FLOAT: **C**SS.Attribute
Float^: java.lang
　—fields: **T**extAttribute^ < JUSTIFICATION_FULL,
　　JUSTIFICATION_NONE, POSTURE_OBLIQUE, POSTURE_REGULAR,
　　WEIGHT_BOLD, WEIGHT_DEMIBOLD, WEIGHT_DEMILIGHT,
　　WEIGHT_EXTRA_LIGHT, WEIGHT_EXTRABOLD,
　　WEIGHT_HEAVY, WEIGHT_LIGHT, WEIGHT_MEDIUM,
　　WEIGHT_REGULAR, WEIGHT_SEMIBOLD, WEIGHT_ULTRABOLD,
　　WIDTH_CONDENSED, WIDTH_EXTENDED, WIDTH_REGULAR,
　　WIDTH_SEMI_CONDENSED, WIDTH_SEMI_EXTENDED >
FloatControl^: javax.sound.sampled
FloatControl.Type^: javax.sound.sampled
　—passed to: **F**loatControl( )
　—fields: **F**loatControl.Type^ < AUX_RETURN, AUX_SEND,
　　BALANCE, MASTER_GAIN, PAN, REVERB_RETURN,
　　REVERB_SEND, SAMPLE_RATE, VOLUME >
FlowLayout: java.awt
FlowView^: javax.swing.text
　—subclasses: javax.swing.text.**P**aragraphView^
　—descendents: javax.swing.text.html.**P**aragraphView^
　—passed to: **F**lowView.FlowStrategy < adjustRow( ),
　　changedUpdate( ), createView( ), getLogicalView( ),
　　insertUpdate( ), layout( ), layoutRow( ), removeUpdate( ) >
FlowView.FlowStrategy: javax.swing.text
　—fields: **F**lowView^.strategy
flush( ): *DataLine*^ **H**TMLEditorKit.ParserCallback **I**mage⌐
　　ImageInputStream⌐ **I**mageInputStreamImpl⌐
flushAttributes( ): javax.swing.text.html.parser.**P**arser⌐
flushBefore( ): *ImageInputStream*⌐ **I**mageInputStreamImpl⌐
flushBits( ): **I**mageOutputStreamImpl⌐
flushedPos: **I**mageInputStreamImpl⌐
flushRequirementChanges( ): **A**syncBoxView^
FOCUS_ACCELERATOR_KEY: **J**TextComponent⌐

FOCUS_EVENT_MASK: **A**WTEvent⌐
FOCUS_FIRST: **F**ocusEvent^
FOCUS_GAINED: **F**ocusEvent^
FOCUS_LAST: **F**ocusEvent^
FOCUS_LOST: **F**ocusEvent^
FOCUS_MANAGER_CLASS_PROPERTY: **F**ocusManager⌐
FOCUS_PAINTED_CHANGED_PROPERTY: **A**bstractButton⌐
FOCUSABLE: **A**ccessibleState^
FocusAdapter: java.awt.event
FOCUSED: **A**ccessibleState^
FocusEvent^: java.awt.event
　—passed to: **A**WTEventMulticaster < focusGained( ), focusLost( ) >
　　Component⌐.processFocusEvent( ) **C**omponent⌐
　　.AccessibleAWTComponent.AccessibleAWTFocusHandler
　　< focusGained( ), focusLost( ) > **D**efaultCaret^ < focusGained( ),
　　focusLost( ) > **F**ocusAdapter < focusGained( ),
　　focusLost( ) > *FocusListener*^ < focusGained( ),
　　focusLost( ) > **J**Component.AccessibleJComponent⌐
　　.AccessibleFocusHandler < focusGained( ), focusLost( ) >
　　JFormattedTextField^.processFocusEvent( )
　　JPopupMenu^.processFocusEvent( )
focusGained( ): **A**WTEventMulticaster **C**omponent⌐
　　.AccessibleAWTComponent.AccessibleAWTFocusHandler
　　DefaultCaret^ *FocusListener*^ **J**Component⌐
　　.AccessibleJComponent.AccessibleFocusHandler
FocusListener^: java.awt.event
　—passed to: *AccessibleComponent*⌐ < addFocusListener( ),
　　removeFocusListener( ) > **A**WTEventMulticaster
　　< add( ), remove( ) > **C**omponent⌐
　　< addFocusListener( ), removeFocusListener( ) >
　　Component.AccessibleAWTComponent⌐
　　< addFocusListener( ), removeFocusListener( ) >
　　JList.AccessibleJList.AccessibleJListChild^
　　< addFocusListener( ), removeFocusListener( ) >
　　JTable.AccessibleJTable.AccessibleJTableCell^ **J**TableHeader⌐
　　.AccessibleJTableHeader.AccessibleJTableHeaderEntry^
　　< addFocusListener( ), removeFocusListener( ) >
　　JTree.AccessibleJTree.AccessibleJTreeNode^
　　< addFocusListener( ), removeFocusListener( ) >
　　MenuComponent.AccessibleAWTMenuComponent⌐
　　< addFocusListener( ), removeFocusListener( ) >
　—returned by: **A**WTEventMulticaster < add( ), remove( ) >
　　Component⌐.getFocusListeners( )
　—implemented by: **A**WTEventMulticaster **C**omponent⌐
　　.AccessibleAWTComponent.AccessibleAWTFocusHandler
　　DefaultCaret^ **F**ocusAdapter **J**Component⌐
　　.AccessibleJComponent.AccessibleFocusHandler
　—fields: **C**omponent.AccessibleAWTComponent⌐⌐
　　.accessibleAWTFocusHandler
　　JComponent.AccessibleJComponent⌐.accessibleFocusHandler
focusLost( ): **A**WTEventMulticaster **C**omponent⌐
　　.AccessibleAWTComponent.AccessibleAWTFocusHandler
　　DefaultCaret^ **F**ocusAdapter *FocusListener*^ **J**Component⌐
　　.AccessibleJComponent.AccessibleFocusHandler
FocusManager^: javax.swing
　—subclasses: **D**efaultFocusManager^
　—passed to: **F**ocusManager^.setCurrentManager( )
　—returned by: **F**ocusManager^.getCurrentManager( )
focusNextComponent( ): **K**eyboardFocusManager⌐
focusPreviousComponent( ): **K**eyboardFocusManager⌐
FocusTraversalPolicy⌐: java.awt
　—subclasses: **C**ontainerOrderFocusTraversalPolicy^
　　InternalFrameFocusTraversalPolicy^
　—descendents: **D**efaultFocusTraversalPolicy^
　　LayoutFocusTraversalPolicy^ **S**ortingFocusTraversalPolicy^
　—passed to: **C**ontainer^.setFocusTraversalPolicy( )
　　KeyboardFocusManager⌐.setDefaultFocusTraversalPolicy( )
　—returned by: **C**ontainer^.getFocusTraversalPolicy( )
　　KeyboardFocusManager⌐.getDefaultFocusTraversalPolicy( )
FOLIO: **M**ediaSize.Other **M**ediaSizeName^
　　PageAttributes.MediaType^

G

HashAttributeSet, InputMap, RenderingHints, Track
UIDefaults^ UIManager
getAccelerator( ): JMenuItem^
getAcceptAllFileFilter( ): FileChooserUI^ JFileChooser^
getAccessibleAction( ): AccessibleContext,
getAccessibleActionAnchor( ): AccessibleHyperlink,
getAccessibleActionCount( ):
AbstractButton.AccessibleAbstractButton^ *AccessibleAction*
AccessibleHyperlink, Button.AccessibleAWTButton^
Checkbox.AccessibleAWTCheckbox^
Choice.AccessibleAWTChoice^
JComboBox.AccessibleJComboBox^
JTextComponent.AccessibleJTextComponent^
JTree.AccessibleJTree.AccessibleJTreeNode^
MenuItem.AccessibleAWTMenuItem^
getAccessibleActionDescription( ):
AbstractButton.AccessibleAbstractButton^ *AccessibleAction*
AccessibleHyperlink, Button.AccessibleAWTButton^
Checkbox.AccessibleAWTCheckbox^
Choice.AccessibleAWTChoice^
JComboBox.AccessibleJComboBox^
JTextComponent.AccessibleJTextComponent^
JTree.AccessibleJTree.AccessibleJTreeNode^
MenuItem.AccessibleAWTMenuItem^
getAccessibleActionObject( ): AccessibleHyperlink,
getAccessibleAt( ): *AccessibleComponent*, *AccessibleTable*,
Component.AccessibleAWTComponent^
JList.AccessibleJList.AccessibleJListChild^
JTable.AccessibleJTable.AccessibleJTableCell^
JTableHeader.AccessibleJTableHeader ⊋
.AccessibleJTableHeaderEntry^
JTree.AccessibleJTree.AccessibleJTreeNode^
MenuComponent.AccessibleAWTMenuComponent^
SwingUtilities
getAccessibleCaption( ): *AccessibleTable*,
JTable.AccessibleJTable^
getAccessibleChild( ): AccessibleContext, ComponentUI,
SwingUtilities
getAccessibleChildrenCount( ): AccessibleContext,
ComponentUI, SwingUtilities
getAccessibleColumn( ): *AccessibleExtendedTable*^
JTable.AccessibleJTable^
getAccessibleColumnAtIndex( ): JTable.AccessibleJTable^
getAccessibleColumnCount( ): *AccessibleTable*,
JTable.AccessibleJTable^
getAccessibleColumnDescription( ): *AccessibleTable*,
JTable.AccessibleJTable^
getAccessibleColumnExtentAt( ): *AccessibleTable*,
JTable.AccessibleJTable^
getAccessibleColumnHeader( ): *AccessibleTable*,
JTable.AccessibleJTable^
getAccessibleComponent( ): AccessibleContext,
getAccessibleContext( ): *Accessible*
Component, HTMLEditorKit^ ImageIcon
JList.AccessibleJList.AccessibleJListChild^
JTable.AccessibleJTable.AccessibleJTableCell^
JTableHeader.AccessibleJTableHeader ⊋
.AccessibleJTableHeaderEntry^
JTree.AccessibleJTree.AccessibleJTreeNode^
List.AccessibleAWTList.AccessibleAWTListChild^
MenuComponent,
getAccessibleDescription( ): AccessibleContext,
getAccessibleEditableText( ): AccessibleContext,
getAccessibleIcon( ): AccessibleContext,
getAccessibleIconDescription( ): *AccessibleIcon*,
ImageIcon.AccessibleImageIcon^
getAccessibleIconHeight( ): *AccessibleIcon*,
ImageIcon.AccessibleImageIcon^
getAccessibleIconWidth( ): *AccessibleIcon*,
ImageIcon.AccessibleImageIcon^
getAccessibleIndex( ): *AccessibleExtendedTable*^
JTable.AccessibleJTable^

getAccessibleIndexAt( ): JTable.AccessibleJTable^
getAccessibleIndexInParent( ): AccessibleContext,
SwingUtilities
getAccessibleKeyBinding( ):
AccessibleExtendedComponent^ *AccessibleKeyBinding*
JComponent.AccessibleJComponent^
getAccessibleKeyBindingCount( ): *AccessibleKeyBinding*
getAccessibleName( ): AccessibleContext,
getAccessibleParent( ): AccessibleContext,
getAccessibleRelationSet( ): AccessibleContext,
getAccessibleRole( ): AccessibleContext,
getAccessibleRow( ): *AccessibleExtendedTable*^
JTable.AccessibleJTable^
getAccessibleRowAtIndex( ): JTable.AccessibleJTable^
getAccessibleRowCount( ): *AccessibleTable*,
JTable.AccessibleJTable^
getAccessibleRowDescription( ): *AccessibleTable*,
JTable.AccessibleJTable^
getAccessibleRowExtentAt( ): *AccessibleTable*,
JTable.AccessibleJTable^
getAccessibleRowHeader( ): *AccessibleTable*,
JTable.AccessibleJTable^
getAccessibleSelection( ): AccessibleContext,
AccessibleSelection
getAccessibleSelectionCount( ): *AccessibleSelection*
JComboBox.AccessibleJComboBox^ JList.AccessibleJList^
JMenu.AccessibleJMenu^ JMenuBar.AccessibleJMenuBar^
JTabbedPane.AccessibleJTabbedPane^
JTable.AccessibleJTable^ JTree.AccessibleJTree^
JTree.AccessibleJTree.AccessibleJTreeNode^
List.AccessibleAWTList^
MenuComponent.AccessibleAWTMenuComponent^
getAccessibleStateSet( ): AccessibleContext, SwingUtilities
getAccessibleSummary( ): *AccessibleTable*,
JTable.AccessibleJTable^
getAccessibleTable( ): AccessibleContext,
getAccessibleText( ): AccessibleContext,
getAccessibleValue( ): AccessibleContext,
getAccessory( ): JFileChooser^
getACHuffmanTables( ): JPEGImageReadParam^
JPEGImageWriteParam^
getAction( ): AbstractButton^ JComboBox^ JTextField^
Keymap
getActionCommand( ): AbstractButton^ ActionEvent^ Button^
ButtonModel^ DefaultButtonModel^ JComboBox^
MenuItem^
getActionForKeyStroke( ): JComponent^
getActionListeners( ): AbstractButton^ Button^
DefaultButtonModel^ JComboBox^ JFileChooser^
JTextField^ java.awt.List^ MenuItem^ TextField^ Timer
getActionMap( ): JComponent^
getActions( ): EditorKit,
JFormattedTextField.AbstractFormatter, JTextComponent^
getActiveWindow( ): KeyboardFocusManager,
getAdjustable( ): AdjustmentEvent^
getAdjustmentListeners( ): JScrollBar^ Scrollbar^
ScrollPaneAdjustable
getAdjustmentType( ): AdjustmentEvent^
getAdvance( ): GlyphMetrics, GraphicAttribute, TextLayout
getAdvanceBetween( ): TextMeasurer
getAdvanceX( ): GlyphMetrics
getAdvanceY( ): GlyphMetrics
getAfterIndex( ): AbstractButton.AccessibleAbstractButton^
AccessibleText, JLabel.AccessibleJLabel^
JTextComponent.AccessibleJTextComponent^
TextComponent.AccessibleAWTTextComponent^
getAlignedSizeRequirements( ): SizeRequirements
getAlignment( ): FlowLayout, GraphicAttribute, Label^
StyleConstants, TabStop, View,
getAlignmentX( ): Component,
getAlignmentY( ): Component,
getAllAttributeKeys( ): CSS, HTML

getBestCursorSize( ): Toolkit
getBevelType( ): BevelBorder^
getBidiLevel( ): StyleConstants‿
getBidiRootElement( ): AbstractDocument‿
getBitDepth( ): DisplayMode
getBitMasks( ): SinglePixelPackedSampleModel^
getBitOffset( ): ImageInputStream⌒ ImageInputStreamImpl‿
    MultiPixelPackedSampleModel^
getBitOffsets( ): SinglePixelPackedSampleModel^
getBitRate( ): ImageWriteParam⌒
getBitsPerBand( ): ImageTypeSpecifier
getBlackBoxBounds( ): TextLayout
getBlackLineBorderUIResource( ): BorderUIResource
getBlinkRate( ): Caret DefaultCaret^
getBlockIncrement( ): Adjustable⌒ JScrollBar⌒ Scrollbar^
    ScrollPaneAdjustable
getBlue( ): Color‿ ColorModel‿
getBlueMask( ): DirectColorModel^
getBlues( ): IndexColorModel^
getBoolean( ): UIDefaults^ UIManager
getBorder( ): JComponent⌒ TitledBorder⌒ UIDefaults^
    UIManager
getBorderInsets( ): AbstractBorder‿ Border
    BorderUIResource
getBorderSelectionColor( ): DefaultTreeCellEditor
    DefaultTreeCellRenderer
getBorderTitle( ): JComponent.AccessibleJComponent⌒
getBottomComponent( ): JSplitPane^
getBottomInset( ): AsyncBoxView⌒ CompositeView⌒
getBoundActions( ): Keymap
getBoundedPosition( ): GlyphView.GlyphPainter
getBoundingBox( ): Polygon
getBoundKeyStrokes( ): Keymap
getBounds( ): AbstractLayoutCache‿
    AccessibleComponent‿ Area Component‿
    Component.AccessibleAWTComponent⌒ CubicCurve2D‿
    GeneralPath GraphicAttribute GraphicsConfiguration
    JList.AccessibleJList.AccessibleJListChild^
    JTable.AccessibleJTable.AccessibleJTableCell^
    JTableHeader.AccessibleJTableHeader⌐
    .AccessibleJTableHeaderEntry^
    JTree.AccessibleJTree.AccessibleJTreeNode^ Line2D‿
    MenuComponent.AccessibleAWTMenuComponent⌒ Polygon
    QuadCurve2D‿ Raster‿ RectangularShape‿ Shape
    TextLayout
getBounds2D( ): AffineTransformOp‿ Area
    BandCombineOp BufferedImageOp ColorConvertOp
    ContextualRenderedImageFactory^ ConvolveOp
    GeneralPath GlyphMetrics LookupOp Polygon RasterOp
    RescaleOp‿ Shape‿
getBoundsAt( ): JTabbedPane^
getBoundsForIconOf( ): DefaultDesktopManager
getBoxPainter( ): StyleSheet^
getBreakLocation( ): Utilities
getBreakWeight( ): View‿
getBufferCapabilities( ): GraphicsConfiguration
getBufferedImageOp( ): BufferedImageFilter^
getBufferedImageType( ): ImageTypeSpecifier
getBufferSize( ): DataLine⌒
getBufferStrategy( ): Canvas^ Window⌒
getButton( ): MouseEvent
getButtonCount( ): ButtonGroup
getByteLength( ): AudioFileFormat MidiFileFormat
getByteOrder( ): ImageInputStream⌒ ImageInputStreamImpl‿
getByteParameter( ): ParameterBlock
getCacheDirectory( ): ImageIO
getCalendarField( ): SpinnerDateModel^
getCanWrapLines( ): AbstractWriter‿
getCapabilities( ): BufferStrategy‿ VolatileImage^
getCaret( ): InputMethodEvent⌒ JTextComponent⌒
    NavigationFilter.FilterBypass
getCaretColor( ): JTextComponent⌒

getCaretInfo( ): TextLayout
getCaretListeners( ): JTextComponent⌒
getCaretPosition( ): AbstractButton.AccessibleAbstractButton⌒
    AccessibleText‿ JLabel.AccessibleJLabel^
    JTextComponent⌒
    JTextComponent.AccessibleJTextComponent⌒
    TextComponent⌒
    TextComponent.AccessibleAWTTextComponent⌒
    TextComponentPeer⌒
getCaretShape( ): TextLayout
getCaretShapes( ): TextLayout
getCategories( ): ServiceRegistry‿
getCategory( ): Attribute⌒ Chromaticity^ ColorSupported^
    Compression^ Copies^ CopiesSupported^
    DateTimeAtCompleted^ DateTimeAtCreation^
    DateTimeAtProcessing^ Destination^
    DocumentName^ Fidelity^ Finishings^ JobHoldUntil^
    JobImpressions^ JobImpressionsCompleted^
    JobImpressionsSupported^ JobKOctets^
    JobKOctetsProcessed^ JobKOctetsSupported^
    JobMediaSheets^ JobMediaSheetsCompleted^
    JobMediaSheetsSupported^ JobMessageFromOperator^
    JobName^ JobOriginatingUserName^ JobPriority^
    JobPrioritySupported^ JobSheets^ JobState^
    JobStateReason^ JobStateReasons^
    Media⌒ MediaPrintableArea MediaSize^
    MultipleDocumentHandling^ NumberOfDocuments^
    NumberOfInterveningJobs^ NumberUp^
    NumberUpSupported^ OrientationRequested^
    OutputDeviceAssigned^ PageRanges^ PagesPerMinute^
    PagesPerMinuteColor^ PDLOverrideSupported^
    PresentationDirection^ PrinterInfo^ PrinterIsAcceptingJobs^
    PrinterLocation^ PrinterMakeAndModel^
    PrinterMessageFromOperator^ PrinterMoreInfo^
    PrinterMoreInfoManufacturer^ PrinterName^
    PrinterResolution^ PrinterState^ PrinterStateReason^
    PrinterStateReasons^ PrinterURI^ PrintQuality^
    QueuedJobCount^ ReferenceUriSchemesSupported^
    RequestingUserName^ Severity^ SheetCollate^ Sides^
getCellBounds( ): JList^ ListUI^
getCellEditor( ): JTable JTree TableColumn
getCellEditorListeners( ): AbstractCellEditor‿
    DefaultTreeCellEditor
getCellEditorValue( ): CellEditor‿
    DefaultCellEditor.EditorDelegate DefaultTreeCellEditor
getCellRect( ): JTable^
getCellRenderer( ): JList^ JTable^ JTree^ TableColumn
getCellSelectionEnabled( ): JTable^
getCenterPoint( ): GraphicsEnvironment
getCenterX( ): RectangularShape‿
getCenterY( ): RectangularShape‿
getChange( ): AbstractDocument.DefaultDocumentEvent^
    DocumentEvent
getChanged( ): HierarchyEvent^
getChangedParent( ): HierarchyEvent^
getChangeFlags( ): HierarchyEvent^
getChangeListeners( ): AbstractButton⌒
    AbstractSpinnerModel DefaultBoundedRangeModel
    DefaultButtonModel‿ DefaultCaret‿
    DefaultColorSelectionModel DefaultSingleSelectionModel
    JProgressBar^ JSlider^ JSpinner^ JTabbedPane^
    JViewport^ MenuSelectionManager StyleContext‿
    StyleContext.NamedStyle
getChannel( ): ShortMessage^
getChannelPressure( ): MidiChannel
getChannels( ): AudioFormat Synthesizer^
getCharacterAttribute( ):
    AbstractButton.AccessibleAbstractButton⌒
    AccessibleText‿ JLabel.AccessibleJLabel^
    JTextComponent.AccessibleJTextComponent⌒
    TextComponent.AccessibleAWTTextComponent⌒
getCharacterAttributeRun( ): StyledEditorKit⌒

G

getCharacterAttributes(): JTextPane^
getCharacterBounds():
   AbstractButton.AccessibleAbstractButton°
   AccessibleText JLabel.AccessibleJLabel^
   JTextComponent.AccessibleJTextComponent°
   TextComponent.AccessibleAWTTextComponent°
   TextComponentPeer°
getCharacterCount(): TextLayout
getCharacterElement(): DefaultStyledDocument°
   StyledDocument^
getCharacterLevel(): TextLayout
getCharCount(): AbstractButton.AccessibleAbstractButton°
   AccessibleText JLabel.AccessibleJLabel^
   JTextComponent.AccessibleJTextComponent°
   TextComponent.AccessibleAWTTextComponent°
getCharIndex(): TextHitInfo
getCharParameter(): ParameterBlock
getChars(): *AbstractDocument.Content* GapContent^
   StringContent
getCharSetSpec(): ChangedCharSetException^
getCheckboxGroup(): Checkbox^
getChild(): ContainerEvent^ DefaultTreeModel FileSystemView
   TreeModel
getChildAfter(): DefaultMutableTreeNode
getChildAllocation(): AsyncBoxView.ChildLocator View
getChildAt(): AbstractDocument.AbstractElement
   DefaultMutableTreeNode *TreeNode*
getChildBefore(): DefaultMutableTreeNode
getChildCount(): AbstractDocument.AbstractElement
   DefaultMutableTreeNode DefaultTreeModel *TreeModel*
   TreeNode
getChildIndices(): TreeModelEvent^
getChildNames(): *IIOMetadataFormat* IIOMetadataFormatImpl
getChildNodes(): IIOMetadataNode
getChildPolicy(): *IIOMetadataFormat* IIOMetadataFormatImpl
getChildren(): TreeModelEvent^
getChildrenAdded(): AbstractDocument.ElementEdit^
   DocumentEvent.ElementChange
getChildrenRemoved(): AbstractDocument.ElementEdit^
   DocumentEvent.ElementChange
getChildState(): AsyncBoxView^
getChildView(): AsyncBoxView.ChildState
getChoosableFileFilters(): JFileChooser^
getChooserPanels(): JColorChooser^
getClassName(): UIManager.LookAndFeelInfo
getClickCount(): MouseEvent°
getClickCountToStart(): DefaultCellEditor^
getClientProperty(): JComponent°
getClip(): Graphics
getClipBounds(): Graphics
getClipRect(): Graphics
getClosedIcon(): DefaultTreeCellRenderer^
getClosestPathForLocation(): JTree TreeUI^
getClosestPositionTo(): javax.swing.text.ParagraphView°
getClosestRowForLocation(): JTree^
getCodeBase(): Applet° *AppletStub*
getColor(): Color DefaultHighlighter.DefaultHighlightPainter^
   Graphics JColorChooser^ PageAttributes UIDefaults^
   UIManager
getColor1(): GradientPaint
getColor2(): GradientPaint
getColorComponents(): Color
getColorFromModel(): AbstractColorChooserPanel^
getColorModel(): BufferedImage^ Component
   ComponentPeer GraphicsConfiguration
   ImageTypeSpecifier *PaintContext* PixelGrabber
   RenderedImage Toolkit
getColorSelectionModel(): AbstractColorChooserPanel^
getColorSpace(): Color ColorModel
getColorSpaceType(): ICC_Profile
getColumn(): DefaultTableColumnModel JTable^
   TableColumnModel TableModelEvent^

getColumnClass(): AbstractTableModel JTable^ *TableModel*
getColumnCount(): DefaultTableColumnModel JTable^
   TableColumnModel *TableModel* TableView.TableCell^
getColumnHeader(): JScrollPane^ ScrollPaneLayout
getColumnIndex(): DefaultTableColumnModel
   TableColumnModel
getColumnIndexAtX(): DefaultTableColumnModel
   TableColumnModel
getColumnMargin(): DefaultTableColumnModel
   TableColumnModel
getColumnModel(): JTable JTableHeader^
getColumnModelListeners(): DefaultTableColumnModel
getColumnName(): AbstractTableModel JTable *TableModel*
getColumns(): DefaultTableColumnModel GridLayout
   JTextArea JTextField *TableColumnModel* TextArea^
   TextField^
getColumnSelectionAllowed(): DefaultTableColumnModel
   JTable^ *TableColumnModel*
getColumnWidth(): JTextArea^ JTextField°
getCommand(): ShortMessage^
getCommitsOnValidEdit(): DefaultFormatter°
getCommittedCharacterCount(): InputMethodEvent^
getCommittedText(): *InputMethodRequests*
getCommittedTextLength(): *InputMethodRequests*
getComparator(): SortingFocusTraversalPolicy°
getComponent(): AncestorEvent^ ComponentEvent°
   ComponentInputMap° ComponentView° Container°
   DefaultCaret^ DefaultCellEditor^ DragGestureEvent^
   DragGestureRecognizer DragSourceContext DropTarget
   DropTargetContext HierarchyEvent^ *MenuElement*
   Renderer StyleConstants
getComponentAfter(): DefaultFocusManager^
   FocusTraversalPolicy
getComponentAt(): Component
getComponentAtIndex(): JMenuBar^ JPopupMenu^
   JToolBar^
getComponentBefore(): DefaultFocusManager^
   FocusTraversalPolicy
getComponentCount(): Container°
getComponentCountInLayer(): JLayeredPane°
getComponentGraphics(): JComponent°
getComponentIndex(): JMenuBar^ JPopupMenu^ JToolBar^
getComponentListeners(): Component
getComponentOrientation(): Component
getComponents(): Color ColorModel Container°
getComponentsInLayer(): JLayeredPane°
getComponentSize(): ColorModel
getComponentToLayer(): JLayeredPane°
getComposite(): Graphics2D^
getCompressionMode(): ImageWriteParam^
getCompressionQuality(): ImageWriteParam°
getCompressionQualityDescriptions(): ImageWriteParam°
getCompressionQualityValues(): ImageWriteParam°
getCompressionThreshold(): StyleContext
getCompressionType(): ImageWriteParam°
getCompressionTypes(): ImageWriteParam°
getConditionForKeyStroke(): JComponent°
getConfigurations(): GraphicsDevice
getConstraint(): SpringLayout SpringLayout.Constraints
getConstraints(): GridBagLayout SpringLayout
getContainer(): ContainerEvent^ View
getContainerListeners(): Container°
getContent(): AbstractDocument
   javax.swing.text.html.parser.Element
getContentPane(): JApplet^ JDialog^ JFrame^
   JInternalFrame^ JRootPane^ JWindow^
   RootPaneContainer
getContents(): AccessibleResourceBundle^ Clipboard
getContentType(): EditorKit JEditorPane°
getContextualShaper(): NumericShaper
getControl(): Line
getControlButtonsAreShown(): JFileChooser^

G

G

getFields(): InternationalFormatter⌒
getFile(): FileDialog⌒
getFileFilter(): JFileChooser⌒
getFileName(): JobAttributes
getFilenameFilter(): FileDialog⌒
getFiles(): FileSystemView
getFileSelectionMode(): JFileChooser⌒
getFileSuffixes(): ImageReaderWriterSpi⌒
getFileSystemView(): FileSystemView JFileChooser⌒
getFileView(): FileChooserUI⌒ JFileChooser⌒
getFilterInstance(): ImageFilter
getFirstChild(): DefaultMutableTreeNode IIOMetadataNode
getFirstColumn(): *AccessibleTableModelChange*
  JTable.AccessibleJTable.AccessibleJTableModelChange
getFirstComponent(): DefaultFocusManager⌒
  FocusTraversalPolicy
getFirstIndex(): ListSelectionEvent⌒
getFirstLeaf(): DefaultMutableTreeNode
getFirstLineIndent(): StyleConstants
getFirstRow(): *AccessibleTableModelChange*
  JTable.AccessibleJTable.AccessibleJTableModelChange
  TableModelEvent⌒
getFirstVisibleIndex(): JList⌒
getFixedCellHeight(): JList⌒
getFixedCellWidth(): JList⌒
getFlatness(): CubicCurve2D FlatteningPathIterator
  QuadCurve2D
getFlatnessSq(): CubicCurve2D QuadCurve2D
getFlavorMap(): DragSource DropTarget
getFlavorsForNative(): *FlavorTable*⌒ SystemFlavorMap
getFlavorsForNatives(): *FlavorMap* SystemFlavorMap
getFlipContents(): BufferCapabilities
getFloatParameter(): ParameterBlock
getFlowAxis(): FlowView⌒
getFlowSpan(): FlowView⌒
getFlowStart(): FlowView⌒
getFlushedPosition(): *ImageInputStream*⌒
  ImageInputStreamImpl
getFocusableWindowState(): Window⌒
getFocusAccelerator(): JTextComponent⌒
getFocusCycleRootAncestor(): Component
getFocusedComponent(): TextAction
getFocusedWindow(): KeyboardFocusManager
getFocusListeners(): Component
getFocusLostBehavior(): JFormattedTextField⌒
getFocusOwner(): JInternalFrame⌒ KeyboardFocusManager
  Window⌒
getFocusTraversalKeys(): Component
getFocusTraversalKeysEnabled(): Component
getFocusTraversalPolicy(): Container⌒
getFont(): *AccessibleComponent* Component
  Component.AccessibleAWTComponent⌒
  DefaultStyledDocument⌒ DefaultTreeCellEditor
  Font FontMetrics GlyphVector GlyphView⌒
  Graphics JList.AccessibleJList.AccessibleJListChild⌒
  JTable.AccessibleJTable.AccessibleJTableCell⌒
  JTableHeader.AccessibleJTableHeader ₂
  .AccessibleJTableHeaderEntry⌒
  JTree.AccessibleJTree.AccessibleJTreeNode⌒
  MenuComponent
  MenuComponent.AccessibleAWTMenuComponent⌒
  MenuContainer StyleContext StyledDocument⌒
  TitledBorder⌒ UIDefaults⌒ UIManager
getFontFamily(): StyleConstants
getFontList(): Toolkit
getFontMetrics(): *AccessibleComponent* Component
  Component.AccessibleAWTComponent⌒
  ComponentPeer FieldView⌒ Graphics
  JList.AccessibleJList.AccessibleJListChild⌒
  JTable.AccessibleJTable.AccessibleJTableCell⌒
  JTableHeader.AccessibleJTableHeader ₂
  .AccessibleJTableHeaderEntry⌒

  JTree.AccessibleJTree.AccessibleJTreeNode⌒ LabelView⌒
  MenuComponent.AccessibleAWTMenuComponent⌒
  StyleContext Toolkit
getFontName(): Font
getFontPeer(): Toolkit
getFontRenderContext(): GlyphVector Graphics2D⌒
getFontSize(): StyleConstants
getFontTable(): *OpenType*
getFontTableSize(): *OpenType*
getForeground(): *AccessibleComponent* Component
  Component.AccessibleAWTComponent⌒
  DefaultStyledDocument⌒ GlyphView⌒
  JList.AccessibleJList.AccessibleJListChild⌒
  JTable.AccessibleJTable.AccessibleJTableCell⌒
  JTableHeader.AccessibleJTableHeader ₂
  .AccessibleJTableHeaderEntry⌒
  JTree.AccessibleJTree.AccessibleJTreeNode⌒
  MenuComponent.AccessibleAWTMenuComponent⌒
  StyleConstants StyleContext *StyledDocument*⌒
getForegroundAt(): JTabbedPane
getFormat(): AudioFileFormat AudioInputStream⌒ *DataLine*⌒
  InternationalFormatter⌒ JSpinner.DateEditor⌒
  JSpinner.NumberEditor⌒
getFormatName(): ImageReader
getFormatNames(): ImageReaderWriterSpi⌒
getFormats(): DataLine.Info⌒
getFormattedTextField():
  JFormattedTextField.AbstractFormatter
getFormatter(): JFormattedTextField⌒
  JFormattedTextField.AbstractFormatterFactory
getFormatterFactory(): JFormattedTextField⌒
getFrame(): RectangularShape
getFrameForComponent(): JOptionPane⌒
getFrameIcon(): JInternalFrame⌒
getFrameLength(): AudioFileFormat AudioInputStream⌒ *Clip*⌒
getFramePosition(): *DataLine*⌒ LineEvent⌒
getFrameRate(): AudioFormat
getFrames(): Frame⌒
getFrameSize(): AudioFormat
getFromIndex(): TableColumnModelEvent⌒
getFromPage(): JobAttributes
getFrontBufferCapabilities(): BufferCapabilities
getFullScreenWindow(): GraphicsDevice
getGamma(): ICC_ProfileGray⌒ ICC_ProfileRGB⌒
getGapEnd(): GapVector
getGapStart(): GapVector
getGestureModifiers(): DragSourceDragEvent⌒
getGestureModifiersEx(): DragSourceDragEvent⌒
getGlassPane(): JApplet⌒ JDialog⌒ JFrame⌒ JInternalFrame⌒
  JRootPane⌒ JWindow⌒ *RootPaneContainer*
getGlobalActiveWindow(): KeyboardFocusManager
getGlobalCurrentFocusCycleRoot():
  KeyboardFocusManager
getGlobalFocusedWindow(): KeyboardFocusManager
getGlobalFocusOwner(): KeyboardFocusManager
getGlobalPermanentFocusOwner(): KeyboardFocusManager
getGlyphCharIndex(): GlyphVector
getGlyphCharIndices(): GlyphVector
getGlyphCode(): GlyphVector
getGlyphCodes(): GlyphVector
getGlyphJustificationInfo(): GlyphVector
getGlyphLogicalBounds(): GlyphVector
getGlyphMetrics(): GlyphVector
getGlyphOutline(): GlyphVector
getGlyphPainter(): GlyphView⌒
getGlyphPixelBounds(): GlyphVector
getGlyphPosition(): GlyphVector
getGlyphPositions(): GlyphVector
getGlyphTransform(): GlyphVector
getGlyphVisualBounds(): GlyphVector
getGraphics(): Component *ComponentPeer* Image
  PrintJob View

G

G

getIOException( ): PrinterIOException^
getItalicAngle( ): Font
getItem( ): Choice^ *ComboBoxEditor* ItemEvent^ JMenu^
  java.awt.List^ Menu˯
getItemAt( ): JComboBox^
getItemCount( ): Choice^ JComboBox^ JMenu^ java.awt.List^
  Menu˯
getItemListeners( ): AbstractButton˯ Checkbox^
  CheckboxMenuItem^ Choice^ DefaultButtonModel˯
  JComboBox^ java.awt.List^
getItems( ): java.awt.List^
getItemSelectable( ): ItemEvent^
getIterator( ): HTMLDocument^
getJMenuBar( ): JApplet^ JDialog^ JFrame^ JInternalFrame^
  JRootPane^
getJobName( ): PrinterJob
getJustificationInfo( ): GraphicAttribute˯
getJustifiedLayout( ): TextLayout
getKernel( ): ConvolveOp
getKernelData( ): Kernel
getKey( ): AccessibleRelation^ MenuShortcut
getKeyChar( ): AWTKeyStroke KeyEvent˯
getKeyCode( ): AWTKeyStroke KeyEvent˯
getKeyEventDispatchers( ): KeyboardFocusManager˯
getKeyEventPostProcessors( ): KeyboardFocusManager˯
getKeyEventType( ): AWTKeyStroke˯
getKeyListeners( ): Component˯
getKeyLocation( ): KeyEvent˯
getKeymap( ): JTextComponent˯
getKeyModifiersText( ): KeyEvent˯
getKeys( ): AbstractAction
getKeySelectionManager( ): JComboBox^
getKeyStroke( ): KeyStroke
getKeyStrokeForEvent( ): KeyStroke^
getKeyStrokesForAction( ): *Keymap*
getKeyText( ): KeyEvent˯
getLabel( ): AbstractButton˯ Button^ Checkbox^
  JPopupMenu^ MenuItem˯ Option
getLabelFor( ): JLabel^
getLabelTable( ): JSlider^
getLargeDisplayIcon( ): AbstractColorChooserPanel^
getLastColumn( ): *AccessibleTableModelChange*
  JTable.AccessibleJTable.AccessibleJTableModelChange
getLastComponent( ): DefaultFocusManager^
  FocusTraversalPolicy
getLastDividerLocation( ): JSplitPane^
getLastIndex( ): ListSelectionEvent^
getLastLeaf( ): DefaultMutableTreeNode˯
getLastPathComponent( ): TreePath
getLastRow( ): *AccessibleTableModelChange*
  JTable.AccessibleJTable.AccessibleJTableModelChange
  TableModelEvent^
getLastSelectedPathComponent( ): JTree^
getLastVisibleIndex( ): JList^
getLatency( ): *Synthesizer*^
getLateReflectionDelay( ): ReverbType
getLateReflectionIntensity( ): ReverbType
getLayer( ): JInternalFrame^ JLayeredPane^
getLayeredPane( ): JApplet^ JDialog^ JFrame^
  JInternalFrame^ JRootPane^ JWindow^
  RootPaneContainer
getLayeredPaneAbove( ): JLayeredPane˯
getLayout( ): Container˯ TextMeasurer
getLayoutAlignmentX( ): BorderLayout BoxLayout
  CardLayout GridBagLayout JRootPane.RootLayout
  LayoutManager2^ OverlayLayout SpringLayout
getLayoutAlignmentY( ): BorderLayout BoxLayout
  CardLayout GridBagLayout JRootPane.RootLayout
  LayoutManager2^ OverlayLayout SpringLayout
getLayoutDimensions( ): GridBagLayout
getLayoutFlags( ): GlyphVector

getLayoutInfo( ): GridBagLayout
GetLayoutInfo( ): GridBagLayout
getLayoutOrientation( ): JList^
getLayoutOrigin( ): GridBagLayout
getLayoutQueue( ): AsyncBoxView^
getLayoutView( ): javax.swing.text.ParagraphView˯
getLayoutViewCount( ): javax.swing.text.ParagraphView˯
getLayoutWeights( ): GridBagLayout
getLeader( ): TabStop
getLeading( ): FontMetrics LineMetrics TextLayout
getLeadSelectionIndex( ): DefaultListSelectionModel JList^
  ListSelectionModel
getLeadSelectionPath( ): DefaultTreeSelectionModel˯ JTree^
  TreeSelectionModel
getLeadSelectionRow( ): DefaultTreeSelectionModel˯ JTree^
  TreeSelectionModel
getLeafCount( ): DefaultMutableTreeNode˯
getLeafIcon( ): DefaultTreeCellRenderer^
getLeftComponent( ): JSplitPane^
getLeftIndent( ): StyleConstants˯
getLeftInset( ): AsyncBoxView^ CompositeView˯
getLength( ): AbstractDocument˯
  AbstractDocument.DefaultDocumentEvent^
  DefaultStyledDocument.ElementSpec
  javax.swing.text.Document˯ *DocumentEvent* IIOByteBuffer
  IIOMetadataNode MidiMessage˯
getLengths( ): JPEGHuffmanTable
getLevel( ): *DataLine*^ DefaultMutableTreeNode˯
getLimit( ): UndoManager^
getLine( ): AudioSystem LineEvent^ *Mixer*^
getLineBreakIndex( ): TextMeasurer
getLineBuffer( ): PlainView˯ WrappedPlainView^
getLineClass( ): Line.Info˯
getLineColor( ): LineBorder˯
getLineCount( ): JTextArea^
getLineEndOffset( ): JTextArea^
getLineIncrement( ): Scrollbar^
getLineInfo( ): *Line*
getLineJoin( ): BasicStroke
getLineLength( ): AbstractWriter˯
getLineMetrics( ): Font˯ FontMetrics
getLineOfOffset( ): JTextArea^
getLineSeparator( ): AbstractWriter˯
getLineSpacing( ): StyleConstants˯
getLineStartOffset( ): JTextArea^
getLineWidth( ): BasicStroke
getLineWrap( ): JTextArea^
getLink( ): *AccessibleHypertext*^
  JEditorPane.JEditorPaneAccessibleHypertextSupport^
getLinkCount( ): *AccessibleHypertext*^
  JEditorPane.JEditorPaneAccessibleHypertextSupport^
getLinkCursor( ): HTMLEditorKit^
getLinkIndex( ): *AccessibleHypertext*^
  JEditorPane.JEditorPaneAccessibleHypertextSupport^
getLinkText( ):
  JEditorPane.JEditorPaneAccessibleHypertextSupport^
getList( ): SpinnerListModel^
getListCellRendererComponent( ): DefaultListCellRenderer˯
  ListCellRenderer
getListDataListeners( ): AbstractListModel˯
getListenerCount( ): EventListenerList
getListenerList( ): EventListenerList
getListeners( ): AbstractDocument˯ AbstractListModel˯
  AbstractSpinnerModel˯ AbstractTableModel˯
  AWTEventMulticaster Component˯
  DefaultBoundedRangeModel DefaultButtonModel˯
  DefaultCaret˯ DefaultListSelectionModel
  DefaultSingleSelectionModel DefaultTableColumnModel
  DefaultTreeModel˯ DefaultTreeSelectionModel˯ DragSource
  EventListenerList MenuItem˯ StyleContext.NamedStyle
  Timer
getListPainter( ): StyleSheet^

getListSelectionListeners( ): DefaultListSelectionModel JList^
getLoadedInstruments( ): *Synthesizer*^
getLoadingImageIcon( ): ImageView^
getLoadsSynchronously( ): ImageView^
getLocalBounds( ): SwingUtilities
getLocale( ): *AccessibleContext* Component ImageReader
   ImageWriteParam^ ImageWriter InputContext *InputMethod*
   TextSyntax
getLocalGraphicsEnvironment( ): GraphicsEnvironment
getLocalizedCompressionTypeName( ): ImageWriteParam^
getLocalName( ): IIOMetadataNode
getLocation( ): *AccessibleComponent* Component
   Component.AccessibleAWTComponent^ DragSourceEvent^
   DropTargetDragEvent^ DropTargetDropEvent^
   JList.AccessibleJList.AccessibleJListChild^
   JTable.AccessibleJTable.AccessibleJTableCell^
   JTableHeader.AccessibleJTableHeader⌐
   .AccessibleJTableHeaderEntry^
   JTree.AccessibleJTree.AccessibleJTreeNode^
   MenuComponent.AccessibleAWTMenuComponent^ Point^
   Rectangle^
getLocationInJTree( ):
   JTree.AccessibleJTree.AccessibleJTreeNode^
getLocationOffset( ): *InputMethodRequests*
getLocationOnScreen( ): *AccessibleComponent* Component
   Component.AccessibleAWTComponent^ *ComponentPeer*
   JList.AccessibleJList.AccessibleJListChild^
   JTable.AccessibleJTable.AccessibleJTableCell^
   JTableHeader.AccessibleJTableHeader⌐
   .AccessibleJTableHeaderEntry^
   JTree.AccessibleJTree.AccessibleJTreeNode^
   MenuComponent.AccessibleAWTMenuComponent^
getLockingKeyState( ): Toolkit
getLogicalBounds( ): GlyphVector
getLogicalHighlightShape( ): TextLayout
getLogicalRangesForVisualSelection( ): TextLayout
getLogicalStyle( ): DefaultStyledDocument^ JTextPane^
   StyledDocument^
getLogicalView( ): FlowView.FlowStrategy
getLogTimers( ): Timer
getLongParameter( ): ParameterBlock
getLookAndFeel( ): UIManager
getLookAndFeelDefaults( ): UIManager
getLoweredBevelBorderUIResource( ): BorderUIResource
getLSB( ): GlyphMetrics
getMagicCaretPosition( ): *Caret* DefaultCaret^
getMajorAxis( ): AsyncBoxView^
getMajorOffset( ): AsyncBoxView.ChildState
getMajorSpan( ): AsyncBoxView.ChildState
getMajorTickSpacing( ): JSlider^
getMajorVersion( ): ICC_Profile
getMapSize( ): IndexColorModel
getMargin( ): AbstractButton^ JMenuBar^ JPopupMenu^
   JTextComponent^ JToolBar^
getMark( ): *Caret* CaretEvent^ DefaultCaret^
getMask( ): MaskFormatter^ PackedColorModel^
getMasks( ): PackedColorModel^
getMasterSyncMode( ): *Sequencer*^
getMasterSyncModes( ): *Sequencer*^
getMatrix( ): AffineTransform BandCombineOp
   ICC_ProfileRGB^ PageFormat
getMatteColor( ): MatteBorder^
getMaxAdvance( ): FontMetrics
getMaxAscent( ): FontMetrics
getMaxBufferSize( ): DataLine.Info^
getMaxCharactersPerLineCount( ): JOptionPane^
getMaxCharBounds( ): Font FontMetrics
getMaxDecent( ): FontMetrics
getMaxDescent( ): FontMetrics
getMaximizedBounds( ): Frame^
getMaximum( ): *Adjustable* *BoundedRangeModel*
   DefaultBoundedRangeModel FloatControl^

InternationalFormatter^ JProgressBar^ JScrollBar^ JSlider^
   ProgressMonitor Scrollbar^ ScrollPaneAdjustable
   SpinnerNumberModel^
getMaximumAccessibleValue( ):
   AbstractButton.AccessibleAbstractButton^
   AccessibleValue Button.AccessibleAWTButton^
   Checkbox.AccessibleAWTCheckbox^
   JInternalFrame.AccessibleJInternalFrame^
   JInternalFrame.JDesktopIcon.AccessibleJDesktopIcon^
   JProgressBar.AccessibleJProgressBar^
   JScrollBar.AccessibleJScrollBar^ JSlider.AccessibleJSlider^
   JSplitPane.AccessibleJSplitPane^
   MenuItem.AccessibleAWTMenuItem^
   Scrollbar.AccessibleAWTScrollBar^
getMaximumCursorColors( ): Toolkit
getMaximumDividerLocation( ): JSplitPane^ SplitPaneUI^
getMaximumRowCount( ): JComboBox^
getMaximumSize( ): Component ComponentUI
getMaximumSpan( ): View
getMaximumValue( ): Spring
getMaximumWindowBounds( ): GraphicsEnvironment
getMaximumZoneSize( ): ZoneView^
getMaxLabel( ): FloatControl^
getMaxLines( ): *Mixer*^
getMaxPage( ): JobAttributes
getMaxPolyphony( ): *Synthesizer*^
getMaxReceivers( ): *MidiDevice*
getMaxSelectionIndex( ): DefaultListSelectionModel JList^
   ListSelectionModel
getMaxSelectionRow( ): DefaultTreeSelectionModel JTree^
   TreeSelectionModel
getMaxTransmitters( ): *MidiDevice*
getMaxValue( ): ColorSpace
getMaxWidth( ): TableColumn
getMaxX( ): RectangularShape
getMaxY( ): RectangularShape
getMaxZonesLoaded( ): ZoneView^
getMedia( ): PageAttributes
getMediaSizeForName( ): MediaSize^
getMediaSizeName( ): MediaSize^
getMediaSubtype( ): DocFlavor
getMediaType( ): DocFlavor
getMediaWhitePoint( ): ICC_ProfileGray^ ICC_ProfileRGB^
getMemberControls( ): CompoundControl
getMembers( ): SetOfIntegerSyntax
getMenu( ): JMenuBar^ MenuBar^
getMenuBar( ): Frame^ JInternalFrame^ JRootPane^
getMenuComponent( ): JMenu^
getMenuComponentCount( ): JMenu^
getMenuComponents( ): JMenu^
getMenuCount( ): JMenuBar^ MenuBar^
getMenuDragMouseListeners( ): JMenuItem^
getMenuKeyListeners( ): JMenuItem^
getMenuListeners( ): JMenu^
getMenuSelectionManager( ): MenuDragMouseEvent^
   MenuKeyEvent^
getMenuShortcutKeyMask( ): Toolkit
getMessage( ): JOptionPane^ MidiEvent MidiMessage
getMessageType( ): JOptionPane^
getMetadata( ): IIOImage
getMetadataFormat( ): IIOMetadata
getMetadataFormatNames( ): IIOMetadata
getMicrosecondLength( ): Clip^ MidiFileFormat Sequence
   Sequencer^
getMicrosecondPosition( ): DataLine^ *MidiDevice*
getMidiDevice( ): MidiSystem
getMidiDeviceInfo( ): MidiSystem
getMidiFileFormat( ): MidiFileReader MidiSystem
getMidiFileTypes( ): MidiFileWriter MidiSystem
getMidLabel( ): FloatControl^
getMillisToDecideToPopup( ): ProgressMonitor
getMillisToPopup( ): ProgressMonitor

G

getMimeType( ): DataFlavor DocFlavor
getMIMETypes( ): ImageReaderWriterSpi
getMinBufferSize( ): DataLine.Info
getMinimum( ): *Adjustable BoundedRangeModel*
  DefaultBoundedRangeModel FloatControl
  InternationalFormatter JProgressBar JScrollBar JSlider
  ProgressMonitor Scrollbar ScrollPaneAdjustable
  SpinnerNumberModel
getMinimumAccessibleValue( ):
  AbstractButton.AccessibleAbstractButton
  AccessibleValue Button.AccessibleAWTButton
  Checkbox.AccessibleAWTCheckbox
  JInternalFrame.AccessibleJInternalFrame
  JInternalFrame.JDesktopIcon.AccessibleJDesktopIcon
  JProgressBar.AccessibleJProgressBar
  JScrollBar.AccessibleJScrollBar JSlider.AccessibleJSlider
  JSplitPane.AccessibleJSplitPane
  MenuItem.AccessibleAWTMenuItem
  Scrollbar.AccessibleAWTScrollBar
getMinimumDividerLocation( ): JSplitPane SplitPaneUI
getMinimumSize( ): Component *ComponentPeer*
  ComponentUI TitledBorder
getMinimumSpan( ): View
getMinimumValue( ): Spring
getMinIndex( ): ImageReader
getMinLabel( ): FloatControl
getMinorAxis( ): AsyncBoxView
getMinorOffset( ): AsyncBoxView.ChildState
getMinorSpan( ): AsyncBoxView.ChildState
getMinorTickSpacing( ): JSlider
getMinorVersion( ): ICC_Profile
getMinPage( ): JobAttributes
getMinSelectionIndex( ): DefaultListSelectionModel JList
  ListSelectionModel
getMinSelectionRow( ): DefaultTreeSelectionModel JTree
  TreeSelectionModel
getMinSize( ): GridBagLayout
getMinSize( ): GridBagLayout
getMinTileX( ): BufferedImage *RenderedImage*
getMinTileY( ): BufferedImage *RenderedImage*
getMinValue( ): ColorSpace
getMinWidth( ): TableColumn
getMinX( ): BufferedImage Raster RectangularShape
  RenderableImage RenderableImageOp *RenderedImage*
getMinY( ): BufferedImage Raster RectangularShape
  RenderableImage RenderableImageOp *RenderedImage*
getMissingGlyphCode( ): Font
getMiterLimit( ): BasicStroke
getMixer( ): AudioSystem MixerProvider
getMixerInfo( ): AudioSystem *Mixer* MixerProvider
getMnemonic( ): AbstractButton AbstractColorChooserPanel
  ButtonModel DefaultButtonModel
getMnemonicAt( ): JTabbedPane
getMode( ): FileDialog
getModel( ): AbstractButton AbstractLayoutCache
  JComboBox JList JProgressBar JScrollBar JSlider
  JSpinner JSpinner.DateEditor JSpinner.ListEditor
  JSpinner.NumberEditor JTabbedPane JTable JTree
getModelIndex( ): TableColumn
getModifier( ): javax.swing.text.html.parser.AttributeList
getModifiers( ): ActionEvent AWTKeyStroke InputEvent
getModifiersEx( ): InputEvent
getModifiersExText( ): InputEvent
getMono( ): *MidiChannel*
getMostRecentEventTime( ): EventQueue
getMostRecentFocusOwner( ): JInternalFrame Window
getMouseListeners( ): Component
getMouseModifiersText( ): MouseEvent
getMouseMotionListeners( ): Component
getMouseWheelListeners( ): Component
getMultiClickThreshhold( ): AbstractButton
getMultiDocPrintServices( ): PrintServiceLookup

getMultipleDocumentHandling( ): JobAttributes
getMute( ): *MidiChannel*
getName( ): AbstractDocument.AbstractElement
  Attribute javax.swing.text.html.parser.AttributeList
  Chromaticity Clipboard ColorSpace
  ColorSupported Component Compression Copies
  CopiesSupported Cursor DateTimeAtCompleted
  DateTimeAtCreation DateTimeAtProcessing Destination
  DocumentName DTD *javax.swing.text.Element*
  javax.swing.text.html.parser.Element
  javax.swing.text.html.parser.Entity Fidelity
  FileView Finishings Font JobHoldUntil
  JobImpressions JobImpressionsCompleted
  JobImpressionsSupported JobKOctets
  JobKOctetsProcessed JobKOctetsSupported
  JobMediaSheets JobMediaSheetsCompleted
  JobMediaSheetsSupported JobMessageFromOperator
  JobName JobOriginatingUserName JobPriority
  JobPrioritySupported JobSheets JobState
  JobStateReason JobStateReasons *Keymap*
  LookAndFeel Media MediaPrintableArea MediaSize
  MenuComponent MidiDevice.Info Mixer.Info
  MultipleDocumentHandling NumberOfDocuments
  NumberOfInterveningJobs NumberUp
  NumberUpSupported OrientationRequested
  OutputDeviceAssigned PageRanges PagesPerMinute
  PagesPerMinuteColor PDLOverrideSupported
  Port.Info PresentationDirection PrinterInfo
  PrinterIsAcceptingJobs PrinterLocation
  PrinterMakeAndModel PrinterMessageFromOperator
  PrinterMoreInfo PrinterMoreInfoManufacturer
  PrinterName PrinterResolution PrinterState
  PrinterStateReason PrinterStateReasons PrinterURI
  PrintQuality *PrintService* QueuedJobCount
  ReferenceUriSchemesSupported RequestingUserName
  Severity SheetCollate Sides *Soundbank*
  SoundbankResource *Style* StyleContext.NamedStyle
  UIManager.LookAndFeelInfo
getNamespaceURI( ): IIOMetadataNode
getNativeContainer( ): Toolkit
getNativeImageMetadataFormatName( ):
  ImageReaderWriterSpi
getNativeMetadataFormatName( ): IIOMetadata
getNativesForFlavor( ): *FlavorTable* SystemFlavorMap
getNativesForFlavors( ): *FlavorMap* SystemFlavorMap
getNativeStreamMetadataFormatName( ):
  ImageReaderWriterSpi
getNavigationFilter( ): JFormattedTextField.AbstractFormatter
  JTextComponent
getNewLeadSelectionPath( ): TreeSelectionEvent
getNewState( ): WindowEvent
getNext( ): javax.swing.text.html.parser.AttributeList
getNextEastWestVisualPositionFrom( ): CompositeView
getNextEvent( ): EventQueue
getNextFocusableComponent( ): JComponent
getNextLeaf( ): DefaultMutableTreeNode
getNextLeftHit( ): TextLayout
getNextMatch( ): JList JTree
getNextNode( ): DefaultMutableTreeNode
getNextNorthSouthVisualPositionFrom( ): CompositeView
getNextRightHit( ): TextLayout
getNextSibling( ): DefaultMutableTreeNode IIOMetadataNode
getNextValue( ): JSpinner *SpinnerModel*
getNextVisualPositionFrom( ): GlyphView.GlyphPainter
  NavigationFilter TextUI View
getNextWord( ): Utilities
getNodeDimensions( ): AbstractLayoutCache
  AbstractLayoutCache.NodeDimensions
getNodeName( ): IIOMetadataNode
getNodeType( ): IIOMetadataNode
getNodeValue( ): IIOMetadataNode
getNoImageIcon( ): ImageView

G

G

getPlaceholder(): MaskFormatter^
getPlaceholderCharacter(): MaskFormatter^
getPluginClassName(): ImageReaderWriterSpi‿
getPoint(): MouseEvent‿
getPoint1(): GradientPaint
getPoint2(): GradientPaint
getPoint2D(): AffineTransformOp BandCombineOp
    BufferedImageOp ColorConvertOp ConvolveOp
    LookupOp *RasterOp* RescaleOp
getPointSize(): StyleSheet^
getPolyPressure(): *MidiChannel*
getPopup(): PopupFactory PopupMenuUI^
getPopupMenu(): JMenu^
getPopupMenuListeners(): JComboBox^ JPopupMenu‿
getPopupMenuOrigin(): JMenu^
getPosition(): JLayeredPane‿ LineBreakMeasurer
    SizeSequence TabStop
getPositionAbove(): Utilities
getPositionBelow(): Utilities
getPositionsInRange(): GapContent^ StringContent
getPrecision(): FloatControl
getPredefinedCursor(): Cursor
getPreferredHeight(): AbstractLayoutCache‿
getPreferredScrollableViewportSize(): JList^ JTable^
    JTextComponent‿ JTree^ *Scrollable*
getPreferredSize(): Component‿ *ComponentPeer*‿
    ComponentUI‿
getPreferredSpan(): View‿
getPreferredThumbnailSizes(): ImageWriter
getPreferredTileSizes(): ImageWriteParam‿
getPreferredValue(): Spring
getPreferredWidth(): AbstractLayoutCache‿ TableColumn
getPrefix(): IIOMetadataNode
getPresentationName(): AbstractUndoableEdit‿ *UndoableEdit*
getPreservesUnknownTags(): HTMLDocument^
getPressedIcon(): AbstractButton‿
getPreviewPanel(): ColorChooserComponentFactory
    JColorChooser
getPreviousBounds(): DefaultDesktopManager
getPreviousLeaf(): DefaultMutableTreeNode‿
getPreviousNode(): DefaultMutableTreeNode‿
getPreviousSibling(): DefaultMutableTreeNode‿
    IIOMetadataNode
getPreviousValue(): JSpinner^ *SpinnerModel*
getPreviousWord(): Utilities
getPrimaryType(): DataFlavor
getPrintable(): Book *Pageable*
getPrintableArea(): MediaPrintableArea
getPrintData(): *Doc* SimpleDoc
getPrinter(): JobAttributes
getPrinterJob(): *PrinterGraphics* PrinterJob
getPrinterResolution(): PageAttributes
getPrintEventType(): PrintJobEvent^
getPrintJob(): *PrintGraphics* PrintJobAttributeEvent^
    PrintJobEvent^ Toolkit
getPrintQuality(): PageAttributes
getPrintService(): *DocPrintJob* PrinterJob
    PrintServiceAttributeEvent^ *StreamPrintServiceFactory*
getPrintServices(): PrintServiceLookup
getProfile(): ICC_ColorSpace^
getProfileClass(): ICC_Profile‿
getProgram(): *MidiChannel* Patch
getProgressiveMode(): ImageWriteParam‿
getProgressMonitor(): ProgressMonitorInputStream^
getProperty(): AbstractDocument‿
    ContextualRenderedImageFactory^
    javax.swing.text.Document‿ Image‿ *RenderableImage*
    RenderableImageOp *RenderedImage*‿ Toolkit
getPropertyChangeListeners(): AbstractAction‿ Component‿
    DefaultTreeSelectionModel‿ KeyboardFocusManager‿
    TableColumn Toolkit UIDefaults^ UIManager

getPropertyNames(): BufferedImage^
    ContextualRenderedImageFactory^ *RenderableImage*
    RenderableImageOp *RenderedImage*‿
getPrototypeCellValue(): JList^
getPrototypeDisplayValue(): JComboBox^
getPSName(): Font
getQTables(): JPEGImageReadParam^
    JPEGImageWriteParam^
getRaisedBevelBorderUIResource(): BorderUIResource
getRanges(): NumericShaper
getRaster(): BufferedImage^ IIOImage *PaintContext*
getRawImageType(): ImageReader
getReader(): HTMLDocument^
getReaderFormatNames(): ImageIO
getReaderForText(): DataFlavor *Doc* SimpleDoc
getReaderMIMETypes(): ImageIO
getReaderServiceProviderName(): ImageTranscoderSpi^
getReason(): URIException
getReceiver(): *MidiDevice*‿ MidiSystem *Transmitter*
getRecursionLimit(): FlatteningPathIterator
getRed(): Color‿ ColorModel‿
getRedMask(): DirectColorModel^
getRedoPresentationName(): AbstractUndoableEdit‿
    UndoableEdit
getReds(): IndexColorModel^
getRefreshRate(): DisplayMode
getRegisteredKeyStrokes(): JComponent‿
getRenderableSource(): ParameterBlock
getRenderedImage(): IIOImage
getRenderedSource(): ParameterBlock
getRenderer(): JComboBox^
getRenderingHint(): Graphics2D^
getRenderingHints(): AffineTransformOp BandCombineOp
    BufferedImageOp ColorConvertOp ConvolveOp
    Graphics2D^ LookupOp *RasterOp* RenderContext
    RescaleOp
getReorderingAllowed(): JTableHeader^
getRepresentationClass(): DataFlavor
getRepresentationClassName(): DocFlavor‿
getReshowDelay(): ToolTipManager^
getResizable(): TableColumn
getResizeWeight(): JSplitPane^ View‿
getResizingAllowed(): JTableHeader^
getResizingColumn(): JTableHeader^
getResolution(): MidiFileFormat ResolutionSyntax‿ Sequence
getResolveParent(): AbstractDocument.AbstractElement‿
    javax.swing.text.AttributeSet *Keymap* SimpleAttributeSet
    StyleContext.NamedStyle StyleContext.SmallAttributeSet
getResourceBaseName(): IIOMetadataFormatImpl
getResources(): *Soundbank*
getRGB(): BufferedImage^ Color‿ ColorModel‿
getRGBColorComponents(): Color‿
getRGBComponents(): Color‿
getRGBdefault(): ColorModel‿
getRGBPixel(): *RobotPeer*
getRGBPixels(): *RobotPeer*
getRGBs(): IndexColorModel^
getRightComponent(): JSplitPane^
getRightIndent(): StyleConstants‿
getRightInset(): AsyncBoxView^ CompositeView‿
getRolloverIcon(): AbstractButton‿
getRolloverSelectedIcon(): AbstractButton‿
getRoot(): DefaultMutableTreeNode‿ DefaultTreeModel
    SwingUtilities *TreeModel*
getRootElement(): DefaultStyledDocument.ElementBuffer
getRootElements(): AbstractDocument‿
    javax.swing.text.Document
getRootFrame(): JOptionPane^
getRootName(): *IIOMetadataFormat* IIOMetadataFormatImpl
getRootPane(): JApplet^ JComponent‿ JDialog^ JFrame^
    JWindow^ *RootPaneContainer* SwingUtilities
getRoots(): FileSystemView

getRootView( ): TextUI^
getRotateInstance( ): AffineTransform
getRoundedCorners( ): LineBorder‿
getRowBounds( ): JTree^
getRowCount( ): AbstractLayoutCache‿ JTable^ JTree^
   TableModel TableView.TableCell^ TreeUI^
getRowEnd( ): Utilities
getRowForLocation( ): JTree^
getRowForPath( ): AbstractLayoutCache‿ JTree^ TreeUI^
getRowHeader( ): JScrollPane^ ScrollPaneLayout‿
getRowHeight( ): AbstractLayoutCache‿ JTable^ JTextArea^
   JTree^
getRowMapper( ): DefaultTreeSelectionModel‿
   TreeSelectionModel
getRowMargin( ): JTable^
getRows( ): GridLayout JTextArea‿ java.awt.List^ TextArea^
getRowSelectionAllowed( ): JTable^
getRowsForPaths( ): AbstractLayoutCache‿ *RowMapper*
getRowStart( ): Utilities
getRSB( ): GlyphMetrics
getRule( ): AlphaComposite StyleSheet^
getSample( ): Raster‿ SampleModel‿
getSampleDouble( ): Raster‿ SampleModel‿
getSampleFloat( ): Raster‿ SampleModel‿
getSampleModel( ): BufferedImage^ ImageTypeSpecifier
   Raster‿ *RenderedImage‿*
getSampleModelTranslateX( ): Raster‿
getSampleModelTranslateY( ): Raster‿
getSampleRate( ): AudioFormat
getSamples( ): Raster‿ SampleModel‿
getSampleSize( ): SampleModel‿
getSampleSizeInBits( ): AudioFormat
getScaledInstance( ): Image‿ JPEGQTable
getScaleFactors( ): RescaleOp
getScaleInstance( ): AffineTransform
getScaleX( ): AffineTransform
getScaleY( ): AffineTransform
getScanlineStride( ): ComponentSampleModel^
   MultiPixelPackedSampleModel^
   SinglePixelPackedSampleModel^
getScreenDevices( ): GraphicsEnvironment
getScreenInsets( ): Toolkit
getScreenResolution( ): Toolkit
getScreenSize( ): Toolkit
getScrollableBlockIncrement( ): JList^ JTable^
   JTextComponent^ JTree^ *Scrollable*
getScrollableTracksViewportHeight( ): JList^ JTable^
   JTextComponent^ JTree^ *Scrollable*
getScrollableTracksViewportWidth( ): JList^ JTable^
   JTextComponent^ JTree^ *Scrollable*
getScrollableUnitIncrement( ): JList^ JTable^
   JTextComponent^ JTree^ *Scrollable*
getScrollAmount( ): MouseWheelEvent^
getScrollbarDisplayPolicy( ): ScrollPane^
getScrollbarVisibility( ): TextArea^
getScrollMode( ): JViewport^
getScrollOffset( ): JTextField^
getScrollPosition( ): ScrollPane^
getScrollsOnExpand( ): JTree^
getScrollType( ): MouseWheelEvent^
getSelectedAccessibleColumns( ): *AccessibleTable‿*
   JTable.AccessibleJTable^
getSelectedAccessibleRows( ): *AccessibleTable‿*
   JTable.AccessibleJTable^
getSelectedCheckbox( ): CheckboxGroup
getSelectedColor( ): *ColorSelectionModel*
   DefaultColorSelectionModel
getSelectedColumn( ): JTable^
getSelectedColumnCount( ): DefaultTableColumnModel
   JTable^ *TableColumnModel*
getSelectedColumns( ): DefaultTableColumnModel JTable^
   TableColumnModel

getSelectedComponent( ): JTabbedPane^
getSelectedFile( ): JFileChooser^
getSelectedFiles( ): JFileChooser^
getSelectedFrame( ): JDesktopPane^
getSelectedIcon( ): AbstractButton^
getSelectedIndex( ): Choice^ DefaultSingleSelectionModel
   JComboBox^ JList^ JTabbedPane^ java.awt.List^
   SingleSelectionModel
getSelectedIndexes( ): java.awt.List^ *ListPeer^*
getSelectedIndices( ): JList^
getSelectedItem( ): Choice^ *ComboBoxModel‿*
   DefaultComboBoxModel JComboBox^ java.awt.List^
getSelectedItems( ): java.awt.List^
getSelectedObjects( ): AbstractButton^ Checkbox^
   CheckboxMenuItem^ Choice^ DefaultButtonModel‿
   ItemSelectable‿ JComboBox^ java.awt.List^
getSelectedPath( ): MenuSelectionManager
getSelectedRow( ): JTable^
getSelectedRowCount( ): JTable^
getSelectedRows( ): JTable^
getSelectedText( ): AbstractButton.AccessibleAbstractButton^
   AccessibleText‿ InputMethodRequests‿
   JLabel.AccessibleJLabel^ JTextComponent^
   JTextComponent.AccessibleJTextComponent^
   TextComponent^
   TextComponent.AccessibleAWTTextComponent^
getSelectedTextColor( ): JTextComponent^
getSelectedValue( ): JList^
getSelectedValues( ): JList^
getSelection( ): ButtonGroup
getSelectionBackground( ): JList^ JTable^
getSelectionColor( ): JTextComponent^
getSelectionCount( ): DefaultTreeSelectionModel‿ JTree^
   TreeSelectionModel
getSelectionEnd( ): AbstractButton.AccessibleAbstractButton^
   AccessibleText‿ JLabel.AccessibleJLabel^
   JTextComponent^
   JTextComponent.AccessibleJTextComponent^
   TextComponent^
   TextComponent.AccessibleAWTTextComponent^
   *TextComponentPeer^*
getSelectionForeground( ): JList^ JTable^
getSelectionMode( ): DefaultListSelectionModel
   DefaultTreeSelectionModel‿ JList^ *ListSelectionModel*
   TreeSelectionModel
getSelectionModel( ): AbstractLayoutCache‿
   DefaultTableColumnModel JColorChooser^ JList^
   JMenuBar^ JPopupMenu^ JTable^ JTree^
   TableColumnModel
getSelectionPainter( ): DefaultCaret^
getSelectionPath( ): DefaultTreeSelectionModel‿ JTree^
   TreeSelectionModel
getSelectionPaths( ): DefaultTreeSelectionModel‿ JTree^
   TreeSelectionModel
getSelectionRows( ): DefaultTreeSelectionModel‿ JTree^
   TreeSelectionModel
getSelectionStart( ): AbstractButton.AccessibleAbstractButton^
   AccessibleText‿ JLabel.AccessibleJLabel^
   JTextComponent^
   JTextComponent.AccessibleJTextComponent^
   TextComponent^
   TextComponent.AccessibleAWTTextComponent^
   *TextComponentPeer^*
getSelectionValues( ): JOptionPane^
getSeparatorSize( ): JToolBar.Separator^
getSequence( ): MidiFileReader MidiSystem *Sequencer^*
getSequencer( ): MidiSystem
getServiceProviderByClass( ): ServiceRegistry‿
getServiceProviders( ): ServiceRegistry‿
getServiceUIFactory( ): *PrintService‿*
getShadowColor( ): EtchedBorder^
getShadowInnerColor( ): BevelBorder^

G

Cross-Ref

getShadowOuterColor() / getTabCount()

getShadowOuterColor(): BevelBorder^
getShaper(): NumericShaper
getSharedAncestor(): DefaultMutableTreeNode
getSharedInstance(): PopupFactory
getShearInstance(): AffineTransform
getShearX(): AffineTransform
getShearY(): AffineTransform
getShortcut(): MenuItem^
getShortcutMenuItem(): MenuBar^
getShortParameter(): ParameterBlock
getShowHorizontalLines(): JTable^
getShowsRootHandles(): JTree^
getShowVerticalLines(): JTable^
getSiblingCount(): DefaultMutableTreeNode
getSides(): JobAttributes
getSize(): AccessibleComponent_ Component_
    Component.AccessibleAWTComponent^
    DataBuffer_ Dimension_ Font_
    JList.AccessibleJList.AccessibleJListChild^
    JTable.AccessibleJTable.AccessibleJTableCell^
    JTableHeader.AccessibleJTableHeader₂
    .AccessibleJTableHeaderEntry^
    JTree.AccessibleJTree.AccessibleJTreeNode^ ListModel_
    MenuComponent.AccessibleAWTMenuComponent^
    Rectangle^ Size2DSyntax_ SizeSequence
getSize2D(): Font_
getSizes(): SizeSequence
getSlaveSyncMode(): Sequencer^
getSlaveSyncModes(): Sequencer^
getSmallDisplayIcon(): AbstractColorChooserPanel^
getSnapshot(): VolatileImage^
getSnapToTicks(): JSlider^
getSolo(): MidiChannel
getSoundbank(): MidiSystem SoundbankReader
    SoundbankResource
getSource(): Image_ ParameterBlock
getSourceActions(): DragGestureRecognizer_
    DragSourceContext DropTargetDragEvent^
    DropTargetDropEvent^ TransferHandler
getSourceAsDragGestureRecognizer(): DragGestureEvent^
getSourceBands(): IIOParam
getSourceElement(): HyperlinkEvent^
getSourceEncodings(): FormatConversionProvider
getSourceLineInfo(): AudioSystem Mixer^
getSourceLines(): Mixer^
getSourceMaxProgressivePass(): ImageReadParam^
getSourceMinProgressivePass(): ImageReadParam^
getSourceNumProgressivePasses(): ImageReadParam^
getSourceRegion(): IIOParam_ ImageReader
getSourceRenderSize(): ImageReadParam^
getSources(): BufferedImage^ ParameterBlock
    RenderableImage RenderableImageOp RenderedImage_
getSourceXSubsampling(): IIOParam_
getSourceYSubsampling(): IIOParam_
getSpaceAbove(): StyleConstants_
getSpaceBelow(): StyleConstants_
getSpan(): BoxView^ GlyphView.GlyphPainter
getSpinner(): JSpinner.DefaultEditor^
getStandardChromaNode(): IIOMetadata
getStandardCompressionNode(): IIOMetadata
getStandardDataNode(): IIOMetadata
getStandardDimensionNode(): IIOMetadata
getStandardDocumentNode(): IIOMetadata
getStandardFormatInstance(): IIOMetadataFormatImpl
getStandardTextNode(): IIOMetadata
getStandardTileNode(): IIOMetadata
getStandardTransparencyNode(): IIOMetadata
getStandardTree(): IIOMetadata
getStart(): SpinnerDateModel^
getStartIndex(): AccessibleHyperlink_

getStartOffset(): AbstractDocument.AbstractElement_
    AbstractWriter_ javax.swing.text.Element_
    Highlighter.Highlight HTMLDocument.Iterator View_
getStartPoint(): Arc2D^
getStartPosition(): AbstractDocument_
    javax.swing.text.Document_
getState(): Checkbox^ CheckboxMenuItem^ Frame^
    FramePeer^ InputMethodHighlight JCheckBoxMenuItem^
getStateChange(): ItemEvent^
getStateLabel(): BooleanControl^
getStaticAttribute(): StyleContext_
getStaticAttributeKey(): StyleContext_
getStatus(): MidiMessage_ PixelGrabber
getStepSize(): SpinnerNumberModel^
getStream(): AppletContext JEditorPane^
getStreamForBytes(): Doc SimpleDoc
getStreamKeys(): AppletContext
getStreamMetadata(): ImageReader
getStreamMetadataFormat(): ImageReaderWriterSpi^
getStreamPosition(): ImageInputStream^
    ImageInputStreamImpl_
getStrikethroughOffset(): LineMetrics
getStrikethroughThickness(): LineMetrics
getString(): AbstractDocument.Content
    javax.swing.text.html.parser.Entity GapContent^
    JProgressBar^ StringContent UIDefaults^ UIManager
getStringBounds(): Font_ FontMetrics
getStringTable(): EnumSyntax
getStroke(): Graphics2D^
getStrongCaret(): TextLayout.CaretPolicy
getStyle(): DefaultStyledDocument^ Font_
    InputMethodHighlight JTextPane^ StyleContext_
    StyledDocument^
getStyledDocument(): JTextPane^
    StyledEditorKit.StyledTextAction^
getStyledEditorKit(): JTextPane^
    StyledEditorKit.StyledTextAction^
getStyleNames(): DefaultStyledDocument^ StyleContext_
getStyleSheet(): BlockView^ HTMLDocument^
    HTMLEditorKit^ ImageView^ InlineView^
    javax.swing.text.html.ParagraphView^
getStyleSheets(): StyleSheet^
getSubElements(): JMenuBar^ JMenuItem^ JPopupMenu^
    MenuElement
getSubimage(): BufferedImage^
getSubsamplingXOffset(): IIOParam_
getSubsamplingYOffset(): IIOParam_
getSubType(): DataFlavor
getSupportedAttributeCategories(): PrintService_
getSupportedAttributeValues(): PrintService_
getSupportedDocFlavors(): PrintService_
    StreamPrintServiceFactory
getSupportsWindowDecorations(): LookAndFeel
getSurrendersFocusOnKeystroke(): JTable^
getSynthesizer(): MidiSystem
getSystemClipboard(): Toolkit
getSystemCustomCursor(): Cursor
getSystemDisplayName(): FileSystemView
getSystemEventQueue(): Toolkit
getSystemEventQueueImpl(): Toolkit
getSystemIcon(): FileSystemView
getSystemLookAndFeelClassName(): UIManager
getSystemSelection(): Toolkit
getSystemTypeDescription(): FileSystemView
getTab(): TabSet
getTabAfter(): TabSet
getTabBase(): javax.swing.text.ParagraphView^
getTabbedSpan(): GlyphView^ TabableView^
getTabbedTextOffset(): Utilities
getTabbedTextWidth(): Utilities
getTabBounds(): TabbedPaneUI^
getTabCount(): JTabbedPane^ TabSet

G

getYOrigin( ): Kernel
GIF: DocFlavor.BYTE_ARRAY^ DocFlavor.INPUT_STREAM^
DocFlavor.URL^
GLASS_PANE: AccessibleRole^
GLASS_PANE_PROPERTY: JInternalFrame^
glassPane: JRootPane^
GlyphJustificationInfo: java.awt.font
—returned by: GlyphVector.getGlyphJustificationInfo( )
GraphicAttribute.getJustificationInfo( )
GlyphMetrics: java.awt.font
—returned by: GlyphVector.getGlyphMetrics( )
GlyphVector: java.awt.font
—passed to: GlyphVector.equals( )
Graphics2D^.drawGlyphVector( )
—returned by: Font. < createGlyphVector( ), layoutGlyphVector( ) >
GlyphView: javax.swing.text
—subclasses: LabelView^
—descendents: InlineView^
—passed to: GlyphView.GlyphPainter < getAscent( ),
getBoundedPosition( ), getDescent( ), getHeight( ),
getNextVisualPositionFrom( ), getPainter( ), getSpan( ),
modelToView( ), paint( ), viewToModel( ) >
GlyphView.GlyphPainter: javax.swing.text
—passed to: GlyphView.setGlyphPainter( )
—returned by: GlyphView.getGlyphPainter( )
GlyphView.GlyphPainter.getPainter( )
GoodBreakWeight: View
GOPHER: ReferenceUriSchemesSupported^
GOT_FOCUS: Event
gotFocus( ): Component
grabFocus( ): JComponent^
grabPixels( ): PixelGrabber
GradientPaint: java.awt
GraphicAttribute: java.awt.font
—subclasses: ImageGraphicAttribute^ ShapeGraphicAttribute^
Graphics: java.awt
—subclasses: DebugGraphics^ Graphics2D^
—passed to: AbstractBorder.paintBorder( )
AbstractButton^.paintBorder( )
AsyncBoxView.ChildLocator.paintChildren( ) BevelBorder^
< paintLoweredBevel( ), paintRaisedBevel( ) >
Border.paintBorder( ) BorderUIResource.paintBorder( )
BoxView^.paintChild( ) Caret.paint( )
CellRendererPane^.paintComponent( ) Component < paint( ),
paintAll( ), print( ), printAll( ), update( ) > ComponentPeer
< paint( ), print( ) > ComponentUI < paint( ), update( ) >
Container^ < paintComponents( ), printComponents( ) >
DebugGraphics( ) DefaultCaret^.paint( ) FontMetrics
< getLineMetrics( ), getMaxCharBounds( ), getStringBounds( ) >
GlyphView.GlyphPainter.paint( ) Highlighter.paint( )
Highlighter.HighlightPainter.paint( ) Icon.paintIcon( )
IconUIResource.paintIcon( ) ImageIcon.paintIcon( )
JComponent^ < getComponentGraphics( ),
paintBorder( ), paintChildren( ), paintComponent( ),
printBorder( ), printChildren( ), printComponent( ) >
JInternalFrame^.paintComponent( ) JMenuBar^.paintBorder( )
JPopupMenu^.paintBorder( ) JProgressBar^.paintBorder( )
JSplitPane^.paintChildren( ) JToolBar^.paintBorder( )
LayeredHighlighter.paintLayeredHighlights( )
LayeredHighlighter.LayerPainter.paintLayer( )
ListView^.paintChild( ) PasswordView^ < drawEchoCharacter( ),
drawSelectedText( ), drawUnselectedText( ) > PlainView^
< drawLine( ), drawSelectedText( ), drawUnselectedText( ) >
Printable.print( ) java.beans.PropertyEditor.paintValue( )
java.beans.PropertyEditorSupport.paintValue( )
SplitPaneUI^.finishedPaintingChildren( )
StyleSheet.BoxPainter.paint( ) StyleSheet.ListPainter.paint( )
SwingUtilities.paintComponent( ) Utilities.drawTabbedText( )
View^.WrappedPlainView < drawLine( ),
drawSelectedText( ), drawUnselectedText( ) >
—returned by: BufferStrategy.getDrawGraphics( )
Component.getGraphics( ) ComponentPeer.getGraphics( )

Graphics.create( ) Image.getGraphics( )
JComponent^.getComponentGraphics( ) PrintJob.getGraphics( )
View.getGraphics( )
Graphics2D: java.awt
—passed to: GraphicAttribute.draw( ) TextLayout.draw( )
—returned by: BufferedImage.createGraphics( )
GraphicsEnvironment.createGraphics( )
VolatileImage^.createGraphics( )
GraphicsConfigTemplate: java.awt
—passed to: GraphicsDevice.getBestConfiguration( )
GraphicsConfiguration: java.awt
—passed to: Canvas( ) Dialog( ) Frame( )
GraphicsConfigTemplate < getBestConfiguration( ),
isGraphicsConfigSupported( ) > JDialog( ) JFrame( )
JWindow( ) ServiceUI.printDialog( ) Toolkit.getScreenInsets( )
VolatileImage^.validate( ) Window( )
—returned by: Component.getGraphicsConfiguration( )
ComponentPeer.getGraphicsConfiguration( )
Graphics2D^.getDeviceConfiguration( )
GraphicsConfigTemplate.getBestConfiguration( )
GraphicsDevice < getBestConfiguration( ), getConfigurations( ),
getDefaultConfiguration( ) >
GraphicsDevice: java.awt
—passed to: Robot( )
—returned by: GraphicsConfiguration.getDevice( )
GraphicsEnvironment < getDefaultScreenDevice( ),
getScreenDevices( ) >
GraphicsEnvironment: java.awt
—returned
by: GraphicsEnvironment.getLocalGraphicsEnvironment( )
gray: Color
GRAY: Color
GrayFilter^: javax.swing
GREEN: Color
green: Color
GREENCOMPONENT: ICC_ProfileRGB^
GridBagConstraints: java.awt
—passed to: GridBagLayout < adjustForGravity( ),
AdjustForGravity( ), setConstraints( ) >
—returned by: GridBagLayout < getConstraints( ),
lookupConstraints( ) >
—fields: GridBagLayout.defaultConstraints
GridBagLayout: java.awt
—passed to: GridBagLayout < getMinSize( ), GetMinSize( ) >
—returned by: GridBagLayout < getLayoutInfo( ),
GetLayoutInfo( ) >
—fields: GridBagLayout.layoutInfo
gridColor: JTable^
gridheight: GridBagConstraints
GridLayout: java.awt
gridwidth: GridBagConstraints
gridx: GridBagConstraints
gridy: GridBagConstraints
group: DefaultButtonModel
GROUP_BOX: AccessibleRole^
grow( ): Rectangle^
growAbsorb: GlyphJustificationInfo
growLeftLimit: GlyphJustificationInfo
growPriority: GlyphJustificationInfo
growRightLimit: GlyphJustificationInfo
GUJARATI: NumericShaper
GURMUKHI: NumericShaper
GZIP: Compression^
H1: HTML.Tag
H2: HTML.Tag
H3: HTML.Tag
H4: HTML.Tag
H5: HTML.Tag
H6: HTML.Tag
HALFWIDTH_KATAKANA: InputSubset^
HALIGN: HTML.Attribute
HAND_CURSOR: Cursor Frame^

handleComment( ): **H**TMLEditorKit.ParserCallback‿
  javax.swing.text.html.parser.**P**arser‿
handleEmptyTag( ): javax.swing.text.html.parser.**P**arser‿
handleEndOfLineString( ): **H**TMLEditorKit.ParserCallback‿
handleEndTag( ): **H**TMLEditorKit.ParserCallback‿
  javax.swing.text.html.parser.**P**arser‿
handleEOFInComment( ): javax.swing.text.html.parser.**P**arser‿
handleError( ): **H**TMLEditorKit.ParserCallback‿
  javax.swing.text.html.parser.**P**arser‿
handleEvent( ): **C**omponent‿ *ComponentPeer*‿
handleJustify( ): **T**extLayout
handleSimpleTag( ): **H**TMLEditorKit.ParserCallback‿
handleStartTag( ): **H**TMLEditorKit.ParserCallback‿
  javax.swing.text.html.parser.**P**arser‿
handlesWheelScrolling( ): *ComponentPeer*‿
handleText( ): **H**TMLEditorKit.ParserCallback‿
  javax.swing.text.html.parser.**P**arser‿
handleTitle( ): javax.swing.text.html.parser.**P**arser‿
HANGING_BASELINE: **F**ont‿ **G**raphicAttribute‿
HANJA: **I**nputSubset^
hasAlpha( ): **C**olorModel‿
hasAttribute( ): **I**IOMetadataNode
hasAttributeNS( ): **I**IOMetadataNode
hasAttributes( ): **I**IOMetadataNode
hasBeenExpanded( ): **J**Tree^
hasChildNodes( ): **I**IOMetadataNode
hasChildren: **J**Tree.DynamicUtilTreeNode^
hasController( ): **I**IOMetadata **I**IOParam‿
hasDynamicLocaleList( ): *InputMethodDescriptor*
hasFocus: **D**efaultTreeCellRenderer^
hasFocus( ): **C**omponent‿
HashAttributeSet‿: javax.print.attribute
  —subclasses: **H**ashDocAttributeSet^ **H**ashPrintJobAttributeSet^
  HashPrintRequestAttributeSet^ **H**ashPrintServiceAttributeSet^
hashCode( ): *javax.print.attribute.AttributeSet*‿ **P**rintService‿
HashDocAttributeSet^: javax.print.attribute
HashMap‿: java.util
  —subclasses: **P**rinterStateReasons^
HashPrintJobAttributeSet^: javax.print.attribute
HashPrintRequestAttributeSet^: javax.print.attribute
HashPrintServiceAttributeSet^: javax.print.attribute
HashSet‿: java.util
  —subclasses: **J**obStateReasons^
Hashtable‿: java.util
  —subclasses: **U**IDefaults^
  —passed to: **B**ufferedImage( ) *ImageConsumer*.setProperties( )
  ImageFilter.setProperties( ) **J**Tree( ) **M**emoryImageSource( )
  PixelGrabber.setProperties( ) *StateEditable* < restoreState( ),
  storeState( ) >
  —returned by: **J**LayeredPane‿.getComponentToLayer( )
  JSlider^.createStandardLabels( )
  —fields: **D**TD < elementHash, entityHash >
  GridBagLayout.comptable **J**Table^
  < defaultEditorsByColumnClass, defaultRenderersByColumnClass >
  StateEdit^ < postState, preState >
hasRaster( ): **I**IOImage
hasThumbnails( ): **I**mageReader
hasTileWriters( ): **B**ufferedImage^ *WritableRenderedImage*^
hasUniformLineMetrics( ): **F**ont‿ **F**ontMetrics‿
head: **D**TD
HEAD: **H**TML.Tag‿
HEADER_RENDERER_PROPERTY: **T**ableColumn
HEADER_ROW: **T**ableModelEvent‿
HEADER_VALUE_PROPERTY: **T**ableColumn
headerRenderer: **T**ableColumn
headerValue: **T**ableColumn
HeadlessException^: java.awt
  —thrown by: **A**pplet( ) **B**utton( ) **C**heckbox( )
  CheckboxMenuItem( ) **C**hoice( )
  Cursor.getSystemCustomCursor( ) **D**ragSource( ) **D**ropTarget( )
  Frame( ) **G**raphicsEnvironment < getCenterPoint( ),
  getDefaultScreenDevice( ), getMaximumWindowBounds( ),

getScreenDevices( ) > **J**Applet( ) **J**ColorChooser^
  < createDialog( ), showDialog( ) > **J**Dialog( ) **J**FileChooser^
  < createDialog( ), showDialog( ), showOpenDialog( ),
  showSaveDialog( ) > **J**Frame( ) **J**OptionPane^ < createDialog( ),
  getFrameForComponent( ), getRootFrame( ), showConfirmDialog( ),
  showInputDialog( ), showMessageDialog( ), showOptionDialog( ) >
  Label( ) java.awt.**L**ist( ) **M**enu( ) **M**enuBar( )
  MenuComponent( ) **M**enuItem( ) **P**opupMenu( ) **P**rinterJob
  < pageDialog( ), printDialog( ) > **S**crollbar( ) **S**crollPane( )
  ServiceUI.printDialog( ) **T**extArea( ) **T**extField( ) **T**oolkit
  < createButton( ), createCheckbox( ), createCheckboxMenuItem( ),
  createChoice( ), createCustomCursor( ), createDialog( ),
  createFileDialog( ), createFrame( ), createLabel( ),
  createList( ), createMenu( ), createMenuBar( ),
  createMenuItem( ), createPopupMenu( ), createScrollbar( ),
  createScrollPane( ), createTextArea( ), createTextField( ),
  createWindow( ), getBestCursorSize( ), getColorModel( ),
  getMaximumCursorColors( ), getMenuShortcutKeyMask( ),
  getScreenInsets( ), getScreenResolution( ), getScreenSize( ),
  getSystemClipboard( ), getSystemSelection( ),
  isDynamicLayoutActive( ), isDynamicLayoutSet( ),
  isFrameStateSupported( ), loadSystemColors( ),
  mapInputMethodHighlight( ), setDynamicLayout( ) >
HEADPHONE: **P**ort.Info^
heavyWeightPopupEnabled: **T**oolTipManager^
height: **A**rc2D.Double^ **A**rc2D.Float^
  Component.BltBufferStrategy^ **D**imension‿
  Ellipse2D.Double^ **E**llipse2D.Float^ **R**aster‿
  Rectangle‿ **R**ectangle2D.Double^ **R**ectangle2D.Float^
  RoundRectangle2D.Double^ **R**oundRectangle2D.Float^
  SampleModel‿
HEIGHT: **C**SS.Attribute **H**TML.Attribute *ImageObserver*
hide( ): **C**omponent‿ *ComponentPeer*‿ **P**opup
HIDE_ON_CLOSE: *WindowConstants*
hidePopup( ): **J**ComboBox‿
hideWindows( ): *InputMethod*
HIERARCHY_BOUNDS_EVENT_MASK: **A**WTEvent‿
HIERARCHY_CHANGED: **H**ierarchyEvent^
HIERARCHY_EVENT_MASK: **A**WTEvent‿
HIERARCHY_FIRST: **H**ierarchyEvent^
HIERARCHY_LAST: **H**ierarchyEvent^
HierarchyBoundsAdapter: java.awt.event
HierarchyBoundsListener^: java.awt.event
  —passed to: **A**WTEventMulticaster < add( ), remove( ) >
  Component‿ < addHierarchyBoundsListener( ),
  removeHierarchyBoundsListener( ) >
  —returned by: **A**WTEventMulticaster < add( ), remove( ) >
  Component‿.getHierarchyBoundsListeners( )
  —implemented by: **A**WTEventMulticaster
  HierarchyBoundsAdapter
hierarchyChanged( ): **A**WTEventMulticaster *HierarchyListener*^
HierarchyEvent^: java.awt.event
  —passed to: **A**WTEventMulticaster < ancestorMoved( ),
  ancestorResized( ), hierarchyChanged( ) > **C**omponent‿
  < processHierarchyBoundsEvent( ), processHierarchyEvent( ) >
  HierarchyBoundsAdapter < ancestorMoved( ),
  ancestorResized( ) > *HierarchyBoundsListener*^
  < ancestorMoved( ), ancestorResized( ) >
  HierarchyListener^.hierarchyChanged( )
HierarchyListener^: java.awt.event
  —passed to: **A**WTEventMulticaster < add( ),
  remove( ) > **C**omponent‿ < addHierarchyListener( ),
  removeHierarchyListener( ) >
  —returned by: **A**WTEventMulticaster < add( ), remove( ) >
  Component‿.getHierarchyListeners( )
  —implemented by: **A**WTEventMulticaster
HIGH: **P**ageAttributes.PrintQualityType^ **P**rintQuality^
highestLayer( ): **J**LayeredPane‿
highlight: **E**tchedBorder‿
Highlighter: javax.swing.text
  —passed to: **J**TextComponent‿.setHighlighter( )
  —returned by: **J**TextComponent‿.getHighlighter( )

H

HTMLEditorKit.HTMLFactory: javax.swing.text.html
HTMLEditorKit.HTMLTextAction^: javax.swing.text.html
—subclasses: **H**TMLEditorKit.InsertHTMLTextAction^
HTMLEditorKit.InsertHTMLTextAction^: javax.swing.text.html
HTMLEditorKit.LinkController^: javax.swing.text.html
HTMLEditorKit.Parser: javax.swing.text.html
—subclasses: **P**arserDelegator^
—passed to: **H**TMLDocument^.setParser( )
—returned by: **H**TMLDocument^.getParser( )
  HTMLEditorKit^.getParser( )
HTMLEditorKit.ParserCallback: javax.swing.text.html
—subclasses: **H**TMLDocument.HTMLReader^
—passed to: **D**ocumentParser^.parse( )
  HTMLEditorKit.Parser^.parse( )
—returned by: **H**TMLDocument^.getReader( )
HTMLFrameHyperlinkEvent^: javax.swing.text.html
—passed to: **H**TMLDocument^.processHTMLFrameHyperlinkEvent( )
HTMLWriter^: javax.swing.text.html
HTTP: **R**eferenceUriSchemesSupported^
HTTPEQUIV: **H**TML.Attribute
HTTPS: **R**eferenceUriSchemesSupported^
HYPERLINK: **A**ccessibleRole^
HyperlinkEvent: javax.swing.event
—subclasses: **H**TMLFrameHyperlinkEvent^
—passed to: *HyperlinkListener*^.hyperlinkUpdate( )
  JEditorPane^.fireHyperlinkUpdate( )
HyperlinkEvent.EventType: javax.swing.event
—passed to: **H**TMLFrameHyperlinkEvent( ) **H**yperlinkEvent( )
—returned by: **H**yperlinkEvent^.getEventType( )
—fields: **H**yperlinkEvent.EventType < ACTIVATED, ENTERED, EXITED >
HyperlinkListener^: javax.swing.event
—passed to: **J**EditorPane^ < addHyperlinkListener( ), removeHyperlinkListener( ) >
—returned by: **J**EditorPane^.getHyperlinkListeners( )
hyperlinkUpdate( ): *HyperlinkListener*^
I: HTML.Tag
icAbsoluteColorimetric: ICC_Profile
ICC_ColorSpace^: java.awt.color
ICC_Profile: java.awt.color
—subclasses: **I**CC_ProfileGray^ **I**CC_ProfileRGB^
—passed to: **C**olorConvertOp( ) **I**CC_ColorSpace( )
—returned by: **C**olorConvertOp.getICC_Profiles( )
  ICC_ColorSpace^.getProfile( ) **I**CC_Profile.getInstance( )
ICC_ProfileGray^: java.awt.color
ICC_ProfileRGB^: java.awt.color
icCurveCount: ICC_Profile
icCurveData: ICC_Profile
icHdrAttributes: ICC_Profile
icHdrCmmId: ICC_Profile
icHdrColorSpace: ICC_Profile
icHdrCreator: ICC_Profile
icHdrDate: ICC_Profile
icHdrDeviceClass: ICC_Profile
icHdrFlags: ICC_Profile
icHdrIlluminant: ICC_Profile
icHdrMagic: ICC_Profile
icHdrManufacturer: ICC_Profile
icHdrModel: ICC_Profile
icHdrPcs: ICC_Profile
icHdrPlatform: ICC_Profile
icHdrRenderingIntent: ICC_Profile
icHdrSize: ICC_Profile
icHdrVersion: ICC_Profile
icon: **J**OptionPane^
ICON: **A**ccessibleRole^
Icon: javax.swing
—passed to: **A**bstractAction( ) **A**bstractButton^ < init( ), setDisabledIcon( ), setDisabledSelectedIcon( ), setIcon( ), setPressedIcon( ), setRolloverIcon( ), setRolloverSelectedIcon( ), setSelectedIcon( ) > **B**orderFactory.createMatteBorder( )
  BorderUIResource.MatteBorderUIResource( )

DefaultTreeCellRenderer^ < setClosedIcon( ), setLeafIcon( ), setOpenIcon( ) > **I**conUIResource( ) **J**Button( ) **J**CheckBox( )
JCheckBoxMenuItem( ) **J**InternalFrame^.setFrameIcon( )
JLabel^ < JLabel( ), setDisabledIcon( ), setIcon( ) > **J**MenuItem^
< init( ), JMenuItem( ) > **J**OptionPane^ < JOptionPane( ),
setIcon( ), showConfirmDialog( ), showInputDialog( ),
showInternalConfirmDialog( ), showInternalInputDialog( ),
showInternalMessageDialog( ), showInternalOptionDialog( ),
showMessageDialog( ), showOptionDialog( ) >
JRadioButton( ) **J**RadioButtonMenuItem( )
JTabbedPane^ < addTab( ), indexOfTab( ), insertTab( ),
setDisabledIconAt( ), setIconAt( ) > **J**TextPane^.insertIcon( )
JToggleButton( ) **M**atteBorder( ) **S**tyleConstants.setIcon( )
SwingUtilities.layoutCompoundLabel( )
—returned by: **A**bstractButton^ < getDisabledIcon( ),
getDisabledSelectedIcon( ), getIcon( ), getPressedIcon( ),
getRolloverIcon( ), getRolloverSelectedIcon( ), getSelectedIcon( ) >
AbstractColorChooserPanel^ < getLargeDisplayIcon( ),
getSmallDisplayIcon( ) > **D**efaultTreeCellRenderer^
< getClosedIcon( ), getDefaultClosedIcon( ),
getDefaultLeafIcon( ), getDefaultOpenIcon( ), getLeafIcon( ),
getOpenIcon( ) > **F**ileSystemView.getSystemIcon( )
FileView.getIcon( ) *ImageView*^ < getLoadingImageIcon( ),
getNoImageIcon( ) > **J**FileChooser^.getIcon( )
JInternalFrame^.getFrameIcon( ) **J**Label^
< getDisabledIcon( ), getIcon( ) > **J**OptionPane^.getIcon( )
JTabbedPane^ < getDisabledIconAt( ), getIconAt( ) >
MatteBorder^.getTileIcon( ) **S**tyleConstants.getIcon( )
TransferHandler.getVisualRepresentation( )
UIDefaults^.getIcon( ) **U**IManager.getIcon( )
—implemented by: **I**conUIResource **I**mageIcon
—fields: **D**efaultTreeCellEditor.editingIcon
  DefaultTreeCellRenderer^ < closedIcon, leafIcon, openIcon >
  JInternalFrame^.frameIcon **J**OptionPane^.icon
  MatteBorder^.tileIcon
ICON_CHANGED_PROPERTY: **A**bstractButton^
ICON_PROPERTY: **J**OptionPane^
iconable: **J**InternalFrame^
IconAttribute: **S**tyleConstants
IconElementName: **S**tyleConstants
ICONIFIED: **A**ccessibleState^ **F**rame^
iconifyFrame( ): **D**efaultDesktopManager *DesktopManager*
IconUIResource: javax.swing.plaf
IconView^: javax.swing.text
icPerceptual: ICC_Profile
icRelativeColorimetric: ICC_Profile
icSaturation: ICC_Profile
icSigAbstractClass: ICC_Profile
icSigAToB0Tag: ICC_Profile
icSigAToB1Tag: ICC_Profile
icSigAToB2Tag: ICC_Profile
icSigBlueColorantTag: ICC_Profile
icSigBlueTRCTag: ICC_Profile
icSigBToA0Tag: ICC_Profile
icSigBToA1Tag: ICC_Profile
icSigBToA2Tag: ICC_Profile
icSigCalibrationDateTimeTag: ICC_Profile
icSigCharTargetTag: ICC_Profile
icSigChromaticityTag: ICC_Profile
icSigCmyData: ICC_Profile
icSigCmykData: ICC_Profile
icSigColorSpaceClass: ICC_Profile
icSigCopyrightTag: ICC_Profile
icSigCrdInfoTag: ICC_Profile
icSigDeviceMfgDescTag: ICC_Profile
icSigDeviceModelDescTag: ICC_Profile
icSigDeviceSettingsTag: ICC_Profile
icSigDisplayClass: ICC_Profile
icSigGamutTag: ICC_Profile
icSigGrayData: ICC_Profile
icSigGrayTRCTag: ICC_Profile
icSigGreenColorantTag: ICC_Profile

H

I

—thrown by: **A**bstractButton˅.setDisplayedMnemonicIndex( )
JLabel˅.setDisplayedMnemonicIndex( )
PageFormat.setOrientation( ) **P**opupFactory.getPopup( )
IllegalComponentStateException^: java.awt
—thrown by: **A**ccessibleContext˅.getLocale( )
IllegalPathStateException: java.awt.geom
IllegalStateException: java.lang
—subclasses: **I**llegalComponentStateException^
InvalidDnDOperationException^
image: **I**IOImage
Image˅: java.awt
—subclasses: **B**ufferedImage^ **V**olatileImage^
—passed to: **C**omponent˅ < checkImage( ), imageUpdate( ),
prepareImage( ) > **C**omponentPeer˅ < checkImage( ),
prepareImage( ) > **D**ragGestureEvent^.startDrag( )
DragSource < createDragSourceContext( ), startDrag( ) >
DragSourceContext( ) **F**rame˅.setIconImage( )
FramePeer^.setIconImage( ) **G**raphics˅.drawImage( )
Graphics2D^.drawImage( ) **G**rayFilter^.createDisabledImage( )
ImageGraphicAttribute( ) **I**mageIcon < ImageIcon( ),
loadImage( ), setImage( ) > **I**mageObserver.imageUpdate( )
MediaTracker < addImage( ), removeImage( ) > **P**ixelGrabber( )
Toolkit < checkImage( ), createCustomCursor( ),
prepareImage( ) >
—returned by: **A**pplet^.getImage( ) **A**ppletContext.getImage( )
java.beans.**B**eanInfo˅.getIcon( ) **C**omponent˅.createImage( )
Component.FlipBufferStrategy^.getBackBuffer( )
ComponentPeer˅ < createImage( ),
getBackBuffer( ) > **F**rame^.getIconImage( )
GrayFilter^.createDisabledImage( ) **I**mage˅.getScaledInstance( )
ImageIcon.getImage( ) **I**mageView^.getImage( )
InputMethodDescriptor.getInputMethodIcon( )
RepaintManager < getOffscreenBuffer( ),
getVolatileOffscreenBuffer( ) > java.beans.**S**impleBeanInfo
< getIcon( ), loadImage( ) > **T**oolkit < createImage( ),
getImage( ) >
—fields: **C**omponent.FlipBufferStrategy^.drawBuffer
JViewport^.backingStoreImage
IMAGE_INCOMPATIBLE: **V**olatileImage^
IMAGE_OK: **V**olatileImage^
IMAGE_RESTORED: **V**olatileImage^
IMAGEABORTED: *ImageConsumer*
ImageCapabilities: java.awt
—passed to: **B**ufferCapabilities( )
Component˅.createVolatileImage( )
GraphicsConfiguration.createCompatibleVolatileImage( )
—returned by: **B**ufferCapabilities
< getBackBufferCapabilities( ), getFrontBufferCapabilities( ) >
GraphicsConfiguration.getImageCapabilities( )
VolatileImage^.getCapabilities( )
imageComplete( ): *IIOReadProgressListener*^
IIOWriteProgressListener^ *ImageConsumer* **I**mageFilter˅
PixelGrabber
ImageConsumer: java.awt.image
—passed to: **F**ilteredImageSource < addConsumer( ),
isConsumer( ), removeConsumer( ),
requestTopDownLeftRightResend( ), startProduction( ) >
ImageFilter˅.getFilterInstance( ) *ImageProducer*
< addConsumer( ), isConsumer( ), removeConsumer( ),
requestTopDownLeftRightResend( ), startProduction( ) >
MemoryImageSource < addConsumer( ), isConsumer( ),
removeConsumer( ), requestTopDownLeftRightResend( ),
startProduction( ) > **R**enderableImageProducer
< addConsumer( ), isConsumer( ), removeConsumer( ),
requestTopDownLeftRightResend( ), startProduction( ) >
—implemented by: **I**mageFilter˅ **P**ixelGrabber
—fields: **I**mageFilter˅.consumer
IMAGEERROR: *ImageConsumer*
ImageFilter˅: java.awt.image
—subclasses: **B**ufferedImageFilter^ **C**ropImageFilter^
ReplicateScaleFilter^ **R**GBImageFilter^
—descendents: **A**reaAveragingScaleFilter^ **G**rayFilter^

—passed to: **F**ilteredImageSource( )
—returned by: **I**mageFilter˅.getFilterInstance( )
imageFlavor: **D**ataFlavor
ImageGraphicAttribute^: java.awt.font
—passed to: **I**mageGraphicAttribute^.equals( )
ImageIcon: javax.swing
—passed to: **I**mageIcon.AccessibleImageIcon( )
ImageIcon.AccessibleImageIcon^: javax.swing
ImageInputStream^: javax.imageio.stream
—extended by: *ImageOutputStream*^
—passed to: **I**mageIO.read( )
—returned by: **I**mageInputStreamSpi^.createInputStreamInstance( )
ImageIO.createImageInputStream( )
—implemented by: **I**mageInputStreamImpl˅
ImageInputStreamImpl˅: javax.imageio.stream
—subclasses: **F**ileCacheImageInputStream^
FileImageInputStream^ **I**mageOutputStreamImpl^
MemoryCacheImageInputStream^
—descendents: **F**ileCacheImageOutputStream^
FileImageOutputStream^
MemoryCacheImageOutputStream^
ImageInputStreamSpi: javax.imageio.spi
ImageIO: javax.imageio
ImageObserver: java.awt.image
—passed to: **C**omponent˅ < checkImage( ), prepareImage( ) >
ComponentPeer˅ < checkImage( ), prepareImage( ) >
Graphics˅.drawImage( ) **G**raphics2D^.drawImage( )
Image˅ < getHeight( ), getProperty( ), getWidth( ) >
ImageIcon.setImageObserver( ) **T**oolkit < checkImage( ),
prepareImage( ) >
—returned by: **I**mageIcon.getImageObserver( )
—implemented by: **C**omponent˅
ImageOutputStream^: javax.imageio.stream
—passed to: **I**mageIO.write( )
—returned by: **I**mageIO.createImageOutputStream( )
ImageOutputStreamSpi^.createOutputStreamInstance( )
—implemented by: **I**mageOutputStreamImpl^
ImageOutputStreamImpl^: javax.imageio.stream
—subclasses: **F**ileCacheImageOutputStream^
FileImageOutputStream^
MemoryCacheImageOutputStream^
ImageOutputStreamSpi^: javax.imageio.spi
ImageProducer: java.awt.image
—passed to: **C**omponent˅.createImage( )
ComponentPeer˅.createImage( ) **F**ilteredImageSource( )
ImageFilter˅.resendTopDownLeftRight( ) **P**ixelGrabber( )
Toolkit.createImage( )
—returned by: **I**mage˅.getSource( )
—implemented by: **F**ilteredImageSource **M**emoryImageSource
RenderableImageProducer
imageProgress( ): *IIOReadProgressListener*^
IIOWriteProgressListener^
ImageReader: javax.imageio
—passed to: *IIOReadProgressListener*^ < imageComplete( ),
imageProgress( ), imageStarted( ), readAborted( ),
sequenceComplete( ), sequenceStarted( ), thumbnailComplete( ),
thumbnailProgress( ), thumbnailStarted( ) >
IIOReadUpdateListener^ < imageUpdate( ),
passComplete( ), passStarted( ), thumbnailPassComplete( ),
thumbnailPassStarted( ), thumbnailUpdate( ) >
IIOReadWarningListener^.warningOccurred( ) **I**mageIO
< getImageTranscoders( ), getImageWriter( ) >
ImageReaderSpi^.isOwnReader( )
—returned by: **I**mageIO.getImageReader( )
ImageReaderSpi^.createReaderInstance( )
ImageReaderSpi^: javax.imageio.spi
—passed to: **I**mageReader( )
—returned by: **I**mageReader.getOriginatingProvider( )
—fields: **I**mageReader.originatingProvider
ImageReaderWriterSpi^: javax.imageio.spi
—subclasses: **I**mageReaderSpi^ **I**mageWriterSpi^
ImageReadParam^: javax.imageio

—passed to: **A**WTEventMulticaster
< caretPositionChanged( ), inputMethodTextChanged( ) >
Component⌄.processInputMethodEvent( ) *InputMethodListener*^
< caretPositionChanged( ), inputMethodTextChanged( ) >
JTextComponent⌄.processInputMethodEvent( )
InputMethodHighlight: java.awt.im
—passed to: **T**oolkit.mapInputMethodHighlight( )
—fields: InputMethodHighlight
< SELECTED_CONVERTED_TEXT_HIGHLIGHT,
SELECTED_RAW_TEXT_HIGHLIGHT,
UNSELECTED_CONVERTED_TEXT_HIGHLIGHT,
UNSELECTED_RAW_TEXT_HIGHLIGHT >
InputMethodListener^: java.awt.event
—passed to: **A**WTEventMulticaster < add( ),
remove( ) > **C**omponent < addInputMethodListener( ),
removeInputMethodListener( ) >
—returned by: **A**WTEventMulticaster < add( ), remove( ) >
Component⌄.getInputMethodListeners( )
—implemented by: **A**WTEventMulticaster
InputMethodRequests⌄: java.awt.im
—extended by: *InputMethodContext*^
—returned by: **C**omponent⌄.getInputMethodRequests( )
inputMethodTextChanged( ): **A**WTEventMulticaster
InputMethodListener^
InputStream⌄: java.io
—subclasses: **A**udioInputStream^
—descendents: **P**rogressMonitorInputStream^
—passed to: *AppletContext*.setStream( ) **A**udioFileReader
< getAudioFileFormat( ), getAudioInputStream( ) >
AudioInputStream( ) **A**udioSystem < getAudioFileFormat( ),
getAudioInputStream( ) > **E**ditorKit⌄.read( )
FileCacheImageInputStream( ) **F**ont⌄.createFont( )
ICC_Profile⌄.getInstance( ) **I**mageIO.read( )
JEditorPane^.read( ) **M**emoryCacheImageInputStream( )
MidiFileReader < getMidiFileFormat( ), getSequence( ) >
MidiSystem < getMidiFileFormat( ), getSequence( ),
getSoundbank( ) > **P**rogressMonitorInputStream( )
Sequencer^.setSequence( ) **S**oundbankReader.getSoundbank( )
—returned by: *AppletContext*.getStream( )
Doc.getStreamForBytes( ) **J**EditorPane^.getStream( )
SimpleDoc.getStreamForBytes( )
InputSubset^: java.awt.im
—fields: **I**nputSubset^ < FULLWIDTH_DIGITS, FULLWIDTH_LATIN,
HALFWIDTH_KATAKANA, HANJA, KANJI, LATIN, LATIN_DIGITS,
SIMPLIFIED_HANZI, TRADITIONAL_HANZI >
inputTypes: **I**mageReaderSpi^
inputValue: **J**OptionPane^
InputVerifier: javax.swing
—passed to: **J**Component^.setInputVerifier( )
—returned by: **J**Component^.getInputVerifier( )
inRange( ): **A**bstractWriter⌄
INSERT: *AccessibleTableModelChange*
DocumentEvent.EventType **E**vent **T**ableModelEvent^
insert( ): **C**hoice^ **D**efaultMutableTreeNode⌄
DefaultStyledDocument⌄
DefaultStyledDocument.ElementBuffer **J**Menu^
JPopupMenu^ **J**TextArea^ **M**enu^ *MutableTreeNode*^
TextArea^ *TextAreaPeer*^ **V**iew⌄
insertAfterEnd( ): **H**TMLDocument^
insertAfterStart( ): **H**TMLDocument^
insertAtBoundary( ): **H**TMLEditorKit.InsertHTMLTextAction^
insertAtBoundry( ): **H**TMLEditorKit.InsertHTMLTextAction^
insertBefore( ): **I**IOMetadataNode
insertBeforeEnd( ): **H**TMLDocument^
insertBeforeStart( ): **H**TMLDocument^
insertBreakAction: **D**efaultEditorKit⌄
insertChar( ): **L**ineBreakMeasurer **T**extMeasurer
insertComponent( ): **J**TextPane^
insertContentAction: **D**efaultEditorKit⌄
insertElementAt( ): **D**efaultComboBoxModel^
DefaultListModel^ *MutableComboBoxModel*^
insertEntries( ): **S**izeSequence

insertHTML( ): **H**TMLEditorKit^
HTMLEditorKit.InsertHTMLTextAction^
insertIcon( ): **J**TextPane^
insertIndexForLayer( ): **J**LayeredPane⌄
insertIndexInterval( ): **D**efaultListSelectionModel
ListSelectionModel
insertItemAt( ): **J**ComboBox^
insertNodeInto( ): **D**efaultTreeModel
insertRow( ): **D**efaultTableModel^
insertSeparator( ): **J**Menu^ **M**enu⌄
insertString( ): **A**bstractDocument *AbstractDocument.Content*
javax.swing.text.*Document*⌄ **D**ocumentFilter
DocumentFilter.FilterBypass **G**apContent^ **S**tringContent
insertTab( ): **J**TabbedPane^
insertTabAction: **D**efaultEditorKit⌄
insertText( ): **T**extArea^ *TextAreaPeer*^
insertTextAtIndex( ): *AccessibleEditableText*^
JTextComponent.AccessibleJTextComponent⌄
insertUpdate( ): **A**bstractDocument
DefaultStyledDocument.ElementBuffer
DocumentListener^ **F**lowView.FlowStrategy
JTextComponent.AccessibleJTextComponent⌄ **V**iew⌄
insets: **G**ridBagConstraints
Insets⌄: java.awt
—subclasses: **I**nsetsUIResource^
—passed to: **A**bstractBorder⌄.getBorderInsets( )
AbstractButton⌄.setMargin( )
BorderUIResource.EmptyBorderUIResource( )
EmptyBorder( ) **G**ridBagConstraints( )
JComponent^.getInsets( ) **J**MenuBar^.setMargin( )
JTextComponent^.setMargin( ) **J**ToolBar^.setMargin( )
MatteBorder( )
—returned by: **A**bstractBorder⌄.getBorderInsets( )
AbstractButton^.getMargin( ) *Autoscroll*.getAutoscrollInsets( )
Border.getBorderInsets( ) **B**orderUIResource.getBorderInsets( )
Container < getInsets( ), insets( ) > *ContainerPeer*⌄
< getInsets( ), insets( ) > **E**mptyBorder^.getBorderInsets( )
JComponent^.getInsets( ) **J**MenuBar^.getMargin( )
JPopupMenu^.getMargin( ) **J**TextComponent^.getMargin( )
JToolBar^.getMargin( ) **T**oolkit.getScreenInsets( )
UIDefaults^.getInsets( ) **U**IManager.getInsets( )
—fields: **G**ridBagConstraints.insets
insets( ): **C**ontainer^ *ContainerPeer*⌄
InsetsUIResource^: javax.swing.plaf
inside( ): **C**omponent⌄ **P**olygon **R**ectangle⌄
insideBorder: **C**ompoundBorder⌄
install( ): *Caret* **D**efaultCaret^ **E**ditorKit *Highlighter*
JFormattedTextField.AbstractFormatter⌄
installAncestorListener( ): **J**ComboBox^
installBorder( ): **L**ookAndFeel
installChooserPanel( ): **A**bstractColorChooserPanel^
installColors( ): **L**ookAndFeel
installColorsAndFont( ): **L**ookAndFeel
installLookAndFeel( ): **U**IManager
installUI( ): **C**omponentUI
InstantiationException: java.lang
—thrown by: **U**IManager.setLookAndFeel( )
Instrument^: javax.sound.midi
—passed to: *Synthesizer*^ < loadInstrument( ), remapInstrument( ),
unloadInstrument( ) >
—returned by: *Soundbank* < getInstrument( ),
getInstruments( ) > *Synthesizer*^ < getAvailableInstruments( ),
getLoadedInstruments( ) >
insureRowContinuity( ): **D**efaultTreeSelectionModel⌄
insureUniqueness( ): **D**efaultTreeSelectionModel⌄
Integer^: java.lang
—passed to: **J**InternalFrame^.setLayer( )
—returned by: **J**LayeredPane^.getObjectForLayer( )
—fields: **J**LayeredPane^ < DEFAULT_LAYER, DRAG_LAYER,
FRAME_CONTENT_LAYER, MODAL_LAYER, PALETTE_LAYER,
POPUP_LAYER > **T**extAttribute^ < SUPERSCRIPT_SUB,
SUPERSCRIPT_SUPER, UNDERLINE_LOW_DASHED,

selectContent( ), startTag( ), text( ), textAreaContent( ), write( ), writeAttributes( ), writeEmbeddedTags( ), writeLineSeparator( ), writeOption( ) > ICC_Profile < getInstance( ), write( ) > *ImageInputStream* < close( ), flush( ), flushBefore( ), getBitOffset( ), getStreamPosition( ), length( ), read( ), readBit( ), readBits( ), readBoolean( ), readByte( ), readBytes( ), readChar( ), readDouble( ), readFloat( ), readFully( ), readInt( ), readLine( ), readLong( ), readShort( ), readUnsignedByte( ), readUnsignedInt( ), readUnsignedShort( ), readUTF( ), reset( ), seek( ), setBitOffset( ), skipBytes( ) > ImageInputStreamImpl < checkClosed( ), close( ), flush( ), flushBefore( ), getBitOffset( ), getStreamPosition( ), read( ), readBit( ), readBits( ), readBoolean( ), readByte( ), readBytes( ), readChar( ), readDouble( ), readFloat( ), readFully( ), readInt( ), readLine( ), readLong( ), readShort( ), readUnsignedByte( ), readUnsignedInt( ), readUnsignedShort( ), readUTF( ), reset( ), seek( ), setBitOffset( ), skipBytes( ) > ImageInputStreamSpi^.createInputStreamInstance( ) ImageIO < createImageInputStream( ), createImageOutputStream( ), read( ), write( ) > *ImageOutputStream^* < flushBefore( ), write( ), writeBit( ), writeBits( ), writeBoolean( ), writeByte( ), writeBytes( ), writeChar( ), writeChars( ), writeDouble( ), writeDoubles( ), writeFloat( ), writeFloats( ), writeInt( ), writeInts( ), writeLong( ), writeLongs( ), writeShort( ), writeShorts( ), writeUTF( ) > ImageOutputStreamImpl^ < flushBits( ), write( ), writeBit( ), writeBits( ), writeBoolean( ), writeByte( ), writeBytes( ), writeChar( ), writeChars( ), writeDouble( ), writeDoubles( ), writeFloat( ), writeFloats( ), writeInt( ), writeInts( ), writeLong( ), writeLongs( ), writeShort( ), writeShorts( ), writeUTF( ) > ImageOutputStreamSpi^.createOutputStreamInstance( ) ImageReader < getAspectRatio( ), getFormatName( ), getHeight( ), getImageMetadata( ), getImageTypes( ), getNumImages( ), getNumThumbnails( ), getRawImageType( ), getStreamMetadata( ), getThumbnailHeight( ), getThumbnailWidth( ), getTileGridXOffset( ), getTileGridYOffset( ), getTileHeight( ), getTileWidth( ), getWidth( ), hasThumbnails( ), isImageTiled( ), isRandomAccessEasy( ), read( ), readAll( ), readAsRenderedImage( ), readRaster( ), readThumbnail( ), readTile( ), readTileRaster( ) > ImageReaderSpi^ < canDecodeInput( ), createReaderInstance( ) > ImageWriter < canInsertEmpty( ), canInsertImage( ), canRemoveImage( ), canReplaceImageMetadata( ), canReplacePixels( ), canReplaceStreamMetadata( ), canWriteEmpty( ), endInsertEmpty( ), endReplacePixels( ), endWriteEmpty( ), endWriteSequence( ), prepareInsertEmpty( ), prepareReplacePixels( ), prepareWriteEmpty( ), prepareWriteSequence( ), removeImage( ), replaceImageMetadata( ), replacePixels( ), replaceStreamMetadata( ), write( ), writeInsert( ), writeToSequence( ) > ImageWriterSpi^.createWriterInstance( ) JEditorPane^ < getStream( ), JEditorPane( ), read( ), setPage( ) > JTextComponent^ < read( ), write( ) > MidiFileReader < getMidiFileFormat( ), getSequence( ) > MidiFileWriter.write( ) MidiSystem < getMidiFileFormat( ), getSequence( ), getSoundbank( ), write( ) > MinimalHTMLWriter^ < endFontTag( ), startFontTag( ), text( ), write( ), writeAttributes( ), writeBody( ), writeComponent( ), writeContent( ), writeEndParagraph( ), writeEndTag( ), writeHeader( ), writeHTMLTags( ), writeImage( ), writeLeaf( ), writeNonHTMLAttributes( ), writeStartParagraph( ), writeStartTag( ), writeStyles( ) > *MultiDoc* < getDoc( ), next( ) > javax.swing.text.html.parser.Parser_ < parse( ), parseDTDMarkup( ), parseMarkupDeclarations( ) > *Sequencer^*.setSequence( ) SimpleDoc < getPrintData( ), getReaderForText( ), getStreamForBytes( ) > SoundbankReader.getSoundbank( ) StringSelection.getTransferData( ) StyleContext_ < readAttributes( ), readAttributeSet( ), writeAttributes( ), writeAttributeSet( ) > StyleSheet^.loadRules( ) *Transferable*.getTransferData( )

ipadx: GridBagConstraints

ipady: GridBagConstraints

IS_CLOSED_PROPERTY: JInternalFrame^

IS_ICON_PROPERTY: JInternalFrame^

IS_MAXIMUM_PROPERTY: JInternalFrame^

IS_SELECTED_PROPERTY: JInternalFrame^

isAccelerated(): ImageCapabilities

isAcceptAllFileFilterUsed(): JFileChooser^

isAccessibleChildSelected(): *AccessibleSelection*
JComboBox.AccessibleJComboBox^ JList.AccessibleJList^
JMenu.AccessibleJMenu^ JMenuBar.AccessibleJMenuBar^
JTabbedPane.AccessibleJTabbedPane^
JTable.AccessibleJTable^ JTree.AccessibleJTree^
JTree.AccessibleJTreeNode^
List.AccessibleAWTList^
MenuComponent.AccessibleAWTMenuComponent_

isAccessibleColumnSelected(): *AccessibleTable*_
JTable.AccessibleJTable^

isAccessibleRowSelected(): *AccessibleTable*_
JTable.AccessibleJTable^

isAccessibleSelected(): *AccessibleTable*_
JTable.AccessibleJTable^

isActionKey(): KeyEvent_

isActive(): Applet^ AppletStub DataLine_ DropTarget Window^

isAddedPath(): TreeSelectionEvent^

isAfter(): CompositeView_

isAllocationValid(): BoxView^

isAlphaPremultiplied(): BufferedImage^ ColorModel_

isAltDown(): InputEvent_

isAltGraphDown(): InputEvent_

isAncestorOf(): Container_

isAntiAliased(): FontRenderContext

isArmed(): *ButtonModel^* DefaultButtonModel_ JMenuItem_

isAttributeCategorySupported(): *PrintService*_

isAttributeRequired(): *IIOMetadataFormat*
IIOMetadataFormatImpl

isAttributeValueSupported(): *PrintService*_

isAutoWaitForIdle(): Robot

isBackgroundSet(): Component_

isBackingStoreEnabled(): JViewport^

isBefore(): CompositeView_

isBigEndian(): AudioFormat

isBlock(): HTML.Tag

isBlockTag(): HTMLWriter^

isBold(): Font_ StyleConstants_

isBorderOpaque(): AbstractBorder_ *Border* BorderUIResource

isBorderPainted(): AbstractButton_ JMenuBar^ JPopupMenu^ JProgressBar^ JToolBar^

isBorderPaintedFlat(): JCheckBox^

isCached(): *ImageInputStream*_ ImageInputStreamImpl_

isCachedFile(): *ImageInputStream*_ ImageInputStreamImpl_

isCachedMemory(): *ImageInputStream*_ ImageInputStreamImpl_

isCanceled(): ProgressMonitor

isCancelled(): PrinterJob

isCellEditable(): AbstractCellEditor_ AbstractTableModel_ *CellEditor*_ DefaultCellEditor.EditorDelegate DefaultTreeCellEditor JTable^ *TableModel*

isCellSelected(): JTable^

isClosable(): JInternalFrame^

isClosed: JInternalFrame^

isClosed(): JInternalFrame^

isCoalesce(): Timer

isCollapsed(): JTree^

isColumnSelected(): JTable^

isCombining(): GlyphMetrics

isCompatibleRaster(): ColorModel_

isCompatibleSampleModel(): ColorModel_

isCompatibleValue(): RenderingHints.Key

isCompletelyDirty(): RepaintManager

isComponent(): GlyphMetrics

isComponentPartOfCurrentMenu(): MenuSelectionManager

isCompositionEnabled(): InputContext *InputMethod*

I

isLocal: DropTargetContext.TransferableProxy
isLocallyDefined( ): *Keymap*
isLocalTransfer( ): DropTargetDropEvent^
isManagingFocus( ): JComponent⌣
ISMAP: HTML.Attribute
isMaximizable( ): JInternalFrame^
isMaximum: JInternalFrame^
isMaximum( ): JInternalFrame^
isMaximumSizeSet( ): JComponent⌣
isMenuComponent( ): JMenu^
isMetaDown( ): InputEvent⌣
isMiddleMouseButton( ): SwingUtilities
isMimeTypeEqual( ): DataFlavor
isMimeTypeSerializedObject( ): DataFlavor
isMinimumSizeSet( ): JComponent⌣
isMixerSupported( ): MixerProvider
isModal( ): Dialog⌣
isMultiBufferAvailable( ): BufferCapabilities
isMultipleMode( ): java.awt.List^
isMultiSelectionEnabled( ): JFileChooser^
isNativeLookAndFeel( ): LookAndFeel
isNodeAncestor( ): DefaultMutableTreeNode⌣
isNodeChild( ): DefaultMutableTreeNode⌣
isNodeDescendant( ): DefaultMutableTreeNode⌣
isNodeRelated( ): DefaultMutableTreeNode⌣
isNodeSibling( ): DefaultMutableTreeNode⌣
ISO_2A0: PageAttributes.MediaType^
ISO_4A0: PageAttributes.MediaType^
ISO_A0: MediaSizeName^ PageAttributes.MediaType^
ISO_A1: MediaSizeName^ PageAttributes.MediaType^
ISO_A10: MediaSizeName^ PageAttributes.MediaType^
ISO_A2: MediaSizeName^ PageAttributes.MediaType^
ISO_A3: MediaSizeName^ PageAttributes.MediaType^
ISO_A4: MediaSizeName^ PageAttributes.MediaType^
ISO_A4_TRANSPARENT: MediaName^
ISO_A4_WHITE: MediaName^
ISO_A5: MediaSizeName^ PageAttributes.MediaType^
ISO_A6: MediaSizeName^ PageAttributes.MediaType^
ISO_A7: MediaSizeName^ PageAttributes.MediaType^
ISO_A8: MediaSizeName^ PageAttributes.MediaType^
ISO_A9: MediaSizeName^ PageAttributes.MediaType^
ISO_B0: MediaSizeName^ PageAttributes.MediaType^
ISO_B1: MediaSizeName^ PageAttributes.MediaType^
ISO_B10: MediaSizeName^ PageAttributes.MediaType^
ISO_B2: MediaSizeName^ PageAttributes.MediaType^
ISO_B3: MediaSizeName^ PageAttributes.MediaType^
ISO_B4: MediaSizeName^ PageAttributes.MediaType^
ISO_B4_ENVELOPE: PageAttributes.MediaType^
ISO_B5: MediaSizeName^ PageAttributes.MediaType^
ISO_B5_ENVELOPE: PageAttributes.MediaType^
ISO_B6: MediaSizeName^ PageAttributes.MediaType^
ISO_B7: MediaSizeName^ PageAttributes.MediaType^
ISO_B8: MediaSizeName^ PageAttributes.MediaType^
ISO_B9: MediaSizeName^ PageAttributes.MediaType^
ISO_C0: MediaSizeName^ PageAttributes.MediaType^
ISO_C0_ENVELOPE: PageAttributes.MediaType^
ISO_C1: MediaSizeName^ PageAttributes.MediaType^
ISO_C10: PageAttributes.MediaType^
ISO_C10_ENVELOPE: PageAttributes.MediaType^
ISO_C1_ENVELOPE: PageAttributes.MediaType^
ISO_C2: MediaSizeName^ PageAttributes.MediaType^
ISO_C2_ENVELOPE: PageAttributes.MediaType^
ISO_C3: MediaSizeName^ PageAttributes.MediaType^
ISO_C3_ENVELOPE: PageAttributes.MediaType^
ISO_C4: MediaSizeName^ PageAttributes.MediaType^
ISO_C4_ENVELOPE: PageAttributes.MediaType^
ISO_C5: MediaSizeName^ PageAttributes.MediaType^
ISO_C5_ENVELOPE: PageAttributes.MediaType^
ISO_C6: MediaSizeName^ PageAttributes.MediaType^
ISO_C6_ENVELOPE: PageAttributes.MediaType^
ISO_C7: PageAttributes.MediaType^
ISO_C7_ENVELOPE: PageAttributes.MediaType^

ISO_C8: PageAttributes.MediaType^
ISO_C8_ENVELOPE: PageAttributes.MediaType^
ISO_C9: PageAttributes.MediaType^
ISO_C9_ENVELOPE: PageAttributes.MediaType^
ISO_DESIGNATED_LONG: MediaSizeName^
    PageAttributes.MediaType^
ISO_DESIGNATED_LONG_ENVELOPE:
    PageAttributes.MediaType^
isObscured( ): *ComponentPeer*⌣
isOneTouchExpandable( ): JSplitPane^
isOnKeyRelease( ): AWTKeyStroke⌣
isOpaque( ): Component
isOpen( ): *Line* *MidiDevice*⌣
isOptimizedDrawingEnabled( ): JComponent⌣
isOwnReader( ): ImageReaderSpi^
isOwnWriter( ): ImageWriterSpi^
isPageFlipping( ): BufferCapabilities
isPaintingTile( ): JComponent⌣
isPaintPending( ): *ContainerPeer*⌣
isParameter( ): javax.swing.text.html.parser.Entity
isParent( ): FileSystemView
isPartialReturn( ): Segment
isPathEditable( ): JTree^
isPathSelected( ): DefaultTreeSelectionModel⌣ JTree^
    TreeSelectionModel
isPlain( ): Font⌣
isPolygonal( ): Area
isPopupMenuVisible( ): JMenu^
isPopupTrigger( ): JPopupMenu^ MouseEvent⌣
    PopupMenuUI^
isPopupVisible( ): ComboBoxUI^ JComboBox^
isPreferredSizeSet( ): JComponent⌣
isPreformatted( ): HTML.Tag^ TagElement
isPressed( ): *ButtonModel*^ DefaultButtonModel⌣
isRandomAccessEasy( ): ImageReader
isReadOnly( ): IIOMetadata
isRecording( ): *Sequencer*^
isRectangleContainingRectangle( ): SwingUtilities
isRectangular( ): Area
isRepeats( ): Timer
isReplacing: DefaultStyledDocument.AttributeUndoableEdit^
isRepresentationClassByteBuffer( ): DataFlavor
isRepresentationClassCharBuffer( ): DataFlavor
isRepresentationClassInputStream( ): DataFlavor
isRepresentationClassReader( ): DataFlavor
isRepresentationClassRemote( ): DataFlavor
isRepresentationClassSerializable( ): DataFlavor
isRequestFocusEnabled( ): JComponent⌣
isResizable: TableColumn
isResizable( ): Dialog⌣ Frame⌣ JInternalFrame^
isRightMouseButton( ): SwingUtilities
isRollover( ): *ButtonModel*^ DefaultButtonModel⌣ JToolBar^
isRolloverEnabled( ): AbstractButton⌣
isRoot( ): DefaultMutableTreeNode⌣ FileSystemView
isRootPaneCheckingEnabled( ): JApplet^ JDialog^ JFrame^
    JInternalFrame^ JWindow^
isRootVisible( ): AbstractLayoutCache⌣ JTree^
isRowSelected( ): DefaultTreeSelectionModel⌣ JTable^ JTree^
    TreeSelectionModel
isRunning( ): *DataLine*⌣ *Sequencer*^ Timer
isSeekForwardOnly( ): ImageReader
isSelected: JInternalFrame^
isSelected( ): AbstractButton⌣ ButtonGroup *ButtonModel*^
    DefaultButtonModel⌣ DefaultSingleSelectionModel
    InputMethodHighlight JInternalFrame^ JMenuBar^
    java.awt.List^ Option *SingleSelectionModel*
isSelectedIndex( ): DefaultListSelectionModel JList^
    ListSelectionModel
isSelectionEmpty( ): DefaultListSelectionModel
    DefaultTreeSelectionModel⌣ JList^ JTree^
    ListSelectionModel *TreeSelectionModel*
isSelectionVisible( ): *Caret* DefaultCaret^

—passed to: **J**Button.AccessibleJButton( )
JRootPane^.setDefaultButton( )
JToolBar^.createActionChangeListener( )
—returned by: **J**RootPane^.getDefaultButton( ) **J**ToolBar^ < add( ),
createActionComponent( ) >
—fields: **J**RootPane^.defaultButton
JButton.AccessibleJButton^: javax.swing
JCheckBox^: javax.swing
—passed to: **D**efaultCellEditor( )
JCheckBox.AccessibleJCheckBox( )
JCheckBox.AccessibleJCheckBox^: javax.swing
JCheckBoxMenuItem^: javax.swing
—passed
to: **J**CheckBoxMenuItem.AccessibleJCheckBoxMenuItem( )
JCheckBoxMenuItem.AccessibleJCheckBoxMenuItem^:
javax.swing
JColorChooser^: javax.swing
—passed to: **A**bstractColorChooserPanel^ < installChooserPanel( ),
uninstallChooserPanel( ) > **J**ColorChooser^.createDialog( )
JColorChooser.AccessibleJColorChooser( )
JColorChooser.AccessibleJColorChooser^: javax.swing
JComboBox^: javax.swing
—passed to: **C**omboBoxUI^ < isFocusTraversable( ),
isPopupVisible( ), setPopupVisible( ) > **D**efaultCellEditor( )
JComboBox.AccessibleJComboBox( )
JComboBox.AccessibleJComboBox^: javax.swing
JComboBox.KeySelectionManager: javax.swing
—passed to: **J**ComboBox^.setKeySelectionManager( )
—returned by: **J**ComboBox^ < createDefaultKeySelectionManager( ),
getKeySelectionManager( ) >
—fields: **J**ComboBox^.keySelectionManager
JComponent^: javax.swing
—subclasses: **A**bstractButton^ **B**ox^ **B**ox.Filler^
JColorChooser^ **J**ComboBox^ **J**FileChooser^
JInternalFrame^ **J**InternalFrame.JDesktopIcon^ **J**Label^
JLayeredPane^ **J**List^ **J**MenuBar^ **J**OptionPane^ **J**Panel^
JPopupMenu^ **J**ProgressBar^ **J**RootPane^ **J**ScrollBar^
JScrollPane^ **J**Separator^ **J**Slider^ **J**Spinner^ **J**SplitPane^
JTabbedPane^ **J**Table^ **J**TableHeader^ **J**TextComponent^
JToolBar^ **J**ToolTip^ **J**Tree^ **J**Viewport^
—descendents: **A**bstractColorChooserPanel^
DefaultListCellRenderer^
DefaultListCellRenderer.UIResource^
DefaultTableCellRenderer^
DefaultTableCellRenderer.UIResource^
DefaultTreeCellEditor.DefaultTextField^
DefaultTreeCellRenderer^ **J**Button^ **J**CheckBox^
JCheckBoxMenuItem^ **J**DesktopPane^ **J**EditorPane^
JFormattedTextField^ **J**Menu^ **J**MenuItem^
JPasswordField^ **J**PopupMenu.Separator^ **J**RadioButton^
JRadioButtonMenuItem^ **J**ScrollPane.ScrollBar^
JSpinner.DateEditor^ **J**Spinner.DefaultEditor^
JSpinner.ListEditor^ **J**Spinner.NumberEditor^
JTextArea^ **J**TextField^ **J**TextPane^ **J**ToggleButton^
JToolBar.Separator^
—passed to: **A**ncestorEvent( ) **C**omponentInputMap( )
ComponentInputMapUIResource( ) **C**omponentUI^
< contains( ), createUI( ), getAccessibleChild( ),
getAccessibleChildrenCount( ), getMaximumSize( ),
getMinimumSize( ), getPreferredSize( ),
installUI( ), paint( ), uninstallUI( ), update( ) >
DebugGraphics( ) **D**efaultDesktopManager
< beginDraggingFrame( ), beginResizingFrame( ),
dragFrame( ), endDraggingFrame( ), endResizingFrame( ),
resizeFrame( ), setBoundsForFrame( ) > *DesktopManager*
< beginDraggingFrame( ), beginResizingFrame( ), dragFrame( ),
endDraggingFrame( ), endResizingFrame( ), resizeFrame( ),
setBoundsForFrame( ) > **I**nputVerifier < shouldYieldFocus( ),
verify( ) > **J**ColorChooser^.setPreviewPanel( )
JComponent.AccessibleJComponent( )
JFileChooser^.setAccessory( ) **J**LayeredPane^ < getLayer( ),
putLayer( ) > **J**Spinner^.setEditor( ) **J**ToolTip^.setComponent( )

LookAndFeel < installBorder( ), installColors( ),
installColorsAndFont( ), makeComponentInputMap( ),
uninstallBorder( ) > **R**epaintManager < addDirtyRegion( ),
addInvalidComponent( ), currentManager( ), getDirtyRegion( ),
isCompletelyDirty( ), markCompletelyClean( ),
markCompletelyDirty( ), removeInvalidComponent( ) >
SwingUtilities < calculateInnerArea( ), getUIActionMap( ),
getUIInputMap( ), layoutCompoundLabel( ), replaceUIActionMap( ),
replaceUIInputMap( ) > **T**oolTipManager^ < registerComponent( ),
unregisterComponent( ) > **T**ransferHandler < canImport( ),
createTransferable( ), exportAsDrag( ), exportDone( ),
exportToClipboard( ), getSourceActions( ), importData( ) >
UIDefaults^.getUI( ) **U**IManager.getUI( )
—returned by: **A**ncestorEvent^.getComponent( )
ColorChooserComponentFactory.getPreviewPanel( )
ComponentInputMap^.getComponent( )
JColorChooser^.getPreviewPanel( )
JFileChooser^.getAccessory( ) **J**Spinner^ < createEditor( ),
getEditor( ) > **J**ToolTip^.getComponent( )
—fields: **D**efaultCellEditor^.editorComponent
JComponent.AccessibleJComponent^: javax.swing
—subclasses: **A**bstractButton.AccessibleAbstractButton^
JColorChooser.AccessibleJColorChooser^
JComboBox.AccessibleJComboBox^
JDesktopPane.AccessibleJDesktopPane^
JFileChooser.AccessibleJFileChooser^
JInternalFrame.AccessibleJInternalFrame^
JInternalFrame.JDesktopIcon.AccessibleJDesktopIcon^
JLabel.AccessibleJLabel^
JLayeredPane.AccessibleJLayeredPane^
JList.AccessibleJList^ **J**MenuBar.AccessibleJMenuBar^
JOptionPane.AccessibleJOptionPane^
JPanel.AccessibleJPanel^
JPopupMenu.AccessibleJPopupMenu^
JProgressBar.AccessibleJProgressBar^
JRootPane.AccessibleJRootPane^
JScrollBar.AccessibleJScrollBar^
JScrollPane.AccessibleJScrollPane^
JSeparator.AccessibleJSeparator^
JSlider.AccessibleJSlider^ **J**SplitPane.AccessibleJSplitPane^
JTabbedPane.AccessibleJTabbedPane^
JTable.AccessibleJTable^
JTableHeader.AccessibleJTableHeader^
JTextComponent.AccessibleJTextComponent^
JToolBar.AccessibleJToolBar^ **J**ToolTip.AccessibleJToolTip^
JTree.AccessibleJTree^ **J**Viewport.AccessibleJViewport^
—descendents: **J**Button.AccessibleJButton^
JCheckBox.AccessibleJCheckBox^
JCheckBoxMenuItem.AccessibleJCheckBoxMenuItem^
JEditorPane.AccessibleJEditorPane^
JEditorPane.AccessibleJEditorPaneHTML^
JEditorPane.JEditorPaneAccessibleHypertextSupport^
JMenu.AccessibleJMenu^
JMenuItem.AccessibleJMenuItem^
JPasswordField.AccessibleJPasswordField^
JRadioButton.AccessibleJRadioButton^
JRadioButtonMenuItem.AccessibleJRadioButtonMenuItem^
JTextArea.AccessibleJTextArea^
JTextField.AccessibleJTextField^
JToggleButton.AccessibleJToggleButton^
—passed to: **J**Component.AccessibleJComponent₂
.AccessibleContainerHandler( ) **J**Component₂
.AccessibleJComponent.AccessibleFocusHandler( )
**JComponent.AccessibleJComponent₂
.AccessibleContainerHandler**: javax.swing
**JComponent.AccessibleJComponent₂
.AccessibleFocusHandler**: javax.swing
JCOMPONENT_UI: **S**erviceUIFactory
JDesktopPane^: javax.swing
—passed to: **J**DesktopPane.AccessibleJDesktopPane( )

—returned by: **J**InternalFrame^.getDesktopPane( )
JInternalFrame.JDesktopIcon^.getDesktopPane( )
JOptionPane^.getDesktopPaneForComponent( )
JDesktopPane.AccessibleJDesktopPane^: javax.swing
JDialog^: javax.swing
—passed to: **J**Dialog.AccessibleJDialog( )
—returned by: **J**ColorChooser^.createDialog( )
JFileChooser^.createDialog( ) **J**OptionPane^.createDialog( )
JDialog.AccessibleJDialog^: javax.swing
JDIALOG_UI: **S**erviceUIFactory
JEditorPane^: javax.swing
—subclasses: **J**TextPane^
—passed to: **E**ditorKit_ < deinstall( ), install( ) >
HTMLEditorKit.HTMLTextAction_ < getHTMLDocument( ),
getHTMLEditorKit( ) > **H**TMLEditorKit.InsertHTMLTextAction^
< insertAtBoundary( ), insertAtBoundry( ), insertHTML( ) >
HTMLEditorKit.LinkController^.activateLink( )
JEditorPane.AccessibleJEditorPane( )
JEditorPane.AccessibleJEditorPaneHTML( )
JEditorPane.JEditorPaneAccessibleHypertextSupport( )
StyledEditorKit.StyledTextAction_ < getStyledDocument( ),
getStyledEditorKit( ), setCharacterAttributes( ),
setParagraphAttributes( ) >
—returned by: **S**tyledEditorKit.StyledTextAction_.getEditor( )
JEditorPane.AccessibleJEditorPane^: javax.swing
—subclasses: **J**EditorPane.AccessibleJEditorPaneHTML^
JEditorPane.JEditorPaneAccessibleHypertextSupport^
JEditorPane.AccessibleJEditorPaneHTML^: javax.swing
JEditorPane.JEditorPaneAccessibleHypertextSupport^:
javax.swing
—passed to: **J**EditorPane_
.JEditorPaneAccessibleHypertextSupport.HTMLLink( )
JEditorPane.JEditorPaneAccessibleHypertextSupport_
.HTMLLink^: javax.swing
JFileChooser^: javax.swing
—passed to: **F**ileChooserUI^ < ensureFileIsVisible( ),
getAcceptAllFileFilter( ), getApproveButtonText( ),
getDialogTitle( ), getFileView( ), rescanCurrentDirectory( ) >
JFileChooser.AccessibleJFileChooser( )
JFileChooser.AccessibleJFileChooser^: javax.swing
JFormattedTextField^: javax.swing
—passed to: **J**FormattedTextField.AbstractFormatter_.install( )
JFormattedTextField.AbstractFormatterFactory_.getFormatter( )
—returned by: **J**FormattedTextField.AbstractFormatter_
.getFormattedTextField( ) **J**Spinner.DefaultEditor^.getTextField( )
JFormattedTextField.AbstractFormatter_: javax.swing
—subclasses: **D**efaultFormatter^
—descendents: **D**ateFormatter^ **I**nternationalFormatter^
MaskFormatter^ **N**umberFormatter^
—passed to: **D**efaultFormatterFactory^ < DefaultFormatterFactory( ),
setDefaultFormatter( ), setDisplayFormatter( ),
setEditFormatter( ), setNullFormatter( ) > **J**FormattedTextField^
< JFormattedTextField( ), setFormatter( ) >
—returned by: **D**efaultFormatterFactory^ < getDefaultFormatter( ),
getDisplayFormatter( ), getEditFormatter( ),
getNullFormatter( ) > **J**FormattedTextField^.getFormatter( )
JFormattedTextField.AbstractFormatterFactory_.getFormatter( )
JFormattedTextField.AbstractFormatterFactory_: javax.swing
—subclasses: **D**efaultFormatterFactory^
—passed to: **J**FormattedTextField^ < JFormattedTextField( ),
setFormatterFactory( ) >
—returned by: **J**FormattedTextField^.getFormatterFactory( )
JFrame^: javax.swing
—passed to: **J**Frame.AccessibleJFrame( )
—returned by: *InputMethodContext*^.createInputMethodJFrame( )
JFrame.AccessibleJFrame^: javax.swing
JInternalFrame^: javax.swing
—passed to: **D**efaultDesktopManager < activateFrame( ),
closeFrame( ), deactivateFrame( ), deiconifyFrame( ),
getBoundsForIconOf( ), getPreviousBounds( ),
iconifyFrame( ), maximizeFrame( ), minimizeFrame( ),
openFrame( ), removeIconFor( ), setPreviousBounds( ),

setWasIcon( ), wasIcon( ) > *DesktopManager*
< activateFrame( ), closeFrame( ), deactivateFrame( ),
deiconifyFrame( ), iconifyFrame( ), maximizeFrame( ),
minimizeFrame( ), openFrame( ) > **I**nternalFrameEvent( )
InternalFrameFocusTraversalPolicy^.getInitialComponent( )
JDesktopPane^.setSelectedFrame( )
JInternalFrame.AccessibleJInternalFrame( )
JInternalFrame.JDesktopIcon^ < JInternalFrame.JDesktopIcon( ),
setInternalFrame( ) >
—returned by: **I**nternalFrameEvent^.getInternalFrame( )
JDesktopPane^ < getAllFrames( ),
getAllFramesInLayer( ), getSelectedFrame( ) >
JInternalFrame.JDesktopIcon^.getInternalFrame( )
JOptionPane^.createInternalFrame( )
JInternalFrame.AccessibleJInternalFrame^: javax.swing
JInternalFrame.JDesktopIcon^: javax.swing
—passed to: **J**InternalFrame^.setDesktopIcon( )
JInternalFrame.JDesktopIcon.AccessibleJDesktopIcon( )
—returned by: **J**InternalFrame^.getDesktopIcon( )
—fields: **J**InternalFrame^.desktopIcon
JInternalFrame.JDesktopIcon.AccessibleJDesktopIcon^:
javax.swing
JIS_B0: **M**ediaSizeName^ **P**ageAttributes.MediaType^
JIS_B1: **M**ediaSizeName^ **P**ageAttributes.MediaType^
JIS_B10: **M**ediaSizeName^ **P**ageAttributes.MediaType^
JIS_B2: **M**ediaSizeName^ **P**ageAttributes.MediaType^
JIS_B3: **M**ediaSizeName^ **P**ageAttributes.MediaType^
JIS_B4: **M**ediaSizeName^ **P**ageAttributes.MediaType^
JIS_B5: **M**ediaSizeName^ **P**ageAttributes.MediaType^
JIS_B6: **M**ediaSizeName^ **P**ageAttributes.MediaType^
JIS_B7: **M**ediaSizeName^ **P**ageAttributes.MediaType^
JIS_B8: **M**ediaSizeName^ **P**ageAttributes.MediaType^
JIS_B9: **M**ediaSizeName^ **P**ageAttributes.MediaType^
JLabel^: javax.swing
—subclasses: **D**efaultListCellRenderer^
DefaultTableCellRenderer^ **D**efaultTreeCellRenderer^
—descendents: **D**efaultListCellRenderer.UIResource^
DefaultTableCellRenderer.UIResource^
—passed to: **J**Label.AccessibleJLabel( )
JLabel.AccessibleJLabel^: javax.swing
JLayeredPane^: javax.swing
—subclasses: **J**DesktopPane^
—passed to: **J**Applet^.setLayeredPane( ) **J**Dialog^.setLayeredPane( )
JFrame^.setLayeredPane( ) **J**InternalFrame^.setLayeredPane( )
JLayeredPane.AccessibleJLayeredPane( )
JRootPane^.setLayeredPane( ) **J**Window^.setLayeredPane( )
RootPaneContainer.setLayeredPane( )
—returned by: **J**Applet^.getLayeredPane( )
JDialog^.getLayeredPane( ) **J**Frame^.getLayeredPane( )
JInternalFrame^.getLayeredPane( )
JLayeredPane^.getLayeredPaneAbove( )
JRootPane^ < createLayeredPane( ),
getLayeredPane( ) > **J**Window^.getLayeredPane( )
RootPaneContainer.getLayeredPane( )
—fields: **J**RootPane^.layeredPane
JLayeredPane.AccessibleJLayeredPane^: javax.swing
JList^: javax.swing
—passed
to: **D**efaultListCellRenderer^.getListCellRendererComponent( )
JList.AccessibleJList( )
JList.AccessibleJList.AccessibleJListChild( )
ListCellRenderer.getListCellRendererComponent( ) **L**istUI^
< getCellBounds( ), indexToLocation( ), locationToIndex( ) >
JList.AccessibleJList^: javax.swing
—passed to: **J**List.AccessibleJList.AccessibleJListChild( )
JList.AccessibleJList.AccessibleJListChild^: javax.swing
JMenu^: javax.swing
—passed to: **J**Menu.AccessibleJMenu( ) **J**Menu.WinListener( )
JMenuBar^ < add( ), setHelpMenu( ) >
—returned by: **J**MenuBar^ < add( ), getHelpMenu( ), getMenu( ) >
JMenu.AccessibleJMenu^: javax.swing
JMenu.WinListener^: javax.swing

J

—returned by: **J**Menu^.createWinListener( )
—fields: **J**Menu^.popupListener
JMenuBar^: javax.swing
—passed to: **J**Applet^.setJMenuBar( ) **J**Dialog^.setJMenuBar( )
  JFrame^.setJMenuBar( ) **J**InternalFrame^ < setJMenuBar( ),
  setMenuBar( ) > **J**MenuBar.AccessibleJMenuBar( )
  JRootPane^ < setJMenuBar( ), setMenuBar( ) >
—returned by: **J**Applet^.getJMenuBar( ) **J**Dialog^.getJMenuBar( )
  JFrame^.getJMenuBar( ) **J**InternalFrame^ < getJMenuBar( ),
  getMenuBar( ) > **J**RootPane^ < getJMenuBar( ), getMenuBar( ) >
—fields: **J**RootPane^.menuBar
JMenuBar.AccessibleJMenuBar^: javax.swing
JMenuItem^: javax.swing
—subclasses: **J**CheckBoxMenuItem^ **J**Menu^
  JRadioButtonMenuItem^
—passed to: **J**Menu^ < add( ), createActionChangeListener( ),
  insert( ), remove( ) > **J**PopupMenu^ < add( ),
  createActionChangeListener( ) >
—returned by: **J**Menu^ < add( ), createActionComponent( ),
  getItem( ), insert( ) > **J**PopupMenu^ < add( ),
  createActionComponent( ) >
JMenuItem.AccessibleJMenuItem^: javax.swing
—subclasses: **J**CheckBoxMenuItem
  .AccessibleJCheckBoxMenuItem^ **J**Menu.AccessibleJMenu^
  JRadioButtonMenuItem.AccessibleJRadioButtonMenuItem^
JOB_CANCELED: **P**rintJobEvent^
JOB_CANCELED_AT_DEVICE: **J**obStateReason^
JOB_CANCELED_BY_OPERATOR: **J**obStateReason^
JOB_CANCELED_BY_USER: **J**obStateReason^
JOB_COMPLETE: **P**rintJobEvent^
JOB_COMPLETED_SUCCESSFULLY: **J**obStateReason^
JOB_COMPLETED_WITH_ERRORS: **J**obStateReason^
JOB_COMPLETED_WITH_WARNINGS: **J**obStateReason^
JOB_DATA_INSUFFICIENT: **J**obStateReason^
JOB_FAILED: **P**rintJobEvent^
JOB_HOLD_UNTIL_SPECIFIED: **J**obStateReason^
JOB_INCOMING: **J**obStateReason^
JOB_INTERPRETING: **J**obStateReason^
JOB_OUTGOING: **J**obStateReason^
JOB_PRINTING: **J**obStateReason^
JOB_QUEUED: **J**obStateReason^
JOB_QUEUED_FOR_MARKER: **J**obStateReason^
JOB_RESTARTABLE: **J**obStateReason^
JOB_TRANSFORMING: **J**obStateReason^
JobAttributes: java.awt
—passed to: **J**obAttributes < JobAttributes( ), set( ) >
  Toolkit.getPrintJob( )
JobAttributes.DefaultSelectionType^: java.awt
—passed to: **J**obAttributes < JobAttributes( ),
  setDefaultSelection( ) >
—returned by: **J**obAttributes.getDefaultSelection( )
—fields: **J**obAttributes.DefaultSelectionType^ < ALL, RANGE,
  SELECTION >
JobAttributes.DestinationType^: java.awt
—passed to: **J**obAttributes < JobAttributes( ), setDestination( ) >
—returned by: **J**obAttributes.getDestination( )
—fields: **J**obAttributes.DestinationType^ < FILE, PRINTER >
JobAttributes.DialogType^: java.awt
—passed to: **J**obAttributes < JobAttributes( ), setDialog( ) >
—returned by: **J**obAttributes.getDialog( )
—fields: **J**obAttributes.DialogType^ < COMMON, NATIVE,
  NONE >
JobAttributes.MultipleDocumentHandlingType^: java.awt
—passed to: **J**obAttributes < JobAttributes( ),
  setMultipleDocumentHandling( ) >
—returned by: **J**obAttributes.getMultipleDocumentHandling( )
—fields: **J**obAttributes.MultipleDocumentHandlingType^
  < SEPARATE_DOCUMENTS_COLLATED_COPIES,
  SEPARATE_DOCUMENTS_UNCOLLATED_COPIES >
JobAttributes.SidesType^: java.awt
—passed to: **J**obAttributes < JobAttributes( ), setSides( ) >
—returned by: **J**obAttributes.getSides( )

—fields: **J**obAttributes.SidesType^ < ONE_SIDED,
  TWO_SIDED_LONG_EDGE, TWO_SIDED_SHORT_EDGE >
JobHoldUntil^: javax.print.attribute.standard
JobImpressions^: javax.print.attribute.standard
JobImpressionsCompleted^: javax.print.attribute.standard
JobImpressionsSupported^: javax.print.attribute.standard
JobKOctets^: javax.print.attribute.standard
JobKOctetsProcessed^: javax.print.attribute.standard
JobKOctetsSupported^: javax.print.attribute.standard
JobMediaSheets^: javax.print.attribute.standard
JobMediaSheetsCompleted^: javax.print.attribute.standard
JobMediaSheetsSupported^: javax.print.attribute.standard
JobMessageFromOperator^: javax.print.attribute.standard
JobName^: javax.print.attribute.standard
JobOriginatingUserName^: javax.print.attribute.standard
JobPriority^: javax.print.attribute.standard
JobPrioritySupported^: javax.print.attribute.standard
JobSheets^: javax.print.attribute.standard
—fields: JobSheets^ < NONE, STANDARD >
JobState^: javax.print.attribute.standard
—fields: **J**obState^ < ABORTED, CANCELED, COMPLETED,
  PENDING, PENDING_HELD, PROCESSING,
  PROCESSING_STOPPED, UNKNOWN >
JobStateReason^: javax.print.attribute.standard
—fields: **J**obStateReason^ < ABORTED_BY_SYSTEM,
  COMPRESSION_ERROR, DOCUMENT_ACCESS_ERROR,
  DOCUMENT_FORMAT_ERROR, JOB_CANCELED_AT_DEVICE,
  JOB_CANCELED_BY_OPERATOR, JOB_CANCELED_BY_USER,
  JOB_COMPLETED_SUCCESSFULLY,
  JOB_COMPLETED_WITH_ERRORS,
  JOB_COMPLETED_WITH_WARNINGS, JOB_DATA_INSUFFICIENT,
  JOB_HOLD_UNTIL_SPECIFIED, JOB_INCOMING,
  JOB_INTERPRETING, JOB_OUTGOING, JOB_PRINTING,
  JOB_QUEUED, JOB_QUEUED_FOR_MARKER,
  JOB_RESTARTABLE, JOB_TRANSFORMING,
  PRINTER_STOPPED, PRINTER_STOPPED_PARTLY,
  PROCESSING_TO_STOP_POINT, QUEUED_IN_DEVICE,
  RESOURCES_ARE_NOT_READY, SERVICE_OFF_LINE,
  SUBMISSION_INTERRUPTED, UNSUPPORTED_COMPRESSION,
  UNSUPPORTED_DOCUMENT_FORMAT >
JobStateReasons^: javax.print.attribute.standard
JOIN_BEVEL: **B**asicStroke
JOIN_MITER: **B**asicStroke
JOIN_ROUND: **B**asicStroke
JoinFractureDirection: **D**efaultStyledDocument.ElementSpec
JoinNextDirection: **D**efaultStyledDocument.ElementSpec
JoinPreviousDirection: **D**efaultStyledDocument.ElementSpec
JOptionPane^: javax.swing
—passed to: **J**OptionPane.AccessibleJOptionPane( )
  OptionPaneUI^ < containsCustomComponents( ),
  selectInitialValue( ) >
JOptionPane.AccessibleJOptionPane^: javax.swing
JPanel^: javax.swing
—subclasses: **A**bstractColorChooserPanel^
  JSpinner.DefaultEditor^
—descendents: **J**Spinner.DateEditor^ **J**Spinner.ListEditor^
  JSpinner.NumberEditor^
—passed to: **J**Panel.AccessibleJPanel( )
JPanel.AccessibleJPanel^: javax.swing
JPasswordField^: javax.swing
—passed to: **J**PasswordField.AccessibleJPasswordField( )
JPasswordField.AccessibleJPasswordField^: javax.swing
JPEG: **D**ocFlavor.BYTE_ARRAY^ **D**ocFlavor.INPUT_STREAM^
  DocFlavor.URL^
JPEGHuffmanTable: javax.imageio.plugins.jpeg
—passed to: **J**PEGImageReadParam^.setDecodeTables( )
  JPEGImageWriteParam^.setEncodeTables( )
—returned by: **J**PEGImageReadParam^ < getACHuffmanTables( ),
  getDCHuffmanTables( ) > **J**PEGImageWriteParam^
  < getACHuffmanTables( ), getDCHuffmanTables( ) >
—fields: **J**PEGHuffmanTable < StdACChrominance,
  StdACLuminance, StdDCChrominance, StdDCLuminance >

J

—returned by: **D**efaultCaret^.getComponent( ) **T**extAction¸
< getFocusedComponent( ), getTextComponent( ) >
JTextComponent.AccessibleJTextComponent¸: javax.swing.text
—subclasses: **J**EditorPane.AccessibleJEditorPane¸
JTextArea.AccessibleJTextArea^
JTextField.AccessibleJTextField¸
—descendents: **J**EditorPane.AccessibleJEditorPaneHTML^
JEditorPane.JEditorPaneAccessibleHypertextSupport^
JPasswordField.AccessibleJPasswordField^
JTextComponent.KeyBinding: javax.swing.text
—passed to: **J**TextComponent¸.loadKeymap( )
—returned by: **L**ookAndFeel.makeKeyBindings( )
JTextField¸: javax.swing
—subclasses: **D**efaultTreeCellEditor.DefaultTextField^
JFormattedTextField^ **J**PasswordField^
—passed to: **D**efaultCellEditor( )
JTextField.AccessibleJTextField( )
JTextField.AccessibleJTextField¸: javax.swing
—subclasses: **J**PasswordField.AccessibleJPasswordField^
JTextPane^: javax.swing
JToggleButton¸: javax.swing
—subclasses: **J**CheckBox^ **J**RadioButton^
—passed to: **J**ToggleButton.AccessibleJToggleButton( )
JToggleButton.AccessibleJToggleButton¸: javax.swing
—subclasses: **J**CheckBox.AccessibleJCheckBox^
JRadioButton.AccessibleJRadioButton^
JToggleButton.ToggleButtonModel^: javax.swing
JToolBar^: javax.swing
—passed to: **J**ToolBar.AccessibleJToolBar( )
JToolBar.AccessibleJToolBar^: javax.swing
JToolBar.Separator^: javax.swing
JToolTip^: javax.swing
—passed to: **J**ToolTip.AccessibleJToolTip( )
—returned by: **J**Component¸.createToolTip( )
JToolTip.AccessibleJToolTip^: javax.swing
JTree^: javax.swing
—passed to: **D**efaultCellEditor^.getTreeCellEditorComponent( )
DefaultTreeCellEditor < DefaultTreeCellEditor( ),
determineOffset( ), getTreeCellEditorComponent( ), setTree( ) >
DefaultTreeCellRenderer^.getTreeCellRendererComponent( )
JTree.AccessibleJTree( )
JTree.AccessibleJTree.AccessibleJTreeNode( )
JTree.TreeModelHandler( ) **J**Tree.TreeSelectionRedirector( )
TreeCellEditor^.getTreeCellEditorComponent( )
TreeCellRenderer.getTreeCellRendererComponent( ) **T**reeUI^
< cancelEditing( ), getClosestPathForLocation( ), getEditingPath( ),
getPathBounds( ), getPathForRow( ), getRowCount( ),
getRowForPath( ), isEditing( ), startEditingAtPath( ),
stopEditing( ) >
—fields: DefaultTreeCellEditor.tree
JTree.AccessibleJTree^: javax.swing
—passed to: **J**Tree.AccessibleJTree.AccessibleJTreeNode( )
JTree.AccessibleJTree.AccessibleJTreeNode^: javax.swing
JTree.DynamicUtilTreeNode^: javax.swing
JTree.EmptySelectionModel^: javax.swing
—returned by: **J**Tree.EmptySelectionModel^.sharedInstance( )
—fields: **J**Tree.EmptySelectionModel^.sharedInstance
JTree.TreeModelHandler: javax.swing
JTree.TreeSelectionRedirector: javax.swing
—fields: **J**Tree^.selectionRedirector
JUSTIFICATION: **T**extAttribute^
JUSTIFICATION_FULL: **T**extAttribute^
JUSTIFICATION_NONE: **T**extAttribute^
JViewport^: javax.swing
—passed to: **J**ScrollPane^ < setColumnHeader( ), setRowHeader( ),
setViewport( ) > **J**Viewport.AccessibleJViewport( )
JViewport.ViewListener( )
—returned by: **J**ScrollPane^ < createViewport( ),
getColumnHeader( ), getRowHeader( ), getViewport( ) >
ScrollPaneLayout¸ < getColumnHeader( ), getRowHeader( ),
getViewport( ) >

—fields: **J**ScrollPane^ < columnHeader, rowHeader,
viewport > **J**ScrollPane.AccessibleJScrollPane^.viewPort
ScrollPaneLayout¸ < colHead, rowHead, viewport >
JViewport.AccessibleJViewport^: javax.swing
JViewport.ViewListener^: javax.swing
—returned by: **J**Viewport^.createViewListener( )
JWindow^: javax.swing
—passed to: **J**Window.AccessibleJWindow( )
JWindow.AccessibleJWindow^: javax.swing
K1Div2Luminance: **J**PEGQTable
K1Luminance: **J**PEGQTable
K2Chrominance: **J**PEGQTable
K2Div2Chrominance: **J**PEGQTable
KAKU_0: **M**ediaSize.JIS
KAKU_1: **M**ediaSize.JIS
KAKU_2: **M**ediaSize.JIS
KAKU_20: **M**ediaSize.JIS
KAKU_3: **M**ediaSize.JIS
KAKU_4: **M**ediaSize.JIS
KAKU_5: **M**ediaSize.JIS
KAKU_6: **M**ediaSize.JIS
KAKU_7: **M**ediaSize.JIS
KAKU_8: **M**ediaSize.JIS
KAKU_A4: **M**ediaSize.JIS
KANJI: **I**nputSubset^
KANNADA: **N**umericShaper
KBD: **H**TML.Tag¸
Kernel: java.awt.image
—passed to: **C**onvolveOp( )
—returned by: **C**onvolveOp.getKernel( )
key: **A**ccessibleBundle¸ **E**vent **J**TextComponent.KeyBinding
KEY_ACTION: **E**vent
KEY_ACTION_RELEASE: **E**vent
KEY_ALPHA_INTERPOLATION: **R**enderingHints
KEY_ANTIALIASING: **R**enderingHints
KEY_COLOR_RENDERING: **R**enderingHints
KEY_DITHERING: **R**enderingHints
KEY_EVENT_MASK: **A**WTEvent¸
KEY_FIRST: **K**eyEvent¸
KEY_FRACTIONALMETRICS: **R**enderingHints
KEY_INTERPOLATION: **R**enderingHints
KEY_LAST: **K**eyEvent¸
KEY_LOCATION_LEFT: **K**eyEvent¸
KEY_LOCATION_NUMPAD: **K**eyEvent¸
KEY_LOCATION_RIGHT: **K**eyEvent¸
KEY_LOCATION_STANDARD: **K**eyEvent¸
KEY_LOCATION_UNKNOWN: **K**eyEvent¸
KEY_PRESS: **E**vent
KEY_PRESSED: **K**eyEvent¸
KEY_RELEASE: **E**vent
KEY_RELEASED: **K**eyEvent¸
KEY_RENDERING: **R**enderingHints
KEY_STROKE_CONTROL: **R**enderingHints
KEY_TEXT_ANTIALIASING: **R**enderingHints
KEY_TYPED: **K**eyEvent¸
KeyAdapter: java.awt.event
KeyboardFocusManager¸: java.awt
—subclasses: **D**efaultKeyboardFocusManager¸
—descendents: **D**efaultKeyboardFocusManager^ **F**ocusManager¸
—passed to: **K**eyboardFocusManager¸
.setCurrentKeyboardFocusManager( )
—returned by: **K**eyboardFocusManager¸
.getCurrentKeyboardFocusManager( )
keyDown( ): **C**omponent¸
keyEqualsCharSet( ): **C**hangedCharSetException^
KeyEvent¸: java.awt.event
—subclasses: **M**enuKeyEvent^
—passed to: **A**WTEventMulticaster < keyPressed( ), keyReleased( ),
keyTyped( ) > **A**WTKeyStroke¸.getAWTKeyStrokeForEvent( )
Component¸.processKeyEvent( )
JComboBox^.processKeyEvent( ) **J**Component¸
< processComponentKeyEvent( ), processKeyBinding( ),

processKeyEvent( ) > **J**Menu^.processKeyEvent( )
JMenuBar^ < processKeyBinding( ),
processKeyEvent( ) > **J**MenuItem^.processKeyEvent( )
JPopupMenu^.processKeyEvent( ) **J**Table^.processKeyBinding( )
KeyAdapter < keyPressed( ), keyReleased( ),
keyTyped( ) > **K**eyboardFocusManager.
< dispatchKeyEvent( ), postProcessKeyEvent( ),
processKeyEvent( ) > *K*eyEventDispatcher.dispatchKeyEvent( )
*K*eyEventPostProcessor.postProcessKeyEvent( )
*K*eyListener^ < keyPressed( ), keyReleased( ),
keyTyped( ) > **K**eyStroke^.getKeyStrokeForEvent( )
*M*enuElement.processKeyEvent( )
MenuSelectionManager.processKeyEvent( ) **S**wingUtilities
< notifyAction( ), processKeyBindings( ) >
KeyEventDispatcher: java.awt
—passed to: **K**eyboardFocusManager. < addKeyEventDispatcher( ),
removeKeyEventDispatcher( ) >
—implemented by: **K**eyboardFocusManager.
KeyEventPostProcessor: java.awt
—passed to: **K**eyboardFocusManager.
< addKeyEventPostProcessor( ), removeKeyEventPostProcessor( ) >
—implemented by: **K**eyboardFocusManager.
KeyListener^: java.awt.event
—passed to: **A**WTEventMulticaster < add( ), remove( ) >
Component. < addKeyListener( ), removeKeyListener( ) >
—returned by: **A**WTEventMulticaster < add( ), remove( ) >
Component..getKeyListeners( )
—implemented by: **A**WTEventMulticaster **K**eyAdapter
Keymap: javax.swing.text
—passed to: **J**TextComponent^ < addKeymap( ), loadKeymap( ),
setKeymap( ) > *K*eymap.setResolveParent( )
—returned by: **J**TextComponent^ < addKeymap( ), getKeymap( ),
removeKeymap( ) > *K*eymap.getResolveParent( )
keyPress( ): **R**obot *R*obotPeer
keyPressed( ): **A**WTEventMulticaster **K**eyAdapter
*K*eyListener^
keyRelease( ): **R**obot *R*obotPeer
keyReleased( ): **A**WTEventMulticaster **K**eyAdapter
*K*eyListener^
keys( ): **A**ctionMap. **I**nputMap.
keySelectionManager: **J**ComboBox^
keySet( ): **R**enderingHints
KeyStroke^: javax.swing
—passed to: **I**nputMap. < get( ), put( ), remove( ) > **J**Component^
< getActionForKeyStroke( ), getConditionForKeyStroke( ),
processKeyBinding( ), registerKeyboardAction( ),
unregisterKeyboardAction( ) > **J**MenuBar^.processKeyBinding( )
JMenuItem^.setAccelerator( ) **J**Table^.processKeyBinding( )
JTextComponent.KeyBinding( ) *K*eymap
< addActionForKeyStroke( ), getAction( ), isLocallyDefined( ),
removeKeyStrokeBinding( ) > **S**wingUtilities.notifyAction( )
—returned by: **I**nputMap. < allKeys( ), keys( ) >
JComponent^.getRegisteredKeyStrokes( )
JMenuItem^.getAccelerator( ) *K*eymap < getBoundKeyStrokes( ),
getKeyStrokesForAction( ) > **K**eyStroke^ < getKeyStroke( ),
getKeyStrokeForEvent( ) >
—fields: **J**TextComponent.KeyBinding.key
keyTyped( ): **A**WTEventMulticaster **K**eyAdapter *K*eyListener^
keyUp( ): **C**omponent.
KHMER: **N**umericShaper
LABEL: **A**ccessibleRole^
Label^: java.awt
—passed to: **L**abel.AccessibleAWTLabel( ) **T**oolkit.createLabel( )
Label.AccessibleAWTLabel^: java.awt
LABEL_FOR: **A**ccessibleRelation^
LABEL_FOR_PROPERTY: **A**ccessibleRelation^
LABELED_BY: **A**ccessibleRelation^
LABELED_BY_PROPERTY: **A**ccessibleRelation^
labelFor: **J**Label^
LabelPeer^: java.awt.peer
—returned by: **T**oolkit.createLabel( )
LabelUI^: javax.swing.plaf

—passed to: **J**Label^.setUI( )
—returned by: **J**Label^.getUI( )
LabelView^: javax.swing.text
—subclasses: **I**nlineView^
LANDSCAPE: **O**rientationRequested^
PageAttributes.OrientationRequestedType^ **P**ageFormat
LANG: **H**TML.Attribute
LANGUAGE: **H**TML.Attribute
LAO: **N**umericShaper
LARGE_CAPACITY: **M**ediaTray^
LARGE_MODEL_PROPERTY: **J**Tree^
largeModel: **J**Tree^
last( ): **C**ardLayout **S**egment
LAST_DIVIDER_LOCATION_PROPERTY: **J**SplitPane^
LAST_LINE_END: **G**ridBagConstraints
LAST_LINE_START: **G**ridBagConstraints
lastAlloc: **A**syncBoxView.ChildLocator
lastColumn:
JTable.AccessibleJTable.AccessibleJTableModelChange
lastDividerLocation: **J**SplitPane^
lastEdit( ): **C**ompoundEdit^
lastElement( ): **D**efaultListModel^
lastIndexOf( ): **D**efaultListModel^
lastPageFirst( ): **P**rintJob
lastPaintPosition: **J**Viewport^
lastPath: **D**efaultTreeCellEditor
lastRow: **D**efaultTreeCellEditor
JTable.AccessibleJTable.AccessibleJTableModelChange
TableModelEvent^
lastValidOffset: **A**syncBoxView.ChildLocator
LATIN: **I**nputSubset^
LATIN_DIGITS: **I**nputSubset^
LAYER_PROPERTY: **J**LayeredPane^
LAYERED_PANE: **A**ccessibleRole^
LAYERED_PANE_PROPERTY: **J**InternalFrame^
LayeredHighlighter.: javax.swing.text
—subclasses: **D**efaultHighlighter^
LayeredHighlighter.LayerPainter.: javax.swing.text
—subclasses: **D**efaultHighlighter.DefaultHighlightPainter^
—fields: **D**efaultHighlighter^.DefaultPainter
layeredPane: **J**RootPane^
layout( ): **B**oxView^ **C**omponent. **F**lowView.FlowStrategy
LAYOUT_LEFT_TO_RIGHT: **F**ont.
LAYOUT_NO_LIMIT_CONTEXT: **F**ont.
LAYOUT_NO_START_CONTEXT: **F**ont.
LAYOUT_RIGHT_TO_LEFT: **F**ont.
layoutChanged( ): **B**oxView^
layoutColumns( ): **T**ableView^
layoutCompoundLabel( ): **S**wingUtilities
layoutContainer( ): **B**orderLayout **B**oxLayout **C**ardLayout
FlowLayout **G**ridBagLayout **G**ridLayout
JRootPane.RootLayout **J**Spinner.DefaultEditor^
*L*ayoutManager. **O**verlayLayout **S**crollPaneLayout.
SpringLayout **V**iewportLayout
LayoutFocusTraversalPolicy^: javax.swing
layoutGlyphVector( ): **F**ont.
layoutInfo: **G**ridBagLayout
layoutMajorAxis( ): **B**oxView^
LayoutManager.: java.awt
—extended by: *L*ayoutManager2^
—passed to: **C**ontainer^.setLayout( ) **J**Panel( ) **P**anel( )
—returned by: **C**ontainer^.getLayout( )
JRootPane^.createRootLayout( )
JViewport^.createLayoutManager( )
—implemented by: **F**lowLayout **G**ridLayout
JSpinner.DefaultEditor. **S**crollPaneLayout. **V**iewportLayout
LayoutManager2^: java.awt
—implemented by: **B**orderLayout **B**oxLayout **C**ardLayout
GridBagLayout **J**RootPane.RootLayout **O**verlayLayout
SpringLayout
layoutMinorAxis( ): **B**oxView^
layoutPool: **F**lowView^

—passed to: **A**bstractListModel˛ < addListDataListener( ),
removeListDataListener( ) > *ListModel*˛ < addListDataListener( ),
removeListDataListener( ) >
—returned by: **A**bstractListModel˛.getListDataListeners( )
—implemented by: **J**ComboBox^ **J**List.AccessibleJList^
listenerList: **A**bstractCellEditor˛ **A**bstractDocument˛
AbstractListModel˛ **A**bstractSpinnerModel˛
AbstractTableModel˛ **D**efaultBoundedRangeModel
DefaultButtonModel˛ **D**efaultCaret^
DefaultColorSelectionModel **D**efaultListSelectionModel
DefaultSingleSelectionModel **D**efaultTableColumnModel
DefaultTreeModel **D**efaultTreeSelectionModel˛
EventListenerList **J**Component^ **M**enuSelectionManager
StyleContext.NamedStyle **T**imer
listeners: **U**ndoableEditSupport
ListModel˛: javax.swing
—extended by: *ComboBoxModel*^
—descendents: *MutableComboBoxModel*^
—passed to: **J**List^ < JList( ), setModel( ) >
—returned by: **J**List^.getModel( )
—implemented by: **A**bstractListModel˛
ListPeer˛: java.awt.peer
—returned by: **T**oolkit.createList( )
ListResourceBundle^: java.util
—subclasses: **A**ccessibleResourceBundle^
ListSelectionEvent^: javax.swing.event
—passed to: **D**efaultTableColumnModel
< fireColumnSelectionChanged( ), valueChanged( ) >
JList.AccessibleJList^.valueChanged( ) **J**Table^
< columnSelectionChanged( ), valueChanged( ) >
JTable.AccessibleJTable^ < columnSelectionChanged( ),
valueChanged( ) > **J**TableHeader^.columnSelectionChanged( )
ListSelectionListener^.valueChanged( )
TableColumnModelListener^.columnSelectionChanged( )
ListSelectionListener^: javax.swing.event
—passed to: **D**efaultListSelectionModel
< addListSelectionListener( ), removeListSelectionListener( ) >
JList^ < addListSelectionListener( ),
removeListSelectionListener( ) > *ListSelectionModel*
< addListSelectionListener( ), removeListSelectionListener( ) >
—returned
by: **D**efaultListSelectionModel.getListSelectionListeners( )
JList^.getListSelectionListeners( )
—implemented by: **D**efaultTableColumnModel
JList.AccessibleJList^ **J**Table^ **J**Table.AccessibleJTable^
listSelectionModel: **D**efaultTreeSelectionModel˛
ListSelectionModel: javax.swing
—passed to: **D**efaultTableColumnModel.setSelectionModel( )
JList^.setSelectionModel( ) **J**Table^ < JTable( ),
setSelectionModel( ) > *TableColumnModel*.setSelectionModel( )
—returned by: **D**efaultTableColumnModel < createSelectionModel( ),
getSelectionModel( ) > **J**List^ < createSelectionModel( ),
getSelectionModel( ) > **J**Table^ < createDefaultSelectionModel( ),
getSelectionModel( ) > *TableColumnModel*.getSelectionModel( )
—implemented by: **D**efaultListSelectionModel
—fields: **D**efaultTableColumnModel.selectionModel
JTable^.selectionModel
ListUI^: javax.swing.plaf
—passed to: **J**List^.setUI( )
—returned by: **J**List^.getUI( )
ListView^: javax.swing.text.html
LIVE_DRAG_MODE: **J**DesktopPane^
LOAD: **F**ileDialog^
LOAD_FILE: **E**vent
loadAllInstruments( ): *Synthesizer*^
loadChildren( ): **A**syncBoxView^ **C**ompositeView^
JTree.DynamicUtilTreeNode^
loadedChildren: **J**Tree.DynamicUtilTreeNode^
loadImage( ): **I**mageIcon
LOADING: **M**ediaTracker
loadInstrument( ): *Synthesizer*^
loadInstruments( ): *Synthesizer*^

loadKeyBindings( ): **L**ookAndFeel
loadKeymap( ): **J**TextComponent˛
loadRules( ): **S**tyleSheet^
loadSystemColors( ): **T**oolkit
localControl( ): *MidiChannel*
locale: **I**mageReader **I**mageWriteParam^ **I**mageWriter
Locale: java.util
—passed to: **A**ccessibleBundle˛.toDisplayString( )
Component˛.setLocale( )
ComponentOrientation.getOrientation( ) **D**ocumentName( )
Font˛ < getFamily( ), getFontName( ) >
GraphicsEnvironment.getAvailableFontFamilyNames( )
IIOMetadataFormat < getAttributeDescription( ),
getElementDescription( ) > **I**IOMetadataFormatImpl
< getAttributeDescription( ), getElementDescription( ) >
IIOServiceProvider˛.getDescription( ) **I**mageReader.setLocale( )
ImageWriteParam( ) **I**mageWriter.setLocale( )
InputContext.selectInputMethod( ) *InputMethod*.setLocale( )
InputMethodDescriptor < getInputMethodDisplayName( ),
getInputMethodIcon( ) > **J**Component^.setDefaultLocale( )
JobMessageFromOperator( ) **J**obName( )
JobOriginatingUserName( ) **J**PEGImageWriteParam( )
OutputDeviceAssigned( ) **P**rinterInfo( ) **P**rinterLocation( )
PrinterMakeAndModel( ) **P**rinterMessageFromOperator( )
PrinterName( ) **R**equestingUserName( ) **T**extSyntax( )
UIDefaults^ < get( ), getBoolean( ), getBorder( ), getColor( ),
getDimension( ), getFont( ), getIcon( ), getInsets( ), getInt( ),
getString( ), setDefaultLocale( ) > **U**IManager < get( ),
getBoolean( ), getBorder( ), getColor( ), getDimension( ),
getFont( ), getIcon( ), getInsets( ), getInt( ), getString( ) >
—returned by: **A**ccessibleContext˛.getLocale( )
Component˛.getLocale( ) **I**mageReader < getAvailableLocales( ),
getLocale( ) > **I**mageWriteParam^.getLocale( )
ImageWriter < getAvailableLocales( ), getLocale( ) >
InputContext.getLocale( ) *InputMethod*.getLocale( )
InputMethodDescriptor.getAvailableLocales( )
JComponent^.getDefaultLocale( ) **T**extSyntax˛.getLocale( )
UIDefaults^.getDefaultLocale( )
—fields: **I**mageReader < availableLocales, locale >
ImageWriteParam^.locale **I**mageWriter < availableLocales,
locale >
locate( ): **C**omponent˛
location( ): **C**omponent˛ **G**ridBagLayout
locationToIndex( ): **J**List^ **L**istUI^
locator: **A**syncBoxView^
LOG_OPTION: **D**ebugGraphics^
LOGICAL_STYLE_ACTION: **H**TMLEditorKit^
logStream( ): **D**ebugGraphics^
LONG_DESCRIPTION: *Action*^
LookAndFeel: javax.swing
—passed to: **U**IManager < addAuxiliaryLookAndFeel( ),
removeAuxiliaryLookAndFeel( ), setLookAndFeel( ) >
—returned by: **U**IManager < getAuxiliaryLookAndFeels( ),
getLookAndFeel( ) >
lookupConstraints( ): **G**ridBagLayout
lookupDefaultPrintService( ): **P**rintServiceLookup
lookupMultiDocPrintServices( ): **P**rintServiceLookup
LookupOp: java.awt.image
lookupPixel( ): **L**ookupTable˛
lookupPrintServices( ): **P**rinterJob **P**rintServiceLookup
lookupProviders( ): **S**erviceRegistry˛
lookupStreamPrintServiceFactories( ):
StreamPrintServiceFactory
lookupStreamPrintServices( ): **P**rinterJob
LookupTable˛: java.awt.image
—subclasses: **B**yteLookupTable^ **S**hortLookupTable^
—passed to: **L**ookupOp( )
—returned by: **L**ookupOp.getTable( )
loop( ): **A**udioClip *Clip*^
LOOP_CONTINUOUSLY: *Clip*^
LOST_FOCUS: **E**vent
lostFocus( ): **C**omponent˛

lostOwnership( ): *ClipboardOwner* **S**tringSelection
LOWER_LEADING_CORNER: *ScrollPaneConstants*
LOWER_LEFT_CORNER: *ScrollPaneConstants*
LOWER_RIGHT_CORNER: *ScrollPaneConstants*
LOWER_TRAILING_CORNER: *ScrollPaneConstants*
LOWERED: **B**evelBorder˄ **E**tchedBorder˄
lowerLeft: **J**ScrollPane˄ **S**crollPaneLayout˗
lowerRight: **J**ScrollPane˄ **S**crollPaneLayout˗
lowestLayer( ): **J**LayeredPane˄
LOWSRC: **H**TML.Attribute
MAGENTA: **C**olor˗
magenta: **C**olor˗
MAIN: **M**ediaTray˄
MAIN_UIROLE: **S**erviceUIFactory
majorRequirementChange( ): **A**syncBoxView˄
majorTickSpacing: **J**Slider˄
makeBounds( ): **A**rc2D˄
makeComponentInputMap( ): **L**ookAndFeel
makeIcon( ): **L**ookAndFeel
makeInputMap( ): **L**ookAndFeel
makeKeyBindings( ): **L**ookAndFeel
makeTag( ): javax.swing.text.html.parser.**P**arser˗
makeVisible( ): **J**Tree˄ java.awt.**L**ist˄ *ListPeer*˄
MALAYALAM: **N**umericShaper
MANUAL: **M**ediaTray˄
MAP: **H**TML.Tag˗
Map: java.util
— passed to: **F**ont˗ < deriveFont( ), **F**ont( ), getFont( ) >
  Graphics2D˄ < addRenderingHints( ), setRenderingHints( ) >
  InputMethodHighlight( ) **P**rinterStateReasons( )
  RenderingHints < putAll( ), RenderingHints( ) > **T**extLayout( )
— returned by: *FlavorMap*˗ < getFlavorsForNatives( ),
  getNativesForFlavors( ) > **F**ont˗.getAttributes( )
  InputMethodHighlight.getStyle( ) **S**ystemFlavorMap
  < getFlavorsForNatives( ), getNativesForFlavors( ) >
  Toolkit.mapInputMethodHighlight( )
— implemented by: **R**enderingHints
— fields: **T**oolkit.desktopProperties
mapInputMethodHighlight( ): **T**oolkit
mapRenderContext( ): *ContextualRenderedImageFactory*˄
MARGIN: **C**SS.Attribute
MARGIN_BOTTOM: **C**SS.Attribute
MARGIN_CHANGED_PROPERTY: **A**bstractButton˄
MARGIN_LEFT: **C**SS.Attribute
MARGIN_RIGHT: **C**SS.Attribute
MARGIN_TOP: **C**SS.Attribute
MARGINHEIGHT: **H**TML.Attribute
MARGINWIDTH: **H**TML.Attribute
mark( ): *ImageInputStream*˄ **I**mageInputStreamImpl˗
markCompletelyClean( ): **R**epaintManager
markCompletelyDirty( ): **R**epaintManager
MARKER_SUPPLY_EMPTY: **P**rinterStateReason˄
MARKER_SUPPLY_LOW: **P**rinterStateReason˄
MARKER_WASTE_ALMOST_FULL: **P**rinterStateReason˄
MARKER_WASTE_FULL: **P**rinterStateReason˄
markFirstTime( ): javax.swing.text.html.parser.**P**arser˗
MaskFormatter˄: javax.swing.text
MASTER_GAIN: **F**loatControl.Type˄
match( ): **D**ataFlavor
matches( ): **A**udioFormat **L**ine.Info˗
matchNameAttribute( ): **H**TMLWriter˄
MatteBorder˄: javax.swing.border
— subclasses: **B**orderUIResource.MatteBorderUIResource˄
— returned by: **B**orderFactory.createMatteBorder( )
max( ): **S**pring
MAXGRIDSIZE: **G**ridBagLayout
maximizable: **J**InternalFrame˄
MAXIMIZED_BOTH: **F**rame˗
MAXIMIZED_HORIZ: **F**rame˗
MAXIMIZED_VERT: **F**rame˗
maximizeFrame( ): **D**efaultDesktopManager *DesktopManager*
maximum: **S**izeRequirements

maximumLayoutSize( ): **B**orderLayout **B**oxLayout **C**ardLayout
  GridBagLayout **J**RootPane.RootLayout *LayoutManager2*˄
  OverlayLayout **S**pringLayout
maximumRowCount: **J**ComboBox˄
MAXLENGTH: **H**TML.Attribute
maxWidth: **T**ableColumn
MD: *DTDConstants*
Media˄: javax.print.attribute.standard
— subclasses: **M**ediaName˄ **M**ediaSizeName˄ **M**ediaTray˄
MEDIA_EMPTY: **P**rinterStateReason˄
MEDIA_JAM: **P**rinterStateReason˄
MEDIA_LOW: **P**rinterStateReason˄
MEDIA_NEEDED: **P**rinterStateReason˄
MediaName˄: javax.print.attribute.standard
— fields: **M**ediaName˄ < ISO_A4_TRANSPARENT, ISO_A4_WHITE,
  NA_LETTER_TRANSPARENT, NA_LETTER_WHITE >
MediaPrintableArea: javax.print.attribute.standard
MediaSize˄: javax.print.attribute.standard
— returned by: **M**ediaSize˄.getMediaSizeForName( )
— fields: **M**ediaSize.Engineering < A, B, C, D, E >
  MediaSize.ISO < A0, A1, A10, A2, A3, A4, A5, A6, A7, A8,
  A9, B0, B1, B10, B2, B3, B4, B5, B6, B7, B8, B9, C3,
  C4, C5, C6, DESIGNATED_LONG > **M**ediaSize.JIS < B0, B1,
  B10, B2, B3, B4, B5, B6, B7, B8, B9, CHOU_1, CHOU_2,
  CHOU_3, CHOU_30, CHOU_4, CHOU_40, KAKU_0, KAKU_1,
  KAKU_2, KAKU_20, KAKU_3, KAKU_4, KAKU_5, KAKU_6,
  KAKU_7, KAKU_8, KAKU_A4, YOU_1, YOU_2, YOU_3,
  YOU_4, YOU_5, YOU_6, YOU_7 > **M**ediaSize.NA < LEGAL,
  LETTER, NA_10x13_ENVELOPE, NA_10x14_ENVELOPE,
  NA_10X15_ENVELOPE, NA_5X7, NA_6X9_ENVELOPE,
  NA_7X9_ENVELOPE, NA_8X10, NA_9x11_ENVELOPE,
  NA_9x12_ENVELOPE, NA_NUMBER_10_ENVELOPE,
  NA_NUMBER_11_ENVELOPE, NA_NUMBER_12_ENVELOPE,
  NA_NUMBER_14_ENVELOPE, NA_NUMBER_9_ENVELOPE >
  MediaSize.Other < EXECUTIVE, FOLIO, INVOICE,
  ITALY_ENVELOPE, JAPANESE_DOUBLE_POSTCARD,
  JAPANESE_POSTCARD, LEDGER, MONARCH_ENVELOPE,
  PERSONAL_ENVELOPE, QUARTO >
MediaSize.Engineering: javax.print.attribute.standard
MediaSize.ISO: javax.print.attribute.standard
MediaSize.JIS: javax.print.attribute.standard
MediaSize.NA: javax.print.attribute.standard
MediaSize.Other: javax.print.attribute.standard
MediaSizeName˄: javax.print.attribute.standard
— passed to: **M**ediaSize˄ < getMediaSizeForName( ), MediaSize( ) >
— returned by: **M**ediaSize˄ < findMedia( ), getMediaSizeName( ) >
— fields: **M**ediaSizeName˄ < A, B, C, D, E, EXECUTIVE, FOLIO,
  INVOICE, ISO_A0, ISO_A1, ISO_A10, ISO_A2, ISO_A3,
  ISO_A4, ISO_A5, ISO_A6, ISO_A7, ISO_A8, ISO_A9, ISO_B0,
  ISO_B1, ISO_B10, ISO_B2, ISO_B3, ISO_B4, ISO_B5,
  ISO_B6, ISO_B7, ISO_B8, ISO_B9, ISO_C0, ISO_C1, ISO_C2,
  ISO_C3, ISO_C4, ISO_C5, ISO_C6, ISO_DESIGNATED_LONG,
  ITALY_ENVELOPE, JAPANESE_DOUBLE_POSTCARD,
  JAPANESE_POSTCARD, JIS_B0, JIS_B1, JIS_B10, JIS_B2,
  JIS_B3, JIS_B4, JIS_B5, JIS_B6, JIS_B7, JIS_B8, JIS_B9,
  LEDGER, MONARCH_ENVELOPE, NA_10X13_ENVELOPE,
  NA_10X14_ENVELOPE, NA_10X15_ENVELOPE,
  NA_5X7, NA_6X9_ENVELOPE, NA_7X9_ENVELOPE,
  NA_8X10, NA_9X11_ENVELOPE, NA_9X12_ENVELOPE,
  NA_LEGAL, NA_LETTER, NA_NUMBER_10_ENVELOPE,
  NA_NUMBER_11_ENVELOPE, NA_NUMBER_12_ENVELOPE,
  NA_NUMBER_14_ENVELOPE, NA_NUMBER_9_ENVELOPE,
  PERSONAL_ENVELOPE, QUARTO, TABLOID >
MediaTracker: java.awt
— fields: **I**mageIcon.tracker
MediaTray˄: javax.print.attribute.standard
— fields: **M**ediaTray˄ < BOTTOM, ENVELOPE, LARGE_CAPACITY,
  MAIN, MANUAL, MIDDLE, SIDE, TOP >
MEMBER_OF: **A**ccessibleRelation˄
MEMBER_OF_PROPERTY: **A**ccessibleRelation˄
MemoryCacheImageInputStream˄: javax.imageio.stream
MemoryCacheImageOutputStream˄: javax.imageio.stream

MemoryImageSource: java.awt.image
menu: SystemColor^
MENU: AccessibleRole^ HTML.Tag⌄ SystemColor^
Menu^: java.awt
— subclasses: PopupMenu^
— passed to: Menu.AccessibleAWTMenu( ) MenuBar^
< add( ), setHelpMenu( ) > *MenuBarPeer*^ < addHelpMenu( ),
addMenu( ) > Toolkit.createMenu( )
— returned by: MenuBar^ < add( ), getHelpMenu( ), getMenu( ) >
Menu.AccessibleAWTMenu^: java.awt
— subclasses: PopupMenu.AccessibleAWTPopupMenu^
MENU_BAR: AccessibleRole^
MENU_BAR_PROPERTY: JInternalFrame^
MENU_ITEM: AccessibleRole^
MENU_TEXT: SystemColor^
menuBar: JRootPane^
MenuBar^: java.awt
— passed to: Frame^.setMenuBar( ) *FramePeer*^.setMenuBar( )
MenuBar.AccessibleAWTMenuBar( ) Toolkit.createMenuBar( )
— returned by: Frame^.getMenuBar( )
MenuBar.AccessibleAWTMenuBar^: java.awt
MenuBarPeer^: java.awt.peer
— returned by: Toolkit.createMenuBar( )
MenuBarUI^: javax.swing.plaf
— passed to: JMenuBar^.setUI( )
— returned by: JMenuBar^.getUI( )
menuCanceled( ): *MenuListener*^
MenuComponent^: java.awt
— subclasses: MenuBar^ MenuItem^
— descendents: CheckboxMenuItem^ Menu^ PopupMenu^
— passed to: Component⌄.remove( )
Menu^.remove( ) MenuBar^.remove( )
MenuComponent.AccessibleAWTMenuComponent( )
MenuContainer.remove( )
MenuComponent.AccessibleAWTMenuComponent^: java.awt
— subclasses: MenuBar.AccessibleAWTMenuBar^
MenuItem.AccessibleAWTMenuItem^
— descendents: CheckboxMenuItem⌄
.AccessibleAWTCheckboxMenuItem^
Menu.AccessibleAWTMenu^
PopupMenu.AccessibleAWTPopupMenu^
MenuComponentPeer⌄: java.awt.peer
— extended by: *MenuBarPeer*^ *MenuItemPeer*^
— descendents: *CheckboxMenuItemPeer*^ *MenuPeer*^
PopupMenuPeer^
— returned by: MenuComponent⌄.getPeer( )
MenuContainer: java.awt
— returned by: MenuComponent⌄.getParent( )
— implemented by: Component⌄ Menu^ MenuBar^
menuDeselected( ): *MenuListener*^
menuDragMouseDragged( ): *MenuDragMouseListener*^
menuDragMouseEntered( ): *MenuDragMouseListener*^
MenuDragMouseEvent^: javax.swing.event
— passed to: JMenuItem^ < fireMenuDragMouseDragged( ),
fireMenuDragMouseEntered( ), fireMenuDragMouseExited( ),
fireMenuDragMouseReleased( ), processMenuDragMouseEvent( ) >
MenuDragMouseListener^ < menuDragMouseDragged( ),
menuDragMouseEntered( ), menuDragMouseExited( ),
menuDragMouseReleased( ) >
menuDragMouseExited( ): *MenuDragMouseListener*^
MenuDragMouseListener^: javax.swing.event
— passed to: JMenuItem^ < addMenuDragMouseListener( ),
removeMenuDragMouseListener( ) >
— returned by: JMenuItem^.getMenuDragMouseListeners( )
menuDragMouseReleased( ): *MenuDragMouseListener*^
MenuElement: javax.swing
— passed to: JMenuBar^ < processKeyEvent( ),
processMouseEvent( ) > JMenuItem^ < processKeyEvent( ),
processMouseEvent( ) > JPopupMenu^ < processKeyEvent( ),
processMouseEvent( ) > MenuDragMouseEvent( )
MenuElement < processKeyEvent( ), processMouseEvent( ) >
MenuKeyEvent( ) MenuSelectionManager.setSelectedPath( )

— returned by: JMenuBar^.getSubElements( )
JMenuItem^.getSubElements( ) JPopupMenu^.getSubElements( )
MenuDragMouseEvent^.getPath( )
MenuElement.getSubElements( ) MenuKeyEvent^.getPath( )
MenuSelectionManager.getSelectedPath( )
— implemented by: JMenuBar^ JMenuItem^ JPopupMenu^
MenuEvent^: javax.swing.event
— passed to: *MenuListener*^ < menuCanceled( ), menuDeselected( ),
menuSelected( ) >
MenuItem^: java.awt
— subclasses: CheckboxMenuItem^ Menu^
— descendents: PopupMenu^
— passed to: Menu^ < add( ), insert( ) >
MenuItem.AccessibleAWTMenuItem( ) *MenuPeer*^.addItem( )
Toolkit.createMenuItem( )
— returned by: Menu^ < add( ), getItem( ) >
MenuBar^.getShortcutMenuItem( )
MenuItem.AccessibleAWTMenuItem^: java.awt
— subclasses: CheckboxMenuItem⌄
.AccessibleAWTCheckboxMenuItem^
Menu.AccessibleAWTMenu^
— descendents: PopupMenu.AccessibleAWTPopupMenu^
MenuItemPeer^: java.awt.peer
— extended by: *CheckboxMenuItemPeer*^ *MenuPeer*^
— descendents: *PopupMenuPeer*^
— returned by: Toolkit.createMenuItem( )
MenuItemUI^: javax.swing.plaf
— passed to: JMenuItem^.setUI( )
MenuKeyEvent^: javax.swing.event
— passed to: JMenuItem^ < fireMenuKeyPressed( ),
fireMenuKeyReleased( ), fireMenuKeyTyped( ),
processMenuKeyEvent( ) > *MenuKeyListener*^
< menuKeyPressed( ), menuKeyReleased( ), menuKeyTyped( ) >
MenuKeyListener^: javax.swing.event
— passed to: JMenuItem^ < addMenuKeyListener( ),
removeMenuKeyListener( ) >
— returned by: JMenuItem^.getMenuKeyListeners( )
menuKeyPressed( ): *MenuKeyListener*^
menuKeyReleased( ): *MenuKeyListener*^
menuKeyTyped( ): *MenuKeyListener*^
MenuListener^: javax.swing.event
— passed to: JMenu^ < addMenuListener( ),
removeMenuListener( ) >
— returned by: JMenu^.getMenuListeners( )
MenuPeer^: java.awt.peer
— extended by: *PopupMenuPeer*^
— returned by: Toolkit.createMenu( )
menuSelected( ): *MenuListener*^
menuSelectionChanged( ): JMenuBar^ JMenuItem^
JPopupMenu^ *MenuElement*
MenuSelectionManager: javax.swing
— passed to: JMenuBar^ < processKeyEvent( ),
processMouseEvent( ) > JMenuItem^ < processKeyEvent( ),
processMouseEvent( ) > JPopupMenu^ < processKeyEvent( ),
processMouseEvent( ) > MenuDragMouseEvent( )
MenuElement < processKeyEvent( ), processMouseEvent( ) >
MenuKeyEvent( )
— returned by: MenuDragMouseEvent^.getMenuSelectionManager( )
MenuKeyEvent^.getMenuSelectionManager( )
MenuSelectionManager.defaultManager( )
MenuShortcut: java.awt
— passed to: MenuBar^ < deleteShortcut( ),
getShortcutMenuItem( ) > MenuItem^ < MenuItem( ),
setShortcut( ) > MenuShortcut.equals( )
— returned by: MenuItem^.getShortcut( )
menuText: SystemColor^
mergeTree( ): IIOMetadata
message: JOptionPane^
MESSAGE_PROPERTY: JOptionPane^
MESSAGE_TYPE_PROPERTY: JOptionPane^
messageType: JOptionPane^
meta: DTD

M

META: HTML.Tag, MetaMessage^
meta(): *MetaEventListener*^
META_DOWN_MASK: InputEvent*
META_MASK: ActionEvent* Event InputEvent*
metadata: IIOImage
metaDown(): Event
MetaEventListener^: javax.sound.midi
—passed to: *Sequencer*^ < addMetaEventListener( ),
  removeMetaEventListener( ) >
MetaMessage^: javax.sound.midi
—passed to: *MetaEventListener*^.meta( )
METHOD: HTML.Attribute
metrics: PlainView*
MICROPHONE: Port.Info^
microsecondLength: MidiFileFormat
MIDDLE: MediaTray^
MIDI_SYNC: Sequencer.SyncMode
MIDI_TIME_CODE: Sequencer.SyncMode ShortMessage^
MidiChannel: javax.sound.midi
—returned by: *Synthesizer*^.getChannels( )
MidiDevice: javax.sound.midi
—extended by: *Sequencer*^ *Synthesizer*^
—returned by: MidiDeviceProvider.getDevice( )
  MidiSystem.getMidiDevice( )
MidiDevice.Info: javax.sound.midi
—passed to: MidiDeviceProvider < getDevice( ),
  isDeviceSupported( ) > MidiSystem.getMidiDevice( )
—returned by: *MidiDevice*.getDeviceInfo( )
  MidiDeviceProvider.getDeviceInfo( )
  MidiSystem.getMidiDeviceInfo( )
MidiDeviceProvider: javax.sound.midi.spi
MidiEvent: javax.sound.midi
—passed to: Track < add( ), remove( ) >
—returned by: Track.get( )
MidiFileFormat: javax.sound.midi
—returned by: MidiFileReader.getMidiFileFormat( )
  MidiSystem.getMidiFileFormat( )
MidiFileReader: javax.sound.midi.spi
MidiFileWriter: javax.sound.midi.spi
MidiMessage: javax.sound.midi
—subclasses: MetaMessage^ ShortMessage^ SysexMessage^
—passed to: MidiEvent( ) *Receiver*.send( )
—returned by: MidiEvent.getMessage( )
MidiSystem: javax.sound.midi
MidiUnavailableException: javax.sound.midi
—thrown by: *MidiDevice* < getReceiver( ), getTransmitter( ),
  open( ) > MidiSystem < getMidiDevice( ), getReceiver( ),
  getSequencer( ), getSynthesizer( ), getTransmitter( ) >
MimeTypeParseException: java.awt.datatransfer
MIMETypes: ImageReaderWriterSpi*
MinimalHTMLWriter^: javax.swing.text.html
minimizeFrame(): DefaultDesktopManager *DesktopManager*
minimum: SizeRequirements
minimumLayoutSize(): BorderLayout BoxLayout
  CardLayout FlowLayout GridBagLayout GridLayout
  JRootPane.RootLayout JSpinner.DefaultEditor*
  LayoutManager OverlayLayout ScrollPaneLayout
  SpringLayout ViewportLayout
minimumSize(): Component, *ComponentPeer*
minIndex: ImageReader
minorRequirementChange(): AsyncBoxView^
minorTickSpacing: JSlider^
minProgressivePass: ImageReadParam*
MINSIZE: GridBagLayout
minus(): Spring
minWidth: TableColumn
minX: Raster*
minY: Raster*
Mixer^: javax.sound.sampled
—returned by: AudioSystem.getMixer( ) MixerProvider.getMixer( )
Mixer.Info: javax.sound.sampled

—passed to: AudioSystem.getMixer( ) MixerProvider < getMixer( ),
  isMixerSupported( ) >
—returned by: AudioSystem.getMixerInfo( ) *Mixer*^.getMixerInfo( )
  MixerProvider.getMixerInfo( )
MixerProvider: javax.sound.sampled.spi
MM: MediaPrintableArea Size2DSyntax,
mnemonic: DefaultButtonModel,
MNEMONIC_CHANGED_PROPERTY: AbstractButton*
MNEMONIC_KEY: Action^
MODAL: AccessibleState^
MODAL_LAYER: JLayeredPane^
MODE_COPY_FROM_METADATA: ImageWriteParam*
MODE_DEFAULT: ImageWriteParam*
MODE_DISABLED: ImageWriteParam*
MODE_EXPLICIT: ImageWriteParam*
MODEL: *DTDConstants*
model: AbstractButton* JProgressBar^ JScrollBar*
  JTabbedPane^
MODEL_CHANGED_PROPERTY: AbstractButton*
ModelAttribute: StyleConstants,
modelIndex: TableColumn
modelToView(): GlyphView.GlyphPainter JTextComponent*
  TextUI^ View,
modifier: javax.swing.text.html.parser.AttributeList
modifiers: Event
MONARCH: PageAttributes.MediaType^
MONARCH_ENVELOPE: MediaSize.Other MediaSizeName^
  PageAttributes.MediaType^
MONGOLIAN: NumericShaper
MONOCHROME: Chromaticity^ PageAttributes.ColorType^
MOUSE_CLICKED: MouseEvent*
MOUSE_DOWN: Event
MOUSE_DRAG: Event
MOUSE_DRAGGED: MouseEvent*
MOUSE_ENTER: Event
MOUSE_ENTERED: MouseEvent*
MOUSE_EVENT_MASK: AWTEvent*
MOUSE_EXIT: Event
MOUSE_EXITED: MouseEvent*
MOUSE_FIRST: MouseEvent*
MOUSE_LAST: MouseEvent*
MOUSE_MOTION_EVENT_MASK: AWTEvent*
MOUSE_MOVE: Event
MOUSE_MOVED: MouseEvent*
MOUSE_PRESSED: MouseEvent*
MOUSE_RELEASED: MouseEvent*
MOUSE_UP: Event
MOUSE_WHEEL: MouseEvent*
MOUSE_WHEEL_EVENT_MASK: AWTEvent*
MouseAdapter: java.awt.event
—subclasses: FormView.MouseEventListener^
  HTMLEditorKit.LinkController^ ToolTipManager^
mouseClicked(): AWTEventMulticaster DefaultCaret^
  MouseAdapter, MouseDragGestureRecognizer^
  MouseInputAdapter *MouseListener*
mouseDown(): Component,
mouseDrag(): Component,
mouseDragged(): AWTEventMulticaster
  DefaultCaret^ HTMLEditorKit.LinkController^
  MouseDragGestureRecognizer^ MouseInputAdapter
  MouseMotionAdapter *MouseMotionListener*
  ToolTipManager^
MouseDragGestureRecognizer^: java.awt.dnd
mouseEnter(): Component,
mouseEntered(): AWTEventMulticaster DefaultCaret^
  MouseAdapter, MouseDragGestureRecognizer^
  MouseInputAdapter *MouseListener*
MouseEvent^: java.awt.event
—subclasses: MenuDragMouseEvent^ MouseWheelEvent^
—passed to: AWTEventMulticaster < mouseClicked( ),
  mouseDragged( ), mouseEntered( ), mouseExited( ),
  mouseMoved( ), mousePressed( ), mouseReleased( ) >

Component, < processMouseEvent( ),
processMouseMotionEvent( ) > **D**efaultCaret^ < mouseClicked( ),
mouseDragged( ), mouseEntered( ), mouseExited( ),
mouseMoved( ), mousePressed( ), mouseReleased( ),
moveCaret( ), positionCaret( ) > **H**TMLEditorKit.LinkController^
< mouseDragged( ), mouseMoved( ) > **J**Component:
< getToolTipLocation( ), getToolTipText( ),
processMouseEvent( ) > **J**MenuBar^.processMouseEvent( )
JMenuItem:.processMouseEvent( ) **J**PopupMenu^
< isPopupTrigger( ), processMouseEvent( ) >
MenuElement.processMouseEvent( )
MenuSelectionManager.processMouseEvent( )
MouseAdapter < mouseClicked( ), mouseEntered( ),
mouseExited( ), mousePressed( ), mouseReleased( ) >
MouseDragGestureRecognizer^ < mouseClicked( ),
mouseDragged( ), mouseEntered( ), mouseExited( ),
mouseMoved( ), mousePressed( ), mouseReleased( ) >
MouseInputAdapter < mouseClicked( ),
mouseDragged( ), mouseEntered( ), mouseExited( ),
mouseMoved( ), mousePressed( ), mouseReleased( ) >
MouseListener: < mouseClicked( ), mouseEntered( ),
mouseExited( ), mousePressed( ), mouseReleased( ) >
MouseMotionAdapter < mouseDragged( ), mouseMoved( ) >
MouseMotionListener: < mouseDragged( ), mouseMoved( ) >
PopupMenuUI^.isPopupTrigger( ) **S**wingUtilities
< convertMouseEvent( ), isLeftMouseButton( ),
isMiddleMouseButton( ), isRightMouseButton( ) >
ToolTipManager^ < mouseDragged( ), mouseMoved( ) >
— returned by: **S**wingUtilities.convertMouseEvent( )
mouseExit( ): Component,
mouseExited( ): **A**WTEventMulticaster **D**efaultCaret^
MouseAdapter, **M**ouseDragGestureRecognizer^
MouseInputAdapter *MouseListener:*
MouseInputAdapter: javax.swing.event
MouseInputListener^: javax.swing.event
— implemented by: **M**ouseInputAdapter
MouseListener: java.awt.event
— extended by: *MouseInputListener^*
— passed to: **A**WTEventMulticaster < add( ), remove( ) >
Component, < addMouseListener( ), removeMouseListener( ) >
— returned by: **A**WTEventMulticaster < add( ), remove( ) >
Component,.getMouseListeners( )
— implemented by: **A**WTEventMulticaster **D**efaultCaret^
MouseAdapter, **M**ouseDragGestureRecognizer^
MouseMotionAdapter: java.awt.event
MouseMotionListener: java.awt.event
— extended by: *MouseInputListener^*
— passed to: **A**WTEventMulticaster < add( ), remove( ) >
Component, < addMouseMotionListener( ),
removeMouseMotionListener( ) >
— returned by: **A**WTEventMulticaster < add( ), remove( ) >
Component,.getMouseMotionListeners( )
— implemented by: **A**WTEventMulticaster
DefaultCaret^ **H**TMLEditorKit.LinkController^
MouseDragGestureRecognizer^ **M**ouseMotionAdapter
ToolTipManager^
mouseMove( ): Component, **R**obot *RobotPeer*
mouseMoved( ): **A**WTEventMulticaster
DefaultCaret^ **H**TMLEditorKit.LinkController^
MouseDragGestureRecognizer^ **M**ouseInputAdapter
MouseMotionAdapter *MouseMotionListener:*
ToolTipManager^
mousePress( ): **R**obot *RobotPeer*
mousePressed( ): **A**WTEventMulticaster **D**efaultCaret^
MouseAdapter, **M**ouseDragGestureRecognizer^
MouseInputAdapter *MouseListener:*
mouseRelease( ): **R**obot *RobotPeer*
mouseReleased( ): **A**WTEventMulticaster **D**efaultCaret^
MouseAdapter, **M**ouseDragGestureRecognizer^
MouseInputAdapter *MouseListener:*
mouseUp( ): Component,
mouseWheel( ): **R**obot *RobotPeer*

MouseWheelEvent^: java.awt.event
— passed to: **A**WTEventMulticaster.mouseWheelMoved( )
Component,.processMouseWheelEvent( )
*MouseWheelListener^*.mouseWheelMoved( )
ScrollPane^.processMouseWheelEvent( )
MouseWheelListener^: java.awt.event
— passed to: **A**WTEventMulticaster < add( ),
remove( ) > Component, < addMouseWheelListener( ),
removeMouseWheelListener( ) >
— returned by: **A**WTEventMulticaster < add( ), remove( ) >
Component,.getMouseWheelListeners( )
— implemented by: **A**WTEventMulticaster
mouseWheelMoved( ): **A**WTEventMulticaster
*MouseWheelListener^*
MOVE: **T**ransferHandler
move( ): Component, **P**oint^ **R**ectangle:
MOVE_CURSOR: **C**ursor **F**rame:
moveCaret( ): **D**efaultCaret^
moveCaretPosition( ): **J**TextComponent:
moveColumn( ): **D**efaultTableColumnModel **J**Table^
TableColumnModel
moveDot( ): *Caret* **D**efaultCaret^ **N**avigationFilter
NavigationFilter.FilterBypass
moveRow( ): **D**efaultTableModel^
moveTo( ): **G**eneralPath
moveToBack( ): **J**InternalFrame^ **J**LayeredPane:
moveToFront( ): **J**InternalFrame^ **J**LayeredPane:
MOVING_TO_PAUSED: **P**rinterStateReason^
MS: *DTDConstants*
MULTI_LINE: AccessibleState^
MULTI_SELECTION_ENABLED_CHANGED_PROPERTY:
JFileChooser^
MultiDoc: javax.print
— passed to: *MultiDocPrintJob^*.print( )
— returned by: *MultiDoc*.next( )
MultiDocPrintJob^: javax.print
— returned by: *MultiDocPrintService^*.createMultiDocPrintJob( )
MultiDocPrintService^: javax.print
— returned by: **P**rintServiceLookup < getMultiDocPrintServices( ),
lookupMultiDocPrintServices( ) >
MultiPixelPackedSampleModel^: java.awt.image
MULTIPLE: **H**TML.Attribute
MULTIPLE_INTERVAL_SELECTION: *ListSelectionModel*
MultipleDocumentHandling^: javax.print.attribute.standard
— fields: **M**ultipleDocumentHandling^
< SEPARATE_DOCUMENTS_COLLATED_COPIES,
SEPARATE_DOCUMENTS_UNCOLLATED_COPIES,
SINGLE_DOCUMENT, SINGLE_DOCUMENT_NEW_SHEET >
MultipleMaster: java.awt.font
MULTISELECTABLE: AccessibleState^
MutableAttributeSet: javax.swing.text
— extended by: *Style^*
— passed to: **H**TMLDocument.HTMLReader^
< addSpecialElement( ), blockOpen( ) >
HTMLDocument.HTMLReader.TagAction,.start( )
HTMLEditorKit^.createInputAttributes( )
HTMLEditorKit.ParserCallback, < handleSimpleTag( ),
handleStartTag( ) > **S**tyleConstants, < setAlignment( ),
setBackground( ), setBidiLevel( ), setBold( ), setComponent( ),
setFirstLineIndent( ), setFontFamily( ), setFontSize( ),
setForeground( ), setIcon( ), setItalic( ), setLeftIndent( ),
setLineSpacing( ), setRightIndent( ), setSpaceAbove( ),
setSpaceBelow( ), setStrikeThrough( ), setSubscript( ),
setSuperscript( ), setTabSet( ), setUnderline( ) >
StyleContext, < readAttributes( ), readAttributeSet( ) >
StyledEditorKit:.createInputAttributes( ) **S**tyleSheet^
< addCSSAttribute( ), addCSSAttributeFromHTML( ) >
— returned by: **J**TextPane^.getInputAttributes( )
StyleContext,.createLargeAttributeSet( )
StyledEditorKit^.getInputAttributes( )
StyleSheet^.createLargeAttributeSet( )

M

—implemented by: **A**bstractDocument.AbstractElement⌣
SimpleAttributeSet
—fields: **H**TMLDocument.HTMLReader^.charAttr
MutableComboBoxModel^: javax.swing
—implemented by: **D**efaultComboBoxModel^
MutableTreeNode^: javax.swing.tree
—passed to: **D**efaultMutableTreeNode⌣ < add( ), insert( ),
remove( ), setParent( ) > **D**efaultTreeModel < insertNodeInto( ),
removeNodeFromParent( ) > ***MutableTreeNode***^ < insert( ),
remove( ), setParent( ) >
—implemented by: **D**efaultMutableTreeNode⌣
—fields: **D**efaultMutableTreeNode⌣.parent
MUTE: **B**ooleanControl.Type^
MYANMAR: **N**umericShaper
N: **H**TML.Attribute
N_RESIZE_CURSOR: **C**ursor **F**rame^
NA_10X13_ENVELOPE: **M**ediaSizeName^
PageAttributes.MediaType^
NA_10x13_ENVELOPE: **M**ediaSize.NA
NA_10X14_ENVELOPE: **M**ediaSizeName^
PageAttributes.MediaType^
NA_10x14_ENVELOPE: **M**ediaSize.NA
NA_10X15_ENVELOPE: **M**ediaSize.NA **M**ediaSizeName^
PageAttributes.MediaType^
NA_5X7: **M**ediaSize.NA **M**ediaSizeName^
NA_6X9_ENVELOPE: **M**ediaSize.NA **M**ediaSizeName^
PageAttributes.MediaType^
NA_7X9_ENVELOPE: **M**ediaSize.NA **M**ediaSizeName^
PageAttributes.MediaType^
NA_8X10: **M**ediaSize.NA **M**ediaSizeName^
NA_9X11_ENVELOPE: **M**ediaSizeName^
PageAttributes.MediaType^
NA_9x11_ENVELOPE: **M**ediaSize.NA
NA_9X12_ENVELOPE: **M**ediaSizeName^
PageAttributes.MediaType^
NA_9x12_ENVELOPE: **M**ediaSize.NA
NA_LEGAL: **M**ediaSizeName^ **P**ageAttributes.MediaType^
NA_LETTER: **M**ediaSizeName^ **P**ageAttributes.MediaType^
NA_LETTER_TRANSPARENT: **M**ediaName^
NA_LETTER_WHITE: **M**ediaName^
NA_NUMBER_10_ENVELOPE: **M**ediaSize.NA
MediaSizeName^ **P**ageAttributes.MediaType^
NA_NUMBER_11_ENVELOPE: **M**ediaSize.NA
MediaSizeName^ **P**ageAttributes.MediaType^
NA_NUMBER_12_ENVELOPE: **M**ediaSize.NA
MediaSizeName^ **P**ageAttributes.MediaType^
NA_NUMBER_14_ENVELOPE: **M**ediaSize.NA
MediaSizeName^ **P**ageAttributes.MediaType^
NA_NUMBER_9_ENVELOPE: **M**ediaSize.NA **M**ediaSizeName^
PageAttributes.MediaType^
name: javax.swing.text.html.parser.**A**ttributeList **C**ursor
DTD javax.swing.text.html.parser.**E**lement
javax.swing.text.html.parser.**E**ntity **F**ont⌣
NAME: **A**ction^ **D**TDConstants **H**TML.Attribute
name2type( ): javax.swing.text.html.parser.**A**ttributeList
javax.swing.text.html.parser.**E**lement
javax.swing.text.html.parser.**E**ntity
NameAttribute: *javax.swing.text.***A**ttributeSet⌣ **S**tyleConstants⌣
NamedNodeMap: org.w3c.dom
—returned by: **I**IOMetadataNode.getAttributes( )
names: **I**mageReaderWriterSpi⌣
NAMES: *DTDConstants*
NATIVE: **J**obAttributes.DialogType^
nativeImageMetadataFormatClassName:
ImageReaderWriterSpi⌣
nativeImageMetadataFormatName: **I**mageReaderWriterSpi⌣
nativeMetadataFormatClassName: **I**IOMetadata
nativeMetadataFormatName: **I**IOMetadata
nativeStreamMetadataFormatClassName:
ImageReaderWriterSpi⌣
nativeStreamMetadataFormatName: **I**mageReaderWriterSpi⌣
NavigationFilter: javax.swing.text

—passed to: **J**TextComponent⌣.setNavigationFilter( )
—returned by: **D**efaultFormatter⌣.getNavigationFilter( )
JFormattedTextField.AbstractFormatter⌣.getNavigationFilter( )
JTextComponent⌣.getNavigationFilter( )
NavigationFilter.FilterBypass: javax.swing.text
—passed to: **N**avigationFilter < moveDot( ), setDot( ) >
NE_RESIZE_CURSOR: **C**ursor **F**rame^
needsCacheFile( ): **I**mageInputStreamSpi^
ImageOutputStreamSpi^
newAttributes: **D**efaultStyledDocument.AttributeUndoableEdit^
newAudioClip( ): **A**pplet⌣
newDataAvailable( ): **D**efaultTableModel^
newLeadSelectionPath: **T**reeSelectionEvent^
NEWLINE: **A**bstractWriter⌣
newmodel: **R**GBImageFilter⌣
newPixels( ): **M**emoryImageSource
newRowsAdded( ): **D**efaultTableModel^
NEWS: **R**eferenceUriSchemesSupported^
next: javax.swing.text.html.parser.**A**ttributeList **C**ontentModel
NEXT: *SwingConstants*
next( ): **C**ardLayout **E**lementIterator **F**latteningPathIterator
HTMLDocument.Iterator *MultiDoc PathIterator* **S**egment
SetOfIntegerSyntax⌣
nextFocus( ): **C**omponent
nextLayout( ): **L**ineBreakMeasurer
nextOffset( ): **L**ineBreakMeasurer
nextTabStop( ): javax.swing.text.**P**aragraphView⌣ **P**lainView⌣
TabExpander **W**rappedPlainView^
nextWordAction: **D**efaultEditorKit⌣
NMTOKEN: *DTDConstants*
NMTOKENS: *DTDConstants*
NNTP: **R**eferenceUriSchemesSupported^
NO_MORE_EVENTS: **P**rintJobEvent^
NO_OPTION: **J**OptionPane^
NO_ORIENTATION: *Adjustable*
NO_SUCH_PAGE: *Printable*
NO_SYNC: **S**equencer.SyncMode
NOBUTTON: **M**ouseEvent⌣
Node: org.w3c.dom
—passed to: **I**IOInvalidTreeException( ) **I**IOMetadata
< mergeTree( ), setFromTree( ) > **I**IOMetadataNode
< appendChild( ), insertBefore( ), removeChild( ), replaceChild( ) >
—returned by: **I**IOInvalidTreeException^.getOffendingNode( )
IIOMetadata.getAsTree( ) **I**IOMetadataNode < appendChild( ),
cloneNode( ), getFirstChild( ), getLastChild( ), getNextSibling( ),
getParentNode( ), getPreviousSibling( ), insertBefore( ), item( ),
removeChild( ), replaceChild( ) >
—fields: **I**IOInvalidTreeException^.offendingNode
nodeChanged( ): **D**efaultTreeModel
nodeDimensions: **A**bstractLayoutCache⌣
NodeList: org.w3c.dom
—returned by: **I**IOMetadataNode < getChildNodes( ),
getElementsByTagName( ), getElementsByTagNameNS( ) >
—implemented by: **I**IOMetadataNode
nodesChanged( ): **D**efaultTreeModel
nodeStructureChanged( ): **D**efaultTreeModel
nodesWereInserted( ): **D**efaultTreeModel
nodesWereRemoved( ): **D**efaultTreeModel
noFocusBorder: **D**efaultListCellRenderer⌣
DefaultTableCellRenderer⌣
NOFRAMES: **H**TML.Tag⌣
NOHREF: **H**TML.Attribute⌣
NONE: **C**ompression^ **F**inishings^ **G**ridBagConstraints
JobAttributes.DialogType^ **J**obSheets^ **J**RootPane^
TransferHandler
NONE_OPTION: **D**ebugGraphics^
NoninvertibleTransformException: java.awt.geom
—thrown by: **A**ffineTransform < createInverse( ),
inverseTransform( ) >
NORESIZE: **H**TML.Attribute
NORMAL: **F**rame⌣ **P**ageAttributes.PrintQualityType^
PrintQuality^

O

DefaultComboBoxModel^ < addElement( ),
DefaultComboBoxModel( ), getIndexOf( ), insertElementAt( ),
removeElement( ), setSelectedItem( ) > DefaultListCellRenderer^
< firePropertyChange( ), getListCellRendererComponent( ) >
DefaultListModel^ < add( ), addElement( ), contains( ),
copyInto( ), indexOf( ), insertElementAt( ), lastIndexOf( ),
removeElement( ), set( ), setElementAt( ) >
DefaultMutableTreeNode_ < DefaultMutableTreeNode( ),
setUserObject( ) > DefaultTableCellRenderer^
< firePropertyChange( ), getTableCellRendererComponent( ),
setValue( ) > DefaultTableColumnModel.getColumnIndex( )
DefaultTableModel^ < addColumn( ), addRow( ),
convertToVector( ), DefaultTableModel( ), insertRow( ),
setColumnIdentifiers( ), setDataVector( ) > DefaultTreeCellEditor
< determineOffset( ), getTreeCellEditorComponent( ) >
DefaultTreeCellRenderer^ < firePropertyChange( ),
getTreeCellRendererComponent( ) > DefaultTreeModel
< fireTreeNodesChanged( ), fireTreeNodesInserted( ),
fireTreeNodesRemoved( ), fireTreeStructureChanged( ),
getChild( ), getChildCount( ), getIndexOfChild( ), isLeaf( ),
nodesWereRemoved( ), valueForPathChanged( ) >
*javax.swing.text.Document_* < getProperty( ), putProperty( ) >
DragGestureEvent^.toArray( ) DTD.defContentModel( )
EnumControl^ < EnumControl( ), setValue( ) > Event( )
GapVector_.replace( ) Graphics2D^.setRenderingHint( )
GridBagLayout.addLayoutComponent( ) *Highlighter*
< changeHighlight( ), removeHighlight( ) >
HTMLDocument^.getElement( ) HTMLFrameHyperlinkEvent( )
HyperlinkEvent( ) IIOMetadataFormatImpl.addObjectValue( )
IIOMetadataNode.setUserObject( )
ImageInputStreamSpi^.createInputStreamInstance( )
ImageIO < createImageInputStream( ),
createImageOutputStream( ), getImageReaders( ) >
ImageOutputStreamSpi^.createOutputStreamInstance( )
ImageReader.setInput( ) ImageReaderSpi^ < canDecodeInput( ),
createReaderInstance( ) > ImageWriter.setOutput( )
ImageWriterSpi^.createWriterInstance( ) InputMap^.put( )
InvocationEvent( ) ItemEvent( ) JApplet^.addImpl( )
JComboBox^ < addItem( ), configureEditor( ), insertItemAt( ),
JComboBox( ), removeItem( ), setPrototypeDisplayValue( ),
setSelectedItem( ) > JComponent^ < firePropertyChange( ),
fireVetoableChange( ), getClientProperty( ), putClientProperty( ) >
JDialog^.addImpl( ) JEditorPane^.read( )
JFormattedTextField^ < JFormattedTextField( ), setValue( ) >
JFormattedTextField.AbstractFormatter_.valueToString( )
JFrame^.addImpl( ) JInternalFrame^.addImpl( )
JLayeredPane^.addImpl( ) JList^ < JList( ), setListData( ),
setPrototypeCellValue( ), setSelectedValue( ) > JOptionPane^
< JOptionPane( ), setInitialSelectionValue( ), setInitialValue( ),
setInputValue( ), setMessage( ), setOptions( ),
setSelectionValues( ), setValue( ), showConfirmDialog( ),
showInputDialog( ), showInternalConfirmDialog( ),
showInternalInputDialog( ), showInternalMessageDialog( ),
showInternalOptionDialog( ), showMessageDialog( ),
showOptionDialog( ) > JRootPane^.addImpl( )
JRootPane.RootLayout.addLayoutComponent( )
JSpinner^.setValue( ) JSplitPane^.addImpl( )
JTable^ < getColumn( ), JTable( ), setValueAt( ) >
JTextComponent^.read( ) JToolBar^.addImpl( )
JTree^ < convertValueToText( ), createTreeModel( ),
JTree( ) > JTree.DynamicUtilTreeNode^
< createChildren( ), JTree.DynamicUtilTreeNode( ) >
JViewport^ < addImpl( ), firePropertyChange( ) >
JWindow^.addImpl( ) KeyboardFocusManager_
< firePropertyChange( ), fireVetoableChange( ) >
LayoutManager2^.addLayoutComponent( )
ListCellRenderer.getListCellRendererComponent( )
ListDataEvent( ) ListSelectionEvent( )
LookAndFeel < getDesktopPropertyValue( ),
loadKeyBindings( ), makeComponentInputMap( ),
makeInputMap( ), makeKeyBindings( ) > MenuEvent( )
MutableAttributeSet^ < addAttribute( ), removeAttribute( ) >

MutableComboBoxModel^ < addElement( ), insertElementAt( ),
removeElement( ) > *MutableTreeNode*^.setUserObject( )
OverlayLayout.addLayoutComponent( ) ParameterBlock
< add( ), addSource( ), set( ), setSource( ) >
PopupMenuEvent( ) PrintEvent( ) *PrintService*_.equals( )
ProgressMonitor( ) ProgressMonitorInputStream( )
Raster_.getDataElements( ) *Renderer*.setValue( )
RenderingHints < containsKey( ), containsValue( ),
get( ), put( ), remove( ), RenderingHints( ) >
RenderingHints.Key.isCompatibleValue( ) SampleModel_
< getDataElements( ), setDataElements( ) >
ScrollPane^.addImpl( ) ServiceRegistry_ < contains( ),
deregisterServiceProvider( ), registerServiceProvider( ),
setOrdering( ), unsetOrdering( ) > *ServiceRegistry.Filter*.filter( )
SimpleAttributeSet < addAttribute( ), containsAttribute( ),
getAttribute( ), isDefined( ), removeAttribute( ) > SimpleDoc( )
SpinnerListModel( ) *SpinnerModel*.setValue( )
SpringLayout.addLayoutComponent( ) StyleContext_
< addAttribute( ), getStaticAttribute( ), getStaticAttributeKey( ),
registerStaticAttributeKey( ), removeAttribute( ) >
StyleContext.NamedStyle < addAttribute( ), containsAttribute( ),
getAttribute( ), isDefined( ), removeAttribute( ) >
StyleContext.SmallAttributeSet < containsAttribute( ),
getAttribute( ), isDefined( ), StyleContext.SmallAttributeSet( ) >
SwingPropertyChangeSupport( ) SwingUtilities.notifyAction( )
TableCellEditor^.getTableCellEditorComponent( )
TableCellRenderer.getTableCellRendererComponent( )
TableColumn < setHeaderValue( ), setIdentifier( ) >
TableColumnModel.getColumnIndex( ) *TableModel*.setValueAt( )
TextEvent( ) Toolkit.setDesktopProperty( )
TreeCellEditor^.getTreeCellEditorComponent( )
TreeCellRenderer.getTreeCellRendererComponent( )
TreeExpansionEvent( ) *TreeModel* < getChild( ),
getChildCount( ), getIndexOfChild( ), isLeaf( ),
valueForPathChanged( ) > TreeModelEvent( ) TreePath
< pathByAddingChild( ), TreePath( ) > TreeSelectionEvent^
< cloneWithSource( ), TreeSelectionEvent( ) > UIDefaults^
< firePropertyChange( ), get( ), getBoolean( ), getBorder( ),
getColor( ), getDimension( ), getFont( ), getIcon( ), getInsets( ),
getInt( ), getString( ), putDefaults( ), UIDefaults( ) >
UIDefaults.LazyInputMap( ) UIDefaults.ProxyLazyValue( )
UIManager < get( ), getBoolean( ), getBorder( ), getColor( ),
getDimension( ), getFont( ), getIcon( ), getInsets( ),
getInt( ), getString( ), put( ) > UndoableEditEvent( )
UndoableEditSupport( ) WritableRaster^.setDataElements( )

— returned by: AbstractAction_ < clone( ), getKeys( ),
getValue( ) > AbstractButton^.getSelectedObjects( )
AbstractDocument_.getProperty( )
AbstractDocument.AbstractElement_.getAttribute( )
AccessibleHyperlink_ < getAccessibleActionAnchor( ),
getAccessibleActionObject( ) >
AccessibleKeyBinding.getAccessibleKeyBinding( )
AccessibleRelation^.getTarget( )
AccessibleResourceBundle^.getContents( ) *Action*^.getValue( )
ActionMap_ < allKeys( ), keys( ) > AffineTransform.clone( )
Area.clone( ) *javax.swing.text.AttributeSet*_.getAttribute( )
AWTKeyStroke_.readResolve( ) BufferCapabilities.clone( )
BufferedImage^.getProperty( ) *CellEditor*_.getCellEditorValue( )
Checkbox^.getSelectedObjects( )
CheckboxMenuItem^.getSelectedObjects( )
Choice^.getSelectedObjects( )
ColorModel_.getDataElements( ) *ComboBoxEditor*.getItem( )
ComboBoxModel^.getSelectedItem( )
Component_.getTreeLock( )
ContextualRenderedImageFactory^.getProperty( )
CubicCurve2D_.clone( ) DataFlavor.clone( )
DefaultButtonModel_.getSelectedObjects( )
DefaultCellEditor.EditorDelegate.getCellEditorValue( )
DefaultComboBoxModel^.getSelectedItem( )
DefaultFormatter^.clone( ) DefaultListModel^ < elementAt( ),
firstElement( ), get( ), lastElement( ), remove( ), set( ),
toArray( ) > DefaultListSelectionModel.clone( )

DefaultMutableTreeNode‿ < clone( ), getUserObject( ),
getUserObjectPath( ) > DefaultTreeCellEditor.getCellEditorValue( )
DefaultTreeModel < getChild( ), getRoot( ) >
DefaultTreeSelectionModel‿.clone( ) Dimension2D‿.clone( )
Doc.getPrintData( ) javax.swing.text.Document‿.getProperty( )
DragGestureEvent^.toArray( )
DropTargetContext.TransferableProxy.getTransferData( )
EditorKit‿.clone( ) ElementIterator.clone( ) EnumControl^
< getValue( ), getValues( ) > EnumSyntax < clone( ),
readResolve( ) > EventListenerList.getListenerList( )
GapContent^.allocateArray( ) GapVector‿ < allocateArray( ),
getArray( ) > GeneralPath.clone( ) GlyphView^.clone( )
Graphics2D^.getRenderingHint( ) GridBagConstraints.clone( )
Highlighter.addHighlight( ) ICC_Profile‿.readResolve( )
IIOMetadataFormat < getObjectDefaultValue( ),
getObjectEnumerations( ) > IIOMetadataFormatImpl
< getObjectDefaultValue( ), getObjectEnumerations( ) >
IIOMetadataNode.getUserObject( ) Image‿.getProperty( )
ImageCapabilities.clone( ) ImageFilter‿.clone( )
ImageReader.getInput( ) ImageWriter.getOutput( )
InputContext.getInputMethodControlObject( )
InputMap‿.get( ) InputMethod.getControlObject( )
Insets‿.clone( ) ItemEvent^.getItem( )
ItemSelectable‿.getSelectedObjects( ) JComboBox^
< getItemAt( ), getPrototypeDisplayValue( ), getSelectedItem( ),
getSelectedObjects( ) > JComponent^.getClientProperty( )
JFormattedTextField^.getValue( )
JFormattedTextField.AbstractFormatter‿ < clone( ),
stringToValue( ) > JList^ < getPrototypeCellValue( ),
getSelectedValue( ), getSelectedValues( ) > JobAttributes.clone( )
JOptionPane^ < getInitialSelectionValue( ), getInitialValue( ),
getInputValue( ), getMessage( ), getOptions( ),
getSelectionValues( ), getValue( ), showInputDialog( ),
showInternalInputDialog( ) > JSpinner^ < getNextValue( ),
getPreviousValue( ), getValue( ) > JTable^.getValueAt( )
JTree^.getLastSelectedPathComponent( ) Kernel.clone( )
Line2D.clone( ) java.awt.List^.getSelectedObjects( )
ListModel‿.getElementAt( ) LookAndFeel
< getDesktopPropertyValue( ), makeIcon( ) >
MediaTracker < getErrorsAny( ), getErrorsID( ) >
MenuComponent‿.getTreeLock( ) MidiMessage‿.clone( )
PageAttributes.clone( ) PageFormat.clone( )
Paper.clone( ) ParameterBlock < clone( ),
getObjectParameter( ), getSource( ), shallowClone( ) >
PixelGrabber.getPixels( ) Point2D‿.clone( ) PrintService‿
< getDefaultAttributeValue( ), getSupportedAttributeValues( ) >
QuadCurve2D‿.clone( ) Raster‿.getDataElements( )
RectangularShape‿.clone( ) RenderableImage.getProperty( )
RenderableImageOp.getProperty( ) RenderContext.clone( )
RenderedImage‿.getProperty( ) RenderingHints < clone( ),
get( ), put( ), remove( ) > SampleModel‿.getDataElements( )
Segment.clone( ) ServiceRegistry‿.getServiceProviderByClass( )
ServiceUIFactory.getUI( ) SimpleAttributeSet
< clone( ), getAttribute( ) > SimpleDoc.getPrintData( )
SoundbankResource‿.getData( ) SpinnerModel‿
< getNextValue( ), getPreviousValue( ), getValue( ) >
StringSelection.getTransferData( ) StyleContext‿
< getStaticAttribute( ), getStaticAttributeKey( ) >
StyleContext.NamedStyle.getAttribute( )
StyleContext.SmallAttributeSet < clone( ), getAttribute( ) >
TableColumn < getHeaderValue( ), getIdentifier( ) >
TableModel‿.getValueAt( ) TextAttribute^.readResolve( )
TextLayout.clone( ) TextMeasurer.clone( ) Toolkit
< getDesktopProperty( ), lazilyLoadDesktopProperty( ) >
Transferable.getTransferData( ) TreeModel < getChild( ),
getRoot( ) > TreeModelEvent^ < getChildren( ), getPath( ) >
TreePath < getLastPathComponent( ), getPath( ),
getPathComponent( ) > TreeSelectionEvent^.cloneWithSource( )
UIDefaults^.get( ) UIDefaults.ActiveValue.createValue( )
UIDefaults.LazyInputMap.createValue( )
UIDefaults.LazyValue.createValue( )

UIDefaults.ProxyLazyValue.createValue( ) UIManager < get( ),
put( ) >
—fields: javax.swing.text.AttributeSet‿ < NameAttribute,
ResolveAttribute > ContentModel.content
DefaultCellEditor.EditorDelegate.value
DefaultMutableTreeNode‿.userObject
javax.swing.text.html.parser.Element.data Event
< arg, target > EventListenerList.listenerList
HTMLEditorKit.ParserCallback‿.IMPLIED
Image‿.UndefinedProperty ImageReader.input
ImageWriter.output InvocationEvent^.notifier
JComboBox^.selectedItemReminder JOptionPane^
< initialSelectionValue, initialValue, inputValue, message,
options, selectionValues, UNINITIALIZED_VALUE,
value > JTree.DynamicUtilTreeNode^.childValue
RenderingHints < VALUE_ALPHA_INTERPOLATION_DEFAULT,
VALUE_ALPHA_INTERPOLATION_QUALITY,
VALUE_ALPHA_INTERPOLATION_SPEED,
VALUE_ANTIALIAS_DEFAULT, VALUE_ANTIALIAS_OFF,
VALUE_ANTIALIAS_ON, VALUE_COLOR_RENDER_DEFAULT,
VALUE_COLOR_RENDER_QUALITY,
VALUE_COLOR_RENDER_SPEED, VALUE_DITHER_DEFAULT,
VALUE_DITHER_DISABLE, VALUE_DITHER_ENABLE,
VALUE_FRACTIONALMETRICS_DEFAULT,
VALUE_FRACTIONALMETRICS_OFF,
VALUE_FRACTIONALMETRICS_ON,
VALUE_INTERPOLATION_BICUBIC,
VALUE_INTERPOLATION_BILINEAR,
VALUE_INTERPOLATION_NEAREST_NEIGHBOR,
VALUE_RENDER_DEFAULT, VALUE_RENDER_QUALITY,
VALUE_RENDER_SPEED, VALUE_STROKE_DEFAULT,
VALUE_STROKE_NORMALIZE, VALUE_STROKE_PURE,
VALUE_TEXT_ANTIALIAS_DEFAULT, VALUE_TEXT_ANTIALIAS_OFF,
VALUE_TEXT_ANTIALIAS_ON > ReplicateScaleFilter^.outpixbuf
StyleConstants‿ < Alignment, Background, BidiLevel, Bold,
ComponentAttribute, ComposedTextAttribute, FirstLineIndent,
FontFamily, FontSize, Foreground, IconAttribute, Italic,
LeftIndent, LineSpacing, ModelAttribute, NameAttribute,
Orientation, ResolveAttribute, RightIndent, SpaceAbove,
SpaceBelow, StrikeThrough, Subscript, Superscript,
TabSet, Underline > StyleConstants.CharacterConstants^
< Background, BidiLevel, Bold, ComponentAttribute,
Family, Foreground, IconAttribute, Italic, Size,
StrikeThrough, Subscript, Superscript, Underline >
StyleConstants.ColorConstants^ < Background, Foreground >
StyleConstants.FontConstants^ < Bold, Family, Italic,
Size > StyleConstants.ParagraphConstants^ < Alignment,
FirstLineIndent, LeftIndent, LineSpacing, Orientation,
RightIndent, SpaceAbove, SpaceBelow, TabSet > TableColumn
< headerValue, identifier > TreeModelEvent^.children
UndoableEditSupport.realSource

ObjectInput^: java.io
— passed to: DataFlavor.readExternal( )
ObjectInputStream^: java.io
— passed to: StyleContext‿ < readAttributes( ), readAttributeSet( ) >
ObjectOutput^: java.io
— passed to: DataFlavor.writeExternal( )
ObjectOutputStream^: java.io
— passed to: AWTEventMulticaster < save( ), saveInternal( ) >
StyleContext‿ < writeAttributes( ), writeAttributeSet( ) >
ObjectStreamException^: java.io
— thrown by: AWTKeyStroke‿.readResolve( )
EnumSyntax‿.readResolve( ) ICC_Profile‿.readResolve( )
ObjectView^: javax.swing.text.html
oEnd: javax.swing.text.html.parser.Element
offendingNode: IIOInvalidTreeException^
offset: DataBuffer‿ DefaultTreeCellEditor Segment
offsetRequested( ): BadLocationException
offsets: DataBuffer‿
OK_CANCEL_OPTION: JOptionPane^
OK_OPTION: JOptionPane^

O

OL: **H**TML.Tag⌄
oldLeadSelectionPath: **T**reeSelectionEvent^
omitEnd( ): javax.swing.text.html.parser.**E**lement
omitStart( ): javax.swing.text.html.parser.**E**lement
onDeregistration( ): **I**IOServiceProvider⌄ *RegisterableService*
ONE_SIDED: **J**obAttributes.SidesType^ **S**ides^
ONE_TOUCH_EXPANDABLE_PROPERTY: **J**SplitPane^
oneTouchExpandable: **J**SplitPane^
onRegistration( ): **I**IOServiceProvider⌄ *RegisterableService*
OPAQUE: **A**ccessibleState^ *Transparency*⌄
OPC_LIFE_OVER: **P**rinterStateReason^
OPC_NEAR_EOL: **P**rinterStateReason^
OPEN: **A**rc2D⌃ **L**ineEvent.Type
open( ): *Line*⌄ *MidiDevice*⌄
OPEN_DIALOG: **J**FileChooser^
openFrame( ): **D**efaultDesktopManager *DesktopManager*
openIcon: **D**efaultTreeCellRenderer^
OpenType: java.awt.font
OPTION: **H**TML.Tag⌄
Option: javax.swing.text.html
—passed to: **H**TMLWriter^.writeOption( )
OPTION_PANE: **A**ccessibleRole^
OPTION_TYPE_PROPERTY: **J**OptionPane^
OptionPaneUI^: javax.swing.plaf
—passed to: **J**OptionPane^.setUI( )
—returned by: **J**OptionPane^.getUI( )
options: **J**OptionPane^
OPTIONS_PROPERTY: **J**OptionPane^
optionType: **J**OptionPane^
orange: **C**olor⌄
ORANGE: **C**olor⌄
orientation: **J**ProgressBar^ **J**ScrollBar⌃ **J**Slider^ **J**SplitPane^
Orientation: **S**tyleConstants⌄
ORIENTATION_PROPERTY: **J**SplitPane^
OrientationRequested^: javax.print.attribute.standard
—fields: **O**rientationRequested^ < LANDSCAPE, PORTRAIT, REVERSE_LANDSCAPE, REVERSE_PORTRAIT >
OriginateDirection: **D**efaultStyledDocument.ElementSpec
originatingProvider: **I**mageReader **I**mageWriter
origmodel: **R**GBImageFilter⌃
ORIYA: **N**umericShaper
oStart: javax.swing.text.html.parser.**E**lement
OTHER: **P**rinterStateReason^
OUT_BOTTOM: **R**ectangle2D⌃
OUT_LEFT: **R**ectangle2D⌃
OUT_RIGHT: **R**ectangle2D⌃
OUT_TOP: **R**ectangle2D⌃
outcode( ): **R**ectangle2D⌃
OUTLINE_DRAG_MODE: **J**DesktopPane^
outpixbuf: **R**eplicateScaleFilter⌃
output: **I**mageWriter
output( ): **A**bstractWriter⌄
OUTPUT_AREA_ALMOST_FULL: **P**rinterStateReason^
OUTPUT_AREA_FULL: **P**rinterStateReason^
OUTPUT_TRAY_MISSING: **P**rinterStateReason^
outputClass: **I**mageOutputStreamSpi^
OutputDeviceAssigned^: javax.print.attribute.standard
OutputStream: java.io
—passed to: **A**udioFileWriter.write( ) **A**udioSystem.write( )
EditorKit⌄.write( ) **F**ileCacheImageOutputStream( )
ICC_Profile⌄.write( ) **I**mageIO.write( )
MemoryCacheImageOutputStream( ) **M**idiFileWriter.write( )
MidiSystem.write( ) **S**treamPrintService( )
StreamPrintServiceFactory.getPrintService( )
—returned by: **S**treamPrintService.getOutputStream( )
outputTypes: **I**mageWriterSpi^
outsideBorder: **C**ompoundBorder⌃
OVER: **D**ragSourceContext
OverlayLayout: javax.swing
owner: **C**lipboard
P: **H**TML.Tag⌄
p: **D**TD

pack( ): **J**InternalFrame^ **J**PopupMenu^ **W**indow⌃
PackedColorModel^: java.awt.image
—subclasses: **D**irectColorModel^
PADDING: **C**SS.Attribute
PADDING_BOTTOM: **C**SS.Attribute
PADDING_LEFT: **C**SS.Attribute
PADDING_RIGHT: **C**SS.Attribute
PADDING_TOP: **C**SS.Attribute
PAGE_AXIS: **B**oxLayout
PAGE_END: **B**orderLayout **G**ridBagConstraints
PAGE_EXISTS: *Printable*
PAGE_START: **B**orderLayout **G**ridBagConstraints
PAGE_TAB: **A**ccessibleRole^
PAGE_TAB_LIST: **A**ccessibleRole^
PAGEABLE: **D**ocFlavor.SERVICE_FORMATTED^
Pageable: java.awt.print
—passed to: **P**rinterJob.setPageable( )
—implemented by: **B**ook
PageAttributes: java.awt
—passed to: **P**ageAttributes < PageAttributes( ), set( ) >
Toolkit.getPrintJob( )
PageAttributes.ColorType^: java.awt
—passed to: **P**ageAttributes < PageAttributes( ), setColor( ) >
—returned by: **P**ageAttributes.getColor( )
—fields: **P**ageAttributes.ColorType^ < COLOR, MONOCHROME >
PageAttributes.MediaType^: java.awt
—passed to: **P**ageAttributes < PageAttributes( ), setMedia( ) >
—returned by: **P**ageAttributes.getMedia( )
—fields: **P**ageAttributes.MediaType^ < A, A0, A1, A10, A2, A3, A4, A5, A6, A7, A8, A9, B, B0, B1, B10, B2, B3, B4, B5, B6, B7, B8, B9, C, C0, C1, C10, C2, C3, C4, C5, C6, C7, C8, C9, D, E, ENV_10, ENV_10X13, ENV_10X14, ENV_10X15, ENV_11, ENV_12, ENV_14, ENV_6X9, ENV_7X9, ENV_9, ENV_9X11, ENV_9X12, ENV_INVITE, ENV_ITALY, ENV_MONARCH, ENV_PERSONAL, EXECUTIVE, FOLIO, INVITE, INVITE_ENVELOPE, INVOICE, ISO_2A0, ISO_4A0, ISO_A0, ISO_A1, ISO_A10, ISO_A2, ISO_A3, ISO_A4, ISO_A5, ISO_A6, ISO_A7, ISO_A8, ISO_A9, ISO_B0, ISO_B1, ISO_B10, ISO_B2, ISO_B3, ISO_B4, ISO_B4_ENVELOPE, ISO_B5, ISO_B5_ENVELOPE, ISO_B6, ISO_B7, ISO_B8, ISO_B9, ISO_C0, ISO_C0_ENVELOPE, ISO_C1, ISO_C10, ISO_C10_ENVELOPE, ISO_C1_ENVELOPE, ISO_C2, ISO_C2_ENVELOPE, ISO_C3, ISO_C3_ENVELOPE, ISO_C4, ISO_C4_ENVELOPE, ISO_C5, ISO_C5_ENVELOPE, ISO_C6, ISO_C6_ENVELOPE, ISO_C7, ISO_C7_ENVELOPE, ISO_C8, ISO_C8_ENVELOPE, ISO_C9, ISO_C9_ENVELOPE, ISO_DESIGNATED_LONG, ISO_DESIGNATED_LONG_ENVELOPE, ITALY, ITALY_ENVELOPE, JIS_B0, JIS_B1, JIS_B10, JIS_B2, JIS_B3, JIS_B4, JIS_B5, JIS_B6, JIS_B7, JIS_B8, JIS_B9, LEDGER, LEGAL, LETTER, MONARCH, MONARCH_ENVELOPE, NA_10X13_ENVELOPE, NA_10X14_ENVELOPE, NA_10X15_ENVELOPE, NA_6X9_ENVELOPE, NA_7X9_ENVELOPE, NA_9X11_ENVELOPE, NA_9X12_ENVELOPE, NA_LEGAL, NA_LETTER, NA_NUMBER_10_ENVELOPE, NA_NUMBER_11_ENVELOPE, NA_NUMBER_12_ENVELOPE, NA_NUMBER_14_ENVELOPE, NA_NUMBER_9_ENVELOPE, NOTE, PERSONAL, PERSONAL_ENVELOPE, QUARTO, STATEMENT, TABLOID >
PageAttributes.OrientationRequestedType^: java.awt
—passed to: **P**ageAttributes < PageAttributes( ), setOrientationRequested( ) >
—returned by: **P**ageAttributes.getOrientationRequested( )
—fields: **P**ageAttributes.OrientationRequestedType^ < LANDSCAPE, PORTRAIT >
PageAttributes.OriginType^: java.awt
—passed to: **P**ageAttributes < PageAttributes( ), setOrigin( ) >
—returned by: **P**ageAttributes.getOrigin( )
—fields: **P**ageAttributes.OriginType^ < PHYSICAL, PRINTABLE >
PageAttributes.PrintQualityType^: java.awt
—passed to: **P**ageAttributes < PageAttributes( ), setPrintQuality( ) >
—returned by: **P**ageAttributes.getPrintQuality( )

Class *Interface* ^—has superclass ⌄—has subclass package—see other volume

—fields: **P**ageAttributes.PrintQualityType^ < DRAFT, HIGH, NORMAL >
pageDialog(): **P**rinterJob
pageDownAction: **D**efaultEditorKit⌇
PageFormat: java.awt.print
—passed to: **B**ook < append( ), setPage( ) > **P**rintable.print( )
 PrinterJob < defaultPage( ), pageDialog( ), setPrintable( ),
 validatePage( ) >
—returned by: **B**ook.getPageFormat( ) **P**ageable.getPageFormat( )
 PrinterJob < defaultPage( ), pageDialog( ), validatePage( ) >
PageRanges^: javax.print.attribute.standard
PagesPerMinute^: javax.print.attribute.standard
PagesPerMinuteColor^: javax.print.attribute.standard
pageUpAction: **D**efaultEditorKit⌇
PAINT: **P**aintEvent^
Paint^: java.awt
—passed to: **G**raphics2D^.setPaint( )
—returned by: **G**raphics2D^.getPaint( )
—implemented by: **C**olor⌇ **G**radientPaint **T**exturePaint
paint(): **C**aret **C**omponent⌇ *ComponentPeer*⌇ **C**omponentUI⌇
 DefaultCaret^ **G**lyphView.GlyphPainter **H**ighlighter
 Highlighter.HighlightPainter **S**tyleSheet.BoxPainter
 StyleSheet.ListPainter **V**iew
PAINT_EVENT_MASK: **A**WTEvent⌇
PAINT_FIRST: **P**aintEvent^
PAINT_LAST: **P**aintEvent^
paintAll(): **C**omponent⌇
paintBorder: **J**ProgressBar^
paintBorder(): **A**bstractBorder⌇ *Border* **B**orderUIResource
 JComponent⌇
paintChild(): **B**oxView⌇
paintChildren(): **A**syncBoxView.ChildLocator **J**Component⌇
paintComponent(): **C**ellRendererPane^ **J**Component⌇
 SwingUtilities
paintComponents(): **C**ontainer⌇
PaintContext: java.awt
—returned by: **C**olor⌇.createContext( )
 GradientPaint.createContext( ) *Paint*^.createContext( )
 TexturePaint.createContext( )
paintDirtyRegions(): **R**epaintManager
PaintEvent^: java.awt.event
—passed to: *ComponentPeer*⌇.coalescePaintEvent( )
paintIcon(): *Icon* **I**conUIResource **I**mageIcon
paintImmediately(): **J**Component⌇
paintLayer(): **L**ayeredHighlighter.LayerPainter⌇
paintLayeredHighlights(): **L**ayeredHighlighter⌇
paintLoweredBevel(): **B**evelBorder⌇
paintRaisedBevel(): **B**evelBorder⌇
paintString: **J**ProgressBar^
PALETTE_LAYER: **J**LayeredPane⌇
PAN: **F**loatControl.Type^
PANEL: **A**ccessibleRole^
Panel⌇: java.awt
—subclasses: **A**pplet⌇
—descendents: **J**Applet^
—passed to: **P**anel.AccessibleAWTPanel( ) **T**oolkit.createPanel( )
Panel.AccessibleAWTPanel⌇: java.awt
—subclasses: **A**pplet.AccessibleApplet⌇
—descendents: **J**Applet.AccessibleJApplet^
PANEL_UI: **S**erviceUIFactory
PanelPeer^: java.awt.peer
—returned by: **T**oolkit.createPanel( )
PanelUI^: javax.swing.plaf
—passed to: **J**Panel⌇.setUI( )
—returned by: **J**Panel⌇.getUI( )
Paper: java.awt.print
—passed to: **P**ageFormat.setPaper( )
—returned by: **P**ageFormat.getPaper( )
PARA_INDENT_LEFT: **H**TMLEditorKit^
PARA_INDENT_RIGHT: **H**TMLEditorKit^
ParagraphElementName: **A**bstractDocument⌇
ParagraphView⌇: javax.swing.text

—subclasses: javax.swing.text.html.**P**aragraphView^
ParagraphView^: javax.swing.text.html
—passed to: javax.swing.text.**P**aragraphView⌇.adjustRow( )
PARAM: **H**TML.Tag⌇
param: **D**TD
PARAMETER: *DTDConstants*
ParameterBlock: java.awt.image.renderable
—passed to: *ContextualRenderedImageFactory*^ < create( ),
 getBounds2D( ), getProperty( ), mapRenderContext( ) >
 RenderableImageOp < **R**enderableImageOp( ),
 setParameterBlock( ) > *RenderedImageFactory*⌇.create( )
—returned by: **P**arameterBlock < add( ), addSource( ), set( ),
 setSource( ) > **R**enderableImageOp < getParameterBlock( ),
 setParameterBlock( ) >
parameters: **P**arameterBlock
paramString(): **A**WTEvent⌇ **C**omponent⌇ **E**vent
 MenuComponent⌇ **M**enuShortcut **S**crollPaneAdjustable
parent: **D**efaultMutableTreeNode⌇ **R**aster⌇
PARENT_CHANGED: **H**ierarchyEvent^
parentTag: **H**TMLEditorKit.InsertHTMLTextAction^
parse(): **H**TMLEditorKit.Parser⌇
 javax.swing.text.html.parser.**P**arser⌇
parseBuffer: **H**TMLDocument.HTMLReader^
parseDTDMarkup(): javax.swing.text.html.parser.**P**arser⌇
ParseException: java.text
—thrown by: **J**FormattedTextField^.commitEdit( )
 JFormattedTextField.AbstractFormatter⌇ < stringToValue( ),
 valueToString( ) > **J**Spinner^.commitEdit( )
 JSpinner.DefaultEditor^.commitEdit( ) **M**askFormatter^
 < **M**askFormatter( ), setMask( ) >
parseMarkupDeclarations():
 javax.swing.text.html.parser.**P**arser⌇
Parser⌇: javax.swing.text.html.parser
—subclasses: **D**ocumentParser^
ParserDelegator^: javax.swing.text.html.parser
passComplete(): *IIOReadUpdateListener*^
passStarted(): *IIOReadUpdateListener*^
PASSWORD_TEXT: **A**ccessibleRole^
PasswordView: javax.swing.text
paste(): *AccessibleEditableText*^ **J**TextComponent⌇
 JTextComponent.AccessibleJTextComponent⌇
pasteAction: **D**efaultEditorKit⌇
Patch: javax.sound.midi
—passed to: **I**nstrument( ) *Soundbank*.getInstrument( )
 Synthesizer^ < loadInstruments( ), unloadInstruments( ) >
—returned by: **I**nstrument^.getPatch( ) **S**equence.getPatchList( )
path: **T**reeExpansionEvent^ **T**reeModelEvent^
pathByAddingChild(): **T**reePath
pathFromAncestorEnumeration(): **D**efaultMutableTreeNode⌇
PathIterator: java.awt.geom
—passed to: **F**latteningPathIterator( ) **G**eneralPath.append( )
—returned by: **A**rea.getPathIterator( )
 CubicCurve2D⌇.getPathIterator( )
 GeneralPath.getPathIterator( ) **L**ine2D⌇.getPathIterator( )
 Polygon.getPathIterator( ) **Q**uadCurve2D⌇.getPathIterator( )
 RectangularShape⌇.getPathIterator( ) *Shape*.getPathIterator( )
—implemented by: **F**latteningPathIterator
paths: **T**reeSelectionEvent^
PAUSE: **E**vent
PAUSED: **P**rinterStateReason^
pcdata: **D**TD
PCL: **D**ocFlavor.BYTE_ARRAY^ **D**ocFlavor.INPUT_STREAM^
 DocFlavor.URL^
PCM_SIGNED: **A**udioFormat.Encoding
PCM_UNSIGNED: **A**udioFormat.Encoding
PDF: **D**ocFlavor.BYTE_ARRAY^ **D**ocFlavor.INPUT_STREAM^
 DocFlavor.URL^
PDLOverrideSupported^: javax.print.attribute.standard
—fields: **P**DLOverrideSupported^ < ATTEMPTED,
 NOT_ATTEMPTED >
peekEvent(): **E**ventQueue
PENDING: **J**obState^

P

PENDING_HELD: **J**obState^
performDefaultLayout(): **G**lyphVector
Permission: java.security
—descendents: **A**udioPermission^ **A**WTPermission^
PERSIST: **J**FormattedTextField^
PERSONAL: **P**ageAttributes.MediaType^
PERSONAL_ENVELOPE: **M**ediaSize.Other **M**ediaSizeName^
   PageAttributes.MediaType^
PGDN: **E**vent
PGUP: **E**vent
PHYSICAL: **P**ageAttributes.OriginType^
PI: **D**TDConstants
PIE: **A**rc2D^
PINK: **C**olor
pink: **C**olor
PITCH_BEND: **S**hortMessage^
pixel_bits^: **C**olorModel
PixelGrabber: java.awt.image
PixelInterleavedSampleModel^: java.awt.image
pixelStride: **C**omponentSampleModel^
PLAIN: **F**ont
PLAIN_DIALOG: **J**RootPane^
PLAIN_MESSAGE: **J**OptionPane^
PlainDocument^: javax.swing.text
plainTextFlavor: **D**ataFlavor
PlainView^: javax.swing.text
—subclasses: **F**ieldView^
—descendents: **P**asswordView^
play(): **A**pplet^ *AudioClip*
pluginClassName: **I**mageReaderWriterSpi^
PNG: **D**ocFlavor.BYTE_ARRAY^ **D**ocFlavor.INPUT_STREAM^
   DocFlavor.URL^
Point^: java.awt
—passed to: **A**bstractButton.AccessibleAbstractButton^
  .getIndexAtPoint() *AccessibleComponent*
  < contains(), getAccessibleAt(), setLocation() >
  AccessibleText.getIndexAtPoint() *Autoscroll*.autoscroll()
  Caret.setMagicCaretPosition() **C**omponent < contains(),
  getComponentAt(), getLocation(), setLocation() >
  Component.AccessibleAWTComponent^ < contains(),
  getAccessibleAt(), setLocation() > **C**ontainer.findComponentAt()
  DefaultCaret^.setMagicCaretPosition() **D**ragGestureEvent^
  < DragGestureEvent(), startDrag() >
  DragGestureRecognizer.fireDragGestureRecognized()
  DragSource < createDragSourceContext(),
  startDrag() > **D**ragSourceContext() **D**ropTarget
  < createDropTargetAutoScroller(), initializeAutoscrolling(),
  updateAutoscroll() > **D**ropTarget.DropTargetAutoScroller
  < DropTarget.DropTargetAutoScroller(),
  updateLocation() > **D**ropTargetDragEvent()
  DropTargetDropEvent() **I**IOParam.setDestinationOffset()
  JLabel.AccessibleJLabel^.getIndexAtPoint()
  JList^.locationToIndex()
  JList.AccessibleJList.AccessibleJListChild^
  < contains(), getAccessibleAt(), setLocation() >
  JTable^ < columnAtPoint(), rowAtPoint() >
  JTable.AccessibleJTable.AccessibleJTableCell^
  < contains(), getAccessibleAt(), setLocation() >
  JTableHeader^.columnAtPoint() **J**TableHeader
  .AccessibleJTableHeader.AccessibleJTableHeaderEntry^
  < contains(), getAccessibleAt(), setLocation() >
  JTextComponent^.viewToModel() **J**TextComponent
  .AccessibleJTextComponent^.getIndexAtPoint()
  JTree.AccessibleJTree.AccessibleJTreeNode^
  < contains(), getAccessibleAt(), setLocation() >
  JViewport^ < computeBlit(), setViewPosition(),
  toViewCoordinates() > **L**istUI^.locationToIndex()
  MenuComponent.AccessibleAWTMenuComponent^
  < contains(), getAccessibleAt(), setLocation() >
  MenuSelectionManager.componentForPoint() **P**oint^
  < Point(), setLocation() > **P**olygon.contains() **R**aster
  < createBandedRaster(), createInterleavedRaster(),

createPackedRaster(), createRaster(), createWritableRaster(),
Raster() > **R**ectangle^ < add(), contains(), Rectangle(),
setLocation() > **S**crollPane^.setScrollPosition()
SwingUtilities < convertPoint(), convertPointFromScreen(),
convertPointToScreen(), getAccessibleAt() > **T**extComponent
.AccessibleAWTTextComponent^.getIndexAtPoint()
TextUI^ < getToolTipText(), viewToModel() >
Toolkit.createCustomCursor() **W**ritableRaster()
—returned by: *AccessibleComponent* < getLocation(),
getLocationOnScreen() > **B**ufferedImage^.getWritableTileIndices()
Caret.getMagicCaretPosition() **C**omponent
< getLocation(), getLocationOnScreen(), location() >
Component.AccessibleAWTComponent^
< getLocation(), getLocationOnScreen() >
ComponentPeer.getLocationOnScreen()
DefaultCaret^.getMagicCaretPosition()
DragGestureEvent^.getDragOrigin()
DragSourceEvent^.getLocation()
DropTargetDragEvent^.getLocation()
DropTargetDropEvent^.getLocation()
GraphicsEnvironment.getCenterPoint()
GridBagLayout < getLayoutOrigin(),
location() > **I**IOParam.getDestinationOffset()
JComponent^.getToolTipLocation() **J**List^.indexToLocation()
JList.AccessibleJList.AccessibleJListChild^ < getLocation(),
getLocationOnScreen() > **J**Menu^.getPopupMenuOrigin()
JTable.AccessibleJTable.AccessibleJTableCell^
< getLocation(), getLocationOnScreen() > **J**TableHeader
.AccessibleJTableHeader.AccessibleJTableHeaderEntry^
< getLocation(), getLocationOnScreen() >
JTree.AccessibleJTree.AccessibleJTreeNode^
< getLocation(), getLocationInJTree(),
getLocationOnScreen() > **J**Viewport^ < getViewPosition(),
toViewCoordinates() > **L**istUI^.indexToLocation()
MenuComponent.AccessibleAWTMenuComponent^
< getLocation(), getLocationOnScreen() >
MouseEvent.getPoint() **P**oint^.getLocation()
Rectangle^.getLocation() **S**crollPane^.getScrollPosition()
SwingUtilities.convertPoint()
WritableRenderedImage^.getWritableTileIndices()
—fields: **I**IOParam.destinationOffset **J**Viewport^.lastPaintPosition
Point2D: java.awt.geom
—subclasses: **P**oint^ **P**oint2D.Double^ **P**oint2D.Float^
—passed to: **A**ffineTransform < deltaTransform(),
inverseTransform(), transform() >
AffineTransformOp.getPoint2D() **A**rc2D^ < setAngles(),
setAngleStart(), setArc(), setArcByTangent() >
Area.contains() **B**andCombineOp.getPoint2D()
BufferedImageOp.getPoint2D() **C**olorConvertOp.getPoint2D()
ConvolveOp.getPoint2D() **C**ubicCurve2D^
< contains(), setCurve() > **G**eneralPath.contains()
GlyphVector.setGlyphPosition() **G**radientPaint()
Line2D < contains(), ptLineDist(), ptLineDistSq(),
ptSegDist(), ptSegDistSq(), relativeCCW(), setLine() >
Line2D.Double() **L**ine2D.Float() **L**ookupOp.getPoint2D()
Point2D < distance(), distanceSq(), setLocation() >
Polygon.contains() **Q**uadCurve2D^ < contains(),
setCurve() > *RasterOp*.getPoint2D() **R**ectangle2D^
< add(), outcode() > **R**ectangularShape < contains(),
setFrame(), setFrameFromCenter(), setFrameFromDiagonal() >
RescaleOp.getPoint2D() *Shape*.contains()
—returned by: **A**ffineTransform < deltaTransform(),
inverseTransform(), transform() >
AffineTransformOp.getPoint2D() **A**rc2D^ < getEndPoint(),
getStartPoint() > **B**andCombineOp.getPoint2D()
BufferedImageOp.getPoint2D() **C**olorConvertOp.getPoint2D()
ConvolveOp.getPoint2D() **C**ubicCurve2D^ < getCtrlP1(),
getCtrlP2(), getP1(), getP2() > **G**eneralPath.getCurrentPoint()
GlyphVector.getGlyphPosition() **G**radientPaint
< getPoint1(), getPoint2() > **L**ine2D^ < getP1(), getP2() >
LookupOp.getPoint2D() **Q**uadCurve2D^ < getCtrlPt(), getP1(),
getP2() > *RasterOp*.getPoint2D() **R**escaleOp.getPoint2D()

PRINTER_STOPPED: **J**obStateReason^
PRINTER_STOPPED_PARTLY: **J**obStateReason^
PrinterAbortException^: java.awt.print
PrinterException: java.awt.print
— subclasses: **P**rinterAbortException^ **P**rinterIOException^
— thrown by: *Printable*.print( ) **P**rinterJob < print( ),
setPrintService( ) >
PrinterGraphics: java.awt.print
PrinterInfo^: javax.print.attribute.standard
PrinterIOException^: java.awt.print
PrinterIsAcceptingJobs^: javax.print.attribute.standard
— fields: **P**rinterIsAcceptingJobs^ < ACCEPTING_JOBS,
NOT_ACCEPTING_JOBS >
PrinterJob: java.awt.print
— returned by: *PrinterGraphics*.getPrinterJob( )
PrinterJob.getPrinterJob( )
PrinterLocation^: javax.print.attribute.standard
PrinterMakeAndModel^: javax.print.attribute.standard
PrinterMessageFromOperator^: javax.print.attribute.standard
PrinterMoreInfo^: javax.print.attribute.standard
PrinterMoreInfoManufacturer^: javax.print.attribute.standard
PrinterName^: javax.print.attribute.standard
PrinterResolution^: javax.print.attribute.standard
PrinterState^: javax.print.attribute.standard
— fields: **P**rinterState^ < IDLE, PROCESSING, STOPPED,
UNKNOWN >
PrinterStateReason^: javax.print.attribute.standard
— fields: **P**rinterStateReason^ < CONNECTING_TO_DEVICE,
COVER_OPEN, DEVELOPER_EMPTY, DEVELOPER_LOW,
DOOR_OPEN, FUSER_OVER_TEMP, FUSER_UNDER_TEMP,
INPUT_TRAY_MISSING, INTERLOCK_OPEN,
INTERPRETER_RESOURCE_UNAVAILABLE,
MARKER_SUPPLY_EMPTY, MARKER_SUPPLY_LOW,
MARKER_WASTE_ALMOST_FULL, MARKER_WASTE_FULL,
MEDIA_EMPTY, MEDIA_JAM, MEDIA_LOW, MEDIA_NEEDED,
MOVING_TO_PAUSED, OPC_LIFE_OVER, OPC_NEAR_EOL,
OTHER, OUTPUT_AREA_ALMOST_FULL, OUTPUT_AREA_FULL,
OUTPUT_TRAY_MISSING, PAUSED, SHUTDOWN,
SPOOL_AREA_FULL, STOPPED_PARTLY, STOPPING,
TIMED_OUT, TONER_EMPTY, TONER_LOW >
PrinterStateReasons^: javax.print.attribute.standard
printerStateReasonSet( ): **P**rinterStateReasons^
PrinterURI^: javax.print.attribute.standard
PrintEvent^: javax.print.event
— subclasses: **P**rintJobAttributeEvent^ **P**rintJobEvent^
PrintServiceAttributeEvent^
PrintException: javax.print
— thrown by: *CancelablePrintJob*^.cancel( ) *DocPrintJob*.print( )
MultiDocPrintJob^.print( )
PrintGraphics: java.awt
PrintJob: java.awt
— returned by: *PrintGraphics*.getPrintJob( ) **T**oolkit.getPrintJob( )
PrintJobAdapter: javax.print.event
PrintJobAttribute^: javax.print.attribute
— passed to: **H**ashPrintJobAttributeSet( )
— implemented by: **C**hromaticity^ **C**opies^
DateTimeAtCompleted^ **D**ateTimeAtCreation^
DateTimeAtProcessing^ **D**estination^ **F**idelity^ **F**inishings^
JobHoldUntil^ **J**obImpressions^ **J**obImpressionsCompleted^
JobKOctets^ **J**obKOctetsProcessed^ **J**obMediaSheets^
JobMediaSheetsCompleted^ **J**obMessageFromOperator^
JobName^ **J**obOriginatingUserName^ **J**obPriority^
JobSheets^ **J**obState^ **J**obStateReasons^ **M**edia^
MediaPrintableArea **M**ultipleDocumentHandling^
NumberOfDocuments^ **N**umberOfInterveningJobs^
NumberUp^ **O**rientationRequested^ **O**utputDeviceAssigned^
PageRanges^ **P**resentationDirection^ **P**rinterResolution^
PrintQuality^ **S**heetCollate^ **S**ides^
PrintJobAttributeEvent^: javax.print.event
— passed to: *PrintJobAttributeListener*.attributeUpdate( )
PrintJobAttributeListener: javax.print.event

— passed to: *DocPrintJob* < addPrintJobAttributeListener( ),
removePrintJobAttributeListener( ) >
PrintJobAttributeSet^: javax.print.attribute
— passed to: **A**ttributeSetUtilities < synchronizedView( ),
unmodifiableView( ) > *DocPrintJob*.addPrintJobAttributeListener( )
HashPrintJobAttributeSet( ) **P**rintJobAttributeEvent( )
— returned by: **A**ttributeSetUtilities < synchronizedView( ),
unmodifiableView( ) > *DocPrintJob*.getAttributes( )
PrintJobAttributeEvent^.getAttributes( )
— implemented by: **H**ashPrintJobAttributeSet^
printJobCanceled( ): **P**rintJobAdapter *PrintJobListener*
printJobCompleted( ): **P**rintJobAdapter *PrintJobListener*
PrintJobEvent^: javax.print.event
— passed to: **P**rintJobAdapter < printDataTransferCompleted( ),
printJobCanceled( ), printJobCompleted( ), printJobFailed( ),
printJobNoMoreEvents( ), printJobRequiresAttention( ) >
PrintJobListener < printDataTransferCompleted( ),
printJobCanceled( ), printJobCompleted( ), printJobFailed( ),
printJobNoMoreEvents( ), printJobRequiresAttention( ) >
printJobFailed( ): **P**rintJobAdapter *PrintJobListener*
PrintJobListener: javax.print.event
— passed to: *DocPrintJob* < addPrintJobListener( ),
removePrintJobListener( ) >
— implemented by: **P**rintJobAdapter
printJobNoMoreEvents( ): **P**rintJobAdapter *PrintJobListener*
printJobRequiresAttention( ): **P**rintJobAdapter
PrintJobListener
PrintQuality^: javax.print.attribute.standard
— fields: **P**rintQuality^ < DRAFT, HIGH, NORMAL >
PrintRequestAttribute^: javax.print.attribute
— passed to: **H**ashPrintRequestAttributeSet( )
— implemented by: **C**hromaticity^ **C**opies^ **D**estination^ **F**idelity^
Finishings^ **J**obHoldUntil^ **J**obImpressions^ **J**obKOctets^
JobMediaSheets^ **J**obName^ **J**obPriority^ **J**obSheets^
Media^ **M**ediaPrintableArea **M**ultipleDocumentHandling^
NumberUp^ **O**rientationRequested^ **P**ageRanges^
PresentationDirection^ **P**rinterResolution^ **P**rintQuality^
RequestingUserName^ **S**heetCollate^ **S**ides^
PrintRequestAttributeSet^: javax.print.attribute
— passed to: **A**ttributeSetUtilities < synchronizedView( ),
unmodifiableView( ) > *DocPrintJob*.print( )
HashPrintRequestAttributeSet( ) *MultiDocPrintJob*^.print( )
PrinterJob < pageDialog( ), print( ), printDialog( ) >
ServiceUI.printDialog( )
— returned by: **A**ttributeSetUtilities < synchronizedView( ),
unmodifiableView( ) >
— implemented by: **H**ashPrintRequestAttributeSet^
PrintService: javax.print
— extended by: *MultiDocPrintService*^
— passed to: **P**rinterJob.setPrintService( )
PrintServiceAttributeEvent( )
PrintServiceLookup.registerService( ) **S**erviceUI.printDialog( )
— returned by: *DocPrintJob*.getPrintService( ) **P**rinterJob
< getPrintService( ), lookupPrintServices( ) >
PrintServiceAttributeEvent^.getPrintService( )
PrintServiceLookup < getDefaultPrintService( ),
getPrintServices( ), lookupDefaultPrintService( ),
lookupPrintServices( ) > **S**erviceUI.printDialog( )
— implemented by: **S**treamPrintService
PrintServiceAttribute^: javax.print.attribute
— passed to: **H**ashPrintServiceAttributeSet( )
— returned by: *PrintService*.getAttribute( )
— implemented by: **C**olorSupported^ **P**agesPerMinute^
PagesPerMinuteColor^ **P**DLOverrideSupported^
PrinterInfo^ **P**rinterIsAcceptingJobs^ **P**rinterLocation^
PrinterMakeAndModel^ **P**rinterMessageFromOperator^
PrinterMoreInfo^ **P**rinterMoreInfoManufacturer^
PrinterName^ **P**rinterState^ **P**rinterStateReasons^
PrinterURI^ **Q**ueuedJobCount^
PrintServiceAttributeEvent^: javax.print.event
— passed to: *PrintServiceAttributeListener*.attributeUpdate( )
PrintServiceAttributeListener: javax.print.event

P

P

provideErrorFeedback( ): LookAndFeel
ptLineDist( ): Line2D
ptLineDistSq( ): Line2D
ptSegDist( ): Line2D
ptSegDistSq( ): Line2D
PUBLIC: *DTDConstants*
push( ): EventQueue
PUSH_BUTTON: AccessibleRole^
pushCharacterStyle( ): HTMLDocument.HTMLReader^
put( ): ActionMap InputMap RenderingHints UIManager
putAll( ): RenderingHints
putClientProperty( ): JComponent^
putConstraint( ): SpringLayout
putDefaults( ): UIDefaults^
putDTDHash( ): DTD
putLayer( ): JLayeredPane^
putProperty( ): AbstractDocument
  javax.swing.text.Document
putValue( ): AbstractAction *Action*^
QuadCurve2D: java.awt.geom
  —subclasses: **Q**uadCurve2D.Double^ **Q**uadCurve2D.Float^
  —passed to: **Q**uadCurve2D < setCurve( ), subdivide( ) >
QuadCurve2D.Double^: java.awt.geom
QuadCurve2D.Float^: java.awt.geom
quadTo( ): GeneralPath
QUARTO: MediaSize.Other MediaSizeName^
  PageAttributes.MediaType^
QUESTION_DIALOG: JRootPane^
QUESTION_MESSAGE: JOptionPane^
QUEUED_IN_DEVICE: JobStateReason^
QueuedJobCount^: javax.print.attribute.standard
RADIO_BUTTON: AccessibleRole^
RAISED: BevelBorder^ EtchedBorder^
RandomAccessFile: `java.io`
  —passed to: **F**ileImageInputStream( ) **F**ileImageOutputStream( )
RANDOMPIXELORDER: *ImageConsumer*
RANGE: JobAttributes.DefaultSelectionType^
raster: IIOImage
Raster: java.awt.image
  —subclasses: **W**ritableRaster^
  —passed to: **A**ffineTransformOp < createCompatibleDestRaster( ),
    filter( ), getBounds2D( ) > **B**andCombineOp
    < createCompatibleDestRaster( ), filter( ), getBounds2D( ) >
    BufferedImage^.setData( ) **C**olorConvertOp
    < createCompatibleDestRaster( ), filter( ),
    getBounds2D( ) > **C**olorModel.isCompatibleRaster( )
    CompositeContext.compose( ) **C**onvolveOp
    < createCompatibleDestRaster( ), filter( ),
    getBounds2D( ) > **I**IOImage < IIOImage( ),
    setRaster( ) > **I**mageWriter.replacePixels( )
    IndexColorModel^.convertToIntDiscrete( ) LookupOp
    < createCompatibleDestRaster( ), filter( ), getBounds2D( ) >
    Raster( ) *RasterOp* < createCompatibleDestRaster( ), filter( ),
    getBounds2D( ) > **R**escaleOp < createCompatibleDestRaster( ),
    filter( ), getBounds2D( ) > **W**ritableRaster^ < setDataElements( ),
    setRect( ) > *WritableRenderedImage*^.setData( )
  —returned by: **B**ufferedImage^ < getData( ), getTile( ) >
    IIOImage.getRaster( ) ImageReader < readRaster( ),
    readTileRaster( ) > *PaintContext*.getRaster( ) **R**aster
    < createChild( ), createRaster( ), createTranslatedChild( ),
    getParent( ) > *RenderedImage* < getData( ), getTile( ) >
  —fields: IIOImage.raster Raster.parent
RasterFormatException: java.awt.image
RasterOp: java.awt.image
  —implemented by: **A**ffineTransformOp **B**andCombineOp
    ColorConvertOp **C**onvolveOp LookupOp **R**escaleOp
RAW_TEXT: InputMethodHighlight
RCDATA: *DTDConstants*
RCSID: StateEdit^ *StateEditable*
read( ): DTD EditorKit *ImageInputStream*^
  ImageInputStreamImpl ImageIO ImageReader
  JTextComponent^ *TargetDataLine*^

readAborted( ): *IIOReadProgressListener*^
readAll( ): ImageReader
readAsRenderedImage( ): ImageReader
readAttributes( ): StyleContext
readAttributeSet( ): StyleContext
readBit( ): *ImageInputStream*^ ImageInputStreamImpl
readBits( ): *ImageInputStream*^ ImageInputStreamImpl
readBoolean( ): *ImageInputStream*^ ImageInputStreamImpl
readByte( ): *ImageInputStream*^ ImageInputStreamImpl
readBytes( ): *ImageInputStream*^ ImageInputStreamImpl
readChar( ): *ImageInputStream*^ ImageInputStreamImpl
readDouble( ): *ImageInputStream*^ ImageInputStreamImpl
Reader: `java.io`
  —passed to: **D**ocumentParser^.parse( ) **E**ditorKit.read( )
    HTMLEditorKit.Parser.parse( ) **J**TextComponent^.read( )
    javax.swing.text.html.parser.**P**arser.parse( )
    StyleSheet^.loadRules( )
  —returned by: **D**ataFlavor.getReaderForText( )
    Doc.getReaderForText( ) **S**impleDoc.getReaderForText( )
readerSpiNames: ImageWriterSpi^
readerSupportsThumbnails( ): ImageReader
readExternal( ): DataFlavor
readFloat( ): *ImageInputStream*^ ImageInputStreamImpl
readFully( ): *ImageInputStream*^ ImageInputStreamImpl
readInt( ): *ImageInputStream*^ ImageInputStreamImpl
readLine( ): *ImageInputStream*^ ImageInputStreamImpl
readLock( ): AbstractDocument
readLong( ): *ImageInputStream*^ ImageInputStreamImpl
readOnlyAction: DefaultEditorKit^
readRaster( ): ImageReader
readResolve( ): **A**WTKeyStroke EnumSyntax ICC_Profile
  TextAttribute^
readShort( ): *ImageInputStream*^ ImageInputStreamImpl
readThumbnail( ): ImageReader
readTile( ): ImageReader
readTileRaster( ): ImageReader
readUnlock( ): AbstractDocument
readUnsignedByte( ): *ImageInputStream*^
  ImageInputStreamImpl
readUnsignedInt( ): *ImageInputStream*^
  ImageInputStreamImpl
readUnsignedShort( ): *ImageInputStream*^
  ImageInputStreamImpl
readUTF( ): *ImageInputStream*^ ImageInputStreamImpl
realEditor: DefaultTreeCellEditor
realSource: UndoableEditSupport
recalcWidthCache( ): DefaultTableColumnModel
Receiver: javax.sound.midi
  —passed to: *Transmitter*.setReceiver( )
  —returned by: *MidiDevice*.getReceiver( )
    MidiSystem.getReceiver( ) *Transmitter*.getReceiver( )
reclaim( ): *AbstractDocument.AttributeContext* StyleContext
reconvert( ): InputContext *InputMethod*
recordDisable( ): *Sequencer*^
recordEnable( ): *Sequencer*^
Rectangle^: java.awt
  —subclasses: DefaultCaret^
  —passed to: **A**bstractLayoutCache < getBounds( ),
    getNodeDimensions( ), getPreferredWidth( ) >
    AbstractLayoutCache.NodeDimensions.getNodeDimensions( )
    AccessibleComponent.setBounds( ) BoxView^
    < childAllocation( ), getViewAtPoint( ), isAfter( ),
    isBefore( ), paintChild( ) > **B**ufferedImage^.getData( )
    CellRendererPane.paintComponent( ) **C**olor.createContext( )
    Component < getBounds( ), setBounds( ) >
    Component.AccessibleAWTComponent^.setBounds( )
    CompositeView^ < childAllocation( ), getViewAtPoint( ),
    getViewAtPosition( ), isAfter( ), isBefore( ) >
    DefaultCaret^ < adjustVisibility( ), damage( ) >
    DefaultDesktopManager.setPreviousBounds( )
    FlowView.FlowStrategy < changedUpdate( ), insertUpdate( ),
    removeUpdate( ) > **F**rame^.setMaximizedBounds( )

P

ReferenceUriSchemesSupported^:
  javax.print.attribute.standard
  —fields: **R**eferenceUriSchemesSupported^ < FILE, FTP,
  GOPHER, HTTP, HTTPS, NEWS, NNTP, WAIS >
REFRESH_RATE_UNKNOWN: **D**isplayMode
RegisterableService: javax.imageio.spi
  —implemented by: **I**IOServiceProvider
registerApplicationClasspathSpis( ): **I**IORegistry^
registerComponent( ): **T**oolTipManager^
registerEditorKitForContentType( ): **J**EditorPane;
registerKeyboardAction( ): **J**Component;
registerListeners( ): **D**ragGestureRecognizer
registerService( ): **P**rintServiceLookup
registerServiceProvider( ): **P**rintServiceLookup
  ServiceRegistry
registerServiceProviders( ): **S**erviceRegistry
registerStaticAttributeKey( ): **S**tyleContext
registerSubclass( ): **A**WTKeyStroke
registerTag( ): **H**TMLDocument.HTMLReader^
rejectDrag( ): **D**ropTargetContext **D**ropTargetDragEvent^
rejectDrop( ): **D**ropTargetContext **D**ropTargetDropEvent^
REL: **H**TML.Attribute
relations: **A**ccessibleRelationSet
RELATIVE: **G**ridBagConstraints
relativeCCW( ): **L**ine2D
releaseWritableTile( ): **B**ufferedImage^
  WritableRenderedImage^
reload( ): **D**efaultTreeModel
REMAINDER: **G**ridBagConstraints
remapInstrument( ): *S*ynthesizer^
REMOVE: **D**ocumentEvent.EventType
remove( ): **A**bstractDocument *AbstractDocument.Content*
  AccessibleRelationSet **A**ccessibleStateSet **A**ctionMap
  javax.print.attribute.AttributeSet **A**WTEventMulticaster
  ButtonGroup *ChoicePeer* **C**omponent
  DefaultListModel^ **D**efaultMutableTreeNode
  DefaultStyledDocument.ElementBuffer
  javax.swing.text.Document **D**ocumentFilter
  DocumentFilter.FilterBypass **E**ventListenerList **G**apContent^
  HashAttributeSet **I**nputMap **M**enu; **M**enuBar^
  MenuContainer **M**utableTreeNode^ **R**enderingHints
  StringContent **T**rack **V**iew
removeAccessibleSelection( ): *AccessibleSelection*
  JComboBox.AccessibleJComboBox^ **J**List.AccessibleJList^
  JMenu.AccessibleJMenu^ **J**MenuBar.AccessibleJMenuBar^
  JTabbedPane.AccessibleJTabbedPane^
  JTable.AccessibleJTable^ **J**Tree.AccessibleJTree^
  JTree.AccessibleJTree.AccessibleJTreeNode^
  List.AccessibleAWTList^
  MenuComponent.AccessibleAWTMenuComponent;
removeActionListener( ): **A**bstractButton; **B**utton^
  ButtonModel *ComboBoxEditor* **D**efaultButtonModel
  JComboBox^ **J**FileChooser^ **J**TextField; java.awt.**L**ist^
  MenuItem; **T**extField^ **T**imer
removeAdjustmentListener( ): *Adjustable* **J**ScrollBar;
  Scrollbar **S**crollPaneAdjustable
removeAll( ): **C**hoice^ *ChoicePeer*^ **C**ontainer; java.awt.**L**ist^
  ListPeer^ **M**enu; **V**iew
removeAllChildren( ): **D**efaultMutableTreeNode
removeAllElements( ): **D**efaultComboBoxModel^
  DefaultListModel^
removeAllHighlights( ): *Highlighter*
removeAllIIOReadProgressListeners( ): **I**mageReader
removeAllIIOReadUpdateListeners( ): **I**mageReader
removeAllIIOReadWarningListeners( ): **I**mageReader
removeAllIIOWriteProgressListeners( ): **I**mageWriter
removeAllIIOWriteWarningListeners( ): **I**mageWriter
removeAllItems( ): **J**ComboBox^
removeAncestorListener( ): **J**Component;
removeAttribute( ): **A**bstractDocument.AbstractElement
  AbstractDocument.AttributeContext **I**IOMetadataFormatImpl

IIOMetadataNode *MutableAttributeSet*^ **S**impleAttributeSet
  StyleContext **S**tyleContext.NamedStyle
removeAttributeNode( ): **I**IOMetadataNode
removeAttributeNS( ): **I**IOMetadataNode
removeAttributes( ): **A**bstractDocument.AbstractElement
  AbstractDocument.AttributeContext *MutableAttributeSet*^
  SimpleAttributeSet **S**tyleContext **S**tyleContext.NamedStyle
removeAuxiliaryLookAndFeel( ): **U**IManager
removeAWTEventListener( ): **T**oolkit
removeBindings( ): *Keymap*
removeCaretListener( ): **J**TextComponent;
removeCellEditorListener( ): **A**bstractCellEditor *CellEditor*
  DefaultTreeCellEditor
removeChangeListener( ): **A**bstractButton;
  AbstractSpinnerModel *BoundedRangeModel*
  ButtonModel **C**aret *ColorSelectionModel*
  DefaultBoundedRangeModel **D**efaultButtonModel
  DefaultCaret^ **D**efaultColorSelectionModel
  DefaultSingleSelectionModel **J**ProgressBar;
  JSlider; **J**Spinner **J**TabbedPane; **J**Viewport^
  MenuSelectionManager *SingleSelectionModel*
  SpinnerModel *Style*^ **S**tyleContext
  StyleContext.NamedStyle
removeChild( ): **I**IOMetadataNode
removeChoosableFileFilter( ): **J**FileChooser^
removeChooserPanel( ): **J**ColorChooser^
removeColumn( ): **D**efaultTableColumnModel **J**Table^
  TableColumnModel
removeColumnModelListener( ): **D**efaultTableColumnModel
  TableColumnModel
removeColumnSelectionInterval( ): **J**Table^
removeComponentListener( ): **C**omponent
removeConsumer( ): **F**ilteredImageSource *ImageProducer*
  MemoryImageSource **R**enderableImageProducer
removeContainerListener( ): **C**ontainer;
removeControllerEventListener( ): *Sequencer*^
removeDescendantSelectedPaths( ): **J**Tree^
removeDescendantToggledPaths( ): **J**Tree^
removeDocumentListener( ): **A**bstractDocument
  javax.swing.text.Document
removeDragGestureListener( ): **D**ragGestureRecognizer
removeDragSourceListener( ): **D**ragSource
  DragSourceContext
removeDragSourceMotionListener( ): **D**ragSource
removeDropTargetListener( ): **D**ropTarget
removeEditor( ): **J**Table^
removeElement( ): **D**efaultComboBoxModel^ **D**efaultListModel^
  IIOMetadataFormatImpl *MutableComboBoxModel*^
removeElementAt( ): **D**efaultComboBoxModel^
  DefaultListModel^ *MutableComboBoxModel*^
removeEntries( ): **S**izeSequence
removeFocusListener( ): *AccessibleComponent*
  Component **C**omponent.AccessibleAWTComponent;
  JList.AccessibleJList.AccessibleJListChild^
  JTable.AccessibleJTable.AccessibleJTableCell^
  JTableHeader.AccessibleJTableHeader
  .AccessibleJTableHeaderEntry^
  JTree.AccessibleJTree.AccessibleJTreeNode^
  MenuComponent.AccessibleAWTMenuComponent;
removeFromParent( ): **D**efaultMutableTreeNode
  MutableTreeNode^
removeHierarchyBoundsListener( ): **C**omponent
removeHierarchyListener( ): **C**omponent
removeHighlight( ): *Highlighter*
removeHyperlinkListener( ): **J**EditorPane;
removeIconFor( ): **D**efaultDesktopManager
removeIIOReadProgressListener( ): **I**mageReader
removeIIOReadUpdateListener( ): **I**mageReader
removeIIOReadWarningListener( ): **I**mageReader
removeIIOWriteProgressListener( ): **I**mageWriter
removeIIOWriteWarningListener( ): **I**mageWriter
removeImage( ): **I**mageWriter **M**ediaTracker

R

RenderContext.getRenderingHints( )
RescaleOp.getRenderingHints( )

RenderingHints.Key: java.awt
 —passed to: **G**raphics2D^ < getRenderingHint( ),
 setRenderingHint( ) > **R**enderingHints( )
 —fields < **R**enderingHints < KEY_ALPHA_INTERPOLATION,
 KEY_ANTIALIASING, KEY_COLOR_RENDERING, KEY_DITHERING,
 KEY_FRACTIONALMETRICS, KEY_INTERPOLATION,
 KEY_RENDERING, KEY_STROKE_CONTROL,
 KEY_TEXT_ANTIALIASING >
reorderingAllowed: **J**TableHeader^
repaint( ): **C**omponent_ *ComponentPeer*_ **D**efaultCaret^
RepaintManager: javax.swing
 —passed to: **R**epaintManager.setCurrentManager( )
 —returned by: **R**epaintManager.currentManager( )
replace( ): **A**bstractDocument_
 AbstractDocument.BranchElement^ **D**ocumentFilter
 DocumentFilter.FilterBypass **G**apVector_ **V**iew_
replaceChild( ): **I**IOMetadataNode
replaceEdit( ): **A**bstractUndoableEdit_ *UndoableEdit*
replaceImageMetadata( ): **I**mageWriter
replaceItem( ): java.awt.**L**ist^
replacePixels( ): **I**mageWriter
replaceRange( ): **J**TextArea^ **T**extArea^ *TextAreaPeer*
replaceSelection( ): **J**TextComponent^
replaceStreamMetadata( ): **I**mageWriter
replaceText( ): *AccessibleEditableText*^
 JTextComponent.AccessibleJTextComponent^ **T**extArea^
 TextAreaPeer^
replaceUIActionMap( ): **S**wingUtilities
replaceUIInputMap( ): **S**wingUtilities
ReplicateScaleFilter^: java.awt.image
 —subclasses: **A**reaAveragingScaleFilter^
REPORT^: **S**everity^
requestDefaultFocus( ): **J**Component^
requestFocus( ): *AccessibleComponent*_ **C**omponent_
 Component.AccessibleAWTComponent^ *ComponentPeer*_
 JList.AccessibleJList.AccessibleJListChild^
 JTable.AccessibleJTable.AccessibleJTableCell^
 JTableHeader.AccessibleJTableHeader **2**
 .AccessibleJTableHeaderEntry^
 JTree.AccessibleJTree.AccessibleJTreeNode^
 MenuComponent.AccessibleAWTMenuComponent^
requestFocusInWindow( ): **C**omponent_
RequestingUserName^: javax.print.attribute.standard
requestTopDownLeftRightResend( ): **F**ilteredImageSource
 ImageProducer **M**emoryImageSource
 RenderableImageProducer
REQUIRED: *DTDConstants* **G**raphicsConfigTemplate
REQUIRES_ATTENTION: **P**rintJobEvent^
RescaleOp: java.awt.image
rescanCurrentDirectory( ): **F**ileChooserUI^ **J**FileChooser^
resendTopDownLeftRight( ): **I**mageFilter_
RESERVED_ID_MAX: **A**WTEvent^
RESERVED_UIROLE: **S**erviceUIFactory
RESET: **F**ormView^
reset( ): **A**rea **G**eneralPath **I**IOMetadata *ImageInputStream*^
 ImageInputStreamImpl_ **I**mageReader **I**mageWriter
 Polygon
resetAllControllers( ): *MidiChannel*
resetChoosableFileFilters( ): **J**FileChooser^
resetKeyboardActions( ): **J**Component^
resetMarksAtZero( ): **G**apContent^
resetRecognizer( ): **D**ragGestureRecognizer_
resetRowSelection( ): **D**efaultTreeSelectionModel_
 TreeSelectionModel
resetToPreferredSizes( ): **J**SplitPane^ **S**plitPaneUI^
resetViewPort( ): **J**ScrollPane.AccessibleJScrollPane^
reshape( ): **C**omponent_ *ComponentPeer*_ **R**ectangle^
RESIZABLE: **A**ccessibleState^
resizable: **J**InternalFrame^
resize( ): **C**omponent_ **R**ectangle^

RESIZE_WEIGHT_PROPERTY: **J**SplitPane^
resizeAndRepaint( ): **J**Table^ **J**TableHeader^
resizedPostingDisableCount: **T**ableColumn
resizeFrame( ): **D**efaultDesktopManager *DesktopManager*
resizingAllowed: **J**TableHeader^
resizingColumn: **J**TableHeader^
resolution: **M**idiFileFormat **S**equence
ResolutionSyntax_: javax.print.attribute
 —subclasses: **P**rinterResolution^
 —passed to: **R**esolutionSyntax_.lessThanOrEquals( )
ResolveAttribute: *javax.swing.text.AttributeSet*_
 StyleConstants_
ResourceBundle: java.util
 —descendents: **A**ccessibleResourceBundle^
 —passed to: **C**omponentOrientation.getOrientation( )
 Window^.applyResourceBundle( )
RESOURCES_ARE_NOT_READY: **J**obStateReason^
restart( ): **T**imer
restoreState( ): *StateEditable*
restoreSubcomponentFocus( ): **J**InternalFrame^
REV: **H**TML.Attribute
revalidate( ): **C**omponent.BltBufferStrategy^
 Component.FlipBufferStrategy^ **J**Component^
REVERB: **E**numControl.Type^
REVERB_RETURN: **F**loatControl.Type^
REVERB_SEND: **F**loatControl.Type^
ReverbType: javax.sound.sampled
REVERSE_LANDSCAPE: **O**rientationRequested^ **P**ageFormat
REVERSE_PORTRAIT: **O**rientationRequested^
REVERT: **J**FormattedTextField^
RGBImageFilter^: java.awt.image
 —subclasses: **G**rayFilter^
RGBtoHSB( ): **C**olor_
right: **E**mptyBorder^ **I**nsets
RIGHT: **E**vent **F**lowLayout **J**SplitPane^ **L**abel^
 SwingConstants **T**itledBorder^
RIGHT_ALIGNMENT: **C**omponent_
RIGHT_TO_LEFT: **C**omponentOrientation
rightComponent: **J**SplitPane^
RightIndent: **S**tyleConstants_
Robot: java.awt
RobotPeer: java.awt.peer
ROLLOVER: **D**efaultButtonModel
ROLLOVER_ENABLED_CHANGED_PROPERTY:
 AbstractButton^
ROLLOVER_ICON_CHANGED_PROPERTY: **A**bstractButton^
ROLLOVER_SELECTED_ICON_CHANGED_PROPERTY:
 AbstractButton^
ROMAN_BASELINE: **F**ont_ **G**raphicAttribute_
root: **D**efaultTreeModel^
ROOT_PANE: **A**ccessibleRole^
ROOT_PANE_PROPERTY: **J**InternalFrame^
ROOT_VISIBLE_PROPERTY: **J**Tree^
rootPane: **J**Applet^ **J**Dialog^ **J**Frame^ **J**InternalFrame^
 JWindow^
rootPaneCheckingEnabled: **J**Applet^ **J**Dialog^ **J**Frame^
 JInternalFrame^ **J**Window^
RootPaneContainer: javax.swing
 —implemented by: **J**Applet^ **J**Dialog^ **J**Frame^
 JInternalFrame^ **J**Window^
RootPaneUI^: javax.swing.plaf
 —passed to: **J**RootPane^.setUI( )
 —returned by: **J**RootPane^.getUI( )
rootVisible: **A**bstractLayoutCache **J**Tree^
rotate( ): **A**ffineTransform **G**raphics2D^
roundedCorners: **L**ineBorder^
RoundRectangle2D^: java.awt.geom
 —subclasses: **R**oundRectangle2D.Double^
 RoundRectangle2D.Float^
 —passed to: **R**oundRectangle2D^.setRoundRect( )
RoundRectangle2D.Double^: java.awt.geom
RoundRectangle2D.Float^: java.awt.geom

ROW_HEADER: **A**ccessibleRole^ *ScrollPaneConstants*
ROW_HEIGHT_PROPERTY: **J**Tree^
rowAtPoint(): **J**Table^
rowHead: **S**crollPaneLayout⌄
rowHeader: **J**ScrollPane^
rowHeight: **A**bstractLayoutCache⌄ **J**Table^ **J**Tree^
rowHeights: **G**ridBagLayout
rowMapper: **D**efaultTreeSelectionModel⌄
RowMapper: javax.swing.tree
—passed to: **D**efaultTreeSelectionModel⌄.setRowMapper()
   TreeSelectionModel.setRowMapper()
—returned by: **D**efaultTreeSelectionModel⌄.getRowMapper()
   TreeSelectionModel.getRowMapper()
—implemented by: **A**bstractLayoutCache⌄
—fields: **D**efaultTreeSelectionModel⌄.rowMapper
rowMargin: **J**Table^
ROWS: **H**TML.Attribute
rowSelectionAllowed: **J**Table^
ROWSPAN: **H**TML.Attribute
rowsRemoved(): **D**efaultTableModel^
rowWeights: **G**ridBagLayout
RTFEditorKit^: javax.swing.text.rtf
run(): **A**syncBoxView.ChildState **R**enderableImageProducer
RUN_DIRECTION: **T**extAttribute^
RUN_DIRECTION_LTR: **T**extAttribute^
RUN_DIRECTION_RTL: **T**extAttribute^
runnable: **I**nvocationEvent^
Runnable: java.lang
—passed to: **A**bstractDocument⌄.render()
   javax.swing.text.Document⌄.render() **E**ventQueue
   < invokeAndWait(), invokeLater() > **I**nvocationEvent()
   LayoutQueue.addTask() **S**wingUtilities < invokeAndWait(),
   invokeLater() >
—returned by: **L**ayoutQueue.waitForWork()
—implemented by: **A**syncBoxView.ChildState
   RenderableImageProducer
—fields: **I**nvocationEvent^.runnable
RuntimeException⌄: java.lang
—subclasses: **C**annotRedoException **C**annotUndoException
   CMMException **I**llegalPathStateException
   ImagingOpException **P**rofileDataException
   RasterFormatException **U**nmodifiableSetException
—descendents: **H**eadlessException^
   IllegalComponentStateException^
   InvalidDnDOperationException^
S: **H**TML.Tag⌄
S_RESIZE_CURSOR: **C**ursor **F**rame⌄
SADDLE_STITCH: **F**inishings^
SAMP: **H**TML.Tag⌄
SAMPLE_RATE: **F**loatControl.Type^
sampleModel: **I**mageTypeSpecifier **R**aster⌄
SampleModel⌄: java.awt.image
—subclasses: **C**omponentSampleModel^
   MultiPixelPackedSampleModel^
   SinglePixelPackedSampleModel^
—descendents: **B**andedSampleModel^
   PixelInterleavedSampleModel^
—passed to: **C**olorModel⌄.isCompatibleSampleModel()
   ImageTypeSpecifier() **R**aster⌄ < createRaster(),
   createWritableRaster(), **R**aster⌄ > **W**ritableRaster()
—returned by: **B**ufferedImage^.getSampleModel()
   ColorModel⌄.createCompatibleSampleModel()
   ImageTypeSpecifier.getSampleModel()
   Raster⌄.getSampleModel() *RenderedImage*⌄.getSampleModel()
   SampleModel⌄ < createCompatibleSampleModel(),
   createSubsetSampleModel() >
—fields: **I**mageTypeSpecifier.sampleModel **R**aster⌄.sampleModel
sampleModelTranslateX: **R**aster⌄
sampleModelTranslateY: **R**aster⌄
sampleRate: **A**udioFormat
sampleSizeInBits: **A**udioFormat
SAVE: **F**ileDialog^

save(): **A**WTEventMulticaster
SAVE_DIALOG: **J**FileChooser^
SAVE_FILE: **E**vent
saveInternal(): **A**WTEventMulticaster
scale(): **A**ffineTransform **G**raphics2D^
SCALE_AREA_AVERAGING: **I**mage⌄
SCALE_DEFAULT: **I**mage⌄
SCALE_FAST: **I**mage⌄
SCALE_REPLICATE: **I**mage⌄
SCALE_SMOOTH: **I**mage⌄
scanForPlugins(): **I**mageIO
scanlineStride: **C**omponentSampleModel^
SCRIPT: **H**TML.Tag⌄
SCROLL_ABSOLUTE: **E**vent
SCROLL_BAR: **A**ccessibleRole^
SCROLL_BEGIN: **E**vent
SCROLL_END: **E**vent
SCROLL_LINE_DOWN: **E**vent
SCROLL_LINE_UP: **E**vent
SCROLL_LOCK: **E**vent
SCROLL_PAGE_DOWN: **E**vent
SCROLL_PAGE_UP: **E**vent
SCROLL_PANE: **A**ccessibleRole^
SCROLL_TAB_LAYOUT: **J**TabbedPane^
Scrollable: javax.swing
—implemented by: **J**List^ **J**Table^ **J**TextComponent^ **J**Tree^
scrollbar: **S**ystemColor^
SCROLLBAR: **S**ystemColor^
Scrollbar^: java.awt
—passed to: **S**crollbar.AccessibleAWTScrollBar()
   Toolkit.createScrollbar()
Scrollbar.AccessibleAWTScrollBar^: java.awt
ScrollbarPeer^: java.awt.peer
—returned by: **T**oolkit.createScrollbar()
SCROLLBARS_ALWAYS: **S**crollPane^
SCROLLBARS_AS_NEEDED: **S**crollPane^
SCROLLBARS_BOTH: **T**extArea^
SCROLLBARS_HORIZONTAL_ONLY: **T**extArea^
SCROLLBARS_NEVER: **S**crollPane^
SCROLLBARS_NONE: **T**extArea^
SCROLLBARS_VERTICAL_ONLY: **T**extArea^
ScrollBarUI^: javax.swing.plaf
—passed to: **J**ScrollBar^.setUI()
—returned by: **J**ScrollBar^.getUI()
SCROLLING: **H**TML.Attribute
ScrollPane^: java.awt
—passed to: **S**crollPane.AccessibleAWTScrollPane()
   Toolkit.createScrollPane()
ScrollPane.AccessibleAWTScrollPane^: java.awt
ScrollPaneAdjustable: java.awt
ScrollPaneConstants: javax.swing
—implemented by: **J**ScrollPane^ **S**crollPaneLayout⌄
ScrollPaneLayout⌄: javax.swing
—subclasses: **S**crollPaneLayout.UIResource⌄
ScrollPaneLayout.UIResource^: javax.swing
ScrollPanePeer^: java.awt.peer
—returned by: **T**oolkit.createScrollPane()
ScrollPaneUI^: javax.swing.plaf
—passed to: **J**ScrollPane^.setUI()
—returned by: **J**ScrollPane^.getUI()
scrollPathToVisible(): **J**Tree^
scrollRectToVisible(): **J**Component^
scrollRowToVisible(): **J**Tree^
SCROLLS_ON_EXPAND_PROPERTY: **J**Tree^
scrollIsOnExpand: **J**Tree^
scrollToReference(): **J**EditorPane^
scrollUnderway: **J**Viewport^
SDATA: *DTDConstants*
SE_RESIZE_CURSOR: **C**ursor **F**rame⌄
SectionElementName: **A**bstractDocument⌄
SecurityException: java.lang

S

—thrown by: **F**ocusManager‸.setCurrentManager( )
KeyboardFocusManager **<** getGlobalActiveWindow( ),
getGlobalCurrentFocusCycleRoot( ), getGlobalFocusedWindow( ),
getGlobalFocusOwner( ), getGlobalPermanentFocusOwner( ),
setCurrentKeyboardFocusManager( ) **>**
UIManager.setInstalledLookAndFeels( )
seek( ): *I*mageInputStream‸ **I**mageInputStreamImpl↓
seekForwardOnly: **I**mageReader
SEG_CLOSE: *P*athIterator
SEG_CUBICTO: *P*athIterator
SEG_LINETO: *P*athIterator
SEG_MOVETO: *P*athIterator
SEG_QUADTO: *P*athIterator
Segment: javax.swing.text
—passed to: **A**bstractDocument↓.getText( )
AbstractDocument.*Content*.getChars( )
*javax.swing.text.D*ocument↓.getText( ) **G**apContent‸.getChars( )
StringContent.getChars( ) **U**tilities **<** drawTabbedText( ),
getBreakLocation( ), getTabbedTextOffset( ),
getTabbedTextWidth( ) **>**
—returned by: **G**lyphView‸.getText( ) **P**lainView‸.getLineBuffer( )
WrappedPlainView‸.getLineBuffer( )
SELECT: **H**TML.Tag↓
select( ): **C**hoice‸ *ChoicePeer*‸ **J**TextComponent↓
java.awt.**L**ist‸ *ListPeer*‸ **T**extComponent↓
TextComponentPeer↓
SELECTABLE: **A**ccessibleState‸
selectAll( ): *C*omboBoxEditor **J**Table‸ **J**TextComponent↓
TextComponent↓
selectAllAccessibleSelection( ): *A*ccessibleSelection
JComboBox.AccessibleJComboBox‸ **J**List.AccessibleJList‸
JMenu.AccessibleJMenu‸ **J**MenuBar.AccessibleJMenuBar‸
JTabbedPane.AccessibleJTabbedPane‸
JTable.AccessibleJTable‸ **J**Tree.AccessibleJTree‸
JTree.AccessibleJTree.AccessibleJTreeNode‸
List.AccessibleAWTList‸
MenuComponent.AccessibleAWTMenuComponent↓
selectAllAction: **D**efaultEditorKit↓
selectBestTextFlavor( ): **D**ataFlavor
selectContent( ): **H**TMLWriter‸
selected: **D**efaultTreeCellRenderer‸
SELECTED: **A**ccessibleState‸ **D**efaultButtonModel↓
HTML.Attribute **I**temEvent‸
SELECTED_CONVERTED_TEXT_HIGHLIGHT:
InputMethodHighlight
SELECTED_FILE_CHANGED_PROPERTY: **J**FileChooser‸
SELECTED_FILES_CHANGED_PROPERTY: **J**FileChooser‸
SELECTED_ICON_CHANGED_PROPERTY: **A**bstractButton‸
SELECTED_RAW_TEXT_HIGHLIGHT: **I**nputMethodHighlight
selectedItemChanged( ): **J**ComboBox‸
selectedItemReminder: **J**ComboBox‸
selectInitialValue( ): **J**OptionPane‸ **O**ptionPaneUI‸
selectInputMethod( ): **I**nputContext
selection: **D**efaultTreeSelectionModel↓
SELECTION: **J**obAttributes.DefaultSelectionType‸
SELECTION_MODE_PROPERTY: **D**efaultTreeSelectionModel↓
SELECTION_MODEL_PROPERTY: **J**ColorChooser‸ **J**Tree‸
SELECTION_VALUES_PROPERTY: **J**OptionPane‸
selectionBackground: **J**Table↓
selectionBackwardAction: **D**efaultEditorKit↓
selectionBeginAction: **D**efaultEditorKit↓
selectionBeginLineAction: **D**efaultEditorKit↓
selectionBeginParagraphAction: **D**efaultEditorKit↓
selectionBeginWordAction: **D**efaultEditorKit↓
selectionDownAction: **D**efaultEditorKit↓
selectionEndAction: **D**efaultEditorKit↓
selectionEndLineAction: **D**efaultEditorKit↓
selectionEndParagraphAction: **D**efaultEditorKit↓
selectionEndWordAction: **D**efaultEditorKit↓
selectionForeground: **J**Table↓
selectionForKey( ): *J*ComboBox.*KeySelectionManager*
selectionForwardAction: **D**efaultEditorKit↓

selectionMode: **D**efaultTreeSelectionModel↓
selectionModel: **D**efaultTableColumnModel↓ **J**Table‸ **J**Tree‸
selectionNextWordAction: **D**efaultEditorKit↓
selectionPreviousWordAction: **D**efaultEditorKit↓
selectionRedirector: **J**Tree‸
selectionUpAction: **D**efaultEditorKit↓
selectionValues: **J**OptionPane‸
selectLineAction: **D**efaultEditorKit↓
selectParagraphAction: **D**efaultEditorKit↓
selectText( ): *A*ccessibleEditableText‸
JTextComponent.AccessibleJTextComponent↓
selectWithKeyChar( ): **J**ComboBox‸
selectWordAction: **D**efaultEditorKit↓
send( ): *R*eceiver
SENTENCE: *A*ccessibleText↓
SEPARATE_DOCUMENTS_COLLATED_COPIES:
JobAttributes.MultipleDocumentHandlingType‸
MultipleDocumentHandling‸
SEPARATE_DOCUMENTS_UNCOLLATED_COPIES:
JobAttributes.MultipleDocumentHandlingType‸
MultipleDocumentHandling‸
SEPARATOR: **A**ccessibleRole↓
SeparatorUI‸: javax.swing.plaf
—passed to: **J**Separator‸.setUI( )
—returned by: **J**Separator‸.getUI( )
Sequence: javax.sound.midi
—passed to: **M**idiFileWriter **<** getMidiFileTypes( ),
isFileTypeSupported( ), write( ) **>** **M**idiSystem
< getMidiFileTypes( ), isFileTypeSupported( ), write( ) **>**
Sequencer‸.setSequence( )
—returned by: **M**idiFileReader.getSequence( )
MidiSystem.getSequence( ) *Sequencer*‸.getSequence( )
sequenceComplete( ): *I*IOReadProgressListener‸
Sequencer‸: javax.sound.midi
—returned by: **M**idiSystem.getSequencer( )
Sequencer.SyncMode: javax.sound.midi
—passed to: *Sequencer*‸ **<** setMasterSyncMode( ),
setSlaveSyncMode( ) **>**
—returned by: *Sequencer*‸ **<** getMasterSyncMode( ),
getMasterSyncModes( ), getSlaveSyncMode( ),
getSlaveSyncModes( ) **>**
—fields: **S**equencer.SyncMode **<** INTERNAL_CLOCK, MIDI_SYNC,
MIDI_TIME_CODE, NO_SYNC **>**
sequenceStarted( ): *I*IOReadProgressListener‸
Serializable↓: java.io
—extended by: *Attribute*↓
—implemented by: **A**bstractAction↓ **A**bstractBorder↓
AbstractButton.ButtonChangeListener **A**bstractCellEditor↓
AbstractDocument↓ **A**bstractDocument.AbstractElement↓
AbstractListModel↓ **A**bstractTableModel↓
AbstractUndoableEdit↓ **A**ctionMap↓ **A**ffineTransform↓
javax.swing.text.html.parser.**A**ttributeList **A**WTKeyStroke
BorderLayout **B**orderUIResource **B**oxLayout **B**uttonGroup
CardLayout **C**heckboxGroup **C**olor↓ **C**olorSpace↓
Component↓ **C**omponent.AccessibleAWTComponent↓
ComponentOrientation **C**ontainerOrderFocusTraversalPolicy↓
ContentModel **C**SS **C**ursor **D**ateTimeSyntax↓
DefaultBoundedRangeModel **D**efaultButtonModel↓
DefaultCellEditor.EditorDelegate
DefaultColorSelectionModel **D**efaultDesktopManager
DefaultFormatterFactory‸ **D**efaultListSelectionModel↓
DefaultMutableTreeNode↓ **D**efaultSingleSelectionModel↓
DefaultStyledDocument.ElementBuffer
DefaultTableColumnModel↓ **D**efaultTreeModel↓
DefaultTreeSelectionModel↓ **D**imension↓ **D**ocFlavor↓
DragGestureRecognizer↓ **D**ragSource **D**ragSourceContext
DropTarget **D**ropTargetContext **E**ditorKit↓
javax.swing.text.html.parser.**E**lement **E**numSyntax↓ **E**vent
EventListenerList **F**lowLayout **F**ont↓ **F**ontMetrics↓
GapVector↓ **G**raphicsConfigTemplate↓ **G**ridBagConstraints↓
GridBagLayout **G**ridLayout **H**ashAttributeSet↓
HTML.UnknownTag‸ **H**TMLEditorKit.LinkController‸

ICC_Profile, IconUIResource ImageIcon
ImageIcon.AccessibleImageIcon^ InputMap, Insets,
IntegerSyntax, JFormattedTextField.AbstractFormatter,
JMenu.WinListener^ JRootPane.RootLayout
JTabbedPane.ModelListener JTree.TreeSelectionRedirector
JViewport.ViewListener^ LayoutFocusTraversalPolicy^
MediaTracker MenuComponent,
MenuComponent.AccessibleAWTMenuComponent,
MenuShortcut NumericShaper OverlayLayout
ParameterBlock ParserDelegator^ Point^ Polygon
Rectangle, ResolutionSyntax, ScrollPaneAdjustable
ScrollPaneLayout, SetOfIntegerSyntax, SimpleAttributeSet
Size2DSyntax, SizeRequirements SpinnerDateModel^
SpinnerListModel^ SpinnerNumberModel^
StringContent StyleContext, StyleContext.NamedStyle
StyleSheet.BoxPainter StyleSheet.ListPainter TableColumn
TabSet TabStop TextSyntax, Timer TransferHandler
TransformAttribute TreePath UIManager URISyntax,
ViewportLayout

SERVICE_OFF_LINE: JobStateReason^
ServiceRegistry: javax.imageio.spi
—subclasses: IIORegistry^
—passed to: IIOServiceProvider, < onDeregistration( ),
onRegistration( ) > RegisterableService < onDeregistration( ),
onRegistration( ) >
ServiceRegistry.Filter: javax.imageio.spi
—passed to: ServiceRegistry,.getServiceProviders( )
ServiceUI: javax.print
ServiceUIFactory: javax.print
—returned by: PrintService,.getServiceUIFactory( )
Set^: java.util
—passed to: Component,.setFocusTraversalKeys( ) ImageReader
< getImageMetadata( ), getStreamMetadata( ) >
KeyboardFocusManager,.setDefaultFocusTraversalKeys( )
—returned by: Component,.getFocusTraversalKeys( )
KeyboardFocusManager,.getDefaultFocusTraversalKeys( )
PrinterStateReasons^.printerStateReasonSet( ) RenderingHints
< entrySet( ), keySet( ) >
set( ): DefaultListModel^ JobAttributes PageAttributes
ParameterBlock
setAccelerator( ): JMenuItem,
setAcceptAllFileFilterUsed( ): JFileChooser^
setAccessibleCaption( ): AccessibleTable,
JTable.AccessibleJTable^
setAccessibleColumnDescription( ): AccessibleTable,
JTable.AccessibleJTable^
setAccessibleColumnHeader( ): AccessibleTable,
JTable.AccessibleJTable^
setAccessibleDescription( ): AccessibleContext,
setAccessibleIconDescription( ): AccessibleIcon
ImageIcon.AccessibleImageIcon^
setAccessibleName( ): AccessibleContext,
setAccessibleParent( ): AccessibleContext,
setAccessibleRowDescription( ): AccessibleTable,
JTable.AccessibleJTable^
setAccessibleRowHeader( ): AccessibleTable,
JTable.AccessibleJTable^
setAccessibleSummary( ): AccessibleTable,
JTable.AccessibleJTable^
setAccessory( ): JFileChooser^
setAction( ): AbstractButton, JComboBox^ JTextField,
setActionCommand( ): AbstractButton, Button^ ButtonModel^
DefaultButtonModel, JComboBox^ JTextField, MenuItem,
setActionMap( ): JComponent,
setActive( ): DropTarget
setAlignment( ): FlowLayout Label^ LabelPeer^
StyleConstants,
setAlignmentX( ): JComponent,
setAlignmentY( ): JComponent,
setAllocation( ): AsyncBoxView.ChildLocator
setAllowsChildren( ): DefaultMutableTreeNode,
setAllowsInvalid( ): DefaultFormatter,

setAnchorSelectionIndex( ): DefaultListSelectionModel
ListSelectionModel
setAnchorSelectionPath( ): JTree^
setAngleExtent( ): Arc2D,
setAngles( ): Arc2D,
setAngleStart( ): Arc2D,
setAnimated( ): MemoryImageSource
setApproveButtonMnemonic( ): JFileChooser^
setApproveButtonText( ): JFileChooser^
setApproveButtonToolTipText( ): JFileChooser^
setArc( ): Arc2D,
setArcByCenter( ): Arc2D,
setArcByTangent( ): Arc2D,
setArcType( ): Arc2D,
setAreaOfInterest( ): RenderContext
setArmed( ): ButtonModel^ DefaultButtonModel, JMenuItem,
setAsksAllowsChildren( ): DefaultTreeModel
setAsynchronousLoadPriority( ): AbstractDocument,
setAttribute( ): IIOMetadataNode
setAttributeNode( ): IIOMetadataNode
setAttributeNodeNS( ): IIOMetadataNode
setAttributeNS( ): IIOMetadataNode
setAttributes( ): AccessibleEditableText^
JTextComponent.AccessibleJTextComponent,
setAutoCreateColumnsFromModel( ): JTable^
setAutoDelay( ): Robot
setAutoResizeMode( ): JTable^
setAutoscrolls( ): JComponent,
setAutoWaitForIdle( ): Robot
setAxis( ): BoxView,
setBackground( ): AccessibleComponent, Component,
Component.AccessibleAWTComponent, ComponentPeer,
Graphics2D^ JList.AccessibleJList.AccessibleJListChild^
JTable.AccessibleJTable.AccessibleJTableCell^
JTableHeader.AccessibleJTableHeader ,
.AccessibleJTableHeaderEntry^
JTree.AccessibleJTree.AccessibleJTreeNode^
MenuComponent.AccessibleAWTMenuComponent,
StyleConstants,
setBackgroundAt( ): JTabbedPane^
setBackgroundNonSelectionColor( ): DefaultTreeCellRenderer^
setBackgroundSelectionColor( ): DefaultTreeCellRenderer^
setBackingStoreEnabled( ): JViewport^
setBase( ): HTMLDocument StyleSheet^
setBaseFontSize( ): StyleSheet^
setBidiLevel( ): StyleConstants,
setBitOffset( ): ImageInputStream, ImageInputStreamImpl
setBlinkRate( ): Caret DefaultCaret^
setBlockIncrement( ): Adjustable JScrollBar, Scrollbar^
ScrollPaneAdjustable
setBold( ): StyleConstants,
setBorder( ): JComponent, TitledBorder,
setBorderPainted( ): AbstractButton, JMenuBar^
JPopupMenu^ JProgressBar^ JToolBar^
setBorderPaintedFlat( ): JCheckBox^
setBorderSelectionColor( ): DefaultTreeCellEditor
DefaultTreeCellRenderer^
setBottomComponent( ): JSplitPane^
setBottomInset( ): AsyncBoxView^
setBounds( ): AccessibleComponent, Component,
Component.AccessibleAWTComponent, ComponentPeer,
JList.AccessibleJList.AccessibleJListChild^
JTable.AccessibleJTable.AccessibleJTableCell^
JTableHeader.AccessibleJTableHeader ,
.AccessibleJTableHeaderEntry^
JTree.AccessibleJTree.AccessibleJTreeNode^
MenuComponent.AccessibleAWTMenuComponent,
Rectangle,
setBoundsForFrame( ): DefaultDesktopManager
DesktopManager
setByteOrder( ): ImageInputStream, ImageInputStreamImpl,
setCacheDirectory( ): ImageIO

S

setCalendarField(): SpinnerDateModel^
setCanWrapLines(): AbstractWriter
setCaret(): JTextComponent^
setCaretColor(): JTextComponent^
setCaretPosition(): JTextComponent^ TextComponent^
  TextComponentPeer^
setCellEditor(): JTable^ JTree^ TableColumn
setCellRenderer(): JList^ JTree^ TableColumn
setCellSelectionEnabled(): JTable^
setChannelPressure(): *MidiChannel*
setCharacterAttributes(): DefaultStyledDocument^ JTextPane^
  StyledDocument^ StyledEditorKit.StyledTextAction^
setCharacterSubsets(): InputContext *InputMethod*
setCheckboxGroup(): Checkbox^ *CheckboxPeer*^
setChooserPanels(): JColorChooser^
setClickCountToStart(): DefaultCellEditor^
setClip(): Graphics
setClosable(): JInternalFrame^
setClosed(): JInternalFrame^
setClosedIcon(): DefaultTreeCellRenderer^
setCoalesce(): Timer
setColor(): Graphics JColorChooser^ PageAttributes
setColorModel(): *ImageConsumer* ImageFilter PixelGrabber
setColumnCount(): DefaultTableModel^
setColumnHeader(): JScrollPane^
setColumnHeaderView(): JScrollPane^
setColumnIdentifiers(): DefaultTableModel^
setColumnMargin(): DefaultTableColumnModel
  TableColumnModel
setColumnModel(): JTable^ JTableHeader^
setColumns(): GridLayout JTextArea^ JTextField^ TextArea^
  TextField^
setColumnSelectionAllowed(): DefaultTableColumnModel
  JTable^ *TableColumnModel*
setColumnSelectionInterval(): JTable^
setCommitsOnValidEdit(): DefaultFormatter^
setComparator(): SortingFocusTraversalPolicy^
setComponent(): DragGestureRecognizer DropTarget
  JToolTip^ StyleConstants
setComponentAt(): JTabbedPane^
setComponentOrientation(): Component
setComposite(): Graphics2D^
setCompositionEnabled(): InputContext *InputMethod*
setCompressionMode(): ImageWriteParam^
setCompressionQuality(): ImageWriteParam^
setCompressionType(): ImageWriteParam^
setConstraint(): SpringLayout.Constraints
setConstraints(): GridBagLayout
setContentAreaFilled(): AbstractButton^
setContentPane(): JApplet^ JDialog^ JFrame^
  JInternalFrame^ JRootPane^ JWindow^
  RootPaneContainer
setContents(): Clipboard
setContentType(): JEditorPane^
setContinuousLayout(): JSplitPane^
setControlButtonsAreShown(): JFileChooser^
setController(): IIOMetadata IIOParam
setCopies(): JobAttributes PrinterJob
setCopiesToDefault(): JobAttributes
setCorner(): JScrollPane^
setCurrent(): CheckboxGroup
setCurrentAccessibleValue():
  AbstractButton.AccessibleAbstractButton^
  AccessibleValue Button.AccessibleAWTButton^
  Checkbox.AccessibleAWTCheckbox^
  JInternalFrame.AccessibleJInternalFrame^
  JInternalFrame.JDesktopIcon.AccessibleJDesktopIcon^
  JProgressBar.AccessibleJProgressBar^
  JScrollBar.AccessibleJScrollBar^ JSlider.AccessibleJSlider^
  JSplitPane.AccessibleJSplitPane^
  MenuItem.AccessibleAWTMenuItem^
  Scrollbar.AccessibleAWTScrollBar^

setCurrentDirectory(): JFileChooser^
setCurrentKeyboardFocusManager():
  KeyboardFocusManager
setCurrentLineLength(): AbstractWriter
setCurrentManager(): FocusManager^ RepaintManager
setCursor(): *AccessibleComponent* Component
  Component.AccessibleAWTComponent^ DragSourceContext
  JList.AccessibleJList.AccessibleJListChild^
  JTable.AccessibleJTable.AccessibleJTableCell^
  JTableHeader.AccessibleJTableHeader
  .AccessibleJTableHeaderEntry^
  JTree.AccessibleJTree.AccessibleJTreeNode^
  MenuComponent.AccessibleAWTMenuComponent^
setCurve(): CubicCurve2D QuadCurve2D
setData(): BufferedImage ICC_Profile IIOByteBuffer
  WritableRenderedImage
setDataElements(): SampleModel WritableRaster^
setDataVector(): DefaultTableModel^
setDebugGraphicsOptions(): JComponent^
setDebugOptions(): DebugGraphics
setDecodeTables(): JPEGImageReadParam^
setDefaultAction(): *Keymap*
setDefaultActions(): DropTarget
setDefaultButton(): JRootPane^
setDefaultCapable(): JButton^
setDefaultCloseOperation(): JDialog^ JFrame^
  JInternalFrame^
setDefaultCursor(): HTMLEditorKit^
setDefaultDTD(): ParserDelegator^
setDefaultEditor(): JTable^
setDefaultFocusTraversalKeys(): KeyboardFocusManager
setDefaultFocusTraversalPolicy(): KeyboardFocusManager
setDefaultFormatter(): DefaultFormatterFactory^
setDefaultLightWeightPopupEnabled(): JPopupMenu^
setDefaultLocale(): JComponent^ UIDefaults^
setDefaultLookAndFeelDecorated(): JDialog^ JFrame^
setDefaultQueue(): LayoutQueue
setDefaultRenderer(): JTable^ JTableHeader^
setDefaultSelection(): JobAttributes
setDelay(): JMenu^ Timer
setDescription(): ImageIcon
setDesktopIcon(): JInternalFrame^
setDesktopManager(): JDesktopPane^
setDesktopProperty(): Toolkit
setDestination(): ImageReadParam^ JobAttributes
setDestinationBands(): ImageReadParam^
setDestinationOffset(): IIOParam^
setDestinationType(): IIOParam
setDialog(): JobAttributes
setDialogTitle(): JFileChooser^
setDialogType(): JFileChooser^
setDimensions(): *ImageConsumer* ImageFilter PixelGrabber
setDirection(): DefaultStyledDocument.ElementSpec
setDirectory(): FileDialog^ *FileDialogPeer*^
setDisabledIcon(): AbstractButton^ JLabel^
setDisabledIconAt(): JTabbedPane^
setDisabledSelectedIcon(): AbstractButton^
setDisabledTextColor(): JTextComponent^
setDismissDelay(): ToolTipManager^
setDisplayedMnemonic(): JLabel^
setDisplayedMnemonicIndex(): AbstractButton^ JLabel^
setDisplayedMnemonicIndexAt(): JTabbedPane^
setDisplayFormatter(): DefaultFormatterFactory^
setDisplayMode(): GraphicsDevice
setDividerLocation(): JSplitPane^ SplitPaneUI^
setDividerSize(): JSplitPane^
setDocument(): JTextComponent^
setDocumentFilter(): AbstractDocument^
setDocumentProperties(): AbstractDocument
setDot(): *Caret* DefaultCaret^ NavigationFilter
  NavigationFilter.FilterBypass
setDoubleBuffered(): JComponent^

S

S

Cross-Ref

setImageObserver( ): ImageIcon
setImplicitDownCycleTraversal( ):
    ContainerOrderFocusTraversalPolicy⌒
    SortingFocusTraversalPolicy⌒
setIndentSpace( ): AbstractWriter⌄
setIndeterminate( ): JProgressBar⌒
setIndex( ): Segment
setInitialDelay( ): Timer ToolTipManager⌒
setInitialSelectionValue( ): JOptionPane⌒
setInitialValue( ): JOptionPane⌒
setInnerHTML( ): HTMLDocument⌒
setInput( ): ImageReader
setInputMap( ): JComponent⌒
setInputMethodContext( ): *InputMethod*
setInputValue( ): JOptionPane⌒
setInputVerifier( ): JComponent⌒
setInsets( ): CompositeView⌒
setInstalledLookAndFeels( ): UIManager
setIntercellSpacing( ): JTable⌒
setInternalFrame( ): JInternalFrame.JDesktopIcon⌒
setInvalidCharacters( ): MaskFormatter⌒
setInverted( ): JSlider⌒
setInvoker( ): JPopupMenu⌒
setInvokesStopCellEditing( ): JTree⌒
setItalic( ): StyleConstants⌄
setItem( ): *ComboBoxEditor*
setJMenuBar( ): JApplet⌒ JDialog⌒ JFrame⌒ JInternalFrame⌒
    JRootPane⌒
setJobName( ): PrinterJob
setJustification( ): javax.swing.text.ParagraphView⌒
setKeyChar( ): KeyEvent⌒
setKeyCode( ): KeyEvent⌒
setKeymap( ): JTextComponent⌒
setKeySelectionManager( ): JComboBox⌒
setLabel( ): AbstractButton⌒ Button⌒ *ButtonPeer* Checkbox⌒
    CheckboxPeer⌒ JPopupMenu⌒ MenuItem⌒ *MenuItemPeer*⌒
    Option
setLabelFor( ): JLabel⌒
setLabelTable( ): JSlider⌒
setLargeModel( ): JTree⌒
setLastDividerLocation( ): JSplitPane⌒
setLayer( ): JInternalFrame⌒ JLayeredPane⌒
setLayeredPane( ): JApplet⌒ JDialog⌒ JFrame⌒
    JInternalFrame⌒ JRootPane⌒ JWindow⌒
    RootPaneContainer
setLayout( ): Container⌒
setLayoutOrientation( ): JList⌒
setLeadAnchorNotificationEnabled( ):
    DefaultListSelectionModel⌒
setLeadSelectionIndex( ): DefaultListSelectionModel
    ListSelectionModel
setLeadSelectionPath( ): JTree⌒
setLeafIcon( ): DefaultTreeCellRenderer⌒
setLeftComponent( ): JSplitPane⌒
setLeftIndent( ): StyleConstants⌄
setLeftInset( ): AsyncBoxView⌒
setLength( ): IIOByteBuffer
setLightWeightPopupEnabled( ): JComboBox⌒ JPopupMenu⌒
    ToolTipManager⌒
setLimit( ): UndoManager⌒
setLine( ): Line2D⌒
setLineIncrement( ): Scrollbar⌒ *ScrollbarPeer*⌒
setLineLength( ): AbstractWriter⌄
setLineSeparator( ): AbstractWriter⌄
setLineSpacing( ): javax.swing.text.ParagraphView⌒
    StyleConstants⌄
setLineWrap( ): JTextArea⌒
setLinkCursor( ): HTMLEditorKit⌒
setList( ): SpinnerListModel⌒
setListData( ): JList⌒
setLoadsSynchronously( ): ImageView⌒

setLocale( ): Component⌄ ImageReader ImageWriter
    InputMethod
setLocation( ): *AccessibleComponent*⌄ Component⌄
    Component.AccessibleAWTComponent⌒
    JList.AccessibleJList.AccessibleJListChild⌒
    JTable.AccessibleJTable.AccessibleJTableCell⌒
    JTableHeader.AccessibleJTableHeader⌄
    .AccessibleJTableHeaderEntry⌒
    JTree.AccessibleJTree.AccessibleJTreeNode⌒
    MenuComponent.AccessibleAWTMenuComponent⌒
    Point2D⌄ Rectangle⌒
setLocationRelativeTo( ): Window⌒
setLockingKeyState( ): Toolkit
setLogicalStyle( ): DefaultStyledDocument⌒ JTextPane⌒
    StyledDocument⌒
setLogStream( ): DebugGraphics⌒
setLogTimers( ): Timer
setLookAndFeel( ): UIManager
setLoopPoints( ): *Clip*⌒
setMagicCaretPosition( ): *Caret* DefaultCaret⌒
setMajorOffset( ): AsyncBoxView.ChildState
setMajorTickSpacing( ): JSlider⌒
setMargin( ): AbstractButton⌒ JMenuBar⌒ JTextComponent⌒
    JToolBar⌒
setMask( ): MaskFormatter⌒
setMasterSyncMode( ): *Sequencer*⌒
setMaximizable( ): JInternalFrame⌒
setMaximizedBounds( ): Frame⌒ *FramePeer*⌒
setMaximum( ): *Adjustable* *BoundedRangeModel*
    DefaultBoundedRangeModel InternationalFormatter⌒
    JInternalFrame⌒ JProgressBar⌒ JScrollBar⌒ JSlider⌒
    ProgressMonitor Scrollbar⌒ ScrollPaneAdjustable
    SpinnerNumberModel⌒
setMaximumRowCount( ): JComboBox⌒
setMaximumSize( ): JComponent⌒
setMaximumZoneSize( ): ZoneView⌒
setMaxPage( ): JobAttributes
setMaxWidth( ): TableColumn
setMaxZonesLoaded( ): ZoneView⌒
setMedia( ): PageAttributes
setMediaToDefault( ): PageAttributes
setMenuBar( ): Frame⌒ *FramePeer*⌒ JInternalFrame⌒
    JRootPane⌒
setMenuLocation( ): JMenu⌒
setMessage( ): JOptionPane⌒ MidiMessage⌄
setMessageType( ): JOptionPane⌒
setMetadata( ): IIOImage
setMicrosecondPosition( ): *Clip*⌒ *Sequencer*⌒
setMillisToDecideToPopup( ): ProgressMonitor
setMillisToPopup( ): ProgressMonitor
setMinimum( ): *Adjustable* *BoundedRangeModel*
    DefaultBoundedRangeModel InternationalFormatter⌒
    JProgressBar⌒ JScrollBar⌒ JSlider⌒ ProgressMonitor
    Scrollbar⌒ ScrollPaneAdjustable SpinnerNumberModel⌒
setMinimumSize( ): JComponent⌒
setMinorTickSpacing( ): JSlider⌒
setMinPage( ): JobAttributes
setMinWidth( ): TableColumn
setMnemonic( ): AbstractButton⌒ *ButtonModel*⌒
    DefaultButtonModel⌄
setMnemonicAt( ): JTabbedPane⌒
setModal( ): Dialog⌒
setMode( ): FileDialog⌒
setModel( ): AbstractButton⌒ AbstractLayoutCache⌄
    JComboBox⌒ JList⌒ JProgressBar⌒ JScrollBar⌒ JSlider⌒
    JSpinner⌒ JTabbedPane⌒ JTable⌒ JTree⌒
setModelIndex( ): TableColumn
setModifiers( ): KeyEvent⌒
setMono( ): *MidiChannel*
setMultiClickThreshhold( ): AbstractButton⌒
setMultipleDocumentHandling( ): JobAttributes
setMultipleDocumentHandlingToDefault( ): JobAttributes

S

setScrollsOnExpand(): JTree^

setSelected(): AbstractButton^ ButtonGroup *ButtonModel*^ DefaultButtonModel_ JInternalFrame^ JMenuBar^ JPopupMenu^

setSelectedCheckbox(): CheckboxGroup

setSelectedColor(): *ColorSelectionModel* DefaultColorSelectionModel

setSelectedComponent(): JTabbedPane^

setSelectedFile(): JFileChooser^

setSelectedFiles(): JFileChooser^

setSelectedFrame(): JDesktopPane^

setSelectedIcon(): AbstractButton_

setSelectedIndex(): DefaultSingleSelectionModel JComboBox^ JList^ JTabbedPane^ *SingleSelectionModel*

setSelectedIndices(): JList^

setSelectedItem(): *ComboBoxModel*_ DefaultComboBoxModel^ JComboBox^

setSelectedPath(): MenuSelectionManager

setSelectedTextColor(): JTextComponent_

setSelectedValue(): JList^

setSelection(): Option

setSelectionBackground(): JList^ JTable^

setSelectionColor(): JTextComponent_

setSelectionEnd(): JTextComponent_ TextComponent_

setSelectionForeground(): JList^ JTable^

setSelectionInterval(): DefaultListSelectionModel JList^ JTree^ *ListSelectionModel*

setSelectionMode(): DefaultListSelectionModel DefaultTreeSelectionModel_ JList^ JTable^ *ListSelectionModel* *TreeSelectionModel*

setSelectionModel(): AbstractLayoutCache_ DefaultTableColumnModel JColorChooser^ JList^ JMenuBar^ JPopupMenu^ JTable^ JTree^ *TableColumnModel*

setSelectionPath(): DefaultTreeSelectionModel_ JTree^ *TreeSelectionModel*

setSelectionPaths(): DefaultTreeSelectionModel_ JTree^ *TreeSelectionModel*

setSelectionRow(): JTree^

setSelectionRows(): JTree^

setSelectionStart(): JTextComponent_ TextComponent_

setSelectionValues(): JOptionPane^

setSelectionVisible(): *Caret* DefaultCaret^

setSeparatorSize(): JToolBar.Separator^

setSequence(): *Sequencer*^

setSharedInstance(): PopupFactory

setShortcut(): MenuItem_

setShowGrid(): JTable^

setShowHorizontalLines(): JTable^

setShowsRootHandles(): JTree^

setShowVerticalLines(): JTable^

setSides(): JobAttributes

setSidesToDefault(): JobAttributes

setSize(): *AccessibleComponent*_ Component_ Component.AccessibleAWTComponent_ DefaultListModel^ Dimension2D_ JList.AccessibleJList.AccessibleJListChild^ JTable.AccessibleJTable.AccessibleJTableCell^ JTableHeader.AccessibleJTableHeader_ .AccessibleJTableHeaderEntry^ JTree.AccessibleJTree.AccessibleJTreeNode^ MenuComponent.AccessibleAWTMenuComponent_ Paper Rectangle_ SizeSequence View_

setSizes(): SizeSequence

setSlaveSyncMode(): *Sequencer*^

setSnapToTicks(): JSlider^

setSolo(): *MidiChannel*

setSource(): AWTEvent_ ParameterBlock

setSourceActions(): DragGestureRecognizer_

setSourceBands(): IIOParam_

setSourceProgressivePasses(): ImageReadParam_

setSourceRegion(): IIOParam_

setSourceRenderSize(): ImageReadParam_

setSources(): ParameterBlock

setSourceSubsampling(): IIOParam_

setSpaceAbove(): StyleConstants_

setSpaceBelow(): StyleConstants_

setStart(): SpinnerDateModel^

setState(): Checkbox^ CheckboxMenuItem^ *CheckboxMenuItemPeer* *CheckboxPeer* Frame_ *FramePeer* JCheckBoxMenuItem^

setStepSize(): SpinnerNumberModel^

setStream(): *AppletContext*

setStrikeThrough(): LabelView_ StyleConstants_

setString(): JProgressBar^

setStringPainted(): JProgressBar^

setStroke(): Graphics2D^

setStub(): Applet_

setStyledDocument(): JTextPane^

setStyleSheet(): HTMLEditorKit^

setSubscript(): LabelView_ StyleConstants_

setSuperscript(): LabelView_ StyleConstants_

setSurrendersFocusOnKeystroke(): JTable^

setTabLayoutPolicy(): JTabbedPane^

setTable(): JTableHeader^

setTableHeader(): JTable^

setTabPlacement(): JTabbedPane^

setTabSet(): StyleConstants_

setTabSize(): JTextArea^

setTarget(): AccessibleRelation

setTargetActions(): DropTargetContext

setTempoFactor(): *Sequencer*^

setTempoInBPM(): *Sequencer*^

setTempoInMPQ(): *Sequencer*^

setText(): AbstractButton_ JLabel_ JTextComponent_ Label^ *LabelPeer*^ TextComponent_ *TextComponentPeer*_

setTextContents(): *AccessibleEditableText*^ JTextComponent.AccessibleJTextComponent_

setTextNonSelectionColor(): DefaultTreeCellRenderer^

setTextSelectionColor(): DefaultTreeCellRenderer^

setThumbnails(): IIOImage

setTick(): MidiEvent

setTickPosition(): *Sequencer*^

setTiling(): ImageWriteParam_

setTilingMode(): ImageWriteParam_

setTipText(): JToolTip^

setTitle(): Dialog_ *DialogPeer*_ Frame_ *FramePeer*^ JInternalFrame^ TitledBorder_

setTitleAt(): JTabbedPane^

setTitleColor(): TitledBorder_

setTitleFont(): TitledBorder_

setTitleJustification(): TitledBorder_

setTitlePosition(): TitledBorder_

setToggleClickCount(): JTree^

setToIdentity(): AffineTransform

setTokenThreshold(): HTMLDocument^

setToolTipText(): JComponent_

setToolTipTextAt(): JTabbedPane^

setToPage(): JobAttributes

setTopComponent(): JSplitPane^

setTopInset(): AsyncBoxView^

setToRotation(): AffineTransform

setToScale(): AffineTransform

setToShear(): AffineTransform

setToTranslation(): AffineTransform

setTrackMute(): *Sequencer*^

setTrackSolo(): *Sequencer*^

setTransferHandler(): JComponent_

setTransform(): AffineTransform Graphics2D^ RenderContext

setTree(): DefaultTreeCellEditor

setType(): DefaultStyledDocument.ElementSpec

setUI(): JComponent_

setUndecorated(): Dialog_ Frame_

setUnderline(): LabelView_ StyleConstants_

S

S

—passed to: **J**Spinner˄.setUI( )
—returned by: **J**Spinner˄.getUI( )
SPLIT_PANE: **A**ccessibleRole˄
SplitPaneUI˄: javax.swing.plaf
—passed to: **J**SplitPane˄.setUI( )
—returned by: **J**SplitPane˄.getUI( )
SPOOL_AREA_FULL: **P**rinterStateReason˄
Spring: javax.swing
—passed to: **S**pring < max( ), minus( ), sum( ) >
SpringLayout.putConstraint( ) **S**pringLayout.Constraints
< setConstraint( ), setHeight( ), setWidth( ), setX( ), setY( ),
SpringLayout.Constraints( ) >
—returned by: **S**pring < constant( ), max( ), minus( ), sum( ) >
SpringLayout.getConstraint( ) **S**pringLayout.Constraints
< getConstraint( ), getHeight( ), getWidth( ), getX( ), getY( ) >
SpringLayout: javax.swing
SpringLayout.Constraints: javax.swing
—returned by: **S**pringLayout.getConstraints( )
Src: **A**lphaComposite
SRC: **A**lphaComposite **H**TML.Attribute
SRC_ATOP: **A**lphaComposite
SRC_IN: **A**lphaComposite
SRC_OUT: **A**lphaComposite
SRC_OVER: **A**lphaComposite
SrcAtop: **A**lphaComposite
srccols: **R**eplicateScaleFilter˄
srcHeight: **R**eplicateScaleFilter˄
SrcIn: **A**lphaComposite
SrcOut: **A**lphaComposite
SrcOver: **A**lphaComposite
srcrows: **R**eplicateScaleFilter˄
srcWidth: **R**eplicateScaleFilter˄
STANDARD: **G**lyphMetrics **J**obSheets˄
STANDARD_INPUT_TYPE: **I**mageReaderSpi˄
STANDARD_OUTPUT_TYPE: **I**mageWriterSpi˄
standardFormatSupported: **I**IOMetadata
standardMetadataFormatName: **I**IOMetadataFormatImpl
STANDBY: **H**TML.Attribute
STAPLE: **F**inishings˄
STAPLE_BOTTOM_LEFT: **F**inishings˄
STAPLE_BOTTOM_RIGHT: **F**inishings˄
STAPLE_DUAL_BOTTOM: **F**inishings˄
STAPLE_DUAL_LEFT: **F**inishings˄
STAPLE_DUAL_RIGHT: **F**inishings˄
STAPLE_DUAL_TOP: **F**inishings˄
STAPLE_TOP_LEFT: **F**inishings˄
STAPLE_TOP_RIGHT: **F**inishings˄
START: **H**TML.Attribute **L**ineEvent.Type **S**hortMessage˄
start: **A**rc2D.Double˄ **A**rc2D.Float˄
start( ): **A**pplet˄ *DataLine*˄
HTMLDocument.HTMLReader.TagAction᷂ *Sequencer*˄
Timer
startCellEditing( ): **D**efaultCellEditor.EditorDelegate
startDrag( ): **D**ragGestureEvent˄ **D**ragSource
startEditingAtPath( ): **J**Tree˄ **T**reeUI˄
startEditingTimer( ): **D**efaultTreeCellEditor
startFontTag( ): **M**inimalHTMLWriter˄
startGrabbing( ): **P**ixelGrabber
startProduction( ): **F**ilteredImageSource *ImageProducer*
MemoryImageSource **R**enderableImageProducer
startRecording( ): *Sequencer*˄
STARTTAG: *DTDConstants*
startTag( ): **H**TMLWriter˄ javax.swing.text.html.parser.**P**arser᷂
StartTagType: **D**efaultStyledDocument.ElementSpec
stateChanged( ): **A**bstractButton.ButtonChangeListener
ChangeListener˄ **J**MenuItem.AccessibleJMenuItem᷂
JScrollPane.AccessibleJScrollPane˄ **J**Spinner.DefaultEditor᷂
JTabbedPane.AccessibleJTabbedPane˄
JTabbedPane.ModelListener
StateEdit˄: javax.swing.undo
StateEditable: javax.swing.undo
—passed to: **S**tateEdit˄ < init( ), StateEdit( ) >

—fields: **S**tateEdit˄.object
stateMask: **D**efaultButtonModel᷂
STATEMENT: **P**ageAttributes.MediaType˄
states: **A**ccessibleStateSet
STATICIMAGEDONE: *ImageConsumer*
status( ): **P**ixelGrabber
STATUS_BAR: **A**ccessibleRole˄
statusAll( ): **M**ediaTracker
statusID( ): **M**ediaTracker
StdACChrominance: **J**PEGHuffmanTable
StdACLuminance: **J**PEGHuffmanTable
StdDCChrominance: **J**PEGHuffmanTable
StdDCLuminance: **J**PEGHuffmanTable
STOP: **L**ineEvent.Type **S**hortMessage˄
stop( ): **A**pplet˄ *AudioClip* *DataLine*᷂
DropTarget.DropTargetAutoScroller *Sequencer*˄ **T**imer
stopCellEditing( ): **A**bstractCellEditor᷂ *CellEditor*᷂
DefaultCellEditor.EditorDelegate **D**efaultTreeCellEditor
stopEditing( ): **J**Tree˄ **T**reeUI˄
STOPPED: **P**rinterState˄
STOPPED_PARTLY: **P**rinterStateReason˄
STOPPING: **P**rinterStateReason˄
stopRecording( ): *Sequencer*˄
storeState( ): *StateEditable*
strategy: **F**lowView᷂
StreamDescriptionProperty: javax.swing.text.**D**ocument᷂
streamPos: **I**mageInputStreamImpl᷂
StreamPrintService: javax.print
—returned by: **S**treamPrintServiceFactory.getPrintService( )
StreamPrintServiceFactory: javax.print
—returned by: **P**rinterJob.lookupStreamPrintServices( )
StreamPrintServiceFactory.lookupStreamPrintServiceFactories( )
strict: javax.swing.text.html.parser.**P**arser᷂
STRIKE: **H**TML.Tag᷂
STRIKETHROUGH: **T**extAttribute˄
StrikeThrough: **S**tyleConstants᷂
STRIKETHROUGH_ON: **T**extAttribute˄
StringBuffer: java.lang
—passed to: javax.swing.text.html.parser.**P**arser᷂ ₂
.parseMarkupDeclarations( )
StringContent: javax.swing.text
stringFlavor: **D**ataFlavor
StringSelection: java.awt.datatransfer
stringToColor( ): **S**tyleSheet˄
stringToValue( ): **J**FormattedTextField.AbstractFormatter᷂
stringWidth( ): **F**ontMetrics
STROKE: **S**hapeGraphicAttribute˄
Stroke: java.awt
—passed to: **G**raphics2D˄.setStroke( )
—returned by: **G**raphics2D˄.getStroke( )
—implemented by: **B**asicStroke
STRONG: **H**TML.Tag᷂
STYLE: **H**TML.Attribute **H**TML.Tag᷂
style: **F**ont᷂
Style˄: javax.swing.text
—passed to: **D**efaultStyledDocument᷂ < addStyle( ),
setLogicalStyle( ), styleChanged( ) > **J**TextPane˄
< addStyle( ), setLogicalStyle( ) > **S**tyleContext᷂.addStyle( )
StyleContext.NamedStyle( ) *StyledDocument*˄ < addStyle( ),
setLogicalStyle( ) >
—returned by: **D**efaultStyledDocument᷂ < addStyle( ),
getLogicalStyle( ), getStyle( ) > **J**TextPane˄ < addStyle( ),
getLogicalStyle( ), getStyle( ) > **S**tyleContext᷂ < addStyle( ),
getStyle( ) > *StyledDocument*˄ < addStyle( ), getLogicalStyle( ),
getStyle( ) > **S**tyleSheet˄.getRule( )
—implemented by: **S**tyleContext.NamedStyle
styleChanged( ): **D**efaultStyledDocument᷂
StyleConstants: javax.swing.text
—subclasses: **S**tyleConstants.CharacterConstants˄
StyleConstants.ColorConstants˄
StyleConstants.FontConstants˄
StyleConstants.ParagraphConstants˄

S

StyleConstants.CharacterConstants^: javax.swing.text
StyleConstants.ColorConstants^: javax.swing.text
StyleConstants.FontConstants^: javax.swing.text
StyleConstants.ParagraphConstants^: javax.swing.text
StyleContextˌ: javax.swing.text
— subclasses: **S**tyleSheet^
— passed to: **D**efaultStyledDocument( )
   StyleContext.NamedStyle( ) **S**tyleContext.SmallAttributeSet( )
— returned by: **S**tyleContextˌ.getDefaultStyleContext( )
StyleContext.NamedStyle: javax.swing.text
StyleContext.SmallAttributeSet: javax.swing.text
— returned by: **S**tyleContextˌ.createSmallAttributeSet( )
   StyleSheet^.createSmallAttributeSet( )
StyledDocument^: javax.swing.text
— passed to: **J**TextPane^ < JTextPane( ), setStyledDocument( ) >
   MinimalHTMLWriter( )
— returned by: **J**TextPane^.getStyledDocument( )
   StyledEditorKit.StyledTextAction^.getStyledDocument( )
— implemented by: **D**efaultStyledDocument^
StyledEditorKit^: javax.swing.text
— subclasses: **H**TMLEditorKit^ **R**TFEditorKit^
— returned by: **J**TextPane^.getStyledEditorKit( )
   StyledEditorKit.StyledTextAction^.getStyledEditorKit( )
StyledEditorKit.AlignmentAction^: javax.swing.text
StyledEditorKit.BoldAction^: javax.swing.text
StyledEditorKit.FontFamilyAction^: javax.swing.text
StyledEditorKit.FontSizeAction^: javax.swing.text
StyledEditorKit.ForegroundAction^: javax.swing.text
StyledEditorKit.ItalicAction^: javax.swing.text
StyledEditorKit.StyledTextAction^: javax.swing.text
— subclasses: **H**TMLEditorKit.HTMLTextAction^
   StyledEditorKit.AlignmentAction^ **S**tyledEditorKit.BoldAction^
   StyledEditorKit.FontFamilyAction^
   StyledEditorKit.FontSizeAction^
   StyledEditorKit.ForegroundAction^
   StyledEditorKit.ItalicAction^ **S**tyledEditorKit.UnderlineAction^
— descendents: **H**TMLEditorKit.InsertHTMLTextAction^
StyledEditorKit.UnderlineAction^: javax.swing.text
StyleSheet^: javax.swing.text.html
— passed to: **H**TMLDocument( ) **H**TMLEditorKit^.setStyleSheet( )
   StyleSheet^ < addStyleSheet( ), removeStyleSheet( ) >
— returned by: **B**lockViewˌ.getStyleSheet( )
   HTMLDocument^.getStyleSheet( )
   HTMLEditorKit^.getStyleSheet( )
   ImageViewˌ.getStyleSheet( ) **I**nlineView^.getStyleSheet( )
   javax.swing.text.html.**P**aragraphView^.getStyleSheet( )
   StyleSheet^.getStyleSheets( )
StyleSheet.BoxPainter: javax.swing.text.html
— returned by: **S**tyleSheet^.getBoxPainter( )
StyleSheet.ListPainter: javax.swing.text.html
— returned by: **S**tyleSheet^.getListPainter( )
SUB: **H**TML.Tagˌ
subdivide( ): **C**ubicCurve2Dˌ **Q**uadCurve2Dˌ
SUBMISSION_INTERRUPTED: **J**obStateReason^
SUBMIT: **F**ormView^
submitData( ): **F**ormView^
subsamplingXOffset: **I**IOParamˌ
subsamplingYOffset: **I**IOParamˌ
Subscript: **S**tyleConstantsˌ
substituteColorModel( ): **R**GBImageFilterˌ
subtract( ): **A**rea
suffixes: **I**mageReaderWriterSpiˌ
sum( ): **S**pring
SUP: **H**TML.Tagˌ
Superscript: **S**tyleConstantsˌ
SUPERSCRIPT: **T**extAttribute^
SUPERSCRIPT_SUB: **T**extAttribute^
SUPERSCRIPT_SUPER: **T**extAttribute^
SUPPORTED: **C**olorSupported^
SupportedValuesAttribute^: javax.print.attribute
— implemented by: **C**opiesSupported^
   JobImpressionsSupported^ **J**obKOctetsSupported^

JobMediaSheetsSupported^ **J**obPrioritySupported^
   NumberUpSupported^
supportsStandardImageMetadataFormat:
   ImageReaderWriterSpiˌ
supportsStandardStreamMetadataFormat:
   ImageReaderWriterSpiˌ
SW_RESIZE_CURSOR: **C**ursor **F**rameˌ
SWAP_COLORS: **T**extAttribute^
SWAP_COLORS_ON: **T**extAttribute^
SWING_COMPONENT: **A**ccessibleRole^
SwingConstants: javax.swing
— implemented by: **A**bstractButton^ **J**Label^ **J**ProgressBar^
   JSeparatorˌ **J**Sliderˌ **J**TabbedPane^ **J**TextFieldˌ **J**ToolBar^
   SwingUtilities **V**iew
SwingPropertyChangeSupport^: javax.swing.event
— fields: **A**bstractActionˌ.changeSupport
   DefaultTreeSelectionModelˌ.changeSupport
SwingUtilities: javax.swing
sync( ): **T**oolkit
synchronize( ): *Mixer*^
synchronizedView( ): **A**ttributeSetUtilities
syncWithScrollPane( ): **S**crollPaneLayoutˌ
synthesizedElement( ): **H**TMLWriter^
Synthesizer^: javax.sound.midi
— returned by: **M**idiSystem.getSynthesizer( )
SysexMessage^: javax.sound.midi
SYSTEM: *DTDConstants*
SYSTEM_EXCLUSIVE: **S**ysexMessage^
SYSTEM_RESET: **S**hortMessage^
SystemColor^: java.awt
— fields: **S**ystemColor^ < activeCaption, activeCaptionBorder,
   activeCaptionText, control, controlDkShadow, controlHighlight,
   controlLtHighlight, controlShadow, controlText, desktop,
   inactiveCaption, inactiveCaptionBorder, inactiveCaptionText, info,
   infoText, menu, menuText, scrollbar, text, textHighlight,
   textHighlightText, textInactiveText, textText, window,
   windowBorder, windowText >
SystemFlavorMap: java.awt.datatransfer
TAB: **E**vent
TabableView: javax.swing.text
— implemented by: **G**lyphViewˌ
TabbedPaneUI^: javax.swing.plaf
— passed to: **J**TabbedPane^.setUI( )
— returned by: **J**TabbedPane^.getUI( )
TabExpander: javax.swing.text
— passed to: **G**lyphViewˌ.getTabbedSpan( )
   GlyphView.GlyphPainter.getSpan( )
   TabableView.getTabbedSpan( ) **U**tilities < drawTabbedText( ),
   getBreakLocation( ), getTabbedTextOffset( ),
   getTabbedTextWidth( ) >
— returned by: **G**lyphView^.getTabExpander( )
— implemented by: javax.swing.text.**P**aragraphView^ **P**lainViewˌ
   WrappedPlainView^
tabForCoordinate( ): **T**abbedPaneUI^
TABLE: **A**ccessibleRole^ **H**TML.Tagˌ
table: **J**TableHeader^
TableCellEditor^: javax.swing.table
— passed to: **J**Table^ < prepareEditor( ), setCellEditor( ),
   setDefaultEditor( ) > **T**ableColumn < setCellEditor( ),
   TableColumn( ) >
— returned by: **J**Table^ < getCellEditor( ), getDefaultEditor( ) >
   TableColumn.getCellEditor( )
— implemented by: **D**efaultCellEditor^
— fields: **J**Table^.cellEditor **T**ableColumn.cellEditor
TableCellRenderer: javax.swing.table
— passed to: **J**Table^ < prepareRenderer( ), setDefaultRenderer( ) >
   JTableHeader^.setDefaultRenderer( ) **T**ableColumn
   < setCellRenderer( ), setHeaderRenderer( ), TableColumn( ) >
— returned by: **J**Table^ < getCellRenderer( ), getDefaultRenderer( ) >
   JTableHeader^ < createDefaultRenderer( ), getDefaultRenderer( ) >
   TableColumn < createDefaultHeaderRenderer( ),
   getCellRenderer( ), getHeaderRenderer( ) >

—implemented by: **D**efaultTableCellRenderer^
—fields: **T**ableColumn < cellRenderer, headerRenderer >
tableChanged( ): **J**Table^ **J**Table.AccessibleJTable^
  TableModelListener^
TableColumn: javax.swing.table
—passed to: **D**efaultTableColumnModel < addColumn( ),
  removeColumn( ) > **J**Table^ < addColumn( ), removeColumn( ) >
  JTableHeader^ < setDraggedColumn( ), setResizingColumn( ) >
  TableColumnModel < addColumn( ), removeColumn( ) >
—returned by: **D**efaultTableColumnModel.getColumn( )
  JTable^.getColumn( ) **J**TableHeader^ < getDraggedColumn( ),
  getResizingColumn( ) > *TableColumnModel*.getColumn( )
—fields: **J**TableHeader^ < draggedColumn, resizingColumn >
TableColumnModel: javax.swing.table
—passed to: **J**Table^ < **J**Table( ), setColumnModel( ) >
  JTableHeader^ < JTableHeader( ), setColumnModel( ) >
  TableColumnModelEvent( )
—returned by: **J**Table^ < createDefaultColumnModel( ),
  getColumnModel( ) > **J**TableHeader^
  < createDefaultColumnModel( ), getColumnModel( ) >
—implemented by: **D**efaultTableColumnModel
—fields: **J**Table^.columnModel **J**TableHeader^.columnModel
TableColumnModelEvent^: javax.swing.event
—passed to: **D**efaultTableColumnModel < fireColumnAdded( ),
  fireColumnMoved( ), fireColumnRemoved( ) > **J**Table^
  < columnAdded( ), columnMoved( ), columnRemoved( ) >
  JTable.AccessibleJTable^ < columnAdded( ),
  columnMoved( ), columnRemoved( ) > **J**TableHeader^
  < columnAdded( ), columnMoved( ), columnRemoved( ) >
  TableColumnModelListener^ < columnAdded( ),
  columnMoved( ), columnRemoved( ) >
TableColumnModelListener^: javax.swing.event
—passed to: **D**efaultTableColumnModel
  < addColumnModelListener( ), removeColumnModelListener( ) >
  TableColumnModel < addColumnModelListener( ),
  removeColumnModelListener( ) >
—returned
  by: **D**efaultTableColumnModel.getColumnModelListeners( )
—implemented by: **J**Table^ **J**Table.AccessibleJTable^
  JTableHeader^
tableColumns: **D**efaultTableColumnModel
tableHeader: **J**Table^
TableHeaderUI^: javax.swing.plaf
—passed to: **J**TableHeader^.setUI( )
—returned by: **J**TableHeader^.getUI( )
TableModel: javax.swing.table
—passed to: **J**Table^ < **J**Table( ), setModel( ) > **T**ableModelEvent( )
—returned by: **J**Table^ < createDefaultDataModel( ), getModel( ) >
—implemented by: **A**bstractTableModel↓
—fields: **J**Table^.dataModel
TableModelEvent^: javax.swing.event
—passed to: **A**bstractTableModel↓.fireTableChanged( )
  DefaultTableModel^ < newDataAvailable( ), newRowsAdded( ),
  rowsRemoved( ) > **J**Table^.tableChanged( )
  JTable.AccessibleJTable^ < tableChanged( ),
  tableRowsDeleted( ), tableRowsInserted( ) >
  TableModelListener^.tableChanged( )
TableModelListener^: javax.swing.event
—passed to: **A**bstractTableModel↓ < addTableModelListener( ),
  removeTableModelListener( ) > *TableModel*
  < addTableModelListener( ), removeTableModelListener( ) >
—returned by: **A**bstractTableModel↓.getTableModelListeners( )
—implemented by: **J**Table^ **J**Table.AccessibleJTable^
tableRowsDeleted( ): **J**Table.AccessibleJTable^
tableRowsInserted( ): **J**Table.AccessibleJTable^
TableUI^: javax.swing.plaf
—passed to: **J**Table^.setUI( )
—returned by: **J**Table^.getUI( )
TableView^: javax.swing.text
—passed to: **T**ableView.TableCell( ) **T**ableView.TableRow( )
—implemented by: **T**ableView.TableCell^
TableView.TableCell^: javax.swing.text

—returned by: **T**ableView^.createTableCell( )
TableView.TableRow^: javax.swing.text
—returned by: **T**ableView^.createTableRow( )
TABLOID: **M**ediaSizeName^ **P**ageAttributes.MediaType^
tabPlacement: **J**TabbedPane^
TabSet: **S**tyleConstants↓
TabSet: javax.swing.text
—passed to: **S**tyleConstants↓.setTabSet( )
—returned by: javax.swing.text.**P**aragraphView^.getTabSet( )
  StyleConstants↓.getTabSet( )
tabSizeAttribute: **P**lainDocument^
TabStop: javax.swing.text
—passed to: **T**abSet < getTabIndex( ), TabSet( ) >
—returned by: **T**abSet < getTab( ), getTabAfter( ) >
TAG_ACNT: *OpenType*
TAG_AVAR: *OpenType*
TAG_BASE: *OpenType*
TAG_BDAT: *OpenType*
TAG_BLOC: *OpenType*
TAG_BSLN: *OpenType*
TAG_CFF: *OpenType*
TAG_CMAP: *OpenType*
TAG_CVAR: *OpenType*
TAG_CVT: *OpenType*
TAG_DSIG: *OpenType*
TAG_EBDT: *OpenType*
TAG_EBLC: *OpenType*
TAG_EBSC: *OpenType*
TAG_FDSC: *OpenType*
TAG_FEAT: *OpenType*
TAG_FMTX: *OpenType*
TAG_FPGM: *OpenType*
TAG_FVAR: *OpenType*
TAG_GASP: *OpenType*
TAG_GDEF: *OpenType*
TAG_GLYF: *OpenType*
TAG_GPOS: *OpenType*
TAG_GSUB: *OpenType*
TAG_GVAR: *OpenType*
TAG_HDMX: *OpenType*
TAG_HEAD: *OpenType*
TAG_HHEA: *OpenType*
TAG_HMTX: *OpenType*
TAG_JSTF: *OpenType*
TAG_JUST: *OpenType*
TAG_KERN: *OpenType*
TAG_LCAR: *OpenType*
TAG_LOCA: *OpenType*
TAG_LTSH: *OpenType*
TAG_MAXP: *OpenType*
TAG_MMFX: *OpenType*
TAG_MMSD: *OpenType*
TAG_MORT: *OpenType*
TAG_NAME: *OpenType*
TAG_OPBD: *OpenType*
TAG_OS2: *OpenType*
TAG_PCLT: *OpenType*
TAG_POST: *OpenType*
TAG_PREP: *OpenType*
TAG_PROP: *OpenType*
TAG_TRAK: *OpenType*
TAG_TYP1: *OpenType*
TAG_VDMX: *OpenType*
TAG_VHEA: *OpenType*
TAG_VMTX: *OpenType*
TagElement: javax.swing.text.html.parser
—passed to: **D**ocumentParser^ < handleEmptyTag( ),
  handleEndTag( ), handleStartTag( ) >
  javax.swing.text.html.parser.**P**arser↓ < handleEmptyTag( ),
  handleEndTag( ), handleStartTag( ), startTag( ) >
—returned by: javax.swing.text.html.parser.**P**arser↓.makeTag( )
TAMIL: **N**umericShaper

target: **E**vent
TARGET: **H**TML.Attribute
TargetDataLine^: javax.sound.sampled
—passed to: **A**udioInputStream( )
TD: **H**TML.Tag‿
TELUGU: **N**umericShaper
text: **S**ystemColor^
TEXT: **A**ccessibleRole^ **H**TML.Attribute **S**ystemColor^
text( ): **A**bstractWriter‿
TEXT_ALIGN: **C**SS.Attribute
TEXT_CHANGED_PROPERTY: **A**bstractButton↲
TEXT_CURSOR: **C**ursor **F**rame↲
TEXT_DECORATION: **C**SS.Attribute
TEXT_EVENT_MASK: **A**WTEvent↲
TEXT_FIRST: **T**extEvent^
TEXT_HIGHLIGHT: **S**ystemColor^
TEXT_HIGHLIGHT_TEXT: **S**ystemColor^
TEXT_HTML: **D**ocFlavor.CHAR_ARRAY^ **D**ocFlavor.READER^
  DocFlavor.STRING^
TEXT_HTML_HOST: **D**ocFlavor.BYTE_ARRAY^
  DocFlavor.INPUT_STREAM^ **D**ocFlavor.URL^
TEXT_HTML_US_ASCII: **D**ocFlavor.BYTE_ARRAY^
  DocFlavor.INPUT_STREAM^ **D**ocFlavor.URL^
TEXT_HTML_UTF_16: **D**ocFlavor.BYTE_ARRAY^
  DocFlavor.INPUT_STREAM^ **D**ocFlavor.URL^
TEXT_HTML_UTF_16BE: **D**ocFlavor.BYTE_ARRAY^
  DocFlavor.INPUT_STREAM^ **D**ocFlavor.URL^
TEXT_HTML_UTF_16LE: **D**ocFlavor.BYTE_ARRAY^
  DocFlavor.INPUT_STREAM^ **D**ocFlavor.URL^
TEXT_HTML_UTF_8: **D**ocFlavor.BYTE_ARRAY^
  DocFlavor.INPUT_STREAM^ **D**ocFlavor.URL^
TEXT_INACTIVE_TEXT: **S**ystemColor^
TEXT_INDENT: **C**SS.Attribute
TEXT_INSET_H: **T**itledBorder↲
TEXT_LAST: **T**extEvent^
TEXT_PLAIN: **D**ocFlavor.CHAR_ARRAY^ **D**ocFlavor.READER^
  DocFlavor.STRING^
TEXT_PLAIN_HOST: **D**ocFlavor.BYTE_ARRAY^
  DocFlavor.INPUT_STREAM^ **D**ocFlavor.URL^
TEXT_PLAIN_US_ASCII: **D**ocFlavor.BYTE_ARRAY^
  DocFlavor.INPUT_STREAM^ **D**ocFlavor.URL^
TEXT_PLAIN_UTF_16: **D**ocFlavor.BYTE_ARRAY^
  DocFlavor.INPUT_STREAM^ **D**ocFlavor.URL^
TEXT_PLAIN_UTF_16BE: **D**ocFlavor.BYTE_ARRAY^
  DocFlavor.INPUT_STREAM^ **D**ocFlavor.URL^
TEXT_PLAIN_UTF_16LE: **D**ocFlavor.BYTE_ARRAY^
  DocFlavor.INPUT_STREAM^ **D**ocFlavor.URL^
TEXT_PLAIN_UTF_8: **D**ocFlavor.BYTE_ARRAY^
  DocFlavor.INPUT_STREAM^ **D**ocFlavor.URL^
TEXT_SPACING: **T**itledBorder↲
TEXT_TEXT: **S**ystemColor^
TEXT_TRANSFORM: **C**SS.Attribute
TEXT_VALUE_CHANGED: **T**extEvent^
TextAction↲: javax.swing.text
—subclasses: **D**efaultEditorKit.BeepAction^
  DefaultEditorKit.CopyAction^ **D**efaultEditorKit.CutAction^
  DefaultEditorKit.DefaultKeyTypedAction^
  DefaultEditorKit.InsertBreakAction^
  DefaultEditorKit.InsertContentAction^
  DefaultEditorKit.InsertTabAction^
  DefaultEditorKit.PasteAction^
  StyledEditorKit.StyledTextAction↲
—descendents: **H**TMLEditorKit.HTMLTextAction↲
  HTMLEditorKit.InsertHTMLTextAction^
  StyledEditorKit.AlignmentAction^ **S**tyledEditorKit.BoldAction^
  StyledEditorKit.FontFamilyAction^
  StyledEditorKit.FontSizeAction^
  StyledEditorKit.ForegroundAction^
  StyledEditorKit.ItalicAction^ **S**tyledEditorKit.UnderlineAction^
TEXTAREA: **H**TML.Tag‿
TextArea^: java.awt

—passed to: **T**extArea.AccessibleAWTTextArea( )
  Toolkit.createTextArea( )
TextArea.AccessibleAWTTextArea^: java.awt
textAreaContent( ): **H**TMLDocument.HTMLReader^
  HTMLWriter^
TextAreaPeer^: java.awt.peer
—returned by: **T**oolkit.createTextArea( )
TextAttribute^: java.awt.font
—fields: **T**extAttribute^ < BACKGROUND, BIDI_EMBEDDING,
  CHAR_REPLACEMENT, FAMILY, FONT, FOREGROUND,
  INPUT_METHOD_HIGHLIGHT, INPUT_METHOD_UNDERLINE,
  JUSTIFICATION, NUMERIC_SHAPING, POSTURE,
  RUN_DIRECTION, SIZE, STRIKETHROUGH, SUPERSCRIPT,
  SWAP_COLORS, TRANSFORM, UNDERLINE, WEIGHT, WIDTH >
TextComponent↲: java.awt
—subclasses: **T**extArea^ **T**extField^
—passed to: **T**extComponent.AccessibleAWTTextComponent( )
TextComponent.AccessibleAWTTextComponent↲: java.awt
—subclasses: **T**extArea.AccessibleAWTTextArea^
  TextField.AccessibleAWTTextField^
TextComponentPeer↲: java.awt.peer
—extended by: ***T**extAreaPeer*^ ***T**extFieldPeer*^
TextEvent^: java.awt.event
—passed to: **A**WTEventMulticaster.textValueChanged( )
  TextComponent↲.processTextEvent( ) **T**extComponent₂
  .AccessibleAWTTextComponent↲.textValueChanged( )
  ***T**extListener*^.textValueChanged( )
TextField^: java.awt
—passed to: **T**extField.AccessibleAWTTextField( )
  Toolkit.createTextField( )
TextField.AccessibleAWTTextField^: java.awt
TextFieldPeer^: java.awt.peer
—returned by: **T**oolkit.createTextField( )
textHighlight: **S**ystemColor^
textHighlightText: **S**ystemColor^
TextHitInfo: java.awt.font
—passed to: ***I**nputMethodContext*^.dispatchInputMethodEvent( )
  InputMethodEvent( ) ***I**nputMethodRequests*↲.getTextLocation( )
  TextHitInfo.equals( ) **T**extLayout < getCaretInfo( ),
  getCaretShape( ), getLogicalRangesForVisualSelection( ),
  getNextLeftHit( ), getNextRightHit( ), getVisualHighlightShape( ),
  getVisualOtherHit( ) > **T**extLayout.CaretPolicy.getStrongCaret( )
—returned by: **I**nputMethodEvent^
  < getCaret( ), getVisiblePosition( ) >
  ***I**nputMethodRequests*‿.getLocationOffset( ) **T**extHitInfo
  < afterOffset( ), beforeOffset( ), getOffsetHit( ), getOtherHit( ),
  leading( ), trailing( ) > **T**extLayout < getNextLeftHit( ),
  getNextRightHit( ), getVisualOtherHit( ), hitTestChar( ) >
  TextLayout.CaretPolicy.getStrongCaret( )
textInactiveText: **S**ystemColor^
TextLayout: java.awt.font
—passed to: **T**extLayout.equals( )
  TextLayout.CaretPolicy.getStrongCaret( )
—returned by: **L**ineBreakMeasurer.nextLayout( )
  TextLayout.getJustifiedLayout( ) **T**extMeasurer.getLayout( )
TextLayout.CaretPolicy: java.awt.font
—passed to: **T**extLayout < getCaretShapes( ), getNextLeftHit( ),
  getNextRightHit( ) >
—fields: **T**extLayout.DEFAULT_CARET_POLICY
textListener: **T**extComponent↲
TextListener^: java.awt.event
—passed to: **A**WTEventMulticaster < add( ), remove( ) >
  TextComponent↲ < addTextListener( ), removeTextListener( ) >
—returned by: **A**WTEventMulticaster < add( ), remove( ) >
  TextComponent↲.getTextListeners( )
—implemented by: **A**WTEventMulticaster
  TextComponent.AccessibleAWTTextComponent↲
—fields: **T**extComponent↲.textListener
TextMeasurer: java.awt.font
textNonSelectionColor: **D**efaultTreeCellRenderer^
textSelectionColor: **D**efaultTreeCellRenderer^
TextSyntax‿: javax.print.attribute

T

—subclasses: **D**ocumentName˄ **J**obMessageFromOperator˄
JobName˄ **J**obOriginatingUserName˄
OutputDeviceAssigned˄ **P**rinterInfo˄ **P**rinterLocation˄
PrinterMakeAndModel˄ **P**rinterMessageFromOperator˄
PrinterName˄ **R**equestingUserName˄
textText: **S**ystemColor˅
TextUI˄: javax.swing.plaf
—descendents: **D**efaultTextUI˄
—passed to: **J**TextComponent˅.setUI( )
—returned by: **J**TextComponent˅.getUI( )
TexturePaint: java.awt
textValueChanged( ): **A**WTEventMulticaster
TextComponent.AccessibleAWTTextComponent˅
TextListener˄
TH: **H**TML.Tag˅
THAI: **N**umericShaper
thickness: **L**ineBorder˅
Thread: java.lang
—returned by: **A**bstractDocument˅.getCurrentWriter( )
Throwable: java.lang
—descendents: **A**WTError **A**WTException
BadLocationException **C**annotRedoException
CannotUndoException **C**hangedCharSetException˄
CMMException **E**xpandVetoException
FontFormatException **H**eadlessException˄
IIOException˅ **I**IOInvalidTreeException˄
IllegalComponentStateException˄ **I**llegalPathStateException
ImagingOpException **I**nvalidDnDOperationException˄
InvalidMidiDataException **L**ineUnavailableException
MidiUnavailableException **M**imeTypeParseException
NoninvertibleTransformException **P**rinterAbortException˄
PrinterException˅ **P**rinterIOException˄ **P**rintException
ProfileDataException **R**asterFormatException
UnmodifiableSetException **U**nsupportedAudioFileException
UnsupportedFlavorException
UnsupportedLookAndFeelException
—passed to: **I**IOException( ) **I**IOInvalidTreeException( )
—thrown by: **A**bstractDocument.AbstractElement˅.finalize( )
Cursor.finalize( ) **F**ont˅.finalize( ) **F**rame˅.finalize( )
ImageInputStreamImpl˅.finalize( ) **S**erviceRegistry˅.finalize( )
Window˅.finalize( )
thumbnailComplete( ): *IIOReadProgressListener*˄
IIOWriteProgressListener˄
thumbnailPassComplete( ): *IIOReadUpdateListener*˄
thumbnailPassStarted( ): *IIOReadUpdateListener*˄
thumbnailProgress( ): *IIOReadProgressListener*˄
IIOWriteProgressListener˄
thumbnails: **I**IOImage
thumbnailStarted( ): *IIOReadProgressListener*˄
IIOWriteProgressListener˄
thumbnailUpdate( ): *IIOReadUpdateListener*˄
TIBETAN: **N**umericShaper
ticks( ): **T**rack
tileGridXOffset: **I**mageWriteParam˅
tileGridYOffset: **I**mageWriteParam˅
tileHeight: **I**mageWriteParam˅
tileIcon: **M**atteBorder˅
TileObserver: java.awt.image
—passed to: **B**ufferedImage˄ < addTileObserver( ),
removeTileObserver( ) > *WritableRenderedImage*˄
< addTileObserver( ), removeTileObserver( ) >
tileUpdate( ): *TileObserver*
tileWidth: **I**mageWriteParam˅
tilingMode: **I**mageWriteParam˅
tilingSet: **I**mageWriteParam˅
TIMED_OUT: **P**rinterStateReason˄
timer: **D**efaultTreeCellEditor
Timer: javax.swing
—fields: **D**efaultTreeCellEditor.timer
TIMING_CLOCK: **S**hortMessage˄
title: **D**TD **J**InternalFrame˄ **T**itledBorder˅
TITLE: **H**TML.Attribute **H**TML.Tag˅

TITLE_PROPERTY: **J**InternalFrame˄
titleColor: **T**itledBorder˅
TitledBorder˅: javax.swing.border
—subclasses: **B**orderUIResource.TitledBorderUIResource˄
—returned by: **B**orderFactory.createTitledBorder( )
titleFont: **T**itledBorder˅
titleJustification: **T**itledBorder˅
titlePosition: **T**itledBorder˅
TitleProperty: javax.swing.text.**D**ocument˅
toArray( ): **A**ccessibleRelationSet **A**ccessibleStateSet
javax.print.attribute.AttributeSet˅ **D**efaultListModel
DragGestureEvent˄ **H**ashAttributeSet˅
toBack( ): **J**InternalFrame˄ **W**indow˅ *WindowPeer*˄
TOBOTTOM_TOLEFT: **P**resentationDirection˄
TOBOTTOM_TORIGHT: **P**resentationDirection˄
toCIEXYZ( ): **C**olorSpace˅
toDisplayString( ): **A**ccessibleBundle˅
toFront( ): **J**InternalFrame˄ **W**indow˅ *WindowPeer*˅
TOGGLE_BUTTON: **A**ccessibleRole˄
TOGGLE_CLICK_COUNT_PROPERTY: **J**Tree˄
toggleClickCount: **J**Tree˄
toIndex: **T**ableColumnModelEvent˄
TOLEFT_TOBOTTOM: **P**resentationDirection˄
TOLEFT_TOTOP: **P**resentationDirection˄
TONER_EMPTY: **P**rinterStateReason˄
TONER_LOW: **P**rinterStateReason˄
TOOL_BAR: **A**ccessibleRole˄
TOOL_TIP: **A**ccessibleRole˄
TOOL_TIP_TEXT_KEY: **J**Component˅
ToolBarUI˄: javax.swing.plaf
—passed to: **J**ToolBar˄.setUI( )
—returned by: **J**ToolBar˄.getUI( )
Toolkit: java.awt
—returned by: **C**omponent˅.getToolkit( )
ComponentPeer˅.getToolkit( ) **T**oolkit.getDefaultToolkit( )
ToolTipManager˄: javax.swing
—passed to: **T**oolTipManager.insideTimerAction( )
ToolTipManager.outsideTimerAction( )
ToolTipManager.stillInsideTimerAction( )
—returned by: **T**oolTipManager˄.sharedInstance( )
ToolTipManager.insideTimerAction: javax.swing
ToolTipManager.outsideTimerAction: javax.swing
ToolTipManager.stillInsideTimerAction: javax.swing
ToolTipUI˄: javax.swing.plaf
—returned by: **J**ToolTip˄.getUI( )
TooManyListenersException: java.util
—thrown by: **D**ragGestureRecognizer˅.addDragGestureListener( )
DragSourceContext.addDragSourceListener( )
DropTarget.addDropTargetListener( )
TOP: **J**SplitPane˄ **M**ediaTray˄ *SwingConstants* **T**itledBorder˅
top: **E**mptyBorder˄ **I**nsets˅
TOP_ALIGNMENT: **C**omponent˅ **G**raphicAttribute˅
TOPDOWNLEFTRIGHT: *ImageConsumer*
toRGB( ): **C**olorSpace˅
TORIGHT_TOBOTTOM: **P**resentationDirection˄
TORIGHT_TOTOP: **P**resentationDirection˄
toString( ): **M**ediaPrintableArea **R**esolutionSyntax˅
Size2DSyntax˅
totalColumnWidth: **D**efaultTableColumnModel
TOTOP_TOLEFT: **P**resentationDirection˄
TOTOP_TORIGHT: **P**resentationDirection˄
toViewCoordinates( ): **J**Viewport˄
TR: **H**TML.Tag˅
TRACK: **A**djustmentEvent˄
Track: javax.sound.midi
—passed to: **S**equence.deleteTrack( ) *Sequencer*˄
< recordDisable( ), recordEnable( ) >
—returned by: **S**equence < createTrack( ), getTracks( ) >
tracker: **I**mageIcon
tracks: **S**equence
TRADITIONAL_HANZI: **I**nputSubset˄
TRAILING: **F**lowLayout *SwingConstants* **T**itledBorder˅

T

trailing( ): TextHitInfo
transferable: DropTargetContext.TransferableProxy
Transferable: java.awt.datatransfer
— passed to: Clipboard.setContents( )
  ClipboardOwner.lostOwnership( )
  DataFlavor.getReaderForText( ) DragGestureEvent^.startDrag( )
  DragSource < createDragSourceContext( ),
  startDrag( ) > DragSourceContext( )
  DropTargetContext.createTransferableProxy( )
  StringSelection.lostOwnership( ) TransferHandler
  < exportDone( ), getVisualRepresentation( ), importData( ) >
— returned by: Clipboard.getContents( )
  DragSourceContext.getTransferable( ) DropTargetContext
  < createTransferableProxy( ), getTransferable( ) >
  DropTargetDropEvent^.getTransferable( )
  TransferHandler.createTransferable( )
— implemented by: DropTargetContext.TransferableProxy
  StringSelection
— fields: Clipboard.contents
  DropTargetContext.TransferableProxy.transferable
transferablesFlavorsChanged( ): DragSourceContext
transferFocus( ): Component
transferFocusBackward( ): Component
transferFocusDownCycle( ): Container^
transferFocusUpCycle( ): Component
TransferHandler: javax.swing
— passed to: JComponent^.setTransferHandler( )
— returned by: JComponent^.getTransferHandler( )
transferType: ColorModel
TRANSFORM: TextAttribute^
transform( ): AffineTransform Area GeneralPath Graphics2D^
TransformAttribute: java.awt.font
TRANSIENT: AccessibleState^
translate( ): AffineTransform Event Graphics Point^ Polygon
  Rectangle^
translateHTMLToCSS( ): StyleSheet^
translatePoint( ): MouseEvent
TRANSLUCENT: Transparency
Transmitter: javax.sound.midi
— returned by: MidiDevice.getTransmitter( )
  MidiSystem.getTransmitter( )
Transparency: java.awt
— extended by: Paint^
— implemented by: ColorModel
tree: DefaultTreeCellEditor
TREE: AccessibleRole^
TREE_MODEL_PROPERTY: JTree^
TreeCellEditor^: javax.swing.tree
— passed to: DefaultTreeCellEditor( ) JTree^.setCellEditor( )
— returned by: DefaultTreeCellEditor.createTreeCellEditor( )
  JTree^.getCellEditor( )
— implemented by: DefaultCellEditor^ DefaultTreeCellEditor
— fields: DefaultTreeCellEditor.realEditor JTree^.cellEditor
TreeCellRenderer: javax.swing.tree
— passed to: JTree^.setCellRenderer( )
— returned by: JTree^.getCellRenderer( )
— implemented by: DefaultTreeCellRenderer^
— fields: JTree^.cellRenderer
treeCollapsed( ): JTree.AccessibleJTree^
  TreeExpansionListener^
treeDidChange( ): JTree^
treeExpanded( ): JTree.AccessibleJTree^
  TreeExpansionListener^
TreeExpansionEvent^: javax.swing.event
— passed to: ExpandVetoException( ) JTree.AccessibleJTree^
  < treeCollapsed( ), treeExpanded( ) > *TreeExpansionListener*^
  < treeCollapsed( ), treeExpanded( ) > *TreeWillExpandListener*^
  < treeWillCollapse( ), treeWillExpand( ) >
— fields: ExpandVetoException.event
TreeExpansionListener^: javax.swing.event
— passed to: JTree^ < addTreeExpansionListener( ),
  removeTreeExpansionListener( ) >

— returned by: JTree^.getTreeExpansionListeners( )
— implemented by: JTree.AccessibleJTree^
treeModel: AbstractLayoutCache JTree^
TreeModel: javax.swing.tree
— passed to: AbstractLayoutCache.setModel( ) JTree^ < JTree( ),
  setModel( ) >
— returned by: AbstractLayoutCache.getModel( ) JTree^
  < createTreeModel( ), getDefaultTreeModel( ), getModel( ) >
— implemented by: DefaultTreeModel
— fields: AbstractLayoutCache.treeModel JTree^.treeModel
TreeModelEvent^: javax.swing.event
— passed to: AbstractLayoutCache < treeNodesChanged( ),
  treeNodesInserted( ), treeNodesRemoved( ),
  treeStructureChanged( ) > JTree.AccessibleJTree^
  < treeNodesChanged( ), treeNodesInserted( ),
  treeNodesRemoved( ), treeStructureChanged( ) >
  JTree.TreeModelHandler < treeNodesChanged( ),
  treeNodesInserted( ), treeNodesRemoved( ),
  treeStructureChanged( ) > *TreeModelListener*^
  < treeNodesChanged( ), treeNodesInserted( ),
  treeNodesRemoved( ), treeStructureChanged( ) >
treeModelListener: JTree^
TreeModelListener^: javax.swing.event
— passed to: DefaultTreeModel < addTreeModelListener( ),
  removeTreeModelListener( ) > *TreeModel*
  < addTreeModelListener( ), removeTreeModelListener( ) >
— returned by: DefaultTreeModel.getTreeModelListeners( )
  JTree^.createTreeModelListener( )
— implemented by: JTree.AccessibleJTree^
  JTree.TreeModelHandler
— fields: JTree^.treeModelListener
TreeNode: javax.swing.tree
— extended by: *MutableTreeNode*^
— passed to: AbstractDocument.AbstractElement.getIndex( )
  DefaultMutableTreeNode < getChildAfter( ), getChildBefore( ),
  getIndex( ), getPathToRoot( ), isNodeAncestor( ), isNodeChild( ),
  isNodeSibling( ), pathFromAncestorEnumeration( ) >
  DefaultTreeModel < DefaultTreeModel( ), getPathToRoot( ),
  nodeChanged( ), nodesChanged( ), nodeStructureChanged( ),
  nodesWereInserted( ), nodesWereRemoved( ), reload( ),
  setRoot( ) > JTree( ) *TreeNode*.getIndex( )
— returned by: AbstractDocument.AbstractElement
  < getChildAt( ), getParent( ) > DefaultMutableTreeNode
  < getChildAfter( ), getChildAt( ), getChildBefore( ),
  getFirstChild( ), getLastChild( ), getParent( ), getPath( ),
  getPathToRoot( ), getRoot( ), getSharedAncestor( ) >
  DefaultTreeModel.getPathToRoot( ) *TreeNode* < getChildAt( ),
  getParent( ) >
— implemented by: AbstractDocument.AbstractElement
— fields: DefaultTreeModel.root
treeNodesChanged( ): AbstractLayoutCache
  JTree.AccessibleJTree^ JTree.TreeModelHandler
  TreeModelListener^
treeNodesInserted( ): AbstractLayoutCache
  JTree.AccessibleJTree^ JTree.TreeModelHandler
  TreeModelListener^
treeNodesRemoved( ): AbstractLayoutCache
  JTree.AccessibleJTree^ JTree.TreeModelHandler
  TreeModelListener^
TreePath: javax.swing.tree
— passed to: AbstractLayoutCache < getBounds( ),
  getExpandedState( ), getRowForPath( ), getRowsForPaths( ),
  getVisibleChildCount( ), getVisiblePathsFrom( ),
  invalidatePathBounds( ), isExpanded( ), setExpandedState( ) >
  DefaultTreeModel.valueForPathChanged( )
  DefaultTreeSelectionModel < addSelectionPath( ),
  addSelectionPaths( ), arePathsContiguous( ), canPathsBeAdded( ),
  canPathsBeRemoved( ), isPathSelected( ), notifyPathChange( ),
  removeSelectionPath( ), removeSelectionPaths( ),
  setSelectionPath( ), setSelectionPaths( ) > JTree^
  < addSelectionPath( ), addSelectionPaths( ), collapsePath( ),
  expandPath( ), fireTreeCollapsed( ), fireTreeExpanded( ),

fireTreeWillCollapse( ), fireTreeWillExpand( ),
getDescendantToggledPaths( ), getExpandedDescendants( ),
getPathBounds( ), getRowForPath( ), hasBeenExpanded( ),
isCollapsed( ), isExpanded( ), isPathEditable( ), isPathSelected( ),
isVisible( ), makeVisible( ), removeDescendantSelectedPaths( ),
removeSelectionPath( ), removeSelectionPaths( ),
scrollPathToVisible( ), setAnchorSelectionPath( ),
setExpandedState( ), setLeadSelectionPath( ), setSelectionPath( ),
setSelectionPaths( ), startEditingAtPath( ) >
JTree.AccessibleJTree.AccessibleJTreeNode( )
RowMapper.getRowsForPaths( ) TreeExpansionEvent( )
TreeModel.valueForPathChanged( ) TreeModelEvent( )
TreePath < isDescendant( ), TreePath( ) > TreeSelectionEvent^
< isAddedPath( ), TreeSelectionEvent( ) > *TreeSelectionModel*
< addSelectionPath( ), addSelectionPaths( ), isPathSelected( ),
removeSelectionPath( ), removeSelectionPaths( ),
setSelectionPath( ), setSelectionPaths( ) > TreeUI^
< getPathBounds( ), getRowForPath( ), startEditingAtPath( ) >
— returned by: AbstractLayoutCache. < getPathClosestTo( ),
getPathForRow( ) > DefaultTreeSelectionModel.
< getLeadSelectionPath( ), getSelectionPath( ),
getSelectionPaths( ) > JTree^ < getAnchorSelectionPath( ),
getClosestPathForLocation( ), getEditingPath( ),
getLeadSelectionPath( ), getNextMatch( ), getPathBetweenRows( ),
getSelectionPaths( ) > TreeExpansionEvent^.getPath( )
TreeModelEvent^.getTreePath( ) TreePath < getParentPath( ),
pathByAddingChild( ) > TreeSelectionEvent^
< getNewLeadSelectionPath( ), getOldLeadSelectionPath( ),
getPath( ), getPaths( ) > *TreeSelectionModel*
< getLeadSelectionPath( ), getSelectionPath( ),
getSelectionPaths( ) > TreeUI^ < getClosestPathForLocation( ),
getEditingPath( ), getPathForRow( ) >
— fields: DefaultTreeCellEditor.lastPath
DefaultTreeSelectionModel. < leadPath, selection >
TreeExpansionEvent^.path TreeModelEvent^.path
TreeSelectionEvent^ < newLeadSelectionPath,
oldLeadSelectionPath, paths >

TreeSelectionEvent^: javax.swing.event
— passed to: DefaultTreeCellEditor.valueChanged( )
DefaultTreeSelectionModel.fireValueChanged( )
JTree^.fireValueChanged( )
JTree.AccessibleJTree^.valueChanged( )
JTree.TreeSelectionRedirector.valueChanged( )
TreeSelectionListener^.valueChanged( )

TreeSelectionListener^: javax.swing.event
— passed to: DefaultTreeSelectionModel.
< addTreeSelectionListener( ), removeTreeSelectionListener( ) >
JTree^ < addTreeSelectionListener( ),
removeTreeSelectionListener( ) > *TreeSelectionModel*
< addTreeSelectionListener( ), removeTreeSelectionListener( ) >
— returned
by: DefaultTreeSelectionModel.getTreeSelectionListeners( )
JTree^.getTreeSelectionListeners( )
— implemented by: DefaultTreeCellEditor JTree.AccessibleJTree^
JTree.TreeSelectionRedirector

treeSelectionModel: AbstractLayoutCache.

TreeSelectionModel: javax.swing.tree
— passed to: AbstractLayoutCache.setSelectionModel( )
JTree^.setSelectionModel( )
— returned by: AbstractLayoutCache.getSelectionModel( )
JTree^.getSelectionModel( )
— implemented by: DefaultTreeSelectionModel.
— fields: AbstractLayoutCache.treeSelectionModel
JTree^.selectionModel

treeStructureChanged( ): AbstractLayoutCache.
JTree.AccessibleJTree^ JTree.TreeModelHandler
TreeModelListener^

TreeUI^: javax.swing.plaf
— passed to: JTree^.setUI( )
— returned by: JTree^.getUI( )

treeWillCollapse( ): *TreeWillExpandListener*^

treeWillExpand( ): *TreeWillExpandListener*^

TreeWillExpandListener^: javax.swing.event
— passed to: JTree^ < addTreeWillExpandListener( ),
removeTreeWillExpandListener( ) >
— returned by: JTree^.getTreeWillExpandListeners( )

trimEdits( ): UndoManager^

trimForLimit( ): UndoManager^

trimToSize( ): DefaultListModel^

TRUETYPE_FONT: Font.

tryToLoadClass( ): DataFlavor

TT: HTML.Tag.

TUMBLE: Sides^

TUNE_REQUEST: ShortMessage^

TWO_SIDED_LONG_EDGE: JobAttributes.SidesType^ Sides^

TWO_SIDED_SHORT_EDGE: JobAttributes.SidesType^ Sides^

type: javax.swing.text.html.parser.AttributeList
ContentModel javax.swing.text.html.parser.Element
javax.swing.text.html.parser.Entity
JTable.AccessibleJTable.AccessibleJTableModelChange
MidiFileFormat TableModelEvent^

TYPE: HTML.Attribute

type2name( ): javax.swing.text.html.parser.AttributeList

TYPE_2CLR: ColorSpace.

TYPE_3BYTE_BGR: BufferedImage^

TYPE_3CLR: ColorSpace.

TYPE_4BYTE_ABGR: BufferedImage^

TYPE_4BYTE_ABGR_PRE: BufferedImage^

TYPE_4CLR: ColorSpace.

TYPE_5CLR: ColorSpace.

TYPE_6CLR: ColorSpace.

TYPE_7CLR: ColorSpace.

TYPE_8CLR: ColorSpace.

TYPE_9CLR: ColorSpace.

TYPE_ACLR: ColorSpace.

TYPE_BCLR: ColorSpace.

TYPE_BILINEAR: AffineTransformOp

TYPE_BYTE: DataBuffer.

TYPE_BYTE_BINARY: BufferedImage^

TYPE_BYTE_GRAY: BufferedImage^

TYPE_BYTE_INDEXED: BufferedImage^

TYPE_CCLR: ColorSpace.

TYPE_CMY: ColorSpace.

TYPE_CMYK: ColorSpace.

TYPE_CUSTOM: BufferedImage^

TYPE_DCLR: ColorSpace.

TYPE_DOUBLE: DataBuffer.

TYPE_ECLR: ColorSpace.

TYPE_FCLR: ColorSpace.

TYPE_FLIP: AffineTransform

TYPE_FLOAT: DataBuffer.

TYPE_GENERAL_ROTATION: AffineTransform

TYPE_GENERAL_SCALE: AffineTransform

TYPE_GENERAL_TRANSFORM: AffineTransform

TYPE_GRAY: ColorSpace.

TYPE_HLS: ColorSpace.

TYPE_HSV: ColorSpace.

TYPE_IDENTITY: AffineTransform

TYPE_IMAGE_BUFFER: GraphicsDevice

TYPE_INT: DataBuffer.

TYPE_INT_ARGB: BufferedImage^

TYPE_INT_ARGB_PRE: BufferedImage^

TYPE_INT_BGR: BufferedImage^

TYPE_INT_RGB: BufferedImage^

TYPE_Lab: ColorSpace.

TYPE_Luv: ColorSpace.

TYPE_MASK_ROTATION: AffineTransform

TYPE_MASK_SCALE: AffineTransform

TYPE_NEAREST_NEIGHBOR: AffineTransformOp

TYPE_PRINTER: GraphicsDevice

TYPE_QUADRANT_ROTATION: AffineTransform

TYPE_RASTER_SCREEN: GraphicsDevice

TYPE_RGB: ColorSpace.

T

Cross-Ref

T

V

getDataVector( ) > **G**apContent^.getPositionsInRange( )
ParameterBlock < getParameters( ),
getSources( ) > *R*enderableImage.getSources( )
RenderableImageOp.getSources( )
*R*enderedImage_.getSources( )
StringContent.getPositionsInRange( )
— fields: **A**ccessibleRelationSet.relations
AccessibleStateSet.states
javax.swing.text.html.parser.**A**ttributeList.values
ButtonGroup.buttons   **C**ompoundEdit^.edits
DefaultMutableTreeNode_.children
DefaultTableColumnModel.tableColumns   **D**efaultTableModel^
< columnIdentifiers,   dataVector >   **D**TD.elements
HTMLDocument.HTMLReader^.parseBuffer   **P**arameterBlock
< parameters,   sources >   **S**equence.tracks   **T**rack.events
UndoableEditSupport.listeners
vendorName: **I**IOServiceProvider_
verify( ): **I**nputVerifier
verifyAttributeCategory( ): **A**ttributeSetUtilities
verifyAttributeValue( ): **A**ttributeSetUtilities
verifyCategoryForValue( ): **A**ttributeSetUtilities
version: **I**IOServiceProvider_
VERSION: **H**TML.Attribute
VERTICAL: **A**ccessibleState^   *A*djustable   **G**ridBagConstraints
JList^   **S**crollbar^   *SwingConstants*
VERTICAL_ALIGN: **C**SS.Attribute
VERTICAL_ALIGNMENT_CHANGED_PROPERTY:
AbstractButton^
VERTICAL_SCROLLBAR: *ScrollPaneConstants*
VERTICAL_SCROLLBAR_ALWAYS: *ScrollPaneConstants*
VERTICAL_SCROLLBAR_AS_NEEDED: *ScrollPaneConstants*
VERTICAL_SCROLLBAR_NEVER: *ScrollPaneConstants*
VERTICAL_SCROLLBAR_POLICY: *ScrollPaneConstants*
VERTICAL_SPLIT: **J**SplitPane^
VERTICAL_TEXT_POSITION_CHANGED_PROPERTY:
AbstractButton^
VERTICAL_WRAP: **J**List^
verticalScrollBar: **J**ScrollPane^
verticalScrollBarPolicy: **J**ScrollPane^
VetoableChangeListener^:   java.beans
— passed to: **J**Component^ < addVetoableChangeListener( ),
removeVetoableChangeListener( ) >
KeyboardFocusManager_ < addVetoableChangeListener( ),
removeVetoableChangeListener( ) >
— returned by: **J**Component^.getVetoableChangeListeners( )
KeyboardFocusManager_.getVetoableChangeListeners( )
View_: javax.swing.text
— subclasses: **A**syncBoxView^   **C**omponentView^
CompositeView^   **G**lyphView^   **I**conView^   **I**mageView^
PlainView^
— descendents: **B**lockView^   **B**oxView^   **F**ieldView^   **F**lowView^
FormView^   **I**nlineView^   **L**abelView^   **L**istView^
ObjectView^   javax.swing.text.**P**aragraphView^
javax.swing.text.html.**P**aragraphView^   **P**asswordView^
TableView^   **T**ableView.TableCell^   **T**ableView.TableRow^
WrappedPlainView^   **Z**oneView^
— passed to: **A**syncBoxView.createChildState( )
AsyncBoxView.ChildState( )
LayeredHighlighter_.paintLayeredHighlights( )
LayeredHighlighter.LayerPainter_.paintLayer( )
StyleSheet^.getViewAttributes( )   **S**tyleSheet.BoxPainter
< getInset( ),   paint( ) >   **S**tyleSheet.ListPainter.paint( )
View_ < append( ),   forwardUpdateToView( ),   insert( ),
preferenceChanged( ),   replace( ),   setParent( ) >   **Z**oneView^
< isZoneLoaded( ),   unloadZone( ),   zoneWasLoaded( ) >
— returned by: **A**syncBoxView.ChildState.getChildView( )
BoxView^.getViewAtPoint( )   **C**ompositeView^
< getViewAtPoint( ),   getViewAtPosition( ) >
FlowView^.createRow( )   **F**lowView.FlowStrategy < createView( ),
getLogicalView( ) >   **H**TMLEditorKit.HTMLFactory.create( )
javax.swing.text.**P**aragraphView^ < breakView( ),   createRow( ),
getLayoutView( ) >   **T**ableView^.getViewAtPosition( )

TableView.TableRow^.getViewAtPosition( )
TextUI^.getRootView( )   **V**iew_ < breakView( ),   createFragment( ),
getParent( ),   getView( ) >   *ViewFactory*.create( )
ZoneView^.createZone( )
— fields: **F**lowView^.layoutPool
ViewFactory^:   javax.swing.text
— passed to: **A**syncBoxView^.loadChildren( )
BoxView^.forwardUpdate( )   **C**ompositeView^.loadChildren( )
FlowView^.loadChildren( )   **P**lainView^.updateDamage( )
TableView^.forwardUpdate( )   **V**iew_ < changedUpdate( ),
forwardUpdate( ),   forwardUpdateToView( ),
insertUpdate( ),   removeUpdate( ),   updateChildren( ) >
WrappedPlainView^.loadChildren( )   **Z**oneView^ < loadChildren( ),
updateChildren( ) >
— returned by: **E**ditorKit_.getViewFactory( )   **V**iew_.getViewFactory( )
— implemented by: **H**TMLEditorKit.HTMLFactory
viewport: **J**ScrollPane^   **S**crollPaneLayout_
VIEWPORT: **A**ccessibleRole^   *ScrollPaneConstants*
viewPort: **J**ScrollPane.AccessibleJScrollPane^
ViewportLayout: javax.swing
ViewportUI^: javax.swing.plaf
— passed to: **J**Viewport^.setUI( )
— returned by: **J**Viewport^.getUI( )
viewToModel( ): **G**lyphView.GlyphPainter   **J**TextComponent^
TextUI^   **V**iew_
VISIBLE: **A**ccessibleState^
VISIBLE_ROW_COUNT_PROPERTY: **J**Tree^
visibleRowCount: **J**Tree^
VK_0: **K**eyEvent^
VK_1: **K**eyEvent^
VK_2: **K**eyEvent^
VK_3: **K**eyEvent^
VK_4: **K**eyEvent^
VK_5: **K**eyEvent^
VK_6: **K**eyEvent^
VK_7: **K**eyEvent^
VK_8: **K**eyEvent^
VK_9: **K**eyEvent^
VK_A: **K**eyEvent^
VK_ACCEPT: **K**eyEvent^
VK_ADD: **K**eyEvent^
VK_AGAIN: **K**eyEvent^
VK_ALL_CANDIDATES: **K**eyEvent^
VK_ALPHANUMERIC: **K**eyEvent^
VK_ALT: **K**eyEvent^
VK_ALT_GRAPH: **K**eyEvent^
VK_AMPERSAND: **K**eyEvent^
VK_ASTERISK: **K**eyEvent^
VK_AT: **K**eyEvent^
VK_B: **K**eyEvent^
VK_BACK_QUOTE: **K**eyEvent^
VK_BACK_SLASH: **K**eyEvent^
VK_BACK_SPACE: **K**eyEvent^
VK_BRACELEFT: **K**eyEvent^
VK_BRACERIGHT: **K**eyEvent^
VK_C: **K**eyEvent^
VK_CANCEL: **K**eyEvent^
VK_CAPS_LOCK: **K**eyEvent^
VK_CIRCUMFLEX: **K**eyEvent^
VK_CLEAR: **K**eyEvent^
VK_CLOSE_BRACKET: **K**eyEvent^
VK_CODE_INPUT: **K**eyEvent^
VK_COLON: **K**eyEvent^
VK_COMMA: **K**eyEvent^
VK_COMPOSE: **K**eyEvent^
VK_CONTROL: **K**eyEvent^
VK_CONVERT: **K**eyEvent^
VK_COPY: **K**eyEvent^
VK_CUT: **K**eyEvent^
VK_D: **K**eyEvent^
VK_DEAD_ABOVEDOT: **K**eyEvent^
VK_DEAD_ABOVERING: **K**eyEvent^

VK_DEAD_ACUTE: KeyEvent
VK_DEAD_BREVE: KeyEvent
VK_DEAD_CARON: KeyEvent
VK_DEAD_CEDILLA: KeyEvent
VK_DEAD_CIRCUMFLEX: KeyEvent
VK_DEAD_DIAERESIS: KeyEvent
VK_DEAD_DOUBLEACUTE: KeyEvent
VK_DEAD_GRAVE: KeyEvent
VK_DEAD_IOTA: KeyEvent
VK_DEAD_MACRON: KeyEvent
VK_DEAD_OGONEK: KeyEvent
VK_DEAD_SEMIVOICED_SOUND: KeyEvent
VK_DEAD_TILDE: KeyEvent
VK_DEAD_VOICED_SOUND: KeyEvent
VK_DECIMAL: KeyEvent
VK_DELETE: KeyEvent
VK_DIVIDE: KeyEvent
VK_DOLLAR: KeyEvent
VK_DOWN: KeyEvent
VK_E: KeyEvent
VK_END: KeyEvent
VK_ENTER: KeyEvent
VK_EQUALS: KeyEvent
VK_ESCAPE: KeyEvent
VK_EURO_SIGN: KeyEvent
VK_EXCLAMATION_MARK: KeyEvent
VK_F: KeyEvent
VK_F1: KeyEvent
VK_F10: KeyEvent
VK_F11: KeyEvent
VK_F12: KeyEvent
VK_F13: KeyEvent
VK_F14: KeyEvent
VK_F15: KeyEvent
VK_F16: KeyEvent
VK_F17: KeyEvent
VK_F18: KeyEvent
VK_F19: KeyEvent
VK_F2: KeyEvent
VK_F20: KeyEvent
VK_F21: KeyEvent
VK_F22: KeyEvent
VK_F23: KeyEvent
VK_F24: KeyEvent
VK_F3: KeyEvent
VK_F4: KeyEvent
VK_F5: KeyEvent
VK_F6: KeyEvent
VK_F7: KeyEvent
VK_F8: KeyEvent
VK_F9: KeyEvent
VK_FINAL: KeyEvent
VK_FIND: KeyEvent
VK_FULL_WIDTH: KeyEvent
VK_G: KeyEvent
VK_GREATER: KeyEvent
VK_H: KeyEvent
VK_HALF_WIDTH: KeyEvent
VK_HELP: KeyEvent
VK_HIRAGANA: KeyEvent
VK_HOME: KeyEvent
VK_I: KeyEvent
VK_INPUT_METHOD_ON_OFF: KeyEvent
VK_INSERT: KeyEvent
VK_INVERTED_EXCLAMATION_MARK: KeyEvent
VK_J: KeyEvent
VK_JAPANESE_HIRAGANA: KeyEvent
VK_JAPANESE_KATAKANA: KeyEvent
VK_JAPANESE_ROMAN: KeyEvent
VK_K: KeyEvent
VK_KANA: KeyEvent
VK_KANA_LOCK: KeyEvent

VK_KANJI: KeyEvent
VK_KATAKANA: KeyEvent
VK_KP_DOWN: KeyEvent
VK_KP_LEFT: KeyEvent
VK_KP_RIGHT: KeyEvent
VK_KP_UP: KeyEvent
VK_L: KeyEvent
VK_LEFT: KeyEvent
VK_LEFT_PARENTHESIS: KeyEvent
VK_LESS: KeyEvent
VK_M: KeyEvent
VK_META: KeyEvent
VK_MINUS: KeyEvent
VK_MODECHANGE: KeyEvent
VK_MULTIPLY: KeyEvent
VK_N: KeyEvent
VK_NONCONVERT: KeyEvent
VK_NUM_LOCK: KeyEvent
VK_NUMBER_SIGN: KeyEvent
VK_NUMPAD0: KeyEvent
VK_NUMPAD1: KeyEvent
VK_NUMPAD2: KeyEvent
VK_NUMPAD3: KeyEvent
VK_NUMPAD4: KeyEvent
VK_NUMPAD5: KeyEvent
VK_NUMPAD6: KeyEvent
VK_NUMPAD7: KeyEvent
VK_NUMPAD8: KeyEvent
VK_NUMPAD9: KeyEvent
VK_O: KeyEvent
VK_OPEN_BRACKET: KeyEvent
VK_P: KeyEvent
VK_PAGE_DOWN: KeyEvent
VK_PAGE_UP: KeyEvent
VK_PASTE: KeyEvent
VK_PAUSE: KeyEvent
VK_PERIOD: KeyEvent
VK_PLUS: KeyEvent
VK_PREVIOUS_CANDIDATE: KeyEvent
VK_PRINTSCREEN: KeyEvent
VK_PROPS: KeyEvent
VK_Q: KeyEvent
VK_QUOTE: KeyEvent
VK_QUOTEDBL: KeyEvent
VK_R: KeyEvent
VK_RIGHT: KeyEvent
VK_RIGHT_PARENTHESIS: KeyEvent
VK_ROMAN_CHARACTERS: KeyEvent
VK_S: KeyEvent
VK_SCROLL_LOCK: KeyEvent
VK_SEMICOLON: KeyEvent
VK_SEPARATER: KeyEvent
VK_SEPARATOR: KeyEvent
VK_SHIFT: KeyEvent
VK_SLASH: KeyEvent
VK_SPACE: KeyEvent
VK_STOP: KeyEvent
VK_SUBTRACT: KeyEvent
VK_T: KeyEvent
VK_TAB: KeyEvent
VK_U: KeyEvent
VK_UNDEFINED: KeyEvent
VK_UNDERSCORE: KeyEvent
VK_UNDO: KeyEvent
VK_UP: KeyEvent
VK_V: KeyEvent
VK_W: KeyEvent
VK_X: KeyEvent
VK_Y: KeyEvent
VK_Z: KeyEvent
VLINK: HTML.Attribute
VoiceStatus: javax.sound.midi

V

—returned by: *Synthesizer*^.getVoiceStatus( )
VolatileImage^: java.awt.image
—returned by: **C**omponent.createVolatileImage( )
ComponentPeer..createVolatileImage( )
GraphicsConfiguration.createCompatibleVolatileImage( )
—fields: **C**omponent.BltBufferStrategy^.backBuffers
Component.FlipBufferStrategy^.drawVBuffer
volume: **V**oiceStatus
VOLUME: **F**loatControl.Type^
vsb: **S**crollPaneLayout.
vsbPolicy: **S**crollPaneLayout.
VSPACE: **H**TML.Attribute
W_RESIZE_CURSOR: **C**ursor **F**rame^
WAIS: **R**eferenceUriSchemesSupported^
WAIT_CURSOR: **C**ursor **F**rame^
waitForAll( ): **M**ediaTracker
waitForID( ): **M**ediaTracker
waitForIdle( ): **R**obot
waitForWork( ): **L**ayoutQueue
WANTS_INPUT_PROPERTY: **J**OptionPane^
wantsInput: **J**OptionPane^
WARNING: **S**everity^
WARNING_DIALOG: **J**RootPane^
WARNING_MESSAGE: **J**OptionPane^
warningListeners: **I**mageReader **I**mageWriter
warningLocales: **I**mageReader **I**mageWriter
warningOccurred( ): *IIOReadWarningListener*^
IIOWriteWarningListener^
wasIcon( ): **D**efaultDesktopManager
WAVE: **A**udioFileFormat.Type
WEIGHT: **T**extAttribute^
weight: **G**lyphJustificationInfo
WEIGHT_BOLD: **T**extAttribute^
WEIGHT_DEMIBOLD: **T**extAttribute^
WEIGHT_DEMILIGHT: **T**extAttribute^
WEIGHT_EXTRA_LIGHT: **T**extAttribute^
WEIGHT_EXTRABOLD: **T**extAttribute^
WEIGHT_HEAVY: **T**extAttribute^
WEIGHT_LIGHT: **T**extAttribute^
WEIGHT_MEDIUM: **T**extAttribute^
WEIGHT_REGULAR: **T**extAttribute^
WEIGHT_SEMIBOLD: **T**extAttribute^
WEIGHT_ULTRABOLD: **T**extAttribute^
weightx: **G**ridBagConstraints
weighty: **G**ridBagConstraints
WEST: **B**orderLayout **G**ridBagConstraints **S**pringLayout
SwingConstants
WHEEL_BLOCK_SCROLL: **M**ouseWheelEvent^
WHEEL_UNIT_SCROLL: **M**ouseWheelEvent^
when: **E**vent
WHEN_ANCESTOR_OF_FOCUSED_COMPONENT:
JComponent^
WHEN_FOCUSED: **J**Component^
WHEN_IN_FOCUSED_WINDOW: **J**Component^
white: **C**olor.
WHITE: **C**olor.
WHITE_SPACE: **C**SS.Attribute
WHITESPACE: **G**lyphMetrics
WIDTH: **C**SS.Attribute **H**TML.Attribute *ImageObserver*
TextAttribute^
width: **A**rc2D.Double^ **A**rc2D.Float^
Component.BltBufferStrategy^ **D**imension^
Ellipse2D.Double^ **E**llipse2D.Float^ **R**aster.
Rectangle. **R**ectangle2D.Double^ **R**ectangle2D.Float^
RoundRectangle2D.Double^ **R**oundRectangle2D.Float^
SampleModel. **T**ableColumn
WIDTH_CONDENSED: **T**extAttribute^
WIDTH_EXTENDED: **T**extAttribute^
WIDTH_REGULAR: **T**extAttribute^
WIDTH_SEMI_CONDENSED: **T**extAttribute^
WIDTH_SEMI_EXTENDED: **T**extAttribute^
WIND_EVEN_ODD: **G**eneralPath *PathIterator*

WIND_NON_ZERO: **G**eneralPath *PathIterator*
window: **S**ystemColor^
WINDOW: **A**ccessibleRole^ **S**ystemColor^
Window^: java.awt
—subclasses: **D**ialog^ **F**rame^ **J**Window^
—descendents: **F**ileDialog^ **J**Dialog^ **J**Frame^
—passed to: **F**ocusTraversalPolicy..getInitialComponent( )
GraphicsDevice.setFullScreenWindow( ) **J**Window( )
KeyboardFocusManager. < setGlobalActiveWindow( ),
setGlobalFocusedWindow( ) > **T**oolkit.createWindow( ) **W**indow( )
Window.AccessibleAWTWindow( ) **W**indowEvent( )
—returned by: **G**raphicsDevice.getFullScreenWindow( )
InputMethodContext^.createInputMethodWindow( )
KeyboardFocusManager. < getActiveWindow( ),
getFocusedWindow( ), getGlobalActiveWindow( ),
getGlobalFocusedWindow( ) > **S**wingUtilities
< getWindowAncestor( ), windowForComponent( ) > **W**indow^
< getOwnedWindows( ), getOwner( ) > **W**indowEvent^
< getOppositeWindow( ), getWindow( ) >
Window.AccessibleAWTWindow^: java.awt
—subclasses: **D**ialog.AccessibleAWTDialog^
Frame.AccessibleAWTFrame^
JWindow.AccessibleJWindow^
—descendents: **J**Dialog.AccessibleJDialog^
JFrame.AccessibleJFrame^
WINDOW_ACTIVATED: **W**indowEvent^
WINDOW_BORDER: **S**ystemColor^
WINDOW_CLOSED: **W**indowEvent^
WINDOW_CLOSING: **W**indowEvent^
WINDOW_DEACTIVATED: **W**indowEvent^
WINDOW_DEICONIFIED: **W**indowEvent^
WINDOW_DEICONIFY: **E**vent
WINDOW_DESTROY: **E**vent
WINDOW_EVENT_MASK: **A**WTEvent^
WINDOW_EXPOSE: **E**vent
WINDOW_FIRST: **W**indowEvent^
WINDOW_FOCUS_EVENT_MASK: **A**WTEvent^
WINDOW_GAINED_FOCUS: **W**indowEvent^
WINDOW_ICONIFIED: **W**indowEvent^
WINDOW_ICONIFY: **E**vent
WINDOW_LAST: **W**indowEvent^
WINDOW_LOST_FOCUS: **W**indowEvent^
WINDOW_MOVED: **E**vent
WINDOW_OPENED: **W**indowEvent^
WINDOW_STATE_CHANGED: **W**indowEvent^
WINDOW_STATE_EVENT_MASK: **A**WTEvent^
WINDOW_TEXT: **S**ystemColor^
windowActivated( ): **A**WTEventMulticaster **W**indowAdapter.
WindowListener^
WindowAdapter.: java.awt.event
—subclasses: **J**Menu.WinListener^
windowBorder: **S**ystemColor^
windowClosed( ): **A**WTEventMulticaster **W**indowAdapter.
WindowListener^
windowClosing( ): **A**WTEventMulticaster **W**indowAdapter.
WindowListener^
WindowConstants: javax.swing
—implemented by: **J**Dialog^ **J**Frame^ **J**InternalFrame^
windowDeactivated( ): **A**WTEventMulticaster **W**indowAdapter.
WindowListener^
windowDeiconified( ): **A**WTEventMulticaster **W**indowAdapter.
WindowListener^
WindowEvent^: java.awt.event
—passed to: **A**WTEventMulticaster < windowActivated( ),
windowClosed( ), windowClosing( ), windowDeactivated( ),
windowDeiconified( ), windowGainedFocus( ), windowIconified( ),
windowLostFocus( ), windowOpened( ), windowStateChanged( ) >
JDialog^.processWindowEvent( ) **J**Frame^.processWindowEvent( )
Window^. < processWindowEvent( ), processWindowFocusEvent( ),
processWindowStateEvent( ) > **W**indowAdapter.
< windowActivated( ), windowClosed( ), windowClosing( ),
windowDeactivated( ), windowDeiconified( ),

windowGainedFocus( ), windowIconified( ), windowLostFocus( ),
windowOpened( ), windowStateChanged( ) >
WindowFocusListener^ < windowGainedFocus( ),
windowLostFocus( ) > *WindowListener*^ < windowActivated( ),
windowClosed( ), windowClosing( ), windowDeactivated( ),
windowDeiconified( ), windowIconified( ), windowOpened( ) >
WindowStateListener^.windowStateChanged( )

WindowFocusListener^: java.awt.event
—passed to: **A**WTEventMulticaster < add( ), remove( ) > **W**indow͜
< addWindowFocusListener( ), removeWindowFocusListener( ) >
—returned by: **A**WTEventMulticaster < add( ), remove( ) >
Window͜.getWindowFocusListeners( )
—implemented by: **A**WTEventMulticaster **W**indowAdapter͜

windowForComponent( ): **S**wingUtilities
windowGainedFocus( ): **A**WTEventMulticaster
WindowAdapter͜ *WindowFocusListener*^
windowIconified( ): **A**WTEventMulticaster **W**indowAdapter͜
WindowListener^
windowInit( ): **J**Window^
WindowListener^: java.awt.event
—passed to: **A**WTEventMulticaster < add( ), remove( ) >
Window͜ < addWindowListener( ), removeWindowListener( ) >
—returned by: **A**WTEventMulticaster < add( ), remove( ) >
Window͜.getWindowListeners( )
—implemented by: **A**WTEventMulticaster **W**indowAdapter͜
windowLostFocus( ): **A**WTEventMulticaster **W**indowAdapter͜
WindowFocusListener^
windowOpened( ): **A**WTEventMulticaster **W**indowAdapter͜
WindowListener^
WindowPeer^: java.awt.peer
—extended by: *DialogPeer*͜ *FramePeer*^
—descendents: *FileDialogPeer*^
—returned by: **T**oolkit.createWindow( )
windowStateChanged( ): **A**WTEventMulticaster
WindowAdapter͜ *WindowStateListener*^
WindowStateListener^: java.awt.event
—passed to: **A**WTEventMulticaster < add( ), remove( ) > **W**indow͜
< addWindowStateListener( ), removeWindowStateListener( ) >
—returned by: **A**WTEventMulticaster < add( ), remove( ) >
Window͜.getWindowStateListeners( )
—implemented by: **A**WTEventMulticaster **W**indowAdapter͜
windowText: **S**ystemColor^
WORD: *AccessibleText*͜
WORD_SPACING: **C**SS.Attribute
WRAP_TAB_LAYOUT: **J**TabbedPane^
WrappedPlainView^: javax.swing.text
writableAction: **D**efaultEditorKit͜
WritableRaster^: java.awt.image
—passed to: **A**ffineTransformOp.filter( ) **B**andCombineOp.filter( )
BufferedImage^ < copyData( ) >
ColorConvertOp.filter( ) **C**olorModel͜ < coerceData( ),
getAlphaRaster( ) > *CompositeContext*.compose( )
ConvolveOp.filter( ) **L**ookupOp.filter( ) *RasterOp*.filter( )
RenderedImage͜.copyData( ) **R**escaleOp.filter( )
WritableRaster( )
—returned by: **A**ffineTransformOp < createCompatibleDestRaster( ),
filter( ) > **B**andCombineOp < createCompatibleDestRaster( ),
filter( ) > **B**ufferedImage^ < copyData( ), getAlphaRaster( ),
getRaster( ), getWritableTile( ) > **C**olorConvertOp
< createCompatibleDestRaster( ), filter( ) > **C**olorModel͜
< createCompatibleWritableRaster( ), getAlphaRaster( ) >
ConvolveOp < createCompatibleDestRaster( ),
filter( ) > **L**ookupOp < createCompatibleDestRaster( ),
filter( ) > **R**aster͜ < createBandedRaster( ),
createCompatibleWritableRaster( ), createInterleavedRaster( ),
createPackedRaster( ), createWritableRaster( ) >
RasterOp < createCompatibleDestRaster( ),
filter( ) > *RenderedImage*͜.copyData( ) **R**escaleOp
< createCompatibleDestRaster( ), filter( ) >
WritableRaster^ < createWritableChild( ),
createWritableTranslatedChild( ), getWritableParent( ) >
WritableRenderedImage^.getWritableTile( )

WritableRenderedImage^: java.awt.image
—passed to: *TileObserver*.tileUpdate( )
—implemented by: **B**ufferedImage^
write( ): **A**bstractWriter **A**udioFileWriter **A**udioSystem
EditorKit͜ **I**CC_Profile **I**mageIO *ImageOutputStream*^
ImageOutputStreamImpl͜ **I**mageWriter **J**TextComponent͜
MidiFileWriter **M**idiSystem *SourceDataLine*^
writeAborted( ): *IIOWriteProgressListener*^
writeAttributes( ): **A**bstractWriter **S**tyleContext͜
writeAttributeSet( ): **S**tyleContext͜
writeBit( ): *ImageOutputStream*^ **I**mageOutputStreamImpl͜
writeBits( ): *ImageOutputStream*^ **I**mageOutputStreamImpl͜
writeBody( ): **M**inimalHTMLWriter^
writeBoolean( ): *ImageOutputStream*^
ImageOutputStreamImpl͜
writeByte( ): *ImageOutputStream*^ **I**mageOutputStreamImpl͜
writeBytes( ): *ImageOutputStream*^ **I**mageOutputStreamImpl͜
writeChar( ): *ImageOutputStream*^ **I**mageOutputStreamImpl͜
writeChars( ): *ImageOutputStream*^ **I**mageOutputStreamImpl͜
writeComponent( ): **M**inimalHTMLWriter^
writeContent( ): **M**inimalHTMLWriter^
writeDouble( ): *ImageOutputStream*^ **I**mageOutputStreamImpl͜
writeDoubles( ): *ImageOutputStream*^
ImageOutputStreamImpl͜
writeEmbeddedTags( ): **H**TMLWriter^
writeEndParagraph( ): **M**inimalHTMLWriter^
writeEndTag( ): **M**inimalHTMLWriter^
writeExternal( ): **D**ataFlavor
writeFloat( ): *ImageOutputStream*^ **I**mageOutputStreamImpl͜
writeFloats( ): *ImageOutputStream*^ **I**mageOutputStreamImpl͜
writeHeader( ): **M**inimalHTMLWriter^
writeHTMLTags( ): **M**inimalHTMLWriter^
writeImage( ): **M**inimalHTMLWriter^
writeInsert( ): **I**mageWriter
writeInt( ): *ImageOutputStream*^ **I**mageOutputStreamImpl͜
writeInts( ): *ImageOutputStream*^ **I**mageOutputStreamImpl͜
writeLeaf( ): **M**inimalHTMLWriter^
writeLineSeparator( ): **A**bstractWriter͜
writeLock( ): **A**bstractDocument͜
writeLong( ): *ImageOutputStream*^ **I**mageOutputStreamImpl͜
writeLongs( ): *ImageOutputStream*^ **I**mageOutputStreamImpl͜
writeNonHTMLAttributes( ): **M**inimalHTMLWriter^
writeOption( ): **H**TMLWriter^
Writer: java.io
—passed to: **A**bstractWriter( ) **E**ditorKit͜.write( ) **H**TMLWriter( )
JTextComponent͜.write( ) **M**inimalHTMLWriter( )
—returned by: **A**bstractWriter͜.getWriter( )
writerSpiNames: **I**mageReaderSpi^
writeShort( ): *ImageOutputStream*^ **I**mageOutputStreamImpl͜
writeShorts( ): *ImageOutputStream*^ **I**mageOutputStreamImpl͜
writeStartParagraph( ): **M**inimalHTMLWriter^
writeStartTag( ): **M**inimalHTMLWriter^
writeStyles( ): **M**inimalHTMLWriter^
writeToSequence( ): **I**mageWriter
writeUnlock( ): **A**bstractDocument͜
writeUTF( ): *ImageOutputStream*^ **I**mageOutputStreamImpl͜
x: **A**rc2D.Double^ **A**rc2D.Float^ **E**llipse2D.Double^
Ellipse2D.Float^ **E**vent **P**oint^ **P**oint2D.Double^
Point2D.Float^ **R**ectangle^ **R**ectangle2D.Double^
Rectangle2D.Float^ **R**oundRectangle2D.Double^
RoundRectangle2D.Float^
x1: **C**ubicCurve2D.Double^ **C**ubicCurve2D.Float^
Line2D.Double^ **L**ine2D.Float^ **Q**uadCurve2D.Double^
QuadCurve2D.Float^
x2: **C**ubicCurve2D.Double^ **C**ubicCurve2D.Float^
Line2D.Double^ **L**ine2D.Float^ **Q**uadCurve2D.Double^
QuadCurve2D.Float^
X_AXIS: **B**oxLayout **V**iew͜
Xor: **A**lphaComposite
XOR: **A**lphaComposite
xpoints: **P**olygon

X

y: **A**rc2D.Double^ **A**rc2D.Float^ **E**llipse2D.Double^ **E**llipse2D.Float^ **E**vent **P**oint^ **P**oint2D.Double^ **P**oint2D.Float^ **R**ectangle⌄ **R**ectangle2D.Double^ **R**ectangle2D.Float^ **R**oundRectangle2D.Double^ **R**oundRectangle2D.Float^

y1: **C**ubicCurve2D.Double^ **C**ubicCurve2D.Float^ **L**ine2D.Double^ **L**ine2D.Float^ **Q**uadCurve2D.Double^ **Q**uadCurve2D.Float^

y2: **C**ubicCurve2D.Double^ **C**ubicCurve2D.Float^ **L**ine2D.Double^ **L**ine2D.Float^ **Q**uadCurve2D.Double^ **Q**uadCurve2D.Float^

Y_AXIS: **B**oxLayout **V**iew⌄

yellow: **C**olor⌄

YELLOW: **C**olor⌄

YES_NO_CANCEL_OPTION: **J**OptionPane^

YES_NO_OPTION: **J**OptionPane^

YES_OPTION: **J**OptionPane^

YOU_1: **M**ediaSize.JIS

YOU_2: **M**ediaSize.JIS

YOU_3: **M**ediaSize.JIS

YOU_4: **M**ediaSize.JIS

YOU_5: **M**ediaSize.JIS

YOU_6: **M**ediaSize.JIS

YOU_7: **M**ediaSize.JIS

ypoints: **P**olygon

ZoneView^: javax.swing.text

zoneWasLoaded( ): **Z**oneView^

W